Modern Europe

Modern Europe

PETER GAY

R. K. WEBB

AMERICAN HISTORICAL ASSOCIATION

HARPER & ROW, PUBLISHERS
New York, Evanston, San Francisco, London

Cartography by Harold K. Faye

MODERN EUROPE
Copyright © 1973 by Harper & Row, Publishers, Inc.

STANDARD BOOK NUMBER: 06-042285-8
LIBRARY OF CONGRESS CATALOG CARD NUMBER: 72-84327

To the memory of
Richard Hofstadter

Contents

Maps

Preface

All histories are works of collaboration, and this history is a work of collaboration in three ways. It is, first, a collaboration between two authors. For fifteen years we were colleagues at Columbia University, working in allied fields with steadily converging interests. We have criticized each other's manuscripts, talked much about historical problems, and in the process have come to a considerable identity of views, if not always precisely the same conclusions, about history. We planned this book together as a whole. With some exchange of jurisdiction, we have independently drafted those sections in which our chief competence lies, but we have read and criticized our individual efforts so often and so thoroughly that the book has become a truly joint venture.

We have underscored the collaborative nature of this enterprise in a second way, by acknowledging as far as possible our obligations to other scholars. Even the author of a highly specialized monograph must lean heavily on the work of others; all the more, the authors of a general textbook go to school to many specialists. We have used our footnotes to indicate the sources of quotations in the text, and the essays on selected readings, which we have attached to each chapter, record our main debts. Most works in foreign languages have had to be omitted, even though some of them have been of first importance to us; the authors of such works must be collectively acknowledged. Still, we trust that in these ways we have told the student of history something about the nature of the craft he is engaged with. And our dedication will indicate that such a book can owe a sum beyond reckoning to a historian from an entirely different field, whose contribution is the friendship he gave us and the example—scholarly, critical, humane—he set to all of us in a generation, at Columbia and beyond.

This is a more traditional book than the one we set out to write. We have devoted a considerable amount of space to the lives of ordinary people and to popular taste and culture, but even more to the high culture of our Western past—its painting and building, its religious convictions, and its scientific achievements. This difference is to some extent owing to the still tentative stage in which social history finds itself: many of the old sources and forms are no longer quite satisfactory or convincing, and the promising new materials and techniques have not yet yielded up the results in some fields that will allow authoritative generalizations. We had to reckon as well with the insistent and proper claims of traditional political history—reigns and battles and political struggles. We have tried to turn to account the remarkable results of research in these fields in the past couple of decades, and to go, as far as possible, beyond mere narrative to analysis. We have sought synthesis, not compromise.

There has been a third collaboration, a largely invisible debate with our critics. Of those whom we know and can thank by name for their mixture of severity and encouragement, we want particularly to thank Professors John A. Garraty, Orest Ranum, and Gordon Wright, Dr. Patricia Kennedy Grimsted, and Mr. Christopher Thorne. Ruth Gay collaborated not only as a critic but as a contributor in her own right.

PETER GAY
R. K. WEBB

A NOTE ON THE USE OF THIS BOOK. To permit the orderly progression of historical argument and a comprehensive view of European civilization, we have organized our chapters and subsections around relatively short spans of time. The maps are grouped together to form small atlases. The index contains the birth and death dates of all persons mentioned in the text, as well as dates for the reigns of monarchs and popes.

Modern Europe

Prologue

Europe was made, not born. From the clashes of tribes and creeds, after waves of conquest and migration, through the coalescence of peoples and their reluctant adaptation of parochial customs to a larger pattern, there emerged in the course of the Middle Ages a single European civilization. Of all the lies that men have told about themselves, that of "racial purity" is at once the most pernicious and most absurd: European civilization was a tapestry woven from distinct ethnic, religious, and cultural strands, but none of these strands itself was pure. Europe was a mixture of mixtures.

In that tapestry, two strands predominate: the classical and the Christian. Since the Renaissance there have been fond classicists and anti-Christian polemicists who have seen the true antecedent of Europe in the classical age alone. "The Greeks were the teachers of the Romans," one of those anti-Christians, the philosophe Denis Diderot, told the Tsarina Catherine of Russia, "the Greeks and Romans have been ours."[1] In contrast, pious scholars and historians saw Europe as the product of what they called the Judaeo-Christian

---

[1] Diderot, *Œuvres complètes,* ed. Assézat and Tourneux (1875–1877), III, 477.

tradition—a set of ethical and religious beliefs grafted on to classical literature and thought. Neither of these schools does Europe full justice; indeed, both together, though closer to the truth, fail to account for the whole of Europe's making. Nineteenth-century writers like Heinrich Heine and Matthew Arnold saw Europe poised between "Hellenes and Hebrews," sometimes in collaboration, sometimes in tension, with one another. That view is useful. But it is worth reiterating that both the "Graeco-Roman" and the "Judaeo-Christian" strands of European civilization were complex mixtures. The first included the sophisticated superstitions of Alexandria quite as much as the serene classicism of Athens—astrology *and* astronomy, mysticism *and* philosophy. The second was a volatile combination of Oriental mystery religion, Jewish legalism, and Greek philosophy. Indeed, it was precisely the composite character of the classical and the Christian strains that permitted the peculiar blending of customs that made Europe: unlike as they were, each offered something to the other. In the third and fourth centuries after Christ, devout church fathers were reluctant to give up pagan classical learning (see p. 20). In the 1660s, the great Italian sculptor and architect Gian Lorenzo Bernini designed a church, piously named for Saint Mary of the Assumption, that clearly derived from the pagan Roman Pantheon—yet Bernini was a devout Roman Catholic. [2]

It is not extravagant, then, to think of European civilization as a compromise between compromises, with all the inner tensions and dissonances inescapable in such an arrangement. And, often enough, both smaller and larger compromises failed. There were times, as this book will abundantly show, when classicists and Christians felt themselves torn apart by the incompatible elements; there were times also when classicists faced Christians in sheer and uncomprehending hostility. If, by the fourteenth century, educated clerics and laymen increasingly used the name "Europe" for the culture they all shared, [3] the widespread perception that theirs was a single civilization did not inhibit deep, often lasting divisions. If the struggles of prince against prince, empire against church, class against class became, in a very real sense, family quarrels, this did not make them any less destructive. The history of Europe abounds with economic rivalry, religious persecutions, pitiless warfare. Emerging unity did not preclude diversity.

But, though diversity was often a source of trouble and suffering, it was also a source of Europe's achievement. "European civilization," the French medievalist Marc Bloch has observed, "arose and flowered, until in the end it covered the face of the earth, among those who dwelt between the Tyrrhenian, the Adriatic, the Elbe, and the Atlantic Ocean. It had no other homeland." [4] This achievement is all the more impressive in the light of the relatively scanty resources Europe had at its command. As historians have rarely failed to

[2] Howard Hibbard, *Bernini* (1965), 148–150. See p. 227.
[3] See Denys Hay, *Europe: The Emergence of an Idea* (Torchbook ed., 1966).
[4] Marc Bloch, *Feudal Society* (1961), I, xix.

observe, the homeland seems remarkably insignificant. Europe is a mere peninsula, attached to the vastness of Asia and today containing no more than a fifth of the population and a tenth of the land mass of the world. As Americans traveling in Europe sense immediately, Europe, geographically no larger than the United States, is an intimate theater. Trips between major cities or from one frontier to another are strikingly short. The distance from the western tip of Ireland to the Ural Mountains in Russia (commonly taken as the eastern frontier of Europe) is shorter than the distance from San Francisco to New York; the distance from Paris to Berlin or Milan to Warsaw is shorter than the distance from Denver, Colorado, to Lincoln, Nebraska. And still, severely limited in size, numbers, and resources, vulnerable for many centuries to invasions by land and sea, Europe conquered the world, and the conquerors brought their culture with them, for good and ill.

While the history of the modern world is not the history of Europe, it is the history of its Europeanization—or, to use a more comprehensive name, its Westernization. The giant powers of the late twentieth century—the United States, the Soviet Union, and China—are wholly or largely non-European in location and population, but they are wholly (or, despite all protestations, striving to become wholly) Western in their civilization. Their grandiose and terrifying power rests on scientific ideas, military technology, public administration, and styles of thinking invented or perfected in that mere peninsula. The mysterious East of romantic novels is growing less mysterious year by year. All the emerging nations of Asia and Africa, though they retain, revive, and sometimes manufacture distinctive traditions, are becoming more like one another, and more Western, in the process of modernization. The so-called "new" nations resent and often battle their old Western overlords, but they do so with Western weapons and for Western stakes: widespread literacy, high standards of living, a share in world trade and world power. Their very resistance to waning Western imperialism clothes itself in Western slogans: self-determination, nationalism, socialism. The world civilization now emerging in great travail and through repeated explosions will not be European or Western exclusively. The struggle of American blacks for self-respect and self-definition that marks the United States in our time is no mere fad; it is part of that great battle for the right to diversity that will make the world—if it does not destroy the world first—a more interesting and more companionable place than it has ever been. But even in this historic moment, Europe—the West—continues to play a part far greater than its share in land, people, or resources. Europe may be in political decline; ironically, the ever more insistent call for its political unification is a consequence of that decline. But the historical importance of Europe remains unimpaired. It made us—even non-Europeans—what we are today.

Introduction:
The Making of Europe

THE GREEK ACHIEVEMENT

The Greek "Miracle"

The first, and in many respects the finest, exemplars of the mixture that Europe would become were the Greeks. Our enthusiastic, often exclusive preoccupation with the "Greek miracle" is understandable but unjustified. For several thousand years before Homer—the first European immortal—composed or collected the *Iliad* and the *Odyssey*[1] non-European peoples had constructed complex civilizations. Well before 3000 B.C., the Sumerians had mastered the art of cultivating the soil by tapping the waters of the Euphrates. They founded

---

[1] Disputes about the identity of Homer go back to the Alexandrian period, but it was not until 1795, when the German classical philologist Friedrich August Wolf published his *Prolegomena ad Homerum,* that the theory of the multiple authorship of these two epics first gained wide currency. Today scholars agree that there was a single poet named Homer who lived before A.D. 700 and who incorporated into his imperishable poems a number of traditional elements.

5

walled cities and erected looming temples, introduced the division of labor and an esoteric form of writing. Their successors in the Mesopotamian river valley complicated the political institutions they had inherited, developed higher mathematics, made astronomical observations, and in the Babylonian era—a thousand years before Homer—codified their laws. Their celebrated epic, the *Gilgamesh,* though dominated by myths and strewn with prodigies, offers philosophical reflections on human mortality; the code of Hammurabi shows, by its provisions, that the Babylonians had by this time established a fairly sophisticated and well-defined class system, ranging from slaves to commoners to aristocrats.

Egyptian civilization, which emerged at about the same time, was quite as advanced. Visiting Egypt about 450 B.C., Herodotus shrewdly perceived the country's gravest problem and greatest victory when, in a famous epigram, he called Egypt "the gift of the Nile." The taming of the Nile by irrigation made Egyptian civilization possible, and it was an impressive civilization. In the first dynasties, before 2500 B.C., Egyptians had invented (or perhaps borrowed) a system of writing, devised a relatively reliable calendar, formulated an elaborate set of myths to account for natural events and political rulership, and developed a characteristic style of art. The most imposing of their pyramids—those solemn, seemingly immortal stone monuments rising from the desert sands to celebrate and commemorate the dead—date from the third millennium B.C. They are a triumph of technology: "The Great Pyramid," in particular, the Egyptologist John A. Wilson writes, "is a tremendous mass of stone finished with the most delicate precision. Here were six and a quarter million tons of stone, with casing blocks averaging as much as two and a half tons each; yet those casing blocks were dressed and fitted with a joint of one-fiftieth of an inch—a scrupulous nicety worthy of the jeweler's craft. Here the margin of error in the squareness of the north and south sides was 0.09 per cent and of the east and west sides, 0.03 per cent. This mighty mass of stone was set upon a dressed-rock pavement which, from opposite corners, had a deviation from a true plane of only 0.004 per cent." [2] One need not admire the theology that inspired or the slave system that built the pyramids to recognize the organization and skill required to sustain such an enterprise.

Yet, interesting and impressive as these early civilizations are, their influence on the making of Europe was indirect, largely through the Greeks. These civilizations were, by and large, static; their thinking was wholly dominated by myth; their world was governed by the gods, capricious and demanding deities who needed to be appeased and could never be understood. Whatever science the Egyptians or Babylonians developed was practical, devised to aid in the measurement of land or the celebration of religious ritual. These people reasoned, but their reasoning was, as it were, intransitive; it led nowhere beyond itself. The Greeks were different; the Greeks, in a phrase, invented critical thinking.

[2] John Albert Wilson, *The Burden of Egypt* (1951), 54–55.

To speak in this summary fashion is to invite two misunderstandings. By the time the Greeks had emerged into the classical period—that great epoch of versatile and intense productivity that was to become an object of awe and idealization to modern Europeans—they had experienced a long history of invasions and migrations, of dark ages and renaissances: the Greeks of the sixth and fifth centuries B.C. were an old and thoroughly mixed people. And they did not leap into civilization unaided: the Greek miracle was not a miracle. As they were not reluctant to acknowledge, the Greeks borrowed heavily from their neighbors: artistic motifs and medical learning from the Egyptians, mathematics and astronomy from the Babylonians, the alphabet from the seafaring Phoenicians. What mattered was that they transformed what they borrowed and made it their own.

The precise process of this transformation is obscure, but its meaning for history is decisive; the invention of critical thinking changed the face of the world as profoundly as the mastery over fire and the emergence of writing. Literally, of course, critical thinking was not a deliberate invention; nor was it the monopoly of one man or even of a school. But it came, when it did come, with such stunning rapidity and with such an avalanche of consequences that we can see why the ancients should honor one man, Thales, with the enviable title, Father of Philosophy. Early in the sixth century B.C., Thales of Miletus dared to inquire into the nature of the universe. He thought the world was made up of water; his successors—like Thales, Greeks living on the Ionian islands or on the west coast of Asia Minor—asked the same question Thales had asked and arrived at different theories: Anaximander taught that the universe was composed of opposing elements; Anaximenes, that its basic element was air. These theories, in some degree dependent on Egyptian and Babylonian myths, matter less than the mental set that made the inquiry possible. No Egyptian, no Babylonian, however intelligent or independent, would have enjoyed the mental freedom that allowed escape from the overwhelming weight of his creation myths. Thales' question was a revolution in men's ways of thinking simply because it dared to be a question that had no predetermined answer. Instead of humbly accepting authoritative and tradition-hallowed oracular or priestly pronouncements, the Greeks embarked on a restless search for new knowledge. This search meant an unsparing criticism of accepted stories and implied a new confidence in human powers.

The revolution, as we have seen, came quickly. Thales is said to have predicted the eclipse of the sun in 585 B.C.; Aristotle, the last of the Greek philosophers of the classical age, died in 322 B.C. In these two-and-a-half centuries—a mere moment in time even in the brief history of civilization—the Greeks had laid the foundations not merely of philosophy, but of history, biology, and anatomy, and had enormously advanced the study of geography, mathematics, and astronomy. The names of these modern disciplines, and of others like aesthetics, logic, and metaphysics, are tributes to these pioneers of the mind: they are all Greek words.

This unprecedented and unrepeated explosion of knowledge had a single root: the organization of curiosity into methodical, fearless, often self-corrective inquiry. Nothing, not even a god, was safe from the questioning spirit of the Greeks; while earlier and elsewhere the learned classes had bent their best efforts to celebrate their kings, worship their divinities, and keep their knowledge hidden, the Greeks were ready to criticize all existing forms of government, to attribute the origin of religion to human invention, and thus to make man, rather than the gods, the measure of all things. The two most celebrated Greek philosophers, Plato and Aristotle, were in a sense latecomers; much of their work was a reply to their predecessors. Yet, of course, they matter most to the historian of modern Europe, for their writings, often in fragmentary form, exercised a powerful and almost continuous influence on Western thought. Alfred North Whitehead's oft-repeated remark that all philosophy is a series of footnotes to Plato is an exaggeration that contains a significant kernel of truth. Indeed, a survey of those among Plato's and Aristotle's writings that have come down to us gives a good idea of the comprehensive inquiry into man and nature that the Greeks initiated: politics, ethics, logic, theology, aesthetics, the nature of life and the meaning of death, and perhaps most important, the very nature of thinking itself.

While it would be impossible to expound the philosophical work of Plato and Aristotle in a few paragraphs, even a brief summary will suggest its overwhelming importance for all subsequent European thought. Plato was born in 428 B.C., near the end of the Golden Age of Greek culture, and studied with Socrates, the great gadfly of official Greek philosophy. We shall never know what, if anything, Socrates wrote; we shall never even be sure just what he was like: the descriptions of him that have survived vary enormously. Plato's account is merely the most famous and the most favorable. Socrates' method was ironic questioning; he troubled the souls of complacent thinkers by showing them to be more ignorant than they had thought they were—more ignorant, certainly, than Socrates, who went about proclaiming his ignorance. Plato adopted this technique of clarifying areas of knowledge and ignorance by persistent questioning and of rising inductively to valid generalizations—the dialectic, the Greeks called it—as his literary and dramatic style: all his works are dialogues, and many of these dialogues use Socrates as their witty, eloquent, and always triumphant protagonist. Not surprisingly, Socrates made himself very unpopular, and in 399 B.C. at the age of seventy, he was sentenced to death for blasphemy and for corrupting the youth of Athens. Plato's account of his trial and his courageous death, the *Apology* and the *Phaedo*, both extraordinarily moving works, gave Socrates immortality and transmitted his reputation to Europe as the first martyr to philosophy.[3]

---

[3] In the Enlightenment, Condorcet, in his essay on progress, called the conviction of Socrates "the first crime announcing the war between philosophy and superstition, which still continues today." See Peter Gay, *The Enlightenment: An Interpretation*, vol. I, *The Rise of Modern Paganism* (1966), 82.

While Plato immortalized Socrates and imitated his irony, in other respects he departed from his master: Socrates had turned his attention to the nature of man and the need to understand right conduct; he had been skeptical and even derisive about the ambitious scientific inquiries typical of Greek philosophy in the Golden Age. Plato, on the other hand, inquired into everything. After the death of Socrates, he traveled widely; when he returned to Athens around 387 B.C., he founded a school, the Academy, and wrote works on a wide variety of subjects, including the theory of knowledge, love and friendship, art, ethics, and politics. His great speculative dialogue, the *Timaeus,* which attempts to explain the nature of the universe, ventures into territory Socrates would have disdained to enter. But Plato's most famous dialogue is the *Republic,* which defines an ideal commonwealth in which the able—the philosopher-kings— rule, the brave fight, and the masses of men work and obey.

Plato died in 347 B.C.; he lived long enough to have as his pupil the other great philosopher of the age, Aristotle. Teacher and student have often been contrasted; in fact, much of Europe's intellectual history can be written as a combat between the disciples of Plato and the disciples of Aristotle. But in fact there was more of Plato in Aristotle than later partisans would admit. Their difference was mainly one of mental style. Plato was the poet of philosophy; his dialogues would delight even those who did not fully understand them. He was the playful explorer. Aristotle was more sober, more patient, more prosaic: he was interested in ordering and classifying available knowledge and in establishing conclusions soundly based on factual inquiry. A comparison of his main political work, the *Politics,* with its platonic counterpart, the *Republic,* is instructive: the *Republic* is a bold inquiry into fundamental principles that does not hesitate to use the state and its hierarchical organization as a grand metaphor for the divisions in man's soul; the *Politics,* in contrast, offers carefully differentiated definitions of forms of government derived from a thorough inquiry into the constitutions under which the one hundred and fifty odd Greek city-states lived. But Aristotle, the father of empiricism, was something better than a compiler; his speculations on general principles, the *Metaphysics* (that which lies beyond physics), his writings on biology, on morals, on aesthetics, were as imaginative as they were fact-bound. Plato and Aristotle were indeed latecomers: both thought the world of the city-state to be the ideal, indeed the only possible, world, and this at a time when the city-state was already fading. Aristotle was born in 384 B.C. and lived long enough—to 322—to become tutor to Alexander of Macedon, the prince who would in fact make the world of Aristotle's *Politics* impossible (see p. 12). Yet Plato and Aristotle display not merely the limited vision, but also the vast achievements, of the Greek intellectual revolution.

The historical writings of the Greeks offer added evidence for the profundity and originality of that revolution. Neither the Babylonians nor the Egyptians had developed true history; they had feasted off conventional tales about superhuman kings and active deities, tales uncritically accepted and endlessly retold.⁴ The Greeks changed this in its essence. Down to early modern times, those pious Christians who accepted the Bible as literally true celebrated Moses as the first historian. More properly this title belongs to Herodotus, an inquisitive traveler and accomplished geographer, who late in the fifth century B.C. recorded the great clash between the Greeks and the Persians that had taken place a few decades before; with his insatiable curiosity and love of anecdote, Herodotus put down some improbable tales, but his history remains the first coherent and critical report on the past we possess. Only a few years later Thucydides, a cool, masterly analyst of men and events, wrote the history of the internecine war between Sparta and Athens in which he had served; his book remains a model of political history, with man at the center of the stage. It has been suggested that Thucydides borrowed some of his devices from the Greek theater, but he remains a true historian, writing in obedience to the events he has investigated and, in part, experienced.

The Greek elevation of man did not mean the one-sided celebration of man's most distinctive characteristic—his reason—or of his most exalted quality—his heroism. Nineteenth-century scholars, persistent and learned but often genteel, fabricated a sunny Greece, serene, rational, measured in its politics, its art, its ethics. They knew—how could they avoid it?—that the Greek tragedies we have⁵ deal with incest, murder, and pitiless divine revenge, but they interpreted these searing plays as appeals to *sophrosyne*—the splendid classical Greek ideal of wholeness, balance, temperance. So they were, but Greek classicism was not cold, remote, dispassionate. On the contrary, it was the hard-won victory over pain and disillusionment and the recognition of man's limitations; it was passionate.⁶ What is more, the loftiness of the Greek theater and of Greek speculation in general was punctuated and relieved by irreverence and ribaldry. The tragedies were accompanied by performances of satyr plays filled with scatological language and barracks humor. The Greeks who emerge from the scholarship of our day retain their value as guides to civilized ideals of rationality and moderation, but they are less serene, more earthy, than they had seemed in Victorian dress. And they are also more human and more comprehensible.

The political history of Greece after it emerged from its dark age in the eighth century B.C. accords well with this realistic portrait. The characteristic

---

⁴ The ancient Hebrews, on the other hand, were profoundly concerned with history; their very religion is a historical religion. God created the world at a certain moment; the experiences of the Chosen People took place in historical time and receive historical treatment in the sacred records; the Jewish prophets never tire of reminding their people of that history and its lessons. On the other hand, this passion for the past—*their* past—was accompanied by many of the characteristics that marked the mythical thinking of the Hebrews' neighbors: acceptance of conflicting stories, reliance on creation myths, appeal to God as chief actor and cause in history.

⁵ The losses are stunning: we have only 7 plays of Aeschylus, although he wrote more than 80; only 7 plays by Sophocles, although he is credited with more than 120; only 19 plays of Euripides, although more than 90 are attributed to him.

⁶ This view is now gaining wide acceptance; it informs such a popularization as H. D. F. Kitto's *The Greeks* (rev. ed., 1957).

political unit, the *polis,* dotted the Greek peninsula and was reproduced wherever the Greeks established their colonies.[7] The *polis* might have been the protagonist in one of their tragedies: a noble creature doomed to final disaster by its fatal flaw, a great success ending in a dismal failure.[8] Not merely for classical scholars later, but for its own contemporaries, the *polis* was far more than a political entity. It was a comprehensive community that demanded and deserved men's utmost loyalty; it was the fount of law, the guarantor of social order, the repository of political ideals. This is the meaning of Aristotle's famous definition of man as a *zoon politikon*: man is a being whose nature it is to live in a *polis*. But which *polis?* Like political theorists in later centuries, so the Greeks wavered between two possibilities represented by the two most powerful among their city-states, Sparta and Athens. Sparta, a tight-lipped dictatorship with no nonsense about art and with a passionate devotion to military discipline, came to stand for order; Athens, with its "democracy"[9] and its brilliant cultural life, came to stand for freedom. Those who would later rhapsodize over "the glory that was Greece," normally had the Athens of the fourth century B.C. in mind; it was then that Aeschylus, Sophocles, and Euripides poured out their tragedies; Aristophanes rudely ridiculed what was most sacred; Socrates incensed his fellow citizens with his uncomfortable and unanswerable questions; Phidias sculpted and helped to decorate that newly risen temple, the Parthenon.

Yet the passion that had made the *polis* great—local patriotism—also encompassed its downfall. Early in the fifth century B.C. Greeks had transcended parochial loyalties to beat back a massive Persian invasion; Spartans and Athenians alike had distinguished themselves with brave sacrificial deaths and ingenious naval strategies. But with the threat gone, Sparta and Athens turned on each other in a prolonged and exhausting conflict; the Peloponnesian War ended in 404 B.C. with the total defeat of Athens and with the Greek political structure in danger. Sparta's attempt to play an imperial role in Greece proved a failure, as did all attempts at union in the face of renewed Persian threats, of Rome rising in the west, and of Macedonia in the north. Through much of the fourth century, internecine warfare continued. Thus, by the 340s, Philip II of Macedonia found the Greeks easy prey for his shrewd policy of diplomacy, bribery, war—and patience. By 336 B.C., the year of his death, Philip was master

---

[7] Almost as soon as they entered the light of history, Greek states sent out energetic sailors to western Asia Minor, to the Black Sea, to Sicily and the tip of the Italian boot, and to what is today southern France. Wherever they went they built a *polis:* Syracuse was a *polis* founded about 734 B.C.; Massilia (which we know under the name of Marseilles) was a *polis* founded about 600 B.C. Self-confidence and imperialism, it seems, went hand in hand.

[8] The development of these "city-states" (as we translate that resonant Greek word, *polis,* a little lamely) differed greatly. Most of them began under the rule of tight aristocratic clans and then, in the seventh and sixth centuries, underwent periods of civil strife as the traditional rulers were challenged by popular leaders, the "tyrants."

[9] It hardly needs pointing out that this antique form of popular rule is quite different from our modern ideal: it excluded resident foreigners, women, and slaves—although the Athenians' relatively decent treatment of their slave population astounded and dismayed the Spartans.

of Greece. Alexander, his son and successor, continued and expanded his father's work. The age of the *polis* was over.

The Alexandrian Bridge

After more than two thousand years, Alexander remains an enigma. He was quick, energetic, inordinately ambitious—that much is clear. But was his imagination that of a historic leader or a mere adventurer, his cosmopolitanism the product of ecumenical thinking or simply a love of Oriental luxury?— these remain a matter for controversy. In a series of swift and brilliant campaigns, he defeated the powerful Persians decisively; by 327 B.C. he was at the gates of India. The pupil of Aristotle and the son of a king who, though a "barbarian," had deeply loved Greek culture, Alexander extended the reach of that culture through the scores of encampments and cities, including Alexandria, that he founded all across his vast, if ephemeral, empire. As he extended the sway of Greek civilization, he also diluted its quality. This cosmopolitanism had two faces: it meant not solely the export of one culture, but also the importation of others. And this was to be the quality, too, of the Hellenistic Age that began with Alexander: it was cosmopolitan and eclectic. Yet the age was also a bridge of transmission; much of what later came to be hailed as classical—like the Pergamum Altar or the Laocoön statue—were products of this autumn of Greek civilization.

Alexander died in 323, and with his early death the inevitable happened: lesser men struggled over the great empire that the Conqueror had left behind. After much confused and bloody squabbling for the spoils, three sizable dynasties emerged: the Ptolemies in Egypt, the Seleucids in Asia Minor, the Antigonids in Macedonia. Alexandria stood out as a center of culture with its great libraries and museum, but Athens and Rhodes, too, had schools of rhetoric and philosophy where ambitious barbarians went to polish their manners and expand their knowledge. Hellenistic culture, which dates roughly from the death of Alexander in 323 B.C. to the Roman conquest of the Mediterranean around 150 B.C., was wide if not deep, subtle if not original. In Alexandria especially, urban and urbane poets wrote pastorals proclaiming the virtues of the simple bucolic life they professed to miss but did their utmost to avoid; scholars perfected textual and literary criticism, collected vast libraries, and quarreled over the Greek classics in poetry and drama. It was an age of editors, of commentators, of disciples. Even today the word "Alexandrian" conjures up the precious, the overripe, the slightly tired.

Yet the Hellenistic Age was also a flowering. In the sixth century B.C., Pythagoras and his disciples had developed a mystery cult around mathematics and made some fruitful guesses about numbers; in the fifth century, Leucippus and Democritus had speculated on the atomic constitution of matter. Their tentative but pioneering ideas were carried further by Hellenistic scientists: between 300 and 200 B.C., Euclid laid the foundations of geometry with his immortal *Elements;* Aristarchus of Samos argued that the earth revolves around the sun; Eratosthenes mapped the earth using longitudinal and latitudinal lines and calculated its size with astounding accuracy; Apollonius of Perga studied conic sections and invented such indispensable mathematical terms as ellipse and parabola; and Archimedes of Syracuse discovered specific gravity—hardly an unimpressive list of accomplishments. Of equal importance for posterity—indeed, of particular importance to European civilization in the sixteenth and seventeenth centuries, those centuries of profound intellectual readjustment—were the philosophers of the Hellenistic Age, chief among them the Stoics and the Epicureans.

Stoicism and Epicureanism have been extensively misunderstood. The Stoics were not merely "stoical"; the Epicureans rarely "epicurean." Appropriately enough, both philosophies originated in Athens: Zeno of Cyprus, the founder of Stoicism, came to Athens around 314 B.C.; Epicurus of Samos arrived there about a decade later. The Greek Stoics developed a comprehensive system in which nature and man, physics and ethics, found their appointed places. God is the animating force, the reason, of the universe. He governs the world through comprehensible and unalterable natural laws; and men, who hold in themselves a bit of the divine flame, have the supreme obligation to understand the divine legislation and obey it: "Live according to nature" was the Stoics' central injunction. In this way, they argued, man would gain mastery over his life by gaining mastery over himself. To live according to nature meant to desire only what could be obtained, to regret nothing that was inaccessible, to face pain and loss with courage and resignation, above all, to conquer the fear of death—that was the Stoics' way to man's freedom. The Epicureans, like the Stoics the disciples of the Greek atomists, expressed similar ideas in rather different language. To Epicurus, the aim of life was happiness, but happiness consisted not in swinish self-indulgence and drunken sensuality: that notion was imposed on the Epicureans later by their enemies. The most desirable state was the absence of pain, *ataraxia*—serenity, a kind of sublime indifference to external discomforts or internal turmoil. And Epicurus, whatever others might later charge, exalted the pleasures of the mind over the pleasures of the body.

Stoicism, Epicureanism, and an associated school, Pyrrhonist skepticism,[10] were landmarks in the history of European thought. But they were also symptoms of a society growing weary of the burdens of survival. Plato and Aristotle had thought man's participation in his *polis* his highest duty; the Stoics, the Epicureans, and the Skeptics, living in vast, impersonal empires in which the individual was so obviously without political influence of any sort, taught that man's highest good lies in withdrawal—escape from the world into oneself. Plato and Aristotle had taught men to act; the Hellenistic schools taught them to endure. A civilization dominated by such systematic passivity sooner or later was bound to fall to the energetic, self-confident barbarians at the gate. They were the Romans.

[10] It derives its name from Pyrrho of Elis, contemporary of Zeno and Epicurus, who taught that nothing can be known with certainty and that the only sensible position man can adopt is one of suspended judgment.

ROME: CLASSICS AND CHRISTIANS

The Republic

The Romans were a surprising people who left the modern world a vast legacy. A tribe of peasants and soldiers given to costly civil wars, energetically devoted to imperial expansion, addicted to blood sports, they turned, in their peaceful years, to administration and the law. Our debt to their political arrangements and legal doctrines is obvious. Words we use every day—senator, censor, dictator, empire—are reminders of what the Romans did best. But this is not all: supremely unoriginal in the arts, literature, and science, the Romans were at the same time remarkably willing to learn. Horace put the situation candidly: *"Graecia capta ferum victorem cepit et artes intulit agresti Latio*—Captive Greece captured her savage conqueror and brought the arts to the rustic Latins." [11] The Greeks, of course, had made their varied contributions to literature and science in Greek, and Greek became the obligatory second language of every civilized Roman for centuries after Greek power had been permanently broken. But the Greek heritage survived into the Middle Ages and into modern times mainly in Latin guise. The Greeks had invented rhetoric, but it was Cicero's treatises on rhetoric, little better than compilations of what he had learned from his Greek teachers, that survived—and these treatises were in Latin. Similarly, the first great "Roman" historian was Polybius, a Greek hostage living in Rome. He wrote in Greek, but the subject of his history was Rome's greatness. Once again, in the transmission of an incalculable and invaluable cultural heritage, Europe proved itself a mixture.

The Romans were latecomers among the nations of the Mediterranean. The Italian peninsula had been settled by Indo-European tribes from the Alps and the Danube Valley around 2000 B.C.; their settlements were eclipsed by the appearance of the mysterious Etruscans, probably transplanted from Asia Minor, before 800 B.C. The Romans themselves later dated the founding of their city in 753 B.C., but this, like much else of their early history, is legend: there is evidence that the city of Rome was populated by about 1000 B.C. At first, it seems, the city was governed by Etruscan kings, but then, around 500 or perhaps later (tradition, with characteristic false precision, says 509 B.C.) the Romans rose, expelled their kings, and founded a republic.

The history of the Roman Republic is the history of expansion abroad and class struggle at home. The two, of course, were related: the need for large

[11] Epistles II, 1, 156–157. For Horace, see p. 16.

standing armies, for officials and colonists for the conquered territories, put a premium on the kind of leadership the patrician landowners seemed best equipped to provide and checked all possibility of experimenting with democracy. The expansion of Rome from city-state to world power proceeded first slowly, then rapidly; inexorably, the Roman legions subdued the Italian peninsula, the Mediterranean islands, Spain, Greece, then North Africa and Asia Minor, and later, Gaul, southern Britain, and central Europe. By the end of the Pyrrhic Wars in 272 B.C., Rome controlled all of Italy; beginning in 264, with the first Punic War, Rome turned against its great Mediterranean rival, the North African city of Carthage. It took more than a century and three major wars before Carthage was reduced; in 218 B.C. the Carthaginian general Hannibal even succeeded briefly in invading Italy with his elephants. But in 146 it was all over; Carthage was defeated and the city razed to the ground. In the same year, Macedonia became a Roman province.

None of these triumphs brought social peace; on the contrary. At the beginning, the Roman Republic was an oligarchy of patrician families who drew their power from their ownership of land. These landowners had a monopoly of membership in the senate and over its two chief executives, the consuls. Gradually the small farmers, the plebeians, organized themselves, won access to the senate; they made their voice heard as well through their own assembly and their elected representatives, the tribunes of the people. But the centuries of war, in which the plebeians served in the army, reduced their grip on the machinery of government; when they came home from service, they found their farms devastated by campaigns or neglected through their absence, while the patricians, already rich, had grown richer. Class distances grew wider, and the oligarchs consolidated their hold: of the 200 consuls who served Rome between 233 and 133 B.C., 159 came from 20 senatorial families.[12] The self-centeredness and unmitigated greed of the patricians reduced many of the Roman farmers to poverty-stricken tenants or serfs, or brought them to the cities as rootless proletarians. Slavery was widespread; it became the favorite method of recruiting domestic servants and menial laborers on city and farm. In 136 B.C. and again in 101, slaves rose in Sicily, but both rebellions were put down with barbaric severity. And beginning with 133, endemic urban and rural unrest brought social experiments, demagoguery, conspiracies, and for the first time, assassination as an instrument of politics. The brothers Gracchi, who attempted to redress the social balance by a radical redistribution of land, both died violent deaths: Tiberius Gracchus was killed in 133 B.C., Gaius Gracchus in 122 B.C. And Julius Caesar—skillful general, shrewd author, superb politician, a poor but enormously ambitious patrician who had conquered Gaul and invaded Britain—was assassinated in 44 B.C., while he exercised dictatorial control over the dying republic. When in 31 B.C. Octavianus took supreme power, he ended more than a century of civil strife.

[12] Tom B. Jones, *Ancient Civilization* (1960), 347.

The Empire

Caesar Augustus (to give him the name by which Octavianus is best known to history) created an empire in the name of preserving the republic. His long and peaceful reign, which lasted from 31 B.C. to A.D. 14, was a golden age of political calm and literary excellence, and it has come to be known as the Augustan Age with much justice. Every part of Rome's history would continue to dominate man's imagination into modern times: "Rome," wrote Gibbon at the end of the eighteenth century, "is familiar to the schoolboy and the statesman." Tales of the early, legendary kings; the powerful evocation of nature and diatribe against superstition, *De rerum natura,* by the Epicurean poet Lucretius, who died in 55 B.C.; the speeches, letters, the philosophical and rhetorical treatises of Cicero, who was regarded, down to the nineteenth century, as one of the greatest writers of all time—these relics, and others, were the staples on which every educated European could draw with ease. But it was the Augustan Age that furnished posterity with the richest food. This was the time of Vergil, who idealized rural life in his *Eclogues,* gave a more realistic though equally poetic portrayal of that life in his *Georgics,* and created a national, deliberately patriotic epic, the *Aeneid,* about the mythical founder of Rome, which many cultivated readers for many centuries thought greater than Homer's *Iliad.* It was the time of Ovid, who raised erotic poetry to a new high level of wit and grace, and of Horace, the self-confessed Epicurean whose brilliant odes, satires, and epistles celebrate the middle way, the life of good sense and calm enjoyment. And it was the time of Livy, historian and propagandist, whose history of Rome incorporated and immortalized the most fascinating legends surrounding Rome's origins.

Perhaps the greatest work of art the Augustan Age produced was Caesar Augustus himself, coupled with his empire and the peace he began to force on a Mediterranean world gradually being Romanized, the *pax Romana.* Wily, supple, more eager to have the substance of power than its trappings, Augustus set the direction for a unified empire that would last, through many vicissitudes, as a political reality down to the fifth century, and as a dream, a myth, an ideal, down to 1806, when it was finally dispatched by another shrewd man of power, Napoleon Bonaparte (see p. 514). How solidly Augustus had built became evident in the decades after his death: his successors, who included such bizarre psychotics as Caligula and Nero, were so insecure on the imperial throne that they spent more energy despatching their enemies—real or imagined—than governing their state; yet Rome flourished. Around 100, Tacitus, the last of the great classical historians, recorded the antics of these emperors in his powerful, austerely eloquent *Annals* and *Histories.* In the second century after Christ, strictly speaking between 96 and 180, the empire was governed by a succession of five "good emperors"—Nerva, Trajan, Hadrian, Antoninus Pius, and Marcus Aurelius—honest administrators, good soldiers, patrons of the arts, and (for Romans) humane men. In their time the empire reached its greatest extent, the provinces were increasingly brought under the control of Roman law, confidence in the state gradually returned as reigns of terror ceased, and Roman civilization experienced a second flowering. It was a Silver Age, generally thought inferior to the Golden Age that had flourished under Augustus, yet not without merit of its own. But after 180, with the death of Marcus Aurelius, the Stoic on the throne, and the accession of his son, Commodus, these splendid years rapidly came to seem a mere interlude. The third century saw the precipitous decline of Roman civilization and the decisive degeneration of Roman politics. As mystery cults from all over the empire competed for the languid attention of the rich and the passionate devotion of the soldiers, the state itself became more and more an affair of naked force. The army, itself increasingly barbarized, ruled through its chosen vessel, the emperor, whose tenure was precarious and whose life expectancy was short. The year 476 when the barbarian invader Odoacer deposed Romulus Augustulus, the last Roman emperor of the West, is often taken as the end of the empire. But it is no more than a convenient date. On the one hand, the event only confirmed what Romans had long anticipated; and on the other hand, the barbarians embraced much of the Roman civilization. Roman law, the most enduring heritage that the Romans left the European world (see p. 26), went underground in the West but remained a powerful shaping force for the thinking of lawyers, ecclesiastics, and statesmen for many centuries. Even the religion that was to dominate the history of Europe for over a thousand years— presumably worldly and pagan Rome's most implacable enemy—anchored its most influential branch in Rome and spoke, and disseminated, the language of the Romans. Greece, Horace had observed, had conquered Rome, her conqueror. Rome, in turn, would conquer *its* conquerors, and civilize them.

The Origins of Christianity

Probably the least heralded yet most portentous event in the reign of Caesar Augustus was the birth of Christianity. Its founder, Jesus, was born in or before 4 B.C., in the Roman province of Palestine, where he acquired a devoted following with his popular preaching, his bold defiance of religious dignitaries, and reports of his miraculous powers. Like all great innovators, Jesus was a profound threat to established institutions, and his claim to more than human stature opened him to the charge of blasphemy. Around A.D. 30 he was crucified by the Roman authorities. A cult rapidly grew around his sayings, his miracles, and his death. The Jews—of whom Jesus was one—taught that a Messiah, a savior, would come; Jesus proclaimed himself that Messiah and his disciples accepted and propagated his word. From just another Jewish sect the doctrine woven around Jesus, the Christ,[13] developed into a new religion. Like European

---

[13] The name *Jesus* is the Greek version of the Hebrew name Joshua, which means "savior"; the name *Christ* is also Greek, a translation of the Hebrew word *Messiah*, which means "anointed."

civilization Christianity was a gathering of many strands, and its doctrines did not arise ready-made, but developed through several centuries.

The first, in many ways the most important, of these strands was Judaism. Not Jesus alone, but Paul, the organizer and codifier of primitive Christianity, and the other early Christians were Jews. A small nomadic tribe that had finally settled in Palestine in the thirteenth century B.C., the ancient Hebrews had experienced military defeats and long exile, lived in republics and monarchies, built temples and a striking religious system. Indeed, what gives the Hebrews world-historical importance is their religion, which was unique in antiquity: unlike all others, Judaism was monotheistic, legalistic, and historical. According to Jewish teaching, there was one God, who had made a covenant with his people—the Hebrews—and was jealous of their flirtations with other gods. He had created the world and would intervene in the historical process to reward or punish the Jews, to lay down their laws and enforce their obedience. By the time of Jesus, the Jews had developed a sizable historical and legal literature that recorded God's work, the history of the Jewish people, and the hundreds of rules governing diet and prayer and marriage and hospitality by which the Jews obsessively thought themselves bound. Not all was harmony; Jesus' vehement outbursts against the "scribes and Pharisees" were, at least in his mind and the minds of his followers, the rebellion of authentic religion against a legalism that reduced religion to the scrupulous observation of sacred rules. "The letter killeth," St. Paul said, "the spirit giveth life." Yet despite this quarrel (which was, after all, a quarrel within the Jewish family), Christianity as it emerged retained much of the Jewish tradition and of Jewish doctrine. Despite attempts by zealous radical Christians to uproot all Jewish teachings, Christianity would retain the Jewish books of the Bible as divinely inspired authority, and thus the Jewish account of a single God-Father, of his creation, and of his historic work; Christians would come to read much of the Old Testament, especially the Song of Solomon and the sayings of the major prophets, as prefigurations of their own dispensation. The ironic spectacle of Christians despising and persecuting Jews, to whom they owed so much, including their Savior, began fairly early in the history of Christianity. "When I see Christians, cursing Jews," Voltaire wrote in the eighteenth century, "me thinks I see children beating their fathers." [14]

Gradually, Christianity grew beyond the Jewish community. It was Paul, a Jew dramatically converted to Christianity not long after the death of Jesus, who became the first and most significant apostle to the gentiles. On numerous missionary voyages and in eloquent epistles he expounded the new faith and insisted on its universality. When around A.D. 50 the original followers of Jesus met to decide whether all Christians should be circumcised—that is, to profess themselves a Jewish sect—Paul vehemently opposed this policy and carried the day. His voluminous writings soon became, and have remained, a fertile source for Christian doctrine. By the second century, the age of the good Roman

[14] In English, in *Notebooks,* 2 vols., ed. Theodore Besterman (1952), I, 31.

emperors, Christians had formed rudimentary religious communities comprehending laymen and priest, the outlines of a creed and of a sacred service. Jesus' sayings, treasured by his disciples, had made no distinction between rich and poor; if anything, Jesus was more skeptical about the former than about the latter. The first gentile Christians, therefore, were among the deprived, the dispossessed, those to whom the material and cultural glories of the Roman Empire meant little. Then, repelled by the confusing welter of religious fanaticisms, Oriental superstitions, and philosophical nostrums that crowded the empire, a number of educated Romans found the new doctrine more convincing and more consoling than all the others.

Christianity had a concrete and fascinating tale to tell, which explained everything from the creation of the world to its end. The central tale, the martyrdom of Jesus, the Son of God, incarnated among men to take away their sins with his sacrifice and to bring love and the promise of eternal salvation, had an irresistible attraction. While Christian clerics anathematized one another on fine points of doctrine, their sect acquired converts, first among the lower orders, then among the educated. The Roman authorities, annoyed by Christian exclusiveness, subjected the new and growing sect to intermittent persecutions. These persecutions, which reached their peak at the end of the third century under the Emperor Diocletian, were severe enough to give the Christians martyrs to celebrate, not severe enough to inhibit their progress among the imperial population. Early in the fourth century, almost certainly in 312, Christianity won its most important convert: the Emperor Constantine himself. The future of Christianity was assured: in 325, Constantine called an unprecedented ecumenical council at Nicaea, which settled disputed questions of Christian doctrine; in 330, on the site of the ancient city of Byzantium, he dedicated a new city in the eastern part of his empire, Constantinople, to the Virgin Mary. Christianity became the favored religion, and by the fifth century the only religion, of the Roman Empire. The old tolerant attitude that had marked the pagan empire was gone: the upholders of Christian doctrine were nothing less than doctrinaire. In earlier days, the devotee of one religion was content to regard the devotee of another as a benighted outsider; with the ascendancy of Christianity there came a new spirit: the unbeliever was a sinner, to be reproved, corrected, and if necessary, eliminated. This was the price of universality.

The first centuries of Christianity were marked by continuous squabbles over church organization and religious doctrine. This is not surprising. At the heart of Christianity lay a dogma that the Christians themselves announced to be absurd: the Trinity. Against the vehement objections of an articulate minority, the Arians,[15] the Council of Nicaea had laid it down that Jesus, the

[15] The most controversial issue animating and exacerbating early debates among Christians was the nature of Jesus. The Arians, named after their founder, the Libyan theologian Arius (ca. 256-336), held that Jesus was the Son and creature of God the Father, neither eternal nor equal in substance with his creator. Arianism was widely popular among the German tribes invading the Roman Empire (see p. 22) and after its condemnation, went underground in Catholic Christendom.

Son of God, was consubstantial with His Father, and thus an equal partner in the Trinity which included as its third component the Holy Spirit. These three components of the Trinity were miraculously separate and united at the same time: three in one. This was to become the orthodox doctrine. Nor is this all: in its totality, Christianity demanded an entirely new conception of man and the universe, life and death, private and public life. The teachings of Jesus and Paul, as developed through four centuries, left no aspect of human activity untouched. The classical world, with all its mysticism and unworldly moments, had celebrated man, this life, and (in the best of times at least) political activity. Christians, too, were ready to live in this world and assign to work its importance and its dignity. While the first Christians had still lived in the vivid hope that the end of the world would come within their lifetime, later Christians resigned themselves to waiting and working and praying. In its essence, though, Christianity reversed the classical order of things: it exalted heaven over earth, eternal life over this life, universal love over patriotism, suffering over success, humility over pride, self-abnegation over sensuality. Perhaps most significant of all, Christianity made belief, not reason, central. The very absurdity of the Trinity, the improbability of Jesus' miracles and resurrection, the great demand made on men's imagination by the conception of a universal God who had made the world and who alone was entitled to worship—all this the Christians proclaimed not apologetically but triumphantly. Some of the church fathers, as later many of the leading Christian clerics, were powerful intellects, but they humbled their reason before their overriding urge to believe the mysteries that Scripture and its chosen interpreters offered them. As St. Anselm was to sum it all up late in the eleventh century: "*Credo ut intelligam*—I believe that I may understand." Here was the great reversal in a phrase: not understanding for the sake of belief, but belief for the sake of understanding.

Such a reversal could only come through and after considerable inner turmoil, and the writings of the greatest church fathers give plain, often moving witness to that turmoil. Classical culture—its philosophy, its poetry, its rhetoric—was a powerful presence to an educated Christian; it was a precious possession as well as a dangerous temptation to put the things of this world above the things of heaven. What was one to do with such an ambiguous legacy? The answer the church fathers gave to this question was to prove of decisive importance to early modern Europe, for it determined the way in which the classical inheritance was to be passed on through the centuries. Origen, in the early third century, and St. Jerome in the late fourth century—both men of wide classical erudition—offered a drastic solution that they had drawn from an Old Testament text: "When thou goest forth to war against thine enemies, and the Lord thy God hath delivered them into thine hands, and thou hast taken them captive, and seest among the captives a beautiful woman, and hast a desire unto her, that thou wouldst have her to thy wife; Then thou shalt bring her home to thine house; and she shall shave her head, and pare her nails; And she shall put the raiments of her captivity from off her, and shall remain in thine house." [16] In other words, shun classical civilization insofar as it provides enjoyment or a philosophy of life; exploit it for Christian purposes and nothing else. Jerome himself, in translating parts of the Old Testament and all of the New Testament into Latin, [17] followed his own prescription to the letter: he used his secular learning for devout purposes.

St. Augustine, the most influential of all the church fathers, whose writings left their mark on the course of Roman Catholicism and on the thinking of the Protestant rebels of the Reformation, solved the same problem with a different metaphor, also from the Old Testament: the children of Israel had left Egypt laden with the treasures of the country that had so long enslaved them; in the same way, he thought, Christians must loot classical culture of what they needed. Augustine was an extraordinary man. Born in Roman North Africa in 354, of a Christian mother, Augustine at first embraced varying forms of pagan belief and lived a worldly life. Then, as he records it in his magnificent *Confessions,* he had a dramatic conversion and put the world behind him. In a long lifetime—he died in 430—he wrote immensely, on dogma, against heretics, about organization, and became bishop of the city of Hippo, not far from where he was born. His main doctrinal opponents were the Pelagians, who took a sunny view of human nature and denied both man's fall and his original sin. In reply, Augustine developed a pessimistic view of man that stressed man's utterly lost condition after his fall, his helplessness without God, and the supreme importance of divine grace, which God could bestow without, as it were, giving his reasons. Calvin, as we shall see, would find this teaching particularly congenial. No one exemplified the great reversal more dramatically than Augustine: in *The City of God,* his greatest and best-known work, he developed the notion of the two cities—the one worldly, corrupt, and lost; the other divine, pure, and saved. Augustine, in his own way a good Roman, thought the Roman Empire to be the finest example of the city of man. But it too was of the devil; it too could make no absolute claim on man's ultimate loyalties—it was too wicked for that. Only the City of God, imperfectly realized on earth by the saintly Christian church and perfectly embodied in God's rule over all the saved, had a right to man's final allegiance. It is only natural that pagans should find such thinking not merely ridiculous, but disloyal and politically subversive as well.

Augustine's *City of God* is a substantial book, but it began as a polemic: in 410 the city of Rome had been sacked by the Visigothic king Alaric, a depressing demonstration of Rome's decay. Hunting for reasons, many pagans charged that the Christians, with their doctrines of humility and unworldliness, had sapped the will to fight. It was against this charge that Augustine wrote, and

[16] Deut. 21: 11–13.
[17] This became the basis of the Vulgate version of the Bible that remains the authoritative version of Scriptures for Roman Catholics.

it was in the course of his defense that he developed the conception of the two cities, which would reverberate through the Middle Ages, as popes and emperors struggled for supremacy (see p. 41). Whatever date a historian may choose to signalize the end of the Roman Empire, *The City of God* may serve as a premature, though wholly deserved, epitaph.

INTO THE "DARK AGES"

The Great Restlessness:
Migrations and Invasions, 400–700

Ever since Augustine, the decline and fall of the Roman Empire has exercised the ingenuity of commentators. The accusation that prompted Augustine to his strenuous rebuttal found persuasive spokesmen as late as the eighteenth century, but it has few defenders today: historians now treat the triumph of Christianity not as a cause of the decline but as a consequence. The same holds true of the event that provoked this charge against the Christians in the first place: a more effective state system than the empire had become by the early fifth century could have turned back or absorbed the barbarian invasions. The very size of the empire, the long peace, the precarious political structure, the economic decline of once prosperous provincial cities, the endemic unrest among an exploited servile labor force, all these and more doubtless played their part. But it is perhaps more pertinent to ask not why Rome fell, but how, given the inescapable vicissitudes of empires, it could have stood for so long.

Whatever our conclusion, it is clear that the Germanic invasions would have taxed the resources of the most resilient of political organizations. Since the first century after Christ, relations between Rome and its northern neighbors had been intermittently peaceful, sometimes even cordial. Some of the Germanic tribes were steadily on the move and harassed the frontiers of the Roman Empire. But many "barbarians" served in the Roman army, settled in imperial territory, intermarried freely, took positions in the public service, and became good Romans. One of these, the gifted, wily Vandal Stilicho, married the niece of Emperor Theodosius I and around 400 led the troops that prevented a Visigothic invasion of the Italian peninsula. The spread of Christianity after Constantine increased tensions between Rome and the Germanic tribes; partially and superficially Christianized, these tribes normally adopted Arianism (see p. 19) at a time when Arianism was being proscribed in Rome as a heinous heresy. Then, in the 370s, their sporadic wanderings became a general, almost panic-stricken movement. The reasons for these migrations were pressure on the food supply and pressure from the Huns in the East. The Huns were an Asian people, nomadic by habit, formidable cavalrymen. Earlier they had terrorized the Chinese in the East; in the fourth century, probably driven by hunger, they turned westward. Their hordes streamed first into the Volga basin and then into the Danube Valley, then into central Europe. Rome dealt with the menace by paying tribute and employing Hun troops as mercenaries; but by the middle of the fifth century the formidable Hunnish ruler, Attila, invaded Gaul and, in 452, Italy itself. He died the next year, and the Huns disappeared from the European scene as precipitously as they had come, but their legacy—large-scale shifts of populations—remained. One by one, the Germanic tribes wandered across the old imperial terrain. The Visigoths (or Western Goths) were at war with Roman emperors throughout the fourth century, took Rome in 410, then moved to southern Gaul and northern Spain, and established a short-lived kingdom with Toulouse as its first, and Toledo as its second, capital. Meanwhile the Ostrogoths (or Eastern Goths), settled in what is Hungary today and invaded Italy in the late 480s. The Vandals, whose ruthless exploitation of conquered lands became proverbial, came out of central Germany in the fifth century to conquer remote regions; by 406 they were in Gaul, in 409 they entered Spain, and in 429, North Africa; they took Carthage in 435, controlled the Mediterranean trade from African strongholds with their pirate ships, and forced Rome to acknowledge their independence. The Franks moved in the fifth century from the Rhineland into Gaul. And the Saxons, settled on the shores of northern Gaul, with their neighbors, the Angles, invaded the British Isles, first in marauding bands and then, in the middle of the fifth century, as permanent settlers. After Odoacer deposed Romulus Augustulus in 476, a chronicler sadly noted: "And so the Western Empire of the Roman people perished with this Augustulus—and from now on the Gothic kings possessed Rome and Italy."[18] The migrations slowed down, but political turmoil continued. In 489, the Ostrogoth Theodoric overthrew Odoacer; he was acting with the approval of the emperor at Constantinople, but, it turned out, in his own behalf: entrenched by 493, Theodoric made himself ruler of Italy. Then, early in the sixth century, Justinian, greatest of Byzantine emperors (see p. 26) tried to reunite in fact what was still united in law. His success was impressive though temporary: he reconquered North Africa from the Vandals and Italy from the Ostrogoths, and when he died in 565, much of the territory of the old Roman Empire was again under a single command. But three years later, in 568, another Germanic tribe, the Lombards, invaded Italy and undid most of Justinian's work. The barbarian rulers of the West were, by their lights, Christians and Romans, but from Constantinople, by its lights the capital of Rome and of civilization, they looked like upstarts and usurpers. As a military and political, even as a linguistic entity—Greek gradually replaced Latin—

---

[18] Quoted in J. M. Wallace-Hadrill, *The Barbarian West: The Early Middle Ages,* A.D. 400–1000 (Torchbook ed., 1962), 32.

Byzantium was separate from Rome; by tradition, and in legal fiction, the two remained one. [19]

Then, early in the seventh century, Byzantium was challenged by a new and far more formidable enemy—the Arabs. Their emergence and expansion constitute one of the extraordinary moments in Western history. No one seemed less likely to unite and conquer than the Arab tribes, nomadic for the most part, and even if settled, fiercely particularistic. But there was restlessness and spreading hunger, and among many Arabs, a certain urge toward unity and—the inescapable consequence of unity—expansion. As one ninth-century Arab poet was to put it, candidly:

> No, not for Paradise didst thou the nomad life forsake;
> Rather, I believe, it was thy yearning after bread and dates. [20]

Mahomet was a religious leader whom many followed for religious reasons, but much of the energy that underlay the triumph of his cause sprang from discontent that he galvanized and channeled. Born around 570 in Mecca, Mahomet heard the call to be prophet to the Arabs; his conversion was followed by a series of visions—some ecstatic, most of them supremely convenient—which supplied the outlines of his doctrines and of the political organization it implied. He made converts and enemies; when, in 622, he discovered a plot against his life, he moved from Mecca to the more sympathetic environment of Medina. This "departure"—the *hegira*—was the decisive event in the creation of Islam; the Arab calendar honors it by dating events from that year. In Medina, under the prodding of his followers and critics, Mahomet put his amalgam of prophetic and apocalyptic notions into some sort of order; later, his disciples gathered his revelation in the Koran, the Muslim's sacred book.

As Christianity was the ungrateful child of Judaism, Islam was the ungrateful child of Judaism and Christianity—in particular, Islam took up ideas popular but heretical in Rome and Byzantium alike. Mahomet was a severe, even fanatical monotheist: there is one god, and all the local Arab gods, or the various persons in the Christian Trinity, are chimeras; Jesus, Mahomet insisted, was a prophet, not a divinity. The good Muslim praises his God—Allah—and unconditionally submits himself to his will, recognizes in the terrible history of the world the wickedness of mankind, and prepares himself for the last judgment, which is near at hand, and for the future life, which will be heaven for the believer, hell for the infidel. It is not surprising that Christians should

---

[19] "There are higher things than facts; the Byzantine theory, fanciful as it sounds, was accepted for many centuries by friends and foes alike, and its influence in preserving the very existence of the Empire is incalculable." H. St. L. B. Moss, in Norman H. Baynes and H. St. L. B. Moss, *Byzantium: An Introduction to East Roman Civilization* (1948), 1.

[20] Quoted in Philip K. Hitti, *History of the Arabs from the Earliest Times to the Present* (5th ed., 1951), 144.

think of this "new" faith as just another heresy or that Mahomet should at first seek the cooperation of Jews and Christians living in the Arab world. It was only when they firmly rejected him that he furiously rejected them. Yet Mahomet's fury did not compromise the administrative flexibility of his successors: as in its origins Islam sought to be a comprehensive religion, later, as a conquering imperial power, Islam proved remarkably tolerant of other cultures and other sects.

Mahomet soon controlled Medina, and by 630, Mecca had fallen to him. Two years later he died, to be succeeded by able politicians and ambitious military leaders. The Arab conquest began with the conquest of Arabia itself. Then the world lay open; neither the Persian nor the Roman Empire was in any condition to resist united and energetic soldiers. Syria fell to Islam in 636, Palestine in 638, Egypt in 640, Persia in the 640s; by 669 all of North Africa was in Muslim hands; in 711 they invaded Spain and moved northward. It was not until 732, at the famous battle of Tours, that Charles Martel halted the assault and the wave of Islam receded.

From Justinian to Charlemagne

By the eighth century, then, the Mediterranean world, still the center of civilization, was divided among three large clusters of states, three more or less united empires. The Arabs, with their sprawling new acquisitions, rapidly adapted to, and even refined, the civilizations they found as they spread their soldiers and settlers across the Near East, Africa, and the southwest tip of Europe. Land warriors, they learned how to sail from the Syrians; tribal individualists, they learned how to administer large territories from all the Roman provinces they subdued. And in Alexandria, in Antioch, in Jerusalem, in southern Spain, they found Hellenistic learning and science and fell upon it with a fresh appetite. For the preservation of Greek philosophy, for the elaboration of Hellenistic mathematics, the Arab conquests, far from being a disaster, were a blessing.

In contrast, the German states of the north and west did little to preserve the political, economic, and cultural institutions they had inherited. Far less flexible than the Arabs, they kept up their tribal organization with its stress on local law, personal loyalty, and war as the most highly prized occupation. Cities that had been the pride of the old Roman provinces decayed, trade dried up, and for the most part, each region was reduced to economic self-sufficiency— which is to say, to poverty. In this unpromising soil, the higher arts could scarcely be expected to grow: the number of literate men dwindled with the general depression, and the number of memorable works produced in these centuries was vanishingly small. The most distinguished, perhaps the only, immortal book of those centuries is Boethius' *De consolatione philosophiae,* composed in prison after 510 by a Roman statesman unjustly accused of treason. The work was highly popular with Christian readers for centuries. The *Etymologiae*, by Bishop Isidore of Seville, an encyclopedia composed early in the seventh century in the Visigothic kingdom of Spain, reveals the cultural poverty of the Christian West. Wholly unoriginal, extremely credulous, intently pious, the *Etymologiae* is a crude, unreliable compilation of what little Isidore knew and understood of classical culture. The most lasting contribution the Germans of those centuries made to history was a myth—the myth of democratic self-government which corresponded only very roughly to their tribal elections.

Byzantium, the self-conscious guardian of civilization and Christendom alike, preserved much but created little. Its capital, Constantinople, was a magnificent city, heavily fortified, with splendid churches, palaces and public monuments, and a population that may have approached a million in the tenth century. The most enduring creation to emerge from the Byzantine Empire was characteristically Roman—the Justinian code, which brought together the mass of statutes and edicts, incoherent, inconsistent, often unclear, that together made up Roman law. Justinian acceded to power in 527, and in the next year, at his command, a commission began the great work of sorting out the so-called "new law"—the statutes of the late empire, followed in 530 by another commission detailed to master all the rest, the "old law," which went back into republican times. The result, flawed but immensely impressive, was the *Digest* or *Pandects*, a vast, many-volumed ordering of all the available material, magnificently summarized in a relatively brief textbook, the *Institutes.* If the immediate impact of this labor was negligible, its long-range effect was incalculable: however mixed up with later and irrelevant notions, the Justinian code enshrined the classical ideals of the sovereign ruler and of a public order under law—a set of ideas of great value to the states as they began to emerge from the feudal order, or disorder, from the thirteenth and fourteenth centuries onward.

In religious matters, Byzantium and Rome engaged in what we might call a hostile collaboration. The doctrine of the Trinity, laid down as orthodox at Nicaea and later, confronted wide and continuous challenges: according to orthodox teaching Jesus was a single being with a double nature, divine and human. The Nestorians argued that He was two persons, while the Monophysites would grant Jesus only one nature, the divine. Rome and Byzantium managed to defeat these and other heresies. But then, a series of issues arose to divide the eastern and western branches of the Roman Empire. Byzantine emperors—in this, as in so much else, the heirs of classical Rome—dismissed conflicts between church and state as unthinkable. In practice this meant subjection of clerical to imperial power: in the great iconoclastic controversy that raged in Byzantium from the eighth century on, emperors directly interfered with the popular worship of images, an interference vigorously denounced in the West. [21] Caesaropapism, the political theory that dominated Byzantium, was a sensible reflection of political realities: as the name implies, the ruler was, in his own way, pope. In Rome, meanwhile, different realities produced a different political theory. One by one, the Germanic tribes gave up their Arian heresy or converted directly from paganism to Roman Catholicism. In the 430s and 440s, St. Patrick brought Ireland into the Roman fold; later in that century (tradition says 496) Clovis, king of the Franks, took his tribe from Arianism and paganism into Catholicism; in 596, Augustine of Canterbury came on a mission from Rome to England and effected widespread conversions there; early in the seventh century, the Lombards in Italy, too, chose the Roman persuasion. While at Constantinople clerics continued to assert their equality with Rome, in the West the primacy of the bishop of Rome seemed secure. After all, it was in Rome that St. Peter was reported to have been martyred, and St. Peter was, in Jesus' celebrated pun, the rock on which His church was to be built. The disorders in the western reaches of the empire exposed the bishop of Rome to military and political threats, but it also freed him from imperial domination.

In the fifth century, Pope Gelasius laid down the doctrine of the "two swords." It would have been unthinkable in Byzantium, but it became the rallying point for political controversy in the West for centuries: God, Gelasius argued, had given man two swords, the secular and the religious, each to the proper personage. Now, since spiritual concerns are more exalted than worldly ones, the sword wielded by the religious powers had higher authority. And even before Gelasius wrote, Pope Innocent I had claimed that the popes held the apostolic succession in their hands and that Rome had jurisdiction over Christians everywhere. Self-serving legends strengthened this case: when Attila first approached, then turned back from Rome, pious Christians ascribed Attila's retreat not to the plague among his troops or shortage of supplies, but to the eloquence of Pope Leo I. But stories, no matter how affecting, were not enough: Roman Catholicism profited immensely from the rule of men like Gregory the Great (590–604), the first pontiff to make really serious claims for papal supremacy over all of Christendom and over secular powers alike. Gregory was a courageous statesman, vigorous administrator, scourge of heresy, and enemy to classical culture, and besides, the first monk to be pope. His elevation cemented a long-lasting alliance between monastic orders and the papacy. Ascetic monasticism—the organized retreat from a corrupt world— dated back to the early fourth century; it had received strong intellectual support from the leading church fathers. Early in the sixth century, Benedict founded a new and effective monastic order at Monte Cassino in central Italy,

---

[21] The iconoclasts—literally, the breakers of images—argued that realistic representations of the Virgin Mary and of Christ were a form of vulgar heresy in which the sheer humanity of sacred figures was unduly stressed; the opponents argued that to forbid representations of Christ was to deny the Incarnation.

and around 529, he laid down what came to be known as the Rule of St. Benedict. It provided for the governance of each monastery by an abbot and imposed monastic discipline and monastic duties—mainly prayer and work— with such clarity and eloquence that other orders soon followed its lead. With Pope Gregory, monasticism entered as a new, powerful element into the amalgam of papal influence. When on Christmas Day, in the year 800, Pope Leo III crowned the Frankish king Charles as emperor, this act reflected the prestige of Rome in the West—the prestige, though not the power: as long as Charles lived, the power was his.

Charles the Great, as he came to be called, had inherited a sizable estate: when he assumed sole rule over the Frankish territories in 771, he was master of what is today France, Belgium, the Netherlands, southern Germany, and Austria. Like his predecessors, Charlemagne cooperated with the papacy, and like them, he mobilized his resources for territorial expansion. In a series of strenuous campaigns, he subdued Lombard Italy all the way to Rome, extended his empire across northern and central Germany to the Elbe, reduced Bavaria to obedience, invaded pagan terrain on the lower Danube, crossed the Pyrenees into the Muslim Empire, took Barcelona, and incorporated a broad strip of northern Spain into his sprawling dominions. Wherever he went, he brought some measure of administrative centralization and Roman Catholicism with him, and for his lifetime at least, there was unity in the West once more, Christian and imperial. The man who came to Rome in 800 to be crowned came as a conqueror, not as a suppliant.

Charlemagne fostered the arts of peace quite as much as the arts of war. His measures to restore trade were rudimentary and paled before the exactions in money and men that his endless wars necessitated. In matters of higher culture he was more successful, though the popular name for his reign, "the Carolingian renaissance," considerably overstates his achievement. Scarcely literate himself, he surrounded himself with literary lights. The intellectual eminence of his reign is a comment on the flatness of the surrounding landscape; still, scholars from all across Europe flocked to his court at Aix-la-Chapelle. And there the palace school under the brilliant direction of the English cleric, Alcuin, and schools set up elsewhere sought to recall the fading glories of classical literature and a pure Latinity. But Charlemagne died in 814, and his "renaissance" died with him: the fire he had tried to light was only a spark, brilliant but ephemeral. When the Frankish historian Einhard wrote Charlemagne's life some time after the emperor's death, he looked back at the last reign with the nostalgia of one who has been expelled from a paradise of learning and greatness.

Charlemagne's empire, indeed, went the way of Alexander's: his son, Louis the Pious, could not hold his inheritance together, and before the ninth century was over, the West was divided once again among a series of small dynasties, which began to define, however roughly, such future states as France and Bavaria. Charlemagne's establishment of a new center of gravity in the north seems now, in long retrospect, the first glimmering of a European civilization, as distinct from the older civilization centered on the Mediterranean. But Europe would have to wait, both as an idea and as a reality. As Charlemagne's empire disintegrated, a new wave of restlessness swept across eastern and central Europe to disturb the tentative balance of powers. In the ninth century, the Magyars moved from the Caucasus across southern Russia into what are today Rumania and Hungary. Like the Huns before them, the Magyars were formidable horsemen and ruthless raiders. They were not stopped until the middle of the ninth century in a series of clashes with Saxonian emperors: Henry I, "the fowler," beat the Magyars at Riade in 933; his successor, Otto I, routed them decisively at the Lechfeld in 955. Confined to Hungary, the Magyars settled there and, around 1000, accepted Roman Catholicism.

The other wanderers were closely associated, though distinct, northern tribes—Danes, Swedes, Norwegians—who began to roam about the year 800. Their terrified victims called them Northmen or Vikings. They were inventive and intrepid sailors, as fierce on land as at sea. With their celebrated long ships, capable of carrying thirty oarsmen and swiftly driven on under huge square sails, the Vikings covered unprecedented distances. They raided Scotland, Ireland, the coast of France, Spain, and Italy. They penetrated deep into Russia, they sailed up the Seine and looted Paris, they briefly took and sacked Cologne and London. They ventured westward into unknown seas, discovered Iceland and Greenland; around 1000 they touched land in America. By the end of the ninth century, they began to settle down in some of the lands they had raided and terrorized before—mainly in Britain and in Normandy. And slowly, almost, one might say, reluctantly, they accepted the civilization about them by accepting baptism in the Roman Church. Yet the Romanization of Western Europe did not in itself produce a revival of civilization. The economic decay and political fragmentation had been too great, the strain imposed by incessant warfare and fearful migrations too severe, to permit such a revival quickly. When historians later looked back on these centuries and called them Dark Ages, they had some reason for using this derogatory epithet.

CHRISTIAN CENTURIES: 1000–1350

Early in the eleventh century, the West began to enjoy a great recovery. For three centuries or more, down to the 1340s, an emerging Europe confronted life with less gloom and more security than before. These are the centuries historians have called the High Middle Ages. The migrations were over. Population increased, and its gradual but uninterrupted growth was at once a cause and a consequence of the slow healing in economic, social, and political life. While the overwhelming mass of Europeans were, and remained, poor peasants, even they found conditions of existence less unstable than they had been. Towns flourished as they had not flourished since the decline of the Roman Empire. Old towns made good their losses in population and trade; new towns were born at strategic spots. Great rulers established great dynasties. In 987, Hugh Capet was elected king of the Western Franks, and his Capetian dynasty, which lasted to 1328, laid the foundations of what is France today. In 1066, William, duke of Normandy, called the Conqueror, invaded England, wrested control from the Anglo-Saxons, and established a particular version of feudal government that would remain unchallenged for a century and a half. This, too, was the age of parliaments—of representative bodies, mainly staffed by magnates, lay and clerical, meeting on occasion to advise the king and vote taxes: the Spanish *cortes,* the French estates, the German diets, the English parliament, date from the twelfth century onward. From being mere servants of the central government, the parliaments would become centers of aristocratic (and, to a lesser degree, urban) power and spokesmen for grievances; the great struggles of early modern history between kings and parliaments, which will mark succeeding chapters of this book, began in the High Middle Ages.

After centuries of dismal desolation, Christian scholarship bloomed once again, with significant assistance from savants but to the greater glory of the Christian god. Men of learning and letters found havens in cities, at courts, and in those new centers of scholarship and professional training, the universities. Architecture and the visual arts, chiefly though not exclusively ecclesiastical in inspiration, brought forth masterpieces and developed distinct styles. The Crusades, which engrossed the attention of secular and religious leaders from the early twelfth century on, were in part disasters and in part cruel farces, but they were also commercial ventures and played their part in that relentless economic and cultural expansion of Europe that would characterize the early modern period. The two swords of church and state, papacy and empire, were often in conflict, but their verbal and sometimes physical combat produced a rich literature in political theory.

The continual and effective threat that heresy posed to the Church of Rome brought persecutions, polemics on faith and obedience, and intermittent efforts at internal reform. In the eighteenth century, anti-Christian historians would deride the High Middle Ages as a time of chaos and credulity; in the early nineteenth century, Romantic historians would look back to the epoch as a time of glory and splendor, of religious unity and exciting personal adventure. Both these characterizations are partial: the High Middle Ages were neither as dismal nor as magnificent as that. But this much is certain: Europe had emerged from the Dark Ages.

Feudal Society

The type of social organization most prevalent in the West in these centuries was feudalism. "A subject peasantry"—this is how Marc Bloch defines its essential qualities—"widespread use of the service tenement (i.e., the fief) instead of a salary, which was out of the question; the supremacy of a class of specialized warriors; ties of obedience and protection which bind man to man and, within the warrior class, assume the distinctive form called vassalage; fragmentation of authority—leading inevitably to disorder; and, in the midst of all this, the survival of other forms of association, family and State."[22] Two terms require explanation here: "fief" and "vassalage." Feudalism was the child of disorganization and decay; later its critics would argue that it was also their father. The Roman political order had rested on the theory, and in its better days the fact, of sovereignty: the sovereign ruler, though responsible for, was not responsible to, the ruled, and the state he governed was a legal, bureaucratic, impersonal entity. As imperial administration collapsed, the sovereign power collapsed with it, and a personal contract emerged as a substitute. This contract was the heart of feudalism; it was a formal acknowledgment of differences in power among men and the need of the weak to obtain security and protection from the strong. The successful—a baron lording it over a province, a military adventurer holding a small castle, or merely the most prosperous farmer in the neighborhood—offered, often imposed, both. As time went by, this system of mutual aid developed into an elaborate ritualized ceremony: the "lord" granted land—a fief or benefice—to his "vassal," who in turn, swore fealty and homage. Both partners in this contract were free men, each had obligations to the other: one to dispense justice and give protection; the other to pay fixed dues, perform stated services, and do military duty.

Feudalism engendered an enormously intricate network of dependence: nearly all lords were also vassals of other, greater lords; nearly all vassals were also lords over other, less powerful vassals. Feudal kings were simply great lords standing in a contractual relationship to their lesser lords: Hugh Capet and his successors ruled not over subjects but over vassals. Thus vassalage tied together areas small and large and imposed obligations on the proudest of men. With the decline (though not disappearance) of a money economy and the increased parochialism of life, feudalism seemed a natural expression of the great fragmentation of authority. Yet feudal institutions differed from region to region. They emerged first in the area of Charlemagne's Empire—Burgundy, central France, and the German Rhineland—and remained most characteristic there. Elsewhere, in England, northern Italy, Spain, central Germany, they assumed special forms; beyond those frontiers, in Scandinavia and Byzantium, they never sank deep roots. The whole system, it can be imagined, was a lawyer's paradise.

Feudal society was larger than the feudal contract. As Marc Bloch's definition makes plain, a subject peasantry was indispensable to the system: someone had to till the soil and weave the cloth that others might carouse and fight and pray at leisure. The peasant did not have the privilege of offering homage: that was reserved to the small elite of landowners and military men.

---

[22] Marc Bloch, *Feudal Society* (1961), II, 446.

Nor was the manor—the kind of organized village in which most of Europe's peasants lived—a feudal institution: manorialism antedated and outlived feudalism. Yet the two, feudalism and manorialism, had enough in common to sustain and support one another in these medieval centuries. The manor was a large estate, usually comprising several small villages and perhaps a hundred peasant households, held by a lord or a monastery. It included the land reserved for the proprietor—the demesne—which the villagers farmed for him; the land held by the peasants;[23] and the land—forest and pasture—enjoyed in common by all. The lord or his representative normally lived nearby and administered justice over his domain: jurisdiction was strictly local.

The status of the peasant varied from place to place and even within a given manor; few peasants were formally slaves, but most were serfs, bound to the soil by grinding obligations. They had to labor a number of stated days on the lord's land, pay fees for the equipment the lord compelled them to use, work on the roads, repair bridges and buildings, hand over part of their harvest to the lord or the local cleric. In Catholic Europe, the manor was not merely a social, economic, and judicial, but also a religious, unit. The peasant formed a distinct dependent class—he was called villein, *vilain, Holde,* rustic—and he lived in steady fear of losing what little freedom he had. Poverty was built into his life; escape was hard. The peasant was a beast of burden with a host of duties and a handful of rights—the victim of nature, of his crude superstitions, and of his endemic undernourishment. It is true that medieval agriculture made significant improvements. Humble innovations had great consequences. The introduction of a heavy plough permitted reduction of effort and the exploitation of strips of land and types of soil hitherto inaccessible. The harness, another medieval contribution, made horsepower widely available for heavy-duty labor. The three-field system, which appeared in Europe in the time of Charlemagne, by leaving one third of the land fallow for a year, brought more land into cultivation and improved general productivity.[24] But the peasant's life was, for the most part, nasty, brutish, and short. No wonder that on the rare occasion when he rose up, in those brief moments of triumph against the feudal elite—they were never more than brief—he was pitiless in his primitive rage.

The Recovery of Urban Life

Feudalism was in its essence a recognition, indeed a celebration, of decentralization. But the towns that grew up during the feudal centuries were the mark and agent of concentration. In its legal order, its economic pursuits, its styles of

---

[23] Though at the beginning of the feudal age, peasant tenure of land had been "precarious," by the twelfth century it was in effect in hereditary possession. See Henri Pirenne, *Economic and Social History of Medieval Europe* (tr. 1936), chap. III.

[24] For details, see Lynn White, Jr., *Medieval Technology and Social Change* (1962).

thinking, the medieval town was a rival, often an enemy, to the agricultural world around it.

There is no single rule for this urban recovery. Some medieval towns grew on ancient foundations, some clustered near natural harbors, at crossroads, close to natural resources, on navigable rivers, around fortified castles. Towns were the knots formed by the necessities of medieval life: they were the seats of bishops, marketplaces, banking centers, hostels for traveling merchants, bastions of defense, headquarters for officials governing the surrounding region. They were also, notoriously, hospitable to innovation. The townsman was less tied to tradition than the peasant who lived only a few steps away from him—he talked to visiting merchants, his occupational specialization impelled him into literacy, strangers made the strange familiar and thus acceptable. The hatred of novelty and modernity that has characterized conservatives through the centuries has always been accompanied by hatred of the town.

Not unexpectedly, the growth of medieval towns followed the establishment of security and the patterns of trade. Byzantium boasted Constantinople, in which most of its wealth, talent, and urban population were concentrated; the Muslims built cities wherever they went—from Cordova to Cairo and beyond. In Roman Catholic Europe, the first impressive towns grew up in the Mediterranean, on the North Sea, and in Flanders: by around 1300, Milan and Venice surpassed one hundred thousand inhabitants, while leading Flemish cities like Bruges and Ghent rarely exceeded forty thousand. Paris, already a great commercial and intellectual center in those years, had eighty thousand inhabitants, twice as many as London.[25] Clearly, our judgment of what is impressive is a relative one.

Many European towns began as fortified centers of defense—*bourgs*—against invaders or marauders. Then, when life became more secure and commerce more active, settlers burst the bounds of the wall and moved beyond the *bourg* itself to the suburb or *faubourg*. And this suburb, as the Belgian historian Henri Pirenne long insisted, was the real nucleus of most medieval towns: it was in the *faubourg* that traveling merchants or migratory craftsmen settled down to a new kind of stable existence; the great medieval fairs that formed such a distinctive feature of economic life were ways of organizing the migration of goods instead of men.

Once formed and dynamically expanding, the towns developed their own political needs. Their relations with the surrounding countryside and with their feudal neighbors were normally tense, but all needed one another too much to permit unmitigated isolation or incessant warfare. Townsmen, increasingly specialized in their activities, needed food and raw materials from the countryside; the countryside could use some of their finished goods; local lords

[25] See John H. Mundy, "Medieval Urbanism," in John H. Mundy and Peter Riesenberg, *The Medieval Town* (1958), 30.

needed assistance in their struggle against greater, more remote lords. What the towns wanted most was what they called "freedom"—freedom from feudal obligations to neighboring lords, freedom to arrange their own commercial affairs, to regulate apprenticeship, to supervise merchandise, to levy tariffs on incoming merchants or merchandise. *"Stadtluft macht frei*—town air gives freedom" was a celebrated slogan, and it was true enough that once towns won their charters of liberty from a feudal magnate, they could control their own affairs, raise their own taxes, and protect their own residents—even "rustics" who had fled to the town to escape their duties elsewhere. "If a villein come to reside in the borough," so ran a typical twelfth-century declaration of Newcastle-upon-Tyne, "and shall remain as a burgess in the borough for a year and a day, he shall thereafter always remain there, unless there was a previous agreement between him and his lord for him to remain there for a certain time." [26]

Though tearing at the feudal network and jealously ready to fight for all its privileges, the medieval town was by no means destructive of authority. It simply built up its own distinctive structure of authority. Most towns were dominated by small patriciates, open to recruitment from outside or from below, but small in number and authoritarian in temper. From the beginning of the eleventh century, these ruling groups organized themselves into gilds. Some gilds, mainly in the Mediterranean region, were specialized interest groups guarding the privileges of merchants, bankers, clothmakers; others, mainly in the north, were comprehensive social organizations with functions not merely economic but social, political, and even military. Gradually, the southern pattern prevailed: gilds grew into authorized instruments bringing apprentices into the system; regulating the wages, hours, and quality of work; and influencing local government for their own particular purposes. In the early thirteenth century, there was one gild for the cloth industry of Toulouse, and at the end of the century there were five. In the middle of the thirteenth century, there were 101 gilds in the city of Paris alone. [27] The gilds were pressure groups, training centers, monopolies. They were also, in those towns in which lesser trades and industries managed to organize themselves, the way to social status and a certain degree of political influence for the lower orders. Urban life in the Middle Ages was in most respects corporate: men lived huddled together within ever-expanding walls, walked on narrow streets, prayed in crowded churches, with the sounds, sights, and smells of the town all about them. Churches, monasteries, hospitals, orphanages, boastful gild halls—these were the crowded backdrop for colorful festivals, sanguinary uprisings, fervent religious revivals. The medieval town was one center of intellectual ferment. The church was the other.

[26] "The Customs of Newcastle-Upon-Tyne in the Time of Henry I, 1068–1135," in ibid., 138.
[27] Ibid., 64, 65.

The Christian Style

The Middle Ages pursued secular interests as strenuously as one might expect from any advanced complex civilization. But it does not follow that it was hypocritical in its religious professions. Commerce had its uses: the great fairs at Champagne or at Frankfurt, where merchants from across Europe gathered all the year round, the weaving cities of Flanders, or the banking centers in northern Italy underscore the importance that medieval men attached to trade. Work had its dignity: pious sculptors carved representations of handicrafts on cathedral doors. Power on earth was worth fighting for: even pious popes recognized that. The most ascetic of churchmen never thought to turn all Christians into monks and nuns. But in the great chain of being, the universal hierarchy with God at the top and inanimate matter at the bottom, religious concerns had a higher place than secular ones; philosophy was a science, but theology was the queen of the sciences and philosophy its servant. Christianity was not a superstition; in fact it acted, with its bold missions into pagan territory, as the enemy of primitive superstitions. But religion was the overriding, dominant purpose of life, even—perhaps especially—the life of the learned. All important social institutions and private events—birth, marriage, death, holidays (the name is significant), even war—stood under the sign of the sacred. The vogue of giving natural phenomena and literary works an allegorical interpretation illustrates this pervasive turn of mind: all, the book of nature and the books of men alike, were reflections of the divine handiwork, which manifested itself in the world in many marvelous guises. Reason had its part to play but revelation was a purer, more reliable source of knowledge. Science was the devout search for God's traces in the natural world—no wonder it accomplished so little (see p. 232). As St. Thomas Aquinas would put it later in the thirteenth century, in his characteristic Aristotelian fashion: "The natural end of a people formed into a society is to live virtuously; for the end of any society is the same as that of the individuals composing it. But, since the virtuous man is also determined to a further end, the purpose of society is not merely that man should live virtuously, but that by virtue he should come to the enjoyment of God."[28] The church, with its lofty spires and its cruciform shape, dominated the medieval landscape, literally as well as figuratively.

Despite all the energetic, often desperate attempts of Rome to impose unity and uniformity, medieval modes of religious thinking and feeling were often a jangling discord. Many historians have found it convenient to assert, and many students convenient to repeat, that heretics and fanatics were little more than occasional and unwelcome intrusions on the happy and united family of Christendom. But a Roman Catholic Europe, at one in its piety, each

[28] *De regimine principum,* quoted by E. F. Jacob, "Political Thought," in C. G. Crump and E. F. Jacob, *The Legacy of the Middle Ages* (1926), 518. For Aquinas and Aristotelianism see p. 39.

believer secure in his place, each worshipping in the same way with the same fervor in the same kind of Gothic edifice, is no more than a picturesque myth. To begin with, the schism between East and West—between the Greek Orthodox and the Roman Catholic churches—which had had its inception in the physical division of the Roman Empire and intensified with the iconoclast controversy (see p. 26) became official and final in 1054. And within Western Christianity itself, heresies were ever-present perils to Catholic claims.

In the twelfth century, two large-scale movements, the Albigensians and the Waldensians, arose in southern and central France and spread their teachings to neighboring Spanish and Italian territories. The Albigensians were an offshoot of the old Manichean tradition that no amount of Christian propaganda and pious persecution had ever wholly silenced: they taught that the world is divided between two forces, good and evil, the first of the spirit and the second of the flesh. Rome, an organized clergy, and the sacraments, the Albigensians insisted, belonged to the wicked world of the flesh; the "perfect" church, in contrast, was in the heart of pure men. In accord with such doctrines, the Albigensians exacted celibacy, pacifism, and communism. The Waldensians, less metaphysical, were almost as ascetic: in their yearning for the simple purity of the primitive Church, they called for poverty and continence. Such unworldly perfection was intolerable, especially since the two movements mustered a following of alarming size; early in the thirteenth century, after a "crusade" called by Pope Innocent III (see p. 43) they were forced underground by vigorous military action and ruthless repression.

But the triumphant conclusion of this crusade was not the end of heresy. There were many preachers like Peter Waldo, the Lyon merchant whose itinerant sermons had given the impetus for the Waldensians—inspired, self-appointed men of God who wandered across Europe, exhorting their followers to reject the flesh and prepare for the end of the world. The line between exceptional sanctity and damnable heresy was thin and shifting. St. Francis and St. Dominic, who early in the thirteenth century founded two great orders of friars who lived in the world by begging, remained firmly within the Roman communion, as did most of their followers; and, by remaining, they validated some of the papacy's claim to spiritual preeminence. But the ostentatious piety and purity of the Franciscans and the Dominicans were an ambiguous support for Catholicism; many troubled believers saw them as a standing reproach to clerical wealth and worldliness, and as a standing invitation to reform.

In the midst of this ferment, the bishop of Rome tightened his hold on the imagination and the religious institutions of the West. In the time of Charlemagne, and for nearly two centuries after, the papacy had been politically impotent, spiritually corrupt, and religiously insignificant; the holders of St. Peter's Chair practiced most of the sins in the calendar, from sexual incontinence to the cynical sale of sacred office, and all in the glare of public indifference or disapproval. Whatever moral and institutional authority the Western church retained rested with a handful of competent and honest bishops. It is significant that the revival of the papacy and the restoration of Western Christendom should begin not at Rome but in eastern France, at Cluny. The Cluniac reform was initiated in 910, with the founding of a Benedictine house. There was nothing novel about its aims and regulations, but in the tenth century a conscientious return to the Rule of St. Benedict (see p. 28) was nothing less than a radical reformation. Soon there were hundreds of monastic houses that followed Cluny and acknowledged its authority, while other independent, new foundations imitated Cluny's pious severity. Monastic celibacy and visible abhorrence of clerical corruption became popular slogans and even popular practices. The papacy, with which Cluny and its daughter houses maintained direct and cordial relations, would benefit enormously from the Cluniac reform. In the midst of papal corruption and impotence, the Cluniacs proclaimed their confidence in Rome. It was a self-fulfilling prophecy: the Cluniacs' confident assertion of papal purity and power helped to secure both. [29]

Other new institutions, the universities, were a rather more ambivalent source of strength to Catholic Christendom. In typical medieval fashion, the universities started as, or quickly turned into, corporations; and, like other corporations, they struggled to obtain charters and jealously watched over the "liberties" they had won. Bologna, founded before 1100 and soon celebrated for its preeminence in the canon law, was organized by the students, who treated their professors strictly as employees; Paris, formally founded around 1200, and the chosen center for theology, was organized by its professors. The universities were battlefields, and the battles did not confine themselves to words: town-gown riots, which claimed numerous victims, were frequent; student-faculty clashes, equally frequent, led to boycotts of classes and migrations of scholars. Students from Bologna set up the University of Pisa; after riots in Paris in 1228 and 1229, students wandered far afield to found new universities elsewhere or, as in Oxford and Cambridge, to swell the tiny number of students already there. There were other battles: between the doctors who were the real professors but few in number, and the masters of arts, lower in prestige, less well trained than the doctors, but numerous and popular within their special provinces—philosophy and science. [30] And there were continuous struggles with the outside world, which supported the universities and sought their support in turn: breeders of bureaucrats and bishops, they fed the spreading apparatus of religious and secular government; centers of debate and new ideas, they were a threat to cautious or autocratic conservatives. "For the popes," Friedrich Heer has written, "the universities were the object of their highest hopes and the occasion of their deepest

---

[29] For later relations of Cluny and the papacy, see p. 42.
[30] It was the masters of arts who were in charge of the seven liberal arts—the *trivium* (logic, rhetoric, grammar) and the *quadrivium* (music, geometry, arithmetic, astronomy).

disappointment."[31] The very qualities that made the universities indispensable also made them dangerous.

From the eleventh century on, and during the intellectually vigorous twelfth and thirteenth centuries, Western Christendom had much to debate about. With the intellectual revival, independent spirits began to object, not to the truth of Christian revelation—that everyone accepted—but to a naive or slavish reliance on authority. A small but influential band of "school philosophers"—the Scholastics—boldly began to approach theological issues with philosophical questions, thus bringing reason into areas from which Augustine and his followers had banished it long before. Scholasticism goes back to the ninth century, to John Scotus Erigena, part mystic, part metaphysician, heir of the Neoplatonists, and for all his mysticism a doughty defender of the place of reason in religious inquiry. In the eleventh century St. Anselm, an Italian cleric who ended his long career as archbishop of Canterbury in England, offered a philosophical proof for the existence of God—the so-called "ontological proof," which holds that since we can conceive of God, God must indeed exist. Anselm, like all the Scholastics, was a devout believer, and he placed belief first—was he not author of that saying, *"credo ut intelligam*—I believe that I may understand"? (See p. 20.) But it is significant that he thought it useful, and possible, to approach one of the profoundest of religious mysteries by the avenue of philosophical inquiry.

After the Scholastics had fallen into discredit in later centuries, it was easy to make fun of their abstruse concerns. "How many angels can dance on the head of a pin?" This is the kind of question that sarcastic critics would consider typical of Scholastic hair-splitting. Actually, in the High Middle Ages, Scholastic disputes had powerful theological and political reverberations. The great debate between Realists and Nominalists is one instance of such a dispute that now interests only the specialist in medieval philosophy but then exercised educated men everywhere. The Realists argued that universal terms like "humanity" or "church" referred to real substances, so that individual men or particular clerics were instances of a greater whole. The Nominalists, on the other side, held such words to be mere names, linguistic conveniences, and that individual entities alone were real. While there were Nominalists who were orthodox, it was Realism that was most serviceable to Roman Catholic doctrine: it permitted men to accept that strange universal, the Trinity; and that perfect institution, the church, amidst overwhelming evidence that it was corrupt, incompetent, or worldly. With Peter Abelard, one of the most inventive of the Scholastics, whose debating techniques did much to advance the Scholastic method of argumentation, the practical consequences of such thinking began to emerge: sometime around 1122, Abelard published his *Sic et Non*, a treatise that listed statements on 158 questions from the Scriptures and the church fathers, statements that patently contradicted one another. The lesson Abelard

[31] *The Medieval World* (tr. 1962), 241.

wished to impart was plain: however great the authority of Augustine and Jerome and the other fathers, they had not said the final word on the True Faith; that Faith, indeed, deserved the most scrupulous and most intelligent examination that Christians could bring to bear on it. "By doubting," Abelard said, "we come to examine, and by examining we reach the truth." Here was the new spirit at work. It is not an accident that Abelard should have spent much time in Paris and have been a most popular lecturer there.

Abelard died in 1142. Not long after his death the Christian West received the writings of Aristotle, largely through the mediation of Arabic and Jewish commentaries. The center of diffusion was Muslim Spain. There, by the 1150s, most of Aristotle's chief works, including his *Metaphysics* and his writings on ethics and logic, had been translated into Latin. Aristotle provided exhilarating but also unsettling reading: he was unmistakably a pagan, but his encyclopedic knowledge and his rigorous logic impressed themselves deeply on learned men who, however devout, thirsted for rational discussion. The very source of the Aristotelian revival was suspect: the Arabic translators and commentators, among whom Averroes of Cordova, Abelard's younger contemporary, was only the most recent and most persuasive, proclaimed doctrines wholly unacceptable to Roman orthodoxy. His Christian disciples interpreted Averroes' reading of Aristotle as an invitation to separate philosophy from theology, and thus to complete autonomy for rational inquiry. No school of Christian thought could tolerate that: it was the road to heresy if not outright secularism. Yet the intellectual power of Aristotle and his Arab commentators would not be denied. The first response of the official guardians of Roman Christendom was rejection: in 1210, the University of Paris was enjoined from reading any work of Aristotle or his interpreters; in the 1230s, when it became evident that Aristotle was irresistible, theologians made attempts to prune his writings and to keep what might be useful. But in 1277, there was a great purge at Paris: the Latin Averroists were proscribed, and even the great work of accommodation performed by St. Thomas Aquinas came under severe censure.

By that date, Aquinas had been dead for three years. Like his teacher and colleague, Albert the Great, a Dominican and a professor at Paris, Aquinas was a great controversialist but, beyond that, a great compromiser. The old question that had plagued Christian thinkers as far back as St. Augustine and beyond— what is the place of classical philosophy in the Christian religion? or, more generally, what is the place of reason in theology?—stood at the forefront of his philosophizing. Aquinas opened his most celebrated treatise, the *Summa theologiae*, with an elaborate discussion of just that issue. His conclusion was perfectly orthodox: Thomas was a rationalist in the service of Christianity. The "philosophical sciences," he wrote, "investigated by reason," are fruitful but inferior to the "sacred science of God and the blessed," which discovers its truths through revelation. Hence, he concluded, using a familiar metaphor, theology uses other disciplines, including philosophy, as its *ancillae*—its handmaidens.

Yet Thomas Aquinas was profoundly suspicious of the anti-intellectualism of those who denigrated secular learning, classical philosophy, or rational argumentation as instances of an impious worldliness. Reason and revelation, far from contradicting, complement and support one another. Thus Thomas found it possible to offer rational proofs for most of the truths of Christianity, including the existence of God, the supremacy of the Roman Church, and the hierarchical character of the universe. Through careful dialectical exposition, Thomas states all the objections to the position he wishes to defend and first examines, then refutes them, to allow the Christian truth to stand forth, triumphant and reasonable. Only the central mysteries—the Trinity and the miraculous event of transubstantiation in the mass—were beyond such rational demonstration.

The work of Thomas Aquinas was the finest achievement of Scholasticism: St. Thomas was a moderate without being a waverer. On the delicate question of universals, he was a moderate Realist; on the equally delicate question of political authority, he was a moderate royalist. In explicating the hierarchy of laws under which the world is governed, he put Eternal Law—God's rational wisdom—first and gave prominence to what he called Divine Law—God's special manifestations to man, His revelations. But he found a place also for Natural Law, the divinely prescribed but rationally comprehensible set of unchanging rules by which men and nature live, and for Human Law. Thomas' task was reconciliation.

But after the death of Aquinas, Scholasticism declined. What had been a scrupulous search for distinctions and logical affinities indeed degenerated into a pedantic splitting of hairs. In part, this was because Thomas had built his system so well. But also a new extreme distrust of reason and pagan thinking pervaded the church, and its leading theologians gave reasons for the impotence of reason. Thomism did not revive until the late fifteenth and early sixteenth centuries, just in time to aid those Roman Catholics who sought to preserve learning and rational argumentation amidst the storms of the Reformation and against the pressures of arch-conservatives in the time of the Counter-Reformation (see p. 164). If it took until 1879 for Thomas' system to become the official theology of the Roman Catholic Church [32] it had been the favored philosophical system of Catholic theologians for some centuries before.

The architectonic grandeur of Thomas Aquinas' life work has tempted some historians to liken it to a Gothic cathedral. But all attempts to discover affinities or mutual influences between Scholasticism and Gothic architecture remain speculation. The Christian art of those centuries has a grandeur all its own. Of that art, the Gothic cathedrals are only the most celebrated. Actually, the Gothic style was a relatively late achievement; it emerged with dramatic suddenness around 1140 at the Abbey of St. Denis, near Paris. We do not know the name of its architect; we do know who was responsible for the building:

---

[32] It was Pope Leo XIII who so declared it, in his encyclical *Aeterni patris.*

Abbé Suger, lover of the arts, biographer, influential advisor to Louis VI and Louis VII of France. There, at St. Denis, Suger's architect brought together the characteristics that other architects had been tentatively and separately employing in churches in and around Paris. The Gothic style, with its flying buttress and, above all, its pointed arch and rib vault[33] was an instant success. Within a few decades tall cathedrals sprang up in central France and in England: Notre Dame of Paris was begun around 1163; Lincoln around 1192; the new Gothic cathedral of Chartres around 1194; Rheims in 1211; Amiens and Salisbury in 1220. The Romanesque style, which the Gothic replaced with such unaccustomed rapidity, had been impressive in its own way: one need only stand in the lofty Romanesque nave of the cathedral at Durham, begun at the end of the eleventh century, or of La Madeleine at Vézelay, built slightly later, to recognize the Romanesque style as something better than pedestrian or earth-bound. With its strong barrel vaults held up by its sturdy piers, the Romanesque church was powerful, stable, secure. The Gothic church in contrast, with its thin piers, its walls pierced by glass, its soaring towers or spires, was a spectacular expression of energy. Everything was calculated to move the eye eastward and upward. Those who commissioned and built them (if not perhaps all those who worshiped there) saw the cathedrals as a spiritual triumph, a symbol of faith, and quite literally, a foretaste of heaven. With the art of cathedral building, the arts of sculpture and of stained-glass making advanced apace: doors, walls, pillars needed decoration that would support and enhance the general impression of lofty sanctity. It has become a commonplace to call these Gothic masterpieces sermons in stones, but this is what they were.

Literature, despite many digressions into worldliness, expressed what the church buildings suggested. Dante's *Divine Comedy*, as imperishable an achievement in poetry as Chartres cathedral is in architecture, was, of course, primarily a poem: Dante, the scholar who wrote his treatises in Latin, put his greatest work into Italian, into the splendid music of the *terza rima.* But the *Commedia* is more than a poem: it is the account of a religious pilgrimage, the voyage of a human sinner through the inferno and purgatory into paradise. It was the destination medieval men all devoutly prayed for.

The Two Swords Drawn: Papacy Against Empire

But men must live. They must work, forget their sorrows in drinking and raucous humor, express their sensuality. Much of the literature of the Middle Ages, though all of it necessarily stood under the sign of Christendom, toyed with heresy and with proscribed notions. The Goliard poets—mainly wandering students and rootless priests—spread their ribald songs, their celebrations

---

[33] For the most convenient definition, see amidst a vast literature, Nikolaus Pevsner, *An Outline of European Architecture* (7th ed., 1962), 89.

of women and drinking, and their impudent assaults on orthodox religion, across Europe from the middle of the eleventh century on. The rich literature of chivalry, composed and sung by the troubadours, though professing piety and soaked in mystical meanings, sang of the complex ritual of courtly love and of heroism in war. Even Dante, perhaps the greatest architect that Christian poetry has ever had, gave respectful hospitality in the *Divine Comedy* to most of the heretical ideas that the popes and the clergy were doing their utmost to extirpate. Nor is this all. The popes, the vicars of Christ on earth, were wholly engaged in the struggle for worldly power. This was doubtless inevitable: power is a limited and scarce commodity, and papal attempts to control territories in Italy, bishops in outlying districts, and nominations to high clerical posts affronted the competing interests of other men. So the papacy, endowed with the spiritual sword, stood with sword drawn through most of the Middle Ages.

The resurgence of the papacy dates from the middle of the eleventh century. Some vigorous Cluniacs became vigorous popes (see p. 37), and the Italian Benedictine cardinal Hildebrand, who became Pope Gregory VII in 1073, had cordial relations with the Cluniac reformers. Hildebrand had been a powerful cardinal in Rome and an effective reformer for decades before his accession. Like his early predecessor and chosen model, Gregory the Great (see p. 27), Gregory VII was one of those rare historical personages who do more than merely embody current tendencies—he set his seal indelibly on Catholic Christendom. But his was a long-range, largely posthumous triumph; the twelve years of his papacy were marked by great claims and great defeats.

In 1059, under Hildebrand's prodding, Pope Nicholas II had decreed that the election of the pope must be taken out of the hands of the Roman nobility and placed into the hands of a college of cardinals; in the same year, under the same prodding, he forbade clerics to marry and declared the appointment to bishoprics to be wholly the pope's business. After his election to the papacy, Gregory VII reiterated these policies. A man of great vigor and great courage, of moderate but useful learning, Hildebrand insisted that the Church of Rome is the guardian of the Christian faith—infallible now and always. The pope, it followed, is sovereign ruler over the church and, being judge of all men, including emperors, can have no earthly judge. Thus, Gregory VII held, the pope alone can call a general synod and alone appoint, depose, or transfer bishops. He can even depose emperors. The emperor of the day, Henry IV, was hardly inclined to bow to such principles. When in 1075 the Synod of Rome officially reiterated the prohibition against lay investiture of bishops, Henry balked. Like many other rulers after him, the emperor was unwilling to surrender the rich patronage and the influence that his right to invest bishops gave him. In 1076, he called a counter-synod at Worms, which obediently deposed Pope Gregory; and, in a strong letter to the pope, he developed his own political theory: the emperor, like the pope, is immediately responsible only to God. Gregory in turn excommunicated the emperor. The great investiture controversy had begun. Faced with a rebellion of German nobles, Henry IV decided to make concessions; he crossed the Alps in midwinter into Italy, and in January 1077, at Canossa, after reputedly standing in the snow for three days, he obtained absolution. "Going to Canossa" was a profound, and became a proverbial, humiliation of the secular before the religious power. But it was Henry's last concession: until Gregory's death in 1085, the emperor made war on the pope and eventually drove him from Rome to die in exile, part guest, part prisoner of his Norman allies. The war of words and arms continued, temporarily appeased in 1122 with a compromise, the Concordat of Worms, which kept the right of investing bishops and abbots in the hands of the church, but specified that insofar as these princes of the church were also feudal landowners—and they all were—their feudal obligations to the secular power, the emperor, would continue in force. It was not until over a century after Gregory's death, with the accession of Pope Innocent III, that his claims were reiterated once again with a sound of real authority.

The importance of Innocent's pontificate lay not in its length—it lasted only from 1198 to 1216—but in its vigor. Innocent did not invent new ideas but acted effectively on old ones. Like Gregory VII, he was tenacious and courageous, an incomparable administrator. He recaptured and enlarged the central Italian lands that had intermittently belonged to the papacy. He reorganized his administration to serve the purposes of a multifarious regime with interests all across Europe. He recognized the potential value of the Franciscans and Dominicans—two orders that had their inception during his reign. He intervened in imperial elections and in domestic politics in several countries as far away as England: by 1213 he had compelled King John, "John Lackland," to grant the lands of England to the Holy See of Rome and receive them back as the pope's vassal. The baronial rebellion that compelled John to affix his seal to the Magna Carta at Runnymede in 1215 grew directly from these concessions to Rome. And in the year of Magna Carta, Innocent assembled the Fourth Lateran Council in Rome, a vast affair crowded with hundreds of princes of the church and representatives of the secular sword; it was at this council that the Church of Rome reiterated its spiritual supremacy over the Christian world. Once again, old ideas received new and definitive formulation: the council declared the sacraments to be "the channels of grace" and the Eucharist—the mass—to be the chief of these channels. It proclaimed the miraculous event of the mass, transubstantiation, as dogma binding on all Christians. It regulated traffic in relics, tightened regulations of monastic life, condemned heresy, and declared the Church of Rome to be one and universal: Gregory VII's political claims were here put into sacred language.

The only conspicuous failure of Innocent III's papacy was the Fourth Crusade, undertaken at the pope's urging. This, too, was an old idea: the notion of crusades had originated in penitential pilgrimages undertaken by Christians to the holy places in Palestine. The early Muslims, tolerant, permitted these pious incursions, but when news came that the Muslim occupants of Jerusalem were persecuting pilgrims and desecrating the Holy Sepulchre, the papacy invited the fighting elite of Europe to take the cross and recapture the Holy Land for Christianity. The First Crusade, preached by Pope Urban II, began in 1095; the Ninth Crusade ended in 1272 with the fall of the last Christian stronghold to Muslim troops. In between, there were official and unofficial crusades, preached and undertaken for a wide variety of reasons. The papacy had religious reasons for seeking the recapture of holy Jerusalem but, as cynics have not failed to point out, some popes at least thought it useful to be publicly identified as the leading champion of Christendom, while other popes, it seems, were pleased to have unemployed and restless European noblemen vent their energies on infidels in the Near East rather than on Christians nearer home. The crusaders themselves ranged across the spectrum of human motivation: sincere believers jostled those lusting for adventure and others hungering for land. Most of the Crusades marched under the highest auspices and were undertaken as military fortunes in the Near East shifted and European settlements there were threatened or reduced. The Fourth Crusade, which briefly marred the rule of Pope Innocent III, is characteristic of their baser aspects. Under pressure from the Venetians, who financed most of the venture, the crusading army first undertook to recapture some Venetian territory in the Balkans, and then in 1204, veered toward Constantinople, took this Christian capital and sacked it, mainly for the Venetians' benefit. Only a few years later, in 1212, another Crusade, this one unofficial, began to assemble in France. Led by a visionary peasant boy, the Children's Crusade gathered thousands of children on the way, but those among them who were not sold into slavery died of hunger and exposure. By that time, the name "crusade" had been perverted to other purposes: it was Innocent III who pressed the military campaign against the Albigensian heretics (see p. 36) and called it a crusade. Thus the very idea of crusades had been widely discredited before the Crusades themselves came to an end in the 1270s. Their part in the expansion of Europe is undoubted; their value, even in that expansion, remains dubious.

The papacy lost more from these excursions than it gained. Innocent III died in 1216 and was succeeded by a number of intelligent and strong-minded popes. But this was the time of the powerful Hohenstaufen Emperor Frederick II, called *Stupor Mundi,* who, in his long reign from 1211 to 1250, vigorously battled the papacy in diplomatic and military arenas alike. The most imperialistic of popes was still to come: Boniface VIII, who succeeded to the Papal Chair in 1294 and promptly asserted papal supremacy over worldly rulers. In 1302, he issued the defiant bull *Unam Sanctam,* which restated, for the last time, the ambitious vision that Gregory VII and Innocent III had seen before him. But Boniface had a redoubtable enemy in Philip IV, the Fair, of France, who threatened to bring the pope to trial. Boniface eluded him: humiliated, helpless, the pope died in 1303. Soon after, in 1309, the papacy moved to the town of Avignon, a papal enclave in southern France, where it was to stay for seven papal reigns, to 1378. It was a shameful interlude, the "Babylonian captivity of the Church," widely interpreted as papal surrender to the power of France and as an abandonment of its spiritual office for the sake of security and splendor. It meant all those things, doubtless, but it also marked a shift in the temper of Europe, the rise of new and powerful entities—the states of the West—and the emergence of that time of glory and trouble, the Renaissance.

SELECTED READINGS

In a field as vast as that covered by this introductory chapter, we can send the reader to only a handful of titles. For antiquity in general, see Tom B. Jones, *Ancient Civilization* (1960). See also Henri Frankfort, ed., *The Intellectual Adventure of Ancient Man* (1946), which deals with the ancient Near East in lucid chapters (the paperback version, titled *Before Philosophy* [1949], omits the ancient Hebrews); Edward Chiera, *They Wrote on Clay* (1938); and Otto Neugebauer, *The Exact Sciences in Antiquity* (2nd ed., 1962), which is excellent. For Egypt, there are Henri Frankfort, *Ancient Egyptian Religion: An Interpretation* (1948), and John A. Wilson, *The Burden of Egypt* (1951). For the early history of the Jews, Salo Wittmayer Baron, *A Social and Religious History of the Jews,* vols. 1 and 2, *Ancient Times* (2nd rev. ed., 1952), is indispensable.

C. M. Bowra, *The Greek Experience* (1957), Hugh Lloyd-Jones, ed., *The Greek World* (1965), and H. D. F. Kitto, *The Greeks* (rev. ed., 1957), are accessible introductions. The emergence of thought in ancient Greece is analyzed in Bruno Snell, *The Discovery of the Mind: The Greek Origins of European Thought* (tr. 1953), and in earlier books by F. M. Cornford: *From Religion to Philosophy: A Study in the Origins of Western Speculation* (1912) and *Principium Sapientiae: The Origins of Greek Philosophical Thought* (1952). For early Greece, see M. I. Finley, *The World of Odysseus* (1954). For economics and politics, see H. Michell, *The Economics of Ancient Greece* (2nd ed., 1957); Victor Ehrenberg, *The Greek State* (tr. 1960), a brilliant treatise; and A. Andrewes, *The Greek Tyrants* (1956). E. R. Dodds, *The Greeks and the Irrational* (1951), is a pioneering study. Werner Jaeger, *Paideia: The Ideals of Greek Culture,* 3 vols. (tr., 2nd ed., 1945), is an aristocratic view of that culture. On Greek science, see George Sarton's exhaustive but pedestrian *A History of Science: Ancient Science Through the Golden Age of Greece* (1952); it should be supplemented by S. Sambursky, *The Physical World of the Greeks* (tr. 1956). On religion, see W. K. C. Guthrie, *The Greeks and Their Gods* (1950), and Martin P. Nilsson, *Greek Folk Religion* (1940). Good introductions to the Greek achievement also include C. M. Bowra, *Ancient Greek Literature* (1933), and H. D. F. Kitto, *Greek Tragedy: A Literary Survey* (3rd ed., 1961). For the Hellenistic world, see M. I. Rostovtzeff, *Social and Economic History of the Hellenistic World,* 3 vols. (1941), a classic; W. W. Tarn, *Hellenistic Civilization* (3rd ed., 1952), a fine survey to be read with Tarn, *Alexander the Great* (1948); Moses Hadas, *Hellenistic Culture: Fusion and Diffusion* (1959), which is, in part, a "democratic" response to Jaeger's *Paideia.*

A good introduction to Roman history remains M. I. Rostovtzeff, *A History of the Ancient World,* vol. II, *Rome* (tr. 1928). Add to this H. H. Scullard, *A History of the Roman World from 753 to 146 B.C.* (3rd ed., 1961); Scullard, *From the Gracchi to Nero: A History of Rome from 138 B.C. to A.D. 68,* (3rd ed., 1970); and Michael Grant, *The World of Rome* (1960). The political transition from republic to empire is brilliantly analyzed in Ronald Syme, *The Roman Revolution* (1939). For the empire, see M. I.

Rostovtzeff, *Social and Economic History of the Roman Empire* (1926), and the more recent A. M. H. Jones, *The Later Roman Empire, 284–602,* 2 vols. (1964). Cyril Bailey, *Phases in the Religion of Ancient Rome* (1932), is very useful; so is H. J. Rose, *Ancient Roman Religion* (1948). M. L. W. Laistner, *The Greater Roman Historians* (1947); S. Sambursky, *The Physical World of Late Antiquity* (1962); and Samuel Dill, *Roman Society from Nero to Marcus Aurelius* (2nd ed., 1911) are all illuminating.

Amid a vast literature on the Fall of Rome and the emergence of Christianity, the following stand out: T. R. Glover, *The Conflict of Religions in the Early Roman Empire* (1909), and Ferdinand Lot, *The End of the Ancient World and the Beginnings of the Middle Ages* (tr. 1931)—both, though old, still full of vitality; Andrew Alföldi, *The Conversion of Constantine and Pagan Rome* (tr. 1948), to be read with Ramsay MacMullen, *Constantine* (1969); A. D. Nock, *Conversion: The Old and the New in Religion from Alexander the Great to Augustine of Hippo* (1933), elegant and comprehensive; Peter Brown, *Augustine of Hippo: A Biography* (1967) and *The World of Late Antiquity from Marcus Aurelius to Muhammad* (1971). In addition to Brown's last-named volume, which moves into the beginnings of the Middle Ages, see H. R. Trevor-Roper, *The Rise of Christian Europe* (1965); H. St. L. B. Moss, *The Birth of the Middle Ages, 395–814* (1935); William C. Bark, *Origins of the Medieval World* (1958); R. W. Southern, *The Making of the Middle Ages* (1953); and, on a special topic, J. M. Wallace-Hadrill, *The Barbarian West, A.D. 400–1000* (1952).

For medieval history in general, see C. W. Previté-Orton, *The Shorter Cambridge Mediaeval History,* 2 vols. (rev. ed., 1952), which, despite its breathlessness, manages to be sound and authoritative. And see Denys Hay, *Europe: The Emergence of an Idea* (1957). See also, Henri Pirenne, *A History of Europe from the Invasions to the XVIth Century* (tr. 1955). Marc Bloch's masterpiece, *Feudal Society,* 2 vols. (tr. 1961), is indispensable. So is Bloch, *Land and Work in Medieval Europe* (tr. 1967). Social and economic history are well treated in Robert S. Lopez, *The Birth of Europe* (1967); the older, briefer study by Henri Pirenne, *Economic and Social History of Medieval Europe* (tr. 1936), remains useful; see also Pirenne's *Medieval Cities: Their Origins and the Revival of Trade* (tr. 1939), which should be compared with John H. Mundy and Peter Riesenberg, *The Medieval Town* (1958). Among other surveys of more restricted scope, Christopher Brooke, *Europe in the Central Middle Ages, 962–1154* (1964), is outstanding, as is Friedrich Heer, *The Medieval World: Europe, 1100–1350* (tr. 1962). Sir Maurice Powicke, *Medieval England* (1931); F. M. Stenton, *English Society in the Early Middle Ages* (1951); Geoffrey Barraclough, *Origins of Modern Germany* (2nd ed., 1947); R. Fawtier, *The Capetian Kings of France* (tr. 1960); and Charles Petit-Dutaillis, *The Feudal Monarchy in France and England: From the Tenth to the Thirteenth Century* (tr. 1964) are excellent introductions for their respective regions. For the Crusades, Steven Runciman, *History of the Crusades,* 3 vols. (1951–1954), is analytical and narrative.

For religious and intellectual life in the Middle Ages, H. O. Taylor, *The Medieval Mind,* 2 vols. (2nd ed., 1925), remains a valuable introduction. Two books by M. L. W. Laistner, *Thought and Letters in Western Europe, A.D. 500 to 900* (2nd ed., 1957) and *The Intellectual Heritage in the Early Middle Ages* (1957), deal with the early period. C. H. McIlwain, *The Growth of Political Thought in the West: From the Greeks to the Middle Ages* (1932), may be supplemented with Fritz Kern, *Kingship, Law and the Constitution in the Middle Ages* (tr. 1939); Ernst H. Kantorowicz's provocative study, *The King's Two Bodies* (1957); Sidney Painter, *French Chivalry* (1940); David Knowles, *The Evolution of Medieval Thought* (1962); and Etienne Gilson, *History of Christian Philosophy in the*

Middle Ages (tr. 1955). Among G. G. Coulton's many books, *Five Centuries of Religion,* 4 vols. (1923–1950), gives a scholarly, if secularist survey. Cuthbert Butler, *Benedictine Monachism* (2nd ed., 1961), is valuable, as is Gerd Tellenbach, *Church, State and Christian Society at the Time of the Investiture Contest* (tr. 1940). See also Geoffrey Barraclough, *The Medieval Papacy* (1968); C. H. Haskins, *The Renaissance of the Twelfth Century* (1927); and vol. II, *The Thousand Years of Uncertainty,* A.D. *500 to* A.D. *1500,* of Kenneth S. Latourette's monumental *History of the Expansion of Christianity,* 7 vols. (1937–1945).

Among several valuable surveys of the Byzantine Empire, Norman H. Baynes and H. St. L. B. Moss, eds., *Byzantium: An Introduction to East Roman Civilization* (1948), is highly recommended; other good introductions include Baynes, *The Byzantine Empire* (2nd ed., 1946); J. M. Hussey, *The Byzantine World* (1957); and the outstanding longer work by Georgije Ostrogorsky, *History of the Byzantine State* (tr. 1956). D. J. Geanakoplos, *Byzantine East and Latin West: Two Worlds of Christendom in Middle Ages and Renaissance* (1966), considers cultural and social relationships.

For the Muslim world, see the economical study by Bernard Lewis, *The Arabs in History* (2nd ed., 1958); Philip K. Hitti, *History of the Arabs from the Earliest Times to the Present* (5th ed., 1951); and the controversial Henri Pirenne, *Mohammed and Charlemagne* (tr. 1939). And see G. E. von Gruenebaum, *Medieval Islam: A Study in Cultural Orientation* (1946).

1

The Renaissance
in Italy

The Renaissance was everything its name implies: a true rebirth. While it kept alive many ties to the Christian Middle Ages, it renewed ties, dimly remembered or wholly forgotten, with classical antiquity and thus laid the groundwork for modern civilization. The claim the great Swiss historian, Jacob Burckhardt, made for the period over a century ago remains valid: the civilization of the Renaissance was "the mother of our own."[1] The chronological and intellectual distance between that age and our modern age may be considerable, but the connection between the two ages is intimate.

The first to celebrate the dawn of a new day were themselves men of the Renaissance—the Humanists, a new breed of scholars and poets. Passionate antiquarians and reform-minded educators, they saw the revolution they helped to make as a revolution; this awareness in itself gave the Renaissance its distinct character and unique vitality. From the middle of the fifteenth century on, the Humanists proclaimed their own time as an era of renewal in the arts,

[1] Burckhardt, who "discovered" the Renaissance as a distinct historical period in his classic *The Civilization of the Renaissance in Italy* (1860), remains the indispensable guide to that age.

in literature, and in learning that rivaled, and perhaps surpassed, the classical ages of Greece and Rome they worshiped. Giovanni Boccaccio hailed the revival of poetry and Coluccio Salutati the restoration of literature; Filippo Villani, like the other two a well-known Florentine Humanist, congratulated the painters of his native city on rescuing their art from extinction. [2] It became a commonplace of educated opinion that the world was awakening to a new age of light after nearly a thousand years of barbarous darkness. What Wordsworth said about the French Revolution, the Humanists said about their very different revolution in Italy three and four centuries before him: "Bliss was it in that dawn to be alive, but to be young was very heaven."

The Humanists' pronouncements, with their single-minded exuberance, capture a great moment in the history of Europe. Since the end of the Roman Empire in the West there had been several revivals of the classics, notably at the court of Charlemagne early in the ninth century and in urban centers in the twelfth century. Beginning around 1100, literature, the arts, and philosophy had prospered impressively. But these so-called "renaissances" did not step beyond the circle of traditional culture and styles of thought. The Renaissance that had its inception around the 1330s in Italy was different in kind: it evolved a way of looking at the world and at man in which we may recognize our own.

While it was important and instructive, the confidence of the Humanists tells only part of the story. And the conventional picture of the Renaissance— glittering courts, prosperous cities, sensual paintings, expansiveness every-where—wholly fails to capture the complexity of the age. The peasants and the urban poor, the bulk of Italy's population, lived on in misery; their unvarying routine was broken only by war and famine, and their superstitions survived as though nothing had happened among the educated. Even the educated sometimes saw the novelty around them with deep uneasiness. While the Humanists joyfully rediscovered ancient manuscripts, enjoyed the world of nature and man's inner life, gave voice to such secular passions as the desire for fame and glory, and experimented with a new individualism, there were many who feared all this innovation as a threat to traditional ways of thinking, standards of value, and ideals of conduct. The Renaissance was an age of heroism and crimes, of extravagant hopes and equally extravagant despair; the new individualism proved a source of pleasure and of anxiety. "True tragedy," Burckhardt noted, "which then found no place on the stage, stepped mightily through palaces, streets, and public squares." As Burckhardt also noted, it was in this mixture of freedom and fear, as much as in anything else, that the Renaissance was the mother of our modern age.

[2] Federico Chabod, *Machiavelli and the Renaissance* (1958), 152–153.

THE SETTING

———··❦··——

Economics and Politics

In striking contrast with the customary view of the Renaissance, the period began in a time of economic decline and physical devastation. During the very decades in which the Renaissance emerged, a commercial and agricultural depression settled over Europe that did not lift for over a hundred years. Prices declined, popular unrest grew, trade contracted, merchants failed; the Renaissance was the golden age of bankruptcies. Not everyone suffered, of course; some merchants waxed rich in the midst of the general decline, and the shrewd and lucky moneylenders of the fourteenth century, like the Fuggers of Augsburg, became the proud princely banking houses of the fifteenth. Laborers, becoming scarce, sought higher wages, though they rarely got them. But in general, in town and country alike, these were decades of constricted markets, low profits, and widespread famine. The drop in population, which, following three centuries of marked expansion, set in at the same time, was part consequence and part cause of this depression. Neither agricultural techniques nor medical technology could keep pace with the rising population, and so nature did, as it were, wholesale what individuals could only accomplish in small measure through birth control: population was checked and cut back by old scourges—famine, pestilence, and war—raging, it seemed to dismayed onlookers, with unheard-of fury.

The consequences for the Italian cities, and for all of Europe, were catastrophic. In 1347, Italian ships, swarming with infected rats, imported the plague into Sicily. With stunning speed, the Black Death spread.[3] By the end of that year, many thousands had died in the Italian peninsula; by 1348 the disease had reached Spain and France and by 1350 no European state, from England to Poland, was safe. The plague played with Europe as a cat plays with a mouse: it would rise in waves of devastation and then let up, raising false hopes only to dash them as it resumed its lethal work. While the Black Death was at its worst in the fourteenth century, it broke out several times in the fifteenth century as well, and remained an ever-present menace right into the eighteenth century. Its mortal effects were, and remain, incalculable. In

---

[3] The two most prominent forms of the plague were bubonic—named for the buboes, or swellings, produced when it attacked the lymph glands—and pneumonic, which attacked the lungs. Both were highly contagious, the latter more than the former, and both were almost invariably deadly.

Florence, which had reached a population of about ninety thousand during the prosperous 1330s, perhaps fifty thousand died in the single year 1348, and as late as 1380, the population had not yet climbed back to sixty thousand.[4] Boccaccio's celebrated *Decameron* reflects the ravages of the plague in Florence in more than one way: the ostensible reason for the meeting of the storytellers whose one hundred tales make up the book is the plague from which they have fled to a country estate; the preface of the book contains a graphic description of the sufferings in the city itself. Nearby, in the Tuscan city of Pistoia, the population dropped from about eleven thousand to six thousand in 1351; by 1400, it was below four thousand.[5] Elsewhere, in Italy and in other countries, in cities and in the countryside, the devastations were quite as bad: in Bremen and Hamburg perhaps half the population died; England, with a population of about 3,700,000 in the critical year 1348, could count no more than 2,000,000 souls in 1400. Some areas were untouched, some suffered only slightly. But the over-all loss of life across Europe in the first thirty years of the Black Death was no less than 40 percent. The time came when men omitted the regular rites for the dead; they were too dangerous to the survivors.

The mundane consequences were, among other things, an economic decline. At the beginning of the fifteenth century, the total imports and exports at Genoa were down to a fifth of what they had been at the end of the thirteenth century, while the Florentine production of cloth dropped from one hundred thousand bolts a year to about thirty thousand by 1500.[6] The economic depression and the drop in morale were rapid; economic and spiritual recovery were slow. For even when the plague subsided, wars and civil wars continued their own deadly work.

Italy in the fourteenth and fifteenth centuries was a congeries of competing states, often at war. The "Babylonian captivity" of the papacy in Avignon (see p. 44) was a political advantage even if it was a disgrace to the church: "For the first extended period in its history Italy in the fourteenth century was able to go her own way largely undisturbed by the conflict which had troubled her from the eleventh century between the claims of the Roman emperor of the west and those of the leader of the Western Christian church, the pope."[7] The empire was just as impotent. The city-states were therefore on their own to strive for power by seeking allies and plotting the destruction of their rivals. This was the atmosphere that nourished the disillusioned political philosophy of Machiavelli. Many of the states were small towns fighting desperately for a

---

[4] Gene A. Brucker, *Florentine Politics and Society, 1343–1378* (1962), 9, 15n.

[5] See Eugene F. Rice, Jr., in John A. Garraty and Peter Gay, eds., *The Columbia History of the World* (1972), 486–487.

[6] Ibid.; Robert S. Lopez, "Hard Times and Investment in Culture," in Wallace K. Ferguson et al., *The Renaissance, Six Essays* (1962), 40; Karl F. Helleiner, "The Population of Europe from the Black Death to the Eve of the Vital Revolution," in E. E. Rich and C. H. Wilson, eds., *The Cambridge Economic History of Europe*, vol. IV (1967), 1–95 passim.

[7] Denys Hay, *The Italian Renaissance in Its Historical Background* (1961), 58.

measure of independence: in the fourteenth century, the territory of Tuscany alone was divided into the states of Florence, Pisa, Lucca, Siena, Volterra, Arezzo, San Giminiano, and Cortona, to say nothing of the smaller cities.[8] The city-states found themselves trapped in an inexorable cycle. Too small to guarantee food for the laboring masses and to build an army of defense, they were driven to endless wars of expansion to secure land, subjects, and raw materials. These in themselves imposed heavy financial burdens; for since the states could not supply adequate manpower, they relied on mercenaries led by *condottieri*. But these military adventurers, by profession ruthless and by preference rootless, posed new threats; more than one ambitious *condottiere* attempted to take power over the city he had been hired to protect; more than one succeeded. Like the Greek city-states of antiquity, the Italian city-states never solved their most pressing problem: the relation of resources to power.[9]

This tension among the Italian states could not be sustained forever. By the fifteenth century, though wars continued, the Italian peninsula was substantially divided up among five major powers—Venice, Florence, despotic Milan, the Papal States, and the feudal monarchy of Naples—each with its satellites, connected by alliances and divided by implacable rivalries. In addition, a few tough military principalities survived to complicate the situation. The number was small enough to ensure a certain degree of stability—imperialist Milan was the main disturber of the peace in fifteenth-century Italy—but too large to permit hegemony to any single state. A balance of power was purchased at the expense of unity, and the continuing, incurable division of Italy was to make it the victim, at the end of the fifteenth century, of European power politics (see p. 115).

While the pressure of the power struggle drove Italian states toward alliances that would control international conflict, the pressure of the social struggle drove them toward strong-man governments that would control domestic conflict. All across the peninsula, from the fourteenth to the fifteenth century, the drift was from republic to despotism. The pattern was everywhere the same: the city-states lived by trade and were dominated by great merchant families. These mercantile dynasties were united in gilds, allied by marriage, and held together by common interest against common adversaries. But they were also divided by family feuds, commercial rivalries, and competing allegiances to papacy and empire, and these divisions were expensive and exhausting. Factional conflict was exacerbated by class conflict: the great families were in perpetual battle with lesser merchants. They lived in an uneasy, unstable truce with the working masses recruited from the countryside, who inhabited the stinking workers' quarters in the city, and who on occasion, when their grievances became insupportable or when they found an articulate

[8] Ibid., 60–62.

[9] William J. Bouwsma, "Politics in the Age of the Renaissance," in *Western Civilization*, vol. I (3rd rev. ed., 1961), 215.

leader, vented their endemic discontent in riots and general uprisings. The poor of Florence, miserable and oppressed and indispensable, never found their poet as did the English poor, but the vision of *Piers Plowman,* that fourteenth-century allegory, probably by William Langland, would have aptly applied to them:

> The poor may plead and pray in the doorway;
> They may quake for cold and thirst and hunger;
> None receives them rightfully and relieves their
> suffering.
> They are hooted at like hounds and ordered off.

The great merchants and the middling people thought they could safely disregard the plebs and concentrated instead on fighting one another. The leading families valued security above freedom—or rather, were content to let other freedoms go as long as they were free to make money—and, weary of costly strife, they appealed to outsiders, or to one dominant local family, to establish a temporary dictatorship, which, more often than not, turned into a permanent despotism.

The labels despotism and republic, which go back to Renaissance Italy, must be applied circumspectly: despotisms could be benign, republics oppressive. Yet there were despots of melodramatic villainy, adventurers who followed their impulses unchecked by religious scruples or institutional controls. Some were madmen who let loose their dogs on the population or rolled stones at them from high hills; others were self-willed sensualists or sybarites who indulged their tastes at the expense—literally—of their cities and silenced all criticism by putting their critics to death. Since most rulers had no legitimate claim to rulership and governed simply because they held power, political life was poisoned by plots and counterplots, by rumors, informers, and an air of universal suspicion that invaded even the family. An ambitious brother or son was a potential enemy for the despot, to be watched and, if necessary, eliminated. Inevitably, moral confusion, a sense that everything is permitted, infected subjects as much as rulers. "Once the burghers of a city," Burckhardt reports, "had a general who had freed them from foreign pressure; they consulted daily how to reward him, and concluded that no reward in their power was large enough, not even if they made him lord of the city. At last one of them rose up and suggested: 'Let us kill him and worship him as our patron saint.' And so, we are told, they did." [10]

This chilling story may not be literally true, but it nicely conveys the atmosphere, not merely in smaller states but also in great cities like Milan. Late in the thirteenth century, its leading families turned over the government to a single aristocratic family, the Visconti, who ruled Milan with an iron hand for

---

[10] Burckhardt, *Die Kultur der Renaissance in Italien: Ein Versuch* (ed. 1958), 21–22, translated by Peter Gay.

a century and a half until they were replaced in 1450 by Francesco Sforza, a brilliant and audacious *condottiere*. The reign of the Visconti was marked by deadly family feuds, enormous cruelty, and successful wars of expansion; it was endurable only because the regime gave the merchants what they wanted—protection and prosperity. The greatest of the Visconti clan, Gian Galeazzo, took power in 1378, embarked on a policy of expansion, and in 1395 bought the coveted title of "duke" from the emperor, giving his rule new legitimacy and prestige. Ten years before, in 1385, he had assumed sole rulership by having his uncle Bernabo murdered, to the surprise of no one—this was Renaissance politics.

Yet some of the despots were men of taste, true men of the Renaissance; Humanists did not have to be hirelings to say that the arts and sciences flourished best under an absolute ruler. There were Renaissance princes who protected painters and scholars for the sake of painting and scholarship. Francesco Sforza of Milan took an informed interest in architecture, imported Humanists to educate his children, and, reversing the bellicose policy of the Visconti before him, made peace with Florence. Federigo da Montefeltro, who governed Urbino from 1444 to 1482, was a characteristic *condottiere* who hired himself and his troops to other Italian rulers and enhanced the fortunes of his family and his small state by adroit diplomatic moves, not excluding marriage. But, as his contemporary biographer, the Florentine bookseller Vespasiano, said of him, Federigo was as brilliant in the arts of peace as in the arts of war. He was a good classical scholar; an amateur theologian; a well-informed patron of architects, sculptors, and painters; a generous supporter of impecunious Humanists; and best of all, a mild duke: his treatment of his subjects "suggested that they were rather his children." His Urbino "was a wondrous sight: all his subjects were well-to-do and waxed rich through labor at the works he had instituted, and a beggar was never seen." [11] Even if we take this panegyric at some discount, Federigo remains the model of the good Renaissance despot.

Conversely, republics were normally tightly constricted oligarchies: in Venice, where nobles alone formed the active political public, the nobility made up less than 5 percent of the population; in Florence, the active citizenry was no larger. [12] Venice, the richest of Italian cities, secure on its remote lagoons since its founding in the sixth century and superbly placed for trade with the East, was run by, and for, its aristocratic merchant families. True, early in the fourteenth century, Petrarch had noted about Venice with some disapproval: "Much freedom reigns there in every respect, and what I should call the only evil prevailing—but also the worst—far too much freedom of speech." [13] But this freedom was possible because the Venetian government secured domestic

---

[11] Vespasiano, *Renaissance Princes, Popes and Prelates* (Torchbook ed., 1963), 107–108.

[12] William J. Bouwsma, *Venice and the Defense of Republican Liberty: Renaissance Values in the Age of the Counter Reformation* (1968), 60; Felix Gilbert, *Machiavelli and Guicciardini: Politics and History in Sixteenth Century Florence* (1965), 20.

[13] Bouwsma, *Venice,* 93.

peace and boundless wealth; criticism was relatively free because relatively few found grounds for criticism. Besides, the notorious Council of Ten, established in the fourteenth century as a temporary adjunct to its other governing councils, became a permanent watchdog over the political health of the Venetian republic.[14] Operating with commendable dispatch, employing informers and a secret police force, the Council of Ten discovered plots in their incipient stages and sent dangerous men beyond reach—into exile or death. With its doge—that powerless, ceremonial head of state elected for life—with its rotating councils where all were equal, the Venetian constitution symbolized the omnipotence, fulfilled the purposes, and expressed the will of the merchant aristocracy to perfection. Venice secured the kind of loyalty that cannot be bought by fear and lies deeper than mere self-interest.

Florence

Florence was, or liked to think it was, different. While ingenious politicians used the republican Florentine constitution as a screen behind which merchant magnates manipulated the machinery of power, the prevalence of republican rhetoric acted as a check on the oligarchy. Republicanism was an ideal to which the dissident could appeal and which the most ambitious Florentines found it convenient to respect. Even the Medici were too shrewd and too attached to this Florentine ideal to subvert it wholly. At the beginning of the fifteenth century, stung to self-awareness by the aggressive designs of Visconti Milan, Florentine Humanists reexamined their boasted republican tradition: Leonardo Bruni, an impressive polemicist and responsible public official, set the tone with his "civic humanism"—a defense of the active as against the contemplative life. He advocated public service, extolled liberty, and recalled the long-neglected virtues of the ancient Roman Republic.[15] Bruni's civic humanism, developed in the face of foreign danger and in the midst of magnificent artistic vitality, was a characteristic local product. In political theory as in the arts, literature, and philosophy, Florence contributed far more than its share to the making and the glory of the Renaissance.

This contribution was the result of hard work in unpromising circumstances. Florence enjoyed an appealing but insecure geographical situation. Surrounded by the lovely Tuscan hills, bathed in the warm, clear Tuscan sun, the city was cut off from the sea by the hostile republics of Lucca and Pisa. Much of its energy was consumed by wearing, inconclusive wars with these neighbors, too weak to resist Florentine expansion, too strong wholly to succumb to it: while Pisa was added to Florentine territory in 1406, a disastrous campaign against Lucca led to a grave domestic crisis in 1433.

---

[14] Ibid., 62.
[15] Hans Baron, *The Crisis of the Early Italian Renaissance: Civic Humanism and Republican Liberty in an Age of Classicism and Tyranny* (2nd ed., 1966).

While in the course of centuries Florence experienced political upheavals, the shape of its government down to the end of the fifteenth century was set early in the twelfth, when the gilds emerged as the distinctive political institution of the republic. In 1282, the seven greater gilds—with the bankers, wool merchants, and cloth importers in the vanguard—tightened their grip on power and devised a constitution that, for all practical purposes, excluded nobles from politics and gave the members of the fourteen lesser gilds—the shopkeepers and artisans—token representation. The ruling oligarchy was active, energetic, shrewd; in the course of the fourteenth century, it made Florence into one of the leading banking and trading centers in Europe. For all its internal strains and undeniable thirst for profit and power, the oligarchy was also, in its way, public spirited: in 1427, at a time of public need, it devised a tax assessment, the *catasto,* astonishing in its equity and unprecedented in the burdens it placed on the rich. Twice in the fourteenth century the oligarchs found themselves obliged to make concessions, first, in 1343, to the lesser gilds after an economic crash, then, in 1378, to the disfranchised workers when the wool workers went into the streets to protest increasing pressure from the greater on the lesser gilds. The Revolt of the Ciompi,[16] as the rising of 1378 came to be called, was an experiment in democratizing the oligarchy; it succeeded only for a moment. By 1381, the old families were back to rule undisturbed and to indulge their own rivalries; when in the 1430s the government fell into the hands of the Medici, the event meant a change of personnel but not of policy or political structure.

The history of the Medici dynasty is the history of the Renaissance itself: ruthless, admirable and terrifying, filled with contradictions. The family made its mark in Florentine affairs in the fourteenth century by acquiring wealth and a reputation for liberalism—one Medici had supported the Ciompi—but it was not until 1397 that the family began the ascendancy it would keep for a century, with the founding of the Medici Bank. Giovanni de' Medici, the founder, was a gifted businessman, a bountiful philanthropist, and a popular political leader with a taste for opposition to the oligarchy. His impressive son, Cosimo de' Medici, who assumed management in 1429 after his father's death, used his immense wealth and his father's prestige to equal advantage; he made the family enterprise into a European power and himself into the ruler of Florence. The bank had branches in major Italian and foreign cities, as far away as London; the enormously profitable branch in Rome handled the business of the papacy and of the great Roman families. In 1434, Cosimo took control over Florence, control that ended only with his death thirty years later. His power rested not on any official position but on his wealth, his adroit use of the firm, his manipulation of elections coupled with well-timed sentences of imprison-

---

[16] *Ciompi* is a corruption of the French word *compère,* which the Florentines had heard from French soldiers; it referred to the wool workers and then, by extension, to the working classes as a whole.

ment or exile for recalcitrant opponents, his eminently personal and eminently successful pacific foreign policy, his lavish public benefactions, and—a surprising modern touch—a natural, tactful simplicity that gave him the affection of wide circles in the republic. When the Humanist Pope Pius II visited Florence he noted: "Though Cosimo is practically lord of the city, he carries himself so as to appear as a private citizen." [17] On his death in 1464, Cosimo's fellow citizens placed a short eloquent epitaph on his tombstone: *pater patriae.*

Cosimo de' Medici was a Renaissance man in his vigor and versatility, his genial association with Humanists and earnest study of philosophy, his ambition, and his highly individualistic religious convictions. He was a worldly businessman who went on silent retreats to refresh his soul, a fervent reader of Plato who was also a devout servant of Christ. These qualities, with all their splendor and complexity, reappeared in his grandson, Lorenzo de' Medici, called "the magnificent." Even the legends that soon formed around Lorenzo are typical of his age, for the Renaissance was fertile soil for biography; it reveled in making idols of mere mortals. Cosimo's son, Piero, though sickly, had beaten back a challenge to his family's rule over Florence, but Piero died in 1469, and Lorenzo was called upon to take charge, in business and politics, at the age of twenty. He was young but he was ready: he had absorbed a thoroughgoing Humanist education and the Medici tradition at home, and he had already demonstrated a precocious cool temper and diplomatic skill on a variety of missions. The family business was passing the peak of its prosperity and influence, and Lorenzo did little to arrest the downward trend; his bank declined in company with a general decline in Florentine prosperity and was saved from open bankruptcy only by the French invasions of 1494.

The legends surrounding Lorenzo de' Medici—part invention, part embroidery, part fact—concentrate on his humanism. Like his grandfather before him, he surrounded himself with men of brilliance, generously lent the Humanists books and gave them access to his table, employed painters, architects, and sculptors to embellish his country houses, and fostered talent. Beyond this, he readily gave advice on architecture that other magnates adroitly begged him to give. The list of his friends and employees is practically coextensive with achievement in Florentine culture of his day: the painters Sandro Botticelli and Domenico Ghirlandaio, the philosopher Marsilio Ficino, the poet Angelo Poliziano, the sculptor Andrea Verocchio are only the most famous members of the Medici circle. And Lorenzo was more than a consumer of Renaissance culture: the advice he gave on architecture was worth hearing, he was informed enough in philosophy to discuss it sensibly with the most learned of his Humanist friends, and he wrote verses of which a professional poet would not have been ashamed.

[17] Nicolai Rubinstein, ed., *Florentine Studies: Politics and Society in Renaissance Florence* (1968), 128n, translated by Peter Gay.

Yet Lorenzo's main skill lay in political leadership, his greatest triumphs in foreign policy. His techniques of control were the techniques his ancestors had used: an increasing concentration of power in his hands coupled with attempts to preserve republican appearances, a pacific diplomacy pursued in person with great alertness and physical courage, the forging of family alliances through arranged marriages, and the use of his powerful and attractive presence to bind men to his person. He needed all the skills at his command: the international situation was increasingly unstable, and at home there were rumblings against the "Medici tyrants," partly motivated by authentic republican leanings, but fanned by rival banking factions anxious for power and greedy for profits. In 1478, the Pazzi family, an old dynasty of Florentine bankers, resentful and vindictive, devised a conspiracy to murder Lorenzo and his popular brother Giuliano. The Pazzi conspiracy reads like a Renaissance plot out of a romance, but it was reality: after some changes of plan, and after obtaining qualified assent from the pope, Sixtus IV, who had his own reasons for hating Lorenzo, the conspirators decided to murder the Medici brothers at mass, in the cathedral of Florence. The plot failed: while Giuliano was stabbed to death, Lorenzo, though wounded, escaped with his life. Justice was summary and terrible: more than eighty persons were hanged, including prominent church-men and some innocent bystanders. But Lorenzo came out of the conspiracy and the brief war that followed it with increased power and prestige, more determined than ever to restore and preserve peace in Italy. For the years that remained to him, he devoted himself to this diplomatic task. He succeeded brilliantly; when he died in 1492, the peace of Italy, though precarious, was still intact.

There is something autumnal about Lorenzo's life and work, a sense that nothing, not even the dominance of the Medici, is secure. His most famous verses poignantly capture this feeling of evanescence:

> "Quant' e bella giovinezza
> Che si fugge tuttavia!
> Chi viol esser lieto, sia;
> Di doman non c'e certezza.—

How lovely is youth, how quickly it flies! Let him who will be merry, of tomorrow nothing is sure." [18] This trivial-sounding quatrain accurately predicted the future. Two years after his death, the French invaded Italy, and Lorenzo's son, Piero, fled the city. This was not the end of the Medicis. They reappeared in early sixteenth-century Florence to govern a domain much diminished in importance; but among the newly styled dukes, one, Cosimo, was a ruler of great competence. Others married into royal houses; they appear

[18] Cecilia M. Ady, *Lorenzo dei Medici and Renaissance Italy* (1962), 125, translated by Peter Gay.

prominently in the history of France. And two Medicis filled the papal throne: Lorenzo's son Giovanni as Leo X, from 1513 to 1521; Lorenzo's nephew Giulio as Clement VII, from 1523 to 1534. Their tenure seems an ironic commentary on the ambiguous achievement of the Medici dynasty and the pathetic end of the Renaissance: Leo X was, as a true Medici, a great patron of the arts, but he also enjoyed the dubious distinction of presiding over Catholic Christendom at the beginning of its irrevocable splintering by Martin Luther. And Clement VII, though diligent, was inept, and it was during his papacy, in 1527, that Rome was brutally sacked by German and Spanish mercenaries in the employ of Emperor Charles V (see p. 117). The Italian Renaissance ended as it had begun two centuries before in Petrarch's mind—in turmoil.

THE HUMANISTS

Makers of a Style: Petrarch and His Followers

The old view that revolutions are made by great men is now discredited, but a look at the beginnings of the Renaissance almost tempts the historian to rehabilitate it. [19] Petrarch was not the first of the Humanists, but he was for long years the only great Humanist, and others felt impelled to follow his path by the sheer force of his example. Petrarch, eager for fame, would have been gratified at his influence, but astonished also: he aimed to be a poet and a moralist, to follow his talent as he understood it—or rather, as he painfully, all his life, tried to understand it. "You make a orator of me, a historian, philosopher, and poet, and finally even a theologian," he wrote to a friend in 1362. "But," he protested, "let me tell you, my friend, how far I fall short of your estimation. . . . I am nothing of what you attribute to me. What am I then? I am a fellow who never quits school, and not even that, but a backwoodsman who is roaming around through the lofty beech trees all alone, humming to himself some silly little tune, and—the very peak of presumption and assurance—dipping his shaky pen into his inkstand while sitting under a bitter laurel tree. . . . I am not so very eager to belong to a definite school of thought; I am striving for truth." [20] The charm and candor of this self-appraisal made Petrarch into a revolutionary. But he did not quite know it, as Boccaccio would know it soon after. Petrarch was a wanderer by choice, a seeker by temperament, a maker largely by inadvertence.

[19] Hay, *Italian Renaissance*, 68–69.
[20] Petrarch to Francesco Bruni, quoted in Ernst Cassirer et al., eds., *The Renaissance Philosophy of Man* (1948), 34.

The Florentine Francesco Petrarca [21] began his restless life, appropriately enough, in exile. He was born in 1304 near Arezzo, where his father had taken refuge after being banished from Florence for political reasons. Petrarch's contemporary fame rested largely on his poetry—on his Italian sonnets and lyrics, his rhymed Latin letters, and the epic about Scipio Africanus, *Africa,* which he circulated but never finished: in 1341 he was crowned in Rome as poet laureate. But his historical significance lies in two discoveries—his discovery of antiquity and of himself. He was, as Gibbon said four centuries later, "the eloquent Petrarch" who, "by his lessons and his example, may justly be applauded as the first harbinger of day." [22]

Petrarch's discovery of antiquity began with his discovery of some ancients. Forced to study law at Montpellier in France, he found himself instead passionately devouring Cicero and, soon after, St. Augustine; these two writers remained Petrarch's favorite classics all his life. His choice is significant both for what it excludes and what it includes. Petrarch, the great Humanist, never acquired more than a smattering of Greek; to a friend who had sent him a copy of Homer's work he replied sadly: "Your Homer is dumb with me, or rather I am deaf to him." [23] And by giving Cicero and Augustine equal claim to his admiration, Petrarch underscored the religious compromise that most Humanists were to adopt: a continued unquestioning loyalty to the Christian faith coupled with a new understanding for the classics of pagan, especially Roman, antiquity.

Petrarch studied his beloved ancients devoutly but not uncritically. In 1345, in the cathedral library of Verona, he discovered the long-forgotten letters Cicero had sent to his man of business Atticus, to his brother Quintus, and to Brutus. [24] These letters greatly enlarged Petrarch's familiarity with Cicero, who had been up to then a somewhat shadowy figure, a remote if eloquent rhetorician. Cicero's letters elated and depressed Petrarch: Petrarch deplored Cicero's obvious compromises with the sordid business of this world; the unmatched Roman Republican turned out to be in his letters a politician among politicians, a man with ordinary qualities. Petrarch expressed his disappointment quite directly, in a letter to Cicero, which was one of the many bridges to antiquity Petrarch sought to build.

Petrarch's effort to see Cicero honestly, unadorned, is a noteworthy achievement and a revision of scholarly ideals prevalent in his day. The effort implied and exacted the search for more classical manuscripts, the open-eyed study and the meticulous purification of manuscripts already known and of

[21] Petrarch's father was known as Petracco; Petrarch himself appears first to have spelled his name Petracchi and then adopted the more familiar version Petrarca. In English he has always been Petrarch.

[22] Edward Gibbon, *Decline and Fall of the Roman Empire* (1902), VII, 117.

[23] Ernest Hatch Wilkins, *Life of Petrarch* (1961), 136.

[24] Ibid., 51.

those coming to light. In 1428, Leonardo Bruni, Petrarch's admirer and biographer, could justly boast that Florence had restored Latin and even Greek learning and made it possible "to see face to face, and no longer through the veil of absurd translations, the greatest philosophers and admirable orators and all those other men distinguished by their learning." [25] Petrarch's ideal was also a historian's ideal: it was his intent to see Cicero as a man in his own time. He addressed his beloved ancients with easy intimacy across the centuries, but he was aware that it was across the centuries that he was addressing them. Familiarity did not preclude distance; on the contrary, the more accurately the ancient texts came to be edited, and the more texts became available, the more antiquity appeared to be what it had been: a different age, far away in time. This notion was an intellectual innovation of far-reaching significance. For medieval theologians and lawyers the writings of the past, whether clerical or secular, existed in a timeless void, in a pantheon of immortals. Until Petrarch it was understood that Rome had never fallen. Petrarch restored to Europe the historian's priceless gift: the sense of distance and of time. The ancients were intellectually near, historically far; Rome had indeed fallen and given way to a cultural decline from which Europe was only now beginning to emerge. This was the meaning of Petrarch's celebrated claim that between the fall of Rome and his own time a "dark age" had intervened—it was not an assault on Christianity but a historian's attempt to see the past as past.

Petrarch, indeed, had no reason to assail Christianity. His vehement denunciations of the Avignon papacy show him, not an unbeliever, but a lover of Rome and an Italian patriot. St. Augustine was ever with him, even on that famous excursion to Mont Ventoux, not far from Avignon, in April 1336, a date that some historians have offered as the birth of the Renaissance. With his brother, purely for the sake of the adventure and the view from the top, Petrarch climbed the mountain and marveled at the sight below. No medieval man before Petrarch had expressed such secular affection for nature. But as he rested at the summit, he pulled his copy of St. Augustine's *Confessions* from his pocket, and read: "And men go about wondering at mountain heights and the mighty waves of the sea and broad flowing streams and the circuit of the sea and the wheeling of the stars: and to themselves they give no heed." [26] Even his piety led Petrarch to self-absorption.

Petrarch's preoccupation with himself was almost as consequential for the Renaissance as his classical learning. In his letters to the ancients, to friends, and to posterity, in dialogues and in a remarkable self-analysis, the *Secretum,* he explored his motives and his gifts, his vices and virtues, his religious and scholarly vocation. He turned the love of his life into imperishable poetry and thus made the name "Laura" immortal. He recorded his most domestic activities, including the planting of trees, landscaping of gardens, and visits of

[25] Baron, *Crisis of the Early Italian Renaissance,* 417.
[26] Wilkins, *Life of Petrarch,* 13.

friends, thus proclaiming, without even pretending to do so, the importance of the individual. If, as Burckhardt has argued, man in the Renaissance pierced the veil of medieval "illusion and infantile preconceptions," discovered himself, and became "a self-conscious *individual*," [27] it is in Petrarch that this process is most patent. And it was the individual with all his contradictions on view: Petrarch was the inordinately ambitious poet who decried worldliness, a dweller at courts who proclaimed the pleasures of solitude, a proud political pamphleteer and humble pilgrim, a medieval Christian cherishing the life of contemplation and a Renaissance individualist who embodied the life of action, an enthusiastic proponent of personal and political freedom who spent most of his years with despots like the Visconti in Milan, a perpetual student whose own Greek was rudimentary but who did much to encourage the study of classical Greek in Italy. If modernity is the frank recognition of inner contradictions, Petrarch was a pioneer in modernity.

When Petrarch died in 1374, he was a famous man—the intimate of scholars, the correspondent of emperors, the favorite of princes, the critic of popes. The Humanists of the late fourteenth and early fifteenth centuries were all his followers, including Giovanni Boccaccio, Coluccio Salutati, the Florentine statesman, and Leonardo Bruni. When Bruni wrote his life of Petrarch in 1436, he gave the reason for Petrarch's reputation: he had been the pioneer. "Petrarch was the first who called back to light the gracefulness of the lost and extinguished ancient manner of writing." Even if his effort was imperfect, "still it was he who discovered and opened the path to this perfection . . . surely he did enough by merely pointing the way for those who were to follow after him." [28]

The Recovery of Antiquity

What Petrarch began others completed. In the course of the late fourteenth and early fifteenth centuries, Humanists ransacked the monastery libraries of Europe and found ancient manuscript after ancient manuscript. Petrarch had enlarged the known corpus of Cicero's works; his followers enlarged it further. Salutati found Cicero's *Epistulae ad familiares;* Poggio Bracciolini, the most avid and most successful collector of manuscripts the Renaissance was to know, found a substantial number of Cicero's legal speeches; and in 1421 Gerardo Landriani, the bishop of Lodi, found the complete manuscripts of Cicero's *Brutus, Orator,* and *De oratore.* Bracciolini also brought to light Lucretius' *De rerum natura,* almost unknown for centuries and apparently surviving in a single manuscript. Tacitus, Catullus, Propertius, known only from fragments and by reputation, now took on living form. And with the recovery of

---

[27] Burckhardt, *Die Kultur der Renaissance in Italien,* 252, translated by Peter Gay.
[28] Baron, *Crisis of the Early Italian Renaissance* (2nd ed., 1966), 267.

manuscripts went care for them. Petrarch was famous for his love of books—he called his thirst for them his "one insatiable passion,"[29] and his disciples were as passionate as he. Boccaccio accumulated a magnificent library, and wealthy amateurs like the Medici eventually made such libraries into public treasures. Nor was accumulation all: the Humanists, in their thirst for the pure classical word, edited what they found. Again Petrarch showed the way: while he was still a young man, he collected all available fragments of Livy's history of Rome, collated them and commented upon them, to restore, as much as possible, Livy's own words.[30]

Strictly speaking, the Humanists' discoveries were not discoveries—what has not been lost cannot be found. But the Humanists' editorial labors, their joyful announcements of their discoveries to their friends, and their diligent, patient copying of long and often difficult manuscripts all prove that their search for books was something more than the idle sport of antiquarians. For all practical purposes, these ancient manuscripts had indeed been lost: they had lain unattended and untouched in filthy libraries, often for many centuries. No one had bothered to read these works, few had bothered even to keep them clean or keep them intact: when Boccaccio visited the Benedictine monastery at Monte Cassino, he found its "library" an open space without a door, with grass growing on the window sills; manuscripts lay about in disorderly piles, covered with dust, many of them torn and shredded. When Boccaccio, appalled to see such desecration, asked how this was possible, the monks told him that they had been in the habit of tearing off strips of parchment and selling them as psalters or amulets, just to make some money.[31]

The Humanists changed all that; they made these manuscripts accessible and thus part of general high culture. They did more: they inculcated respect for learning and for accuracy. Some pagan classical writings had survived the Middle Ages through the accretion of legends around them and through allegorical interpretations that turned lascivious poets like Ovid into proper reading for Christian clerics. If a classical author could not be converted into an anticipator of Christian doctrine by means of allegory, some obliging monk would forge the texts that made him so: the Stoic philosopher Seneca, for one, was supplied with a correspondence with St. Paul—a forgery that Petrarch still accepted as authentic. All sorts of stories were told of Vergil: he was turned into a sorcerer, and there were learned theologians who took the *Aeneid* as an allegory of man's pilgrimage on earth, almost as if the classical poet, born just a little too soon, had fathomed the kind of teaching Christ would bring. Gradually, with some missteps and wrong guesses, the Humanists dismantled such allegories and discredited such legends. The classics were permitted to

[29] Wilkins, *Life of Petrarch*, 57.
[30] Ibid., 16–17.
[31] See Peter Gay, *The Enlightenment: An Interpretation*, vol. I, *The Rise of Modern Paganism* (1966), 262.

speak in their own voice once again, as ancients and as pagans. This scholarship enormously enriched the culture of the Renaissance and threw doubt on devout efforts to protect the Christian dispensation from pagan impurities. The Humanists' erudition had political consequences: in 1361, Petrarch used his classical learning to discredit claims by Duke Rudolf IV that Austria was a sovereign state. Rudolf offered in evidence privileges granted by Caesar and Nero, but Petrarch proved these charters to be later forgeries.[32] In 1440, in a dazzling display of erudition that had reverberations among historians for centuries, the Florentine Humanist Lorenzo Valla proved that the so-called "donation of Constantine," a gift of the empire that the converted Roman emperor had purportedly made to the pope in the fourth century, was actually composed in the eighth century. Moreover, the Humanists' recovery of ancient works of literature and their affectionate reading of all classics gave unprecedented importance to purity of expression; it became fashionable to condemn the style of theologians and poets who had written before the advent of humanism as mere barbarian efforts. Since manner easily shades into matter, this too had practical consequences: the Humanists were calling attention to new—that is, old—ways of looking at man and the world. The recovery of antiquity was therefore more than the rediscovery of literary masters, interesting storytellers, and matchless poets. It was a prelude to new ways of thinking.

Philosophies and Theologies

There was no single philosophy of the Renaissance, any more than there was a single vision of antiquity. The Humanists placed antiquity into history, but they did not yet know enough about the ancients to give antiquity itself a history—the discrimination among ancient styles in philosophy or in art, or the discrimination between an original doctrine and the commentaries and interpretations of disciples, both familiar exercises to us today, were still impossible in the Renaissance. Those Humanists who wrote on philosophy gave themselves respectable party labels: they were "Platonists" or "Aristotelians" or in the midst of intellectual combat, "Antischolastics." But, in fact, in the time of the Renaissance ancient thought was still incompletely known and often ill-digested. While, from the middle of the fourteenth century on, Greek scholars swarmed across Renaissance Italy, bringing with them knowledge of the classical Greek language and thought, a leading Aristotelian like Pietro Pomponazzi could, in 1516, publish an important treatise on the *Immortality of the Soul* without knowing any Greek.[33] And there were "Platonists" who had never read Plato in the original.

[32] Wilkins, *Life of Petrarch*, 176.
[33] Paul Oskar Kristeller, *Renaissance Thought: The Classic, Scholastic, and Humanist Strains* (1961), 42.

Ignorance was compounded by confusion. There had been a good deal of Plato in Aristotle, but after many centuries of philosophical polemics, and since down to the fourteenth century almost nothing of Plato was in Latin, Plato's own teachings had been overlaid by what modern scholars have called Neoplatonism. The Neoplatonists, who began their work at Alexandria in the third century after Christ, concentrated on the mystical and theological implications of Plato's thought at the expense of the rest, and their version of Plato was therefore highly congenial to Christians. Renaissance Humanists did not yet distinguish Neoplatonism from Platonism, and often thought they were expounding the latter when they were expounding the former: Marsilio Ficino, who enjoyed celebrating Plato's birthday with his fellow philosophers of the Platonic "Academy" and holding philosophical discussions on the model of Plato's dialogues, was a conscientious translator of Plato, but his main philosophical treatise, significantly entitled *Platonic Theology,* was a rich and curious mixture of some aspects of Platonism, Neoplatonism, and Thomistic theology—a characteristic product of the Renaissance mentality.

Aristotle was little better off. His writings had remained far better known than Plato's, in part through redactions and commentaries by Arab scholars, and he had been incorporated into Scholastic philosophy by the systematizing mind of St. Thomas Aquinas. But this led some Humanists to attack Aristotle, for to strike at him was to strike at the philosophy of the Scholastics. In the fifteenth century, as the works of Aristotle were carefully disentangled from the writings of his interpreters, there were Humanists who found it possible to despise Scholasticism and to worship Aristotle at the same time, although even then the Aristotle they worshipped was hardly recognizable: Pomponazzi's "Aristotelianism" owes far more to medieval commentators than to the Greek master himself. [34] Beyond all this, the Humanists who criticized the Scholastics for their "barbarism"—by which, incidentally, they did not mean the content of their religious teaching but their style—found themselves in debate with other Humanists who were perfectly content with Scholasticism. In this welter of claims and counterclaims, Paul Kristeller's almost irritated verdict that "the Italian humanists on the whole were neither good nor bad philosophers, but no philosophers at all," [35] seems only slightly too harsh. Not content with losing themselves among ancient doctrines and medieval commentators, many of the Humanists found elements of ancient lore—astrology, magic, mysticism—highly intriguing. A darker, obscurantist tradition, largely borrowed from Hellenistic sources, competed with what we have come to think of as the classical heritage. As the German art historian Aby Warburg felicitously said of Renaissance thought: Athens had to be rescued from the hands of Alexandria. [36]

[34] Ibid.
[35] Ibid., 100.
[36] See Gay, *Enlightenment,* I, 259.

In the midst of this profusion, the Humanists' thought circled around a single problem: how to absorb the rich, bewildering heritage of pagan antiquity into the inherited body of Christian philosophy and theology. Modern historians seeking to differentiate the Renaissance from the Middle Ages have greatly exaggerated the paganism of fifteenth- and sixteenth-century Italy. They have pointed to Valla's Epicurean tract on pleasure, *De voluptate,* and to the immoralities of Renaissance despots. But Valla did not want to exchange Christianity for Epicureanism, he wanted to reconcile the two—it is not an accident that he should have ended his career as a papal secretary. And the lustful, proud, and vicious Renaissance despots were immoral not because they were pagans, but because they were immoral and because there was no one to restrain their appetites. The Humanists were not unbelievers, and they did not do their work for the sake of unbelief, but they made unbelief accessible. Even so, pagan philosophies did not really become significant forces in European culture until the late sixteenth and seventeenth centuries, long after the Renaissance had passed. The Renaissance was not an irreligious or a non-Christian age; it was an age of widening secular concerns. It shows, as Kristeller has put it, a "steady and irresistible growth of nonreligious intellectual interests which were not so much opposed to the content of religious doctrine, as rather competing with it for individual and public attention." [37]

Humbly aware that man is less than the angels but confident that he occupies a worthy place in the scheme of things, the Humanists concentrated their philosophizing on man. Again and again, whatever their particular intellectual loyalty, whether they believed that man's actions are determined by fate or (as some of them did) by the stars or that they are free, whether they were optimistic about man's prospects or pessimistic, the Humanists insistently returned to man's value, man's dignity. Petrarch had given the lead with his life and his writings, and a century later the Florentine Humanist Giannozzo Manetti showed that this was a controversial matter indeed: his sizable treatise on *The Dignity and Excellence of Man* was quite explicitly directed against a treatise on man's misery by Pope Innocent III. Pomponazzi urged that it was man's central task in this world to seek the sphere of moral action most appropriate to him, and in 1486 Giovanni Pico della Mirandola, a precocious disciple of Ficino's, summarized this central concern of humanistic philosophizing in a famous *Oration* on the dignity of man: God, he argued, had created man last of all, after all of the divine gifts had been distributed among God's other creatures. But this was a fortunate fate: it meant that man was free to move freely among all possibilities, to shape himself as he pleased. This unique opportunity imposed a unique duty: to choose the best possible way of life open to mortal man.

One way in which the question of man's place and proper activity presented itself to the Humanists was through the old debate about styles of

[37] Kristeller, *Renaissance Thought,* 72.

life. The ancient Greeks had been the first to confront two conflicting styles—the active and the contemplative life—and to debate the relative merits of each. For the Christian, the choice was not hard; while Christian societies had their secular side—they too needed their peasants, workers, merchants, scribes, and soldiers—the highest form of existence was embodied in monastic withdrawal which symbolized the unquestioned preeminence of heavenly over earthly things. Petrarch had still been enmeshed in this view of life; had he not been dismayed to find Cicero in the midst of incessant political activity? But here was one issue on which Petrarch's disciples abandoned their master: they praised Cicero for his willingness to concentrate his philosophizing on practical issues—that is, ethics and politics—and to participate in the political strife of the dying republic. It is this view of Cicero as the practical philosopher that helps to explain his enormous reputation in the Renaissance, a reputation that survived, and largely for this reason, into the Enlightenment. The Humanists who wrote about Cicero—Coluccio Salutati and Leonardo Bruni among others—admired him as the embodiment of the civic ideal and sought to emulate him in their own manner of life. But life itself intervened to complicate the matter. In the middle of the sixteenth century, Marsilio Ficino and his fellow Humanists in Florence turned their minds to things remote from political action and counseled withdrawal for the sake of contemplation. But this victory of the contemplative over the active style was not a purely philosophical victory; civic humanism was a casualty of the Medici ascendancy. By 1460 in Florence, a call to political participation would have been interpreted either as a utopian flight or as an attempt at treachery. Just as philosophy has its effect on life, life has its effect on philosophy.

Humanist Eloquence and Humanist Education

The Humanists were not—or not primarily—philosophers; they were above all educators. The very name Humanist originally meant a teacher concerned with the *studia humanitatis,* the "humanities," which included the study of grammar, poetry, history, ethics, and significantly, rhetoric. [38] To the Humanists, rhetoric was never "mere" rhetoric; it was clear and convincing speaking and writing for the sake of worthwhile instruction. The Humanists liked to quote the ancient Roman rhetorician Quintilian to the effect that the good orator is a good man experienced in the art of speech. All subjects lent themselves to eloquence: Valla's exposure of the "donation of Constantine" (see p. 65) was cast in the form of a declamation, composed as a formal speech with formal rhetorical arguments, and larded with shorter speeches inserted into the whole. [39] To be

[38] Hanna H. Gray, "Renaissance Humanism: The Pursuit of Eloquence," in Paul Oskar Kristeller and Philip P. Wiener, eds., *Renaissance Essays* (1968), 201.
[39] Ibid., 213–214.

eloquent was to be effective, to be effective was to educate. Many Humanists were in fact professional educators, and their posts in schools and universities were the pulpits for their ideas. And a number of them, including Leonardo Bruni, published treatises on pedagogy that laid down their ideal and their method.

The moral intentions of this ideal are obvious; after all, educators are, almost by definition, moralists. What was distinctive about the educational ideal of the Humanists was their intense classicism. They argued that all subjects, whether grammar or ethics, must be taught through the classics—a body of writings, it must always be remembered, that included such "classical" Christian writers as St. Augustine and St. Jerome. The Humanists did not believe in progress: the study of morals, of eloquence, of politics, had been brought to such heights among the Greeks and the Romans that all the moderns could do was to find what the ancients had said.

The Humanists' indefatigable efforts at collecting and copying manuscripts, at editing and translating inaccessible classics, were therefore part of their educational program: it was to make available to all civilized men the whole treasure of ancient reflections on all possible subjects. Liberal education—the education worthy of a free man—was thus classical education, a view of schooling that continued to dominate Europe until the advent of democracy and universal schooling in our time.

Posted in their strategic places, the Humanists spread their doctrines through Renaissance society, among the learned and the rich. Technical philosophy, the sciences, mathematics—subjects in which the Humanists did not take great interest—all profited from the Humanists' scholarship, their rescue of texts, and their ideal of clarity. Even manners benefited: Renaissance society was nothing if not sociable, and by the fifteenth century it was clear that social conduct was a moral matter quite as much as a matter of mere "form." Among the moral treatises on manners, the most important and most influential was Baldassarre Castiglione's *Book of the Courtier,* published toward the end of the Italian Renaissance in 1528. Castiglione's courtier lacks the robust directness that had characterized the Florentine ideal of civic humanism, and embodied instead the ideal of the polished universal man who is well read in the classics without showing his learning as a pedant would, who is polite in conduct and entertaining in conversation, who is adept at the arts of music and painting without falling into professional specialization, who presents himself to the world as casual and self-controlled, and who is considerate of others. Burckhardt said that Renaissance rulers had made their states into works of art; Castiglione sought to make man himself into a work of art.

THE ARTS

Art in the Renaissance as Renaissance Art

Art remains, quite literally, the most visible achievement of the Renaissance. Italian cities offer inexhaustible reminders of its magnificence. To walk through Florence is to walk past buildings designed by Brunelleschi, ornamental doors carved by Ghiberti, a cathedral bell tower built by Giotto, statues sculpted by Cellini; to enter its churches is to encounter frescoes by Masaccio and sculptures by Michelangelo. Appropriately enough, modern historians seeking to define the distinctive qualities of this period have appealed to Italian artistic practice and aesthetic theory. This, as we have seen, is not a new idea. The Italians of the Renaissance liked to offer the painting, sculpture, and architecture of their day as proof that theirs was an age of glorious renewal. In the *Decameron*, written between 1348 and 1353, Boccaccio singled out Giotto, who had died only a few years before, for having "restored to light" the art of painting that had languished in darkness for many centuries. This interpretation of the death and rebirth of art, as the distinguished art historian Erwin Panofsky has pointed out,[40] echoes the interpretation that Petrarch had earlier offered for literature; thus, by assimilating the career of painting to that of literature, Boccaccio was postulating a single Renaissance among all the arts. This view became almost a commonplace; it reappears in the *Reminiscences* of the great Florentine sculptor Lorenzo Ghiberti in the middle of the fifteenth century, and was codified in Giorgio Vasari's much-quoted collection of biographies, the *Lives of the Artists,* which first appeared in 1550 and then, in a greatly enlarged edition, in 1568. Vasari prefaces his book with an extensive history of art, recounting how it had risen "from the smallest beginnings" to "the greatest height" in classical antiquity, only to "decline from its noble position to the most degraded status" after the triumph of Christianity and the barbarian invasions of Italy, now at last to be "reborn" and to have "reached perfection in our own times."[41]

The notion that the arts somehow express the style of a whole culture— the spirit of the times or *Zeitgeist*—is far from self-evident and has often been misused. But it seemed obvious at the time that art was indeed an expression of a wider rebirth, and modern research supports the contention that there was a free interplay between painting and poetry, sculpture and classical learning,

[40] Erwin Panofsky, *Renaissance and Renascences in Western Art* (2nd ed., 1965), 15.
[41] Giorgio Vasari, *The Lives of the Artists* (Penguin ed., 1965), 46–47.

in the Renaissance. Painters, sculptors, and architects were classical enthusiasts. Ghiberti and Brunelleschi, Donatello and Masaccio, Alberti and Mantegna, went to Rome, sometimes for years, to study classical ruins; like so many Humanists, they pondered and measured the bits of architecture and fragments of sculpture recovered from the earth. Such passionate antiquarianism was still an oddity at the beginning of the fifteenth century; the remains in the Roman Forum, like the classical manuscripts in monastery libraries, had been grossly neglected. But this amateur archeology was contagious; in the 1440s, Flavio Biondo, Humanist and papal secretary, "the father of modern archeology," compiled a catalogue of surviving monuments in Rome, and after him ancient fragments exercised a pervasive influence on artists and scholars alike.

Renaissance artists talked a great deal about imitation. Even a superficial comparison between ancient and Renaissance art shows, however, that their passion for antiquity resulted not in slavish copying, but in a certain inner freedom that permitted them to take up antique and more recent styles in an entirely new way. Filippo Brunelleschi's Foundling Hospital in Florence is one of the finest and most characteristic buildings of the Renaissance, with its slender Corinthian columns, its generous arches, its lucid organization of space throughout. But its inspiration, as Nikolaus Pevsner has shown, came from local buildings of fairly recent vintage, like the facade of the church of San Miniato al Monte, right outside Florence, begun in the second half of the eleventh century. "The Tuscans, unconsciously of course, prepared themselves for the reception of the Roman style by first going back to their own Romanesque Proto-Renaissance." [42] Classicism was the road to artistic independence and, as the artists themselves often proudly said, to nature.

This inner freedom manifested itself in many areas. For centuries, Christian art had turned its back on the beauty of the human body; the rare nudes in medieval art are faint reminiscences of antique figures; they are awkward and seem out of place. Then, in the trecento [43] the antique figure of the winged naked little boy reappeared as the *putto,* the little angel, [44] and at the beginning of the quattrocento, Ghiberti carved a small nude Isaac for a door panel (see p. 76). In 1434, Donatello fully restored the claim of the naked body to man's admiration with his statue of the young David. With its graceful posture, its frank, almost aggressive nudity, the Donatello *David* is a radical break with the Christian tradition. [45] From then on, the nude was domesticated in Renaissance art; later, particularly in Venice, it came to express a voluptuous,

[42] Nikolaus Pevsner, *An Outline of European Architecture* (5th ed., 1957), 130.

[43] The Italian way of calling centuries by hundreds—so that the fourteenth century (the thirteen hundreds) is the trecento, the fifteenth century the quattrocento, and the sixteenth century the cinquecento—has been universally adopted by art historians.

[44] Panofsky, *Renaissance and Renascences in Western Art,* 147 ff.

[45] It is a break with antiquity as well; although it is alive with reminiscences of antique bronzes, it is a work of striking originality. Kenneth Clark, *The Nude: A Study in Ideal Form* (1956), 54–55.

single-minded pleasure in the flesh that was wholly alien to the Christian view of man.

With the new readiness to glory in the human body came a new interest in the human face: the Renaissance is a great age of portraiture as it is—and for the same reason—a great age of biography. Patrons had themselves painted on the walls of their studies or into sacred scenes as donors, or carved in heroic poses for their tombs. While these portraits strove for idealization (not because the patron needed to be flattered, but because the classical ideal called for beauty), they were highly individualized and did not shrink from including unflattering detail. Even when they were done after the sitter's death—as was Verrocchio's equestrian statue of the *condottiere* Bartolomeo Colleoni in Venice, or Ghirlandaio's touching painting of an old man with his grandson— they strive for characterization, realism, life.[46] Fully participating in this new individualism, artists depicted themselves with confidence and candor; they smuggled themselves into group scenes or cast medals of their features for posterity to admire. Ghiberti, who could say in his *Reminiscences,* boastfully but accurately, that in his time there were few things in Florence he had not planned or made,[47] put his portrait into the frame of his bronze doors for the Baptistry in Florence. There it remains: the bald head surrounded by a fringe of hair, the shrewd witty face with its compressed lips, distinctive, unique. Portraits are everywhere in Renaissance art, if we could only read them: Masaccio's frescoes in Florence are crowded with the features of Humanists, sculptors, merchants, many of them still awaiting definitive identification. For the Renaissance artists, pride was not a sin but an inducement to accurate and virile portrayals.

As Burckhardt noted over a century ago, the discovery of man was accompanied by the discovery of nature. In medieval art, convincing depictions of nature were exceedingly rare, and notable because they were so rare; the loving, accurate representations of vines and leaves on the capitals in Rheims cathedral have few counterparts. The exploration of nature as a source of aesthetic pleasure begins with the Renaissance, with Petrarch's excursions and his meticulous observations on his property. Landscape backgrounds for a Crucifixion or, as glimpsed through a window, in a portrait or in a depiction of Virgin with Child came to be exquisitely painted, luminous with brilliant sunlight and contrasting shade (see p. 87 for Northern, Flemish influences). In the quattrocento, landscape backgrounds developed into full-scale landscape paintings; in Renaissance art, the world reappears for its own sake.

Renaissance artists, then, were steeped in the attitudes they found around them, recorded, and helped to perpetuate. But they participated in the Renaissance in an even more direct way; many of their works are representations of literary programs drawn up by Humanists, classical myths revived by

[46] John Pope-Hennessy, *The Portrait in the Renaissance* (1966), 56–57.
[47] Michael Levey, *Early Renaissance* (1967), 23–25.

Humanists, and philosophical notions propagated by Humanists. Botticelli's two most celebrated paintings, *The Birth of Venus* and *Primavera*, which still strike the viewer with their combination of gravity, grace, and mystery, derive from a poem on the reign of Venus by Poliziano, who, like Botticelli, was part of the Medici circle. [48] Other works of art give pictorial form to contemporary Neoplatonism or accounts of primitive culture. In all respects, art in the Renaissance was Renaissance art.

Art was part of its culture also in its continued dependence on religion. While much patronage came from merchants and princes, the princes of the church remained influential patrons; the Renaissance papacy employed architects to build spacious churches, painters to cover their walls, and sculptors to adorn their chapels. And secular patrons continued to order works of a religious nature—it seemed a good investment in salvation. Giotto's frescoes in the Arena Chapel at Padua were commissioned by Enrico Scrovegni, probably to atone for the vast fortune he had inherited from his father, a usurer. [49] The monastery of San Marco in Florence was restored through the munificence of Cosimo de' Medici, who had Michelozzi rebuild, and Fra Angelico decorate it. Religious themes dominated the arts down to the very end of the Renaissance: Michelangelo's most famous architectural commission is St. Peter's in Rome, his most famous panel painting a Holy Family, his most famous fresco a Last Judgment, and his most famous pieces of sculpture a David, a Moses, a Pietà— the sorrowing Virgin holding the body of her crucified son. Raphael's Madonnas hang in all the major museums of the world; and while Leonardo da Vinci's finest paintings include secular portraits, they include also several Madonnas and, of course, a Last Supper. It is true that the quality of religion changed in the course of centuries; in restless spirits like Michelangelo, Christian belief was infused with Neoplatonic speculations, and the new pleasure in earthly things—in the beauty of bodies, the quality of light, or the vigor of classical stories—gave Renaissance art a pagan quality that sets it off, unmistakably, from earlier Christian art. It has become a commonplace that the supposedly religious art of the Renaissance was pervaded by anachronisms and by worldliness: Adorations of the Kings are set in a Tuscan landscape, Crucifixions are bathed in the light of Umbria, Virgins look like Venetian ladies. It is just as commonplace to say—and just as true—that the loveliest girls in Renaissance art are Madonnas. But this secularization was not a turning away from Christianity; it represented, rather, an enlargement and an enrichment of experience, a certain displacement of emphasis. The antique intrudes more than ever, carnal beauty invades sacred precincts, but for most, if not all, artists in the Renaissance, this meant simply that there were more, and more glorious, ways now of celebrating God's work than ever before. In the early

[48] See Warburg as summarized by Panofsky, *Renaissance and Renascences in Western Art*, 191–200.
[49] John White, *Art and Architecture in Italy, 1250–1400* (1966), 204; see p. 74.

twelfth century, St. Bernard had denounced the natural forms he saw carved in cloisters as impermissible worldliness; they were, he said in a striking phrase, "deformed beauty and beautiful deformity—*deformis formositas ac formosa deformitas.*" [50] Two and three hundred years later, the most devout among Renaissance artists did not hesitate to portray the evidence of God's hand in the world—a face, a flower, a tree—with the utmost fidelity. Although sometimes a little unorthodox, and sometimes not very strict in their piety, Renaissance artists remained Christians. Some of them in fact, like Botticelli, were mystics.

Whatever secularization there was in Renaissance art became marked only in the quattrocento; the trecento remains wholly at the service of the Christian story. The painter who dominates the fourteenth century, Giotto, did only sacred scenes. Yet he was in his own way a revolutionary: it is with him that Renaissance art takes its beginning. Giotto's admirers, like Boccaccio, recognized his eminence early; his close friend, Dante, said that Giotto's fame had obscured that of his teacher, Cimabue. For Boccaccio, the revolutionary quality of Giotto's work was an uncanny naturalism: face to face with one of his paintings, "the human sense of sight was often deceived by his works and took for real what was only painted." [51] Like Boccaccio, Vasari saw Giotto as a unique agent—"Giotto alone, by God's favor," had restored painting—and, like Boccaccio, he credited Giotto with a miraculous naturalism: "In my opinion, painters owe to Giotto, the Florentine painter, exactly the same debt they owe to nature, which constantly serves them as a model and whose finest and most beautiful aspects they are always striving to imitate and reproduce." He thought this achievement all the more a "miracle" since Giotto had been born into a "gross and incompetent age." [52] For the men of the Renaissance, Giotto was the Petrarch of painting.

These are only slight exaggerations. Cimabue and Duccio of Siena, both working late in the thirteenth century, had begun to liberate painting from the rigid postures and decorative detail of Byzantine art; their Madonnas appear freer, more natural, than those of their predecessors. But Giotto, an artist of great intuitive invention, moved far beyond his teachers. Compared with their work, his scenes are simple, his dominant figures expressive, his spaces three-dimensional. Giotto achieved his effects by radical means: he places his scenes into a room framed by foreshortened architectural features like columns and roofs; his main actors sometimes appear in the rear of the painting faced by figures shown from the back—both cunning devices to create the illusion of depth. Again, Giotto gives his figures natural postures and, through careful modeling, rounded shapes; the Christ child may hold on to his mother by grasping a finger, and there are real bodies beneath Giotto's draperies. Finally, he composes his scenes with an impressive economy of means, reducing the

[50] Quoted in Levey, *Early Renaissance,* 18.
[51] Quoted in Panofsky, *Renaissance and Renascences in Western Art,* 12–13.
[52] Vasari, *Lives of the Artists,* 57.

number of figures, giving each a simple and expressive gesture, and by means of light and shade, placing each solidly within the frame and into appropriate relation to all other figures. Up to Giotto's time, art had striven to express high religious truth symbolically; in Giotto, divine figures, though they are handled no less devoutly than before, appear human. The gain in power and plasticity was enormous.

Giotto's fame matched his pioneering role. He did the Arena Chapel in Padua, a compact group of over forty scenes on four walls, between 1304 and 1313; later he worked in Rome, in Assisi, and in Florence, where in addition to painting, he designed the *campanile* of the cathedral, and where he died, much honored, in 1337.

Civic Art: The Early Quattrocento in Florence

Giotto's genius hovers over the rest of the trecento; meritorious disciples all across Italy—some, like Andrea Orcagna, remarkably gifted—retained Giotto's devices and worked within his limits. The art historian Millard Meiss has conjectured that the Black Death of 1348 awakened a sense of guilt and fear in the fortunate survivors, discouraging experimentation and inviting religious conservatism; certainly, the plague decimated the young, promising artists. [53] Whatever the reasons, it was not until the beginning of the quattrocento that artists outdistanced Giotto. But then change came in a rush: Florence witnessed a concentrated outpouring of creativity in all the arts, which made Giotto's earlier radicalism seem tame.

This beneficent explosion aroused such passionate interest and was so dependent on public participation, that it is not too much to call it a moment of civic art. Florentines had taken pride in their great buildings for centuries; all their art was somehow involved with public events—the gilds' assumption of political power or deliverance from Milanese aggression. The Baptistry, the place not merely of baptisms but of important celebrations and processions, had been started in the middle of the eleventh century, probably on earlier foundations; the legends that formed around this octagonal structure vividly testify to its prominent place in Florentine consciousness. It was the cloth-importers' gild—the most prominent, most powerful, and most affluent of the greater gilds—that was in charge of decorating and preserving the Baptistry. In 1296 the foundations were laid for a new cathedral, next to the Baptistry, and three years later, in 1299, for what is today called the Palazzo Vecchio—both designed by Arnolfo di Cambio. Other structures, only less prominent than these, grew in the city in the course of the trecento, and with all of them the

[53] Millard Meiss, *Painting in Florence and Siena After the Black Death: The Arts, Religion, and Society in the Mid-Fourteenth Century* (1964).

Florentine public—and not the great patrons alone—was intimately engaged; it earnestly debated these buildings, used them for business or worship, paid for them through special taxes. When the artistic explosion came around 1400, Florence was ready—Florence had, in a sense, prepared the way.

In 1401, there was a competition in Florence that brilliantly illuminates the civic nature of its art. In the middle of the trecento, Andrea Pisano had cast two bronze doors for the south entrance of the Baptistry; now the east doors were to be decorated in the same fashion. The gild set the theme for the competition, the sacrifice of Isaac, and seven artists, most of them young, all of them Tuscans, submitted their designs. The debate among the judges seems to have been heated; their verdict was later confirmed by the vote of the whole gild. The judges chose the young Ghiberti, then about twenty, to do the east doors. The only other design that survives, by Brunelleschi, demonstrates that the decision must have been hard, but that it was just. Ghiberti's panels were such a triumph that they were moved to the less conspicuous north entrance, to give Ghiberti room for an even more splendid set of panels. These latter, soon called with pardonable hyperbole, "the doors of paradise," remain in place today, a marvel of refined detail, dramatic clarity, skillful perspective, and a reminder of the importance that Florentine art had for its city.

Filippo Brunelleschi (who, Ghiberti proudly recalled, urged the judges to pass over his design in Ghiberti's favor) went to Rome after this competition and returned years later, a master of the classical idiom and an innovator of genius. One instance of his technical powers was the great dome over the crossing of the cathedral, completed in 1434. His Foundling Hospital, begun in 1419, became a model of the new style (see p. 71); Brunelleschi himself followed it in his designs for the Medici church of San Lorenzo, the Pazzi chapel, and other buildings, while Michelozzi adopted the same combination of slim, virile columns and firm, round arches for his restoration of San Marco. Brunelleschi's Renaissance buildings were vigorously anti-Gothic, a revival of Romanesque with new clarity and delicacy, a renewal, therefore, of a domestic style.

Florentine art of the quattrocento was a collective enterprise; Ghiberti employed over twenty workmen, while artists of lesser stature and renown carried forward what the pioneers had set before them. But two giants deserve individual attention—Donatello and Masaccio. Like the others, Donatello was an eminently public performer: his most popular piece of sculpture, the St. George, was designed for an outside niche at the church of Or San Michele and placed practically at eye level. The young warrior stands, not quite squarely, his shield before him negligently held by the left hand, his finely chiseled features expressive of youth, dignity, alertness, and an almost unbearable tension. As in his many other statues, busts, and reliefs—he was an extraordinarily prolific artist—Donatello here achieves a conquest of reality it would be inadequate to call mere "realism": classical in inspiration, Christian in theme, Donatello's work is modern in its mixture of passion and control, its variety, and its expressiveness, proof of Donatello's freedom to do precisely what he wanted with his materials. Donatello was widely admired, and he influenced painters quite as much as sculptors. Even Masaccio learned from Donatello's early work.

Masaccio's genius invites and defies explanation. His life was as short (1401 to 1428?) as his achievement was unparalleled. He was not a classicist, although antique conceptions reached him indirectly, through his friend Brunelleschi; he was not a medievalist, but he had the wit to learn from Giotto. A comparison of Giotto's work with Masaccio's shows the moment when a change in quantity amounts to a change in quality: Giotto had known tricks of foreshortening and of lending his figures a certain roundness. Masaccio moved beyond tricks to mastery; his paintings are the first statement of the modern vision in art that remained valid for five centuries. Masaccio mastered perspective and anatomy, and design as well: he does not merely copy what he sees, but arranges it with a sure feeling for drama and significance. "To Masaccio especially we are indebted for the good style of modern painting," Vasari wrote, "for it was Masaccio who perceived that the best painters follow nature as closely as possible."[54] It was not nature as the artist found it, but nature artistically shaped—as Alexander Pope would say in the eighteenth century, nature methodized. Masaccio's admirable frescoes in the Brancacci Chapel have a presence, a movement, a convincing naturalness that induced painters from all over Italy to come to Florence, to marvel at Masaccio's work and imitate it. But it is his fresco of the Trinity in the Florentine church of Santa Maria Novella— a work of decisive historical importance—that most eloquently sums up Masaccio's revolutionary achievement. The crucified Christ appears surmount- ed by the Holy Spirit and God the Father, framed by the standing figures of the Virgin and St. John the Evangelist, and outside the action, by two kneeling donors; the sacred figures are contained within a kind of chapel, beneath a barrel vault of breathtaking depth. The observed perspective is perfect. From then on, whether the debt to Masaccio was direct or indirect, mastery of perspective formed part of the artist's equipment. In Florence itself, such interesting painters as Paolo Uccello continued to experiment with foreshort- ening, while the wonderfully crowded yet wonderfully organized paintings of the Paduan Andrea Mantegna show how much clear narration and plastic power perspective permitted. With Masaccio and his followers, the old problem of how to make a two-dimensional surface appear three-dimensional had been solved, not in dry academic exercises, but in paintings and plaques of enduring beauty and vitality.

The High Renaissance

While the great Florentine generation passed from the scene at midcentury (Brunelleschi died in 1446, Ghiberti in 1455, and the long-lived Donatello in 1466), a younger generation, only slightly less remarkable than the pioneers,

[54] Vasari, *Lives of the Artists,* 124.

ably took its place: Verrocchio, with his energetic nervous line, recognizable in sculpture and painting alike; Domenico Ghirlandaio, with his cheerful, beautifully painted frescoes which give delight without arousing any complicated feelings and which sometimes suffer from sheer prettiness; Filippino Lippi, son of Fra Filippo Lippi, the distinguished Florentine master, with his charming Madonnas and restless, crowded, almost baroque frescoes; and Sandro Botticelli with his Madonnas, his *Annunciation,* his great allegorical paintings, unmistakable in their sinuous line, their attenuated figures, and their pale, solemn faces.

Then, toward the end of the quattrocento and the beginning of the cinquecento—the period that art historians call the High Renaissance—other cities, mainly Rome, Milan, and Venice, began to produce great artists of their own and attract with irresistible commissions artists born elsewhere. Yet Florence continued to be a setter of styles; the three towering figures of the High Renaissance—Leonardo da Vinci, Raphael, and Michelangelo—all went to school there.

It seems to be impossible to speak of these masters without sounding banal. Even Heinrich Wölfflin, a pioneer of modern art history and a master of cool analytical perception, found it necessary to exclaim: "The progress of Michelangelo through Italian art was like that of a mighty mountain torrent, at once fertilizing and destructive; irresistibly carrying all before him, he became a liberator to a few and a destroyer to many more." [55] Let us grant these artists their titanic stature and summarize their work.

Leonardo da Vinci was the oldest of the three. Born in 1452, he went to Florence in 1466 to study with Verrocchio. His gifts emerged early: Vasari reports that the angel young Leonardo painted for Verrocchio's *Baptism of Christ* was so superior to Verrocchio's own work that the master, conceding the pupil's superiority, never touched paint again. [56] Stylistic evidence alone makes the story appear well founded: the angel has the kind of beauty no other artist, save Raphael, could capture. After working on important Florentine commissions Leonardo moved to Milan in 1482 and stayed there, at the court of Lodovico Sforza, for sixteen years. It was a period of exceptional productivity; it was there that Leonardo painted his *Madonna of the Rocks* and his *Last Supper.* When the Sforzas were overthrown in 1499 by the French invasion, Leonardo left Milan, and, after some wandering, returned to Florence in 1503. This was the decade of the *Mona Lisa.* He died in France in 1519, after some productive years in Milan and Rome, painting, drawing, experimenting, writing (see p. 87).

The range and technical facility of Leonardo's work stretch the vocabulary of the reporter. When Burckhardt sought for an example of the ideal Renaissance man, that universal man who in addition to doing everything did

[55] Heinrich Wölfflin, *Classic Art: An Introduction to the Italian Renaissance,* (2nd ed. tr., 1953), 39.
[56] "Life of Leonardo." See Kenneth Clark, *Leonardo da Vinci: An Account of his Development as an Artist* (1939), 258.

everything well, he singled out Leone Battista Alberti, a member of the great generation in Florence—architect, art theorist, athlete, musician, scientist, prose stylist in Italian and Latin. But then he adds, "Leonardo da Vinci was to Alberti as the completer is to the beginner, the master to the dilettante. . . . The gigantic outlines of Leonardo's being will forever be merely glimpsed from afar." His caricatures are savage and telling; his anatomical renderings, remarkable for their accuracy, are obviously the result of diligent dissections; his drawings of leaves and plants would be at home in a modern book on botany; his architectural designs reveal a major talent in yet another discipline; his brilliant drawings of faces, figures, animals, riders in combat are unexcelled for their tough-minded realism and plastic power: his self-portrait—the full-bearded bald old man, with full lips drawn down, vigorous nose jutting out, and keen eyes peering from beneath bushy eyebrows—is a marvel of candor, old age turned into beauty. Leonardo was a great artist and a great inventor; his mind a marriage of exuberant scientific imagination disciplined by constant experimentation and a severe sense of form.

His paintings, which support this estimate, are perhaps too famous: it is hard to see now that they were innovations in their day or that they realized an unexpected perfection. The *Mona Lisa* is a portrait of a handsome young woman with plucked eyebrows, translucent skin, firm posture, the mysterious hint of a smile, and round though elegant hands—but it is more than that. Leonardo said that "relief is the principal aim and the soul of painting." [57] In this portrait, his principal aim is realized. The *Last Supper* takes a familiar subject into unfamilar regions. Leonardo is so intent on rendering the dramatic impact of Christ's announcement, "One of you will betray me," that the table he uses is too small for thirteen people to sit at—not until Cézanne would art again exact such subordination of realistic detail to painterly purposes. Leonardo sweeps away the traditional ways of rendering Christ or Judas; he bunches the disciples into four gesticulating groups, visibly shocked by the announcement; Christ is absolutely central in the design, serene and alone, lit by the middle window; Judas is marked as the betrayer by the simple device of having his face entirely in the shadows. Damaged as the painting is, it still speaks of its creator's genius.

If Leonardo is universality, Raphael is concentration. No one painted more Madonnas, or lovelier Madonnas, that he. Born in 1483 in Urbino, Raffaello Santi first studied with Perugino, whose orderly, lyrical, somewhat sentimental style dominates Raphael's early work. Then, around 1504, he went to Florence and came under the kind of influence he deserved. Raphael must have known the cartoon Leonardo had exhibited in 1501 of *The Virgin and Child with St. Anne,* a daring, odd, triangular composition with the head of St. Anne forming the apex, and the lamb that the Christ child is straddling, the acute angle at the right. Raphael's Madonnas, which he began to pour out mainly after his move

---

[57] Quoted in Wölfflin, *Classic Art,* 23.

to Rome in 1508 or early 1509, are alive with a cunning architectural freedom; Raphael organizes the Virgin and Child, or the groupings around the Mother of God, in complex and ever varied triangles: the *Sistine Madonna,* probably his most famous painting, compels the viewer to complete the implicit triangle by moving his eyes from her two worshippers to the Virgin, who stands above them. Raphael was not a master of design alone, he was a master also of color, and his faces, which have won him his enduring popularity, are expressive but calm, beautiful but rarely sentimental.

Raphael was concentrated but not monotonous; in his short life—he died in 1520, at the age of thirty-seven—he designed buildings in Rome; painted some distinguished portraits, including a half-length of Castiglione (see p. 69); and designed a set of ten large cartoons for tapestries which depict scenes from the Acts of the Apostles. And at Rome he decorated the Stanza della Segnatura as well as other rooms in the Vatican; two of his finest murals there are the *School of Athens* and the *Disputation,* both vast, firmly organized compositions classical in their environment and their temper. The first depicts Greek philosophers and their disciples in a fantastic building of lofty receding barrel vaults—the vault of Masaccio's *Trinity* multiplied—the second portrays the fathers of the church in various postures of debate, reading, contemplation, and ecstasy.

Michelangelo lacked Leonardo's scientific passion and Raphael's appealing serenity; he was a tormented genius who converted his sufferings into art, an art that openly discloses the torments its creator has undergone. Michelangelo was a Tuscan; he was born in 1475 not far from Florence and was trained there in the workshop of Ghirlandaio, and under the protection of Lorenzo de' Medici who discovered the young sculptor's talent. While his first, youthful *Pietà,* a brilliant, highly polished, life-size composition of a young woman holding a dead body lightly on her lap, was done in Rome, it was in Florence, on commission from the city, that Michelangelo sculpted his *David,* an outsize statue of a proud young man with huge hands and feet. The details are modeled with superb clarity, the body stands in an awkward posture; the whole is at once impressive and repellent. In spite of this ugliness, Wölfflin has said, "it has become the most popular statue in Florence,"[58] and, one might add, not in Florence alone. Like Leonardo, Michelangelo never descended to mere prettiness. In 1505, Pope Julius II called him to Rome, where Michelangelo sculpted his sitting *Moses* and several *Slaves,* and painted the Sistine Chapel. This chapel is one of the most famous sights in Rome, but it is a sight hard to see: the distant ceiling practically compels the viewer to lie on his back, and the huge *Last Judgment,* which Michelangelo imposed on the chapel wall later, between 1534 and 1541, overpowers the ceiling and the lunettes, with their smaller scenes from the Old Testament, their sibyls and prophets. The whole is rather like his *David*: masterly in every technical detail, impressive in individual scenes, but in many ways unpleasant—an ungainly miracle.

[58] Wölfflin, *Classic Art,* 47–48.

By 1520 Michelangelo was back in Florence on a commission to design and decorate the funeral chapel of the Medici in the church of San Lorenzo. Michelangelo labored on this task until 1534 without quite completing it. His seated sculptures of two minor Medici princes sit in their niches, complete; the Medici Madonna is a perfect specimen of his later style in its harsh beauty; the four recumbent figures of the *Times of Day* are finished enough to compel admiration for their monumentality, the strength of their modeling, and once again, the artist's refusal to make things pretty. In his last years, back in Rome, he turned his attention to architecture and redesigned Bramante's plan for St. Peter's. Upon his death in 1564, he was the most famous artist in the Western world, a legend in his own time.

This legend, based largely on reality, centers around the conflict between genius and society, the free artist in a world of patrons. Michelangelo was an artist difficult to employ and impossible to pass over. The works he completed (and even more, the works he did not complete) testify to his need for vast masses, for twisted postures, and for trying the untried. To organize the curved Sistine ceiling into an articulate whole, to sculpt a group that seems alive and individualized while retaining the general shape of the stone almost undisturbed: these were the problems Michelangelo set himself precisely because they seemed to be insoluble. Dukes and popes treated this prickly genius as an equal, and sometimes as a superior, but never with adequate comprehension. Pope Julius II, who had the wit to employ Raphael, Bramante, and Michelangelo at the same time allowed the last to walk out on him, and begged him to return. He had called Michelangelo to Rome to do his tomb, and then changed his mind. Michelangelo made representations and when he got no satisfaction, simply left for Florence. Julius II, Michelangelo later recalled, sent horsemen after him ordering him to return, but the artist coolly told the pope that he would come back only if he discharged the obligation he had undertaken. It was only to oblige the city of Florence that Michelangelo went back to Rome.[59] In this attitude, as in his art, the ordered relationships of the Renaissance have been disturbed, and a new age, of Mannerism and Baroque, has dawned. The greatest of the Renaissance men, Michelangelo, was also the last.

SELECTED READINGS

Good general treatments of the period are Myron P. Gilmore, *The World of Humanism, 1453-1517* (1952); the informative textbook by Wallace K. Ferguson, *Europe in Transition, 1300-1520* (1963); and G. R. Potter, ed., *The Renaissance, 1493-1520* (1957), the opening volume of *The New Cambridge Modern History.* Denys Hay, *The Italian Renaissance in Its Historical Background* (1961), analyzes the age as a historical and historiographical problem. Among collections of essays, the following may be recommended: E. F. Jacob, ed., *Italian Renaissance Studies: A Tribute to the Late Cecilia M. Ady* (1960); Wallace K. Ferguson et al., *The Renaissance: Six Essays* (1962), which

[59] Rudolf Wittkower and Margot Wittkower, *Born Under Saturn: The Character and Conduct of Artists—A Documented History from Antiquity to the French Revolution* (1963), 38-40.

includes an important essay by Robert S. Lopez, "Hard Times and Investment in Culture"; and Ferguson et al., *Facets of the Renaissance* (1963).

Florence has been much written about. Ferdinand Schevill, *History of Florence*, 2 vols. (1936), can now be supplemented by such modern analyses as Gene A. Brucker, *Florentine Politics and Society, 1343-1378* (1962) and *Renaissance Florence* (1969); Nicolai Rubinstein, *The Government of Florence Under the Medici (1434 to 1494)* (1966); and Raymond de Roover, *The Rise and Decline of the Medici Bank, 1397-1494* (1966). Cecilia M. Ady, *Lorenzo dei Medici and Renaissance Italy* (1962), is short, popular, but reliable.

For Venice, somewhat neglected, there is the fine, exhaustive study by William J. Bouwsma, *Venice and the Defense of Republican Liberty: Renaissance Values in the Age of the Counter Reformation* (1968).

For the Humanists, see especially Eugenio Garin, *Italian Humanism: Philosophy and Civic Life in the Renaissance* (tr. 1965), and Paul Oskar Kristeller, *Renaissance Thought: The Classic, Scholastic, and Humanist Strains* (1961), a revised and expanded version of his earlier *The Classics and Renaissance Thought*. Kristeller's shorter essays, collected in *Renaissance Thought II, Papers on Humanism and the Arts* (1965), and his *Eight Philosophers of the Italian Renaissance* (1964), are also extremely valuable. Kristeller, with Philip P. Wiener, has edited *Renaissance Essays, from the Journal of the History of Ideas* (1968), which contains, among many excellent papers, Hanna H. Gray, "Renaissance Humanism: The Pursuit of Eloquence" (pp. 199-216), which places the Humanists into the rhetorical tradition. For lengthy excerpts from the writings of Humanist thinkers, see Ernst Cassirer, Paul Oskar Kristeller, and John Herman Randall, Jr., eds., *The Renaissance Philosophy of Man* (1948), supplied with excellent introductions. Cassirer's *The Individual and the Cosmos in Renaissance Philosophy* (tr. 1963), is a difficult but rewarding survey. For Petrarch, see Ernest Hatch Wilkins, *Life of Petrarch* (1961). Humanist education is well treated in the older but still dependable book by William Harrison Woodward, *Vittorino da Feltre and Other Humanist Educators*, with a Foreword by Eugene F. Rice, Jr. (1897, ed. 1963).

The classical revival in the Renaissance was first placed into its proper context by Jacob Burckhardt, *The Civilization of the Renaissance in Italy;* this book, first published in 1860 and translated in 1878, remains the indispensable classic for this subject, as well as for the idea of "Renaissance" in general. Wallace K. Ferguson, *The Renaissance in Historical Thought: Five Centuries of Interpretation* (1948), surveys the scholarship before, by, and after Burckhardt. See also the reading by Peter Gay, "Burkhardt's Renaissance: Between Responsibility and Power," in Leonard Krieger and Fritz Stern, eds., *The Responsibility of Power: Historical Essays in Honor of Hajo Holborn* (1967), 183-198. One important aspect of Renaissance classicism, "Civic Humanism," has been extensively canvassed in the splendid, though still controversial, volume by Hans Baron, *The Crisis of the Early Renaissance: Civic Humanism and Republican Liberty in an Age of Classicism and Tyranny* (2nd ed., 1966). And see R. R. Bolgar, *The Classical Heritage and Its Beneficiaries* (2nd ed., 1964).

Renaissance art continues to evoke scholarly attention. Michael Levey, *Early Renaissance* (1967), is a suggestive essay; Cecil Gould, *An Introduction to Italian Renaissance Painting* (1957), is a reliable survey. Three volumes in the Pelican series on history of art are indispensable: John White, *Art and Architecture in Italy: 1250-1400* (1966); Charles Seymour, Jr., *Sculpture in Italy: 1400-1500* (1966); and Sydney Joseph Freedberg, *Painting in Italy: 1500-1600* (1971). Erwin Panofsky, *Renaissance and*

Renascences in Western Art (2nd ed., 1965), persuasively connects art history and general history to sustain the idea of a distinct "Renaissance." Heinrich Wölfflin, *Classic Art: An Introduction to the Italian Renaissance* (tr. from 8th German ed., 2nd ed., 1953) remains informative. Vasari's all-important *Lives of the Artists,* first published in the middle of the sixteenth century, has often been presented in excerpts; the recent selection by George Bull (1965) is excellent. Among a vast number of more specialized treatises, the following are perhaps the most important: Millard Meiss, *Painting in Florence and Siena After the Black Death: The Arts, Religion and Society in the Mid-Fourteenth Century* (1964); Kenneth Clark, *Landscape into Art* (1961), especially chaps. I–III, and Clark's spendid essay, *The Nude: A Study in Ideal Form* (1956), which is relevant throughout. John Pope-Hennessy, *The Portrait in the Renaissance* (1966); Sir Anthony Blunt, *Artistic Theory in Italy, 1450–1600* (1962); and Rudolf Wittkower, *Architectural Principles in the Age of Humanism* (3rd ed., 1962) are all valuable. For Leonardo, see Kenneth Clark, *Leonardo da Vinci: An Account of His Development as an Artist* (rev. ed., 1958); for Michelangelo, the bulky volumes by Charles de Tolnay, beginning with *The Youth of Michelangelo* (1943), are indispensable.

For late Renaissance figures like Machiavelli, and for the Renaissance in the North, see the Selected Readings following Chapter 2.

2

The Rise of the Atlantic States

Beginning in the second half of the fifteenth century, while the artistic and intellectual Renaissance in Italy was at its height, the center of European power shifted from the Mediterranean to the Atlantic states, from the South to the West and, later, to the North. Trade and population began to recover all across Europe, but Italy benefited less than its rivals. This shift was both comprehensive and decisive, embracing economic as much as political affairs, leadership in the realm of the intellect as much as in the realm of belief, and setting a pattern of power that remained relatively undisturbed for over a century.

The most spectacular and, in the long run, most significant evidence for the emergence of the Atlantic states was, of course, the voyages of discovery. The names of the discoverers, their dates and routes, are justly memorable. For many centuries, Western men had been intrepid adventurers, traveling wherever their equipment and an often hostile environment would permit. The motives for exploration had always been mixed, or rather, many. They included the search for souls to save through the Word of the Gospel, the search for spectacular new continents or legendary cities, the search for profits in trade or piracy: for God (as the old saying had it), glory, and gold. Now a fourth motive was added: government. Most of the early expeditions were financed, or at least claimed, by the rulers of the Atlantic states who recognized that control of overseas territories and of their scarce resources could play a part in the struggle for power in Europe.

The first to find spiritual, financial, and political profit in Atlantic exploration were the Portuguese. In the first half of the fifteenth century Prince Henry the Navigator organized meticulous geographical and astronomical studies and financed frequent expeditions, thus markedly increasing reliable knowledge of the eastern Atlantic and the coast of West Africa. Prince Henry, one of his associates said, "had caused seas to be navigated which had never before been sailed, and had discovered the lands of many strange races, where marvels abound."[1] His ambition was greater than his achievement: he had hoped to reach India by sea, but when he died in 1460, his explorers had only reached the Cape Verde Islands off the West African coast. This hardly diminished the importance of Prince Henry's activities; he had laid down the program and pioneered in the marriage of inquiry and practice, astronomy and navigation.[2] But Henry's legacy, like the legacy of European expansion in general, was an ambiguous one: Henry gave the impetus to the formation of a world market in ideas and goods, but while this meant a magnificent enlargement of European horizons, it also meant the organized inception of a great crime for which the West continues to pay today. In the 1440s some of Henry's voyagers to Africa began to trade in slaves.[3]

Occupied nearer home in the 1460s, the Portuguese let Henry's efforts lapse for a few years, only to take them up again in the 1470s; they intensified them further after 1481, with the accession of John II. Their careful accumulation of knowledge and piecemeal reconnaissance now paid gratifying dividends: Bartolomeu Dias rounded the Cape of Good Hope early in 1488, and between 1497 and 1499 Vasco da Gama made a spectacular voyage to India; he returned, two of his four ships and many of his crew gone, but with a cargo of spices estimated at sixty times the cost of his venture.[4] The Portuguese were not slow to apply the lesson of da Gama's profitable expedition. Nor were they alone. When around 1483 King John of Portugal refused to finance Christopher Columbus' projected voyage to the East by means of going westward—a proposal based on the assumption that the earth is round—Columbus turned to the Spanish court for help and finally persuaded Queen Isabella to sponsor his voyage. On October 12, 1492, Columbus' expedition sighted land—not Asia, as he fondly believed, but America, specifically the Bahamas. This was only the first of his four voyages to the Americas; in later expeditions Columbus

---

[1] Myron P. Gilmore, *The World of Humanism, 1453–1517* (1952), 24.

[2] Ibid., 23.

[3] This was not the *absolute* beginning, since after A.D. 1000 slaves were brought to Europe by Crusaders. See E. E. Rich, "Colonial Settlement and Its Labour Problem," in *Cambridge Economic History of Europe,* vol. IV (1967), chap. 6.

[4] Gilmore, *World of Humanism,* 26.

discovered Puerto Rico, Jamaica, and other Caribbean islands; Trinidad and portions of South America; and Central America. Like many other pioneers, Columbus, Admiral of the Ocean Sea, did not quite know what he had done. To the day of his death in 1506, he thought he had been exploring the easternmost coast of Asia. Perhaps there is a certain rough justice in the fact that America was to be named not after her discoverer but after Amerigo Vespucci, a Florentine who had made two voyages to America around 1500 and seems to have been the first to assert in print that it was a new continent and not India.

England and France entered the competition for discovery a little later, timidly at first, allowing merchants to finance the expensive voyages: under Henry VII of England, before 1500, John Cabot and his son Sebastian discovered Newfoundland and New England; by the 1520s, the French took an interest in Canada. But it was Spain, for a century the greatest power in Europe, that supported the most decisive of the voyages. The name Christopher Columbus will forever be attached to that of Queen Isabella; in 1513, the Spaniard Vasco Nuñez de Balboa discovered the Pacific Ocean; and between 1519 and 1522, the Portuguese Fernão de Magalhães, better known by his English name Magellan, in the Spanish service, led an expedition that circumnavigated the globe. From then on the expansion of European culture into a world culture—for good or ill—was only a matter of time.

But it *was* a matter of time. The full significance of the discoveries did not immediately appear: their economic, social, and intellectual effects belong not to the history of the late fifteenth, but to that of the late sixteenth century (see p. 206). This was a time of fundamental change on the European scene, but its direct impulse came in and from the realms of ideas, technology, economics, and politics. "The three great elements of modern civilization," Thomas Carlyle observed in the nineteenth century, were "Gunpowder, Printing, and the Protestant Religion." The first of these, a medieval invention, symbolized military power in political affairs; the second and third of these originated not in Italy but in the North, and were in part the instruments, in part a repudiation, of the Northern Renaissance.

THE NORTHERN RENAISSANCE

The Arts

The Northern Renaissance flourished later than the Renaissance in Italy. Its most celebrated Humanist, artist, and scientist—Erasmus, Dürer, and Copernicus—did their enduring work after 1500 (for early modern science, see p. 233). This late date suggests that the Renaissance originated in Italy and expanded northward, to spawn a Renaissance there. The evidence in favor of this view is impressive. Leonardo da Vinci, who died in France, and lies buried at the French château of Amboise, did little in his last years in the service of Francis I, but the French king's eagerness to have this great Italian with him indicates how much prestige the Italian Renaissance had for its northern admirers. Albrecht Dürer was only one, and the greatest, among northern painters to enter the ambiance of Italian artists and theoreticians; when he said, in perfect candor, that the rebirth of the arts had begun in Italy, with Giotto, he was voicing an accepted opinion.[5] English and French Humanists traveled to Italy, Italian Humanists traveled to France and England, and in these exchanges it was understood that the Italians were the teachers, the northerners their disciples.

But there were areas where the flow of influence also went in the opposite direction. Vasari credited the early fifteenth-century Flemish painter Jan van Eyck with the invention of oil-painting, and even if Vasari is not literally right, it remains true that Italian artists welcomed and imitated van Eyck's technical improvements. And the Flemish painters of the early quattrocento were more than technicians for the Italians: they learned a great deal from van Eyck's powers of accurate pictorial observation and meticulous brushwork. When in the 1450s the Genoese Humanist Bartolommeo Fazio compiled his collection of famous men, he included two Flemings among the four painters on his list and called one of these—Jan van Eyck—"the first painter of our century."[6] This, from an Italian, was high praise.

Apart from these exchanges, the arts of the Northern and Southern Renaissances also developed with a certain independence of one another. Dürer's woodcuts reflect the religious turmoil in Germany perhaps even more than the artistic principles he studied on his Italian visits. The Flemish painters of the fifteenth century employed their newly found pleasure in light, landscape, and three-dimensional modeling to depict traditional subjects in traditional ways: it is impossible and in fact meaningless to decide whether a Deposition by Rogier van der Weyden, or a Crucifixion by Rogier's greatest pupil, Hans Memling, should be called a late Gothic or an early Renaissance work. The world of nature invaded these luminous Flemish paintings, but their religious feeling seems more conservative, more continuous with medieval piety, than contemporary Italian feeling.

In Italian art, religious sentiment emerges most forcefully in the quiet figures of Fra Angelico and the pale Madonnas of Botticelli; but in the North some painters dwelled on the horrible glory of Christ's Passion with such fervor and such ecstasy that their work has been called, without any sense of anachronism, "expressionist."[7] The best known document of this frenzy is the Isenheim altarpiece by Mathis Gothardt-Neithart, better known as Matthias Grünewald, painted between 1513 and 1515. It consists of several panels, the

[5] See Erwin Panofsky, *Renaissance and Renascences in Western Art* (2nd ed., 1965), 30.

[6] Erwin Panofsky, *Early Netherlandish Painting: Its Origins and Character,* 2 vols. (1953), 1–2.

[7] Otto Benesch, *The Art of the Renaissance in Northern Europe: Its Relation to the Contemporary Spiritual and Intellectual Movements* (rev. ed., 1965).

most famous a Crucifixion which shows the crucified Christ noticeably larger than his swooning mother and St. John the Baptist; His twisted body is riddled with wounds and beginning to assume the color of decay; His blood flows freely; His head, lacerated by the crown of thorns, lolls helplessly on one side; His mouth is open; His hands are cruelly contorted. The whole seems like an aggression against the spectator, a pressing invitation to participate in the Lord's sufferings that will not be denied. This altarpiece, glorious and disturbing, records the religious travail of the North, to which the Reformation was a response and a resolution (see p. 127).

In portraiture, too, the North reached independent heights that rivaled those of Italy. Thanks to Lucas Cranach the Elder, Hans Holbein the Younger, and Albrecht Dürer, we vividly know what the leading actors on the stage of German and English history in these times looked like—we have splendid portraits of reformers, kings, and scholars. Erasmus' personal vanity in particular—he greatly enjoyed having his features fixed in pencil, brush, or metal—served the curiosity of later historians: Massys, Dürer, and Holbein portrayed him over and over again. And these artists sought their models not in the great alone, but among the humble as well, with their careworn faces and workworn hands—pious, ordinary men and women made immortal because immortal artists took the trouble to record their features.

It is in the art of Albrecht Dürer that the divergent streams of the Northern Renaissance flow together, harnessed by one man's technical skill and sheer talent. Dürer owed to the Italians his discovery of pagan antiquity and instruction in proportion, but his inspiration is pure German piety in the time of Luther; he was a scientist in art and a seeker in religion: he inquired after the laws of perspective and the true faith with equal earnestness. Born in 1471 in Nuremberg, the son of a goldsmith, Dürer early acquired, and on his travels rapidly extended, the professional deftness to which his engravings and woodcuts still testify. He did series of woodcuts on religious subjects, painted altarpieces, and drew portraits. But his most enduring works are his great engravings, like his *Knight, Death and the Devil,* or his still mysterious *Melancholia I.* Dürer's copperplate is crowded with incident, but rarely overwhelmed by detail; he boldly captures his figures in vehement motion and in difficult foreshortening. Not all of Dürer's work was tempestuous: his engraving *St. Jerome in His Study* depicts the saint reading serenely in a large, sunlit room, his lion somnolent at his feet, the whole breathing a tranquility, order, and saintly industriousness that contrast with the turmoil of Dürer's agitated portrayals of the horsemen of the Apocalypse.

Printing

When Dürer died in 1528, artists, scholars, and the educated lay public were living in a new world, transformed beyond recall by the advent of printing. Dürer himself illustrated printed books, and so did other leading artists. But the aesthetic appeal of books, although pleasing, was a secondary element in the printing revolution—its primary significance lay in the rapid multiplication and distribution of information, which produced rapid decay of the handicraft of copying and a decisive decline in the oral tradition.

Like the discovery of America and the circumnavigation of the globe, the invention of printing was a great moment in man's history whose revolutionary import became evident only with the passing of years. "The coming of the printed book did not immediately produce substantial changes in taste and outlook." [8] Resistance on the part of many Humanists, mainly on aesthetic grounds, was vigorous: in his biography of Federigo da Montefeltro, duke of Urbino (see p. 55), the Florentine bookseller Vespasiano spends several pages listing the duke's books, and then adds: "In this library all the books are superlatively good, and written with the pen, and had there been one printed volume it would have been ashamed in such company." [9] The Humanists had not developed their celebrated handwriting for nothing, and it is not an accident that the first printing types were careful imitations of these Renaissance hands. "The weary copyists . . ., not those who made a living copying, but the many who had to copy a book to possess it," Burckhardt observes, "were jubilant at the German invention." At the same time, as Burckhardt does not neglect to note as well, the new invention inevitably produced a fearful reaction on the part of the powerful; printing brought preventive censorship in its train. [10] Every instrument of human progress, it seems, exacts its price.

When Johann Gensfleisch zum Gutenberg of Mainz perfected or invented printing by movable type in the 1440s—the precise sequence of events and influences remains, and must always remain, somewhat obscure—the idea of multiplying information mechanically was not new. But in the hands of Gutenberg and of the financiers and printers associated with him, the convenient new device spread rapidly. The Gutenberg Bible, set from 1452 on and published in 1456, remains the most precious relic of these heroic days. While the cultural effects were not immediate, the technical transformation was indeed nothing less than a revolution; this was not handwriting speeded up, it was a new mode of communication altogether: "A hard-working copyist," Elizabeth L. Eisenstein has said, "turned out two books in little less than a year. An average edition of an early printed book ranged from two hundred to one thousand copies. Chaucer's clerk longed for twenty books to fill his shelf; ten copyists had to be recruited to serve each such clerk down to the 1450s, whereas one printer was serving twenty before 1500." [11]

The phenomenal growth of the printing industry reflects the widespread hunger for books. The spread of lay learning, at once cause and effect of the

[8] Hans Baron, "Fifteenth-Century Civilisation and the Renaissance," in *The New Cambridge Modern History,* vol. I, *The Renaissance, 1493–1520* (1957), 53.

[9] Vespasiano, *Renaissance Princes, Popes, and Prelates* (Torchbook ed., 1963), 104.

[10] See Jacob Burckhardt, *The Civilization of the Renaissance in Italy* (1860, ed. 1945), 118.

[11] "Some Conjectures about the Impact of Printing on Western Society and Thought: A Preliminary Report," *Journal of Modern History,* XL, 1 (March 1968), 3.

Renaissance mentality, called for reading material in ever larger quantities, and printers across Europe soon supplied it. Mainz, Gutenberg's home city, was the first center; before 1460, there were printers in Bamberg and Strasbourg; by the early 1470s, the major German and Italian cities all had printing presses, and by the early 1480s, so did Stockholm and Valencia, Budapest and Antwerp, Cracow and Paris. [12] Printing was an industry calling for considerable capital; it was part not merely of the intellectual, but also of the commercial, revolution of the age.

For the Humanists who accepted printing—and gradually more and more of them did—it meant a wide public for their editions of classical authors and for their writings: Erasmus, who in his wandering life spent eight months in 1508 with the Venetian printer Aldus Manutius, was thoroughly modern in his quick recognition and shrewd exploitation of movable type. He wrote quite deliberately for the press, with gratifying results. His European reputation, already established, grew with the thirty-four editions of his *Adages* and the many thousands of copies that were sold all over Europe of his *Praise of Folly* (see p. 94). The ancients—both the pagan and the Christian classics—became available to a new reading public, and as scholars enjoyed the new audience printing gave them, this audience in turn provided a stimulus for further scholarly efforts.

But this was by no means all. As today so at its very beginning, printing mainly served a public that had no interest in scholarship. Printers turned out textbooks, books of devotion, collections of saints' lives, and political tracts in impressive quantities. "Printing," Luther said, "was God's highest act of grace," [13] and this single observation, made about half a century after printing had been invented, illuminates its cultural possibilities. The printing press, after all, was a docile and neutral instrument. It could produce a learned edition of St. Jerome but also, and with far less trouble, an inflammatory broadside or a papal indulgence. Printing made information immeasurably easier to produce and disseminate; truths and lies traveled faster and further than ever before. In the long run, the invention radically altered the tone and even the content of political and social life, the mode and matter of education, the distribution of fashion, and man's very way of perceiving the world. The effects were incalculable and, in the early modern centuries, no one even tried to calculate them. All one could say was said by Bacon early in the 1600s: the three inventions that the ancients had not known and that had "changed the appearance and state of the whole world," he wrote, were gunpowder, the compass, and printing. [14]

---

[12] S. H. Steinberg, *Five Hundred Years of Printing* (Penguin rev. ed., 1966), 44–45.
[13] Quoted in Eisenstein, "Conjectures about the Impact of Printing," 34.
[14] Aphorism 129 of *Novum Organum*. Quoted in Eisenstein, "Conjectures about the Impact of Printing," motto on p. 1.

Northern Humanism

If printing was a unique contribution of the North to the Renaissance, northern humanism, although not unique, was distinctive. Its single-minded campaign to purify religion has earned it an epithet of doubtful validity: "Christian humanism." It is doubtful because the Italian Humanists, for all their flirtations with esoteric doctrines, remained Christians too; it is doubtful also because the northern Humanists, for all their intentions, sometimes strayed perilously close to infidelity.

Moreover, it is plain that French, British, German, and Netherlands scholars acted under the impress of ideas and personalities native to the Mediterranean regions. By the 1480s, Paris was saturated with Italian and Greek Humanists teaching Greek and denigrating Scholastic philosophy. The two most influential figures in the French Renaissance, Guillaume Budé and Jacques Lefèvre d'Etaples, eagerly consumed these southern dispensations; Lefèvre in fact absorbed Italian teachings quite directly in Florence and Padua. The same is true of English Humanists: William Caxton, the most distinguished printer in the country—and in this movement, printers were not simply technicians or businessmen but influential molders of learned opinion as well—resorted to Italian scholars in England as editors and advisers;[15] and the leading English Humanists—John Tiptoft, William Grocyn, Thomas Linacre, John Colet—all studied in Italy during the second half of the fifteenth century and bore the marks of Italian tastes and Italian scholarship. Sir Thomas More, the exemplar of English humanism—the English Erasmus—is only an apparent exception. He never set foot in Italy, but he acquired the methods and aims of the Mediterranean Renaissance through his circle of learned friends and through Italians resident in England.

The German Humanists, too, beginning early in the fifteenth century with the versatile theologian Nicolas of Cusa and ending a century later with the political knight Ulrich von Hutten (see p. 133), looked to the South for instruction and inspiration; they disseminated their new learning at courts and in universities, in literary societies and academies. The members of these societies encouraged the study of antiquity, the writing of Latin verse, the study of the German past—and one another.[16] Perhaps the best known of these informal but influential groups centered around Mutianus Rufus at Erfurt, and Rufus was a disciple of the Florentine Neoplatonists.

Yet all across northern Europe the Humanists applied what they had acquired on their memorable journeys—the doctrines of Neoplatonism, the restored works of Aristotle, respect for precise scholarship, and Greek—in their

[15] R. Weiss, *Humanism in England During the Fifteenth Century* (2nd ed., 1957), 139, 172, 176.

[16] See R. Weiss, "Learning and Education in Western Europe from 1470 to 1520," in *The New Cambridge Modern History*, vol. I, *The Renaissance, 1493-1520* (1957), 117.

own way and for their own purposes. The German movement nourished, and was nourished by, a series of new Humanist universities—between 1450 and 1510 there were eight new foundations, including Wittenberg in 1502—and fed the stream of religious discontent that was to become the German Reformation.[17] Elsewhere, too, northern Humanists wrote treatises and founded institutions in the service of a purified Christian faith. Their very ideal of learned piety—*docta pietas*—had first been proclaimed by the Italian Petrarch, but in the North it acquired special force. The northern Humanists were certain that the shortest and perhaps the only path to true religion was through scholarship. Accurate learning alone could clear away the trivia, the superstitions, and the worldliness that had accumulated around Christianity and that were threatening to choke it. The truth would make men pious, and the truth lay in the sacred texts themselves; in the Scriptures carefully read, devoutly interpreted, and accurately translated; and in the writings of the church fathers, printed and edited with religious care. Secular learning—the study of languages, the law, and the natural sciences—were forms of, and often preparations for, authentic piety. The northern Humanists did not denigrate religious feeling and did not doubt miracles; they were not unbelievers in clerics' disguise. But they saw danger in the general sway of ignorance, and a place for the exercise of the intellect—was not reason itself, honestly and humbly used, a divine gift?

Since these scholars were as eager to disseminate their knowledge as they were to acquire it, they were all educators. And their energetic pedagogy was anything but remote or neutral: in the inflamed political and religious situation around 1500, it was a force for reform, even toward revolution. "We should actively rejoice at the felicity of this age," Robert Gaguin exclaimed in France in 1496, "in which, although many other things have perished, many men of genius are nevertheless incited, like Prometheus, to seize the splendid torch of wisdom from the heavens."[18] Guillaume Budé was one of Gaguin's Prometheuses: his treatises and commentaries on Roman law and money, his translations from Plutarch, are filled with calls to remember prudence in the pursuit of wisdom, to heed the lessons of history, and to reform contemporary institutions in accord with intelligence. His most direct contribution to education, however, was his persistent lobbying with Francis I in behalf of a new university that would break with the traditional restrictive, corporate organization of the medieval university in behalf of an open and free pursuit of knowledge. First broached in 1517, the Collège de France was established about 1530, with its chairs first in Greek and Hebrew, later in mathematics and Latin; it was a tribute to Budé's patient nagging and Humanist ideals. Lefèvre d'Etaples, meanwhile, inspired by Italian Aristotelians, lectured on Aristotle in Paris and published a commentary on him. Urged on by the desire to make available authentic texts, he translated church fathers and portions of the Bible

---

[17] Hajo Holborn, *A History of Modern Germany*, vol. I, *The Reformation* (1959), 106.
[18] Eugene F. Rice, Jr., *The Renaissance Idea of Wisdom* (1958), 94.

into Latin and brought out a French version of the New Testament in 1523. A prolific writer and editor, he also wrote commentaries on the Epistle of Paul and the Four Gospels. Lefèvre was a characteristic transitional figure. He was a sound scholar prone to mystical experiences; he exposed some pious forgeries but perpetuated others; several years before Luther, he placed special weight on faith and encouraged the reading of Scriptures, but he would have nothing to do with Luther or other reformers. Lefèvre d'Etaples, like many other northern Humanists, was a heretic but not a Protestant; his scholarly contributions are undeniable, but others, more radical than he, would reap the benefits of his labors and draw the conclusions he had only implied.

In England, Humanist learning penetrated the court and the church. It even touched the universities: this was a time of college foundations, mainly at Cambridge, devoted to the study of the ancient languages, including Hebrew. The Humanist message was carried to wide reaches of society by an impressive collection of scholars, nearly all of them in holy orders. The career of John Colet is representative. Born in London around 1467 of a substantial family, he became a priest, but while his eyes were on higher things, he did not neglect the blessings of reason. With inherited money he opened St. Paul's School in 1512, dedicated to the realization of *docta pietas* (see p. 92). Even more significant, perhaps, for the cause of Christian learning were his public lectures on the Epistles of St. Paul, which he delivered to large and distinguished audiences at Oxford in 1496. One modern student has not hesitated to call these lectures on 1 Corinthians and Romans, "a milestone in the history of Christian scholarship."[19] Medieval exegetes, delighting in number mysticism, allegorical readings, and obscure depths beyond obscure depths, had treated sacred texts as material for elegant or esoteric dialectical games. Colet broke with all this, and the effect was electrifying. He was not a modern rationalist or a radical philologist; compared with other Humanists of his time he was not even much of a classicist. But his devotion, which has something mystical about it, was directed at the plain sense of the texts; he cut through logic-chopping and the manufacture of allegories to the meaning of St. Paul's message, its historical context, and the moral lesson it held for the time of Colet and his hearers. And this reform of method led to a demand, by Colet and his friends and disciples, for larger reform—in church and state alike. More than in the Mediterranean world, Humanism in the North was thoroughly political.

Erasmus and More: Two Humanists in the World

John Colet made memorable contributions to Christian scholarship, but his greatest achievement was doubtless Desiderius Erasmus.[20] He found Erasmus

---

[19] E. Harris Harbison, *The Christian Scholar in the Age of the Reformation* (1956), 58.
[20] For what follows, see Harbison, *Christian Scholar*, 61, 69–78; Johan Huizinga, *Erasmus of Rotterdam* (tr. 1952).

a brilliant classicist without inner direction; he left him launched on a career of scholarly productivity and humane propaganda unequaled in his time.

Erasmus was born at Rotterdam, probably in 1466, an illegitimate child. Educated by an influential lay fraternity, the Brethren of the Common Life (see p. 128), he early made a misstep that took many years to rectify: around 1488 he took monastic vows. Until he met Colet he was not certain of his vocation, but he was certain that he had no vocation for the clerical life. He secured permission to study at the University of Paris, and with his first long stay there, beginning in 1495, he moved from one center of scholarship to another. Erasmus' peripatetic career testifies to the cosmopolitan quality of the Renaissance style; where there was a Humanist, Erasmus was at home. He visited England three times, he stayed at Louvain and Venice, and he ended his years at Basel, where he died in 1536, one of the most famous men in Europe, a private citizen of doubtful ancestry who had made his fame with his pen alone.

When Erasmus met Colet and other English Humanists on his first English visit in 1499, his erudition was already impressive. What Colet did for him was to channel his talents, to prove to him that learning and piety, even wit and piety, were by no means incompatible. Every reader of Erasmus has been impressed by his cool temper, that almost ostentatious moderation which he erected practically into a philosophy. If there were deep crises in his emotional and spiritual life, Erasmus knew how to keep them private. In his adolescence, he had been passionately attached to a friend and been rebuffed; from then on his letters contain no more intimate revelations. He was fastidious beyond the normal, but if his passion for cleanliness is indeed a neurotic symptom, he turned his neurosis to good purpose. He spent his life seeking to cleanse thinking, to purify texts, to bring the fresh air of decency and good sense into the affairs of the world.

Erasmus was both a scholar and a popularizer, and sometimes both at once. His first major work, the *Adages (Adagiorum collectanea),* published in 1500 and often reprinted and greatly enlarged, consisted of a vast collection of sayings from the classical writers supplied with full annotations—all, of course, in Latin. The work made Erasmus famous and humanism popular. "Until this time the humanists had, to some extent, monopolized the treasures of classic culture," Johan Huizinga has written, "in order to parade their knowledge of which the multitude remained destitute, and so to become strange prodigies of learning and elegance. With his irresistible need of teaching and his sincere love for humanity and its general culture, Erasmus introduced the classic spirit, in so far as it could be reflected in the soul of a sixteenth-century Christian, among the people." [21] The phrase "the people" should be taken in a restricted sense; the many were still illiterate, and to many who could barely read, Latin was still an alien tongue. Still, Erasmus pioneered in making classical education general by taking the classics out of the realm of mystery open to a few initiates

[21] Huizinga, *Erasmus,* 39.

alone. The vast success of his book was a tribute at once to the powers of the printing press and to his lively Latin style. Erasmus' great edition of St. Jerome and his corrected edition of the Greek New Testament, both published in 1516, reached a smaller public, but they were daring appeals to the text in defiance of tradition, all the more so as Erasmus joined to his Greek text of the Scriptures a Latin translation that varied considerably from the accepted Vulgate version.

Erasmus sought to disseminate his religious and social ideas in a wide variety of ways: his vast correspondence with publishers, cardinals, kings, and Humanists and his didactic treatises, like the *Manual for a Christian Knight* of 1503 and the *Education of a Christian Prince* of 1515. The most celebrated of these writings, the one book by Erasmus that is still widely read, is *The Praise of Folly* (1509), a lighthearted satire that says humorously what his other writings say, though with wit, gravely. Its original title, *Moriae encomium,* with its punning reference to Thomas More, reveals its origin: Erasmus conceived the book on his way to More's house, and wrote it there. Cast, like Valla's critique of the Donation of Constantine (see p. 65), in the form of a declamation, *The Praise of Folly* once again displays the hold of classical rhetoric on the Humanists. Cheerfully speaking in its own behalf, Folly declares itself necessary to human happiness, indeed human existence, and in the course of its demonstration surveys the contemporary world with a keen eye for its failings. All professions are legitimate targets for Erasmus' gentle yet biting scorn, but most of all the clergy, with their worldliness, their ignorance, their elevation of ritual over faith.

In *The Praise of Folly,* we penetrate to the core of Erasmus' thought. As the aim of scholarship must be to free texts from corrupt readings and ignorant misinterpretations, so in life the aim is to find the essence of things by discarding its trappings. This is what Erasmus meant by what he called "the philosophy of Christ"; his religious thought is a distillation of Christian morality at its purest. This set him apart from mystics or from unquestioning followers of Rome—some thought, in fact, from religion altogether. It is undeniable that the perfect marriage of antiquity and Christianity, consummated in Erasmus' mind, made him a stranger to religious fervor. Eventually, his way of thinking set him apart from the Reformers as well. He prized Christian unity too highly to participate in its destruction, cultivation and moderation too highly to enjoy the coarse fanaticism of Luther and his followers. While at first he welcomed Luther as a surgeon called by God to cure the corruptions of the Renaissance papacy, he later polemicized against him. It was this moderation that led Erasmus even to ridicule fellow Humanists for demonstrating the "purity" of their Humanism by slavishly imitating Cicero.

Strong spirits have always found Erasmus too mild for their tastes, but there is something vastly appealing about this self-made scholar and moralist, inveighing against corruption, superficiality, fanaticism, stupidity, and the love of war, and championing tolerance, reasonableness, accuracy, generosity of mind, and decency. Yet in the world of the Reformation, Erasmus was in the end a misfit, distrusted by Catholics for the tepidness of his support and detested by Protestants (whose cause he had done so much to advance with his criticisms and his scholarship) for his refusal to join them. In immoderate times, moderate men are sadly out of place.

Just as sadly, in an unprincipled world a man of principle is out of place. This is the lesson that forces itself on the student of Sir Thomas More. In the extravagant portrait Erasmus drew of him in a letter to Hutten, he appears a man "born for friendship," simple in his tastes, a charming and witty host, a generous husband and father, "the common advocate of all those in need," an excellent speaker, a consummate classicist versed in Greek, Latin, pagan and Christian writers alike, a splendid stylist, a good man even at court—"and then there are those who think that Christians are to be found only in monasteries!"[22] Born in 1478, More came under the beneficent influence of Colet; the passionate humanitarianism of his *Utopia* owes much to Colet's articulate practical charity. Unlike most of the other English Humanists, More was not a cleric but a lawyer; yet his piety was as fervent and his scholarship as accurate as that of any priest. And he wrote, both English and Latin, better than anyone else in his day. His rise was rapid and his career, first as a lawyer and then as a statesman, was distinguished; Henry VIII employed him on diplomatic missions and in 1529 appointed him to his highest post, lord chancellor. But in the midst of his legal and public activities More never forgot his humanism; at Oxford, his university, he defended the teaching of Greek against detractors who feared that such Humanist interests would lead to impiety.

More's greatest work, a fine late flower of Renaissance humanism, is *Utopia,* published in 1516, a satire and program that has given its name and form to a large genre of writings for four and a half centuries. Erasmus, who had reason to know its author's intentions, said that it "was published with the aim of showing the causes of the bad condition of states; but was chiefly a portrait of the British State, which he has thoroughly studied and explored."[23] The first book, written last, is a vehement indictment of war, the idle rich, an unjust social system that first turns men into thieves and then cruelly punishes them, and the enclosure movement which has led the mild sheep of England to grow voracious and wild, so that (in More's savage simile) they eat men, and "devour whole fields, houses, and cities."[24] The second book, written first, portrays a perfect commonwealth, rationally divided into regions and cities, reasonably and justly governed, tolerant of religious dissent, and above all, free from the curse of private property. Some critics have dismissed these utopian proposals as a Humanist's intellectual pastime or as the longing of a reactionary for the medieval communal ideal that was being destroyed by nascent capitalism. On the other side, Socialists have hailed them as an early version of

---

[22] July 23, 1519, in selected letters appended to Huizinga, *Erasmus,* 231-239 passim.
[23] Letter in Huizinga, *Erasmus,* 238.
[24] *Utopia,* 175.

their own designs. While there is some point to the Socialist view of More, both parties are wrong: More was neither a belated Scholastic nor a premature Marxist, but a keenly observant student of his own time and a radical reformer. [25] And his satire was not a game; it was serious—satires usually are.

As soon as he accepted employment under Henry VIII in 1518, More was compelled to recognize that he could not act in government and realize the principles he had so seriously advocated; neither toleration nor communism seemed a possibility in the world of sixteenth-century England. Then came Henry VIII's divorce and his break with Rome (see p. 154), both incompatible with More's legal and religious principles. He retired from office, refused to take the required oath of supremacy, and paid for his principles with his life. In 1535 he went to his execution, his wit unimpaired to the end. Speaking from the scaffold, he told the throng that he "died the King's good servant but God's first." [26] They were brave and potent words, but they could not hide the reality that had brought him to his fall. Politics was made by ideas, but in the clash of the two, politics must win.

THE ORGANIZATION OF POLITICAL ENERGIES: THE GREAT POWERS

Among the forces that gave France, Spain, and England preeminence in Europe around 1500, the weightiest was the capacity of their rulers to consolidate their hold and their holdings. Most of the institutions they manipulated and modified were centuries old; ancient rivalries were scarcely appeased; competing centers of power at home and implacable enemies abroad continued to limit their range of action; economic and, soon enough, religious divisions threatened to disrupt precarious order. But amid the confusion of old and new and the endemic conflicts, there began to emerge in these great powers, still faint yet recognizable, the lineaments of the modern state.

The state, to put it baldly, exists for two purposes: to keep order and to make war. Of course, neither of these is as simple as it sounds. Keeping order is something more than the mere repression of the poor and the rebellious; it includes the administration of justice, the distribution of charity, the supervision of the economy, and until quite recent times, the safeguarding of the dominant religion. Similarly, making war is not merely the search for territory or supremacy by force of arms; it includes economic penetration and diplomatic maneuvering. To trade and to negotiate, one might say, playing a variation on

[25] We here agree with the position of J. H. Hexter, *More's "Utopia": The Biography of an Idea* (1952), and dissent from Gilmore, *World of Humanism,* 136–137.
[26] Raymond Wilson Chambers, *Thomas More* (1958), 349.

a famous saying of Clausewitz's, are to carry on war by other means. To complicate things further, the precise relationship between the two purposes of the state is far from obvious and continues to be a subject of vigorous controversy among historians: Ranke and his followers have insisted on the primacy of foreign over domestic policy, Marx and *his* followers on the primacy of domestic over foreign. No dogmatic answer will hold in all situations. War, even successful war, may produce famine, tax revolts, or political crises at home. Besides, the state may keep order for the sake of making war—an obedient kingdom is the best possible base for the raising of money and men; or it may make war for the sake of keeping order—foreign distractions can usefully divert attention and energies from domestic troubles, and foreign conquest often brings welcome booty. Finally it is worth noting that the instrumentalities of the state—the military machine or the bureaucracy—feed upon their own prosperity. An army increasing in size and competence, far from giving the desired security, may spur statesmen on to more ambitious plans and bigger wars than ever before; a growing bureaucracy, designed to master complex problems of administration, will create even greater complexities to administer. No general ever cheerfully dismissed his troops; few bureaus have abolished themselves. Solutions turn out to be problems.

The emerging Atlantic powers confronted all these difficulties; they rose to preeminence because they had solved earlier difficulties. They were large enough, rich enough, and unified enough to conduct their business. This, precisely, was what the political entities of medieval Europe had been unable to do. Feudal units were normally manors with a few farms attached, overgrown villages, clusters of villages, or in a few instances, sizable baronies—centers of resistance to effective centralization. They were too small or too unruly to curb international anarchy; in many respects, indeed, they were its cause. In contrast, the great units, empire and papacy, were too large to curb internal anarchy, too loosely organized and too weak, especially in the extremities, to control their rebellious vassals (see p. 112). The great powers of the fifteenth century redistributed power to their own advantage by curbing the independence of the small manorial lords, defeating and disarming proud feudal barons, disregarding or manipulating the empire, and defying the claims of the papacy to sole control over clerical organization. The power these states got was power they took away from others.

Historians have given the great powers of 1500 a single name: "the new monarchies." But both their prehistories and their organization were quite different. France, the originator of feudalism, gathered the large domains it controlled at the end of the Renaissance through war, diplomacy, purchase, inheritance, and adroit marriages. Spain emerged from the laborious reconquest of the peninsula from the Muslims and a marital union of two dynasties; it was united only in policy, not in law. In contrast, England, though rent by persistent civil conflict, was unified in territory and institutions. And while there *was* something new about these monarchies—the sheer weight of their power abroad, the tightening control over the feudal nobility at home—at least the French and English monarchs who wielded that power and exercised that control did not lack for precursors: Edward I of England and Philip the Fair of France, contemporaries and rivals at the end of the thirteenth and the beginning of the fourteenth centuries, gathered as much executive power into their hands, and asserted as much sovereignty[27] as poor roads, slow communications, stubborn aristocrats, and entrenched ecclesiastics would permit. "Through his whole existence," writes Leopold von Ranke about Philip the Fair, "there already blows the piercing draft of modern history."[28]

France: Consolidation of a Kingdom

Philip the Fair died in 1314, after a long and effective reign, marked by acquisition of territory, centralization of government, defeat of papal claims to rights over the French church, ruthless tax exactions, and vicious but profitable persecutions of the Templars[29] and the Jews. Louis XI, the first of the new monarchs, came to the throne in 1461, and completed what Philip the Fair had begun. But the line connecting these two kings is a long, sagging curve, for in that century and a half royal authority and the French economy gravely declined, only to be restored, gradually and painfully, in the first half of the fifteenth century.

The most visible disaster of this period was the intermittent conflict that occupied England and France from 1338 to 1453, the so-called Hundred Years War. English kings laid claim to territory controlled or coveted by France, and to give weight to that claim, to the crown of France itself. The war fluctuated through four distinct phases. The first, ending in 1360, was a period of English victories, well-meaning but futile attempts at administrative reform in France, the ravages of the Black Death (see p. 51), and the great peasant revolt of 1358, the *jacquerie,* a protest against the exactions of the war. The second phase began with the accession of Charles V, who anticipated Louis XI by his capable administration in fiscal and military matters. But his reign proved a mere interlude; with his death in 1380 came the third and, for the French, most disastrous phase of the war, lasting until 1422, when Henry V, their most formidable invader, suddenly died. This was a period of civil war, of bloody feuds among great nobles proving, if further proof were needed, that feudalism

---

[27] The thing, not the word—that was not invented, or revived from Roman law, until the late sixteenth century.

[28] *Französische Geschichte,* vol. I (ed. 1957), 26.

[29] The Templars were a military religious order, called, from their Jerusalem foundation, Knights of the Temple of Solomon. They emerged early in the twelfth century, during the Crusades, and rapidly grew rich and powerful, a favorite with chivalric nobles. Solidly established across the Christian world, and increasingly worldly, they acted as bankers and aroused both genuine disapproval and envy. Philip the Fair's proceedings against them between 1308 and 1314 claimed a religious basis, but the results were eminently rewarding, largely in a financial sense.

bred anarchy. As usual, the poor paid for the sport of the rich; starvation, always endemic, became epidemic in these years: "And on the dunghills of Paris . . . you could have found ten, twenty, or thirty children, boys and girls alike, dying there of hunger and cold, and no heart could be so hard as to hear their cries at night—'Ah! I die of hunger'—without pitying them; but the poor administrators were not able to help them, for they had no bread, nor wheat, nor fuel." [30] It was only in the final phase that France recovered her vigor and her territory and paved the way for the work of Louis XI.

Charles VII, a weak man whose only strength was the strength of others, was crowned at Rheims in 1429 under the watchful eye of Joan of Arc, who had so miraculously rallied French morale and presided over the French relief of Orléans in the same year. Joan was captured in 1430, turned over to the English, tried, and burned at the stake in 1431; and the king she had raised from a despised puppet to a real monarch did nothing to save her. On the other hand, he discarded the favorites who had been so ruinous to him in earlier years and now followed sound advice—having been called the King of Bourges he was now called Charles the Well-Served. In his long reign—he died in 1461—the decay of the medieval political system was, as it were, made official. The great nobles, the rich cities, and the representative estates were brought to heel. Charles VII took the collection of taxes into his own hands, made the beginnings of a permanent army under royal control, and proclaimed, in the Pragmatic Sanction of Bourges, [31] in 1438, the superiority of church councils over the papacy and the right of French ecclesiastics to select their own bishops. This bold declaration of independence of the French church from Rome was, in actuality, a declaration of the submission of French clerics to the French crown. It was also a firm statement of what came to be known as Gallicanism: the claim that in Catholic Christendom, the French crown had special privileges, amounting almost to sovereignty, over the clerical establishment in its own boundaries. [32]

The test of these vigorous policies came in 1440, with a rebellion of great dukes. It was crushed, and Charles VII used the opportunity to enlarge his domains with the lands of the rebels. Class society, even caste society, remained alive, but an elite of lawyers, merchants and petty nobles acquired a new political prominence. Feudalism as a force was dying. "To be sure," writes the French historian Georges Duby, "there remain some dependencies, groups of armed men, private castles, and powerful habits of insubordination, and for a long time to come these will make themselves known through rebellions and

---

[30] Georges Duby and Robert Mandrou, *A History of French Civilization from the Year 1000 to the Present* (1964), 171.

[31] The term "pragmatic sanction," which recurs in European history, originated in Roman law; it refers to a ruler's decision of vital importance claiming the status of a fundamental law; among later pragmatic sanctions, that of 1713, modifying the Hapsburg succession, is possibly the best known (see p. 389).

[32] Gallicanism punctuates French history; it reemerged with special force in the reign of Louis XIV (see p. 306).

outbursts of impatience running from end to end of the kingdom. . . . But henceforth these rebellions are merely short-lived, unimportant clashes, *guerres folles*. No longer is France the sum of her manors: now the realm belongs, truly, to the king." [33]

The reign of Louis XI confirms this assessment. The feudal barons, several of them connected by ties of blood to the royal house, continued to hold sizable territories, harbor undiminished aspirations, and cherish unappeasable resentments. The most considerable of these barons was the duke of Burgundy. His land was rich and his territory extensive: in the reign of Louis XI, it stretched from Dijon in the south northward across what is today Lorraine, Luxemburg, and most of Holland and Belgium. Endowed with fertile farm lands and opulent trading cities, the duchy, although an appanage of the French crown, was in effect an independent state and a real threat to France. This threat increased in 1467, when Charles le Téméraire succeeded to his sprawling duchy. He is usually called Charles the Bold in English, but his French appellation is more justly rendered as Charles the Rash. In the dazzling constellation of major European monarchs, Charles of Burgundy is a star of a lesser order, but for the decade of his reign—he was killed in 1477 by Swiss troops in French pay—he flashes across history like a meteor, proud, unbending, with a rage for magnificent show and an unquenchable thirst for immortality: "He desired great glory," the historian Philippe de Comines, his contemporary, reports, "which more than anything else led him to undertake his wars; and longed to resemble those ancient princes who have been so much talked of after their death." [34] His intention was nothing less than to establish a "middle kingdom" by rounding out his territories in the center of his thin, stretched-out domain.

Compared with this glittering dreamer, Louis XI of France seemed at a decisive disadvantage. Charles the Rash gave him the nickname "the universal spider"; that it should have gained general currency is a commentary on the impression Louis XI made on the men of his day. Impatient for power, he had participated in the Praguerie and had been exiled to the provinces for his share in the revolt against his own father. Ill-favored in body and unprepossessing in appearance, he compensated for his physical defects, and confirmed his bad reputation by exploiting his resourceful and ruthless intelligence. The contradictions that haunt all men haunted him more than most. He was characterized (as Ranke aptly puts it) by "generosity and greed, incautious trust and an ever-active, unappeasable suspiciousness, a nervous timidity under pressure and an absolute confidence, in fortunate moments, that they would last. Respect for the individual vanished in the face of his concern for the whole; justice and cruelty became one." He did great things, but no one was grateful to him, for he was without "all higher moral qualities. He made a kingdom great, but he lacked all personal greatness." [35]

[33] Duby and Mandrou, *History of French Civilization*, 187.
[34] Johan Huizinga, *The Waning of the Middle Ages* (ed. 1956), 72.
[35] Ranke, *Französische Geschichte*, 43.

In foreign policy, his skill and determination served Louis well. The end of the Hundred Years' War, and the Wars of the Roses, which kept the English occupied at home, were favorable preconditions for expansion. Charles of Burgundy left only a female heir upon his death in 1477, and after some fighting and much negotiating, Louis managed to add the province of Burgundy and, later, Artois and Franche-Comté, to the domains of France. In 1481, when the Angevin line died out, Louis inherited the rich provinces that had belonged to the house of Anjou: Maine, Bar, Anjou, and Provence. The territories Louis acquired for France were not simply favors that timely deaths and childless rivals threw into his lap: he had to fight for every inch of land in the field and at the conference table.[36] Such luck comes only to the able.

In domestic matters, Louis followed and developed the policies of his father. Characteristically, he called the Estates, first called by his great predecessor Philip the Fair in 1302, only once, in 1468, and for the same reason: not to participate in his government but to give him support and ratify his policies. He staffed his council with petty nobles and lawyers who would give him sound advice without seeking to circumscribe his authority. He imperiously supervised the courts and refused to countenance any independence on the part of judges, let alone grant them the share in the making of policy they liked to claim as a right. He controlled church appointments more firmly than any of his predecessors and dispensed this lucrative patronage himself. He vigorously protected industry and trade—not always to the satisfaction of those he presumed to protect, for his policies always were expensive. He encouraged trading companies, supported mining, and in some respects anticipated the policies of mercantilism—the use of state power to encourage the economy for the sake of increasing state power—that was to become so typical of seventeenth-century policy (see p. 300). When Louis XI said on his deathbed in 1483, "Under us the crown has not been diminished, but rather it has gained and grown," he could with justice apply this remark to domestic as well as to foreign affairs.

How solidly he had built emerged most clearly after his death. His son and successor, Charles VIII, was a boy of thirteen, and unappeased nobles and restless subjects alike thought the regency a good time to reverse the trend toward absolutism. They were wrong: the confused intrigues and uprisings, derisively called *guerres folles,* and an inconclusive meeting of the Estates General in 1484, only left the crown more firmly entrenched than ever. In 1491, three years after the death of the duke of Brittany, Charles VIII married the duke's daughter, Anne, thus adding another coveted territory to France. When he invaded Italy in 1494, the resources of a large, populous kingdom, heavily taxed and in general obedient, were at his disposal.

[36] But note the warning of Gilmore not to modernize Louis XI too much *(World of Humanism,* 82–83).

Spain: The Marriage of Castile and Aragon

One of Louis XI's most galling failures in foreign policy was his inability to prevent the marriage between Ferdinand of Aragon and Isabella of Castile in 1469. If anything, his aggressive posture did much to speed it. With that marriage, hastily concluded to circumvent widespread opposition to the match, Spain was launched on its march to the status of a great power. The union of Ferdinand and Isabella was dictated by reason; it joined the heirs to the two largest, richest, and most populous portions of the peninsula. There was about it, as the English historian J. H. Elliott has written, "a dynastic logic which reached back to a period long before they were born."[37] That logic, as Elliott says, was dynastic rather than modern: the marital union of the two houses united only those two houses, not the territories they controlled. Like the other "new monarchs," Ferdinand and Isabella did not set out to destroy traditional patterns of kingship; they joined patrimonies, but kept their portions distinct. Domestic and even foreign affairs continued to be regarded as mainly the business of Castile or Aragon, and the institutions of these realms were untouched. When the couple acted in concert, as they often did, they acted like intimate allies, never as rulers of a single state. The marriage was an effective way of joining two branches of a single Castilian dynasty[38] and of freeing the energies of militant Christians to complete a long-delayed crusade; it was the signal for the final *reconquista* of Spain.

At the time of the marriage the Muslim holdings in Spain consisted of the Kingdom of Granada, a modest patch of ground just east of the southern tip of the peninsula. Early in the tenth century, the Moors had held practically all of Iberia, but in the twelfth and thirteenth centuries, Christian troops had slowly pushed them toward the south: the compact Kingdom of Granada was the last remnant of the great Moorish offensive in Europe. The shape of the Spanish map had remained unaltered for over a century and a half; while Castilians and Aragonese were busy with foreign adventures and domestic conflicts they paid little attention to the infidel in the south. Nor did the efforts made in the 1450s to renew the *reconquista* come to very much. The idea of a crusade against unbelievers was in the air, but it needed vigor, intelligence, resources, and common action to become a reality.

Ferdinand and Isabella supplied all four. Upon the death of her brother Henry IV in 1474, Isabella styled herself Queen of Castile, but she had to fight a civil war, sometimes of serious dimensions, before her title was honored; opposition was not eliminated until 1479. In the same year Ferdinand succeeded to the throne of Aragon. The two crowns now turned to the *reconquista* in earnest. They achieved it in piecemeal but rapid fashion. In ten years, between

[37] *Imperial Spain, 1469–1716* (1963), 6.
[38] The house of Aragon had died out in 1410, and in 1412 a member of a Castilian house had ascended the Aragonese throne.

1482 and 1492, the Kingdom of Granada was overpowered. The defeated Moors, at least for the moment, were left in peace, to live their lives and practice their religion.[39]

The Spanish Jews were not so fortunate. In March 1492, shortly after their victory over the Moors at Granada, Ferdinand and Isabella issued a decree that ordered all Jews expelled from Castile and Aragon within four months. Perhaps as many as one hundred fifty thousand Jews left the Spanish lands, among them a number of Jewish converts to Roman Catholicism (known as *conversos* or *maranos*) whose sincerity had come into question.[40]

The Jews of medieval Spain had participated actively and constructively in the cultural and economic life of their countries; many of them had converted to Catholicism from conviction not fear, some of them had intermarried— Ferdinand himself was partly Jewish—and found Spanish society and professional life open to them. There had been sporadic anti-Jewish outbursts; during the Black Death and in times of economic distress fanatical priests had aroused general hatred for the outsiders, and in 1391 there had been a massacre of Spanish Jews across the peninsula. By the middle of the fifteenth century, the first racial laws requiring *limpieza de sangre* (pure blood) had excluded Jews from office in the city of Toledo.[41] The triumph of Ferdinand and Isabella over the Moors strengthened the feeling—scarcely national, partly racial, wholly irrational—that Spain must be purged to reach its true greatness; it was a signal not to relax, but to intensify, this great crusade for religious and racial purity. At least in part, the Spanish monarchs were driven to the expulsion of the Jews by their own successes.

This was the first irony of the expulsion. The second was that by depriving Spain of loyal merchants, bankers, and physicians, it threatened Spanish economic, intellectual, and scientific life at the very moment Spain was launching its great career as an empire.[42] There was yet a third irony: one instrument of the anti-Jewish policy was the Tribunal of the Holy Office, the Inquisition, an old institution put on a regular footing in Spain in 1478. It was designed to guard the purity of the Christian religion in Ferdinand and Isabella's domains, and at least one group favoring the institution had been influential *conversos*, anxious lest their position be imperiled by false converts.[43]

---

[39] For later Morisco policy, see pp. 174, 198.

[40] The familiar distinction between Sephardic and Ashkenazic Jews has its origins in the expulsion. The descendants of the Spanish Jews, who settled across Europe, northern Africa, and the Near East, came to be known as Sephardim, and to be contrasted with the Ashkenazim—a word of obscure and disputed origins that acquired the meaning of "German" and, by extension, "eastern European."

[41] Elliott, *Imperial Spain*, 95.

[42] Ibid., 99.

[43] The precise role of the Inquisition in Spain remains a matter of some discussion. It now seems doubtful that, as some earlier historians used to assert, the rulers of Spain designed the

The expulsion of the Jews was an act of politics, but it was also an act of piety. In these years as later, Spain was the proverbial bastion of the faith: in view of the worldliness that infected the Renaissance papacy (see p. 110), the old cliché about being more papist than the pope applies quite literally to Spain. But their fervent religious feelings did not stop Ferdinand and Isabella from acting decisively against the Spanish clergy. As in other kingdoms, quite as Christian or nearly as Christian as Castile and Aragon, in Spain, too, the state treated the church as a powerful rival to be mastered before it could be considered a congenial ally to be aided and a spiritual guide to be followed. The Spanish church was enormously rich, exceptionally privileged, and hence extraordinarily independent. It enjoyed an annual income of more than six million ducats, while individual prelates, like the archbishop of Toledo, had an income of eighty thousand ducats a year;[44] it owned vast tracts of land for the most part free from taxation; its great dignitaries acted precisely like feudal nobles, with their castles, their private armies, their "dynastic" ambitions. After prolonged and often embittered controversy, reaching all the way to the pope, Ferdinand and Isabella reduced the independence of these proud and powerful clerics, more barons than bishops: they assumed the right to name bishops, first in the conquered kingdom of Granada, later in the conquered territories overseas;[45] diverted part of the exactions of the church to their own treasury; intervened in the administration of clerical affairs; and supervised the conduct of clerical personnel, who, for all of Spanish piety, badly needed supervision.

This ecclesiastical policy, which the Spanish monarchs enforced with consistent vigor, was part of a general effort at mastering their sprawling and disparate domains. To achieve this mastery, they revived and transformed some old institutions. They reduced the anarchy rampant in the cities by strengthening the *corregidor,* a royal official who supervised municipal government; they further brought order into local chaos by reviving the *santa hermandad.* In the Middle Ages, these holy brotherhoods had been strictly local police forces; with the decree of 1476, they were staffed by the localities but controlled by the crowns. In a land overrun with brigands and robbers, the *hermandades*—at the same time policeman, judge, and executioner—armed with wide powers, animated by fresh zeal, and acting with notorious ferocity, appeared necessary and were soon effective. As elsewhere, so in the Spanish world, the united

---

Inquisition as a political weapon to tighten the crown's control over their lands or to speed the unification of their territories. The ostensible purpose of the Inquisition—to supervise the purity of the faith—was also its actual purpose. But, as Elliott has said, "in a country so totally devoid of political unity as the new Spain, a common faith served as a substitute, binding together Castilians, Aragonese, and Catalans, in the single purpose of ensuring the ultimate triumph of the Holy Church." Thus it compensated, "in some respects for the absence of a Spanish nationhood" (*Imperial Spain,* 97).

[44] Elliott, *Imperial Spain,* 88.

[45] It was not until 1523 that the process was completed, when Charles V won the privilege of naming bishops all across Spain.

crowns firmly believed in an aristocratic, steeply graded society, but they asserted their authority over great nobles, sought and found sources of taxation that needed approval from no assembly, and chose able men from the middling strata to serve them: "They took care," one contemporary wrote, "to appoint discreet and capable officials, even though they were only of middling rank, rather than important figures from the principal houses." [46]

Ferdinand and Isabella's proceedings against the Spanish church were thus anything but a sign of impiety. Machiavelli thought Ferdinand acted "under the pretext of religion," [47] but Machiavelli, although he understood a great deal, could never understand the complexity of the religious mind. It cannot be repeated too often that men could be truly devout and yet attack the church; indeed—and this was to become a pervasive theme during the Reformation— men could attack the church *precisely because* they were truly devout.

Historians of Spain like to point to the year 1492 as a decisive year for their country. They are right: the defeat of the Moors, the expulsion of the Jews, and the discovery of America were linked by more than coincidence. They were steps in the precarious unification of Spain around the conquest of territory, fanatical religious convictions, and the search for empire, and it was the last of these that was made realistic by the first two. Ferdinand and Isabella enjoyed a long reign—the queen of Castile died in 1504, the king of Aragon in 1516— and in their time they molded the institutions and gathered the resources that would make Spain into the first power in Europe. [48] Modernity comes in strange ways. These monarchs made a country they did not envisage and conquered an empire they could not oversee; they were new monarchs acting on traditional principles and medieval ideals.

England: The Triumph of the Tudors

When Henry Tudor usurped the throne of England in 1485, he could look back on nearly two centuries of political instability. For ordinary Englishmen and women, doing their daily chores, the interminable squabbles among nobles may have seemed remote and even trivial—the kind of game aristocrats, trained only for fighting and professionally incapable of working, would play to pass the time. Even the long and wearisome Wars of the Roses (1455–1485) scratched only the surface of English society. "The fighting was sporadic," as the English historian S. T. Bindoff puts it, "the armies small, the material losses inconsiderable." Yet, he adds, "anarchy is a dangerous pastime," as "four centuries of heroic efforts by kings and statesmen to establish the reign of law seemed in danger of being brought to nought amid a surfeit of kings and a

---

[46] This is from Elliott, *Imperial Spain*, 80, quoting other sources.
[47] *The Prince* (1532), chap. xxi. For Machiavelli, see p. 118.
[48] For the Spanish Empire, see p. 170.

shortage of statesmen."[49] Dangerous as it was to society, anarchy was particularly dangerous to kings and aspirants: of the nine Plantagenets who had reigned in England after the death of the great Edward I in 1307, only four died a natural death.

Let us read the dismal roll: Edward II, deposed in 1327 and murdered; Edward III, died of natural causes in 1377; Richard II, forced to abdicate in 1399, died a year later in prison, murdered; Henry IV and his son Henry V, the hero of Agincourt, died natural deaths, the first in 1413, the second in 1422; Henry VI, deposed in 1461, imprisoned, and finally murdered in 1471; Edward IV, died of natural causes in 1483; Edward V, a twelve-year-old boy, deposed and murdered, under circumstances that still exercise historians and amateur detectives, in 1483; Richard III, died on Bosworth Field in battle against Henry Tudor, in 1485. This catalogue, dismaying as it is, does not even tell the whole story of vendettas, the abuse of Parliament for purely partisan purposes, slanders, plots, poisonings. Shakespeare's famous line, which he lends to Henry IV, "Uneasy lies the head that wears a crown," was true in a more literal sense than its author had meant to convey. It was a cruel world of proud men and women, of bellicose landowners and ambitious officials who knew that defeat exacted only one price: death. The Wars of the Roses were essentially a family feud between two branches of the Plantagenet dynasty, the white rose of the Yorkists and the red rose of the Lancastrians. The triumph of Henry Tudor was the triumph of Lancaster.

But it did not bring immediate peace. As Henry could not help seeing in the light of recent history and current challenges, his greatest problem was survival itself. His title to the throne, like everyone else's, was doubtful, and Yorkist claimants did not give up their pretensions. For the first half of his reign—down to 1499, when the main Yorkist pretender, young Warwick, was executed for treason—Henry VII faced invasions and melodramatic conspiracies. He surmounted them by a combination of intelligence, adroitness, and hard work. His marriage to a member of the competing house, Elizabeth of York, typical of his shrewdness, was not enough to appease those who felt hungry for, and cheated out of, power.

Hence Henry used other means, all of critical importance for the rise of the modern English state. One of these, a welcome departure, was relative clemency: in more than one uprising, the king brought only the leaders to the scaffold and sent the followers back to their ordinary lives. But beyond this, Henry laid hands on time-honored institutions. Characteristically, he kept their name but changed their role. He did not destroy the common law, local government, or the Parliament, but instead bent them to his purposes. The chief menaces to political stability were the great feudal nobles, equipped, as wealthy landowners, with the means and the manpower to form private armies of the retainers they maintained and who wore their masters' livery. The

[49] *Tudor England* (1950), 8.

common law courts, which had been used against them in the past, were unwilling and unable to control these magnates: the courts were mired in legalism, ridden with corruption, and enfeebled by fear of the great. Henry VII was both willing and able. He restored local government, badly neglected under his predecessors, by strengthening the justices of the peace, carefully and diligently supervising the appointment of these magistrates. This duty of appointment, among all his duties, Henry took most seriously of all.[50] He centralized executive power in his councils—the flourishing of conciliar government, which marks the Tudor epoch, begins with him—and increasingly staffed them not with great lords but with lesser aristocrats and landed squires. By surrounding himself with men who owed him everything and on whose unwavering loyalty he could count, Henry VII employed a technique of absolute government that was becoming widespread (in Spain, for example; see p. 105), and that Louis XIV of France would bring to perfection a century and a half later. He created a court of the Star Chamber,[51] an offshoot of the judicial work of his council, defined by act of Parliament in 1487. The court settled disputes among the great, gave judgment in riots and other unlawful assemblies, and enforced the prohibitions against "livery and maintenance".[52] It acted, that is, against the powerful subjects before whom the common law courts had stood in awe. Hated as it came to be under the Stuarts (see p. 272), under the early Tudors the Star Chamber was popular, at least with the people. Finally, Henry VII adroitly used Parliament. He called it when he needed it—between 1485 and 1497 it met ten times—and sent it home when it had passed the legislation he wanted and when he was militarily and financially secure: After 1497 it met only once more during his reign, in 1504.[53]

To break the power of the feudal aristocracy was a notable achievement, but Henry was not satisfied with that. He wanted a prosperous crown and a prosperous country, and he produced both. A poor crown is a dependent crown, and Henry wanted independence. He managed the crown lands to yield greater returns, enlarged his patrimony by confiscating the lands of nobles partisan to Richard III, diligently collected feudal dues, effectively collected taxes, and derived large profits from customs duties and court sentences imposing fines and granting pardons: Henry VII, quite literally, made justice pay. At his accession, the crown took in £52,000; twenty-four years later, at his death, its income had nearly tripled to £142,000.[54] But Henry also took care of his subjects, especially the merchants. In 1496, he granted a charter to John

[50] Ibid., 58.

[51] So called after a chamber in the palace of Westminster, where it met, under a ceiling decorated with stars.

[52] "Livery" was the practice of keeping uniformed retainers, small private armies; "maintenance" was the equally obnoxious practice of the powerful to press unjust claims in court by means of threats and outright violence.

[53] Bindoff, *Tudor England*, 63.

[54] Sir David Lindsay Keir, *The Constitutional History of Modern Britain, 1485-1951* (5th ed., 1955), 12.

Cabot to explore, and take possession of, territories in North America; in the same year, he concluded a trade treaty with the Netherlands that hardened the monopoly of London merchants on the profitable cloth trade with Antwerp; and he further protected and regulated domestic manufacture. These enactments were less a system of economic policy than the groping of an intelligent monarch with an emerging commercial capitalism;[55] as such, they are another element in Henry's successful campaign to restore England to order, centralize political power, and make the country prosperous. Not even Henry VIII, his flamboyant and neurotic son, could undo it all (see p. 154).

THE ORGANIZATION OF POLITICAL ENERGIES: PAPACY AND EMPIRE

The Papacy as a Political System

While France, Spain, and England took the center of the political stage late in the fifteenth century, other political systems continued to play considerable roles in the making of history. Events in Rome or at Wittenberg reverberated across Europe.

One of the most remarkable of these systems was the papacy. In the eyes of European statesmen, no matter how devout, it was a state like any other. It is true that the church had a special hold on men's minds in medieval and early modern Europe, but when its kingdom was evidently of this world, secular princes could not afford to overlook its activities. And from the thirteenth century on, precisely as the involvement of the church in the world—in its politics, its luxuries, its corruptions—became overwhelming and disturbing, the capacity of the papacy to influence events markedly declined. This combination of visibility and impotence was irresistible: ruler after ruler deprived Rome of the right to appoint bishops, tax the local clergy, or take appeals from local courts.

By 1417, when a comparatively united church agreed to elect the Roman cardinal Otto Colonna to the papal chair, the long decline of the papacy seemed to have been arrested. For over a century it had undergone humiliation at the hands of grasping princes, a glittering captivity at Avignon under French pressure, and most dismaying of all, a discreditable schism in which two, and later three, clerics had claimed to be the sole vicar of Christ (see p. 44). The Council of Constance, convoked in 1414 to deal with disorders in the church, combat heresy, and restore unity, had three popes on its hands: the aged Gregory XII, the Avignon claimant Benedict XIII, and the egregious John XXIII,

---

[55] See Bindoff, *Tudor England,* 64.

"the most profligate of mankind," as Gibbon, with malicious accuracy, describes him. Gregory resigned, Benedict was deposed, and John imprisoned: "He fled," Gibbon writes, "and was brought back a prisoner; the most scandalous charges were suppressed; the vicar of Christ was only accused of piracy, murder, rape, sodomy, and incest."[56] After such leadership, the resumption of papal residence at Rome and the elimination of rivals seemed the most far-reaching of reforms. But the Renaissance popes who followed the Great Schism resisted the drastic purge that was so obviously essential for the health of organized Christendom. For the first half of the fifteenth century, a series of church councils made solemn efforts to assert their superiority over the pope: "This synod," the Council of Constance affirmed and, in 1432, the Council of Basel reaffirmed, "lawfully assembled in the Holy Ghost, and forming a general council representing the Catholic Church, has its power directly from Christ, and everyone, of whatever rank and office, even the Pope, is obliged to obey it in matters touching the faith, in the removal of the Schism, and in the reformation of the church in head and members."[57] Clerical vices were prevalent and palpable: simony—the selling of church offices; indulgences—the selling of salvation;[58] pluralism—the profitable occupancy of several benefices; and concubinage—the widespread practice of priests too weak (or too strong) to obey the church's rule demanding celibacy. The conciliar movement enlisted some of the finest minds of Christendom, including Nicolas of Cusa, but after an effort of thirty years, it failed. The popes temporized: they agreed on the need for reform but rejected the political theory of the reformers. When the acrimonious Council of Basel was dissolved in 1449, the papacy had reasserted its sovereignty over the church. Flushed with victory, it staged a jubilee in 1450, and the need for concessions being over, made no reforms. Precisely like other states, the papacy sought to secure its hold on its territories and absolute authority over its constituencies. Half a century later, Martin Luther would make the papacy pay, not so much for its monarchical aspirations as for its self-confident and short-sighted neglect of its spiritual office.

While few of the Renaissance popes were admirable spiritual guides to Christians across Europe, many of them were characteristic Renaissance men, with all the good and evil consequences this implies. Nicholas V, a Humanist who had been librarian to Cosimo de' Medici, founded the Vatican Library and surrounded himself with such fellow Humanists as Lorenzo Valla and Leone Battista Alberti. Pius II, who is one of the heroes of Burckhardt's *Civilization of the Renaissance in Italy*, was a reformed worldling and poet who distinguished

---

[56] *Decline and Fall of the Roman Empire* (1787, ed. J. B. Bury), VII, 288, 289.

[57] George H. Sabine, *A History of Political Theory* (rev. ed., 1950), 323.

[58] This, of course, is what the Protestants later came to call it; precisely and officially, indulgences, first introduced in 1300 by Boniface VIII to raise money, were considered supplementary expiations of sin, added to the sacrament of penance. To gain an indulgence, by prayer or by purchase, was to "make satisfaction."

his tenure with a fine autobiography and an elegant correspondence. Sixtus IV was one of the most lavish among Renaissance patrons; he began construction of the Sistine Chapel and brought painters like Botticelli and Ghirlandaio to Rome. But with the reign of Sixtus, the worldly papacy added to the innocuous patronage of artists the vicious patronage of relatives. Sixtus' midcentury predecessors—Pius II's reign had ended in 1464—had still taken their responsibilities with the utmost seriousness. The Turks' capture of Constantinople in 1453 had moved the vicars of Christ to proclaim a crusade against the infidel at the gates, and Pius II, disappointed in the poor response his call for a crusade received among Christian princes, even outfitted his own fleet. But Sixtus cared more for his family than for larger issues; he made nepotism, one of the most glaring vices of the papacy, into a system. Six of Sixtus' cardinals were close relatives, three of them his nephews. "One alone—Giuliano della Rovere—" the Catholic historian Philip Hughes exclaims, scandalized, "held eight bishoprics in four different countries, besides various abbeys!" [59] Giuliano's influence in Rome was almost unparalleled. After his uncle's death in 1484, he remained to dominate his successor and finally obtained the papal tiara himself in 1503. As Julius II, he proved to be as energetic and militant as a *condottiere.* "He would have been a pope worthy of the highest renown," the great sixteenth-century Florentine historian Guicciardini said of him, "if he had been a secular prince or if the care and diligence he showed in glorifying the church in the temporal sphere and through the art of war had been used to glorify it in the spiritual sphere through the arts of peace." [60] Even to Italians hardened in the ways of the world, the spectacle of warrior-diplomat-popes seemed a little inappropriate.

The lust for political power, artistic display, and family influence reached its climax with Alexander VI, the Borgia pope, Giuliano's rival and predecessor. Among Alexander's unusual distinctions is the fame—or the notoriety—achieved, with his active support, by two of his illegitimate children, Lucrezia and Cesare Borgia. Alexander made no secret of his sensuality and his greed, even as pope. While the most scandalous rumors about his conduct, like his supposed incest with his daughter Lucrezia, have been traced to the malicious gossip of disappointed office seekers, the truth about Alexander's debauchery and abuse of office for political purposes and private gain was dramatic enough. "Of all the pontiffs who ever reigned," Machiavelli coolly appraised him, "Alexander VI best showed how a Pope might prevail both by money and by force." [61] It was popes like Alexander VI and Sixtus IV who moved Erasmus to excoriate, in *The Praise of Folly,* the "scourges of the human race."

[59] *A Popular History of the Catholic Church* (Image Book ed., 1954), 157; note to Pazzi conspiracy in chap. I.

[60] Quoted by R. Aubenas, "The Papacy and the Catholic Church," in *The New Cambridge Modern History,* vol. I, *The Renaissance, 1493–1520* (1957), 84.

[61] *The Prince,* chap. XI.

By and large, the Renaissance popes were an effective group of men, normally with exquisite taste, consummate diplomatic skill, and, like Julius II, personal bravery. But, especially from Sixtus IV on, they walked like dreamers through an earthquake. In the midst of outbursts of popular fanaticism, large-scale heresy, foreign invasion, and the Turkish menace to Christendom, they looked to their property and haggled with painters. In the century and a half after the Great Schism had been healed, the popes regained some of their political power, firmly secured the papal states around Rome, amassed immense wealth for their families, and procured for the world imperishable works of art. But the papacy was not to recover much of its spiritual authority until the second half of the sixteenth century, with the austere and militant Counter-Reformation (see p. 164).

The Empire: Decline and Recovery

The decline and recovery of the empire—the Holy Roman Empire—preceded those of the papacy, but its capacities never matched its claims, not even in the early sixteenth century under the Emperor Charles V. Voltaire's famous quip that the Holy Roman Empire was neither holy, nor Roman, nor an empire was absolutely on target. The empire was a confused conglomerate. It contained more than two thousand imperial knights who held anything from a tiny patch of land to a castle with surrounding terrain and owed allegiance to none but the emperor himself; dozens of ecclesiastical principalities usually dominating a wealthy city and its hinterland; perhaps three score free cities; and a few small independent countries like Bavaria or Saxony or Brandenburg. The political, geographical, and constitutional confusion that characterized this patchwork is illustrated by the sheer impossibility of giving precise numbers for these constituent parts and by the arbitrary way in which some were represented in the imperial parliament, the Reichstag, and others not. In the hands of exceptional emperors, this miserable memory of a greater past might muster some political unity and military strength, but such exceptional emperors were just that—exceptional. The emperor could call on his Reichstag to vote him financial supplies or troops against foreign enemies, but if no money or troops came, he was powerless to compel their presence. The very procedure for choosing an emperor—determined in the Golden Bull of 1356 to be by majority vote of seven electors—[62] underscored the intentions of the emperor's great subjects to keep the substance of power in their own hands and leave their overlord with its trappings.

Then, in 1438, though not at first by design, this elective aristocracy became something like a hereditary monarchy, when the king of Bohemia and

[62] The archbishops of Mainz, Cologne, and Trier; the king of Bohemia; the elector of Saxony; the margrave of Brandenburg; and the count palatine of the Rhine.

Hungary, a Hapsburg, was elected Emperor Albert II. From then on, to the ignominious end of the empire in 1806, Hapsburgs were chosen as emperors. [63] They brought to the imperial crown the kind of authority that only extensive lands and impressive wealth can bestow.

The Hapsburg dynasty emerges into the light of history in the tenth century, with family holdings in Switzerland and Alsace. By the thirteenth century Hapsburgs had amassed great estates in Austria, Bohemia, Carinthia, and Styria, and in succeeding centuries these domains, with Hungary added, became the heartland of Hapsburg power. When Albert II died in 1439, his distant cousin Frederick became Emperor Frederick III and was succeeded, after a long reign, by his son Maximilian I in 1493. As king of Rome, he had already been wielding considerable power since 1486; as emperor—intelligent, impressive, and popular—he first aroused, and soon disappointed, great expectations. But what he could not do for his realm, he did for his family, and significantly enough, he did so by pursuing the policies and methods that his ancestors had used: he made advantageous marriages. The Hapsburgs' adroitness in adding desirable territory by uniting their house with eligible heirs and heiresses gave rise to envious jokes. Every self-respecting textbook quotes the famous Latin quip: "*Bella gerant alii, tu felix Austria nube*—Let others wage war, you, happy Austria, marry," a quip that concludes with the observation that what others obtained through Mars, the Hapsburgs obtained through Venus. But marriage is no joke; for the Hapsburgs, in any event, it was a favorite means of enlarging domains with a minimum of cost. Albert II had acquired Hungary by marrying the daughter of the king of that country. Frederick III gave the Hapsburgs a grip on Western Europe by marrying his son Maximilian to Mary of Burgundy, daughter of Charles the Rash (see p. 101). When Maximilian became emperor, he brought this pacific dynastic imperialism to a climax with a spectacular union between his son Philip and Joanna, the daughter and heiress of Ferdinand and Isabella. Charles, the eldest son of this couple, was to become Emperor Charles V, holding, overseeing, if not wholly controlling, lands stretching from Central America to the gates of Turkey. Spanish America, Spain, the Netherlands, Italian territory, Austria, Bohemia, Hungary, all gathered into a single, if somewhat tenuous family property by means of marriage: it was a great tribute to the institution.

Besides covering Europe with his family and his in-laws, Maximilian laid the foundations for the Austrian state. In several provinces he set up governing councils responsible to the crown, and he reorganized and strengthened the central administration. He liked to say that he preferred being a powerful duke of Austria to being the impotent emperor of the Germans. [64] One can see what

[63] For the record we must note a single brief interlude: from 1742 to 1745, Charles Albert, elector of Bavaria, of the house of Wittelsbach, was emperor as Charles VII.

[64] See R. G. D. Laffan, "The Empire under Maximilian I," in *The New Cambridge Modern History*, vol. I, *The Renaissance, 1493–1520* (1957), 210.

he meant: the constituent elements of the empire were too strong, and in consequence the empire itself was too weak, to make real imperial government possible.

The reasons for this impossibility lay in the course of German history. With the death of Emperor Frederick II in 1250, the German territories had fallen into an anarchy lasting a century or more; it was a time of foreign interventions and domestic disorders. As French and English history testifies, feudalism had been a centrifugal force everywhere; in the German lands its divisive power was greater than anywhere else. When in the fourteenth and fifteenth centuries German rulers and statesmen painfully restored a measure of order, they did so by strengthening local territories, coming to terms with local estates, raising local armies. Reform meant a stronger state of Saxony or a stronger city of Frankfurt, rather than a united Germany. There was an emerging sense of Germanness everywhere, a consciousness that found its expression in that odd term "German nation" that was appended to the older name "Holy Roman Empire" in the fifteenth century.[65] But this was, if anything, a cultural rather than a political nationalism; no one, no matter how far-seeing, drew the consequence that Europeans of the nineteenth century would have found inescapable: that cultural unity implies and demands political unity. Despite these obstacles, Maximilian preserved the empire largely if not wholly intact. His Swiss subjects escaped imperial control by their rebellion of 1499, and other lands, like Holstein in the north and those controlled by the Teutonic knights in the east, came under foreign domination. And he preserved a certain imperial influence in European affairs.

But the future lay with France, Spain, and England; with states growing within the empire (like Prussia); with the Hapsburg domains themselves (lying partly within and partly outside the empire); and with the looming giant of the East, Russia. This was so not because these states were modern or national while the empire was medieval and dynastic. The emerging states, too, derived their authority from traditional sources, and their royal houses were firmly committed to the principle of dynasticism. But the empire was too scattered in its territories, too diverse in its populations, too indefensible in the flatlands, surrounded by too many voracious neighbors, and subdivided too finely into thousands of units, each jealous of its prerogatives, to forge the parts into a whole. What marriage had done, diplomacy, rebellion, and war would in the long run undo. Mars was not wholly powerless in the hands of Venus after all.

[65] Ibid., 194.

WAR AND REALISM IN ITALY

Italy as Battleground

The Italian wars demonstrate how vulnerable small states had become to the ambitions of great powers. And—an illustration to warm the hearts of moralists—the conduct of Italian statesmen during these wars demonstrates that selfishness and cynicism often have disastrous consequences.

When in 1494 Charles VIII of France crossed into Italy with an army of forty thousand men, he set a pattern for French foreign policy that he and his two immediate successors, Louis XII and Francis I, would follow for half a century. Italy (to use language Machiavelli might have used) was like a beautiful young woman—too seductive to be left intact, too weak to defend herself, a temptation irresistible to rulers trained not to resist but to yield to such temptations. The reasons for Charles' intervention were old: a combination of claims to Naples by the house of Anjou and pressing invitations to the French by Italian politicians to rescue them from other Italian politicians. What was new was the capacity of France for large-scale adventures, mobilized by young Charles VIII, whose chivalric imagination was unchecked by intelligence. Charles was dazzled by grandiose plans to seize Naples as a base for a crusade against the Turk, and there were disturbing, well-founded reports that he meant to retake Constantinople, liberate Jerusalem, and make himself emperor of East and West. [66] Political refugees at the French court stirred him into action. The embittered Cardinal Giuliano della Rovere, whose bid for the papacy had been defeated by the Borgia faction, urged Charles into Italy; other exiles told him that the Angevin party at Naples was being persecuted and ardently hoped for his coming. Then Lodovico Sforza of Milan, fearful of Neapolitan intervention in his affairs, declared himself the ally of France and associated himself with those Italians interested in seeing Charles seize the crown of Naples to which the French had such a dubious claim. Lodovico's precise expectations remain unclear. He thought either that the mere threat of the French presence would deter his enemies or that the French, having done his work for him, would limit their Italian intervention to Naples itself.

In either case he was mistaken. Backed by agreements with Ferdinand of Aragon and Emperor Maximilian, both expensive to France, Charles invaded

---

[66] J. R. Hale, "International Relations in the West: Diplomacy and War," in *The New Cambridge Modern History*, vol. I, *The Renaissance, 1493-1520* (1957), 263-264, 295-296.

Italy in September 1494. The internal divisions that bedeviled most Italian states materially aided his campaign; each ruler treated him in accord with his own partisan interest. Accordingly, Charles met with little resistance, and by February 1495 he was in Naples. His triumph was his undoing: alarmed at French dominance over Italy, and outraged by the conduct of French troops and military governors, his enemies formed the Holy League in 1495, designed to expel the invader. Even Charles' former supporters, the emperor and Spain, joined the league, which also included Milan, Venice, the papacy, and in the following year, the English. It rapidly achieved its objectives: by 1496 all Italy was free of French troops.

In 1499, the French were back in Italy. The second scenario was reminiscent of the first, only this time the French king was Louis XII, who had ascended the throne the year before, and his claim was to Milan. But once again, the Italians thought only of their immediate interests. "Before 1494," the English historian Cecilia M. Ady has said, "they were confident that the French would not come; after Charles' withdrawal they flattered themselves that the French would not stay; the chief thought in their minds was how Louis's intervention could best be used to their individual advantage." [67] The Venetians supported the far-fetched French claim in the hope of territorial gains at the expense of Milan; Florence favored French designs to advance its own design of retaking Pisa; most cynical of all, Pope Alexander VI abetted Louis' Italian plans and his desire for a divorce in return for French support for the ambitious secular career of his son, Cesare Borgia, that impious cardinal turned ruthless duke. Power politics could go no further, and sink no lower, than this.

For a time they French did well. By 1500, after shifting fortunes, they held Milan; Lodovico Sforza was taken and spent the rest of his days in French captivity. In the same year, Louis agreed with Ferdinand of Aragon to divide up the Neapolitan kingdom between France and Spain, and in 1501, French troops were in Naples once again. But the allies fell out, as allies will, and by 1504, Naples was in Spanish hands. After complex fighting across the peninsula, a second coalition finally compelled the French to yield their Italian holdings. By 1512, the French had evacuated Milan, and a last desperate attempt to recoup their losses led to a French defeat at Novara in 1513, and to tenuous peace. In consequence, the Sforzas returned to Milan, and the Medici, who had been expelled in the wake of the first invasion of 1494, to Florence. The lesson was inescapable: domestic power in Italy depended on the fortunes of war, and those depended on foreign states.

Where Charles VIII and Louis XII had failed, Francis I failed as well. Three successive invasions of Italy—in 1515, the very year of his accession, in 1524, and in 1527—only ended in 1529 with the Treaty of Cambrai, in which the French gave up all their Italian claims, a renunciation confirmed, after further

---

[67] "The Invasions of Italy," in *The New Cambridge Modern History*, vol. I, *The Renaissance, 1493–1520* (1957), 355.

tentative probes, in 1559, with the Treaty of Cateau-Cambrésis (see p. 163). Meanwhile, Italy had turned into one theater of war among several, as two great dynasties, Valois and Hapsburg, battled for hegemony. Reduced to a battleground, Italy suffered the ultimate humiliation of becoming, by the 1520s, merely a secondary battleground (see p. 60).

The New Realism: Machiavelli

Though in many respects more a symptom than a cause of transformation, the wars that began in 1494 and ended, more or less, in 1529, stimulated far-reaching changes in styles of warfare and diplomacy and modes of thinking about international and domestic affairs. The rise of the infantry and the increasing importance of portable firearms diminished the relevance (while it increased the beauty) of armor and reduced (while it did not eliminate) the work of cavalrymen in battle. The shift to infantry had been pioneered by the Swiss, who continued to export their able-bodied men to mercenary contingents all across Europe. "The Swiss, whose defeat of the Burgundian cavalry at Grandson and Morat in 1476 had caused such general concern among military men, fought in compact squares of about 6,000 men, eighty-five shoulder to shoulder, on a hundred-yard long front, and seventy ranks deep. The success of this formation depended on rigid discipline and strict drill. Nothing could be allowed to divert the pressure or resistance of the square till it was crippled or victorious; no prisoners could be taken, the wounded were ignored. A cavalry charge at such a square met first a solid hedge of steel, the pike heads of the first four ranks, then halberds, taking advantage of broken order to stab at close quarters or to grapple from the flank and hook a horseman down, then at the centre of the square broadswords which could swing at a man still mounted or be grasped below the hilt to thrust at those unhorsed. An infantry charge was met first by ranks of halberds which struck down the points of the pikes, then by row after row of pikes in front and in the flanks by swordsmen and crossbows and arquebusiers issuing from the centre and rear of the phalanx." [68] These tactics, as contemporaries noted, came into their own in, and through, the Italian wars. "Before 1494," writes Guicciardini, with Machiavelli the keenest observer of his day, "wars were long, campaigns were relatively bloodless, and methods of conquest were slow and difficult. And although artillery was already in use, it was handled so unskillfully that it did little damage. Thus, those who held power stood in little danger of losing it. When the French came to Italy, they introduced such efficiency into war that, up to 1521, the loss of a campaign meant the loss of a state." But, as Guicciardini also observed, new tactics of attack produced new ingenuity in defense: "Rulers now have the same security they had before 1494, but for a different reason.

---

[68] Hale, "International Relations in the West," 284.

Then, it was due to the fact that men were unskilled in the art of offense; now, to the fact of knowing well the art of defense." [69]

Like the art of war, the art of diplomacy was greatly refined during these decades. The old method of handling international relations through special envoys and the occasional meeting of princes was simply inadequate in a Europe bound together by a network of alliances, intricate dynastic arrangements, shifting enmities that might engage troops far from home, and commercial relations as complex and sometimes as acrimonious as political competition. The period of the Italian wars saw the proliferation of permanent missions, which had been tried by a few states before and now became general practice. Sir Henry Wotton's celebrated definition of an ambassador—"an honest man sent to lie abroad for the good of his country"—dates from 1604, but it might well have been coined a hundred years before.

Modern historians think of these decades as the end of an epoch and the beginning of another. Acute observers at the time obviously thought the same thing. The Italian wars raised old questions in a new and most acute form: What are the stakes of fighting and negotiating? What are proper moral and constitutional constraints on political action? What is the place of self-interest in politics? What, indeed, is the function of state and the state system? Princes of the church had appealed to the sword, secular princes had blatantly placed private profit above public good. And it was sadly plain that the Italian state system had failed. True, the French had been expelled from Italy, but this was no cause for rejoicing: Italians had connived at their coming; Spaniards, Swiss, and Germans had engineered their going. In the second half of the fifteenth century the Italian powers had worked out a relatively pacific arrangement among its five largest constituent states, a miniature balance of power. That balance was a foretaste of the larger balance at which European statesmen would aim for centuries, and which would dictate the formation of coalitions against those—from Louis XIV to Adolf Hitler—who would seek to destroy that balance in search of hegemony. But the smaller Italian balance had proved inadequate to keep Italy from being victimized by larger, more powerful states. It was not until the second half of the nineteenth century that Italy would once again control her own affairs.

These were all agonizing matters, and these are the raw material that Machiavelli worked into his political theory. Niccolò Machiavelli wrote for the sake of practice, out of a fund of personal experience, enriched by purposeful reading in the classics. He was born in 1469, to a poor but patrician family and was tied all his life to the turbulent affairs of his beloved Florence. From 1498 to 1512, while the Medicis were in exile, he held a post in the chancellery in Florence. He went on diplomatic missions—his low estimate of human nature rests on intimate and lengthy experience with statesmen and rulers. He raised

[69] Francesco Guicciardini, *Maxims and Reflections of a Renaissance Statesman* (tr. 1965), 57–58.

troops for the defense of Florence, acting on his conviction that mercenaries are the death of republics and that only militiamen preserve freedom. Then, when the Medicis returned in 1512, he was dismissed, imprisoned, and sent out of the city.

This was dreadful exile for him. He would rise early (as he describes his life in his most famous letter), inspect his estate, talk with farmers, do desultory reading. "When evening comes, I return home and go into my study. On the threshold I strip off the muddy sweaty clothes of everyday, and put on the robes of court and palace, and in this graver dress I enter the antique courts of the ancients where, being welcomed by them, I taste the food that alone is mine, for which I was born. And there I make bold to speak to them and ask the motives of their actions. And they, in their humanity, reply to me. And for the space of four hours I forget the world, remember no vexation, fear poverty no more, tremble no more at death: I am wholly absorbed in them. And as Dante says that there can be no understanding without the memory retaining what it has heard, I have written down what I have gained from their conversation, and composed a small work *De Principatibus,* where I dive as deep as I can into ideas about this subject, discussing the nature of princely rule, what forms it takes, how these are acquired, how they are maintained, why they are lost." [70] To his death in 1527, the rest of his life, filled with talk about political theory and restless activity, was one long effort to find employment suitable to his talents. He wrote his books—his comedies, his history of Florence, his long essay on the art of war, and his two classics in political theory, *The Prince* and *The Discourses on the First Ten Books of Livy,* all distinguished by his virile mind and brilliant style—as a substitute for, and a way back into, the action he craved. However he felt about his later years, we have reason to be grateful to the political fortunes that gave him the unwelcome leisure to do his immortal work. [71]

The controversy over the meaning of Machiavelli's political thought has raged for over four centuries. He has been portrayed as a scientist, a patriot, and a devil. Some of his admirers, pained by the harsh tone and ruthless prescriptions of *The Prince,* have read it, not as a handbook for tyrants but as a satire on tyranny. There have been desperate admissions that the teachings of *The Prince* and those of *The Discourses* are irreconcilable, and ingenious efforts to reconcile them. But, as Gilbert has said, "Machiavelli's contemporaries would have found the seeming disparity of his subject matter less astounding and less objectionable than we do. . . . The contrast between *The Prince* and *The Discourses* is more apparent than fundamental; in both works the problem of political leadership is clearly a basic issue." [72] Machiavelli's political thinking reflects the sober response of a disillusioned, clear-eyed

[70] Quoted by J. R. Hale, *Machiavelli and Renaissance Italy* (1963), 130.

[71] See Felix Gilbert, *Machiavelli and Guicciardini: Politics and History in Sixteenth-Century Florence* (1965).

[72] Ibid., 188.

observer witnessing a new rootless age. His two masterpieces deal with Machiavelli's greatest, his only love: politics, or more precisely, human nature in politics. As a Humanist, Machiavelli is ready to apply the lessons that classical antiquity has to teach; as an innovator, proudly aware that his enterprise is unprecedented—"I have resolved to open a new route," he said, "which has not yet been followed by anyone"[73]—he sought for the laws that would make politics into a science. Clearly he preferred a republic to a tyranny; *The Discourses* breathe his distaste for plutocracies and his admiration for sturdy, self-governing commonwealths. He knew, as all men of the Renaissance knew, that fortune is fickle and powerful, and that the most resolute vigor and the most cunning foresight will fail if fortune frowns. But this was no excuse for passivity; it was, on the contrary, a call for the exercise of *virtù*—of energy, of patient, vigorous, and intelligent action. He was convinced that men are by nature bad: Machiavelli shows that one does not have to be a Christian to be a pessimist about human nature. *The Prince,* with its imaginative transformation of Cesare Borgia into a kind of ideal ruler and its cold advice on how to succeed in the jungle of the political world, voices this pessimism on every page. "Men must either be caressed or else annihilated; they will revenge themselves for small injuries, but cannot do so for great ones."[74] And again, "A prince being thus obliged to know well how to act as a beast must imitate the fox and the lion, for the lion cannot protect himself from traps, and the fox cannot defend himself from wolves. One must therefore be a fox to recognize traps, and a lion to frighten wolves. Those that wish to be only lions do not understand this. Therefore, a prudent prince ought not to keep faith when by doing so it would be against his interest, and when the reasons which made him bind himself no longer exist. If men were all good, this precept would not be a good one; but as they are bad, and would not observe their faith with you, so you are not bound to keep faith with them."[75] And yet this clinical intelligence that could draw such lessons and give such advice also had its passions. In the last chapter of *The Prince,* which remains as controversial as the rest of the book, Machiavelli suddenly draws yet another lesson from the dreadful time of the Italian wars. In a passionate outburst, reaching back to the very beginning of the Renaissance, to Petrarch, he calls for a liberator who will drive the barbarians from Italy. "This barbarous domination stinks in the nostrils of everyone."[76]

If Machiavelli's world of grasping princes, immoral popes, craven peoples, wholly ruled by self-interest and always ready for murder, does not awaken our admiration, Machiavelli's effort to portray and penetrate it does. His political theory belongs with the magisterial achievements of the Renaissance, with

---

[73] "Introduction," First Book of *The Discourses* (Modern Library ed.), 103.
[74] *The Prince,* chap. III.
[75] Ibid., chap. XVIII.
[76] Ibid., chap. XXV.

Leonardo's portraits or Michelangelo's sculptures. In Machiavelli's books the modern world stands before us; political power has been secularized, freed from religious direction and moral restraint, become an end in itself. *The Prince* and *The Discourses,* sometimes explicitly, always implicitly, are involuntary tributes to the rising Atlantic states. They are heralds of the age to come. Yet in one respect they are curiously incomplete: with all his gift for observation, Machiavelli treated religion as merely a mode of manipulating superstitious populaces. There is no sign in his work of the upheaval through which he was living, the greatest revolution the Christian church had known until then, or has known to this day.

SELECTED READINGS

For the expansion of Europe, see the magisterial volume by Samuel Eliot Morison, *The European Discovery of America,* vol. I, *The Northern Voyages, A.D. 500-1600* (1971). Morison's biography of Columbus, *Admiral of the Ocean Sea* (1942), is definitive. Other excellent titles include Boies Penrose, *Travel and Discovery in the Renaissance, 1420-1620* (1955); John B. Brebner, *The Explorers of North America, 1492-1806* (1933); and J. H. Parry, *The European Reconnaissance* (1968), with selected documents and a fine bibliography. J. H. Elliott, *The Old World and the New, 1492-1650* (1970), traces the interaction of conqueror and conquered.

For the arts in the Northern Renaissance, see Otto Benesch, *The Art of the Renaissance in Northern Europe* (rev. ed., 1965); John Pope-Hennessy, *The Portrait in the Renaissance* (1966), which contains material on Holbein, Dürer, and other northern artists; the brilliant studies by Erwin Panofsky: *The Life and Art of Albrecht Dürer* (4th ed., 1965) and *Early Netherlandish Painting: Its Origins and Character,* 2 vols. (1953); and Theodor Müller, *Sculpture in the Netherlands, Germany, France, Spain: 1400-1500* (1966).

Northern Humanists are well treated in E. Harris Harbison, *The Christian Scholar in the Age of the Reformation* (1956). For more, see Raymond Wilson Chambers, *Thomas More* (1958), and J. H. Hexter, *More's "Utopia": The Biography of an Idea* (1952). Johan Huizinga, *Erasmus of Rotterdam* (tr. 1952), and the fuller biography by Preserved Smith, *Erasmus: A Study of His Life, Ideals and Place in History* (1923), may be supplemented with John C. Olin, ed., *Christian Humanism and the Reformation: Selected Writings of Desiderius Erasmus* (1965), and Roland M. Bainton, *Erasmus of Christendom* (1969). R. Weiss, *Humanism in England During the Fifteenth Century* (2nd ed., 1957), sets the background. Equally interesting is Fritz Caspari, *Humanism and the Social Order in Tudor England* (1954). For French humanism, above all, Eugene F. Rice, Jr., *The Renaissance Idea of Wisdom* (1958). Louis Battifol, *The Century of the Renaissance* (1916), on France, is now rather antiquated. For the importance of printing, see S. H. Steinberg, *Five Hundred Years of Printing* (2nd ed., 1966), and polemical articles by Elizabeth L. Eisenstein, notably "Some Conjectures about the Impact of Printing on Western Society and Thought: A Preliminary Report," *Journal of Modern History,* 40 (March 1968), 1-56.

For the rise of the Great Powers see, for France, the relevant chapters in Georges Duby and Robert Mandrou, *A History of French Civilization from the Year 1000 to the Present* (tr. 1964); vol. I of Charles Guignebert, *A Short History of the French People,*

2 vols. (1930); and J. Russell Major, *Representative Institutions in Renaissance France* (1960). For England, A. R. Myers, *England in the Late Middle Ages* (1964); the opening chapters of S. T. Bindoff, *Tudor England* (1950); J. D. Mackie, *The Earlier Tudors* (1952); V. H. H. Green, *The Later Plantagenets: A Survey of English History Between 1307 and 1485* (1955); and Lacey Baldwin Smith, *Tudor Prelates and Politics* (1953). For Spain, the best coverage is in the early chapters of J. H. Elliott, *Imperial Spain, 1469–1716* (1963). See also, H. Mariéjol, *The Spain of Ferdinand and Isabella* (tr. 1961). J. Vincent Vives, *An Economic History of Spain from the Earliest Times to the End of the Nineteenth Century* (tr. 1969), is brilliant.

General treatments of politics and culture in these decades have been listed in the Selected Readings for Chapter 1. Most relevant here are Myron P. Gilmore, *The World of Humanism, 1453–1517* (1952), and G. R. Potter, ed., *The Renaissance, 1493–1520* (1957). See also Denys Hay, *Europe in the Fourteenth and Fifteenth Centuries* (1966). To these should be added the splendid survey by Garrett Mattingly, *Renaissance Diplomacy* (1965).

The decline and revival of the empire is traced in Hajo Holborn, *A History of Modern Germany*, vol. I, *The Reformation* (1959). Two books by F. L. Carsten bring modern scholarship to bear on early modern Germany: *The Origins of Prussia* (1954) and *Princes and Parliaments in Germany* (1959). For Machiavelli the best among a large literature is Felix Gilbert, *Machiavelli and Guicciardini: Politics and History in Sixteenth-Century Florence* (1965); see also J. R. Hale's sketch, *Machiavelli and Renaissance Italy* (1963).

3

The Shattering of Christian Unity

Outsize figures—Martin Luther, John Calvin, Emperor Charles V, Henry VIII of England—loom over the age of the Reformation like so many giants. Yet the Reformation was not the work of a few individuals, no matter how titanic their stature. Fortune was on their side. There had been self-willed rulers before, but they had always somehow remained within the communion of Rome. There had been uncompromising religious rebels before, but they had never produced the effective and irremediable[1] shattering of Christian unity. Luther, Calvin, Zwingli, and their followers were the right men at the right time; economic, political, and social developments gave them what had been denied their predecessors: the opportunity to construct a viable alternative to Roman Catholicism.

---

[1] It seems safe to say now, more than four centuries later.

PRECONDITIONS FOR RELIGIOUS REVOLUTION

From Wyclif to Hus

To speak of the Reformation as a shattering of Christian unity is in an important sense misleading. As we have noted in some detail, Christendom had been deeply, often furiously, divided for centuries, long before Martin Luther made that division final (see p. 35). To say this is not to diminish Luther's historical importance—to the extent that an individual can ever change the course of events, he did—but simply to place him into the stream of time. Luther himself never denied that he had ancestors and allies in his great enterprise.

Among these ancestors, John Wyclif in England played a decisive part; he was John the Baptist to the Reformation. Wyclif's shift from orthodoxy to heresy, motivated as it was by a peculiar mixture of religious rage and private interest, of desire for institutional reform and theological purification, prefigures the life and work of Martin Luther. Wyclif's very ideas—his stress on faith and on man's direct relation to God—are early versions of Protestant doctrines. Born in Yorkshire around 1328, Wyclif first achieved prominence as a prolific, wholly respectable scholar, with close ties to Oxford. He entered religious controversy as a propagandist for the antipapalism of the English Crown in the early 1370s. But this was a financial rather than doctrinal squabble. The government wanted good reasons why money should not leave England, and Wyclif supplied them. Politics led into theology, as in that time it often did; by the mid-1370s, Wyclif was defending the right of the laity to control the property of the church. Then, at the end of the 1370s and the beginning of the 1380s, Wyclif became a thoroughgoing theological revolutionary.

Advancing age, ill health, frustrated ambitions, and the scandal of the Great Schism, then in its inception, probably all contributed to Wyclif's growing radicalism. But his teaching was greater than his motives. As Wyclif himself insisted—this was a favorite argument of reformers, radicals, and revolutionaries down to the eighteenth century—he had no wish to innovate and every wish to restore. His model was the pure early church of primitive Christendom, unencumbered by complex organization or doctrinal accretions of dubious origins and equally dubious worth. The heart of Christian faith was the Scriptures. This heretical doctrine was to find loud echoes in sixteenth-century Protestantism. The Bible alone has divine authority. By devout and careful reading, a Christian layman can work toward goodness and even hope for salvation. "He who reads the Scriptures of God," one of his followers said, speaking for them all, "will find God, and his good living is like the light of the lamp before the eyes of his heart, and will open the way to truth."[2] The supremacy of the Bible meant the fallibility of all clerical institutions, including the papacy; the true church, Wyclif reasoned, is invisible. He went further. While he was neither consistent nor clear in his writings—his mind has been called both academic and unsystematic—and worked out only some of the implications of his ideas, he laid hands (profane hands, Rome thought) on some of the most cherished ideas of Catholic Christendom: free will and the mass. The true invisible church consists of the saved, the "elect," and God has chosen them in advance. And what happens during mass, though miraculous, is not precisely what Rome said. Wyclif seems to have become so hostile to Rome, so suspicious of the manner in which articles of faith had been manipulated to the profit of sinful men masquerading as humble servants of Christ, that he could no longer accept the doctrine of transubstantiation. Faith was more important than ritual (see p. 132). Indeed, to Wyclif and his excitable disciples, the visible church, disfigured by monks across Europe and the pope in Rome, was a gathering of antichrists.

That the lords and beneficiaries of the visible church should have taken offense at Wyclif's teaching is only human. In a Christian world no one, especially not the man who occupies the papal chair as Christ's vicar, likes to be called antichrist. But while the papacy condemned Wyclif's doctrines as heretical, it could not get its hands on him. He had loyal support among the clerics at Oxford and across England; he had strong, if, in his last years, waning, support at the court. "Heresy," V. H. H. Green has aptly said, "is a more dangerous ally than anti-clericalism, both in this world and . . . in the next."[3] Hence Wyclif died peacefully enough, at home, in 1384. Roman Catholicism took posthumous if ineffectual revenge: the Council of Constance solemnly condemned Wyclif's teachings (see p. 109), and in 1428 his bones were dug up and burned. But his teaching, though more or less underground, survived through the fifteenth and into the sixteenth century with the Lollards; they form part of the stream of heresy that was to swell into the broad river of the Reformation.

The Lollards, Wyclif's disciples, are as interesting as he.[4] Down to the seventeenth century, when documentation becomes more abundant, the poor erupt into historical visibility mainly in riots, rebellions, and religious upheavals. Lollardy began, not as a poor man's movement, but at Oxford, under the direct influence of Wyclif's lectures and books. But academics are rarely

[2] Put into modern English, slightly paraphrased, from V. H. H. Green, *The Later Plantagenets: A Survey of English History Between 1307 and 1485* (1955), 199.

[3] *Later Plantagenets*, 195.

[4] The name "Lollard," writes A. G. Dickens, was applied "to the sect in a sermon by the Irish Cistercian Henry Crump" in 1382. "A Middle Dutch word meaning 'mumbler' or 'mutterer' of prayers, it had long been applied to the Beghards and other Netherlandish pietists whose orthodoxy was suspect" (*The English Reformation* [1964], 23–24).

persistent revolutionaries; one learned Lollard after another recanted and rejoined the orthodox communion. But what Lollardy lost in intellect it gained in vehemence and tenacity. It soon spread to the country, to receptive squires, urban merchants, even members of the House of Commons, and a few aristocrats. Finally, early in the fifteenth century, itinerant preachers enlisted segments of the urban and rural proletariat. Support for Lollard doctrine was as varied as the doctrine itself; some followed it because they wanted clerical reform; others because they saw profit, both to themselves and the common-wealth, in the expropriation of the wealthy English church; still others, the most radical and least tractable, fervently hoped for a reform of the articles of faith and the restoration of primitive Christianity, when men had faced God as humble children, without priestly intermediaries. Lollardy was confined to no single class: Sir John Oldcastle, who plotted a pathetic Lollard uprising in 1414, was a close associate of King Henry V. But in the end most of the Lollards were poor, rescued from total anonymity only in the town records that list their names and the price of the faggots needed to burn them. The movement went underground but not out of existence: there are records of sporadic burnings of Lollards right into the time of the English Reformation.

Wyclif's influence spread from England to the Continent; the other great heresiarch before Luther, Jan Hus, was obviously and deeply in Wyclif's debt. Hus, born around 1369, was, like Wyclif, a prominent priest and scholar—for a time he served as rector of his University of Prague. Like Wyclif, he was an orthodox believer for much of his life, and once again like Wyclif, he was moved to heresy by clerical abuses. Soon Hus's rhetoric grew extreme: he applied the favorite epithet of heretics—antichrist—to Rome. In 1410 he was excommunicated, but his local popularity, in which nascent Bohemian nation-alism and anti-German sentiment played a prominent part, remained undimin-ished, and Hus continued his provocative preaching. On matters of doctrine, Hus was less radical than Wyclif: while he insisted on the fallibility of the pope—those who proclaimed his infallibility were also antichrists—and on the primacy of Scriptures, he conceded that a pure clergy or a pure written tradition could have their uses.[5] On the mass, too, Hus was relatively cautious: his moderate followers, the Utraquists,[6] whose views did not markedly differ from Roman Catholic teachings, accurately preserve his own views.

Hus was both a political and a religious storm center. He stood for Bohemian particularism quite as much as for independence from the papacy. His fate was certainly shaped by the exigencies of politics. Emperor Sigismund first protected Hus and then betrayed him: he lured Hus to the Council of

[5] See Heiko Augustinus Oberman, *The Harvest of Medieval Theology: Gabriel Biel and Late Medieval Nominalism* (1963), 376.

[6] The name derives from the Latin term for their demand for the mass "in both kinds"—*sub utraque specie.*

Constance with an imperial safe-conduct, which induced Hus to leave the safety of Bohemia for the treacherous soil of Constance. At the council, Hus found himself in a difficult position. He refused to repudiate Wyclif but refused, at the same time, to admit he was a heretic. Reasonably enough, he was willing to reformulate many of his ideas, but he insisted that Christ, not Peter, was the rock on which the church had been built, and he would not submit to the humiliating conditions his examiners sought to force upon him. The end was inevitable: in July 1415 he was burned at the stake, with the heretic's hat on his head.

The execution was stupid as well as vicious. Its consequence was not an end to heresy in central Europe, but war. In a series of brilliant forays, Bohemian troops defeated all crusading armies sent against them; the Hussite wars, fought sporadically from 1418 on, finally ended with a compromise, the so-called Compactata of 1436, which largely excluded Germans from Bohemian affairs and gave the Hussites the kind of Utraquist mass they had asked for. And this was not all. By handing the Wyclifite heresy a martyr on the Continent, the papacy had given the forces of reform a figure to admire and to exploit when the time of the Reformation came.

Piety Beyond the Pale

The great heresies that beset fourteenth- and fifteenth-century Europe were expressions of class hatreds, economic distress, local particularism, and political aspirations, but the dominant component of these movements was what the heretics claimed it to be—religious. To put it in another, perhaps more precise way, in the centuries preceding the Reformation, social, economic, and political discontents took religious forms. They could hardly do anything else: with the rare—extremely rare—exceptions of a few disenchanted intellectuals like Marsiglio of Padua (see p. 128), all men saw the world in religious terms. Utopians cast their visions of social regeneration in religious language, not from convenience but from conviction. Economics and politics were not yet separated from religion, even in thought.

It is only in recent years that historians like Johan Huizinga have taught us to appreciate the extent and intensity of the religious malaise that darkened the face of Europe in the time before the Reformation. Ecstatic visions of the blessed kingdom on earth alternated with gloomy preoccupations with death; art historians have singled out the emergence of obsessions with the Dance of Death, social historians the witch craze which held in its deadly grip both the poor deranged beings who actually believed themselves to be witches and the inquisitors who ferreted them out and burned them by the thousands. Christians translated their helplessness and despair into the conviction that the land was overrun by devils who conjured up plagues and crop failures—there was nothing abstract in this late medieval quest for scapegoats. The Jews were the most prominent victims of this displacement, and it was not the illiterate alone who persecuted them: learned theologians denounced the Jew as Anti-Christ, called for his conversion or, more often, his extirpation, and manufactured charges of ritual murder that would never wholly disappear from the popular mythology of the Western world.

The range of religious belief was enormously varied—from naive credence in tales about witchcraft to involved theories about the influence of the stars, from primitive visions of heaven on earth to abstruse philosophical speculations about the nature of reality and the course of history. Among the most modern of heretics was Marsiglio of Padua, whose *Defensor Pacis* of 1324 anticipates secular political ideas of the seventeenth century. A polemic serving Emperor Louis the Bavarian in his controversy with Pope John XXII, *Defensor Pacis,* like other tracts of the time, defends imperial institutions against papal claims to supremacy in worldly as well as spiritual matters. But Marsiglio went beyond his time. Almost alone in using rationalistic methods in inquiry, he argued for the total autonomy of the secular power, a monopoly of legal and coercive authority for the state, the equality of all priests, the equation of the church with the whole body of Christendom, and—an idea that Wyclif and Hus would take up—the supremacy of Christ, rather than the pope, in and over the church. For centuries after, Marsiglio's bold propositions served not merely the anticlerical assertions of pious men, but the wider claims of secularists.

The English Franciscan William of Occam, Marsiglio's ally in the antipapal cause, fed the stream of heresy also in another way. In the early fourteenth century the dominant philosophical direction in Western Christianity was Scholasticism, a school which placed considerable trust in the power of reason to prove the existence of God and the necessity of Catholic institutions. Occam—to use modern words for him—was a nominalist and an empiricist. He denied substantive reality to universal terms like "Church" and held that they were but names. Only individual things are real. This was of considerable philosophical importance, but it was his empiricism, his insistence that our knowledge comes from experience alone, that helped to undermine the confidence of Christian believers in the power of reason to prove the existence of things that were higher than reason. Nothing, not even the existence of God, could be demonstrated.

William of Occam should not be read through modern spectacles. He was not an unbeliever. Quite the contrary: Occam sought not to discredit God but to exalt him by vastly widening the gulf between the creator and his creatures, a gulf the Scholastics had tried to bridge with their rational arguments. Only a handful took Occam's skepticism as a guide to irreligion; most of his readers—and his influence was enormous and lasting—interpreted his assault on the powers of reason as an invitation to practical piety, to mysticism, and to a new trust in a sheer faith that operated without, and often against, the evidence of reason. In 1349, Occam, like so many thousands of others, succumbed to the Black Death, but a century and a half later Martin Luther hailed him as "my dear master."[7]

Most troubled Christians needed headier fare than disputes over the theory of knowledge. In the fourteenth century, in England, the German states, Flanders, and northern Italy above all, but elsewhere as well, individual believers turned away from formal theology to establish personal relations with the deity through mystic union. One of these, Johann Tauler, later exercised significant influence on young Martin Luther struggling for light. By definition, the mystical experience is intimate and private, but the mystics did not disdain to record their visions in ecstatic writings, and these induced others to reexperience them. The church found it hard to establish a consistent policy for these exceptional believers; Christianity, after all, insisted on the essentially nonrational character of religious experience, but an organized church that proclaimed itself, as Roman Catholicism proclaimed itself, the chosen intermediary between God and man, could only view with some suspicion the devout who took their own road to God. Hence Rome excommunicated some of the mystics and canonized others.

One offshoot of mysticism relatively safe to the established clerical order— "mysticism by retail," it has been called[8]—was the tendency among devout Christians before the Reformation to reject theological controversy to concentrate on charity. The best known of these were the Brethren of the Common Life, founded late in the fourteenth century. The brethren lived in common quarters but, not being monks, remained in the world; they devoted themselves to doing charitable works, nursing the sick, studying the Scriptures, and teaching the young. Their fervent, practical piety, which came to be called the *devotio moderna,* was only an indirect precursor of Protestantism: where Luther and his followers would stress faith, the practitioners of the "modern devotion," though their faith was ardent, stressed works. But they, too, prepared the way for religious upheaval; they laid the foundations, as Huizinga has said, both "in the northern Netherlands and in lower Germany, for a generally diffused culture among the middle classes; a culture of a very narrow, strictly ecclesiastical nature, indeed, but which for that very reason was fit to permeate broad layers of the people."[9] Many famous men went through their schools, including Nicolas of Cusa, Thomas à Kempis, and Erasmus, all of whom studied at the brethren's school at Deventer. The most familiar work to emerge from their circle, *The Imitation of Christ,* perhaps by Kempis, perhaps by Gerhard Groote, the founder of the movement, is the most widely read devotional tract ever written; in lucid and simple language and without recourse to theological quibbles and doctrinal subtleties, it calls Christians to pious communion with their Savior.

[7] G. G. Coulton, *Studies in Medieval Thought* (1940), 190.
[8] Johan Huizinga, *The Waning of the Middle Ages* (ed. 1956), 225.
[9] Johan Huizinga, *Erasmus of Rotterdam* (tr. 1952), 4.

Other spirits in these terrifying times could not respond to the world by devotion and charity. Finding their life unbearable, Christians by the thousands thirstily consumed prophecies of a new world to come.[10] Extravagant pessimism invited and produced extravagant optimism. The first Christians had expected the return of Christ within their lifetime; sporadically after that, century after century, prophets had prophesied the end of history, the Second Coming. In the late twelfth century, this vision found authoritative expression in the writings of Joachim of Flore, a Calabrian priest who was at once a hermit and the friend of popes. No millenarian either before or after him has ever been so orderly in his system. Neatly, everything fell into three parts: there were, Joachim taught, three ages of man. The first reached from the creation to the coming of Christ—roughly 1260 years. The second began with Christ and would end around 1260, to give way to the third period in which mankind would witness the great struggles that must precede the victory foretold in the Apocalypse. Each of these three periods had its characteristics: the first, the age of the Old Testament, was under the sign of the Father; it was the reign of law, and thus of men's fear and servitude. The second, the age of the New Testament, was under the sign of the Son; it was the reign of faith, and thus of filial obedience and belief. The third, the age to come, would be the age of what Joachim called, from a passage in Revelation, the "everlasting gospel." It would be under the sign of the Spirit and would usher in the reign of charity. This was the glorious future, a time of universal poverty, spirituality, and freedom when the bonds of human institutions like church and empire and marriage would be cast off. Mankind would unite in a universal monastery and live in joy and spiritual happiness to the Last Judgment.

These Joachimite notions spread from country to country and survived refutations and persecutions. In the German states, Emperor Frederick Barbarossa and his grandson, Frederick II, became the subjects of hopeful legends: they would rise again and lead Christendom to a future of untold bliss. Extremists among the Franciscans in the fourteenth century, the radical wing of the Hussites in the fifteenth century, saw the world ready for the Second Coming; in 1501, Christopher Columbus proclaimed himself the "Joachimite messiah."[11] The vision never disappeared—the English Puritans in the seventeenth century entertained hopes of the Messiah, and in our own time the Nazis would enact a hideous parody of the "Third Reich" that Joachim of Flore had foretold, with wholly different intentions, almost eight centuries before. Men in deep trouble will believe almost anything. The period of the Reformation itself was marked by these expectations: the Anabaptists and their most pitiless adversary, Martin Luther, shared, if they shared little else, millenarian visions (see p. 143).

---

[10] On this point see H. G. Koenigsberger and G. L. Mosse, *Europe in the Sixteenth Century* (1968), 87.
　[11] Ibid., 94.

Lighting the Fuse: Luther's Europe to 1517

It is the most extraordinary quality in that extraordinary man, Martin Luther, that he contained within himself most of the strands of thought and passion traversing Europe in the fifteenth and early sixteenth centuries. He joined, at least for some years, in the mystics' millenarian hopes: the fantasy that Christ's thousand-year reign was about to begin. He had his own personal encounters with the devil, suffered fearful attacks of indecision, absorbed the humble skepticism of Occam, shared in northern Humanist learning, longed for the cleansing of his church, and became involved—somewhat against his will—in the social struggles of which the Reformation was in part the cause, in part the expression. The miracle is that after long and heartrending suffering Luther brought coherence to this diversity of ideas, fears, and hopes.

Martin Luther was born in the Saxon town of Eisleben, in 1483, the son of a peasant grown prosperous in the mining of copper. He became an educated man—few Germans more than he—but he always retained the impress of his background; his pungent, often rude speech, his coarse humor, his delight in proverbs, his vehement prejudices and quick calls for violent remedies contrast sharply, indeed painfully, with the urbanity of his great contemporary, Erasmus. His schooling, at Eisleben and at the University of Erfurt, was sound and conventional. He was destined for the law, but in 1505, after a bolt of lightning threw him to the ground as he was walking to Erfurt, he vowed to become a monk. His father was dismayed and infuriated, but Luther was firm. The lightning was no more than the dramatic occasion of his conversion; he had long been wrestling with the state of his soul.

Luther entered the Augustinian order at Erfurt and proved, by all reports, a brilliant but troublesome brother. He insisted on confessing, at great length and on every possible occasion; his fellow clerics, no cynics, thought his search for holiness extravagant and almost absurd. But Luther was in earnest: the sense of his unworthiness and of the chasm that inexorably divided him from his angry God, haunted and terrified him. "Though I lived as a monk without reproach," he recalled much later, "I felt that I was a sinner before God with an extremely disturbed conscience. . . . I did not love, yes, I hated the righteous God who punishes sinners, and secretly, if not blasphemously, certainly murmuring greatly, I was angry with God." [12] He was certain he was damned. It is too easy to say he was a guilt-ridden neurotic—many people are, and do not achieve what Luther achieved. Luther translated his sufferings into a new vision that changed the face of Europe.

The precise course of Luther's religious development, his liberation from despair, remains a matter of some debate. It is certain that it involved prayer, philosophizing, profound and private religious experiences, and above all

---

[12] "Preface to Latin Writings" (1545), in John Dillenberger, ed., *Martin Luther: Selections from His Writings* (1961), 11.

reflection on the Scriptures. Despite his obtrusive anguish, his superiors trusted him. In 1508 they sent him to the University of Wittenberg as a lecturer; in 1512 he took the doctorate in theology there and began his celebrated lectures on the Bible: on the Psalms, on Romans, and on Galatians. Whatever they taught others, these lectures taught Luther what he desperately needed to know. The book that had plunged him into despair now gave him relief. "At last, by the mercy of God, meditating day and night," he recalled later, "I gave heed to the context of the words, namely, 'In it the righteousness of God is revealed, as it is written; He who through faith is righteous shall live.' [13] There I began to understand that the righteousness of God is that by which the righteous lives by a gift of God, namely by faith. . . . Here I felt that I was altogether born again and had entered paradise itself through open gates." [14] The traditional Catholic faith, which stressed the conjunction of faith and works and insisted that man seek to earn salvation, now was confronted by the sublime passivity of the believer who puts himself into the hands of the Savior: the Protestant doctrine of justification by faith alone—*sola fide*—was born, and with it a new era in European history. Probably by 1516, certainly a year or two later, Luther's new vision was clear and, despite recurring bouts of despairing uncertainty, secure.

The world in which young Luther was laboring to attain religious light was, as usual, in turmoil, but perhaps in graver turmoil than usual. We have pointed to the destructive effects of the Italian wars, the unmeasured ambitions of secular rulers, the disruptive consequences of heresy, and the much-criticized conduct of Renaissance popes (see p. 110). But there were some new and explosive ingredients in the familiar mixture. The Renaissance popes were perhaps no worse than earlier popes, but they were more open about their political and financial manipulations than their predecessors, and they alienated many ambitious men by their very successes against the Councils and their very concentration on Italian affairs. Complaints against the laziness of priests, their lust, their ignorance, their greed for lucrative offices, were very old indeed; there are texts from clerical reformers of the thirteenth century that sound like the inflammatory tracts written in Luther's day. What was new was the general virulence of antipapal and anticlerical sentiment; what was new was the printing press, which distributed manifestos, tracts, pictures with unprecedented effectiveness. Both the makers and the critics of scandals were more public than ever before.

As the strange interlude of Savonarola shows, discontent with the papacy was not a monopoly of the North. The Dominican friar Girolamo Savonarola, one of the most remarkable religious zealots of all time, first came to Florence in 1482, but his first preaching mission there was not a success. When he returned to preach in 1490, he had learned to trust his charismatic presence, developed his oratorical powers, and hit upon his single theme. That theme was

---

[13] Rom. 1:17.
[14] Dillenberger, *Martin Luther*, 11.

sin: the wicked luxury of the laity, the unforgivable corruption of the church, the need for universal reform, and the opportunity for such reform—now. In 1494, when Charles VIII invaded Italy, Savonarola hailed him as "an instrument in the hands of the Lord who has sent you to cure the ills of Italy." [15] In that year, as the Medici fled, Savonarola identified himself with the popular regime in Florence; in his short ascendancy—many have called it a dictatorship—religion and politics fused to perfection. The same combination would destroy him: Florentine plutocrats and, once he had become sufficiently aroused, Pope Alexander VI cordially hated the gaunt, fierce-eyed preacher who wanted to deprive laymen of pleasure and clergymen of wealth.

Like other preachers of humility, Savonarola had his share of pride: if Florence was now entering the millennium of purity, who, after all, was the savior who had stood up to antichrist? Like other saintly reformers, he was intolerant—certainly he enjoyed his hold over his audiences. His short reign produced some rather peculiar spectacles in luxury-loving Florence. Smarting under his words and afraid of his supporters who were as fanatical as he, the elegant and the vicious assumed simple dress and abandoned, or concealed, their pleasures. In 1497, and once again in the following year, Savonarola presided over a "burning of the vanities," big public bonfires in which dice, carnival dresses, lascivious pictures, and other symbols of sin were solemnly consigned to the flames. [16] But in the long run Savonarola could not hold his public; his support dwindled as rapidly as it had grown, and he was first excommunicated, and then, in 1498, burned at the stake, his two chief lieutenants by his side.

The Savonarola intermezzo is richly instructive. It illustrates, once again, the fatal conjunction of politics and religion, the persistent appeal of traditional rhetoric, and the height of passion that millenarian appeals could arouse—even in Italy. This is a useful reminder of a neglected fact. A look at the religious map of Europe, say in 1600, suggests a generalization about the course of the Reformation that would in fact be wrong. Because Italy and the regions nearest it retained—or in some instances regained—their loyalty to Rome, this does not mean that unrest and heresy were weakest in Italy and strongest in the outermost reaches of Christendom. Both were everywhere; the eventual disposition of religious allegiance depended on other forces.

Yet it remains true that in the North, particularly in the German states, discontent with the church was closest to the point of revolutionary action. German Humanists, in the new universities and in their polemical writings, inveighed against the papacy, lampooned the Scholastics, defended the new learning, and proudly felt themselves to be German imperialists tired of Roman domination. With Ulrich von Hutten, the wandering knight who put his chivalrous values in the service of German humanism, the search for religious

[15] Ferdinand Schevill, *Medieval and Renaissance Florence*, 2 vols. (Torchbook ed., 1963), 444.
[16] Ibid.

purification grew from outspoken, often scatological criticism of the clergy and from vehement support of the "German" emperor, to acceptance of religious revolution. "While Hutten," Hajo Holborn has written, "merged the popular resentment against Rome . . . with the humanistic opposition to the theologians, he was in his heart not unmindful of the need for a more comprehensive spiritual power to broaden the basis of the struggle with the Romanists."[17] Once he had grasped the meaning of Luther's cause, Hutten ranged himself on Luther's side.

Luther was to find many other allies, among them, to his embarrassment, the German peasantry. Peasant unrest was endemic in early modern Germany; in 1502, there was a large-scale peasant rising in the southwest, the *Bundschuh*.[18] The peasants fondly recalled earlier days when taxes were lower, income was higher, and respect for the peasant was greater. In their minds nostalgia for the past and millenarian hopes for the future coalesced. Corrupt priests must be driven out, life under the old divine law where men were equal must be restored. Credulous, ill-organized, and ill-equipped, the rebels were no match for the troops sent against them, but they did not give up easily. In 1517 famine conditions brought a new *Bundschuh* rising, more alarming than any before. It was a fateful year. Politically, religiously, socially, Germany was ready for rebellion. The wood was dry, the tinder was laid. All that was needed was someone to light it.

THE LUTHERAN REFORMATION

From Rebel to Revolutionary

On October 31, 1517, Martin Luther affixed ninety-five theses to the door of the castle church at Wittenberg. They were a protest against the Dominican commissary Johann Tetzel, who was traveling about the country selling indulgences. The issue of indulgences had long been the subject of ill-tempered debate; objections to the practice had multiplied since the reign of Pope Sixtus IV, who had extended it in 1476 to apply to the time that sinners would have to spend in purgatory. The old logic of indulgences—that Christ and the saints had built up a "treasure of merits" on which ordinary mortals could draw—now became a blatant excuse for collecting money for all sorts of secular purposes: Tetzel was circulating around Wittenberg as an agent of Prince

---

[17] *A History of Modern Germany*, vol. I, *The Reformation* (1959), 112.
[18] The *Bundschuh* is the low shoe the peasant wore, laced above the ankle with a string, in contrast with the riding boots favored by the aristocracy (see Holborn, *History of Modern Germany*, vol. I, 62). This is not the last time that an article of clothing gave a name to a revolutionary group: for the *sans-culottes* in the French Revolution see p. 480.

Albert of Brandenburg, archbishop of Mainz and thus primate of Germany, to raise funds for the rebuilding of St. Peter's in Rome. [19] For Luther the issue was particularly sensitive. He knew, from his own harrowing experience, that the road to redemption was hard, and here was a scandalous preacher collecting money on the pretense that redemption was easy—and cheap. [20]

Luther's theses—the "Disputation on the Power and Efficacy of Indulgences"—were moderate in tone. They were an invitation to a scholarly disputation in the traditional manner, written "out of love and concern for the truth, and with the object of eliciting it." [21] They argued that "the entire life of believers" should be one of "penitence," and that ways of evading this obligation, like the treasure of merit, were invalid. "Any Christian whatsoever, who is truly repentant, enjoys plenary remission from penalty and guilt, and this is given him without letters of indulgence." [22] Perhaps Luther was being offensive when he suggested that the pope should "liberate everyone from purgatory for the sake of love (a most holy thing)," rather than "for money, a most perishable thing, with which to build St. Peter's church, a very minor purpose." [23] But Luther's theses were only implicitly heretical. And they were in Latin.

But then translators put the ninety-five theses into German and printers distributed them by the thousands. Almost overnight, a scholar's protest grew into a popular cause. In October 1518, Luther was ordered to discuss his views with the Dominican Cajetan, the cardinal legate, but the conversation broke up in disagreement and ill-feeling over the meaning of the word "treasure." Luther and his friends realized that Pope Leo X would soon act against him, but in December 1518 Frederick the Wise, elector of Saxony, told the papacy that Luther was under his protection. Luther was fortunate in the timing of his rebellion: Emperor Maximilian was dying (he was, in fact, to die in January 1519), and neither the imperial nor the papal party could afford to antagonize Frederick, whose vote they wanted. The election of Maximilian's successor took place in June 1519; Charles of the house of Hapsburg became emperor, "after an election conducted with the publicity of an auction and the morals of a gambling hell." [24]

---

[19] Frivolous as this ostensible purpose was, the actual reason for the indulgences proclaimed by Albert was more frivolous still. His drive to collect posts had involved him in huge expenditures for fees and placed him in debt to the Fuggers. By a secret agreement with the Roman curia which did not become public until much later, Albert agreed to repay the Fuggers with half of the proceeds from the indulgences and hand over the other half to Leo X for St. Peter's. One can imagine how Luther would have couched his theses if he had known *this*.

[20] On this point, see E. G. Rupp, "Luther and the German Reformation to 1529," in *The New Cambridge Modern History*, vol. II, *The Reformation, 1520–1559* (1958), 77.

[21] Theses, introductory paragraph, in Dillenberger, *Martin Luther*, 490.

[22] Thesis No. 36, in Dillenberger, *Martin Luther*, 494.

[23] Thesis No. 82, in Dillenberger, *Martin Luther*, 498.

[24] R. H. Tawney, *Religion and the Rise of Capitalism* (1929), 79; quoted in Joel Hurstfield, ed., *The Reformation Crisis* (1965), 2.

The undignified wrangle made the case of Luther recede into the background, but the issues he had raised were too inflammatory to remain dormant for long. In July 1519, at Leipzig, Luther engaged in a fundamental and seemingly interminable debate with Johann Eck, a formidable theologian and an adroit antagonist who drove Luther into admission of heresy. Under the pressure of events, Luther's religious thinking had been evolving rapidly. What he had called "our theology" in Wittenberg before 1517 was still compatible with orthodox belief, and his rebelliousness against clerical authority in 1517 and 1518 smacked of a Conciliarist position—out of favor but not precisely heretical. Now, with Eck, Luther went beyond anything he had said or written before. Eck charged Luther with following "the damned and pestiferous errors of John Wyclif," and "the pestilent errors of Johann Hus." [25] In reply, Luther vehemently denied "the charge of Bohemianism," and criticized the Hussites for creating a schism in the church. But he acknowledged that "among the articles" of Hus he found "many which are plainly Christian and evangelical." [26] Neither councils nor popes could establish articles of faith—"these," Luther argued, "must come from Scripture." [27] This was true particularly because the papacy was a human, not a divine, institution. Papal decretals purportedly dating back to the early days of Christianity and asserting the opposite were, Luther asserted, plain forgeries. It was equally plain that Luther had read himself out of the Roman communion. Nor did he stop with the fragmentary theology he had developed at Leipzig under the prodding of Eck. By February 1520 he could say: "We are all Hussites without knowing it." [28]

Rome knew it. In June 1520 Leo X issued a bull condemning his writings. If he did not recant within sixty days, he would stand an obstinate heretic, a withered branch on the tree of Christendom. The proscribed man did not waver. In December, in a flamboyant gesture of defiance, he publicly burned the papal bull, together with books on canon law. In the months before, he had set down his new-won clarity for the world to read in a trio of tracts which, different as they are in tone and purpose, belong together. The whole of the Reformation is in them. The first of these tracts, *An Appeal to the Christian Nobility of the German Nation,* rehearses the grievances of German Christians against Rome and the familiar list of complaints against clerical conduct— boldly, plainly, effectively, and it must be added, exhaustively. But, beyond that, in his *Appeal* Luther advanced his uncompromising doctrine of the priesthood of all believers. "The Romanists," he wrote in the slashing polemical manner characteristic of him, have "very cleverly" protected their privileged position with three paper walls, so far impregnable. They have argued that secular power has no jurisdiction over clerical institutions, that there is no point

[25] See Roland H. Bainton, *Here I Stand: A Life of Martin Luther* (1962), 89.
[26] Ibid.
[27] Ibid., 90.
[28] Ibid., 92.

in citing Scriptures against them since the pope alone is competent to expound Holy Writ, and that the threat of a council is empty since after all only the pope can convene such a council. What was inscribed on these three walls was the separation of Christendom into two distinct classes, the secular and the religious. But this separation, Luther insisted, was only "a specious device invented by certain time-servers." In fact, "all Christians whatsoever really and truly belong to the religious class, and there is no difference among them except in so far as they do different work." This is so because "we have one baptism, one gospel, one faith, and are all equally Christian." Baptism "consecrates us all without exception, and makes us all priests." [29] Since in its sublime arrogance, Rome has failed to observe this essential principle of true Christianity and continues to manipulate believers to its own profit, the time has now come for German Christians to turn to the only true source of authority— Scriptures—and take the cause of reform into their own hands. Luther's copious list of "twenty-seven proposals for improving the state of Christendom" calls for the dismantling of nearly the whole structure of "Romanism" including indulgences, the Holy Office, the pope's assertion of authority over secular affairs, pilgrimages, unbreakable vows, excessive masses and holidays. Centuries-old longings of pious heretics are here gathered into one grand, impressive program.

Luther had addressed the first tract to the German nobility in German. He addressed the second, *The Babylonian Captivity of the Church,* to the clergy, in Latin. In the opening paragraph, he testified to the rapid and decisive shift in his thinking; as late as 1518, only two years before, he had still been "entangled in the gross superstitions of a masterful Rome." [30] Now he had thrown them off. In his address to the German nobility he had sought to destroy Roman institutions; in his address to the clergy he sought to destroy Roman beliefs. He denied that there were seven sacraments (the Catholic complement); instead, "for the present," he propounded three: "baptism, penance, and the Lord's Supper." [31] Of these, as Luther recognized, the Lord's Supper was "the most important of all." By eliminating such sacraments as ordination and extreme unction, Luther was reaffirming his doctrine that all believers are priests and that therefore no special qualities inhere in professional clerics. But while retaining the Lord's Supper, Luther took care to distinguish his interpretation of that sacrament from the Roman version. First of all, the laity must have restored to it what the Roman curia had so wickedly taken away: the mass in both kinds. The communicant must receive not merely the bread, but the wine as well: "To deny both kinds to the laity is impious and oppressive." [32]

---

[29] In Dillenberger, *Martin Luther,* 406–408.

[30] Ibid., 250.

[31] Actually, as Luther writes later in this tract, only two of these, baptism and the Lord's Supper, are divinely instituted. Penance is merely "a means of reaffirming our baptism" (in Dillenberger, *Martin Luther,* 359).

[32] In Dillenberger, *Martin Luther,* 263.

Secondly, the mass is not a sacrifice but a testament, and the sole precondition for its worthy observation is faith: "Of all for whom the mass has been provided, only those partake of it worthily whose consciences make them sad, humble, disturbed, confused, and uncertain." The mass is the testament of Christ which takes away sin only if men "cling to Him with unwavering faith. . . . If you do not believe this, then never, nowhere, by no good works, and by no kinds of efforts, can you gain peace of conscience."[33] Finally, what happens at mass is not transubstantiation; that notion is a "human invention" defended by overly clever Scholastics like Thomas Aquinas who base themselves on a misunderstanding of Aristotle—"thus building an unfortunate superstructure on an unfortunate foundation." Christ, Luther believed, is mysteriously present in communion—"consubstantiation." But at the same time, Luther was concerned to allay the tender consciences of those who thought, following the plain meaning of the Scriptures, that bread remained bread, and wine, wine. "Here I shall be called a Wycliffite and six hundred times a heretic. But what does it matter? Now that the Roman bishop has ceased to be a bishop and has become a dictator, I fear none of his decrees at all; for I know that he has no power to make a new article of faith, nor has a general council."[34] Luther squarely placed the burden of faith on the conscience of the individual Christian.

Luther completed this structure of argument in his third great tract of 1520, *Of the Liberty of a Christian.* Shaped as a letter to Pope Leo X, it is far shorter than the other two and more pacific in tenor. But, however edifying its tone and conciliatory its intention, its doctrine is clearly heretical. Men must live among ceremonies and do good works, but both are the consequences and not the conditions of faith. Works produce hypocrites; faith alone justifies. Works have no power to give men the healing belief in God, or honor Him, or unite men with Christ; faith alone can do all three. "Works, being inanimate things, cannot glorify God, although they can, if faith is present, be done to the glory of God."[35] The liberty of a Christian—that is, of a man of faith—brings glorious works in its train: "Behold, from faith thus flow forth love and joy in the Lord, and from love a joyful, willing, and free mind that serves one's neighbor willingly and takes no account of gratitude or ingratitude, of praise or blame, of gain or loss."[36] All else, no matter what learned theologians might argue, is bondage. It was Luther's purpose in these three tracts to free man from such bondage.

This was precisely what the clerical authorities feared. Luther had apostrophized Leo X as "most excellent Leo" and hailed Charles V as "a young

---

[33] Ibid., 291.
[34] Ibid., 265–267.
[35] Ibid., 62.
[36] Ibid., 75–76.

man of noble ancestry" whom God had given to the world, but neither pope nor emperor was appeased by Luther's rare excursions into diplomatic manners. On January 3, 1521, Luther was excommunicated. But he was not without protection. The papal nuncio in Germany reported that nine tenths of all Germans cried "Luther," and the other tenth, "Death to the pope." [37] After complex maneuverings on all sides, Luther was bidden to appear at Worms, at the first imperial diet of Charles' long reign. Luther was courageous and tenacious, but he could go to Worms confident that he would not share Hus' fate; the attention of the world—and, more important, of sympathetic German princes—was centered on him, guaranteeing that the imperial safe-conduct would be honored. In April, Luther presented himself before a crowded assembly including princes and bishops and the emperor himself. Sternly, he was asked two questions: Did he acknowledge the books that were heaped up on a table before him? He did. Did he defend what he had written there? He wanted time to think it over. His examiners gave him one day, and Luther's second hearing has remained, in history and in myth, one of the decisive moments in European history. With the skill of a politician, Luther turned a trial into a triumph. He distinguished among his many writings, regretted the personal attacks he had permitted himself, and appealed to the Germans in the audience by inveighing against the foreign tyranny that was devouring his nation. And he sturdily refused to recant any of his theological opinions: "Unless I am convicted by Scripture and plain reason—I do not accept the authority of popes and councils, for they have contradicted each other—my conscience is captive to the Word of God. I cannot and will not recant anything, for to go against conscience is neither right nor safe. God help me. Amen." [38] Adroitly, Luther had spoken in German, but upon request he reiterated his stand in Latin, and walked out.

Luther, his safe-conduct intact, underwent further private hearings, but in May, after he had left, the diet voted the Edict of Worms accusing him of Bohemianism, denying the sacraments, sullying sacred institutions, and encouraging rebellion. By decree of the governing body of the empire he was an outlaw. His temporal overlord, Elector Frederick of Saxony, saw it otherwise; while Luther was on his way home, Frederick's men kidnapped him and hid him at a remote stronghold, the Wartburg. Isolated in the castle—for a time his anxious supporters feared him dead—and released from almost unbearable strain, Luther experienced some terrible depressions and terrifying confrontations with evil spirits. The wall against which he hurled his ink-well at the devil was to become a tourist attraction. But he soon regained his spirits and began

---

[37] Bainton, *Here I Stand*, 130.

[38] These are the words quoted in the report of the meeting. Ironically enough, his most famous words, which have given titles to books and been endlessly repeated—*"Hier stehe ich, ich kann nicht anders*—Here I stand, I can do no other"—were added later to the printed account of the day.

to write again—letters, tracts, and most important, his German translation of the New Testament.

His cause was prospering. The rich mixture of religious, social, and political elements that had distinguished the Reformation from the beginning became, if anything, richer than before. True, some leading Humanists fell away; drawn at first by Luther's undeniable good will and reforming zeal, they were soon put off by his unwillingness to compromise, his growing impatience with disagreement—the occupational hazard of the prophet—and his invectives. Erasmus, to whose scholarship Luther was considerably indebted, temporized on Lutheranism for years and thus lent it some of his enormous prestige, but in 1524 his distaste for, and disagreements with, Luther came into the open. Ostensibly the break came over the philosophical issue of free will versus determinism; actually, it was a clash of temperaments and essential aims. The bull-headed, assertive dogmatist with a single cause could not peacefully coexist for long with the urbane skeptic and compromiser.

On the other hand, Luther found fanatical and often unwanted supporters all across Germany. In 1522, the year Luther emerged from hiding and returned to Wittenberg to preach, a band of imperial knights waged a scattered series of feuds against the "Romanists" in Germany, raiding monasteries, plundering abbeys, and assaulting well-fortified ecclesiastical cities. The princes crushed their efforts, and their leaders died—Franz von Sickingen in battle in 1523, Ulrich von Hutten in exile in the same year. Romantic anachronisms that they were, the knights in their last flickering bid for power courted, and found, disaster.

The imperial cities and the princes induced to join Lutheranism fared much better. For them, power, profits, and piety harmonized splendidly. To assume full sovereign rights over one's territory—to gather ecclesiastical establishments into a state church that would obey the dictates not of pope or emperor but of the local patriciate or local prince—made it possible to eliminate Roman influence, expropriate the property of monasteries or cathedral chapters, and keep at home the money the faithful had been sending to Rome for centuries. By the mid-1520s, two imperial electors—of Saxony and Hesse—had joined the Lutheran cause. So had Albert of Hohenzollern, grand master of the Catholic Order of the Teutonic Knights, who converted at Luther's urging and took the territories under his control—East Prussia and Brandenburg—into the Protestant camp. Many of the imperial cities, including Nuremberg, Bremen, Erfurt, and Gotha, all populated by literate and independent-minded men who were a receptive audience for the outpouring of Luther's prolific pen, turned Protestant as well. But by 1525, its very success had brought Lutheranism to the edge of disaster: the peasants, inflamed by Luther's teachings, had risen to claim their share of the new dispensation at hand. [39]

[39] For Lutheranism after 1525, see p. 144.

The Radical Reformation

In 1521, while the Diet of Worms was weighing its edict against Luther, the city was plastered with placards bearing the symbol of peasant rebelliousness, the *Bundschuh*. In 1524 and 1525, with the short-lived, ill-starred Peasants' War, the emerging alliance between religious reformation and social rebellion briefly flourished and quickly collapsed.

"The French Revolution," as Hajo Holborn has observed, "was not caused by the philosophy of the Enlightenment, nor was the so-called Great Peasants' War caused by Lutheranism." Despite frequent defeats and ferocious reprisals, peasants had continued to engage in sporadic protest ever since the *Bundschuh* had first unfurled its defiant flag. "But," Holborn continues, "the new ideas gave the peasants' movement principles that enabled it to organize beyond the local sphere and to present its aims as part of a universal and national reform." [40] The regions in which the great war originated in 1524 are significant: southwest Germany, in the Black Forest, near the Swiss territories that were rapidly falling into the hands of reformers, and near the walls, in the shadow, of imperial cities that had embraced Protestantism. Soberly, the rural rebels held greed, cruelty, even millenarian hopes in check. The best known formulation of their demands, the *Twelve Articles of the Peasantry,* began, in good Lutheran fashion, with the pacific salutation, "To the Christian Reader Peace and the Grace of God through Christ," and concluded with the modest proviso that if any of the demands "should not be in agreement with the word of God," the peasants would "willingly recede" from them. What the rebels asked for was reasonable enough: a clergy elected by, and responsible to, its congregation and capable of preaching the Divine Word plainly, "pure and simple, without any human addition, doctrine or ordinance"; an end to excessive services, fees, and rents exacted by the lords; an end as well to the nobles' appropriation of woodlands and to their burdensome monopoly on hunting and fishing rights; an end above all to serfdom. This was the way the Swabian tanner, Sebastian Lotzer, who wrote the *Twelve Articles,* chose to understand Luther's doctrine of Christian freedom.

For a time the conciliatory attitude of the rebels, coupled with the craven fears of the lesser rulers, produced an aura of possible compromise and peaceful social adjustment. But the social fear drove the greater princes not toward concessions but into resistance. As men with great privileges to defend and the power to defend them, they refused to deal with the rebels at all or dealt with them only to gain time to raise their own armies. As princely resistance stiffened, the revolt spread northward, mainly in the Rhineland, grew more violent in its methods and more radical in its aims. The peasants never had a chance for victory. Though filled with brave and experienced soldiers, their

[40] *History of Modern Germany,* vol. I, 170–171.

forces were scattered and amateurish; they had no horses, no alliances, no long-range aims. While by April 1525 the number of rebellious peasants exceeded a quarter of a million, by May and June their movement was in disarray. First came routs, then came retribution, an outburst of wilful mass slaughter that blighted the German lands for decades. The traditional devices of criminal procedure—torture, mutilation, hanging, burning, decapitation—were applied in city after city with wanton energy and on an unprecedented scale. When Würzburg was recaptured by Bishop Conrad, "the event was celebrated with the execution of 64 citizens and peasants. Then the bishop made a tour of his diocese, accompanied by his executioner, who took care of 272 persons." [41] The ruling orders, back in control, were repaying their hapless victims for the months of shameful panic in which they had lived. No reliable figures exist or can exist, but it is estimated that a hundred thousand peasants were killed in battle and after; the number of cripples who survived is incalculable. It was, as Hajo Holborn has said, "one of the most shameful chapters in German history" [42]—one of the most shameful chapters, but not the most shameful.

Infatuated with Luther, whom they regarded as one of their own, the peasants did not anticipate that Luther would turn against them. They should have anticipated it. In his published writings he had always insisted, with perfect consistency, that the political authorities must be obeyed. Late in April 1525, when the peasants seemed on the verge of victory, Luther assailed both princes and rebels in his *Friendly Admonition to Peace Concerning the Twelve Articles of the Swabian Peasants.* He urged the princes, whom he blamed for the outbreak of the revolt, to grant the peasants what they deserved to allay their "intolerable grievances." At the same time, he berated the peasants for taking the sword. "Because you boast of the divine law and act against it, He will let you fall and be punished terribly, as men who dishonor His name." [43] Then, in May, after his attempts to calm rebellious peasants in Thuringia had embarrassingly failed, Luther dashed off a far more one-sided and far coarser exhortation to the princes, *Against the Murderous and Thieving Hordes of Peasants,* in which he declared the rebels "outside the law," worse than murderers, who had brought "murders and bloodshed" to the land, "made widows and orphans," and turned the social order upside down. "Therefore, let everyone who can, smite, slay, and stab, secretly or openly. . . . It is just as when one must kill a mad dog; if you don't strike him, he will strike you, and the whole land with you." [44] The princes had been unwilling to listen to Luther's call for social reform; they cheerfully obeyed his call to vengeance.

As by 1525 Luther had vehemently repudiated the social radicalism that had been encouraged by his example, so he had divorced himself from the

---

[41] Bainton, *Here I Stand,* 220.
[42] *History of Modern Germany,* vol. I, 170–171.
[43] Quoted in Hans J. Hillerbrand, ed., *The Protestant Reformation* (1968), 74.
[44] Bainton, *Here I Stand,* 217.

religious extremism that had for some years drawn inspiration from his work. The most interesting of his early extremist adversaries was Thomas Münzer, like Luther a Saxon and, like Luther, a well-educated cleric. For a time he professed himself Luther's disciple, but by 1524, he was denouncing Luther as a sensualist, a false prophet, and a servile truckler to temporal authority. He rejected all authority including Scriptures—"Bible, Babel, bubble!"—and insisted that the true Christian must wait, as the first Christians had waited, for direct divine inspiration. "The letter killeth, but the spirit giveth life."[45] Wherever Münzer preached, he attracted a fierce following among the disinherited of the world, urging them to turn their back on the fat, self-satisfied compromiser Luther and to overthrow the oppressive social order. His presence in Saxony helped to precipitate the peasant uprisings there; Luther's brutal accents in his diatribe against the "murderous and thieving hordes" were partly an expression of his rage against Münzer. Finally, in May 1525, following a decisive defeat of his peasant troops, Münzer was captured, tortured, and beheaded.

In Thomas Münzer religious extremism and social protest coalesced. In other sectaries of the time, like the Anabaptists, religious enthusiasm predominated.[46] The precise early history of the Anabaptists remains somewhat uncertain; Münzer, who rejected all baptism, seems to have had some influence on the discussions about infant baptism that divided Wittenberg in 1521. But the first significant center for the doctrine was Zurich (see p. 147). The reformer Ulrich Zwingli had gained control there in 1523 and found himself almost instantly in debate with the Protestant left wing. Some new Protestants, led by the "noble and learned young" Conrad Grebel,[47] insisted that baptism be given only upon profession of faith. Their following was considerable; numerous troubled citizens of Zurich refused to have their children baptized, although the city council, dominated by Zwingli's views, ordered them to comply with infant baptism. By 1525, the Anabaptist leaders were in prison or in exile. But the movement, cruelly persecuted wherever it went, spread and flourished, a sincere and touching Christian underground.[48]

The religious program of the Anabaptists was simple and straightforward. But the turmoil of the Reformation cast up other preachers, other sects, each with his own particular version of Christianity. The confusion of tongues against which Roman Catholic partisans had warned, once the Protestant contagion was allowed to spread, was not long in showing itself. Andreas Karlstadt, Luther's colleague at the University of Wittenberg and for some time his rival in popularity, developed a stridently anti-intellectual, populist Protes-

---

[45] 2 Cor. 3:6.

[46] The word is derived from the Greek prefix *ana*, meaning again or anew, marking the central doctrine of the sect, that true baptism can be administered only to adults.

[47] See Ernest A. Payne, "The Anabaptists," in *The New Cambridge Modern History,* vol. II, *The Reformation, 1520–1559* (1958), 120.

[48] For its development after 1525, see p. 144.

tantism: he professed to prefer the wisdom of illiterate peasants to the disputations of scholars and sought to banish images and music from the churches. Other sectarians excluded outsiders from the blessings of their teachings. Still others wandered about the countryside foretelling the millennium. Like many revolutionaries, Luther would discover that he could not confine the revolution he had made within the boundaries he himself had chosen; like many revolutionaries, he found his own extreme left—those who wanted to drive his logic to its conclusion—troublesome, detestable, and dangerous.

Spreading the Word: Luther's Europe After 1525

The year 1525 was decisive for Martin Luther. In that year his breach with Erasmus, with social radicals, and with religious extremists became final and irreparable. In that year, too, he put an end to monasticism in his church: he married. The time that was left him—he died in 1546, after some ill-health—was a time of significant and tireless activity: he defined the relations between church and state, wrote hymns and catechisms that became the classics of his confession, watched the travail of Lutheranism within, and the expansion of Lutheranism beyond, the frontiers of his Germany.

Anabaptism continued to be a holy plague. Driven from Zurich, the sect took refuge in Moravia, in some Hapsburg territories and some German cities, and found new supporters. The authorities hounded these pious rebaptizers, exiling them, burning them, and in an unconscious form of poetic justice—or, rather, injustice—drowning them. In 1527, a group of Anabaptists met in Switzerland and adopted what came to be called the Schleitheim Confession, which reiterated the Anabaptists' insistence on baptizing only those who "walk in the resurrection of Jesus Christ"; reduced the Lord's Supper to a "memorial" occasion and restricted it to the baptized; and abjured the use of violence for themselves. [49] This profession of faith remained the heart of the Anabaptists' program across northern Europe. A large-scale tragedy awaited them. In 1533, Anabaptists had managed to secure control of the German city of Münster. Sympathizers from the Netherlands, hearing the good news, tried to join their brethren, in vain; they were rounded up and judicially murdered. While the city was besieged, the holy remnant within expelled Catholics and Lutherans, baptized adults, preached community of property, and at the urging of their young leader John of Leyden, began to practice polygamy. John of Leyden, whose sanity gave way under the pressure of events, took a total of sixteen wives, had one of them executed, and finally had himself crowned king. In the early summer of 1535, this modern caricature of an Old Testament common-

---

[49] The seven points are summarized in *The New Cambridge Modern History*, vol. II, *The Reformation, 1520-1559* (1958), 125.

wealth was taken. Most of the defenders were butchered, the leaders tortured and executed in leisurely and edifying fashion. In the late 1520s Luther had still urged the authorities to deal mercifully with harmless Anabaptists; now, his patience gone, he said nothing.

Not all was turmoil and trouble. Lutheranism spread. In the 1530s other German cities, including Frankfurt am Main and Augsburg, joined the earlier converts. There were many states now, large and small, with a stake in the new order: they had confiscated church properties that they would on no account surrender. In 1530, Charles V called an imperial diet at Augsburg to clarify the religious situation of the empire. It was clarified beyond his desires. The Lutherans, led by the moderate Humanist Philip Melanchthon, drew up the Augsburg Confession which, despite its compromising tone, made the division between Catholics and Protestants obvious and irreparable. For some years there was confessional peace. It is a token of the complex political situation that German Protestant rulers, conscious of their membership in a Holy Roman Empire headed by a Roman Catholic prince, supported Charles V during the early 1530s to ward off a new threat from the Turks. True, in 1531 German Protestant princes, joined by German Protestant cities, set up the Schmalkaldic League which undertook to defend their faith in all their lands.[50] But war within the empire did not erupt until 1546, the year of Luther's death, only to be settled nine years later, in 1555, with the Peace of Augsburg, which gave the Lutherans what they wanted—the right to determine their own religion in their own states (see p. 164).

Other countries, meanwhile, had swelled the Lutheran avalanche. Lutherans made many converts and exerted widespread influence in France and England although neither was to become a Lutheran country (see pp. 177 and 184). The Swiss reformers were inspired by Luther's ideas and heartened by Luther's success, though they remained an independent strain of Protestantism (see p. 147). In Luther's lifetime, there were to be Lutheran settlements in Transylvania, the Baltic regions, small areas of Poland, and far more significantly, in Scandinavia. Before 1525 preachers who had been in direct touch with Luther himself preached in Denmark, and by 1537 the Danish crown established a Lutheran state church. Having taken full control of Norway the year before, King Christian III of Denmark also gradually introduced Lutheranism into his Norwegian lands. In Sweden, which had secured independence from Danish overlordship in 1521 under the leadership of Gustavus Vasa, Lutheranism was imposed by Gustavus (crowned king in 1523). A Lutheran preacher, Olaus Petri, who married in 1525 (the year his model Martin Luther took the same step), exercised enormous influence over his country and his king. Petri

---

[50] The name of the league is drawn from the town of Schmalkalden, where the negotiations for its formation took place in late 1530 and early 1531. Its most prominent members were Landgrave Phillip of Hesse, the duke of Brunswick, the elector of Saxony, the cities of Strasbourg, Bremen, and Ulm, joined later by Göttingen, Hamburg, and Rostock, and in 1537, by the major city-states of Frankfurt, Hanover, and Augsburg. See *New Cambridge Modern History*, vol. II, 350.

published popular books of Lutheran devotion, preached endless Lutheran sermons, participated in a Swedish translation of the New Testament, and wrote a Swedish mass. While Gustavus Vasa largely expropriated the church in 1527, Lutheranism proved a slow growth confronting sturdy resistance. It took decades, punctuated by rebellions and interminable efforts at persuasion, before Lutheranism was really established in Sweden. But once it was secure, it was unassailable.

The Lutheran Paradox

It was the essential aim of Luther's reformation to restore the direct, primitive Christian relationship between God and man. Man was to feel all the weight of his sin, all the terror of his perdition, all the glory of his faith, unencumbered by mere human intermediaries. Luther's attack on the Roman Catholic hierarchy was only in small part, and mainly at the beginning of his mission, an attack on secularism, corruption, nepotism, bureaucratic stupidity. It was an attack, rather, on a human institution that had dared to interpose itself between God and man and to claim the right of mediating in a situation in which no mediator, except Christ, was welcome. The political and economic profits accruing to those confessing themselves Lutherans—and they were, for many, considerable—should not obscure the profound inwardness of Luther's teachings. The extremists who arose so widely, and so wildly, in the wake of Luther's break with Rome, testify to the emotions that his preaching, his writing, his very presence unloosed in pious and disoriented men. If—as many reasoned after 1517—there was to be no pope, no separate priesthood, no pilgrimages, no interceding saints, there was no need for formal clerical institutions at all. Faith in God and a divine sign in man were all a true Christian needed; or, as others, less individualistic, put it: the communion of saints was sufficient unto itself.

But this was not Luther's view, even though some of his early pronouncements could be interpreted in this way. His lifelong ideal was the communion of saints, united in the invisible church of the faithful. But the experiences of 1524 and 1525, as well as inexorable political realities, drove Lutheran rulers, and Luther himself, into a less exalted conception of church and state. In a world of hostile Catholic neighbors and excitable fanatics at home, the secular princes and city governments came to assume the position of little popes within their territories. No longer a universal autocracy governed by Rome, the church became a local autocracy governed by its duke or city council. As Luther's political thought developed in response to external events, it became clear that the state must assume certain functions, notably education and welfare, that had once been the province of the church, and must supervise, moreover, the good conduct and uniform practice of churchmen. Luther did not think rulers free from sin; on the contrary, he frankly told them over and over again how subject they too were to human failings and how liable they too were to damnation. But Luther took seriously St. Paul's injunction that the powers that be are ordained of God; it followed that a Christian owed his state obedience, and nothing but obedience. A true Christian man was a free man, but Luther interpreted this freedom in a subjective sense. He was free in his heart, no matter how oppressive the regime under which he might live and suffer. Thus Luther, the great liberator, became the great proponent of state churches subservient to state governments. And so, when Protestantism began its march across Europe, Lutheranism traveled far less well than Calvinism. It was Calvinism, not Lutheranism, that seemed made for export. [51]

THE SWISS REFORMATION

Zwingli: Protestantism in Zurich

The Swiss Reformation, dominated by that austere logician, John Calvin, arose partly on its own impulsion, largely as a response to Luther. The precise proportions of its independence and dependence are, like all such subtle affairs, impossible to settle with precision; nor does it much matter: the ideas were in the air. Ulrich Zwingli, who set the Swiss Reformation in motion, was an Erasmian Humanist and a learned student of the Old Testament; he knew the Neoplatonists of Florence and the church fathers. He later claimed that he had taken the road to reform before he had heard of Luther: "I object to being called Lutheran by the papists; for I did not learn Christ's teaching from Luther but from the very word of God." [52] The claim can neither be substantiated nor refuted, but it is certain that Zwingli studied Luther's progress closely and admired it greatly. Born in 1484, Zwingli entered the priesthood in 1506; in 1518 he was called to Zurich. When he began to preach there on January 1, 1519, his heresy was dramatically obvious. In his sermons and his writings, he rapidly developed his Protestant theology until, in 1525, he was ready to summarize his teachings in his main work, the *Commentary on True and False Religion:* scriptures are the sole authority a Christian must accept; Roman sacraments, festivals, institutions are devilish inventions; the spirit is essential, trappings like church music are nothing. By the time he wrote the *Commentary,* he and his party had been in control of Zurich's political and religious affairs for two years. The clergy were allowed to marry; Catholic religious houses were closed;

---

[51] Holborn, *History of Modern Germany,* vol. I, chap. 8.
[52] Quoted in Hurstfield, *Reformation Crisis,* 35.

local churches were cleansed of relics and organs; the mass was abolished; and Zwingli instituted a new order of preaching, a new church service, a new ritual of baptism.

All this, a few details apart, was compatible with Luther's teachings. Only one issue remained, and that an important one: the meaning of the Lord's Supper. In his *Commentary,* as in many sermons, Zwingli employed a good deal of metaphysical and philological ingenuity to prove that the bread and wine of the mass were simply a commemoration, a symbol of God's covenant with man. Zwingli was so intent on asserting the distance between matter and spirit that he rejected, almost with disgust, any intimation that merely physical things like bread and wine could ever embody, even vaguely, such spiritual things as the body and blood of Christ. Thus he repudiated not merely transubstantiation, but also Luther's teaching of the "real presence"—consubstantiation.

This issue occupied Zwingli above all others. It is true to say, with Owen Chadwick, that "in his early years as a Reformer he and his friend Oecolampadius of Basle were so engaged upon saying what the Lord's Supper was not, that they rarely and reluctantly attempted to describe what it was."[53] His single-minded zeal led Zwingli into direct confrontation with Luther. In 1529, Landgrave Philip of Hesse, anxious to forge a united Protestant front, brought together a glittering galaxy of reformers: Zwingli and Luther came, as did Oecolampadius, Melanchthon, Bucer of Strasbourg, and some others. They settled much and at least did not break up in mutual animosity. But on the Lord's Supper, on which Luther in earlier years had been so pliable, no agreement proved possible: Luther strongly insisted on reading supernatural meaning into Jesus's words, "This is my body"; Zwingli insisted, quite as strongly, that they meant simply, "This signifies my body." The union of Protestants, however desirable politically, failed to materialize. The Lutheran, and what came to be called the Reformed church, continued to coexist, compete, and often enough, conflict with one another. In 1531, two years after this Colloquy of Marburg, Zwingli died, "sword and battle-ax in hand,"[54] at Kappel, in a battle between Zurich and Catholic Swiss cantons. The Zurich Reformation was fortunate: Zwingli's long-lived successor, Henry Bullinger, kept Zwingli's work alive, both in Zurich and, largely by correspondence, elsewhere. But Zwingli's and Bullinger's dream of an all-Protestant Switzerland never became reality.

Calvin: Protestantism in Geneva

What Zwingli failed to do in Switzerland, another Swiss reformer—or, rather French reformer active in Switzerland—succeeded in doing across much of

---

[53] Owen Chadwick, *The Reformation* (1964), 79.
[54] Ibid., 80.

northern Europe.[55] John Calvin developed a rigorous theology, a widely admired church, a persuasive moral doctrine, and a set of justifications for his faith that impressed the scholar and moved the plain man. Calvin was a remarkable theologian, but he was not a theologian alone; he was, in addition, a Humanist and a lawyer, and his extensive, versatile philological and legal training gave his thought on divine things its unique strength. He read the Scriptures with the eyes of a scholar;[56] he served Protestantism as learned counsel, as if it were a case he must win.

He found his opportunity in permanent exile. Probably in 1533, Calvin had turned Protestant; he remembered his conversion as a sudden experience, a blinding insight that dispelled his obstinate adherence to error and calmed his fear that apostasy might destroy the church. Once he was a heretic, his life was in danger, and he left France to settle at Basel. There he wrote and, in 1536, published *The Institutes of the Christian Religion,* destined to become a classic of Protestantism. In the same year, Guillaume Farel, who was leading the Reformation in Geneva, imperiously invited Calvin to apply his administrative talents to the Protestant cause in that divided city-state. "When I first came into this Church," Calvin recalled later, "there was almost nothing there. They preached and that was all. They sought out the idols indeed, and burnt them, but there was no reformation. Everything was in tumult."[57] It was a muddle only a lawyer could have loved, or resolved.

In the Geneva of 1536, the Protestants were a dominant and embattled minority. In the embittered disputations between Catholic and Reformed theologians that had brought the republic to the verge of civil war, reformers had carried the day; in 1533, the Catholic bishop had left; by 1535, against the objections of the Catholic majority, the city government had abolished the mass. But staunchly Catholic Savoy (a powerful and aggressive neighbor), Roman Catholics within Geneva, and a desperate shortage of qualified leadership in Farel's party placed the Reformation in Geneva in a precarious position. Then Calvin began to organize the Protestant forces with all the subtlety of a scholar, decisiveness of an attorney, and self-assurance of a believer who knows that he is right. Calvin was everywhere; the outlines of a city of the saints, which he would later impose on Geneva, rapidly emerged.

[55] Calvin was born in 1509 at Noyon in Picardy as Jean Cauvin, but it is by the abbreviated version of his Latin name Calvinus that he is universally known.

[56] Calvin insisted that the Scriptures were God's inestimable gift to man, superseding all merely human efforts at comprehending His will. The authority of the Bible is therefore nothing less than divine, and Calvin made much—more than Luther did—of the Old Testament. Accordingly he condemned both the Roman Catholics, who relied on tradition and priestly interpretation, and the radical enthusiasts, who relied on inspiration. At the same time, "he accepted like any other humanist the need for historical and textual criticism" (A. G. Dickens, *Reformation and Society in Sixteenth-Century Europe* [1966], 156).

[57] Quoted in François Wendel, *Calvin: The Origins and Development of his Religious Thought* (1963), 49n.

Too rapidly. While Calvin's aims pleased the city, his speed and his methods did not; in 1538, accordingly, he was asked to leave Geneva. Farel left with him.

For three years, Calvin lived in Strasbourg, watched the Reformation at work there, read and wrote extensively including a second much enlarged version of his *Institutes,* and elaborated his theological, ecclesiastical, and political views. Then, in 1541, after abject appeals by the Genevan council, once again controlled by his friends, he returned, on his own terms, not quite, but seeking to become, a holy dictator. Once installed, Calvin moved without hesitation. His clerical ordinances setting up a Calvinist church appeared in the same year; other ordinances, penetrating into every aspect of life, appeared soon after. Calvin preached and wrote, recast his *Institutes,* decimated and gradually silenced his opponents. When he died in 1564, his mastery over his republic absolute, Geneva had become the headquarters for spreading his militant faith.

The three rocks on which Calvin built his church were the majesty of God, the mercy of Christ, and the vigilance of the faithful. The rigor of Calvin's logic, the harshness of his doctrines, and the dour aspect of his Geneva, have impelled many of his later readers to visualize him as a gloomy Scholastic obsessed by the rage to dominate and by man's utter, sinful wretchedness. But, it has rightly been said, "No summary does Calvin justice." While it will not do to "soften the message of Calvin," it is essential to remember that Calvin was "vitally concerned with divine mercy and redemptive power, as well as with the more fearful aspects of the divine plan. To neglect these moving, impressive passages would be to barbarize a great theologian and reduce him to the level of his least enlightened followers." [58] This much said, Calvin's God remains an awesome, remote, terrifying, wholly self-willed paternal figure. In man's fallen state, the direct consequence of Adam's sin in Eden, he cannot encompass his salvation or even understand God's decrees. He cannot earn heaven: like Luther, Calvin firmly rejected the notion that works could in any way influence man's ultimate fate. Among God's dark decrees, inaccessible to human reason and unchangeable by human action, the one that aroused most discussion in his day was Calvin's doctrine of election and reprobation. It was important to him, though not nearly so important as it would become to his disciples, the Puritans. God, Calvin reasoned, had decided from all eternity to elect some to salvation and assign others to eternal damnation. While God had conceived this decree in perfect foreknowledge of man's conduct, foreknowledge was not the cause of His decree: to explain God's permanent and irrevocable decision by foreknowledge was to infringe on His majesty by reducing His freedom. "If we ask why God takes pity on some, and why he lets go of the others and leaves them, there is no other answer but that it pleases him to do so." [59] This, in all its stark simplicity, was Calvin's famous doctrine of predestination; it had been implied

[58] Dickens, *Reformation and Society,* 157–159.
[59] Quoted from Calvin's Sermon on Ephesians 1:3–4, in Wendel, *Calvin,* 272–273.

or obliquely stated by many other earlier theologians, notably St. Augustine, but never with such uncompromising precision.

Yet it is worth noting—and this brings us to the second aspect of Calvin's doctrine—that the chapters of the *Institutes* in which Calvin discusses election and reprobation are in Book III, which deals not with the majesty of God but with the grace of Christ. It was not a matter of lamentation that most men should be damned, but a matter for rejoicing that a few men should be saved, for by his original sin man had forfeited all claim to divine consideration. The salvation of any was therefore an act of superhuman mercy; it could be justified only by the sacrifice Christ had made on the cross. Christ had died for the elect. While "the whole human race perished in the person of Adam," Christ, the sole mediator, had, through his death, taken away "penalty and guilt"[60] from some.

The psychological and social consequences of this doctrine were not apathy but incessant labor, not heedless sinning but austerity; far from drawing lessons of despair or libertinism, Calvinists drew instead incentives for strenuous efforts and a sturdy (it seemed, to their many adversaries, smug) self-confidence. The reason for this perhaps surprising result lay in Calvin's conception of outward signs. Not even Calvin was arrogant enough to claim that he and his followers were definitely saved. But it seemed at least highly probable. While no one could be certain of his own, or anyone else's, fate, there were indications, divinely bestowed hints, on which men could place some reliance. To lead a sober Christian life, work hard, dress quietly, eschew giddy entertainments, worship God in the correct—that is to say, the Calvinist—manner, was to confirm, as much as mere mortals could confirm, one's sense of being among the elect. Calvin's social and religious thought here join: man could be godly in his worldly calling, in his profession as a merchant, quite as much as a minister was godly in his preaching.

As historians have not failed to note, in the effort to turn Geneva into a city of saints, Calvin made it into something of an armed camp. As a Humanist, Calvin respected literature and the arts, but he was wholly without patience for a life of pleasure or self-indulgence. From the beginning he insisted that the community must control the moral life of Genevans in the most minute detail and guarantee observance of the orthodox faith in the most rigid fashion. As his power grew, the association of ministers, the consistory, followed his lead. The reports of repression sound like tendentious stories invented by Calvin's enemies, but they are fully documented. The consistory disciplined Genevans for dancing, for making noise or laughing during divine service, for speaking out on touchy issues (one Genevan was penalized for complaining that the influx of French refugees had raised the cost of living, another for objecting to the death penalty imposed on religious dissenters), or even for owning a copy of the romance *Amadis of Gaul.*[61] Calvin might have to contend with a

<hr>

[60] *Institutes of the Christian Religion,* II, 6, 1; and III, 4, 30; ed. John T. McNeill (1960), 340, 657.
[61] For these and similar cases see Wendel, *Calvin,* 84, and Williston Walker, *John Calvin: The Organizer of Reformed Protestantism* (1906), 304 ff.

recalcitrant city government—despite his reputation as a dictator he always found vigorous local opposition—but at least he could act with a high hand against moral offenders and theological dissenters. His reign in Geneva is punctuated by acts of repression, at least unpleasant and at worst tyrannical. After a long controversy in the mid-1540s, Calvin succeeded in procuring the expulsion of the French reformer Sebastian Castellio with whom he had become embroiled over the canonical status of the Song of Songs. Far grimmer was the case of the Spaniard Michael Servetus, a provocative, somewhat unbalanced religious radical who professed antitrinitarian views as offensive to the Calvinists as they were to the Roman Catholics to whom they were originally addressed. In 1553, seeking refuge, Servetus made the mistake of entering Genevan territory. He behaved as offensively as he could; he was arrested at Calvin's instigation, tried for blasphemy at Calvin's urging, and put to death with Calvin's approval, though at the end Calvin objected to the mode of executing Servetus—burning alive—in vain. The incident shows, if it shows anything, that Calvin's hold over his city was not complete even as late as 1553, and it shows, also, that Calvin was a man of his day.

Calvinism for Export

Despite all this, and partly because of all this, Calvinism was a faith with a future, and not in Geneva alone. Geneva was deluged with Protestants from all across Europe, curious scholars and desperate refugees, from Scotland and Poland, France and England, the Netherlands and Germany. When they returned home, they were fired with the determination to make other Genevas. In 1559, the bishop of Winchester spoke for chagrined Roman Catholics everywhere: "The wolves be coming out of Geneva and other places of Germany," he said, "and have sent their books before, full of pestilent doctrines, blasphemy and heresy to infect the people." [62] Wherever else the Protestant wolves might come from, Geneva was evidently first, and worst. Thucydides had proudly called Athens the school of Greece; John Knox, the great Scottish Calvinist, proudly called Geneva "the most perfect school of Christ that ever was on earth since the days of the Apostles." [63]

One influential source of Calvinist instruction was Calvin's masterpiece, *The Institutes of the Christian Religion*. With its lucid Latin and perspicuous organization, it found many grateful readers. In 1541, Calvin himself translated the second edition into French, thus greatly enlarging its public, and the definitive version of 1559, also in Latin, was immediately translated as well. The second source was the example of the Calvinist community, sober, self-

[62] Quoted from J. E. Neale, *Elizabeth I and Her Parliaments* (1953), 57, by J. H. Elliott, *Europe Divided, 1559-1598* (1968), 31–32.
[63] Quoted in Hurstfield, *Reformation Crisis*, 43.

respecting, dominated by preachers and merchants and craftsmen confident in their calling; here was a community at once pious and worldly, a model to those who wanted to follow Christ without quite turning their backs on Mammon. Finally, there was the Calvinist church organization; it had a definite shape in Geneva itself, but Calvin, in his discussions and correspondence with foreigners, showed himself reasonable and flexible: he was persuaded that local differences might require differences in structure. It has often been observed, and with justice, that while Calvinism was far from democratic in its political and ecclesiastical ideas, it promoted, however indirectly, the progress of democracy. While Calvin himself sought to convert Geneva into a theocracy, his doctrine that church and state govern separate spheres induced, in many Calvinist communities, a congregational system, in which the church members chose their ministers and in which the ministers were subject, in worldly matters, to the magistrates. These were local variations which Calvin himself sanctioned and encouraged.

But there was one respect in which Calvinism survived and flourished abroad not because it obeyed, but because it abandoned, Calvin's explicit teachings—in the area of political theory. Calvin himself had taught passive obedience. The exceptions to his severe injunction, duly recorded in his *Institutes,* were so exceptional as to be, for Calvin himself, almost meaningless. In a political order equipped with magistrates whose explicit duty it was to resist tyranny, such resistance was permissible. And there might be an inspired individual, obeying God's direction, overthrowing the tyrant. But in general, men must bear even the infidel—only God should punish the wicked king. This was an obvious political theory for a party in power; Calvinists in a minority position must revise this theory or perish. They chose to revise it: John Knox in Scotland and a series of Calvinist writers in France laid down the conditions under which resistance to the wicked king was not merely permitted but commanded. This tenacious will to live was among Calvinism's most appealing traits.

THE ENGLISH REFORMATION

The Dynastic Issue

On the Continent, the Reformation began with religion and ended in politics; in England, it began with politics and ended in religion. In 1509, when Henry VIII ascended the throne to succeed his father, Henry VII, Lollard piety, Erasmian philosophy, and popular anticlericalism were in the air; they were soon joined, first by Lutheran, then by Calvinist, heresies. Doubtless these religious forces would have compelled some form of rebellion against Rome in

England, but the English Reformation took its particular course because the king of England wanted—needed—a divorce.

Henry VIII is a curious, and remains a controversial, figure. Profligate, lecherous, cultivated but not civilized, eager to govern but impatient with the routine of administration, imprudently militant in foreign affairs, and incapable of sustaining frustration, he was nevertheless thoroughly alert to his situation. He was the second of a disputed line, heir to a throne his father had usurped, and his primary concern was to sustain the Tudor dynasty. For this purpose he needed a son, but his queen, Catherine of Aragon, the victim of repeated disasters—miscarriages, stillbirths, infants dying—had given him only a daughter, Mary. It was, Henry feared, not good enough. He was not above toying with Lutheran ideas and negotiating with Lutheran leaders to frighten Catholic clerics from whom he wished to extract concessions. But he was not a Lutheran or any kind of Protestant. Indeed, in 1521 he published a polemic against Luther in defense of the Catholic sacraments, for which the Pope granted him and his successors the title of *defensor fidei*.[64] The irony is too obvious to have gone unnoticed: whatever Protestantism was to come to England would come against his intentions. Next to the Renaissance popes, Henry VIII of England was the most effective unwitting agent the Reformation had.

When Henry married Catherine in 1509, he had earlier obtained a papal dispensation, for his chosen wife was the widow of his brother Arthur, a marital union explicitly forbidden in the Old Testament. It had been a strictly political choice: Henry VII had insisted on it because he was intent on retaining the Spanish dowry and the Spanish alliance for England. As Catherine failed and failed to produce a viable heir to the throne, the grim prohibition of Leviticus seemed nothing less than prophetic: "If a man takes his brother's wife, it is impurity; he has uncovered his brother's nakedness, they shall be childless."[65] It is naive to suppose that Henry wanted a divorce because he wanted to gratify his lust; as he had repeatedly demonstrated during his marriage, he did not need a divorce for that. He was brooding over his dynasty, and he came to regard Catherine's tribulations as divine punishment. Accordingly, in 1527 he applied to Pope Clement VII for a dispensation; the marriage that one pope had legitimized, another pope was now to dissolve.

Clement was in a difficult position. There was no question of his competence in the matter; it was common practice to release the powerful and the rich from marriages that did not suit them. But the pope was in the hands of Charles V, and Catherine of Aragon was the emperor's niece and under his

---

[64] He published, but did not write it by himself. "There is not much proof that the King had either learning or leisure enough to produce the *Assertio Septem Sacramentorum Adversus Martin Lutherum*. It is probable that the royal author had considerable assistance from More, Fisher and Lee and that the texts of Scripture, the linguistic evidence from Hebrew and Greek, the patristic citations and much of the argument were supplied by others" (E. G. Rupp, *Studies in the Making of the English Protestant Tradition* [1947], 90).

[65] Lev. 20:21; Revised Standard Version.

protection. Thus Cardinal Wolsey, Henry's much-feared, much-hated chief minister maneuvered and remonstrated in vain: the pope delayed and prevaricated. Henry lost his patience and Wolsey his post, and in November 1529, Parliament met to encompass at home what the king had failed to obtain abroad. The legislation that the Reformation Parliament passed in its long existence—it met in numerous protracted sessions until 1536—was like an avalanche, moving less by a deliberate plan than by its own growing momentum. Down to 1532, its acts were mostly directed at controlling the English clergy and intimidating the pope. Then Anne Boleyn, Henry's long-time mistress, became pregnant. In April 1533, Thomas Cranmer, recently appointed archbishop of Canterbury and one of the king's most assiduous servants, became the last court of appeal in clerical matters—the tie with Rome was loosened. And in May Cranmer gave the king what Clement had refused: he annulled Henry's marriage to Catherine. In June, Anne was crowned queen of England, and in September she gave birth. It was a girl: Elizabeth. But Henry persevered in his course. In 1534 he induced Parliament, astutely managed by Thomas Cromwell, to pass a whole series of enactments culminating in the Act of Supremacy which laid down that the king of England "is and ought to be the supreme head of the Church of England." [66] There was scattered, but only scattered, resistance: the two most prominent Englishmen to refuse to take the oath of supremacy—Sir Thomas More and John Fisher, bishop of Rochester— were beheaded in 1535. The king was supreme in more than name.

In 1536, Henry demonstrated this supremacy by adopting a policy profitably pursued on the Continent by princes won over to Protestantism: he expropriated the monasteries. In the previous year Cromwell had ordered inquiries into the financial position and the moral conduct of the English church, and to no one's surprise, he found what he was seeking and what he did not find he invented. Using the revelations as a convenient pretext, the king had about four hundred smaller monasteries dissolved, and in the next three years, in gradual but rapid steps, he put his hands on the larger houses. Monks were pensioned off, many of the nuns found husbands, abbots and priors obtained often lucrative posts in the English church. But the ultimate social consequences of the dissolutions were vast and unforeseen; they far transcended the shift of some ten thousand regular clergy from one place, or post, to another. The dissolution eliminated centers of resistance to royal policy and gave the crown undreamed-of wealth. Wasting his substance in splendor, gifts, and war, Henry could not hold on to what he had grasped, and in the end the Crown was as dependent on Parliament for supplies as before. But between 1536 and 1547, the year of Henry's death, he had realized more than £1.5 million from the sale of church properties. [67] The most far-reaching consequence of the dissolution, however, was its aid in creating and fostering a class

[66] See S. T. Bindoff, *Tudor England* (1950), 95.
[67] Ibid., 114.

of middling landed proprietors, the gentry. The courtiers and speculators who acquired church lands in the earliest distributions rapidly sold them, chiefly to prosperous farmers and younger sons of country gentlemen.[68] Thus the Henrician dissolution produced a subterranean social revolution that its author had not foreseen and would hardly have liked.

The Infiltration of Protestantism

It was obvious to all but Henry VIII that he could not for long contain, let alone throttle, the religious revolution he had unloosed. To deny the supremacy of the pope, to erase the monasteries and nunneries after first thoroughly maligning them, to conduct talks with Luther and Melanchthon, and to marry again and again for an impressive total of six marriages, was to act like anything but a Catholic king, to give public support to antipapal passions, and awaken the impression that the king of England was in company with rebellious Protestant princes on the Continent.[69] Such conduct could only give English reformers a certain measure of hope.

Henry did his best to disappoint it. He made it painfully clear that while he had departed from Rome he had little intention of departing from the Catholic faith. True, he responded violently to Catholic unrest. In 1536, in Lincolnshire and Yorkshire and the whole northeast of England, a mixture of parochial resistance to London and nostalgia for medieval monasticism produced a confused and short-lived series of risings, the Pilgrimage of Grace, which the government repressed with little difficulty; the rebels' leader, Robert Aske, was executed in 1537 despite a royal promise of pardon—Henry was nothing if not unscrupulous. But on the other side and, to the king, just as alarming, there was a marked drift toward Protestantism: powerful public figures like Thomas Cromwell and Thomas Cranmer found themselves in sympathy with Luther's teachings. English Bibles, tendentiously translated by William Tyndale and Miles Coverdale and pointedly patronized by Cromwell and Cranmer, became influential agents in the dissemination of Protestant

---

[68] See David Knowles, *The Religious Orders in England,* vol. III, *The Tudor Age* (1961), 399.

[69] Henry's six marriages were more than a tragicomedy, although they were also that. They were part of the great political and religious struggle that went on in his realm during his long reign. In 1536, after she had had a stillbirth, Anne Boleyn was tried for adultery (on trumped-up charges, it would seem) and beheaded. Henry's third wife, Jane Seymour, finally gave him the son he longed for, Edward, but she died in bearing him. Free to marry again, Henry this time chose (or was persuaded by his chief minister, Thomas Cromwell, to choose) for diplomatic reasons. Anne of Cleves, daughter of the duke of Cleves, was the symbol of a Protestant alliance against the powerful Catholic Emperor Charles V, but Henry found Anne distasteful and the alliance unprofitable, and so he divorced his fourth wife soon after marrying her, in 1540. Cromwell, the architect of the king's Protestant policy, fell with the divorce and was executed shortly after. Catherine Howard, Henry's fifth wife, marked the decline of the Protestant faction and the rise of the Catholic clan of Norfolk, but when Henry had her executed in 1542 for "treasonable unchastity," this meant the end of the "conservatives." Henry's final marriage, to Catherine Parr, a devout and moderate Protestant, was peaceful and lasting—Catherine had the unique experience of outliving her dangerous husband.

ideas. The king liked none of it; in the early 1530s a few of the Cambridge reformers and a number of hapless Anabaptists were burned at the stake, and in 1539, at the king's insistence, Parliament passed the Act of Six Articles. It was uncompromisingly Catholic. It declared transubstantiation, mass in one kind, celibacy for the clergy, the vow of chastity, and auricular confession to be the belief and practice of all Englishmen and threatened to enforce those doctrines with savage penalties. Anyone caught denying transubstantiation was to be burned at the stake and have his property confiscated, with no pardon for recantation.[70] But Henry VIII was a king of England before he was a champion of orthodoxy; in his last years he proceeded cautiously against Protestant dissent and protected Cranmer, for all his Lutheran leanings, against his vocal enemies. The Protestants moved ahead cautiously, in private Bible readings, in discussions about a new prayer book, awaiting their opportunity.

It came in 1547, with Edward VI, Henry's son by Jane Seymour. Edward was ten at his accession and had been raised, on his father's command, by distinguished reformers. Like all minorities, Edward's short reign—the young king died in 1553—was marred by the jockeying of great families greedy for power. The king's first protector, the duke of Somerset, held control until 1549 when he was supplanted and eventually brought to the scaffold by his rival, the earl of Warwick.[71] But neither the political squabbles of the magnates nor Warwick's short-lived return to the repressive policies of Henry VIII slowed down the impetus of the reformers. Among Somerset's first acts was the repeal of Henry's treason laws, the Six Articles, and of all restrictions on the dissemination of the English Bible. Cranmer, now a little freer to maneuver, cautiously imposed a new service on all English churches; in the following year, somewhat more boldly, he got Parliament to accept a new *Booke of the common prayer and administracion of the Sacramentes, and other rites and ceremonies of the Church after the use of the Churche of England.* Imposed on the country, and then drastically revised in 1552 to catch up with the revolutionary reformist mood of much of the country, the Book of Common Prayer, even in its celebrated second version, remains typical of the Anglican attitude toward doctrinal questions: majestic and memorable in tone, it was conveniently obscure about important doctrinal details, claiming to be truly Catholic while incorporating many significant features of the Protestant revolt on the Continent. The austere monopoly of that book was part of the great dismantling of Catholic observances that characterized Edward's short reign: Catholic images and books were ordered destroyed, the service was given new simplicity, the mass was translated into communion, priests were transformed from vessels of grace into appointed officials. All was still flux; the building of Anglicanism, still incomplete, was on its way to completion. But Edward was dying, and after a mad, abortive scheme to substitute Jane Grey for Mary Tudor predictably

[70] See Dickens, *English Reformation,* 177.
[71] Warwick is perhaps better known by the title he acquired in 1551, as the duke of Northumberland.

failed, Mary became queen of England, and the course of the English Reformation was dramatically reversed.

From Mary to Elizabeth

In company with other celebrated epithets, the name Bloody Mary, bestowed on Mary Tudor in pure hatred, is only three quarters deserved. Protestant propagandists aside, historians agree that Mary was kindly in her personal life and on numerous occasions generous with mortal enemies. But like her half-brother, she brought her education into her reign and, being the proud daughter of Catherine of Aragon, she was half Spanish and all Catholic. And unlike her father she acted from religious rather than political principles—she was doctrinaire rather than flexible. Her own father-in-law, Charles V, who married her to his son Philip in 1554, disapproved of the persecutions she unloosed on her realm: as Catholic as Mary, but more politic, he distrusted a policy that would divide and weaken a country that could be useful to him.

Heedless and pious, Mary persecuted the Protestants with all the calm confidence of a believer doing the Lord's work. By the end of 1554, her Parliaments had repealed the reform legislation[72] enacted by Henry VIII and Edward VI, while her distant kinsman, Cardinal Reginald Pole, returned to England as papal legate bringing the pope's absolution with him. Her Parliament under control, her political enemies dead, her predecessor's spiritual guides in the Tower, Mary could now undertake her purification in all earnest. Cranmer and other Protestant bishops died by burning, disdaining to take flight; about three hundred others, most of them humble workmen and artisans, some sixty of them women, died with them, for the most part with exemplary courage, stubbornly loyal to their heresies and saying memorable things at the stake. Around eight hundred Protestants fled abroad, settling in Frankfurt, in Strasbourg, in Geneva, to celebrate the English martyrs, hammer out their theological doctrines, and quarrel with one another.

To our century, stained by vaster horrors, the number of Mary's victims seems modest. The persecution was, in fact, too small to eradicate Protestantism in England.[73] But what made it so notorious, what gave Mary her unenviable epithet, was its solitary prominence in the queen's policy. She seemed untouched by the Catholic spirituality burgeoning abroad in response to the Protestant challenge; her burnings at the stake were unaccompanied by any inner fire that might rekindle traditional Catholic religion in England. Men might be intimidated by the threat of the stake; it did not turn them into fervent believers. Besides, the queen found herself powerless to reverse the policy that

---

[72] For the single exception, the land settlement, see p. 155.

[73] In the century and a quarter before 1529, some one hundred Lollards had been burned for their religion; in the first twenty years of the English Reformation, the figure was sixty; and during Elizabeth's reign there were about two hundred Roman Catholic victims. The rate of executions was thus noticeably higher. For the figures, see Bindoff, *Tudor England*, 177.

had despoiled the monasteries under her father. No effort on her part could induce Parliament to return the church lands to their original owners. It was technically impossible to trace properties to their original owners, and in any event present owners would give up nothing. With his dissolution of the monasteries Henry had, without wishing it, given thousands a stake in Reformed England. And finally, by burning some Protestants and allowing others to escape, Mary gave those others a rich opportunity for celebrating the martyrs she had made. In 1559, the year after Mary's death, John Foxe, one of the exiles, published a Latin account of the sufferings his fellow Protestants had undergone; in 1563, he published the first English version of his *Actes and Monumentes.* It became widely known as Foxe's Book of Martyrs and remained for many years the most popular book—for some people, aside from the Bible, the only book—they read.[74] In the course of her reign, Mary had made herself generally hateful with her Spanish marriage even among those whom the persecutions left indifferent. After her death, Foxe, with his lurid woodcuts, his circumstantial, stirring reports of the burnings, and his placement of the Marian interlude amidst the eternal struggle between God and the devil, made Mary into a byword of satanic cruelty. Her reputation helped to determine English policies for centuries after. With such an enemy, Protestantism scarcely needed a friend.

Still, English Protestants were delighted to see Mary die in 1558; the bonfires they lit in the streets were perhaps as much for her disappearance as for the advent of her half-sister, Anne Boleyn's daughter. Elizabeth's precise religious position was unknown—it still is—and she had good military and diplomatic reasons for proceeding with caution. Her very hold on the throne was uncertain and needed to be secured. She was a woman and (at least Catholics professed to believe and soon began to murmur) of illegitimate birth. But there was no doubt that her accession would make the Marian return to Rome a mere interlude. In 1559, she moved, and by 1563, the shape of what has come to be called the Elizabethan Settlement had emerged. The English crown was "the only supreme governor" in ecclesiastical as well as temporal matters.[75] The exiles had come home, not, it turned out, to be quiet but to agitate for the purification of the Anglican church and to eradicate from it all traces of what appeared to them, not without justice, Roman beliefs and practices. In 1563, a convocation passed the Thirty-Nine Articles of the Church of England; they

[74] Foxe is one of the first beneficiaries of printing to celebrate its vast merits: "The Lord began to work for His Church not with sword and target to subdue His exalted adversary, but with printing, writing and reading. . . . How many printing presses there be in the world, so many blockhouses there be against the high castle of St. Angelo, so that either the pope must abolish knowledge and printing or printing at length will root him out" (quoted in William Haller, *The Elect Nation: The Meaning and Relevance of Foxe's Book of Martyrs* [1963], 110).

[75] Note that Henry VIII had proclaimed himself "the only supreme head" rather than "governor." "This qualitative difference in the wording, be it noted, sacrificed nothing of the substance of power, but it was intended to soften the impact of the measure on the catholic conscience, and to make the transference of ecclesiastical power to the Crown as little obtrusive as possible" (J. B. Black, *The Reign of Elizabeth, 1558–1603* [2nd ed., 1959], 16).

became the law of the land eight years later—Elizabeth was the most circumspect of monarchs. This statement of Anglican belief has often been called ambiguous. The charge is true but the ambiguity was deliberate; it was designed to invite as large a number of Englishmen as possible to join the Anglican communion. Ambiguity was an act of statesmanship, a typical expression of Elizabeth's canny political sense. It was typical as well for the time, a time of groping for settlements that would make the stake and the hangman unnecessary. Yet it was not wholly a success. Far too many Englishmen, including a variety of Puritans and permanently disgruntled English Catholics, wanted only clarity. As Elizabeth would discover in her long and glorious reign (see p. 183), for the truly devout, compromise was at best unacceptable, at worst the work of the devil.

SELECTED READINGS

The preconditions for the religious revolution are set out in a variety of studies. Paul Vignaux, *Philosophy in the Middle Ages: An Introduction* (1959), and G. G. Coulton, *Studies in Medieval Thought* (1940), are two of many volumes exploring the medieval background. To these should be added Meyrick H. Carré, *Realists and Nominalists* (1946); David Knowles, *The English Mystical Tradition* (1961); and Heiko Augustinus Oberman, *The Harvest of Medieval Theology: Gabriel Biel and Late Medieval Nominalism* (1963). The prehistory of the German Reformation can be followed in Ulrich von Hutten and others, "Letters of Obscure Men," collected in *On the Eve of the Reformation* (tr. 1909 and ed. 1964, with an introduction by Hajo Holborn). From the Roman Catholic point of view, Philip Hughes, *The Revolt Against the Church: Aquinas to Luther* (1947), says the essential.

Among many general treatments of the Reformation, see above all, Owen Chadwick, *The Reformation* (1964); A. G. Dickens, *Reformation and Society in Sixteenth-Century Europe* (1966); G. R. Elton, ed., *The Reformation, 1520–1559* (1958), the second volume in *The New Cambridge Modern History;* and Elton, *Reformation Europe, 1517–1559* (1963). Hans J. Hillerbrand, ed., *The Protestant Reformation* (1968), is a judicious collection of documents; Joel Hurstfield, ed., *The Reformation Crisis* (1965), has some helpful essays. H. G. Koenigsberger and G. L. Mosse, *Europe in the Sixteenth Century* (1968), though a general text, has some excellent chapters on the Reformation. E. Harris Harbison, *The Christian Scholar in the Age of the Reformation* (1956), lucidly surveys Luther, Calvin, and other leading thinkers. The old study by Karl Holl, *The Cultural Significance of the Reformation* (tr. 1959), retains its value. See also J. S. Whale, *The Protestant Tradition* (1955). From a Roman Catholic perspective, see especially Josef Lortz, *How the Reformation Came* (1964), and Philip Hughes, *A Popular History of the Reformation* (1957).

Martin Luther has attracted numerous biographers. Roland H. Bainton, *Here I Stand: A Life of Martin Luther* (1962), is comprehensive, but neglects Luther's connections with the apocalyptic tradition. Heinrich Boehmer, *Martin Luther: Road to Reformation* (tr. 1946), treats the young Luther in detail, as does E. G. Rupp, *The Progress of Luther to the Diet of Worms* (1951), and, from a psychoanalytical perspective, Erik H. Erikson, *Young Man Luther: A Study in Psychoanalysis and History* (1958). A. G. Dickens, *Martin Luther and the Reformation* (1967), is short and excellent.

So is V. H. H. Green, *Luther and the Reformation* (1964). Lucien Febvre's biography, first published in 1929, repays reading. So does the fine biography by Ernest B. Schwiebert, *Luther and His Times* (1950). Hajo Holborn, *A History of Modern Germany*, vol. I, *The Reformation* (1959), places Luther into his age and his times. Clyde Leonard Manschreck, *Melanchthon, The Quiet Reformer* (1958), ably sums up the career of Luther's powerful associate. It should be read in conjunction with Lewis Spitz, *The Religious Renaissance of the German Humanists* (1963). For the radical German reformation, see Hajo Holborn's biography, *Ulrich von Hutten and the German Reformation* (tr. 1937); George H. Williams, *The Radical Reformation* (1962), a massive treatise; and Franklin H. Littell, *The Anabaptist View of the Church* (1958). Norman Cohn, *The Pursuit of the Millennium* (rev. ed., 1964), begins with the Middle Ages, but does much with extremists in the sixteenth century.

For the Swiss reformers the literature is less ample than for Luther, but ample enough. S. M. Jackson, *Huldreich Zwingli* (1901), is now old but remains important; Oskar Farmer, *Zwingli, The Reformer* (1952), is a skimpy condensation of an authoritative biography available in German in three volumes (1943, 1946, 1960). For Bucer, see Hastings Eells, *Martin Bucer* (1931). The best modern biography of Calvin is François Wendel, *Calvin: The Origins and Development of His Religious Thought* (tr. 1963). R. N. Carew Hunt, *John Calvin* (1933), is also worth reading. The early chapters of John Thomas McNeill, *The History and Character of Calvinism* (1954), are relevant here. For Calvin's state, see William Monter, *Calvin's Geneva* (1966), and Robert Kingdon's important monograph, *Geneva and the Coming of the Wars of Religion in France, 1555–1563* (1956). For Calvin's victim, Servetus, see Roland H. Bainton, *Hunted Heretic: The Life and Death of Michael Servetus* (1953). John Calvin and Jacopo Sadoleto, *A Reformation Debate* (ed. John C. Olin, 1966), is an interesting document.

The history of the English Reformation begins with the dynastic issue. Among many general histories of the period, S. T. Bindoff, *Tudor England* (1950), is crisp and accurate. See also F. M. Powicke, *The Reformation in England* (1941). Garrett Mattingly, *Catherine of Aragon* (1942), is an elegant biography that reaches wider and deeper than its ostensible subject. G. R. Elton, *The Tudor Revolution in Government: Administrative Changes in the Reign of Henry VIII* (1959), is controversial but useful. Among general surveys, A. G. Dickens, *The English Reformation* (1964), is masterly. To this one may add E. G. Rupp, *Studies in the Making of the English Protestant Tradition* (1947), which concentrates on the reign of Henry VIII. For that ruler, we are fortunate in two recent biographies: the general account by J. J. Scarisbrick, *Henry VIII* (1968), and the penetrating psychological study by Lacey Baldwin Smith, *Henry VIII: The Mask of Royalty* (1971). Another approach to the English Reformation is through the leading figures (normally the victims) of Henry's reign. See Jasper Ridley, *Thomas Cranmer* (1962); A. G. Dickens, *Thomas Cromwell and the English Reformation* (1959); and above all Raymond Wilson Chambers, *Thomas More* (1958). Among a large literature on More, see J. H. Hexter, *More's "Utopia": The Biography of an Idea* (1952). David Knowles, *The Religious Orders in England*, vol. III, *The Tudor Age* (1961), deals authoritatively with the dissolution of the monasteries. James Kelsey McConica, *English Humanists and Reformation Politics* (1965), is a general account. Christopher Morris, *Political Thought in England: Tyndale to Hooker* (1953), surveys the ideas dominating English politics in the critical decades, while William Haller, *The Elect Nation: The Meaning and Relevance of Foxe's Book of Martyrs* (1963), brilliantly treats English Protestants under Bloody Mary.

4

Dominance
and Decline
of Spain

EUROPE AFTER THE REFORMATION

A Moment of Settlement and Regrouping

The Europe of 1560 was a Europe at peace. The diplomatic and religious settlements that ended half a century of fighting among and within states were little better than truces, soon to be broken by bigger and better conflicts. But especially in the sphere of religion, these settlements represented the dawning of an awareness—no more—that all attempts at reunion were bound to fail, that Protestants and Catholics, Calvinists and Lutherans, would have to learn to live together in some fashion. Many rulers and statesmen continued to act in defiance of this insight; many whose profession it was to preach the true religion would insist that the truth could survive only if falsehood were extirpated. But their failures in the next decades would prove that the pose of crusader was outmoded, the time of crusades, over. The Spaniards would be the last to know this.

The Spaniards' tenacious desire to impose Catholic uniformity on their world reflected their particular national and religious experience and their powerful position in Europe. The Treaty of Cateau-Cambrésis, concluded in 1559, ratified Spanish victories on the diplomatic and military battlefield. It settled, or at least controlled, the endemic warfare between Europe's two greatest dynasties, Hapsburg and Valois. It put an end to France's Italian ambitions for two centuries and a half, until the advent of Napoleon Bonaparte. Francis I had been badly beaten at Pavia in 1525, and checked in 1529 by the Treaty of Cambrai (see p. 116), but to the end of his reign in 1547, he had made intermittent forays against Hapsburg possessions in the Italian peninsula. The slightest pretext, the smallest opportunity, mobilized French troops and French greed: in 1536, Francis I had managed to take and hold Savoy and Piedmont. His son and successor, Henri II, continued the anti-Hapsburg policy, mainly in Germany. But while an exhausted Spain went bankrupt in 1557, France, just as bankrupt, was even more exhausted, and Cateau-Cambrésis mirrored their respective resources. While the French held on to the imperial cities of Toul, Metz, and Verdun, which they had occupied in 1552, they conceded to Spain continued control over its Italian territories, evacuated Piedmont, and left the Spaniards in possession of Franche-Comté.[1] Thus the Spanish Hapsburgs, closely allied with the Austrian Hapsburgs, straddled Europe while France was left weakened and confined.

Emperor Charles V, in many respects the architect of Cateau-Cambrésis, did not live to see his triumph. Aged beyond his years and excessively disheartened, he had abdicated his many posts in 1555 and 1556, retired to the country in Spain, and died there in 1558. Charles was a tragic figure, a missionary for two anachronisms—universal empire and universal Catholicism. He was intelligent without being brilliant, impressive solely by an act of will, ridden with his duty, and imbued with his imperial destiny. The very size of his empire worked against him: it was too large, too diverse, to be kept easily under control, and his enemies were too numerous and too formidable to be permanently kept down. As a Hapsburg, Charles held Spain, the Netherlands, Naples and Milan, and the Austrian lands; as emperor, he held the Germanies. Hence he had to fight everyone: the Ottomans on the eastern frontier, rebellious coalitions of German states, restive Spaniards who thought him a Burgundian foreigner, to say nothing of France. The way Charles disposed of his dominions in 1555–1556 (he handed his Spanish possessions to his son, Philip II, and the imperial lands to his brother, Ferdinand I) suggests that he had become aware just how unmanageable his sprawling domains were.

Among the most intractable problems of Charles' beleaguered reign was the German problem, which was, in large part, a Protestant problem. Intermit-

---

[1] The Treaty of Cateau-Cambrésis also included an agreement between France and England under which the French would keep Calais, England's last continental foothold, which the French had retaken in Mary Tudor's reign.

tently, Charles offered concessions German Protestants deeply desired—the communion in both kinds and the right of priests to marry—but by about 1540 he recognized that his attempts at conciliation did not appease the Protestants and only aroused devout Catholics against him. From that time on he schemed to close out his wars elsewhere that he might crush German resistance. By 1546 he was ready. In a short war, ending in 1547, he easily defeated the Schmalkaldic League (see p. 145). But his victory was inconclusive. While it weakened the military and political power of German states for a time, it left Protestant inroads unaffected: neither the defeated states nor those Protestant states that did not belong to the league returned to Catholicism. The great banking firm, the Fuggers, who had helped to elect Charles with enormous loans in 1519, now warned that their patience with him was wearing thin. And in 1552, when war flared up again in Germany, he had insufficient resources to win it. Significantly, Charles' Protestant enemies had Roman Catholic allies, among them Henri II of France, proving, if further proof be needed, that religion was no longer the sole determinant of a nation's foreign policy. [2] At last, reluctantly, Charles agreed to the Diet of Augsburg in 1555, which produced a far-reaching religious settlement. The Peace of Augsburg granted each Lutheran and Catholic prince the right to determine the religion of his own country, a policy later summarized in a famous Latin phrase: *cuius regio, eius religio*. True, the peace excluded the Calvinists and included pious hopes of fostering religious unity in the German lands. But in effect, claiming to be a step to unity, the peace guaranteed the persistence of political and religious fragmentation in Germany for a long time to come. And there were forces in Roman Catholicism that would not accept the new religious realities as permanent.

Catholic Reform and Counter-Reformation [3]

Even before Martin Luther's rebellion there had been voices demanding institutional reforms in the Roman communion; after Luther's cause had proved indestructible, these voices redoubled in volume and anxiety. Urbane

---

[2] Francis I had made this painfully clear earlier, in the late 1520s, when he had negotiated and achieved a cordial understanding with the Ottomans, whose aid he wanted in his struggle against his fellow Catholic, Charles V.

[3] It is important to note that the very names historians use for this epoch are controversial. For Roman Catholic historians, the Protestant Reformation is the Protestant Revolt and the Catholic Counter-Reformation the Catholic Reformation. The implications of such names should be obvious: Roman Catholicism, they argue, was faced early in the sixteenth century with a major rebellion which was not a reform but a departure from the truth; and the efforts of Catholic rulers and ecclesiastics to bring order into their affairs was not a *counter*-reformation because it sprang from internal impulses. We have retained the traditional names because they seem to us to do justice to the historical realities. Some recent historians have offered a useful terminological amendment: they speak of Catholic Reformation or Catholic reform when these internal reforms are in question, and use the old term Counter-Reformation when Catholic actions seem to be a response to Protestant pressures. We have adopted this device here. See G. R. Elton, *Reformation Europe, 1517–1559* (1963), 176–197; and J. H. Elliott, *Europe Divided, 1559–1598* (1968), 145–174.

disciples of Erasmus and strict followers of old, long-neglected vows alike pressed for an internal purification that would equip the faithful for battle with the Protestant rebels while leaving the essentials of the Roman theology and Roman hierarchy untouched. The urgency of reform was indeed obvious: Lutheranism was making inroads even in Italy; some old and some new heresies were gaining adherents among troubled and intelligent men; there was remarkably widespread interest in the radical antitrinitarian heresy of Socinianism (so-called after two Italians, Lelio Sozzini and Fausto Sozzini), which denied the divinity of Jesus. Beginning in 1522, with Adrian VI, the age of the Renaissance papacy was over; the new popes were more austere, more purposeful, than their flamboyant predecessors. True, during his long reign (1534-1549), Pope Paul III revived in some measure both worldliness and nepotism, but even he could not deny the call for reform; while he was intensely interested in advancing the fortunes of his family, he also appointed scholars and clerical reformers to the highest posts and sympathetically supervised their work.

Sincere as they were, the efforts at self-criticism and amendment were scarcely radical. The reformers were high-minded, hard-working, unimpeachably pious, and their notions conformed to their character: they were eager to cleanse the church of abuses but defensive in the face of heresy all about them. Their conservatism emerges plainly from one of the most famous documents the Catholic reform produced, the *Consilium de Emendanda Ecclesia*, a report published in 1537 by a commission that Paul III had appointed in the previous year. It included such distinguished men as Reginald Pole (see p. 158); Gasparo Contarini, a devout Venetian aristocrat, a diplomat of wide learning and generous spirit; and Gian Pietro Carafa, an energetic, fiercely aggressive cardinal whose later pontificate as Paul IV (1555-1559) was to mark a high point in the repressive Counter-Reformation. The rhetoric of the *Advice on Reforming the Church* was brave and bold; it pleased the Protestants enormously. It excoriated corruption, evil counselors, lazy priests, and profiteering bishops and did not exempt the papacy from its strictures. But beyond calling for an end to such abuses (and what candid churchman could do less?) the *Consilium* also called for the censorship of books, tight control over philosophical speculation, and elimination from the schools of such pernicious works as Erasmus' *Colloquia*. For these reformers freedom was as great a vice as corruption.

Purity, piety, and control, the governing themes of the *Consilium*, also were, or soon became, the moving forces behind the new orders that were to furnish the shock troops of the Counter-Reformation. The history of Roman Catholicism is dotted with the founding of new clerical orders and the decay and regeneration of old orders. While the picture was far from uniform, during the age of the Reformation religious orders were generally in disarray; the worldliness of the papacy had not left them untouched. Hence in the first years of the Catholic Reformation there was much doubt which policy would best advance the cause of purification: the creation of new or the suppression of old orders. [4] The enthusiasm, patience, and devotion of a few, driven by the fervent desire for a holy life and the accompanying desire to win others to it, wore down the skepticism of the popes and their advisors. Soon the few became many, and the first half of the sixteenth century saw the creation of several new orders destined to affect the religious history of Europe in the most profound way. All these orders had difficulty being accepted and accredited; conservative supporters of the old hierarchy saw them as dangerously independent, given to private interpretations of important doctrinal issues and possibly schismatic. Yet all of them managed to convince the authorities that their intention was pure, their faith correct, and their organization effective.

One of these new orders, the Capuchins, grew out of an older one, the Franciscans. Its founders, Italian priests, vowed to take St. Francis' precepts seriously, to live in absolute poverty and do charitable works. Founded in the 1520s, ridden with internal strife, and endangered in 1542 by the desertion of their superior, Bernardino Ochino, to the Lutherans, the Capuchins survived these trials to establish themselves as an independent order and, by the 1570s, to spread abroad from Italy. In contrast, the Theatine order was too strenuous and inward-looking to achieve the Capuchins' popularity: leading lives of intense piety, forming centers of exalted discussion, and doing works of difficult charity, the Theatine priestly communities remained a small elite of Catholic Puritans. [5] New as these orders were, the religious impulse that animated them was conservative: it was to restore an earlier unblemished ideal. Their institutional arrangements were also forced into a conservative pattern; thus the Ursuline community, founded in 1535 by and for women to lead lives of good works and exemplary piety in the world, was before long transformed into a regular order of nuns with habits and houses.

The most famous and most significant of the new orders was the Society of Jesus, founded not (like all the others) by an Italian, but by a Spaniard, Ignatius Loyola. [6] Born in 1491 into an aristocratic family, he led the life of the typical worldling—soldiering and womanizing—until he was laid low in 1521 by a painful, slow-healing leg wound received in battle. During his extensive and involuntary leisure he avidly read devotional books and experienced a religious conversion. When he emerged from his hospital bed he was an avowed servant of God. Loyola, who never did things by halves, prepared himself meticulously for his new vocation. He confessed his sins—as he said later, he had many sins to confess—and spent eight months buried in the small Catalonian town of Manresa, doing severe penance and having religious visions. His self-discipline became absolute; later he imposed the same discipline on others.

The earliest expression of Jesuit discipline dates from this period: the first

---

[4] See *The New Cambridge Modern History*, vol. II, *The Reformation, 1520-1559* (1958), 277.
[5] Ibid., 287.
[6] Loyola's original name was Don Inigo Lopez de Loyola; his origins were, strictly speaking, Basque.

draft of a handbook, the *Spiritual Exercises,* which Loyola periodically revised, put into final shape in 1541, and published in 1548, eight years before his death. "It is not a book to be read," Owen Chadwick has said. "If it is not used experimentally, it is nothing."[7] Its point is to train the mind, to direct attention to man's sinfulness, and, by contrast, to God's grace. From solitary, silent contemplation will come the decision to live for Christ, in total self-denial and total obedience. If the church teaches that white is black, the Jesuit must believe it. This phrase, all too famous, was unfortunate: designed to dramatize the need for absolute obedience, it instead gave generations of hostile critics the impression that Jesuits were a band of trained liars and sworn enemies of rationality—which is to say, a wrong impression.

Loyola was still groping. In 1523 he went to Jerusalem on a pilgrimage and sought to join the Franciscans, in vain. On his return to Barcelona, he considered various courses; ever alert and self-critical, he saw that he must first get the education he had neglected in his worldly days; he attended Spanish universities and then, in 1528, went to Paris, where he studied for seven years. It was there, in 1534, that he took a vow to live in poverty and chastity and to serve God wherever He should need him. Six of his disciples took the vow with him: Loyola, from his youth, had exercised charismatic power over men. Finally, in 1540, Pope Paul III, after some hesitation, established Loyola's band as the Society of Jesus. It was different from all other orders. Its sole head, the general, was chosen for life. Its members had to pass through several stages— a two-year novitiate, an indefinite period of training, the "scholasticate," and another one-year probationary period—before they were admitted to formal membership. Its purposes were to spread the word of Christ through missions, to counter the threat of Protestantism, and to serve as the educators of the young—this last, the least of Loyola's aims, actually became the most prominent as time went on. It produced an odd paradox: "No one could be less truly called a 'child of the Renaissance' than Ignatius who had early and decisively rejected the Erasmian outlook; but it was the Jesuits with their high academic standards in Latin and Greek who incorporated much of the scholarship and not a little of the humanistic spirit of the classical Renaissance into orthodox Catholic education."[8] Jesuits would educate much of Europe for over two centuries, including, in the eighteenth century, their wittiest and deadliest enemies (see p. 441). Their cultivation and urbanity throw serious doubts on the ubiquitous metaphor of the Jesuit "soldier of Christ." The Jesuits were not monastics, of course, and they took an active role in the world; but their rhetoric to the contrary, they were not military but militant.[9] Yet the

---

[7] Owen Chadwick, *The Reformation* (1964), 257.

[8] H. O. Evennett, "The New Orders," in *The New Cambridge Modern History,* op. cit., 297.

[9] "Yet the conception of Jesuit obedience as essentially military is not the whole truth. The amount of care for individual temperaments which the constitutions specifically require to be shown by superiors, and which is exemplified in Ignatius's own skill in dealing with his subjects, is very remarkable, and many early Jesuits showed a truly Renaissance variety and independence of character within the society's prudent and elastic framework" (Evennett, "New Orders," 295-296).

Jesuits were, without doubt, energetic and highly visible. There were Jesuits at the shoulders of kings and chancellors, Jesuits on the ships that conquered distant territories, Jesuits on the frontiers of the Protestant North and in the midst of religiously divided lands. Unafraid of the world, seeking prominence, and always, in all things, fiercely loyal to the popes and their policies, they would gather unto themselves a special admiration and a concentrated hatred, neither of which they wholly deserved.

From Reform to Repression

As Catholic morale recovered from the first shocks of the Lutheran assault, the desire to extirpate dissent or to treat mere dissent as outright heresy recovered with it. The reform proposals of 1537, the *Consilium* (see p. 165), had shown the reformers in no way averse to censorship, but they had at least been willing to see the sources of Catholic distress in themselves. As time went by, the balance of policy shifted away from self-criticism to the suppression of others, from compromise to dogmatism, from reform to repression. To be sure, Lutherans, Calvinists, Anglicans were no less hostile to the idea of toleration than the Catholics: toleration implied, after all, that the doctrines of heretics might be correct or that the full truth was not known—two ideas that all but a handful of philosophers found unthinkable. But it was the Catholics who developed the best-known of all repressive agencies, the Inquisition. It alone became proverbial for its ruthlessness, its cruelty, its unrelieved bigotry.

The idea of an inquisition into belief, backed by the power to extract confessions of heresy, dates back to the great waves of Waldensian and Albigensian heresies in the twelfth and thirteenth centuries, but it was put on a regular footing in Spain, under Ferdinand and Isabella, in 1478 (see p. 104). It employed spies and informers, customary tortures, and unaccustomed pressures—endless delays, sowing of universal distrust, and the weapon of disgrace for whole families—to check on, and to check, suspected religious disloyalty among recent converts to the true faith, whether former Jews or Muslims. In 1542, upon the urging of Cardinal Carafa, a papal bull established an Inquisition in Rome, the Holy Office, which centralized all local tribunals under a single committee of six inquisitors-general, all cardinals. Carafa was among them. Its powers were extensive: they included the right to imprison suspects and to execute heretics. [10] Centralization of the Inquisition brought uniformity and effectiveness. It also brought control over publications. In 1543, Carafa listed books and publishers he thought dangerous, though it was not until 1559, while he held supreme power as Pope Paul IV, that the full-fledged Index, the notorious *Index Librorum Prohibitorum,* was inaugurated. It was to be often revised and republished, to keep up with new heresies; one of its entries

[10] Chadwick, *Reformation,* 269.

prohibited the reading of the *Consilium* of 1537 in which Carafa had participated.[11]

The course of the Council of Trent, convened after many delays in 1545, testifies to the hardening of the Catholic position. Its calling was a victory of Charles V over a reluctant Paul III; the emperor hoped it might bring reform and, perhaps, accommodation with Protestantism; the pope feared it might mark a return to conciliarism and compromise with the devil. Both hopes and fears were groundless. In three protracted, often adjourned sessions—the council met from 1545 to 1547, 1551 to 1552, and 1562 to 1563—the Italian prelates, ably seconded by the Jesuits, dominated the proceedings. Except for pushing through some perfectly traditional resolutions against financial and organizational abuses, the reforming party was outgeneraled and outvoted on every point. When in January 1564 the Tridentine decrees were published, there was rejoicing among dogmatists everywhere: the Roman church had refused to compromise on any of its crucial doctrines—whether transubstantiation or the importance of works, the denial of private judgment or insistence on clerical celibacy—and, on the contrary, firmly reiterated and meticulously clarified the Catholic position on these and other points of doctrine, discipline, and organization. The papacy emerged stronger than ever, having now the added authority of conciliar confirmation. While there was some resistance in Spain and France to those provisions of the Tridentine decrees that seemed to infringe the rights of the crown over its churches, the confirmation of the old doctrine and the old church was welcome throughout all the Catholic territories. Religious reunion of Christendom was now impossible, and only two courses were open: a crusade to impose a single faith on the other half of Europe, or the decision to live together somehow, permanently divided.

SPAIN'S ASCENDANCY

During much of the sixteenth century, relations between Spain and the papacy were strained; they improved only in the 1560s, when common interests outweighed causes for conflict. Despite these strains, Spain never ceased to regard herself as the supreme fortress of Christendom; while at home the Spanish Inquisition solicitously shielded the faithful from the contamination of modern ideas, abroad Spain played the role of defender and disseminator of the true faith.

[11] See Elton, *Reformation Europe,* 189–192. The Protestants, it is worth repeating, had their own inquisitions into belief and their own lists of forbidden books, but the great variety of practice in the Protestant territories and the often decentralized organization of the churches permitted thought far greater latitude than it was to have in the Italy and the Spain of the Counter-Reformation.

The Spanish Overseas Empire

From the beginning of their overseas explorations (see p. 85) Spaniards had found their solemn religiosity a problem. To be the privileged bearers of the Christian message to the heathen was an excuse for imperialism, but it was also an obstacle—a cover for, but also a restraint on, cupidity. The Spanish conquerors were unused to manual labor and reluctant to do in the Caribbean what they would scorn to do in Aragon and Castile. Hence, on the West Indian islands discovered and settled by Columbus, they enlisted the Indian natives in a system of forced labor much like slavery—much, but not quite: it was disguised by a legal device called the *encomienda,* an adaptation of the Spanish experience with conquered territories on the Iberian peninsula. *Encomienda* was in legal theory a system of mutual obligation, a distant cousin of feudal relationships. The Spanish overlord, or *encomendero,* could exact labor and commodities from "his" Indians, and owed them in return military protection and religious instruction. There were pious Spaniards, including Queen Isabella herself, who insisted on decent treatment for Spain's new subjects,[12] but it can be imagined how little her instructions meant in remote territories. There, only the conquered were compelled to fulfill their side of the "bargain."

Equally grave, perhaps graver, problems of conscience arose when the Spaniards moved to the American mainland. In 1519, Hernando Cortes, the first and greatest of the Spanish *conquistadores,* began the conquest of Aztec Mexico. By 1520, the Aztec emperor, Montezuma II, was dead; by 1521, Mexico City was in Cortes' hands, and Mexico became not a foreign country to be conquered but a Spanish territory to be administered. Francisco Pizarro, after some unsuccessful attempts in the 1520s, reached Peru in the early 1530s and undertook the protracted "pacification" of the Inca empire. These conquests were extended romantic tales, glorious and terrible, in which fact rivals fiction. Like all men, the *conquistadores* were rent with inner contradictions; unlike other men, they gloried in them. Their mentalities had been shaped by romances, and their hunger for conquest overseas was sharpened by social and financial aspirations at home. Once in the Americas, they acted out a high drama of adventure in which piety and treachery, an unmeasured appetite for life and a reckless courtship of death, kindness and cruelty, high ideals and the most sordid scramble for profit, were curiously intermingled. "We came here," wrote Bernal Díaz del Castillo, historian and Cortes' friend, "to serve God and the king, and also to get rich."[13] When Cortes and his men encountered

---

[12] The good queen should not be sentimentalized. "Her condemnation of Indian slavery—a condemnation frequently cited by her modern admirers—" writes Charles Gibson, the leading modern authority on Spanish America, "was neither uncompromising nor disinterested. On a number of occasions the queen countenanced, and even demanded a share in, the trade of Indian captives as slaves" (*Spain in America* [1966], 51).

[13] Quoted by J. H. Elliott, *Imperial Spain 1469–1716* (1963), 53, from Lewis Hanke, *Bartolome de las Casas* (1951), 9.

Montezuma's envoys, they received the Indians' gifts with unmasked excitement: "When they were given these presents," one Indian contemporary reported, "the Spaniards burst into smiles. . . . They picked up the gold and fingered it like monkeys. . . . Their bodies swelled with greed, and their hunger was ravenous. They hungered like pigs for that gold." [14]

Their hunger was not always so unconcealed. The *conquistadores* carried with them a legal document much like an injunction, the *requerimiento*, which they were supposed to read aloud to the opposing Indians before battle. It is a classic in man's long history of rationalization: the Indians could usually not hear the reading of this "requirement," nor would they have understood it. But the mere reading of its provisions calmed the Spaniards' conscience. It enjoined the Indians to submit themselves to Spain, the papacy, and the Roman Catholic church; if they refused, the death and devastation that would follow were their own responsibility.

This was not all. The Spaniards settled and exploited the territories they conquered and, for the most part, though they supplemented the local pool of labor with black African slaves, they relied heavily on the natives to till the fields and work the mines. The *conquistadores* decisively subdued the native populations. They had weapons on which the Indians could look only with superstitious awe: firearms, horses, superb military discipline, seemingly unlimited self-confidence, and alcohol. Moreover, the empires that the Spaniards overthrew were themselves relative latecomers and often deeply divided internally; hence the *conquistadores* could count on native allies. Nor were the Incas and Aztecs particularly beloved: they too had taken slaves, and they practiced human sacrifices. In consequence, many Indians humbly, but with justification, asked the Spanish crown to recognize and reward their services. The Spaniards brought disease and the Inquisition, but they also brought techniques of raising food and governing territories, universities and Christian humanity, all unknown in the Americas. Thus the history of the Spanish overseas empire is part of a larger history: the expansion of the West over the rest of the world.

While the bestiality of the Aztec rulers served many Spaniards as an excuse for their expansion into Latin America, there were Spanish Christians whom the conquests made profoundly uneasy. As early as 1511 the Dominican friar Antonio de Montesinos had startled his fellow Spaniards on the Caribbean island of Hispaniola with his bold rhetorical question: "Are these Indians not men? Do they not have rational souls? Are you not obliged to love them as you love yourselves?" [15] Others disagreed, but the Christian conscience of Spain was awakened, and in 1550 Charles V actually ordered a cessation of all further conquests while Bartolome de las Casas, bishop in Mexico and for many years

---

[14] Miguel Leon-Portilla, ed., *The Broken Spears: The Aztec Account of the Conquest of Mexico* (tr. 1962); quoted in Gibson, *Spain in America*, 37.

[15] Quoted in Lewis Hanke, *Aristotle and the American Indian* (1959), 15.

the spokesman for the Indians, debated the question with Juan Gines de Sepulveda, an Aristotelian scholar, who used arguments that later advocates of slavery would also find enormously convenient: the Indians were specimens of what Aristotle had called "natural slaves," and wicked idolators and inhuman cannibals to boot. Moreover, being conquered by Spaniards exposed them to the blessings of the true religion, legitimate government, and humane treatment. Las Casas won the debate; the atmosphere was in any case favorable to his side: Indian slavery had already been outlawed in the Spanish territories, and while exploitation continued and the reduced availability of Indians for the most unsavory labor only led to a rise in the importation of African Negroes, there was at least some easing of the Indians' lot by midcentury. But even this modest claim must be kept modest indeed: mistreatment of natives continued, and epidemics swept the Indian populations vulnerable to the ravages of smallpox and other scourges. In 1548, when the Indian population in Spain's American territories had already been much reduced, it was estimated at 6.3 million; in 1580 it was down to 1.9 million. [16] Nor was the government's attack on the *encomienda* system purely a humane reflex. The crown was concerned to secure its control over its remote outposts, and it could do so only if it permanently weakened the semifeudal, relatively independent centers of power that the *encomiendas* became. [17]

The Spanish Empire in Europe

Spanish expansion overseas was to have profound consequences at home. Those *conquistadores* who survived the rigors of the New World—the risks of battle, the climate, and treachery—came home to claim titles for their services. Then, from the 1530s on, the settlers began to send home silver from the rich American mines; the greatest of these, Potosí in what is today Bolivia, was discovered in 1545. Despite its almost inaccessible site twelve thousand feet above sea level, the Spaniards exploited it heavily. Potosí silver changed the economic fate of Spain and the economic face of Europe—but not immediately. It was not until the reign of Philip II that the effects of Spain's overseas possessions became apparent.

Philip II, who accepted the crown of Spain and Spain's possessions in 1556 (see p. 163), seemed, but only seemed, in every respect the antithesis of Charles V. Actually Philip II and his father, whom he revered, were alike in what counted: both were driven by their religious fervor and by an overwhelming sense of public duty. They differed mainly in their attitude toward Spain. Charles V (who was Charles I in Spain) was a Burgundian who at the beginning

---

[16] See J. H. Parry, *The Spanish Seaborne Empire* (1966), 219-220. As Parry points out (p. 220), the epidemic of 1576-1579 "destroyed one optimistic illusion about labour in the Tropics: the mortality among Negroes was at least as severe as that among Indians."

[17] This point has been persuasively argued most recently by Elliott, *Imperial Spain*, 63-64.

of his reign spoke no Spanish and had few Spaniards in his entourage; he aroused mainly hostility when he arrived to take over his Spanish realm, and in 1520 and 1521, he was compelled to crush a revolt against him in Castile. He won the trust of his Spanish subjects gradually, over the years, with his undisputed diligence, his obvious religious sincerity, and his equally obvious respect for Spanish culture and Spanish power. Yet, as emperor, he had obligations to his many disconnected territories, and during his nearly forty years of kingship, he spent more than twenty-four years outside Spain; indeed, from 1543 to his abdication in 1556, he was steadily occupied elsewhere. [18] Spain, though ostensibly central in Charles' mind, was no more than a good place to visit.

Philip II, on the other hand (apart from the years 1556 to 1559, which he spent in Flanders), lived in Spain as though it were one vast protective citadel. This long physical presence in Spain—he died there, after a long reign, in 1598—did not merely reflect his sense of himself as a Spaniard. Nor did it reflect sedentary habits. Rather, Philip II conceived his task as king to be one of assiduous application to paper work, for the sake of his subjects. Almost two centuries before Frederick II of Prussia spoke of himself, in a famous phrase, as "the first servant of his people," Philip II thought of himself as such a servant and acted accordingly. The heroic age of Spanish kingship was over; the time for bureaucratic regularity had come. In 1561, Philip moved his court from Toledo to Madrid, which was in the mathematical center of his Iberian realm, and after some years, Madrid gained ascendancy over other cities to become the capital of Spain. [19] It was near Madrid that Philip built his enormous retreat, the Escorial, which with its immense walls, its austere gridiron shape, and its symmetrical, uninviting facades, symbolized and guaranteed the king's isolation from the subjects he strove to serve.

Whatever later historians—many of them Protestant—may have said, most Spaniards thought Philip II served them well. Yet his successes were never easy: they were hard-won victories, wrested from continual travail. Philip's life was marred by a succession of private tragedies—the deaths of wives and children, and the bizarre episode of his strange wild son, Don Carlos, whom his father felt compelled to arrest and who died in detention. If Philip seemed aloof, a stranger to emotions, a victim of self-imposed courtly ritual, these characteristics point not to an absence of feelings but to a desperate and iron-willed search for control over feelings.

At home and abroad, enemies loomed large. At home, with the aid of the Inquisition, Philip II routed the small minority of Protestants, silenced Catholic cosmopolitans attracted by the urbane, tolerant philosophy of Erasmus, encouraged the growth of fanatical racist doctrines demanding pure blood—*limpieza de sangre*—directed against Catholic Spaniards of Jewish ancestry (see

[18] See Elliott, *Imperial Spain,* 154.
[19] The best treatment of this development is in Elliott, *Imperial Spain,* 242–251.

p. 104),[20] and ended what he regarded as a continuing source of infection and possible treason by moving decisively against the Moriscos.[21] For decades, no one had troubled to take these poor and insignificant "new Christians" of Muslim antecedents seriously. But in 1566, in the midst of his campaign to continue the purification of Spain, Philip II issued a "pragmatic," or decree, that reiterated standing prohibitions against the Moriscos' traditional dress, custom, and Arabic language.[22] The Moriscos protested: they had evaded these regulations before, but they were good Christians, and loyal Spaniards. Philip's officials, decree in hand, zealously chose to enforce what their predecessors had wisely ignored, and by 1568 the Moriscos had been goaded into revolt. After fierce and ugly fighting, the rebellion was crushed, and Philip (in this as in so many other things anticipating twentieth-century practices) ordered the wholesale removal of Moriscos from Andalusia to all parts of Castile. This ended a concentration of a population separatist in habits and perhaps in loyalty, which threatened a possible Morisco-Turkish alliance. At the same time, while Philip's drastic policy lessened the intensity of the Morisco problem, it widened its impact. The problem was finally solved by Philip III with a ruthlessness worthy of his father: in 1609, he ordered all Moriscos expelled from Spain, and by 1614 the process was reported complete. Crusades are rarely the work of one king, or one generation.

Abroad, too, the Spaniards triumphed over the Infidel and in spectacular fashion. The year was 1571. It was a tense moment in the history of international Catholicism: France was in the midst of civil war (see p. 178). England, under Queen Elizabeth, if not quite at war with itself, was torn among Anglicans, Puritans, and Catholics; besides, the pope had excommunicated Elizabeth in 1570 and thus declared her, to her Roman Catholic subjects, an outlaw (see p. 185). The Protestant movement, notably its Calvinist wing, proved as international in scope and busy in correspondence as its Roman adversary. The Infidel—as defined by Rome—was distinctly on the defensive. Then came the Spanish confrontation with the Ottomans, and the victory that had so long eluded Philip II's father now fell into his hands: in May 1571, Pope Pius V, the very pontiff who had recently excommunicated the queen of England, organized a Holy League—a naval coalition of Western powers, chiefly Venice and Spain—to expel the Turks from the eastern Mediterranean, where they had just taken Cyprus. On October 7, 1571, the opposing forces, vaster than any within memory, drew up at Lepanto, in the Gulf of Corinth. It was the battle of the century, and when the day was over, the victory of the

---

[20] This unsavory development to which we, after Hitler, have become particularly sensitive, deserves more attention than historians have hitherto given it. Once again, Elliott has given the matter lucid treatment; see his *Imperial Spain*, 213-217.

[21] This was the name applied to Spanish subjects of Moorish ancestry who, after the *reconquista* of the peninsula, had chosen to stay in Spain at the price of conversion to Roman Catholicism. They kept their own communities, practically all in the south, in the province of Andalusia around the city of Granada.

[22] The decree was actually published on January 1, 1567, and this is generally known as its official date.

century: Ottoman ships were dispersed, captured, and destroyed in impressive numbers. Don John of Austria, natural son of Charles V and half-brother of Philip II, who had commanded the Spanish troops against the Moriscos, now commanded the allied navy against the Moriscos' cousins. Among the Spaniards who fought at Lepanto was Miguel de Cervantes. [23]

While the Ottoman fleet had been routed in the battle, the response of Catholics all over Europe and the reputation that Spain reaped, or confirmed, through her victory were the triumph of appearance over reality. Cervantes himself later proudly described the battle as "the noblest occasion that past or present ages have seen or future ones may hope to see," [24] but the long-range advantages to Spain or to Christendom were slim indeed. Unable to agree on a future course of action, the allies dissipated their immediate advantage; the Ottomans repaired their losses with impressive speed; and the Spanish-Turkish confrontation ended in most unspectacular fashion in 1578, when the two powers entered a truce. But before then, Lepanto became a symbol and a legend: it was proof that the formidable Ottomans were not invincible, proof that Spain was foremost in Europe, proof above all that the Catholic crusade might be more than brave talk. In 1580, while Spain was still enjoying its reputation, Philip II claimed the throne of Portugal, which had just fallen empty and was subject to confused and multiple claims, and successfully reinforced his claim by invading the country and defeating its defending army. In the same year, he annexed Portugal and made himself, as Philip I, its king.

Yet in the midst of all these signs of prosperity, at the height of his glory, Philip II could look about him and discern threatening signs: France in the midst of civil war was of doubtful help in his Catholic crusade; England under Elizabeth was proving a determined adversary; the Spanish dependencies in the Netherlands were in open revolt; and the economy was showing signs of strain. Philip's proverbial gloom was a reflection not merely of his temperament or his dour piety, but of reality.

LIMITS ON SPAIN'S POWER: FRANCE AND ENGLAND

France: The Age of Fanatics

For most of Philip II's long reign, France was too near anarchy to be either a dependable ally for Spain's Catholic crusade or an effective challenger to Spain's hegemony. From the early 1560s to the early 1590s France was torn apart by civil wars, the Wars of Religion. Some historians have called these

---

[23] For the glorious days of Spanish culture, see p. 220.
[24] *Don Quixote,* introduction, part II; see Reginald Trevor Davies, *The Golden Century of Spain* (1965), 174.

decades "the age of fanatics."[25] It is an apt name, for while these mutual massacres were also class and regional and political and even family wars, Frenchmen killed Frenchmen with that special pleasure, that peculiar sense of righteousness associated with religious war. Others have called these decades the "age of Catherine de' Medici."[26] This, too, is an apt name, for Catherine, that wily, often cruel Florentine politician, dominated the French scene for thirty years, practically to the day of her death in 1589.

In her earlier years, as wife to King Henri II of France, Catherine had displayed mainly her talent for self-control and self-abasement: she was all too aware of her "low" mercantile origins. Thus she countenanced her husband's lasting infatuation with Diane de Poitiers, a grasping, aging beauty who was twenty years older than her royal lover. Then a grotesque accident precipitated Catherine from the wings of affairs into the center: in June 1559, at a tournament celebrating the dynastic marriages agreed upon at Cateau-Cambrésis (see p. 163), Henri II entered the lists in person; a few days later he was dead, mortally wounded by one of his great nobles. Francis II, the eldest of Catherine's surviving sons, aged fifteen and sickly, took the throne, while his mother took the power. When Francis died the next year, his younger brother succeeded him as Charles IX; he reigned for fourteen years, until 1574, but he did not rule—his mother ruled in his place. She could hardly do anything else: Charles was only ten when he assumed the throne and proved neither stable nor competent. The last of her surviving brood, Henri III, was far more intelligent than his brothers; but his fifteen-year reign, to 1589, proved him, too, incapable of ruling: a striking combination of self-denying penitent and self-indulgent homosexual, half flagellant and half debauchee, he furnishes material more interesting to the psychoanalyst than to the student of monarchy.

Seeking to rule the country as she ruled her sons, Catherine faced a formidable task. France was financially bankrupt, politically fragmented, and religiously divided. It had barely emerged from feudalism and was hesitantly constructing the rudiments of a national government against the stubborn resistance of local privilege—against cities, provinces, nobles, each with some special right to defend, some special tax exemption to protect. In this volatile situation, court intrigues acquired general political significance, and the court of Catherine was a snake pit of intrigues.

Three superb families, each with considerable territories at its disposal and each a great aristocratic clan, struggled for preeminence. The feebleness of Catherine's sons made the greatest prize of all—the crown of France, or at the least, control over the king of France—appear not too remote. None of these miserable kings seemed capable of, or interested in, producing heirs, and if the

[25] See Georges Duby and Robert Mandrou, *A History of French Civilization from the Year 1000 to the Present* (tr. 1964), 284.
[26] See J. E. Neale, *The Age of Catherine de' Medici* (1943).

house of Valois died out, who should succeed? The extensive Guise clan, from Lorraine, enormously rich and solidly entrenched in high positions in church and state, was one powerful court party. The Montmorency clan, tied to the French crown through distinguished public service, was a second. The Bourbons, ostensibly headed by Anthony, king of Navarre, but actually headed by his younger brother, the prince of Condé, of royal blood and with the most authentic claim to the succession, was the third—it would, in the end, prove the first.

Family rivalries were exacerbated by religious hatreds. True, not all Frenchmen were equally firm in their religious beliefs—Henri Bourbon of Navarre, who was to become the great King Henri IV of France, changed his confession several times. But often religious loyalties were powerful and fiercely held. Religious convictions sometimes even took precedence over family solidarity: the head of the Montmorency clan, Anne de Montmorency, constable of France, remained faithful to the Roman Catholic confession, but the constable's three nephews, including Gaspard de Coligny, admiral of France, became sincere converts to Protestantism. Regions, cities, families were torn apart in this painful way.

Calvinism—a sect, after all, with a French father—exercised a strong appeal among wide circles. As elsewhere, so in France, this appeal was a mixture of revulsion against Catholic practice and attraction to Calvinist piety. The concordat that Francis I had concluded with Rome in 1516 had been, in Neale's vivid phrase, "a deal in the spoils of the Gallican Church." By giving the French crown the power to nominate (which meant, in practice, to appoint) clerics to practically all posts, it gave the crown a splendid instrument of patronage. Courtiers, dependents of influential nobles, friends of the king's mistress, even foreigners, were made abbots and bishops: "Not a single French bishop," as Neale summarizes it, "obtained his post because of religious zeal or spiritual worthiness." [27] Pluralists, absentee holders of great sees, indifferent, ignorant (and it was said, in some districts, illiterate) clerics were in charge of French souls; as the scandals continued to grow, the influence of the reformers grew with them. At first, there had been Lutherans around Francis I; later, with the rise of militant French Calvinism, indulgence toward Protestants in high quarters gave way to impatience; by the 1550s, impatience had given way to persecution. The Calvinists, with their tight congregational, local, regional, and eventually national organization, with their firm beliefs and obvious popularity, constituted a real danger to central authority. The more energetic and more learned among the lower clergy, professors and lawyers, a considerable sprinkling of merchants, and with the passage of years, a growing number of the lesser nobility, made up the army of Huguenots. [28] And the nobles among

[27] Ibid., 11.

[28] This name, first applied to the French Calvinists around 1562, is of uncertain origins; it may come from the Swiss-German *Eidgenoss,* a confederate bound to his fellows with an oath.

them were armed, imbued with notions of feudal obligation and with resentment against authority centered in Paris. While they always remained in a minority, the Huguenots made up for their limited numbers with energy, fervor, intelligence, and a collection of grievances—part religious, part social, part economic—that forged them into a formidable political force. And they were not quite that insignificant numerically; by the 1560s perhaps one out of every two French nobles was a declared Calvinist, and by 1561 there were over two thousand Huguenot congregations in France. [29]

In 1559, the year of Francis'—or, rather, Catherine's—accession, the Huguenots convened their first national synod in Paris. Hundreds of their sympathizers had fled to Geneva, and while Calvin himself still frowned on armed resistance against authority, his Geneva was headquarters of the French Protestant movement. The scores of French printers who had fled to Calvin's City of the Saints poured out pamphlets, and Calvin poured out directions. In 1560 and 1561, after the accession of Charles IX, the Huguenots came out into the open. All across France, Calvinist preachers, protected by faithful body-guards, expelled Catholic priests and preached the Word, in French, according to the German dispensation. The younger Montmorencys, and the Bourbons, were on their side. The tinderbox was ready to explode.

Two conspiracies served as prologue to the Wars of Religion; both were led by Condé from a safe, protected position and directed against Guise influence at court. Both were beaten back. Then, in 1562, the Huguenots, emboldened but not appeased by Catherine's conciliatory policies, responded to the bloody Massacre of Vassy with a general call to arms. [30] From then on, a series of sometimes large-scale, often fitful, always brutal encounters—nine in all—punctuated by truces, kept France in a turmoil from which it emerged only in the 1590s, with the triumph of Henri of Navarre.

For several years, Catherine veered among the parties. She offered the Huguenots a measure of toleration—not enough to suit them, too much to suit the Catholics. She toyed with dynastic marital arrangements including Protes-tant houses, and even, for a time, with war against Spain. The Catholic party was strong and united: in 1561, before open violence had erupted, the leaders of the Montmorency and the Guise clans had joined to form what was to become the Catholic League; it would play a formidable part for over thirty years. But the Huguenots were quite as determined. Catherine cared chiefly for the perpetuation of the French monarchy, and threatened by one party, she would approach the other. Her statesmanship, marred at this point not by its aims but by its vacillations, found support among a small but articulate group of Catholic moderates, the *politiques*, who included such distinguished figures

[29] See Neale, *Age of Catherine de' Medici*, 29.

[30] On March 1, 1562, a group of the duke de Guise's men fell on Protestant worshipers at Vassy, in Champagne, slaughtering more than seventy of them, and wounding more than a hundred. The duke did not object.

as Catherine's chancellor de l'Hôpital, the political theorist Jean Bodin, and that imperishable explorer of the self, the essayist Michel de Montaigne. The *politiques* preferred peace to salvation; in a time of fanaticism, they raised the improbable standard of reason and decency.

The influence of the *politiques* was short-lived; in 1572, Catherine abruptly abandoned conciliation and tried a new policy: murder. Looking back, Huguenots later asserted that she had long planned her moves. They recalled a meeting at Bayonne, in 1565, at which Catherine had discussed—who knew what?—with the Spaniards. In fact, Catherine's shift was quite impulsive. After 1570, with the close of the third War of Religion, the Huguenots had been in the ascendancy, and their most prominent leader, Coligny, was energetically pushing for war with Spain.[31] To everyone's surprise, young King Charles IX, charmed by Coligny, and without consulting his mother, agreed to support Coligny's policy. Wounded maternal pride and shrewd political calculation moved Catherine to sabotage Coligny's plans. Ironically, she chose an occasion of reconciliation, the wedding of her daughter Margaret to Henri of Navarre, to have Coligny murdered. Paris was full of Huguenot nobles come to help their favorite celebrate his marriage. On August 22, 1572, an agent of the duke of Guise tried to kill Coligny and failed; faced with exposure, Catherine decided to cover her guilt by converting a single murder into a general slaughter. By the evening of August 23, she had won over her feeble son; early the next morning, the St. Bartholomew's Day massacre began. A few days later, after the provinces had loyally followed the example of Paris, many thousands of Huguenots were dead—perhaps four thousand had been killed in Paris alone. Coligny was among the victims; Henri of Navarre one of the few Huguenot leaders who escaped.

Like all major incidents in the French Wars of Religion, the St. Bartholomew's Day massacre was an international event. All over Europe, Catholics rejoiced and celebrated. The pope announced the news to his cardinals and had a Te Deum chanted in honor of the event; Catholic powers sent their congratulations to France; Philip II told Catherine that the "punishment" she had meted out to Coligny and his "sect" was "of such value and prudence and of such service, glory, and honor to God and universal benefit to all Christendom that to hear of it was for me the best and most cheerful news which at present could come to me."[32] Protestants for their part excoriated the massacre as a characteristic expression of Catholic fanaticism. They forgot that they had earlier hailed one of their own number for murdering the duke of Guise, and that their troops had murdered women and children without mercy or compunction, violated truces, and invented bestial tortures for hapless

---

[31] Here, as everywhere, the international situation must be taken into account. In 1572, the Dutch rebels had scored a great success against Spanish troops, and news of their victory suggested an opportunity for breaking the grip of a power that surrounded France on practically all sides.

[32] Neale, *Age of Catherine de' Medici*, 80.

priests. The St. Bartholomew's Day massacre was unusual only in the number of its victims. During the Wars of Religion, the Christian virtue of charity was in short supply on both sides.

As the impenitent Catherine de' Medici soon discovered, the massacre had been, to paraphrase a famous modern epigram, both a crime and a blunder.[33] It solved nothing and exacerbated everything. War resumed and went on, getting more atrocious and involving more and more foreign troops. The reign of Henri III was in this respect no better than the reigns of his brothers. In other respects it was worse; the king disfigured it with extravagant and ostentatious pleasures, enjoyed in the company of his young men, his *mignons,* who were his partners in piety, politics, and debauchery alike. The house of Valois was dying, not with a bang, but a whimper. Henri's end was strangely apt: in 1588, the current duke of Guise had taken over the city of Paris in defiance of his king. The Catholic League seemed to be master of France. Henri III, defying his ailing, aging mother, took revenge. In December 1588, he had the duke of Guise and his powerful brother, the cardinal of Lorraine, murdered. He did not enjoy his new-found independence long. Early in 1589, his mother died, and on August 2, Henri III himself was murdered by a fanatical Dominican. The way for Henri of Navarre was now open, in law if not yet in fact.

France: The Age of Henri IV

Henri IV, the first Bourbon king of France, is a striking and enigmatic figure. A compulsive womanizer, a man of impressive charm effective with proud nobles, substantial burghers, and ordinary people alike, Henri was above all a consummate politician and a statesman who shared the *politiques'* vision for France: peace, prosperity, religious forbearance. His task in 1589 was far from easy. The dying Henri III had recognized him as his rightful heir, provided he turn Catholic—which remained, after all, the religion of most Frenchmen. But Henri of Navarre could not simply shift his confession once again. His earlier shifts had been too opportune not to be opportunistic, and a timely conversion now, in 1589, would only have aroused unanimous skepticism. He had been born a Catholic, but his mother, a powerful and intelligent woman, had taught him the Calvinism he adopted in his youth; then, in 1572, in semicaptivity after the St. Bartholomew's Day massacre, he had announced his reconversion to Rome, a return he annulled in 1576, when he placed himself at the head of Huguenot forces.

Henri faced other claimants to the throne, with dubious legal standing but with the appropriate religion; besides, in 1589 much of France, including devout

---

[33] "This is worse than a crime, it is a blunder," is what Talleyrand is quoted as saying in 1804, when he learned of Napoleon's execution of the duke of Enghien (see p. 511).

Catholic Paris, was in the hand of League troops and Spain was intervening in the League's behalf: domestic and international politics were once again wholly intertwined. As a true *politique,* Henri made religion serve his politics. In July 1593, after a prudent wait, he turned Catholic, for the sake of France. In February 1594 he was crowned at Chartres, and in March he entered Paris in triumph; in 1595 Pope Clement VIII gave the old heretic absolution, and the League dissolved, and with it all serious resistance. Paris had been worth a mass. [34]

Henri governed as he had fought: with a realistic sense of his France, with an eye to reconstruction. His treatment of even the most prominent Leaguers was clement in the extreme. Henri would rather bribe men than kill them, and all but his most fanatical Huguenot followers agreed with him: there had been too much killing already. His first task as king of a united France was the elimination of a Spanish threat, which took Henri three years to accomplish. In 1595 he declared war on Spain, and by 1598, with English and Dutch help, he had fought that greatest of European powers to a standstill. The Peace of Vervins guaranteed France Brittany, Calais, and the strips of northern France that the Spaniards had occupied. It was Cateau-Cambrésis all over again, but with the meaning reversed. Cateau-Cambrésis had marked France's defeat and the end of its Italian adventures; Vervins marked Spain's defeat and the end of its French adventures.

In the same year, 1598, Henri IV issued his edict of toleration, the Edict of Nantes, which is his claim to immortality. Like other men who rise from being party chiefs to a position of national leadership, Henri IV found himself compelled to be more generous with his enemies than with his friends. The Huguenots, whose leader he had been and without whose loyalty he would never have become king, grumbled at Henri's "apostasy" and feared for their future in a land officially, overwhelmingly, and in many quarters intolerantly, Catholic. After more than a year of tense discussions, Henri devised an edict of concord, a truce that would last, with certain modifications, for ninety years. [35] While it excluded the Huguenots from Paris and episcopal seats, the edict granted them the right to worship in the households of nobles who were professing Calvinists, and in designated towns. And it recognized that the Huguenots were a minority, scattered all across the land, in need of some protection. It guaranteed them their own *places fortes*—perhaps a hundred fortified towns under their control—and gave them special courts of justice

---

[34] Henri's most celebrated saying, "Paris is well worth a mass," the staple of all textbooks and biographies, has been attributed to him since the early seventeenth century but is unfortunately not satisfactorily documented. It is a remark, though, he might well have made.

[35] For the revocation of the Edict of Nantes, see p. 307; for an interpretation, see Elliott, *Europe Divided,* 363.

staffed by Huguenots and Catholics to protect their interests. Finally, the edict provided that the Huguenots had the same right as Catholics to hold public office or to attend university.

It was a measure of its evenhandedness that all parties should receive the Edict of Nantes with disclaimers and detestation. The Huguenots wanted more toleration, but, having shrunk to perhaps a tenth of the population, they could scarcely ask anyone, not even their old leader, to give them more. The Catholics wanted one religion, but Henri was determined to have the *politiques'* conception of the state prevail. It was a new idea, pregnant with possibilities for the future of a Europe that must remain religiously divided not only among, but within nations. And it worked better than its original reception might have led anyone to believe; after a time of protest, especially by the powerful *parlements,*[36] Henri forced the edict on his reluctant country.

Once Spain had been turned back and religious turmoil quieted, Henri IV could concentrate on domestic reconstruction. He was determined, he said, to serve *l'utilité publicq*—the public good.[37] After more than thirty years of ferocious slaughter, royal indifference, and general incompetence, France was in disrepair, almost in dissolution. Houses, cities, roads, rivers, the government, the very economy bore the marks of strife, hatred, and neglect. During the Wars of Religion, the town of Vienne had changed hands twenty times, and whoever took it pillaged what was left; three times during these years, as if war had not been enough, it had been attacked by the plague. When it finally surrendered to Henri IV in 1595 it was "a mass of ruins and half deserted."[38] In the reign of Henri IV there were many Viennes in France. Henri IV knew this. He was ubiquitous: in depending on his ministers and his emissaries instead of appealing to local estates or the Estates General, Henri IV was one of the first of modern kings, a true predecessor of Louis XIV. But he did not rule in obedience to some abstract theoretical principle; he governed as he did, by himself and through his agents, because no one else was capable of bringing a devastated country back to a semblance of order and a government in disarray

---

[36] The identity of the English word "parliament" with the French word "parlement" discloses the identity of their origins. England's Parliament, now the supreme legislature, began as a court; the French parlements, wiped out during the French Revolution, never lost their original character, though in the seventeenth and eighteenth centuries the judges who sat in them claimed the right to participate in the making of laws. As we shall see, much of the political history of France during these centuries was dominated by rival interpretations of the French past, notably the position of the parlements in the state. The first of the parlements was that of Paris, which emerged in the thirteenth century. It was soon joined by other, provincial parlements; by the seventeenth century, the number had risen to a dozen. But the parlement of Paris retained its central position; it had the highest prestige, the largest jurisdiction, and the most articulate spokesmen. The judges who sat in these parlements were ennobled, forming the "nobility of the robe." With its caste pride, the robe nobility sought marital alliances with other, older nobles, especially among the ancient "nobility of the sword."

[37] See Orest Ranum, *Paris in the Age of Absolutism* (1968), 59.

[38] Karl F. Helleiner, "The Population of Europe from the Black Death to the Eve of the Vital Revolution," in *Cambridge Economic History of Europe*, vol. IV (1967), 33.

back into working effectiveness. In his feverish but purposeful and consistent activity, Henri placed the stamp of the state on manufactures, trades, and the arts.

Capable of arousing fervent loyalties, Henri IV found intelligent and outspoken public servants, many of them, significantly enough, Huguenots. The duke de Sully, soldier and economist, became superintendent of finances before 1600 and carried through a far-reaching program of fiscal reform. It was one thing to demand taxes; it was another to collect them and keep the hands of officials off the revenues. Within the limits imposed by early seventeenth-century communications, Sully did all that. An ancestor of the eighteenth-century Physiocrats (see p. 363), Sully was a fanatical supporter of agriculture and did all he could to encourage farmers by clearing land, draining marshes, and securing property from marauders or greedy creditors. After 1599, he turned to the rebuilding of roads and waterways and bridges: he took his mission to reconstruct France quite literally.

His associate, Barthélemy de Laffemas, seconded Sully's efforts. Like all economists of the time a mercantilist (see p. 300), he strove for a surplus of exports over imports, encouraged new luxury industries that would make the importation of silk unnecessary, and sponsored French expansion into the New World, notably Quebec. Whatever the disadvantages of such authoritarian interventions into economic life, whatever the inevitable disparity between glorious dreams and harsher realities, Henri's interference with the economy and restoration of governmental efficiency had rapid and remarkable success. The public debt was converted into a surplus; a second-rate economic power turned into a first-rate one; for the first time in many decades French population markedly increased, and prosperity was widespread.

But Henri's work was cut short: in May 1610, he was stabbed to death by François Ravaillac, a pious paranoiac who heard voices and felt it necessary to kill a king who, he feared, would lead the Huguenots in a mass slaughter of Roman Catholics. A century and a half later, reflecting on the untimely end of his favorite French king, Voltaire, who detested the death penalty, wrote that he would make Ravaillac the one exception to his humane convictions.

England: Elizabethan Policies

Henri IV's most impressive, if inconstant, ally against the menace of Spain was Elizabeth I of England. The two monarchs in fact had much in common beyond an enemy. Both were courageous, shrewd, exceptionally humane for their age; both believed in a kind of practical toleration. Both used their sexuality in politics; Henri his undisputable virility to offer himself to fellow Frenchmen as a model of kingly strength, Elizabeth her celebrated virginity to dangle the throne of England before the hungry suitors of Europe as a prize too valuable to give up despite repeated rebuffs. Elizabeth, one might say, reversed the marital diplomacy of the Hapsburgs: she achieved her political and diplomatic aims not by marrying, but by not marrying. Both, in short, were *politiques;* both, great statesmen. But they were also very different: Henri was the activist, Elizabeth the scholar who had mastered several languages and liked nothing so much as a theological disputation. And where Henri was profligate, Elizabeth was parsimonious—from need as much as from inclination. Besides, her overriding problems, though much like Henri's, were not identical with his: she had, not to heal the wounds of civil war, but to prevent one.

The first five years after her accession in 1558 were frantic with activity, not all of it conclusive. Elizabeth had to find a husband that she might give her country an heir, but she postponed and postponed her decision, carrying on for over a year an unpromising and still obscure affair with Lord Robert Dudley, and later listening to proposals without accepting any of them. The queen's need for a husband, and her reluctance to acquire one, furnished her reign with suspense and surrounded her throne with danger. In economic matters these early years were more productive. In 1563, as part of a series of parliamentary enactments, a statute of apprentices set long terms of apprenticeship, encouraged (or rather, enforced) the entry of the young and able-bodied into agriculture (economically the most useful, if not, among laborers, the favorite kind of work), and made local justices of the peace responsible for setting decent wage scales adjusted to the locality and the season. [39] And in these years, as all through her reign, Elizabeth found the religious passions that divided her country a formidable obstacle to social peace: the so-called Elizabethan Settlement (see p. 159) turned out to be a patchwork of compromises that few liked and many tried to undo.

Quite like Henri IV, Elizabeth I treated religion as a political question. She had her own convictions, but after a brief time of candor, she kept those convictions to herself and tried instead to impose rules that would make the state the master of the church and guarantee public order. But religious peace was as scarce as international peace. The exiles Bloody Mary had made had come back from the Continent accustomed to speaking their minds and filled with the Calvinist's confidence that theirs was the only true way. In characteristic sixteenth-century fashion, the toleration they demanded for themselves they were wholly unwilling to grant others, on the perfectly logical ground that their doctrine was the truth while the doctrines of their rivals were abysses of error. A few of the most intransigent of the Puritans sought to separate themselves from the Church of England, but most of them refused to become Separatists and worked for reform with the Church of England; these "moderate" Puritans found that church "but halfly reformed" [40]—neither pure enough to be acceptable without serious amendment, nor wicked enough to

---

[39] This enactment, which later came to be called the Statute of Artificers, was a codification of a mass of traditional and regional regulations and customs.

[40] See Patrick Collinson, *The Elizabethan Puritan Movement* (1967), 29 ff.

call for its eradication. The Puritans' grievances were real and extensive; their demands were far-reaching. They were hostile to episcopacy, the "Romish" Anglican hierarchy with its bishops and archbishops, though they were far from unanimous about the shape of the purified church they wanted. The religious "parties," whose debates would enliven and embitter the political life of England in the early seventeenth century, were present under Elizabeth in rudimentary form, though without the names they would later acquire. Some Puritans were tending toward Presbyterianism, a form of church government by elders and with a certain centralized structure, the synods, that held the congregations together. Other Puritans were tending toward Independency, or Congregationalism, which (as the names make clear) demanded the self-government of each congregation. On matters other than organization, however, the Elizabethan Puritans were at one. They wanted a clergy less corrupt, less ignorant, less inarticulate; they wanted a further simplification—"purification"—of doctrine and preaching. Elizabeth's parliaments, which she hoped to call more rarely than her steady need for money and support compelled her to do, became sounding boards for Puritan demands. At first she handled the vigorous protest with forbearance; only later, when Puritan spokesmen remained persistent and became even more offensive, did she grow severe.

Elizabeth's Catholic policy had a similar career. In the 1560s, the hostility English Catholics encountered was mainly rhetorical; the crown and in general the country allowed them to exist in peace, demanding only some superficial marks of conformity to the established religion. "There was no mention then of factions in religion," one Catholic later recalled, "neither was any man much noted or rejected for that cause; so otherwise his conversations were civil and courteous." [41] Then foreign aggressiveness and domestic anxiety forced the queen's hand. In 1570, by excommunicating Elizabeth, Pius V invited her Roman Catholic subjects to see her as a rebellious heretic who deserved no obedience and might deserve assassination. While most English Catholics rejected the sinister implications of the Papal Bull of Excommunication, a number of them left the country, some to found Catholic seminaries to prepare for an eventual recapture of England for the Church of Rome, others to plot against the queen's life. In the 1570s, there were several such plots—all real enough, none of them trumped up for public consumption—and in 1580 the most militant of Catholics, the Jesuits, sent missionaries to England. And the queen was still unmarried, still without an heir. The danger of a Catholic succession, produced either by natural death or (since by and large Elizabeth was in excellent health) by assassination, worried the country greatly. Then in the early 1580s, relations with Spain, already strained, worsened. Parliament, which loved the queen better than she loved it, pressed legislation on Elizabeth; her advisors urged action, her dependable Sir William Cecil (later Lord Burghley) at their head. In 1581, Edmund Campion, the head of the Jesuit

---

[41] S. T. Bindoff, *Tudor England* (1950), 234.

mission, was executed, and other executions followed. The realm was in danger, both from war abroad and subversion at home.

England: Confrontation with Catholicism

The long encounter of Elizabeth Tudor and Mary Stuart gains its significance from this concatenation of threatening circumstances. It has been dramatized by playwrights and novelists—beyond need; the reality was dramatic enough. Mary Stuart, for a time queen of the Scots, was in all respects the opposite of her great adversary: Catholic, irresponsible, cruel, and anything but virginal. As a granddaughter of one of Henry VIII's sisters, she had an undisputed claim to the English throne upon Elizabeth's death; when she arrived in England in 1568, she had already occupied and lost two thrones, one through misfortune, the other through misconduct. As the young wife of Francis II, she had been briefly queen of France, from 1559 to 1560; as the daughter of James V of Scotland, she assumed the Scottish crown in 1561. Charming and clever, she held her place for some time, a Catholic queen in a Protestant country, but a series of unsavory adventures which included the murder of her second husband presumably with her connivance and her marriage to the man who had been in charge of the murder, aroused the Scots against her. She was compelled to abdicate in favor of her son, James VI, [42] and to flee the country. Her arrival in England made her a nuisance to Elizabeth; her stay, which gradually changed into semi-imprisonment, made her a danger. Swearing by all that was holy that she was innocent, she was involved in nearly every foreign machination against England and nearly every plot against Elizabeth's life. Elizabeth's advisors and parliaments grew frantic, but for years Elizabeth temporized; she was reluctant to execute a royal personage who had been twice a queen, and might be queen yet a third time, no matter how guilty or duplicitous she might be. In the end, Mary's involvement in still another assassination plot broke down Elizabeth's resistance, and she agreed to have Mary tried. In February 1587, Mary was decapitated. Queen Elizabeth, whether from grief or from policy no one can say, mourned her dead rival and berated her rash officials. But England, delivered, rejoiced.

Deliverance was brief. The execution of Mary moved Philip II of Spain, who had been deeply engaged in Mary's plans, to go forward with his Enterprise of England. For years the English had been as provocative as Spain was powerful. The Spanish annexation of Portugal in 1580, which added Portuguese ports and Portuguese colonies to the Spanish arsenal, only increased the Spanish menace to English eyes, and the English, who had for years harassed Spain, mainly through privateers, stepped up their aggressive activities on sea and land alike. In 1584, the English government expelled the

[42] He was to succeed Elizabeth I in 1603 as James I; see p. 262.

Spanish ambassador for his part in a plot to murder Queen Elizabeth. In 1585 England concluded a treaty with the Dutch, who had been in rebellion against their Spanish masters since the 1560s (see p. 190). This was a drastic step, for while the rebels were Protestants and natural allies for England, they *were* rebels, and Elizabeth was as reluctant to support rebels, no matter how sympathetic, as she was reluctant to cause the death of a queen, no matter how dangerous. In 1587—the year of Mary Stuart's execution—Sir Francis Drake, slave trader and flamboyant sailor, made a brilliant raid on Spanish territory. He swooped down on Cadiz, destroying more than thirty vessels and invaluable cargo; later, cruising near the Azores, he took a Portuguese ship, the *San Felipe*, laden with spices, ivory, silk, gold, silver, and jewels, worth over £100,000: "All the barrel staves and all the fishing-boats in Spain could not have been sold for such a figure."[43]

Philip II retorted by pushing his plans for an invasion of England. But the greatest of all armadas suffered the greatest of all disasters. It sailed in late spring of 1588, under rigid and incomplete instructions to meet Spanish troops stationed in Flanders and protect their invasion. The Armada was huge, totaling one hundred thirty ships, of which only forty were proper men-of-war; it was an awkward procession vulnerable to accidents in timing, to intelligent opposition, and to bad weather. Much as in 1812 the Russians would let Napoleon reach Moscow, only to destroy his army on its retreat, the English navy, brilliantly led and bravely joined by private vessels, allowed the Armada to pass through the English Channel. Then, the English fleet fell on the Spaniards, burned some of their vessels, sank others, disabled and scattered the rest. What they did not do on that day, the winds and English harassment did in following days, as the surviving Spanish vessels struggled northward, through hostile waters and against stormy seas. The invaders who did not drown were slaughtered in remote isles off Scotland or in Ireland, and many of those who reached safety in Spain died at home of typhus and of exhaustion. English losses were insignificant. The Enterprise of England was over.

England: A Good Queen in Hard Times

Once again, as after the death of Mary Stuart, England rejoiced, but the breathing space that the shattering of the Armada gave Elizabeth in foreign affairs only called attention to domestic problems. Elizabeth's reign would end, as it had begun, amid widespread distress. The queen's trusted counselors died one by one—Burghley in 1598—and among their potential successors there was strident, often undignified competition for the queen's attention. The Elizabethan religious settlement was more threatened than it had been in decades, with Puritan Separatists noisier than ever—after 1590 a number of Puritan

[43] Garrett Mattingly, *The Armada* (1959), 120.

leaders were jailed and a few extremists were executed—and with Catholics, especially in remote Ireland, restless and rebellious. The rise of commercial monopolies under royal approval—over foreign trade and domestic manufacture—stimulated commercial activity, but led to fraud, influence-peddling, intimidation of independent merchants, and widespread public complaints. Bad harvests brought high prices for bread, and in the late 1590s there were bread riots of a violence that England had not seen for fifty years. First in 1597 and then, more comprehensively in 1601, earlier legislation was supplemented by the Elizabethan Poor Law, a law which, as S. T. Bindoff has said, "was as much the offspring of fear as of pity, of hatred as of charity." [44] It provided local relief for those who could not work, and local compulsion—work houses or whippings—for those who could, but would not, work.

And with the queen's person quite as much as with her realm, the last decade of her reign echoed its first. In the late 1590s, as long before in the 1560s, Elizabeth found her affections engaged, much to the distress of her realm. Her early infatuation with Robert Dudley had almost led to a disastrous marriage; it had ended happily in mutual indifference and in Dudley's service (as earl of Leicester) in the Netherlands. Her late infatuation, with the earl of Essex, ended less happily. Essex, handsome, undisciplined, inordinately ambitious, rapidly rose in the aging queen's favor and, wielding patronage, soon exercised great influence in the realm. He wanted more. Sent to subdue rebellious Ireland, he played with treasonous plots, possibly designed to oust his rivals from the court, possibly to impose his will on the queen. Elizabeth had loved Essex, but she could not save him from the end that his rashness and the standards of the time dictated. In 1601 he was executed. Two years later Elizabeth, too, died, melancholy and alone. The Tudor line died with her.

The pathos of her end is the kind of shadow the Elizabethans would have taken as a reminder of human frailty in the midst of splendor. In poetry, in music, in architecture (see p. 216), as in politics and, despite all the endemic distress, in economic affairs, the age of Elizabeth was a memorable age—vigorous, expansive, the stuff from which legends are made. And the queen herself was the cause and center of that legend. Behind all the great impersonal and often invisible forces of social and economic change there stands her figure, a queen who loved her subjects as much as her subjects loved her, and who spent many hours wooing her subjects as though she needed their votes. In one of her many stately progresses through her realm, when the city fathers of Coventry handed her the customary cup with the customary donation in it, Elizabeth thanked the lords of the city: "It was a good gift, £100 in gold; I have but few such gifts." The mayor replied, "If it please your Grace, there is a great deal more in it." "What is that?" she asked. "It is," he told her, "the hearts of all your loving subjects." To which the queen, consummate politician that she was, gave answer: "We thank you, Mr. Mayor; it is a great deal more indeed." [45]

[44] *Tudor England,* 293.
[45] See J. E. Neale, *Queen Elizabeth I* (rev. ed., 1966), 205.

SPAIN IN DIFFICULTIES

The Birth of the Dutch Republic

During the decades that Spain disastrously failed to subdue England by marriage, diplomacy, or invasion, it suffered another failure, in the north, equally disastrous. After prolonged, confused fighting, some of the lands that had come into Hapsburg hands a century before detached themselves from Spanish overlordship and secured their independence. Both the war itself and the eventual loss proved expensive to Spain.

The Netherlands was a conglomerate of seventeen provinces divided by particularism, economic interest, and language; they were united, or at least drawn together, by geography, common experiences with their Burgundian masters, and later, military accident. The southern, Walloon population spoke French; northerners spoke a Germanic language that was assuming, in these years, the lineaments of Dutch. But this was not a divisive force in an age that was still a stranger to nationalism. The Reformation further complicated matters: there were for many years more Protestants in the south than in the north, and during the revolt, the great city of Amsterdam, in Holland, stubbornly remained a Catholic island in a Calvinist sea. It was a prosperous region fiercely concentrated on perpetuating that prosperity, a region of commercial cities, grown fat on fishing, shipping, small manufacture, banking. It lived by, and from, the sea. Its old aristocratic families were influential but not dominant. The culture and the politics of the region were urban, and the decisive power was exercised by commercial oligarchies reigning unchallenged in the cities which, in turn, controlled the provincial estates. The favorite political slogan of the Netherlands was "liberty," which they defined in good medieval fashion as freedom from interference by central authorities or outside powers. It was another name for local custom, local law, local privileges. There were two possible rallying points for common action, the States General and that rather peculiar institution, the Stadholderate. The first was simply an assembly of delegates from each province, shackled by instructions from home; it could act only if it could obtain unanimity, and thus reflected, with its relative impotence, the centrifugal nature of power in the Netherlands. The role of the second depended on the vagaries of history. The king of Spain had stadholders—lieutenants, representatives—in each of his Netherlands provinces; in the sixteenth century, the house of Orange had been granted the stadholderate of several provinces and was to keep its hold through the rebellion into the republic. But the stadholder was not (and after the revolt only sometimes became) the chief executive of the state. Thus "liberty" was preserved, and liberty meant that each merchant oligarch, in his own city, could grow rich in his own way.

With the accession of Philip II, this liberty was in danger. "Turk like," wrote Sir Walter Raleigh with more passion than justice, Philip II was seeking "to tread under his feet all their national and fundamental laws, privileges, and ancient rights." [46] In the course of the fourteenth and fifteenth centuries, parts of the Netherlands had been acquired by the dukes of Burgundy, and upon the death of Charles the Rash in 1477, his daughter Mary had brought to her husband, Maximilian of Hapsburg, most of the region as dowry (see p. 113). Her grandson, Charles I of Spain—Emperor Charles V—eventually inherited and rounded out his Netherlands possessions, and in 1548, he gathered the seventeen provinces into the Burgundian circle of his empire. But while the emperor's policies were dictated mainly by his imperial and his Spanish concerns, he governed these provinces with a relatively light hand. When, in October 1555, in Brussels, Charles handed over his northern domains to his son, Philip II, the delegates of the seventeen provinces, witnessing the solemn occasion, broke into tears. They would soon know they had been right to weep.

The revolt of the Netherlands, with its dashing raiders, its savage Spanish oppressors, its dramatic battles, and its patient leader, William the Silent, has often been simplified and sentimentalized as a struggle between Protestants and Catholics, or (which for many historians has been the same thing) between good and evil. In fact, especially in the early years, there were as many Catholics among the rebels as there were Protestants, and progress lay probably more with the policies of Philip II than with those who resisted them. "The rebellion against the Spanish authorities," Johan Huizinga has noted, "was a conservative revolution and could not have been otherwise—in those days, it was not the rebels but the lawful governments who were the reformers and innovators." [47] Nor was the revolt a nationalistic struggle against foreign oppression: the sentiment of Dutch nationality was the consequence, not the cause, of the rebellion. Nor, finally, was the outcome predestined by political or ethnic or religious realities; it was the result of military fortunes.

Philip II alienated his northern subjects first of all by what he was, not by what he did. He was as unmistakably Spanish as his father had been Burgundian, as ignorant of Dutch as Charles V had been, at the outset, of Spanish (see p. 172). But he soon added the irritant of policy to the accident of birth. Operating through his half-sister, Margaret of Parma, as regent, and through Cardinal Granvelle, Philip sought to introduce some administrative centralization. In 1559, he ordered a massive reorganization of the churches which would place the nomination to bishoprics into the hands of the crown,

[46] Quoted by Sir George Clark, "The Birth of the Dutch Republic" (1946), in Lucy S. Sutherland, ed., Studies in History (1966), 121.

[47] "Dutch Civilisation in the Seventeenth Century," in Huizinga, Dutch Civilisation in the Seventeenth Century and Other Essays (Torchbook ed., 1968), 26.

increase the number of bishops, insist on proper qualifications for high church officials, and rationalize the boundaries of the dioceses. It was, as one Dutch historian has put it, "a very great measure; its bold logic and symmetry and its vigorous attack on historic development and ancient rights were thoroughly characteristic of the spirit of the monarchy and its rationalistic lawyer servants"; altogether it was a "striking instance of what the monarchy could do in the way of state building." [48] The measure was utterly reasonable, thoroughly progressive, and vastly unpopular. It offended Catholics and Calvinists alike, for it constituted an invasion of cherished rights over patronage, and it was an ominous sign that Philip would enforce the uncompromising decrees of the Council of Trent against his "heretical" subjects in the north (see p. 169).

Unrest grew. At first, protests against the Spanish policy were the work of prominent nobles—of the vain, vacillating, self-deluded count of Egmont, who was stadholder of Flanders; of the count of Hoorne, who was a Knight of the Golden Fleece and admiral-general; and of that puzzling statesman, William of Nassau, who was prince of Orange, the most influential and clear-sighted statesman the rebellion was to produce. He came later to be called William the Silent, not because he was taciturn but because he had shown himself a wily diplomat from his youth. [49] It is a sign of the deep feelings stirred by the new policy that William of Orange should participate in the movement at all. He was a prince imbued with dynastic loyalty, an aristocrat of immense wealth, a prominent servant of Philip II, and stadholder of Holland, Zeeland, and Utrecht since 1559.

By 1564, the Protestants had won their first victory: Philip had abandoned his plan and sent Granvelle into exile. A year later, riding the crest of this precarious triumph, more than four hundred nobles from practically all of the Netherlands joined to form the "compromise," a league of the nobility led by Protestants but open to Catholics.

The league's first step was to plead with the government to mitigate the edicts against heresy. Representatives went to Spain, and in April 1566, a group of about two hundred nobles appeared in Brussels to present their petition to Margaret of Parma. The occasion gave the rebellion its most enduring slogan: looking at the petitioners, the count of Berlaymont, one of Margaret's closest advisors, derisively referred to them as *gueux*—beggars. As is so often true of party names, so here: the name *beggar*, bestowed in contempt, was soon flaunted with pride.

[48] Pieter Geyl, *The Revolt of the Netherlands, 1555–1609* (rev. ed., 1958), 71, 74.

[49] Perhaps, as more than one historian has suggested, the epithet "silent" is apt because William's private religious convictions and some of his aspirations remained unclear to those who knew him, as they have remained unclear to historians since. Yet, writes H. G. Koenigsberger, who makes this point, "it was always clear what he fought against: despotic government and religious persecution" ("Western Europe and the Power of Spain," in *The New Cambridge Modern History*, vol. III [1968], 281). A cosmopolitan among patriots, an urbane believer in toleration among religious fanatics, such reserve was perhaps not only useful, but essential.

The nobles could not contain what they had begun; in the summer of 1566, the lower orders took the rebellion into their own hands. They were impatient with passivity, harassed by widespread unemployment and high prices, and thus ripe for provocative Calvinist preachers. The Calvinists were still a small minority of the population, but unlike other Protestant sects, they were energetic, bellicose, and well organized; since 1560, their ranks had been strengthened and their passions inflamed by Huguenot refugees from France. They had begun to hold public services, and in August 1566 they indulged themselves in an orgy of iconoclasm. In city after city—the contagion spread like a wave—Calvinist mobs invaded Catholic churches to "purge" houses of the Lord of all symbols of hateful image worship. They toppled statues and broke windows. "It is a small matter, or revenge," wrote one Calvinist apologist at the time, "thus to have destroyed the images, which are only a species of idolatry, since the ecclesiastics have done us a thousand times more hurt and hindrance through their persecutions which broke those statues which God Himself had made and for which He once shed His precious blood, namely, our dearest friends, fathers and mothers, sisters and brothers."[50] To justify one's own violence by blaming others for starting it is special pleading common among those who are perhaps a little ashamed of their actions, but truculence was the attitude of a militant and powerful minority in the Netherlands. The outlook for compromise was dark.

Philip II responded to these Calvinist outrages with uncharacteristic speed and rare determination. Some of the leading nobles, helpless to check a movement whose fanaticism they detested, had left the country; William of Orange was stripped of his posts under the crown. Now Philip, in effect superseding Margaret, reinforced the Spanish garrisons with crack troops drawn from his Italian possessions. They were commanded by the duke of Alva, who had long deplored his sovereign's indulgence with the northern heretics. Indifferent to local customs and contemptuous of time-honored rights, Alva speedily instituted a reign of terror. *"Non curamus privilegios vestros,"* he coldly told delegates from the University of Louvain who had come to protest his arbitrary proceedings: "We don't care about your privileges."[51] By the fall of 1567, only a few months after his arrival, Alva had arrested dozens of leading nobles; by the following summer, he had executed hundreds of them, Egmont and Hoorne among them. Alva's tribunal, the Council of Troubles—quickly labeled the Council of Blood—terrorized the population and thus minimized the possibility of revolt.[52] Then, after death, taxes: in 1569, Alva demanded that

[50] Quoted in Geyl, *Revolt of the Netherlands*, 93.

[51] Ibid., 102.

[52] The actual figures are less terrible than the reputation of the council: in six years, between 1567 and 1573, it convicted around nine thousand persons out of the twelve thousand who came before it, but only one thousand were actually executed. The number of those, however, who avoided the executioner's axe by emigration—about sixty thousand—may explain this relatively moderate figure. For the precise figures, see A. L. E. Verheyden, *Le Conseil des Troubles: Liste des condamnés, 1567-1573* (1961).

the States General approve a 10 percent impost on all goods sold—the notorious "tenth penny." The Netherlanders were outraged. It was a thoroughly Spanish tax, reminding them, once again, that they were in the hands of Spaniards; besides, it struck directly at their commercial prosperity. Unrest spread further. Undeterred, Alva continued his executions and his exactions and confiscated the properties of wealthy rebels, including William of Orange.

The result was disaster—for Spain. The rebels were by no means united: William of Orange never gave up his dream of unity and toleration, while the Calvinists, determined to win the right to practice their religion, had no intention of extending the same right to others. But before Alva retired from his post in November 1573, he had managed to arouse in aristocrats and merchants, Calvinists and Catholics, one fierce desire: to be rid of the Spaniards. In April 1572, a bold band of sea-Beggars had captured the strategic port of The Brill, which made them masters of the lower Rhine; the two northern provinces of Holland and Zeeland now took the lead in the rebellion. But it was in no way a purely Protestant cause: there were many Catholics in Brabant and Flanders quite as determined as the Protestants to do without Spanish troops, Spanish governors, and Spanish taxes.

In 1576, this determination acquired new firmness. Late in the previous year, the Spanish government had gone bankrupt, an event fatal for a war in which most soldiers, "mercenaries" in the literal sense, died only for money. Alva's successor, Requesens, had fought ably in the field, but after his death in March 1576, his lieutenants could no longer restrain their impatient and irritable troops. They mutinied, and in November, they vented their "Spanish fury" on Antwerp, in a week of pillage, murder, and wanton cruelty. Calvinists had committed atrocities against priests, but their ferocity was mildness compared with this systematic, unrestrained savagery. The response was an agreement among the seventeen provinces, the Pacification of Ghent, published in November 1576. It was an alliance concluded to drive out the Spaniard, and it foresaw an eventual settlement of that most troublesome of questions, the religious question, which threatened to undermine the precarious understanding almost as soon as it had been reached.

But, as elsewhere in Europe in these years, in the emerging Netherlands the religious question could not be settled simply because most of the disputants did not want to settle it. They wanted not to tolerate error, but destroy it. William the Silent was a *politique,* but like his French counterparts (see p. 178) he found his ideals unpopular and his vision premature. While he cast about for some foreign sovereign who would take the united provinces under his protection, intransigent Calvinists entered city after city, expelled Catholic officials, and drove out priests and monks. Don John of Austria, Requesens' successor, agreed to make peace with the States General on condition that the Catholic religion be everywhere restored, but the Beggar-dominated provinces, Holland and Zeeland, with their Calvinist allies elsewhere, frustrated this possible compromise. When the intelligent and able

Alexander Farnese, duke of Parma, was made governor-general over the rebellious regions in 1578, he found it possible to divide by diplomacy and the judicious application of military pressure what his predecessors had united with their rashness, cruelty, and lack of realism.

The decisive year was 1579. In that year, the southern provinces joined in the Union of Arras, and proclaimed their continued loyalty to the Spanish crown, while the seven northern provinces formed their own alliance, the Union of Utrecht, the germ of the modern Dutch state. Neither side precisely foresaw, or intended to produce, the future. "The treaty of union," Huizinga reminds us, "was not expressly concerned with political freedom and independence, nor was it intended to be the constitution of a free state." Rather, "the Union of Utrecht was, in principle, no more than an *ad hoc* military alliance." [53] Indeed, the future was to be determined by the fortunes of war. When two years later, in 1581, the States General abjured its allegiance to the Spanish crown and called its members the United Provinces of the Netherlands, a number of cities now in Belgium—Antwerp, Bruges, Brussels, Ghent—still formed part of the newly born state. The three provinces, Holland, Zeeland, and Utrecht, over which William of Orange had been stadholder, now honored him, once again, with that title and made it hereditary. But Farnese vigorously and patiently reconquered the major centers in the south by winning strategic sieges and making strategic concessions. By 1585, Brussels and Antwerp had surrendered to him, and the shape of the Dutch Republic was, in all essentials, final. William the Silent, the leader of the republic, had been assassinated the year before, in July 1584, shot down at Delft by a fanatic encouraged, no doubt, by the outlawry Philip II had proclaimed four years before. The States General, mourning William's loss, called him the father of the fatherland. It was a tribute to his aims and his eventual influence. The manner of his death, the legends surrounding his life and end, were no substitute for his diplomacy and his skill, but they remained a force in Dutch affairs. His son, Maurice, who succeeded him, inherited his father's titles and much of his father's authority.

Now definitively divided, the Spanish Netherlands and the United Provinces began to sort themselves out religiously, with Catholics migrating southward and Protestants northward. By 1585, when Queen Elizabeth, after maddening hesitations, finally committed some troops to the rebels' cause (see p. 187), a Protestant front against the Spanish crusade had taken shape. The English intervention in the revolt of the Netherlands, led by Elizabeth's favorite, the earl of Leicester, was more a burden on the Dutch than a help, and Parma for some years extended Spanish military gains. But by the 1590s, after the defeat of the Spanish Armada, and in the declining years of Philip II, the Spaniards found themselves unable to reconquer the lost territories. Thus, in 1609, after extended and tedious negotiations, the belligerents concluded a

[53] "Dutch Civilisation," 28.

twelve-year truce which, in effect, recognized the existence of a new Dutch state.[54]

It was inevitable that the young Dutch Republic should undergo strains. The truce with Spain gave abundant room for internal dissension: nothing is so productive of domestic quarrels as international peace. Doctrinaire Calvinists, who never ceased reminding themselves and others of the noble part they had played in winning independence, found themselves beleaguered far less by Catholic or nonconformist Protestant minorities than by theological currents within the Calvinist persuasion itself. Soon religious quarrels, exacerbated by new opportunities for settling old political scores and by bitter differences over economic policy, brought the United Provinces to the edge of civil war.

The ascendancy of strict Calvinism had never gone wholly unchallenged. William the Silent himself, and Jan van Oldenbarneveldt, William's closest associate in the rebellion and, after William's death, the undisputed political leader of the United Provinces, both believed in toleration and obviously had their doubts about the stark Calvinist doctrine of predestination. In 1602, with the appointment of Jacobus Arminius to a chair at Leyden, this explosive theological issue assumed new prominence, for while Arminius stressed man's original sin, he insisted that man at least participated in shaping his eternal destiny. After his death in 1609, his partisans among the professors, the commercial oligarchy, and the ministry kept his teachings very much alive. They had distinguished support, including the brilliant scholar Hugo Grotius (see p. 230) and Oldenbarneveldt himself. The orthodox charged the Arminians with denigrating God's majesty and with wishing to reintroduce the noxious doctrine of free will—in a word, with secretly favoring popery. The Arminians charged the orthodox with insulting God's goodness by making Him the father of sin.

In a society as small and as intensely engrossed in religious matters as the seventeenth-century Dutch Republic, the state could hardly allow this theological squabble to go on unchecked. In 1610, a group of Arminian ministers addressed a Remonstrance to the States of Holland, in which they stated their side of the theological issue and asked for protection. Oldenbarneveldt was only too ready to give it. As advocate of the Province of Holland, as spokesman for its delegation to the States General, as one of the architects of independence, simply by the force of his person, Oldenbarneveldt exercised enormous political authority. And he was certain—he had insisted on it as early as 1586— that the state must not be ruled by the church, even by the most godly of ministers.

Sound as Oldenbarneveldt's policy was, his position progressively weakened. He had been at the head of affairs too long not to make enemies. The war party detested him for concluding a truce with Spain; there were merchants

[54] The official recognition had to await the general European settlement that followed the Thirty Years' War in 1648 (see p. 254).

who disliked his championship of the East India Company (see p. 211); the Contra-Remonstrants tried to ruin his reputation by spreading slanders and resorting to the lowest demagogy, while Oldenbarneveldt, in retaliation, only alienated wider circles by aiding the Remonstrants in high-handed ways. Then, in 1617, Maurice of Nassau, with whom he had clashed before, openly joined the orthodox Calvinists. Nibbling away at Oldenbarneveldt's basis of support, Maurice filled clerical and governmental posts all across the country with extreme Calvinists; in 1618, with a show of force, he took over Holland and had Oldenbarneveldt arrested. After interminable and humiliating questioning before a court illegally constituted and packed with men lusting to revenge themselves on the aging statesman, Oldenbarneveldt was condemned to death and executed in May 1619. He went to his death resigned but uncomprehending, after a lifetime of brilliant service. He was seventy-two years old.

Maurice's coup d'état brought a time of decreased influence of the provinces on Dutch affairs, and a time of persecution of Arminians, censoring of intellectuals, and a new harshness of life in the Genevan fashion. The packed Synod of Dort, held in 1619, confirmed the hold of the Contra-Remonstrants on the ministry and the universities. But not for long. When Maurice died in 1625, his younger brother and successor, Frederick Henry, rapidly moved to suspend the persecutions, and by 1630 Remonstrants found themselves once again in pulpits and in city governments. These years were years of real troubles, and they issued in real crimes, but Dutch prosperity soon dimmed memory of them.

There are Dutch historians who deplore to this day the settlement that produced a truncated republic, small in population, poor in resources, incapable in the long run of competing with the great powers of Europe. They have called it a disaster. [55] If it was a disaster, the naval prowess, imperial acquisitions, commercial profits, and cultural glories of the seventeenth-century Dutch Republic managed to conceal it well. The Spanish Netherlands bore the scars of the conflict far more visibly: far more than remote Holland, southern provinces like Flanders and Brabant had been theaters of war for years; their cities had been despoiled by Calvinists, by Spanish troops obeying the orders of their general or—which was far more devastating—by Spanish troops disobeying the orders of their general. Antwerp, once the most splendid commercial metropolis of the north, lost half its population and all its splendor during the Dutch wars, undergoing, first the Spanish fury, later Parma's siege which led to massive emigration of Calvinists, and finally, loss of access to the sea (see p. 210). The implacable Dutch throttled Antwerp in 1585 by blockading the mouth of the Scheldt and kept the river closed to ocean-going shipping during the truce and after; when peace was concluded in 1648, they wrote the economic death sentence of Antwerp into the treaty. It was the enemies of the

[55] See Geyl, *Revolt of the Netherlands*, 256–259.

Dutch, the Spanish Netherlands and Spain itself, that seemed to have suffered the disaster.

The Erosion of Spanish Power

Despite all its setbacks, Spain remained a power to be reckoned with. Its vast empire in Europe and America, the flow of precious metals from its mines overseas, the sheer resiliency of what had once been the arbiter of European affairs, combined with the troubles that continued to beset its rivals, sustained the strength, or the reputation, of Spain for some decades. True, by the time Philip II died in 1598, some Spaniards had noticed symptoms of decay, yet the country could still muster considerable energy in the 1620s and 1630s, in the reign of Philip IV, under the leadership of the count-duke Olivares. But in 1640, Spain's decay was palpable and, as it were, official, with the outbreak of a long-drawn-out rebellion in Catalonia, and the short, successful revolt, in the same year, of Portugal, which recaptured the independence it had lost in 1580 (see p. 175).

The decline of Spain in the early seventeenth century is often taken as a salutary lesson; it is cited as proof that intolerant crusading zeal, excessive political ambition, and disdain for the humble virtues of work and thrift must bring punishment in their train. The moralizing is beside the point, but there is some merit in the diagnosis. Spain was by no means alone in keeping up its intolerance, overextending itself abroad, and rewarding the holy idleness of the priest and the secular idleness of the courtier. It is only that Spain could afford such policies and such ideals less than other states, and pursued them more vigorously. As the events of 1640 were to prove, Spain was far from united; in 1591–1592 there had been a brief, bizarre rebellion in Aragon, and Spaniards outside Castile resented its dominance in Spanish affairs. Castile, which had over six million of Spain's eight millions, was undergoing plague, famine, and an untoward shift of population from the countryside to the towns—a sign not of urban prosperity, but of the intolerable exactions to which the peasants were subject. By 1600, Castile was importing grain and its industries were stagnant. "The nature of the economic system was such," writes J. H. Elliott, who has convincingly suggested that the decline of Spain was first a decline of Castile, "that one became a student or a monk, a beggar or a bureaucrat. There was nothing else to be." [56] The Spanish crown offered an equally depressing picture. The kings of Spain were inordinately expensive; what Philip II had spent on war (the Invincible Armada had cost a fortune), his successor, Philip III, spent on the court. The bankruptcy of the first, in 1596, was followed by the bankruptcy of the second, in 1607.

[56] "The Decline of Spain," in Trevor Aston, ed., *Crisis in Europe* (1965), 183.

But Spain was bankrupt in more than funds. Philip III, passive and patient, let himself be duped by a grasping, smooth aristocrat, whom he created duke of Lerma and made master in his house. The result was that the gap between the privileged and the unprivileged grew wider, that pressing problems went unsolved, and that a host of desirable offices were filled with Lerma's relatives. The most memorable policy of Lerma's reign was the expulsion of the Moriscos (see p. 174) which, by removing nearly three hundred thousand people from a population already stationary or perhaps declining, only weakened an already shaky economy. The enormous amounts of silver that flowed through the port of Seville into Spain actually reached their maximum around 1600, but they did not remain in the country to support industry despite all official efforts to keep silver at home (see p. 208). While there were more who strove for advancement in the church or at court or in the army than in other countries, their chances for mercantile ventures or industrial investment were correspondingly smaller. What was missing, more than in France or the Dutch Republic or in England, was an urban middle class. This was apparent as early as 1600: in that year a perceptive public official, Gonzalez de Cellorigo, invidiously compared the Spain of 1492, with its harmonious balance among the classes, with the Spain of 1600, which had come, he wrote, "to be an extreme contrast of rich and poor," with "no means of adjusting them to one another." The condition of Spain, he added, "is one in which we have rich who loll at ease, or poor who beg, and we lack people of the middling sort, whom neither wealth nor poverty prevents from pursuing the rightful kind of business enjoined by natural law" [57]—by which he meant the kind of productive effort that was making the Dutch so rich.

Beneath all this was a fatal loss in morale. The terrible tragedy of the Armada and the humiliating spectacle of a truce with the Dutch contrasted bitterly with the glorious legend of the *reconquista;* the concentration on further military adventures in the early seventeenth century was less a commitment to glory than a final admission of incompetence and a failure of will, a confession of inability to use the breathing space of peace. If more and more Spaniards sought courtier's jobs or clerical benefices, this was less from conviction than from despair, not a gratification but a refuge. The age that was dawning was the age in which the inglorious—the merchant, the scientist, the engineer—would achieve glory. It was an age in which the Spain of the Counter-Reformation, despite its great painters and writers, would have no place.

SELECTED READINGS

For sixteenth- and early seventeenth-century Spain, see, J. H. Elliott, *Imperial Spain, 1469–1716* (1963); H. Mariéjol, *The Spain of Ferdinand and Isabella* (tr. 1961); and J. Lynch, *Spain Under the Hapsburgs,* vol. I, *Empire and Absolutism, 1516–1598* (1964).

[57] Quoted in Elliott, *Imperial Spain,* 305.

Lynch's second volume, *Spain and America, 1598-1700* (1969), continues his lucid account. The standard biography of Charles V remains Karl Brandi, *The Emperor Charles V* (tr. 1939). Reginald Trevor Davies, *The Golden Century of Spain, 1501-1621* (rev. ed., 1965), remains useful for this period.

For the age of the Counter-Reformation, see J. H. Elliott, *Europe Divided, 1559-1598* (1969); R. B. Wernham, ed., *The Counter Reformation and Price Revolution, 1559-1610* (1958), a volume in *The New Cambridge Modern History;* and H. O. Evennett, *The Spirit of the Counter Reformation* (1968). See also the magisterial account by Hubert Jedin, *The Council of Trent* (1957-1961). A. G. Dickens, *The Counter Reformation* (1969), is popular and accurate. Amidst a controversial literature on the Jesuits, one may single out René Fülöp-Miller, *The Power and the Secret of the Jesuits* (1930), and Christopher Hollis, *The Jesuits* (1968). Hollis has also written a biography of Loyola (1931), which may be read in conjunction with James Brodrick, *The Origin of the Jesuits* (1956).

For Spain overseas, see in addition to the books on Spain just cited, J. H. Parry, *The Spanish Seaborne Empire* (1966), to be supplemented by Parry's earlier monograph, *The Spanish Theory of Empire in the Sixteenth Century* (1940); Lewis Hanke's, *The Spanish Struggle for Justice in the Conquest of America* (1949) and his *Aristotle and the American Indian* (1959), which ably sums up the moral and theological problems of conquest. Charles Gibson, *Spain in America* (1966), is a dependable synthesis. For the economic impact of Spanish expansion, see the pioneering, still controverted E. J. Hamilton, *American Treasure and the Price Revolution in Spain, 1501-1650* (1934); on this point see J. Vincent Vives, *An Economic History of Spain from the Earliest Times to the End of the Nineteenth Century* (tr. 1969).

J. E. Neale, *The Age of Catherine de' Medici* (1943), is a clear but very short history of France in the second half of the sixteenth century; it should be supplemented with the old yet still useful study by James Westfall Thompson, *Wars of Religion in France, 1559-1576* (1909); Jean Héritier's biography, *Catherine de Medici* (tr. 1963); and A. J. Grant's *The Huguenots* (1934). Among many biographies of Henri IV none is wholly satisfactory; the best in English is perhaps Hesketh Pearson, *Henry of Navarre, The King Who Dared* (1963). See also Davis Bitton, *The French Nobility in Crisis, 1560-1640* (1969). David Buissert, *Sully and the Growth of Centralized Government in France, 1598-1610* (1968), ably deals with Henri's great minister, while Raymond F. Kierstead, *Pomponne de Bellièvre: A Study of the King's Men in the Age of Henry IV* (1968), ably deals with another. See also the opening chapters of Orest Ranum, *Paris in the Age of Absolutism* (1968).

The Elizabethan reign is best approached through J. E. Neale, *Queen Elizabeth I* (rev. ed., 1966); see also the judicious survey by J. B. Black, *The Reign of Queen Elizabeth, 1558-1603* (1936). The politics in the early part of her reign are lucidly examined in Wallace MacCaffrey, *The Shaping of the Elizabethan Regime* (1968). Joel Hurstfield, *Elizabeth I and the Unity of England* (1966), is short and clear. For Elizabeth's ministers there are the splendid volumes by Conyers Read: *Mr. Secretary Walsingham,* 3 vols. (1925), *Mr. Secretary Cecil* (1955), and *Lord Burghley and Queen Elizabeth* (1960); for her parliaments there are the equally splendid volumes by J. E. Neale: *Elizabeth I and Her Parliaments, 1559-1581* (1953), and *Elizabeth I and Her Parliaments, 1584-1601* (1957). For the Elizabethan Settlement, see J. V. P. Thompson, *Supreme Governor* (1940). Lawrence Stone, *The Crisis of the Aristocracy, 1558-1641* (1965, abridged ed., 1967), profoundly analyzes the social history of England's peerage. Louis B. Wright analyzes a lower social stratum in *Middle Class Culture in Elizabethan England* (1935). The failure of the attempt of Philip II to overthrow Queen Elizabeth is told in Garrett Mattingly's superb narrative and analysis, *The Armada* (1959).

On English religious history, see Patrick Collinson, *The Elizabethan Puritan Movement* (1967); see also Marshall Moon Knappen, *Tudor Puritanism* (1939); William Haller, *The Rise of Puritanism* (1938); and J. F. H. New, *Anglican and Puritan: The Basis of Their Opposition, 1558–1640* (1964). Christopher Hill, *Economic Problems of the Church: From Archbishop Whitgift to the Long Parliament* (1956), is an excellent survey of a neglected subject. J. H. Pollen, *The English Catholics in the Reign of Queen Elizabeth* (1920), and Wilbur K. Jordan, *The Development of Religious Toleration in England to the Death of Queen Elizabeth* (1931), are both very useful.

For English commercial enterprise in those decades, see J. A. Williamson, *The Ocean in English History* (1941); Williamson's biography, *Sir Francis Drake* (1951); G. D. Ramsay, *English Overseas Trade During the Centuries of the Emergence* (1957); and the modern, technical essay by Theodore W. Rabb, *Enterprise and Empire: Merchant and Gentry Investment in the Expansion of England, 1575–1630* (1967). D. B. Quinn, *Raleigh* (1947), is a good biography.

The best known work on the birth of the Dutch Republic is Pieter Geyl, *The Revolt of the Netherlands, 1555–1609* (rev. ed., 1958), which revises earlier views of the revolt as a purely Protestant rebellion against Catholics. Geyl continued his history with *The Netherlands in the Seventeenth Century*, Part One (tr. 1961). Johan Huizinga, "Dutch Civilisation in the Seventeenth Century," in Huizinga, *Dutch Civilisation in the Seventeenth Century and Other Essays* (tr. 1968), is suggestive. *William the Silent*, by C. V. Wedgwood (1944), is the best biography in English. The early chapters of Charles Wilson, *The Dutch Republic and the Civilisation of the Seventeenth Century* (1968), are short and authoritative. See also Book I of G. J. Renier, *The Dutch Nation: An Historical Study* (1944), which draws extensively on pamphlet literature.

5

Commerce and Culture

COMMERCE: THE EXPANSION OF THE EUROPEAN ECONOMY

Commercial Capitalism

In 1721, in his speech from the throne at the opening of Parliament, George I of England observed that it was the nation's commerce upon which "the riches and grandeur of this nation chiefly depend."[1] A quarter of a century later, David Hume praised merchants as "one of the most useful races of men."[2] Neither of these remarks was startling, nor were they intended to be. The benefits of commerce and the value of commercial men had long been

---

[1] Quoted in C. H. Wilson, "Trade, Society and the State," in *Cambridge Economic History of Europe,* vol. IV (1967), 516. The author of this speech, of course, was not the king but his chief minister, Sir Robert Walpole.

[2] "Of Interest," *Philosophical Works,* III, 324.

recognized, certainly since the middle of the fifteenth century—such matters are impossible to date with any precision—when the more advanced sectors of the European economy had entered the era of commercial capitalism.[3]

Historians seeking to define capitalism normally throw up their hands in despair and then bravely list some characteristics they hope may point the reader in the right direction. Certainly trade and greed—two of its indispensable ingredients—are as old as civilization itself. And the medieval centuries that directly precede the capitalist era displayed many of its qualities; they too had known far-flung commercial activities like international fairs and the long-range hauling of goods. What distinguishes early modern capitalism from previous phases is that it vastly extended the range and intensity of economic relations, gave them a complex organization, eased them with a series of novel techniques, and made a revolution in credit. And these changes were accompanied and rationalized by a change in attitude: "Capitalism," the influential German sociologist Max Weber wrote half a century ago, "is identical with the pursuit of profit, and forever *renewed* profit, by means of continuous, rationalistic, capitalistic enterprise."[4] Medieval economic life was severely circumscribed; goods were produced principally for direct use or local sale and, if sold, paid for generally in kind; in commercial capitalism goods came to be produced primarily for exchange and were paid for in currency. What had been parochial, occasional, difficult, dangerous, and primitive became international, customary, easy, safe, and complicated.

While the coming of capitalism was anything but a sudden irruption, its eventual triumph remade the face of Europe so decisively that its origins, its "causes," have held considerable fascination for historians. One ingenious and comprehensive interpretation that long captured historians' imagination and continues to have its adherents is associated with Max Weber. Impressed by the extraordinary share of Protestants, and especially Calvinists, in capitalist enterprise, Weber postulated a direct relationship between the Calvinist idea of "calling" and the "spirit of capitalism." Calvinism, Weber suggested, propagated a "worldly asceticism," which prized sobriety, thrift, and upright conduct in secular affairs as part of the Christian's duty. Calvinists therefore, far more than other Christians, would be inclined to postpone gratification, save money, and see worldly success as one of the signs of election.[5] Surely, someone who

---

[3] The very name "capitalism" had and in many quarters continues to have, tendentious overtones; similarly, the various adjectives that describe its "stages"—commercial, industrial, financial—have been part of the long debate over the role of capitalism as a necessary stage on the road to socialism. None of them wholly fits, since in the stage with which we are here concerned finance played a very significant part, as did private small-scale industry. Yet the adjectives are not wholly without value; they tell us which aspect of capitalist enterprise was dominant.

[4] *The Protestant Ethic and the Spirit of Capitalism* (1904–1905, tr. 1930), 17.

[5] It will be recalled that Calvin offered his sectaries no guarantees; God had chosen or rejected them before they had ever been born, and their fortunes in life were at best a sign of election, never a means to it. Still, far from inducing apathy, the Calvinist doctrine of predestination produced a race of responsible and hard-working men (see p. 151).

would work rather than play, and invest rather than spend, was precisely the kind of person useful for capitalist accumulation.

The difficulty with the Weber thesis, attractive as it appears, is twofold, and ultimately it must be rejected as an explanation. Many capitalists, both before and during the reign of capitalism, were not Calvinists; and many Calvinists were not capitalists. In fact, on the crucial moral issue on which Roman Catholic teaching can be said to have been anticapitalist—its insistence on the "just price" and its associated condemnation of "usury"—Christians of all persuasians were of the same mind. Medieval theologians had thought it evident and right that a product should be sold for what it cost to produce, a cost calculated to include the wage of the producer. They thought it just as evident, and just as right, that since money was "sterile," merely a medium of exchange, lending should be without profit. Thomas Aquinas formulated and reinforced this hostility to interest-taking by associating the word of Aristotle to the explicit text from Scriptures. The prohibition entered the canon law and was occasionally enforced by secular courts; in 1179 the Third Lateran Council denied "usurers" access to communion. But Luther was quite as scathing against the Fuggers and their money-lending, Calvin himself took little interest in the question, and Calvinist divines in the commercial Dutch Republic down to the seventeenth century inveighed against usurers with the same aversion, and even the same arguments, that St. Thomas Aquinas had expended upon them four centuries earlier. What made interest-taking finally acceptable was not the Calvinist spirit but the practical necessity of extending credit, the recognition that the lender should be compensated for his risks, the drop in the interest rate, and the rise of dependable and respectable banks.

This much seems clear: the capitalist style was above all urban, cosmopolitan, impatient with traditional constraints. A remarkable early capitalist was Francesco Di Marco Datini, a fourteenth-century merchant from the city of Prato, near Florence, who pyramided a minute inheritance into a vast fortune. Datini made money at anything from which money could be made: spices and wool, slaves and lead, oranges and wine. His ledgers (all of them, with his memoranda and his enormous business correspondence meticulously preserved for posterity) bear the telling motto: "In the name of God and profit." He lived, his modern biographer tells us, in a "small, busy earthy society" and was strangely like a modern capitalist: "In the extent and variety of his ventures, in his powers of organization, in his international outlook, in his swift adaptability to the changes of a society in turmoil, as in his own ambition, shrewdness, tenacity, anxiety, and greed, he is a forerunner of the businessman of today."[6] In the 1360s, in Avignon, he sold arms both to the pope and to his enemies. The Dutch merchants who, in the midst of their desperate struggle for independence, sold goods to Spain, and later, during the Dutch war with England, munitions to the English, were Datini's spiritual offspring.

___

[6] Iris Origo, *The Merchant of Prato, Francesco Di Marco Datini, 1335-1410* (1957), introduction, passim.

This striking freedom from patriotic, religious, and ethical shackles has long given socialists and other critics of capitalism rich material for derision. But these vices were virtues essential to the system. Medieval thought was dominated by ruminations about the just price, by conservative legal and professional institutions, which all stood in the way of the massive accumulation of capital without which capitalism would have been unthinkable. It is therefore anything but surprising that capitalism in recognizable form should first have taken shape in the Italian city-states, and that Italians should have retained a strong grip on trading and banking firms all across Europe for centuries, even after Flemings and Englishmen had risen to compete with them. The Italian cities were schools of cosmopolitans, freer than their counterparts elsewhere from feudal habits; while, by the sixteenth century, their gilds obstructed necessary innovation and healthy competition, the early gilds were machines of economic progress. Italians invented all the techniques that were to mark commercial capitalism, including double-entry bookkeeping, a rationalistic device on which Luca Pacioli published a classic treatise in 1494, soon imitated in other countries. Similarly, the Italians were the first to develop maritime insurance, which spread the risks of expensive trading voyages among large numbers of investors, and the first, or at least the most active, in transforming themselves from money-lenders into commercial bankers—organizers of usury. The bankers from Milan became proverbial; it is a reminiscence of these early itinerant Italians from Lombardy that the financial district in London should be centered in Lombard Street. Flanders, the second center of capitalist enterprise, was crowded with, and dominated by, representatives of Florentine, Genoese, and Venetian firms. As rapidly and as aptly as they could, northerners acknowledged Italian superiority and copied Italian techniques for their own profit: when the Augsburg banking house of Fugger wanted to expand its operations, it sent one of its family to Venice to live there and study the Italian methods. And the Italians also excelled in manufacture: Florence in particular was preeminent in the weaving and finishing of cloth.

Capitalism, of course, was not simply a matter of the "capitalist spirit." It was a conjunction of mentality with opportunity. The Italian cities, notably Venice, profited enormously from the commercial stimulation the Crusaders had given them on their way to and from the Holy Land; and the Italian republics were splendidly situated to participate in the Mediterranean grain trade and the trade in luxury goods with the Orient. Flanders, which came to rival Italy in the fifteenth century, followed the Italian lead: its commercial cities served as entrepots, transhipping grain and lumber from the Baltic and spices and textiles from the Mediterranean. And, also on the Italian model, the Flemish cities developed their own cloth industries.

While it is of the essence of capitalism that private traders and private manufacturers enter the market for the sake of private gain, competition among capitalists was not confined to rivalry among individuals or houses. In order to raise capital for large-scale ventures and to secure protection for representatives abroad, capitalists often leagued together. Competition then simply reappeared on a larger and more vicious scale, among cities or regions. The history of the Hanseatic League is a vivid instance of this sort of collective capitalism. Formed in the fourteenth century by an association of German merchants from trading cities like Hamburg, Leipzig, Bremen, Danzig, Stettin, and Lübeck, it achieved official standing as a league in 1370 and henceforth acted as a political and military entity, flying its own flag and concluding its own treaties. The Hanse established "factories," settlements in foreign cities which served as protected enclaves where Hanse merchants settled or visited and lived by their own regulations. In the fifteenth and sixteenth centuries the Hanse was a powerful force, dominating trade in the Baltic region, and spreading its factories from the Norwegian town of Bergen to the Russian town of Novgorod, participating in the Netherlands trade with its factory in Bruges and the English trade with its factory, the "Steelyard," in London. Then, with the rise of the political power of the English and the Dutch, the Hanse found formidable and in the long run fatal rivals. The Dutch, with their incomparable ships, began to interfere with the Hanse monopoly in the Baltic Sea; Dutch fishermen began to outstrip their Hanseatic competitors; the English, in search of independence, established their own small Hanse, the Merchant Adventurers. In 1611, this English association set up its factory at Hamburg, a sign that the great days of the Hanse were over.

The drastic decline of the Hanse, however, was not merely the consequence of economic warfare among rival traders; it was symptomatic of a more general and more fundamental shift in the patterns of trade and centers of economic power that took place in the late sixteenth century. Much went into that shift: the fortunes of war, the recovery of population, and above all the belated effects of the expeditions of Columbus, Vasco da Gama, and Magellan. The discoveries made their economic impact slowly, but when it came, it was stunning.

Commerce and Prices: Two Revolutions

Historians are coming to be as embarrassed with the word "revolution" as they have long been with the word "capitalism," and with justice. Surely the French Revolution and the Russian Revolution, with their explosive speed, bloody action, and drastic and permanent overturn of authority, are authentic specimens; to call the enlargement of trade and the inflation of the early modern period "revolutions," as historians have normally done, is to lend an aura of rapidity and violence to developments that were slow, devious, and so complicated that their contemporaries often could hardly describe them. Yet the changes in commerce and prices were so vast and so irreversible that we may perhaps, if we are duly cautious, speak of the "commercial revolution" and the "price revolution."

By 1600, long-distance trade was an old story. As early as the second half of the thirteenth century, the Polos, a Venetian family, among whom Marco Polo is only the most famous, had reached China on several expeditions, and thereafter the European market had enjoyed highly coveted spices from the East. Later, toward the end of the fifteenth century, Portuguese explorers sought and found a direct route to India by sea, around the Cape of Good Hope, and the Spaniards explored America, bringing back its sugar, tobacco, and silver (see p. 84).

Yet the obvious did not happen, certainly not immediately and not simply. Portuguese and Spanish ports—Lisbon and Seville above all—were the direct beneficiaries of the empires their governments were establishing in India and in Central and South America. For a few heady decades, Lisbon became the dominant port for the Oriental spice trade—pepper, cinnamon, nutmeg—and Seville the receiving center for bullion from the seemingly inexhaustible American mines. But the pouring in of unknown commodities or of unprecedented quantities of precious metals was beyond the capacity of the Portuguese and Spanish governments to cope with. The commercial potential uncovered by the voyages seemed more frightening than exhilarating. In any event, the Spanish and Portuguese way of managing them—royal protection and close state supervision—turned out to be unfortunate. With the rise of the early modern state, simultaneous and associated with the age of discovery and commercial revolution, every government took a consuming interest in economic affairs.[7] But the Iberian governments depended on control almost entirely, at the expense of private investment and commercial independence. The Portuguese monarchy granted some monopoly rights to favored individuals, but kept monopolies over bullion and over the most desirable of commodities, the spice imports; and it owned, or tightly controlled, Portuguese merchant fleets. The Spanish government, far from avoiding Portugal's mistakes, simply repeated them: it organized commerce under royal officials, arbitrarily granted away monopolies, and engaged in trade directly. The short-run consequence was the rapid amassing of wealth; the long-range consequence, the conquest of trade by more flexible nations.

The inability of Portugal and Spain to convert their discoveries and their conquests into lasting economic advantage supports the dictum of the English historian, Charles Wilson, that it was "not merely coincidence" that trade after 1500 should flourish above all in the northern Italian and in the Flemish cities. These were "areas where the tradesmen of the cities had been most successful in emancipating themselves from feudal interference and in keeping at bay the newer threat of more centralized political control offered by the new monarchies," and where men "glimpsed the material advance that was possible when tradesmen were left in peace unflattered by the attentions of strategists who regarded their activities as sinews of war."[8] The Italian cities, therefore, never

---

[7] For a discussion of mercantilism, see p. 300.
[8] Wilson, "Trade, Society, and the State," 492.

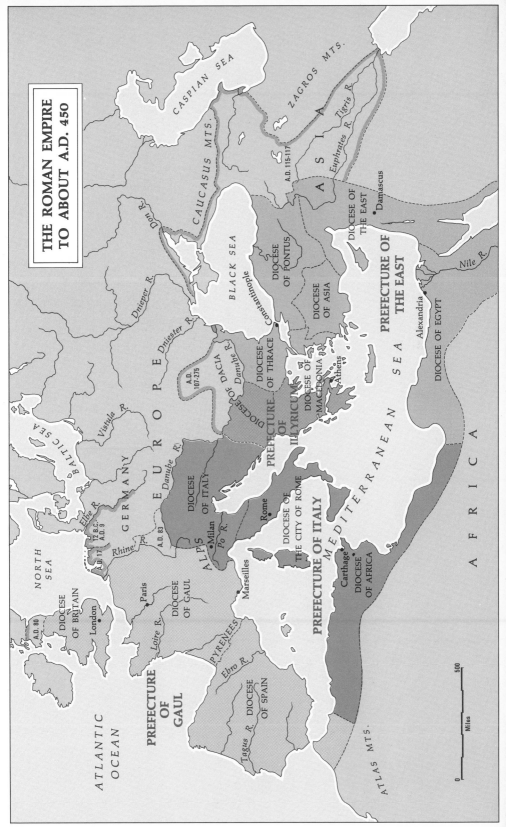

**THE ROMAN EMPIRE
TO ABOUT A.D. 450**

ATLANTIC
OCEAN

NORTH
SEA

A.D. 80

DIOCESE
OF BRITAIN

London

BALTIC SEA

Elbe R.

Vistula R.

GERMANY

E U R O P E

Rhine R.

A.D. 83

A.D. 17
T.B.C.
A.D. 9

Dnieper R.

Dniester R.

A.D. 107-275

DIOCESE OF DACIA

Danube R.

Danube R.

ALPS

DIOCESE
OF ITALY

Milan

Po R.

Rome

Paris

Loire R.

DIOCESE
OF GAUL

Marseilles

**PREFECTURE
OF GAUL**

PYRENEES

Ebro R.

DIOCESE
OF SPAIN

Tagus R.

CASPIAN SEA

CAUCASUS MTS.

Don R.

BLACK SEA

Constantinople

DIOCESE
OF PONTUS

ZAGROS MTS.

A.D. 115-117

Tigris R.

Euphrates R.

A S I A

DIOCESE OF
THE EAST

Damascus

DIOCESE
OF ASIA

DIOCESE OF THRACE

**PREFECTURE
OF
ILLYRICUM**

DIOCESE OF
MACEDONIA

Athens

DIOCESE OF
THE CITY OF ROME

PREFECTURE OF ITALY

Carthage

DIOCESE
OF AFRICA

M E D I T E R R A N E A N   S E A

**PREFECTURE OF
THE EAST**

Nile R.

Alexandria

DIOCESE OF EGYPT

A F R I C A

ATLAS MTS.

0   500

Miles

Plate 1

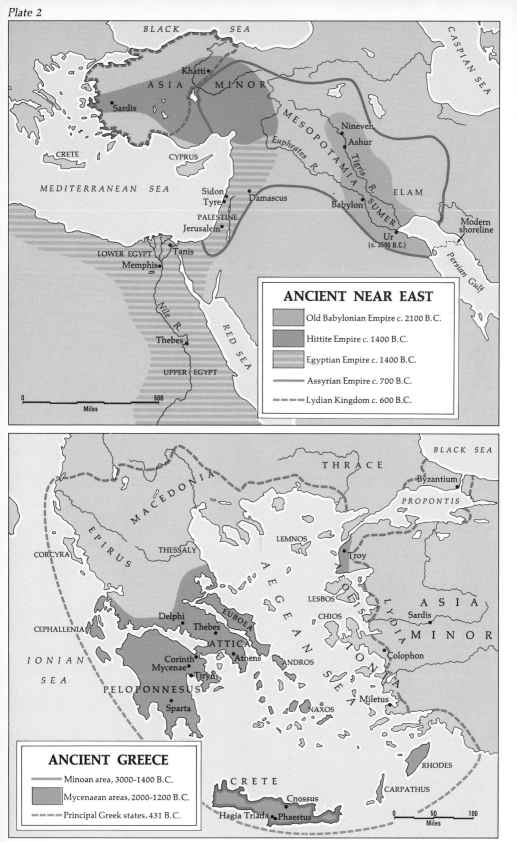

Plate 2

ANCIENT NEAR EAST

Old Babylonian Empire c. 2100 B.C.
Hittite Empire c. 1400 B.C.
Egyptian Empire c. 1400 B.C.
Assyrian Empire c. 700 B.C.
Lydian Kingdom c. 600 B.C.

ANCIENT GREECE

Minoan area, 3000–1400 B.C.
Mycenaean areas, 2000–1200 B.C.
Principal Greek states, 431 B.C.

Plate 3

Ancient Near East

Sumer. The first Mesopotamian civilizations emerged at Sumer c. 4000 B.C. City-states developed theocracies with a rich culture and ceremonial religion; writing appeared c. 3000. Akkadians from north of Sumer led by Sargon I conquered Sumer c. 2300. His dynasty, which lasted until 2150 when the Sumerians regained independence, was followed by a succession of kings who ruled until c. 2000 when Elamite invaders captured the capital, Ur.

Assyria. In the third millennium the city of Ashur was ruled by Sumer and shared its culture. As Sumer waned, Assyria rose and in 1380 Ashur-uballit I became the first great king of Assyria. Under a series of aggressive rulers, Assyria conquered most of Mesopotamia and dominated it until defeated in 612.

Babylonia. Rival to Assyria and Sumer, Babylonia developed an independent theocracy c. 2000. While the Gilgamesh epic reveals a despairing religion, materially Babylonia's centralized irrigation system made it the breadbasket of Mesopotamia. In the 1700s Hammurabi, Babylon's great lawgiver, took Sumer and Akkad, but c. 1000 Babylon was overrun by Bedouins and declined. After subjection to Assyria, Babylon joined Persia to destroy Assyria in 612 but in 538 fell to the Persians.

Egypt. About 3000 B.C. King Menes of Upper Egypt conquered the delta kingdom of Lower Egypt and founded an empire that lasted to 332 B.C., though the Hyksos invaded and held Egypt briefly from c. 1700 to 1570. The pharaohs consolidated their power under Amenhotep III (c. 1411) and extended their empire around the Mediterranean. Later, Egypt was defeated by the Hittites and lost its Syrian cities. Rameses II (1299–1232) tried to win back the cities and hold the Hittites off by signing a treaty of friendship with them. After his death invaders appeared; wars with Libya, Canaan, and raiders from Asia Minor sapped Egypt's strength. From c. 1100 the country declined further as weak kings poured wealth into sterile religious ceremonials and neglected the needs of the state.

Ancient Greece

Crete. The island was occupied in 4000 B.C. and by 2000 developed a rich civilization sustained by Mediterranean trade. Farmers, artisans, and traders were prominent in Crete's economy while at Cnossus, Phaestus, and Hagia Triada the architecture of the palaces suggest a relatively egalitarian society. This brilliant Minoan civilization came to an end when sea raiders destroyed Cnossus and Phaestus in 1400.

Mycenae. On the mainland c. 2000 B.C., Greek-speaking invaders began to establish settlements, of which Mycenae was the most prominent. In the 1600s they traded extensively across the Mediterranean and built impressive palaces at Mycenae. Mycenean civilization lasted until the city fell to the Dorians in 1200. Four centuries of barbarism followed, yet later Greeks regarded the Myceneans as their ancestors.

Greece. In the 700s Greek life began to develop as trading increased and the city-states evolved more organized forms of government. Contacts with Asia Minor introduced writing, new religions, and new forms of art. Sparta and Athens emerged as the most powerful Greek states and bore the brunt of the Persian War. After the Greek victory at Plataea in 479, Athens led the other states, except Sparta, into a permanent defensive alliance. When, in 468 several states tried to withdraw from it, Athens attacked and made vassals of its former allies. At its height, the Athenian empire extended over 200 cities. By 450 Pericles presided over Athens' greatest development, following twin policies of imperialism and peace, but by 431 Athens and Sparta were at war. This Peloponnesian War lasted until 404 ending in the total defeat of Athens. The city never regained its political and cultural supremacy.

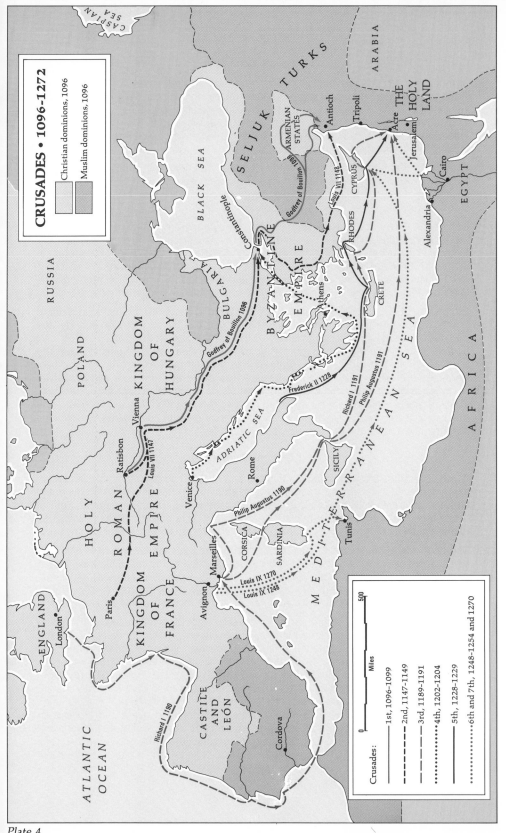

Plate 4

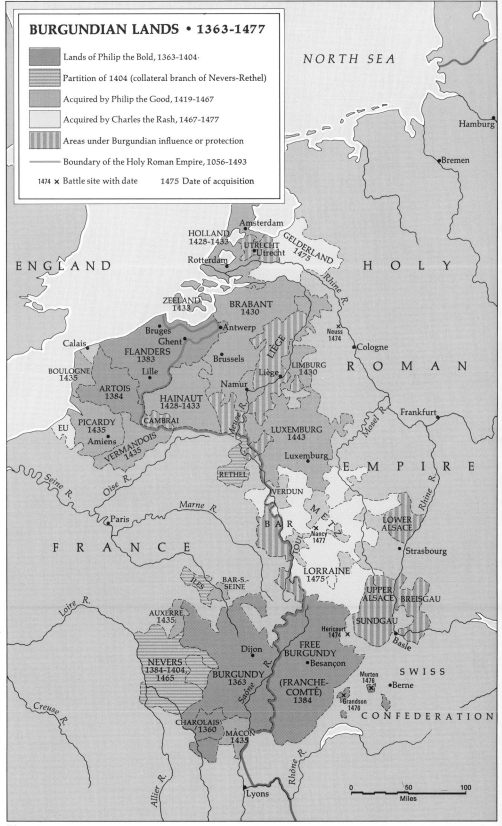

BURGUNDIAN LANDS • 1363-1477

Lands of Philip the Bold, 1363-1404·

Partition of 1404 (collateral branch of Nevers-Rethel)

Acquired by Philip the Good, 1419-1467

Acquired by Charles the Rash, 1467-1477

Areas under Burgundian influence or protection

Boundary of the Holy Roman Empire, 1056-1493

1474 ✕ Battle site with date   1475 Date of acquisition

NORTH SEA

Hamburg

Bremen

ENGLAND

HOLY

Amsterdam

HOLLAND
1428-1433

GELDERLAND
1475

UTRECHT
Utrecht

Rotterdam

Rhine R.

ZEELAND
1433

BRABANT
1430

Antwerp

Bruges

Ghent

Calais

FLANDERS
1383

Brussels

LIÈGE

Neuss
1474

Cologne

ROMAN

BOULOGNE
1435

Lille

Liège

LIMBURG
1430

ARTOIS
1384

Namur

HAINAUT
1428-1433

EU

PICARDY
1435

CAMBRAI

LUXEMBURG
1443

Frankfurt

Amiens

VERMANDOIS
1435

Meuse R.

RETHEL

EMPIRE

Mosel R.

Luxemburg

Seine R.

Oise R.

VERDUN

Marne R.

Paris

BAR

METZ

TOUL

Nancy
1477

LOWER
ALSACE

Rhine R.

FRANCE

Strasbourg

LORRAINE
1475

BAR-S.-
SEINE

ILES

UPPER
ALSACE BREISGAU

Loire R.

AUXERRE
1435

SUNDGAU

Hericourt
1474 ✕

Basle

Dijon

FREE
BURGUNDY

Besançon

SWISS

Creuse R.

NEVERS
1384-1404,
1465

BURGUNDY
1363

Saône R.

(FRANCHE-
COMTÉ)
1384

Murten
1476

Berne

Grandson
1476

CONFEDERATION

CHAROLAIS
1360

MÂCON
1435

Allier R.

Rhône R.

Lyons

0   50   100
Miles

Plate 7

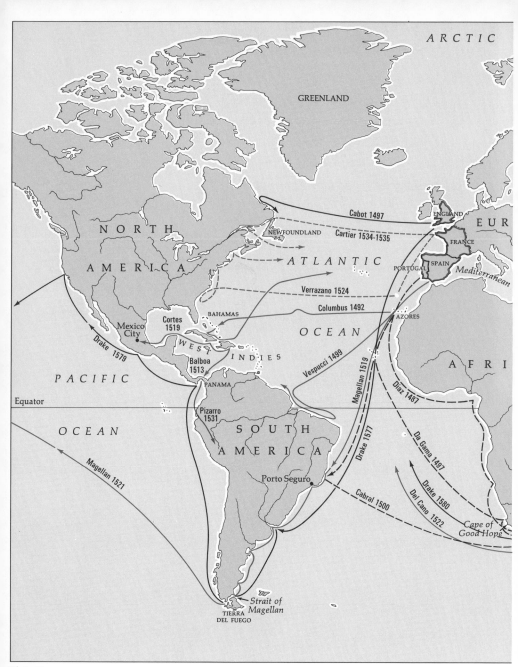

Plate 8

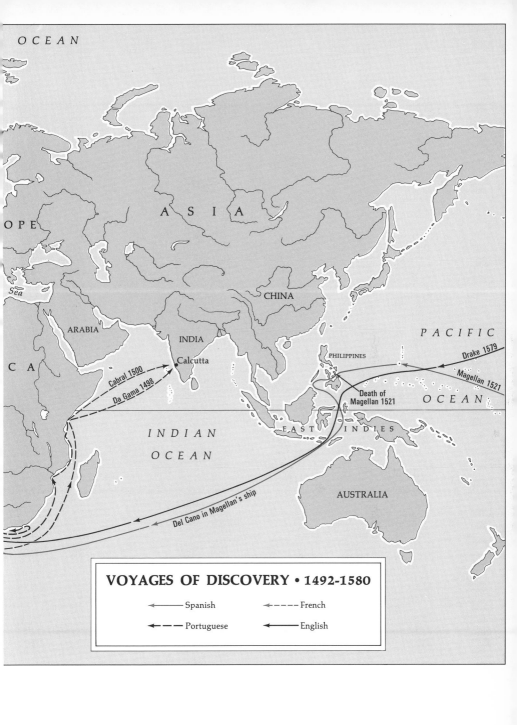

OCEAN

ASIA

OPE

Sea

ARABIA

CA

INDIA

Calcutta

CHINA

PHILIPPINES

PACIFIC

Drake 1579

Magellan 1521

Cabral 1500

Da Gama 1498

Death of
Magellan 1521

OCEAN

INDIAN

OCEAN

EAST INDIES

Del Cano in Magellan's ship

AUSTRALIA

VOYAGES OF DISCOVERY • 1492-1580

Spanish   French

Portuguese   English

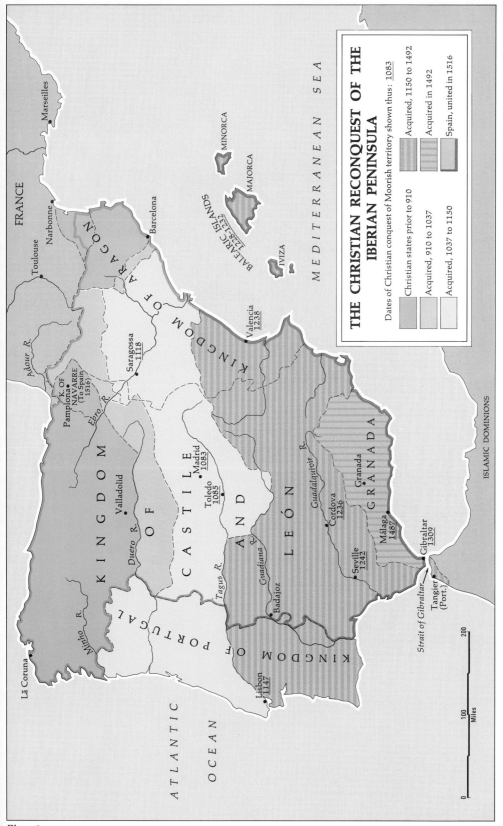

THE CHRISTIAN RECONQUEST OF THE IBERIAN PENINSULA

Dates of Christian conquest of Moorish territory shown thus: 1083

Christian states prior to 910
Acquired, 910 to 1037
Acquired, 1037 to 1150
Acquired, 1150 to 1492
Acquired in 1492
Spain, united in 1516

FRANCE

Marseilles
Toulouse
Narbonne
Adour R.

KINGDOM OF ARAGON
Barcelona

K. OF NAVARRE
Pamplona
K. OF NAVARRE (To Spain, 1516)
Ebro R.
Saragossa 1118

MINORCA
MAJORCA
BALEARIC ISLANDS 1229-1232
IVIZA

MEDITERRANEAN SEA

Valencia 1238

KINGDOM OF CASTILE AND LEÓN

Valladolid
Duero R.
Madrid 1083
Toledo 1085
Tagus R.
Guadiana R.
Badajoz

KINGDOM OF PORTUGAL

Minho R.
La Coruña

Guadalquivir R.
Cordova 1236
Seville 1242
Granada
GRANADA
Málaga 1487
Gibraltar 1309
Strait of Gibraltar
Tangier (Port.)

ISLAMIC DOMINIONS

Lisbon 1147

ATLANTIC OCEAN

0   100   200
Miles

Plate 9

Plate 10

In the 1400s Russia was changed by strong rulers from a land of independent princes into a powerful central monarchy. Ivan the Great (1462–1505) began the process by victories over foreign powers and by subordinating other Russian princes; he annexed Novgorod, Tver, and most of Ryazin. In 1480 he repulsed a Tartar advance on Moscow and established an armed truce and partial alliance with them. His marriage to Sophia in 1472 brought Byzantine manners to Russia. Ivan established a formal court, emphasizing his position as a monarch above his nobles. To show his supremacy, Ivan adopted the titles Tsar and Sovereign of All Russia and stressed his sense of divine mission by referring to his conquests not as new land but as his "patrimony of old," now regained. His son, Vasily (Basil) III (1505–1533) continued the expansion.

On Vasily's death in 1533, his 3-year-old son Ivan IV succeeded. His bloody regime of 50 years (earning him the epithet the Terrible) was marked by a policy of internal subjection: he weakened the power of provincial rulers and checked the noble families who had tried to regain their old strength. Ivan organized a personal arm of government, the *oprichnina,* whose original 1000 members were settled on lands taken by Ivan from their hereditary owners. With the conquest of Kazan and Astrakhan, Ivan pushed his borders further south and east, beyond the Volga River. He successfully invaded Siberia, but defeats in wars with Poland and Sweden meant the loss of territory and important ports in the Baltic.

The expansion of Russia gave the peasants room to move; and as wars, famine, and plague were rife in the 1570s and 1580s, many peasants fled east and south. By the 1580s the lords forced the passage of laws binding the peasant to the land: he became a serf—a chattel unable to move and subject to sale with the estate to which he belonged. When Ivan died in 1584, a series of weak rulers or aspirants with unclear titles brought the old aristocratic families back to power.

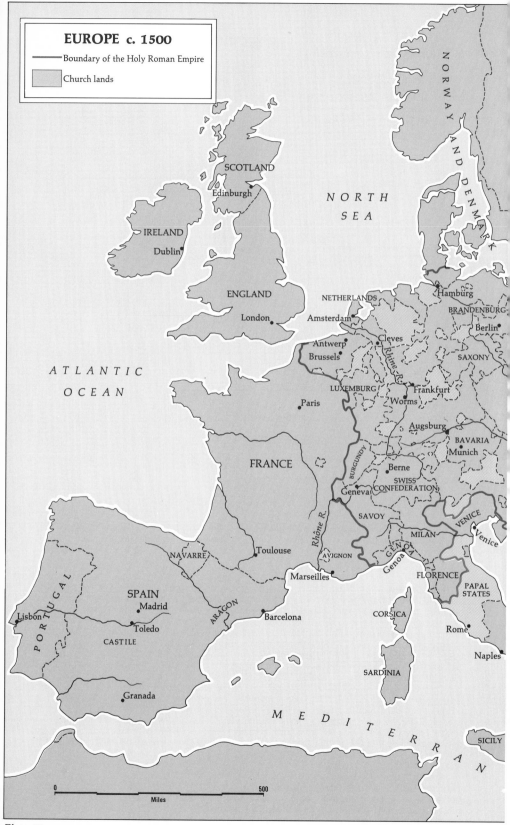

Plate 11

1560

Spanish Hapsburgs

Austrian Hapsburgs

SWEDEN

BALTIC SEA

TEUTONIC ORDER

Danzig

TEUTONIC ORDER

PRUSSIA

LITHUANIA

RUSSIA

POLAND

SILESIA

Prague

BOHEMIA

Cracow

Dnieper R.

Vienna

Buda

AUSTRIA

HUNGARY

MOLDAVIA

CRIMEA

WALLACHIA

BLACK SEA

BOSNIA

O T T O M A N

BULGARIA

NAPLES

Constantinople

E M P I R E

Athens

CYPRUS

CRETE

E A N

S E A

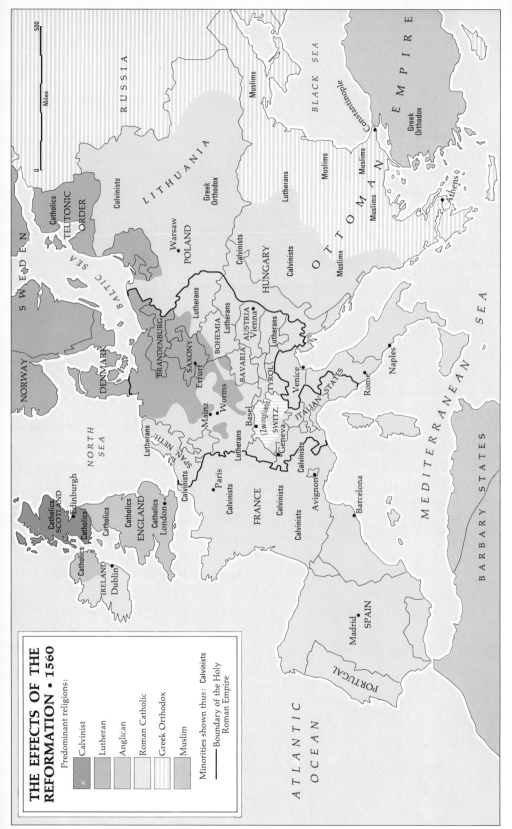

THE EFFECTS OF THE
REFORMATION · 1560

Predominant religions:

Calvinist

Lutheran

Anglican

Roman Catholic

Greek Orthodox

Muslim

Minorities shown thus: Calvinists

—— Boundary of the Holy
Roman Empire

500

Miles

RUSSIA

SWEDEN

NORWAY

TEUTONIC ORDER

Catholics

LITHUANIA

Greek Orthodox

Warsaw
POLAND

Calvinists

HUNGARY

Calvinists

Calvinists

OTTOMAN EMPIRE

Muslims

Muslims

Muslims

Muslims

Muslims

Muslims

Constantinople

Greek Orthodox

Athens

BLACK SEA

BALTIC SEA

DENMARK

BRANDENBURG

Lutherans

SAXONY

Erfurt

BOHEMIA

Lutherans

Lutherans

BAVARIA

AUSTRIA

Vienna

Lutherans

TYROL

Lutherans

Venice

Rome

Naples

ITALIAN STATES

Lutherans

SPAN. NETH.

Lutherans

Mainz

Worms

Basel

(Zwinglians)

SWITZ.

Geneva

Calvinists

Avignon

Barcelona

NORTH SEA

Lutherans

Paris

FRANCE

Calvinists

Calvinists

Calvinists

Calvinists

Calvinists

SCOTLAND

Catholics

Edinburgh

Catholics

Catholics

IRELAND

Dublin

Catholics

ENGLAND

Catholics

London

MEDITERRANEAN SEA

BARBARY STATES

Madrid

SPAIN

PORTUGAL

ATLANTIC OCEAN

Plate 12

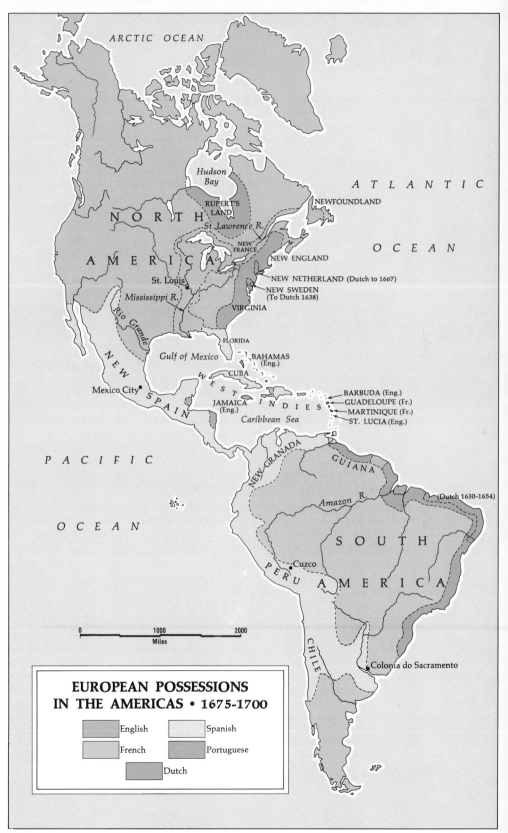

ARCTIC OCEAN

Hudson Bay

RUPERT'S LAND

St. Lawrence R.

NEWFOUNDLAND

ATLANTIC

OCEAN

NORTH

AMERICA

NEW FRANCE

NEW ENGLAND

St. Louis

NEW NETHERLAND (Dutch to 1667)

NEW SWEDEN (To Dutch 1638)

Mississippi R.

VIRGINIA

Rio Grande

FLORIDA

Gulf of Mexico

BAHAMAS (Eng.)

NEW

CUBA

WEST

BARBUDA (Eng.)
GUADELOUPE (Fr.)
MARTINIQUE (Fr.)
ST. LUCIA (Eng.)

Mexico City

SPAIN

JAMAICA (Eng.)

INDIES

Caribbean Sea

PACIFIC

NEW GRANADA

GUIANA

(Dutch 1630-1654)

OCEAN

Amazon R.

SOUTH

PERU

AMERICA

Cuzco

0   1000   2000
Miles

CHILE

Colonia do Sacramento

EUROPEAN POSSESSIONS IN THE AMERICAS • 1675–1700

	English		Spanish
	French		Portuguese
	Dutch		

Plate 13

NETHERLANDS • 1555-1609

Union of Arras, 1579

Lands under Spanish control, 1607

United Provinces, formed 1581

Approximate linguistic boundary

NORTH SEA

Leeuwarden
GRONINGEN
FRIESLAND
DRENTHE
ZUIDER ZEE
Amsterdam
OVERYSSEL
Leyden
The Hague
Utrecht
GELDERLAND
HOLLAND
Brill
Rotterdam
ZEELAND
UPPER GELDERLAND
Bruges
Ghent
Scheldt R.
Antwerp
FLANDERS
Lys
Flemish
Walloons
LIÈGE
LIMBURG
Rhine R.
Brussels
Flemish
Walloons
Lille
Liège
BRABANT
Artois
Arras
HAINAUT
CAMBRAI
NAMUR
Somme R.
LUXEMBURG
Luxemburg
FRANCE
Aisne R.
Meuse R.
Moselle R.

0   50   100
Miles

Plate 14

had to fear their Iberian rivals as their gravest threat. The Venetian spice trade, though it dropped briefly early in the sixteenth century, revived later. Plainly the economic decay so evident in Italian life in the seventeenth century, resulted mainly from the ossification of Italian economic institutions, unwise governmental policies, and the ruthless competition offered by areas in the north—England and the Dutch Republic—that had once been so dependent on their Mediterranean teacher.

The decline of Italian manufacturing, shipping, and trade was only one consequence of the commercial revolution. That revolution changed the face of Europe. Along with political power, economic power gradually but decisively shifted northward. As the volume of trade grew, commodities that had been rare became common, and new commodities, hitherto wholly unknown, changed habits of consumption. By the middle of the seventeenth century, thousands of Europeans were drinking tea and coffee and smoking tobacco. Other exotic items, like china, remained luxuries, while such strange new products as quinine and opium gave European physicians new opportunities for experimenting with their patients. A new world, quite literally, had opened for European culture, supplying it with materials for unheard-of profits, new myths, and troublesome reflections—what *was* one to make of a highly civilized country like China which was obviously living so well without the blessings of Christianity?

One unmistakable characteristic of the commercial revolution, there for all to see, was the rise of large cities. While in 1500, only four European cities—Paris, Milan, Venice, and Naples—had over one hundred thousand inhabitants, by 1600, the number had risen to twelve and had come to include, in addition, Palermo and Messina, Lisbon and Seville, Rome and London, Antwerp and Amsterdam. Smaller cities like Florence and Hamburg and Danzig were not far behind.[9] This urbanization both followed and caused new manufactures and larger consumption, radical ideas and social problems. The city, a microcosm of the economic changes then overtaking Europe, was proof of the mixed quality of "progress": life in the city was more colorful, but also shorter; men were as open to new notions there as they were vulnerable to the plague.

The other economic upheaval of the time, the price revolution, was inextricably tied to the growth of European commerce. With our present state of historical information, it remains, despite diligent research, hard to assess the significance of the inflation that engulfed Europe in the sixteenth century, especially from the 1560s on. We still know too little about real wage rates; prices rose differently in different areas and for different commodities. This much we may say with confidence: the inflation Europe had been experiencing since the late fifteenth century was greatly intensified as precious metals, first gold and then silver, began to pour into Europe after the conquests of Mexico and Peru. While there was widespread puzzlement over the phenomenon,

---

[9] See maps in *The New Cambridge Modern History,* vol. III (1968), 35. Paris and Naples actually had over two hundred thousand inhabitants.

some writers acutely diagnosed it on the spot. In the late 1560s, Jean Bodin (see p. 179) attributed inflation to several minor causes but chiefly to the influx of precious metals from overseas. And it *was* an overwhelming experience. In Spain, the first recipient of the metals, prices trebled in a century; in France and England they more than doubled. Nor do these figures tell the whole story: the price of grain was far more subject to inflation than that of other commodities. By around 1600, wholesale grain prices (a sensitive indicator for the price of food) were roughly five times what they had been a century before, while in France in the same period they had increased about seven times.

Spain, to be sure, had not intended to produce this effect. Officially, the gold and silver received at Seville were to stay in the country in obedience to the generally accepted notion that the possession of precious metals was equivalent to the possession of wealth. But, while prohibiting the export of bullion, the Spanish government made its export unavoidable. There was smuggling, which the Spaniards did little to prevent. Worse than that, there was Spain's unfavorable balance of trade: while the country exported salt and oil, it needed large infusions of wheat and cloth, for consumption both at home and in Spanish America. All this had to be paid for mainly in silver. Worst of all, Spain insisted on its ruinously expensive foreign policy, which meant the shipment of bullion, mainly to Antwerp, to pay for troops and war supplies. Thus gold and silver spread, became commodities for speculators, and fed manufacturing and trade alike.

Bodin's explanation for the impressive inflation of his day has much plausibility, but it does not seem to be the whole truth. The rapid rise or, rather, recovery of population also played its part. Precise population estimates are impossible in the absence of reliable statistics, but the fairly well-documented growth of towns in this period is only one of several strong indications of a remarkable rise: by no means all the new city dwellers were migrants from the land. Population increase (like so much else in social history) was both a blessing and a curse: it showed that the plague was receding and health improving; it gave the prosperous farmer the manpower he needed, and the merchant new customers. But increased population also exercised pressure on scarce food resources, which did not grow as rapidly as the number of people, and helped to depress wages, which did not rise as rapidly as did prices. The result was that peasants found themselves subdividing land among their children, laborers found themselves working longer hours for less real income, and all the poor (which is to say, the bulk of Europe's population) found themselves closer to sheer hunger through the rise in food prices. Thus the pressure of population—that is, increased demand—is likely to have been an element in the great inflation of the sixteenth century.

The consequences of these far-reaching and fundamental economic changes are as hard to assess as their causes; they remain the subject of intense investigation and vociferous controversy. The continuing debate among English historians over the rise (or decline) of the English gentry in the seventeenth century should warn us against rash generalizations. This much we can say: those, like much of the French lower nobility, whose income was in fixed rents, found their income cut in half and were compelled, for the most part, to seek employment in the army or at court. Those landlords who could force their tenants off the land and farm it with servile labor, profited from the inflation; so did most merchants, whose investments in goods and equipment rose with rising prices, and who could hedge against losses by diversifying their activities and speculating in economic fluctuations. Normally, especially where governments were too feeble to repress the exploiters, the real sufferers were the peasants; especially in eastern Europe, the growing distance between lord and serf, and the increasing dependency of the serf, dates from these years (see p. 259). But everywhere, the revolution in economic affairs brought increased social mobility, with some rising and many falling in the scale. And the poor on the whole got poorer; even the skilled laborers discovered that their wages rose more slowly than prices—there were many self-respecting journeymen in those years who fed the endemic revolutionary mood with their discontent. Hardship and misery were general. The West has never been free of them, but the late sixteenth century, it seems, was a time conspicuous for beggars. In the midst of wealth and luxury, thousands starved, millions hungered.

Two Commercial Giants: Antwerp and Amsterdam

The expansion and shifting fortunes of the European economy in the sixteenth century are lucidly reflected in the history of two of its leading commercial cities, Antwerp and Amsterdam.[10] The spectacle of Brabant's chief city, Antwerp, aroused the admiration, almost the awe, of visitors. In the 1560s, the Florentine traveler Ludovico Guicciardini noted: "Many goodly buildings there are in Andwerp, as well private as publike, but the publike especiallie are very sumptuous," including "the Butchery, the Waighhouse, the English house," as well as the "newe lodging for the discharging of marchandise that commeth to the towne by land," yet all of these, and others, are "farre surmounted by the townhouse, the building whereof cost almost 100,000 crowns." Antwerp, he added, "is marvelouslie wel furnished both out of their own countrey and out of forren countreyes, of all kinde of victuals and dainties, both for the necessary use of man, and also for wantonnesse."[11] Active in banking, manufacture, and trade, Antwerp was supreme in northern commerce, the center through which activity flowed both north and south. Bruges, in Flanders, had been the first commercial city in the Netherlands in the fifteenth century, only to be overtaken, early in the sixteenth century, by Antwerp. A fine harbor (equipped,

[10] We are indebted, for the former, to S. T. Bindoff, "The Greatness of Antwerp," in *The New Cambridge Modern History*, vol. II (1958), 50–69; for the latter, to Violet Barbour, *Capitalism in Amsterdam in the 17th Century* (1950).

[11] Lodovico Guicciardini, *The Description of the Low Countryes and of the Provinces thereof, gathered into an Epitome out of the Historie of L. G.* (1593), 26r, 26v.

Guicciardini wrote, with "eight principall chanels within the towne,"[12] the biggest of which could accommodate a hundred ships) and a sensibly liberal policy toward merchants and bankers gave the city a splendid position for rapid growth. Perhaps the chief single impulse for its rise came with the decision of the Portuguese crown to make Antwerp its spice staple. In 1499, the royal factor, the official representative of the king, settled in Antwerp, and two years later the first shipment of goods, including precious pepper, reached the city from Lisbon. By 1504, Antwerp was receiving Portuguese consignments regularly, in increasing number and volume. In return, Antwerp supplied the royal factor with commodities that Portugal needed, notably metal goods and cloth. Even before the Portuguese had favored Antwerp with their business, traders from other nations, mainly England and southern Germany, had established themselves in Antwerp to enliven the scene and enrich the city. In its far-flung international markets, Antwerp traded in an impressive range of commodities: cloth from England and Italy and Germany, wines from Germany and France and Spain, spices from Portugal, salt from France, wheat from the Baltic. The city was more than an entrepot. With its sizable and growing population, it was a large-scale customer for food, textiles, and luxury goods. With its skilled labor force, it was a significant center for the processing of raw materials: the making of soap, the curing of fish, the refining of sugar, and above all, the finishing of cloth were flourishing local industries. Banking— including the extending of large loans to the Netherlands government—and speculation flourished side by side with the carrying trade and the processing industry.

Appropriately enough for a capitalist center, Antwerp was a cosmopolitan city. While domestic traders and manufacturers kept a hand in all profitable affairs, German and Italian financiers, Portuguese and English merchants, visited or settled there, encouraged by Antwerp's marked and unusual hospitality toward foreigners. When the great Antwerp bourse was founded in 1531, an inscription proudly proclaimed it to be open "to the merchants of all nations."[13]

But decline came, far more precipitously than anyone might have guessed. The Portuguese factor, as though sensing trouble, left the city in 1549, and the spice trade took other routes; the English cloth industry sought independence from its continental entrepot. Beginning in 1557, a series of bankruptcies—of Spain and France, and then of Portugal—were so many blows against the financial houses of the city. The disasters that were to strike the city during the revolt of the Netherlands (see p. 196) only confirmed and hastened the decline that had begun in the 1550s. Antwerp did not collapse, but it abdicated its part as master of northern commerce.

---

[12] Ibid., 22r.
[13] Henri Sée, *Modern Capitalism: Its Origin and Evolution* (tr. 1928), 30.

By the turn of the century, Amsterdam had inherited the glory of Antwerp, and its profits. The exclamations of mingled astonishment and envy that foreign visitors had expended on the one they now expended on the other. In 1601 an English visitor characterized Amsterdam as one of the "new upstarte townes in Holland,"[14] and it is true that while Amsterdam had long been a trading town, its rise to a position of European dominance came swiftly, in the course and partly by the agency of the rebellion against Spain. All the institutions that mark a great commercial center came into being within a few years: a "chamber of assurance" which regulated marine insurance policies in 1598; the East India Company in 1602; the bourse—designed, of course, in the Italian style—in 1608; an exchange bank in 1609; a lending bank in 1614. By that year, or a little later, Amsterdam joined the handful of European cities with over one hundred thousand inhabitants; it had more than trebled its population in the course of fifty years. With its bustling traffic, its aura of steady activity, and its network of canals, Amsterdam reminded everyone of Venice; it was an epithet of praise.

Much like Antwerp before it, Amsterdam's greatness sprang from its versatility. It was an impressive center of shipping, harboring large numbers of vessels of all nations and supplying ships to all with its burgeoning ship-building industry. It was an equally impressive center of trade, superintending an unceasing flow of merchandise of all kinds; the city's merchants and (which was much the same thing) the city's government did their best to make Amsterdam into the inescapable marketplace of northern Europe: its warehouses, its wholesale dealers, its insurance agents, its brokerage houses, its official lists of prices were proverbial for efficiency and reliability. In addition, Amsterdam grew into the industrial capital of the Dutch Republic; trade brought capital for local investment, and imported raw materials gave opportunities to processing industries. Thus, like Antwerp, Amsterdam developed plants for finishing silk, leather, wool, sugar, wood, tobacco, metal. Amsterdam's printing presses, gun foundries, and lens grinders had customers across the Western world. Finally, and not surprisingly in view of all this intense activity, Amsterdam became a financial capital. Its banks were the depositories, and the causes, of immense wealth; its bourses the centers of large-scale, often anxious speculation. The fortunes of war, or of a trading expedition, were reflected on the faces of the traders milling about its stock exchanges.

Inevitably, most of these activities made themselves felt all across Europe. The exchange bank of Amsterdam was, for many decades, a model for all other banks; none could duplicate the cool rationality of its operations and its exemplary trustworthiness; princes and merchant princes alike deposited their fortunes in it. Moreover, its dependable coins and credit operations helped to simplify and stabilize the money markets of commercial cities everywhere. Similarly, Amsterdam merchants and financiers took dominant roles in the

[14] Quoted in Barbour, *Capitalism in Amsterdam*, 17n.

economic ventures that made the Dutch Republic rich and formidable. When in 1602 a number of Dutch merchants founded the United East India Company, more than half its starting capital of 6.5 million florins came from Amsterdam. The importance of that company, and with it of Amsterdam, for enlarging and maintaining Dutch prosperity and power can hardly be overestimated.

From its formation on, the East India Company, founded just two years after its English counterpart, was partly public and partly private, at once an engine for economic and for military operations. It organized the exploits of armed Dutch merchants in areas that had traditionally "belonged" to the Portuguese, especially India and the Spice Islands in the East Indies. It insinuated itself into the confidence of local potentates, destroyed the old Portuguese monopoly and set up its own. Whenever necessary, it reinforced economic pressure with military force, capturing Portuguese trading posts, founding fortified cities, massacring people suspected of favoring the "enemy," building an empire—at the expense, of course, of the local populations, whom the Dutch treated with unrelieved contempt and cruelty. The avidity for total monopoly even brought into conflict in the East powers that were at peace in Europe: while the Dutch government for political reasons explicitly forbade the East India Company to use force against English settlers and traders in the Spice Islands, the Dutch commanders on the spot resented and defied these orders. In 1623, officials of the company came to suspect that English settlers on the island of Amboyna were planning "treason" against them. They confirmed their suspicions, mainly by torturing the suspects, and then executed ten English traders and, with them, ten Japanese soldiers presumably implicated in the affair. There is no evidence that the "massacre of Amboyna" troubled any consciences back home. The Amsterdammers who invested in the company, lent it money, and solicitously watched over its profits, cared little about Asiatics or even about Englishmen.

The Amsterdam merchant who emerges from this brief portrait is much like other merchants, only more intensely so: a trading animal, calculating, greedy, tight-fisted, and implacable. If the Weber thesis has any validity, it might be demonstrated here: "Their common Riches," said Sir William Temple of the seventeenth-century Dutch, "lye in every Man's having more than he spends; or, to say it properly, In every Man's spending less than he has coming in, be that what it will." [15] Such a man, ready to furnish munitions to all sides, ready to forego immediate for the sake of remote pleasure, ready to forget all teachings of religion if profit is at stake, was, in Violet Barbour's words, an "international capitalist," and "where business was concerned, a Man without a Country." The "seventeenth-century Amsterdammer, though by no means a man without a city, was strikingly uninhibited by abstract considerations of patriotism or by theories of economic nationalism." [16]

---

[15] Ibid., 29.
[16] Ibid., 130.

But there is another, more positive way of expressing the same thing: one may call the capitalist a cosmopolitan. And this is of great importance, in the career of Amsterdam as in the career of capitalism in general. Rumors to the contrary, economic behavior is by no means always rational. Over and over again, history shows that traditional ways of conducting business often prevail over demonstrably more profitable new ways, that religious injunctions against profitable activities often act to inhibit them, and that an anxious and hidebound preoccupation with immediate returns and cosy security, as in the gild system, often delays or prevents the kind of innovation that purely economic rationality would call for. It is for this reason that capitalism, which demands contempt for tradition and security above all, has depended to such a great extent on outsiders. For the outsider—the religious pariah, the political refugee, the ambitious climber—has played a central role in capitalism. He has done jobs that were necessary but unpalatable to traditional society—like taking usury—and he has brought much-needed skills to his new home. In Amsterdam, the first to do serious money lending were Lombards, and when the exchange bank was founded in 1609, over half of its biggest depositors were refugees from the southern provinces, now in Spanish hands. Besides this, Jews from Spain and Portugal brought trading skills and financial resources, Walloons and Flemings brought new or improved techniques for the processing industries. None of this would have been to Amsterdam's economic benefit if its leading circles, with all their rigidity and conservatism, has not seen the good sense of tolerance. It was this good sense, after all, that was to move Karl Marx, in the *Communist Manifesto,* to his much-quoted tribute to the capitalist bourgeoisie: "The bourgeoisie . . ." he wrote, "has created enormous cities, has greatly increased the urban population as compared with the rural, and has thus rescued a considerable part of the population from the idiocy of rural life." [17]

Marx's ambiguous tribute suitably complicates matters. To generalize easily about the bourgeoisie, or about merchants, or even about Amsterdam merchants may be a tempting, but it is a perilous, exercise. There were many kinds of Amsterdam merchants, divided by occupation, wealth, and personal predilection. And there is abundant evidence that wealth-getting was by no means their only activity. Certainly by the 1620s and 1630s, when their wealth and their state were relatively secure, they spent a good deal of time and money on culture. When John Evelyn came to Rotterdam in 1641, he observed that Dutchmen bought pictures because they did not have land to invest in, and then sold them "at their Kermas'es to very great gains." But the year before another English visitor, Peter Mundy, was less cynical about the burghers of Amsterdam. "As for the art of painting and the affection of the people for pictures, I think no other goes beyond them, there having been in this country many excellent men in that faculty, some at present, as Rimbrantt, etc., all in

[17] Karl Marx and Friedrich Engels, *Communist Manifesto* (tr. 1964), 9.

general striving to adorn their houses, especially the outer or streetroom, with costly pieces, butchers and bakers not much inferior in their shops, which are fairly set forth; yea, many times blacksmiths, cobblers, etc., will have some picture or other notion, inclination and delight that the natives of this country have to paintings."[18] Inclination and delight—these bourgeois took to art not for investment but for pleasure.

CULTURE: AN AGE OF GOLDEN AGES

If Dutch burghers, and their counterparts elsewhere, bought a great deal of art, there was a great deal of art to buy. The century beginning before 1550 and ending after 1650 was an age that produced giants worthy to stand beside Leonardo da Vinci or Michelangelo, an age of golden ages in literature and art alike. In a rough way, these renaissances coincided with economic and political power. But only in a rough way, for there was also cultural splendor in the midst of decline. Thus, by the 1520s the Italian states had become mere puppets on the stage of European politics, but Italy continued to generate artists and ideas to export for another century and more. Italians originated, or played a leading part in, all the dominant styles that followed upon the High Renaissance. When Bernini, the greatest, most versatile of Baroque artists, came to Paris in 1665 to serve Louis XIV, he found nothing in France he liked, except the paintings of Poussin, who had, of course, lived in Italy; with superb self-assurance he advised French painters to study in Rome before they ruined their style by staying at home.[19] Cultivation may be a substitute for power, as much as its expression.

Mannerism: An International Italian Style

Mannerism, the first of the post-Renaissance styles, was largely an Italian style—but not wholly, for the early Mannerists greatly admired the "primitivism" of Dürer. Born in Rome and Florence around 1520, Mannerism rapidly spread across Italy and then the rest of Europe, where its evolution and convolutions were followed, more or less faithfully.

It is tempting but inaccurate to see Mannerism simply as a reaction against the Renaissance. Actually, the Mannerists worked out the implications of the High Renaissance to their logical (and sometimes their illogical) conclusions.

---

[18] Both quotations from Jakob Rosenberg, Seymour Slive, and E. H. Ter Kuile, *Dutch Art and Architecture, 1600–1800* (1966), 9; modernized.

[19] Howard Hibbard, *Bernini* (1965), 171, and see p. 227. For a definition of Baroque, see p. 225.

The founders of Mannerism in painting—Pontormo, Rosso, and Parmigiani-no—and the leading Mannerist sculptors—Benvenuto Cellini and Giovanni Bologna—took the giants of the High Renaissance not as adversaries to be overcome but as inspirations to be exploited. They emphasized elegance, virtuosity, artificiality, all in the best senses of these now ambiguous words: "mannered" and "artificial" had not yet become pejorative terms. They called attention to their technical facility with sinuous lines, distorted bodies, and crowded, nervous, deliberately unharmonious compositions. They replaced the Renaissance goal of the figure that follows nature, or the figure that purifies nature, by the artist's free vision. [20] Mannerist paintings seem restless; Mannerist buildings, strained: Michelangelo's oddly ungraceful anteroom to the Laurentian Library in Florence or the violent activity in Rosso's *Deposition* reject the serenity of the High Renaissance. Mannerism was a civilized style, and it held the interest of European artists for a long time—El Greco, in many respects a Mannerist, painted his finest canvases in the 1580s and after. But the exaltation of style over content, which makes Mannerism interesting, also made its decline inevitable.

Half a century ago, Mannerism as a distinct style was unknown. Today there is a tendency to describe European art from 1520 to 1590 simply as Mannerist. This excess is as regrettable as the earlier neglect: anti-Mannerist artists continued to flourish, especially in Venice, where painters of genius made their own adaptation of the High Renaissance style. The father of the sixteenth-century Venetian school was Giovanni Bellini, in whom the characteristic Venetian qualities—sensuality, the free disposition of figures on canvas, and an almost self-indulgent love of color—found brilliant expression. His pupils, Titian and Giorgione, brought the Venetian style to perfection. But the love of life in no way excluded deep piety: Bellini chose subjects mainly from the New Testament, and Titian, that long-lived master who died in 1576 (some say at the age of ninety-nine), painted voluptuous Venuses, virile portraits, classical allegories, but also powerful Assumptions of the Virgin and affecting Pietàs. And Titian's tragically short-lived contemporary, Giorgione, who died in 1510 in his early thirties of the plague, painted an altarpiece and a Virgin, along with his dream-like genre scenes. Giorgione is the most mysterious great painter in the history of painting: canvases in many styles have been attributed to him; canvases probably from his hand have been attributed to Titian. The very subject matter of his most famous paintings remains unexplained: his *Fête champêtre* shows four principal figures in a landscape—two young Venetian gallants, elegantly attired and most impolitely inattentive to two young women, one about to play music, the other getting water from a well, and both entirely nude. His *Tempesta* portrays similar detachment: the center of the painting is taken up with a bizarre landscape with unexplained and useless architectural detail; a bolt of lightning strikes in the distance; at the right a young woman,

[20] See Walter Friedlaender, *Mannerism and Anti-Mannerism in Italian Painting* (ed. 1965), 8.

naked, nurses a child, while at the left a young man, dressed, stands rigid, barely looking on. Whatever these pictures mean—and they mean, probably, just themselves, conveying a mood, no more and no less—they have nothing in common with Mannerism. The same was true of architecture: Palladio, the greatest Italian architect of the second half of the cinquecento, who has been called, with justice, "the most imitated architect in history,"[21] built his exemplary villas and churches almost in defiance of the Mannerist activity around him. What made Palladio great and so influential was his ability to learn from ancient Roman architecture and to apply his lessons freely to a new, lucid, beautifully proportioned classicism.

Yet, since Mannerism was dominant, it was against Mannerism that artists explicitly rebelled before 1600. The most imitated of the early Baroque painters, another striking instance of Italy's continuing cultural vitality, was Michelangelo Merisi, called Caravaggio after his native town, the Palladio of painting. Born in 1573, his career was short and violent; it included charges of manslaughter, flights from the police, and feverish creative activity, and ended abruptly in 1610, with his early death from malaria. His choice of religious subjects (Christ at Emmaus and The Conversion of St. Paul) was traditional; his genre paintings, showing a fat, pampered, effeminate youth lolling at his ease as Bacchus, or a young man gulled by a gypsy fortune teller, were new. But whatever his subject, his technique was revolutionary. Caravaggio broke with Mannerist contortions and distortions and rendered his figures in what appeared to be massive realism. But the realism—and this is the real secret of his power—was only apparent. Caravaggio modeled his figures with great ingenuity, gave them emphatic gestures to enhance their emotional impact, and placed them into sharp light contrasted with deep shadows—his famous *tenebroso*. Caravaggio was a master of the technique of chiaroscuro, the play of light and dark in the service of pictorial drama. The impact of his paintings was enormous and unmeasurable: practically all Italian painters of the early Baroque, even those who never met him and responded only to his pictures, became his disciples, and the school of Caravaggisti spread all across Europe. No one, not even Rembrandt, wholly escaped him.

The Elizabethan Renaissance

The diversity of artistic styles that marks the age reflected not merely resistance to, or rebellions against, Mannerism, but also the burgeoning of national styles in the midst of international currents. The Elizabethan Renaissance is a brilliant instance of this emergent cultural independence, and, as well, of the coincidence of culture with power. During the reign of Elizabeth, England acquired unprecedented prominence in international politics, and Englishmen respond-

[21] James S. Ackerman, *Palladio* (1966), 19.

ed with a new self-confidence—some would say, self-satisfaction—that was nurtured by the nation's writers. In ancient Rome, Vergil and Horace had sung the glory of Caesar Augustus; they had helped his reign by praising it. In Elizabethan England, playwrights, historians, and poets sang the glory of the Tudors, the humiliations that doughty English sailors had inflicted on the Spaniards, and the astonishing efflorescence of "civility"; and they too hoped to perpetuate what they praised, by praising it. "Plays are writ with this aim," the dramatist and essayist Thomas Haywood said around 1608, "to teach their subjects obedience to their king, to show the people the untimely ends of such as have moved . . . insurrections, to present them with the flourishing estate of such as live in obedience, exhorting them to allegiance, dehorting them from all traitorous and felonious stratagems."[22] When Haywood wrote these candid words, James I was already on the throne; the momentum that had been gained in Elizabeth's glorious decades, in the 1570s and 1580s, had survived the troubles of her last years and her death in 1603. Petrarch's poems, Palladio's writings and sketches, Castiglione's *Courtier,* were admirable models, but especially in literature, England was developing her own classics, second to none—not even to the Italians.

The giant looming over this literary Renaissance is, of course, William Shakespeare. Indeed, Shakespeare's place in the history of literature, and in our consciousness, is so secure and so exalted that it seems impertinent even to praise him. But it is worth remembering that while he was, in Ben Jonson's words, "for all time," he was also very much of his time, an Elizabethan among Elizabethans. Considering how much we admire, quote, and even read him, it is tantalizing how little we know of his life. He was born in 1564, at Stratford-on-Avon, of prosperous yeoman stock; he seems to have had adequate schooling—adequate surely to read Plutarch, and Hakluyt's *Voyages,* and his other sources, and to write his own plays. The old remark, "The plays of William Shakespeare were written by an actor named William Shakespeare," is certainly apt. Sometime in the mid-1580s he went to London as an actor, and by about 1589 he had begun to write. Judging from his dedications and other scanty evidence, he moved in noble circles and enjoyed distinguished patronage. The theatrical companies in which he was prominent—the Lord Chamberlain's Men in the Globe Theater and later the King's Men in the Blackfriars Theater—were fashionable and profitable ventures. Around 1610, evidently comfortably off, he retired to Stratford, where he died in 1616, already something of a legend.

It is impossible to date his work with precision, but it may be roughly divided into four periods: The first five years of his production, beginning around 1589, were years of apprenticeship, in which he wrote comedies like

---

[22] *An Apology for Actors* (ca. 1608); quoted in L. G. Salingar, "The Elizabethan Literary Renaissance," in Boris Ford, ed., *The Age of Shakespeare,* vol. II of *The Pelican Guide to English Literature* (1956), 65.

The Taming of the Shrew and history chronicles like his trilogy on King Henry VI. Then, from around 1594 to 1600, the time of his sonnets and other poems, he perfected the dramatic genres he had explored earlier: the late 1590s saw such mature comedies as *Twelfth Night* and such historical dramas as *Henry V* and *Julius Caesar*. The third period, dating down to about 1609, established his claim to immortality; it is the period of his incomparable tragedies—*Hamlet, King Lear, Othello, Macbeth, Antony and Cleopatra*—and of those strange dramas, the "dark comedies" *Troilus and Cressida* and *Measure for Measure,* that have strained his interpreters to the utmost. His last plays are distinctly autumnal; Prospero's farewell in *The Tempest* reads like Shakespeare's own valedictory:

> I'll break my staff,
> Bury it certain fathoms in the earth,
> And deeper than did ever plummet sound
> I'll drown my book.

It is perilous to discover Shakespeare's "philosophy" in his plays and vulgar to reduce them to some scheme of thought. They are poems, works of the imagination, in which the personality of the poet disappears behind his creations. The shifting assessments of Shakespeare through three centuries are tributes to the wealth and profundity of his invention. *Hamlet* (1601) is only the most puzzling of his many puzzling creations; it can be read as a revenge tragedy derived from an earlier version by Thomas Kyd; or as a psychological drama of a young man who could not make up his mind; or as a metaphysical exploration of a world unhinged by unnatural crime; or as all of these, and more, together. *Hamlet* was instantly popular, but it is new for each reader or spectator. *King Lear,* probably Shakespeare's most overpowering creation, is quite as multifaceted; while we may trace its sources and explore its world view, as a total poem it remains elusive, awesome, and unique. Yet there are some things we may say with some confidence. Like his fellow writers, Shakespeare borrowed from his contemporaries, expressed current attitudes toward life, and made political propaganda. His chronicle plays are part of a larger literature which includes John Stow's patriotic chronicles of London and of England, and Edmund Spenser's vast allegorical *Faerie Queene,* a modernized version of the Arthurian legend in which Queen Elizabeth I appears transmuted into Queen Gloriana. *Richard III,* one of Shakespeare's earliest plays, echoes the official Tudor version by making Richard into a melodramatic and murderous villain (see p. 107). *Henry V* invidiously contrasts the snobbishness, cowardice, and treachery of foreigners with the geniality, courage, and straightforwardness of Englishmen. Such plays are more than propagandistic exercises; they are memorable because they contain memorable poetry and memorable characters, but they fit perfectly into the Elizabethan scheme, in which the "Tudor myth"[23] and general self-congratulation played a significant part. Moreover,

---

[23] The term is E. M. W. Tillyard's; see his *Shakespeare's History Plays* (ed. 1962), 39–42.

Shakespeare, whatever his private feelings, beautifully articulated fundamental Elizabethan ideas about order: the old medieval vision of a hierarchical universe in which each star and each man obeys and governs according to his proper place had survived into the sixteenth century with few modifications. Hamlet returns to Denmark to find the time "out of joint" and laments, and yet accepts, his obligation "to set it right." A famous speech, which Shakespeare puts into the mouth of Ulysses in his *Troilus and Cressida,* sums up this Renaissance view to perfection:

> The heavens themselves, the planets, and
>   this centre
> Observe degree, priority, and place
> Insisture, course, proportion, season, form
> Office, and custom, in all line of order;

This heavenly arrangement is mirrored in human institutions, in orders of rank or "degree."

> But when the planets
> In evil mixture to disorder wander,
> What plagues and what portents, what mutiny,
> What raging of the sea, shaking of earth . . .
> Take but degree away, untune that string,
> And hark what discord follows.

The political implications of such cosmic doctrine were inescapable.

Yet, it is worth repeating, Shakespeare's plays are above all great literature, and as his London audiences were the first to recognize, great theater. In fact, Shakespeare's contemporaries were particularly fortunate in their theater, for while poets and historians and translators were publishing impressive work, it was on the stage that the Elizabethans shone most brightly. It was there that the culture of the people and the humanism of the educated clashed and coalesced: Shakespeare was not alone in marrying low comedy to high tragedy, and in pleasing groundlings and courtiers at the same time. The profusion of dramatists was so great, indeed, that such fine playwrights as Tourneur and Webster and Middleton, who would have stood out in any age but this, recede before the immortal trio, Shakespeare, Marlowe, and Jonson.

Christopher Marlowe, born like Shakespeare in 1564, was, unlike Shakespeare, a university man. A master of blank verse, which he domesticated in England with his powerful dramas, he compressed his output into a few years: *Tamburlaine the Great, The Jew of Malta,* and the greatest of them all, *Doctor Faustus,* were written between 1587 and 1589 or perhaps 1591. He did not have much longer to live: in 1593 Marlowe was stabbed to death in a drunken tavern brawl. His plays are filled with blood and destruction, with boast and rant and sonorous speeches, but their precise nature remains a matter of dispute: T. S. Eliot provocatively called *The Jew of Malta,* with its "savage comic humour," a "farce." Yet the speeches of Marlowe's gigantic figures wrestling with their ambitions and their fate continue to resound in the ear of those who love the

English language. Like Marlowe, Ben Jonson was an educated man: he professed to despise the mob, and he dedicated his *Volpone* to Oxford and Cambridge, "the most noble and most equal sisters." He was scholar and wit, educator and entertainer, classicist and Englishman, and he fused these disparate elements into that vigorous and pure diction that is perhaps the most impressive contribution of the Elizabethan Renaissance to world literature. Yet, while the particular and permanent attractiveness of Jonson seems Elizabethan, he lived into a new world, with new literary luminaries. Born in 1572, he had Shakespeare acting in his *Every Man in His Humor* in 1598, but his most enduring comedies, *Volpone* and *The Alchemist,* date from the reign of James I, and he lived on to 1637, well into the reign of Charles I. This was already the time of the metaphysicals: of John Donne and his fellow Baroque poets, and of John Milton's early verse. England's cultural efflorescence did not abate, it only changed expression.

Spain and the Dutch Republic: Two Golden Ages

Even more than England, both Spain and the Dutch Republic derived impulses for their cultural flowering from Italy. The Spanish *Siglo de Oro* began in the 1540s, in the reign of Charles V, with a volume of poems by two Spanish writers, Juan Boscán and Garcilaso de la Vega, who brought Italian verse forms to Spanish literature, and thus liberated Spanish poetry from timeworn shackles. Similarly, Spanish painting enormously profited from Italian Mannerists either imported into Spain by royal patrons or studied on the spot: El Greco, the greatest of them, was a Greek, born Domenicos Theotocopulos in 1541, who, before he settled in Spain around 1576, spent profitable years in Venice and Rome.

Like Italy, Spain enjoyed a cultural flowering during the years of its decline; its finest writers did their best work after the failure of the Armada. Lope de Vega, poet and playwright, has been called "the greatest literary improviser ever seen." [24] In his long lifetime (he was born in 1562 and died in 1635) he wrote innumerable poems and over fifteen hundred plays, many of them dashed off in two or three days. His fluency made much of his work trivial and trite, but his best plays are full of brilliance, wit, naturalness, and a fresh dramatic sense. Calderón belongs to a later generation and to a later style, the Baroque. Born in 1600, he lived to 1681, almost to the nadir of Spanish power. He borrowed ideas and incidents from Lope de Vega, and he wrote worldly comedies and melodramas, but his strength lay in aristocratic tragedies depicting the clash of love and honor, and in religious allegory. To read the latter, with their deep feeling and their disdain for all secular virtues, is to be

---

[24] Gerald Brenan, *The Literature of the Spanish People* (2nd ed., 1962), 204.

back in the world of the Counter-Reformation, a world Spain had never left—except perhaps for Cervantes.

Don Quixote breathes a freer spirit. Cervantes took to writing after an adventurous career, which included service at the battle of Lepanto and five years of slavery in a Moorish prison. Impecunious and neglected, Cervantes wrote romances, plays, and poems, but his first success came with Part One of *Don Quixote*, published in 1605, when he was fifty-eight. Part Two, which takes Don Quixote to disenchantment and death, came out in 1615, a year before Cervantes' own death. *Don Quixote* is the *Hamlet* of novels: it invites, and has survived, many interpretations. Cervantes himself insisted that he had written the book to expose popular novels of chivalry, and its first claim to fame was its humor. The mad don was irresistible: riding out on his nag Rozinante, accompanied by his squire Sancho Panza, to restore true chivalry to the country, tilting at windmills, and taking inns for castles. But the novel is far subtler than that: Quixote and Sancho Panza are not merely polar opposites but, in many respects, parallels; as their adventures proceed, they learn from one another, and sometimes exchange roles. The don is mad only on the subject of chivalry; he is sane, kind, observant in all other respects. And when he discards his fantasy at the end, he dies. In our own century, it has been tempting to take the don as the sane critic of a mad world and the common sense of Sancho Panza as complacency or resignation in the face of horror and evil. This is a permissible reading. But it is likely that Cervantes himself did not have such polemical intentions. Only the greatness of his masterpiece remains beyond question.

In painting as in literature, the Spanish seventeenth century is more interesting than the sixteenth. El Greco, it is true, had mastered his characteristic style as early as the 1570s, but his celebrated *View of Toledo,* and his religious compositions, angular, harsh in color, distorted in their figures—the work of a religious visionary, subjective and fervent—date from the decade before his death in 1614. And the other major Spanish painters belong wholly to the age of decline: Ribera was born around 1590, Zurbarán in 1598, Murillo in 1617. All these, the first two quite directly, the last through his Spanish masters, learned much from Caravaggio. Their Madonnas and beggars, spiritual, colorful, perhaps a little cheap in their search for effects, hang in many museums and retain some of their luster; only Velázquez (born in 1599, a year after Zurbarán) retains it all. Like Rubens, whom he met, Velázquez associated with princes, popes, and nobles, and wasted much valuable time in official tasks for the kings of Spain. While his debt to Caravaggio is clear, his portraits have a controlled realism, his still lifes a palpable vitality, that are quite distinctive: labels like "poetic realist" and "religious realist," which betray the helplessness of words in the face of great art, do capture something of his particular quality. Velázquez' best known paintings—the portraits of Philip IV of Spain and of Pope Innocent X, the candid and touching depictions of Spanish court fools, the celebrated *Venus and Cupid,* lovely and chaste at the same time—are obviously masterly in their control. But there is something more in them—a kind of democratic openness to experience and a search for meanings behind surfaces. In Velázquez' century, only Rembrandt saw deeper into his subjects than this.

The Dutch Golden Age, more than the others, was concentrated on the visual arts, especially on painting, drawing, and etching. [25] All the Dutch painters, including Hals, Rembrandt, and Vermeer, were attuned to the international Baroque style; there was a whole school of painters called the Haarlem Mannerists; early seventeenth-century artists closely followed Caravaggio with their anecdotal subjects and their experiments in chiaroscuro—witness Gerrit van Honthorst's *Supper Party* and Dirck van Baburen's *The Procuress*. And down to midcentury, Italianate painters like Nicholas Berchem were immensely popular, and in consequence prosperous, with scenes of Italian peasants riding on their mules past antique ruins, bathed in a golden sunlight the Dutch knew only from travel or from such pictures as these.

Yet there is also an unmistakable Dutch style, as there are unmistakable Dutch interests. Everyone likes to have his face immortalized; the Dutch, it seems, liked it even more than others. It is not an accident that Dutch painters were among the most accomplished and most prolific of portrait painters: Jan van Miereveldt, almost legendary among his contemporaries, did nothing but face painting after a short, shaky start as a history painter, and is reported to have turned out over ten thousand portraits. Military companies, syndics of gilds, regents of old men's homes had themselves portrayed in groups, and the most famous among Dutch artists sought the substantial fees and enjoyed the technical problems that these vast pictorial machines brought them. In addition, as avid consumers of paintings, prosperous Dutch burghers called for landscapes, still lifes, and genre scenes, and in all these subjects their painters reached true distinction. Jacob van Ruisdael and Jan van Goyen painted waterfalls shadowed by majestic trees, canals dominated by old castles, windmills in a field under the vast cloudy Dutch sky—the first with vigorous, dense brushwork of greens and browns; the second with a delicate touch and harmonious palette. The humblest objects served the purposes of art: Pieter Claesz posed a glass of wine and a loaf of bread (not forgetting the crumbs) on a white tablecloth; Willem Kalf beautifully composed combinations of silver vessels, Delft bowls, and fruit. Aert van der Neer specialized in nocturnal landscapes bathed in moonlight; Hendrick Avercamp in cheerful, brilliantly painted snow scenes showing Dutch villagers disporting themselves on the ice.

---

[25] The Dutch produced important theologians and philosophers, and one poet of distinction, Joost van den Vondel, a prolific and versatile translator, a political poet who lent his pen to the Remonstrant cause, and a Baroque, often verbose dramatist. But he is strictly a local classic. "We Dutchmen know," Johan Huizinga sadly observes, "that Vondel must be counted among the finest writers of all time. We also realise, and are resigned to the fact, that the world neither knows him nor is ever likely to do so." Nor is this, Huizinga concedes, because he wrote in Dutch—other writers, like Cervantes, have enjoyed and survived translation. See *Dutch Civilisation in the Seventeenth Century* (1968), 69.

A considerable number of painters, of whom Willem van de Velde the Younger was only the most accomplished, painted Dutch ships under full sail, becalmed at sea, or in the midst of battle. Jan Steen and Adriaen van Ostade reproduced the simple charm of domestic and the rowdy vigor of tavern life with their carousing peasants, playing children, reflective pipe smokers. Gerard ter Borch lovingly recaptured interior scenes in which elegant ladies dressed in satin read love letters. And Pieter de Hooch painted luminous Dutch interiors, with the light streaming through the window onto those obsessively clean Dutch tiles. This catalogue seems long, but it offers only a selection of names and subjects. Never in history has one country—and so small a country!—produced so many painters of such high caliber in such a short time.

Amid this wealth of talents, Frans Hals, Rembrandt van Rijn, and Jan Vermeer tower as painters of genius. Hals was one of many benefits the northern Netherlands received from its southern neighbors during the great migration. Born in Antwerp around 1580, Hals came to Haarlem with his parents after the fall of his native city to the Spaniards (see p. 194). He lived to a ripe age—to 1666—and tried his hand at a variety of subjects. But he early recognized that his true talent lay in portraiture, individual and collective; as he grew older, and his mood more subdued, he gave up genre painting altogether. He brought radical, almost revolutionary techniques to a traditional genre. His life-size portraits of militia companies and other respectable groups—he did nine of them, more than any of his competitors—completely loosened up the old, stiff, soldiers-all-in-a-row kind of portrait. Hals' companies are informal, animated, wholly individualized, yet so beautifully composed that the eye may calmly travel from one figure to another, or rest with pleasure on the painting as a whole. Even more perhaps than these group portraits, Hals' portraits of individuals display his gift for life-like rendering, for capturing the animation and the unique quality of his subject. In his attempt to give a convincing representation of fleeting emotion he is very much the Baroque artist; in his darting, casual-looking but wholly deliberate brushwork, he seems like an Impressionist.[26] Hals was very much a man of his time, and of the future.

Rembrandt, like Shakespeare, is "for all time." A true genius, he converted the elements around him—late Mannerism, the Baroque, the Dutch predilection for landscape—into a profoundly personal expression. Like other Dutch painters, Rembrandt loved to do portraits; unlike most of them, he constantly returned to biblical subjects: some of his greatest etchings show scenes from the life of Christ. We know much about him, and yet not enough: he did more than a hundred self-portraits, a moving record of his development from confident youth to tragic old age, rendered with an unsurpassed eye and no sentimentality whatever. We know also that in the 1630s, in Amsterdam, he grew rich and famous, that gradually he became unfashionable, went bankrupt in 1656, and was compelled to auction off a fine and varied art collection. But most

---

[26] See Rosenberg et al., *Dutch Art and Architecture*, 37–38.

conjecture about his spiritual life is sheer speculation, prompted by his somber masterpieces.

Rembrandt was born in 1606 at Leyden, the son of a comfortably situated miller. By 1625, he had set up on his own. From his earliest paintings onward, Rembrandt showed himself master of chiaroscuro, and his particular use of it became his signature. Caravaggio and the Caravaggisti had used alternations of light and dark in sharply delimited regions, achieving drama by stark contrast. Rembrandt, on the other hand, graduated his tones to create a single, highly expressive atmosphere. [27] With the Caravaggisti, a single look establishes the configuration of the painting; with Rembrandt, long and repeated viewing yields surprising dividends, as figures emerge from the darkness. In his Leyden years, Rembrandt became not merely an accomplished painter, but a prolific etcher—etching, indeed, was an art in which he was to become supreme.

In 1632, he moved to Amsterdam, where he spent the rest of his life, down to 1669. He married, moved in cosmopolitan circles, enjoyed his fame. Gradually he discarded the shock techniques of the early Baroque and participated in the current fashion of landscape painting. But it is as a portrait painter that he gained his fame; indeed, the picture that made his reputation, *The Anatomy Lesson of Dr. Tulp* (1632), is one of the most active, most brilliantly composed group portraits ever painted: it shows Dr. Tulp lecturing to an intent group of seven observers and dissecting a corpse which lies, brightly lit, in full view.

Fashions changed in the 1640s, and Rembrandt changed too, though, to his cost, in his own way. The tale of Rembrandt's sudden fall from favor is a legend; gradually, as his vision grew more private and his canvases darker, many of the most desirable commissions went elsewhere. Yet he continued to have customers: Rembrandt executed the *Night Watch* [28] and the *Syndics of the Cloth Drapers' Guild,* the two most famous group portraits ever painted, in 1642 and 1661–1662, respectively. They are, of course, wholly different pictures, solving wholly different problems: the first shows an animated group striding out in the open, with brilliant light falling on the captain and his lieutenant; the second depicts a composed smaller group of five syndics and one servant, unified by the table at which they are seated and by their alert looking at the same point, perhaps at a person just entering the room. These last decades of Rembrandt's life are also the years of his most powerful self-portraits and some of his finest religious etchings. He never gave up portraiture; late and early, he liked to dress up his subjects in extravagant finery, to create a harmony, or a contrast, between accessory and face—witness his late *The Man in the Gilt Helmet,* in which a somber, strong elderly man, his fact deeply lined and his mouth tightly

[27] Ibid., 51–52.
[28] The name is a complete misreading of the painting, but it has stuck. Its proper, though admittedly clumsier, title is *The Company of Captain Frans Banning Cocq and Lieutenant Willem van Ruytenburch.*

drawn, grimly poses with a shining, plumed helmet on his head. And, just as he had liked to paint his wife Saskia until her death in 1642, so he later painted Hendrickje Stoffels, who came to live with him, and his one surviving child, his son Titus. He painted wrinkled old women, elderly philosophic-looking Jews, Jesus at Emmaus—his output, though increasingly concentrated on portraits and religious subjects, remained varied. And his achievement is universal, for his gifts were not confined to the play of light and shadow. "Throughout his career," Rudolf Wittkower has noted, "chiaroscuro remained his most powerful means of expression." But there were also "other important features of his art: his colouristic treatment, his draughtsmanship, his brushwork, his compositional devices." [29] It was Rembrandt's genius to unite these gifts in the paintings and etchings we know so well.

If the mystery of Rembrandt is his internal development, the mystery of Vermeer is his external career. He was born at Delft in 1632, became prominent in the painters' gild at Delft, and died at Delft in 1675; little else is known about him. Not surprisingly, his greatest landscape, one of the greatest landscapes ever painted, depicts his city serenely stretched out by its river under the typical Dutch sky—part sunny, largely cloudy. Like all painters, Vermeer incurred his debts: his early *Procuress* is an essay in the Caravaggisti tradition, a restatement of Baburen's earlier treatment of the same theme. He learned much from Carel Fabritius, Rembrandt's most talented pupil, who settled in Delft after 1650. But his later paintings, of the 1660s and early 1670s, could only have been painted by one man. They are nearly all genre paintings, mainly indoor scenes with one or two figures—a woman reading a letter, a servant pouring out milk, a man and woman drinking and talking—all of them bathed in Vermeer's unique light, organized with supreme clarity, and painted with blues and yellows that remain unsurpassed in their luminous beauty. Vermeer's art has been called simple and accessible, and we respond to it today with sheer pleasure. Yet Vermeer, whose output was small, was nearly forgotten and was rescued from obscurity only about a century ago. And nothing in his color or his composition is accidental: the simplicity of his mature work is the result of supreme artistic intelligence, the work of an individualist to whom the extravagance of Baroque meant nothing.

Two Baroque Masters: Rubens and Bernini

The term Baroque, which has already appeared on these pages, is a vexed and vexing name; it is easier to point to Baroque works of art than to define the Baroque itself, partly because it differed in different hands and different arts, partly because it underwent a distinct internal development, normally distinguished as Early, High, and Late Baroque. The Baroque style, which grew out

[29] *Art and Architecture in Italy, 1600–1750* (1958), 52.

of, and in response to, an enfeebled Mannerism at the end of the sixteenth century, was in part a return to the Renaissance ideal of order, rendered with verve and through a magnificent massiveness. Baroque artists sought to control and portray emotions, especially religious emotions; the tricks for which they are famous—the false perspective in architecture, the gesture that attacks the viewer out of the canvas, the general air of theatricality—are not tricks for their own sake, but attempts at making these emotions palpable and, if possible, overwhelming.

Yet inspection is superior to definition. A refined portrait painter like Anthony van Dyck, who could make peasants look like gentlemen, and a boisterous religious painter like Jacob Jordaens, who could make gentlemen look like peasants, both belong to the Baroque. So, in his way, does the great neoclassical painter Nicolas Poussin (see p. 297). But the enormous vitality of the Baroque is most distinctly embodied in two universal men, Peter Paul Rubens and Gian Lorenzo Bernini. Both were men of the world, consorting with dukes and popes. Both were supremely energetic. Both possessed an uncanny versatility: Rubens was a good classical scholar, an accomplished linguist, a professional diplomat, a remarkable letter writer, and a shrewd businessman, who liked to display his multiple talents by painting while he was dictating a letter, conducting a conversation, or listening to a reader. Bernini for his part could do anything; as John Evelyn noted: Bernini "gave a public opera wherein he painted the scenes, cut the statues, invented the engines, composed the music, writ the comedy, and built the theatre." [30] It is in their art that they diverge: Rubens was exclusively a draftsman and painter; Bernini a sculptor and architect who could have been, had he wanted to be, a remarkable painter.

Though a Brabanter in origin, Rubens was born in Germany in 1577 and raised in Cologne. As an adolescent he moved to Antwerp, his parents' city, and despite prolonged absences on diplomatic missions and painter's commissions, the Spanish Netherlands were his home. His legendary facility and his characteristic style (despite some change and some growth) evidenced themselves early. He was a vigorous draftsman, a natural colorist, and a genius at crowded large-scale compositions that obeyed, with all their movement, the ideal of Baroque order. He made power palatable, even graceful. Prosperity came early, and commissions poured down on him from across Europe; Rubens soon found himself compelled to open a large workshop. Many "Rubenses" are so largely by courtesy: planned by Rubens in a quick sketch, perhaps touched up by the master at the end. But only his most discriminating patrons ever knew the difference: he surrounded himself with talented young men and seems to have been an inspiring teacher who imparted some of his touch to his assistants.

It is impossible to single out any one work from an output which has been estimated at over two thousand paintings. Rubens did everything: portraits,

[30] Quoted in Hibbard, *Bernini*, 19.

landscapes, hunting scenes, religious subjects, allegories. In the late 1620s he did a series of twenty-four huge allegorical paintings for Marie de' Medici, widow of Henri IV and queen mother of France. Some of his smaller paintings are the best known: the elegant wedding picture showing himself and his first wife Isabella Brant, the exuberant *Italian Straw Hat* showing his lovely young second wife Helena Fourment, and for obvious reasons, a number of canvases depicting classical legends concerning buxom nude young women being abducted by virile young men—Rubens rivaled Titian in his flesh tones. Our own time perhaps responds most readily, less to his elaborate productions than to his preparatory essays—to his quick oil sketches (called *bozzetti*) and to his drawings, which demonstrate his daring and his unsurpassed eye with their bold foreshortening, esoteric subjects, and complicated postures, and with their triumphant sense not of difficulty felt, but of difficulty overcome. Nor was his art simply an outpouring of spontaneity. As the French critic Roger de Piles put it some thirty years after Rubens' death: Rubens' works are "full of a beautiful imaginative fire, profound erudition, and intelligence in painting."[31]

Bernini was, if anything, even more prodigious than Rubens. He was born in Naples in 1598, the son of a Florentine sculptor who mercilessly drove his son, as Leopold Mozart was to drive *his* son a century and a half later, and with the same remarkable results. Only, unlike Wolfgang Amadeus Mozart, Bernini lived on to a ripe and productive old age: when he died in 1680 he had just ceased sculpting. His virtuosity emerged early; long before he was twenty, he was a famous sculptor. His early Mannerist works are still a little forced, as though the sculptor is trying to squeeze drama out of his marble. By the 1620s, his style was ripe and his aim clear: he sought to connect the piece of sculpture to its environment, and make the whole a single experience, so cunningly devised that the spectator would be compelled to see the total precisely as the designer had planned it. His *Ecstasy of St. Teresa,* which is the centerpiece of the Cornaro chapel in the Roman church of Santa Maria della Vittoria, dates from the late 1640s, but everything he had done before then leads up to this celebrated work. The saint lies swooning back as a smiling angel, who has stabbed her before, is about to stab her once more with his arrow. The whole composition is crowned by golden rods representing the rays of the sun, and light actually comes from behind and above the niche; the niche itself, with its tense curves and crowded columns, seems like a door forced open; the side walls of the chapel are populated by lively representations of the Cornaro family. The composition is a single whole, a *Gesamtkunstwerk.*[32] Much play has been made with the expression on St. Teresa's face, and to profane eyes she indeed appears to be in the throes of orgasm. But in fact Bernini was seeking

---

[31] Quoted in H. Gerson, and E. H. Ter Kuile, *Art and Architecture in Belgium, 1600–1800* (1960), 71–72.

[32] This notion of the "total work of art" in which several arts collaborate to create a single experience, is an idea attributed to Richard Wagner, but Bernini had some such idea, without the word, two hundred years before Wagner.

to reproduce as faithfully as he could St. Teresa's graphic report of her religious experiences; besides, we know that Bernini was a devout Catholic, and whatever his worldly connections, anything but a worldling in religious matters. His Cornaro chapel is theatrical Christianity at its most theatrical, but there is no reason to doubt that it is Christian.

A sculptor with Bernini's gift of expression and passion for environment could be supposed to excel in portraiture and in architecture. Bernini in fact did both superbly well. His busts, mainly but not exclusively of popes and cardinals, are among the supreme achievements of portrait sculpture: convincing, vivid, and penetrating. His achievement as an architect is no less distinguished; among his many works, probably the best known is the piazza before St. Peter's, a cunning embrace inviting the masses of worshipers to receive the papal blessing. Nor is this all. No one who has been to Rome can forget those among Bernini's works that combine sculpture and architecture: his many charming fountains and that eloquent monument to Catholic piety, the canopy over St. Peter's grave under the dome of St. Peter's. The *baldacchino* consists of four twisted columns topped by four curving volutes meeting high in the center—a splendid invention, but a reminder, too, that Bernini stood at the end of an age, looking back to Christian glories that had passed rather than the modern world to come.

CULTURE: ANCIENT DOCTRINES AND NEW PHILOSOPHY

The Revival of Classical Philosophy

This age of artistic creativity was also an age of extraordinary intellectual vitality. The impulse of the Renaissance was by no means exhausted; the currents of thought set in motion by Erasmian humanism and fed by the turbulent torrent of the Reformation continued to work in the minds of Europeans, to confuse and trouble, but also to liberate them. Medieval conceptions of life were slowly eroding, although the temper of the times then emerging can scarcely be called secular. These were Christian times, as their predecessors had been. But the process of widening the intellectual horizons of Christendom, begun in the twelfth century with the rediscovery of Aristotle and the influx of Arab philosophy and greatly advanced in the Renaissance, now reached new intensity. Ancient doctrines, dusted off and purged by the Humanists of centuries of pious misreadings, found learned modern supporters and, disseminated by printed books and skillful popularizers, a wide public. This was the age of Christian Humanists, Christian Stoics, even Christian Epicureans.

It was Michel de Montaigne, *politique* and essayist, who demonstrated in his famous essays the variety and vitality of antique thought and its relevance to the sixteenth century. Born in 1533 in a merchant family and rising to property, office, and noble status, Montaigne made garrulity into an art and self-absorption into the foundations of modern individuality. Like a pedant, Montaigne filled his essays with frequent, often interminable quotations from the classics; like a bore, he dwelled lovingly on anecdotes. But he was neither a pedant nor a bore; he was an explorer of the meaning of man, the inventor of introspection. His radical innovation was to use himself as his favorite witness. When he looked inward he did not pray or seek mystical union with God, he recorded his feelings candidly and clearly; with the aid of ancient pagan writers—Epictetus, Cicero, Seneca, Plutarch—he thought his way to a ripe philosophy of man. Montaigne is best known as a skeptic; his query, *"Que sais-je?,"* suggests that he knows nothing and that by acknowledging his ignorance he has demonstrated, as Socrates had demonstrated long before him, the greater ignorance of other men. But there is more to Montaigne than this. As a young man he had been much taken with Roman Stoics like Seneca and Marcus Aurelius; his essay entitled "To Philosophize Is To Learn How To Die" was characteristic of this early mood. Then his Stoic detachment gave way gradually to explorations in skepticism, and this, in turn, to the humane, almost relaxed thought of his last years, which holds that "our great and glorious masterpiece is to live appropriately." When he died in 1592, he died, as he had been born, a Catholic; but (as a good *politique*) he hated fanaticism and preferred living in peace with error to exterminating heretics. Thus—and this was his meaning to his readers—he was not a sectarian theologian but a cosmopolitan moralist, not so much a pagan as an urbane Christian offering, in his copious essays, a splendidly usable anthology of classical philosophy.

Montaigne's popularity was instantaneous and his following wide. John Florio translated the *Essais* into florid English in 1603, but even before then, such cultivated Englishmen as Sir William Cornwallis had borrowed from Montaigne. In his own essays, published two years before the Florio translation appeared, Cornwallis examined himself much in Montaigne's fashion; his observation, "Montania and my selfe . . . doe sometimes mention our selves,"[33] is a charming understatement. Critical introspection had come to stay.

Yet, influential as Montaigne's catalogue of humanism proved to be, another current of thought, nourished like Montaigne by antiquity, was even more influential: Stoicism. The church fathers had found much that was admirable in Stoicism, especially Roman Stoicism. Its natural piety, its insistence on social service, its praise of such virtues as patience in adversity, had tempted the most classically trained among the early Christians to welcome

---

[33] Quoted in Douglas Bush, *English Literature in the Earlier Seventeenth Century, 1600–1660* (1945), 188.

Stoicism as a groping anticipation of Christian truth. In the Renaissance, as the writings of Roman Stoics and their allies—Cicero and Seneca—became once more widely available, Stoicism exercised wide appeal: Epictetus' noble manual was rendered from its original Greek into Latin and, in 1567, into French. Gradually, scholars disentangled Stoic doctrine from Christian admixtures and presented it not as a rival but an auxiliary to Christian philosophy, an elevating guide to life. The Renaissance Stoics insisted that Stoicism was no danger to the sacred truth—that was the ultimate monopoly of Christianity. As the Flemish scholar Justus Lipsius, the leading popularizer of Christian Stoicism, wrote around 1600, in his book On Constancy, and elsewhere: it was a rare thing for Stoicism and Christianity to conflict, but when they did, as with the Stoics' defense of suicide and the idea of fate, Stoicism was in error and Christianity was in the right. Yet, despite such occasional clashes of doctrine, Stoicism was the best philosophy the best of pagan philosophers had been able to devise. In the late sixteenth century, a time of warring fanaticisms and destructive civil conflict, the reasonableness and cosmopolitanism of Stoic teachings seemed a possible way out of turmoil.

The assertions of modern Stoics that Stoicism was no danger to Christianity must be taken more or less at face value; it was not until later, in the eighteenth century, that pagan reason became a direct threat to Christian revelation. But the classicizing tendencies of seventeenth-century thinkers were hardly innocuous; consider the writings of Hugo Grotius, diplomat, theologian, patriotic Hollander, and by general consent, the founder of modern international law. Grotius was prominent among the Dutch Arminians (see p. 195) and, late in life, found Roman Catholicism, with its universality and its vision of comprehensive peace, most appealing. In his epoch-making De jure belli ac pacis of 1625, Grotius, the declared disciple of Seneca and Cicero, sought to derive the rules of international law not from man's dependence on God but from his nature and his place in the natural universe. Even assuming that God does not exist, he wrote, the rules of natural law would remain valid, and again: "Natural law is so unalterable that God himself cannot change it." Seeking to give substance and authority to the law of nations, Grotius returned to the ideas of classical philosophy and liberated natural law from its subordination to theology. This was not secularism, but it helped to widen the road to secularism that was being constructed, slowly and largely unintentionally, by the philosophers and scientists of the seventeenth century.

"New Philosophy Calls All in Doubt"

The return to antiquity took many forms: Romans and Greeks—especially Greeks—had, after all, speculated on all aspects of nature and man. And one antique current, Epicureanism, entered into the rising tide of scientific inquiry, which had been quickening since mid-sixteenth century. Unlike Stoicism,

Epicureanism was almost impossible to reconcile with Christianity; even in antiquity, their shocked opponents had stigmatized the Epicureans as atheists for teaching that the world is essentially composed of material atoms and for denying that the gods, remote and serene spectators, had any power over man. Yet, perhaps partly from caution, certainly largely from conviction, the leading modern Epicurean, Pierre Gassendi, earnestly proclaimed his piety: he was, like the ancient Epicureans, an atomist, but as a priest he found it both politic and persuasive to argue that God had made the atoms. Friend and correspondent to most of the leading scientists and philosophers of his day, Gassendi lived at a time critical for the scientific revolution. He was born in 1592 and died in 1655, which makes him the contemporary of Bacon, Galileo, and Descartes; his writings and his letters are a bridge between ancient doctrines of materialism and the distinctly modern enterprise of the seventeenth century—the making of a scientific universe—an enterprise we have come to call the "scientific revolution." Among Gassendi's distinguished admirers, the most distinguished was Isaac Newton: Gassendi, Newton thought, had been entirely right about the critically important questions of God, space, and time.[34]

The scientific revolution was a long and slow process. But once it had taken final shape in the work of Newton, man's way of looking at the world and man's relation to nature had changed forever, beyond recognition. Newton would bring the worlds of the heavens and of the earth under a single rubric, a single set of natural laws; Newton himself would hint that what he had done for physics and astronomy might be done for chemistry, and even for what the eighteenth century would call the sciences of man. The old dream that man might gain dominion over nature now seemed near realization. And yet, the revolution took place within a Christian context: John Donne's much-quoted— too much quoted—lament of 1612, that "new philosophy calls all in doubt," mirrored the dismay of a small minority. For most seventeenth-century natural philosophers—pious Christians, nearly all of them—the study of nature was the devout tracing of God's handiwork. It is not an accident that Newton should have spent as much time and effort on establishing biblical chronologies as he did on finding equations for gravity. In 1692, five years after he had published his epoch-making *Principia* (see p. 341), he wrote to the classicist Richard Bentley, who had used arguments from Newton to defend the Christian dispensation: "When I wrote my treatise about our system, I had an eye upon such principles as might work with considering men for the belief of a Deity, and nothing can rejoice me more than to find it useful for that purpose." This was the voice of the majority. The scientific revolution was a revolution, but its anti-Christian and, beyond that, antireligious implications troubled only a few theologians and philosophers in the seventeenth century and became the mainstay of Enlightenment propaganda only in the eighteenth century. They did not really pervade European culture until the nineteenth century.

[34] This is what Voltaire reports in his well-informed study of Newton, published in 1738.

While the religious consequences of the scientific revolution manifested themselves slowly, its roots were deep. To dismiss medieval civilization as simply antiscientific would be to oversimplify a complicated story. The twelfth-century revival of philosophy had given room for speculation on the phenomena of nature; especially in optics and biology, medieval scientists did respectable work. Much like the seventeenth-century scientists, these medieval scientists were devoutly certain that their studies could only confirm and enhance man's awe for God's truly marvelous creation. They did much: in the thirteenth century two English Franciscans, Robert Grosseteste and Roger Bacon, spread Greek and Roman scientific thought among learned circles with their voluminous writings and laid down canons of scientific procedure that read like passages from a modern textbook. Bacon prophetically argued for the use of mathematics, defended experimentation, called for the classification of the various sciences by their objects of study, and sounding much like his seventeenth-century namesake, Francis Bacon, proclaimed the aim of science to be power over nature.[35]

Despite all this, the scientific revolution remains just that—a revolution: Roger Bacon might speak highly of experiments, but neither he nor any of his admiring readers performed them; he might advocate the classification of the sciences, but for centuries after him, astrology and astronomy, alchemy and chemistry, magic and mathematics cheerfully coexisted. The very motive for studying nature in the Middle Ages inescapably limited the conclusions such study might reach: Christian theology laid down rigid boundaries beyond which the most brilliant medieval mind did not dare go—quite literally could not think of going. Since the only aim of science was to serve religious purposes—to settle the precise dates of holidays or to confirm once again the glory of God—it was not science that benefited or progressed. Methodological pronouncements remained empty; reliance on authority remained practically universal. And then, with the decline of fresh thinking in the fourteenth and fifteenth centuries, with the logic-chopping and sublime irrelevance of late Scholastic philosophy, whatever energies Grosseteste and Bacon might have generated dissipated themselves. Not even the Renaissance markedly changed this. While the philosophical preoccupations of the Humanists had some indirect effect on the temper of inquiry, and while their scholarly efforts restored indispensable scientific texts, the Humanists themselves were more interested in philology and literature, and in purely speculative natural theology, than in science proper. Leonardo da Vinci, as we have noted (see p. 78) was a remarkably fertile and precise scientific observer, experimenter, and discoverer, but his achievements were uncharacteristic of his age and in

[35] Grosseteste (ca. 1168–1253) became a bishop, Bacon (ca. 1214–1292) was Grosseteste's student. It is worth adding that only lack of space prevents a longer discussion: these two Franciscans were by no means alone in their passion for God's handiwork in the natural world.

any event, hidden as they were in his notebooks, remained unknown. It took a drastic shift in the intellectual temper of Europe before Roger Bacon's bold prophecies could become realities.

Sixteenth-Century Revolutionaries

The first evidence, and indispensable cause, of this shift came in the year 1543, with two books: Copernicus' *Concerning the Revolutions of the Celestial Spheres* and Vesalius' *On the Fabric of the Human Body*. Two years later, the French physician Jean Fernel hailed the dawn of a new age: "The world sailed round, the largest of the Earth's continents discovered, the compass invented, the printing-press sowing knowledge, gun-powder revolutionizing the art of war, ancient manuscripts rescued and the restoration of scholarship, all witness to the triumph of our New Age."[36] Fernel was a follower of Vesalius and could appreciate his master's work. But the epoch-making discovery of his day, the one that marked the first real breach in the medieval conception of the world— the Copernican revolution—he passed by in silence. That was only natural: it took some years to disseminate Copernicus' theory and many more years before it was generally accepted.

Nicholas Copernicus, a Polish mathematician and astronomer, was born in 1473, studied first at Cracow and then at Bologna, and spent his life pondering his subversive ideas. For decades he kept his convictions to himself—too long for worldly glory, for his book came out in the year of, but after, his death. Like many revolutionaries, Copernicus was a conservative, a careful student of the scientific tradition, respectful of its teachings. What drove him to dissent was the mathematical difficulties surrounding the prevailing view of the world, the "uncertainty," as he put it, "of the mathematical tradition in establishing the motions of the systems of the spheres."[37] That mathematical tradition was the legacy of the Greek-Egyptian mathematician and astronomer Ptolemy, who had collated and summarized one school of ancient astronomy early in the second century after Christ in his *Almagest*, which was eagerly studied in manuscript and printed in the sixteenth century. Ptolemy's central assertion, that the earth is the stationary center of the universe, was not the unanimous view of ancient astronomers, but Ptolemy's authority choked off debate for over a millennium; it was, of course, a welcome theory for Christians who could hardly be expected to believe that God would place man, made in His image (or that Jesus Christ, God's only begotten son, would take the trouble to be incarnated) on a relatively minor planet. One half of this theory, that the earth is stationary, had not gone unchallenged: a few medieval scholars had tried to reduce the difficulties in Ptolemy's theory by suggesting that the earth, though

---

[36] Quoted in Marie Boas, *The Scientific Renaissance, 1450-1630* (1962), 17.
[37] Ibid., 69.

the center of the universe, rotated on its axis. Copernicus took the next and far more important step: he argued that the earth indeed revolves on its axis but, in addition, revolves around the sun, in a circular orbit.

Like all astronomers of his day, Copernicus began with Ptolemy, but, precisely like Ptolemy a mathematician, Copernicus could not rest content with him. He found Ptolemy's account of planetary motion too clumsy and ultimately unconvincing. The observed paths of the planets are maddeningly irregular, and the better the observation of the planets became, the more maddening the irregularities. For mathematicians since Plato and Pythagoras, the ideal had been lucidity and simplicity, but Ptolemaic astronomers found themselves compelled to be at once obscure and complex: to give a persuasive explanation of planetary motion, they developed an extremely involved system of epicycles—little circles which together make up a large circle in which the planets travel around the earth. The center of all this planetary motion—this was another desperate attempt to "save the appearances"—was not precisely at the earth, but near it. While Copernicus did not wholly give up the epicycles, and while his heliocentric hypothesis had obscurities and complexities of its own, he explained some of the more embarrassing eccentricities of the planetary orbits. Copernicus himself, in any event, was convinced of his theory largely on rationalistic and mathematical grounds. To reduce irregularities to mere apparent motion, and to place the sun into the center of the universe, were to serve the ideals of simplicity, harmony, reason, and beauty. "In the middle of all," he wrote, almost ecstatically, "sits the Sun enthroned. How could we place this luminary in any better position in this most beautiful temple from which to illuminate the whole at once? He is rightly called the Lamp, the Mind, the Ruler of the Universe."[38]

Copernicus' heliocentric astronomy was a scientific accomplishment of the first order, even if his argumentation for it has an antique aura. His proposal required enormous daring and imagination: it was nearly impossible even for advanced spirits of the sixteenth century to conceive an earth that moved, and the psychological and religious consequences (though they were not immediately perceived by anyone) were bound to be enormously troubling. As Sigmund Freud was to observe almost four centuries later, here was the first of three scientific discoveries to humble man's pride: Copernicus expelled man from the center of the universe, Darwin would deprive man of his unique privileged place in creation, while Freud would show the frailty of human reason by demonstrating the power of the unconscious.[39]

Such penetrating interpretations of Copernicus' work were still far off, though its theological implications began to worry thoughtful natural philoso-

[38] Ibid., 81.
[39] There had been three blows that science had dealt man's narcissism, Freud wrote, the first cosmological, the second biological, the third psychological. The first of these, normally associated with Copernicus, had actually been hinted at before by the ancient Greeks. See "A Difficulty in the Path of Psycho-Analysis," in *Standard Edition of the Complete Psychological Works of Sigmund Freud*, vol. XVII (1953), 137–144.

phers in the generation after his death. The great controversy over the possibly subversive character of the Copernican system did not break out until the time of Galileo, early in the seventeenth century (see p. 238), but it already figured in the thought of the Danish astronomer Tycho Brahe, indisputably the greatest student of the stars in the late sixteenth century. Brahe, who spent his life observing planets and comets, constructing calculations and charts, and vastly improving man's knowledge of the heavens, admired Copernicus as a great man and a powerful mathematician; he wholeheartedly accepted Copernicus' criticism of the Ptolemaic system. That system, Brahe said, is hopelessly inelegant and accounts for far too little of celestial motion. However, both on physical and theological grounds, Brahe rejected the notion of an earth in motion; this, he argued, ran counter to what we know of the "sluggishness" of our earth and counter to explicit passages in Scriptures. His own substitute system was perhaps less offensive than Copernicus', but no more elegant and far less convincing.

Johannes Kepler, on the other hand, briefly Brahe's assistant, accepted Copernicus' revolution and, in his own astronomical work, confirmed and extended it. Characteristically, and wholly in tune with Copernicus' own aesthetic, classical, and philosophical preoccupations, Kepler assented to Copernicus' views because he found them more imposing, more beautiful, than those of his rivals: "I have confessed to the truth of the Copernican view, and contemplate its harmonies with incredible rapture." In general, Kepler went through life in a condition of religious excitement. He sought, and found, mystical correspondences between the heavenly bodies and the Holy Trinity; like a modern Pythagoras, he saw enchanting harmonies in the laws of the universe. At the same time, he respected Tycho Brahe, the observer, and made meticulous calculations; at the dawn of the scientific era, mysticism and precision were not yet enemies.

Kepler was born in Germany in 1571, and was among the first to be thoroughly trained in both the Ptolemaic and the Copernican astronomy. After some years of teaching mathematics in the Austrian town of Graz, he moved to Prague in 1600, where Tycho Brahe was installed as imperial mathematician. Kepler became Brahe's assistant and, after Brahe's death in the following year, his successor. He had already published a defense of the Copernican system. Indeed, despite his private musings and subjective insights, Kepler distinctly belonged to a scientific tradition then developing: he proclaimed he had taken most of his ideas from others—"I have built all Astronomy on the Copernican Hypothesis of the World; the Observations of Tycho Brahe; and the Magnetic Philosophy of the Englishman William Gilbert."[40] Such collaboration was becoming a widespread experience: William Gilbert, whom Kepler here singles out, exercised considerable influence on Kepler with his *De Magnete* of 1600, which gave Kepler the idea that the sun emits a magnetic force as it emits light

---

[40] Quoted in Boas, *Scientific Renaissance*, 301.

and thus animates the planets in their orbits; Gilbert in turn singled out Copernicus as the restorer of true astronomy.

Fame came to Kepler after Brahe's death, with his famous three laws of celestial motion. These laws are a triumph of science over aesthetics: reluctantly, and after many attempts at rescuing Copernicus' circular orbits, Kepler came to the conclusion that in fact the planets move not in circles, but in ellipses. Fortunately for him, the ellipsis too was a harmonious figure, testifying to the mathematical loveliness of God's creation. He published the first two of his laws in 1609. They held, first, that planets travel around the sun in elliptical orbits, with the sun in one focus; and second, that the speed of the planets varies with their distance from the sun so that the planet's path sweeps out equal areas in equal times. But ten years later, in 1619, in a work significantly entitled *The Harmony of the World,* Kepler announced his third law: the squares of the revolution of any two planets are proportional to the cubes of their mean distance from the sun. And it was this third law that made his astronomy complete, and harmonious, and thus satisfying almost beyond Kepler's power to express. He himself testified to his ecstasy: "Eighteen months ago the first dawn rose for me, a very few days ago the sun, most wonderful to see, burst upon me." And he spoke of his "divine rage"—which is to say his overpowering pleasure—at his discovery. Kepler, this frenzied mathematical philosopher, was saying that Aristotle was dead; he had been put to rest forever by Plato, that divine mathematician. It is a mistake to think of the scientific revolution as a rebellion of the new against the old: it was the creation of the new by means of the rebellion of one ancient philosophy against another.

Galileo: The Making of Modern Dynamics

The most extraordinary of these modern Platonists was Galileo Galilei, but he was not simply that: Galileo was also supremely endowed with the curiosity that is the true scientific spirit. Sometime in May or June 1609, he heard of a Flemish "spyglass" which, it was reported, brought distant objects near. To hear of the device was enough: Galileo instantly set about constructing a telescope, and then trained it on the heavens. The radical reconstruction in method that Francis Bacon was calling for in England (see p. 240) was about to take place in Italy. What Galileo saw in his telescope, and what he deduced from it, enormously enriched scientific knowledge and prepared the way for Newton.

Early in 1610, Galileo reported his discoveries in the *Sidereal Messenger:* the mountains of the moon, the starry composition of the Milky Way, four moons of Jupiter, the phases of Venus, and spots on the sun. His report made him famous overnight. Born in Pisa in 1564, he had displayed his talents and, more than that, his intellectual independence, early; at twenty-five he secured the chair of mathematics in Pisa, and soon after he moved to Padua. When he made his astronomical discoveries, he was forty-five, the correspondent of Kepler and other scientific pioneers; he had long before satisfied himself that dominant Aristotelian theories of motion were wholly wrong. But few knew of his work. Now he became embroiled in controversy which he would have been wise, but loved too much, to avoid.

Many scientists accepted Galileo's observations, and, about this time, Copernicus' heliocentric theory enjoyed wide support. But in 1616 the Holy Office condemned that theory as absurd, false, and heretical. Galileo was in a dangerous position; his experiments reinforced his early support of Copernicus. Then, in 1623, his old acquaintance, Cardinal Barberini, a humane, civilized intellectual, was elected Pope Urban VIII. Galileo therefore felt safe in pursuing his path. His *Dialogue of the Two Chief Systems of the World,* published after long delays in 1632, gave Galileo's convictions clear—all too clear—expression. What followed was a personal quarrel raised to historic importance by the stature of the participants and the stakes of the controversy. Urban had encouraged Galileo to proceed with his investigations, but warned him to stay clear of theological questions and to present the Copernican view as nothing more than a plausible hypothesis: the intellectual freedom Barberini could permit himself and his friends as cardinal was unavoidably circumscribed by the obligations he had accepted as pope. Galileo supplied his *Dialogues* with disclaimers, but they were obviously disingenuous; no one could read his delightful exposition without recognizing that the Copernican had all the good lines. The sequel is known to everyone: Urban VIII felt betrayed and was furious. In June 1633, the Inquisitors found Galileo guilty of disobedience and condemned him to abjure his errors, confess his rebelliousness, and go to prison. His *Dialogue* was placed on the Index, but his judges commuted the prison sentence to house arrest. In house arrest Galileo remained until his death in 1642; he published only one more book, the *Discourses on Two New Sciences.* Hearing of Galileo's fate, Descartes decided to withhold a treatise on cosmology from publication.

To place the trial of Galileo into proper perspective is important but difficult; it is easy to overestimate or, by reaction, to slight its effects on scientific inquiry. In Italy certainly, and in other countries in which the Counter-Reformation and, more specifically, the Inquisition were influential, science languished. It was not wholly stifled: Galileo abjured his heresies and went on holding them, and other Catholic scientists were converted to his views. But by and large scientific activity moved northward, to Protestant countries. The trial of Galileo suggests a dawning realization that the scientific revolution might bring a religious and intellectual revolution in its train. But these attendant revolutions were still far in the future; what matters most about Galileo is not the implications of his trial, but the implications of his work. It amounted to a revolution in dynamics—the science of motion—which was to find its culmination in Newton's laws half a century later. It was on the matter of motion that the authority of Aristotle would be finally overthrown.

Controversies over motion go back to the earliest Greek philosophers, and not all Greeks reasoned like Aristotle. But with the Roman Catholics' adoption of Aristotle as their official classical ancestor, Aristotle's authority over science was absolute. Now, Aristotle had postulated two qualitatively different kinds of motion: celestial motion proper to the perfect beings of the heavens, and terrestrial motion proper to the imperfect beings here on earth. This was not the only myth the slavish reading of Aristotle had fastened on scientific thought: Aristotle had held that the "natural" condition of bodies is rest, so that they will persist in motion only as long as they are being pushed. Finally, Aristotle taught that "light" bodies tend upward while "heavy" bodies tend downward, so that bodies must fall at a speed proportionate to their weights.

The point about such thinking was not simply that its ultimate conclusions were wrong, but that its underlying methods were unscientific, for what persuaded Aristotle to hold these views, and his followers to perpetuate them, were philosophical, religious, and aesthetic considerations—considerations, that is to say, important in themselves but irrelevant to scientific inquiry. Kepler had already drawn some of this kind of thinking into question by discovering that the orbits of the planets around the sun were not "perfect" circles but ellipses—a mathematical figure universally considered to be inferior to the circle in beauty and perfection, though also harmonious. Kepler was a mystic and an enthusiast, but he allowed his discoveries to override his preferences.

This was the road to scientific thinking, and Galileo continued on it. Proceeding with care, Galileo formulated the principle of inertia, which holds that a body at rest, or in motion at a constant speed on a straight line, will persist either at rest or in its course without alteration. Aristotle was wrong: a force was required not to keep a body in motion, but to stop it or to change its speed or its course. This formulation was the critically important distinction between velocity and acceleration. Galileo also refuted Aristotle with his discovery that bodies will drop at speeds proportionate to their time of fall, not to their weight. It is true that Galileo, like his predecessors, was prompted in his discoveries by philosophical convictions: his rejection of Aristotle led him to Plato, to the view that the universe is governed by uniform, universal laws that can be expressed in the lovely and precise language of mathematics. But, at least in Galileo's hands, Plato was a far more dependable guide to science than Aristotle had ever been.

Galileo's scientific work—his astronomical discoveries, his formulation of the laws of inertia, his empirical and mathematical proofs for Copernicus' heliocentric theories—is of the most far-reaching significance. But the importance of Galileo's discoveries is overshadowed by that of his method. He was observer, experimenter, mathematician together, and he taught that true science is possible only through the conjunction of observation, experiment, and mathematics. By ridiculing those doctrinaires who would not look through his telescope, he exalted the open-minded inquirer who is willing to learn from experience over the dogmatic traditionalist who persists in deriving his knowledge from ancient authoritative books. And by showing, finally, that theological or aesthetic considerations have no place in scientific findings, Galileo widened the domain of scientific thinking and made way for the reign of quantity and objectivity, on which all real science must depend. When he died in 1642, the year Newton was born, Galileo had delineated the possibility of a unified physical science that would explain the orbit of a planet and the fall of an apple by the same overarching law. It was Isaac Newton who would turn the possibility into reality (see p. 340).

The Emergence of Scientific Philosophy

Copernicus and Kepler had been revolutionaries in their discoveries, but not in their method or their rhetoric; Galileo was a revolutionary in what he found, how he found it, and the way he defended his findings. He was not alone. The subversive potential of early modern science emerged with fair clarity in the antiauthoritarianism of physiologists like Vesalius and William Harvey, and in the codification of the new mentality by philosophers like Francis Bacon and Descartes.

Like astronomy, the science of the human body had been mired for many centuries in the adoration of the past. Galen, a Greek scholar like Ptolemy active in the second century after Christ, had left behind a large number of treatises on anatomy, physiology, and medicine, and Renaissance scientists treated these documents as Holy Writ, as the Scriptures of physiology, devoutly to be followed and never to be questioned. The difficulty for science was not Galen's errors, but Galen's authority; the habit of "proving" a point by appealing to ancient texts, which was the method of theology, remained prevalent in the natural sciences as well. It was notorious that when these scientists performed dissections and their findings differed from the received text, they made light of their own observations and kept the authority of the text intact. Down to the sixteenth century, medical students would attend dissections and look at the cadaver while a standard work—Galen, or perhaps a treatise by the fourteenth-century anatomist, Mondino—would be read aloud to them. How heavily this kind of thinking weighed on scientists appears plainly enough in the career of the great sixteenth-century physiologist Andreas Vesalius. Born in 1514 in Flanders, trained at Louvain, Paris, and—most significantly—Padua, Vesalius was enormously ambitious and insatiably curious: unlike his predecessors, he insisted on seeing for himself and on drawing his own conclusions. His masterpiece of 1543, *On the Fabric of the Human Body,* and associated writings of the same period were spirited attacks on his teachers; they marked a revolutionary advance over man's previous knowledge of the human skeleton, muscles, arteries, veins, nerves, inner organs including the brain, and the relation of the part to the whole. The splendid illustrations that accompanied Vesalius' work remain striking evidence of how much the method of strenuous and uninhibited empiricism could discover. Yet not even Vesalius could wholly free himself from the past; the organization of his book was a deliberate restatement of Galen's main concerns, and much of what Vesalius found he found with an eye to the master he sought to replace: he advertised some of his discoveries as insights the great Galen had missed, and on many fundamental principles of physiology he simply followed that ancient authority who had been dead for fourteen centuries.

In the seventeenth century, the English anatomist William Harvey laid down what had become a commonplace among scientists, thanks in large part to Vesalius: "I profess to learn and teach anatomy not from books but from dissections, not from the tenets of philosophers but from the fabric of nature."[41] Yet not even Harvey wholly dispensed with books or even with Galen. Trained in Padua and practicing in London as a prosperous physician, Harvey carefully stored up what he had learned from his professors in Italy, piously quoted Galen, but also patiently experimented in the laboratory for many years. Finally, in 1628, he published his *On the Movement of the Heart and Blood,* which established firmly what some Italian physiologists had already partly understood: the circulation of the blood. However imperfect Harvey's empiricism, however adroit his obeisances to established authority, his work proved how far the scientific method had advanced in the course of less than a hundred years, and how much it produced in the way of tangible and permanent results.

Ironically, the man who drew out all the implication of the new philosophy and the new method, Francis Bacon, was curiously insensitive to the magnificent scientific work that was being done around him. Bacon rejected Copernicus, underestimated Harvey, misread Galileo, and slighted the importance of mathematics in scientific inquiry. He has been called, with much justice, the prophet and the poet, of science; essayist, lawyer, statesman, utopian philosopher, Bacon understood the meaning of science without understanding science itself. While this anomaly resists explanation, his role in the scientific revolution is clear and was central; he was right to think of himself as a pioneer, the first to see with total clarity a new vision of man's ways of thinking and of his ultimate possibilities: Bacon was, as he said, with that vivid lucidity of his unsurpassed English style, "a bellringer which is first up to call others to church."

He did his bell-ringing in the midst of feverish political activity. Bacon was born in 1561 and entered Parliament in 1584, but despite his obvious brilliance rose slowly and rather tortuously into higher government circles. His associ-

[41] Ibid., 280.

ation with the unfortunate Essex (see p. 188) and later, his opportunistic repudiation of Essex on trial, held him back. It was not until the reign of James I that his political talents found an appropriate outlet. James knighted Bacon in 1603, the year of his accession, named him attorney general in 1613, Baron Verulam and lord chancellor in 1618, and Viscount St. Albans in 1621. Yet in the same year, he was indicted for taking bribes (which meant probably doing what everyone else was doing, but that his enemies were powerful); he was convicted and disgraced. In his last five years—he died in 1626—Bacon wrote a history of Henry VII, his scientific utopia, the *New Atlantis,* and recast and expanded what he regarded as his life's work, the *Instauratio Magna*—The Great Renewal, which he left incomplete. The first part of that ambitious project designed to lay out a wholly new way of studying and mastering the world, *The Advancement of Learning,* had already appeared in 1605; the second part, the *Novum Organum,* in 1620. While historians have tended to belittle these efforts as naive in method and vulgar in aim, their influence proved enormous, and their merit is perhaps greater than is commonly recognized.

Bacon's case must be understood as part of a great polemic against the survivals of Aristotelianism and what was generally called "Scholasticism" in scientific inquiry. "The knowledge whereof the world is now possessed," he argued, "especially that of nature, extendeth not to magnitude and certainty of works. The Physician pronounceth many diseases incurable and faileth oft in the rest. The Alchemists wax old and die in hopes. The Magicians perform nothing that is permanent and profitable. The mechanics take small light from natural philosophy, and do but spin on their own little threads." What was needed, therefore, was a complete housecleaning; mankind, Bacon said in his ringing tones, must "commence a total reconstruction of sciences, arts, and all human knowledge, raised upon proper foundations." Bacon's central effort was to discover, and to disseminate knowledge of, these foundations. What he sought to do, then, was to find knowledge that all reasonable men could accept and use: "I am labouring to lay the foundation, not of any sect or doctrine, but of human utility and power." The much-debated Baconian method was simply the spelling out of this labor.

The method meant, first of all, the diagnosis and cure of the kinds of judgments that confuse and mislead men, the so-called "idols"—the loose language, entrenched prejudices, unfounded judgments, that keep man from true knowledge. The "Idols of the Tribe" have "their foundation in human nature itself"; the "Idols of the Cave" are "the idols of the individual man"; the "Idols of the Market-place" are "formed by the intercourse and association of men with each other"; and the "Idols of the Theatre" are "received into the mind from the playbooks of philosophical systems." All must be exposed before the reconstruction of rational inquiry and social policy can begin. Second, the Baconian method stressed induction, the painstaking collection and skeptical sifting of facts, which give rise to preliminary hypotheses which in turn can be expanded into general theories. [42] Associated with this method was, in the third place, experimentation, the deliberate construction of situations in which notions could be tested and could serve as confirmations of, and guides to, observation. Bacon did not stop there; perhaps his most significant contribution to scientific procedure—the one that had the most immediate and most visible results—was his clearheaded view of inquiry. He, more than most, saw the complexity of scientific investigation, and he insisted that henceforth natural philosophers must agree to divide their labors that they may know well the subjects in which they specialize. And it followed also that this division of labor must be organized: the new learning should be public, cooperative, and cumulative—cooperation was the clue to scientific progress. It was out of this insistence, largely, that the Royal Society of London for Improving Natural Knowledge was to grow (see p. 341).

Bacon never wearied of insisting that the new method he was advocating was above all practical—knowledge, as he said in a celebrated aphorism, is power. He hoped to lay down the grounds of a science that would produce "a line and race of inventions that may in some degree subdue and overcome the necessities and miseries of humanity." He was eager to make man the architect of his fortune. With all its obvious limitations, then, Bacon's thought points to a new civilization in which men would be masters rather than victims of their world.

Descartes essentially had the same program in view. Beginning in the eighteenth century, later generations would pit Bacon against Descartes as though their philosophies were wholly irreconcilable. In the seventeenth century, their convergence was far more important than their differences. Like Bacon, Descartes developed a thoroughgoing and systematic impatience with all earlier modes of inquiry: the quibbling logic of Scholastic philosophers, the far-flung speculations of ancient thinkers, and the pretentious claims of theologians had perpetuated ignorance and sowed confusion. "As for the other sciences," Descartes added, "since after all they borrow their principles from philosophy, I decided that nothing solid could have been built on such unstable foundations." From this dissatisfaction Descartes derived his program: to construct solid knowledge on solid foundations. Like Bacon he was convinced that one could do this only by beginning at the beginning.

---

[42] It is at this point that the charge of naivete is most commonly leveled. A scientist, it is often and rightly pointed out, does not arrive at his discoveries by piling up facts one by one; he has insights, hunches, wild guesses, which he then substantiates or drops in the course of systematic testing. And much scientific discovery has significant irrational components: aesthetic appreciation, say, or the need for applause. Certainly Bacon's insistence on induction and practicality slight the playfulness of much scientific thinking. But Bacon was not a dogmatic advocate of induction. He hoped, rather, for a "true and lawful marriage between the empirical and the rational faculty." Mere reasoners, he suggested, are spiders "who make cobwebs out of their own substance," but mere experimenters are ants, who "only collect and use." The ideal natural philosopher is like the bee, which gathers its material and then digests it "by a power of its own." If Baconian is mere vulgar empiricism, then Bacon was not a Baconian.

Descartes was more than a mere methodologist or a utopian dreamer. Born in 1596 at La Haye, in Touraine, he spent much of his life in retirement, almost seclusion, abroad; when he died in 1650, he was, significantly enough, in Sweden as Queen Christina's guest. Descartes wrote widely on philosophical and psychological subjects, and was the first to apply algebra to geometry. His invention of analytical geometry has been immortalized by what are still called, after him, "Cartesian coordinates." But his most celebrated and most influential contribution to the reconstruction of inquiry and the spread of the scientific method was his *Discourse on Method,* all the more influential for being written in lucid French. It was published in 1637 and explicitly designed as a guide for "correctly conducting the reason and seeking truth in the sciences." Precisely like Bacon, Descartes offered his method full of optimism about the new learning, and of irritation against the old: "It is possible to obtain knowledge highly useful in life. . . . Instead of the speculative philosophy taught in the Schools we can have a practical philosophy with which . . . we may make ourselves the masters and possessors of nature." All that men know, Descartes insisted, "is almost nothing compared to what remains to be known; we could be freed from innumerable maladies, of body and mind alike, and perhaps even from the infirmities of old age, if we had sufficient knowledge of their causes and of all the remedies with which nature has provided us."

Descartes made his revolution in method by turning to himself; since no previous way of inquiry had brought certain truth or reliable information, introspection was all that was left. It is not an accident that the *Discourse* should be largely an autobiography detailing Descartes' early confusion, growing restlessness, and decisive intellectual discoveries. Whatever Descartes' debt to medieval schools of thought, this self-reliance was a radical step, a triumph of self-confident rationalism. Seeking to avoid the old traps in the way of reasoning, Descartes devised a set of four rules that would clear all obstacles and produce dependable knowledge. These rules were, first, to accept only clear, distinct, self-evidently true ideas; second, to divide each difficulty into "as many parts as may be necessary for its adequate solution"—that is, to analyze; third, to arrange each acceptable idea in a sequence beginning with the simplest and moving on to the more complicated ones, and thus to propel human reason forward cautiously but surely, step by step; and four, to make the enumeration of instances and the review of one's way of thinking as complete as they could be.

By rigorously following this program and by looking into himself, determined to trust nothing that was not wholly trustworthy, Descartes established his famous first truth: *"Cogito, ergo sum*—I think, therefore I am." It was a slender foundation, and later thinkers would question its adequacy, but for Descartes it was enough to construct a world. Nothing else was certain, but even the most radical doubt required a doubter: thinking, therefore, implied the existence of a thinker. Moving forward from this first step, with the caution he had prescribed, Descartes proved the existence of God, of matter, and of motion. His proof for the existence of God infuriated such devout thinkers as Pascal who suspected (rightly enough, it turned out in the eighteenth century) that Descartes' conception of a remote God, coupled as it was with his rigidly mechanistic philosophy, was first cousin to sheer materialism. Descartes said that animals are machines—how far was this from the atheist's assertion that men, too, are machines? But for Descartes this chain of reasoning was ground for true philosophical piety: since man can conceive of something higher, more perfect, than himself, something higher, more perfect, must have inspired this conception—and that is God.

Reasoning in this way, from clear ideas to clear ideas, Descartes constructed a mental and physical world that contained a number of indefensible notions: since space, in the Cartesian system, means extension, and extension presupposes matter, there can be no void; consequently, the universe must be filled with impalpable matter. Newton was to refute this view half a century later. But while Descartes' scientific ideas were to come under decisive attack before long, his *Principles of Philosophy* (1644), which outlined them, seemed to his many admirers a powerful and coherent account of the universe. Much of Descartes' power lay, doubtless, in his eclecticism: in his willingness to move from deductive reasoning to an appeal to experience, and from mathematics to experimentation. It lay, also, in his rationalism: no one before Descartes had so effectively assailed authoritarian ways of thinking and so elegantly asserted the autonomy of the rational self. For a hundred and fifty years or more, even his severest critics were to some degree his disciples (see p. 340n). But it lay, above all, in his vision. Descartes, much like Bacon, offered a hope that was as grandiose as it was—or was proclaimed to be—realistic: man could lengthen life, abolish the terrors of old age, improve health, and do away with onerous labor. Yet one thing was clear, even to those who read these scientific prophets with excitement and sought to put their ideas into practice: the realities of their time were quite different—they were, as they had always been, and perhaps even more so, the old realities of war, pestilence, and hunger.

SELECTED READINGS

In two long essays of 1904-1905, *The Protestant Ethic and the Spirit of Capitalism* (tr. 1930), the great German sociologist Max Weber argued that Calvinist "worldly asceticism" was a powerful agent in the creation of a capitalist "spirit." In his *Religion and the Rise of Capitalism* (1926), the English economic historian R. H. Tawney takes up and modifies Weber's argument. Amid a considerable controversial literature, the outstanding recent polemic, which seeks to disprove the "Weber thesis" root and branch, Kurt Samuelsson, *Religion and Economic Action: A Critique of Max Weber* (tr. 1961), is the most persuasive; it contains a survey of the literature. H. M. Robertson, *Aspects of the Rise of Economic Individualism: A Criticism of Max Weber and His School* (1933), is an earlier, less incisive critique.

For the rise of capitalism and the "commercial revolution," see Henri Sée, *Modern Capitalism: Its Origin and Evolution* (1928); John U. Nef, *Industry and Government in*

France and England, 1540-1640 (1940); and many excellent articles in E. E. Rich and C. H. Wilson, eds., *The Economy of Expanding Europe in the Sixteenth and Seventeenth Centuries,* vol. IV, *Cambridge Economic History of Europe* (1967), notably Wilson's own long essay, "Trade, Society and the State," pp. 487–575. Among monographs, Bernard Bailyn, *The New England Merchants in the 17th Century* (1955); Stella Kramer, *The English Craft Gilds: Studies in Their Progress and Decline* (1927); and Louis B. Wright, *Religion and Empire: The Alliance Between Piety and Commerce in English Expansion, 1558-1625* (1943), are particularly useful. For Antwerp, see S. T. Bindoff, "The Greatness of Antwerp," in G. R. Elton, ed., *New Cambridge Modern History,* vol. II (1958), 50–69; H. Van Der Wee, *The Growth of the Antwerp Market and the European Economy,* 3 vols. (1963). For Amsterdam, see especially Violet Barbour, *Capitalism in Amsterdam in the 17th Century* (1950); John J. Murray, *Amsterdam in the Age of Rembrandt* (1967); and C. R. Boxer, *The Dutch Seaborne Empire, 1600-1800* (1965).

For Mannerism, see the intelligent recent essay by John Shearman, *Mannerism* (1967); see also Guiliano Briganti, *Italian Mannerism* (1962), and the civilized study by Walter Friedlaender, *Mannerism and Anti-Mannerism in Italian Painting* (ed. 1965). For the most influential architect of the age, see James S. Ackerman, *Palladio* (1966). And for Titian, see the splendid study by Erwin Panofsky, *Problems in Titian, Mostly Iconographic* (1969).

Boris Ford, ed., *The Age of Shakespeare* (1956), vol. II of *The Pelican Guide to English Literature,* is a handy introduction to the Elizabethan Renaissance. Douglas Bush, *English Literature in the Earlier Seventeenth Century, 1600-1660* (1945), moves into the Jacobean period and beyond. Amid a vast literature on Shakespeare, Mark Van Doren, *Shakespeare* (1939); E. E. Stoll, *Art and Artifice in Shakespeare* (1935); and Henri Fluchère, *Shakespeare* (tr. 1953), may be mentioned. For Ben Jonson, see L. C. Knights, *Drama and Society in the Age of Jonson* (1937); for Christopher Marlowe, Harry Levin, *The Overreacher* (1952). T. S. Eliot has some remarkable essays on Shakespeare, Jonson, Marlowe, and other Elizabethan dramatists brought together in *Selected Essays* (1932).

The Golden Age of Spain is lucidly discussed in Gerald Brenan, *The Literature of the Spanish People* (2nd ed., 1962), and George Kubler and Martin Soria, *Art and Architecture in Spain and Portugal and Their American Dominions, 1500-1800* (1959). For the greatest of Spanish writers, see W. J. Entwistle, *Cervantes* (1940), and the essay by Salvadore de Madariaga, *Don Quixote* (1934). For Velázquez, José López-Rey, *Velázquez: A Catalogue Raisonné of his Oeuvre with an Introductory Study* (1963), is essential.

The best introduction to the Dutch Golden Age is Jakob Rosenberg, Seymour Slive, and E. H. Ter Kuile, *Dutch Art and Architecture, 1600-1800* (1966). H. E. Van Gelder, *Guide to Dutch Art* (1952), is very useful. Ingvar Bergström, *Dutch Still-Life Painting in the Seventeenth Century* (1956), and Wolfgang Stechow, *Dutch Landscape Painting of the Seventeenth Century* (1966), add much of use. For Rembrandt, see Jakob Rosenberg, *Rembrandt,* 2 vols. (1948); Seymour Slive, *Rembrandt and His Critics: 1630-1730* (1953); and Ludwig Goldscheider, *Rembrandt: Paintings, Drawings, and Etchings* (1960), which reprints three early biographies and has excellent notes. The best monograph on Vermeer is P. T. A. Swillens, *Johannes Vermeer, Painter of Delft* (1950).

For the Baroque, see the authoritative surveys by Rudolf Wittkower, *Art and Architecture in Italy, 1600-1750* (2nd ed., 1965); H. Gerson and E. H. Ter Kuile, *Art and Architecture in Belgium, 1600-1800* (1960); and Anthony Blunt, *Art and Architecture in France, 1500-1700* (1954). To this should be added John Pope-Hennessy, *Italian High*

Renaissance and Baroque Sculpture (1963), which sketches the transition between styles; Ellis Waterhouse, *Italian Baroque Painting* (1962); Walter Friedlaender, *Caravaggio Studies* (1955); R. A. M. Stevenson, *Peter Paul Rubens* (1939); and Howard Hibbard, *Bernini* (1965), a brilliant essay to be read in conjunction with Rudolf Wittkower, *Gian Lorenzo Bernini, The Sculptor of the Roman Baroque* (1955).

The best work on the revival of ancient philosophy, by Wilhelm Dilthey, "Weltanschauung und Analyse des Menschen seit Renaissance und Reformation," in *Gesammelte Schriften,* vol. II (5th ed., 1957), has not been translated; we can refer the reader to Chapter 5 of Peter Gay, *The Enlightenment: An Interpretation,* vol. I, *The Rise of Modern Paganism* (1966). And see Chapter 13 of Ernst Cassirer, *The Myth of the State* (1946); Jason Lewis Saunders, *Justus Lipsius: The Philosophy of Renaissance Stoicism* (1956); Donald M. Frame, *Montaigne's Discovery of Man: The Humanization of a Humanist* (1955); and Johan Huizinga, "Grotius and His Time" (1925) reprinted in his *Men and Ideas* (1959). See also William S. M. Knight, *The Life and Works of Hugo Grotius* (1925).

A judicious survey of the early scientific revolution is Marie Boas, *The Scientific Renaissance, 1450-1630* (1962). The early chapters of A. R. Hall, *The Scientific Revolution, 1500-1800: The Formation of the Modern Scientific Attitude* (1954), are also very useful. See also Herbert Butterfield, *The Origins of Modern Science, 1300-1800* (2nd ed., 1966), and the more technical I. Bernard Cohen, *The Birth of a New Physics* (1960). For the evolution of the new cosmology, see Thomas S. Kuhn, *The Copernican Revolution: Planetary Astronomy in the Development of Western Thought* (1957). E. M. W. Tillyard, *The Elizabethan World Picture* (1943), and Theodore Spencer, *Shakespeare and the Nature of Man* (2nd ed., 1955), deal with the mental world in the span between Kepler and Galileo. For the latter, see Giorgio di Santillana, *The Crime of Galileo* (1955). Bacon's relation to the scientific revolution remains controversial. Especially recommended are F. H. Anderson, *The Philosophy of Francis Bacon* (1948), and R. F. Jones, *Ancients and Moderns: A Study of the Background of the Battle of the Books* (1936). Catherine Drinker Bowen, *Francis Bacon* (1963), is less searching but still informative. For Bacon's legacy—the organization of science—see Martha Ornstein, *The Role of Scientific Societies in the Seventeenth Century* (3d ed., 1938). Descartes' "modernity" is also subject to debate. See Norman Kemp Smith, *New Studies in the Philosophy of Descartes: Descartes as Pioneer* (1952), and T. F. Scott, *The Scientific Work of René Descartes* (1952).

6

Times of Troubles: Europe at Mid-Seventeenth Century

Most times in history are times of troubles, but in the middle of the seventeenth century, economic, social, intellectual, religious, and political upheavals were so devastating and so general that historians have come to call this period "the crisis of the seventeenth century." In their love for labels, they may have overstressed the uniqueness and intensity of this particular time of troubles—the middle of the sixteenth century, after all, appeared as a crisis to *its* contemporaries[1]—but there can be no question that the mid-seventeenth century was a difficult time. "These days are days of shaking," an English preacher declared in 1643, "and this shaking is universal: the Palatinate, Bohemia, Germania, Catalonia, Portugal, Ireland, England." The days of shaking were recorded on battlefields, in starving villages, on scaffolds, and in men's minds. Their most striking expression, perhaps, was Thomas Hobbes' *Leviathan,* published in the time of Cromwell's republic, in 1651. The *Leviathan* cannot be summarized in a phrase: it is a masterpiece in the history of political

[1] See J. H. Elliott, "Revolution and Continuity in Early Modern Europe," *Past and Present,* 42 (Feb. 1969).

theory, an icily logical effort to discover how man, the animal that seeks power, can be effectively governed. But it was also a response to its own somber time. Civil war, Hobbes tells his readers, is the worst of times, worse than tyranny, bad though that may be: "The state of man can never be without some incommodity or other," but "the greatest, that in any form of government can possibly happen to the people in general, is scarce sensible in respect of the miseries, and horrible calamities, that accompany a civil war, or that dissolute condition of masterless men, without subjection to laws, and a coercive power to tie their hands from rapine and revenge." Without a civil power strong enough to overawe the boldest, man's condition is a "war of every man against every man" and his life "solitary, poor, nasty, brutish, and short." When Hobbes was writing, many thought this dismal series of adjectives a fitting description, not for some imaginary state of nature, but for their own day (see p. 346). [2]

THE THIRTY YEARS' WAR

The Opening Phases

The earliest manifestation, and in many respects an aggravating cause, of the general crisis was the Thirty Years' War.

The name is somewhat arbitrary: much of the fighting ended well before the peace of 1648, while other fighting broke out, in different constellations, well after 1648; and the events of 1618 that are customarily taken as the beginning of the war were actually the culmination of long-growing religious and political tensions. Nor was it a single war; it was, rather, a series of intermittent and interlocking wars. Still, its traditional name and the traditional subdivisions on which the textbooks are virtually unanimous adequately stress its salient features. The opening years (1618 to 1625) are known as the Bohemian phase after the first theater of war. Between 1625 and 1629 the war was widened by the entry of the Danes, and this second phase was followed (1630 to 1635) by the spectacular intervention of Sweden; finally, the entry of France brought the war to its last and most general phase (1635 to 1648). Other complexities abound. The war began as a relatively local conflict but spread

---

[2] Among the first historians to call attention to the general crisis was Roger B. Merriman in a lecture delivered in 1937; it was expanded into a book in 1938: *Six Contemporaneous Revolutions.* Since then a whole group of historians has considerably advanced and refined the idea and has come up with far more than six revolutions. The fundamental papers have been collected in Trevor Aston, ed., *Crisis in Europe, 1560-1660* (1965), which contains, among others, articles by E. J. Hobsbawm, H. R. Trevor-Roper, J. H. Elliott, Michael Roberts, and Roland Mousnier. The quotation from the English preacher in the text is drawn from Trevor-Roper, "The General Crisis of the Seventeenth Century," in Aston, *Crisis in Europe,* 59.

across nearly all of Europe; the main place of the action, and the main sufferer, was Germany, but far more than Germany's destiny was involved; while the official participants were states and their armies, private military adventurers, *condottieri* of the north, entered and further confused the lineup of forces; the original confessional division of sides—Catholics versus Protestants—gave way to divisions based on sheer considerations of foreign policy. A largely religious war became primarily a power struggle.

The event that precipitated war in 1618 was the Defenestration of Prague. In May, a crowd of Czechs, Protestants all, invaded a council chamber in the Hradschin Castle and threw two imperial officials and their secretary, Catholics all, out of the window. The victims landed safely, bruised but alive, and made their escape through the vast throng that had assembled to witness the incident. "A pile of mouldering filth" had broken their fall: "A holy miracle or a comic accident according to the religion of the beholder." [3] But whether the one or the other, it was signal for revolt in Bohemia and for wider war.

The Bohemian revolt achieved its larger significance through Bohemia's peculiar position. It was a kingdom which took pride in its religious spiritedness—was it not the land of Hus?—and in its right to elect its own king. But in fact the first meant strenuous infighting among Protestant sects—Utraquists, Lutherans, and Calvinists were steadily at one another's throats—and led to effective domination of Hapsburg, that is to say, Catholic, officialdom. And the second amounted to little more than the dubious privilege of endorsing a Hapsburg prince, who was, in addition to being king of Bohemia, ruler of the neighboring Austrian lands, an imperial elector, and Holy Roman Emperor. In 1617, Emperor Matthias, childless, had designated Archduke Ferdinand as king of Bohemia and as his successor in the imperial seat, a succession that, in view of Matthias' advancing age, could not be long delayed. Ferdinand's religious fervor, his energy, and his eagerness to stamp out the Protestant heresy were well known; the victims of the Defenestration of Prague, Ferdinand's representatives, could hardly be popular with the Bohemians. The materials for trouble were therefore gathered well before Ferdinand's "governors'" lives were saved by a pile of dung.

Events moved with uncommon swiftness. The Bohemian rebels purged officials, expelled the Jesuits, and appealed to Protestant Europe for help; Archduke Ferdinand, king-elect of Bohemia, prepared for a crusade. By June of 1618, the Bohemians had enlisted the support of Frederick, imperial elector of the Palatinate, in the German Rhineland. Frederick was young—twenty-two in 1618—charming and optimistic. For reasons of simple arithmetic, he had long had his eyes on the kingdom of Bohemia: there were seven imperial electors— three of them Roman Catholic bishops, three of them Protestant rulers including himself, while the decisive seventh vote was held by the king of Bohemia. In the hands of a Hapsburg the imperial election must fall to a

[3] C. V. Wedgwood, *The Thirty Years' War* (ed. 1944), 79-80.

Catholic; in the hands of a Protestant, a Protestant would become emperor, and part of Hapsburg power would be whittled away. In addition to holding his electoral office, young Frederick was son-in-law to King James I of England and president of the Protestant Union, a loose defensive confederation of German Protestant princes and cities, most of them Calvinist, that had been formed in 1608.

While the Protestant Union timidly rejected Frederick's aggressive plans for aiding the Bohemian rebels, Frederick himself, with the support of the duke of Savoy, equipped an army and placed it under the command of a distinguished general, Ernst von Mansfeld. At first the war went well for the Protestants. When Matthias died in March 1619, Ferdinand seemed ready to recognize new realities: he offered the rebels a compromise. But the moderates were not in control at Prague. In August 1619, confident—or desperate—the Bohemians declared Ferdinand deposed and, to no one's surprise, elected the elector palatine, Frederick, king of Bohemia. Independently, and at the same time, the imperial electors met at Frankfurt and chose Ferdinand as the new emperor. When news reached the electors that the Bohemians had deposed Ferdinand, all possibility of accommodation vanished.

Ferdinand was in serious difficulties; he was helpless in Bohemia and beset by dissidence elsewhere in his sprawling dominions. And Frederick, though reluctantly and prayerfully, accepted the Bohemian crown in September 1619, and was solemnly crowned King Frederick V. He was faced with an implacable enemy, tepid friends, and the ominous prediction of the Jesuits that he would be nothing more than a "winter king." He was: he got little help from his fellow Protestants; they recognized his reign and scanted their aid. Not even his own family thought it wise to commit themselves to his precarious cause: James I from the first had deplored his son-in-law's rashness. Ferdinand, on the other hand, mustered the military and financial resources of Catholic Europe: Maximilian of Bavaria and his Catholic League, Pope Paul V, and Spain sent troops and money. By the middle of 1620, the Spaniards, using troops gathering in the Netherlands, invaded Frederick's own Rhenish domains, and finally, on November 8, 1620, Ferdinand's army decisively won the battle of the White Mountain, outside Prague. The Winter King's short pathetic reign was over.

The emperor's triumph was so complete that Bohemia lay at his mercy; speedily Ferdinand took advantage of his position. He did more than execute leading rebels, expel Protestant officials, or let his troops sack Prague; he confiscated the estates of Bohemian nobles and used the vast domains now in his gift to reward reliable servants and to found monasteries and convents. Many thousands—burghers, scholars, aristocrats—fled into exile, while Jesuits brought their forceful Catholic message to those compelled to stay and listen. The Counter-Reformation triumphed in a largely Protestant land through religious example, economic pressure, and physical compulsion. And while Ferdinand restored Bohemia to the True Catholic Faith, and destroyed

Bohemia's old social structure with his "new nobility," he crushed rebellion elsewhere in his lands.

But the war was not over. The Protestant Union was dead. Frederick had lost his territory and his post as elector; his intrigues, conducted from exile at The Hague, were scarcely important. But in 1625 another Protestant ruler, Christian IV of Denmark, decided to challenge Ferdinand in Germany. Christian's motives were largely dynastic and only incidentally religious: he was anxious to provide new territories for a son. As duke of Holstein, Christian was an imperial prince, and until 1625 he proclaimed his continued loyalty to his emperor, Ferdinand. Then he acted. His prospects were promising: the English, the Dutch, the French were all deeply concerned over Spain's presence in Germany and what appeared to be Spain's formidable power. But while Christian got large promises, he got little help. At the same time, his adversary, Emperor Ferdinand, was fortunate in his generals: he had Tilly, the victor of the White Mountain, and Wallenstein, with his own army.

Albrecht von Wallenstein remains a mysterious figure, a military magnate who took the moderate legacy his wife left him and converted it into one of the greatest fortunes in Europe. A man of violent temper and unpredictable moods, he had been born a Lutheran in 1583 and converted to Catholicism as a young man, but he believed, it seems, only in the stars and in himself. In 1625, when King Christian of Denmark entered the conflict, Wallenstein had acquired vast holdings in Bohemia and elsewhere in the empire, and the emperor was deeply in his debt. Ferdinand had created him prince of Friedland the year before, and now Wallenstein offered to raise an army of fifty thousand men. With some misgivings, Ferdinand accepted, and Wallenstein moved northward. Four years later, his work against Christian was done: collaborating with Tilly at Lutter, he defeated the Danish troops in 1626; in the same year, he defeated Mansfeld at Dessau. And in 1627, marauding through central and northern Germany, Wallenstein effectively put an end to both General Mansfeld's and King Christian's armies. By 1629, Wallenstein's men were in Danish territory, and Wallenstein had taken the duchy of Mecklenburg for himself. In the same year, Christian IV, soundly beaten, agreed in the Treaty of Lübeck to evacuate Germany and stop interfering in imperial (which is to say, Ferdinand's) affairs.

But, as the emperor's Edict of Restitution suggests, victory was dangerous for the victor. The edict was an act of unmeasured self-confidence, when measured self-restraint would have been wiser. The Bohemian incident of 1618 had blown up into a European-wide war partly because the settlement of Germany, attempted in 1555 at the Peace of Augsburg, had settled very little. The fragmentation of the German lands and the principle that the religion of the ruler was the religion of his subjects converted each prince's death into a scramble for territorial gain. Moreover, the Calvinists, who had found no place in the provisions of the Peace of Augsburg, had managed to secure adherents in a number of states. There were numerous incidents, small wars, harbingers of greater wars to come. The formation of the Evangelical League in 1608 and the response of the German Catholics with their own league in the following year, were further signals of turmoil ahead. Now, in 1629, Emperor Ferdinand, master of Germany, sought almost literally to turn back the clock to a time before Augsburg: his edict bluntly declared almost a century of tentative religious and political accommodation null and void. It invalidated Protestant purchases of church lands and grants of church lands to Protestant princes. It held that Calvinism had no legal standing at all. The stakes were high: if the edict were enforced, so contemporaries reckoned, many free cities, including the great Lutheran center of Augsburg, many former bishoprics and other territories would be compelled to return to Catholicism; princes like the duke of Wolfenbüttel in northern Germany would have to surrender the lands once owned by thirteen convents and most of the old bishopric of Hildesheim.[4] It would restore Catholicism in the very heart of Protestant Germany.

In addition, as an imperial edict, Ferdinand's action was the assertion of independent Hapsburg power, an assertion that even Catholic princes like Maximilian of Bavaria greatly resented. Ferdinand could rationalize his edict as a supreme expression of piety, a late fruit of the Counter-Reformation; Ferdinand's victims, Catholics as well as Protestants, could only see it as a typical Hapsburg maneuver, a cynical grab for hegemony in the name of a spiritual cause. Whatever Ferdinand's motives—and they were probably even more complex than he himself knew—the Edict of Restitution revived Protestant energies and dampened the eagerness of Catholic powers to continue service in a religious crusade that appeared more and more like a Hapsburg war. Ferdinand posed a particular threat through Wallenstein, the great general who laid waste territories wherever he went and who obeyed, if he obeyed anyone, the emperor alone. While the debate over the edict raged, Wallenstein's many enemies, fearful—with reason—of his vast and cloudy ambitions, compelled his dismissal. And then, in 1630, the Thirty Years' War entered a new and, for Ferdinand, perilous, phase with the intervention of Sweden.

Competition for Power: The Intervention of Sweden and France

Gustavus II (Gustavus Adolphus) of Sweden could hardly remain indifferent to the threat of an all-powerful Hapsburg empire, the territorial ambitions concealed (or revealed) in the Edict of Restitution, and the implications of Wallenstein's recent title, "Admiral of the Oceanic and Baltic Seas." King since 1611, Gustavus Adolphus had secured overwhelming popularity with all segments of his people, including the nobility, by his friendly bearing, his soldierly courage, his impressive learning, his administrative skills, and his domestic policies. He had encouraged commerce, built schools, improved

[4] Ibid., 243 ff.

justice, pacified the aristocracy, vastly modernized his army. Moreover, he made progress in the seemingly endless war against the Poles. "The lion of the north" is only the best known of the many admiring epithets his astonished contemporaries bestowed on this brilliant statesman and charismatic leader. He got the advisors he deserved, above all his chancellor, Axel Oxenstierna, intellectual, cool, devoted to his master, though independent enough to offer criticism. Nearly from the beginning of his reign, Gustavus Adolphus had been diplomatically and militarily involved in the Baltic shores of Germany; in 1628 he had promised to aid King Christian IV of Denmark; in 1629, after Christian's defeat, he intensified his negotiations with France, which, although a Catholic power, opposed the extension of Hapsburg dominion (whether Spanish or Austrian) across the German lands.[5] In June 1630, Gustavus Adolphus was ready: he invaded Pomerania with his superbly disciplined army. His ulterior motives were, and remain, unclear; there were even rumors that he wished to become emperor. But it is too easy to say that he masked territorial ambitions behind his championship of Lutheranism. Gustavus Adolphus was at once a devout Lutheran and an aggressive statesman, and he obviously had no difficulty in identifying the expansion of Swedish power on North German soil with the interest of German Protestants.

All went as he expected at first. With the financial help of France, officially settled by treaty in 1631, and with the military support of Saxony and Brandenburg, Gustavus Adolphus defeated the imperial army under Tilly at Breitenfeld, near Leipzig, in September 1631. Alarmed, Ferdinand recalled Wallenstein, who, after canny negotiations, agreed to fight once again for the emperor. Gustavus Adolphus, in control of central Germany and ambitious to march to Vienna, now had a worthy adversary. The two confronted one another, indecisively at first, then decisively in mid-November 1632, at Lützen, just west of Leipzig. Gustavus Adolphus, as always in the midst of the fighting, was killed. It was an incalculable loss, but the Protestant cause, in any event, had been saved by his brief and brilliant intervention. The central aim of the Counter-Reformation, to wipe out the Protestant heresy, had been frustrated. But the war went on, mainly because the French wanted it to go on. While the Swedes continued their German campaign under Oxenstierna's leadership, the Saxons made peace with the emperor in 1635. By that time Wallenstein, the emperor's most formidable and least dependable aide, was dead. Pursuing his own devious designs, Wallenstein had privately and treacherously negotiated with the Swedes and probably with other heretics, conducted himself in the field and in territory under his control as a merciless and brutal ruler, and made ready to take his army over to the Protestant side. His plans failed; in January 1634, the emperor dismissed him, and in the following month Wallenstein and his fellow conspirators fell to the swords of assassins. Ferdinand, immensely relieved, rewarded the murderers. It was that kind of war.

[5] Cardinal Richelieu, in fact, helped Gustavus Adolphus to win a favorable truce with Poland in 1629, which gave the Swedes Livonia.

The Great Settlement of 1648

From the mid-1630s, hostilities were punctuated by truces and separate treaties. Emperor Ferdinand II died in 1637 and was succeeded by his relatively pacific son Ferdinand III, but the Spaniards, the Swedes, and the French were bent on further adventures. General negotiations began tentatively in 1641 and then seriously in 1644, at the Westphalian towns of Münster and Osnabrück. Yet even during the negotiations, there was more fighting, more marauding, more destruction; as late as 1648 a French-Swedish army devastated Bavaria. The main antagonists, France and Spain, both Catholic powers, continued their bloody struggle, and in the late 1630s, in a last assertion of her once majestic authority, Spain dealt heavy military blows to the French and brought the war to French territory. But this situation could not, and did not, last: in 1640, the French could take advantage of the revolts of Catalonia and Portugal against Spain (see p. 257), aid the rebels, and briefly invade Spanish soil. Once the French forces were under the generalship of the young prince of Condé and of Marshal Turenne, Spain's eventual defeat was only a matter of time—though the Spaniards did not give up until 1659, when they signed the Peace of the Pyrenees with France. The lineup of forces became positively bizarre: for a brief period (1643–1645) the Swedes even became embroiled in a war with their fellow Lutherans, direct neighbors, and old allies, the Danes. Religion became a minor consideration: the alliance of Catholic France and Lutheran Sweden which, more than anything else kept the war going, continued in force until peace was made.

But peace finally came. In October 1648, after tedious negotiations, the negotiators affixed their signatures, and bells rang in churches of all denominations. There were grown men and women all across central Europe who now saw peace for the first time. The precise toll of despair, devastation, and death will never be known. Their incidence has been exaggerated, and their long-range effects are hard to measure: some areas, such as northwestern Germany, saw little action; others, such as central and southern Germany, sustained repeated sieges and the surging of marauding armies in both directions, and thus suffered far more heavily; some cities, like Magdeburg, and some regions, like Bavaria, may have lost half their population. But not all, perhaps not even most, of these losses were the results of massacres. The indirect effects of war—famine produced by dislocation and migration and an unusual incidence of diseases—were probably worse than the spectacular looting and killing by undisciplined soldiers. [6] But whatever the truth, the Peace of Westphalia, which did not settle everything, at least put an end to most of the fighting.

It did much more. The Peace of Westphalia set the pattern for the

[6] See D. C. Coleman, "Economic Problems and Policies," in *The New Cambridge Modern History*, vol. V (1961), 19–21.

emerging state system of early modern Europe. It exalted the sovereign state at the expense of universal empire, and this meant, before long, the dominance of large powers over small. Few of the provisions of the peace were new; they were important more for what they confirmed than for what they created. The peace confirmed, first of all, the disintegration of Germany, a reality since the early sixteenth century, now officially recognized and thus harder than ever to reverse. At the insistence of the chief victors, Sweden and France, the three hundred or more German states participated in the peacemaking as individual sovereign powers, and the peace itself granted them all the sovereignty they had demanded. Sovereignty meant self-determination in foreign and domestic affairs—the peace specified that the Reichstag, in which all these hundreds of sovereign units participated as equals, alone could levy taxes, raise armies, make treaties. This official recognition of the old "German liberties" reduced the emperor to little more than a ceremonial head of a quarrelsome collection of independent entities.

One of the most highly desired consequences of sovereignty was self-determination in religious matters. The principle of the Peace of Augsburg, now almost a century old, giving each prince the right to dictate the faith of his subjects, was now written into the peace settlement; in addition, the peace recognized the Calvinists and granted the Protestants all the conquests they had made since 1624. This meant that Germany was to be long divided among small free cities, vest-pocket states, and a few larger and voracious units—each Lutheran, Calvinist, Catholic as its master chose. The old principle of *cuius regio, eius religio* benefited not merely the Lutherans and the Calvinists: it meant also that the Protestants promised not to interfere in the vigorous Hapsburg campaign to convert all the subjects in its scattered territories into obedient Catholics. Both the Reformation and the Counter-Reformation had failed in their common aim—the only thing they had in common: their hope of cleansing Europe of heretics.

Since no single German state was powerful enough to overawe and control the others, the assault on the remaining powers of the empire amounted to the elimination of Germany from international politics for a long time to come. This obviously pleased the French, who wanted Germany weak, but it also pleased the German princelings, who wanted to be, or at least appear to be, independent rulers. Since the peace named Sweden and France as guarantors, for more than a century France (for Sweden soon dropped out of the great-power game) happily meddled in German affairs on the excuse of safeguarding the settlement of 1648. And that settlement enfeebled the empire not merely by confirming the sovereignty of German states, but also by recognizing the independence of the Dutch Republic and of the Swiss Cantons (another pair of old realities now signed and sealed) and removing them from the empire. The peace further reduced the empire's territory by giving the French three bishoprics in Lorraine—Metz, Toul, and Verdun—which they had held for almost a hundred years.[7] Sweden, too, was paid off: no victor went empty-handed. While the territories granted to Sweden—the bishopric of Bremen and most of Pomerania—remained within the empire, these acquisitions gave the Swedes control over the mouths of several important German rivers, including the Oder and the Elbe. Since Westphalia also confirmed the Dutch hold over the mouth of the Scheldt (see p. 196), and since the Dutch already held that of the Rhine, the settlement of 1648 left the outlets of all major German rivers in the hands of foreign powers.

The Peace of Westphalia thus exacerbated Germany's weakness and imposed recognition of religious coexistence and of the state system. It also loosened the hold of the Hapsburgs over Europe by weakening each of its branches—the Spanish and the Austrian—and by weakening the bonds between the two. Spain turned inward, Austria turned toward eastern Europe. Thus 1648 brought to the forefront, more than ever before, the states of northwestern Europe: France, England, and to a lesser degree, the Dutch Republic. Yet not even these states escaped the times of troubles that plagued Europe in these decades.

TIMES OF TROUBLES

The Travail of Spain

From a later perspective, Spain's travail in and after the 1640s seemed foreordained. But contemporaries did not see it quite that way. True: Spain was far from prosperous, far from displaying the formidable power it had displayed in the sixteenth century, but the reign of Philip IV began in 1621 with some signs of recovery. The king's chief minister, the count-duke Olivares, vigorously addressed himself to domestic reform. Besides, the presence of Spanish troops in Germany and, for a time, in France itself, forcefully suggested that Spain was still a great power to be feared. Yet what had been true in the sixteenth century was true now: the show of strength abroad revealed, and produced, the reality of weakness at home; one of the causes of Spain's time of troubles was a foreign policy the country could not afford. In 1640, the impression of power proved an illusion.

The first evidence of the real state of affairs came from Catalonia. This northeastern province of Spain, with its indigenous tradition and proud culture, had long viewed its subjection to Madrid with resentment, and Catalans had

---

[7] In the imperial province of Alsace, the French were handed the governance of cities and territories on conditions so unclear that Louis XIV later built claims to absolute control on them (see p. 305).

long asserted a measure of independence. When, in 1639, Richelieu's troops invaded Spain by taking the Catalonian fortress of Salces, the Catalans found themselves in an odd position: they vehemently defended their own territory and asked Madrid for additional help. But it seemed to the Catalans, with much justice, that Olivares was interested more in securing the submission of Catalonia to the central monarchy than in driving out the French. Philip's viceroy, the count of Santa Coloma, though Catalan in origin, found himself compelled to carry out policies that his fellow Catalans found intolerably humiliating: he billeted Castilian troops on Catalonia, disregarded Catalan advice, had distinguished Catalans arrested. In March 1640 there were riots in the streets; in May Catalans forcibly freed their imprisoned leaders; in June there were serious and bloody clashes and Santa Coloma himself was murdered. Civil war began. It did not end until 1659, with a substantial victory for the Catalans. While Spanish troops had taken Barcelona in 1652, this proved a hollow victory for Madrid: the city surrendered on condition that provincial autonomy be respected, and the crown was too weak to disregard its promises. Spain's territorial integrity was preserved, at a price.

In the early stages of the Catalan uprising one great piece of news sustained the rebels: in December 1640 there was a revolt in Portugal, itself stimulated by the events in Catalonia. As in Barcelona, so in Lisbon, Richelieu encouraged unrest; the duke of Braganza was persuaded by his family and his advisors to advance his claim to the Portuguese throne, and on December 1, 1640, with Portugal practically empty of Spanish troops, the rebellion began. It was quick and almost bloodless. Acclaimed as King John IV early in the same month, Braganza officially took the throne in January 1641, and Spain's tepid, conspiratorial efforts to nullify the results of the revolt came to nothing. France and the Protestant powers recognized John as king of Portugal; in 1644, at the battle of Montijo, Portuguese troops decisively defeated a Spanish army, and Portugal's independence was secure.

Even in the distant dependency of Naples, Spain reasserted its authority only at the cost of some concessions. Naples was governed by viceroys with extensive powers and dominated by a narrow oligarchy of local, landowning barons; it was a colony of Spain, existing mainly to support Spain's adventures elsewhere; it suffered, as Merriman put it, "from all the bad consequences of an antiquated feudal system and of modern absolutism" without enjoying any "of the compensating advantages of either."[8] Resentment of Castilian domination and of ever-intensifying exploitation was general, but the revolt that broke out in 1647 was essentially a class war, and thus fatally divided the Neapolitans. It began in early June in consequence of a new and stringent tax on fruit; it was the most regressive impost possible, hard on the poor and insignificant for the rich. The revolt was led by a fisherman, Tommaso Aniello, known as Masaniello, a charismatic leader—young, inexperienced, eloquent, and violent.

[8] *Six Contemporaneous Revolutions*, 19.

In a week of confused fighting, widespread pillaging, and large-scale executions, Masaniello and his irregular troops terrorized the viceroy and wholly alienated the aristocracy. Masaniello himself was murdered after a few days of heady, absolute power, but the popular rebellion continued; in October, the rebels proclaimed a republic and once again (as they had done all summer) begged the French for aid. But French policy was too hesitant, and French affairs were too confused, for French assistance to be effective, and by early 1648, the rebellion had flickered out after some conciliatory gestures on the part of Spain. It stands in history as little more than a dramatic episode in the long history of man's exploitation of other men.

Russia: A Century of Turmoil

Between the death of Ivan the Terrible in 1584 (for the period preceding and following, see p. 323) and the accession of Peter the Great in 1689, Russia was in a state of endemic political and social turmoil. The very name "time of troubles" was first coined for the melodramatic years 1604 to 1613, when the power of the *boyars*—the Russian aristocracy—was at its height. But it can be generalized for the century as a whole. The struggle for the throne bore a certain resemblance to the political struggles elsewhere in Europe: the feudal nobility sought to perpetuate its privileges in the face of timid attempts at assertion of state power. But the uncertainty of the succession and the social consequences for the vast majority of Russians, poor peasants, made the Russian experience particularly bitter.

The dynastic situation may be quickly summarized. Ivan IV was the first Russian ruler to take the title of tsar. His sustained ferocity, notorious even in a country where life was hard and cruelty common, was a deliberate policy to establish some form of central control. But such a policy required time and a succession of effective rulers. These Russia did not enjoy: Ivan's son and successor, Feodor I (1584–1598), allowed power to revert into hands from which Ivan had striven to wrest it: the boyars. The effective ruler, even during Feodor's reign, was his brother-in-law Boris Godunov, whom an assembly of nobles elected tsar upon Feodor's death. Once in power (1598–1605) Boris attempted to secure Ivan's aims, with the same shrewdness and the same ferocity, but his efforts were frustrated a year before his death by the appearance of the "false Dmitri," a pretender claiming to be the son of Ivan IV, who had presumably been murdered on orders of Boris in 1591. A year later, Boris died, and for nine confused and terrible years, the succession to the throne was regulated by assassination: Boris' son Feodor was tsar briefly, until he was murdered; he was succeeded by the false Dmitri, who was murdered in turn; and so it went, amid popular rebellions and Polish invasions. Finally, in February 1613, a national assembly elected as tsar Michael Romanov, Ivan the Terrible's great-nephew; from then on at least the succession was clear: Michael (1613–1645) established a dynasty that was to end only with the Russian Revolution in 1917.

Yet, though Romanov was to follow Romanov, social unrest continued and burst into the open in several memorable rebellions. While boyars plotted and murdered, Russian peasants sank deeper and deeper into dependence, and Russia bled; as the fool says in his moving song in Mussorgski's magnificent opera, *Boris Godunov:*

> Cry, faithful heart,
> cry in deep anguish:
> soon the foe will come—
> and the dark will fall—
> night will blind us all
> and no hope of dawn
> is great Russia's sorrow—
> cry—cry—
> Russian land—
> hungry people—
> cry. [9]

The triumph of serfdom in Russia was the triumph of a vicious circle: rich, noble landlords needed peasants to cultivate their vast and underpopulated lands; miserable overworked peasants often chose to flee their exploiters to the border lands, an outward movement of population that landlords sought to prevent by tightening legal control over "their" peasants; this in turn led to renewed flights, which naturally produced efforts at even tighter controls. The flight of the peasant beyond the borders of Muscovy's effective control—into permanent vagrancy, to Siberia, or to the military bands of the Cossacks in the south or southwest—reached its climax late in the sixteenth century: "Many villages and townes of halfe a mile and a mile long, stande all unhabited," a contemporary English visitor noted, "the people being fled all into other places, by reason of the extreme usage and exactions done upon them." [10] By the seventeenth century, economic pressure and legal enactments had reduced such movement to a minimum. Down to the fifteenth and in many areas the sixteenth centuries, Russian peasants had by and large met their tax, labor, and military obligations as free men; now, in a series of laws passed at the insistence of landlords and as rigorously enforced as was humanly possible, Russian peasants became serfs, practically slaves. They were bound to the land; they had few legal rights against their masters, who in contrast, had almost complete jurisdiction over them; by the end of the seventeenth century, peasants could be bought and sold like so much merchandise. The landlord was employer, father, judge, tsar to the peasant, all in one, and the peasant's lot depended wholly on his master's character and caprice.

This degradation of the vast majority of Russians, exacerbated by continuous warfare, political disorder, and ever-increasing taxation, was fuel for unrest and rebellion. In 1648, there was a merchant-led uprising in Moscow

---

[9] Act IV, scene 3, tr. by John Gutman (1953).
[10] Quoted in Geroid Tanqueray Robinson, *Rural Russia Under the Old Regime* (1932), 16–17.

to protest the harsh imposition and arbitrary collection of a salt tax; in 1662, the debasement of the coinage provoked another urban rebellion. But it was the Cossack-led peasant uprisings that seemed most threatening to the state bureaucracy. Such uprisings were a recurrent theme in Russian history; in the seventeenth century they were only more frequent and more desperate than at other times. In 1668, the Don Cossacks, led by Stenka Razin, started a campaign of terror in the region near the Caspian Sea and along the lower Volga; they resented what they considered the encroachment of Russian landlords on their own free land. As their rebellion spread they appealed to all the nostalgia burgeoning in a time of drastic social change: the longing for the old days when tsars had been good fathers and when *boyars* had been servants not masters. In 1670, Stenka Razin's motley but energetic army, reinforced by runaway serfs, resentful tribesmen, restless nobles, and disaffected government troops, turned northward and took some fortified cities. Yet his reign of terror against the state and against the landlords was short-lived; in September 1670, Stenka Razin, a figure of almost legendary stature, suffered his first defeat, and in April 1671, he was betrayed, captured, and taken to Moscow. In June he was executed with a barbarity still widespread in Europe but particularly characteristic for the Russia of his day: he was tortured, drawn, and quartered. The ferocity with which the Russian state suppressed all these rebellions has been taken as a sign of weakness and fear; that may be so, but its consequence was the confirmation and strengthening of serfdom in Russian society. [11]

Troubles for the Victors

The crisis of the seventeenth century left its mark even on those countries that had profited from the Thirty Years' War. When Gustavus Adolphus of Sweden fell at Lützen in 1632 (see p. 253), his daughter, Christina, was a girl of six; the early years of her reign were therefore years of regency under the governance of Gustavus' trusted chancellor, Axel Oxenstierna. But even after she took command in 1644, Christina proved less interested in ruling than in art, philosophy, and display. Yet it was not her indifference, it was her consistent policy of favoring the nobility, that caused seditious murmurs. In 1650, the Swedish Diet, which had won considerable freedom of action in preceding decades, found its three unprivileged estates—peasants, burghers, and priests—pitted against the nobility; the queen herself lamented that "neither king nor *parlement* have their proper power, but the common man, the *canaille*, rules according to his fancy." [12] It was hardly a just complaint: since before her

---

[11] For cultural and political developments leading to the reign of Peter the Great, see p. 324.
[12] Quoted in Michael Roberts, "Queen Christina and the General Crisis of the Seventeenth Century," in Roberts, *Essays in Swedish History* (1962), 112.

accession, and in greatly increased tempo after 1648, the crown had alienated, by sale and donation, much of its land to the nobility, in part to simplify the Swedish tax structure, in part to reward loyal officers, in part to gratify aristocrats who pleased the queen. In consequence, an exclusive group grew even richer than before and threatened the lower estates, particularly the peasants on their land, with their powers to exploit and tax their dependents. It was against this that the Riksdag protested, demanding that the crown take back some of its lands. The queen was already toying with conversion to Roman Catholicism and was bent on having her cousin, Charles, declared her successor and hereditary prince of Sweden. In 1649 she persuaded the Diet to grant the first; in 1650, offering concessions to the lower orders, she obtained the second. When she abdicated and emigrated in 1654, leaving the country in the hands of Charles X, the crisis was over, and only a pair of victims, executed for sedition, testified to its potentially explosive quality.

In the Dutch Republic, the crisis was less bloody and more consequential. Since its inception, the republic had witnessed a struggle between the centralizing forces led by the house of Orange, and the decentralizing forces represented in the States General. The defeat of Oldenbarneveldt by Prince Maurice (see p. 196) had given the Orangists the ascendancy; Maurice's successor, Frederick Henry, though less militant, was quite as insistent on his authority: stadholder in six of the seven provinces, and addressed after 1637 as Your Highness, he wielded great power. In 1647 he died; his son, William II, succeeded to his father's titles. William was young, headstrong, bellicose, and inordinately ambitious: that he was the husband of Mary Stuart, daughter of Charles I of England, did not help him to recognize his limitations or those of his country. The States were looking toward peace and final recognition of the independence of the Dutch Republic; the stadholder, in secret conversations with France, sought to continue the war against Spain. The States wanted to muster out most of the Dutch army—which was, of course, under the stadholder's command—but William II resisted. Conflict grew sharper month by month; neither of the two greatest powers in the United Provinces was willing to yield more than a few steps. But in late October 1650, William II was stricken with the smallpox; early in November 1650, he died, just in time to avoid civil war. Mary Stuart was pregnant, but she was delivered too late; her son, the future King William III of England, was born after his father's death, and in any event, the Orangist party was leaderless. Province after province decided to forego electing a stadholder, and for twenty-two years, until William III of Orange resumed the office, the provinces looked to their own affairs. But they did not fall into anarchy: in 1653, Jan de Witt became grand pensionary of Holland and, in effect, chief statesman of the Dutch Republic. In this one country, at least, the crisis took a mild, even beneficent form. With the Netherlands' neighbor and rival across the channel, it was to be a far more sanguinary affair.

ENGLAND: FROM RESENTMENT TO REVOLUTION

James I: The Road to Confrontation

In the course of the eighteenth century, Great Britain acquired an enviable reputation for political stability; in the seventeenth, Britain was a byword for turmoil. Its dubious record included one king executed, another king exiled; the monarchical succession interrupted by a republic; the state church torn apart, deposed, reinstated; the nobility discredited, disfranchised, restored; Parliament enlarging its power at the expense of the crown. Fittingly enough, when James VI of Scotland came south in 1603 to assume the English throne as James I, he was greeted by a short, devastating outbreak of the plague in London. But affairs in general seemed prosperous and promising. Two days before her death, Elizabeth I had emphatically silenced all speculation about her successor: "A King," she said, "should succeed me; and who should that be but our cousin of Scotland?" What was more, England was pleased by her choice, and Elizabeth's able advisor, Robert Cecil, the son of her old mentor, Lord Burghley, was ready to serve his new monarch, the first of the Stuart line. Cheered by his reception, James reciprocated the loyal acclaim of his English subjects by diluting the estate of knighthood: in the first four months of his reign, he dubbed 906 knights, thus trebling the size of the order. [13]

Early Stuart England was still a minor power: counting Wales, its population amounted to little more than four million, and as an island protected from invasion, it had a sizable navy but no army. Yet the signs of growth were everywhere. English traders roamed the seas: the Baltic, the Mediterranean, the Atlantic, the rich spice islands of Asia lay open to its adventurous sailors. While most of England's towns were small—Norwich, its second city, had thirty thousand inhabitants—bustling, bursting London, with its cluster of suburbs, boasted (though visitors complained of) its two hundred thousand inhabitants. When James I first saw it, the city controlled seven eighths of England's trade. The yeoman estate was flourishing. The English coal industry could barely satisfy the rapidly growing demand; at the accession of Elizabeth I in 1558, total production had amounted to two hundred thousand tons a year; at the accession of James I, it had risen to 1.5 million, and by the time of the Glorious Revolution, to nearly three million tons.

> England's a perfect world! has Indies too!
> Correct your maps: Newcastle is Peru—

[13] Lawrence Stone, *The Crisis of the Aristocracy, 1558-1641* (1965), 74.

exclaimed the poet John Cleveland in 1651.[14] The woollen industry continued to be, as it had been for a century, England's principal manufacture and England's principal exporter. Though rudimentary in organization and small in size, there were industries in James' reign capitalized at £10,000 and more. Spain and France might disdain England as a second-class power, but its emergence as a first-class power could not be long delayed.

Yet James I had scarcely settled into his office when he confronted a set of problems he was to hand on, unsolved, to his successor: problems above all of religion and finance, exacerbated by England's unsettled foreign relations and by his own awkward personality. And all these problems brought James into conflict with Parliament.

The Elizabethan religious settlement had been not so much a permanent solution as a screen behind which conflicts of conscience might play themselves out in veiled decency. The studied ambiguities of Anglicanism, adroitly captured in the formulas of its Thirty-Nine Articles, had permitted large segments of the English people to live in peace with themselves and their state. But Puritan discontent, both with the organization of the Anglican church and with its doctrine, was endemic and unappeasable—matters of religious principle are notoriously hard to compromise.[15] The Church of England was burdened at the top with wealthy, relatively worldly pluralists, and crowded at the bottom with unlettered and impecunious clerics. And the whole panoply of Anglican ceremonial and discipline remained offensive to Puritan souls intent on confronting their God without intermediaries.

In Scotland, James had been humiliated by the dominant and domineering Presbyterians, but he was not wholly unsympathetic to the complaints that English Puritans now addressed to him. The so-called Millenary Petition[16] that Puritan clerics had presented to James on his way to London seemed to him worth investigating. Puritan grievances, which this petition summarized, were fivefold: Anglican ceremonies were reminiscent of the old popish faith discarded at the Reformation; preaching was perfunctory; Anglican bishops were "pluralists," holding too many livings at once, thus scanting their pastoral duties; the Anglican church was omnipresent and too severe, using its power of excommunication to excess; finally, the Anglicans' neglect of the Sabbath urgently called for correction.

In 1604, James I met at Hampton Court Palace with delegations of churchmen and granted the Puritans some of their demands: he promised to check pluralism and to see to better preaching. He agreed also to secure a "uniform translation" of the Bible—this was the germ of the celebrated, irreplaceable Authorized Version, the "King James Version," of 1611. But the

---

[14] Charles Wilson, *England's Apprenticeship, 1603–1763* (1965), 80.

[15] English "Puritans," it must be remembered, were loyal members of the Anglican church and sought to reshape it from within.

[16] It is called this because its drafters claimed a thousand signatures, a dubious figure.

king had no intention of reorganizing the Anglican church on Presbyterian principles. "A Scottish Presbytery," he said caustically, "agreeth as well with a monarchy as God and the Devil. Then Jack and Tom and Will and Dick shall meet, and at their pleasures censure me and my Council." And in a testy outburst, he warned the Puritans to conform: otherwise he would "harry them out of the land." Every student of American history knows that this is what James actually was to do: some three hundred clergymen who would not accept the Book of Common Prayer were stripped of their livings, and it was a group of Puritan Separatists from Nottinghamshire who, tired of ridicule and harassment, left England for the Dutch Republic in 1607 and finally landed in America in 1620, where they formed Plymouth Colony. There had been English colonists in Virginia since 1607, but the founding legend of the United States— the voyage of the *Mayflower* and the travails of the Pilgrim fathers—had its origins in the Anglican policy of James I. Religion was not a trivial issue for seventeenth-century Englishmen: religion, and the church, impinged on their lives literally every day. James' Anglican policy, which became more stiff-necked with the passage of years, was a touchy political issue. And it incensed many members of Parliament, already in a bellicose mood, for Parliament was filled with men of Puritan sympathies.

It was only James' desperate need for money—"this eating canker of want," he called it—that made this confrontation so consequential. James had inherited a debt of £400,000 from Elizabeth I, a debt that had risen to over £700,000 only three years later; in subsequent years the king, who was nothing if not prodigal, would spend on the average £200,000 a year more than he took in. The medieval principle that the king must live on his own income, often breached before, now was wholly inapplicable: the sources of revenue on which James I could draw were simply inadequate. He had at his disposal anachronistic feudal privileges, like wardships, which brought some income and much irritation; he increased customs duties; like his predecessor, he sold crown lands, a technique that secured immediate but reduced long-term revenues; he sold monopolies to merchants and honors to anyone who could buy them. In 1611 the crown marketed—it is the only word—the new hereditary title of baronet for £1095, with the promise that it would name no more than two hundred, a promise that James kept and his successor would break. All these desperate fiscal expedients brought in less than the king needed, and so James had to go to Parliament for supplies. Thus the epic struggle began.

Liberal historians, imbued with detestation for absolutism and admiration for parliamentary government, have often portrayed this struggle as a virtuous assertion of parliamentary rights endangered by swollen royal pretensions. But this is anachronistic: however much we may wish to applaud the outcome of the struggle, in the Stuart period Parliament was, in fact, the aggressor. Elizabeth had kept her parliaments under tight control, shrewdly exploiting the length and successes of her reign and converting the liability of her sex into an asset. She too had insisted on the royal "prerogative." It was not so much what James I claimed, as when and how he claimed it, that aroused parliamentary opposition.

James' most formidable adversary was his chief justice, Sir Edward Coke, grown into a rigid defender of the common law and Parliament as the source of legislation. The king, Coke insisted, cannot create law, and he angered his royal master by arguing that however great the king's "natural reason," the law must rest on "artificial reason," that is, the judgment of those who were, as the king was not, "learned in the laws of his realm of England." It was against the assertion that the courts must be independent of royal pressure and Parliament the sole source of legislation that the king pitted his claim to absolute authority. It did not help his cause that he should so often and so tactlessly reiterate it. As early as 1598 James had anonymously published a treatise, *The True Law of Free Monarchies,* in which he had committed himself to what was known as the divine right of kings. The theory, for all its formidable name, was merely an extreme statement of a widely accepted idea: that the king is the source of legislation. In 1616, James restated it in a particularly offensive way: "That which concerns the mystery of the King's power is not lawful to be disputed," for to argue about it is "to take away the mystical reverence that belongs unto them that sit in the throne of God."

Obviously the conflict between James I and his parliaments was more than a clash of individuals: it sprang from, and expressed, the growing wealth, power, and self-confidence of the Commons, and it reflected, ironically enough, the increasing safety of England from foreign invasion. But it was also a matter of personalities. True, his popularity was reinforced by the extravagant Catholic Gunpowder Plot of 1605, which aimed at blowing up the king along with Parliament. But James I was a learned man[17] who showed his learning, something few men can tolerate. And he was a homosexual addicted to favorites for qualities irrelevant to statesmanship. The most damaging and most lasting of his attachments was to George Villiers, whom in his infatuation he created duke of Buckingham, and who vastly enriched himself and his family. Greedy and corrupt almost beyond belief, Buckingham shamelessly sold monopolies and honors and pushed his relatives into profitable and conspicuous posts. Buckingham's visibility was as high as his influence was pernicious, and his ascendancy did little to support James' pretensions to more than human stature.

Charles I: The Confrontation

James' son Charles, who succeeded in 1625, was neither learned nor homosexual; but his liabilities were, if anything, more crippling. For one thing, he retained Buckingham as his chief advisor, and between them, the two rapidly plunged the country into political and military folly. Charles was not enough of a statesman to find his way through the maze of international events, not enough of a politician to come to terms with Parliament. He was stubborn,

---

[17] The disdainful epithet of "pedant" is a late and inaccurate invention.

devious, wholly undependable. His father had made peace with Spain in 1604, a peace many Englishmen had resented for economic as much as religious reasons; when in 1623, James had sent Charles, accompanied by Buckingham, to Spain to woo the Spanish infanta, protests were loud. But Charles had come back without a bride, insulted by the treatment he had received and anxious for war with Spain. After his accession, Charles made ready for that war. Like his father he was in need of money and called Parliament. Like his father, he found Parliament intractable.

James had called four parliaments in all and each had gathered strength and experience from its predecessors. His first parliament had sat from 1604 to 1611, accomplishing little but to define the opposing positions; the second sat for two months in 1614 and accomplished nothing except to train new parliamentary leaders including Sir John Eliot and Sir Thomas Wentworth [18] in the art of frustrating royal designs—it is known, from its inaction, as the Addled Parliament. The third sat for a year, from early 1621 to early 1622, and is noted for the Great Protestation of December 1621, which declared "that the liberties, franchises, privileges, and jurisdictions of Parliament are the ancient and undoubted birthright and inheritance of the subjects of England; and that the arduous and urgent affairs concerning the King, State, and defense of the realm, and of the Church of England, and the maintenance and making of laws, and redress of mischiefs and grievances which daily happen within this realm, are proper subjects and matter of counsel and debate in Parliament; and that in the handling and proceeding of those businesses every member of the House of Parliament hath, and of right ought to have, freedom of speech to propound, treat, reason, and bring to conclusion the same." James I, in a fury, tore this offensive declaration from the journal of the House with his own hands. Yet his last parliament, which sat from early 1624 to early 1625, secured a right that English kings had always reserved to themselves: to advise on foreign policy. And this parliament, like its immediate predecessor, used its privilege of impeachment against royal servants to weaken the royal power and enhance its own.

Royal weakness quickly became apparent with Charles I's first parliament, a short affair lasting from June to August 1625. Spain was vastly unpopular, but Buckingham's oily assurances of loyalty to Protestant principles and of his readiness to take advice on policy were so obviously mendacious that the Commons took an unprecedented step. It had been normal practice for centuries to grant a new monarch the revenues from customs duties ("tonnage and poundage") for life; Commons now proposed to grant them for one year. Before it could enact this rebellious measure, Charles I had dissolved Parliament and collected the customs revenues on his own authority. But from the outset his war with Spain (complicated after early 1627 by a rash war with France) went badly: disasters befell the British navy with almost comical

---

[18] In 1639 Charles I would create Wentworth earl of Strafford.

repetitiousness, and most of these were the direct responsibility of Buckingham who was, after all, lord high admiral. When Charles called his second parliament in February 1626, it had a naval fiasco off Cadiz to brood about. Sir John Eliot, once a supporter but now a resolute enemy of Buckingham, an independent country gentleman and an eloquent orator, moved to impeach him: "In reference to the King," Eliot said, Buckingham "must be styled the canker in his treasure; in reference to the State, the moth of all goodness." The king briefly imprisoned Eliot, then released him, and dissolved Parliament in June, continuing to raise revenues without parliamentary assent, largely by collecting forced loans. The expedient, vigorously resented and widely resisted, produced less than Charles needed; when Buckingham once more disgraced his policy, his king, and himself by an incredibly incompetent effort to relieve the French Huguenots, then under siege by Richelieu at La Rochelle (see p. 284), the old tragicomedy repeated itself: in March 1628, Charles I called his third parliament.

Predictably, its members were in an unyielding mood. To appease tempers all around, the government had released seventy-six men imprisoned for refusing to pay the forced loan. But twenty-seven of these, including Sir Thomas Wentworth, sat in the third parliament, and they did their best not to calm, but to inflame the temper of both houses. [19] They refused to vote supplies before the redress of grievances, and upon Coke's suggestion, drew up a Petition of Right, which was agreed upon, after much debate, in May. This concerted attack on the prerogative is a great constitutional document. It declared that forced gifts, benevolences, or loans must not be levied without Parliament's assent; that no one must be arbitrarily imprisoned; and that the billeting of soldiers on private subjects without their consent must henceforth cease. Protesting that the petition would "dissolve the foundation and frame of our monarchy," Charles I nevertheless signed it in June, and obtained, in return, some of the funds he had asked for. But his troubles were not at an end. The Commons, more and more inclined to take the lead in parliamentary business, demanded Buckingham's dismissal: "I think the Duke of Buckingham," said Coke, speaking for them all, "is the cause of all our miseries. . . . That man is the grievance of grievances." Charles, rather than heed the outcry, prorogued Parliament, but indirectly Parliament had its revenge on the hated minister: in August 1628, John Felton, a naval lieutenant, brooding on a fancied failure to receive adequate recognition and adequate pay, and further disoriented by the Commons' denunciations of the royal favorite, stabbed Buckingham to death.

Ironically, the assassination, far from smoothing Charles' relations with Parliament, only exacerbated them; the general outlines of his policy were set in his mind, and Buckingham's abrupt death compelled him to find new men.

[19] See Joseph Robson Tanner, *English Constitutional Conflicts of the Seventeenth Century, 1603–1689* (1962), 61.

These proved more competent, and also more determined, than the friend he had lost. When Charles I confronted a new session of Parliament in January 1629, he had as his chief advisors Thomas Wentworth, now Viscount Wentworth, who, alarmed by the course of events he had helped to shape, had joined the royal service in 1628, and William Laud, bishop of London since the same year. Both were strong and effective men; both have remained controversial. Their policy was vigorous, even merciless, and wholly consistent: to strengthen royal authority by finding revenues if necessary without the aid and against the wishes of Parliament and the interests represented there, and to subject the country to firm Anglican rule. It is from the amicable correspondence of the two statesmen that their policy derives its name of Thorough. It meant resolute government by the king and his ministers and the crushing of opposition.

The first sign of the policy of Thorough came in March 1629, after some rousing sessions in the House of Commons in which three truculent resolutions of Sir John Eliot had been read out, while two strong members of Commons held the Speaker in the chair to prevent adjournment at the king's command. Eliot and other leaders of the opposition were arrested and imprisoned, and Parliament was dissolved. Charles I, it was said, acted as if a weight had been taken from his shoulders. It was, for eleven years: from 1629 to 1640, a time known dramatically and rather inaccurately as the Eleven Years' Tyranny, Charles I and his ministers governed England without benefit of parliamentary advice or consent. And they did so, it must be added, with fair success. By 1630, Charles had made peace with France and Spain, and while he continued a foreign policy of drift, at least two costly ventures were over. And at home, while the rule of Wentworth and Laud was scarcely millennium for the poor, the government did make some effort at efficient administration, caring for the indigent, and controlling greedy monopolists and enclosers of land. The great royalist historian Clarendon was exaggerating when he said later that in 1639 "England enjoyed the greatest measure of felicity it had ever known," [20] but it remains true that the English people did not groan under unprecedented tyranny and did not stage demonstrations for the return of parliamentary government. The forces dominating the House of Commons—self-respecting country squires and lawyers with pronounced leanings toward Puritanism— were prosperous, angry, and articulate, and it was these groups, and their followers, whom Charles I mortally affronted.

For some years the king had things his own way. Eliot, growing feeble and denied leave from the Tower to recover, died in prison in November 1632. As Charles had held Eliot responsible for the death of Buckingham, the parliamentary party now held Charles responsible for the death of Eliot. And in August 1633, Charles named Laud archbishop of Canterbury, thus endorsing, with as much emphasis as he could muster, Laud's ferocious Anglicanism. Laud was

---

[20] Quoted in Maurice Ashley, *England in the Seventeenth Century* (1960), 71.

honest and courageous, but his undisputable virtues came perilously close to being vices: His gravity amounted to humorlessness, his candor to tactlessness, his clarity to imperiousness, his energy to ruthlessness. Besides, he was unlucky, perhaps inescapably so, in being tarred with the papist brush: the king he served so well was married to Henrietta Maria, sister of Louis XIII of France, a Roman Catholic who enjoyed a notorious ascendancy over her husband. Charles was surrounded by Catholic ministers and allowed ambassadors from Roman Catholic countries access to him. Of humble origins but with an excellent Oxford education, Laud was determined to secure uniformity of Anglican observances throughout his domains and obedience of all to the state; James I's celebrated aphorism "no bishop, no king," expressed Laud's ecclesiastical politics to perfection. Laud protected the High Church service from contamination; he assiduously visited churches to see that their furnishings and their preaching accorded with High Church principles and that no unlicensed lecturers—Puritans all—could seduce Anglican flocks from true principles. As chief advisor to the king and as archbishop of Canterbury, Laud had free recourse to the Star Chamber and the ecclesiastical court of High Commission to harass and silence Puritans. He was anything but a papist; he was an Arminian (see p. 195 for the origins of the term), but to his Puritan enemies this was a distinction without a difference: "An Arminian is the spawn of a Papist," one member of Parliament said in 1629, ". . . if you mark it well, you shall see an Arminian reaching out his hand to a Papist, a Papist to a Jesuit, a Jesuit gives one hand to the Pope and the other to the King of Spain."[21]

Charles' campaign for religious conformity struck at the Puritans; his search for fiscal solvency without Parliament systematically offended merchants, gentry, and nobles. Against often courageous resistance, the king continued to levy tonnage and poundage on his own authority and revived a series of obsolete laws as excuses for extorting money from men of wealth and property. He fined gentlemen who refused knighthoods and the expenses that came with them; he forced property owners with land once held as royal forests to pay for the right of continued ownership; he discovered new and obnoxious possibilities for that old abuse, the monopoly. But his most offensive and most profitable expedient was ship money, a tax originally imposed on seaports to supply ships or, failing that, funds to the navy. In 1634, Charles issued a traditional writ for ship money; in 1635, he extended it to inland counties; in 1636, in a third writ, he abandoned all pretense of raising emergency funds for the navy: ship money stood revealed, quite plainly, as a tax, levied, moreover, without parliamentary consent. In the following year, John Hampden, country squire, member of Parliament, and cousin to Oliver Cromwell, challenged the

[21] Quoted in Tanner, *Constitutional Conflicts*, 68n. It is worth noting that what James' Anglican policy began, Laud's policy of Thorough continued: in the 1630s and early 1640s, some sixteen thousand Englishmen, nearly all of them unhappy Puritans, swelled the colony of Massachusetts Bay, which had begun so inconspicuously as Plymouth Colony in 1620.

legality of ship money; by the narrow vote of seven to five, the judges in the Court of the Exchequer found for the crown, in an alarming extension of the royal prerogative. "I never read nor heard, that lex was rex;" one of the judges wrote, "but it is common and most true, that rex is lex, for he is 'lex loquens,' a living, a speaking, an acting law." [22] This meant that in emergencies, the king could do as he pleased, and what was an emergency was defined by the king. It was a great victory for Charles I, but he had soon cause to regret it. Resistance to collection of ship money stiffened, and in the same year, in 1637, rebellion broke out—not over money but over religion, and not in England, but in Scotland.

Charles I: Into Civil War

In 1603, a union of crowns began a process that was completed in 1707 with a union of parliaments; in the intervening century, Scotland played a peculiarly disturbing part in English affairs. [23] Early in his reign, in 1606 and 1607, James I had broached the possibility of a closer union between the two countries, but his plans had collapsed under the concerted prejudice of his English subjects. James still had the support of the Scottish nobility; his son Charles, though born in Scotland, alienated that nobility with an act of revocation by which, at a single stroke, he took back lands his predecessors had handed out for nearly a century. More ominous, he aroused the hatred of the dominant Calvinists with his effort to impose Anglicanism on Scotland. Laud had been making efforts in this direction since 1633, but real riots erupted only in July 1637, when a clergyman in St. Giles Cathedral in Edinburgh read the service from the new prayer book, adapted from the Anglican Book of Common Prayer. "The mass is entered amongst us!" Jenny Geddes shouted, threw her stool at the minister's head, and started a melee which grew into countrywide resistance. Charles, backed by Laud, refused to yield or compromise, and in February 1638, thousands of Scots subscribed to the National Covenant, a vehement repudiation of Laud's attempts to fasten "the Popish religion and tyranny" on Scotland, and a solemn pledge to "recover the purity and liberty of the Gospel." The uncompromising policy of Thorough had produced an uncompromising response. The Scots were the first to arm; the bloodless First Bishops' War proved an embarrassing setback for the royal forces. In June 1639, Charles was compelled to conclude the Treaty of Berwick which gave the Scots the right to call a new assembly of the church. When that assembly insisted on the abolition of episcopacy—a decision Charles could under no circumstances accept—full-scale war was inevitable. But such war was expensive, and so Laud

---

[22] Ibid., 83.
[23] See H. R. Trevor-Roper, "Scotland and the Puritan Revolution" (1963), in his *Crisis of the Seventeenth Century: Religion, the Reformation, and Social Change* (1968).

and Wentworth persuaded Charles to convoke Parliament. What Englishmen anxious about their liberties or their pocketbooks had been unable to do with speeches, lawsuits, or tax evasion, Scottish Calvinists, zealously attached to their beliefs and their ceremonies, did with a show of force. In mid-April 1640, Charles I called his fourth parliament.

It is not called the Short Parliament for nothing: Charles dissolved it after three weeks. The Short Parliament was dominated by an experienced member of the Commons, John Pym, a sensible speaker and skillful parliamentarian. In long and memorable speeches, Pym urged the House to put the redress of grievances before the granting of supplies, and reinforced his position by patiently listing the wrongs to which the country had been subjected in the last fifteen years. Pym carried the House with him; Charles, infuriated, had to find his funds elsewhere. The subservient Irish Parliament and an equally pliant Convocation (the legislative body of the church) had already granted him £300,000; Wentworth (now earl of Strafford) advised the king to appeal to the wealthy merchants of the City of London. But the City refused, and English officers faced the Scots in the field with scant supplies and mutinous troops. In late October, Charles ended the Second Bishops' War, on terms as humiliating as the Treaty of Berwick. He left the Scots in possession of northern England and undertook to pay the Scottish army still under arms. Only a new parliament could fulfill the promises a humiliated king had been compelled to make.

In November, Charles' fifth and last parliament met at Westminster; it was as long as its predecessor had been short. The most dramatic parliament in English history, it was not officially dissolved until 1660. The men who had been masters in its predecessor were masters in the Long Parliament as well. Under Pym's able and implacable leadership, the House of Commons, far from voting supplies, addressed itself to redressing grievances. On its orders, Puritan leaders now in prison were released; then it impeached the king's chief ministers for breaking "fundamental laws"—Strafford in November, Laud in December of 1640. The king himself was still beyond the reach of his rebellious subjects. When it became clear that Strafford would be acquitted in his trial before the House of Lords, the Commons abandoned the impeachment and secured his conviction on a bill of attainder instead; if his guilt could not be adjudicated, it could be legislated. The Lords and Charles, under pressure from conveniently engineered mobs, gave their consent, and Strafford died bravely in May 1641; Laud, harmless in prison, was attainted later and executed in January 1645. Other royal ministers fled.

Having eliminated the agents of absolutism, Pym and his associates now wrecked its machinery. As early as February 1641, Parliament had underscored its new-found power with the Triennial Act, which specified that Parliament must be called into session every three years. Late in the spring and through the summer of 1641, in a burst of frantic activity, the Commons continued on its revolutionary course. In May Parliament declared that it could not be dissolved without its own consent. In June it insisted that taxes could be levied only with parliamentary assent. In July it abolished the Star Chamber, the Court of High Commission, and other prerogative courts, those lethal instruments of the royal will—once beneficent but now perverted. In August it declared the hated ship money unlawful. And also in August it deprived the king of his last fiscal expedients by undoing his manipulations of royal forests and knighthoods. [24] Never before in English history, and never since, has so much power been shifted so easily.

Pym had managed to keep his forces united by concentrating on grievances they all shared and avoiding an issue on which they differed: religion. As religious matters had brought rebellion in 1637, so were they to bring disunity to the parliamentary forces in 1641. Early in the year there had been rumblings among radical Puritans, the "root and branch" men, intent on abolishing episcopacy and drastically revising the Book of Common Prayer. In November 1641, when Parliament addressed a Grand Remonstrance to the king, the principles of root and branch found vivid expression. Much of the Remonstrance, to be sure, was a plain appeal to the public; it catalogued what Charles I had done wrong and what Parliament had already done, and must still do, to set it right. But its demand for a "reformation" in the church caused exhausting debates and sharp divisions, and the Remonstrance carried by only a small majority—159 to 148. It was a great moment in the history of the great events then unrolling, and those present at the debate knew it. "If the Remonstrance had been rejected," Oliver Cromwell said about himself, "he would have sold all he had the next morning, and never have seen England more; and he knew there were many other honest men of the same resolution." [25]

Commons was divided on another issue as well. Late in October a revolt had broken out in Ireland, an unhappy country long colonized—that is to say, systematically exploited—by Englishmen. Strafford, lord deputy of Ireland since 1632, had kept Ireland under firm control; his absence brought relief and rebellion. Charles asked Parliament for troops to suppress the Irish rebels, but Pym, suspicious of a king he thought capable of using troops intended for Ireland against the Parliament, insisted that funds should be granted only if Parliament approved the king's ministers. This was a revolutionary assertion of parliamentary supremacy, and it passed by only 151 to 110.

Charles now made a characteristic mistake: instead of playing on the divisions in Parliament, he united it with a foolish act of force. In January 1642, he tried to have five members of Commons arrested, including Pym and Hampden. The House refused to turn them over to his men, and when the king appeared in person, the five members were gone. When Charles asked the Speaker of the House, once a royal appointee and mere messenger boy, if any of the members were present, Speaker Lenthall fell on his knees and humbly,

[24] For these laws, see Tanner, *Constitutional Conflicts*, 96–99.
[25] Ibid., 111.

but firmly replied: "May it please your Majesty, I have neither eyes to see nor tongue to speak in this place but as this House is pleased to direct me, whose servant I am here."[26] The City of London gave the five members, and Parliament, protection, and Charles I, aware that civil war had become inevitable, left London.

The rebels did not throw off their obedience lightly. Unpopular as a king might be, kingship was still dressed in grave majesty, and there was anguished searching of heart and shedding of tears among those about to take arms against their lawful sovereign. Through the spring and early summer of 1642, king and Parliament continued their negotiations, but Parliament's claims had become the claims of men who wanted nothing less than a parliamentary monarchy, with the making of laws, the levying of taxes, the affairs of the church and the army in the hands of the old High Court of Parliament that had come to see itself as a supreme legislature. Out of harm's reach, Charles I refused, and gathered about him his family and sympathizers frightened by the Puritan rigidity and the rebelliousness of the parliamentary aggressors. Pym's party responded by raising an army. In August 1642, at Nottingham, Charles I raised the standard of war. Few had thought things would go this far. They would go much further.

ENGLAND: FROM REVOLUTION TO RESTORATION

The Great Civil War

The civil war divided the country more sharply than anything else had ever divided it before. Yet, after centuries of historical inquiry, historians have not reached agreement on patterns of partisanship. While, by and large, the south and east of England were parliamentarian, and the west and north royalist, this map of support was dotted with exceptions. The war itself created parties. As the lines of battles shifted and both sides levied troops in the territories under their control, the majority of Englishmen who had hoped to stay remote from civil strife found themselves compelled to take sides. Differences in religion were doubtless of central importance, but it was not simply that a Puritan was a man of the opposition: often a man in opposition for nonreligious reasons found himself being called a Puritan. The aristocracy, the gentry, merchants, cities, even families, were split. The City of London, headquarters and mainstay of the parliamentary rebels, was royalist in sympathies and remained so until Pym's supporters in early 1642 expelled the old loyalists.[27] The familiar names of the adversaries—Cavaliers and Roundheads—derive from, and imply, social

---

[26] Ibid., 114.
[27] See Wilson, *England's Apprenticeship,* 116.

distinctions,[28] and social distinctions were among the causes of the conflict. At the same time, like the name Puritan, the name Roundhead was often applied as a partisan epithet, and sometimes to men of the "better sort."[29] Even the House of Commons split down the middle. Nearly half of its members committed themselves to the king's side and an exhaustive study of the Long Parliament has shown that the only marked differentiation was not wealth or status or regional origins or religious affiliation, but age: the rebels in Parliament, trained in the first years of Charles I, embittered by the Eleven Years' Tyranny, and nurtured in Puritan severity, were on the average some years older than the royalists.[30] In 1642, men took the sword for many reasons.

The war began with deliberate speed, as both sides raised troops and carried on desultory negotiations. In a series of indecisive engagements, Charles I improved his position; by late 1643, Parliament and its forces were mainly clustered around London and the southeast of England. Cavaliers seemed to be getting the advantage of Roundheads. Thoroughly alarmed, Parliament imposed new and unpopular taxes, took steps to reorganize its armed forces and adopted (as it had so often before) a policy long advocated by Pym. In September 1643, only three months before Pym's death, it reluctantly concluded a solemn league and convenant with the Scots, pledging both signatories to extirpate "popery and prelacy" and to establish the reformed religion "according to the Word of God." Subsequently, the parties to the pact were to interpret these words in widely differing ways; many Englishmen, even Puritans, were appalled by the dour clerical discipline of the Scottish Presbyterians. But the parliamentary cause was in peril, and a Scottish army might be useful. It was: in January 1644, a Scottish force crossed the border into England; Charles was now held in a pincer from which he could not extricate himself.

The first tangible reward for these policies came on June 2, 1644, with the parliamentarians' victory of Marston Moor, where the Scots were joined by detachments from England. What mattered about this battle was less its clear outcome than its dubious aftermath. Lacking decisiveness of aim and unity of command, the parliamentarians bickered over the conduct of the war and dissipated their advantage in the summer and fall of 1644; by early winter the need for a thoroughgoing constitution of their armies had become the first order of business. Parliament compelled its generals to lay down their command by passing a self-denying ordinance, and equipped the New Model Army with new leaders: Sir Thomas Fairfax was named commander in chief; Oliver Cromwell, whose cavalry had distinguished itself at Marston Moor, became Fairfax's lieutenant general.

[28] The partisans of Parliament, a contemporary wrote, "were, most of them, men of mean or a middle quality . . . modest in their apparel but not in language. They had the hair of their heads very few of them longer than their ears, whereupon it came to pass that those who usually with their cries attended Westminster were by a nickname called *Roundheads*. The courtiers, again, wearing long hair and locks and always sworded, at last were called by these men *Cavaliers*" (quoted in Christopher Hill and Edmund Dell, eds., *The Good Old Cause* [1949], 245–246).
[29] See Wilson, *England's Apprenticeship,* 110.
[30] See D. Brunton and D. H. Pennington, *Members of the Long Parliament* (1954).

In early 1645, Oliver Cromwell was already a widely known and highly respected figure. Born in 1599 in Huntingdon, he was a landed gentleman of middling rank, a solemn, sober Puritan who had undergone a prolonged and exhausting religious conversion and did nothing without devout appeals to his God. He had sat both in the parliament that preceded and the parliaments that ended King Charles' Eleven Years' Tyranny and proved himself an articulate champion of poor farmers threatened by enclosures and an equally articulate enemy to Laud's Anglicanism. In 1642 he displayed a new talent organizing and leading troops; he had learned much from studying the cavalry tactics of Gustavus Adolphus. His "ironsides"[31] became the model for the New Model Army: composed of "honest, godly men, thoroughly trained, thoughtfully looked after,"[32] firmly disciplined, devoted to their officers, courageous and above all, determined to see the cause of true religion prevail. On June 14, 1645, at the battle of Naseby, the parliamentary troops displayed these qualities, decisively routing the king's troops. By fall, even Charles' hopes for Scotland, pinned insecurely on the brilliant military sallies of the royalist earl of Montrose, were dashed by Montrose's defeat. In June 1646, Oxford, Charles' headquarters since early in the war, surrendered, and the king fled to Scotland. The New Model Army had proved a superb instrument.

But it was not content to remain an instrument, and here Charles, untiring in intrigue, saw his opportunity. Though trained to iron discipline, Cromwell's troops steadily engaged in discussions among themselves and with their officers, and their vision of the future differed markedly from the vision held by the parliament to which they owed their allegiance. Many of the troops were Independents, strongly in favor of a Congregationalist church organization free from the heavy hand of central control, free even from Presbyters. The great poet and pamphleteer John Milton, the most eloquent recruit the Independent cause could boast during the Civil War, bitterly commented on the compromises now in the air: "New Presbyter," he said, "is but old Priest writ large."[33]

[31] The name was first bestowed on Cromwell himself by Prince Rupert, commander of the royalist troops at Marston Moor, and then extended to the troops under Cromwell's command. See Charles Firth, *Oliver Cromwell and the Rule of the Puritans in England* (ed. 1953), 106.

[32] Ibid., 89.

[33] While Milton is remembered as one of the great poets in the English language, his long life included much vigorous political pamphleteering. In the middle of the nineteenth century, the English liberal statesman John Bright told a working-class audience that Milton was "the greatest name in English political history" (quoted in John Gross, *The Rise And Fall of the Man of Letters* [1969], 121). Born in 1608 in London, educated at St. Paul's School and Cambridge, Milton gave up his early intention to join a church he increasingly disliked and devoted himself to poetry. In 1640, returning from an Italian journey, he joined the Presbyterian cause of church reform, but by the middle of the Civil War he had moved to Independency, and wrote brilliant polemics in its behalf. His *Areopagitica* of 1644, which voices his discontent with parliamentary censorship, remains one of the most powerful defenses of a free press ever written; his *The Tenure of Kings and Magistrates* of 1649, which grew out of his commitment to the Cromwellian cause, was an almost equally powerful defense of popular sovereignty taken to its logical conclusion: the right to dispose of the tyrant. Appointed Cromwell's secretary for foreign tongues in 1649, he went completely blind in 1652; his most celebrated poetry, including his finest English sonnets and the epic *Paradise Lost* (published in 1667), date from his last years. When he died in 1674, he was a famous poet.

The epigram reflects the aspiration of solemn seekers intent on forming and governing their own congregations that they might find their own way to God, and the rancor of left-wing Puritans against their more conservative brethren in control of Parliament. After 1646, too, radical political ideas were percolating through the army; there were demands for manhood suffrage, a republic, and annual parliaments. The spokesmen for these new ideas were nicknamed "Levellers," disdainfully and misleadingly, by their enemies. In an animated debate held in October 1647, and attended by Cromwell and his son-in-law General Henry Ireton, a Colonel Rainborough laid down the Leveller principles in a moving speech: "For really I think that the poorest he that is in England hath a life to live, as the greatest he; and therefore truly, sir, I think it's clear, that every man that is to live under a government ought first by his own consent to put himself under that government; and I do think that the poorest man in England is not at all bound in a strict sense to that government that he hath not had a voice to put himself under." [34] Actually, neither Rainborough nor John Lilburne, the leading Leveller publicist, meant "the poorest he" literally; they did not wish to extend the franchise to paupers or servants, but rather to the respectable lower orders, to those who had given up all they had to fight in a righteous cause. But while Cromwell keenly appreciated the part that independent Protestant sectarians had played in his New Model Army, while he pleaded for freedom of conscience and was himself strongly sympathetic to Independency, he had no intention of enlarging the political nation to include those who owned no property—to those who, as a long-popular phrase had it, had no stake in the country.

The struggle within the army was secondary to the struggle between army and Parliament. The Levellers did not prevail, but the effervescence of religious and political ideas they helped to produce radicalized the troops and, to some degree, the generals. In February 1647, after undignified squabbles, the Scots had turned over Charles I to the English Parliament, for a promised payment of £400,000. But what to do with him could hardly be resolved while Parliament and its military arm were at one another's throats. The parliamentary leaders sought to weaken the army by partially demobilizing it and by sending some of it to Ireland, but they only brought its distrust to a new pitch, and its generals shared the rage and the suspicions of their men. In the midst of these verbal skirmishes, Charles I escaped from detention in November 1647 and made a new agreement with the Scots giving them what they wanted; early in 1648, the second Civil War began. It did not last long. Despite political and social strains, the New Model Army continued to fight brilliantly, and by August 1648, Cromwell had put down scattered risings and beaten the royalist forces mustered by the Scots.

The army was now determined to put the king out of the way; Charles I had converted rebellious monarchists into vindictive republicans. Cromwell

---

[34] "The Putney Debates," in A. S. P. Woodhouse, ed., *Puritanism and Liberty* (2nd ed., 1950), 53. In the late 1640s George Fox founded the sect contemporaries unkindly called Quakers.

had long hesitated, but late in 1647 he had made up his mind: Charles, "that man of blood," had subverted the constitution and proved himself slippery, mendacious, and dangerous. But Parliament clearly would not accept the radical implications of the army's program. A show of force resolved the impasse: on December 2, 1648, the army was in London; on December 6 a detachment of troops led by Colonel Pride turned away or arrested most of the members of Parliament; Pride's Purge left a small Rump of presumably dependable men. But when it was moved to try the king for treason and other heinous crimes, the vote was only twenty-six to twenty. Old attachments, and old taboos, die hard.

The trial of Charles I began in mid-January 1649. Of the 135 commissioners named to try their king, only 68 appeared, and not all these could bring themselves to condemn their sovereign to death. Charles steadfastly refused to recognize the jurisdiction of the court, there were disturbances in the hall, and disapproval of the proceedings was widespread. When the expected verdict was given, on January 27, Cromwell had to exercise considerable pressure to obtain 58 signatures. His own was among them. On January 30, 1649, Charles died on the block, bravely, better than he had lived, and with his last words defending the idea of a personal monarch ruling in a balanced constitution.

Cromwell's Republic

The execution of Charles I had solved one problem but it created many others—institutional, political, diplomatic. The government was in the hands of the minority of a minority: of army leaders and of the Rump,[35] an unrepresentative fragment, ranging from fifty to eighty, of a House of Commons which had considerably diminished in size during the course of the Civil War. As Cromwell recognized more clearly than anyone, the new state sorely needed a framework of legality. Rapidly, the Rump set about providing it. In February 1649 Parliament, now sovereign, abolished the monarchy and the House of Lords, and established a Council of State which was essentially an agent of Commons: it numbered forty-one and was chosen for one year; thirty-one of its members were members of Parliament. In May, the Rump declared England to be a "Commonwealth and Free State," and in a gesture foreshadowing the French Revolution, ordered a new great seal bearing the inscription, "In the first year of freedom by God's blessing restored." These were words, symbols, but as Gibbon said two hundred years ago, mankind is governed by names.

[35] The difficulties of classifying the actors in this historic drama are underlined by the composition of the Rump. Presumably, Pride's Purge had eliminated the Presbyterians and left only Independents. But many of these so-called Independents were in fact elders in the Presbyterian church: clearly, the motives of men in history are more complicated than historians are often willing to recognize. See J. H. Hexter, "The Problem of the Presbyterian Independents" (1938), in Hexter, *Reappraisals in History* (1961).

Words were not enough: difficulties multiplied on all sides. The execution of the king had caused horror abroad, even among Protestant powers. At home, mourning royalists, unappeased Presbyterians, discontented soldiers, rebellious Scots and Irishmen plunged England into the semblance of a new civil war. For two years Cromwell, who bore most of the burden, had little time for constructive statesmanship. He performed his tasks with his characteristic and prayerful realism: Cromwell was a Puritan zealot who justified his actions and his arbitrariness by claiming divine guidance, but he was also a statesman, eager to found a republic in law, and at peace, with a degree of toleration narrow perhaps by modern, but generous by seventeenth-century, standards. The Leveller mutiny in the army (complicated by the emergence of the "True Levellers," or Diggers, a small communist sect) was easiest to deal with: Cromwell could understand the grievances, even if he could not honor the demands, of his soldiers. "Freeborn John" Lilburne was confined to the Tower, three leading mutineers were shot, and the rest sent to Ireland.

The Irish and Scottish rebellions demanded more severe action and brought out Puritan self-righteousness in its most repellent form. The Irish, Catholics and Presbyterians alike, proclaimed Charles I's eldest son as King Charles II; so did the Scots, who had veered from hatred of Anglicanism toward devotion to a dynasty that was, after all, Scottish, and toward a young prince who seemed ready to grant them the Presbyterian order they craved. Cromwell took command of the English expedition to Ireland and soundly beat the rebels in August, 1649. In September, he besieged the port of Drogheda; when the defenders refused to surrender, he took the city by storm and had the survivors cut down. In October, his troops took Wexford, and a second massacre ensued. Cromwell was anything but an indiscriminate killer of men, but he thought the Irish massacres authorized not merely by the laws of war, but by the laws of revenge as well. What had happened at Drogheda, he told the Speaker of the House, was "a righteous judgment of God upon these barbarous wretches, who have imbrued their hands in so much innocent blood"—an unmistakable allusion to the Ulster massacre of 1641, when rebellious Irishmen had killed new Protestant settlers wholesale. Thus, as so often, murder begot murder. By spring 1650, Cromwell was back in England; his lieutenants spent two years mopping up the Irish rebels, cruelly starving out the resisters. Cromwell's program for settling Ireland with Protestants was rapidly carried out; all across the land, miserable Irish Catholic peasants confronted substantial Protestant English landlords, nourishing mutual hatreds that have not died down to this day. The Scottish situation was, if anything, more delicate: young Prince Charles was among the Scots, negotiating, promising to uphold their cherished covenant. It was not until September 1651, with the battle of Worcester, that Scotland was subdued and pacified: Worcester was probably Cromwell's most brilliant victory in a career studded with brilliant victories. Charles II, whom the Scots had solemnly crowned at the beginning of the year, made a melodramatic escape; in October, he was in France, to resume his intrigues and wait for a call to take his rightful throne.

In 1651, such a call seemed a remote possibility; the Rump and the generals were in firm control. There was much dissension, but also much able government: "Not only are they powerful by sea and land," one of Mazarin's agents reported back to France, "but they live without ostentation, without pomp, and without mutual rivalry. They are economical in their private affairs, for which each man toils as if for his private interest. They handle large sums of money, which they administer honestly, observing a strict discipline. They reward well and punish severely." [36] The forcible pacification of the British Isles was the first success of the new regime; Cromwell's foreign policy and conduct of war abroad was the second. Late in 1651, Parliament enacted the first Navigation Act, England's most ambitious venture into mercantilist policy so far (see p. 300). It provided that goods imported into England must be carried only in English ships or in ships of the exporting country, a measure directed, more than against any other power, against the Dutch—Protestants, but also the princes of the carrying trade. Trade rivalry between the two countries, already keen and burdened with bitter memories, [37] soon degenerated into war, and from July 1652 on, able English commanders confronted able Dutch admirals in a series of naval engagements. Two years later, when the two countries made peace, the English had won a significant share of Dutch trade, and Cromwell could begin to think of the Dutch Republic less as a rival than as a potential ally.

But by 1654, the Commonwealth had given way to a new experiment in republicanism: the Protectorate. Cromwell did not take this step irresponsibly; his earlier reluctance to put Charles I to death was now repeated in his reluctance to tear apart the flimsy legal fabric of the young English republic. Parliament forced his hand. There was widespread sentiment for new elections, but in 1651 the Commons resolved to stay in being for three more years. There was urgent demand for "reform of the law," and Cromwell strongly supported it: "Relieve the oppressed," he wrote from Scotland in 1650, after he had beaten the Scots at Dunbar, "reform the abuses of all professions, and if there be any one that makes many poor to make a few rich, that suits not a commonwealth." [38] But (as Cromwell realistically noted) the entrenched legal profession and equally entrenched property owners made reform impossible.

There was, finally, growing need for a religious settlement; English religious life was in a state of anarchy, since the abolition of the Anglican church had not been followed by an establishment of a Presbyterian or any other kind of order. Cromwell wanted an established church that would

---

[36] Quoted in Firth, *Cromwell*, 241-242.
[37] For the Dutch massacre of English traders in Amboyna in 1623, see p. 212.
[38] Quoted in Firth, *Cromwell*, 298.

tolerate other Protestant sects, but Parliament, deeply split, remained indecisive. True, in February 1652 Cromwell had induced the Commons to pass an Act of Oblivion for earlier treasons, but it had few practical results. As reforms were stalled and the promised dissolution of Parliament was about to be compromised by parliamentary chicanery, the army pressed Cromwell to act. Finally, on April 20, 1653, in a dramatic scene, Cromwell came to the House of Commons, and after listening to the debate, rose and accused his fellow members present of all sorts of crimes and misdemeanors. "Come, come," he exclaimed, "I will put an end to your prating. You are no parliament, I say you are no parliament." Then he called his musketeers and had the house cleared. If not officially, at least in effect, the Long Parliament was over.

His decisive intervention depressed Cromwell deeply: "It's you that have forced me to this," he shouted after the departing members, "for I have sought the Lord night and day, that he would rather slay me than put me upon the doing of this work." [39] The next five years, the last of Cromwell's life, were years of institutional improvisation. A new council of state was formed, and in the summer of 1653, a small parliament was called together, not elected but appointed by Independent congregations. [40] Respectable, serious, but immobilized by the plethora of reforming projects its members poured forth, it lasted only until December, 1653, when it handed its authority back to Cromwell, who became Lord Protector of the Commonwealth of England, Scotland, and Ireland, under the Instrument of Government, England's first written constitution. It could not provide stability. Two more parliaments came, were purged, and dissolved; Cromwell, offered the crown, refused it in May 1657. While a war with Spain, begun in 1656, went exceedingly well, [41] at home discontent was general: Cromwell was beset by religious fanatics who preached that the end of worldly government had come; by principled republicans who distrusted him, particularly after he accepted the right to name his own successor; by rigid Puritans who detested his tolerance; by monarchists who longed for the day of Charles II's return. Against the continuing pressure of political radicals, Cromwell had moved toward the right, more concerned at the end with the privileges of the propertied than with protection of the poor against the propertied. When he died in September 1658, only a handful mourned, and Cromwell's son, Richard, named Lord Protector, could not hold his father's structure together.

In February 1660, General Monck put an end to the chaos. He marched his army from Scotland into London. Without political ambitions of his own, eager only to restore stability, Monck called together a "free parliament"—the Long

---

[39] Wilbur Cortez Abbott, ed., *The Writings and Speeches of Oliver Cromwell*, vol. II (1939), 643.

[40] This parliament is known as the Little Parliament (for it had only 140 members) or Barebones Parliament, after Praise-God Barbon, member for the City of London.

[41] The great prize was Jamaica.

Parliament as it had been before Pride's Purge in December 1648. Restoration was in the air; Charles II made it a certainty with his statesmanlike Declaration of Breda, issued, he said, to bind up old wounds. It undertook to restore "King, Peers and people to their just, ancient and fundamental rights"; it offered a general pardon, excepting only those whom Parliament itself would single out for punishment; it promised "liberty to tender consciences" in matters of religion; and it reassured those who had acquired land during the upheavals that disposition of their property rights, too, would be determined by Parliament. A freely chosen Convention Parliament voted to accept the declaration and invited the exile home. On May 29, 1660, Charles II entered London: "This day came in his majesty Charles the Second to London," the diarist John Evelyn recorded, "after a sad and long exile and calamitous suffering both of the King and Church, being seventeen years. This was also his birthday, and with a Triumph of about 20,000 horse and foot, brandishing their swords and shouting with unexpressable joy. The ways strewn with flowers, the bells ringing, the streets hung with tapestry, fountains running with wine. The Mayor, aldermen, all the companies in their liveries, chains of gold, banners. Lords and nobles, cloth of silver, gold and velvet everybody clad in; the windows and balconies all set with ladies, trumpets, music; and myriads of people flocking the streets and ways as far as Rochester, so as they were seven hours in passing the city, even from two in the afternoon 'til nine at night. I stood in the Strand and beheld it and blessed God. And all this without one drop of blood, and by that very army which rebelled against him. But it was the Lord's doing, and wonderful to our eyes, for such a Restoration was never seen in the mention of any history ancient or modern, since the return from the Babylonian Capitivity, nor so joyful a day and so bright ever seen in this nation."

In the light of such sentiments, and of Charles' subsequent actions, England's travail over the past decades seems at first glance like so much waste motion. Charles II kept the promises he made at Breda: only some of the surviving regicides, thirteen of them, were executed for their vote to condemn Charles II's father to death. A royalist parliament turned the king's promises to advantage: it returned to royalists the land they had lost by confiscation, though not the land that royalists—a far larger number—had felt compelled to sell during the Civil War. It restored the monarchy, the House of Lords, the Church of England, and drove the nonconformists out of the Anglican communion. But the Puritan Revolution and the regime of Cromwell left a permanent mark on England and on the British Isles. Parliament retained much of the power it had won; the crown surrendered much of its prerogative. Neither the prerogative courts nor the royal claim to a right of taxation without parliamentary consent returned to haunt and divide Englishmen. While France solved the problems of political anarchy by turning to absolutism, England solved these problems by devising a parliamentary monarchy. Nor was Cromwell forgotten. He had made

England into a great power; when Charles II degraded England into a mere client of France (see p. 308), Englishmen began to recall the great days of Cromwell with some nostalgia. "It is strange," Samuel Pepys noted in his diary in July 1667, how "everybody do now-a-days reflect upon Oliver and commend him, what brave things he did, and made all the neighbour princes fear him; while here a prince, come in with all the love and prayers and good liking of his people, who have given greater signs of loyalty and willingness to serve him with their estates than ever was done by any people, hath lost all so soon."

FRANCE: THE REIGNS OF TWO MINISTERS

In the half century between the murder of Henri IV in 1610 and the onset of Louis XIV's personal rule in 1661, France was successively governed by two great statesmen: Richelieu and Mazarin. Yet their statesmanship could not keep France from the ravages of peasant uprisings, political divisions, religious troubles, and civil war. The awesome splendor of Louis XIV, whose power loomed over Europe in the second half of the seventeenth century, was in part a response to the disturbances that marked the first half. But it was also the heir of those years, for it was in the reigns of Richelieu and Mazarin that France achieved enough stability to survive its internal troubles and rise to commanding stature in Europe.

Louis XIII: The Reign of Richelieu

When Louis XIII ascended the throne in 1610 after Henri IV's premature death (see p. 183), he was a boy of nine; this meant a regent, a post held during the next four years with stunning incompetence by Louis' mother, Marie de' Medici. The king's conduct after 1614, when he proclaimed himself officially of age and ended his tutelage, suggests that dependency was a lifelong habit, or necessity, with him: Louis XIII was alert, hard-working, even persistent, but he was moody, spiteful, and perpetually in need of advice. Luckily for him, he had Richelieu to govern him for most of his reign. At the same time, though neurotic and indecisive, Louis was not incapable of action; he even instigated an important political assassination. The queen mother had induced the valued Sully to hand in his resignation early in 1611 and, instead of trusting Henri IV's able ministers, surrounded herself with a camarilla of court favorites. Most conspicuous and most obnoxious among these were Leonora Galigai, Marie's lady-in-waiting and Leonora's husband, Concini, Italians both. The pair were grasping and ostentatious, if intelligent, adventurers, who were not above snubbing the adolescent king. After years of enduring such treatment, Louis induced some of his entourage to murder Concini. The queen mother went into exile, while the young king, weeping with joy, exclaimed: "I am your king. I was king before, but now I am and, God willing, will be king more than ever." [42]

It was harder to be king than Louis fondly believed. The death of his great father had revived the ambitions and quarrels of the feudal princes; rumors that Henri IV's murderer, Ravaillac, was in the pay of the Jesuits raised the tempers of the restless Gallican clergy; French Huguenots organized for the defense of their Protestant faith and of the political privileges secured for them in the Edict of Nantes (see p. 181) which they believed to be in jeopardy. In 1614 the regent convoked an Estates General. It wrangled for half a year and dissolved, leaving tensions as high as before. Its only visible result was the public demonstration of its incapacity to govern. [43] Nor was Marie's departure from the center of power permanent: in 1619, the queen mother made peace with her rebellious son with the aid of a superbly skillful negotiator, Richelieu. Concini's death had brought into prominence young Louis' favorite, the duke de Luynes, advocate of an implacable Catholic policy; Luynes' own death in 1621 gave the queen mother renewed and undue influence. It was not until 1624 that Louis XIII was persuaded to make Richelieu his chief minister. Unrest did not cease, but the French state now had a formidable, purposeful advocate.

Armand Jean du Plessis, Cardinal Richelieu, is a fascinating figure and something of an enigma. He felicitously combined passion and self-control, personal ambition and public service, efficiency in religion and a vocation for politics; he awed others by his very presence and clawed his way to power by a superiority of intellect and a toughness of will that would not be denied. His early path was smoothed by his ancient lineage: born in 1585, he was a bishop by 1608. Once his abilities had brought him to the attention of the queen mother, he had to contend with jealous courtiers; that is why it was not until 1624 that Richelieu held power in his hands. Despite intrigues against his post and his life, he did not relinquish that power until his death in 1642.

Richelieu was at once the characteristic product and the supreme promoter of the early modern state. He subordinated everything to a single purpose: *raison d'état*—reason of state, the securing of the French monarchy against its internal and external rivals. This meant the ordering of the French government for effective action in peace and war and the improvement of the French position in the councils of Europe. Richelieu was not an irreligious man, but he, a cardinal of the Church of Rome since 1622, serenely concluded treaties with Protestant powers when his conception of French interests demanded it Richelieu had no intention of subverting a society built on rank and status, but

[42] Quoted in Jean H. Mariéjol, *Henri IV et Louis XIII (1598–1643)* (1911), 193.

[43] Its failure, coupled with the rise of the absolute monarchy, led to its long sleep; the next Estates General was not called until 175 years later, in the fateful year of 1789 (see p. 463).

he mercilessly repressed French aristocrats who set themselves against the authority of the crown. Richelieu was not a fanatic—his foreign policy proved that—but since, in his judgment, the semiautonomy of French Huguenots was a danger to the state, he found it necessary to curtail their power. All his moves, both in foreign and in domestic policy, were intertwined: that is why Richelieu and *raison d'état* are practically synonymous.

The Huguenots were the first to test Richelieu's view of *raison d'état*. Early in 1625, Protestant nobles staged an uprising, limited in scope but embarrassing to Richelieu, who was occupied elsewhere; a truce gave him time to prepare his forces against possible repetition. When in 1627 there was a Huguenot rebellion centered on La Rochelle, Richelieu took personal charge of the expedition against that western port. For a year the Huguenots held out, encouraged and misled by sporadic help from England; they were to discover that to have the duke of Buckingham as one's ally was as bad as having Richelieu as one's enemy. In late October 1628, a starving La Rochelle surrendered to its determined besieger; the other Huguenot strongholds surrendered soon after. In June 1629, the Peace of Alais brought the first major modification of Henri IV's Edict of Nantes: the Huguenots lost their special towns, their ports and fortresses, and their legal privileges; they retained the right to practice what French Catholics liked to call "the so-called reformed religion." At a stroke, Richelieu had broken the Huguenots' power and guaranteed their docility; a mixture of ruthlessness and leniency, with ruthlessness dominant, was always his favorite technique.

The Huguenot rebellions had been led by the dukes de Soubise and Rohan; other nobles, with their vast estates, small private armies, political independence, and ceaseless intrigues, prevented Louis XIII from playing the role that Richelieu insisted a king of France must play: master in his own house. To that end, Richelieu did not scruple to have rebellious nobles executed— Henri IV would have paid them off instead—or to have their fortified castles razed to the ground. The feudal sport of dueling, a romantic reminder of the old aristocratic privilege of avenging insults, real or fancied, against one's honor, was one of Richelieu's first targets in his campaign to reduce the French nobility into decorative and docile servants of the state. In 1626 he induced his king to outlaw the duel; in the following year, to everyone's surprise, he enforced the law against the count de Montmorency-Bouteville, a notorious offender who had defied Richelieu by fighting a duel under Richelieu's very eyes: "On 22nd June 1627, the indignant and astonished young man mounted the scaffold." [44] Dueling did not cease but it began to go underground. More constructively, Richelieu undertook to domesticate the nobility by increasing the administrative authority of the central government—a difficult task in those days of provincial autonomy, lumbering transport, and slow communications.

[44] C. V. Wedgwood, *Richelieu and the French Monarchy* (1949), 62.

Richelieu strengthened the royal hand in the provinces by charging commissioners, intendants, with superintending royal policy and enforcing royal orders. With the intendants as with his other administrative measures, like his reorganization of royal councils, Richelieu showed himself an effective and sensible reformer: he took old offices and fashioned them into instruments of royal policy. Not surprisingly, the intendants came into conflict with local grandees, who had hitherto exercised so much unchecked power, and with the provincial parlements which found their old privileges as courts of final instance and as leviers of taxes greatly reduced. In France, as elsewhere, the growth of the modern state amounted to a transfer of power from nobility to crown.

The administrative reforms brought some changes in the status of the old aristocracy: Richelieu chose many of the king's chief ministers, and many of his counselors, from relatively obscure, sometimes from nonnoble, families, thus securing "creatures" who usefully combined competence in their work with gratitude to their master. [45] But these innovations did not penetrate into French society as a whole. Richelieu had some fairly rudimentary notions about commercial policy; he improved communications, built canals, supervised the silk industry, protected domestic commerce with a simple (and wholly unenforceable) anticipation of the English navigation acts (see p. 279), and launched trading and colonial companies. But his ideas were too ambitious for his means of realizing them. Moreover, his foreign policy, a policy of intervention in the European wars to the greater glory of France, was, like all such policies, extremely burdensome on the French people. New adventures abroad meant new taxes at home, and these brought rebellions. In 1630 there were riots at Dijon; in 1631, at Paris; in 1632, at Lyons, all against the introduction of new, or the raising of old, taxes. In the countryside, there were sporadic but extremely violent peasant uprisings. Bands of rebels, usually driven by hunger and normally encouraged by their landlords, tore royal officials to pieces. These are the famous revolts of the *nu-pieds*—revolt was the only language the "shoeless" had for their protest and the only language the powerful could understand. Most of these rebellions were put down with unmitigated ferocity; on rare occasions, the government would appease the rebels by withdrawing some obnoxious tax.

Yet from Richelieu's own point of view—power politics—his policies, so burdensome at home, were supremely successful. Power—on this Richelieu agreed with Machiavelli—must increase, lest it decline and the power of one state can increase only at the expense of another. The Hapsburgs were the greatest power in Europe, hence it was against the Hapsburgs that Richelieu directed his most sustained efforts. That is why the Thirty Years' War offered such splendid opportunities for the French; that is why Richelieu did not scruple to ally himself with Protestant Sweden on the principle that the enemy

[45] See Orest A. Ranum, *Richelieu and the Councillors of Louis XIII* (1963).

of your enemy is your friend; that is why, in 1635, when general peace threatened to break out, Richelieu intervened to keep the pot of power politics bubbling. When Richelieu died in December 1642, his aims—to "ruin the Huguenot party," to secure the state against the nobility, and to wrest European hegemony from Spain—had been only partly realized. But his legacy was plain. "The torment and the ornament of his age," an English writer called him upon his death. "France he subdued, Italy he terrified, Germany he shook, Spain he afflicted, Portugal he crowned, Lorraine he took, Catalonia he received, Swethland he fostered, Flanders he mangled, England he troubled, Europe he beguiled." [46] Cardinal Mazarin would find it hard to follow such a man in office.

Young Louis XIV: The Reign of Mazarin

Louis XIII survived his minister and master by five months, and when he died in May 1643, events had a curious familiarity about them. Like Louis XIII, his son, Louis XIV, was a child at his accession—not yet five. Consequently, the reign of Louis XIV, like that of his father before him, began under a regency, and like his father, Louis XIV found his widowed mother in charge. Moreover, Louis XIII and Marie de' Medici had governed with the aid of a wily cardinal-statesman; Louis XIV and Anne of Austria had *their* statesman-cardinal to guide the business of France: Jules Mazarin, who retained his influence unbroken until his death in 1661. In their policies, if not in their characters, the two cardinals were much alike: where Richelieu was pitiless, Mazarin was diplomatic; where Richelieu employed the weapon of fear, Mazarin relied on the persuasiveness of devotion. Anne of Austria, at least, and her young royal son, found him lovable. Louis XIV, indeed would always remember Mazarin with filial fondness.

The country at large did not share this affection. It was bad enough that Mazarin should be a foreigner—he was a Neapolitan, naturalized in 1639; to make things worse, he was obsessively preoccupied with the welfare of his family, including himself: loyalty to his private fortune and to his five nieces was second only to his loyalty to France, and there were times when he had trouble keeping the two apart. And his loyalty to France was, like Richelieu's before him, expensive and unpopular: Mazarin preached absolutism to his king and followed an aggressive anti-Spanish policy abroad; he raised taxes and offended old families with his appointments.

The Frondes,[47] those riots, treacheries, and civil wars that intermittently

---

[46] Quoted in Wedgwood, *Richelieu*, 191.

[47] "The word *fronde* means a child's sling. The police had tried to prevent the *gamins* of Paris from disporting themselves with these playthings in the time of Richelieu, but had conspicuously failed. When the Paris populace successfully defied the government in 1648, men said: 'Ils font comme leurs enfants: ils jouent à la fronde'" (Merriman, *Six Contemporaneous Revolutions*, 61n). This view of the Frondes as a set of irresponsible games overstresses the comical aspects of these events and fails to do justice to their long-range consequences, which became palpable only after 1661, when Louis XIV began his personal reign (see p. 293).

plagued France between 1648 and 1653, were in part responses to Mazarin's policies and Mazarin's conduct. Imitating Richelieu in substance though not in style, Mazarin increased taxes through the 1640s, had them collected by shameless profiteers, and kept France in the war—the cause of, or excuse for, the heaviest exactions. Mazarin's rapacity was real enough, even by the lax standards of his day; rumors that he was exploiting his powerful position to bleed France to death for the sake of his own family made his rapacity appear even worse than it was. But in large part, the Frondes were a delayed response to Richelieu's disappearance from the scene. Since the reign of Louis XI in the late fifteenth century, feudalism had appeared moribund (see p. 101), and Richelieu had done his utmost to unify France and reduce the remaining power of the nobility and the parlements. His death offered an opportunity to undo his work. In the summer of 1648, rural uprisings coalesced with aristocratic dissatisfaction and parlementary rebellions to make the first Fronde, the *Fronde parlementaire*. Failing other spokesmen, the forces arrayed against the regent and her favorite relied upon the Parlement of Paris to speak, and act, for them all. The oldest of the twelve supreme courts of France, the Parlement of Paris, was also the most aggressive. Through the early part of 1648, it had showered remonstrances on the queen mother, demanding the recall of royal intendants and the right to pass on proposed taxes. The parlementary cause was popular, yet it was anything but disinterested: the call for reform meant, in substance, the call for increased authority for itself at the expense of the crown. By March 1649, the first Fronde was over; the parlement secured most of its demands, and Mazarin kept away from the court, in voluntary exile.

But in early 1650 the second Fronde, the *Fronde princière*, took up where the first had left off. It was plain that the crown had no intention of keeping its promises; moreover, the great nobles wanted more power than they had or could reasonably expect. The second Fronde offered a strange spectacle, explicable only by the incomplete unification of France: here were Condé, a royal prince, Turenne, a brilliant general, and the cardinal de Retz, a courtier and prominent churchman, terrorizing the French countryside, battling against other French troops, and making alliances with Spain, even permitting Spanish troops to enter French soil, at a time when France was still officially at war with Spain. Amid this confusion of heedless, wholly self-centered, and conflicting ambitions, Mazarin constructed a loyalist coalition, raised an army to fight the rebels and the Spaniards, and finally carried the day. By September 1653 all rebels were out of commission and all rebellious cities under royal control. Concessions offered under pressure were withdrawn, and the Parlement of Paris remained silent. Nothing seemed to have happened—nothing except more devastation of the countryside, looting, and unpunished murder. But appearances were deceptive. In the years that remained to him, Mazarin kept his control undiminished and triumphantly concluded the war with Spain in 1659, at the Peace of the Pyrenees, which extended French territory in the north and south alike, at Spain's expense. Then in 1661, with Mazarin's death, the real consequences of the Fronde became clear to all. As a young boy, silent and bewildered, Louis XIV had witnessed the disloyalty of the great, of the parlements, and of Paris, and experienced a brief but uncomfortable exile. When he took power into his own hands to begin a long, glorious, and terrible reign, he acted like a man who remembered and like a ruler determined to make all further Frondes impossible.

SELECTED READINGS

The question of the nature and extent of the mid-seventeenth-century crisis remains controversial. The essays that began the debate—mainly by E. J. Hobsbawm and H. R. Trevor-Roper—some responses and criticisms, are in Trevor Aston, ed., *Crisis in Europe, 1560-1660* (1965); Roger B. Merriman, *Six Contemporaneous Revolutions* (1938), anticipated much of the discussion.

The most useful general discussion of the military upheaval is C. V. Wedgwood, *The Thirty Years' War* (ed. 1944), to be supplemented by S. H. Steinberg, *The Thirty Years' War* (1967), and Georges Pagès, *The Thirty Years' War, 1618-1648* (tr. 1971). For three central actors on the European stage at the time, see Francis Watson, *Wallenstein: Soldier Under Saturn* (1938)—though a modern analysis remains desirable; Michael Roberts, *Gustavus Adolphus, A History of Sweden, 1611-1632,* 2 vols. (1953, 1958), to be read with several of Roberts' shorter essays, collected in *Essays in Swedish History* (1966); and, amid a sizable literature, Carl J. Burckhardt, *Richelieu: His Rise to Power* (tr., rev. ed., 1964), and *Assertion of Power and Cold War* (1970). C. V. Wedgwood, *Richelieu and the French Monarchy* (1949), is clear and reasonable. See also, on Richelieu's style of governing men, Orest A. Ranum, *Richelieu and the Councillors of Louis XIII* (1963). For the decline of Spain, see J. Lynch, *Spain and America, 1598-1700* (1969), already cited. To this should be added J. H. Elliott, *The Revolt of the Catalans: A Study in the Decline of Spain, 1598-1640* (1963), a brilliant book, and H. G. Koenigsberger, *The Government of Sicily Under Philip II of Spain* (1952), which shows the seeds of decay under the cover of grandeur.

For the Russia of the time, see the relevant chapters in Michael T. Florinsky, *Russia: A History and an Interpretation,* 2 vols. (1953); Jerome Blum, *Lord and Peasant in Russia from the Ninth to the Nineteenth Century* (1961); the opening chapter of Geroid Tanqueray Robinson, *Rural Russia Under the Old Regime* (1932); and Ian Grey, *Ivan the Terrible* (1964). The travail of the Dutch Republic at midcentury is traced in Pieter Geyl, *The Netherlands in the Seventeenth Century,* 2 vols. (2nd. ed., 1961, 1964).

A good survey of English history from the death of Elizabeth to the Restoration is Godfrey Davies, *The Early Stuarts, 1603-1660* (1937); the first half of Maurice Ashley, *England in the Seventeenth Century (1603-1714)* (3rd ed., 1961), is introductory and clear. See also the early chapters in J. P. Kenyon, *The Stuarts* (1958). Wallace Notestein, *The English People on the Eve of Colonization: 1603-1630* (1954), ably surveys English society; it may be supplemented with Carl W. Bridenbaugh, *Vexed and Troubled Englishmen, 1590-1642* (1968). David Willson, *King James VI and I* (1956), is a scholarly and dependable biography of the first Stuart king. For his successor, see Christopher Hibbert, *Charles I* (1968).

The great "storm over the gentry"—rising or falling?—has been ably anatomized in J. H. Hexter's article of that title, now in Hexter, *Reappraisals in History* (1961). One immensely valuable contribution, to this debate and to English history of the period in general, is Lawrence Stone, *The Crisis of the Aristocracy, 1558-1641* (1965), abridged by the author (1967). For the economic history of these decades, see the appropriate chapters in Charles Wilson, *England's Apprenticeship, 1603-1763* (1965). For the civil war there are the eloquent narratives by C. V. Wedgwood, *The King's Peace, 1637-1641* (1959) and *The King's War, 1641-1647* (1959); her biography, *Oliver Cromwell* (1956), is equally readable. These narratives need to be supplemented by analytical and interpretative works like J. H. Hexter, *The Reign of King Pym* (1941); D. Brunton and D. H. Pennington, *Members of the Long Parliament* (1954); A. S. P. Woodhouse, ed., *Puritanism and Liberty* (2nd ed., 1950), which prefaces Leveller documents with a long informative introduction; Joseph Frank, *The Levellers* (1955); William Haller, *Liberty and Reformation in the Puritan Revolution* (1955); George Yule, *The Independents in the English Civil War* (1958); Christopher Hill, *Society and Puritanism in Pre-Revolutionary England* (1964); and Michael Walzer, *The Revolution of the Saints: A Study in the Origins of Radical Politics* (1965), whose thesis is revealed in its subtitle. Cromwell remains enigmatic; in addition to Wedgwood's biography, see Charles Firth, *Oliver Cromwell and the Rule of the Puritans in England* (ed. 1953), and G. M. Young, *Charles I and Cromwell* (1935), which, though of an earlier vintage, retain their interest.

For France, in addition to the biographies of Richelieu mentioned, see Ernst H. Kossmann, *La Fronde* (1954), which partially supersedes the earlier Paul R. Doolin, *The Fronde* (1935). Davis Bitton, *The French Nobility in Crisis, 1560-1640* (1969), is a study in politics and ideology. A. D. Lublinskaya, *French Absolutism: The Crucial Phase, 1620-1629* (tr. 1968), is a Marxist interpretation by a Soviet historian.

7

The Age
of Louis XIV

In 1751, Voltaire published *Le siècle de Louis XIV,* a masterpiece of historical literature. The title is significant: Voltaire characterized an age with the name of a man. As this chapter will show, Voltaire's historical instincts were sound. Louis XIV was not all of Europe; there were developments in England, in Brandenburg-Prussia, in the Hapsburg domains, in Sweden and Russia that owed little to Louis' plans and were relatively immune to his interventions. Yet Louis XIV dominated half a century of European history. It is in this sense that the years stretching from 1661 to 1715 were what Voltaire called them: "The age of Louis XIV."

THE MAKING OF A MYTH

The Costs of Splendor

The reign of Louis XIV is synonymous with glory, splendor, magnificence. The flattery courtiers lavished on the Sun King was not merely the forced tribute of hirelings greedy for preferment, protection, and pay; it was, for many, the spontaneous expression of awe for a ruler who seemed more than human. The hostility of foreign princes was only another kind of tribute. All across Europe, Louis XIV was specter and model, whom lesser rulers feared and imitated. At the same time, for the vast majority of Frenchmen, Louis XIV was a remote and shadowy being; the golden rays that scattered from his presence did not warm them. Their realities were starvation, pestilence, war, the yield of the harvest, the price of bread. Louis XIV might smile or frown on his courtiers and fight battles in distant lands; most Frenchmen fought their wars with nature and with the tax collector. Out of twenty million Frenchmen over fifteen million were peasants, ranging from the miserable squatter to the small farmer to a small minority of substantial proprietors. Even among the more fortunate minority of the peasants, many lived perilously near the edge of misery and, in bad years, of outright starvation. In the cities, over a million Frenchmen formed a starving proletariat, conscious not of class but of their destitution, dependence, and incurable insecurity. A million more, perhaps, made up a lower middle class of more or less independent craftsmen and small shopkeepers. The rest—around two million—were substantial bourgeois, nobles, and priests. Clerics, like others, showed considerable differences in wealth and status. Few clerics were really poor; many were rich and noble; all were influential whether in their parishes in the provinces or among politicians in Paris; all enjoyed tax exemptions. Finally, at the top of the social and economic pyramid clustered the courtiers; they strove upward toward the king yet took care to keep their distance, for the king insisted on presiding over "his" people in splendor made all the more splendid by his remoteness and uniqueness. "Nine out of ten of King Louis' subjects worked hard and thanklessly with their hands"—so the French historian Pierre Goubert sums it up—"in order to permit the tenth to devote himself comfortably to the life of bourgeois, nobleman or mere idler."[1] A king's splendor—court ritual, mistresses, châteaux, hunts, wars—bore down heavily on those least able to resist and least able to spare what an omnivorous

[1] *Louis XIV and Twenty Million Frenchmen* (tr. 1970), 46.

and insatiable state demanded of them. Generalizations are hard to make, for imposts varied greatly from province to province, even from village to village; but everywhere the peasant found himself paying a good share of his crop, every year, to the local seigneur as feudal dues, to the local church as tithes, and to the local representative of the king as taxes. The overwhelming mass of the peasantry were dependent on good harvests, sturdy laborers in the family, and a fortunate absence of pestilence. But such conjunctions were all too rare. Contrary to the widespread belief, peasant families in the Old Regime were by no means very large. Birth control was infrequent, and women conceived as often as nature permitted them to conceive, but they married late, and the number of children stillborn and dying in infancy was enormous—so enormous, indeed, that it seemed a daily event, "of less moment than a bad storm, a freak tempest, or the death of a horse."[2] The average life expectancy was perhaps twenty-five years; of one hundred children, one fourth died before they were a year old, another fourth before they reached twenty. It took very little—the black death, which periodically recurred in France, as elsewhere, throughout the seventeenth century; a marauding foreign army; a plague of one's own troops; or a disastrous harvest—to carry off ten or fifteen out of a hundred villagers.

Let one case stand for many. There was a family in Beauvais, named Cocu: Jean Cocu, weaver, his wife, and three daughters working for him as spinners of wool—the youngest being nine. Between them, the five ate seventy pounds of bread a week, a diet they could easily afford when bread cost one half sol a pound. But in bad years the price of bread would rise, markedly. In 1693, there was a bad harvest and a shortage of work—two crises that normally came together. The price of bread went up, first to one sol, then to two, then to more than three sols a pound. The Cocu family ate up their meager savings and pawned what they had; then started to eat unwholesome food, moldy cereals, cooked nettles, the entrails of animals. They fell ill, suffering from undernourishment and the diseases attendant upon such a regimen. In December 1693, the Cocus registered at the Office of the Poor—too late; in March 1694 the youngest daughter died, to be followed in May by the eldest daughter and the father. They were fortunate, the Cocus, for the two who survived—the mother and the middle daughter—worked, and they doubtless survived because they worked. All this "because of the price of bread."[3] At Versailles, in the midst of stately court ritual, religious ceremonies, and the making of high policy, Louis XIV heard rare, isolated voices lamenting the lot of his people, but there is no evidence that he listened.

[2] Ibid., 21.
[3] Pierre Goubert, *Beauvais et le Beauvaisis de 1600 à 1730,* vol. I (1960), 76–77. This passage has also been sympathetically noted by Peter Laslett, *The World We Have Lost* (2nd ed., 1971), 112–113.

The Beginning of the Reign

The young Louis XIV of France loved Cardinal Mazarin as a father, but when he had his opportunity, he showed himself more eager to govern than to mourn. On March 9, 1661, Mazarin died; on March 10, Louis entered upon the task which, he said, he had "so longed for, and so feared." He summoned his ministers and advisors and told them, one by one, that he, Louis, was now in charge. "You will assist me with your counsels when I ask for them." He would take advice, but he himself would govern. Until his death in 1715, Louis XIV held to his resolve. For nearly half a century before, France had been governed by two great prime ministers in succession. During the half century of Louis' reign, there was to be no third.

Clearly, Louis XIV enjoyed being king: he often spoke, then and later, of the grandeur and glory that are the lot of kings. Ruling, he confessed, brought out gifts he did not know he had. He was short, but this only made him stand up straight; his famous high heels and high wig were the external supports of an inner sense of command and a need to control, sharpened, no doubt, by his untoward experience in the Frondes with disloyal nobles and rebellious cities. He was superbly healthy, active, and despite his great sexual appetite, eager to master all the details of government; he was, in an age of great courtiers, the greatest courtier of them all, the faultless chief and first member of a dazzling aristocracy.

Assiduous, suspicious, intent on controlling everything, Louis XIV sought to extend his influence into all reaches of French society. Everything became part of his policy—the performance of plays or the building of châteaux no less than the gathering of armies or the supervision of merchants. It was an understandable exaggeration for Bishop Bossuet, the official political theorist of the reign, to say: "The whole state is in him; the will of the whole nation is contained in his." Bossuet's theory that kings rule by divine right—a traditional Christian doctrine brought up to date—seemed realized in this omnipresent young ruler. Certainly it was the impression the king did his best to cultivate. He enjoyed and exploited the mysteries of power. When he was born he was called—in gratitude that his father should have been able to beget him at all—"the God-given," *Louis, Dieu-donné.* That was an assertion of piety. But when panegyrists placed him above Alexander and Caesar, when he took the sun as his device and consciously acted the part of the *roi soleil,* the cult of the king reached, perhaps breached, the bounds of blasphemy. It is probable that Louis XIV never said, "L'état c'est moi," the most famous words attributed to him. But they epitomize his view of himself.

Yet *l'état c'est moi,* whether actual or fictitious, conceals a trap of which the historian should beware. Louis' boundless vanity and extravagant fantasies have induced historians to interpret his reign as the apogee of absolutism. But this view mistakes aspirations for realities. It is possible that Louis XIV wanted to exercise as close a supervision, and as tight a control, over France as

Napoleon I was to exercise a century later—his recorded utterances certainly sound that way. But true absolutism required the kind of administrative machinery, the kind of transportation and communication, and the kind of legal uniformity that seventeenth-century France simply did not provide: "France" was a geographical expression far more than a political or legal, let alone a national, entity. Louis XIV was king of all Frenchmen, but while lawyers fondly dwelled on the loyalty that all his subjects owed him, millions of peasants and thousands of nobles in effect felt their chief loyalty to their immediate, visible lords; if feudalism in the strict sense had long been moribund, local obligations of peasant to landlord, retainer to seigneur, took precedence over obligations to the crown. All across provincial France, the king and his bureaucrats appeared mainly as an intermittent threat to their independence and their income. The civil wars of the late sixteenth and the Frondes of the mid-seventeenth centuries had brought local particularism into some disrepute and had, in the general bloodletting, eliminated some competitors for royal authority. But the country remained a bewildering, almost incomprehensible patchwork of overlapping and conflicting jurisdictions. Understandably, royal authority was at its most effective near the center of the kingdom: in the Ile-de-France around Paris or in the Loire valley to the south. But the "new" acquisitions, Brittany and Provence (which had been French for two centuries) and even Normandy (which had come into the hands of the Capetian dynasty as far back as the thirteenth century), had their own parlements and their own local estates, their own sets of laws, their "liberties," and they clung to them with a tenacity normal for men defending their cherished interests. Every professional corporation and ecclesiastical establishment had its own *coutume,* its set of laws, and its privileges, as though they were so many cities or provinces. There were as many dialects as there were local or provincial tariff barriers; there were competing systems of weights and measures and coinage; there were literally hundreds of *coutumes.* The intendants and other royal agents whom Richelieu had sent into the provinces and the lawyers who had sought to codify this mass of custom, legislation, and privilege had made no more than a beginning when Louis XIV assumed the burden he had wanted and feared. When he began his personal government in March 1661, he found that "disorder reigned throughout the land."

From the outset, Louis acted energetically, often brutally, to reduce that disorder. One plausible instrument of centralizing the government—the Estates General—was hardly suitable for a king determined to bend the traditional order rather than to govern through it. Louis wanted a system responsible—and responsive—directly to him. To that end he acted as his own prime minister and radically reconstituted the royal council; with pitiless consistency, he excluded from the High Council, the *Conseil d'en haut,* the princes of the blood, the princes of the church, the great generals, the great nobles, his younger brother, called Monsieur, and even his mother, Anne of Austria, who had once acted as his regent—all those who had taken their right to advise the king as practically

God-given. Instead, Louis began his reign by retaining three of Mazarin's creatures: Le Tellier, secretary of state for war and later chancellor; Lionne, a well-trained and experienced diplomat for foreign affairs; and Fouquet, superintendent of finances. All were "new men," all belonged to relatively obscure families of bourgeois or unimpressive aristocratic origins. This was what the proud duke de Saint-Simon would call "the reign of the vile bourgeoisie": Louis systematically relied on men who owed their prominence and their power not to ancient lineage but to their master alone. "I had no intention of sharing my authority with them," Louis wrote about his advisors. "It was important that they should not entertain hopes higher than those it pleased me to give them." Before his first year as king–prime minister was over, Louis had shown his intention not merely of humbling the old grandees, but also of keeping the new men in their place. Fouquet, who had grown immensely rich in the 1650s and had built up a personal empire of loyal followers, aspired to the place his old master Mazarin had left vacant. But he built his empire and displayed his wealth too lavishly not to arouse the ire of a young king determined to lead rather than to be led. Too eager to rise, Fouquet had to fall: in September, Louis had him arrested and imprisoned. Fouquet's enemy, Colbert, another new man, entered the king's council in his place (see p. 299).

One by one, French institutions felt the sting of Louis' intentions. The once influential assembly of the clergy found itself under the king's watchful eye; disobedient cities were saddled with rapacious garrisons; old aristocratic army commanders were replaced by obedient professional officers. Above all, Louis XIV reduced the parlements to their judicial functions and, in effect, to silence. "It was necessary," he wrote later, "to humble them less for the wrongs they had done than for the wrongs they could do in the future." The truth was a little different: Louis bitterly remembered what they had done in his youth and wished to keep them from doing it in his reign. A series of decrees culminating in the edict of 1673 commanded the parlements to register all royal decrees without delay; this deprived the parlements' remonstrances of all political importance. Louis neither destroyed institutions nor invented them: he shaped them to his will. He enlarged and disciplined the army, widened the powers of his intendants, and improved his bureaucracy. All France felt the king's rule—but the nobility most of all.

The Politics of Culture

Nothing escaped the king; everything could be converted into a servant or symbol of his dominance. Versailles, probably the most famous royal palace ever built, reflects its builder's purposiveness: it was even more a political than an architectural masterpiece. Yet Versailles, and the social system that Louis XIV perfected there, were of slow growth. In the first years of his reign, the king's court was peripatetic, as all medieval courts had been; it moved with all its gear from château to château, setting up theaters, fireworks, hunts, gambling casinos. While he did not like Paris or the Parisians, Louis did not forget the old palace in the heart of his capital. He imported Bernini to redesign the Louvre, and Bernini made drawings, perfect for a sun king, placing the royal apartments squarely into the center, noisy and uncomfortable but symbolic. Eventually, nothing came of Bernini's plan, and Perrault's classical facade was adopted instead.

In any case, by 1667, the king had another idea: he would convert the simple hunting lodge of Versailles into a complex that would mirror by its magnificence his own. With his sure taste and his customary disregard of cost, Louis enlisted France's leading architects, landscape artists, painters, and sculptors, and by 1686, Versailles was ready for him and his entourage: a microcosm of the great world that Louis XIV adorned and governed. It was at Versailles that the king converted his aristocracy from semi-independent princes into adoring and decorative satellites. The duke de Saint-Simon, whose brilliant and malicious memoirs can still be read with great pleasure although they must be used with some care, records the solemn, unvarying charade on page after page: the king, with his fine sense of discrimination, knew just how to indicate, by the degree of his bow or the width of his smile, the precise rank of the courtier before him, the precise degree of favor he enjoyed. Louis insisted that his nobility attend him at Versailles, a policy that was ruinously expensive for the nobles and politically profitable for the king; it removed the noble from his local base, his landed property, and set him adrift to live by the fickle favor of his master. The most trivial detail of the king's daily existence was invested with dignity; great magnates struggled for the privilege of handing the king his shirt, or at night, his candle. His *lever,* his *souper,* his *coucher* were like so many sacred rituals, minutely subdivided to permit the largest possible number of courtiers to serve the king as he rose, ate, and went to bed. To obtain favor, or favors, required a constant presence—of body and mind alike. If (Saint-Simon reports) a courtier spoke in behalf of a noble who rarely or never appeared at Versailles, the king would say, "I do not know him," or, "He is a man I never see." These were more than comments; they were condemnations. In such an atmosphere, obsequiousness plumbed new depths of servility; intrigues surrounded all acts and pervaded conversation. The court was indispensable for advancement, but its frozen routine became, after a while, infinitely monotonous; the moralist La Bruyère described it as a place where "the joys are visible but false, and the sufferings are hidden but real." The whole seemed like an absurd game, but it worked; by the middle of Louis' reign the old nobility of the sword was domesticated.

Like the nobility, the arts too felt Louis's presence. The king made himself into a munificent patron, distributing pensions, handing out commissions, expressing authoritative opinions. "Without being a scholar," the Prussian ambassador Spanheim said of him, "Louis XIV writes well. He loves the arts and protects them; he knows his way about, especially in music, painting, and architecture."[4] His chief instruments for reducing the arts to order were the academies. In 1672 he became the official protector of the Académie Française, established in 1635 by Richelieu; other academies—of painting and sculpture, of science, of music, of architecture—flourished under his (or Colbert's) benign yet severe eye. The academies had several well-delineated tasks: the Académie Française, with its forty members, honored the great or harbored the well connected of literature and guarded the French language by prescribing what was and was not acceptable. All the academies were busy finding new ways of praising their king and of serving him by submitting ideas and designs for his approval. But most important of all, they trained the younger generation in the accepted style and set standards on which men of taste were supposed to agree. At the same time, as Louis XIV well knew, masterpieces did not arise by command. His reign was a time of great talents, and he had the good judgment to encourage them. It was an age, Voltaire wrote later, "worthy of the attention of ages to come," dominated by "the heroes of Corneille and Racine, the characters of Molière, the symphonies of Lully," the pulpit eloquence of Bourdaloue and of Bishop Bossuet, the greatest rhetorician of his age: "The time will not come again when a duke de La Rochefoucauld, author of the *Maxims,* upon leaving a conversation with Pascal or Arnauld, would go to the theater of Corneille." Voltaire might have added the fables of La Fontaine, the architecture of François and Jules-Hardouin Mansart, and the paintings of Claude Lorrain and Nicolas Poussin.

The dazzling productions of these artists were part of Louis' system; they brought his name and the name of France greater glory, at less cost, than the stratagems of his diplomats and the strategies of his generals. But Louis did not achieve absolute control over the arts; after all, he never achieved that in politics either. Under Louis XIV artists worked under the constraint of the officially approved style: neoclassicism. But its rules were shackles only for the second-rate, or the epigones, who painted or versified according to prescription only because that was all they could do. The masters of the seventeenth century treated neoclassicism as a call to discipline, not as an obstacle to invention. Essentially, neoclassicism[5] was a system of appropriateness; its rules were designed to prescribe what each art can do and how it must do it. Neoclassicists taught that art is a science, capable of discovering objective standards of beauty; that it is moral, designed to improve, as it entertains, the public; that it is dignified, eschewing the vulgar; that it is natural, striving for verisimilitude. This last demand, for the natural, introduced complications. Like the ancients, seventeenth-century critics held that art is mimesis—imitation—but this did

[4] Quoted in Peter France and Margaret McGowan, "Louis XIV and the Arts," in John Cruickshank, ed., *French Literature and Its Background*, vol. II, *The Seventeenth Century* (1969), 85.

[5] It took its name from its origins: its precepts went back to the aesthetic writings of Aristotle and Horace.

not mean plain realism. It meant an idealization and purification of nature—not as we see it around us in individual, imperfect specimens, but as we can glimpse it by long practice and the contemplation of the most beautiful objects we can find. That had been the way, the neoclassicists said, of the ancient Greek sculptors and playwrights; modern men could do no better than to follow them. The whole machinery of neoclassical rules was a logical consequence of these fundamental precepts. Playwrights must observe the three unities of time, place, and action because this lends the play verisimilitude. Paintings have their place in a hierarchy of dignity: historical paintings, with their depiction of heroic postures and exemplary actions, are at the top of that hierarchy; still lifes, with their humble subject matter, are at the bottom; portraits rise in stature as they aspire to universality. Playwrights and poets must work within a single genre: to introduce comic scenes into tragedies (as Shakespeare had done with the gravedigger's scene in *Hamlet*) or common speech into elevated dramas (as Shakespeare had done in play after play) was to fall into barbarism. From this point of view, the paintings of Poussin, with their crowded but orderly scenes from classical mythology or sacred history, calmly posed, their postures copied from antique sculptures, were neoclassicism to perfection.

Not all neoclassicists avoided controversy: Pierre Corneille established his reputation and started a famous quarrel with *Le Cid* in 1637; as his critics pointed out, the play was far too crowded to stay within the "proper" span— one day—and permitted more vehement action on stage than neoclassical doctrine countenanced. In the great tragedies that followed in rapid succession—*Horace, Cinna,* and *Polyeucte*—Corneille accordingly worked more closely within the accepted canon. In these early plays, and in the plays he wrote during the reign of Louis XIV, Corneille populated the stage with outsized heroes who defy, or seek to remake, their world, and who fail, if they fail, with superb nobility. Corneille was not simply an aristocratic moralist anatomizing the trials of ambition; he was above all a dramatist whose announced purpose was to astound and dazzle his audience with the tension of his action and the virtuosity of his language. Jean Racine, Corneille's successor and only rival in the tragic genre, pursued the same ends with similar means. Worldling, courtier, royal historian, and in his last years, devout Jansenist,[6] Racine, like Corneille before him, drew his themes from ancient history, classical myths, and the Old Testament. Like Corneille, too, Racine explicitly aimed to please his audience and to move them, but he achieved these dramatic aims by strictly obeying the canons of neoclassicism. The plots of his plays are notable for their simplicity; all is subordinated to the clash of great passions among, and within, his magnificent personages. His language is elevated: it is rare that a speaker will break away from the measured rhythms of his alexandrines. The emotions Racine portrays—love, ambition, conflict between inclination and duty—are at once elemental and universal, but the elevation of his dramatic style makes his tragedies more than simply psychological dramas;

[6] For the Jansenists, see p. 305.

they are, as critics have often noted, ritual occasions. Yet the tensions are there, all the greater for being concealed under decorous speech. To portray the stirring of passionate, almost unbearably intense life beneath a formal rational surface was the contribution of neoclassicism to literature and the arts. In his *Phèdre* of 1677, among Racine's most famous plays, he follows the doomed guilty love of the queen, Phèdre, for her stepson, Hippolyte, through to its terrible end—an end that has been implicit from the opening scene. Like Corneille, Racine was interested less in surprising his audiences than in making them witness the gradual unfolding of a human destiny.

Racine lived on to 1699, through the grim middle years of Louis' reign. Molière, the comic genius of the age, died young, in 1673, when the reputation of the king for whom he poured out his productions was still untarnished. Molière's plays are a rogue's gallery that portray, not merely types he saw around him, but universal human foibles: miserliness, hypocrisy, snobbery, hypochondria. Not unexpectedly, his victims—or those who chose to see themselves victimized—were furious. At least one of his plays, *Tartuffe* (first version, 1664), in which a religious impostor nearly ruins a credulous family, precipitated him into a quarrel that went beyond the theater; the young Louis XIV, intent on asserting his ascendancy over the church in France, defended Molière against the charge of blasphemy. Molière's genius made him more than the scourge of obvious targets; his plays are brilliantly developed dramatic entities, and his language—the quick turns of phrase, and above all, the repetitions he used to immense comic effect—remains unsurpassed. And Molière's vision, though comic, is complex: many have read his *Misanthrope* as pouring ridicule on a young nobleman who seeks sincerity and, failing to find it in high society, decides to flee to a desert island. Actually, the play is a debate among three incompatible points of view: demanding honesty, pliant sociability, and mature, if lax, common sense. Molière leaves the solution open. Even under Louis XIV, the arts did not teach a single message.

Jean Baptiste Colbert: The Perfect Mercantilist

It was different, of course, in the economic sphere. There, Louis XIV's grand design was perfectly obvious. Fortunately for himself, he had the services of Colbert. Born in 1619 into a merchant family, Jean Baptiste Colbert had entered the royal service early, had impressed Mazarin and been bequeathed to Louis XIV, who rapidly gave him post after post. In 1661, he took Fouquet's post but not his title; in 1664, he became superintendent of buildings; in 1665, he was officially named controller general of finance; in 1668, secretary of state for the navy—critical offices all. French finances were in grave disarray: a quarter century of war and the ruinous financial policies of Mazarin had left their toll. The king's building program, far from a mere private hobby, was central to his search for glory and reputation—and fabulously expensive. And the French navy needed to be increased enormously and improved if France was to compete with her greatest rivals, the seafaring Dutch and English. Colbert set about his many tasks with obsessive, almost legendary energy. But he was not an innovator. His fiscal expedients for raising ever more money from a restive populace and a spoiled aristocracy; his founding of monopolistic companies to exploit the West and East Indies and the Baltic Sea; his attempts to control the quality of manufactured goods and encourage the output of new industries; his programs for improving communications by building roads and canals, went back to Richelieu and beyond him, into the sixteenth century. The "isms" that have been foisted onto Colbert—"mercantilism" and "Colbertism"—are posthumous, undeserved honors. True, Colbert was the most consistent and systematic mercantilist in history; he has been called "perhaps the only true 'mercantilist' who ever lived."[7] But even for Colbert, mercantilism was little more than a loose collection of economic policies, tied together, if at all, by certain fundamental assumptions about economic life in a system of competing states and in a condition of scarcity. The assumptions were that growth in one state required decline in other states and that economic activity was, therefore (like diplomacy), war carried on by peaceful means. Indeed, Colbert said so explicitly, as did other students of economic affairs in his time: "All trade," Colbert's English contemporary, Sir Josiah Child, declared, "is a kind of warfare."[8] This warfare drove states to strive for what was significantly called "a favorable balance of trade"—an excess of exports over imports—by giving bounties to the former, by placing crippling tariffs on the latter, and by hoarding bullion; to put restrictions on the emigration of skilled craftsmen; to superintend the quality of goods and the training of those who made them; to encourage the growth of population; to foster domestic shipping. One implication of these policies was that while prosperity is desirable partly for its own sake, its fundamental importance—at least from the statesman's point of view—is that it serves and enhances political power. As long as profits and power coincided, there was no difficulty; when they clashed, profits must give way. Another implication, more elusive, is this: the policies that go under the names of Colbertism or mercantilism are a search for strength, not its expression. They betoken weakness and recession.[9]

For a decade or so, Colbertism was a success. Like his king and master, Colbert was everywhere. He read, he planned, he composed endless memoranda, for himself and for Louis XIV. He began by saving money: he abolished sinecures, tightened the collection of taxes, investigated false claims to nobility and thus tax exemption, improved the management of the royal estates, and

[7] By D. C. Coleman, "Economic Problems and Policies," in *The New Cambridge Modern History*, vol. V (1961), 46.

[8] Quoted in William Letwin, *The Origins of Scientific Economics* (1963), 44.

[9] For this point, see F. J. Fisher, "16th–17th Centuries: The Dark Age in English Economic History?" *Economica*, new series, 24 (Feb. 1957), 2–18.

squeezed more money out of the privileged provinces and the clergy by inducing them to increase their "voluntary donations." Partly for purely economic reasons (to decrease the need for imports), partly for reasons of state (to increase the show of royal magnificence), he founded new luxury industries and new trading companies. And he moved rapidly: in 1664, he was instrumental in the establishment of the royal tapestry works at Beauvais, founded the East and West India companies, and began simplification of the immensely complex internal tariff structure of France. In 1665, he laid plans for a great canal, the *canal des deux mers,* to link the Mediterranean with the Atlantic. In 1666 he set down new regulations concerning manufactures. In 1667, he converted the Gobelin tapestry works, which he had taken over five years before, into a royal factory; showing what he meant by saying that trade was a species of war, he imposed new high tariffs directed mainly against English and Dutch cloth merchants. He brought in Venetian glassmakers and Flemish clothmakers; he protected the silk industry at Lyons and encouraged iron foundries; he set the port cities of Brest and Toulon humming with activity, building docks and shipyards.

If one judges simply by intentions, this was a decade of unparalleled economic achievement, based on a program of unmatched rationality. But intentions count for little in history. Colbert could decree regulations, establish monopolies, and multiply formulas for apprenticeship or workmanship, but the temper of the country was not on his side. His attempts to rationalize the tax structure, even though they would strike a modern reader as mild indeed, offended powerful vested interests; his tariffs benefited some and hurt others; his regulations were strange to many and, despite all the efforts of his officials, relatively easy to evade. Besides, his policies had a severely restricted goal: to make his king more magnificent and more powerful than any other king anywhere in Europe or, perhaps, in history. Such a policy could wholly delight only a few men—the king himself and those of his subjects, like Colbert, who identified their interests and their welfare with those of Louis XIV. Still, Colbert's achievement in these years was impressive, if only as an effort to counteract the depression that was gripping the country. Then, in 1672, with the great French assault on Holland and the beginning of decades of war, Colbert's policy was wrecked completely. He had formulated it at least in part to make war possible; he had, indeed, enthusiastically supported Louis' early military ventures in 1667. But when war became large-scale and long-lasting, as it did from 1672 on, the paradox built into Colbertism emerged into the light of day: the aggressive policies for whose sake it had been devised were also its nemesis.

LOUIS XIV AT WAR: 1667-1685

War Abroad: The Rectification of Frontiers

Louis' unremitting search for glory was a psychological need with military consequences. It was not that he was ambitious; every self-respecting prince longed to increase his prestige and enlarge his domains. But Louis XIV wanted hegemony over Europe, an aspiration that did not lend itself readily to compromise. It was the unmeasured quality of his desires that brought into being those great coalitions against France—coalitions even he could not defeat. Louis XIV enjoyed humbling foreign ambassadors, compelling smaller powers to send envoys to France and apologize for "insults." That was easy enough. But Louis XIV was after larger game than the Genoese Republic or the Papal States. He hoped to grab Spanish possessions, taking advantage of Spain's obvious military weakness. There has been an inconclusive debate among historians whether the French king and his advisors had a consistent vision of French "natural frontiers" on the Rhine, the Atlantic, and the Pyrenees. But even if his policy did not have the clarity of a vision, as soon as he had mastered the administrative apparatus and had unmistakably taken power, Louis XIV strove to extend French borders by all means at his command.

The diplomatic and the military situations were favorable. England under Charles II was in France's pay. The German princes, including Brandenburg, were France's dependents. And in September 1665, King Philip IV of Spain died, leaving a sickly four-year-old heir and a sprawling, tempting heritage on France's frontiers. From 1662, Louis' lawyers had been busy finding plausible reasons why the king of France was the true heir to most of these territories. In May 1667, Louis was ready; his troops moved east into Franche-Comté and north into the Spanish Netherlands. The War of Devolution had begun.[10]

For a while, it went well, Louis' fine commanders—Turenne in the Netherlands, the great Condé in Franche-Comté—swept all before them. But Louis was frustrated by the joint effort of the Dutch, the English, and the Swedes. To his fury, the Dutch, a mere nation of shopkeepers and simple

---

[10] The war takes its name from the efforts of Louis' lawyers. Seeking to substantiate his flimsy claim to Spanish territory, these lawyers managed to dredge up the "right of devolution," according to which the private possessions of the Spanish crown, which included the territories Louis XIV had invaded, could be passed on only through the children of a first marriage. While Maria Theresa had renounced her inheritance upon marrying the young king of France, Louis' lawyers argued that this renunciation was invalid since the Spaniards had never paid Maria Theresa's dowry. The whole business shows the anxiety with which the greediest of rulers tried to find at least shreds of legal justification for naked aggression.

republicans, had laid aside a war with England to protect their southern borders by engineering this Triple Alliance. In May 1668, at Aix-la-Chapelle, the belligerents made peace. Louis XIV obtained twelve strongholds on the frontiers of the Spanish Netherlands, including Lille, but he restored Franche-Comté to its Spanish owners. Everyone knew the peace was only a truce. The Sun King would not rest content with such meager rewards.

Louis XIV's second war lasted longer, from 1672 to 1678, and had more serious consequences both abroad and at home. Again private motives shaped public policy. Louis XIV could not forgive the Dutch for their role in the War of Devolution. The Dutch War was to be their chastisement. But Louis was not governed by emotion alone; he had meticulously laid the ground for war by breaking up the Triple Alliance. He bribed the Swedes, "senator by senator,"[11] to desert their allies. He made secret arrangements with King Charles II of England at the Treaty of Dover in May 1670. He bought support and troops from German princes. In late March 1672, Charles II of England declared war on the Dutch; in early April, French troops moved into Dutch territory. For a time, domestic discord kept the Dutch from countering the danger, and in June they sent an embassy to Louis XIV offering peace at the expense of the terrain they had already lost and of heavy indemnities. Louis, self-confident to the point of megalomania, made counterdemands so vast and so insulting that the Dutch could only break off negotiations. Beaten as they felt themselves to be, and despite some counsels of despair, they would not give up half their lands, grant the French exorbitant commercial privileges, permit Catholics freedom of worship, and annually humble themselves in solemn ceremonies at Paris. True, the United Provinces were deeply disunited. In August 1672, an excited crowd murdered Jan de Witt, the grand pensionary of Holland, and his brother Cornelius, both firm advocates of resistance to France. The consequence of this mob action was to bring to undisputed command William III, prince of Orange, the most implacable enemy Louis XIV was to face. William gathered authority in his hands and continued the de Witt policy. By 1674, he had made peace with England and cemented the First Coalition, which included the emperor, Brandenburg, Spain, and the duke of Lorraine. One fruit of his policy, which was to be of transcendent importance later, was his arrangement with Charles II to marry the English king's niece, Mary.

For some years the fortunes of war seesawed. In 1675, Turenne was killed in battle; the French navy acquitted itself remarkably well—Colbert's preparatory labors had not been in vain. But by 1678 it was clear that no side could hope for a decisive victory, and negotiations began. They resulted in the Treaties of Nimwegen, signed by the separate belligerents in 1678 and 1679. Dutch territory was integrally preserved, but Franche-Comté, so much coveted by France, finally fell to Louis XIV. In other complicated arrangements, France and Spain exchanged strongholds, but France got the better of the bargain. By

[11] Goubert, *Louis XIV*, 112.

1679, French territory to the north and east was rounded out and strengthened by the addition of fortified towns.

The high point of Louis XIV's reign had been reached and passed, but there were no indications that he, or anyone else, knew it. French expansion continued, and once again legal subterfuge assisted territorial greed. Nimwegen had shown Louis to be less than omnipotent, but at the same time, Spain and the empire were proved almost wholly impotent. The provinces of Alsace and Lorraine, strategically located on France's frontiers to the east and providing access to the Rhine, were ideal subjects for obfuscation and victimization. They consisted of numerous towns and small regions, all standing in complicated feudal relationships to the emperor and to various monarchs. The Treaties of Westphalia, which had settled the Thirty Years' War (see p. 255), only compounded the confusion. Louis perceived the possibilities, and in 1679 he set up four special courts, the *chambres de réunion,* which examined French claims to these desirable lands and, not unexpectedly, found them valid in case after case. Armed with this feeble excuse, French troops through the next four years peacefully annexed Alsace, Lorraine, and some surrounding territories. In 1681, Louis made the most important of these conquests—he moved into the free city of Strasbourg. While German princes and the emperor, either bribed or powerless, were silent as the king of France rounded out his northeastern frontiers, the capture of Protestant Strasbourg, to which he had no right at all, aroused widespread and outraged protests. In vain. In 1684, Louis XIV and the emperor concluded a Twenty Years' Truce at Regensburg, which confirmed French acquisitions, including that of Strasbourg. The truce opened prospects of peace, but meanwhile, at home, Louis XIV was engaging in policies that could only end in renewed war.

War at Home: The Imposition of Religious Uniformity

Like all rulers, Louis XIV found domestic and foreign policy inextricably intertwined. Colbert, as we have seen, discovered that war ruined his most carefully laid plans to rescue the finances of the state. In turn, domestic uprisings diverted troops from duty at the front to duty against French subjects: in 1675, in the midst of the Dutch War, "some of the king's troops had to be spared to carry murder and pillage to the inhabitants of lower Brittany and Rennes who were in violent rebellion against taxes and nobility alike." It took a winter to restore order. Then, "having hanged a few thousands of his subjects, the king was able to send back his troops to face the members of the coalition." [12] Precisely in the same way, foreign policy would both affect, and be affected by, Louis' religious policy. The king's own religious convictions remain somewhat obscure; it seems likely that, as he grew older, he retreated from a

---

[12] Ibid., 135.

certain measure of libertinism to a certain measure of piety. After he moved to Versailles in 1682, the elaborate festivities of his younger years gave way to a more solemn and more boring routine, and he increasingly surrounded himself with *dévots.* The favorite royal mistress of his later years, the widow Scarron, whom he created Madame de Maintenon and probably married in secret after the death of Maria Theresa, was both extremely pious and extremely influential. But whatever his private persuasion might have been, through all his reign he fully intended to be master over all spheres of public life, and that included religion. This intention brought him into intermittent, embittered conflict with the Jansenists, the papacy, the Huguenots—and Europe.

In essence, the Jansenists were Augustinians—serious Catholics who derived their theology from St. Augustine's pessimistic appraisal of man's nature and possibilities. The derisive epithet their enemies applied to them— "Calvinists who go to mass"—though harshly denying them the status of loyal Catholics, aptly captures their severity. The Jesuits and other "relaxed" Catholics of the day were preaching that man plays an active part in securing his salvation; this was not merely far more cheerful than Augustine's doctrine of human corruption and powerlessness, but it also implied what the Jansenists strenuously denied: that all men might be saved. Cornelis Jansen, after whom this French movement was named, was an unimpeachably orthodox Catholic theologian, a professor at Louvain who had died in 1638, as bishop of Ypres. Two years after his death, his lifework, *Augustinus,* appeared, and it restated Augustine's austere position on grace without any mitigation. In the following year, in 1641, the book appeared in Paris, to be taken up by Jansen's friend, Jean Duvergier de Hauranne, abbé of Saint Cyran (he is known as Saint Cyran) and Antoine Arnauld, head of a large and distinguished clan of theologians and ecclesiastical administrators. Saint Cyran went to the convent of Port Royal des Champs, outside Paris, as confessor and found a ready supporter there in Angélique Arnauld, the mother superior, Antoine Arnauld's sister. It was Antoine who precipitated the great controversy in 1643, with his *Concerning Frequent Communion;* the Jesuits, quite rightly, thought this highly offensive polemic aimed at them. The book excoriated priests who winked at worldliness as long as lapses were confessed and "purified" by frequent communion.

The Jesuits had the ear of the papacy, and in 1653 Pope Innocent X condemned in detail five propositions of the Jansenists. They were indeed imprudent in the extreme: the Jansenists argued that it was heretical to assert that man cooperates in achieving grace and that Christ died for all men. But these assertions, the pope countered, were perfectly orthodox. His condemnation placed the Jansenists in a terrifying quandary. Whatever their enemies might say, they were not Calvinists; they wanted to continue enjoying the right to go to mass. So they prevaricated: they humbly agreed with the pope that the five propositions he found objectionable and heretical were indeed both, but they submitted, just as humbly, that *Augustinus* actually did not contain them. This was sheer sophistry, but it was the sophistry of troubled, even desperate men.

In January 1656, Antoine Arnauld was expelled from the faculty of theology at the Sorbonne, and the Jansenists moved from defense to attack. In the same year the brilliant mathematician Blaise Pascal, who had come to Port Royal the year before, published his *Provincial Letters* in Arnauld's defense. They are a savage, telling, and at the same time, amusing attack on Jesuit beliefs and practices—they still make good reading today. But they are not a wholly candid performance: Pascal took the Jesuits' casuistry as expressing their true convictions. Casuistry is a legalistic game, the setting up of hypothetical situations for the sake of examining all eventualities, thus to clarify the muddy region between honest error and mortal sin. True, the Jesuits were sometimes guilty of abusing casuistry in behalf of their highly placed penitents, but Pascal's charge that the Jesuits condoned lying, adultery, and murder, and degraded religion into the observance of empty forms, was hardly justified.

This was the position in 1661, when Louis XIV assumed personal power. The Jansenists were not prospering. Angélique Arnauld died that year, Pascal died in 1662, and the young king was hostile to Jansenism in spite of, and partly because of, its influential supporters. The nuns at Port Royal were subjected to harassment. But other countervailing forces were at work. Eager to assert his authority not merely over France but over all Europe, Louis XIV found himself in a pronounced antipapal mood for over twenty years. And the Jansenists, being anti-Jesuit and thus hostile to ultramontane tendencies, found themselves taken up by the robe nobility of the French parlements. It was as part of this Gallican phase that the Jansenists survived. Jansenist writings appeared in rapid succession: Pascal had compiled voluminous notes for a comprehensive "apology" for Christianity; he had never completed his work, but in 1670 the first edition of his *Pensées* appeared; they explore in lucid, memorable aphorisms man's lost condition after his fall from grace. Then came the writings of Saint Cyran, of Antoine Arnauld, and others, all serious, all Augustinian in doctrine, all, it seemed, superior in style and argumentation to the more relaxed view of their opponents. Louis, meanwhile, left the Jansenists alone while he perfected his version of Gallicanism—that old doctrine (see p. 100) of royal independence from Rome, especially in the appointing power. In the 1670s, the king claimed the right to nominate to certain benefices and certain convents, as well as the right to collect the income from vacant sees all across France, without regard to ancient exemptions. In 1678, Pope Innocent XI, as courageous as his redoubtable adversary, vigorously censured Louis' policies, and in the years that followed he threatened the Sun King with reprisals. This was too much. Employing subservient bishops for the purpose, Louis XIV in 1682 countered the papal threat with four articles, which asserted the king's freedom from ecclesiastical (even papal) jurisdiction in secular matters; the supremacy of general councils over the papacy; the superiority of French law in regulating relations between the Holy See at Rome and the French state; and the need to obtain universal assent to make papal decrees binding. This was strong language, and schism seemed a possibility. But neither the pope nor the French king had any intention of bringing matters to a breach. Innocent XI died in

1689, and his successors found ways to settle the matter peaceably; by 1693, the Gallican articles had been withdrawn, Louis XIV had declared his sympathies with Rome, and the persecution of the Jansenists resumed. [13]

Like the Jansenists, the Huguenots found their fate bound up with events abroad. Louis, in search of uniformity, had little use for the Protestants in his realm. At first he had forsworn the use of violence and instead offered to reward converts to the true faith, but by 1669 there were signs that he was getting ready to revoke the Edict of Nantes (see p. 181) under whose protection the Huguenots continued to shelter. Only his alliances with Protestant princes induced him to wait. Then, beginning around 1679–1680, a combination of circumstances (still incompletely unraveled) allowed him to wait no longer. Colbert, who valued the industrial and commercial skills of the Protestant minority, and especially the Huguenot bankers, found himself increasingly bypassed, as Louis XIV listened more and more to Louvois, [14] who was far more militant at home, and far more aggressive abroad, than Colbert had ever been. Then, in 1683, Colbert died, and this too helped to loose the dogs of persecution in France. These were the years when the king grew more solemn in his religious observances and listened to Madame de Maintenon and to his Jesuit confessors. And abroad all was going well, if not quite so well as Louis had privately hoped. The motives that had held him back, then, no longer operated.

The campaign to eradicate Protestantism from French soil began in all seriousness in 1679 and gained further momentum in 1681. More forceful methods than paid conversions gained in favor. The chief means of pressure were the so-called *dragonnades*—the quartering of dragoons on unwilling Huguenot families, an inconvenience (to put it mildly) that procured thousands of hasty conversions. By 1684, nearly six hundred out of about eight hundred Huguenot churches were closed. Then, in October 1685, the king officially revoked the Edict of Nantes and forbade Huguenots to exercise their faith, to educate their children as Protestants, and to leave the country. The repression was effective, backed up as it was by the demolition of churches, the kidnapping of children, and the expulsion of Huguenots from strategic cities like Paris. The prohibition on emigration failed: of the more than one million Huguenots in France, many went underground at home, but over two hundred thousand left the country to find shelter in hospitable places elsewhere—mainly in England, in the Dutch Republic, and in Brandenburg. The émigrés took with them rare skills and a great anger. The revocation was one of Louis' greatest mistakes. It strengthened France's enemies at its direct expense, united

---

[13] To anticipate: in a series of bulls, notably *Unigenitus* of 1713, the papacy continued its campaign against Jansenist teachings; in France itself, Louis XIV attacked the Jansenists directly. In 1708, Port Royal des Champs was officially suppressed; in 1709, the remaining nuns were expelled; in 1710, the buildings were razed and the graves of distinguished Jansenists desecrated. The Paris foundation suffered the same fate.

[14] François-Michel le Tellier, marquis de Louvois, son of the trusted Le Tellier on whom Louis XIV had relied at the beginning of his reign.

Europe against Louis XIV, and helped to precipitate a revolution in England and turn England into a formidable adversary.

ENGLAND: THE UNEXPECTED ENEMY

From Restoration to Revolution

The transformation of England from a dependent into an enemy was a disconcerting turn of events for Louis XIV. England under Charles II was once more a second-rate power. The rousing mobilization of national energies that had animated the country under Cromwell had come to an abrupt end with the Restoration; the austerity imposed by the Puritans was relaxed. Charles II was ideally suited to lead the country in this cheerful direction: he was witty, charming, tolerant, given to science, mistresses, and bawdy plays. The sonorous Milton was famous, but in retirement. Restoration comedies, with their cynicism, their polish, and their sensuality, accurately reflected both the royal taste and a widespread thirst for a less strenuous mode of living. One victim of the new style was Cromwell's vigorous foreign policy. To make doubly sure of English subservience, Louis XIV did his utmost to put, and keep, Charles II in France's pocket with subsidies and promises. Several times during his reign, Charles was bribed to countenance and even to support Louis' quest for hegemony. But kings, like other blackmailers, do not stay bought: Charles II proved an expensive and not wholly trustworthy ally. After all, he had to reckon with powerful anti-Catholic, anti-French sentiments in his own country. Still, he was more of a help to Louis XIV than an obstacle. Then, in 1685, when Charles II was succeeded by his Roman Catholic brother, James II, the new king immediately asked Louis XIV for money. It looked as if the cordial arrangement between France and England would continue.

But other forces were at work within English society. The Puritan legacy could not be liquidated and would not be denied. The Restoration, as we have seen (p. 281), did not restore the old monarchy, but gave Parliament a continuous, influential voice in public affairs, and by converting the source of the king's income from traditional feudal dues to modern forms of taxation, took yet another step toward the modern state, away from the old conception of the king as the country's greatest feudal landlord. Even more important, the Puritan religious impulse remained a vital force in the country, even in the restored Church of England. The conflicts that marked Charles' long reign mainly erupted over religious issues. Charles II was not only not a Puritan—that was scandalously evident to all—he was, if he was anything at all, a crypto-Catholic. And he was surrounded by Catholics: His brother James, duke of York, converted to the Roman persuasion around 1668; his queen, Catherine of

Braganza, whom he married in 1662, had been born into it. His foreign policy (though the Dutch Wars were largely wars over trade) certainly showed no hostility to Catholic powers. And his religious policy, though devious, appeared calculated to strengthen Catholicism in a country that by and large had hated and feared Catholics for a century.

Charles' divergence from dominant ways of English thinking impelled him into some adroit political maneuverings. The king had spent his youth in exile and, as he later said to his impetuous younger brother, the duke of York: "I am too old to go again to my travels: you may, if you choose it." The elections of 1661 gave Charles a loyal but not wholly pliant parliament; it was filled with staunch Anglicans and equally staunch royalists—its nickname, Cavalier Parliament, was not undeserved. [15] But Parliament's loyalty to the restored monarchy was aggressive, almost embarrassing, and its Anglicanism was accompanied by vindictiveness against Puritans. For four years, this Cavalier Parliament enacted stringent legislation against the Puritan sectaries. Proposals to establish a comprehensive English Protestant church that would at least include Presbyterians were shunted aside with impatience. The Corporation Act of 1661 excluded from municipal office all who did not belong to the Anglican communion or refused to swear an oath of nonresistance to the king. In 1662 an Act of Uniformity drove from their livings all those clergymen who would not use the newly revised Book of Common Prayer. In 1664, the Conventicle Act prohibited religious meetings of more than five persons. Finally, the Five Mile Act of 1665 imposed on all preachers who had not sworn to the Act of Uniformity a new oath of nonresistance and loyalty, and prohibited those who refused to come within five miles of any incorporated town. With this legislation—known, somewhat inaccurately, as the Clarendon Code [16]—the Cavalier Parliament made the split between Anglicans and Puritan Dissenters official and created English Nonconformity. In abandoning the old idea of "comprehension" in a single, truly national church, it at once legalized and disfranchised Dissent and drove a wedge between Englishmen that would shape English history for two centuries.

Charles had other ideas, and the emergence of Nonconformity gave him an opportunity to seek toleration for Catholics by linking their cause to that of the Dissenters. He failed. In 1662, he tried to suspend the Act of Uniformity and issued a Declaration of Indulgence offering to suspend the operation of the laws against Dissenters. Bishops and Parliament together persuaded him to desist. In 1672, he tried again; in his second Declaration of Indulgence, he declared the suspension of "all and all manner of penal laws in matters ecclesiastical against

[15] It also has another nickname: Pension Parliament. Under the management of the earl of Danby, parliamentary corruption became a standard procedure: the crown influenced parliamentary decisions by bribery and the free use of influence.

[16] Edward Hyde, first earl of Clarendon, a distinguished historian and statesman, followed Charles into exile in 1646 and returned in 1660, with the Restoration. For seven years, down to 1667, he was King Charles II's lord chancellor. While Clarendon disliked the stringencies of the laws named after him, he did little to prevent their enactment and loyally enforced them.

whatsoever sort of nonconformists and recusants." But then, early in 1673, Parliament induced him to drop the declaration by offering, in return, a grant of money for the Dutch War then under way. To drive its meaning home, Parliament then passed the Test Act, which specified that Anglicans alone— only those, that is, who took the sacraments according to the rites prescribed by the Church of England—could hold military or civil office. The king's brother James, duke of York, who had been a capable lord high admiral, had to hand in his resignation. This parliamentary victory in no way appeased the religious troubles; victories rarely make the victors content. In September 1673, the duke of York married Mary of Modena, like him a Catholic. Here was a terrible danger to Reformed England. James' first wife had given him two daughters, Mary and Anne. Both were raised as Protestants, both were destined to be queens of England. But in 1673, no one could foresee that: all that seemed obvious, and ominous, was that King Charles II and his queen were not going to have an heir, and that James and his new wife were likely to produce Charles' successor. Englishmen—Nonconformists as much as Anglicans—shuddered at the thought. Charles' evident capacity to govern without parliamentary subventions, at least in times of peace, only fueled the general suspicion. In 1678, suspicion was turned into hysteria by the bizarre Popish Plot. It was completely imaginary, the brainchild of an utterly convincing and utterly unprincipled Anglican cleric named Titus Oates. According to Oates and his associate, Israel Tonge, the Jesuits planned to assassinate King Charles, murder leading Protestants, and put Catholic James on the throne of England. Fortunately for their fiction, a London magistrate named Godfrey, who had heard the charges, was found dead under melodramatic circumstances. To heated imaginations nothing could be more clear-cut: the Jesuits had murdered Godfrey to silence him. Hysteria now burst all bounds. Parliament met in October 1678. This was to be the last session of Charles' Long Parliament—still loyal, but more loyal to the principle of the Protestant succession than to the whims of Charles and his dangerous brother. It unanimously passed a resolution declaring that "there hath been, and still is, a damnable and hellish Plot, contrived and carried on by the Popish recusants for the assassinating and murdering the King, and for subverting the government, and rooting out and destroying the Protestant religion."[17] It impeached Danby, the king's chief minister, for his secret correspondence with the French, and forced his dismissal and imprisonment. It passed an act excluding all papists from both Houses—the duke of York alone excepted. It consigned five Catholic peers to the Tower. It created and exacerbated an atmosphere in which perhaps two score innocent or merely indiscreet persons were executed for "treason."

Persuasive charlatans can do much; their role in history is impressive. Parliament acted entirely under the impress of Oates' impudent charges. And Oates did more. By embittering the already serious divisions within the English

---

[17] Quoted in J. R. Tanner, *English Constitutional Conflicts of the Seventeenth Century, 1603-1689* (1962), 239.

political public, Oates and his Popish Plot spurred the growth of English parties. The Whigs, speaking broadly, were intent on securing a Protestant succession; they were opposed to what they called "the French interest," and harped much on the English constitution. The Tories, for their part, were diehard loyalists, ready to swallow a pro-French policy, and even a Catholic on the throne, for the sake of stability. [18]

In 1679, the Whigs, under the able leadership of the earl of Shaftesbury, brought in an Exclusion Bill that explicitly denied the succession to the duke of York. This became the great goal of the opposition and the leading theme of parliamentary rhetoric in the two years that followed. To save the throne for his brother, Charles II dissolved Parliament early in 1679. Three parliaments followed in rapid succession; each brought up the Exclusion Bill, and each was accordingly dissolved. From March 1681 on, Charles II ruled without Parliament. He had subsidies from France, and beginning in 1682, a royalist reaction on his side. In that year a confused medley of plots, mainly invented but some real enough, gave the king his opportunity. He had some potential rebels sent to the block; his brother, who had gone into exile, returned; leading exclusionists found it prudent to leave the country. Among the exiles was the philosopher John Locke. But Charles did not have long to enjoy his triumphs; he had the pleasure of seeing Oates exposed and in prison, but in February 1685, he died, a Catholic on his deathbed. James succeeded him, fulfilling, indeed exceeding, the worst premonitions of his worst enemies.

At first all went well for the king. James freed the imprisoned peers and took further revenge on Oates and his friends. His Parliament was royalist, patient, and generous. Events helped: in May 1685, the earl of Argyll invaded Scotland; in June, the duke of Monmouth, an illegitimate son of Charles II and a great favorite with the Protestant opposition, landed in western England. This double rebellion rallied the political leadership around James. Argyll was easily beaten in June, taken, and executed. Monmouth was beaten, just as easily, at Sedgmoor, in July. His royal parentage did not save him—he too was executed, and his followers were decimated in the following months with signal brutality by the notorious Jeffreys, lord chief justice, in the Bloody Assizes. James' throne seemed beyond challenge.

But the king rapidly wasted the capital of good will on which an English monarch—*any* monarch—could draw after the unsettling decades of civil war and commonwealth. And Louis XIV powerfully aided the opposition to James with his increasingly ruthless persecution of the French Huguenots. When he officially revoked the Edict of Nantes in October 1685, he gave troubled

[18] Like most party names, these were first words of abuse. "Whig" meant a Scottish Presbyterian outlaw; "Tory" an Irish Catholic bandit. More important than these etymologies is the recognition that these "parties" had almost nothing in common with the modern English party system. They were not disciplined; they were shifting alliances, often rather strange, and their class base was far from clear. While on the whole the Whigs were hospitable to Dissenters and urban merchants, the Tories drew heavily on country squires and Anglican clergymen. But this division was neither firm nor final (see p. 383).

Englishmen much to think about. James' ostentatious piety was annoying, but what mattered more was his public policy. For three years, continuously, impatiently, he did everything he could to remind his subjects that they were not far from Continental despotism, that even the old religious settlement going back to Queen Elizabeth was not safe. He called for repeal of the Clarendon Code to relieve the Dissenters and of the Test Acts to relieve the Catholics. He packed the army, the navy, the public service, and the universities with Roman Catholics, in open and repeated defiance of the law. He was clearly dominated by Roman Catholic advisors. In the face of parliamentary uneasiness, he kept troops stationed around London. In April 1687, he issued his first Declaration of Indulgence, much like his brother's declaration of 1672. A year later, he returned with a second declaration and ordered it read in all churches. Most Anglican clerics, though used to obedience, disobeyed. In addition, Sancroft, the archbishop of Canterbury, and six other bishops remonstrated with him and were sent to the Tower. Late in June, they were tried for seditious libel. It was a decisive trial in English history. On June 30, the seven bishops were acquitted. Revolution was now only a matter of time and of detail.

From the Glorious Revolution to the Grand Coalition

The causes of the Glorious Revolution are transparent. James' policies were tactlessness carried to the point of self-destructive mania. In three years the king had managed to offend and frighten nearly all Englishmen; the Catholics alone were grateful for his attentions. The Dissenters did not value what he planned to do for them. The Whigs saw him as a despot on the model of Louis XIV or Bloody Mary. Even the Tories and the High Anglicans, who were among the most patient of Englishmen, turned against this high-handed autocrat. But the immediate cause of the Glorious Revolution was, quite simply, the birth of a child. In June 1688 Mary of Modena finally had a son. "In the seventeenth century," G. N. Clark comments, "people would believe anything. The Catholics thought it was a miracle and the Protestants said it was an imposture. It was neither." [19] Whatever it was, it was too much. In July, seven distinguished Englishmen, including the old royal servant Danby, calmly invited William of Orange to invade England. William quickly accepted. Late in the summer, James II suddenly veered about; he restored some suspended officials, clerics, and university fellows, promised to call Parliament, and made other concessions—too late. In November, with a favorable wind, William landed at Torbay on the south coast and found the country with him. James II, his queen, and their baby escaped to France.

It was a bloodless invasion; the only victims were the king, his family and friends, and the four hundred or so "nonjurors"—Anglican clerics who refused to swear allegiance to the usurper. But these victims lost only their posts, not

[19] *The Later Stuarts, 1660–1714* (1934), 121.

their lives. In January 1689, a Convention Parliament legalized this Glorious Revolution; it found James guilty of having tried to subvert the constitution "by breaking the original contract between king and people," and, in violation of all constitutional logic, it declared the throne vacant. By February, William and Mary were installed jointly as king and queen of England. Mary died not long after, in 1694, and Dutch William reigned alone until his death in 1702. But in their relatively brief reign a political and religious settlement was patched together that set the stage for the rule of the English oligarchy, with all its grave flaws the most progressive and most widely admired regime of eighteenth-century Europe (see p. 348). In early 1689, Parliament issued the Declaration of Rights and tied it to its offer of joint kingship. The declaration insisted on the right of Parliament to make and unmake all laws. This meant that the royal power to suspend laws or to dispense with their penalties for favorite individuals was unconstitutional and that all money must be raised with the approval of Parliament. To put teeth into this declaration, Parliament provided that standing armies could be raised only with parliamentary consent, enforced by requiring annual renewal of an act authorizing military discipline; that Parliament had the right to petition the crown; that its elections and debates must be free; and that a new parliament must be elected every three years. (In 1701, the Act of Settlement further spelled out the meaning of the Glorious Revolution; it settled the succession specifically in a Hanoverian princess, Sophia, the Protestant granddaughter of James I, and her descendants, and it generally held Roman Catholics ineligible to take the English crown.) A Toleration Act of 1689 granted the Nonconformists relief from the penalties specified in earlier laws for failure to take the Anglican sacraments—a large step in an atmosphere inflamed by the revocation of the Edict of Nantes, but still far short of the comprehension some Englishmen had hoped for and far short of the civil equality Dissenters wanted.

The intervention of a Dutch prince in the affairs of England underscores the Europe-wide view that dominated William's mind. To be sure, William of Orange had dynastic interests in England: he was the grandson of King Charles I and the son-in-law of King James II. But what mattered most to him was to stop Louis XIV, and he was doubtful just what England under James II might do once France moved its superb war machine into the field. William for years had been in a delicate position and conducted himself circumspectly. From 1687 on, however, he became increasingly anxious to secure English resources in the struggle against Louis' unending search for "reputation." It was a sound calculation. In 1686, William had constructed the League of Augsburg—a coalition against France adhered to by Sweden, the emperor, Spain, the Palatinate (to which Louis XIV, in his usual fashion, was laying claim), and the electors of Bavaria and Saxony. Savoy joined in 1687. Then, in October 1688, while William was making ready to invade England and dethrone his father-in-law, Louis XIV attacked the Rhenish Palatinate, laying it waste, not for the first time. And he declared war on the Dutch. In March 1689, the exiled James

II invaded Ireland, whence he was not expelled until July 1690, after the bloody battle of the Boyne. James' move, which would have been impossible without substantial French support, practically guaranteed English adherence to the League of Augsburg. All Europe was now joined against Louis XIV.

The War of the League of Augsburg raged for eight years, bringing financial troubles to the leading allies, devastation to the invaded territories, and depression, unemployment and famine to France; the years 1693-1694 especially were years of drastically declining births and mounting deaths. Many Frenchmen starved (see p. 292). By 1696 the Grand Coalition had broken up with the defection of Savoy, but general peace was not made until late 1697, at Ryswick. Few were wholly happy with it, but William III had achieved most of his objectives. Louis XIV had been checked. He was compelled to recognize William III as king of England, to promise to cease supporting James II and the Jacobites,[20] and to give up most of the conquests gained from the "reunions," with the exception of territory in Alsace, Strasbourg, and Saarlouis.

Louis XIV's armies had been checked; his appetite had not. One prize had long haunted him, and he had no intention of abandoning it: the crown and the domains of Spain. Spain's Hapsburg king, Charles II, had ascended the throne in 1665, but childless and in perpetual ill health, his endlessly imminent death had been arousing the greedy hopes of several European princes for decades. His putative heirs could hardly wait, although contrary to all expectations, Charles II lived until 1700. Louis XIV had a certain claim to the Spanish inheritance, both as the husband of Charles II's older sister and as the grandson of Philip III. Another claimant was Emperor Leopold I, the Austrian Hapsburg, as husband of Charles II's younger sister and as another grandson of Philip III. A third claimant, the young prince-elector of Bavaria, had a much weaker claim, but he became the beneficiary of a partition treaty, signed in 1698, which divided the Spanish inheritance. Barely alive but alive enough to be piqued at not being consulted, Charles II offered Spain and its empire to the prince-elector, but in 1699 the boy suddenly died, and another, more complex, partition treaty was arranged. At last, on November 1, 1700, Charles II died; his will, insisting that the Spanish dominions be left undivided, made Philip of Anjou, second grandson of Louis XIV, sole heir provided he renounce his claim to the throne of France. After serious consideration, Louis XIV accepted in his adolescent grandson's name.

While Frenchmen boasted that there were no more Pyrenees, others were determined to prevent this destruction of the European balance of power. Louis XIV made the Grand Alliance against him a certainty in 1701; he violated his own pledges by asserting that Spain's new Bourbon king, Philip V, had a right

[20] The Jacobites—so called from Jacobus, the Latin form of James—were partisans of the house of Stuart. Down to James II's death in 1701, they conspired to have him restored; after that, they pinned their hopes on his son, James Edward Stuart, the Old Pretender. And after *his* death, they pressed the claim of his son, Charles Edward Stuart—Bonnie Prince Charlie, the Young Pretender—to the English throne. In vain, as we shall see below.

to both the Spanish and the French thrones, and he violated the Peace of Ryswick by attacking the barrier forts in the Spanish Netherlands. These actions silenced the peace party in England and brought together an alliance too formidable even for Louis XIV. William III died in early March 1702, to be succeeded by his wife's younger sister, Anne, but not before he had forged a great coalition against France. By May 1702, the allies were in the field, and the War of the Spanish Succession had begun. The allies were brilliantly led by John Churchill, duke of Marlborough; Prince Eugene of Savoy; and Anthony Heinsius, grand pensionary of Holland—an impressive trio of generals and statesmen. Spain, a puppet of France, and Bavaria, the inveterate adversary of Hapsburg Austria, were Louis' only allies. For some years, the war went badly for France. In a series of memorable battles, the allies repeatedly defeated Louis' forces: in August 1704, Marlborough routed the joint Bavarian-French army at Blenheim; in May 1706, Marlborough reconquered the Spanish Netherlands with a victory at Ramillies; in the same year, Prince Eugene drove the French from Italy with a victory at Turin. In July 1708 at Oudenarde, and again in September 1709 at Malplaquet, Marlborough and Eugene together set back the French. But both battles, especially Malplaquet, were bloodbaths, and by 1710 the bellicose Whigs were out of office in England, and a Tory ministry tried to make peace. Louis XIV, gravely hurt, had offered to negotiate as early as 1708, but the allies, blinded by success, demanded such humiliating terms that Louis felt compelled to withdraw from the talks. He was ready to give up a great deal of territory and to recognize the Hanoverian succession in England, but he could not bring himself to expel his own grandson from Spain. The war resumed, with better fortune for France in the last years. Peace finally came in a series of treaties concluded in 1713 at Utrecht and in 1714 at Rastatt and Baden.

The Peace of Utrecht, as this collection of agreements is summarily called, was a settlement of decisive importance. Whatever the disgruntled Whigs might say, it was a triumph for England. Cromwell's aspiration to make his country into a great power had finally become reality. In 1704, the British navy had captured Gibraltar; Utrecht guaranteed its possession. In addition, Britain gained firm footholds in America, at France's expense: Newfoundland, the Hudson's Bay territory, and Nova Scotia. While the Bourbon king of Spain, Philip V, was confirmed on the throne, the separation of the Spanish and French crowns was written into the peace, and Spanish possessions in the Mediterranean and the Netherlands were handed to the Austrian Hapsburgs and other members of the coalition. The Dutch, too, profited, not so much in territory as in military security. England's triumph was France's defeat. It was not Cromwell's dream alone that was realized; Utrecht was a posthumous vindication of William III. France remained a great power, but Louis' fantasy of hegemony was frustrated, it would seem forever. Even eastern Europe entered into the settlement. Prussia obtained new territories, and the title of "king in Prussia," which the elector Frederick had taken in 1701, was officially confirmed (see p. 323). The Peace of Utrecht reads like a definitive, final judgment on the reign of Louis XIV. The old king died on September 1, 1715, after long suffering, the power of his country diminished, many of his promises unfulfilled, his children and grandchildren dead before him, his lust for conquest and passion for "reputation" a source of bitter regret and self-reproach at the end. But the comprehensive provisions of Utrecht also suggest that the age of Louis XIV cast its shadow wide and far, even into eastern Europe.

EASTERN EUROPE IN THE AGE OF LOUIS XIV

The struggles that convulsed western Europe for the century between the outbreak of the Thirty Years War in 1618 and the death of Louis XIV in 1715 resulted in significant shifts of power—in the weakening of Spain, the containment of France, the flourishing of the Dutch, the emergence of England. But the physical outlines of these states had been, roughly speaking, fixed, and remained relatively stable. In eastern Europe on the other hand, these years saw fundamental changes on the map. Poland, once a sizable empire, shrank into insignificance—first a universal joke, later the hapless victim of its neighbors (see p. 435). The Ottoman Turks, a persistent threat, reached a final paroxysm of aggressiveness and then receded to become "the sick man of Europe" (see Ch. 13). The Austrian Hapsburgs, an old and declining dynasty, regained their position. Brandenburg-Prussia and Russia, both marginal to the West, became great powers and henceforth played a role in all diplomatic calculations and in every major European war.

The Austrian Hapsburgs

The seventeenth century was a time of trial for the Austrian Hapsburgs—a trial they overcame, though at great cost. Relations with Hapsburg Spain grew more distant and, in any event, less rewarding as Spain sank into torpor and political insignificance. And the Peace of Westphalia in 1648 made the imperial crown, traditionally in Hapsburg hands, an ambiguous honor by turning the Holy Roman Empire into a patchwork of hundreds of small sovereign states, hard to rule, impossible to unite (see p. 255). The Thirty Years' War had raised havoc in the Hapsburg domains; many of them had been theaters of battle and objects of pillage. Impoverished and depopulated, they showed the scars of war for many years. The persistent and pitiless Catholicizing policies of the Hapsburgs left other scars: the utter neglect of local culture in Bohemia and the large-scale emigration of Protestants unwilling to convert to the Roman church. By 1660, the Hapsburg monarchy was a disparate collection of inheritances, the uneasy home of several languages: German, Czech, Magyar, and others. In the west and south, there were the "hereditary provinces" of the Austrian house, subject to the ruler in Vienna who united within one person a confusing but, for the age, perfectly typical number of titles. He was duke of Upper and Lower Austria, of Carinthia and Carniola; he was margrave of Styria, and lord of lands in Swabia—the only noncontiguous territories in the Austrian domains. After 1665, he became Landesfürst of the Tyrol as well. In the north, the Hapsburg wore the crown of St. Wenceslas: he was king of Bohemia, margrave of Moravia, and duke of Upper and Lower Silesia. In the east, he was king of Hungary, endowed with the crown of St. Stephen, which had fallen into Hapsburg hands in 1526. It supposedly gave him sovereignty over Hungary, Transylvania, Croatia, Dalmatia, and Slavonia. In actuality, the Austrians held only the northwest quarter of Hungary, and even there, what with the stubborn pride of the local Magyar aristocrats, their control was more nominal than real. They had little influence over the principality of Transylvania in central Hungary, ably led in the first half of the seventeenth century by Bethlen Gabor and George I Rakoczy. Amid the decay of Ottomans to their east and the preoccupations of Hapsburg to their west, these Transylvanian princes had secured virtual autonomy from both and had carved out a Calvinist enclave surrounded by Catholics and Muslims. The eastern parts of Hungary, finally, were firmly in Ottoman hands. Thus, estranged from Spain, enfeebled in Germany, impotent in most of Hungary, Austria in 1660 was both troubled and compact.

Yet the Austrian Hapsburgs turned both their troubles and their compactness to good account. They set about solving manageable tasks: extirpating the Protestant heresy from their lands, concentrating administration in Vienna, and surrendering hopes of a great Germanic empire, creating instead an empire in eastern and southeastern Europe. A succession of competent Hapsburg rulers did all this. When Ferdinand II died in 1637, Bohemia was a pitiful Hapsburg dependency (see p. 250). His son, Ferdinand III, who ruled from 1637 to 1657, participated in the making of general peace in 1648, and in the nine years that remained to him, did something to repair the damages of war and devastation, intensified the Catholicizing of his Bohemian subjects, and worried about the imperial succession. When his second son succeeded him in 1658 as Leopold I, the basis for economic recovery and territorial reconquest seemed secure. Leopold I was an unlikely warrior-king. He had not been expected to succeed to the Hapsburg dominions, but when his older brother Ferdinand died in 1654, Leopold had to give up his study of theology to enter into his heritage. He did so unwillingly; he never lost his religiosity and his shyness. But, unlikely as he was in the role of warrior-king, he filled it, and well, until his death in 1705.

Leopold I faced two enemies: Louis XIV in the west and the Ottoman Turks in the east. These two enemies were not unconnected. Louis XIV resented the king of Spain's parading the title "Catholic majesty" and liked to think of himself as the "most Christian king," the scourge of heretics. Indeed, when he revoked the Edict of Nantes in 1685, the delighted Bishop Bossuet apostrophized him as a "new Constantine." But the exigencies of policy overrode the demands of piety, and in the Turkish wars the French king tacitly supported, or openly encouraged, the Turks (France's traditional ally) against Austria (France's traditional enemy).

Leopold I was put to the test not long after his accession. Since 1648, the prince of Transylvania had been George II Rakoczy, a man with visions of empire. By the mid-1650s, he had concluded an alliance with Sweden and invaded Poland. But his plan for an eastern European domain was ruined, first by the desertion of his Swedish allies and then from an unexpected source: the revitalized Turks. In 1656, a new grand vizier, Mohammed Kuprili, had taken control. Brutal and energetic, he purged his opposition, reorganized economic affairs, and refurbished his army. In July 1657, he defeated George II Rakoczy at Tremblowa and forced Rakoczy's deposition. In defeat, Rakoczy turned to the Hapsburgs for aid, and before his early death in 1660, Austrian and Turkish troops were engaged, though still fitfully.

Sporadic fighting turned into large-scale war soon after. The fall of Transylvania to the Turks brought them perilously close to Austria's hereditary provinces. In 1661, Ahmed Kuprili succeeded his father and extended his father's expansionist policies; in April 1663, he moved his army up the Danube, toward the prize—Vienna. But not yet; in August 1664, at the battle of St. Gotthard in western Hungary, a European, mainly Hapsburg, army defeated the grand vizier and imposed on him a twenty-year truce. Foiled, the Turks attacked elsewhere. They raided Poland and, in the 1670s, Russia, but their aggression bore indifferent fruit: while the Turks took Ukrainian territory from the Poles in 1676, they were obliged to disgorge it to the Russians in 1681. And in any event, Vienna was their real target.

By mid-July 1683, the Turks had closed in on it. They surrounded the city and heavily bombarded its walls. While Emperor Leopold I took himself and his family to safety, the garrison, vastly outnumbered, bravely refused to surrender and waited for relief. Relief finally came, in the shape of a motley army—Austrians, Saxons, Bavarians, Poles—under the leadership of John III (John Sobieski), king of Poland. Here was a critical moment in European affairs: the effects of the heathens conquering Vienna would have been momentous. Louis XIV, the most Christian king, was conspicuously absent; in fact, his emissaries had done their best to dissuade Sobieski from relieving the city. Yet, in mid-September, the allied forces routed the Turks, and the danger was over.

Their defeat ended the Turkish threat to Austria and created an opportunity for a latter-day crusade to expel the infidel from Europe. Financed largely by the pope, a European army of Austrians, Poles, Venetians, and later, Russians, under the command of Prince Eugene, conducted a successful counterattack, the War of the Holy League.[21] It came to an end in January 1699,

---

[21] One casualty of the war was the Parthenon in Athens. Used as a powder magazine by the Turks, in 1687 it was shelled by the Venetian navy and an unlucky hit severely damaged the structure.

with the Treaty of Karlowitz. Prince Eugene had decisively defeated the Turks at Senta, in September 1697, and the peace reflected the military situation. Austria's allies, Venice and Poland, obtained some territory at the Turk's expense, but the Austrians took the prizes: Hungary, Transylvania, Croatia, and Slavonia. The Austrian Empire in southeastern Europe was taking shape.

Leopold and his successors did not disdain the old imperial game in the west. Leopold I died in 1705, to be succeeded by the short-lived Joseph I (1705-1711), and by Joseph's brother, Charles VI (see p. 389). Under Leopold Austria participated in the Grand Alliance against Louis XIV; under Charles it reaped its reward for its work in the War of the Spanish Succession: The Treaty of Rastatt in 1714 converted the old Spanish Netherlands into the Austrian Netherlands and confirmed Austrian occupation of Spanish dominions—Naples, Sardinia, and Milan—in Italy. Between the Peace of Karlowitz and the Peace of Rastatt Austria's glory and might had been restored, but this was not a time for complacency. The Turks remained a threat, though they increasingly tended to turn their attentions northward, against the Russians. And the Hungarians were restive. They resented the increasing interference of Viennese officials in their affairs, the obvious subjugation of Hungarian to Austrian interests, and the settlement of Catholic Austrians in their territory. In 1703, led by Francis II Rakoczy, they rebelled, but the rebels were defeated and in 1711 they agreed to a settlement. Significantly, the Peace of Szatmar was a compromise which reaffirmed Austrian sovereignty over Hungary but granted a general amnesty and promised to respect Hungarian constitutional rights and redress Hungarian grievances. Hapsburg power depended on holding together a motley assortment of peoples and aristocracies, and on making these subjects, to some degree at least, partners in this fragile empire. For the eighteenth century this proved a workable arrangement. But the same century also provided the Hapsburgs with a new and unlooked-for rival in the north, in Prussia.

From Brandenburg to Prussia

The emergence of Prussia as a great power was the triumph of will over nature. Since the establishment of the Hohenzollern dynasty in 1415, Brandenburg had extended its territories with policies reminiscent of the Hapsburgs: the Hohenzollerns negotiated cleverly and married well. They needed to: Brandenburg's soil was sandy, its climate was raw, and its natural resources were scanty; its possessions, moreover, were scattered across the low-lying tableland of northern Germany, vulnerable to invasion.

When Louis XIV ascended to personal power in 1661, Frederick William had been elector of Brandenburg for twenty-one years, decisive years for Brandenburg's growth. Both at Westphalia in 1648 and at Oliva in 1660, Frederick William had acquired important dominions in west and east alike. He had also determined to stake his future on a standing army. This was a momentous decision in Prussian history, indeed for world history. All the proverbial meanings that cluster around the word "Prussian," all the caricatures of snobbish, cruel, bemedaled Junkers, all the widespread fears of Prussian militarism have their roots in that decision. As Freiherr von Schrotter, ex-soldier and liberal minister, would ruefully say around 1800: "Prussia was not a country with an army, but an army with a country which served as headquarters and food magazine."[22] Yet until 1740 (see p. 389) this army was rarely in the field; Frederick William and his successors increased its size, improved its equipment, and maintained its reputation by husbanding its strength. Prussian militarism is the offspring of this irony: it grew formidable by not fighting.

Three aspects of Prussian militarism deserve particular attention: its financial resources, its social base, and its cultural consequences. Both the old dominions of Brandenburg and those it acquired in the seventeenth century had estates jealous of their prerogatives, particularly of their right to vote taxes. But Frederick William, eager to participate in the European power game and to build an effective and loyal armed force, wanted more money and more international involvements than the estates were ready to grant. In his early years, the elector compromised; when the Baltic War[23] erupted in 1655, he rapidly overthrew the constituted order. Illegally, he raised money without the estates' consent, and when the war was over, kept his standing army in being. Soon all power was in his hands and in the hands of his chosen bureaucrats. The estates were broken; while they retained certain privileges, their capacity to resist the elector or sabotage his plans had vanished. Even in the western provinces of Cleves and Mark, where the estates had once been strong, participation in the making of public policy meant little more than solemn ratification of what the elector had dictated. What opposition remained, Frederick William crushed by cajolery and, more often, by brute force. On a scale far smaller than Louis XIV, but in a far more thoroughgoing manner, the elector of Brandenburg welded his disparate territories into a unified country subject to a ruler with absolute power. It has often been noted that in these years, and for long thereafter, the Brandenburg-Prussian state did not even have a name. But it had substance: a full treasury, an impressive army, an efficient bureaucracy, and an obedient populace.

Frederick William's chief instrument of government was, or rather became, the *Generalkriegskommissariat*. As its name suggests, this "general war commissariat" was established during the Northern War of 1655–1660. Its first duties were directly connected with that conflict: it had to raise money for the

---

[22] Quoted in Hans Rosenberg, *Bureaucracy, Aristocracy, and Autocracy: The Prussian Experience, 1660–1815* (1958), 40.

[23] This conflict is sometimes called the Northern War; it should not be confused with the Great Northern War, which began in 1700 (see p. 328).

army and see to its training, equipment, victualling, and all other aspects of supply. During the decade of peace its role was reduced, but in 1672, when Brandenburg joined the Dutch Republic in the war against France, the *Generalkriegskommissariat* grew into the vital center of Brandenburg's bureaucracy. It served as the central treasury and, gradually, without any theoretical pronouncements about "mercantilism," entered the general domain of economic superintendence. It collected the new excise tax in the towns. It supervised the establishment of new industries and commercial ventures. It inspected Brandenburg's gilds and participated in foreign affairs by controlling Frederick William's tentative ventures in navy-building and colonial entrepreneurship. In 1685, after the revocation of the Edict of Nantes, when fourteen thousand Huguenots streamed into Brandenburg, it was the *Generalkriegskommissariat* that was in charge of settling the new immigrants. Directly responsible to the elector, aware of their importance, these new bureaucrats interfered with the estates and were as arrogant with the general public as they were loyal to their chief. It is almost unnecessary to add that practically all higher officials in this body were members of Prussia's rural aristocracy—Junkers. [24]

Though not confined to it, the essential task of the *Generalkriegskommissariat* was to maintain the army, that instrument of policy that became the center of a national cult. After the 1660s, with a population of little over a million, the Brandenburg army stood at twenty-five thousand to forty thousand—an imposing number to be sustained by so small and so poor a population. It has been estimated that Prussians bore more than twice as much in taxes as did contemporary Frenchmen, even though Prussia was poor and France rich. Prussia's poverty, indeed, was the center of a vicious circle: the poverty ostensibly required an expansionist militarist foreign policy; the expansionist militarist foreign policy kept Prussia poor. True, Brandenburg-Prussia's revenues increased threefold in the reign of Frederick William,[25] but for many years the state had no money to squander on luxuries like civilization. Yet Prussians bore these burdens with few murmurs—and when murmurs were heard, they were quickly stilled with methods more familiar in eastern than in western Europe. The most burdened, and the quietest, subject of these exactions was, of course, the Prussian peasant. Like his Russian counterpart, he had sunk into servitude in the sixteenth century and his servile status had been legally confirmed early in the seventeenth century (see p. 259). Here, too, the Brandenburg dominions were moving in the direction of their eastern rather than their western neighbors.

In the army, as in the bureaucracy, leadership was the preserve of the Junker. Practically all officer posts were reserved to Junkers, though there were some branches, notably army engineering, where talent might prevail over birth. The place of the Junkers in the Prussian state was essentially the fruit of

---

[24] The name derives from the Middle High German *junc herre,* young lord.
[25] See F. L. Carsten, *The Origins of Prussia* (1954), 270.

a tacit bargain. In return for surrendering independent political power, the landed aristocracy was granted a monopoly over the higher posts; in return for blind obedience to the dynasty,[26] the Junkers might exact the same obedience from "their" peasants on the land, "their" subordinates in the bureaucracy, or "their" recruits in the army. "Many of these experts in local tyranny," as the historian Hans Rosenberg has put it, "were experienced in whipping the backs, hitting the faces, and breaking the bones of 'disrespectful' and 'disobedient' peasant serfs. Thus they were eminently fitted to be the drillmasters of common Prussian soldiers who, as Frederick II envisaged their proper status, should 'fear their officers more than any danger to which they might be exposed.'"[27] Contrary to their reputation, many Junker landowners had amassed considerable wealth through shrewd estate management and commercial dealings in the sixteenth century. But the dislocations of the Thirty Years' War and the unsettled conditions that followed it left many of them stranded on backward farmlands, with no provision for their numerous progeny. The state made entry into the aristocracy nearly impossible by stringent legislation against the alienation of Junker lands to commoners, and at the same time reserved jobs and prestige for Junkers alone. This was a bargain from which both sides profited.

There were no classes or institutions to challenge or bend this authoritarian structure. The soil was barren not for agriculture alone: Brandenburg-Prussia was no place for intellectuals, journalists, or poets. Nor could the urban bourgeoisie offer any competition. Brandenburg's cities were small, and their local autonomy was ruined during the reign of Frederick William by the ever-present bureaucracy. The Huguenots who populated Berlin after 1685 gave it some color and imported some new trades, but on the whole, burghers were trained to work and obey. The efflorescence of commercial enterprise that had made the Dutch great in the seventeenth century and would make the English great in the eighteenth passed Brandenburg by. Those naive diagrams that would distort and other social system of the time have some application to Brandenburg-Prussia: the ruler ruled, the aristocrats gave orders, the burghers worked, the peasants toiled.

As generations passed, and as King Frederick William I early in the eighteenth century elaborated that pattern his grandfather had laid down (see p. 320), the social structure necessity had created was rationalized into an ideal. This is a delicate matter, and historians today, after the Nazi experience, are still seeking to define a "Germanic" political style and to trace its divergence from a Western style. That style consisted of talk of "service," an exaltation of military over civilian ideas, a bureaucratic temper with its characteristic mixture of probity, efficiency, obsessiveness, and authoritarian arrogance, a contempt for politicians and for "mere" commercial values. Whatever its precise

---

[26] The characteristic German word is *Kadavergehorsam,* that is, the obedience of a corpse.
[27] *Bureaucracy, Aristocracy, and Autocracy,* 60.

contours, it originated well before 1700, in the long reign of Frederick William, whom German historians would soon call the Great Elector.

Frederick William died in 1688, leaving behind an anti-French foreign policy, a legacy of accepting generous subsidies from other countries, and a relatively unified state. His son could hardly be expected to compete with so overwhelming a father. In fact, there was something of a reaction against the Great Elector's austerities. Frederick III built palaces in and near Berlin and an opera house. In 1694 he opened a university at Halle; in 1696 he founded an academy of arts and, four years later, upon Leibniz's plan, an academy of sciences. He spent money on food and festivals, on precious jewelry and magnificent gardens. Contemptuous historians, thinking of his powerful father and equally powerful son, have dubbed Frederick's twenty-five-year reign an "interregnum." But this is hardly accurate. The civilizing amenities he introduced would prove to have more than decorative value in the eighteenth century. And the temporary relaxation of strenuousness had its own salutary effect, though the vastly rising expenditures on baubles and buildings, accompanied by continuing expenditures for the army, led to some uncomfortable, though temporary, deficits.

Besides, in his own way, Frederick did his part to increase his patrimony. Keeping the army in being proved eminently useful in 1700, when Emperor Leopold prepared to enter the War of the Spanish Succession against France. Frederick undertook to support the Hapsburgs in return for a substantial subsidy and—a long-cherished dream—a royal title. Accordingly, in 1701, Frederick III of Brandenburg-Prussia was granted the right to style himself Frederick I, king in Prussia. [28] In 1713, when Frederick I was succeeded by his son, Frederick William I, one of the new king's first acts was to have his royal title confirmed at the settlement that followed the War of the Spanish Succession. Prussia was on its way to greatness.

From Muscovy to Russia

Like Prussia, Russia emerged from remoteness and isolation late in the seventeenth century and, like Prussia, Russia secured great-power status under the driving knout of a single ruler—Peter I. In 1721, a grateful Russian Senate acknowledged the tsar's labors by calling him emperor, father of his country, and "the Great." Peter, the senators declared, had led his subjects "from the darkness of ignorance on to the theatre of glory before the whole world and, so to speak, from non-existence to existence." [29] The label has stuck, but its

---

[28] The "in" of this title was a compromise, agreed upon to pacify Frederick Augustus of Saxony, who had become king of Poland and held western Prussia. It was not until the reign of Frederick the Great that the preposition was changed to "of."

[29] Quoted in B. H. Sumner, *Peter the Great and the Emergence of Russia* (1951), 121.

justification must be modified: it is true that Peter was exigent, inexorable, passionately devoted to bringing his backward country to military, economic, and administrative modernity. But, just as the problems he faced were inherited from his predecessors, so were most of his proposed solutions. What Peter did was to speed up a process already under way with an unprecedented ruthlessness that sometimes achieved its purpose, more often defeated it. An inveterate borrower, Peter was by no means blind to the difficulties of transplanting ideas and institutions from one cultural climate to another. He hounded his advisors to adapt to Russian conditions what they had learned abroad. But in a long and stormy reign, he would discover what all reformers have to discover: styles of thinking—and even more, styles of feeling—have an extraordinary tenacity and resist the most rational refutation. Peter's most effective adversaries were not the Swedes or the Turks, but his own obstinate, conservative people.

Peter was born in 1672. The famous rebel Stenka Razin had been captured and executed the year before (see p. 260). In the West, Muscovy had made significant gains: in 1667, in the Treaty of Andrussavo, Tsar Alexis had acquired large parts of the Ukraine, including the towns of Kiev and Smolensk, from the Poles. But at home there was unrest; the rebellion that Stenka Razin led after 1670 was only one virulent symptom among many. Perhaps most damaging, certainly most persistent, was the schism that divided the Russian Orthodox church and, with it, the Russian people. Ignorance and illiteracy were more widespread in Russia than in the West, but beyond accepting these conditions with perfect complacency, many Russians viewed them with undisguised pride. The intellectual storms that had agitated the West since the Renaissance had passed Russia by, and there was much boasting about Russian resistance to Greek or "German" innovations. [30] This pride in Muscovite uniqueness was a perfectly understandable response to Russia's situation; it translated a defect into a virtue. But it confirmed and worsened a cultural isolation that was to give Peter the Great much trouble. Among the defenders of this cultural chauvinism, the Russian Orthodox church was the most articulate. Since 1589, when the Greek Orthodox patriarch at Constantinople had established a patriarch in Moscow, the Russian Orthodox church had been virtually independent of its Greek mother-church. This led to large claims. Moscow had become the Third Rome, the true center of orthodoxy, and since Constantinople had been in heathen hands since 1453, the only sovereign power to harbor and espouse the faith. But the Russian Orthodox church also produced the antidote to this isolationism. When Alexis came to the throne in 1645, he surrounded himself with Graecophiles intent upon reforming the church and bringing it closer to Greek traditions. The church needed reform: the clergy were ignorant, often illiterate, and mired in casual corruption. To introduce stringent tests of

---

[30] The word "German," it appears, came to be used for any Western invention or idea that such eager reformers as Peter brought back with them from their travels.

performance was to threaten their accustomed ways, and so "Greek innovations" came to be contrasted invidiously with "Muscovite traditions." In 1652, Nikon, an energetic and vastly ambitious man, became patriarch and set about revising the ritual of the Russian Orthodox church; in 1655 he introduced a new liturgy. His changes left dogma intact; most of them, in fact, were trivial: Nikon insisted, for instance, that the proper way to make the sign of the cross was with three fingers instead of two, as the Moscow Council had prescribed in 1551. But to simple religious minds, ritual has vast significance, and every gesture tremendous implications. Nikon had his way: while he was deposed for his secular ambitions, two councils in 1666 and 1667 confirmed his reforms and excommunicated those who persisted in their accustomed ritual. The resulting schism was a defeat for the church and a tragedy for Russia. It showed the church incapable of blending Muscovite traditions with Western innovations.[31] And it divided Russia, more deeply than ever before, along class—or rather, caste—lines. A large and growing number of clerics and laymen, many of them peasants, refused to adopt Nikon's "reforms." These were the Old Believers. They split into sectarian groups, wrestled with their souls, bravely resisted pressure, and suffered persecution. Thousands of them burned themselves to death; thousands of others were saved that exertion by the state. When Peter was born, the schism had assumed violent forms. Old Believers had denounced Peter's father, Tsar Alexis, as Anti-Christ in person; Peter's own persistent efforts to bring his people closer to the West would face the same rhetoric and be resisted on the most unyielding of grounds—religion.

All this was unpromising enough. Peter's personal situation was even more menacing. Peter was a Romanov, and the dynasty itself was secure. But he was the son of Alexis' second wife, and for some time the supporters of the tsar's first wife had the upper hand. When Alexis died in 1676, he was succeeded by Peter's ailing half-brother, Feodor III, who reigned for six years. When he in turn died in 1682, he left no sons. The result was confusion and a bloody struggle for power, issuing in a compromise: Ivan V, Feodor's younger brother, and Peter were proclaimed co-tsars under the regency of Ivan's older sister, Sophia. The terrible scenes in which the *streltsi*[32] rioted murderously in the Kremlin left a permanent mark on Peter, quite similar to that which the Frondes had left on Louis XIV—an abiding hatred of the *streltsi*, an aversion to the Kremlin, and a thirst for sole rule.

Peter had his first opportunity in 1689, though he did not fully seize it for some years. In a brief and sanguinary court revolution, Peter took power, sent the regent Sophia to a convent, and had her advisors exiled or executed. But he left the government to his mother and persisted in his strange self-education:

[31] See Werner Philipp, "Russia: The Beginning of Westernization," in *The New Cambridge Modern History*, vol. V (1961), 589-591.

[32] The *streltsi* were a kind of palace guard, but more sizable and more independent than most such guards. Organized into twenty-two regiments of a thousand men each, they regarded themselves as a privileged force, and their political support was considered of vital importance.

in Moscow he continued to hang about the "German suburb," a quarter in the city populated by foreign Protestants, including Dutchmen and Scots, who brought him news of Western ways. And in the country he continued to play his "war games," exercises with his soldiers which, as he grew to manhood, developed into full-fledged maneuvers. But then Peter's mother died in 1694 followed by his inoffensive co-ruler Ivan in 1696, and the responsibilities of rule could no longer be evaded. Nor did he evade them. But he did not cease his education. In 1697 he went West, on his "great embassy," complete with court chaplains and court dwarfs. The trip has been much romanticized, but it was extraordinary enough. It was, in itself, an unprecedented gesture for a Russian tsar, and while abroad, Peter behaved less like a ruler than like an apprentice. In Amsterdam, he worked in the shipyards of the East India Company; early in 1698, after nearly half a year among the Dutch, he sailed to England. Wherever he went, he asked questions. He looked everywhere: in hospitals, naval installations, carpenters' shops. His thirst for knowledge, above all mechanical knowledge, was insatiable. A tall, powerfully built man, he was coarse in his tastes, brutal in his pleasures, and sadistic in his practical jokes. At the same time, he was capable of simple family affection; Peter was a strange mixture endowed with an incongruous collection of traits, all distorted to gigantic size. He was a dreaded guest: rude in manners, drunken, and destructive. Yet his trip had practical results: he imported over seven hundred Westerners—shipwrights, mathematicians, engineers—and, quite as useful, an ineradicable impression of Russia's need for instruction in all practical things. He saw his country mired in superstitions and ignorant of modern military tactics, naval skills, commercial enterprise. Culture meant nothing to him, but he was certain that he must modernize his Russia in order to give it the formidable army and navy it needed. Charles XII, the observant king of Sweden, plainly saw the meaning of Europe for this Russian tsar: Moscow's power, he said, had "risen so high thanks to the introduction of foreign military discipline."[33]

It was in foreign affairs that Peter's education paid its earliest dividends. But there was one score he needed to settle first. His European tour was cut short in the spring of 1698, when news came that the *streltsi* had revolted in his absence. Peter rushed back to Moscow and put down the rebellion in an orgy of public torture and executions. It was on this occasion, too, that Peter enacted that celebrated scene of shaving off his court nobles' beards with his own hands. Sumptuary laws prescribing European dress and taxing those who kept their beards quickly followed. Peter, it was clear, would tolerate no disloyalty and no delay in bringing Russia into Europe by bringing Europe into Russia. For the nobles, many of them already half Westernized, this was scarcely painful; for the peasants, especially the Old Believers among them, this assault on time-honored dress and appearance was, quite literally, blasphemy.

[33] Quoted in Sumner, *Peter the Great*, 64.

But war was foremost on Peter's mind. Here, too, Peter followed a policy laid down by a predecessor: through most of his short reign, Feodor III had battled the Turks for the territories that lie on the north of the Black Sea; in 1681, he had acquired the Turkish Ukraine. Now, in 1695, just before he went on his "great embassy" to the West, Peter extended Feodor's gains by assaulting the port of Azov, which commands the entrance to the Black Sea. He took it in 1696 and turned it into Russia's first naval stronghold. But the Swedes offered Peter his strongest challenge and provided him with his greatest triumphs.

Sweden's times of troubles had passed with the abdication of Queen Christina in 1654 (see p. 261). Her successor, Charles X, reestablished domestic order, and for the six years of his reign successfully fought in the War of the North. At the peace of Oliva, in 1660, the Poles definitively abandoned all claims to the Swedish throne and ceded the province of Livonia. And by the Treaty of Copenhagen of the same year, the Danes surrendered what is today the southern tip of Sweden. But Sweden's new king, Charles XI, was a boy of four at his accession and his regents proved incompetent. Territorially a satisfied power, Sweden's foreign policy was, quite simply, to keep her gains intact. [34] But isolation was impossible, and Sweden's participation in the wars of the seventies proved a waste of resources. War with Brandenburg brought a resounding defeat at the battle of Fehrbellin in June 1675; and in 1679, when Sweden returned to general peace, the Treaty of St. Germain-en-Laye restored the status quo. Happy to have lost nothing, Sweden also gained nothing. But peace gave Charles XI, who had attained his majority in 1672, the opportunity to assert royal supremacy. In the seventeen years that remained to him— between 1680 and 1697—Charles XI broke the independent power of the Swedish nobility. He did so with a simple device: reversing Queen Christina's openhanded alienation of crown lands, Charles XI energetically resumed those lands, as well as the royal revenues that his prececessors had granted away. This was the famous *reduktion;* it reduced the influence of the Swedish nobility by depriving it of its economic base. Rebuilding the army, improving the navy, reforming the finances, constructing a bureaucracy, subduing the Riksdag and the church, Charles XI built an absolute regime remarkable for its control over the country. He was a pallid man, and shy, and his work seemed plodding labor after the military exploits of Gustavus Adolphus and Charles X. But, as Michael Roberts has rightly noted, Charles XI "was of critical importance in the history of his country: the hinge upon which the whole of modern Swedish history swings." [35] That he had labored well appeared plainly enough in 1697, when his fifteen-year-old son succeeded to the throne as Charles XII and drew on the resources his father had amassed.

[34] For this paragraph, see Michael Roberts, "Charles XI," in Roberts, *Essays in Swedish History* (1966), 226–268.
[35] Ibid., 227.

Charles XII was a strange man, much resembling his great adversary, Peter the Great, in his brute strength and his contradictions. Voltaire, one of his first biographers, called him half Don Quixote, half Alexander the Great, and the epigram captures Charles—his quixotic ambitions, his brilliant generalship, his sublime impatience with common sense. He displayed his gifts shortly after his accession. In the summer of 1700, as soon as Peter had freed his hands by making peace with the Turks, Russia, supported by Poland and Denmark, declared war on Sweden. Charles XII moved swiftly; late in November 1700, his small but disciplined force of eight thousand soldiers routed a Russian army of forty thousand at Narva. The Great Northern War was under way. [36] While the great powers were struggling to redraw the map of western Europe in the War of the Spanish Succession, lesser powers struggled for similar stakes in the north and east.

The defeat at Narva proved a disguised blessing for Peter the Great. It was, as he candidly admitted, a "terrible setback," but at the same time, a vital lesson: he must reconstruct his army completely, in every way. He acted with his customary ruthlessness, drawing, as he always did, on the West, by importing officers and military tactics. And Charles helped him, through his obstinacy. Instead of following up his victory over the Russians—which would have deprived Peter of the time he so badly needed—Charles wasted valuable years fighting an inconclusive war in Poland. Retribution came in 1709, in southern Russia. Charles XII, with his highly trained army, disregarding the length of his lines and the scorched earth that greeted him everywhere, followed Peter deep into Russia. There, in July 1709, at the battle of Poltava, Peter had his revenge. Swedish troops fled and capitulated in droves, and Charles sought refuge in Turkish territory. For Peter, Poltava had special meaning. In 1703, in the frozen north and in the teeth of Swedish forces, he had founded a new city, St. Petersburg, on which he lavished all his organizational energies, enormous amounts of money, and that most expendable material of all—his peasants. Victory over Sweden made his city secure. "Now," with Poltava, Peter said, "the final stone has been laid of the foundation of St. Petersburg." [37]

The Great Northern War dragged on until 1721, but the threat of Charles XII was broken at Poltava. When Charles finally returned to Sweden from Turkey in 1714, he found that the Russians had taken a wide swath of territory to the north: Estonia, Livonia, Finland, Karelia. Stettin had been turned over to Prussia in 1713. Then, in December 1718, while on a military campaign in Norway, Charles XII was shot to death under mysterious circumstances. But he had lived long enough to see Russia beginning negotiations for peace. Finally, in 1721, at the Peace of Nystadt, Russia retained all her northern gains except

---

[36] It is important to distinguish this war from an earlier, less decisive conflict, the Northern War (1655-1660), involving Sweden, Poland, and Prussia (see p. 320).

[37] Quoted in Sumner, *Peter the Great*, 73.

Finland—a minimal concession. It was on the occasion of Nystadt that the Russian Senate endowed Peter with the epithet, "the Great." Russia was now a European power. Nor is this observation mere hindsight: Peter deliberately aimed at this end. In 1717, on a diplomatic mission to Paris, he had explicitly told the French that the European system had changed and that Russia should now take the place of Sweden.

Peter the Great was not a systematic thinker, but this single aim—to make Muscovy into Russia and Russia into a European empire—animated him in all he did, in domestic as much as in foreign policy. The cost of greatness was enormous, but Peter cheerfully imposed it on his country. The building of St. Petersburg alone claimed thousands of lives. The workmen there perished in floods and from fevers; they were overwhelmed by fires and eaten by wolves. "The wretched peasants, soldiers and prisoners—Finns, Swedes, Esthonians, Karelians, Cossacks, Tartars, Kalmucks—who were brought to the Neva in their thousands to build a city of which every foot had to be made on piles, had most of them to sleep in the open air among the marshes. Their labour was inhuman—for long they had no tools and were forced to dig with sticks or with their nails and carry the earth in their coats or in the tails of their shirts; and they were kept perpetually short of food and drank foul water. In consequence they died like flies." One of Peter's jesters gloomily described the position of the new city in these words: "On one side the sea, on the other sorrow, on the third moss, on the fourth a sigh."[38]

War meant conscription, endless military service, further extension of serfdom and intensification of demands on serfs, extortionate taxes (borne, as usual, by those least able to afford it), and a system of informers to report tax evasion. The Old Believers had other grievances: Peter was Satan, who shaved off the beards that God had given man, he was Anti-Christ. There were rebellions, among the volatile Cossacks on the Don, the people of Astrakhan, the Ukrainians. Peter disposed of these revolts with his usual ferocity. His conduct on such occasions was part of his character, but Peter rationalized his predilections into a policy: cruelty, he said, was all this rabble could understand. Even his son, the heir-apparent, felt the full force of Peter's barbarity. Alexis, Peter's oldest son, had been a grievous disappointment to his father from the start: sympathetic to the Old Believers, indifferent to administration and hostile to military affairs, lazy and incompetent, a focus for all opposition to Peter's reform program, Alexis seemed a most improbable heir to all his father's enormous efforts. After renouncing the succession at his father's request, in 1716 Alexis fled to Vienna, but was lured back late in 1717 by Peter's promise of pardon. His suspicions of treason unallayed by his son's protestations, Peter had Alexis interrogated and tortured. Some of Alexis' supporters were

---

[38] Christopher Marsden, *Palmyra of the North: The First Days of St. Petersburg* (1942), 47–48, 51.

executed, and Alexis himself died in prison in July 1718. The coroner's verdict was apoplexy; the popular verdict was murder—certainly instigated, probably witnessed, and some said, personally committed by Peter himself. [39] In October 1721, Peter assumed the title, Emperor of all the Russias. [40] In 1722, he reiterated that he was absolute autocrat by issuing the law of succession, which claimed his right to name his successor. It was a pathetic move: all the sons by his second wife, Catherine, died in infancy, and when Peter himself lay on his deathbed, he scribbled a fragmentary note that read: "I leave all . . ." But to whom he left his Russia was not left for him to say.

Peter the Great died in 1725, at the age of fifty-two. Much of his work was rapidly undone in the aristocratic reaction that normally follows upon the death of an absolute ruler who has destroyed the regular channels of authority. [41] But then much of his work was of doubtful value: the price of transforming a backward Asiatic country into a modern European power was, as we have said, enormous. Yet some of his work, whatever its cost, lasted through the turmoil that followed his disappearance from the scene. To govern his vast empire, Peter in 1711 instituted a senate to make decisions in his absence; during the last years of his reign, when its ineffectiveness became apparent, Peter borrowed from the West the institution of "colleges," boards of bureaucrats charged with specific tasks—the navy or foreign affairs. Western, too, was Peter's administrative division of Russia—at first, in 1708, into eight *gubernii*, and then, in 1719, after these proved too unwieldy, into fifty provinces. His aim was to create a "police state"—a term that has acquired sinister connotations in our time, but which meant in the eighteenth century a rational administrative machinery that would diligently supervise public affairs, deal out justice, and govern under law. In 1721, a law creating the college for municipal affairs ambitiously defined the kind of police state to which Peter was aspiring: police, it said, is "the soul of citizenship and of all good order and the fundamental support of civil security and propriety." It superintends justice, creates good morals, thwarts thieves, prevents disease, keeps the streets clean, helps the poor and the sick, protects widows and orphans. [42] Of course, Peter failed in all this. No rule of law could emerge from a system based on compulsion, forced labor, and arbitrary decision-making by the tsar or his trusted army officers. Yet he did much. He raised much-needed funds by adopting Western mercantilist policies, protecting old or founding new industries, constructing a large navy, and exploiting rich domestic resources like the iron mines in the Urals. He levied new taxes, mainly a poll tax, to finance his endless wars: Peter was at war without interruption for twenty-eight years, between 1695 and 1723, and in

[39] For a strikingly similar story about Frederick William I of Prussia and his son, see p. 391.
[40] For the sake of convenience, we have used the traditional term, "tsar," throughout.
[41] For this general, Europe-wide phenomenon, see p. 376.
[42] See Sumner, *Peter the Great*, 132.

some years his armed forces, including his expensive navy, took as much as four fifths of the entire revenue. His exactions required several censuses of the population, each more stringent than the earlier one, and backed up with the threat of the death penalty for "concealment."

The clergy and the aristocracy were enlisted in Peter's inexorable search for military might. After the patriarch of the Russian Orthodox church died in 1700, Peter managed church affairs with acting patriarchs wholly beholden to him. Then, in 1721, Peter made the political impotence of the church official and permanent by abolishing the patriarchate and establishing in its place the holy governing synod, headed by a procurator, which tied the church into Peter's autocracy. And the nobility was mobilized by the doctrine of "state service," an old device that Peter employed with new vigor. He attempted to force the boyars to send their children to school—a command the Russian aristocracy resisted so fiercely that even Peter moderated it. But while he could not make the young nobles read, he could make them perform in the army or the civil service. In 1722, Peter imposed an elaborate table of ranks which listed the hierarchy of positions both in the military and the civilian service through which all must pass regardless of their birth or their wealth. Thus service to the state, rather than traditional aristocratic status, became the way to prestige and power. Whatever he failed to do, Peter made a social revolution, substituting a new service nobility for the old landed warrior class of boyars.

Our final verdict on Peter the Great's autocracy must be dotted with question marks. Everything, including education, stood under the sign of war and glorification of the tsar. Reforms were hasty and profoundly inorganic. Thus the so-called Westernization of the Russian mind remains a dubious enterprise. Peter set up a printing press to increase the circulation of books in his country and to add to the production of religious tracts already being produced by a theological "publishing house." But the publications of Peter's press were hardly impressive: the bulk was devotional literature, with a liberal sprinkling of technical manuals on such subjects as shipbuilding. The single true work of literature to be published in Peter's reign was a Russian translation of Aesop's fables. [43] Despite all Peter's intentions and declarations, the great movement of enlightenment that was sweeping western Europe made little impact on him and less on his country.

SELECTED READINGS

For the Sun King, see the expansive scholarly biography by John B. Wolf, *Louis XIV* (1968). Pierre Goubert, *Louis XIV and Twenty Million Frenchmen* (tr. 1970), relates the man to his age and his people. Maurice Ashley, *Louis XIV and the Greatness of France* (1953), is an introductory survey; Laurence B. Packard, *The Age of Louis XIV*

[43] See L. R. Lewitter, "Peter the Great, Poland, and the Westernization of Russia," *Journal of the History of Ideas,* 19 (Oct. 1958), 493–506.

(1938), is even briefer. W. H. Lewis, *The Splendid Century* (1953), is chatty but helpful. See also the opening chapters of E. N. Williams, *The Ancien Régime in Europe: Government and Society in the Major States, 1648-1789* (1970). For Louis' dictatorship over French culture, Peter France and Margaret McGowan, "Louis XIV and the Arts," in John Cruickshank, ed., *French Literature and Its Background,* vol. II, *The Seventeenth Century* (1969), is economical but informative. Anthony Blunt, *Art and Architecture in France, 1500-1700* (1954), is valuable on this point. See James E. King, *Science and Rationalism in the Government of Louis XIV, 1661-1683* (1949). Among interpretations of French literature in the age, especially recommended are Martin Turnell, *The Classical Moment: Studies of Corneille, Molière and Racine* (1947); E. B. O. Borgerhoff, *The Freedom of French Classicism,* (1950); and Paul Bénichou's sophisticated social analysis, *Man and Ethics: Studies in French Classicism* (tr. 1971).

Charles W. Cole, *Colbert and a Century of French Mercantilism,* 2 vols. (1939), and its sequel, *French Mercantilism, 1683-1700* (1943), are standard for Louis' great minister. For mercantilism in general, see the great treatise by Eli Heckscher, *Mercantilism,* 2 vols. (2nd ed., 1955), which should be contrasted with Jacob Viner, "Power versus Plenty as Objectives of Foreign Policy in the Seventeenth and Eighteenth Centuries," in Viner, *The Long View and the Short: Studies in Economic Theory and Policy* (1958), and Charles Wilson, *Profit and Power* (1957). See also Paul W. Bamford, *Forests and French Sea-Power, 1660-1789* (1956). On the growth of economic thought, see Edgar A. J. Johnson, *Predecessors of Adam Smith: The Growth of British Economic Thought* (1937), to be read in conjunction with William Letwin, *The Origins of Scientific Economics* (1963). On the Huguenots, see Warren C. Scoville, *The Persecution of the Huguenots and French Economic Development, 1680-1720* (1960), as well as the older study by A. J. Grant, *The Huguenots* (1934), and Guy H. Dodge, *The Political Theories of the Huguenots of the Dispersion* (1947). For the Jansenists, see Nigel Abercrombie, *The Origins of Jansenism* (1936). Two important monographs on French foreign policy are G. N. Clark, *The Dutch Alliance and the War Against French Trade, 1688-1697* (1923), and N. M. Crouse, *The French Struggle for the West Indies, 1665-1713* (1943).

For England after the Restoration, see the later chapters of Maurice Ashley, *England in the Seventeenth Century (1603-1714)* (3rd ed., 1961), and J. P. Kenyon, *The Stuarts* (1958); see also the more detailed G. N. Clark, *The Later Stuarts, 1660-1714* (1934). David Ogg's detailed volumes, *England in the Reign of Charles II,* 2 vols. (1934), and *England in the Reigns of James II and William III* (1955), are very valuable. On William III see the biography by Steven B. Baxter by that title (1966). G. M. Trevelyan's *The English Revolution, 1688-1689* (1939), though brief and Whiggish, says the essential. Trevelyan has also given a detailed account of *England Under Queen Anne,* 3 vols. (1930-1934), distinguished by his usual narrative lucidity. Harry G. Plum, *Restoration Puritanism* (1943), Gerald R. Cragg, *Puritanism in the Age of the Great Persecution* (1957), and R. S. Bosher, *The Making of the Restoration Settlement* (1951), adequately cover religious events. Peter Laslett, *The World We Have Lost* (2nd ed., 1971), is interesting social history.

Eastern Europe in this period is well surveyed in numerous chapters of J. S. Bromley, ed., *The Rise of Great Britain and Russia, 1688-1725* (1970), which is volume VI of *The New Cambridge Modern History.* For the Hapsburgs, see in addition to general histories of Europe, Paul Frischauer, *The Imperial Crown: The Rise and Fall of the Holy Roman and the Austrian Empires* (1939), to be read in conjunction with Adam

Wandruszka, *The House of Hapsburg* (tr. 1964), an authoritative account; L. S. Stavrianos, *The Balkans Since 1453* (1958), disentangles a complex story. For Hungary (in this and other periods), see the magisterial history by C. A. Macartney, *Hungary* (1934).

On the emergence of Prussia, Sidney B. Fay, *The Rise of Brandenburg-Prussia to 1786* (rev. by Klaus Epstein, 1964), is a brief essay; J. A. R. Marriott and C. G. Robertson, *The Evolution of Prussia* (ed. 1946), is longer if superficial. Hajo Holborn, *A History of Modern Germany,* vol. II, *1648-1840* (1964), has already been cited. For Frederick William, see Ferdinand Schevill, *The Great Elector* (1947); for the father of Frederick the Great, see Robert Ergang, *The Potsdam Führer: Frederick William I, Father of Prussian Militarism* (1941), which is rather better than its tendentious title indicates. It should be supplemented with the careful analysis by Reinhold A. Dorwart, *The Administrative Reforms of Frederick William I of Prussia* (1953). The early chapters of Hans Rosenberg's brilliant study of the rise of "bureaucratic absolutism," *Bureaucracy, Aristocracy, and Autocracy: The Prussian Experience, 1660-1815* (1958), are relevant here, as are the equally brilliant chapters in Gordon A. Craig, *The Politics of the Prussian Army, 1640-1945* (2nd ed., 1964). So, finally, is F. L. Carsten, *The Origins of Prussia* (1954).

On Russian developments see, in addition to the general studies by Florinsky, Blum, and Robinson cited in Chapter 6, B. H. Sumner, *Peter the Great and the Emergence of Russia* (1951), brief but informative; it should be supplemented with Vasiliu Kliuchevsky, *Peter the Great* (tr. 1958). For Peter's great enemy to the north, see R. M. Hatton, *Charles XII of Sweden* (1969), and some of Michael Roberts' *Essays in Swedish History* (1967).

8

An Age of Science and Enlightenment

The Enlightenment was a time of hope. The intellectuals who spoke for the movement, the philosophes, looked to the future as a realm in which many possibilities would be realized. And, in the eighteenth century, their many allies—reasonable, humane Christians—used the word "innovation," an old term of abuse, less with fear than with approval. Progress was an expectation, a program, and a reality. It became almost a fad. "The age," Samuel Johnson said in 1783 with some acerbity, "is running mad after innovation; all the business of the world is to be done in a new way; men are to be hanged in a new way; Tyburn itself is not safe from the fury of innovation." The year after Johnson made this caustic observation, Immanuel Kant defined the Enlightenment as "man's emergence from his self-imposed tutelage," and offered as its motto, "*sapere aude*—dare to know."

The philosophes were anything but alienated from their culture. They were subversive on the important matter of religion: whether they were deists, skeptics, or atheists they were certainly not Christians. But they were surrounded by educated Christians who, like them, deplored superstition, idealized science, and aimed at reasonableness and humaneness. Kant thought he discerned a general "revolt against superstition"; many Frenchmen who were not philosophes liked to call their century the *siècle des lumières*. And just as the philosophes were not isolated from their time, they were not cut off from the past. They were radicals, but they were not rootless. Their most admired intellectual ancestors were the philosophers of pagan antiquity, the critical scholars and disenchanted historians of the Renaissance, and the revolutionary political, religious, and scientific thinkers of the seventeenth century. Without them the Enlightenment would have been impossible.

ROADS TO ENLIGHTENMENT: THE SEVENTEENTH CENTURY

Modern Christianity

The world of educated men in the late seventeenth century had changed out of all recognition since the Renaissance and the Reformation. Neither had aimed at the dissolution of religious authority; quite the contrary. But, as we know, the venturesome diligence of Renaissance Humanists and the quarrels of theologians that marked the Reformation inevitably produced a certain degree of independent judgment; where dogmatic authorities conflict, there is room for skepticism. Few even of the boldest spirits stepped beyond the sacred domain of Christian belief, but many insisted on the need to simplify it and to strip it of inessential admixtures.

Seventeenth-century Europe offered many incentives to skepticism. Not that skepticism was rampant or a serious threat to established religions; most scientists did their work, much as medieval scientists had done theirs, to testify to the splendor of God's handiwork. The great chemist Robert Boyle (see p. 341) wrote tracts designed to prove the religious utility of his scientific researches, and left £350 in his will to endow lectures demonstrating the truth of Christianity. But Boyle's very concern was a sign that science was emerging as a threat to religion: one does not bother to defend what is not under attack. The churches themselves showed signs of a changing spirit. Late in the seventeenth century, partially in reaction to the austerity of the Puritans, now overthrown, the Anglican church embraced Latitudinarianism—a mild, rationalistic Christianity purged of emotionalism and improbable beliefs. "Enthusiasm" and "superstition" were decried and proscribed. Anglicanism consequently lost much genuine religious feeling. In France, "modern" Catholics, most strikingly represented by the Jesuits, toned down their sermons on sin, hell, and damnation; cheerfully they concentrated on men's chances of realizing Christian ideals in this life and of obtaining bliss in the next. Catholics and Protestants alike were moving toward a civilized, relatively worldly faith.

The growth of this new spirit has often been called a crisis, but it was too imperceptible, too long-drawn-out, and in a sense too pleasant to be really a crisis. It was the slow readjustment of educated men and women of their world view to new knowledge which led most of them, not to unbelief, but to tepid belief. Many of them pushed religion, once the center of everyone's concern, to the margins of their existence. [1]

Knowledge and Change

Among the many agents of intellectual change culminating in the Enlightenment, three assumed special prominence: travel reports, historical scholarship, and biblical criticism. Travelers—the ancestors of the cultural anthropologists—showed the world to be larger and far stranger than earlier ages had even suspected. Their discoveries in America and, later, in the Far East had made Europeans acquainted with civilizations that were highly developed and functioned well, and all without the blessings of Christianity. This discovery, as the French anthropologist Claude Lévi-Strauss has observed, was profoundly demoralizing: "Never had the human race been faced with such a terrible ordeal." [2] Yet it was also exhilarating; for every pious believer unsettled by the spectacle of civilized pagans, there was a venturesome European ready to treat them as fascinating specimens in the museum of man. But whether demoralizing or exhilarating, advanced Chinese and Indian civilizations compelled Europeans to weigh their own culture against others and relate it to a worldwide spectrum. Travel became an antidote to parochial isolation and a spur to cultural relativism: the discovery that Christianity was not the only "valid" culture led to the further discovery that there was much wrong with Christian culture. And behind cultural relativism there stood religious skepticism. While most of the travelers were unimpeachable Christian missionaries, the consequence of their work was to throw at least some doubt on the received religious wisdom: Christianity was, it seemed, only one of several religions, one story among many.

As travel made the world larger and stranger than it had been, history made it older and richer. The dominant view of history remained scrupulously devout. In 1681, Bishop Bossuet published a *Discours sur l'histoire universelle* which took as its central events the dispersal of Noah's offspring and the coming of Christ, and as the central cause of historical change the will of God. But there were other currents in the widening stream. There was the school of historical Pyrrhonists who, appealing to the ancient skeptic Pyrrho, held all knowledge of the past to be uncertain and rejected most writing about it as a

---

[1] While the materials for the struggle between science and religion were amassed in the eighteenth century, the struggle itself was fought out largely in the nineteenth.

[2] *Tristes Tropiques* (ed. 1964), 78.

set of fables. This view of the past—or rather, assault on the past—had a hint of impiety about it; but even priests sharpened the instruments of historical research and thus, however unwittingly, prepared the way for the Enlightenment. In 1681, the Benedictine monk Jean Mabillon, member of the distinguished scholarly congregation of Saint Maur in Paris, published a Latin treatise that few men have ever read, but that transformed the discipline of history. *De Re Diplomatica—Concerning Charters*—originated as an attempt to vindicate the authenticity of documents in the possession of the Benedictines which their malicious rivals, the Jesuits, had called into question. Mabillon succeeded, and in the process he established the science of diplomatics—the science of reading historical documents, of establishing their authenticity or spuriousness, of detecting emendations and layers of editions.[3] Other scholars, armed with such instruments, weeded out forgeries, extended the scientific examination of documents to coins, wrote dictionaries: Charles Du Cange published a "glossary" of "late" Latin that vastly improved men's grasp on medieval literature. Knowledge multiplied, with bewildering speed.

In this atmosphere, the critical reading of the Bible touched a particularly sensitive spot. In his *Leviathan,* Thomas Hobbes coolly divided religion from superstition with criteria drawn from politics: "Publicly allowed [tales are called] Religion; not allowed, Superstition."[4] And he suggested that the most fruitful way of understanding Scriptures was by means of the higher criticism. Such a reading, he thought, would prove, among other things, that the books of Kings, Chronicles, and Judges had been written later than tradition asserted. Baruch[5] Spinoza took the higher criticism to new heights in his *Tractatus Theologico-Politicus* of 1670, in which he treated the Bible as a book like any other: "The method of interpreting Scripture does not differ greatly from the method of interpreting Nature—in fact, it is almost the same." Spinoza found the ethical teachings of Scriptures to be parochial—written for, and principally applicable to, one people in one age. Moreover, since the natural order is unalterable and the Bible recounts many tales in which divine intervention interferes with that order, Scripture must be full of later interpolations. Finally, Spinoza argued, the Pentateuch, with its duplicate set of narratives and irreconcilable chronologies, must be a conflation of many manuscripts. The intemperate controversialist Richard Simon, a French priest who flaunted his orthodoxy as he undermined it, added to Spinoza's philosophical penetration a sensitive discrimination of styles. If we carefully read the Old Testament,

---

[3] Renaissance erudition, of which the Humanist Lorenzo Valla's exposure of the Donation of Constantine is a fine example, was an ancestor to this scholarly enterprise.

[4] Renaissance scholarship devoted to establishing a reliable and definitive text of the Bible—textual criticism—was called "lower criticism." Historical criticism, which seeks to settle the meaning of biblical passages by reference to the historical context and general probability, was called "higher criticism." It emerged in the Reformation but required many decades of cautious work before it was generally accepted.

[5] Or, after his expulsion from the synagogue, Benedict.

Simon wrote, we can detect the interpolations of medieval scribes and glaring inconsistencies, like the purported claim of Moses to have written the whole Pentateuch, even though these first five books of the Old Testament include an account of his own death.

These secular readings of sacred texts were offensive to religious authorities, but they remained isolated events; specialized, abstruse, technical, they were read in the main only by a few theologians and by the censors who condemned them. Only the deists in England and Pierre Bayle on the Continent won a wide public with their controversial writings, and thus seriously widened the public for secularism. There were deists on the Continent as well, but the headquarters for this philosophical faith was England. One of its most prominent spokesmen was John Locke's self-proclaimed disciple John Toland, who published *Christianity Not Mysterious* in 1696, a year after Locke's *Reasonableness of Christianity*.[6] The two titles are similar, but they enshrine a decisive difference: Locke had wanted to defend the essence of Christianity by reducing its content; Toland wanted to discard its essence by proving that in its origins Christianity had been quite simply a reasonable belief. Mystery-mongering priests, he argued, had tampered with the primitive Christian doctrine. Without the "pretense" of mystery, "we should never hear of the Transubstantiation, and other ridiculous Fables of the Church of Rome; nor of any of the Eastern Ordures, almost all received into the Western sink." Down to the 1730s or so, the small but loquacious tribe of English deists made a good deal of noise. It has been customary to separate them into "critical" and "constructive" deists, but actually each of them was both one and the other. In their criticism, the deists threw doubt on the authenticity of biblical texts; pointed out contradictions, absurdities, and unpalatable doctrines in both the Old and New Testaments; assailed established churches and ecclesiastical authority. In their constructive work, they portrayed God as a blessed watchmaker who had made the world in all its magnificent variety, with unbreakable physical and self-evident moral laws, and then had withdrawn to allow men to work out their own destiny.[7]

Pierre Bayle

Pierre Bayle appealed to the Enlightenment on other grounds; whatever crisis there was in the mind of the seventeenth century is epitomized in his work. Born in 1647, the son of a Huguenot minister and briefly a Catholic convert, he ended up a Pyrrhonist. After the French government began to persecute the Huguenots seriously, Bayle fled to Holland. There, in 1682, he published his *Miscellaneous Thoughts on the Comet of 1680,* a brilliant assault on the

[6] For Locke, see p. 344.
[7] For later applications of this argument, see p. 354.

superstitious fears that had clustered around the appearance of Halley's comet and a proof that superstition, which converts a natural event into a sign of divine wrath, is more dangerous to civilization than atheism. After the revocation of the Edict of Nantes, Bayle continued these polemics with a moving, powerful appeal for toleration. His *Philosophical Commentary on the Words of Jesus Christ, "Compel Them To Come In,"* is a scathing critique of Catholics' persecuting their Protestant brothers. As a consistent skeptic, Bayle argued that persecutors are not merely vicious but unreasonable for they are certain that their faith is correct and that all other faiths are wicked error. Yet all we know is that we are forever ignorant. And to compel belief is the antithesis of, not the road to, religion—it makes men into victims or hypocrites.

Bayle's masterpiece was the *Historical and Critical Dictionary*, first published in 1697. While it parades as a biographical compendium chastely arranged in alphabetical order, it is actually a shrewd, laboriously disguised statement of Bayle's convictions. It luxuriates in footnotes and sidenotes and interminable cross-references which lead the reader to an article denying what an earlier article had asserted, in unexpected criticisms of traditional heroes like King David, and in occasional salacious anecdotes that pique the reader's interest. The *Dictionary* is a full-throated assault on everything Bayle hated: intolerance, dogmatism, superstition, gullibility, persecution. It is an immensely erudite book, but the erudition is in the service of a new vision of man and society: a vision of brothers, ignorant and comradely, who acknowledge their imperfections and live in peace. Bayle's innermost religious convictions vanish before his passionate propaganda in behalf of toleration, but it is clear that his principled modesty, his Socrates-like insistence that all men are utterly ignorant, is far from incompatible with a certain kind of Protestant belief, and may well have had its roots in such belief.[8] Whatever the elusive truth of the matter, the philosophes treated Bayle quite simply as a skeptic: he was the most welcome and most eloquent ally against "superstition" they could find anywhere.

ROADS TO ENLIGHTENMENT: NEWTON AND LOCKE

While the philosophes quoted Bayle, they deified Newton. All the philosophes—Voltaire and d'Alembert, Hume and Jefferson—treated Bacon, Locke, and Newton as a trinity of great minds, and one of these, Newton, as the

---

[8] It has recently become the subject of scholarly controversy; Howard Robinson's standard *Bayle the Skeptic* (1931) has been countered by writers ready to discover a "positive," and positively religious, philosophy in Bayle. See especially W. H. Barber, "Pierre Bayle: Faith and Reason," in Will Moore et al., eds., *The French Mind: Studies in Honour of Gustave Rudler* (1952), 109–125.

greatest man who ever lived. We must examine Newton's work and, to a lesser degree, the work of Locke to understand how the philosophes employed the heritage they claimed. [9]

Newton's World

Isaac Newton was a legendary figure even in his lifetime, and most of the legends about him are true. The adulation the world showered on him was the tribute appropriate to an achievement unmatched in the history of thought. David Hume called him, in his *History of England,* "the greatest and rarest genius that ever rose for the ornament and instruction of the species," and no one accused Hume of flattery or hyperbole. He had stated a simple truth on which every educated man could agree, and not in England alone.

With his well-known eccentricities and his self-imposed isolation, Newton lent plausibility to the stories about the solitary genius, "voyaging," as Wordsworth would put it, "through strange seas of thought alone." It is in no way to disparage his originality to say that while Newton was voyaging through strange seas, he was not alone. He was part, and culmination, of a philosophical and scientific tradition; he was the heir of the ancient Epicureans, the beneficiary of Bacon's distrust of metaphysics, of Galileo's gift for experimentation, of Descartes' inventions in mathematics. When Newton entered the fraternity of natural philosophers, there was vigorous scientific activity in most European capitals. The eighteenth, and even more the twentieth, century would celebrate Blaise Pascal as the lucid, brooding Christian existentialist who, in his fragmentary *Pensées,* confronted man with his fallen and desolate condition; but his contemporaries knew Pascal as a brilliant mathematician who put the theory of probability on a sound footing, and as an equally brilliant physicist who did research on atmospheric pressure and the behavior of fluids. In biology, a group of scientists used that splendid invention, the microscope, to confirm and extend Harvey's discoveries about the circulation of the blood (see p. 240). One of these was Marcello Malpighi, an Italian anatomist, who published his pioneering treatise on the lung, *De Pulmonibus,* in 1661, in which he described the movement of the blood through capillaries. Another was the Dutch naturalist Jan Swammerdam, who discovered red blood corpuscles in 1658 and the valves of the lymphatics in 1664; he greatly improved scientific knowledge of that mysterious progression—caterpillar into butterfly—which he studied with minute attention and faultless precision. Two other great

---

[9] For strict accuracy we must also understand the heritage they did not claim. The French philosophes in particular were much in debt to Descartes, especially to his doctrine of clear ideas and his analytical energies. His physiology could also be used—and was so used—as a basis for downright materialism. But Descartes had been "captured" by the forces of respectable piety late in the seventeenth century, his physics had been disproved by Newton, and his methodology seemed excessively rationalistic. Thus it seemed more profitable for the philosophes to disown and attack Descartes than to acknowledge fully how much they owed him.

scientists, Robert Hooke in England and Antony van Leeuwenhoek in Amsterdam, refined the microscope they used so effectively: in 1665, in his *Micrographia,* Hooke described both his new design and some of his discoveries, including the cells of plant tissues. And Leeuwenhoek, diligent correspondent to the Royal Society of London, astonished his contemporaries with his meticulously designed microscopes and with the minute objects he was the first to see and describe: red blood cells, protozoa, bacteria. Chemistry, too, was gradually being transformed from alchemy into a true science. Robert Boyle, ingenious experimenter, bold theorist, and indefatigable writer, applied mechanical philosophy to fluids and gases; he saw the chemist as a physicist dealing with small material particles. His famous *Skeptical Chymist* of 1661 was a critique of traditional procedure and a program for treating substances as composites which the chemist must resolve into their elements—minute particles. The fruits of his work were many and varied; the best known was Boyle's law, which holds that, if temperature is held constant, the volume of a confined gas will decrease in proportion as the pressure is increased. [10]

Newton, then, did his work in a congenial, even fostering, environment. As in other countries, so in England, serious gentlemen, the *virtuosi,* studied natural philosophy in obedience to Bacon's advice to cooperate in the search for knowledge. They clustered in scientific societies that enabled them to exchange ideas, share instruments, and publish experiments. The first of these ambitious associations to survive infancy was the group of scientific amateurs who gathered at Gresham College in London from the mid-1640s on, not long after Newton was born; they met weekly to discuss "experimental Philosophy." In 1662, shortly after the Restoration of Charles II, the Royal Society of London for Improving Natural Knowledge received its charter. [11] Newton's connection with the Royal Society was intimate if rather intermittent. Averse to the squabbling that invigorated and impeded the gatherings of these pioneers, he joined in 1672 but did not play a major part in its deliberations for some years. Then, in 1687, when he published his greatest work, the *Philosophiae Naturalis Principia Mathematica,* he dedicated it to the Royal Society. This is a symbol of the great collaboration that science had become. The *Principia,* for all its lonely eminence, is the top of a pyramid of thought which had been under construction for a century and a half.

Newton's Principia

Like other scientific geniuses, Newton worked out most of his fundamental ideas early. He was born at Woolsthorpe in Lincolnshire, on Christmas Day, 1642; when he succeeded his Cambridge teacher, Isaac Barrow, as Lucasian

[10] On Boyle's religion, see p. 335.
[11] Its French counterpart, the Académie Royale des Sciences de Paris, protected by Louis XIV and Colbert, was chartered in 1666; it, too, emerged from the gatherings of leading scientific theorists and practitioners.

professor of mathematics in 1669, he was already far advanced on the calculus, had discovered the binomial theorem, had performed path-breaking optical experiments that brought him to his theory of colors, and had settled the fundamentals of his greatest discovery, the theory of gravitation. "All this," he recalled much later, "was in the two plague years of 1665 and 1666, for in those years I was in the prime of my age for invention, and minded Mathematicks and Philosophy more than at any time since." Late in 1665 an outbreak of the plague in Cambridge had driven him to retreat at his mother's house at Woolsthorpe, and it was there, in 1666, that he "began to think of Gravity extending to ye orb of the Moon, & (having found out how to estimate the force with which a globe revolving within a sphere presses the surface of the sphere), from Kepler's rule . . . I deduced that the forces which keep the Planets in the Orbs must [be] reciprocally as the squares of their distances from the centers about which they revolve." The essential idea of gravitation, he remembered, had come into his mind as he watched an apple fall. This is the most famous anecdote about him, and it may even be true. But true or not, Newton withheld his discoveries for years, in part because his calculations were at variance with his postulates for the power of the gravitational force. He kept quietly to himself at Trinity College, Cambridge. Then, stung by the astronomical calculations of Robert Hooke (which came perilously close to the truth as Newton divined it) and encouraged by Edmund Halley, astronomer royal and prominent Fellow of the Royal Society, he emerged from his isolation. By 1684, Newton had begun work on the *Principia;* in 1687, he published it to an astonished world.

It is customary to call the *Principia* the greatest scientific work ever written, and custom is right. It is customary also to call Newton's work a synthesis, and once again custom is right. Newton's *Principia* synthesized the scattered discoveries of the pioneers into a single, comprehensive science of mechanics. It suggested solutions to a number of puzzling phenomena like the precession of the equinoxes and the rhythm of the tides. It united such seemingly diverse theories as Galileo's laws of falling bodies and Kepler's laws of planetary motion. And it demonstrated, once and for all, the mutual service that mathematics and the physical sciences can, indeed must, perform for each other. Not the least remarkable aspect of the Newtonian synthesis was that Newton had to invent a language—called "fluxions" then, differential calculus now—before he could construct his system. [12]

The controversial idea that held Newton's system together was gravitation. The *nature* of this astounding force was a mystery Newton did not pretend to unravel. But this much was clear: his theory contradicted Descartes' theory of

---

[12] The question of priority on the calculus caused one of the celebrated quarrels of the scientific revolution. Newton was doubtless first with the calculus: he wrote of "fluxions" in 1671 and described his method even earlier. Leibniz published his first essay on calculus in 1684. Newton's English admirers then charged Leibniz with plagiarism—a charge of doubtful validity. The ugly controversy simmered for decades.

vortices, which holds that the planets are propelled in their orbits by an impalpable ether in which they rest as they circle around the sun. When the idea of gravitation came to him in 1666, Newton had noted that though the apple was very small and the earth very large, their action must be mutual: "The apple draws the earth, as well as the earth draws the apple." It was precisely this peculiar, almost incredible interaction that permitted Newton to think of gravitation as a universal and uniform force. Every body, every particle, in the universe attracts all other bodies and particles with a power inversely proportional to the square of their distance and proportional to the product of the masses of the bodies involved. These laws of motion show the gravitational pull of the earth on the moon and on an apple to be the same. Bodies terrestrial or celestial, large or small, familiar like planets or rare like comets, moving through an unresisting void or a resisting medium all obey the same law. While the *Principia* was an inordinately inaccessible book, with its Latin and its archaic geometric formulas, its teachings won an instantaneous and complete triumph—at least in England. In France, dominated by the physics and astronomy of Descartes, the conquest took a little longer, but by the 1750s every respectable scientist was a disciple of Newton. What Bacon had hoped for, and scientific societies were advocating, Newton realized with his *Principia:* he made science an international, contentious but cooperative discipline, capable of vast explanatory power.

Newton's Opticks

Once in the public eye, Newton remained there; much of the rest of his life was a diversion from the pursuits that interested him most: theology, chemistry, optics. In 1689, in the midst of the Glorious Revolution, Cambridge elected him to Parliament; in 1693, he suffered a severe breakdown, from which he recovered only gradually; in 1696, he was named warden of the mint; in 1703, he was appointed president of the Royal Society. Two years later, he was knighted—the first scientist to be so honored for his scientific achievement. When he died on March 20, 1727, he was buried in Westminster Abbey with a pomp due a giant among men and hitherto reserved for such dubious benefactors of mankind as princes and generals—"like a king," Voltaire wrote, "who has been good to his subjects."

His many distractions—for fame and fortune are distractions to a speculative mind—did not prevent Newton from completing his early researches on light. The *Opticks: Or a Treatise on the Reflections, Refractions, Inflexions and Colours of Light* appeared in 1704; written in English and attractively argued, it was a relief after the austere complexities of the *Principia*. The *Opticks* gave a precise account of Newton's experiments with the prism and proved the composite nature of colors from the pure colors of the spectrum. While other scientists had known something of the properties of the prism, Newton established the theory of optics on a firm basis and brought it into the range of physics. The results were enormously fruitful. Newton fully explained the color of the rainbow and of soap bubbles and a host of other optical phenomena; his speculative queries opened the tantalizing possibility that light might be both wave and particle; and he successfully demonstrated his incredible contention that white is not a simple color, but a composite of all pure spectral colors.

This in itself was a very great deal. But Newton did more. His historic importance lay in his capacity to move from the substance of science to its method—or rather, to move to its method *through* substance. The theory of gravitation led to a strange paradox: since the nature of gravitation was admittedly unknown, Newton's critics accused him—him, the master empiricist!—of reintroducing into science the "occult qualities" of the Scholastics. Gravitation, after all, supposedly acted across vast distances, through empty space, and how was such a mystery to be accounted for? Newton did not find these difficulties daunting; he denied that his principles were occult in any way. The idea of gravity worked, and the effects of gravitation were clear and measurable; now if the cause of a phenomenon is not known, the scientist must remain content with studying its effects. This disclaimer was a giant step in the emancipation of science from metaphysics. "*Hypotheses non fingo*—I feign no hypotheses," he insisted; this meant not that the "experimental philosopher" can do without imaginative leaps, but that he is always guided by the phenomena, always returns to experience, always checks his results through experimentation. "Whatever is not deduced from the phenomena is to be called a hypothesis; and hypotheses, whether metaphysical or physical, whether of occult qualities or mechanical, have no place in experimental philosophy." It was under the pleasing name of "philosophical modesty" that these methodological principles would become the battle cry and the announced, if not always the actual, method of Newton's self-proclaimed disciples in the eighteenth century (see p. 349).

Newton's Ally: John Locke

From the perspective of the philosophes, the only rival to the immortal Newton was John Locke, the philosopher who, they thought, took the methods of Newton and opened the way to science where there had been nothing but fancy before. Locke himself enormously admired Newton. Although he was born in 1632, and was thus ten years older than Newton, Locke talked of him as a guide, almost a master. Next to "the incomparable Mr. Newton" he wrote in his *Essay Concerning Human Understanding*, he himself was but "an underlabourer in clearing the ground a little and removing some of the rubbish that lies in the way to knowledge."

As a characteristic model for the Enlightenment, John Locke was proficient in many fields and wrote with authority on many matters. He was trained at

Oxford, lectured there on philosophy, studied the sciences, and briefly practiced medicine. He moved all his life among the Whig magnates whose convictions and political fortunes he shared; late in 1683, when the Whig leaders were under suspicion or in exile, he took ship to the Dutch Republic and did not return until early in 1689, in the train of the successful revolutionaries, Dutch William and his queen, Mary (see p. 313). He brought with him the manuscripts of books he had been working on for a number of years: a *Letter Concerning Toleration,* published in the year of his return, *Two Treatises of Government* and the *Essay Concerning Human Understanding,* both published in 1690, all three landmarks in their spheres. Locke's *Some Thoughts Concerning Education* (1693) would be scarcely less epoch-making for the history of pedagogical theory.

John Locke has been called a conservative revolutionary, but in some respects his political ideas reached beyond the boundaries that his own associates, the architects of the Glorious Revolution, set for England. In his *Letter Concerning Toleration,* he argued against religious persecution on both moral and practical grounds. A church is a "voluntary society" with no right to use force against its members; a state may use such force, but not in religious matters. Persecution, whether by the religious or the secular arm, is unlawful. It is also foolish: dissenting sects become seditious and conspiratorial only when they are being persecuted, not otherwise. Locke wanted to exclude only two groups from toleration: Roman Catholics, because their loyalty was to a foreign power, the papacy; and atheists, because they are without a firm foundation for moral conduct, belief in God. Locke's arguments for broad toleration are practical, political, secular. Yet, while Locke's ideas would echo in the writings of the philosophes, his England of the 1690s was not yet ready for them. The toleration Locke desired was what English politicians called "comprehension" and rejected in behalf of a narrower policy—a state church of Anglicans that excluded the dissenting sects from higher education and political participation (see p. 313).

The ideas of Locke's *Two Treatises,* on the other hand, fitted the new conditions to perfection. The accident of their publication after the expulsion of James II, and Locke's own claim in the preface that they were designed "to establish the throne of our great restorer, our present King William; to make good his title, in the consent of the people," gave them the appearance of apologies written for the Glorious Revolution. They could be so used, and Locke, as we have seen, was glad to see them so used. But he had actually written them earlier, as a contribution to the exclusion campaign aimed at keeping the Catholic duke of York from succeeding to the throne.[13] That political tracts written for one occasion could be cited for another is a tribute to their reach for general application.

Actually, the first of these treatises, little read today, is highly specialized. It is a contemptuous refutation of Sir Robert Filmer's posthumous *Patriarcha.*

[13] See the critical edition of the *Two Treatises* by Peter Laslett (2nd ed. 1967).

Filmer, an extreme royalist, had died in 1653, in Cromwell's reign, but his pamphlet conveniently—or inconveniently—appeared in the midst of the exclusion crisis, in 1680. Filmer had argued in behalf of the divine right of kings from the absolute right of fathers over their children. Locke demolished the theory by demolishing the analogy. He pictured man's original condition not as one of natural subjection, but of natural equality and freedom given to all men by God. This is the meaning of Locke's "state of nature." While this portrait seems at first glance cheerful enough, actually Locke's view of man's prepolitical condition was little more cheerful than Hobbes'—with its war of all against all and its vision of the life of man as "solitary, poor, nasty, brutish, and short." Locke suggested that while men might live in peace without any public authority, the absence of impartial judges and the endemic threat of war made the state of nature at best an inconvenience and at worst a hell on earth. Man, Locke reasoned, is driven by these realities into making a social contract, which establishes a society, which in turn establishes an authority to govern. He insisted that this grant of power was conditional: it must rest, no matter how indirectly, on the consent of the governed and act in their interest. While with his characteristic moderation Locke circumscribed the right of revolution, he explicitly recognized conditions when the state invites disobedience and thus makes revolution lawful. The state, Locke wrote in a famous chapter, exists principally to protect the subjects' "property"—an ambiguous term that Locke himself broadly interpreted to include man's physical possessions and his liberty and life as well. When a monarch deprives his subjects of their property without their consent or interferes with the proper functions of the legislature, he has broken the social contract, and the people may form a new state. "The community," Locke insisted, "perpetually retains a supreme power."

In the Enlightenment, these ideas were generalized beyond the English political scene to the Western world. They became principles underlying the demands for constitutional government, for the rule of law, for protected rights—for liberalism. Locke as a liberal did not maintain, "the fewer laws the better"; Locke took care to argue that the executive must be endowed with adequate powers to carry out his duties. He even envisaged occasions when the executive acts outside the laws: "This power to act according to discretion for the public good, without the prescription of the law and sometimes even against it, is that which is called prerogative." But the dominant direction of his thought was in behalf of individual freedom and the rule of law, and this is how his ideas were taken in the eighteenth century.

Influential as Locke's political ideas proved to be, his ideas on philosophical method and the theory of knowledge proved even more influential. Arguing against Descartes and the Cartesians, Locke held in his *Essay* that man has no innate knowledge at birth, but acquires all the materials for knowledge through the senses and then gives his acquisitions shape through reflection. Thus Locke became the patron of modern empiricism—the philosophy that derives all knowledge ultimately from experience and continually sends the inquirer back to experience. This view placed enormous stress on the power of environment over ideas and thus opened the way for an optimistic appraisal of the possibilities for reforming man and society. In his pedagogic treatise, *Some Thoughts Concerning Education,* Locke drew these consequences with perfect consistency: "Of all the men we meet with," he wrote, "nine parts of ten are what they are, good or evil, useful or not, by their education." In his analysis of knowledge, Locke, following Galileo and Newton, divided the qualities of the things we experience into primary and secondary. The primary qualities— extension, shape, motion—inhere in the things themselves; they exist in the outside world independently of the observer. The secondary qualities—smell, color, taste—are supplied by the observer. Thus Locke denied knowledge to be a mere copy of the outside world; it was instead a correspondence established by clear perceptions and careful discriminations. Locke implicitly argued what the philosophes would make explicit: philosophy is scientific method. This, in essence, was the meaning of Locke—and Newton—for the Enlightenment.

THE ENLIGHTENMENT: MAP OF A MOVEMENT

An International Family

The accepted name for the men of the Enlightenment, "philosophe," is French. But there were philosophes in Scotland, England, Geneva, Milan, Prussia, and the British colonies in America as well; while the French representatives of the movement were the most celebrated and the most conspicuous, the type was truly international. [14] The philosophes did not form a disciplined party or a tight school. They were a loose, generally cordial coalition of literary men, academics, public servants, scattered all over the Western world—Voltaire and Lessing were men of letters, Adam Smith and Immanuel Kant were professors, Turgot and Jefferson were statesmen. They were friends, correspondents, members of informal coteries. They might argue, even quarrel, with one another, but they were allies, self-conscious and self-selected, in a great cause. They were an international family. Paris was the headquarters, and French the favored language of these radical intellectuals all across the Western world, but other countries too played their part in the shaping of the Enlightenment. Its first inspiration came, as we have seen, from seventeenth-century England. Until the romance began to fade in the 1760s, the men of the Continental Enlightenment admired, even envied England as the home of philosophy, freedom, and decency, and held up English institutions for imitation. Voltaire, who came to England in 1726 and stayed for over two years, and Montesquieu, who arrived for a long visit in 1729, were indefatigable propagandists for England. They were "Anglomaniacs" and proud of it. Voltaire's sprightly,

---

[14] That is why, instead of italicizing "philosophe," we have naturalized it here.

much-read report on his love affair with England, the *Lettres philosophiques*,[15] is a cardinal document of the Enlightenment. It affectionately surveys English religious diversity, English political freedom, and English cultural wealth. England, Voltaire told his readers, is tolerant, free, and prosperous, and prosperous precisely because it is tolerant and free. "The commerce which has enriched the citizens of England, has contributed to making them free; from this has sprung the greatness of the state." Here was a country that respected merchants, idolized scientists, and rewarded literary men with good incomes, influential positions, and social prestige. This enviable situation of writers was of particular interest to Voltaire, that ambitious and self-respecting man of letters; it was, he wrote, still another consequence of England's political structure. In England, "literature is more highly honored than in France. This advantage is a necessary consequence of their form of government."

While French philosophes were the receptive disciples of English writers and delighted observers of English institutions, they in turn influenced the rest of the Western Enlightenment. The Neapolitan legal reformer Gaetano Filangieri acknowledged that the impetus for his treatise on legislation had come from Montesquieu; Hume in Scotland, Gibbon in England, Madison in America were all deeply in Montesquieu's debt. One of the two best known German *Aufklärer*, Gotthold Ephraim Lessing, learned a great deal from Diderot's aesthetic writings and bourgeois dramas; the other, Immanuel Kant, declared that he owed his respect for the common man to his reading of Rousseau.[16] And while the French Enlightenment imported ideas, it also exported them, through the whole eighteenth century. Cesare Beccaria, the great Milanese legal theorist, traced what he called his "conversion to philosophy" to Montesquieu, d'Alembert, Diderot, Helvétius, Buffon, and Hume—all but the last of these Frenchmen. But his celebrated treatise on legal reform, the essay *On Crimes and Punishments* (1764), had considerable influence in France, especially on Voltaire. The collaboration among the philosophic family was intense and reciprocal.

The terms of that collaboration differed from country to country, and depended on local political realities. England had had its revolution, and the voices of Enlightenment in that country were least demanding, most closely associated with respectable circles. France was on its way to revolution; conservative forces were just tenacious enough to place the philosophes into opposition and to unite them through harassment, but not strong enough to prevent them from disseminating their often subversive views. Further east, in the authoritarian regimes of the German states and beyond, *Aufklärer* for the most part timidly worked within the system as much as they could, as advisors to the ruling house.

---

[15] It was first published, incomplete, in English, in 1733, as *Letters Concerning the English Nation*, and complete, in French, in the following year.

[16] Rousseau was a Genevan, but French in language and largely in culture. In thinking of him, though, we must never forget that he was, first and foremost, a Genevan.

The philosophes, then, differed in their temperament, their tactics, and their hopes. But they were united by a common set of convictions and a common style of thinking. What characterized them all, in the face of their differences, was an aggressive secularism and its accompaniment, a commitment to the critical spirit. Everything—including politics and religion, those two sacrosanct subjects—was open to criticism; everything, including the very methods of inquiry, was open to inquiry. "Facts," Denis Diderot wrote in his *Encyclopédie* (see p. 356), "may be distributed into three classes: the acts of divinity, the phenomena of nature, and the actions of men. The first belong to theology, the second to philosophy, and the last to history properly speaking. All are equally subject to criticism." It was in this spirit that David Hume could write a long essay entitled *The Natural History of Religion:* for the men of the Enlightenment, religion was a psychological disposition and a social institution like any other. The universal criticism of the philosophes led away from piety and to a determined critique of Christianity.

On this crucial issue, of course, men of the Enlightenment repudiated Newton, for Newton had been a devoutly religious man. He had spent a great deal of effort seeking to establish biblical chronologies, and he was piously certain that God actively and continuously governed the universe. The deists' conception of God as the divine watchmaker struck Newton as blasphemous. God supplements and corrects the laws of nature by direct intervention; he had done his scientific work, Newton said in 1692, to establish "such principles as might work with considering men for the belief of a Deity" (see p. 231). The philosophes labored in precisely the opposite direction. Polemics against superstition and fanaticism in general, and Christianity in particular, invaded all their work and compromised some of it: one need only read Voltaire's or Hume's historical writings on the Middle Ages to see that irreligiosity may, in addition to enlarging men's horizons, narrow their sympathies and color their judgment. Not even Locke was an acceptable guide in this touchy field. Locke's little treatise, *The Reasonableness of Christianity,* had proposed that revelation is only an exalted form of reason and that a good Christian must accept only one dogma: the divinity of Christ. But these large concessions to the secular spirit were not enough for the philosophes: "Mr. Lock's reasonableness of christian relligion," Voltaire wrote in one of his notebooks, in English, "is really a new relligion." And if there was anything the philosophes wanted, it was surely not the making of a new religion but an end to the old.

The meaning of Newton for the Enlightenment, to reiterate, lay not in what he believed, but in how he went about his work.[17] Newton—and to a degree his precursor, Bacon, and his ally, Locke—had been an empiricist.

[17] It lay also in what he was—and what Bacon and Locke were. This trinity is interesting not merely in whom it includes, but in whom it excludes. None of these three was a king, a conqueror, a visionary, or a saint. The philosophes greatly preferred merchants to politicians, scientists to generals, secular to religious men, as they preferred pleasure to austerity, prosperity to glory, reasonableness to exaltation. What Nietzsche undertook late in the nineteenth century—a transvaluation of values—was also a significant aspect of the philosophes' work.

Bacon, Voltaire emphatically told his readers, was the "father of experimental philosophy," builder of "the scaffolding with which we have built the new philosophy," a thinker who, if he himself did not know nature, "knew and showed all the paths that led to it." Locke, the sage and practical thinker had refused to write "the romance of the soul," and "modestly wrote its history" instead. And Newton, as Voltaire often reiterated, taught mankind to "examine, weigh, calculate, and measure, and never to conjecture." He had refused to construct futile systems: "He saw and he made people see, but he did not put his fantasies in place of truth." This modesty in the face of impenetrable mysteries, this confession of partial ignorance, was a strategic weapon in the conquest of knowledge; it protected intelligent men from wasting their lives quibbling about mere words and instead helped them to concentrate their energies on what can be known and must be done. The unprecedented triumphs of Newton—on this Voltaire and the other philosophes endlessly insisted—were not simply the unduplicable work of a unique genius. They were the triumphs of a method that lesser men, too, could acquire and apply.

Reason, Passion, and Hope

Since the early nineteenth century, when a number of Romantic critics charged the philosophes with "shallow rationalism" and "facile optimism," these two labels have clung to the Enlightenment. But, as the philosophes' devotion to Newton's "philosophical modesty" should make clear, both are largely unjust. Their Newtonianism pointed the philosophes toward practicality. Somewhat narrowly, they defined philosophy as effective criticism; a century before Marx said it, they held that the task of the philosopher is not merely to understand the world but to change it. The philosophes have been called irresponsible coffeehouse politicians and wide-eyed utopians, but these charges, too, will not stand examination. While few of them held public office, most of them derived their criticisms, proposals, and expectations from the world in which they lived. They were neither isolated nor sheltered. If they were men of good hope, the world pressed such hope upon them. In fact, while optimism was the spreading mood of the age, the philosophes fenced in their hopes with skepticism and pessimism. The theory of progress, which sees improvement inherent in the world's way and inescapable, was not widespread among them. The philosophe Condorcet, whose celebrated *Essay on the Progress of the Human Spirit* has often been treated as a typical expression of the Enlightenment's view of life, actually stood at the rosiest end of the philosophic spectrum. And even he saw most of the world still plunged into darkness, ignorance, suffering, and superstition and pinned his hopes mainly on "the sweet hopes" of the future. For Condorcet, belief in progress was a form of therapy. Most of the other philosophes asserted, with the historian Gibbon, that for much of the past, progress had in fact taken place, but they did not commit themselves to the continuation of such advance. It was pleasing to note, that, in Gibbon's words, "every age of the world has increased, and still increases, the real wealth, the happiness, the knowledge, and perhaps the virtue of the human race." But most philosophes agreed that progress was slow and highly selective: it might take place in the sciences and in the standard of living, but it was improbable in morals and unthinkable in the arts. Besides, many philosophes were convinced that human affairs undergo a certain cycle of growth and decay. "Empires, like men," d'Alembert argued, "must grow, decay, and die." David Hume put it even more strongly: "When the arts and sciences come to perfection in any state, from that moment they naturally, or rather necessarily decline, and seldom or never revive in that nation, where they formerly flourished." In addition, most of the philosophes held the uncomfortable conviction that all progress must be paid for. A civilization that achieves the benefits of politeness acquires the vice of artificiality; improvements in trade and industry often increase the chances of despotic rule. This was not merely the kind of paradox for which Jean Jacques Rousseau was to become notorious; it was the general view of the Enlightenment. "No advantages in this world are pure and unmixed"—it was not Rousseau who wrote these words, but Hume.

The philosophes' attitude toward reason was as nuanced as their optimism. Their commitment to practicality, in fact, led them to repudiate the rationalist philosophies of seventeenth-century thinkers—those grandiose, ambitious systems of thought which, they charged, were derived not from experience but from rumination, and which undertook to explain what sensible men renounced as forever inexplicable. In this sense, the philosophes' philosophy was a revolt against rationalism. The Enlightenment is often called an Age of Reason, but these two names are not contradictory. It is worth repeating that to the philosophes reason meant scientific method: it meant reasonableness and a constant appeal to experience. Voltaire's motto, au fait!—to the facts!—was the motto of the Enlightenment. The methods of theology and metaphysics, which had traditionally dominated men's thinking, had only produced endless squabbles and unresolved contradictions. The new philosophy—science—was showing a way of breaking away from this scandal and promised to produce knowledge that men could agree upon and use.

The philosophes did not merely limit the competence of reason by insisting that there was a great deal man could never know. They also rehabilitated the great competitor of reason in insisting on the power and defending the effects of the passions. Hume's much-quoted remark, "Reason is, and ought only to be the slave of the passions," is less a critique of the Enlightenment's philosophy from within the camp than an expression of confidence in the passions that most of the philosophes shared. "People ceaselessly proclaim against the passions," Diderot wrote, "people impute to the passions all of men's pains, and forget that they are also the source of all his pleasures. It is an element of man's constitution of which we can say neither too many favorable, nor too many unfavorable things. . . . It is only the passions, and the great passions, that can raise the soul to great things." The philosophes recognized the significance of dreams, the driving force of unacknowledged emotions, and even the Oedipus complex [18] because they seriously respected, and scientifically studied, the passions.

It has often been noted, rightly enough, that the Enlightenment assailed Christianity for its supposed hostility to reason. In fact, as the philosophes saw it, Christianity offended against reason in two ways: by harboring superstitions no reasonable man could accept and by constructing ambitious systems (as in Scholasticism) that violated reasonableness in the opposite direction—by excess. But in addition, the philosophes assailed Christianity for what they thought its hostility to innocent or beneficent passions, especially pride and sensuality. They acknowledged that pride, in the form of conceit or snobbery or love of power, had its harmful aspects. But, rejecting the Christian doctrine of original sin in all its forms, they cherished man's proud self-reliance: "One should say to every individual," Voltaire wrote, "'Remember your dignity as a man.'" For the same reason, they offered a sympathetic view of man's sensual nature; to denounce sexual desire as "lust" and to demand "evangelical perfection" was, quite simply, to stifle an essential part of man's nature and to lead him into confusion, misery, and crime. In his *Supplement to Bougainville's Voyage*, part book review, part imaginary dialogue, Diderot pitted reasonable Tahitians, who copulate freely and have no incest taboo, against the hypocritical and immensely damaging doctrine of Christian shame and chastity. Indeed, Christian notions about sensuality irreparably corrupt the mind: "People will no longer know what they must do or not do; guilty in the state of innocence, tranquil in the midst of crime, they will have lost the north star that should guide their course." Diderot's little extravaganza states the Enlightenment's case rather strongly, but his defense of sensuality was characteristic. Enlightened man, who was the philosophes' ideal, would be both more freely reasonable and more freely passionate than the Christian man. The philosophes' program for social, legal, political improvement for which they are best known—their cosmopolitanism, their call for tolerance and humanity—logically followed not merely from their hopes, but from this analysis of reason and the passions.

Three Generations of Philosophes

This definition of the philosophes and summary of their philosophy gives a misleading impression of immobility. In fact, the Enlightenment had its own

---

[18] In his dialogue, *Rameau's Nephew*, Diderot has one of the two speakers say to the other about his child: "If your little savage were left to himself, keeping all his childish foolishness and joining the bit of rationality of the infant in the cradle to the violent passions of the man of thirty, he would strangle his father and sleep with his mother." A hundred and fifty years later, Sigmund Freud delightedly quoted this passage.

internal history; each generation of philosophes confidently built on the work of its predecessors, each could take for granted the critical achievements of its elders and thus be more radical than they.

Broadly speaking, the Enlightenment unfolded within the hundred-year span between the Glorious Revolution and the French Revolution. These dates are, to be sure, only approximate, but they are convenient and evocative: Montesquieu was born in 1689 and Holbach died in 1789. Within this period, we may distinguish three overlapping generations of philosophes. The first of these was dominated by Montesquieu and Voltaire, those two Anglomaniacs who formed their thought while Locke and Newton were still alive. Montesquieu was born into a noble family near Bordeaux; he briefly served in the local parlement in a seat he had inherited from his uncle and was active in the local academy, where he read his earliest philosophical papers. His first important work, the *Lettres persanes,* was published in 1721 during the Regency (see p. 379). It was a witty, sly collection of disenchanted reflections on love, religion, and freedom, with some daring hits at French society and the Christian religion. With its sympathy for slaves, its contempt for persecutors, its impatience with humbug, and its literate way of saying serious things in a light-hearted manner, the *Lettres persanes* set the tone for nearly a century of Enlightenment propaganda. It gave Montesquieu first some notoriety and then, in 1728, a seat in that exclusive club, the Académie Française. After an extended time of travel, Montesquieu sat down in his splendid library at La Brède, and translated his copious notes and omnivorous reading into *De l'esprit des lois,* a vast, disheveled masterpiece, the pioneer of modern sociology. [19] It appeared in 1748, and achieved international influence by the 1750s. When Montesquieu died in 1755, his only rival in the world of wit and intellect was Voltaire.

Voltaire—really François Marie Arouet—was born at Paris in 1694, the son of prosperous bourgeois parents. He was intended for the law, but chose literature instead; in his fashionable Jesuit school, Louis-le-Grand, and in equally fashionable salons which welcomed him as a very young man, he acquired a reputation for his literary gifts and his unmatched wit. His facility with words was almost proverbial, but he disciplined his talents to serve the one virtue he prized above all others—clarity. The wide popularity of the Enlightenment owes as much to his style as to its teachings. His irreverence and his associations soon got him into trouble. In 1717-1718 he spent eleven months in the Bastille (for scurrilous verses against the regent); he emerged with a new name, "de Voltaire," and his first tragedy, *Œdipe.* The name stuck, and the tragedy was an immense success: the public, parched for talent, hailed him as the successor to Corneille and Racine. Buoyed by his triumph, Voltaire tried his hand at a new genre—the epic. He aspired to being the Vergil of France. During the 1720s, he published various versions of the *Henriade,* an overlong and relatively uninspired—though at the time much praised—paean to his favorite

[19] For an appraisal of the book, see p. 361.

French king, Henri IV. The *Henriade,* with its sallies against fanatical priests and praise of the tolerant Henri, suggested certain intellectual and political interests. Events were to force these interests to the fore. In the winter of 1725, Voltaire became involved in a petty quarrel with a dissolute aristocrat, the chevalier de Rohan, who treated his non-noble adversary with superb disdain; early in 1726, Rohan watched from a cab as his footmen gave Voltaire a humiliating beating. The consequence—for Voltaire—was arrest; after some weeks of comfortable imprisonment in the Bastille, Voltaire went to England, where he breathed the air of a free society, nourished his resentments, and strengthened his political and philosophical convictions. When he returned, he had new language for ideas he had held before. The first result was the *Lettres philosophiques* (see p. 348); another was a lucid popularization of Newtonianism, published in 1738. The *Eléments de la philosophie de Newton* was written at Cirey, the château of his mistress, Madame du Châtelet, a scientifically inclined bluestocking. There, at Cirey, conveniently remote from Paris, Voltaire studied science and theology. But his subversive investigations into Scriptures long remained private; instead he published poetry and philosophical tales and campaigned for a seat in the Académie Française. Famous as he was, and assiduously as he flattered his influential friends, he did not achieve that goal until 1746: despite his caution, he could not repress his irreverence. The long Cirey episode ended in 1749, when his mistress died in childbirth, bearing someone else's child. A year later, the disconsolate, displaced Voltaire finally yielded to the entreaties of Frederick II and went to Prussia. By this time the second generation of philosophes was active and had moved, in some respects, beyond its masters.

Midcentury: A Turning Point

Like most of the early philosophes, Voltaire was and always remained a deist. He repudiated the cruel and vengeful God of the Old Testament and the fabulous tales of the New Testament, and instead pictured the divine watchmaker, who had made the world perfectly, giving it unalterable physical and moral laws. Some of the second generation were in sympathy with these doctrines—they certainly permitted a great deal of vocal anticlericalism. And all the philosophes welcomed Voltaire's advocacy of toleration. But some of them went toward skepticism or into outright materialism.

This was a generation rich in talent. Benjamin Franklin, who would later serve as a model for philosophes in search of the enlightened statesman, was born in 1706. Buffon, the greatest natural scientist of the century (the Newton of geology and biology), was born in 1707. La Mettrie, the most amusing of the materialists, was born in 1709. Others followed in a cluster: David Hume was born in 1711, Rousseau in 1712, Diderot in 1713, Condillac and Helvétius in 1715, d'Alembert in 1717. At midcentury, these men had done some striking work. Actually, the most remarkable among all these remarkable men, David Hume, had published his first book, the *Treatise of Human Nature,* a decade before, in 1739-1740. Unlike many of the philosophes, Hume was a technical philosopher: his *Treatise,* and his more accessible revisions of it, developed what he himself called a moderate skepticism—a devastating critique of Christian, deist, and metaphysical dogmatism, and a psychological analysis that traced the roots of human actions and the firmest of convictions to habit. At the same time, like the other philosophes, Hume was a versatile man of letters, polished in manner and persuasive in argumentation. In an impressive burst of creativity, he wrote epoch-making essays on demography, political economy, cultural history, religious sociology (see p. 360). By 1751, when he published the *Enquiry Concerning the Principles of Morals,* his philosophy was familiar to the literate public, though few adopted it; Hume's skepticism, for all its moderation, was an uncomfortable guide even to the enlightened.

In contrast, Jean Jacques Rousseau, born the year after Hume, championed a kind of philosophical faith—an emotional, sentimental deism—all his life. Unlike Hume, who was edgy in his philosophy and amiable in his conduct, Rousseau breathed warmth in his writings and alienated everyone. The son of a watchmaker who abandoned him, Rousseau never shed his Genevan Calvinist background (it marks all his thinking) and never overcame his neurotic dependence. He longed for friendship and he made enemies; yet he was so obviously perceptive, so clearly a man of unprecedented vision, that many men of great talent—Diderot, Voltaire, Hume—were his friends for a time. He broke with them all; indeed, late in life his sense of isolation and fear of persecution overwhelmed him. But in his troubled, wandering life he produced cultural criticism and social theory of great penetration and enduring influence.

In 1750, still Diderot's friend and living in Paris, Rousseau became famous overnight with an essay that won a prize offered by the Academy of Dijon. In this extravagant and eloquent *Discourse on the Arts and Sciences,* Rousseau argued that man, innately good, had been corrupted by the advances of culture. The essay, stronger in rhetoric than in logic or history, gave him a reputation he strenuously repudiated but never quite outgrew—that of a primitivist. Rousseau insisted that one fundamental principle informed all his writings: man is born good and society has depraved him; he can never return to his prepolitical condition, but must rise to a higher civilization. While Rousseau's second discourse, *On the Origin of Inequality,* published in 1754, was far more nuanced than the first, it did not rescue him from the charge of primitivism. In fact, the phrase, "the noble savage," which is often identified with him, does not appear in his writings. In this second discourse, he developed a hypothetical history of civilization in which the invention of private property appears as the clue to most social evils. In these early diagnostic works, Rousseau noted in passing that civilization had brought man suffering, but also inestimable benefits like the rule of law. In the early 1760s he would move from criticism to construction, diagnosis to prescription (see p. 358).

His old friend Denis Diderot, meanwhile, had launched an *Encyclopédie,* an enterprise that marked the increasing radicalism of the Enlightenment and the increasing tension between the philosophes and the Old Regime. The son of a prosperous provincial craftsman, Diderot had at first thought of entering the church, but had lost his faith and drifted to Paris, where he made a precarious living doing translations from the English and occasional writing. He moved from orthodox Catholicism to a vague philosophical religion to materialism, and in the summer of 1749, his philosophical opinions landed him in the dungeon of Vincennes. A place of detention near Paris, it proved far less comfortable than the Bastille. He was released after making an abject apology, and on the insistence of his employers, a consortium of publishers for whom he had been editing an encyclopedia since 1747.

A ponderous, multivolume enterprise like an encyclopedia seems a most unsuitable weapon in an intellectual crusade, but this is what Diderot's *Encyclopédie* in fact became. It was a piece of drudgery as well, and a mine of politically innocuous information; Diderot, who wrote hundreds of the articles himself and supervised a stable of contributors, took care to include informative articles on crafts and the sciences. But his chief associate, the brilliant mathematician Jean le Rond d'Alembert, was a philosophe like himself, and the two brought such philosophes as Montesquieu and Voltaire, Holbach and Rousseau, and others, to write pieces that ridiculed superstition, advocated toleration, and more or less candidly supported the new philosophy of the Enlightenment. A good encyclopedia, Diderot ambitiously announced, should "change the general way of thinking." His *Encyclopédie,* with its thousands of subscribers and thousands of additional readers in public libraries, did nothing less.

At first all went relatively smoothly. The first volume was published in 1751; it aroused some adverse comment and widespread enthusiasm. The turning point—it proved a turning point not merely for the *Encyclopédie* but for the Enlightenment in general—came in 1757, with the seventh volume. It included a long, highly tendentious article on Geneva by d'Alembert: he had praised the Genevan Calvinist clergy for their modernity and freedom from superstition and insinuated that they were practically all deists. This, for a philosophe, was high praise, but the Genevan pastors treated it as an insult or a grave indiscretion. There was a storm, first by Genevans against d'Alembert, then by pious Frenchmen against the *Encyclopédie.* Early in 1758, d'Alembert prudently withdrew from the enterprise and Diderot, though shaken, went on alone. But then, in July of that year, Helvétius published *De l'esprit,* a treatise on psychology and morals that analyzed man as a purely selfish animal. It caused a scandal far greater than d'Alembert's article on Geneva, and the two were linked in the minds of alarmed Christians. *De l'esprit* is hardly a first-rate book, but its frank hedonism suggested how subversive the philosophes had already become. The censor who had approved the book for publication was fired, Helvétius was dismissed from his post at court, and in the general swarm of charges of impiety the *Encyclopédie* was victimized as well. In 1759 it was officially suppressed, and Diderot continued to publish it—underground.

The Mature Enlightenment: The 1760s and Beyond

The suppression of the *Encyclopédie* was a symptom and a sign. Except for Montesquieu, the philosophes of the first two generations were still active—in new fields, with new intensity. And a third generation of philosophes had joined them to add new talents and new lands to the domain of philosophy. After midcentury, the German states could boast a modest but growing Enlightenment. A small, intrepid band of *Aufklärer*, frustrated by the domination of French culture, handicapped by the small size of the reading public, and shackled by stringent censorship, sought to bring the new ideas to a new audience. They, too, were part of the international family of philosophes. The eldest of these, though not the first to distinguish himself, was Immanuel Kant. Born in 1724, a lifelong resident and professor at Königsberg, Kant developed a philosophical system of striking coherence and originality. The problem he posed to himself was a characteristic Enlightenment problem: how are knowledge and morality possible? Nor is it an accident that his three great works were entitled "critiques." All of them—*Critique of Pure Reason, Critique of Practical Reason,* and *Critique of Judgment,* published between 1781 and 1790—sought to establish the possibility of knowledge and morality on grounds that Newton had prepared and in response to problems that Hume and Rousseau had raised. Kant's decisive insight, which he likened to the Copernican revolution, was to reverse the accepted view that the structure of men's knowledge reflects the structure of the outside world. He held instead that the structure of the outside world conforms to the structure of men's minds: we can only know what we know because we, as men, are made as we are. Original though his answer was, his way of asking questions, and his general philosophical orientation, belongs squarely to the Western Enlightenment. It was Kant who gave the aim of the Enlightenment its most comprehensive formulation: it was, he said, human autonomy (see p. 334).

The other *Aufklärer* resembled their Western counterparts perhaps even more closely. Gotthold Ephraim Lessing and his Jewish friend, Moses Mendelssohn, both born in 1729, were men of letters with a most versatile range. Lessing wrote poems; essays on the theater, aesthetics, religion, and freemasonry; and plays advocating reconciliation and toleration. His most famous drama, *Nathan the Wise,* a sermon on brotherhood, took Mendelssohn—a religious thinker, epistemologist, translator, poet, and aesthetician—as its model. A third *Aufklärer*, Christoph Martin Wieland, born in 1733, moved to freethinking on the Voltairian model after a pious youth, and proliferated tales,

novels, essays, poems, and satires. His writings breathe a modern Epicureanism; they preach (if such elegant writings may be said to preach) reasonableness
and responsibility, urbanity and tolerance, worldliness and civilization.

In France, too, younger men entered the field. There was Anne Robert
Jacques Turgot, born in 1727, famous for his youthful discourse on progress, an
economist and public servant who became intendant of Limoges in 1761, and
in 1774, after the accession of Louis XVI, was appointed to the cabinet (see
p. 461). There was the gifted mathematician Condorcet, born in 1743, the
disciple of Turgot, d'Alembert, and Voltaire. There was Baron Holbach, born
earlier, in 1723, but achieving prominence late, in the combat-ridden 1760s. A
rich German nobleman resident in Paris, Holbach copiously entertained the
advanced spirits of the day; at his table men praised materialism, assailed
superstition, and collaborated in their diatribes against God and the godly. His
"factory" produced most of the anticlerical and antireligious literature of the
1760s and 1770s; his own *Système de la nature,* an earnest, wholly uncompromising treatise, summed up the materialism from which most of the older
philosophes vehemently dissented, and which only Diderot found possible to
accept.

Most remarkable of all, perhaps, was the continued vigor of the older men.
Diderot, now nearing fifty, turned to pioneering essays in art theory and art
criticism, and wrote experimental dialogues like *Rameau's Nephew* and novels
like *Jacques le fataliste.* The 1760s also was the decade in which Rousseau,
though increasingly estranged from the other philosophes, produced in rapid
succession his trio of masterpieces—*La nouvelle Héloïse, Emile,* and *Contrat
social.* The first is a sentimental epistolary novel in the style Richardson had
made famous; the second is a philosophical romance on education; the third is
a treatise on political theory in the classical vein. But Rousseau thought of them
together, and they elucidate one another. Civilization, as he saw it around him,
had not merely stifled the passions—or rather, substituted artificial passions
like snobbery for elemental passions like family feeling and candor—it had also
perverted reason. The problem was to rescue both. Far as man had fallen,
Rousseau argued, the possibility for regeneration lies in his hands. The gravest
social evil, doubtless, was the atrophy of the simple emotions—the cooling of
friendship and the fading glow of honesty. When the emotions are starved, cold
calculation, which is only an excuse for reason, must take over, and men
become hypocrites. It is true that Rousseau indulged himself—and invited
countless others to indulge themselves—in sentimental effusions about the
outdoors and about simplicity. At the same time, Rousseau found room for
reason. In his novel, the heroine, who has "sinned" with her lover makes a
rational marriage and substitutes virtue for inclination; in *Emile,* that most
influential of Rousseau's writings, he takes a solitary pupil through a "negative" and "natural" education that avoids the pitfalls of artifice and cultivates
the emotions first and reason last. This sequence, Rousseau argued, displays
not hostility to reason but respect for nature: "Of all man's faculties, reason . . .

is the one that develops last and with the greatest difficulty." If a man is ever to be treated like a man, the child must first have been treated like a child. It is an educational idea stunning in its simplicity.

Emile, in which a single boy is entrusted to a single tutor, was a brilliant thought experiment. The *Contrat social* displays Rousseau's originality in another way. It attempts to answer the ancient question of political obligation—Why should men obey authority?—in a new way, not by delimiting the relative spheres of individual freedom and social power, but by dissolving the two. The citizen of the *Contrat social* is ruler and ruled at once; he obeys willingly because the laws he obeys are the laws he himself has made. The good society is governed by the "general will," a complex notion which Rousseau himself did not do enough to clarify. Essentially, it is the public good, arrived at by a community of rational, public-spirited men. Rousseau was not a blind believer in the multitude; the will of all may contradict the general will. But in the good society, which dominates its agent, the government, through frequent assemblies, the will of all and the general will *are* the same. The relation of the *Contrat social* and *Emile* should now be obvious: only a community of Emiles can make the good society a reality.

While thousands wept over *La nouvelle Héloïse* and reformed their educational practices after reading *Emile,* the *Contrat social* had little immediate influence. Its real impact came later, in the nineteenth century, when its arguments were used to support many political positions, but one position above all: popular sovereignty. And Rousseau himself grew ever more suspicious of his erstwhile friends; the late 1760s and the 1770s were times of deep distress and paranoid episodes. He was lucid enough to write three autobiographies of which one, the *Confessions,* is a psychological masterpiece in its own right. But when he died in 1778, many, even his former friends, thought him little better than a gifted madman.

Voltaire, who died in the same year, left the world with quite a different reputation. The old Voltaire is an astonishing sight. His visit to Frederick of Prussia had ended disastrously in 1752, with a quarrel and Voltaire's departure. He did not settle down until in the late 1750s, first at Les Délices in Geneva, then at Ferney nearby, on French territory. He was rich and famous, but he grew more radical with the years. His aggressive deist tracts, some first noted down at Cirey, now found their way into print, and his fierce slogan, *"écrasez l'infâme!*—crush the infamous one," began to dot his vast correspondence. More and more, Voltaire used his fertile pen to propagate toleration and to pillory persecution. He was a one-man propaganda factory. In essays, stories, dialogues, poems, even plays, he reiterated the same message: work hard, criticize nonsense, tolerate your brothers, hate persecutors, unmask the tellers of religious lies. His passions entered all his work and dominated much of it—his immortal philosophical tale, *Candide,* of 1759, little less than his influential philosophical handbook, the *Dictionnaire philosophique,* of 1764. The infamous thing he exhorted his friends to crush was not simply superstition, or

Catholicism; it was all supernatural religion, for such religion, no matter how bland, contained the germs of infection—rampant fanaticism.

In 1762, Voltaire tied his antireligious to his humanitarian views in the celebrated Calas case. Late in 1761, in Toulouse, a Huguenot cloth merchant named Jean Calas was accused of murdering his son, who had been found hanged in his father's shop. The ostensible motive was that young Calas was supposedly contemplating conversion to Catholicism. While it was likely that the moody young man had actually committed suicide, the father was tortured, convicted, and in March 1762, executed. Voltaire was at first wryly amused at this spectacle of fanaticism: if he was guilty, Jean Calas showed how far Huguenots would go in their hatred of the popish religion; if he was innocent, the case showed how credulous Catholics were willing to be about Protestants. But his amusement gave way to generous rage, and he inundated Europe with tales of the case, pleas for an end to such judicial murder and for general toleration. Jean Calas' good name was in fact rehabilitated three years after his execution, and the effect of Voltaire's campaign—and similar campaigns in behalf of similar victims of French justice—helped to shift the climate of public opinion toward the philosophes. When Voltaire came home to his native Paris in 1778, to be deified and to die, he was hailed not merely as the poet of the century but also as *"l'homme aux Calas."*[20]

THE ENLIGHTENMENT: THE SCIENCE OF MAN

In his *Traité des systêmes* of 1749, a devastating critique of seventeenth-century system-makers, the French psychologist Condillac expressed a hope widespread among the philosophes. "Today," he wrote, "a few physical scientists, above all the chemists, are concentrating on collecting phenomena, for they have recognized that one must possess the effects of nature, and discover their mutual dependence, before one poses principles that explain them. The example of their predecessors has been a good lesson to them; they at least wish to avoid the errors that the mania for systems has brought in its train. If only all the other philosophers would imitate them!" Thus Condillac, like his fellows, expected that Newton's methods might be extended beyond the exact natural sciences to disciplines that had been hitherto mere collections of observations and aphorisms. Newton himself had hinted at this tantalizing possibility in the *Opticks:* "If natural Philosophy, in all its parts, by pursuing this method, shall at length be perfected, the bounds of moral philosophy will also be enlarged." The prospect haunted the philosophes and exhilarated them. David Hume subtitled his *Treatise of Human Nature,* "An Attempt To Introduce

---

[20] For the persistence and revival of religious ideas, see p. 402.

the Experimental Method of Reasoning into Moral Subjects." And in the introduction he expressed his firm conviction that once men had understood human nature, they could construct on that knowledge "a science, which will not be inferior in certainty, and will be much superior in utility, to any other of human comprehension." Hume had no illusions: the science of man would be difficult, but he thought it possible at least in principle. Hence, the Enlightenment was crowded with students of man and society who aspired to Newton's mantle. They did not wholly succeed; there could be only one Newton. Still, the social scientists of the eighteenth century—philosophes, nearly all of them—placed their disciplines on a rational, if not precisely scientific, basis. Condillac and Hartley developed a psychology using what they considered to be Newton's methods, and even using such Newtonian terms as "attraction." David Hume, in a brilliant and learned essay, *Of the Populousness of Ancient Nations,* laid the foundation for modern demography. But the chief of these new sciences were sociology, history, and economics.

Sociology: From Facts to Freedom

While playing their part of social scientists, the philosophes did not abandon their favorite role of educator and—which was the same thing—reformer. They wanted the truth, but for the sake of humanity. "I should think myself the happiest of mortals," Montesquieu wrote, "if I could help men to cure themselves of their prejudices." These words are from the preface to his *De l'esprit des lois.* The book is disorganized, seemingly without direction. It begins with political sociology—the nature and forms of government and the "principles" that underlie them. It goes on to a celebrated if now dated analysis of the relation of environment to politics—the power of climate over government. It concludes with a collection of topics that Montesquieu was interested in, the historical origins of the French state and political economy. Voltaire, who like everyone else learned immensely from the book, called it "a labyrinth without a clue."

Yet it was more than that. Montesquieu argued that "physical causes," like climate, soil, size of country, interact with "moral causes" like religion or form of government. Here was a significant instrument for the understanding of society. In addition, Montesquieu recognized that each formal set of political institutions is underpinned by a set of convictions, a style of public and private life. By emphasizing these subterranean "principles," Montesquieu transformed the study of governments from a formal catalogue into a substantive and critical analysis. The principle of democratic republics, he wrote, is public spirit; the principle of aristocratic republics is the self-restraint of the governing aristocratic clans; the spirit of monarchies is what Montesquieu calls "honor"— an awareness of status and competition for places. The principle of despotism (a government which, to Montesquieu, is always bad) is fear. As long as the appropriate principle rules a given state, its form of government is secure; when other principles invade it, social change or outright revolution are inevitable. It is true that Montesquieu was far from being wholly neutral. In his famous admiring survey of the English constitution, he portrayed king, Parliament, and the courts as each endowed with its distinctive sphere—executive, legislative, and judicial—each separate and each checking the others. The realities were by no means so neat; still, we can grasp Montesquieu's intentions by a look not at England but at France. Montesquieu's insistence on the separation of powers was in actuality a contribution to a great political debate that pervaded his country. He meant to support the claims of the French aristocracy to political power: "No monarch, no nobility," Montesquieu argued, "no nobility, no monarch." Montesquieu was saying that without a strong aristocracy, a king would turn into a despot. This was partisanship in the name of analysis. But Montesquieu's model of the good government went beyond the pretensions of his social group. Simply to call Montesquieu a conservative, or a partisan of the French nobility, is vastly to underestimate him. With all his biases, he was the first political sociologist.

Montesquieu's numerous disciples took his ideas into new fields. Hume's sociological essays aimed destructive criticisms at the myth of the social contract and proposed instead an empirical treatment of social origins and social cohesion. Hume's friend and fellow Scot, Adam Ferguson, published in 1767 an admirable *Essay on the History of Civil Society* that explicitly tried to abandon speculative system-making in favor of an account based on careful observation and careful comparisons. Like Montesquieu, Ferguson argued that "man is born in society" and that it is only through society, including social conflicts, that his nature and his possibilities can be understood. Ferguson's originality lies in his comprehension of the social function of conflict. "He who has never struggled with his fellow-creatures, is a stranger to half the sentiments of mankind." This cool view of human nature, which characterized the social scientists who followed Montesquieu, coupled with the equally characteristic hope that science can be used for progress, also animates the *Federalist* papers, the greatest political tract produced in the eighteenth century. It is worth mentioning here for its symbolic value quite as much as for its intrinsic merits. America was a model for the European philosophes and a great hope; a place where men, free of feudalism and open to new ideas, would arrange things better. And documents like the *Federalist* papers suggested not only how well founded these hopes might be, but how much the Americans had learned from the European Enlightenment.

In the *Federalist,* a reasoned polemic in behalf of the proposed constitution of the United States, Madison, Hamilton, and Jay argued that power must check power because men are men. While men have sociable passions, their dominant passions—"ambition, avarice, personal animosity"—lead to anti-social thoughts and actions. Hence men need government, a bridle they would not need if they were angels. But hence, also, governments need to be controlled, for the rulers are as fallible as the ruled. Arguments like these, like all the arguments of enlightened social science, were attempts to place knowledge in the service of happiness and progress. "An extension of Knowledge," Ferguson wrote, in impeccably Baconian fashion, "is an extension of power."

Political Economy: From Power to Prosperity

What held true for enlightened sociology also held true for enlightened political economy: it was intended to be scientific for the sake of welfare. The mercantilist writers of the seventeenth and early eighteenth centuries had not neglected prosperity, but if the wealth of the subject and the power of the state came into conflict, wealth must give way. In the course of the Enlightenment, mercantilist ideas—and ideals too—were first refined, then overturned. In France the Physiocrats, in Scotland David Hume and his younger friend, the economist Adam Smith, abandoned the protectionist notions of "political arithmetic"; they visualized the world as a single market of peacefully competing traders and set the stage for a scientific political economy.

The Physiocrats were a small band of devoted followers of François Quesnay, physician at the court of Louis XV: the sect included the elder Mirabeau, Pierre Samuel Du Pont, Mercier de la Rivière, and—with some misgivings—the philosophe and statesman Turgot. Quesnay was the master, the "Confucius of Europe"; his famous *Tableau économique*, first circulated in 1758-1759, offered a rather mysterious diagrammatic representation of his views. His most abject admirers admitted that they did not wholly understand the *Tableau*, but Quesnay's basic ideas and those of his disciples are anything but opaque. The economy is a single system composed of the productive class (agricultural laborers and entrepreneurs), the sterile class (merchants, professionals, nonagricultural laborers and entrepreneurs), and the proprietors' class (the owners of land who make income from the land, chiefly through rents). The point of economic policy is to aid the productive class by taxing the proprietors' class, thus improving the lot of those who work the land, and through them, the country as a whole. The notion that taxes can be reduced to one was typical of the Physiocrats' systematizing and reforming spirit. That spirit finds expression in their famous slogan, *laissez faire, laissez passer.*[21] This was a call to the state to reject and repeal that host of crippling survivals from earlier, more primitive times—of regulations, taxes, tariffs, monopolies perhaps appropriate to a medieval economy but crippling to enterprise, initiative, and investment in the new day. Many ridiculed the Physiocrats, but while their claims were extravagant and their language was often pompous, their ideas

[21] The probable author of this phrase was Vincent de Gournay, who anticipated many of the Physiocrats' ideas, but died in 1759, before the school became really influential.

were rational and sensible—not mysticism parading as science, but science dressed up as mysticism.

Adam Smith, who spent some time in France during the early 1760s, has been called the disciple of the Physiocrats. But while he was indebted to them, his essential ideas date back to early lectures he delivered at Glasgow and to the pioneering essays of David Hume. Hume argued for relative economic equality, for high standards of living among the laboring classes, and in the face of prevailing prejudices, for free trade: "I shall therefore venture to acknowledge," he wrote, "that, not only as a man, but as a British subject, I pray for the flourishing commerce of Germany, Spain, Italy, and even France itself." These ideas, brilliantly enunciated but still informal, were ranged into a system in Adam Smith's *An Inquiry into the Nature and Causes of the Wealth of Nations* (1776), a masterpiece of political economy and of the Enlightenment.

Adam Smith was a philosopher; his *Wealth of Nations* does not offer his complete view of human nature, but concentrates on man in one special, though important role, that of the trader. As its title makes clear, the book is primarily a study in economics, but it is economics in a social setting. It begins with a celebrated analysis of the division of labor. Writing at the very dawn of the industrial age, Adam Smith shrewdly perceived that this institution enormously increases "the productive powers of labor" through specialization. But as a philosophe, Smith was alert to the social cost of progress, and his analysis includes a somber portrayal of what happens to workers "confined to a few very simple operations." Such operatives become "as stupid and ignorant as it is possible for a human creature to become." They become "incapable of relishing or bearing a part in any rational conversation" and of "conceiving any generous, noble, or tender sentiment, and consequently of forming any just judgment concerning many even of the ordinary duties of private life."

This mixture of scientific spirit and enlightened compassion characterizes the *Wealth of Nations* as a whole. Smith's chief target was "the mercantile system," and his sarcasms against the mercantilists are biting and, indeed, conclusive. But while he speaks highly of the virtues of private enterprise and lauds the unintended social benefits of self-centered economic behavior, he insists at the same time on the need for regulation. As things are now, he writes almost cynically, "Civil government, so far as it is instituted for the security of property, is in reality instituted for the defence of the rich against the poor, or of those who have some property against those who have none at all." This is not as it should be. The role of government in the economy should be a restricted one—after all, Adam Smith wrote his book to get the state out of regulation, rather than into it—but it should prevent or at least mitigate the antisocial activities, especially the secret conspiracies, of merchants and industrialists. For Adam Smith, it was a point of humanity and of good economic sense to have wages high, and rising: "No society can surely be flourishing and happy, of which the far greater part of the members are poor and miserable" (see also p. 407). However dismal a science political economy might become in the nineteenth century, in the age of the Enlightenment it sought to enlist rational policy in the cause of the population as a whole.

History: The Secularization of Time

The search for science and the urge for reform also pervaded the historical writings of the age of Enlightenment. But here this combination proved something of a problem: the philosophes' passion for polemics invaded their portrait of the past, somewhat to its detriment. They could see, more clearly than their pious predecessors, the failings of the Christian past; they could not see its virtues. The philosophes' historical writings on the Middle Ages are less one-sided than their reputation might suggest, but they can hardly claim to be exercises in historical sympathy. Still, the Enlightenment produced great historians—Voltaire, William Robertson, David Hume, and Edward Gibbon. If their secularism limited their vision, it was also an asset of inestimable value. While these philosophe-historians did little, if anything, to advance scholarly research, they were formidable readers in their own right. Gibbon devoured books in the classical and modern languages like a man starving; Voltaire skeptically examined documents and aspired to make history into a science; Robertson wrote all across Europe for documents; and Hume, in preparing his essay on the populousness of ancient nations, "read over all the classics, both Greek and Latin." Voltaire's two finest histories, the *Siècle de Louis XIV* and the *Essai sur les mœurs,* David Hume's *History of England,* Robertson's *History of America,* and above all, Gibbon's *History of the Decline and Fall of the Roman Empire* were regarded as monumental achievements in their own day and remain splendid reading in ours. Despite their admixture of anticlerical propaganda, they substantiate Hume's claim that his was "the historical Age."

In fact, far from being unhistorical, the philosophe-historians made a revolution in the discipline of history, and they did so because they were philosophes. They secularized the idea of historical causation, they stretched the canvas of history in time, and they broadened its scope from court annals or saints' lives to the history of culture. This freed the historian to study economic, social, geographic, and psychological factors to explain the course of events; by eliminating God as a cause, the philosophes could focus on the events themselves, rather than seek their explanation in theology. It meant, further, that the historian, instead of concentrating on Christianity, its fortunes and its ancestors, could examine the course of non-Western civilizations— appreciatively if not always knowledgeably. It meant, finally, that history-writing gained in depth by abandoning trivia. If the philosophe-historians did not supply all the right answers, they asked most of the right questions: Voltaire, whose history of the reign of Louis XIV included informative chapters on the arts and literature, put it programmatically: "A lock on the canal that joins the two seas, a painting by Poussin, a fine tragedy, are things a thousand times more precious than all the court annals and all the campaign reports put together." The whole modern ideal of social history is contained in these words.

The masterpiece that sums up the achievement of enlightened history-writing is Gibbon's *Decline and Fall of the Roman Empire*. Born in 1737 to a prosperous family, Edward Gibbon spent most of his life as a private scholar in Lausanne, publishing in French before he published in English. Brilliant in style, masterly in detail, malicious in temper, his *Decline and Fall* traces the gradual decay of the Roman Empire from its pinnacle of order and splendor in the second century, through its gradual dissolution, and its later career into the early modern period. As he remembered it, the inspiration to treat this majestic theme came to him on his Italian journey: "It was at Rome, on the 15th of October 1764, as I sat musing among the ruins of the Capitol, while the barefooted friars were singing vespers in the temple of Jupiter, that the idea of writing the decline and fall of the city first started to my mind." It was, almost literally, a life's work: the first volume appeared in 1776, the last in 1788, and Gibbon himself died in 1794. His undertaking was vastly ambitious and wholly successful in execution. The irony of his first discovery—the Christian friars amidst the pagan ruins—sets its tone. Penetrating in his perception, Gibbon presents an all-too-human picture of the past: men with mixed motives—the lower usually predominating—struggling with their ambitions and with one another. His chilly irony was perfectly calculated to offend Christian sensibilities; his two chapters on the rise of Christianity roused much adverse comment among the pious. Yet Gibbon, his reputation to the contrary, did not simply blame the fall of Rome on the enervating effect of Christianity, coupled with the barbarian incursions. He was too good a historian, too much the disciple of Montesquieu, for that. He thought that this long, tragic decline had many causes—the long peace, the unwieldy size of the empire, economic exploitation. But if Gibbon remains worth reading today, it is not simply for his historical sophistication; it is, above all, for his intelligence and his wit. With Gibbon, as with all the philosophes, the most solemn pronouncement somehow turned into literature.

THE CIVILIZED EIGHTEENTH CENTURY

The Power of the Word

The reputation of the eighteenth century as a civilized century is thoroughly deserved. The philosophes were self-conscious and indefatigable pedagogues; it is not an accident that one of their masters, Locke, and one of their luminaries, Rousseau, should have written pioneering tracts on education. Voltaire's pamphlets on deism and legal reform, Diderot's long hard labor on the *Encyclopédie,* Lessing's diatribes on the German theater, were all characteristic expressions of the Enlightenment's passion to civilize its age. There was nothing new in this: the attempt to marry the instructive to the entertaining was a classical ideal, and the classics, especially of ancient Rome, dominated the minds of the philosophes, as they dominated those of other educated persons in their century.

The thirst to teach was matched by the thirst to learn. The eighteenth century saw a marked widening of the reading public; this was the age when municipalities founded public libraries, when publishing became a fairly large-scale industry, when practical works like popular encyclopedias, almanacs, and grammars sold by the hundreds of thousands. In 1762, the German *Aufklärer* Wieland optimistically noted that "the number of readers is growing steadily"; in 1781, Samuel Johnson called the English "a nation of readers." It is notoriously difficult to measure the size of the reading public and the quality of its reading. And it is certain that most readers devoured sentimental novels or religious tracts; the best seller of the eighteenth century in England was probably Bishop Sherlock's *Letter from the Lord Bishop of London to the Clergy and People of London on the Occasion of the Late Earthquakes,* published in the spring of 1750, when London was repeatedly shaken by slight tremors. More than a hundred thousand copies of the Bishop's *Letter* were sold or given away, recommending (in Hume's caustic summary) "fasting, prayer, repentance, mortification, and other drugs, which are entirely to come from his own shop." But the didactic streak of the age took diverse forms; at the other end of the scale were the new periodicals that flourished, first in Britain, then, by imitation, on the Continent. The best known, and the best, of these periodicals were the *Tatler* and the *Spectator,* edited and largely written by Joseph Addison and Richard Steele between 1709 and 1714. Both these journals inculcated decency, good manners, courtesy, urbanity, industry, and humanity. And they did so by following the classical recipe: "I shall spare no pains," Mr. Spectator said of his readers, "to make their instruction agreeable, and their diversion useful. For which reasons I shall endeavor to enliven morality with wit, and to temper wit with morality." His ambition, he wrote, was to follow Socrates, who brought philosophy down from heaven, and to bring "philosophy out of closets and libraries, schools and colleges, to dwell in clubs and assemblies, at tea-tables and in coffee-houses." To judge from their circulation of several thousand and a far larger readership, Mr. Spectator succeeded in leaving his mark on his age.

The best writers of the century were as happy to instruct as they were eager to please. Jonathan Swift, prominent Tory in the last years of Queen Anne and distinguished Anglican cleric, expended his wit on the foibles of his fellowmen—he lampooned religious enthusiasts and empty-headed scientists with impartial spleen. His greatest and most famous book, *Gulliver's Travels* (1726), which every child knows, remains controversial; especially Gulliver's last voyage among the rational horses, the Houyhnhnms, has been variously interpreted. But there can be no question that it is a didactic work castigating man's parochialism, pretentiousness, and pride, his false science and his real vices. Similarly, Swift's friend, Alexander Pope, an elegant satirist whose ear was unsurpassed and whose diction was unrivaled, did not disdain the part of educator. Some of his most famous poems are lessons in verse: his *Essay on Criticism* (1711) is a sprightly yet organized treatise on aesthetic theory and the rules of taste; his *Essay on Man* (1733–1734) is a philosophical survey of man's station in the universal chain of created beings, and a sermon on resignation. The novelists, too, joined the ranks of the educators. The novel, which grew out of medieval romances and picaresque tales like *Don Quixote,* is essentially an eighteenth-century invention, or rather, development. It is impossible to say which was the "first" novel—Daniel Defoe's *Robinson Crusoe* of 1719 or Samuel Richardson's *Pamela* of 1740. But both these works of fiction were addressed to that new and wider reading public, and qualify as literary works designed to instruct as they please. *Robinson Crusoe* taught self-reliance; *Pamela* praised virtue and condemned vice. Indeed, Richardson's many admirers thought him a profound moralist. Henry Fielding, dramatist and magistrate as well as novelist, lampooned sentimentality in *Joseph Andrews* (1742), and his vigorous *Tom Jones* (1749) aspired to portray human nature in all its variety.

It will not do to be too solemn about these works of the imagination. Pope wrote charming poems with no didactic purpose whatever; Fielding enjoyed telling a tale quite as much as teaching a lesson. In fact, lightness of touch, calmness of voice, ease of manner were in themselves educational. Many Englishmen and Frenchmen looked back on the seventeenth century as a time of gravity, solemn theological debates, and competing religious fanaticisms, and thought that the time for urbanity had come. That is why the eighteenth century was such a great age of conversation. It is significant that one of the favorite literary forms of the age should have been the dialogue. The philosophes talked to each other at Holbach's dinner table or through their entertaining and strenuous correspondence; they met the influential at urbane salons in Paris. Others talked at coffeehouses, at scientific societies, in clubs. One of the most famous of these last was The Club, founded in London in 1764; it included among its prominent members such distinguished artists and literary men as Sir Joshua Reynolds, Edward Gibbon, Adam Smith, James Boswell, Edmund Burke, Oliver Goldsmith, and that greatest talker of them all, Samuel Johnson. Born in 1709 at Lichfield, the son of an impecunious bookseller, and for most of his life impecunious himself, Samuel Johnson was an ornament of the civilized eighteenth century. He was a sound classicist, an elegant stylist, an earnest moralist. By profession he was a literary man: his *Dictionary of the English Language,* first published in 1755, was a monument of comprehensiveness, unprecedented in its scope; his edition of Shakespeare (1765) displayed his uncommon common sense; his monumental *Lives of the Poets* (1779–1781) combined criticism and biography and was marked, as was all of Johnson's work, by his sturdy independence. But by avocation Johnson was a talker. He was fortunate in meeting James Boswell in 1763; the younger man, a good friend and a better listener, recorded Johnson's sayings—

combative, witty, profound—for posterity. When Johnson died in 1784, he was a familiar figure on the English literary scene; when Boswell's *Life of Samuel Johnson* appeared in 1791, he became an immortal.

The Arts

Clearly, the age of the Enlightenment was crowded with talent, but there were many, including Voltaire, who thought it a mere "silver age" after the "golden age" of the seventeenth century. And it is true that the eighteenth century produced no Rembrandts, no Berninis. Its characteristic painters were François Boucher, a specialist in female flesh; or Jean Honoré Fragonard, a charming recorder of frivolous high society. But their Rococo grace did not exhaust the painterly productivity of the century. They had after all, been preceded by a master like Antoine Watteau, whose canvases of country festivals or Italian clowns go beyond the surface to capture something deeper: the fragility of life and pleasure. And it could boast a whole school of English painters, trained in the styles of Italy and Flanders but solidly English in their independence: William Hogarth, with his lively portraits and his moralizing series of engravings depicting the London poor or the decline and fall of a rake; Thomas Gainsborough, who raised portraiture and landscape-painting to a high art; and Sir Joshua Reynolds, more monumental in his style than Gainsborough, but a skillful, fertile—and prosperous—portrait artist in his own right. A century that could boast Jean Baptiste Chardin, who turned humble still lifes into luminous and moving works of art with his mastery of color, or Giovanni Battista Tiepolo, who endowed his small wash drawings and gigantic ceilings with dramatic life, can scarcely be dismissed as second-rate.

Indeed, in painting and in the other arts, the age of the Enlightenment was a time of profusion and of rapid change. In their writings on aesthetics, the philosophes powerfully contributed to this change. The official doctrine ruling the arts—and for a time ruling the writing of Diderot and Lessing as well—was neoclassicism (see p. 297). But gradually there was a move toward freedom. Addison had already celebrated the imagination in his *Spectator,* and as the century progressed, aestheticians more and more came to give precedence to the artist's imagination and the audience's taste, and to play down the importance of the rules. By stressing the power and the value of subjectivity, the aestheticians of the eighteenth century were not calling for chaos; they continued to argue that an artist and his public should be calm and well informed in their judgment. They thought to create stability of style and continuity of taste by appealing to the consensus of cultivated men. But the tendency was away from the search for objective laws of beauty toward a psychology of artistic creation and appreciation. Neoclassicism retained its charms: in architecture, notably in England, the model of Palladio (see p. 216) continued to exercise a great fascination over architects and patrons alike; late in the eighteenth century there was to be another wave of neoclassicism, seeking grandeur and powerful spatial organization, and concentrating on themes from Roman antiquity. But other styles jostled for attention, including chinoiserie and bourgeois sentimentality. It was an age richer than many of its participants understood.

It was particularly rich in music. The modern listener is apt to think of the century crowned by Bach and Mozart as a single entity—the age of "classical music." But the composers and listeners of the time thought of their century as a time of movement, reform, even of revolution. Like other eighteenth-century revolutions, the one in music had been prepared in earlier centuries—by the triumph of harmony over polyphony. From the ninth century onward, and with increasing subtlety through the Middle Ages, composers had woven melodic lines into long, complex horizontal patterns, normally for the unaccompanied voice. In the sixteenth-century compositions of Giovanni Pierluigi da Palestrina and Orlando di Lasso, harmonies emerged from the polyphonic interplay of the melodic line. Then harmony gradually became an aim musicians sought for its own sake. In the seventeenth century, the long-lived Claudio Monteverdi, "the first modern composer," wrote operas, cantatas, madrigals, on the new principles. He depicted character by descriptive instrumental accompaniment—agitation by tremolos, serenity by quiet long lines—and gave new prominence to vertical harmonic combinations. At the end of the Baroque era, the keynote of the musical scene was variety, indeed confusion. The fine composers of the late seventeenth and early eighteenth century—Scarlatti and Vivaldi, Telemann and Buxtehude, Couperin and Corelli—composed in a number of genres and loosely employed general names like "concerto" and "sinfonia" without giving them any fixed meaning: a "sonata" could be a composition for a small orchestra or for a single instrument. Bach and Handel, the two giants of the early eighteenth century, were not so much innovators as clarifiers. Their genius has obscured how much they owed to the past.

Johann Sebastian Bach was born in 1685; many of his twenty children became gifted performers and well-known composers in their own right. He began, as most composers did, by listening and copying and by training himself as a versatile instrumentalist. All his life he lived with, and for, music; after holding several positions, he settled at St. Thomas' church in Leipzig and stayed there until his death in 1750. He composed for a wide variety of purposes and a wide variety of instruments: finger exercises for his students (including his children), humorous secular cantatas, religious cantatas, concertos, pieces for the unaccompanied violin, cello, organ; he wrote light-hearted orchestral suites and sonorous masses. His didactic music—his *Well-Tempered Clavier* and his *Art of the Fugue*—are rescued from tedium by his genius; the former stabilized the tempered keyboard, then still new;[22] the latter explored the unsuspected

---

[22] The system of "equal temperament," now standard, still experimental in Bach's day, takes the octave as the stable basis, and divides it equally into twelve semitones. This permits keyboard instruments to play compositions in all keys.

possibilities of counterpoint. His religious music, among which the St. Matthew Passion and the B Minor Mass remain the most famous, reflect his seriousness and his intense, pious desire to make "well ordered music in the honor of God."

George Frideric Handel, born like Bach in 1685, and like him in Saxony, was in contrast a secular-minded composer. After acquiring a thorough grounding in Italy, he began his own abundant musical production with operas in the Italian style. In 1712 he moved to England and remained there until his death in 1759, thoroughly acclimated to his chosen home. Appropriately enough, he was buried in Westminster Abbey among the great of England. His taste ran to gigantic performances, with large orchestras making unprecedented noise. He composed suites like the Firework Music for outdoor performances; his familiar Water Music was designed for a procession of royal barges making their stately progress down the Thames. Much of his music lies unperformed, though his operas, when revived, show remarkable vitality despite their stylistic conservatism. And his suites and concertos have never lost their popularity. Yet for most listeners his fame rests on the sacred oratorio, *Messiah,* first performed in 1742. A worldling, a businessman, a robust figure who was, if he was anything, a deist, Handel survives mainly as a religious composer on the strength of one of his rare religious works. It is one of history's minor ironies.

While Bach and Handel perfected what they had received, Gluck, Haydn, and Mozart broke new ground. Christoph Willibald von Gluck was almost a philosophe in his earnest reforming passion. The object of his ardor was opera, which had reached depths of absurdity by midcentury. Ordinary operas, ground out by the hundreds, mainly in Italy, were mere display pieces for vocal dexterity, and their librettos, generally stilted and ridiculous tales, bore no relation to the music. This is one reason why John Gay's *Beggar's Opera* of 1728 was such a resounding success in London: in addition to portraying recognizable local types and lampooning well-known political figures, it satirized the arid artificiality of Italian opera with so much gusto that the audience cheered, and the Royal Academy of Opera, headquarters for Italian opera, went bankrupt. In France, at midcentury, the philosophes became involved in the battle for reasonable music. French opera was wholly Italianate; when Pergolesi's refreshing, simple, and melodious comic opera, *La Serva Padrone,* came to Paris in 1752, a number of leading philosophes, including Rousseau and Diderot, spoke in its defense. It was this new temper, this search for the natural in opera, that Gluck discovered and satisfied in 1762 with his *Orfeo ed Euridice.*

Gluck, born in Bavaria in 1714, had made a considerable reputation with operas in the old Italian manner. But then, in association with a new librettist, Raniero de' Calzabigi, Gluck put this style behind him. His *Orfeo,* deliberately modeled on a classical Greek myth, explicitly sought naturalness and simplicity. Its music matches the words; its chorus remains in character and forms part of the action; traditional florid declamations give way to simple (and therefore truly eloquent) expressions of feeling. In 1767, when Gluck and Calzabigi collaborated on another masterpiece, *Alceste,* Gluck signed (but Calzabigi probably wrote) a manifesto: "It was my design to divest the music entirely of all those abuses with which the vanity of singers, or the excessive complacency of composers, has so long disfigured Italian opera." Any modern performance will testify that he succeeded.

Gluck specialized in opera; Franz Josef Haydn wrote music in a wide variety of forms, in quantities so large that even today his total output remains uncounted. His symphonies alone number one hundred four. These symphonies and his late string quartets greatly influenced the development of both forms, but while Haydn was an innovator in music, he was a hired hand practically all his life. Born in 1732, he became musical director to two immensely rich Hungarian aristocrats, the brothers Esterhazy, in 1761. He stayed in their service, docile and content, most of his life; it was only a pair of visits to London in 1790 and 1794, that gave him a taste of freedom. He liked it, and he was enormously productive during his English stay. But habit was too strong to be conquered: he returned to his comfortable servitude and died in it, a cheerful old man, in 1809.

The only composer to exceed Haydn's versatility was Wolfgang Amadeus Mozart. It is impossible to guess what Mozart might have done had he lived as long as Haydn, but his life was tragically short—he was born in 1756 and died in 1791. Trained and driven by his gifted martinet of a father, Leopold, young Mozart showed himself a child prodigy. When he was six, he concertized on the harpsichord; when he was twelve, he wrote his first opera. Despite his gifts and his fame, he never held a post he deserved and was pathetically short of commissions. The archbishop of Salzburg, whom Mozart served intermittently as court musician between 1772 and 1781, treated him like a menial servant, almost like a serf. Yet his music belies his poverty and his ill fortune; it sounds, at least at first hearing, easy, light, serene. It is impossib. and happily unnecessary, to choose among his works: the compositions of the la ten years of his life remain, quite simply, unsurpassed. He wrote six fine string quartets dedicated to Haydn between 1782 and 1785; he wrote his last and greatest three symphonies within three months in 1788; he wrote four of his operas, transcendent masterpieces all—The Marriage of Figaro, Don Giovanni, Così fan tutte, and The Magic Flute—between 1786 and 1791. It was in this last year of his life that he wrote the last of his splendid piano concertos and nearly all of his mysterious Requiem. This was a commission from an unidentified aristocrat, but Mozart, feeling low and ill, saw it as his own requiem. He was right; he did not live to finish it.

When Mozart died, he was buried in a pauper's grave; it was unmarked, and no one knows where he lies. Mozart, no less than these other great makers of music of his century, lived in a world of patronage and intrigue, of courts and concert promoters. Some, like Handel, were its masters; others, like Mozart, were its victims. But there was another world in which their part was marginal—the world of war and peace, diplomats and statesmen. It was a wider, if not exactly a better world.

SELECTED READINGS

For a general survey of seventeenth-century intellectual tendencies, see the first volume of Preserved Smith's *A History of Modern Culture* (1930). Franklin L. Baumer's *Religion and the Rise of Skepticism* (1960), keeps the promise of its title. The rise of scientific presuppositions is lucidly traced by E. A. Burtt, *The Metaphysical Foundations of Modern Physical Science* (2nd ed., 1932). Alexandre Koyré, *From the Closed World to the Infinite Universe* (1957), is a sophisticated analysis. E. J. Dijksterhuis, *The Mechanization of the World Picture* (tr. 1961), takes the rise of scientific ideas down to Newton. Richard S. Westfall, *Science and Religion in Seventeenth-Century England* (1958), reports on the emerging divergence between the religious and the scientific world views. Charles C. Gillispie, *The Edge of Objectivity: An Essay in the History of Scientific Ideas* (1960), is important for the scientific revolution and eighteenth-century thought alike. General histories of science in this period include Herbert Butterfield, *The Origins of Modern Science, 1300–1800* (2nd ed., 1966), and A. R. Hall, *The Scientific Revolution, 1500–1800: The Formation of the Modern Scientific Attitude* (1954). See also the splendid summary in Hall, *From Galileo to Newton, 1630–1730* (1963), and the English version of G. Taton, ed., *A General History of the Sciences*, vol. II, *The Beginnings of Modern Science from 1450 to 1899* (tr. 1966).

For Newton, see L. T. More, *Isaac Newton: A Biography* (1934), which is likely to be superseded once the edition of Newton's correspondence by H. W. Turnbull and others, now in progress, is completed. E. N. da C. Andrade, *Sir Isaac Newton* (1954), is very brief. Frank E. Manuel has explored Newton's historical-biblical researches in *Isaac Newton Historian* (1963) and Newton's unconscious in *A Portrait of Isaac Newton* (1968). H. G. Alexander, ed., *The Leibniz-Clarke Correspondence: Together with Extracts from Newton's "Principia" and "Opticks"* (1956), throws much light on Newton's thought. I. Bernard Cohen, *Franklin and Newton: An Inquiry into Speculative Newtonian Experimental Science and Franklin's Work in Electricity as an Example Thereof* (1956), illuminates Newton's use of hypotheses. Marjorie Nicolson's *Newton Demands the Muse* (1946), proves that the Newtonian world view did not ruin the poets' appreciation of nature; Marie Boas lucidly analyzes Newton's great contemporary in *Robert Boyle and Seventeenth-Century Chemistry* (1958). See also A. E. Bell, *Christian Huygens and the Development of Science in the Seventeenth Century* (1947).

H. R. Fox-Bourne's ancient *Life of John Locke,* 2 vols. (1876), has not yet been superseded; Maurice Cranston, *John Locke, a Biography* (1957), effectively uses some recently opened papers but is weak on Locke's ideas. For these one may go to Richard I. Aaron, *John Locke* (2nd ed., 1955), and D. J. O'Connor's brief, introductory *John Locke* (1952). Peter Laslett's critical edition of Locke's *Two Treatises of Government* (2nd ed., 1967), is indispensable; it corrects many misreadings.

The interpretation of the Enlightenment followed in this chapter is drawn from Peter Gay, *The Enlightenment: An Interpretation,* vol. I, *The Rise of Modern Paganism* (1966), which analyzes the philosophes' debts to antiquity and rebellion against Christianity, and vol. II, *The Science of Freedom* (1969). Both volumes have extensive polemical bibliographical essays. In addition, see Gay's *The Party of Humanity: Essays in the French Enlightenment* (1964). Ernst Cassirer, *The Philosophy of the Enlightenment* (tr. 1951), concentrates, as its title indicates, on the philosophy. Other general interpretations are Alfred Cobban, *In Search of Enlightenment: The Role of the Enlightenment in Modern History* (1960), and the economical essay by Norman

Hampson, *A Cultural History of the Enlightenment* (1969). Paul Hazard's *The European Mind: The Critical Years, 1680-1715* (tr. 1953), though brilliant, sees intellectual changes too abruptly and too much in isolation from culture as a whole; Hazard's *European Thought in the Eighteenth Century: From Montesquieu to Lessing* (tr. 1954), has many insights. The second volume of Preserved Smith, *A History of Modern Culture, The Enlightenment, 1687-1776* (1934), is conventional but intelligent. Carl Becker's brilliant and influential essay, *The Heavenly City of the Eighteenth Century Philosophers* (1932), is no longer tenable; it should be read in conjunction with R. O. Rockwood, ed., *Carl Becker's Heavenly City Revisited* (1958).

On the philosophes' presumed "rationalism" and "optimism," see in addition to Gay's books cited above, R. V. Sampson, *Progress in the Age of Reason: The Seventeenth Century to the Present Day* (1956), and, especially, Henry Vyverberg, *Historical Pessimism in the French Enlightenment* (1958). There is a lucid analysis of a celebrated legal case by David D. Bien, *The Calas Affair: Persecution, Toleration and Heresy in Eighteenth Century Toulouse* (1960).

There is a vast literature on individual philosophes; the following selection indicates the range. For Voltaire, see Gustave Lanson, *Voltaire,* now old (it was published in 1906 and translated in 1966) but still remarkably fresh; Theodore Besterman's *Voltaire* (1969) is large-scale, shallow on ideas, but dependable on details. Peter Gay, *Voltaire's Politics: The Poet as Realist* (1959), seeks to rescue Voltaire from his reputation as an abstract and superficial thinker. See also Norman L. Torrey, *The Spirit of Voltaire* (1938). For Diderot, see Arthur M. Wilson's definitive biography *Diderot* (1972). Rousseau has been brilliantly studied in Jean Guéhenno, *Jean Jacques Rousseau,* 2 vols. (tr. 1966). Ernst Cassirer, *The Question of Jean Jacques Rousseau* (tr. 1954), is a splendid brief analysis that connects Rousseau's life with his times; Ronald Grimsley, *Jean Jacques Rousseau: A Study in Self-Awareness* (1961), is a fine psychological (though not psychoanalytical) study, while Grimsley's *Rousseau and the Religious Quest* (1968), dependably surveys Rousseau's complicated religious ideas. And see Charles W. Hendel, *Jean Jacques Rousseau, Moralist,* 2 vols. (1934). For Montesquieu there is Robert Shackleton, *Montesquieu: A Critical Biography* (1961), judicious and comprehensive; it can be supplemented by Franz Neumann's "Introduction" to Montesquieu's *Spirit of the Laws* (ed. 1945). For Holbach, see W. H. Wickwar, *Baron d'Holbach: A Prelude to the French Revolution* (1935); the pivotal philosophe and psychologist Helvétius has been well surveyed in D. W. Smith, *Helvétius: A Study in Persecution* (1965). J. Salvwyn Shapiro, *Condorcet and the Rise of Liberalism* (1934), is well meaning but too adoring. Douglas Dakin does justice to Turgot in *Turgot and the Ancien Régime in France* (1939). Ronald Grimsley's recent biography, *Jean d'Alembert, 1717-83* (1962), is the best in English.

There are few good titles on the German Enlightenment in English. See the relevant pages in Hajo Holborn, *A History of Modern Germany,* vol. II, *1648-1840* (1964); W. H. Bruford, *Germany in the Eighteenth Century: The Social Background of the Literary Revival* (1935), along with Bruford's more recent study, *Culture and Society in Classical Weimar, 1775-1806* (1961). The best biography of Lessing in English is H. B. Garland, *Lessing: The Founder of Modern German Literature* (1937). For Kant, see the useful intelligent biography by A. D. Lindsay, *Kant* (1934), and the brief recent analysis by S. Körner, *Kant* (1955). One other German *Aufklärer* has been fortunate in English: see J. P. Stern's fine long study, *Lichtenberg: A Doctrine of Scattered Occasions* (1959).

For English thought, the old volumes by Leslie Stephen, *English Thought in the*

Eighteenth Century, 2 vols. (1876), and *English Literature and Society in the XVIIIth Century* (1907), though partly dated, retain much of value. See also chapters VI and VII of J. M. Saunders, *The Profession of English Letters* (1964). Among analytical biographies see Mary P. Mack, *Jeremy Bentham: An Odyssey of Ideas* (1963), highly sympathetic to its controversial subject. The most comprehensive biography of Gibbon remains David M. Low, *Edward Gibbon, 1737–1794* (1937); it can be read in conjunction with G. M. Young's brilliant, brief *Gibbon* (1932). Hume, the greatest of the Scots, has an adoring, accurate, and dry biography by E. C. Mossner, *The Life of David Hume* (1954). See also Norman Kemp Smith, *The Philosophy of David Hume: A Critical Study of Its Origins and Central Doctrines* (1941), and J. A. Passmore, *Hume's Intentions* (1952).

On the science of man see, in general, Gladys Bryson, *Man and Society: The Scottish Inquiry in the Eighteenth Century* (1945), and in particular, David Kettler, *The Social and Political Thought of Adam Ferguson* (1965), William C. Lehmann, *Adam Ferguson and the Beginnings of Modern Sociology* (1930), and the same author's *John Millar of Glasgow, 1735–1801* (1960), Glenn R. Morrow, *The Ethical and Economic Theories of Adam Smith: A Study in the Social Philosophy of the Eighteenth Century* (1923), and C. R. Fay, *Adam Smith and the Scotland of His Day* (1956). For history, see the civilized essay by J. B. Black, *The Art of History: A Study of Four Great Historians in the Eighteenth Century* (1926), to be read in conjunction with Nellie N. Schargo, *History in the Encyclopédie* (1947), and J. B. Brumfitt's brief *Voltaire Historian* (1958). For economic thought see, in addition to the titles on Adam Smith, Ronald L. Meek, *The Economics of Physiocracy* (1962), the old but still useful *The Cameralists: The Pioneers of German Social Polity* (1909) by Albion Small, and William Letwin, *The Origins of Scientific Economics: English Economic Thought, 1660–1776* (1963).

For the group around the *Spectator,* see Peter Smithers, *The Life of Joseph Addison* (1954), and Calhoun Winton, *Captain Steele: The Early Years of Richard Steele* (1964).

For the history of eighteenth-century music see the later chapters in Manfred F. Bukofzer, *Music in the Baroque Era from Monteverdi to Bach* (1947); Adam Carse, *The Orchestra in the XVIIIth Century* (1950); and the relevant chapters in Paul Henry Lang, *Music in Western Civilization* (1941). Biographies of leading composers include E. M. and S. Grew, *Bach* (1949); Paul Henry Lang, *George Frideric Handel* (1966); Percy M. Young, *Handel* (1947); Alfred Einstein, *Gluck* (tr. 1936); Karl Geiringer, *Haydn: A Creative Life in Music* (1946); and, among a vast literature on Mozart, W. J. Turner, *Mozart: The Man and His Works* (1938), and the often penetrating if speculative study by Alfred Einstein, *Mozart: His Character, His Work* (tr. 1945).

9

Europe in the Eighteenth Century: 1713-1763

A TIME OF WAITING: EUROPE TO 1740

In 1713 and 1714, after decades of making war, the European powers made peace. The one serious eruption was the War of the Polish Succession, which brought most of Europe into the field in 1733—another episode in the drawn-out, inexorable decline of the Polish kingdom, once so impressive (see p. 435). In the main, however, country after country had time to absorb domestic developments—the change of rulers, the opportunities and ravages of economic change. In 1711, Charles VI acceded to the Hapsburg throne; in 1713, the year of Utrecht, Frederick William I to that of Prussia. In 1714, the year of the supplemental peace treaties at Rastatt and Baden, Queen Anne, the last Stuart ruler of England, gave way to George I, the first Hanoverian; in 1715, Louis XIV finally died, and, while his dynasty survived him, his threatening posture toward Europe did not. In 1718, after the death of Charles XII, Sweden became, in effect, an oligarchic republic with a crowned figurehead; in 1725, Peter the Great left a stage he had so long monopolized, to be followed by a succession of bizarre and inadequate rulers. Indeed, the signature of the quarter-century now beginning was the reaffirmation of aristocratic against autocratic claims—in France, in Sweden, in Russia, as well as in the Dutch Republic and in Spain under Philip V. The most conspicuous exceptions were Prussia, where the aristocracy obeyed, and England, where it shared power with the squirearchy. But in general, all across Europe, "absolutism" was under siege.

The Travail of Authority: Northern Europe

While most of Europe experienced this travail of authority, each country experienced it in its own way. In the emerging age of great powers, the Dutch Republic was in decline. Its international economic position in shipping, manufacturing, and banking remained impressive, but receded from the heights it had reached in the seventeenth century, when the Dutch had routed naval powers like England and defied military giants like France. Its international decline was matched by the triumph of particularism. Dutch history, we know, is a pendulum perpetually swinging between the centralizing tendencies of the house of Orange and the decentralizing tendencies represented chiefly by the richest of the seven provinces, Holland. When the stadholder William III died in 1702, he left no successor, and for over forty years the regent patriciate governed the republic without a stadholder. Republicans everywhere hailed this regime as a model of freedom—a view encouraged by the regents' paid partisans who were bitter about the house of Orange: "Our own prince," one of these propagandists wrote, "made us suffer worse oppression than had the enemy."[1] Others, watching the commercial decline and the obvious military impotence of the Dutch, were not so sure.

As in the Dutch Republic, so in Sweden, the restoration of an aristocratic oligarchy had to await the disappearance of a strong ruler: the effective regime that Charles XI had constructed and Charles XII exploited, collapsed with the latter's sudden death in 1718 (see p. 328). The social and political fissures these two kings had done their utmost to paper over reemerged to plague the kingdom and delight its neighbors. In 1720, the Swedish nobility, cowed into silence for half a century, imposed a constitution on Queen Ulrika Eleonora—Charles XII's sister—which in effect turned power over to the Riksdag and, within that, to the nobility. Until young King Gustavus III boldly seized power in 1772, the Swedish nobility governed the state for well or ill, in its own interest. Like the Dutch, the Swedes had a name for this oligarchic interlude: they called it *Frihetstiden*—the age of freedom. Like other ages so named, it meant freedom for a few, and freedom to indulge in factional infighting. For

---

[1] Quoted in Pieter Geyl, *The Netherlands in the Seventeenth Century*, part II, *1648–1715* (1964), 306.

half a century, Sweden was prey to the acrimonious debates of two parties: the Caps, who favored a cautious, pacific foreign policy, and the Hats, who sought glory through war.[2] For nearly twenty years, while affairs were in the hands of a responsible minister, Count Arvid Horn, the age of freedom was in fact an age of peace and healing for Sweden. But Horn was overthrown in 1738 by the Hats, and after that the irresponsibility of the Swedish oligarchy became truly apparent.

The Russians watched developments in Sweden with keen interest and undisguised pleasure; they firmly supported the new Swedish constitution which they rightly saw as an instrument that would weaken Sweden abroad by dividing it at home. But within a few years, Russia was in danger of going the way of Sweden. Only the size of the country, the extent of its resources, and the surprising competence of some of its ministers preserved it as a great power. There was little talk here about ages of freedom; the single attempt to hedge monarchical authority with a revived Senate and constitutional "conditions" came in 1730, at the accession of the Tsarina Anna. It failed immediately. At the same time, while the Russian nobility did not impose itself on the state with such complete authority as its Swedish counterpart had done, its position in the Russian system grew more and more favorable. Taking advantage of Peter's successors, Russian aristocrats progressively reduced their obligations to the state. In 1736, under Anna, they managed to fix compulsory service at twenty-five years; in practice, this meant that noble families would "inscribe" in service their children at birth, so that young men reached exalted rank and freedom from state service at the same time. And in 1762, Tsar Peter III freed the nobility from service altogether. Thus, the noble landowner gained after, and by, the death of Peter the Great.

In the succession, as in so much else, Peter the Great left an ambiguous legacy. By having his son Alexis murdered and by reserving to the tsar the right to name the successor, he ensured a series of palace intrigues, military interventions by privileged troops, and recourse to assassination as an instrument of policy. It was not until 1762 that Russia would see a monarch worthy of Peter the Great; Catherine II would prove as shrewd, as energetic, as single-minded, and as unscrupulous as he. In contrast, those who reigned between Peter the Great and Catherine the Great were memorable mainly for their vices and their eccentricities. Peter was succeeded by his widow, Catherine I, who, in her two years of authority, proved a tsarina as intelligent as she was uneducated. Unlike Peter the Great, who had died before naming his successor, Catherine lived to name hers: Peter II, the twelve-year-old son of Peter the Great's hapless son Alexis. His was a short reign—from 1727 to 1730—marked

---

[2] The origin of these party names is amusing. The bellicose party called themselves "Hats" to evoke the image of military headgear and gave their adversaries the nickname "Caps" to recall the notion of unheroic men in unheroic nightcaps.

by the court rivalries of two great Russian families. He was followed by Anna, daughter of that Ivan V who had been Peter the Great's complaisant co-ruler for some years (see p. 325). The decade of her rule (1730–1740) was a decade of favorites who withstood all efforts at bridling her authority in the interest of the great magnates. Anna acted, in fact, as a true autocrat: she moved the court back to St. Petersburg, resorted to the secret police and to widespread arbitrary arrests. Her lover, the Courland baron Ernst Johann Bühren, exercised his enormous influence through her good will alone. Bühren brought in his friends, Germans all, and while they were on the whole active and capable men, his rule and that of his friends came to stand for all that was baneful about a regime dominated by foreign favorites. During the short reign of her successor, the infant Ivan VI, Anna's pro-German policies were faithfully followed by Ivan's mother, a duchess of Courland. But then, late in 1741, a palace revolution brought to the throne Elizabeth, daughter of Peter the Great and Catherine I, and she held the throne for twenty-one years, until 1762. Exceedingly ignorant, inordinately vain, she was an attractive, even seductive figure who amused herself and scandalized Western observers by arranging transvestite parties. But her erotic preoccupations did not keep her from throwing her weight into the scales of European diplomacy. With her aggressiveness and her inconsistencies, she was too formidable to be ignored, too erratic to be respected. In 1759, the *Universal Magazine,* an English journal, expressed Western opinion with curt contempt: "The crown of Russia may now be deemed elective, and of the worst kind of elective monarchies."[3]

The Travail of Authority: France

The assault on autocratic pretensions was most dramatic where they had been most far-reaching—in France. Their dismantling took precisely as long as their first assertion—twenty-four hours. Louis XIV had laid claim to full royal authority the day after the death of Mazarin (see p. 293). The symbol of that authority—his will—was broken the day after his own death.

Louis XIV died on September 1, 1715. His successor was Louis XV, his great-grandson, who was then five. The unavoidable regent was Louis' nephew, Philippe, duke of Orléans, an intelligent and debauched worldling. But since Louis XIV did not trust Orléans, he fenced him in with a regency council and assigned to the duke of Maine, one of his bastards, the guardianship of the young king. The Parlement of Paris had the royal testament in its care; Orléans found it easy to persuade the magistrates to break it and to hand sole authority to him. On September 2, in a famous session, the parlement declared portions of the late king's will invalid. In return, the parlement resumed the right it had

[3] Quoted in M. S. Anderson, *Europe in the Eighteenth Century, 1713–1783* (1961), 180.

lost under Louis XIV—to remonstrate, which is to say, to obstruct legislation. Thus the nobility of the robe reasserted its power. The nobility of the sword, reduced to sheer decorativeness in the great reign, also reappeared as a political power under the regency. Orléans set up the Polysynodie, a set of six councils, with ten members each, which for a time shouldered aside the secretaries of state. These councils were a haven and a power base for the old nobility.

The regent's experiment in government failed. As Franklin L. Ford has said, "The results, in administrative terms," of calling into service the most assertive of the nobles, "were about what could be expected from a group of barely literate soldiers and pompous courtiers."[4] By 1718, the councils had been replaced by the old ministers. But the social and political consequences of Orléans' bid for power remained after the Polysynodie had gone the way of other ill-founded ventures in administration. Both segments of the French nobility, robe and sword, were to become centers of power in the French state and sources of resistance to royal policies of reform, notably in finance. The crucial political issue for France, raised in spectacular fashion on September 2, 1715, and kept alive right down to 1789, was this reassertion of noble power, especially of the parlements' right to participate in the making of legislation.

The regent's most intractable problem was, of course, the need for money. Decades of war had saddled France with a vast public debt. Taxes were in time-honored disarray: the two privileged estates, clergy and nobility, were exempt from the most onerous imposts, many towns and well-situated bourgeois managed to make special arrangements, which meant, in practice, evading most if not all taxes. The rolls from which taxes were levied were out of date, and so inequity was piled on inequity. For a time, Orléans permitted a partial repudiation of the public debt, but this halfway bankruptcy rightly struck him as an inadequate solution to France's financial plight. It was his desperate search for remedies that put him into the hands of John Law, a Scottish adventurer and financial wizard, whom he had met in earlier, less responsible days, at the gaming table. What happened now can be understood only if we understand the rudimentary and chaotic condition of public finance in early modern Europe. The line between private and public finance was thin and faint: in many states, France included, the collecting of taxes was "farmed" to private entrepreneurs who contracted to supply the state with a fixed sum. Profiteering, collusive arrangements, and savage treatment of the helpless were almost guaranteed by such a system; nor was tax farming calculated to produce adequate sums for the state's treasury—too much stuck to the fingers of the tax farmer. The balance sheets that ministers of finance occasionally prepared bore little resemblance to the carefully detailed and scrupulously audited budgets of modern states; they were, for the most part, fantasies with figures. Law was by no means a crook or a fool; he was manipulating a complex financial system

---

[4] *Robe and Sword: The Regrouping of the French Aristocracy After Louis XIV* (1953), 176.

with inadequate means and discovering the mysterious power of credit. "Unfortunately," as Alfred Cobban has put it, these "early experiments with its magic were only to be performed by apprentice sorcerers."[5]

In 1716, Law persuaded the regent to set up a central bank, a device that worked well and increased public confidence in his schemes. In 1717, Law established the Company of the Occident holding the monopoly on trade with Louisiana. Two years later, in 1719, this "Mississippi Company" became the Company of the Indies; it superseded all other overseas trading companies and expanded its operations to the whole of France's colonial trade. Armed with public authority, Law's company undertook to underwrite the public debt: all holders of government certificates could trade them in for shares in the company. Nor was this all: in 1718 and 1719, Law took charge of indirect and direct taxes and issued paper money. Law was an entrepreneur, a reformer, and one of the first of modern economists; he was trying to simplify and rationalize a structure long marked by incredible complexity and confusion. In January 1720, the regent signalized his satisfaction with Law by appointing him controller general.[6] But Law's phenomenal success became the cause of his catastrophic failure. The circulation of paper money, the accessibility of shares in the Mississippi Company, and Law's evidently infallible touch, induced the French, normally so prudent, to indulge in a riot of speculation. Speculation brought inflation, inflation the smile of prosperity.

It was a painted smile. No amount of overseas trade could sustain the prices to which the universal hunger for quick profits had driven his shares. Issued at a face value of 500 livres and promising a dividend of 12 percent, they were soon traded at 12,000 livres and above. A few shrewd investors recognized that this could not last, and gradually speculation decreased in intensity. The price of shares dropped. In the course of 1720, the Mississippi Bubble burst.[7] Thousands who had borrowed heavily or mortgaged everything, lost everything. In December 1720, John Law went into exile. His legacy was ruin, shaken confidence in the French state, increased suspicion of credit, some newly rich speculators, and some lasting, if largely invisible, benefits to the French economy.[8]

While the bursting of the Mississippi Bubble appeared at the time as sheer disaster, in his international ventures the regent, ably seconded by Cardinal Dubois, did far better. When he died in December 1723, he left behind a fragile

[5] "The Decline of Divine-Right Monarchy in France," in *The New Cambridge Modern History,* vol. VII (1957), 223.

[6] Like other French statesmen later, Orléans was to find France's restrictive religious policy a burden; only Roman Catholics could hold official posts. Indeed, this would be an issue as late as the reign of Louis XVI, with the Swiss Protestant, Necker (see p. 462). But Law made things easy for the regent: he converted to Catholicism and became a naturalized French citizen.

[7] It was an international bubble; for its impact on England, see p. 384.

[8] ". . . the stimulus given to economic life by the System was not entirely lost. Commerce and industry profited, and the great roads and canals planned by Law were not all abandoned" (Cobban, "Decline of Divine-Right Monarchy," in *The New Cambridge Modern History,* vol. VII [1957], 223).

alliance with France's old enemy, England, and a pacific foreign policy. In the following two decades, France gradually abandoned the first and generally sustained the second.

Orléans' successor was the duke of Bourbon, hag-ridden and demonstrably incompetent. Therefore in 1726, Cardinal Fleury, Louis XV's tutor, found it easy to encompass Bourbon's dismissal and to become, in effect, first minister. Fleury was an old man of seventy-three at his accession; he was moderate and diplomatic. He knew what he wanted or rather, what he did not want. And he had the full confidence of his former charge who, despite intermittent attacks of responsibility and religiosity, preferred hunting and whoring to governing. Married in 1725 to Marie Leszczynska, daughter of Stanislaw, the deposed king of Poland, Louis XV soon plunged into a series of highly public love affairs and left the conduct of government business to Fleury.

Both at home and abroad, Fleury aimed at a policy of pacification for the sake of financial stability and economic progress. He was fortunate in his associates and largely successful in his intentions. He could not wholly silence the religious controversies centering around a revived Jansenism; the lower clergy were in a rebellious mood against the bishops, and popular agitation issued in an irrepressible series of hysterical outbursts and unauthorized, embarrassing miracles in public places. And in foreign affairs, Fleury, much against his will, found himself dragged into the War of the Polish Succession in 1733. But until 1740, three years before his death, when the aged cardinal was finally shunted aside by new favorites, France prospered under his benign hand. Then, with Europe engaged in the War of the Austrian Succession (see p. 389), France, too, joined the general scramble for position and power. Its time for a great duel with England was at hand.

A TIME OF WAITING: BRITAIN TO 1740

1714-1722: A Confusion of Whigs

What France virtually experienced in 1715, Britain had experienced in full force the year before—a change in dynasty. In accord with the Act of Settlement (see p. 313), Queen Anne was succeeded in 1714 by George I, the elector of Hanover. Like the Glorious Revolution, the shift from Stuarts to Hanoverians was bloodless and, for the standards of the time, remarkably easy. Obviously, most Englishmen passionately preferred a Prostestant monarch, even a foreigner and a mediocrity, to a Catholic, no matter how eligible. The most conspicuous victims of the accession of George I were the Tories. A Tory ministry had precariously governed the country since 1710; Viscount Bolingbroke and Robert Harley (later earl of Oxford), its two dominant personalities, had quarreled, and their quarrel paralyzed the Tory leadership. Still, in the face of strident war propaganda by the Whigs, the Tories had managed to make peace with France.[9] It was a good peace: the Whigs' cry of treason at Utrecht was pure demagogy. But while the accusation was unjust, it was telling. When George I came over to England in September 1714, the Tory party was ejected from power. Bolingbroke fled the country to serve the pretender—"James III," as his supporters called him. Oxford was sent to the Tower. Jacobite[10] mobs roamed the London streets, and in September 1715, the earl of Mar raised the standard of revolt in Scotland. By December, the pretender had joined the rebels. The rebellion was easily contained early in 1716, and Oxford was acquitted of treason in 1717. But the fear of a Stuart restoration remained to poison party politics. The abortive "'15," coupled with Bolingbroke's defection, seemed to lend substance to the Whig charge that the Tories were all secret Jacobites.

Both political parties were loose and unstable alliances; the notion of party discipline was far in the future. Whatever the Whigs might say, many Tories were aghast at the thought of a James on the English throne; whatever the Tories might say, not all Whigs were money-grabbing parvenus. Yet, while the party labels were becoming increasingly meaningless, in these years they still designated more than the struggle between ins and outs, or between court and country; they stood for real divisions on matters of principle and of policy.

The Whig rule initiated by the change of dynasty was far from easy. For over seven years—from the accession of George I in 1714 to the accession of Walpole in 1722—there was vehement, often bitter debate among the ruling Whig factions. This internal division, like the larger division between Whig and Tory, was not simply a naked struggle for power: "The groups," J. H. Plumb writes, "differed on how to make the world safe for Whigs and on how far to undo the work of the last Tory ministry. This was their battle-ground."[11] On one side were Lord Stanhope and Marlborough's son-in-law, the earl of Sunderland—aggressive men, eager to play a large role in the councils of Europe. The death of Louis XIV permitted Stanhope, in charge of foreign affairs, to reverse the old Whig anti-Bourbon policy by an alliance with France. By 1718, England was part of a Quadruple Alliance that also included the Dutch and the empire. It was directed against Spain and the machinations of the pretender, and was designed to defend Hanover, whose interests George I never

[9] Since these party labels are used a great deal and formed the staple of political talk at the time, it is worth noting that the groups designated by these names changed policies and character in the reign of Queen Anne. At the time of the Glorious Revolution, the Whigs were critical of monarchical power, anticourt, and depending on Parliament to defend their interests; by 1700, they had countered Tory influence at court by cultivating the crown, and they had become deeply skeptical of parliamentary power in an age when members of Parliament depended so heavily on royal patronage. So by 1700 the roles of Whig and Tory were reversed.

[10] For this term, see p. 314n.

[11] *England in the Eighteenth Century (1714-1815)* (1950), 55.

neglected. But, despite the French alliance, Stanhope was a true Whig: he worked to remove the disabilities placed on English Dissenters during the Restoration and retained after the Glorious Revolution. His success was only partial; resistance to repeal of the Test Act and the Corporation Act (see p. 309) was too tenacious to be overcome. Some disabling acts were dropped, and though the Dissenters remained second-class subjects, they gradually, often surreptitiously, began to rejoin the political nation. The methods of reunion were characteristically English compromises; some Dissenters practiced "occasional conformity," taking the Anglican communion once a year; after 1727, many Dissenters were saved the legal penalties for violating anti-Nonconformist laws by the provisions of an indemnity act.

Sunderland, meanwhile, was in charge of repairing the finances disorganized by the long wars, and finance gave the leaders of the opposing faction, Sir Robert Walpole and his brother-in-law, Charles, second Viscount Townshend, their opportunity. They, too, wanted Whig rule, but not Stanhope's or Sunderland's. As good Whigs they supported the Septennial Act of 1716, which prolonged the life of the sitting Parliament and prescribed general elections every seven instead of every three years. But they wanted a less expensive foreign policy, and they wanted power. As in France, so in England, overseas commerce offered irresistible temptations to get rich. In 1710, a South Sea Company had been formed to trade in South America and the Pacific; in 1717, it proposed to assume a large part of the national debt and sell shares to the general public. Early in 1720, Parliament approved the scheme. The new mood of confidence, encouraged by peace, prosperity, reports of Law's triumphs in France, and the government's low interest policy, produced an orgy of speculation. Everyone was in it, including the king's mistresses. In May 1720, Oxford's brother, Auditor Harley, wrote: "The madness of stock-jobbing is inconceivable. This wildness was beyond my thought." [12] Late in June, shares with a par value of £100 traded at £1050; in July they still stood at over £940. [13] The speculative wildness spawned numerous other companies, each advertising huge dividends and promising huge profits. The capital of new companies floated in a single week in June added up to £224 million. [14] But, as in France, commercial realities could not sustain such inflated prices, and the shares began to drop. By September, they stood at £180; ruin was widespread and scandal loud. Walpole, a well-known critic of the South Sea Company, took charge of rescuing what could be rescued. His task was complicated but not insuperable: the country, including its trade and its bank, was sound. But the bursting of the South Sea Bubble drove the Stanhope-Sunderland faction from office. In April 1721, Walpole became chancellor of the exchequer and first lord of the treasury; his old ally, Townshend, and, after some maneuvering, a new ally, the

[12] Quoted in J. H. Plumb, *Sir Robert Walpole: The Making of a Statesman* (1956), 293.
[13] Ibid., 299.
[14] See Charles Wilson, *England's Apprenticeship (1603-1763)* (1965), 316.

duke of Newcastle, were appointed secretaries of state. Sunderland, though out of office was still dangerous, but then, in April 1722, he suddenly died. The road to Walpole's primacy lay open.

1722-1733: Walpole in Command

"I am no Saint, no Spartan, no Reformer"—thus Sir Robert Walpole on Sir Robert Walpole. The self-appraisal is shrewd; it underscores not merely his liabilities, but his assets. And it explains why Alexander Pope and other literary lights of the Augustan Age who flourished under his hand despised Walpole the man and Walpole the statesman even more. They detested his passion for commercial values. Peace, trade, prosperity—these were Walpole's aims. But the motto first attributed to him by his son—*quieta non movere*—is apt to mislead: Walpole was anything but passive. He had a great appetite for life, great energy for work, great capacity for detail; and he was never content "to let sleeping dogs lie"—he was a manager of men. He needed to be: his enemies were influential and his power rested on two props—the favor of the crown and the support of the House of Commons. He strove mightily to secure both.

The House of Commons that Walpole led with such consummate skill was a microcosm of the minority that dominated Great Britain. After the union with Scotland in 1707, it totaled 558 members—513 for England and Wales, 45 for Scotland. The franchise under which electors sent members to Parliament varied enormously; sizable towns like Birmingham were badly underrepresented, tiny hamlets grossly overrepresented. Many boroughs were owned more or less outright by immensely rich and politically influential peers; some, like Westminster, enjoyed practically manhood suffrage. There were more than six million people in England, Scotland, and Wales; of these perhaps a quarter of a million had the franchise—and many of these voted as they were told to vote. Elections were expensive and avoided whenever possible. Thus, the House of Commons was a tiny oligarchy speaking for a larger oligarchy. The country squires in the Commons boasted of relative independence; they gave Walpole some bad moments. But Walpole remained in control through his personality, his program, and his skillful manipulation of pensions and government jobs—"places"—for obedient members.

Most of the members of the House of Commons knew one another intimately; many were related to one another and to members of the House of Lords. That upper house, too, could be managed by an alert politician who had the ear of the crown. Peerages were, of course, hereditary, and most peers were rich landowners, but, as courtiers or as lord lieutenants of their districts, they too were part of the political machinery. And, especially under Walpole, the twenty-six bishops of the Church of England, who sat in the House of Lords, docilely voted at government orders; they saved Walpole more than once. Parliament was a large, often irritable and intractable family with a common vocabulary, and, by and large, common aims. This made management manageable.

For a dozen years Walpole's control of the political machinery was so complete that he has often been called Britain's first prime minister. The title is an anachronism, but it reflects his mastery. Walpole took care to keep that mastery intact; while he did not resort to violent methods, he purged all opposition and even competition; in 1730, even Townshend had to leave the government. But power was not an aim in itself; Walpole's vision was limited but sensible. He had a passion for stability. In retrospect the threat of a Stuart restoration seems remote. But Walpole did not enjoy hindsight: the Jacobites were active intriguers, and the possibility of foreign aid to their cause was ever present. Walpole therefore feared the Jacobites and frantically worked to keep the Hanoverian settlement secure. When George I died in 1727, to be succeeded by George II, Walpole passed his first test on this score: there was no move to dislodge the dynasty and (which was almost as gratifying) no move to dislodge him. In fact his relation to Queen Caroline approached that of friendship. Until she died in 1737, Walpole might suffer occasional defeats in Parliament, but he need fear no rival.

Walpole enlisted his talent for finance in this search for stability. The bursting of the South Sea Bubble had fastened on England, as it fastened on France, a lasting suspicion of joint stock companies; the Bubble Act, passed at the height of the speculative fever, carefully controlled the activities of joint stock companies and thus continued to channel investment into partnerships. But, while this served as a long-range check on large-scale investment, it did not compromise the prosperity Walpole was determined to impose upon the country. He succeeded splendidly. He rationalized customs rates, abolished export duties, imposed protective tariffs in behalf of domestic industry, and aided the port of London by instituting bonded warehouses that permitted storage of goods to be transshipped. He refused to raise taxes. Since 1717, a sinking fund—Walpole's idea—had served as a permanent reserve to back up the national debt; its reassuring presence guaranteed to the public that the state would meet its obligations. This, too, raised general confidence and brought the interest rate down: by 1727, it stood at 4 percent, and an even lower rate of 3 percent was in the offing.

Walpole was certain these gains could be preserved only if Britain followed a pacific (which is to say, cheap) foreign policy. Townshend had more bellicose ideas; supported by vehemently anti-Spanish sentiments in England, he negotiated expensive alliances and conducted what amounted to an undeclared war against Spain. Walpole superseded his brother-in-law; in 1729 he joined France and Spain in the Treaty of Seville, and in 1731, after he had forced Townshend from the government, he concluded the Treaty of Vienna with the emperor, both leading to general pacification. Thus Britain saved money, and kept Gibraltar, first taken in 1704, into the bargain.

Paradoxically, finance, which had given Walpole his undisputed ascendancy, also gave him his first intimations of fallibility. Part of Walpole's eminently successful warehouse scheme had been the provision of an excise tax to be imposed on such colonial products as coffee, chocolate, and tea, if they were not transshipped but consumed in Britain. It was a workable system, and it raised much-desired revenue. In 1732, seeking to keep taxes low and perhaps abolish the land tax, Walpole announced his intention to extend the excise first to tobacco, then to wine. It was an immensely unpopular move, tailor-made for the opposition in search of an opening against the invulnerable minister. Bolingbroke, who had been permitted to return home in 1723, was too brilliant to miss his opportunity. Joined by an equally brilliant and equally disgruntled Whig, William Pulteney, Bolingbroke, in an unscrupulous propaganda campaign, represented Walpole's new excise as an invasion of the rights of Englishmen and the prelude to new imposts. Undeterred, Walpole introduced his tobacco excise into Parliament in March 1733, but in April, finally aware of the extent and determination of his opposition, he dropped the scheme. It was his first great defeat. Others would follow.

1733-1742: Walpole in Eclipse

Walpole was too formidable to crumble quickly. All the best writers and all the leading politicians were arrayed against him; theirs was a coalition of Tories whom he had kept from office and dissident Whigs whom he had driven from office. What Gibbon said of the Roman Empire, we may say of Walpole's ministry: the very length of his tenure provided the precondition for his fall. Very few of the opposition were principled: they wanted, quite simply, to be where Walpole was. Practically all of them accepted the Glorious Revolution; the Jacobites, who rejected it, were weak and isolated. Talking points against Walpole's supposed subservience to the crown's Hanoverian interests or his resort to corruption carried little conviction; it was obvious that his most vociferous enemies, once in power, would assiduously obey the Hanoverian crown. And their cry for purity in politics was the old story of the sour grapes. Besides, Walpole spoke for much of England. The country could be swayed by chauvinistic appeals, but it was, at the same time, weary of instability at home and ruinous adventures abroad. This was the heart of Walpole's strength with the public and the House of Commons: he gave them something better than glory.

Yet in the end it was glory, shrewdly linked to trade by a rising young politician, William Pitt, that would bring Walpole down. In 1733, Walpole managed to keep Britain out of the War of the Polish Succession, and he boasted of it with some self-satisfaction: in 1734 he told Queen Caroline that of the fifty thousand men killed in Europe that year, not one was an Englishman. The War of the Polish Succession was a short war, but Europe would not remain pacified, and in the general maneuvering, Britain found itself more and more isolated. Walpole's efforts to stay in office and on top of events grew more and more strenuous. In 1734, he barely squeaked through a general election, though he used the financial and influence-peddling talents of Newcastle as unsparingly as he could. The clamor for war—especially for war against Spain—grew in intensity: "When Trade is at stake it is your last Retrenchment," Pitt told the country, "you must defend it, or perish." Pitt was not a greedy man; he thought war part of a nation's destiny. But he did not hesitate to play on the greed of his rapt listeners: "Spain knows the consequences of a war in America. Whoever gains, it must prove fatal to her." Walpole was anything but indifferent to trade, but he judged that war in the interest of a segment of the commercial community—the traders in slaves, in sugar, and in smuggled goods—would be a calamity for the country as a whole. But even timid, neurotic Newcastle was for war, and so, in October 1739, to Walpole's open chagrin, Britain was drawn into the War of Jenkins' Ear against Spain.[15]

"It is your war," Walpole told Newcastle, "and I wish you joy of it." It was the end of Walpole's system. The general elections of 1741 showed that the country was no longer with him, and in February 1742, Walpole resigned and was elevated to the House of Lords as the first earl of Orford. His end is a commentary on the changing locus of political power in Britain and on his own peculiar capacities. Thirty years before, the House of Lords had been so powerful that passage of the unpopular Peace of Utrecht could be secured only be creating twelve Tory peers to swamp the upper chamber. But in mid-eighteenth century, the center of power moved to the Commons. Walpole, whose natural habitat had always been the House of Commons, of course knew this; he took his elevation not as a promotion but as an interment. Meeting his old adversary Pulteney, just created earl of Bath, Walpole told him: "You and I, my lord, are now two as insignificant men as any in England."[16] Three years later Walpole was dead. It was perhaps just as well: his pacific system had grown inappropriate not to Britain alone, but to Europe as well. For by 1740, the time of waiting was over and had given way to a quarter century of war.

---

[15] The war takes its bizarre name from a Captain Robert Jenkins, who testified before the House of Commons in 1738 that the Spaniards had captured his ship, pillaged it, tied him to a mast, and cut off an ear—which he carried about with him in a little box. Asked what he did then, he said that he "committed his soul to God and his cause to the country." The war party could not ask for a better, more inflammatory slogan than this.

[16] Basil Williams, *The Whig Supremacy, 1714–1760* (1939), 201.

A TIME OF WAR: 1740-1763

The War of the Austrian Succession: Rewards of Militarism

In October 1740, Charles VI, the Hapsburg emperor died, leaving his young daughter, Maria Theresa, as his heir. Two months later, in December, Frederick II of Prussia invaded the prosperous Hapsburg province of Silesia. His aggression set off a general conflict that moved across three continents and did not subside until 1763, with the Peace of Paris.

Frederick's action was ungallant but perfectly comprehensible: never before had Prussia, still small, still poor, been given a chance to acquire such desirable loot—and so cheaply. Maria Theresa was married to Francis Stephen of Lorraine, an insignificant and unpopular figure. She was expected to have difficulties with her Bohemian and Hungarian subjects. She was known to be unprepared for the burden her father's death imposed upon her. True, he had attempted to secure the succession. In 1713, he announced a pragmatic sanction [17] regulating that succession; by 1720, when it became evident that his issue would consist of two daughters, no more, Charles VI began to induce all his domains and all of Europe to recognize the succession rights of his eldest daughter. By 1732, the Hapsburg dominions had given their assent; other European powers followed suit after protracted negotiations, usually for a price. But for the powers the pragmatic sanction was a bargaining point and a scrap of paper. When Charles VI died, there were influential voices around Louis XV asking that France tear up the agreement and seize part of the rich Hapsburg territory. To make her plight even more acute, Maria Theresa was confronted with rivals to her inheritance. Philip V, king of Spain, Frederick Augustus II, elector of Saxony, and Charles Albert, elector of Bavaria, related by blood, marriage, or treaty to the Austrian Hapsburgs, hastened to present their claims. But it was the invasion of Silesia that precipitated the general War of the Austrian Succession.

For a ruler, Frederick of Prussia's action was not surprising; for the man he claimed to be, it was nothing less than shocking. After all, Frederick II was a philosophe, whom Voltaire and other assiduous literary flatterers of the time had hailed as the incarnation of the modern philosopher-king. Just before his accession, while he was still crown prince, he had written a relatively high-minded treatise entitled *Anti-Machiavel* with Voltaire's editorial assistance. In December 1740, he coolly disregarded his own precepts. It was this contradic-

---

[17] For the meaning of the term, see p. 100.

tion that Voltaire had in mind when he noted a little sourly in his *Memoirs* of 1759 that if Machiavelli had tutored a prince, he would have begun by advising him to write against Machiavellianism.

Frederick II came by his ambivalence honestly: as a child, at home. His father, Frederick William I, was everything that popular legend and unsympathetic historians have called him: a boor, a tyrant, a drill sergeant as king. A vicious caricature of the Protestant ethic, he thought himself a divine instrument chosen to administer his legacy, Prussia; everyone must serve him blindly, just as he served God. Ostentatiously he saved money by dismantling his father's costly court and by living simply; everything—almost everything— went for his military forces. His only extravagance was his "giants," those tall recruits whom his roving, ruthless agents found in his domains (and, on illegal raids, even in neighboring countries) and "enlisted" in the Prussian army. Frederick William I might have been merely a comic figure, but in his single-minded devotion to Prussia he was, instead, a ruler to be reckoned with. An alert, energetic, and intelligent manager of his country, he beat down the last lingering resistance of the Junkers to royal authority, founded domestic industries like textile and powder factories (significantly related to military requirements), and persistently pursued his ideal of a large, well-manned, well-trained army. With careful attention to detail, he reorganized the financial administration of his state and rationalized the civil service; even as crown prince he had insisted on the need for a central treasury, and as king he brought the reforms of his grandfather, the Great Elector, to their logical conclusion by establishing a general finance directory in charge of all domestic revenues. Finally, in 1723, Frederick William rationalized his administration by creating a single administrative body, the General-Ober-Finanz-Kriegs- und Do-mainen-Direktorium. With justice, he has been called "the father of Prussian bureaucracy."[18]

Frederick William I worked himself unsparingly, but he did not spare his ministers or his people either. The results were gratifying, even astounding: a certain economic independence, a trebling of revenues, a reserve fund of eight million thalers, and an army doubled in strength, from forty thousand men at his accession to eighty thousand at his death. And Frederick William I husbanded his resources by a cautious foreign policy. His armies and his financial resources were a counter, a threat, more effective in reserve than in use. His successor, Frederick II, would deploy this legacy to great advantage and reap the rewards of militarism.

But Frederick William I left his son another legacy as well—a miserable youth and ineradicable inner conflicts. Just as Frederick William I had rejected the civilized ways of his father, his son rejected the barbaric ways of *his* father. Born in 1712, brought up by a cultivated tutor and under the influence of his mother, young Frederick early showed a talent for the flute and an inclination

[18] By Hajo Holborn, in *A History of Modern Germany*, vol. II, *1648-1840* (1964), 196.

for gambling and reading. Like Crown Prince Alexis of Russia, Frederick detested the military drill the king loved above all else and sought to force on him. Conflict between such a father and such a son was foreordained. Like Peter the Great, Frederick William I found it particularly galling to reflect that this shameless creature would some day inherit the realm that he, the hard-working king, was safeguarding with such paternal care. Relations deteriorated; there were violent scenes with the violence all on one side; Frederick William did not hesitate to humiliate or beat his son in public. When the sixteen-year-old boy sent a submissive message to his father, the king curtly replied that he had no use for a "self-willed" child who does not love his father, an "effeminate chap" without "manly leanings," a boy incapable of riding and shooting, who is, at the same time, "personally unclean, wears his hair long and curled like a fool." At eighteen, Frederick could stand it no longer; in 1730, he tried to escape abroad. Easily overtaken and brought back, the king compelled him to watch the execution of his friend, Katte, his confederate in the escapade. This was a gratuitous bit of sadism, but it was also a specimen of *Kabinettsjustiz*—arbitrary justice: a court martial had sentenced Katte to life imprisonment, but Frederick William I tore up the verdict and substituted decapitation. For some time the crown prince himself was in danger of execution, but at length the king relented and instead imposed a long, hard penance of work. Helpless, Frederick submitted and buried his private tastes more deeply than ever. After his accession, however, it became clear that he had not escaped the training his father had willed for him—he became something of a drill sergeant himself, addicted to cruel practical jokes and punishing work, and possessed by a fierce sense of devotion to his post. He would express that sense in a famous phrase: the king, Frederick II said, is the first servant of the state. But his other side, more civilized and more feminine, never wholly disappeared. Beneath the cold, cynical, hard-driving and hard-driven administrator there smoldered an ambitious poet and incurable worldling, a German barbarian who never quite forgave fate for not letting him be born a Frenchman.

In 1740, Frederick II acted as his father's son, only more rashly. He committed the troops and the funds his father had so diligently amassed to a gamble for big-power status. His friends the philosophes were appalled at him. Frederick had no illusions about his legal rights; he knew perfectly well that his claims to Silesia did not bear a moment's candid examination. But he told his lawyers to find good reasons and gave marching orders. To his surprise, Maria Theresa proved a doughty opponent. She fought gallantly to keep what she rightly thought was hers and indignantly rejected Frederick's offer of compromise. Frederick himself was lucky in this war: his first major engagement, at Mollwitz in April 1741, was only narrowly won. But this victory was the signal for the French to enter the war on the Prussian side. In June, France and Prussia concluded an alliance; Saxony and Spain also ranged themselves on the anti-Austrian side. But Maria Theresa persevered. In the summer of 1741 she bravely went to Hungary to claim the crown of St. Stephen and to enlist the loyalty of her wavering subjects. Her youth, her gallantry, her carefully staged emotional scenes won the day and secured substantial military support. Yet Frederick had occupied Silesia, and reluctantly Maria Theresa decided to treat with him. In October 1741, with the secret Convention of Klein-Schnellendorf (soon repudiated), and in July 1742, at Berlin, Hohenzollern and Hapsburg made a separate peace: Prussia was to keep practically all of Silesia. Frederick's negotiations were a clear violation of Prussia's treaty with France. The king of Prussia was acquiring a bad reputation not merely among idealistic philosophes but among hardened diplomats.

Meanwhile Frederick of Prussia had Silesia—a splendid addition to his poor territories. Yet the last months of 1742 and the year 1743 brought Maria Theresa successes that early 1742 had withheld. The English were now active in the war, and the "pragmatic army," consisting of English, Hanoverian, and Hessian troops, defeated the French in June, at Dettingen, while the Austrians took Bavaria and invaded Alsace. By the end of the year, Frederick's hold on Silesia was in jeopardy.

Frederick II had started the First Silesian War in the winter of 1740 to take that rich province. He started the Second Silesian War in the summer of 1744 to keep it. All went as appointed; Frederick's troops took Prague. But once again Maria Theresa proved resourceful: in January 1745, she had constructed an alliance with England, Saxony, and the Dutch Republic. And she was lucky as well; in 1742, after her defeat, she had been unable to prevent the imperial crown from going, for the first time in centuries, out of Hapsburg hands: Charles Albert of Bavaria had become emperor as Charles VII. But now, in January 1745, the emperor died, and his son, the Bavarian elector Maximilian Joseph, was anxious for accommodation. It came in April: Austria agreed to restore her Bavarian conquests while Bavaria promised to vote for Maria Theresa's husband, Francis Stephen, at the forthcoming imperial election. But Frederick II, too, had resources to draw upon. While his French allies defeated the pragmatic army at Fontenoy in May 1745, Frederick scored some notable victories over an Austrian-Saxon army at Hohenfriedberg in June and over an Austrian army at Soor in September. The drill sergeant's son was proving himself to be a tenacious, inspiring, even brilliant general. His protests against the election of Francis Stephen as Emperor Francis I were unavailing, but he drove the Saxons from the war by routing their troops at Kesseldorf in December. On Christmas Day 1745, the Second Silesian War was settled with the Peace of Dresden. It left Silesia in Frederick's hands, gave Prussia indemnities from Saxony, and guaranteed Frederick's acceptance of Francis' coronation. His people were beginning to call Frederick "the Great." The other belligerents fought on, but the sides were too evenly matched to make continuation of hostilities anything but an absurdity.

In October 1748 the Peace of Aix-la-Chapelle offered a general settlement which had something for everyone and satisfied no one, except Prussia. Its occupation of Silesia was generally recognized; certain Italian possessions of

Austria, notably Parma and Piacenza, were handed over to Spain; England and France, the originators of Aix-la-Chapelle, agreed to keep things as they had been before the outbreak of hostilities (see p. 382). One result of Aix-la-Chapelle cast its shadow far forward, into the mid-nineteenth century: there were now two major German powers—Prussia, still vulnerable and anxious but infinitely more powerful than before 1740, and Austria, wounded and reduced, but after years of battering largely intact.

The Diplomatic Revolution

The Peace of Aix-la-Chapelle was not a peace but a truce. It could not be anything else. Maria Theresa was in no position to retake Silesia, but she was wholly unwilling to cease planning for its eventual reconquest. Britain and France had fought to a standoff, but the wars had brought their colonial rivalries into the forefront. For almost a decade there was a deceptive calm that deceived no one. Rulers exploited the breathing space to undertake domestic reforms for the sake of a stronger military posture next time; diplomats, working feverishly, took up where generals had left off.

It was in Hapsburg Austria that these reforms had their strongest impetus. Maria Theresa, the Catholic empress, supreme housewife, loving spouse, and fertile mother,[19] has often been contrasted with her son and successor, Joseph II, enlightened ruler, cool administrator, radical innovator. The contrast should not be overdrawn. Even in matters of government, Joseph was the son of his mother.[20] Maria Theresa's father, Charles VI, had presided over a glittering and cultivated court and turned high government posts over to the magnates of the realm. His administrative machinery was clumsy and in need of clear directives; state intervention in the economy was half-hearted and unimpressive; the army, despite all Prince Eugene's brave efforts, suffered from poor organization, inadequate provisions, and low morale; the state's debt was astronomical and the treasury almost literally empty. What is more, the ill-assorted lands gathered under the Hapsburg crowns enjoyed a good deal of freedom, which only increased the general sense of laxity and made the collection of adequate taxes a near impossibility. If Maria Theresa wanted to take back Silesia, she needed a stronger bureaucratic, economic, and military base than this. With an energy that secured her the reluctant admiration of Frederick II, she set about constructing it. Her reforms took time—many of them were far from complete in 1763—but she began them early.[21] She decided to leave the relative independence of Hungary untouched, and to obtain troops,

---

[19] Her well-known "good heart" did not extend to the Jews in her realm; they were subject to repeated pogroms and, in 1745, they were expelled from Prague.

[20] For Joseph, see p. 426.

[21] For the late reforms including that of serfdom, see p. 426.

money, and general compliance through persuasion; but she deprived the Austrian and Bohemian diets of their right to vote on taxes and abolished the old separate chanceries that had dealt with their respective realms. Instead, in 1749, she established the Directorium in Publicis et Cameralibus, which handled the regions in common. Administrators with instructions from Vienna replaced the old officials, who had taken orders from, and owed their loyalties to, local estates. In a memorandum intended for her children, Maria Theresa shrewdly recognized the main evil in her realm to be that "various *ministri* only regarded each his own land. It was also a great abuse, which weakened the service, that the Capi and Presidents were paid by the Estates and remunerated by them at their pleasure." [22] This she was determined to cure, though slowly and with her customary good sense: distance did not permit the Viennese bureaucracy to dominate the Italian and Netherlands possessions completely. But in the center, chaos gave way to a certain measure of order. Results became visible after 1748, when Vienna took over the collection of taxes from local estates. Maria Theresa invaded the exemptions of the privileged estates and made nobles and clerics pay substantial taxes. The Hapsburg army could now be strengthened. The empress tightened up the recruiting system and founded a military academy in Vienna. In as many ways as possible, Maria Theresa was diligently imitating Frederick of Prussia in order to defeat him.

For the realization of her ambitious if unsystematic program, the empress found the ministers she deserved. The officials left her at her father's death were well-meaning, elderly, and ineffective; she did not have the heart to dismiss them and instead waited for them to die. They did, in rapid succession, and she replaced them with a group of men who, with her active assistance, reshaped the Hapsburg monarchy. One of these was Count Ludwig Haugwitz, a Silesian aristocrat, who proposed many of the early tax measures and became president of the Directorium upon its establishment. Another was Count Rudolph Chotek, a Czech aristocrat, who succeeded Haugwitz in 1761 and devised the tax laws which drew the whole population into the net of contribution. A third and the most remarkable of these public servants was Prince Wenzel Anton von Kaunitz. He had come to Maria Theresa's attention early in her reign as a skillful diplomat; in 1748 he participated in the settlement at Aix-la-Chapelle; in 1750 he went to Paris as ambassador; and in 1753 his ascendancy was confirmed with his appointment as court and state chancellor. An unbeliever and a rationalist in politics who trusted the power of systematic thinking, he was unhampered by traditional preconceptions. This made him a rather dangerous councillor in domestic, and especially in religious affairs. But in foreign affairs his perception was unsurpassed. The Diplomatic Revolution, which forms the prelude to the Seven Years' War, was largely his work.

From 1748 on, Kaunitz consistently argued that old diplomatic alignments no longer corresponded to realities. England, Austria's ally, had proved worse

---

[22] Quoted in C. A. Macartney, "The Hapsburg Dominions," in *The New Cambridge Modern History*, vol. VII (1957), 411. For Prussian administration, see p. 423.

than worthless; it had pushed Hapsburg negotiators into unfavorable treaties and was clearly interested in Austria simply as a makeweight against France. On the other hand, France, Austria's enemy from time immemorial, no longer had any real reason for its hostility. The Austrian Netherlands were in any case indefensible if France should decide to take them. The true, indeed the sole enemy of Austria, Kaunitz continued, was that new power, Prussia. Consequently, the single aim of Austrian foreign policy must be to isolate Prussia and to secure allies who (unlike Britain) would assist Austria in regaining Silesia. France must be won over so that, recognizing Prussia as a threat to the balance of Europe, France would ally itself with Austria. The idea was so simple that most thought it fantastic. Maria Theresa, encouraged by her wily minister to regard the reconquest of Silesia as a religious crusade, rightly thought it brilliant.

When Kaunitz went to Paris in 1750, he found the French-Prussian alliance firm, and for some time his proposals fell on unsympathetic ears. But then circumstances altered the calculations of France and made it more receptive to Kaunitz's idea for a reversal of alliances. One of these was the game Russia was playing on the diplomatic chessboard. Despite weak and mediocre monarchs, Russia retained the active interest in European affairs that Peter the Great had manifested and fostered. Like Austria, Russia saw Prussia as the enemy—or rather, as the friend of its enemies: the Ottoman Empire, Sweden, and Poland. Austria, on the other hand, was a close ally, formally so after 1726. Russian expansionist drives, toward the Black Sea in the south and the Baltic in the northwest, continued. Prussia was thus, in Russian eyes, a potential obstruction. After Elizabeth was proclaimed tsarina in late 1741, Russia grew even more active in foreign policy, and wholly unreliable. Kaunitz, though, thought he could count on Elizabeth to be consistently anti-Prussian and handled her with great tact. He wanted Russian *and* French aid in the reconquest of Silesia, and the forging of such a combination would take time and subtlety. To complicate matters further, the British concluded a subsidy treaty with Russia in September 1755; it stipulated that the Russians would keep a British-paid army of fifty-five thousand men in their northwestern province of Livonia. This open show of hostility alarmed Frederick of Prussia and precipitated him into a miscalculation. Convinced that he could appease the British if he promised to leave Hanover alone, he approached them and, in January 1756, Britain and Prussia signed what is known as the Convention of Westminster.

It seemed harmless enough; all it provided for was peace in Germany. But the French took a grave view of Frederick's diplomatic initiative: the British, they argued, had been fighting an offensive war against French possessions overseas, and for Prussia, France's ally, to come to terms with Britain, France's enemy, was nothing less than treachery. Whatever it was, the Convention of Westminster did reflect Frederick's low opinion of France and his conviction that if Prussia were attacked, France would be of no real assistance. What Kaunitz's words had not achieved, Frederick's actions did: on May 1, 1756,

France and Austria signed the First Treaty of Versailles. It involved a declaration of Austrian neutrality in the Franco-British war and a defensive alliance. But Kaunitz's triumph was only partial. The agreement was a surprise to Europe, but it did not commit France to the destruction of Prussia. The Russians, on the other hand, were ready. Kaunitz had assiduously kept St. Petersburg informed of the Austro-French negotiations; while the Russians were quizzical about close association with France, Kaunitz had maneuvered them into a position where they could hardly retreat. Elizabeth, in fact, became impatient, and Kaunitz had to hold her back: "The Russians," he wrote in some alarm, "are behaving too precipitately."[23] Elizabeth wanted to move against Prussia in 1756; Kaunitz wanted to prepare more carefully and start war in 1757.

The Colonial Stakes

Elizabeth's irresponsible aggressiveness and Frederick's blundering anxiety were two ingredients in the Diplomatic Revolution; the undeclared war that raged between France and Britain overseas was the third. Much eighteenth-century European history was made in Asia and America; in return, valuable colonies in remote areas were prizes for which European armies battled in the field and diplomats haggled at the conference table. By the time of Walpole and Fleury, Europe's political and economic systems were worldwide. William Pitt's celebrated remark, "America was conquered in Germany," captures this development to perfection. And Pitt was not the only European statesman to recognize that colonial trade was worth a war. Colonial possessions were prized as strategic outposts and commercial centers: Voltaire contemptuously dismissed the Anglo-French struggle over Canada as a quarrel over "a few acres of snow," but this was a rare instance when his judgment was obtuse. In fact, the stakes of the colonial system were high; as consumption of luxury goods and exotic raw materials increased in the eighteenth century, they were raised higher still. To the extent that mercantilism was a system of ideas at all, it was in the doctrine of colonies that the system emerged most clearly. Colonies furnished their mother country with rare materials impossible to raise, mine, or capture in Europe—sugar from the West Indies, fur from Canada, tobacco from Virginia, spices from India—and, in return, a protected market for finished goods. This early imperialism aimed not at the conquest of large territories, but at strategic spots that could be used as ports, trading stations, and gathering depots for slaves and other goods. As one French minister put it in 1765, writing to the governor of the French possession of Martinique: "It would be making a great mistake to think of our colonies as French provinces separated only by the sea from the mother-country. They are absolutely nothing but commercial establishments."[24] By the eighteenth century, Euro-

---

[23] Quoted in Herbert Butterfield, *Man on His Past* (1955), 168.
[24] Quoted in Anderson, *Europe in the Eighteenth Century,* 267.

pean colonies stretched across the known world, but they were tiny dots on the map, normally on the sea, and often widely scattered.

As the earliest colonial powers, Spain and Portugal, lost overseas territories and commercial privileges to upstart rivals, two of these upstarts, France and England, engaged all across the world in a titanic struggle for empire. Wherever Englishmen and Frenchmen sailed and settled—in India, the West Indian islands, the North American continent—they competed with one another, sometimes peacefully, often with force of arms. It was possible for rival companies overseas to be in a state of war while the mother countries in Europe enjoyed peaceful relations. At times it was even possible for the colonists to be at peace while the home countries were at war. But both situations were rare: by the eighteenth century the two realms, Europe and the world, could no longer be kept separate.

India, with its vast resources, half-unexplored domains, and political weakness, had been an inviting hunting ground for venturesome European traders since the early sixteenth century, when the Portuguese seized the port of Goa on India's western coast. The great Mogul Empire, with its capital at Delhi in the north, had established Muslim hegemony over most of India's millions; but its ascendancy of the sixteenth century crumbled in the seventeenth. The tolerant and civilized rule of Akbar set high standards of administrative effectiveness and of diplomatic forbearance with the large number of Hindu sects that his successors could not match. When Akbar died in 1605, his empire underwent a period of slow decline: the Taj Mahal, that star of tourist attractions, was built between 1632 and 1653 by Shah Jehan, one of Akbar's successors, as a tomb for his beloved wife—symbol if not of artistic, then of political decadence. It was in Shah Jehan's time, in 1639, that the site of Madras on the east coast was granted to the English East India Company. Aurangzeb, Akbar's last notable successor, devoted much of his long reign— 1659 to 1707—to a reversal of Akbar's policies. He prohibited the exercise of Hindu worship and destroyed Hindu temples, and thus invited widespread Hindu uprisings, led by the militant Sikhs. These uprisings, coupled with incursions across the frontier by Afghan tribes, produced growing disorder and, after Aurangzeb's death, open anarchy. Princes once subservient to the Moguls declared their independence, and India became a mere geographic expression— a patchwork of small and large kingdoms.

While this chaotic, fluid situation held its dangers for the colonial settlements on the coast, it also offered an unprecedented opportunity. Bold officials of the French and English East India companies alike bargained for privileges with local potentates and meddled in local politics. It was this meddling that proved the undoing of the marquis Dupleix, commandant general of the French East India Company. The French had come to India fairly late, in the time of Louis XIV, and had established several prosperous "factories"—commercial settlements—chiefly at Surat, Pondicherry, and Mahé. Part commercial agent, part military commander, part empire-builder, Dupleix, ambitious and sanguine, repeatedly exceeded his instructions. In 1746, while England and France were at war in Europe, he took Madras, but his conquest was annulled in 1748, in the settlement at Aix-la-Chapelle. Peace in Europe did not bring peace in Asia; the idea of a French empire, including an array of native puppet rulers, seems to have grown in Dupleix's inventive mind, and when the rulerships of the Carnatic and the Deccan fell vacant, he intervened. Ably seconded by the generalship of the marquis de Bussy, Dupleix for a time in effect ruled both regions. His first setback came in September 1751 when Robert Clive, Dupleix's English counterpart, took Arcot and, later, other towns in Madras. This held the French troops in check. In 1754, Dupleix was recalled, but the hostilities between French and English forces did not abate. With the coming of general war in 1756, the battles between the French and English East India companies merged into the wider conflict.

Similar confrontations marked the encounter of the British and French in America. At the Peace of Utrecht the British had acquired some valuable French possessions that strengthened their hold on the east coast of the American continent and in the West Indies. They won access to the rich cod fisheries; Hudson Bay, with its share of the Canadian fur trade; Acadia (Nova Scotia), a strategic base for operations against the French; and St. Kitts, another toehold on the rich sugar islands of the West Indies. In the Caribbean the British held several islands, in addition to St. Kitts, Jamaica, Antigua, and Barbados. The French, for their part, despite their losses at Utrecht, were well placed for economic exploitation and military adventure. They built the fortress of Louisbourg in Nova Scotia to counteract a possible threat from the British in the north; they founded New Orleans to gain access to the Mississippi from the sea; they consolidated their alliances with Indian tribes whom they managed with a suppleness and a real understanding that eluded the British.

There was trouble all along this extended frontier. In June 1745, New England militiamen supported by an English naval squadron, took Louisbourg, but, just as Madras in India reverted to the British at Aix-la-Chapelle, so did Louisbourg to the French in the same settlement, to the outrage of the colonists. In the West Indies, there was a similar standoff; British vessels vigorously harassed and successfully disrupted French trade for a time, but Aix-la-Chapelle temporarily restored calm in the islands. On the American mainland the conflict was more extensive and more virulent. The French treated the Ohio valley as private preserve, but British land speculators were eager to challenge this monopoly. Virginians formed the Ohio Company, and British colonists started ambitious settlements in the "French" region. The French quickly responded by strengthening their old forts and building new ones. The core of their military position was Fort Duquesne on the site of what is now Pittsburgh. "It was their absolute Design to take Possession of the *Ohio*," they told the young British officer George Washington, "and by G— they would do it." [25] In

---

[25] Quoted in John A. Garraty, *The American Nation: A History of the United States to 1877* (2nd ed., 1971), 108.

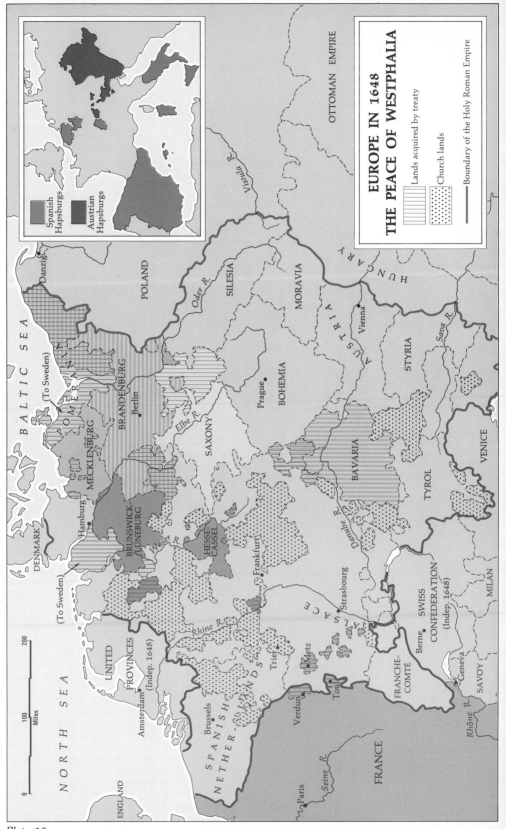

EUROPE IN 1648
THE PEACE OF WESTPHALIA

Lands acquired by treaty
Church lands
Boundary of the Holy Roman Empire

Spanish Hapsburgs
Austrian Hapsburgs

OTTOMAN EMPIRE

Vistula R.

POLAND

SILESIA

Oder R.

MORAVIA

H U N G A R Y

Vienna

AUSTRIA

STYRIA

Sava R.

Prague
BOHEMIA

SAXONY

Elbe R.

BAVARIA

TYROL

VENICE

Berlin

BRANDENBURG

P O M E R A N I A

(To Sweden)

BALTIC SEA

Danzig

MECKLENBURG

Hamburg

BRUNSWICK-LUNEBURG

Weser R.

HESSE-CASSEL

Frankfurt

Danube R.

Strasbourg

SWISS CONFEDERATION (Indep. 1648)

Berne

MILAN

DENMARK

(To Sweden)

Rhine R.

S P A N I S H   N E T H E R - L A N D S

Trier

A L S A C E

Metz

Toul

FRANCHE-COMTÉ

Geneva

SAVOY

Rhône R.

UNITED PROVINCES (Indep. 1648)

Amsterdam

Brussels

Verdun

FRANCE

Seine R.

Paris

NORTH SEA

200

100

Miles

0

ENGLAND

Plate 15

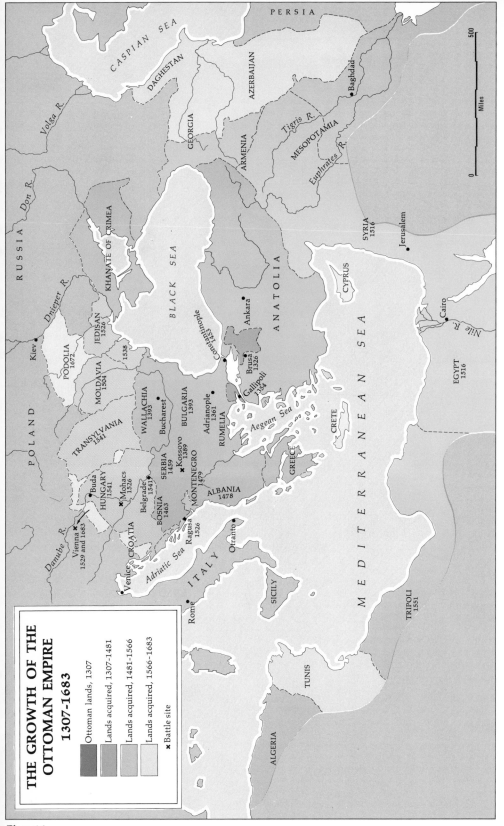

THE GROWTH OF THE
OTTOMAN EMPIRE
1307-1683

Ottoman lands, 1307
Lands acquired, 1307-1481
Lands acquired, 1481-1566
Lands acquired, 1566-1683
× Battle site

PERSIA

CASPIAN SEA

DAGHESTAN

AZERBAIJAN

Baghdad

GEORGIA

ARMENIA

MESOPOTAMIA

Tigris R.

Euphrates R.

Volga R.

Don R.

RUSSIA

KHANATE OF CRIMEA

Dnieper R.

BLACK SEA

ANATOLIA

SYRIA
1516

Jerusalem

Cairo

Nile R.

EGYPT
1516

Kiev

PODOLIA
1672

POLAND

JEDISAN
1526

1538

MOLDAVIA
1504

Ankara

Constantinople
1453

Brusa
1326

CYPRUS

MEDITERRANEAN SEA

TRANSYLVANIA
1541

WALLACHIA
1393

Bucharest

BULGARIA
1393

Adrianople
1361

RUMELIA

Gallipoli
1354

Aegean Sea

CRETE

Buda

Mohacs
1526

HUNGARY
1541

Belgrade
1541

SERBIA
1459

Kossovo
1389

MONTENEGRO
1479

BOSNIA
1463

Ragusa
1526

ALBANIA
1478

GREECE

Vienna
1529 and 1683

Danube R.

CROATIA

Venice

Adriatic Sea

ITALY

Otranto

Rome

SICILY

TRIPOLI
1551

TUNIS

ALGERIA

500

Miles

0

Plate 16

The Growth of the Ottoman Empire • 1307–1683

The Ottomans came out of Central Asia where they had roamed since the sixth century as a subgroup of the Turks, dispersed from Mongolia to the Near East. Although many tribes were called "Turk," they were joined by no ethnic ties but related as a linguistic family. In the ninth and tenth centuries, the Ottomans were converted to Islam. As nomads, they moved westward; by the eleventh century they had conquered their way to lands close to Constantinople and set themselves up in warlike posture at the borders of the Byzantine Empire.

The Ottomans, or Osmanlis, took their name from their first dynastic ruler Osman I who, between 1290 and 1326, chipped away at the Byzantine Empire reaching as far west as Brusa, which fell in 1326. Orkhan I, Osman's successor, consolidated the empire into a self-conscious entity, striking coins and taking the title Sultan of the Ghazis—warrior of the faith. Wars of conquest took on the quality of crusades. In 1354 Orkhan established the first permanent Turkish settlement in Europe at Gallipoli. In 1366, having taken Adrianople, the Turks moved their capital from Asia Minor and continued their pressure into Europe. In a string of victories in Bulgaria, Serbia, and Bosnia during the next century, they subdued the entire Balkan peninsula.

Under Mohammed II, the Ottomans captured Constantinople in May 1453, ending a thousand years of Christian rule in Asia Minor. Mohammed made Constantinople into a flourishing capital; its population grew from 10,000 in 1453 to 70,000 by the end of his reign in 1481. Not content with Constantinople, the Turks continued to push westward, and in a war with Venice, 1463–1479, won most of Albania and Venetian tribute. In 1480, the year before his death, Mohammed took Otranto on the Adriatic.

The legendary brutality of the Turks was not confined to foreigners. It was a long-standing, drastic practice for new rulers to consummate their accession by killing all contenders, that is, their brothers and sons. Mohammed made this practice into law and did, indeed, stabilize the succession. The height of Ottoman power and culture was reached under Suleiman the Magnificent (1520–1566) who penetrated farther into Europe than his predecessors. In 1526 he defeated the Hungarians at Mohacz, and in 1529 he reached and besieged Vienna. But a month of bad weather and determined resistance by the Viennese led him to withdraw. He maintained a foothold in the west, waging war with Venice over the straits of Otranto and with Charles V over Tunis. Within five years after his retreat from Vienna, he conquered Baghdad and Mesopotamia and reached Tabriz.

The fear inspired by Suleiman's Empire, more powerful than any in Europe, led in 1538 to the Holy League which included Charles V, the Pope, and Venice. In 1571, under Selim II (Suleiman's son), Pius V organized a second Holy League, which backed its intentions with an allied fleet under Don John of Austria. The allied victory at Lepanto, October 1571, was thrown away when Spain and Venice fell out, which permitted the Turks to rebuild their fleet. The Turkish Empire began to suffer from the internal weakness produced by its system of succession, which led to puppet emperors; real power was divided between competing viziers and a professional military corps, the Janissaries. It took another century before the Turks once again mustered the strength to mount a last unsuccessful attack on Europe.

SWEDEN UNDER THE VASAS
1523-1660

Under Gustavus Vasa, 1523-1560

Lands acquired by Eric XIV and John III, 1560-1592

Lands acquired by Gustavus II, Adolphus and Christina, 1611-1654

Lands acquired by Charles X, 1654-1660

Seas frozen in winter

ARCTIC OCEAN

ATLANTIC OCEAN

LAPLAND

Tonia

RUSSIA

TRONDHEIM (To Sweden 1658-1660)

HERJEDALEN

Vasa

FINLAND

KARELIA (To Russia 1721)

NORWAY

S W E D E N

Lake Ladoga

Christiana

DALECARLIA

Nystad

Vyborg

GULF OF BOTHNIA

GULF OF FINLAND

INGRIA (To Russia 1721)

Stockholm

DAGÖ

ESTONIA (To Russia 1721)

BOHUS

ÖSEL

RUSSIA

Göteborg

GOTLAND

LIVONIA (To Russia 1721)

HALLAND

Riga

DENMARK

SCANIA

B A L T I C   S E A

Copenhagen

Malmö

Memel

Königsberg

LITHUANIA

Lübeck

Danzig

PRUSSIA

BREMEN (To Hanover 1719)

Hamburg

HITHER POMERANIA (To Prussia 1720)

BRANDENBURG

POLAND

H O L Y   R O M A N   E M P I R E

0 ——— 300
Miles

Plate 17

Sweden Under the Vasas • 1523–1660

In 1397 the three major countries of Scandinavia—Sweden, Norway, and Denmark—formed the Kalmar Union under the leadership of Queen Margaret of Sweden and accepted her nephew, Eric of Pomerania, as their joint king. The Union proved unstable, lasting only until Margaret's death in 1412. The ensuing years were bloody struggles as Eric tried to weld his territories into one kingdom and to push his Danish border south. Popular opposition to a powerful monarch led to his deposition in 1439 by Denmark and Sweden and in 1442 by Norway. In Sweden the state council (later the *Riksdag* or parliament) seized power and reverted to the system of electing a king. Denmark, too, elected its own king, Christian I, who succeeded in establishing a dynasty, while Norway became the vassal of Denmark and remained its subordinate until 1815.

In the sixteenth century, a complex struggle between Sweden and Denmark ensued; it included a period of temporary union, a revolt by Sweden, and a battle in which the regent of Sweden, Sten Sture, was killed. After the Danes' victory, the Danish king, Christian II, grandson of Christian I, was made king of Sweden in 1520. He marked his coronation several months later by a massacre of the nobles attached to the late regent's party, an event known in Swedish history as the Stockholm Bloodbath.

One of those who escaped, Gustavus Eriksson, whose father had been killed in the massacre, continued the struggle for independence. He enlisted the support of the city of Lübeck and the Hanseatic League, whose merchants had a strong interest in Swedish trade. By 1523, having led a peasant army against the Danes, he was elected king of Sweden by the *Riksdag* and took the name of Gustavus I Vasa.

During his long reign from 1523 to 1560 Gustavus presided over the emergence of Sweden as a great Baltic power and its conversion to Lutheranism. In 1526 the New Testament was published in a Swedish translation. In 1527 the state took actions that markedly weakened Catholic power in Sweden: the *Riksdag* made the appointment of bishops the prerogative of the king rather than the church, and simultaneously ceased to send its annual tribute to Rome. Meanwhile, church holdings were confiscated, an action caused in part by the government's need to raise funds for its Lübeck creditors. In 1529 church services were reformed to follow the Protestant order. It was not until 1537, however, following a war with Lübeck that Sweden freed itself from the economic domination of the Hanseatic League.

In addition to winning political and spiritual independence for Sweden, Gustavus persuaded the *Riksdag* to declare his family hereditary monarchs of Sweden, and on his death his crown passed without dispute to his son Eric XIV. Despite the expansion of Swedish territory to include Reval and Estonia under Eric, his reign was clouded by insanity which led to the elevation of his brother John III to the kingship in 1568. John's son, Sigismund, who succeeded him in 1593, was also king of Poland, and attempted to reimpose Catholicism on Sweden. An ensuing rebellion in 1599 led to the regency of Charles IX, Gustavus' youngest son, who took immediate action to have the *Riksdag* declare Lutheranism the state religion. Charles became king in 1604 and during his seven-year reign entered two wars that outlasted his lifetime. A war with Denmark over Lapland ended in defeat in 1613; another with Poland endured until the Peace of Oliva in 1660. On his death in 1611, he was succeeded by his son, Gustavus II Adolphus.

THE ENGLISH CIVIL WAR
1642-1646

Land controlled by Royalists,
Aug. 1642

Land controlled by Parliamentarians,
Aug. 1642

Land controlled by Royalists,
end of 1645

Land controlled by Parliamentarians,
end of 1645

✗ Battles

SCOTLAND

Glasgow
Edinburgh

Philipaugh
1645

Newburn
1640
Newcastle

NORTH
SEA

ISLE OF MAN

IRISH
SEA

IRELAND

Marston
Moor
1644

Hull
1643

Preston
1643

ENGLAND

Trent R.

Lichfield
1643

Naseby
1645

Nen R.

Ouse

WALES

Severn R.

Edge Hill
1642

Cambridge

Monmouth

Pembroke

Thames R.

Turnham
Green
1643

London

Newbury
1643 and 1644

Dover

Langport
1645

ISLE OF WIGHT

Bradock Down
1643

ENGLISH   CHANNEL

FRANCE

0   50   100
Miles

Plate 18

**WARS OF LOUIS XIV
1667-1697**

Treaty of Aix-la-Chapelle, 1668:

To France

Treaty of Nimwegen, 1678-1679:

To France

To Spain

Treaty of Ryswick, 1697:

To France

—— Boundary of France, 1648

◄—— William's invasion of England, 1688

DENMARK

ENGLAND

Amsterdam • UNITED
The Hague • PROVINCES

HOLY

ROMAN

EMPIRE

London

Tor Bay

ENGLISH CHANNEL

FLANDERS
Brussels • Liège
LILLE SPANISH NETHERLANDS • Aix-la-Chapelle
ARTOIS
LUXEMBURG

RHENISH
PALATINATE

Philippsburg •

Rhine R.

Seine R.

LORRAINE ALSACE • Strasbourg

Paris

Nantes •

FRANCHE-
COMTÉ

SWITZERLAND

FRANCE

ATLANTIC

OCEAN

Loire R.

Geneva •

SAVOY

MILAN

Rhône R.

Bordeaux •

Garonne R.

AVIGNON •

Marseilles •

ROUSSILLON
(To France 1659)

SPAIN

0   100   200
Miles

Members of the League of Augsburg:
Austria   Savoy
Brandenburg   Spain
England   Sweden
Holy Roman Empire United
Hungary   Provinces

Plate 19

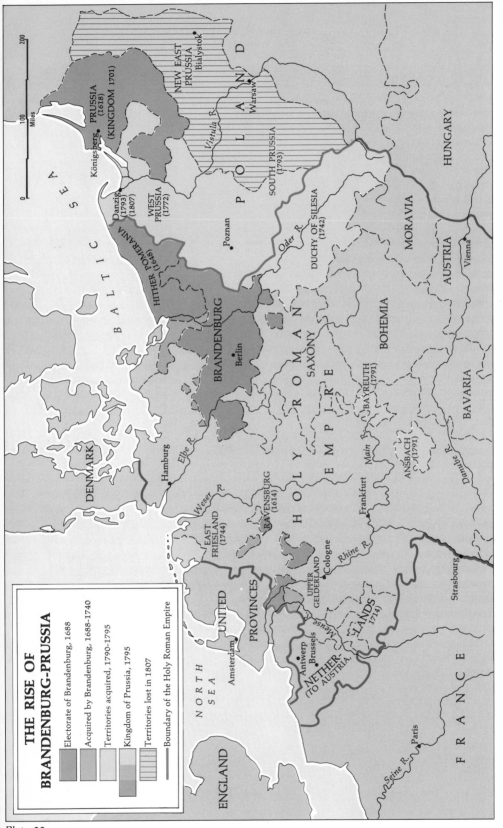

THE RISE OF
BRANDENBURG-PRUSSIA

Electorate of Brandenburg, 1688

Acquired by Brandenburg, 1688–1740

Territories acquired, 1790–1795

Kingdom of Prussia, 1795

Territories lost in 1807

Boundary of the Holy Roman Empire

NORTH SEA

BALTIC SEA

DENMARK

ENGLAND

UNITED PROVINCES

Amsterdam

Antwerp
Brussels
NETHER-LANDS
(TO AUSTRIA) 1714

FRANCE

Paris

Seine R.

Strasbourg

Rhine R.

Cologne

UPPER GELDERLAND

RAVENSBURG (1614)

EAST FRIESLAND (1744)

Hamburg

Weser R.

Elbe R.

Frankfurt

Main R.

ANSBACH (1791)

BAYREUTH (1791)

Danube R.

BAVARIA

BOHEMIA

SAXONY

HOLY ROMAN EMPIRE

BRANDENBURG

Berlin

HITHER POMERANIA (1648)

Danzig (1793) (1807)

WEST PRUSSIA (1772)

Königsberg

PRUSSIA (1618) (KINGDOM 1701)

NEW EAST PRUSSIA

Białystok

Warsaw

POLAND

Vistula R.

SOUTH PRUSSIA (1793)

Poznan

Oder R.

DUCHY OF SILESIA (1742)

MORAVIA

AUSTRIA

Vienna

HUNGARY

Miles
0   100   200

Plate 20

The Rise of Brandenburg-Prussia

Medieval Brandenburg had a mixed population of Slavs and Teutons whose languages showed their mutual distaste. The German word for Slavs referred to their earlier status as slaves, while the Slavic word for Teutons, *Niemtsi,* nonspeaking, reflected on their "barbarism." The Germans prevailed, steadily pushing eastward, overcoming and absorbing the Slavs and converting them to Christianity. The borders of Brandenburg had been roughly set in the tenth century as a diocese between the Elbe and the Oder and widened in succeeding centuries by the Ascanian ruling house to the valley of the Vistula. Here they were repulsed by the Teutonic knights, a militant religious order that was carving a new state out of the lands east of the Vistula in the name of a crusade to convert the Slavs. By the fourteenth century their relentless warfare had won them the districts that make up Prussia.

As the Margraves of Brandenburg, the Ascanian house became one of the seven electors of the Holy Roman Empire in the thirteenth century. When their line died out, the Hohenzollerns succeeded them in 1415; by diplomacy and marriage they built a powerful state out of an unpromising principality. By 1618 the Hohenzollerns straddled northern Europe with territories scattered from the Rhine to the Niemen.

A claim to Pomerania, which did not materialize until 1637, was based on a treaty of 1529 which names the Margraves of Brandenburg as successors to the ruling house should that line fail. Earlier, a marriage in 1591 of John Sigismund of Brandenburg to Princess Anne, eldest daughter of the duke of Prussia, advanced some of the Hohenzollerns' greatest ambitions. In 1609 on the death of Anne's uncle, duke of Cleves and Jülich, both were claimed and won by her husband because the duke had left no heir.

When Anne's father died in 1618, also without male heir, John Sigismund became duke of Prussia; he survived by only two years and was succeeded by his son Georg William. But Georg William's power over his territories was sharply limited by the local Estates, and further weakened during the Thirty Years' War when Imperial troops invaded Brandenburg in 1627 and Swedish troops took Berlin in 1631. Even when he fell heir to Pomerania in 1637 under the terms of the old agreement, he was unable to take it from the Swedes. Paradoxically, during this time the Elector's chief minister tightened his control over the Estates of Brandenburg and Prussia by levying taxes.

On Georg William's death in 1640 his son Frederick William, then 20, succeeded and used his power of taxation so effectively that within several decades he had laid the foundations for an absolutist regime. He expelled the Swedes from Brandenburg; at the Peace of Westphalia in 1648 he received eastern Pomerania and three bishoprics in western Germany. In the Northern War between Sweden and Poland (1655 to 1660), Frederick William fought first with Sweden and then with Poland and managed at the Peace of Oliva to gain general European recognition of Brandenburg's sovereignty over Prussia. By this judicious combination of diplomacy and arms, the Great Elector assembled a territory of 40,000 square miles, second in the Holy Roman Empire only to Austria.

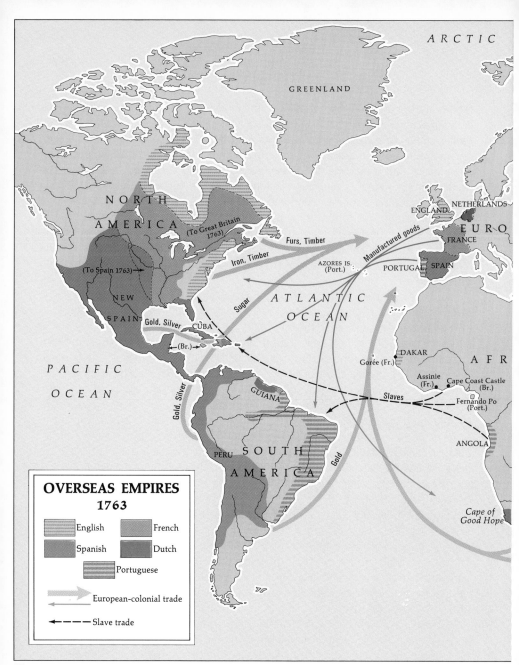

ARCTIC

GREENLAND

NORTH
AMERICA

(To Great Britain 1763)

(To Spain 1763)

NEW
SPAIN

Gold, Silver

CUBA

(Br.)

Gold, Silver

PACIFIC
OCEAN

GUIANA

PERU

SOUTH
AMERICA

Gold

Furs, Timber

Iron, Timber

Sugar

ATLANTIC
OCEAN

Manufactured goods

AZORES IS.
(Port.)

ENGLAND

NETHERLANDS

EURO

FRANCE

PORTUGAL

SPAIN

DAKAR

Gorée (Fr.)

AFR

Assinie
(Fr.)

Cape Coast Castle
(Br.)

Fernando Po
(Port.)

Slaves

ANGOLA

Cape of
Good Hope

OVERSEAS EMPIRES
1763

English   French

Spanish   Dutch

Portuguese

European-colonial trade

- - - - Slave trade

Plate 21

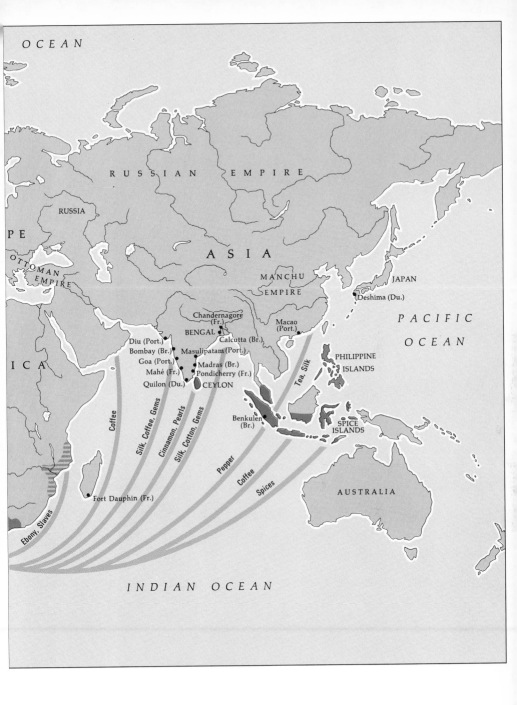

OCEAN

RUSSIAN EMPIRE

RUSSIA

PE

OTTOMAN
EMPIRE

ICA

ASIA

MANCHU
EMPIRE

JAPAN

Deshima (Du.)

PACIFIC

OCEAN

Chandernagore
(Fr.)
BENGAL
Diu (Port.)
Calcutta (Br.)
Bombay (Br.)
Masulipatam (Port.)
Goa (Port.)
Madras (Br.)
Mahé (Fr.)
Pondicherry (Fr.)
Quilon (Du.)
CEYLON

Macao
(Port.)

PHILIPPINE
ISLANDS

Tea, Silk

Coffee

Silk, Coffee, Gems

Cinnamon, Pearls

Silk, Cotton, Gems

Benkulen
(Br.)

SPICE
ISLANDS

Pepper

Coffee

Spices

AUSTRALIA

Fort Dauphin (Fr.)

Ebony, Slaves

INDIAN OCEAN

Plate 23

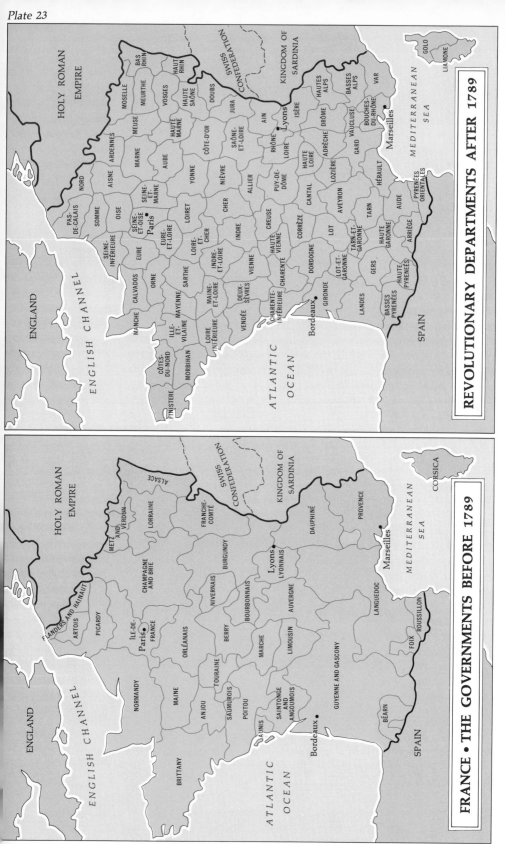

REVOLUTIONARY DEPARTMENTS AFTER 1789

HOLY ROMAN EMPIRE

SWISS CONFEDERATION

KINGDOM OF SARDINIA

GOLO

LIAMONE

MOSELLE

BAS RHIN

HAUT RHIN

MEURTHE

VOSGES

HAUTE SAÔNE

DOUBS

JURA

AIN

HAUTES ALPS

BASSES ALPS

VAR

ARDENNES

MEUSE

HAUTE MARNE

CÔTE-D'OR

SAÔNE-ET-LOIRE

RHÔNE

ISÈRE

Lyons

DRÔME

VAUCLUSE

BOUCHES-DU-RHÔNE

Marseilles

MEDITERRANEAN SEA

NORD

AISNE

MARNE

AUBE

YONNE

NIÈVRE

LOIRE

HAUTE LOIRE

ARDÈCHE

GARD

HÉRAULT

PAS-DE-CALAIS

SOMME

OISE

SEINE-ET-MARNE

ALLIER

PUY-DE-DÔME

LOZÈRE

PYRÉNÉES ORIENTALES

SEINE-INFÉRIEURE

EURE

SEINE-ET-OISE

Paris

LOIRET

CHER

INDRE

CREUSE

HAUTE VIENNE

CANTAL

AVEYRON

TARN

AUDE

CALVADOS

ORNE

EURE-ET-LOIR

LOIRE-ET-CHER

CORRÈZE

LOT

TARN-ET-GARONNE

HAUTE GARONNE

ARIÈGE

MANCHE

MAYENNE

SARTHE

INDRE-ET-LOIRE

VIENNE

DORDOGNE

LOT-ET-GARONNE

GERS

HAUTE PYRÉNÉES

ILLE-ET-VILAINE

MAINE-ET-LOIRE

DEUX-SÈVRES

CHARENTE

Bordeaux

GIRONDE

LANDES

BASSES PYRÉNÉES

CÔTES-DU-NORD

MORBIHAN

LOIRE-INFÉRIEURE

VENDÉE

CHARENTE-INFÉRIEURE

FINISTÈRE

ENGLAND

ENGLISH CHANNEL

ATLANTIC OCEAN

SPAIN

FRANCE • THE GOVERNMENTS BEFORE 1789

HOLY ROMAN EMPIRE

SWISS CONFEDERATION

KINGDOM OF SARDINIA

CORSICA

ALSACE

METZ AND VERDUN

LORRAINE

FRANCHE-COMTÉ

FLANDERS AND HAINAUT

ARTOIS

PICARDY

CHAMPAGNE AND BRIE

BURGUNDY

NIVERNAIS

BOURBONNAIS

Lyons

LYONNAIS

DAUPHINÉ

PROVENCE

Marseilles

MEDITERRANEAN SEA

ÎLE-DE-FRANCE

Paris

ORLÉANAIS

BERRY

MARCHE

AUVERGNE

LIMOUSIN

LANGUEDOC

ROUSSILLON

NORMANDY

MAINE

TOURAINE

ANJOU

SAUMUROIS

POITOU

SAINTONGE AND ANGOUMOIS

GUYENNE AND GASCONY

FOIX

BÉARN

BRITTANY

AUNIS

Bordeaux

ATLANTIC OCEAN

ENGLAND

ENGLISH CHANNEL

SPAIN

Plate 22

ARCTIC
OCEAN

ATLANTIC
OCEAN

NORWAY

SWEDEN

FINLAND

BALTIC SEA

St. Petersburg

Riga

NOVGOROD

N. Dvina R.

SIBERIA

U R A L   M O U N T A I N S

Danzig

W. Dvina R.

Moscow

P R U S S I A

POLAND

Warsaw

R U S S I A

Volga R.

Ural R.

HOLY

ROMAN

EMPIRE

Danube R.

AUSTRIA

Vistula R.

Don R.

Astrakhan

HUNGARY

(Boundary of Poland before
the 1st partition 1772)

CRIMEA

C A U C A S U S   M T S.

CASPIAN
SEA

ITALY

BLACK SEA

Kiev

Constantinople

O T T O M A N   E M P I R E

M E D I T E R R A N E A N   S E A

THE GROWTH OF RUSSIA

Russia in 1682

Acquired, 1682-1762

Acquired, 1762-1796

0   500
Miles

THE PARTITIONS OF POLAND

BALTIC SEA

LITHUANIA

(To Russia)

(To
Prussia)

(To Prussia)

(To Prussia)

(To Russia)

(To Austria)

PODELIA

(To Russia)

(To Austria)

1st partition,
1772

2nd partition,
1793

3rd partition,
1795

0   200
Miles

Plate 24

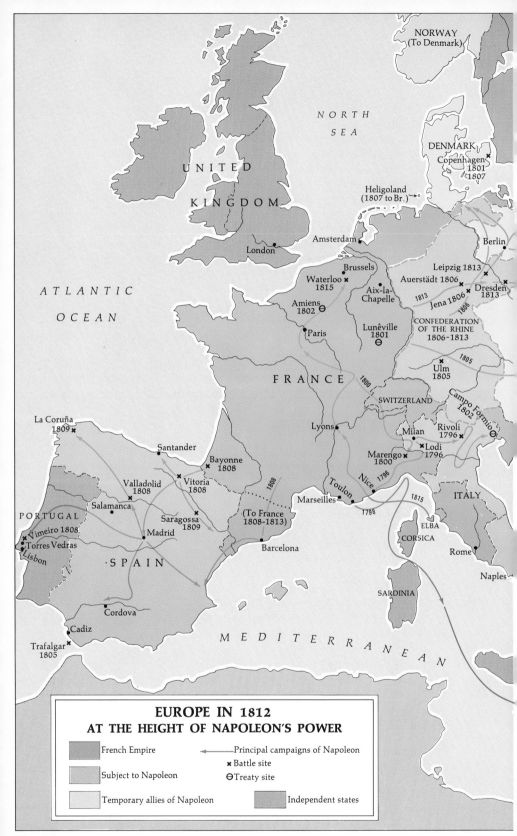

NORWAY
(To Denmark)

*NORTH
SEA*

DENMARK
Copenhagen
1801
1807

Berlin

Heligoland
(1807 to Br.)

UNITED

KINGDOM

Amsterdam

London

Leipzig 1813

Brussels

Auerstädt 1806

Waterloo
1815

Aix-la-
Chapelle

Dresden
1813

ATLANTIC

Amiens
1802

1813

Jena 1806

OCEAN

Paris

Lunéville
1801

CONFEDERATION
OF THE RHINE
1806-1813

1806

1805

Ulm
1805

F R A N C E

1800

SWITZERLAND

Campo Formio
1802

La Coruña
1809

Lyons

Milan

Rivoli
1796

Santander

Bayonne
1808

Marengo
1800

Lodi
1796

Valladolid
1808

Vitoria
1808

1796

1808

Salamanca

Toulon

Nice

1815

ITALY

Saragossa
1809

Marseilles

1798

P O R T U G A L

Madrid

(To France
1808-1813)

ELBA

Vimeiro 1808

CORSICA

Torres Vedras

Barcelona

Rome

Lisbon

S P A I N

Naples

Cordova

SARDINIA

Cadiz

Trafalgar
1805

M E D I T E R R A N E A N

EUROPE IN 1812
AT THE HEIGHT OF NAPOLEON'S POWER

French Empire	Principal campaigns of Napoleon
	✕ Battle site
Subject to Napoleon	⊖ Treaty site
Temporary allies of Napoleon	Independent states

Plate 25

SWEDEN

BALTIC SEA

Tilsit 1807

1812

Vilna

Danzig

Friedland
1807

Eylau 1807

PRUSSIA

DUCHY OF

1806

WARSAW

Warsaw

Austerlitz 1805

Vienna   Wagram 1809

Pressburg 1805

AUSTRIA

Leoben

HUNGARY

RUSSIA

Borodino
1812

Moscow

Smolensk
1812

BLACK   SEA

ILLYRIAN PROVINCES

ADRIATIC SEA

NAPLES

OTTOMAN

EMPIRE

Constantinople

AEGEAN SEA

SICILY

IONIAN ISLANDS
(To Venice to 1797;
to France 1797-1799
and 1807-1815; to
Russia 1799-1807)

SEA

CRETE

CYPRUS

Acre

0   500

Miles

Alexandria
1798

Cairo

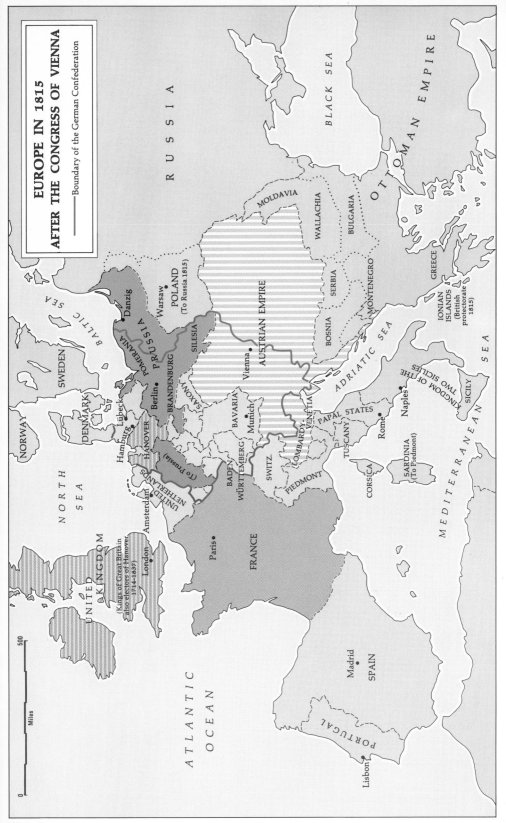

EUROPE IN 1815
AFTER THE CONGRESS OF VIENNA

——— Boundary of the German Confederation

RUSSIA

BLACK SEA

OTTOMAN EMPIRE

MOLDAVIA

WALLACHIA

BULGARIA

SERBIA

BOSNIA

MONTENEGRO

GREECE

IONIAN
ISLANDS
(British
protectorate
1815)

BALTIC SEA

SWEDEN

NORWAY

DENMARK

POMERANIA

PRUSSIA

Danzig

Warsaw

POLAND
(To Russia 1815)

SILESIA

BRANDENBURG

Berlin

SAXONY

Lübeck

Hamburg

HANOVER

(To Prussia)

AUSTRIAN EMPIRE

Vienna

BAVARIA

Munich

WÜRTTEMBERG

BADEN

SWITZ.

PIEDMONT

LOMBARDY

VENETIA

PAPAL STATES

TUSCANY

Rome

SARDINIA
(To Piedmont)

CORSICA

KINGDOM OF THE
TWO SICILIES

Naples

SICILY

ADRIATIC SEA

MEDITERRANEAN SEA

NORTH
SEA

UNITED
KINGDOM

(Kings of Great Britain
also electors of Hanover
1714–1837)

London

Amsterdam

UNITED
NETHERLANDS

Paris

FRANCE

ATLANTIC
OCEAN

Madrid

SPAIN

PORTUGAL

Lisbon

500

Miles

0

Plate 26

1753, they sent a detachment of troops. In June 1754, the British Board of Trade called a conference at Albany, attended by representatives of the Iroquois and of seven colonies. Here, Benjamin Franklin proposed a statesmanlike plan of union, but the colonial legislatures, too parochial for concerted action, had no intention of ratifying it. Military action alone was left. It was a disaster—for the British: in July 1755, the British commander, General Braddock, allowed himself to be surprised near Fort Duquesne. Braddock was killed, his troops fled, and the plan against the French forts was dropped, for a time. American historians like to remember that one officer who distinguished himself in this dismal campaign was Colonel George Washington. Both sides skirmished and constructed fortified places for future use. Action was not long in coming.

The Climax of the Anglo-French Struggle Overseas

After 1756, the continuing Anglo-French struggle was part of a general war, the Seven Years' War.[26] As we know, we cannot separate the action in India and America from that in Europe. At the same time, while the outbreak of the Seven Years' War in Europe was marked by distinct acts of aggression and followed a period of intense diplomacy, overseas the war was simply the continuation of a war that had been going on intermittently for some time. In India, Britain's declaration of war on France simply lent a sheen of legality to Clive's military operations and encouraged him to broaden his activities. In a series of encounters, Clive took Calcutta back from its Indian ruler, conquered the French fort of Chandernagor, and in June 1757, routed the French and their native allies at the decisive battle of Plassey. A brilliant and brooding man, Clive was laying the foundation for British supremacy over the large Bengal region in the northeast and the Carnatic in the south, and for extensive British dominion over most of the Indian subcontinent. Native rulers were puppets moving to Clive's orders. England watched, amazed, impressed, but also a little uneasy: Clive had opened the way to vast power, vast profits, and their inevitable shadow, vast corruption. But these problems were still in the future. When the powers made peace at Paris in 1763, the French retained a few stations in India, including Pondicherry and Chandernagor, but in substance, India became a British dependency. It was to bring Britain profits beyond the dreams of Clive.

In America, the profits were to prove more problematical. The war, after unpromising beginnings, was a series of heady triumphs for Pitt, his army and even more, his navy. By supplying his Prussian ally with generous subsidies, Pitt freed his hand for wide-ranging military action. The British navy concentrated on harassing the French fleet, capturing and sinking as many vessels as it could and bottling up the others in their ports. The British armies, too, fought

---

[26] In America, this war is known as the French and Indian War.

bravely and, by and large, intelligently. In July 1758, General Wolfe took Louisbourg; in November, General Forbes took Fort Duquesne and promptly renamed it Fort Pitt. Early in 1759, the British captured the rich sugar island of Guadeloupe; in November, Hawke permanently disabled the French navy in America with a splendid victory in Quiberon Bay. Meanwhile, in September, the British had taken Quebec, after the romantic battle of the Plains of Abraham, celebrated by historians, poets, and painters. Quebec was a strongly defended citadel, ably manned by French troops under Montcalm. After feints and explorations, Wolfe discovered access to Quebec across the Plains of Abraham just outside the fortifications, and after a pitched battle, took the fortress itself. Both Wolfe and Montcalm died in combat, but victory went to the British. In September 1760, Montreal, too, surrendered to them, and Canada was in their hands. Then, in 1762, the British took Grenada, Martinique, and the other French islands in the West Indies. As we shall soon see, they did not keep them long; but the general settlement of 1763 gave Britain a far larger and far more secure hold on America than it had had before (see p. 401).

War and Peace in Europe

As in 1740, so in 1756, it was Frederick II of Prussia who brought war to Europe. In August he marched into Saxony; early in September he took Dresden, and in October, after he defeated the Austrian army at Lobositz, the Saxon army surrendered. As in 1740, so now, Frederick's move was an act of aggression, but in 1756 he had a real, in place of a trumped-up, excuse: while he did not fully recognize the extent of Tsarina Elizabeth's designs, he knew that his enemies planned to attack and eventually to dismember Prussia. His assault on Saxony was a preventive war; his plan was to win a quick victory campaign of surprise.

But while his early successes gave Frederick significant advantages, victory eluded him and he was forced into the very kind of war he had feared—long-drawn-out and on several fronts. Frederick had a thoroughly trained military machine, a handful of minor allies, and enormous subsidies from Pitt; the allies had vast armies, superior resources, and a thirst for revenge. Frederick fought bravely and brillantly, driving his troops, and himself, to exertions excessive even for him—Frederick veered during these years between elation and depression, confident predictions and suicidal fantasies. His victories became proverbial; every German schoolchild for two centuries after could rattle off such resounding names as Prague, Rossbach, Leuthen—three personal triumphs for the Prussian king, all scored in 1757 over the Austrian and French armies. The defeats at Kolin (June 1757), which compelled Frederick to leave Bohemia to the allies, and at Kunersdorf (August 1759), which gave them Saxony, were less familiar. For all his brilliance, Frederick could do little to stem the allied advance: in October 1760, the Russians succeeded in entering Berlin and setting fire to the city. By 1761, Frederick's Epicureanism had turned sour, and his Stoicism was beginning to give way. [27] Yet when peace came in 1763, his Prussia was intact.

In addition to Frederick's courage and persistence, this improbable outcome had two causes: the steadfast support of Pitt and a lucky accident in Russia. The fall of Walpole in the early 1740s had left Britain in the hands of a coalition unskillful abroad and uncertain at home. George II was reluctant to bring the young, immensely popular, William Pitt into the government—had Pitt not denounced the king's ancestral home, Hanover, as a "despicable electorate"? But by the mid-1740s, Pitt *was* in the government; in 1756 he formed his first cabinet and in the following year, after a few months out of office, he returned, in complete charge of the war. He was a strange man, subject to fits of manic activity and melancholic apathy; especially in his later years he crossed the threshold of madness. But his self-confident boast, "I know that I can save the country and that I alone can" (which every English schoolchild knows as well as every German schoolchild knows Frederick's military exploits), was not the product of mania—it carried conviction. He was bold, original, and charismatic. In 1757 he needed all these qualities; the war was going badly everywhere. By 1759, Pitt's *annus mirabilis,* the world looked brighter: this was the year in which the British took Guadeloupe and Quebec, defeated the French army at Minden in August, and the French navy at Quiberon Bay in November, while continuing their cooperation with Frederick of Prussia. Yet all this would not have been enough to save the Prussian king and the Prussian state. To make things worse, in 1760 George II died and was succeeded by George III, who had little use for Pitt. By 1761, Pitt was out of office, and Lord Bute, the king's great favorite, deserted Prussia in 1762. It was then that Frederick coined the derisive phrase, "perfidious Albion." [28] But it was in the same year that Russia, the source of Frederick's initial distress, became the source of his eventual rescue. In January, the Tsarina Elizabeth died; she was succeeded by the young Tsar Peter III, a fanatical admirer of Frederick the Great. He instantly called off hostilities against Prussia, and thus reduced Frederick's military burdens by half. Prussia was saved.

Since the accession of George III there had been talk of peace: Elizabeth's death hastened negotiations. In May 1762, with the Treaty of St. Petersburg, the Russians settled with Prussia, restoring Prussian territory in Russian hands. In the same month, at Hamburg, the Prussians settled with Sweden. And in February 1763, after some final victories over the Austrians in the field, Frederick concluded the Peace of Hubertusburg with Maria Theresa. It restored Saxony, but—and this is what mattered to Frederick—it kept Silesia in his hands. In the same month, at Paris, Britain and France made peace as well. It was a diplomatic coup for the French, who got back the sugar islands the British

---

[27] For these terms, see p. 13.
[28] For Britain's domestic history in these decades, see p. 443.

had taken, but, abandoning its American holdings in the south to Spain and in the north to the British, the French in effect left the American continent to become part of the growing British Empire. It was a peace of exhaustion; only Pitt and the City merchants of London thought it a disaster.

EIGHTEENTH-CENTURY SOCIETY: PEERS, PIETISTS, AND PEASANTS

The Changing Contours of Religion

While generals maneuvered and ministers intrigued, the essential realities of eighteenth-century European society—habits of piety, patterns of deference, methods of food production, paths of commerce, and techniques of industry— slowly changed. These changes were often anything but radical; in religion especially they represented a return to earlier ways of thinking—or rather, of feeling. The Enlightenment had penetrated wide reaches of educated society; while picturesque tales of atheist bishops in France and deist bishops in England were wild exaggerations, it remains true that especially in the advanced Western countries, the official guardians of piety on the whole favored a tranquil and cultivated religion, derided displays of pious emotion- ality, and concentrated their sermons on the hope of salvation rather than the dread prospects of hell. The Anglican bishop Benjamin Hoadly is doubtless exceptional, but he represents an extreme symptom of a general condition: Hoadly was too busy as Walpole's political agent to attend to his religious duties. When he ascended the pulpit at all, he enunciated a doctrine so worldly and so bland, that the most liberal of Anglicans, the Latitudinarians, were moved to remonstrate with him. In one well-known sermon of 1717, Hoadly argued that since Christ Himself had pronounced His church to be not of this world, it followed that the Church of England had neither the right to meddle with worldly power, nor the obligation to inquire into evidence of religious orthodoxy. This view found apt expression in Joseph Addison's famous ode, which he published in his journal, the *Spectator:*

> The Spacious Firmament on high,
> With all the blue Etherial Sky,
> And spangl'd Heav'ns, a Shining Frame,
> Their great Original proclaim:
> Th' unwearied Sun, from Day to Day,
> Does his Creator's Power display,
> And publishes to every Land
> The Work of an Almighty Hand.

Such tepid, cheerful religiosity, in which respectful contemplation of nature's beauty, benevolence to the unfortunate, and good manners were the keys to heaven, was useful to politicians like Walpole. But it left the traditional religious emotions starved. The striking careers of notorious mountebanks—sellers of medical nostrums, esoteric knowledge, or infallible financial schemes—in the midst of what was supposed to be an age of Enlightenment, testifies to this starvation. So do, even more eloquently, the rise of Pietism and Methodism, the two dominant religions of the heart in the eighteenth century.

Pietism was a response to German Protestantism gone sterile. Luther's complacent heirs had been wholly unable to sustain his crusading spirit and intellectual vitality; they lived comfortably in the certainty that they possessed the truth, and quibbled over trivial theological points. Their congregations were treated to pedantic lectures or vituperative denunciations of heretics; in the parade of erudition and the extravagant name-calling, the meaning of the Reformation withered away for lack of sustenance. Then, in the 1670s, Philipp Jakob Spener spoke, like the proverbial voice in the desert, for a return to a study of the Bible and an increased voice of the laity in church affairs. Not surprisingly, his reforming words, formulated in sermons and, in 1675, in the book *Pia Desideria*, aroused vehement opposition. But Pietism survived the attacks on Spener and Spener's death in 1705; Spener's disciple and successor August Hermann Francke used the University of Halle, which Spener had helped to found in 1694, as a platform from which to preach a revitalized Lutheranism, with an emphasis on practical piety, on works, and on sincere self-searching in contrast with the dry-as-dust scholasticism into which it had fallen.

The impact of Pietism was wide and deep. After Spener's death, its most influential supporter was the count von Zinzendorf, a Saxon nobleman who, under Pietist impulsion, offered refuge to a persecuted Protestant sect, the Moravian Brethren, on his estate at Herrnhut. Under his guidance, the Moravians reconstituted themselves, indulging freely in the very emotional displays that more rational Protestants were apt to regret and ridicule, preaching man's fellowship with man and kinship with Christ. To the Moravians and to Zinzendorf, their bishop after 1737, God was love, His word the Bible, and His injunction to true believers: spread the faith. Accordingly, the Moravians became missionaries, taking their heartfelt, unintellectual Protestantism across Europe and into the British colonies in America. One of their most devoted admirers was the founder of English Methodism, John Wesley.

John Wesley, and his younger brother Charles, first encountered the Moravians in the British colony of Georgia, to which they had gone in 1735 in the company of James Oglethorpe, who was intent on founding a refuge in which graduates of England's debtors prisons could be rehabilitated. Wesley was already a deeply pious, but still a deeply troubled soul; the name Methodist had been conferred on him at Oxford in derision for his forming a club of devout young men intent on praying and studying the Bible. "That such a programme should have provoked ridicule," it has rightly been observed, "is a revealing commentary on the condition of the Hanoverian church."[29] It was not until 1738, a year after his return from Georgia, that John Wesley found the certainty he had prayed for. "In the evening" of May 24, 1738, he noted in his great journal, "I went very unwillingly to a society in Aldersgate Street, where one was reading Luther's preface to the Epistle to the Romans. About a quarter to nine, while he was describing the change which God works in the heart through faith in Christ, I felt my heart strangely warmed. I felt that I did trust in Christ, Christ alone, for salvation; and an assurance was given me that he had taken away *my* sins, even *mine*, and saved me from the law of sin and death." It is a famous moment in religious history, and an important moment in English social history. For Wesley, filled with new knowledge and endowed with enormous energy, discovered that while he trusted in Christ, the Anglican church did not trust in Wesley. Undismayed, and encouraged by the powerful evangelist George Whitefield, Wesley took to the streets and the fields, holding public meetings at any time and in any place that seemed possible. And he traveled, carrying the gospel of his earnest faith across the country; it is not for nothing that his journal has been called a "guidebook to the British Isles." The estimate of two hundred fifty thousand miles traveled, mainly on horseback, and of forty thousand sermons delivered, seems accurate. It was a hard task; crowds were often unfriendly, hurling insults and more damaging missiles as well. Wesley was unafraid and triumphant.

Wesley did not only preach; he organized his followers into societies held together internally by religious seriousness and small dues, and as a group by a network culminating in the Conference. But Wesley had no intention of forming his own church. Like the Anglicanism in which he had grown up, Wesley's Methodism was Arminian in theology; it rejected Calvin's strict doctrine of predestination. Wesley, indeed, was a conservative, both theologically and politically; he wanted to keep his followers in the Anglican communion and away from revolutionary sentiments. He failed in the first: in 1784, he reluctantly constituted the Methodist societies as legal entities, though when he died in 1791, he was still a member of the Church of England. It was only after his death that the English Methodists followed the step already taken in the United States and became an independent church. But Wesley succeeded in the second part of his conservative program. By reaching the unchurched and discontented with his simple and eloquent Christian message, he helped to channel potentially revolutionary sentiments into constructive paths. Methodism, writes the great French historian Elie Halévy, brought "under its influence, first the Dissenting sects, then the Establishment, finally secular opinion." And this helps to explain "the extraordinary stability which English society was destined to enjoy throughout a period of revolutions and crises."[30] Halévy's

---

[29] G. R. Cragg, *The Church in the Age of Reason (1648–1789)* (1960), 142.
[30] *England in 1815* (1913, 2nd English ed., 1949), 387.

famous thesis has recently been disputed, and the essential impact of Methodism remains a matter of debate. But what is clear is that Methodism reached the masses, wholly untouched by the eighteenth-century Church of England. And when Wesley preached, there were more masses in England, and in Europe, than ever before.

Toward the Population Explosion

Probably the most far-reaching of the subterranean changes in eighteenth-century Europe was the increase in its population; the roots of the great population explosion in the nineteenth century go back to the eighteenth. England (with Wales) grew from 5.5 million in 1700 to more than 9 million in 1800; France from 22 million to 28 million in the same period. Other countries offer equally striking figures: the population of the Italian peninsula increased roughly from 13 million to 19 million in the course of the eighteenth century; that of Spain from about 5 million to about 11 million. In Scandinavia, the German States, the American colonies, there were more mouths to feed, more customers to satisfy, more peasants to exploit. All in all, Europe in 1800 had nearly 190 million souls—70 million more than in 1700.

In view of scanty, often maddeningly incomplete statistics, these estimates must remain just that—estimates. The *fact* of population growth remains undisputed; it caused widespread discussion in its own time, and even some dismay, before the Reverend Thomas Malthus painted the grim specter of overpopulation in his famous essay *On Population* (1798). Recent studies suggest that the population of Europe increased nearly 60 percent in the eighteenth century not because the birthrate rose, but because the death rate dropped.[31] The improvements in medicine and sanitation, coupled with the decline of the plague and of smallpox, reduced the number of victims claimed earlier by infant mortality and by epidemics. Improvements in agricultural techniques and in transport reduced the number of victims claimed earlier by famine. Improvements in medicine were chiefly in theory: medical practitioners remained the threat to their patients' lives that they had always been. Smallpox was diminishing, but it haunted men's minds: in 1766, an advertisement offering a consignment of "about 250 fine healthy *Negroes*" duly noted that "the utmost care has already been taken, and shall be continued, to keep them free from the least danger of being infected with the *small-pox*"; indeed, a postscript added, "full one half of the above Negroes have had the *small-pox* in their own country."[32] Nevertheless, in some areas of Europe, notably in England and Flanders, the birthrate actually rose to contribute to the general increase. Even periods of high mortality, caused by bitter winters, bad harvests,

[31] For the controversy, and the population explosion, see Chapter 14.
[32] Reproduced in the picture section of Daniel P. Mannix and Malcolm Cowley, *Black Cargoes: A History of the Atlantic Slave Trade, 1518-1865* (ed. 1965).

or local epidemics, had their part to play: when the times of trouble had subsided, deferred marriages took place in large numbers, and the number of births following upon them swelled the population. One significant factor in eighteenth-century population growth was the call for working hands. "What is essentially necessary to a rapid increase of population," Malthus wrote, "is a great and continued demand for labour." Demographic and economic factors reinforced one another; certainly Europe at the end of the eighteenth century was drastically different from what it had been a hundred years before.

Behind these general observations stand concrete, often terrible experiences. Cruelty, destitution, infanticide (a favorite way of disposing of illegitimate babies) remained wholesale killers. "It is not uncommon, I have frequently been told," Adam Smith reported in 1776, "in the Highlands of Scotland for a mother who has borne twenty children not to have two alive." The death of an infant was as common an occurrence among the rich as among the poor. Goethe, who came from a prosperous patrician family in Frankfurt, later could not recall how many of his younger siblings had died in infancy. And the historian Edward Gibbon, writing near the end of the eighteenth century, coolly noted that "the death of a newborn child before that of its parents may seem an unnatural, but it is strictly a probable event: since of any given number the greater part are extinguished before their ninth year." His own infantile constitution had been so weak, he wrote, that "in the baptism of my brothers, my father's prudence successively repeated the Christian name of Edward, that, in case of the departure of the eldest son, this patronymic appellation might still be perpetuated in the family." Gibbon's story is inaccurate, but it testifies to the power the death of the young had over the imagination of the eighteenth century.[33]

The Persistence of Hierarchy

Whatever else it changed, the growth in population did not materially affect the hierarchical structure of society. All across Europe, and in its outposts overseas, government was in the hands of the few who governed in behalf of the few. Republics and monarchies alike were what they had traditionally been— oligarchies. The gap between rich and poor, powerful and powerless, enfranchised and disfranchised, remained wide. It was spanned by a few narrow and precarious bridges bearing the one-way traffic of charity and the two-way traffic of social mobility: the ruin of old and the rise of new families. But this, though spectacular, was relatively light. Some hundreds of enterprising tradesmen and bankers moved upward, their financial success the ticket to social ascent. But to speak of a "rising bourgeoisie" is to neglect a fact of central significance: by

---

[33] See Gibbon's *Autobiography* (ed. Dero A. Saunders, 1961), 53; for a correction of this report, see D. M. Low, *Gibbon's Journal* to January 28th, 1763 (n.d.), xxix.

buying rural properties and marrying his children into the gentry or the aristocracy, the affluent bourgeois did not rise—he disappeared. He himself might acquire a patent of nobility; many merchants, including prosperous slave traders in the French port cities, did. And if he failed, his offspring succeeded. As Daniel Defoe, the vigorous spokesman for the English bourgeoisie, put it in 1726, in *The Complete English Tradesman:* "Trade in England makes gentlemen, and has peopled this nation with gentlemen; for the tradesmen's children, or at least their grandchildren, come to be as good gentlemen, statesmen, Parliament men, privy counsellors, judges, bishops and noblemen, as those of the highest birth and the most ancient families." Even the elder Pitt, the Great Commoner, accepted a peerage after he resigned in 1761. The phrase, "the people," was on everyone's lips: Samuel Johnson, in a well-known epigram, said that unlike Walpole ("a minister given by the King to the people"), Pitt was "a minister given by the people to the King." In statements like these, "people" referred to the merchants of the City of London, to bankers and tradesmen, to some thousands of politically influential country squires and peers, and to a handful of disinterested patriots impressed with Pitt's gift for leadership. Even in England, where discussion was unusually candid and politics a game played by an unusually large number of persons, the political public was a small minority of the total population. The oligarchic, hierarchical nature of social life and political power was all-pervasive. It was evident in vast empires like Russia and in tiny republics like Geneva, in large tracts of countryside with their local lord and in flourishing cities with their commercial patriciate. The free imperial city of Frankfurt rigidly ranked its population by a nuanced dress code—a *Kleiderordnung*—that instantly placed each citizen into his proper social niche. And in Strasbourg, a typical city, the governing legislature "seemed to be a debating society for brothers, cousins, and brothers-in-law."[34]

Politics and power were family affairs. The majority of Europeans were subjects of condescension, fear, or indifference. There were a few exceptional voices, more audible for being so exceptional. Adam Smith, the most brilliant political economist of the century, flatly urged high wages for the working population: "The liberal reward of labour," he argued, "as it encourages the propagation, so it increases the industry of the common people"; where wages are high, "we shall always find the workmen more active, diligent, and expeditious than where they are low." Nor was such "liberal reward" merely a device for ensuring high productivity; it was sheer "equity" that those "who feed, cloath and lodge the whole body of the people, should have such a share of the produce of their own labour as to be themselves tolerably well fed, cloathed, and lodged." But this was the voice of the radical Enlightenment; other, harsher voices were more representative of the age: "Everyone but an idiot knows," Arthur Young, the influential writer on western European agriculture, said in 1771, "that the lowest classes must be kept poor or they will

---

[34] Franklin L. Ford, *Strasbourg in Transition, 1648–1789* (1958), 15.

never be industrious." Clearly, the time of the "lowest classes" had not yet come.

All across Europe, then, societies were dominated by oligarchies. Nearly everywhere, noblemen monopolized the highest posts in state and church, and there was a tendency for different branches of the aristocracy to coalesce: in France, the old nobility of the sword increasingly intermarried with the new nobility of the robe. Wealth and status attracted each other. In their role as influential courtiers, great landowners, high-ranking bureaucrats, or princes of the church, aristocrats had access to the sources of wealth. While not all nobles were rich—the poor among them were numerous and conspicuous—most of them could afford extensive estates, luxurious styles of life, and impressive gambling debts. And those aristocrats whose resources were failing could replenish them by marrying their sons to bourgeois heiresses. Yet the cosmopolitan splendor of the leading noble houses gives eighteenth-century Europe a misleading appearance of uniformity. In fact, the shape, role, and powers of aristocracies differed from country to country. In Great Britain, the nobility generally lived on the land; though their properties were generally rented to tenant farmers, they kept in touch through their stewards, and many among them actually enjoyed experimenting with new agricultural techniques. These peers governed Britain by superintending local government in association with the local squire and by going to Westminster to sit in the House of Lords. In Britain, only the eldest son inherited his father's title. Thus father and son, older and younger brother, often met one another in Parliament—the one sitting in the Lords, the other in the House of Commons (see pp. 385 and 445). Both in local and national affairs, then, relations between the peerage and the far larger squierarchy were often intimate. This, and a sizable, self-respecting urban bourgeoisie, meant that the higher reaches of English society were not sharply divided, but gently, if subtly, graded and interrelated. One did not have to be a nobleman to get on: the great Sir Robert Walpole was the incarnation of the country squire in politics. As we know, his elevation to the peerage was less a reward for services performed than a sign that his political influence was at an end (see p. 388).

In France, in contrast, the apex of the social hierarchy remained the court nobility. For them, to go back to the provinces was to go into exile. But there were striking and numerous exceptions to this pattern: while French law closed most trades to the nobility as unworthy of their privileged estate, many provincial nobles lived cheerfully enough far from Paris, cultivating their properties and increasing their incomes. For example, at Toulouse, whose nobility has been closely studied, noblemen were thrifty and rational landlords; their "mode of living," writes their historian, "was maintained by adherence to the so-called bourgeois virtues of thrift, discipline, and strict management of the family fortune."[35] High posts were in the hands of aristocrats; by 1789, all

---

[35] Robert Forster, *The Nobility of Toulouse in the Eighteenth Century* (1960), 177.

bishops in France were noblemen, often younger sons combining vast perquisites with no duties, and only one of Louis XVI's thirty-six ministers was a commoner. The French Revolution, as we shall see, had many causes. But one of them was the short-sighted self-centeredness of the French aristocracy, alert mainly to its interests, intent on pleasure, and deaf to the call for social responsibility, let alone social reform. As the marquise de La Tour du Pin, one of the most intelligent survivors of this aristocracy, would later put it in her memoirs: "The Revolution of 1789 was only the inevitable consequence and, I might almost say, the just punishment of the vices of the upper classes, vices carried to such excess that if people had not been stricken with a mortal blindness, they must have seen that they would inevitably be consumed by the very fire they themselves were lighting." The "famous 'douceur de vivre,' of the old regime," as Professor John McManners sums it up, "was concocted from a very simple formula, privilege without responsibility."[36]

Elsewhere, in Prussia, the Hapsburg Empire, Russia, aristocracies were variations on the English and French models. Nearly everywhere, there were too many noble courtiers, doing too many useless things. They organized dances and hunts, they arranged theatricals and card parties, they intrigued to be close to the duke—or, perhaps better, the duchess—who was the center of these little universes. "In the Saxon State Calendar," one historian reminds us, "the list of offices covered fifty-three pages."[37] Most of these aristocracies were supposedly service aristocracies; they enjoyed a monopoly of high offices in the bureaucracy and the army, and an almost undisputed right to treat "their" peasants as they liked, but in return they were obliged to serve their royal masters all their lives, and with unquestioning fidelity. The reality was a little more complicated than this; everywhere, nobles sought to escape, or at least lighten, the burdens that energetic and power-hungry monarchs had imposed upon them. In Russia they wholly succeeded;[38] even in Prussia—though only after the death of the omnipresent Frederick II in 1786—they succeeded in part. Gradually, the Junker bureaucrats became centers of power hard to move and impossible to dislodge. It is not extravagant to call the eighteenth century a century of the rising aristocracy.

Europe: A Rural Society

The basis of aristocratic wealth and power was the land. Economic historians used to date the Industrial Revolution from 1760. There is some reason for their choice. It was in 1769, after long experimentation, that James Watt patented his

[36] "France," in A. Goodwin, ed., *The European Nobility in the Eighteenth Century* (1953), 29.
[37] J. O. Lindsay, "The Social Classes and the Foundations of the States," in *The New Cambridge Modern History*, vol. VII (1957), 55.
[38] See p. 378 and, for developments under Catherine II, p. 432.

steam engine—the decisive invention of that revolution, the source of power vastly greater than men, or horses, or waterwheels could provide. What has been called the "invention of invention" multiplied the number of devices used in the production of goods: while in the century between 1660 and 1760, the average number of patents granted in England was sixty, in the years between 1760 and 1790, that number rose to three hundred twenty-five. This was the period in which the factory began to emerge, and the factory—a central building with machinery, on which workers converged for stated periods of time—was an invention like that of the steam engine. The factory demanded something new: the regular employment of labor. It put a premium on what came to be called "industrial discipline"—the workingman's ability and willingness to report for work on schedule, every day, for the machines were voracious and could not stand idle. These moral and psychological requirements went hand in hand with improvements in commercial and banking techniques which eased the transfer of funds, and with the agglomeration of sprawling industrial cities, in which the working population clustered in increasing numbers—and increasing misery.

In some industries, notably in textiles, these spectacular improvements were truly revolutionary. John Kay's flying shuttle, patented in 1733, cut the number of weavers needed to work the loom from two to one. In about 1764, James Hargreaves invented the spinning jenny, a modern mechanical version of the spinning wheel. His first version permitted the simultaneous working of eight spindles; in 1770, when the jenny was patented, it was capable of handling sixteen. The year before, the gifted Richard Arkwright had patented the water frame, and ten years later, in 1779, Samuel Crompton patented the spinning mule. These two inventions permitted the spinning of fine and coarse yarns in unprecedented, hitherto almost unimaginable quantities. And, significantly enough, in 1785 Watt's steam engine was harnessed to these devices, and factory mass production of cloth was under way. Yet, despite all this, the Industrial Revolution was a slow and uneven growth. It began in England: Germany saw its first steam engine in 1785, and factories in France long remained small. And even in England, the factory town did not spring up overnight: by 1790 there were still fewer than a thousand spinning jennies in operation. The old commercial mentality, the old handicraft industries, and the old small-scale enterprise were tenacious survivals. Through the eighteenth century, Europe remained a predominantly rural society.

This in itself was not a sign of stagnation. There was no rigid separation between agricultural and industrial occupations; before the age of the factory, employers of labor depended largely on the domestic system. They engaged workers, rural and urban, to do their work at home. This held true for England, the mother of industrial society, as well as all across central Europe. In the rural districts of Bohemia, there were more than two hundred thousand domestic workers spinning flax; in the Swiss canton of Glaurus there were more than thirty-four thousand domestic spinners across the countryside. Most of these rural industrial workers were women.[39]

Moreover, like the industrial sector of Europe, rural life, too, felt the bracing breath of innovation. Viscount Townshend acquired the nickname Turnip Townshend for his experiments with introducing turnips, which served as fodder for livestock, fed nitrogen to the soil, and facilitated crop rotation; his dual career—politics and scientific farming—is in many ways characteristic of the style congenial to the English peerage. But not all experimental, "improving" farmers were noblemen. Jethro Tull, a gentleman farmer, was something of a crank and professional inventor, who published an important book on the use of deep and straight ploughing for the thorough tillage of the soil. And Robert Bakewell, a tenant farmer still lower on the social scale, proved the immense utility of controlled, selective stock breeding for sheep and cattle alike. Nearly all these innovations took place on enclosed land. The enclosure of common land, on which the small tenant farmer had traditionally grazed his cattle and the rural poor squatted, consolidated holdings and made farming more efficient. Enclosure had been going on since the Tudors, and called forth protests from reformers appalled at the dislocations it produced. But it went on, at a vastly increased pace in the eighteenth century after 1760, while dislocations and protests increased apace. Like so much else in economic life, the enclosure movement illustrates an experience that is almost a law of progress: procedures that benefit some will hurt others; all improvement must be paid for, and it is normally paid for by those least capable of making their voices heard or their will felt.

In England, agricultural improvements were far more noticeable than on the Continent, but even in England innovations moved slowly against massive resistance. The once popular term, "agricultural revolution," is going out of use: the proverbial conservatism of rural life defeated the most impatient projector. Hierarchies of wealth and status remained intact, and in some areas grew more pronounced. In England, the three hundred or so noble families were also the great landlords; their incomes ranged from a comfortable £5000 to a magnificent £50,000. Next in line were the gentry, less than a thousand of them rich enough to approach the peers; three to four thousand solid squires with incomes ranging from £1000 to £3000 a year; and up to twenty thousand ordinary, middling landed gentlemen whose income was anywhere between £300 and £1000 a year. The least affluent of these gentlemen were little more prosperous than that far larger category, the freeholders, whose farms might bring them as little as £30, or as much as £700 a year. This scale, ranging from £30 to £50,000, offers a prospect of vast economic and social distance, from cottage to palace. Yet even this hierarchy, steep as it appears, does not comprehend the whole spectrum of English rural life: below the petty freeholder with his £50 or £75 a year were the mass of tenant farmers, some of

---

[39] See Anderson, *Europe in the Eighteenth Century,* 65.

them respectable yeomen, many of them sturdy laborers, and many others miserable squatters dependent on casual labor, charity, and poaching.[40]

In France, the hierarchy was steeper still, and the condition of the poor, worse. France's population was far larger than Britain's—about five times larger—and more rural: roughly six out of every seven Frenchmen lived on the land.[41] The church, which made up a vanishingly small minority of the French population—no more than 0.5 percent—owned 15 percent of that land. This was considerably less than aggressive philosophies like to charge, but it was still a great deal, and most church lands were highly desirable soil. The nobility, which totaled 1.5 percent of the French population, owned 20 percent of the land, another striking disproportion. Well-to-do bourgeois, holding farms normally on the outskirts of the towns in which they lived, owned another third. And a final third was in the hands of peasants, a class that made up about 85 percent of France's population.

These bare figures tell only part of the story. A small minority of peasants, the *laboureurs,* were prosperous and proud; a handful of these rural aristocrats could put by enough to finance their children's social ascent; many of them made themselves unpopular with their tight fists and hard hearts, their shrewd dealings with their poorer neighbors and with the government. But many, indeed most, of the peasants who owned land could not really support themselves and their burgeoning families with the returns from their small plots. They therefore hired themselves out to work on the property of *laboureurs* or earned a pittance taking in domestic industry. Nor were these pathetic property owners at the bottom of the economic and social ladder: perhaps eleven million French peasants were sharecroppers at the mercy of their neighbors and the price of bread, and five million more were condemned to a life of intermittent labor, migratory work, banditry, and starvation. Most of these peasants were ridden with onerous obligations: rents to the landlord, tithes to the church, a variety of payments dating back to medieval times for such "privileges" as the use of the local wine press or the local mill, and a host of taxes to the government. When Arthur Young traveled through France in the years from 1787 to 1789 to write his famous comparison between French and English conditions, he was amazed at the low productivity of French agriculture, appalled at the "miserable state of the labouring poor," and constrained to observe that the average French peasant's morale was irremediably low. They were "content merely to live."[42]

If French peasants suffered in comparison with the English yeomanry, they were at least legally better off than the peasants on Prussian, Hapsburg, or Russian lands. While about a million French peasants—less than one in

[40] See G. E. Mingay, *English Landed Society in the Eighteenth Century* (1963).
[41] For the French population of the seventeenth century, see p. 291.
[42] See Robert and Elborg Forster, eds., *European Society in the Eighteenth Century* (1969), 108 ff.

twenty—were serfs, the vast majority of east European peasants lived in legal bondage. In Austria, they suffered under heavy and growing exactions from their noble landlords; the nobility sweated the peasantry for increasing contributions, through a variety of taxes and, above all, through *robot*—compulsory labor service. Here, as everywhere else, there were regional and local variations; the lot of the peasant differed with the laxity or efficiency, kindness or cruelty, of individual landlords and their stewards. But in general, conditions were terrible almost beyond description; travelers' reports are notoriously undependable, but visitor after visitor speaks of Bohemian and Hungarian peasants living more or less like animals. It was not until the 1760s and 1770s, when Maria Theresa turned her attention from Silesia—now definitively lost to her—to domestic affairs, and when peasant revolts jogged her elbow, that she placed these conditions on the agenda for state action. She decreed the abolition of some long-standing obligations which had become burdensome abuses on the peasants, established "maxima" beyond which peasants could not be exploited by their lords, and at least in some measure protected common lands from being converted to the landlords' private use. She did much, but, as C. A. Macartney has observed, her decrees "left the peasant position in the monarchy incompletely solved."[43]

In Russia, too, the condition of the serf, though it varied greatly, was in general a life of incessant toil and total dependence, a routine of exploitation and oppression. The law put the peasant into the hands of the landlord, and the gradual emancipation of the Russian nobility from state service was accompanied by its tightening control over its serfs' labor and their very lives. Peter the Great had made the nobility's right to its serf-estates hereditary, so that Russian peasants were handed down from father to son like so much cattle. The law protected a serf from being tortured to death by his master—an ominous prohibition act whose very existence suggests the prevalence of the practice—but the law did not provide specific penalties for those landlords who violated it. "Where the masters took their returns from the peasants in the form of money-dues or *obrok*," Geroid T. Robinson sums up the life of the Russian serf in the eighteenth century, "the average weight of this obligation seems to have increased considerably between the 'sixties and the 'nineties—perhaps even as much as one hundred per cent. . . . On the estates where the principal exaction was in the form of forced labor or *barshchina*, three days' work per week was the amount usually required of adult peasants of both sexes, but four or five days' work was sometimes exacted, and not infrequently the peasant was forced to work continuously for a considerable period in the manorial fields, while his own plot waited for seeding, or his own harvest rotted on the ground. Furthermore, it was customary to require of the forced-labor peasants certain payments in kind—poultry, eggs, meat, honey, homespun cloth, and the like.

---

[43] *The Hapsburg Empire, 1790–1918* (1969), 66. For the reign of Maria Theresa's son, Joseph II, see p. 427 below.

Again, it was this century that witnessed the first considerable development of mining and manufacturing in Russia, and numbers of private serfs were put to forced labor in these industries. Sick and aged peasants who were unable to render the dues and services required by their masters might be 'liberated'— that is to say, expelled from their villages to go where they could."[44] Not surprisingly, most of the serfs were so beaten down by their existence, so dully accustomed to their misery, that they did not even think of complaining, to say nothing of rebelling. "It appears that the spirit of freedom is so dried up in the slaves," the eighteenth-century Russian educator and reformer Alexander Mikolayevich Radichev observed, that they "have no desire to end their suffering."[45]

Radichev's use of the word "slave" should cause only momentary surprise. The Russian landlord could compel his serfs to increase their contributions in labor or products, move them from field to domestic service, force them to marry or to abstain from marrying, and sell them alone or with the rest of their families, with or without the land on which they toiled—completely at will.[46] Slaves were hardly worse off than this.

Slavery

There were few slaves in Europe proper, but slaves were an indispensable ingredient in the European economy. America—North, Central, and South— was a vitally important extension of the European market, and the slave trade formed the basis for the mercantile greatness of port cities like Nantes and Liverpool, Bordeaux and Bristol. Slavery, as we know (see p. 85), was invented long before the eighteenth century, but the slave trade rose to its climax in that century—a depressing commentary on an age of Enlightenment. The argument for slavery was simple and practical: the gold mines of Brazil, the sugar plantations of the West Indies, the tobacco plantations of the southern colonies, demanded labor so hard, in such heat, that free men would never do the necessary work. In 1764, John Pinney, a prominent Bristol sugar merchant, spoke for the British commercial community: "Negroes," he wrote, "are the Sinews of a Plantation, and it is as impossible for a Man to make Sugar without the assistance of Negroes, as to make Bricks without Straw"—and by Negroes he meant slaves.[47] And in 1789, the chambre de commerce of Bordeaux officially declared: "France needs its colonies to sustain its commerce, and consequently slaves to allow agriculture in that part of the world to flourish, until another way is found to achieve this end."[48] These were the arguments

---

[44] *Rural Russia Under the Old Regime* (1932), 27-28.
[45] Quoted in Forster and Forster, *European Society in the Eighteenth Century,* 136.
[46] See Robinson, *Rural Russia,* 27.
[47] Quoted in C. M. MacInnes, *A Gateway to Empire* (1939), 193.
[48] Quoted in Henri Sée, *La France économique et sociale au XVIIIe siècle* (5th ed., 1952), 121.

of mercantile good sense; they carried weight with a substantial majority of Europeans. Antislavery agitation was rising, but the outraged protest of humane philosophes and conscience-stricken Christians were dismissed as the voices of well-meaning but irresponsible cranks. Most Europeans continued to justify the institution, and its lifeline the slave trade, in James Boswell's words, as a "very important and necessary branch of commercial interest." They rationalized it (again in Boswell's words) as kindness to the "African Savages, a portion of whom it saves from massacre, or intolerable bondage in their own country, and introduces . . . into a much happier state of life." Samuel Johnson thundered that slavery is against nature; Horace Walpole passionately and prophetically exclaimed: "I scarce wish perfect freedom to merchants who are the bloodiest of all tyrants. I should think the souls of the Africans would sit heavy on the swords of the Americans." But the antislavery cause was slow to win converts.

Late in the eighteenth century, philosophes added a new argument to the cause. While slavery had long been attacked as inhuman or un-Christian, two Scottish economists, John Millar and Adam Smith, now suggested that it was uneconomical as well: the slave always remains a reluctant and unskilled workman, and slavery by its very existence keeps managers from introducing labor-saving innovations. "The work done by slaves," Adam Smith wrote, "though it appears to cost only their maintenance, is in the end the dearest of any." Recent studies support these eighteenth-century conjectures. In addition to perpetuating inefficient modes of labor, the profits accruing to what were essentially selected luxury industries were purchased at an exorbitant price in health and life. The high mortality of slaves is widely known. Untold black lives were lost in Africa during slaving expeditions and internecine warfare, untold more in America in an unaccustomed environment of exhausting toil, brutal treatment, and endemic disease. In addition, the mortality rate of slaves on board ship averaged more than 13 percent—often it was much higher. What is less well known is the loss sustained by the whites: again and again, more sailors than slaves died in the long middle passage across the Atlantic. Besides, the soldiers, merchants, and officials who went to the disease-ridden slave depots in West Africa perished in large numbers: one estimate suggests that during the first year there one of two Europeans died. And life in the West Indian plantations was little better. The social cost of slavery—to Africa, Europe, and America, to blacks and whites alike—was thus incalculable. Nor can this cost be measured by wasted lives alone; those who survived suffered irreparable moral damage. Captain John Newton, a reformed eighteenth-century slave trader, insisted late in life that the need for dealing harshly with Negro slaves "gradually brings a numbness upon the heart, and renders most of those who are engaged in it too indifferent to the sufferings of their fellow creatures." [49] Slavery degraded everyone, master and slave alike.

[49] Quoted in Mannix and Cowley, *Black Cargoes,* 145.

Despite these harrowing and familiar realities, the slave trade flourished mightily through the eighteenth century. In the sixteenth century, the number of slaves imported from Africa into all of America—Brazil, Spanish America, and the islands—totaled about[50] two hundred thirty thousand. In the seventeenth century, especially after 1650, when the plantation economies of the Western hemisphere became firmly established, the number rose to over one and a third million, with the largest single contingent, over 40 percent, going to Brazil. In the eighteenth century, the number rose again, and drastically, to about six million, with Brazil still taking the lion's share—almost a third. Most of these imports came from Africa, but by no means all: throughout the eighteenth century, the West Indian island of Jamaica exported as one of its commodities an average of two thousand blacks a year to the English colonies on the mainland. While the trade continued beyond the end of the eighteenth century, it fell off, especially in the north, in the nineteenth. All in all, about ten million black slaves came from Africa to America, to work in the mines and the fields, to enrich the planters and the shipping magnates. The miserable mutilated slave whom Voltaire's innocent voyager, Candide, finds lying on a road sums it all up with bitter felicity: "This is the price at which you eat sugar in Europe."

The price, as we have said, was high, and the trade was risky; but the profits were great. And if there were any doubts, a host of pamphleteers reassured the public: "Our West Indian and African trades," one such writer told his British readers in 1749, "are the most nationally beneficial of any we carry on." The "Negroe-Trade," he concluded, "may be justly esteemed an inexhaustible Fund of the Wealth and Naval Power of this Nation."[51] This is why British merchants fought so hard for the *asiento,* the exclusive agreement that Britain imposed on Spain at Utrecht in 1713, giving British traders a monopoly on the selling of African slaves to the Spanish colonies in America. This, too, is why the British Parliament granted the Royal African Company—a company specializing in the slave trade—a generous subsidy to maintain its forts on the Gold Coast against the unwelcome intrusion of Dutch and French slavers. The profits of the trade were not confined to the returns on slaves alone. What was called the "triangular trade" involved European exports to Africa (payments like beads or firearms to African slave sellers), the transport of African blacks to the West Indies or the Carolinas, and the import of American commodities into Europe. Shipbuilders and importers, therefore, quite as much

---

[50] We use this cautious word advisedly; all discussions on the slave trade, with the complex questions it raises about the origins and destination of slaves, and the fragmentary, often contradictory figures, must depend on intelligent estimates at best. These estimates vary enormously—between 8 million and 25 million as the global figure; detailed estimates (exports from, or imports to, specific areas) differ as well. In this section we are much indebted to Philip D. Curtin, *The Atlantic Slave Trade: A Census* (1969), a brilliant reassessment of all the available evidence, and an invaluable compendium of new estimates.

[51] Quoted in Williams, *Whig Supremacy,* 296.

as shareholders in slaving companies, were deeply involved in the trade and did their utmost to defend it. What with disease, piracy, accident, high costs, and commissions, many expeditions involved losses, but the average profit has been estimated at 30 percent or more—too tidy a sum to permit mere humanitarian or prudential considerations to weigh heavily in the balance. The importance of the trade and its consequences for the mercantile establishment stand revealed in the rising share of Britain's trade with America (which rose from 13 percent in 1700 to 34 percent in 1785) and with Africa (which rose, in the same time span, at the same rate). [52] Only reformers and revolutionaries could make light of such figures.

SELECTED READINGS

For Europe in the quarter century after the Peace of Utrecht, see, in general, M. S. Anderson, *Europe in the Eighteenth Century, 1713-1783* (1961). It largely replaces the older book by Penfield Roberts, *The Quest for Security, 1715-1740* (1947). The appropriate volume (VII) of *The New Cambridge Modern History,* J. O. Lindsay, ed., *The Old Regime, 1713-1763* (1957), is useful.

France after Louis XIV is beautifully and economically summarized in Alfred Cobban, *A History of Modern France,* vol. I, *The Old Regime and Revolution, 1715-1799* (1957). Franklin L. Ford, *Robe and Sword: The Regrouping of the French Aristocracy After Louis XIV* (1953), takes an important sociopolitical problem down to 1748. It can be read in conjunction with Robert Forster's informative essay, *The Nobility of Toulouse in the Eighteenth Century* (1960). On foreign policy, Arthur M. Wilson, *French Foreign Policy During the Administration of Cardinal Fleury, 1726-43* (1936), retains its value. See also the general treatment by G. P. Gooch, *Louis XV: The Monarchy in Decline* (1956). C. B. A. Behrens, *The Ancien Régime* (1967), though up-to-date, is slight; it should be supplemented by Elinor G. Barber, *The Bourgeoisie in 18th Century France* (1955); John Lough, *An Introduction to Eighteenth Century France* (1960); and John McManners, *French Ecclesiastical Society Under the Ancient Regime* (1961)—this last, though it concentrates on the city of Angers, is a masterly account that illuminates life in the France of Louis XV and beyond. For economic history, the brief book by Henri E. Sée, *Economic and Social Conditions in France During the Eighteenth Century* (1927), is useful.

For England during these same decades, see the survey by Basil Williams, *The Whig Supremacy, 1714-1760* (1939), though it is now somewhat old. For a more modern view, the first half of J. H. Plumb, *England in the Eighteenth Century* (1950), short, lucid, and accurate, is excellent; so is Plumb's large-scale biography, *Sir Robert Walpole: The Making of a Statesman* (1956) and *Sir Robert Walpole: The King's Minister* (1960)—these take the great minister down to 1734; a final volume is promised. Plumb's popular *The First Four Georges* (1956) and his brief life of *Chatham* (1953) are also valuable introductions to the period; his *The Growth of Political Stability in England, 1675-1725* (1967) is more technical, but an important reinterpretation. See also John B. Owen, *The*

---

[52] See Jacques Godechot and R. R. Palmer, "Le problème de l'Atlantique du XVIIIe au XXe siècle," *X Congreso Internazionale di Scienze Storiche,* V (1955), 196-197.

Rise of the Pelhams (1957). On social history, M. Dorothy George, *London Life in the XVIIIth Century* (1925), and her *England in Transition* (1931), may be supplemented with Dorothy Marshall's *English People in the Eighteenth Century* (1956) and *The English Poor in the Eighteenth Century* (1926). See also the opening sections of Peter Mathias, *The First Industrial Nation* (1969), and the later sections of Charles Wilson, *England's Apprenticeship, 1603-1673* (1965). John Carswell, *The South Sea Bubble* (1960), explains a complex matter of high finance; Norman Sykes' *Church and State in England in the XVIIIth Century* (1934) is authoritative.

The best survey of the great confrontation after 1740 is Walter L. Dorn, *Competition for Empire, 1740-1763* (1940). Among biographies of Prussia's controversial ruler, G. P. Gooch, *Frederick the Great: The Ruler, the Writer, the Man* (1947), is judicious; Pierre Gaxotte, *Frederick the Great* (tr. 1942), is hostile; D. B. Horn, *Frederick the Great and the Rise of Prussia* (1969), is brief. Hans Rosenberg, *Bureaucracy, Aristocracy, Autocracy: The Prussian Experience, 1660-1815* (1960), and volume II of Hajo Holborn's *History of Modern Germany* (1964), are indispensable here. Chester V. Easum, *Prince Henry of Prussia, Brother of Frederick the Great* (1942), is also useful.

For Frederick's Austrian counterpart, see Edward Crankshaw, *Maria Theresa* (1969), and G. P. Gooch, *Maria Theresa and Other Studies* (1951); for her son, the recent *Joseph II* by Paul P. Bernard (1968) largely supersedes Saul K. Padover, *The Revolutionary Emperor: Joseph the Second, 1741-90* (2nd. ed., 1967). See also Robert J. Kerner, *Bohemia in the Eighteenth Century* (1932), and, also on Bohemia, William E. Wright, *Serf, Seigneur, and Sovereign* (1966), and Edith M. Link, *The Emancipation of the Austrian Peasant, 1740-1798* (1949).

On population increase, see Carlo Cipolla, *The Economic History of World Population, 1750-1918* (1962); M. C. Buer, *Health, Wealth and Population in the Early Days of the Industrial Revolution* (ed. 1968); and above all a number of important essays in D. V. Glass and D. E. C. Eversley, eds., *Population in History: Essays in Historical Demography* (1965). On social structure, in addition to the volumes by Ford, Forster, Barber, and Marshall cited earlier in this chapter, as well as Geroid T. Robinson, *Rural Russia Under the Old Regime* (1932), on the Russian serf, see Albert Goodwin, ed., *The European Nobility in the Eighteenth Century* (1953); G. E. Mingay, *English Landed Society in the Eighteenth Century* (1963); and Robert and Elborg Forster, eds., *European Society in the Eighteenth Century* (1969)—an unusually well-conceived anthology of social history.

On slavery, we (and the historical profession) are much indebted to the researches of Philip D. Curtin, published in *The Atlantic Slave Trade: A Census* (1969). C. M. MacInnes, *A Gateway to Empire* (1939), discusses one slave-trading port, Bristol. Daniel P. Mannix, in collaboration with Malcolm Cowley, *Black Cargoes: A History of the Atlantic Slave Trade, 1518-1865* (ed. 1965), is a sobering survey. For the African side of the trade, see Basil Davidson, *Black Mother* (1961), and Melville J. Herskovits, *The Myth of the Negro Past* (1958). Eric Williams, *Capitalism and Slavery* (1944), treats the question from a Marxist perspective.

10

*Reformers and Revolutionaries:
1763-1789*

THE VARIETIES OF GOOD GOVERNMENT

The age of Enlightenment was also an age of reform. An impressive array of energetic rulers modified institutions and experimented with policies to meet new demands, to fulfill old obligations in a new way, to bring their states into a new age. These parallel developments—enlightenment and reform—were obviously not unrelated, and since the nineteenth century it has been fashionable to group reforming rulers under the single rubric of "enlightened despots." The fashion persists, at the expense of historical precision, for the name is misleading. It unjustly saddles the philosophes with a principled predilection for progressive despots. It wrongly implies that these "despots" heavily depended on the guidance of philosophes. And, by forcing a striking diversity of ideas and practices into a single category, it imposes on the second half of the eighteenth century a specious uniformity. Frederick II of Prussia dominated and prized his nobility, Catherine II of Russia increased the privileges of her nobility, Joseph II of Austria humbled his nobility as much as lay within his power. While Joseph sought to centralize Hapsburg institutions under his authoritarian control, his younger brother Leopold, archduke of Tuscany, fostered local autonomy. And—to give one more instance—while Joseph II and other potentates of the day lightened the burden of the peasantry, Catherine of Russia increased those burdens until Russian serfdom took on the lineaments of slavery. In light of these far-reaching differences, it would be best to characterize the period as an age of good government, eighteenth-century style.

Sweden, Portugal, and Spain

This search for good—that is, effective—government dominated great powers and small, in the centers of Europe and on its periphery. In Sweden, in 1772, young King Gustavus III abruptly terminated half a century of aristocratic misrule with a picturesque coup d'etat. He forced a new constitution on a cowed Riksdag and then, his hands relatively free, he proceeded on an ambitious program of internal reforms. The first laws introduced by his regime demonstrated the king's devotion to enlightened principles: they ended torture and established a free press. Gustavus' legislation made judges irremovable, abolished extraordinary tribunals, and protected, with a habeas corpus act, the rights of accused persons. Abundantly endowed with vitality and liberal principles, Gustavus battled entrenched abuses on all sides. He reformed the currency and the state's finances; he cleansed the scandal-ridden judiciary in a spectacular trial; he brought a measure of equality to the tax system; he proclaimed religious liberty, modernized the poor law, and fostered free trade. Mindful of Sweden's great enemy, Russia, Gustavus also improved his army and constructed a formidable navy. But after a prolonged period of domestic peace, Gustavus found aristocratic opposition reemerging. It was perhaps an inescapable development: Gustavus, proud to be a noble, had no intention of eliminating the aristocracy from its high social position; he only wanted to keep it from exercising political power. But he could not sustain this policy in the long run without either moderating his own claims or violating the very constitution he had pressed on the country in 1772, for in that constitution, he had deliberately kept the power of the purse in the hands of the Riksdag. The Riksdag that convened in 1786 was practically in mutiny and so Gustavus, who was preparing to engage Russia in war, determined to govern on his own. In 1788, he declared war, and in February 1789, with the support of the non-noble estates, he imposed a new constitution, the Act of Union and Security. This made the king practically absolute in his kingdom.

The French Revolution completed Gustavus' move to absolutism. He had surprisingly beaten the Russians, and in 1790 he concluded an advantageous peace with them; this permitted him to concentrate on events in France. With his customary vigor, he attempted to construct a league of princes against the revolutionaries. But the Swedish nobility, humiliated and infuriated, took a revenge more melodramatic than his accession had been: in March 1792, at a midnight masquerade at the Stockholm opera house, Gustavus was shot to death by a masked aristocrat. The Swedish experiment in good government was over.

At the other end of Europe, in the Iberian Peninsula, enlightened government, too, had its moment. In both Portugal and Spain, legislative experimentation was pragmatic; it was undertaken in behalf not of the anti-Christian Enlightenment but of the commercial revival of the country and the political independence of the crown. In Portugal, the legislative program was the monopoly of Sebastião José de Carvalho e Melo, marquis de Pombal. Joseph I had ascended the throne in 1750, but he disliked the business of government and left it to Pombal, his favorite minister. Pombal ruled almost as though *he* were king—almost, but not quite: when Joseph I died in 1777, Pombal was instantly dismissed, and his reform program limped on without him. Pombal's first concern was to crush competing centers of power; to that end he curbed the Inquisition, kept the Jesuits from the court, and curtailed the powers of the nobility. An attempt on the life of his king, in September 1758, gave Pombal the pretext he needed. He had several leading Portuguese nobles tried and, early in 1759, cruelly executed. Later that year, Pombal gained a unique distinction for his Catholic country: Portugal was the first kingdom in Europe to sequester the Jesuits' property and to expel them from the country and from its overseas possessions. Pombal's regime illustrates the essential ambiguities of reform activities undertaken not under a constitution or with widespread popular support but by the will of a single autocrat. Pombal worked with single-minded concentration to free Portugal from its commercial dependence on Britain, a condition that was profitable to the latter and galling to the former. He built silk, wool, glass, paper, and gunpowder factories; he founded chartered companies to compete with British traders; he reorganized the tax structure and encouraged free trade between Portugal and her overseas possessions. Once his hands were untied by his triumph over the nobility and expulsion of the Jesuits, he moved toward reform in other fields. He cut government expenditures by dismissing useless officials from their sinecures. He abolished the distinction between "old and new Christians" and thus, in effect, extended toleration to Portuguese Catholics of Jewish ancestry. And the departure of the Jesuits, who ran the schools in Portugal as they did across Catholic Europe, compelled him to found new schools on new principles. He succeeded: under his close supervision, Portugal saw the rise of commercial schools, schools of art, and a comprehensive system of primary and secondary education. Yet with no apparent perception of incongruity, Pombal stamped out opposition, actual or potential, without regard to the niceties of the law or the commands of charity. He honeycombed the country with informers; when the new monarch, Maria I, dismissed him in 1777, she began her reign by releasing a horde of Pombal's prisoners.

Pombal's greatest claim to enlightened statesmanship, which fastened his hold on the loyalty of his king and the imagination of his contemporaries, was his response to the Lisbon earthquake. On November 1, 1755, a devastating tremor, followed by a tidal wave, leveled much of the city and left thirty thousand dead. Tirelessly and efficiently, Pombal labored to bring the city out of its shock and panic and to restore it to a semblance of normal life. The famous command attributed to him—"bury the dead and feed the living"—appears to be apocryphal, but it is an apt epitome of his work, and of authoritarian eighteenth-century reform in general.

In neighboring Spain, planning and reform were perhaps less spectacular than in Portugal, but more sustained. Spain's first Bourbon king, Philip V, died in 1746, and was succeeded by his son, Ferdinand VI, pacific in foreign policy and mildly interested in domestic reform. Despite his mediocrity and general lack of initiative, Ferdinand superintended the beginnings of tax reform and, in line with other Catholic rulers of his day, curbed the Inquisition. But it was not until his half-brother Charles, king of Naples, ascended the throne in 1759, that Spain entered the main current of eighteenth-century reform. Experienced and popular as he was, Charles' earliest interventions only served to document the tenacity of Spanish conservatism. His favorite minister, the Sicilian marquis di Squillace, aroused a furor of xenophobia. His edicts ordering the cleaning of streets, lighting of roads, and construction of highways seemed reasonable enough, but they were accompanied by rumors of his private rapacity, and all this in a time of high bread prices. In 1766 Squillace prohibited the wearing of the traditional Spanish slouch hat and long cape (on the ground that the former prevented the recognition of bandits, and the latter concealed their weapons). There was a popular riot, and Squillace was forced into exile. His successors, the counts de Aranda and de Floridablanca, Spaniards both, were more diplomatic than the luckless Squillace. Under their regime, loyally supported by Charles III, a measure of Enlightenment came to Spain. Aranda was an admirer of Voltaire and an acquaintance of the Encyclopedists. Under his eye, and at his urging, Spain expelled the Jesuits in 1767 in the wake of widespread reports that they had been behind the anti-Squillace riots and secretly opposed all reform. Aranda, too, converted the Spanish Inquisition into a relatively innocuous office. But Charles III refused to countenance its abolition: "The Spaniards want it," he is reported to have said of the Inquisition, "and it does not bother me."[1]

The royal remark, whether authentic or invented, expresses the conservative tenor of Spanish reform. Only a handful of the philosophes' writings were permitted to enter Spain; in the censoring of books, the Inquisition retained a certain measure of influence. Indeed, when the French Revolution burst over France in 1789, Spain's panic-stricken response was to prevent its contagion from crossing the borders. Charles III had died in 1788, but Floridablanca, who

---

[1] Quoted in Richard Herr, *The Eighteenth Century Revolution in Spain* (1958), 29. For the origins of the Spanish Inquisition, see p. 104.

survived him and retained office under Charles IV, sealed off Spain with a fair degree of effectiveness. Official newspapers reported nothing at all; news of the fall of the Bastille on July 14, 1789, entered Spain underground and became known to a few only later that month. In such an atmosphere, the sphere of reform was severely constricted. The government built roads, simplified and reduced taxes, encouraged local industry, improved the policing of cities and the administration of justice. The primary and secondary school system was radically modernized, and the universities painfully freed themselves from the Scholastic mold in which they had been frozen for centuries. But such reform was always timid; the Enlightenment that the most radical of the reformers could countenance was the kind that in no way questioned the truths of the Roman Catholic church. Characteristically, it was the *amigos del pais*—societies devoted to disseminating information on agricultural and industrial techniques—that spread across Spain's major cities and, of all new institutions, enjoyed the greatest success. They did not, after all, touch on sacred things. Yet even the *amigos del pais,* with their affronts to traditional ways, found their triumphs at best partial. The societies that need change most usually resist it best.

"Old Fritz" and His Prussia

If the name "enlightened despot" has any application at all, it applies to Frederick of Prussia. Except for participating in the dismemberment of Poland (see p. 488) and a brief flurry against Hapsburg Austria over Bavaria in the late 1770s, Frederick II after 1763 cultivated the arts of peace. In the twenty-three years that remained to him—he died in 1786, venerated and feared by his people as Old Fritz—he sought to heal the wounds his own wars had made. He resumed his interrupted friendship with Voltaire, though never on the old intimate footing; the two depended entirely on correspondence—a safe and distant means of communication. Frederick continued to write poetry, essays, history, and memoirs, all in French, and to despise the burgeoning seeds of German culture all around him. None of the German writers of his day—not even Lessing, not even the phenomenally gifted young Goethe—found favor in his eyes. They were, after all, not French neoclassicists. When all was said and done, they did not write like Voltaire.

Frederick II found it relatively easy to concentrate on domestic restoration; unlike many contemporary potentates, he had no factions to appease or rivals to fear at home. His role as "the first servant of the state" was self-imposed. He would do his duty as he saw it, surrounded by obedient servants. Service to the state, in Frederick's view, was service to reason, specifically to *raison d'état;* it included a conscientious attempt to eliminate subjective motives like pride, ambition, and desire for revenge. As he put it in his Political Testament of 1752, the statesman must realistically concentrate on "the strengthening of his state and the growth of its power." Frederick II tried to run Prussia as if he were running a machine; it worked fairly well as long as the supreme engineer was at the controls. How quickly it could fall apart after he left them became promptly and painfully evident during the Napoleonic Wars, only two decades after Frederick II's death (see p. 515). The king governed alone, from the privacy of his study, from which he periodically emerged on his feared tours of inspection. The French minister to Prussia, Lord Tyrconnel, had reported in 1751: "The King is naturally mistrustful and in general thinks ill of all men. He consequently gives his confidence to none and often plays his own Ministers false by misinforming them on the few subjects which he leaves in their hands. He transacts all his business himself, and seldom allows his Ministers to make representations, especially in foreign affairs."[2] His suspiciousness only increased as the reign stretched into the 1770s and 1780s. Voltaire, who knew his Frederick well, had good cause to deplore Frederick's low estimate of human nature and a cynicism that saw mankind solely governed by fear of punishment and hope for reward.

Yet, cynic though he was, Frederick II was philosophe enough (and found enough enjoyment in the publicity the philosophes gave him) to take his duty to provide enlightened government with the utmost seriousness. "My peacetime activity," he wrote to an admirer as early as 1742, after his first Silesian venture, "must be as useful to the state as had been my concern for the war." After 1763, he had the time to stress this aspect of his self-imposed servitude. From his early days he had been hostile to all organized religions, impatient with theology, and contemptuous of priests of all denominations. Shortly after his accession, he had proclaimed freedom of conscience: "Religions must all be tolerated . . . for here everybody must be saved in his own fashion." Frederick's consistent if limited policy of toleration sprang from this attitude: it was a tolerance born of indifference, even of disdain.[3] The secularism implicit in such a view also governed Frederick's other domestic policies. Three days after his accession, he abolished torture in cases of high treason and mass murder; in 1755 he suppressed it altogether. The state must act not to avenge crime, he thought, but to deter it. In the 1740s, he ordered Samuel von Cocceji, the minister of justice, to prepare a new code for Prussia; after Cocceji's death in 1755, younger jurists, notably Karl Gottlieb Suarez and J. H. von Carmer, carried on his work. While they had not completed it by 1786, the year of Frederick II's death, the direction of their thinking, and that of Frederick's, was plain: the state is a legal institution, not a religious one; its ruler and subjects

[2] Quoted in C. A. Macartney, ed., *The Habsburg and Hohenzollern Dynasties in the Seventeenth and Eighteenth Centuries* (1970), 329.

[3] Frederick II's attitude was by no means wholly consistent. Toward the Jews, whom he regarded with even greater contempt than other human beings, he was persistently distrustful; in his Political Testaments he urged his successor to keep the numbers and the economic power of the Jews in check. But Frederick himself used them, as bankers and industrialists, when they suited his own schemes.

have clearly defined rights and obligations; and the whole stands under the sign, not of tradition or churchly regulation, but of reason. It was the reason of Prussian absolutism, not of the philosophes. The code formalized the social structure that Frederick II took so strictly: the nobility, the bourgeoisie, and the peasantry were three distinct estates, with little mobility among them. Thus Prussia's rigid social, political, and legal structures were officially acknowledged and confirmed. This was not what most of the philosophes had had in mind.

Frederick's peculiar mixture of *raison d'état* and enlightened policies emerges most clearly in his economic policy. As a good mercantilist, Frederick gave economic matters high priority and made them, as much as possible, the business of the state. Prussia was poor in resources, in industry, and in population. Frederick husbanded the first, encouraged the second, and enlarged the third. He founded a bank and several trading companies; he offered powerful inducements to foreign workers and capitalists to migrate to Prussia; he improved Prussia's transportation system by constructing a series of canals and new ports. But progress was slow. Frederick was appalled to find Prussian merchants without initiative; yet he would give them neither the economic freedom nor the social prestige that would have developed the kind of high morale their counterparts were displaying in England, France, and the Dutch Republic—the three leading capitalist states of his day. And Frederick faced another difficulty, at the core of his political machine. In his view, the Prussian bureaucracy must be the servant of its ruler just as the ruler was the servant of the state. But actually, bureaucrats, mainly of noble family, generated vested interests and a measure of power of their own. In 1766, not long after the end of the Seven Years' War, Frederick set up an office to superintend the customs and the excise, the *régie;* significantly he entrusted its management to de Launay, a Frenchman. Frederick devised this new institution to bypass the General Directory, which had demurred at levying new taxes in the midst of an economic downturn. In fact, Prussia's bureaucrats affected policies by administrative sabotage. To achieve their aim and protect their colleagues, officials would keep silent about embarrassing incidents, submit misleading reports, manipulate inconvenient figures. However hard Frederick tried to subdue his servants, however furiously he railed at them, they were his "active political copartners" who "limited his powers," for they "possessed, in fact, a tacit veto over royal legislation and executive decrees."[4] Yet, much was accomplished. Frederick had the Oder and the Netze valleys drained and settled thousands of families on the reclaimed lands. In consequence, over fifty-seven thousand families found new homes; by 1786 one in every five Prussians belonged to a settler family. In the last decade of his reign, Frederick could look back on his record with some satisfaction. While industry remained relatively insignificant and foreign trade and shipping small, all were growing at a most gratifying rate.

[4] Hans Rosenberg, *Bureaucracy, Aristocracy, and Autocracy: The Prussian Experience, 1660-1815* (1958), 192-193; the book is a splendid essay to which we are much indebted.

Yet, at the same time, Prussia's collection of revenue, and its war chest, were larger than ever. Even Frederick's detractors could not withhold their admiration from so strenuous a performance.[5] Its hidden, nearly fatal flaws emerged later.

The Hapsburgs: A Family Drama

As in Prussia, so in Austria, too, the rhythm of reform accelerated in the 1760s, but for a different reason—not the end of a war but the death of an emperor. In 1765, after Maria Theresa's amiable, adored, and ineffectual husband, Francis, died, the amble of cautious compromise changed to the gallop of determined innovation. Joseph, Maria Theresa's eldest son, was promptly elected German emperor, and his mother co-opted him as her co-regent. Final authority remained in her capable hands, but Joseph II was far too assertive to remain a mere figurehead. For fifteen years, until Maria Theresa's death in 1780, mother and son argued, cooperated, and clashed. Maria Theresa watched Joseph with motherly tenderness and statesmanlike disapproval; she tried to curb his tongue, give him patience, and teach him tact—in vain. "You are a coquette of wit," she admonished him in a long letter in 1776, "and run after it wherever you think to find it, without discrimination. . . . What I fear is that you will never find a friend, a man attached to Joseph—by which you set such store—for it is neither from the Emperor nor from the co-Regent that these biting, ironical, malicious shafts proceed, but from the heart of Joseph, and this is what alarms me, and what will be the misfortune of your days and will entail that of the Monarchy and of us all."[6] In her fond concern, she exaggerated, but her admonitions were not without point: Joseph's character was at once his greatest asset and his gravest liability. His devotion to work and aversion to frivolity were complete; his supervision of his officials, though effective, approached paranoia; he desired the good of his subjects with a fanatical intensity that ultimately caused great suffering. His edicts, issued from his office in a veritable avalanche, trampled on cherished feelings and ancient, deeply rooted practices. Joseph showed all the callousness of the ruler who combined absolute sincerity with absolute power. He puzzled the philosophes, who watched him with a great deal of interest. "The Emperor is hard to judge," wrote the Physiocrat Du Pont. "When one observes what he has done and is doing daily for his country, he is a prince of the rarest merit. . . . But on the other hand, when one takes a look at his political attitude toward his neighbors, his avidity for war, his desire for aggrandizement, the partition of Poland, the invasion of Bavaria, the plots against the Turkish Empire, his disrespect for old

[5] See Hajo Holborn, A History of Modern Germany, vol. II, 1648-1840 (1964), 262-277.
[6] Quoted in Macartney, Habsburg and Hohenzollern Dynasties, 185-186.

treaties, his inclination to decide everything by force, then the noble-minded eagle is only a terrible bird of prey."[7] After 1780, when he ruled alone, these contradictions became more palpable than ever.

Not surprisingly, a potentate of such single-mindedness could brook no opposition and tolerate no independent centers of power. Joseph II was an avid centralizer. He laid his hands on the court chancellery, reorganized the ministries, and constructed new departments. Yet the result was not efficiency but paralysis: Joseph II was too eager to be everywhere to be able to construct a rational administrative system—even had the resistance of established bureaucrats permitted it. Joseph II, all too readily, confused reason of state with his own will. His policy toward subject peoples was no more tactful. Sweeping aside the anxious warnings of his ministers, he replaced self-governing institutions in Hungary and in the Austrian Netherlands with a uniform bureaucracy centered ultimately on himself. More autocratic than his mother, Joseph II broke more promises than Maria Theresa ever had. He was an indefatigable Germanizer; when, in 1784, he decreed German to be the official language, he gravely affronted the Hungarians and sealed the humiliation of the Czechs, who had endured Hapsburg autocracy since early in the seventeenth century (see p. 250). It was not that Joseph II thought German culture somehow superior to all others, but that his rage for uniformity of laws, rules, and regulations knew no bounds. Ironically enough, Joseph avoided the company of philosophes and, quite literally, went out of his way *not* to meet Voltaire, but with his overriding desire to make everyone happy, in *his* own way, he acted like a caricature of a philosophe in power.[8]

In his hostility to institutions competing with the autocratic authority of the state, Joseph II could hardly overlook the nobility in his sprawling domains. Aristocratic clans held vast estates and kept them intact with a strict system of land entail, the *Fideikommiss.* They had a firm grip on ceremonial court offices and a monopoly of high posts, often sinecures with rich emoluments and no duties, in the government, the army, and the church. And they enjoyed extensive, almost unchecked privileges over their peasants. Like Louis XIV a century before, Joseph II broke these noble monopolies by introducing commoners into positions of power: seven members of his imperial cabinet, and three out of every four officials in the ministry of war were commoners. Even the nobles appointed to public place were expected to give their undivided loyalty to the state and to defend it against intermediate interests and lesser allegiances.[9] A related aspect of Joseph's absolutism, his peasant policy, grew

[7] Quoted in Heinz Holldack, "Der Physiokratismus und die absolute Monarchie," *Historische Zeitschrift,* CVL (1932), 533.

[8] This is not to say that he did not get philosophic counsel. He was particularly open to the advice of Joseph von Sonnenfels, grandson of a rabbi, son of a Catholic convert, professor at the University of Vienna, and distinguished theorist of public administration.

[9] See H. G. Schenk, "Austria," in A. Goodwin, ed., *The European Nobility in the Eighteenth Century* (1953), 109.

beyond a mere attack on aristocratic privilege into a characteristic instance of what came to be known as "Josephinism."

Josephinism

Most peasants in the Hapsburg territories were for all practical purposes serfs. Their legal position differed from province to province and was, for the most part, better than that of their Russian counterparts. Yet in practice their dependence was almost unmitigated and certainly inescapable. Peasants were obliged to perform onerous, back-breaking, compulsory labor service, and stood by powerless if their landlord chose to expel them from their meager holdings because he judged he could cultivate the land more profitably in large enclosed farms. Practically the whole tax burden imposed by the Hapsburg government was either borne directly by or passed on to the peasants, while their noble masters lived increasingly luxurious lives at court or in their splendid local manor houses. Maria Theresa had launched some extensive investigations and instituted some pioneering reforms, setting an upper limit to taxation and to *robot*. But it was not until after 1780, when Joseph II attacked the peasant question with his characteristic impatience, that legislation became systematic. Beginning in November 1781, in a stream of edicts, he addressed himself to the peasant's life and turned him from a pliant instrument in the hands of his omnipotent master into a subject of the Austrian government. Here, as elsewhere, Josephinism directed itself against intermediate powers in the state. Joseph's first edicts erased all remaining traces of the *Leibeigenschaft*—personal servitude—still in force after Maria Theresa's initial reforms. They stipulated the kinds of penalties a court could impose on peasants and gave peasants an elaborate procedure for lodging complaints against their lord or their lord's steward. These were only the first steps, and in practice small ones; they were supplemented by further edicts regulating forced labor and limiting the landlord's other exactions. Yet, for all Joseph's furious energy, resistance to all these enactments, especially to a proposed tax reform of 1789, was powerful and, in the end, triumphant. Joseph's liberal peasant policy remained more an aspiration for the future than a guide to the present.

In the area of religious policy, Josephinism was rather more successful. Its rationale was, as usual, complicated. Joseph was anxious to enlist the church in his campaign to make good—that is, obedient—subjects, to curtail its influence in the state, and to reduce its dependence on Rome. His motives were also intensely personal and are therefore hard to fathom. Suspicious as he was of the philosophes, he shared their distaste for the "wasteful" lives of monks and nuns and their fear of priestly control over education and marriage. Joseph claimed to be a good Catholic and advertised his religious policy as an act of purification wholly consonant with adherence to the Church of Rome. His antipapal policy, in fact, owed much to the German prelate von Hontheim, whose doctrines are generally known as Febronianism.[10] In any event, whatever his true convictions, no issue caused greater controversy between Joseph and his doting mother than religion. He profoundly provoked Maria Theresa by urging that "all sects" enjoy "perfect equality" and by insisting on his essential principle, "liberty of belief."[11] He tried to reassure his mother: "I would give all I possess," he told her, "if all the Protestants of your States would go over to Catholicism." But he argued at the same time that a sound state must not seek to do the work of the Holy Spirit, but must confine itself instead to ensuring punctual obedience to the laws. "The word 'toleration,' as I understand it, means only that I would employ any persons, without distinction of religion, in purely temporal matters, allow them to own property, practice trades, be citizens, if they were qualified and if this would be of advantage to the State and its industries. . . . The undisturbed practice of their religion makes them far better subjects and causes them to avoid irreligion." Maria Theresa was appalled at such lax doctrine. The institution of tolerance, she told Joseph, would be a "misfortune, the greatest which would ever have descended on the Monarchy." Her attitude toward the Jews, another issue that divided mother and son, accurately defines her horizons: "I know of no worse plague than this people, with their swindling, usury, and money-making, bringing people to beggary, practicing all evil transactions which an honest man abhors." To her, a tolerant recognition of cultural variety was a betrayal of the true faith, the child—and the father—of religious indifference.

It was therefore only after her death—but very promptly after—that Joseph II found it possible to translate his convictions into legislation. His famous Toleration Edict was issued in October 1781. It extended considerable religious and full civic rights to Protestants, though retaining a visibly privileged status for Catholic places of worship. Protestant churches, the decree specified, "shall not have any chimes, bells, or towers, unless such already exist, or public entrance from the street signifying a church." These were bearable constraints: Protestants were granted the right to worship in peace, to appoint teachers for their parish schools, to choose their pastors, to raise their children in their faith, to buy houses and real property, to practice as master craftsmen, and to be admitted to "academic appointments and posts in the public service" without being "required to take the oath in any form contrary to their religious tenets." In the course of time, issuing separate decrees for each of his domains between 1781 and 1789, Joseph extended some, though by no means all, of these rights to Jews as well; as Joseph explicitly noted, it was his intention not to raise the Jews in his domains to full equality, but to place them "on a footing of near-equality." In a spirit typical of the Enlightenment, he exacted from the

---

[10] The name derives from the pseudonym "Febronius" which von Hontheim used for his critique of the pope, published in 1763.

[11] Quoted material is from Macartney, *Habsburg and Hohenzollern Dynasties,* 145-169 passim.

Jews, in return, a measure of assimilation: "We do earnestly exhort them to observe strictly all political, civic, and judicial laws of the land. . . . We look to their sense of duty and their gratitude" not to abuse "Our grace and the freedom deriving from it to cause any public scandal by excesses and loose living." Many eighteenth-century free spirits, even sovereigns who professed contempt for old prejudices and advocated freedom, found it hard wholly to escape the first and wholly to grant the second.

Yet, limited though Joseph's radicalism was, the bulk of the Catholic hierarchy in his domains and the papacy in Rome found his edicts of toleration extremely alarming. In 1782, Pope Pius VI took the unprecedented step of visiting Vienna to protest against the Toleration Edict. He got no more than a respectful reception. Indeed, some of Joseph's other interventions were even more disturbing. It was one thing to close down all the contemplative orders in the kingdom—that had been done in other Catholic countries. It was a drastic but not unprecedented step to place the surviving monasteries under state control and to establish a series of "general seminaries" in which future priests would be trained uniformly, free from what Joseph called the "fanatical hydra of ultramontanism." After all, Joseph also decreed in 1783 that in areas of his kingdom "where the parochial clergy are too few in numbers, or too far from the communes which they serve," new priests or curates should be sent, and that all shortages of churches and vicarages be promptly repaired as well. Joseph's insistence that all religious policy-makers, including archbishops, look to Vienna instead of Rome was also familiar; during the eighteenth century, many good Catholic rulers claimed the ultimate supremacy of secular over religious authority. Many of Joseph's decrees, including those concerning monastic orders and religious holidays, had been anticipated by Maria Theresa, whose loyalty to the faith of Rome was never questioned by anyone. But Joseph intervened in Catholic practice, and this aroused vehement opposition not merely among priests, but among his population as well. He produced an "order of divine service," which regulated such petty but cherished details as the number of candles proper on the altar; and, in the interest of purifying and elevating the church, he decreed that his subjects be buried not in coffins but in sheets or linen sacks—an edict that was promptly withdrawn. [12] Down to his pathetic end in 1790, Joseph II never learned that it is easier to curtail the power of the few than to change the habits of the many.

From Joseph II to Leopold II

Joseph had a decade of sole government, and in that time he tried to reform everything. He decreed the institution of civil marriage; he simplified and modernized the legal code, removing from the catalogue of crimes such offenses

---

[12] See Saul K. Padover, *The Revolutionary Emperor: Joseph the Second, 1741-90* (1934), 231.

as apostasy from the Roman church and the practice of magic. He reformed the courts, reducing the jurisdiction of local aristocrats. He wiped out censorship, thus inundating the country with heterodox opinions from abroad. Like his mother, he took an abiding interest in education and in attracting skilled foreigners to his dominions. Yet on balance, as Joseph II himself sadly realized, his rule was a failure. Six thousand edicts in ten years testify to his industry, his energy, and his ubiquity. But he discovered that everything he did aroused opposition, even resistance. It is too easy to criticize his ignorance of human nature and his impatience with the conservatism of custom. Joseph suffered from the dilemma of all radical reformers: he feared that moderate proposals and tactful proceedings would bring no visible results, and he found that the forced pace he set brought only rebellion.

While in the late 1780s there was unrest in his Austrian dominions, Joseph's most pressing problems arose in the south, in Hungary, and in the west, in the Austrian Netherlands. Joseph's rage for centralization and his insensitive disregard for traditional privileges were partly responsible for these rebellions. But in addition Joseph's foreign policy obliged him to raise money from unwilling subjects. In 1778, while Maria Theresa was still alive, Joseph had involved Austria in the brief, almost bloodless War of the Bavarian Succession, which had given him only a small portion of eastern Bavaria—far less than he had plotted to obtain. Later, in 1785, his continued designs on Bavaria led to the formation of the *Fürstenbund,* the League of German Princes, which held Joseph in check. Then, in 1788, Austria joined its ally, Russia, in a war against the Ottomans, and the campaign turned out to be a frustrating and expensive adventure. Hard-pressed for money, Joseph proposed to raise taxes on, among others, the Hungarian nobility, and this without calling the diet that the constitution provided for. Joseph had already mortally offended articulate Hungarians with his language decrees, his refusal to be crowned king of Hungary, and other abrasive measures. In the fall of 1789, the threat of rebellion was very real, while loyal Hungarian officials begged the emperor to change his course. The Austrian Netherlands, meanwhile, were in open revolt, led (in striking distinction from the revolutions all across the Western world) by the forces of conservatism. The application of the Toleration Edict to the Belgian lands and the closing down of the contemplative orders had aroused widespread anger; Joseph's arbitrary, rationalistic intervention in the celebration of religious holidays and time-honored constitutional arrangements brought Brabant to rebellion in late 1787; in December 1789 the Netherlands Estates General proclaimed Joseph deposed. Disheartened, sick, worn out before his time—he was not yet fifty—Joseph II hastened to undo what he had done and, late in January 1790, gave the Hungarians what they had pressed for. He agreed to repeal the most disturbing of his enactments and to convoke a Coronation Diet. He did not live to see it: in February 1790, he died, to be succeeded by his younger brother, Leopold, as Emperor Leopold II. The concessions Joseph had not had time to make, his successor promptly granted.

Leopold II was an extraordinary figure, perhaps the only ruler of the eighteenth century to take the vocation of enlightened monarch seriously. Since 1765, he had governed Tuscany with a consistently progressive program designed to permit the Tuscan people ultimately to determine their own political life. His elder brother's policies, which he derided as "despotism," struck him as the opposite of good government. All his early reforms, he wrote in 1782, had been designed to awaken "in men's hearts the feeling of an honorable civic freedom, and the habit of devotion to, and zeal for, the public good." To that end, he instituted free trade and a humane legal code, reformed local government, and improved the police; then, in 1779, he began to draft a constitution that would sum up his reform work and give the Tuscans political self-determination. His belief in the fundamental rights of the people was exceptional for its radicalism and its consistency. The sovereign, he wrote, is "only the delegate of his people" and must "govern through law alone." If the ruler is granted preeminence, it is for the sake of his subjects, whom he is duty-bound to make happy, "not as he wants it, but as they themselves want it and feel it." This was to take the logic of Enlightenment as education for autonomy to its logical conclusion.

A combination of domestic resistance, administrative sabotage by reluctant officials, and unexpected foreign involvements aborted the scheme for a constitution. And then in 1790, Leopold was called to succeed his brother in Vienna. In his short reign—he died suddenly in March 1792—he repealed much of his brother's hasty and schematic work. He pacified the Hungarians, restored order in the Austrian Netherlands, and withdrew much of the legislation that seemed to him unenforceable or calculated to alienate too many powerful social groups from the monarchy. His partial repeal of Josephinism was based less on fear of the revolutionary forces at work in the West, and less on the growing conservatism of an aging liberal, than on his innate tact, his commitment to constitutional procedures, and his search for stability in a multinational empire. What his role might have been in the decade of the French Revolution is hard to say. He died too soon.

EXTREMES IN EASTERN EUROPE: RUSSIA AND POLAND

Catherine of Russia: At Home

Of all the eighteenth-century monarchs ostensibly devoted to enlightened government, Catherine II of Russia was doubtless the most spectacular and the most disappointing. The philosophes, most of whom she cleverly kept at a distance, greatly overestimated her; Voltaire in particular acted as her unpaid propaganda agent in the West. In her struggle for security, Catherine needed all the help she could get, and the philosophes' all-too-public adulation could be had at bargain rates. It cost a few pensions and generous gestures, some honeyed letters and some well-advertised obeisances to the principles of Montesquieu; in return, it gave her a good press that helped to establish and solidify her reputation before a skeptical world.

It was the manner of her accession that made Catherine need help and the world skeptical. When in June 1762 Catherine deposed her inadequate husband, Peter III, and took the throne, her dependence on her aristocratic co-conspirators seemed so complete that few observers gave her much chance of survival. "It is certain," the Prussian ambassador reported back to Frederick II soon after her coup d'etat, "that the reign of the Empress Catherine is not to be more than a brief episode in the history of the world." [13] The forecast proved wrong, but it was sensible. Catherine had been born a foreigner and a heretic—a German princess of the Lutheran persuasion. Her title to the throne was weaker than that of Prince Ivan, briefly tsar in 1744, or that of her son Paul. She had come to power by means of a palace revolt, and rulers who owe their accession to intrigues live under the threat of being deposed by the same means. Her passion for amorous adventure, which emerged early and lasted her lifetime, exposed her to public scandal and, worse, seemed to put her at the mercy of her many lovers whom she, in her gratitude, endowed with public posts and great estates. Worst of all, when her husband, the deposed tsar, was assassinated in July 1762, she was rumored to have ordered or abetted the murder; she certainly knew of the act and never punished the actors. Rumor also implicated her in the disposition of her other rival, Ivan, murdered in prison in 1764. Western opinion, no longer callous to political assassination, was shocked; even some of the philosophes—always with the exception of Voltaire, who had unlimited indulgence for his "Semiramis of the North"—declared themselves out of patience with her. Yet there was more to Catherine than charm, sensuality, and ambition. She was able, energetic, and in the midst of her pleasures, hard-working. By about 1770 the English *chargé d'affaires* could report that "the power of Her Imperial Majesty increases every day, and is already arrived at such a degree, that this prudent Princess thinks herself strong enough to humble the Guards, who placed her upon the throne." [14]

That might well be: Catherine soon learned to maneuver among rival factions of Russian aristocrats. But she never made the mistake of alienating the aristocracy as a whole. Her intention was to govern. "The monarch must be sovereign," she wrote. "His power cannot be divided." And, while she made far-reaching concessions to the Russian nobility, it remained a service nobility. Catherine followed her late husband's policy of exempting nobles from

---

[13] Quoted in Leo Gershoy, *From Despotism to Revolution, 1763–1789* (1944), 108.
[14] Quoted in Georg Sacke, *Die gesetzgebende Kommission Katherinas II,* in *Jahrbuch für Geschichte Osteuropas,* Beiheft 2 (1940), 156.

compulsory state service, and a number of them took advantage of this new liberality to return to their country estates or to travel abroad. Yet, as Max Beloff has argued, "service to the State in some form continued to be the normal practice among Russian noblemen. It was encouraged by the State, for instance by sumptuary laws which discriminated in favor of nobles who had done their stint. Nobles who had not served were not received at court," so that at the end of the eighteenth century the Russian nobility "was no less a subservient element in the Russian state than it had been under the masterful Peter one hundred years before." [15] Thus in return for service, the nobles had their privileges confirmed. In 1785, Catherine promulgated a charter of nobility that gave it corporate organization in each province, designed to channel noble officials into local government and to serve as a vehicle for grievances. Freedom from compulsory state service was reaffirmed, nobles were explicitly exempted from the billeting of troops, corporal punishment, and perhaps most important, direct taxation. In addition, they were guaranteed trial by their peers and hereditary status, and were granted the right to enter trade and dispose of their land. Best of all, the charter left the vast and increasing power of nobles over their serfs untouched. While Catherine, the philosophe in power, trimmed the remaining privileges of the Russian Orthodox church by extending toleration to minority sects and secularizing church property, she gave the nobility— especially its richest and oldest families—most of what it wanted. Her reward was peace from that difficult, always troublesome quarter.

While Catherine appeased the nobles, she did little for the peasants, beyond fastening the yoke of servitude more securely than ever. Her "enlightened" regime was punctuated by peasant uprisings. The most notable of these was led by the illiterate, charismatic Don Cossack Emelian Pugachev, a new Stenka Razin (see p. 260). Claiming to be Peter III in the flesh, this latest in a long line of pretenders in Russian history enlisted thousands of aggrieved Cossacks, Asiatics subject to Russian hegemony, and embittered peasants conscripted into factory labor. In 1773, Pugachev's casual but fierce army defeated the tsarina's troops in the Volga basin; in 1774 it took the city of Kazan. Pugachev's inflammatory rhetoric embodied a social program: he told his followers to treat the noble landowners as "traitors to the empire, despoilers of the peasants," and to put them to death—instructions his followers cheerfully obeyed. In the end, Catherine's troops were too much for him: in September 1774, after a crushing defeat, he was betrayed and brought to Moscow, where, in January 1775, he was publicly quartered. Clearly, humanitarianism did not extend to social rebels.

Not all of Catherine's reign was maneuver or repression. She reduced tariffs, imported skilled foreigners, and cultivated the iron industry. In this one industry, indeed, she could boast some remarkable results: dozens of new iron works were built, especially in the rich Ural Mountains, and by the end of her

[15] Max Beloff, "Russia," in Goodwin, European Nobility, 181–182, 189.

reign, Russia was exporting pig iron to all of Western Europe, including England. But capital was too scarce, the urban bourgeoisie too timid, and domestic consumption too restricted, to permit Russia to compete for long with the more dynamic economic powers of the West. It remained a land of domestic handicraft and an importer of manufactured goods. Yet in the search for economic growth, Catherine made at least some strenuous, if incomplete and often misguided efforts. In other respects, her domestic policy reads like an exercise in duplicity. In 1767, she convened a legislative commission and supplied it with her famous *Nakaz*—Instruction. This *Instruction,* ostentatiously patterned after Montesquieu and Beccaria, provided guidelines for legislation and for a legal code, and even laid down principles of political theory. The commission, which included representatives from the government, the nobility, the towns, the peasants, the Cossacks and other subject peoples, earnestly debated the *Instruction* and submissively praised Catherine. Admirers called it a monument to liberalism, cynics a charade, and in the end the cynics were right: by 1768, most of the representatives had left to serve in Catherine's first war against the Ottomans (see p. 436), and the noble intentions (or, at least, the noble professions) of the *Instruction* were forgotten. Catherine's comprehensive reform of provincial government displays similar ambiguities. In an ambitious act of 1775, Russia was divided into provinces of roughly equal size, each headed by a governor, and each subdivided into manageable districts. But the measure in effect gave the landed magnates a share in the tsar's autocratic authority; like other reforms, it benefited the privileged by securing them in their privileges. By the end of the reign the process of Europeanization begun by Peter was complete; in trade as in international politics, Russia was a power to be reckoned with. But the cost was very high: a deeply divided society.

Catherine of Russia: Abroad

Catherine never absorbed that old and obvious lesson that foreign conquests cost money. The sums she lavished on her entertainments and her favorites were vast; the sums she poured into her wars were vaster. In the thirty-four years of her reign, the outlay of the Russian state quadrupled; the issuing of paper money had caused ruinous inflation; and taxes rose precipitously. Undeterred, the tsarina pressed on.

Catherine directed her aggressive attentions principally to two of her neighbors: Poland to her west and Turkey to her south. Her adventures were linked: Russia's intervention in Poland brought the Ottomans, alarmed at Russia's growing power, into the field. Poland was easy terrain for manipulation and conquest; it had declined in the course of a hundred and fifty years from stability and even grandeur into an international joke. Poland's Catholic ruling oligarchy, the landed gentry, oppressed, and on occasion actively persecuted, its large ethnic and religious minorities. Poland's elective king was a puppet in the hands of the proud and quarrelsome nobility. The work of the Polish Diet was an exercise in futility; a single deputy could force its dissolution and the cancellation of its earlier decisions by exercising the *liberum veto.*[16]

Voltaire expressed the general contempt when he characterized Poland as the plaything of selfish forces. "The nobility and the clergy defend their liberty against their king, and take it away from the rest of the nation." Such a country virtually invited the intervention of its more powerful neighbors. In 1764, Catherine replied to that invitation. When Poland's Saxon king, Augustus III, died in 1763, Catherine bullied and bought Polish support to secure the election of a former lover, Stanislas Poniatowski. At the same time, in concert with Frederick of Prussia, she insisted on perpetuating the anarchy prevalent in Poland and on posing as the champion of its religious minorities. Things did not go smoothly. Once on the throne, Poniatowski aimed at reform, especially the abolition of the *liberum veto,* an improvement in the Polish state that Catherine had no interest in permitting. And her insistence that Roman Catholic Poland grant toleration to the Dissidents—the Greek Orthodox and the Protestants— brought the formation of the anti-Russian Confederation of Bar.

In 1768, the Ottoman's alarm, shrewdly stimulated by the French ambassador, resulted in a Turkish declaration of war on Russia. Catherine converted the war she had not wanted into a convincing demonstration of Russia's stature. Her Polish intervention had worried the Turks; her rapid and convincing victories, dramatically underscored by the operations of Russian naval squadrons that had sailed from Kronstadt around Europe into the Mediterranean, in turn worried the Austrians. By 1771, war between Austria and Russia seemed only a matter of time. But this would be a general European conflict that the great powers rather dreaded. Frederick of Prussia found the way out. Playing on rising sentiments for the partition of Poland, he convinced both Russia and Austria to annex some Polish territory instead of fighting one another. Catherine still adhered to the traditional Russian view of Poland as a useful buffer in the west, but early in 1772, the bargain was concluded, and in August, the first Partition pitilessly cut into the body of Poland. Roughly one third of Poland's territory, and nearly one half of its population, went to its rapacious neighbors: Prussia acquired most of Polish Prussia; Austria received Red Russia, Galicia, and western Podolia; Russia took the Greek Orthodox eastern sections of the country—White Russia and territories to the Dvina and the Dnieper rivers.

---

[16] The member, presumably speaking for the province that had elected him, but actually open to bribery on other appeals by a local magnate or a foreign power, simply rose and said, *"nie pozwalam—I protest."* This was called "exploding" the Diet; for a century nearly all of them had ended in this way. True, the Poles had devised a constitutional alternative, the Confederation, which could substitute for the Diet; here the *liberum veto* did not hold and simple majority ruled. But in practice this meant virtual civil war among contending aristocratic clans. The whole system, ostensibly designed to protect individual liberty and a symbol of the equality of every Polish gentleman, was organized anarchy.

The Turkish War, meanwhile, continued to go well for the Russians. In 1769, Russian troops had overrun Moldavia and Wallachia, and were stirring up revolt in Greece. In July 1770, the Russian navy annihilated the Turkish navy at the battle of Chesme, and by 1771, the Russians were in the Crimea. The affair of Poland and the Pugachev rebellion slowed Russian operations, but the Peace of Kutchuk-Kainarji of 1774 detached the Crimea from the Ottoman Empire and gave Russia the mouth of the Dnieper, freedom to navigate the Black Sea, and the right to make representations in behalf of Christian subjects of the Turks. This last, a vaguely worded provision, laid the groundwork for future Russian interventions.

Catherine's victory encouraged her further. In 1780, she won Joseph II's assent to the "Greek project," which looked to the expulsion of the Turks from Europe; in 1783, on the pretext of restoring order, she annexed the Crimea. Further deliberate provocations on her part drove the Turks into war once more: in 1788, the second Russo-Turkish War began, ending, much like the first, in Russian gains. In 1792, at the Treaty of Jassy, the Ottomans had to yield up the northern shore of the Black Sea. While Catherine's most ambitious plans had not been realized, the Turkish threat was over. She had four more years to reign, to 1796—and in these final years, though distracted by the French Revolution, she continued Russian expansion in Poland. She had not achieved all she had wanted, but she had wanted much. For the German states, in any event, accustomed in the past to look westward in concern, or for support, Russia was now a formidable neighbor, equal in power perhaps to France.

THE FORTUNES OF FRANCE: 1743-1774

Louis XV: Reign of a Disappointment

In January 1743, the aged Cardinal Fleury died, and Louis XV, sounding much as Louis XIV had sounded in 1661, after the death of Mazarin, announced that he would govern by himself, without a first minister. He did not mean it literally, of course; not even Louis XIV, a far more powerful man than his successor, had been able to forego the counsel of ministers or to overcome the resistance of provincial officials. But Louis XV, though he wished to, was not equipped to lead. He was too indolent, too intent on his pleasure, and despite attacks of energy and independence, too uncertain, to emulate his more energetic contemporaries.

Fleury had given both Louis XV and France what they badly needed: calm leadership, pacific policies, a group of competent and diligent royal officials, and a respite from the costly bellicosity of Louis XIV. True, not long before his death, the war party had dragged Fleury into the War of the Austrian

Succession, and in future years, France would continue the old duel with England in the Seven Years' War (see p. 400). But despite serious losses of territories overseas, France under Louis XV was experiencing economic expansion and widespread prosperity. Fleury's program, though his moderate foreign policy did not in the end prevail, had much to do with this gratifying condition. Peace and the government of able and honest ministers proved good foundations for national well-being. They helped to restore profitable foreign trade and to stabilize a once fluctuating currency. Beginning not long after Fleury's accession, France underwent a long-drawn-out and slow inflation, which acted as a stimulus to the French economy as a whole; it ended about the time Louis XV died, in 1774, and its end, as much as anything else, put France on the road to revolution. Cities boomed, as slave traders, financiers, cotton and silk manufacturers, prosperous judges built their town houses. Roads were improved, new canals speeded the transport of goods. There were gloomy spots in this cheerful picture: tenacious French conservatism, especially strong after Law's schemes had ended in disaster (see p. 380), slowed down the rate of investment and kept alive a host of old-fashioned regulations—internal tariffs, gild regulations—that had long been abandoned in Britain and the Dutch Republic. The poor, as usual, remained poor; as in the course of the century the population increased without a corresponding increase in food production, many of them pressed hard upon the margin of subsistence. And there was unrest in the midst of prosperity. In Lyons, in 1744, the silk workers rose up against their masters, only to be callously repressed by the state: their leaders were tortured and executed or sent to the galleys for life. Prevailing social attitudes precluded the expenditure of pity on such workers; they had risen against their natural place in the social order. And in any case, it was well known that high wages only served to corrupt the poor. "I reflected on the terrible drawbacks of the high cost of labor," Restif de la Bretonne, novelist, pornographer, and social observer, wrote, "and thought of this in terms of the noxious effects on the masses, who, like savage tribes, think only of the present. If they earn enough in three days for necessities, they work for three days only and spend the other four in debauchery." [17] This was in 1788. In the cheerful, prosperous days of the 1740s, such views were, if anything, even more pronounced. Life was good and getting better. Why worry about those whose appointed task in life was to labor and be silent?

Rebellious workers and miserable peasants were objects of religious charity, but they did not constitute a serious problem for the state. The need for an attack on privilege on the other hand, was palpable, even to Louis XV. As a young monarch, he had been called *le bien aimé,* but soon he was widely disliked. As popular opinion turned against the king, he was particularly blamed for his mistresses—for the power they were reputed to hold and the

---

[17] "Les Nuits de Paris or Nocturnal Spectator," in Robert and Elborg Forster, eds., *European Society in the Eighteenth Century* (1969), 264.

money they were reputed to cost. True, the king was an avid womanizer. He had been married in 1725 to Marie Leszczynska, daughter of Stanislas, the deposed king of Poland. But apart from Lorraine, which Stanislas Leszczynski obtained in 1736 as a consolation prize, and which passed to France after his death in 1766, Louis XV had few rewards from his wife. So he occupied himself with hunting and with a shifting gallery of mistresses. The most famous and most interesting of these, Madame de Pompadour, became the king's official mistress in 1745 and remained his friend until her death in 1764, long after Louis' sexual appetites had led him to other mistresses. She was witty and intelligent as well as lovely, and she was a munificent and keen-eyed patron of the decorative arts: the china factory at Sèvres was essentially her idea, and the arts of music, tapestry, weaving, furniture design, and light-hearted painting flourished under her hand. She was doubtless influential and expensive, but her influence was hardly baneful, and her cost, though high, hardly ruinous: "That a lot of money went on palaces, parks, works of art, and even more on places and pensions for courtiers and their hangers-on, is undeniable; but in relation to the whole cost of the government of France the expenditure of the court, excessive as it may have been, does not play a decisive role. The expense, even of a small war, was greater than that of the biggest palace." [18] Still, her reign symbolized a malaise from which Fleury's sensible appointment policies had attempted to rescue France: the prevalence of intrigue, the rule of favorites, the rapid shift of personnel at the top. In such an atmosphere it was hard to devise a rational financial policy, impossible to carry it through.

The Resistance of Privilege

France was a society riddled with privilege—it was burdened with a set of exemptions that Louis XV had not invented, but inherited. Here, more than anywhere else, the legacy of his great predecessor was nothing less than disastrous. The checks on the king's power were not merely personal; many of them were structural. Most official positions—judgeships, army posts, all but the highest government jobs—were private property. They were bought, traded, sold with little interference from the state; their value fluctuated and was regulated by market conditions. This was the so-called "venality of office," an old abuse by which French kings had raised money, but which had become a regular, seemingly irrevocable part of French government early in the seventeenth century. It was rare for the crown to dismiss or to buy out one of its servants; hence judges, bureaucrats, even army officers faced their sovereign with a good deal of independence and with a solid, thoroughgoing esprit de corps which normally put loyalty to one's corporation before disinterested

[18] Alfred Cobban, *A History of Modern France*, vol. I, *Old Regime and Revolution, 1715–1799* (1965), 55.

service to one's country. [19] Resistance to royal decrees was stiffened by appeals for exemptions from this tax or that, granted in the past to nobles, towns, and corporations. The clergy, France's first estate, did not pay taxes, but contributed what it called a "voluntary gift," the *don gratuit,* voted at its quinquennial assemblies. Surviving provincial estates were in perpetual obstructive conflict with royal officials. And while Louis XIV had deprived his parlements of their share in the making of legislation, the regent, as we know, had in effect restored it by restoring their right to remonstrate against royal decrees (see p. 379).

In May 1749, upon the urging of his controller general of finance, Machault d'Arnouville, Louis XV boldly confronted the whole system of privilege. He issued a decree imposing a 5 percent income tax on all his subjects. Machault, former intendant of Valenciennes, had been finance minister since 1745 and had spent the first three years in his office raising money for the War of the Austrian Succession. In 1748, the Peace of Aix-la-Chapelle took that burden off his shoulders and enabled him to address himself to the structure of French taxation. The *vingtième,* that 5 percent income tax, was the result. Resistance was noisy and immediate. The *vingtième* was an equitable tax without exemptions. It thus affronted all those—towns, office holders, nobles, clerics— hitherto exempted, and it endangered the system under which the inequitable indirect taxes were gathered by the farmers general. Worse, it was being levied in peacetime. Under pressure, the parlements registered the decrees, and Louis XV stood firm: Machault, he said, "is the man after my own heart." Officially, the parlements obeyed, but they knew their cause was in capable hands—the clergy. The bishops, highly placed and well connected, mobilized the *dévot* party at court and obliquely threatened to go on strike. Machault, earnest and determined, rallied public opinion in his turn. But his master was too unstable to persevere. In May 1750, the Assembly of the Clergy met in Paris and, in the course of the summer, secured some decisive concessions from a weakening king: in August, he demanded that the clergy deliver up its normal *don gratuit* and add a special gift in the next five years. The principle of a tax without exemptions had been breached. But the clergy wanted more, and in December 1751, Louis XV, thoroughly softened up by the assaults of his own family and of favorite ecclesiastics, withdrew all of his demands. His brave, brief effort at fiscal reform was over.

The parlements had profited from the triumph of the clergy; in the 1750s and 1760s, they took the lead in defending privilege against a vacillating king. In the name of the "French constitution," an unwritten set of precepts with little, if any, legal standing, they preached disobedience and taught it to others. As we shall soon see, their talk led to action, especially in Brittany. With the Parlement of Paris setting the tone, and the provincial parlements providing the

---

[19] Louis XIV had tampered with this system through periodic inquiries into the right of nobles to hold their titles or of office holders to keep their posts. But this had been a kind of blackmail rather than an assertion of absolute power.

echo, the high magistrates sabotaged royal policies and embittered the lives of provincial intendants. The magistrates triumphed all along the line; the expulsion of the Jesuits from France was largely their work, and a sign of their power. The robe nobility of the parlements were Gallican in temper and Jansenist in sympathy; they feared and detested the ultramontane Society of Jesus and schemed to dispose of it, however much Louis XV and his bishops might dislike that. Effective teachers, assiduous collectors of influential personages, subject to stringent military discipline, and slavishly devoted to Rome, the Jesuits, in France as elsewhere, found themselves the targets of dark, unproved, normally untrue charges. The parlements were lucky: the French Jesuits presented them with a solid case. In 1761, a Jesuit commercial house on the island of Martinique had gone bankrupt; a court at Marseilles found the society as a whole financially responsible for the losses its branch had incurred. Whatever possessed them, the Jesuits appealed the verdict to the Parlement of Paris. With unconcealed pleasure, the Paris magistrates seized on the issue and ordered an investigation into the practices and ideas of the Jesuit order. Not surprisingly, they found what they wanted: shocked, they reported that the Jesuits believed in political assassination. In August 1761, the parlement ordered twenty-four Jesuit books burned as irreligious and seditious; in 1762, overcoming royal reluctance, they secured the suppression of the society in France and closed its *collèges;* in 1764, they secured a royal edict officially expelling the Society of Jesus from the country. In 1767, finally, whatever individual Jesuits remained on French soil as secular priests were ordered to leave.

But while they succeeded in their religious politics, in provincial politics the parlements overreached themselves. The parlements' most powerful ally in the royal entourage was the duke de Choiseul, a friend of Madame de Pompadour, who had been secretary of state for foreign affairs since 1758. With his hold on offices and grasp of affairs, Choiseul came closer to rivaling Fleury than anyone else in Louis XV's reign. He had a difficult task: to extricate France from a losing war and to make an acceptable peace. Abler than his British counterparts, tenacious and intelligent, he succeeded to a remarkable degree. Yet, to secure his flank at home, he yielded to the parlements on every point, including the all-important issue of fiscal reform. "Choiseul had willed the end, which was the re-establishment of French power in the world and a war of revenge against England"—to quote Alfred Cobban once again—but "he did not will the necessary means, which was the restoration of royal authority inside France and the reform of royal finances, without which all other reforms would be in vain."[20] Counting on Choiseul, the parlements went too far. In 1764, the provincial estates of Brittany protested against the royal *corvée*—the service due the king for construction and maintenance of roads—as an illegal infringement of its traditional rights; the Breton parlement at Rennes naturally

[20] *History of Modern France*, vol. I, 87.

sustained the estates and suspended the administration of justice. In reply, the royal military commander, d'Aiguillon, had the Breton attorney general, La Chalotais, and five other officials put under arrest. In their newly found unanimity, the other parlements sent vehement remonstrances to Louis XV supporting the strike of their Breton brethren.

The king had had enough. In March 1766, he read the Parlement of Paris a stern lecture on his rights and its duties. He claimed sole sovereign authority and admonished the judges to remember that he was supreme judge as well and that their power depended on his will alone. Besides, the affair of Brittany was none of their business. The magistrates were cowed only for a time. After all, the king had blustered before, only to collapse. In an impudent display of self-confidence, the Breton parlement initiated a prosecution of d'Aiguillon. Paris continued defiant. "This astonishing anarchy," wrote Voltaire, "could not subsist. Either the crown must recover its authority, or the parlement must prevail. In such a critical moment, an enterprising and audacious chancellor was needed. He was found." That chancellor was René Nicolas de Maupeou, a one-time member of the Parlement of Paris, who knew his former colleagues well and detested them thoroughly. Since the mid-1760s, he had enjoyed considerable influence—it is probable that the king's strong language in March 1766 owed something to Maupeou's dour tone and uncompromising views. In September 1768, Louis XV appointed Maupeou his chancellor. In the following year, Maupeou brought the abbé Terray into the government as controller general. Avid for power and intent on his plans, Maupeou knew he could never obtain the former or implement the latter without first ruining his rival, Choiseul. Beginning in September 1770, Maupeou warned the parlements against any further disobedience—in vain. Then, in December, Maupeou and Terray secured Choiseul's dismissal. Maupeou's coup d'etat followed. In January 1771, the members of the Parlement of Paris were dismissed and exiled from the city. In February, Maupeou undertook a far-reaching reform of the judicial system: he abolished venality of office and created six courts in place of the Parlement of Paris, with its extensive jurisdiction. In April, Louis XV publicly declared his unyielding support for Maupeou: "I shall never change."

Actually, the new system, a few minor, much blown-up scandals apart, worked fairly well; gradually, lawyers and judges abated their resistance and agreed to practice before, or sit on, the new courts. At the same time, Terray initiated a reform of French finances as far-reaching as Maupeou's court reforms. His task was, if anything, even harder. He renegotiated the government's contract with the farmers general on better terms for the state, improved the collection and increased the equity of several imposts, and reimposed the old *vingtième*. The aging Louis XV held firm, for once. It seemed as if the counterattack of privilege could be checked and France reformed. Then nature intervened. In May 1774, Louis XV died. He was succeeded by his grandson, Louis XVI. The new king was by no means averse to reform or hostile to reformers, but Maupeou was unpopular, and Louis XVI had no wish to share that "tyrant's" reputation. "What I should like most," he is reported to have said on his accession, "is to be loved."[21] To that end, by late 1774, he had dismissed Maupeou and recalled the parlements. Only a few pessimists recognized that a revolution in France was only a matter of time now. In any event, there was a revolution in the making elsewhere: in America.

THE AMERICAN REVOLUTION

Britain and the American Revolution

In Britain's history, the rebellion of its American colonies stands as a supreme irony. It came after the Hanoverian dynasty had established itself beyond question and after some brilliant British victories in the Seven Years' War. And from the perspective of the colonies, the irony is compounded.

The mercantilist notions of the British government prescribed that the American colonies be subjected to tight economic controls and exploited for the sake of the homeland. But in actuality, the American colonies grew to a measure of political maturity and economic prosperity in an atmosphere of benign neglect. The majority of Englishmen, as J. H. Plumb has put it, "never thought about America at all; to them it was a dumping ground for thieves, bankrupts, and prostitutes," for which England "received tobacco in return."[22] At the same time, British troops defended the American colonies against Indian raids and French incursions, furnishing a far-flung and expensive protective shield that the colonists needed, but ungratefully took for granted.

Colonial government was equally paradoxical. The official powers of each colonial governor were large. He was responsible, and in theory responsive, to the privy council in London, which had the authority to "disallow" colonial laws. When in the 1760s excited demagogues roused up the colonists against the "tyranny" of George III, all these principles were sufficiently denounced. But they did not represent the realities of colonial life. The colonial governor was as much the prisoner of his legislatures as their master; he lived among them and found it politic by and large to listen to them. He had little patronage to dispense, and without patronage, power could rest only on guns, which he did not have and in any event would have been reluctant to use. The board of trade, which from its establishment in 1696 oversaw colonial economic affairs, on occasion placed restrictions on American manufacture and export, but these restrictions were rare and relatively insignificant. And the privy council on the whole left the colonies to themselves and exercised its ultimate veto power with

---

[21] See Gordon Wright, *France in Modern Times, 1760 to the Present* (1960), 42.
[22] *England in the Eighteenth Century* (1950), 124.

the utmost restraint. The impressive growth of American towns, trades, and general prosperity proves that the hand of Britain rested lightly on its American dependencies.

Yet (as subsequent events made abundantly clear) all was not well with Britain's empire overseas, or with Britain's affairs at home. In his long, deliberately undramatic rule, Walpole had given his country deeper tranquility than it had known for over a century (see p. 385). It was only in 1745, three years after Walpole's fall and in the year of his death, that King George II faced one more challenge to his hold on the British crown. Thirty years earlier, in 1715, the son of James II, the Pretender, had launched an invasion to reclaim the throne for the Stuarts. As we know (see p. 383), the "'15" had ignominiously failed. Now the Pretender's son imitated his father, in tactics and in results. The glamorous fables woven around the Young Pretender, Bonnie Prince Charlie and his early successes cannot conceal his ultimate disaster. In July 1745, he landed in Scotland and rallied wide support among the Highlanders. He took Edinburgh, and by fall his rebel troops were on English soil. But while the "'45" enlisted the emotional support of Scotsmen nostalgic for the Stuart dynasty—it was, after all, Scotland's own—the Jacobite cause found practically no supporters among Englishmen. Finally, in April 1746 the Young Pretender's forces were routed by government troops at Culloden, and the Jacobite menace was over. The "'45," intended to overthrow the Hanoverians, only confirmed them on Britain's throne.

From war at home, George II turned his attention to war abroad. And it was foreign war, as we have seen (see p. 401), that compelled George II to turn to Pitt; the outbreak of the Seven Years' War made the immensely popular Pitt the inevitable first minister. Pitt could rightly boast that he had been called into office by his sovereign and "by the Voice of the People." Pitt was first minister during the early months of the Seven Years' War, from November 1756 to April 1757; then, after three months out of office, he returned, with Walpole's old political manager, the duke of Newcastle, as first lord of the treasury. This arrangement remained secure until George II's death in 1760.

The accession of George's grandson as George III changed the shape of Pitt's career and much else in British history besides. George II had disliked Pitt but found he could not do without him for the conduct of the war; George III, who wanted to substitute his old tutor and lifelong favorite, the earl of Bute, for the great war minister, was willing to be consistent. He was ready to close out the war to get rid of Pitt. In 1761, he appointed Bute secretary of state to find ways of making peace; half a year later, Pitt was out of office.

In foreign policy, this turn of events meant the Peace of Paris of 1763, which restored to France at the conference table much that it had lost on the battlefield (see p. 401). At home, it meant a constitutional crisis whose true lineaments did not become clear until a few decades ago, through the magisterial work of Sir Lewis Namier. The critics of George III, and many historians after them, accused the king of seeking to destroy the British

Constitution and to rule absolutely with the aid of his men, the King's Friends. But George III had no wish to subvert the British Constitution; he meant to rule in accord with the constitution established by the Glorious Revolution in 1689. His model was William III, not Charles I. [23]

The king's "aggression" focused new attention on Parliament and on the role of parties in the political life of the nation. While ministers squabbled over the Paris settlement and formed unstable alliances, and while George III envisioned himself as a "patriot king" floating above contending forces, a few perceptive political thinkers reversed the time-honored condemnation of party as mere faction, and praised it instead as an essential element of good government. In 1770, Edmund Burke, a rising Whig politician, articulated this new vision in a famous pamphlet, *Thoughts on the Cause of the Present Discontents*. A party, Burke wrote, "is a body of men united, for promoting by their joint endeavors the national interest, upon some particular principle in which they are all agreed." By implication, a party leader must publicly state his principles and then govern through a firm majority of the House of Commons.

But this raised other and even more pressing problems. When Burke wrote, "parties" were mere coalitions of interest, susceptible to bribery or other pressures from the court. The franchise by which the nation selected its representatives to the House of Commons was notoriously unequal and notoriously open to manipulation. The idea of responsible party government thus could not be divorced from the idea of parliamentary reform, and through the 1760s and 1770s the reform agitation occupied the center of England's political stage. Like all great reform movements, this too enlisted a curious collection of supporters. There was the conservative theoretician Edmund Burke, who believed in "virtual representation"—the government of the rich and powerful in behalf of the lesser orders—but who insisted on the need to eliminate conflicting outside interests among members of Parliament. There was the indefatigable Major John Cartwright, who in contrast to Burke sought to make representation more equal. For fifty years, down to his death in 1824, he campaigned in innumerable pamphlets for the payment of members, for annual elections, for universal male suffrage, for the equalization of parliamentary constituencies, and for the abolition of property qualifications for membership in the House of Commons—the whole program of nineteenth-century English radicals is contained in his energetic writings. And then there was John Wilkes, whose flamboyant style, amorous adventures, and gift for dramatic cases gave the reform agitation a raffish, though by no means absurd, air. Wilkes, known for his ugliness and irresistible attractiveness to women, had

[23] See R. K. Webb, *Modern England from the Eighteenth Century to the Present* (1968), 74. Namier's main work bearing on these years of English politics are the classic *The Structure of Politics at the Accession of George III* (1929) and *England in the Age of the American Revolution* (1930). It must be added, however, that his conception of politics has been criticized for being unduly narrow: see Sir Herbert Butterfield, *George III and the Historians* (1957).

entered Parliament in 1757, but was expelled from it in 1764 for seditious libel. What had aroused the government to this extreme act was the notorious Number 45 of the *North Briton,* a newspaper Wilkes had been publishing since 1762. In that number, Wilkes had so venomously assailed George III's speech from the throne defending the Peace of Paris, that he was thrown into the Tower. Wilkes was released, pleading parliamentary privilege, but once released, he republished the offensive Number 45, and into the bargain an obscene poem entitled *An Essay on Woman.* Facing arrest once more, Wilkes fled to France.

This was only the beginning. In 1768, Wilkes returned, stood for the constituency of Middlesex, was elected, arrested and imprisoned, and once again expelled from the Commons. Obviously enjoying this notoriety, Wilkes stood for reelection for Middlesex four more times, defying the House of Commons which continued to refuse to seat him. But then, in 1774, as Wilkes had some supporters in Parliament, his election was allowed to stand, and the principles of majority rule and free criticism advanced by a step. Stirring events overseas, meanwhile, were engrossing Englishmen including the reformers. The American colonies were filled with unrest; there had been clashes with loss of life. The reformers from all quarters—Burke, Cartwright, Wilkes, and the aging Pitt, now earl of Chatham—called for conciliation with America and voiced their sympathies with the rebels' cause. But the British government, stable once more under the guidance of Lord North, had other ideas and made conciliation impossible.

Foundations of American Identity

It is evident that the American Revolution was a great event in the history of Britain. It was also a great event in the history of Europe, reverberating into the nineteenth and even the twentieth centuries. More immediately, its impact on French finances and, with that, on French politics, was enormous. And in the realm of ideas, it seemed like a fantasy realized. The philosophes had long professed their admiration of the American colonies, and made much of those colonials, like Benjamin Franklin, who came to visit them. In fact, Franklin's enthusiastic European followers used him as a model in two opposite ways. He seemed to embody the simplicity of nature and the sophistication of urbanity; he was philosopher and backwoodsman at the same time. America, wrote Turgot in 1778, must prosper, for the American people are "the hope of the human race; they may well become its model." In the same year, as the aged Voltaire returned to his native Paris to be celebrated and to die, he met Benjamin Franklin in a carefully staged public encounter; while spectators shed tears, Voltaire embraced Franklin and blessed Franklin's grandson in English with the significant words, "God and liberty." For its European well-wishers, the American Revolution was a just cause, but it was also more than that: it was the culmination of a development to which enlightened men could look with hope. America was the Enlightenment in action.[24]

American realities were, of course, much more complicated. The British colonies that rose against their mother country in the 1770s were, though geographically and economically linked, politically and emotionally separate. Their official status was unambiguous: they were colonies, governed from England presumably for its sake. Yet these colonies displayed most of the characteristics one expects from developed states. They had far-flung trade, established elites, social conflicts, colleges, newspapers, and an emerging self-awareness. If European states had their serfs, the American colonies had their slaves. Leading colonial cities had achieved respectable size: in 1775, Philadelphia, America's largest and the British Empire's second largest city, had forty thousand inhabitants; New York followed with twenty-five thousand, then Boston with over sixteen thousand, and Charleston with twelve thousand. Through the seventeenth century, American colonials had looked to England as their home, and their attachment reflected more than economic or political dependence. It was a powerful, unquestioned sentiment, not unmixed with the inferiority feelings of the provincial. England set the tone for the Americans: their religious and political convictions, their cultural styles, their most cherished kind of approval came from there. Nothing could better please the Massachusetts Puritan Cotton Mather, professional theologian and amateur scientist, than to be able to style himself "F.R.S."—Fellow of the Royal Society, London. It was not until the eighteenth century that this began to change. Economic self-interest dictated conduct sharply at variance with the needs of the mother country: during the French and Indian Wars, while the British desperately battled against France on three continents, colonial merchants in America coolly and profitably traded with the enemy. While the colonies squabbled with one another over boundaries, and while frontiersmen argued with "easterners" over Indian policy, the American colonists had enough common interests (intercolonial trade) and common enemies (the Indians, the French, and increasingly, the English government) to develop a certain sense of distance from Europe and a certain sense of identity. Yet it is striking how slowly these feelings grew; Americans became Americans with marked reluctance. Through the 1760s, the most discontented and most radical of the colonists continued to think of themselves as Englishmen[25] and borrowed their most subversive ideas from English political writers. When, on July 4, 1776, the American rebels gave the reasons why it had become necessary for them to "dissolve the political bands" that had hitherto connected them with England,

---

[24] See Peter Gay, *The Enlightenment: An Interpretation,* vol. II, *The Science of Freedom* (1969), 555–568.

[25] The language of the revolution was English, and most revolutionary leaders were of English descent, but by the middle of the eighteenth century, there were numerous settlers of Scotch-Irish and German origins as well. And there were two hundred thirty thousand blacks, practically all of them slaves.

they took care to indict the "tyranny" of "the present King of Great Britain" by citing over a score of "injuries and usurpations." They knew that a declaration of independence was an act of the utmost gravity and, however eager they had become for separation, they felt it as a wrench and needed to explain and justify it.

The special quality of the American experience—what made Americans American—has been debated since the time of the Revolution. "What then is the American, this new man?" J. Hector St. John de Crèvecoeur asked in 1782, in words that have often been quoted. America, he answered his own question, is a land where "individuals of all nations are melted into a new race of men." Anticipating the self-congratulation that would become the envy of Europeans, he added that the Americans' "labors and posterity will one day cause great changes in the world. . . . The American is a new man, who acts upon new principles; he must therefore entertain new ideas, and form new opinions." In good eighteenth-century fashion, Crèvecoeur did not overlook the impact of geography on character: "From involuntary idleness, servile dependence, penury, and useless labor, he has passed to toils of a very different nature, rewarded by ample substance." The American was new in part because America was new. This assertion of American uniqueness itself contributed to the creation of that uniqueness. So did the experience of fighting a war for independence together, under the single command of George Washington.

While, once free and united, Americans strenuously cultivated their sense of a common fate and a common mission, the early history of Britain's colonies on the North American continent differed from colony to colony. Yet some of the common ingredients in the American experience were palpable enough. Settled predominantly on the eastern seaboard and in its adjacent hinterland, migrants to America mainly became farmers. Virgin land was plentiful and agricultural labor scarce—a reversal of the familiar European pattern. Life was isolated, even in the villages of New England or in the Middle Atlantic states; population was thinly scattered, and migrants to America found voyages to their homeland arduous if not perilous. All these factors gave survival value to qualities that Americans later claimed as particularly their own: ingenuity, adaptability, self-reliance, and a certain sense of social freedom, almost egalitarianism. Of course, like the European societies from which they had sprung, the American colonies, too, were socially stratified; the old habits of deference receded slowly. Yet in this vast, largely unexplored and promising new land many traditional guideposts lost their meaning. Social boundaries were more porous, social mobility was easier, sheer ability counted for more than it had at home, in the "old country."

While each colony had its own history, the principal divisions among them were sectional. Indeed, the division that marks (and plagues) the United States to this day—South versus North—emerged early in colonial times. The southern colonies were dominated by large plantations worked by black slaves and white indentured servants. Its great export crop was tobacco; rice and indigo became cash crops only in the eighteenth century. The Middle Atlantic colonies and New England, in contrast, grew tobacco only in a few isolated areas like the southern Connecticut valley. Instead, northern farmers raised corn and wheat and familiar European staples—rye, barley, and oats. In addition, the northern colonies developed a flourishing home industry, weaving linen and making furniture. While the vast majority of Americans even in the North continued to live on, and off, the land, colonial towns grew into flourishing ports, with a lively trade in fish, raw materials, and slaves. In the Middle Atlantic states the iron industry and the export of grain burgeoned. Life here was visibly good and getting better: wages were high, and opportunities for the entrepreneur vast.

In cultural life, too, the distinction between South and North was striking. The South was Anglican and English; the North, far more mixed religiously and ethnically. In New York, Dutch and English settlers learned to live with each other. In Pennsylvania, German settlers (the misnamed Pennsylvania Dutch), descendants of English Quakers, and Scotch-Irish immigrants forged a single society. New England, in contrast, was Puritan, but this much-abused word should be used with care. The Puritans were not puritan. They lived and dressed soberly, they believed in hard work, they taught that few are elected to salvation and many damned. And at least in the early decades, the dominant families kept their communities pure by driving out dissenters. But the Puritans knew how to laugh; they wrote poetry and gave room to sensuality—if normally within narrowly prescribed limits. While the Virginia planter aristocracy produced some educated men in these early times, the center of learning in America was in New England. It is not an accident that Harvard, America's first college, founded in 1636, should be in the Massachusetts Bay Colony.

Despite all opportunities for independent development, the ties between the colonies and the motherland remained intimate to the very edge of revolution. Earthquakes in England caused tremors in America. The Restoration of Charles II in 1660 forced increased tolerance on New England. The Glorious Revolution, after some confusion, produced conditions congenial to the new British government and the colonists alike: James II had briefly experimented with joining New Jersey, New York, and the New England colonies into the single Dominion of New England, but with the accession of William and Mary this unpopular idea vanished, with its author, from the scene. Religious and philosophical movements, too, had their reverberations in the American colonies. As the life of the educated in Europe grew more urbane and secular, so did life in Philadelphia, New York, and even in Congregationalist Boston. By the beginning of the eighteenth century, the survivors of the old Puritan order lamented the disappearance of the fervent sense of mission and charged that Bostonians had grown more interested in making money than in discussing Calvinist doctrine. In England John Wesley had responded to worldliness with his powerful Methodist sermons (see p. 403), and Americans once again followed the home country's lead. In the late 1730s, Wesley's most eloquent disciple, the revivalist orator George Whitefield, toured the colonies to touch off a frenzy of religious enthusiasm and produce thousands of dramatic conversions. The European Enlightenment had a pervasive effect in America; those who would soon lead the American colonies in rebellion were all in some degree philosophes. Benjamin Franklin—printer, moralist, inventor, business promoter, statesman—formed his style on Addison's *Spectator,* his deist philosophy on English writers, his scientific knowledge on Newton, his wit on Voltaire. Thomas Jefferson, principal author of the Declaration of Independence, third president of the United States, and founder of the University of Virginia, was European in every fiber of his intellectual being; John Adams (his predecessor in the presidency) said maliciously of Jefferson that he "drank freely of the French philosophy, in religion, in science, in politics." But Jefferson drank, just as freely, of English sources, too; he was both Francophile and Anglomaniac. And James Madison, the chief architect of the Constitution, and fourth president of the United States, imitated Addison and Voltaire and learned his political theories from Locke, Montesquieu, and Hume. America's separation from England and from Europe came, when it finally did come, with English and with European words and ideas.

From Resistance to Rebellion

Serious tensions began during and because of the Seven Years' War. In 1759, the privy council disallowed several South Carolina and Virginia enactments and announced that henceforth the royal prerogative would be more strictly enforced. Two years later, angered at continued smuggling operations, the government authorized general search warrants in Massachusetts, which permitted searches of warehouses and even private dwellings without court order. Then, in 1763, after peace had come, the British government addressed itself to the Indian "problem" in a manner to anger the colonists further. Beginning with the first settlements, the American Indian tribes had lived sometimes at peace, often at war, with the European invaders. The white newcomers, as in Massachusetts Bay, were sometimes grateful for the help they received; elsewhere, as in Virginia, they accepted help from the local tribes and then unscrupulously despoiled them. A century and a half of experience had taught the American Indians that French masters were preferable to English masters, and when, after their victory over France, the British pressed inland across the Appalachians, Indian tribes, led by the Ottawa chief Pontiac, mounted a vigorous, if futile campaign. "Freed of the restraint imposed by French competition," John A. Garraty sums it up, "Englishman and colonist increased their pressure on the Indians. Cynical fur traders now cheated them outrageously, while callous military men hoped to exterminate them like vermin. The British commander in the west, Lord Jeffrey Amherst, suggested infecting the Indians with smallpox, and another officer expressed the wish that they could be hunted down with dogs." [26] Eventually, caution prevailed over brutality: in a proclamation of 1763, the British government prohibited settlers from crossing the Appalachian divide, an action that was also intended to divert settlement to the colony of Canada, newly acquired from the French. But the English colonists failed to see the statesmanship of the move; speculators in western lands and prospective westerners were furious.

All this was bad enough; the use of general search warrants—the so-called "writs of assistance"—in the absence of a stringent emergency could even be dramatized as an invasion of an Englishman's fundamental rights. But now the British government proposed to invade the colonists' pocketbook, and the outcry became an uproar. For the British, the situation in 1763 was anything but enviable. Victory had brought more problems than it had solved. The national debt had nearly doubled in the course of the war; taxes were high, and the ministry was casting about for ways of reducing them—or at least of avoiding raising the onerous land tax any further. In April 1763, a month after the Peace of Paris was proclaimed, Bute was followed in office by George Grenville, a competent though limited and highly unpopular politician. His course seemed clear to him: across the seas lived nearly two million British subjects who had violated practically every law on the books, manufactured what they were forbidden to manufacture, exported what they were forbidden to export, traded with enemy merchants in time of war, and evaded most taxes for a century. A year after his accession to office, in April 1764, Parliament passed the Revenue Act (popularly called the Sugar Act), which actually reduced tariffs on a number of raw materials but sought to enforce payment. Clearly, the colonists would rather live under high tariffs that were not collected than under moderate ones that were. They exploded, and with a principled argument: the restrictions provided by the Navigation Acts were designed to channel manufacture and trade in prescribed directions, not to raise revenue. The Sugar Act, though, was clearly a money-raising law, and it had been passed without the colonists' consent. In the following year, the same principle was raised by another act, the Stamp Act of 1765, more detested in the colonies even than the Sugar Act. It did not strike Englishmen as a burdensome exaction; they were used to paying small sums on land transfers, licenses, and newspapers. But it so happened that this act, innocuous as it seemed, struck at the most articulate interest groups in America: at lawyers and printers, at editors, notaries, and tavern keepers. With the battle cry, "No taxation without representation," colonists resisted the Stamp Act. Grenville's announced intention to spend all the anticipated revenue on the defense of the colonies made no impression. Popular dema-gogues became popular heroes. In May 1765, Patrick Henry started a great debate in the Virginia legislature by introducing resolutions declaring Parliament powerless to tax the colonies. And in the summer, mobs looted the houses

[26] *The American Nation to 1877* (1966), 78.

of the officials designated to distribute the stamps. But by then Grenville had been dismissed.

For several years the British government, appalled at the outcry in America, vacillated. For a year—from July 1765 to July 1766—the Rockingham Whigs, including Burke, tried to conciliate the Americans: Rockingham repealed the Stamp Act in 1766, but insisted that on principle Parliament had the right to tax the colonies. The American call for representation was confronted with the British doctrine of "virtual representation"—members of Parliament were held to represent not this district or that, but all of Britain's great empire. The interests of colonials were safeguarded by members of Parliament in the same way as were those of English subjects who did not have the right to vote. The Americans were not impressed. They were impressed even less by the "Townshend duties," imposed in 1767 by the young chancellor of the exchequer, Charles Townshend, even though he had dressed up the new imposts under the guise of "indirect taxes," an absurd distinction that meant nothing to Townshend and nothing to the colonists, even if some orators had proclaimed their readiness to pay taxes as long as they were indirect. Colonists were joining forces to an alarming degree: in 1765, a Stamp Act Congress in New York had brought together delegates from nine of the colonies; in 1768, the Massachusetts legislature circularized other legislatures to discover common ground on the new duties. The atmosphere, already inflamed, fed on its own high temperature. Townshend had died in 1767, and was succeeded at the exchequer by Lord North, who favored repeal, but insisted that, simply to dramatize Britain's rights, one tax—that on tea—be retained. He prevailed, and by 1770, all but one of the Townshend taxes were lifted. In the same year, North became prime minister and brought a measure of stability to English affairs. Blood had already been shed: in March 1770, British troops fired on a mob in Boston and killed five persons. Then, in December 1773, Boston was involved in another incident which was less tragic but more consequential. The East India Company, which, thanks to American boycotts, had stores of tea on its hands, persuaded the British government to remit its duties and grant it a monopoly on the American market. A consignment of their tea, low in price and high in quality, arrived in Boston harbor late in November 1773. Samuel Adams and his fellow agitators inflamed excited crowds with their single argument that to permit the tea to land was to submit, abjectly, to tyranny from overseas. On the night of December 16, "patriots" painted like Indians boarded the vessels and dumped their cargo into Boston harbor. The Boston Tea Party provoked stern reprisals in the early spring of 1774. The Boston port was closed, the jurisdiction of the Massachusetts courts was curtailed, the power of the colonial governor was enlarged at the expense of local government. By an unfortunate coincidence, colonists were further incensed by the Quebec Act, a wise and statesmanlike measure that was directed at providing a form of government suitable to the French Canadians, whose ways were alien to the colonists; it seemed both arbitrary and—in its more liberal aspects—a portentous concession to Roman Catholics. The American response to these "Intolerable Acts" was the first Continental Congress; it met in Philadelphia in September, with twelve out of thirteen colonies—all but Georgia—sending delegates. Samuel Adams had been talking of an "American Commonwealth" since 1773, but conciliation seemed, if improbable, still possible to American and British moderates alike. Lord Chatham, Edmund Burke, even Lord North himself suggested far-reaching concessions. But then large-scale violence frustrated such hopes. In April 1775, General Gage received orders in Boston to repress rebellion; on April 19, his troops clashed with American irregulars, the Minute Men, at Lexington and Concord. There were sharp losses on both sides. The call for independence became irresistible. "The revolution was complete, in the minds of the people and the Union of the colonies," John Adams said many years later, "before the war commenced." But not long before.

The British began to gather troops—including German mercenaries—to restore order, and in January 1776, the English polemicist Thomas Paine published his *Common Sense,* an inflammatory, brilliantly lucid attack on the "Royal Brute," George III, in which he denounced monarchy as corrupt and called upon Americans to become independent. It spoke to, and for, America. The second Continental Congress, which had been in session since May 1775, followed Paine's call, which was being echoed with growing fervor through all the colonies. On July 4, 1776, Congress passed Jefferson's draft of a Declaration of Independence, a mixture of natural-law sentiments and specific grievances. To support this declaration, the delegates mutually pledged their lives, their fortunes, and their sacred honor. The fortunes of war vacillated, but George Washington converted his untrained troops into a respectable fighting instrument, while British commanders, incompetent, self-destructive, and far from home, found the colonists far more formidable than they had expected. In October 1777, General John Burgoyne, failing to split the colonies, surrendered his army at Saratoga; in early 1778, Benjamin Franklin and two fellow envoys concluded a treaty with France, which recognized the independence of the rebellious colonies and provided for troops and supplies; in 1779 the beleaguered colonists obtained further support from Spain. Lord North's belated concessions were rejected, and the Americans, through defeat, desertions, and treason, fought on. After the British took Charleston in May 1780, affairs took a turn for the better, and in October 1781, at Yorktown, Virginia, General Cornwallis capitulated to General Washington. The improbable and the unforeseen had become reality: the American colonies were free and independent.

The Peace of Paris, provisionally complete in November 1782, and signed at Paris in September 1783, exceeded all expectations and astounded the most experienced of European diplomats. Britain recognized the sovereign independence of the "United States," set their frontiers just north of Spanish Florida, at the Great Lakes, and on the Mississippi River—a western boundary remote enough to invite westward expansion. It undertook to withdraw British troops rapidly, and granted Americans fishing rights off Newfoundland. All this was impressive enough. But whether this agglomeration of independent colonies— now independent states—would prosper, or even survive, remained an open question.

From Confederation to Federation

In 1778, Turgot had called the rebels "the hope of the human race"; in 1790, Condorcet paid excited tribute to the new nation that was serving as an inspiration to the old nations of Europe: "Men whom the reading of philosophic books had secretly converted to the love of liberty, became enthusiastic over the liberty of a foreign people while they waited for the moment when they could recover their own." The victory of the colonies proved that free men could, after all, defeat a powerful and entrenched imperial power.

At the beginning, however, the American experiment seemed fragile, exposed to constant danger. The young confederation found itself in conflict with Great Britain over the carrying out of peace terms. American manufacturers, swamped by reasonably priced and well-made British imports, entered a period of depression. Money was first too scarce and then too plentiful; the war emergency had induced both the Continental Congress and the individual states to print paper money, which produced severe inflation and then, as governments responded, even more severe deflation. In this uncertain situation, relations between debtors and creditors, never easy, deteriorated; in 1786, a debtors' rebellion in Massachusetts, let by Daniel Shays, brought actual violence. Benjamin Franklin's famous warning, issued on July 4, 1776, "We must all hang together, or assuredly we shall all hang separately," now acquired new urgency.

The ideal of a United States was obvious, its nature was something else again. The colonies had fought the war of independence under articles of confederation ratified in 1778 by eight of the states, and in 1781 by them all. But the articles, which remained in force after the Peace of Paris had been signed, kept the sovereignty of the individual states intact; it ratified a "league of friendship," suitable to an emergency perhaps, when a common enemy overrides all particular interests, but hopelessly inadequate in a world of great powers, with well-organized and well-financed traders, to say nothing of sizable armies and navies. The states were jealous of their independence and wary of a closer union that might compromise their interests. But in the end, after a long and often acrimonious debate, they preferred common survival to parochial pride. From 1786, strong voices for union were heard, and from impressive quarters: from George Washington, from the Virginia legislature. In September, delegates from five states met at Annapolis; the sparse attendance was a sign of obvious failure, but one of the delegates, the brilliant and indefatigable

New York lawyer Alexander Hamilton, persuaded the others to try again. In May 1787, delegates from nine states accordingly met at Philadelphia, elected George Washington as president, and adjourned in September with a draft constitution. Its preamble, in grave and ambitious words, spoke the language of a new age: "We the People of the United States, in order to form a more perfect union, establish justice, insure domestic tranquility, provide for the common defence, promote the general welfare, and secure the blessings of liberty to ourselves and our posterity, do ordain and establish this Constitution for the United States of America." The delegates dispersed, to lobby in their respective states for its adoption. One of the polemics written in its behalf—eighty-five separate articles by James Madison, Alexander Hamilton, and John Jay, and collected as *The Federalist*—was a masterpiece of persuasion, a model of enlightened sociology, and a monument to the ideal of freedom, eighteenth-century style. The authors were thoroughly aware that the eyes of the world were upon them. "It has been frequently remarked," Hamilton wrote in the opening paragraph, "that it seems to have been reserved to the people of this country, by their conduct and example, to decide the important question, whether societies of men are really capable or not, of establishing good government from reflection and choice, or whether they are forever destined to depend, for their political constitutions, on accident and force." Tough-minded and realistic, the authors saw man in need of government, and government in need of checks. "If men were angels," wrote Madison, "no government would be necessary. If angels were to govern men, neither external nor internal controuls on government would be necessary. In framing a government which is to be administered by men over men, the great difficulty lies in this: You must first enable the government to controul the governed; and in the next place, oblige it to controul itself." In the eyes of Madison, Hamilton, and Jay, the proposed constitution admirably met this double requirement.

Public opinion was deeply divided. The Constitution proposed to substitute energetic action for the paralysis into which the confederation had fallen. That is largely why its advocates won out over the opposition. One other important thing helped. The Constitution was a shrewd compromise among conflicting forces. The proposed government was a secular republic, with guarantees for the civil rights of all its citizens. But it was not a democracy; the manner of voting for senators and for president was designed to weaken, if not eliminate, the influence of the mob. Some of its compromises, as between large states and small, were wise; others, above all the retention of slavery, were disastrous and bore the seeds of grave troubles ahead. Still, the advantages of a strong, yet not tyrannical government carried the day. By June 1788, ten ratifying conventions had approved the new constitution; the last, Rhode Island, fell into line in May 1790. By that time, George Washington, architect of victory, remote but trustworthy, a legend in his time, had been serving as the first president of the United States for over a year. He had been in office since April 30, 1789. Four days after his momentous swearing in, which brought the

American Revolution to a close with official solemnity, the French Estates General met in Versailles to inaugurate, with greater pomp, an even more portentous revolution.

SELECTED READINGS

For a recent, brief general survey of good government, eighteenth-century fashion, see John G. Gagliardo, *Enlightened Despotism* (1967), and the relevant chapters in M. S. Anderson, *Europe in the Eighteenth Century, 1718–1783* (1961). A. Goodwin, ed., *The American and French Revolutions, 1763–1793* (1968), vol. VIII of *The New Cambridge Modern History,* has numerous useful articles. See also Geoffrey Bruun, *The Enlightened Despots* (2nd ed., 1967), and, for a historical account of these years, Leo Gershoy, *From Despotism to Revolution, 1763–1789* (1944). The first volume of R. R. Palmer, *The Age of the Democratic Revolution: A Political History of Europe and America, 1760–1800* (1959), has, in addition to its thesis of a general movement toward democracy, a great deal of interesting material.

For specific countries in the time of reform, see in addition to these general titles, for Sweden, Michael Roberts, "The Swedish Aristocracy in the Eighteenth Century," in his *Essays in Swedish History* (1967), and Ingvar Andersson, *A History of Sweden* (tr. 1956); for Spain, Richard Herr, *The Eighteenth Century Revolution in Spain* (1958), and the appropriate chapters in Rafael Altamira, *A History of Spain, from the Beginnings to the Present Day* (tr. 1949). For Germany in general, W. H. Bruford, *Germany in the Eighteenth Century: The Social Background of the Literary Revival* (1935); Bruford's more specialized but illuminating study, *Culture and Society in Classical Weimar, 1775–1806* (1962); the excellent monograph by Helen P. Liebel, *Enlightened Bureaucracy Versus Enlightened Despotism in Baden, 1750–1792* (1965); the opening section of Leonard Krieger, *The German Idea of Freedom* (1957), a searching analysis; and Klaus Epstein's bulky *The Genesis of German Conservatism* (1966). For Josephinism, in addition to the titles by Bernard, Padover, Kerner, and others listed in Chapter 9, see Henrick Marczali, *Hungary in the 18th Century* (tr. 1910), and Robert A. Kann, *A Study in Austrian Intellectual History: From Late Baroque to Romanticism* (1960).

Catherine of Russia is undergoing reappraisal. Meanwhile, there is G. P. Gooch, *Catherine the Great and Other Studies* (1954), conventional but informative; Gladys S. Thomson, *Catherine the Great and the Expansion of Russia* (1947); the recent Paul Dukes, *Catherine the Great and the Russian Nobility* (1968); and the interesting essay by Marc Raeff, *Origins of the Russian Intelligentsia: The Eighteenth Century Nobility* (1966).

In addition to the titles on the regime of Louis XV listed in Chapter 9, see Shelby B. McCloy, *The Humanitarian Movement in Eighteenth Century France* (1957); Vivian R. Gruder, *The Royal Provincial Intendants: A Governing Elite in Eighteenth Century France* (1968); George T. Matthews, *The Royal General Farms in Eighteenth-Century France* (1958); Franklin L. Ford, *Strasbourg in Transition, 1648–1789* (1966); and Jacques L. Godechot, *France and the Atlantic Revolution of the Eighteenth Century, 1770–1799* (tr. 1965), to be read in conjunction with Palmer, *Age of the Democratic Revolution.*

For England under George III, see the opening chapters of R. K. Webb, *Modern England from the 18th Century to the Present* (1968), and J. Steven Watson, *The Reign* of George III, 1760–1815 (1960). Lewis Namier, *The Structure of Politics at the Accession of George III* (2nd ed., 1957), and *England in the Age of the American Revolution* (2nd ed., 1961), are both classics. But see Herbert Butterfield, *George III and the Historians* (1957), a critique of Namier. To these should be added Richard Pares, *King George and the Politicians* (1953); Herbert Butterfield, *George III, Lord North and the People, 1779–80* (1949); and John Brooke, *The Chatham Administration, 1766–1768* (1956). There is stimulating information on English radicals in George Rudé, *Wilkes and Liberty* (1962); see also I. R. Christie, *Wilkes, Wyville and Reform* (1963); Betty Kemp, *Sir Francis Dashwood* (1967); and Lucy Sutherland, *The City of London and the Opposition to Government, 1768–1774* (1959). On economic history, see T. S. Ashton, *The Industrial Revolution, 1760–1830* (2nd ed., 1964), and *An Economic History of England: The Eighteenth Century* (1955). And see J. D. Chambers and G. E. Mingay, *The Agricultural Revolution, 1750–1880* (1966).

Among histories of the American colonies, see the general treatment by John A. Garraty, *The American Nation to 1877* (1966), which includes helpful bibliographies. Richard Hofstadter's posthumous *America at 1750: A Social Portrait* (1971) is a lucid essay. See also John R. Alden, *Pioneer America* (1960). Bernard Bailyn's *The Ideological Origins of the American Revolution* (1967) and *The Origins of American Politics* (1968) offer important interpretations. See also Clarence L. Ver Steeg, *The Formative Years* (1964). For colonial culture in general, L. B. Wright, *The Cultural Life of the American Colonies* (1957), says the essential. For New England civilization, several volumes by Perry Miller remain indispensable, especially *Errand into the Wilderness* (1956), a collection of stimulating essays, and his informal trilogy, *Orthodoxy in Massachusetts* (1933), *The New England Mind: The 17th Century* (1939), and *The New England Mind: From Colony to Province* (1953). In addition, see Carl Bridenbaugh, *Myths and Realities: Societies of the Colonial South* (1952), and two other books by him: *Cities in the Wilderness* (1938) and *Cities in Revolt* (1955). See also L. B. Wright, *The First Gentlemen of Virginia* (1940).

For the revolutionary period, see Lawrence H. Gipson, *The Coming of the Revolution* (1954), which ably summarizes a far more voluminous work; J. C. Miller, *Origins of the American Revolution* (1943); and Edmund S. Morgan, *The Birth of the Republic* (1956). Richard B. Morris, *The American Revolution Reconsidered* (1967), intelligently surveys the field. Arthur M. Schlesinger, Sr., *The Colonial Merchants and the American Revolution* (1918), has not been superseded. See also Benjamin W. Labaree, *The Boston Tea Party* (1964), as well as Edmund S. and Helen M. Morgan, *The Stamp Act Crisis* (1953). The best biographies of revolutionary leaders include Carl Van Doren's *Benjamin Franklin* (1938) and Verner W. Crane's economical *Benjamin Franklin and a Rising People* (1954); Dumas Malone's *Jefferson: The Virginian* (1948) and Merrill D. Peterson's *Thomas Jefferson and the New Nation* (1970); Douglas S. Freeman's *George Washington*, 7 vols. (1948–1957) and Marcus Cunliffe's *George Washington: Man and Monument* (1958); J. C. Miller's *Alexander Hamilton: A Portrait in Paradox* (1959); and Irving Brant's *James Madison: Father of the Constitution* (1950). On the Constitution itself, Charles A. Beard's controversial *An Economic Interpretation of the Constitution* (2nd ed., 1935) long held the field, but has now been successfully challenged by Robert E. Brown, *Charles Beard and the Constitution* (1956). See also Forrest McDonald, *We the People: The Economic Origins of the Constitution* (1958).

11

The French Revolution

Historians are inordinately fond of resounding terms like "turning point" and "epoch making." The French Revolution fully deserves such language. It confirmed the ascendancy of the modern state and gave birth to the modern army; it served to spread ideas of Enlightenment and mass politics across several continents; it signaled the intervention of new sectors of the population in the political process; it served for decades, and continues to serve, as a rallying cry to radicals and a dreadful warning to conservatives. Modern radicalism, indeed, like modern conservatism, takes its rise from the French Revolution. And it was more than a French revolution; it marked an epoch in the history of France, of Europe, and of the world.

DECLINE AND FALL OF
THE OLD REGIME: 1774–1789
————••◁∞▷••————

Anatomy of a Reign

When Louis XVI became king of France in 1774 at the age of twenty, he had only his birth to recommend him for his position. He was well meaning, indolent, and incurious. Even the vivacious Hapsburg princess, Marie Antoinette, to whom he was married at sixteen, did not interest him, although her impetuous character and strong will eventually gave her a baleful influence over him. His amusements consisted of tinkering with locks, working at masonry, and hunting. On that imperishable day in 1789, Bastille Day, when Paris was swept by the first wave of the revolution that would cost him his head, his diary, characteristically preoccupied with his hunting, contained the single entry: "July 14: Nothing."

The country that Louis inherited had all the bloom of prosperity, but it was a bloom ill-rooted and ill-nourished. At the end of the eighteenth century France remained overwhelmingly agricultural, and most of its peasants lived at, and sometimes below, subsistence level. In some areas such as maritime Flanders or in the neighborhood of Versailles three-fourths of the peasants owned no land at all, and in most regions they depended heavily on customary communal grazing and forest rights and on supplementary employment to sustain their minimum standard. Every agricultural crisis reduced hordes of day laborers and small landholders to destitution. In Normandy, Arthur Young reported, "most of the dwellings consist of four posts . . . to which a chimney has been added made up of four poles and some mud." The inhabitants of such hovels, he wrote, were "walking dunghills."

Anachronistic as French agriculture was, the French tax structure, with its age-old inequities, was more anachronistic still. As we have seen, the rich, the most obvious source of revenue, were for the most part exempt; by the time of the Revolution, the nobles, despite their vast holdings, were paying a bare 10 percent of the taxes. The nobility justified its privileges with a convenient feudal theory: in exchange for offering their king (the first of the nobles) support in war, they had a right to be exempt from the *taille* (the land tax) and from the *corvée*. Many prosperous members of the urban bourgeoisie escaped most taxation as well; not even Louis XIV had managed to prevent widespread tax evasion. His successors managed no better. The system of turning over the collection of taxes to tax farmers was an inefficient and desperate way of raising money; by May 1789, 60 percent of the revenue the farmers general collected remained with them. The one national tax that was faithfully collected and universally hated was the salt tax, the *gabelle;* the Paris financiers who bought the right of collecting it for three million livres a year had the right to sentence evaders to the galleys or even to death.

On top of the national taxes were piled the seigneurial dues, the *banalités,* payments to the lord for use of the village bakeovens, winepress, and mill, and payments that fell due when property changed hands. Among other irritating, and sometimes costly, vestiges of feudalism was the lord's retention of hunting rights: game was reserved to the nobility, and hunting parties could ride across tilled fields without paying indemnity for any damage to standing crops. This was not yet all. The church retained its ancient rights to the tithe, theoretically a tenth but actually a thirteenth, of the gross produce of the land. Once again the rich generally evaded this supposedly universal tax, which yielded the church some five million livres a year.

With this chaotic and antiquated system of raising revenue, the government was running progressively deeper into debt. Despite its high and inflammatory visibility, the notorious extravagance of Marie Antoinette and her court was a relatively minor drain on French resources: perhaps 6 percent of French revenue in 1788 went to support the royal family and its palaces.[1] The real burden was the cost of the military establishment and of past wars, which had been financed by loans: almost half the national income in the year before the Revolution went to the payment of principal and interest. One of the heaviest charges on the French exchequer was the cost of the American Revolution: French support of this revolution, given less out of love of liberty than from enmity to England, helped to bring revolution to France. Yet, the burdens of the French national debt and current expenditures were no greater than those encumbering other states.

But public morale was low, resistance to reform entrenched, and, to make matters worse, the French economy was in the midst of a rising tide of unemployment, of inflation and a decline in production. The increase in population that had begun early in the eighteenth century amounted by 1789 to six million. This placed an increasing strain on the resources available in the countryside where methods of cultivation had not improved. Those displaced by unemployment or by endless subdivision of landed property drifted to the towns as unskilled laborers or joined the bands of homeless brigands who infested the countryside. One of the major industries employing day labor was textiles, but with increasing unemployment, purchases of textiles fell; by 1789 the quantity of cloth produced in France was half that of 1787. A disastrous harvest in 1788 followed by an only moderately successful one in 1789 carried the crisis into agriculture, while the wine industry, of central importance, faced similar difficulties as a result of an only fair grape harvest in 1788. The economic decline affected not only the poor and landless, but larger landowning farmers

---

[1] The same, as we saw on p. 439, had held true of Madame de Pompadour.

and master craftsmen as well. The seigneurs, finding their feudal dues worth less and less, sought to recoup by collecting rents in kind rather than in cash or by renegotiating their contracts. The whole century saw a widening gap between the price of food and real wages. After 1730 prices, especially those of necessities, rose while wages limped behind; when prices dropped, as they did in the 1780s, the drop was selective and benefited only a few. Rents and the price of bread remained high.

Population growth, crop failures, cycles of inflation and unemployment: by the 1780s the great question was, Who is to blame? As Frenchmen discussed their hardships in the cafés, they found the cause of the trouble not in the vagaries of nature or the fluctuation of the economy, but in the court. Prices had risen not because of crop failures but because the government did not care for its people—had it not signed a treaty of commerce with the English in 1786 which had let down customs barriers? Other grievances—military service, the burdensome population, the heavy taxes—all seemed to have a political origin, so that the regime itself became the target of popular criticism.

In Search of a Policy

In this lurid light, the reign of Louis XVI appears as a search for the finance minister who would extricate the country from its difficulties and for ways of translating his program into practice. The king's first appointment was his boldest, although his courage did not match his minister's. Anne Robert Turgot, whom Louis XVI appointed controller general of finance only three months after his accession, was a precocious intellectual, a friend of the philosophes, and sympathetic to the physiocratic doctrines of free trade. He had been intendant at Limoges, where he had made a reputation by his attack on old abuses and by a rational road-building program in place of the *corvée*. Now, as controller general, Turgot devised a vigorous plan of reform; radical in its prescriptions and humanitarian in its philosophy, it grew out of his administrative experience and embodied his advanced convictions. He drafted six edicts, which proposed to abolish useless sinecures, internal customs barriers (which had the effect of greatly increasing the price of grain), the gilds (which limited the introduction of both new workmen and new processes) and, most daring of all, the *corvée*, which he planned to replace with a new land tax. In moving language Turgot dwelt both on the irreparable harm to the peasant "who has nothing for his subsistence but his hand," and on the uneconomic nature of the old system.

Louis let himself be persuaded to support Turgot's program; he presented the six edicts to the Parlement of Paris for registration. But he was unwilling to back his minister in the face of outraged criticism. Turgot's edicts did indeed touch upon the practices that were strangling the country, and his recommendations were preparing to overturn usages that had been in effect for centuries.

The members of the parlement were indifferent to the arguments of both humanity and economic theory, and they steadfastly reiterated their belief in the fitness of things as they were: "All public financial burdens," said one member, "should be borne by the lower orders."

The merits of Turgot's policies, combined with his undiplomatic self-confidence, were the causes of their demise and of his downfall. The intransigent Parlement of Paris refused to register the six edicts, and the king, after a brief show of energy, grew tired of the complaints of the nobility and of Turgot's rivals. In May 1776, to restore his own tranquility, he dismissed Turgot. The six edicts were forgotten and the poor continued to labor on the roads, pay most taxes, and accumulate grievances. Voltaire, the gadfly of the nation, then an old man of eighty-two, had followed Turgot's career with passionate interest. When Louis XVI removed Turgot from office, Voltaire saw in it more than the fall of a ministry. "The dismissal of this great man," he wrote, "crushes me. . . . Since that fatal day, I have not followed anything . . . and I am waiting patiently for someone to cut our throats."

There were still some years, and some further changes of ministers, before any throats were cut. Louis temporized. Some of his officials were effective and imaginative administrators: the army, the navy, the church, the Protestants all felt the breath of reform. But reform, where it was not too late, was too little. Essentially uninterested in government, Louis XVI hoped for some magical solution, some sleight of hand that would set all to rights and permit him to pursue, untroubled, his regular pleasures. The minister he chose to perform this miracle was the Swiss banker Jacques Necker, who arrived accompanied by a dazzling reputation as a financial wizard. He assumed the post of director general of finances at the moment when these finances were undergoing particular strain; French support for the American Revolution was placing intolerable burdens on insufficient revenue. The cost of this support was borne by a shaky financial pyramid constructed by borrowing funds for capital outlay and then further borrowing to pay interest on the earlier loans. By the end of hostilities in America in 1781, the French government had accumulated a national debt of 3400 million livres. During Necker's ministry expenditures were outrunning income at the rate of 80 million livres a year; the gap continued to grow until by 1786 it had reached 110 million.

After five years in office, Necker showed his verbal, if not his financial brilliance in a lengthy account of his stewardship, the *Compte Rendu* of 1781, which glossed over the essential structural difficulties of French finances. In his accounting he chose to treat the war debt as an emergency expenditure to be reckoned apart from the regular finances of the country. He could assure the nation, therefore, that there was actually a "normal" annual surplus of some 10 million livres. Having offered this improbable explanation of his "success," his next act of magic was to resign before he could be dismissed.

The most remarkable among Necker's successors was Charles Alexandre de Calonne, an energetic administrator who had gathered valuable experience as intendant at Lille. He was appointed controller general in 1783 and undertook boldly to attack privilege, the disease of the French state, at its source. He proposed to abolish the *corvée,* reduce the salt tax, increase the stamp tax, and above all, replace the inequitable *taille* with a land tax that would finally tap the rich as well as the poor. Calonne was enough of a statesman to know that such measures could succeed only with the consent of the prospective victims. He decided therefore to bypass the parlements and obtained Louis' agreement to convene an Assembly of Notables, a body that had last met a hundred and sixty years before. It met in February 1787. The Assembly was composed of prominent clerics, noblemen, important land-owners, and officers of state. Here was a splendid chance—it turned out to be the last—for the privileged orders to surrender or reduce their privileges voluntarily, as an act of disinterested statesmanship. But once convened, the Assembly developed a surprising independence of spirit; it refused to ratify Calonne's proposals with the docility he had hoped for. And so, intimidated by Calonne's enemies, including Necker and the queen's entourage, the king let Calonne go.

Louis XVI's weakness had left him in the indefensible position of asking as a favor what he might have demanded as a right. The aristocracy responded by reasserting its prerogatives, notable its right to be exempt from taxation. The leader of the opposition to Calonne in the Assembly, Loménie de Brienne, archbishop of Toulouse, succeeded Calonne. Having unseated a minister and rejected his program, the Assembly retired, but Calonne's proposal for a land tax survived his disgrace. Brienne, compelled to advocate what he had helped to defeat, carried it to the Parlement of Paris. This august body found the proposal no less distasteful than the Assembly of Notables; in an attempt to evade the issue, it argued that such a tax could only be approved by the Estates General, an advisory body representative of the three estates of the realm. Instead of raising money, the Assembly of Notables had triggered widespread expressions of dissatisfaction with the crown; and it was used by the provincial parlements to affirm their independence. From April 1787, when Brienne became minister, until August 1788, when he resigned, he struggled with an increasingly intransigent aristocracy who were closing ranks against absolutism. Abusive pamphlets, offensive declarations of rights, and open disobedience became endemic. Having consistently yielded to the privileged, the government now found itself with a virtual revolt of the privileged on its hands.

This "aristocratic revolution" came at a time when the French state was on the verge of bankruptcy. In a desperate move to find money in the face of an uproar across the country and to restablish harmony—the aristocracy refusing to be taxed, the church refusing to make satisfactory *dons gratuits* to the treasury, and parlements aggressively declaiming against "tyranny"—the king was forced at last into motion. Among Brienne's last acts as minister, he agreed to convene the Estates General for May 1, 1789. Necker, the popular miracle-worker whom Louis XVI had reluctantly recalled to office in August, acceded. The king piously hoped to see the meeting of the three estates as an "assembly of a great family headed by a common father," organized with "essential

proportion and harmony in the composition of the three orders." The French
Revolution had many causes—loss of respect for the crown, resistance of the
privileged, long-range economic decline in the face of population increase, high
bread prices in critical moments. But among these causes, the very calling of the
Estates General must rank high. It brought and kept together men who took
ideas and determination from one another and made the revolution they had
been invited to forestall.

The Emergence of the Third Estate

There are times when the tempo of events increases radically; when far-
reaching, irreversible changes take place in a matter of weeks, even of days.
Remote, deep causes lurk in the background, but a single day may bring the
eruption of subterranean forces, long, often silently in the shaping. The French
Revolution was such a time—a time of dramatic, revolutionary *journées*. Hence,
as the pace of events quickens, the speed of the historian slows down, as he
seeks to grasp, and describe, each decisive moment in its turn.

For whom did the three orders speak? How were they to conduct their
business? These proved to be pivotal questions, and their discussion began long
before the assembly convened. Since the Estates had last been convoked under
Louis XIII in 1614, Louis XVI appealed to the learned of the nation to advise him
on procedure. His request unloosed such a flood of pamphlets that the
censorship office was swamped and in a significant retreat from authority
abandoned censorship altogether. Doubtless the most lasting of this literature
was *What Is the Third Estate?* by the supple and ubiquitous Abbé Sieyès,
published in January 1789. The very title of Sieyès' pamphlet framed the
question over which the first revolutionary struggle would be fought. In
phrases as memorable as the catechism, Sieyès answered his own question:
"1st. What is the third estate? Everything. 2nd. What has it been up to now in
the political order? Nothing. 3rd. What does it demand? To become something
in it."

By its nature, he said, the third estate contains "within itself all that is
necessary to constitute a complete nation." If the "privileged orders were
abolished," he continued, somewhat ominously, "the nation would be not
something less but something more." The third estate, he reminded his readers,
"represents twenty-five million persons and deliberates on the interests of the
nation. The two others . . . have the powers of only 200,000 individuals and
think only of their privileges."[2] Sieyès' threatening pamphlet sharpened a

---

[2] The best modern estimates of the composition of the three estates differ only slightly from
those of Abbé Sieyès: the clergy or first estate numbered about one hundred thirty thousand; the
nobility or second estate four hundred thousand. The third estate, twenty-six million strong, thus
accounted for 98 percent of the population.

debate that clarified the conflicts dividing French society. The previous September the Parlement of Paris had decreed that the Estates should vote, as in 1614, by order. With one stroke, the magistrates stood unmasked as the spokesmen of privilege. By their stubborn, self-interested resistance to reform, the privileged orders had compelled the king to convene the Estates General. Now, if the three orders were to vote separately the third estate would obviously be outvoted two to one every time, and the rule of privilege would be saddled on France, perhaps forever. As critical pamphleteers did not fail to point out, even if the voting was to be *par tête,* with each delegate casting one vote in a joint session, the third estate needed to double its allotted representation to equal the other two. In late December 1788 the royal council, acting on Necker's proposal, agreed to the "doubling of the Third"; in the end, the third estate elected 610 representatives, the nobles 291, and the clergy 300. The mode of voting remained in the air, but the third estate had scored its first triumph. *What Is the Third Estate?* did not make, it consolidated, that triumph. It is essential to recognize that the third had not secured its victory alone: the leading propagandists at this early stage were liberal nobles and priests, touched by the doctrines of the Enlightenment, even more than discontented bourgeois.

The election of the 610 representatives of the third estate proceeded by a cumbersome indirect process which did not, however, winnow out local grievances. At each level the deputies were sent on with a statement of the needs of the local population. These *cahiers,* of which twenty thousand survive, took the form of addresses to the king beginning with expressions of loyalty and continuing with particular complaints. Taking advantage of this unusual opportunity for a hearing, the writers of the *cahiers* freely voiced political or philosophical theories, sometimes genuinely representative of a district, often reflecting the ideas of a profession, of a special interest, or of the author himself. As usual, the very poor, the most inarticulate, had few spokesmen.

In addition to the expected chronic complaints about taxation, the *cahiers* offered a rich expression of the prevailing desire for a radical reform of the government. The *cahiers* of the third estate called for nothing less than a recognition that authority had shifted from the king to the people. For three decades or more, the parlements had been swamping the nation with constitutionalist, even democratic rhetoric; it was now employed by other men, in a better cause. The vows of loyalty were accompanied by reiterated demands for the abolition of "feudal" dues, an end to the special status that privilege conferred, and a guarantee of the civil rights of the individual. This meant, in addition to freedom of the press, protection from arbitrary arrest at the pleasure of the king or his ministers using *lettres de cachet.* In sum, the *cahiers* of the third estate asked for the transformation of the absolute into a constitutional monarchy. The *cahiers* of the nobility and clergy were equally representative. While the aristocrats also desired a legislative assembly with a voice in taxation, their main concern was to preserve traditional privileges to as great a degree as possible. At the same time, therefore, that they seemed to be accepting a constitutional monarchy, some *cahiers* of the nobility called for the appointment of official genealogists in each province to investigate and clear noble titles. The *cahiers* of the clergy were defensive: they demanded perpetuation of control over the extensive properties of the church and of its traditional authority over education and the registration of births and deaths. Not unexpectedly, they took a conservative—which is to say, dim—view of the widespread demand for greater freedom of the press.

After months of preliminaries—meetings, elections, drafting sessions for the *cahiers*—the Estates General of France convened at Versailles on May 4, 1789, with all the pageantry of a regime accustomed to splendor. The very opening ceremonies, however, were symptomatic of the troubles that had brought the deputies together—the attachment of the king to hierarchy and privilege, his evident indifference to the national interest. The France of the Old Regime was a status-conscious society. Money and ability mattered; birth mattered more. Precisely in the century in which bourgeois—lawyers, physicians, merchants, manufacturers, civil servants—increased their wealth, acquired new self-confidence, and thought of themselves, not without justice, as doing the nation's business, they found themselves subject to certain taxes from which the nobility was exempt, excluded from high posts they knew they could fill, and snubbed at court or in select social circles. The "aristocratic revolt" of the 1780s was a closing-in upon itself of a caste in danger; resentful bourgeois took this defensiveness as aggression. Now, in the ceremonies of May 4, the delegates of the third estate were being gratuitously exposed to indignities they had no intention of swallowing. They were dressed in plain black—as distinct from the gorgeous plumage of the first and second estates—compelled by ancient ceremonial to remain bareheaded when the privileged orders put on their hats, compelled even to enter the hall by a side door while the others entered in front.

With the verification of the deputies' credentials, the question of status merged into the question of power. The nobility saw no difficulty; they convened separately, formally registered their deputies, and on May 11 declared their estate to be officially constituted. The clergy, heavily represented by village *curés* with radical leanings, proceeded more cautiously by beginning a roll call but keeping open a line of discussion with the third estate. The commons, for their part, were tenacious. Their world was not the world of the Bourbons based on ceremony and adherence to medieval ideas of kingship. The revolution in America for which France had paid so dearly, the ideas of the philosophes which had been fermenting legally and illegally for half a century, the sympathies of radical clerics and aristocrats, had created a new temper and a new set of expectations. The deputies of the third estate were men of education and standing: half were lawyers, and the rest were largely professional men, merchants, and officials. They proposed to use the convocation of the three orders to create an Estates General that spoke for the nation. The issue of credentials, therefore, became critical. While the clergy temporized, the commons met for six consecutive weeks and waited to have their claims recognized.

This long period of calculated resistance heightened tempers; at the same time it gave the members of the third estate an opportunity to develop esprit de corps and find leaders, and time to deliberate as a body on their course of action. Abbé Sieyès, deputy from Paris, was once again the catalyst. On June 10, he proposed that the third estate meet to verify not only its own credentials but also the credentials of those members of the other orders who wished to be counted as "representatives of the French nation." On June 13, as the roll call continued, the impasse was broken when three members of the clergy came over to sit with the third estate. In the next three days, sixteen more clergymen appeared and, intoxicated by a sense of precedent-breaking significance, the third estate, on June 17, concluded its verification by proclaiming itself the National Assembly.

Even Louis XVI could not ignore so bold an action; although in mourning for the dauphin who had died two weeks earlier, he emerged to summon a second convocation of the Estates General for June 22, in the very hall which the third estate was then using. The deputies did not receive this announcement in time to forestall their next meeting which had been set for June 20. They arrived in a heavy rain to find the hall closed and stood around angrily until their president, the distinguished astronomer Bailly, led them to a nearby indoor tennis court. Outraged by an affront that seemed to presage their dismissal, the assembled deputies reaffirmed their function as representatives of the nation. In an emotional meeting, they swore, "to go on meeting whatever circumstances may dictate until the constitution of the realm is set up and consolidated on firm foundations." June 20, the day of the Tennis Court Oath, marks the emergence of a new power that set itself up firmly as a counterweight to privilege, royalty, and tradition.

The king's response to this extraordinary declaration was characteristic: he seemed to yield while insisting all the while on the old ways. By June 23, when the Estates General met again, two archbishops and one hundred fifty other clerical deputies had joined the third estate, and two days later, nearly fifty liberal nobles came over. The separation of orders had become obsolete. Louis obstinately continued to insist on that separation in procedural matters and in all questions touching on the personal rights of the privileged classes; he dismissed the joint assembly to their separate deliberation. It was a stupid, and in the long run fatal, move. Amid vehement protestations, the commons refused to move despite a hint of force. Bailly spoke for their new-found determination: "No one can give orders to the assembled nation." Finally alerted to this defiance, Louis decided by June 27 that it was prudent to order the three orders to meet jointly. Of the 1201 deputies, only 371 abstained from the meetings, and emboldened by such numbers the deputies set to work, appointed a constitutional committee, appropriately adopted the title of

National Constituent Assembly, and addressed themselves to "the regeneration of France."

Bastille Day: The Intervention of Paris

Despite their brave words the deputies had cause for apprehension. The king, in the sly way of a weak man, called up troops to help shore up his authority. As the Assembly began to meet, the king secretly ordered up six regiments to Versailles and stationed another ten in the outskirts of Paris. The court factions ready to use force against the third estate were gaining the upper hand. On July 11 Necker was dismissed, and baron de Breteuil, the queen's favorite, succeeded him.

The king had read the mood of Paris correctly. Economic hardship, reflected in the rising cost of bread in Paris, was compounded as hungry refugees from the countryside flocked to the city seeking work and food. The parliamentary activity in the manicured parks of Versailles found a powerful echo in the streets of Paris. The *menu peuple* of the capital—the small craftsmen, journeymen, day laborers, domestics—became the new center of national agitation. The overturn of the traditional order of things had begun with the aristocrats' repudiation of their responsibility at the Assembly of Notables. A loose confederation of lawyers, public servants, radical nobles, and priests then took the lead with their parliamentary demands at the convocation of the Estates General. Now the working men—and women—of Paris moved to express their indignation. "The patricians," said Chateaubriand succinctly, "began the revolution; the plebeians completed it." The patricians began it, one must add, both by their resistance to, and pressure for, change.

In April 1789, before the Estates General had convened, Paris had been the scene of a sizable riot, directed against the wealthy wallpaper manufacturer, Réveillon. It was followed in succeeding months by other riots. These street actions, with their raids on food shops and bakeries, were less political demonstrations than simple, violent searches for food. The price of a standard four-pound loaf of bread had risen to fourteen and a half sous, nearly twice the usual price of eight to nine sous. This was a desperately serious matter; 1789 was not the first time, and would not be the last, that the price of bread would trigger popular unrest. In normal times, a French worker laid out about half of his income on bread for himself and his family; when the price of this, his staple food, rose above ten or even twelve sous, practically all he earned must go for bread. In practice, this was destitution; in the winter, it meant being hopelessly cold; at all times, it meant going hungry.[3] By mid-July tempers were as high as the price of bread. Rumors inflated the numbers of troops Louis had ordered up to the Champ de Mars, and the demonstrable presence of armed men added

[3] See George Rudé, *The Crowd in the French Revolution* (1959), 21, 43.

to the news of Necker's fall aggravated the anxiety of Parisians who now sought arms as well as bread. Every night thousands of people gathered at the Palais Royale to listen to orators like Camille Desmoulins, who formulated popular demands in inflammatory slogans. Words were soon accompanied by actions; shops of armorers and gunsmiths were broken into and arms removed. Forty of the fifty-four customs posts that ringed the city were burned down, only partly as a protest against duties that raised prices on food, firewood, and livestock. Their symbolic significance was even more important at that moment: they stood as a barrier to the free entry of arms and persons into the city.

By the morning of July 13, the electors of Paris who had sent the deputies to the Estates General formed a committee to govern the city. They also sought to balance the indiscriminate demand for arms by establishing an official citizen's militia. The momentum of popular agitation, however, outran even this aggressive program. Crowds closed in on the Hôtel de Ville—the city hall— demanding and getting arms, and in the early morning of July 14, they plundered the Invalides. Then they marched on the Bastille. This old fortress, which held a paltry seven prisoners, was reported to be well armed and manned and ready to fire into the buildings around it.

At first the crowd of some eight hundred persons—mostly small merchants, craftsmen, and workmen—wanted only to negotiate for the gunpowder stored in the Bastille. Then the citizen's militia arrived. After several hours of confused palaver the governor of the fortress, de Launay, grew nervous as the besiegers lowered the outer drawbridge. He ordered his men to fire their cannon; ninety-eight persons in the courtyard were killed and some seventy wounded. The crowd outside brought up more arms and men and penetrated the inner courtyard. The governor then surrendered, and the citizens of Paris surged into the Bastille, taking the troops prisoner. De Launay himself was murdered on the way to the Hôtel de Ville.

The political consequences of the storming of this antique fortress far outran its military significance. In Paris the committee of electors appointed a council to govern the city, named Bailly mayor, and the marquis de Lafayette, a popular figure since his participation in the American Revolution, commander of the citizen's militia, the National Guard. Within three days the king decided that it would be prudent to acknowledge the new city council as the official government of Paris. He then ordered his mercenaries to decamp, recalled Necker, and on July 17 himself came to Paris to receive the national cockade with the colors of the Revolution: the white of the house of Bourbon ringed by the red and blue for the city of Paris. These events gave the National Assembly new, much-needed strength. The *menu peuple* of Paris had saved their "betters" at Versailles. By August, only two months after the Estates General had convened, the locus of authority had been irrevocably moved from the king to the representatives of the nation. July 14, Bastille Day, remains a memorable day in European history.

Great Fear and Great Expectations

The scarcity of grain had had its effect outside restless Paris as well. Wandering, penniless men and women roamed the countryside in search of bread. Just as the bread riots in Paris had brought the respectable bourgeoisie into action, so in the country the bands of famished poor sent the small property-owning peasants into a panic. Their feeling, which rose to a paroxysm during the summer, sprang from their apprehension that the roving bands were actually the instruments of an aristocratic plot to seize their holdings. These suspicions were built upon an old and settled conviction that the high price of bread and the grain shortages were directly caused by the hoarding and the manipulation of supplies by the aristocrats. The farmers' response was to arm themselves. But once armed and organized, in many regions they broke into the châteaux, less to pillage than to seize and destroy the ancient feudal records that spelled out the terms of their indebtedness and their onerous obligations. This infectious hysteria was *la grande peur*—the Great Fear.

By early August the aristocrats in the Assembly at Versailles were beginning to feel the discomfort attendant upon so much attention to their affairs. They heard of rioting in the cities and attacks upon the châteaux in the country; open defiance of authority—refusal to pay taxes, shooting of protected game, and the seizure of cultivated land—seemed ubiquitous. On July 27, 1789, as these alarming accounts were circulating widely, the constitutional committee presented to the Assembly its draft of the Declaration of the Rights of Man and Citizen, and opened the floor to debate. Then, on August 4, one deputy introduced a resolution to enforce the payment of dues and taxes. A number of aristocrats who had been meeting privately used this as an opportunity to make a dramatic counterproposal. Beginning with the viscount de Noailles and continuing with aristocrats from a variety of regions and ranks, one after another—noble deputies and propertied commoners—rose to renounce their privileges and prerogatives. Cynical historians have sought the source of this moving exhibition in the desire for self-preservation: by giving up what they could no longer hold, the privileged deputies hoped to keep the rest. Whatever the reason, by the time the meeting adjourned in the early hours of the morning, French society had been dramatically transformed, at least on paper. The principal target had been the remnants of feudal privilege: serfdom was abolished, as were all forms of personal obligation. True, the peasants who now became owners of the land they tilled, were required to make redemption payments to their former lords, but the events of the succeeding years made these payments unnecessary. Hunting preserves were abolished, as were tax exemptions. The church was not spared either: its tithes and ecclesiastical dues were cut off. This orgy of renunciation went on until August 11, and although a nation and its economic institutions cannot be transformed overnight, officially at least privilege as the basis of a social order had been legislated out of existence; all offices were declared open to free competition based solely on ability, not rank.

Against this background, the Declaration of the Rights of Man and Citizen could only be received with fervent enthusiasm. A spare, almost laconic document of no more than two thousand words, it was saturated with the ideas and the rhetoric of the Enlightenment, and obviously in debt to Jefferson's Declaration of Independence. It broke completely with the tradition that entrusted government to God's anointed and held the state to be a sacred institution. "Men," declared the first article, "are born, and remain, free and equal in rights." The function of the state is to guarantee the inalienable freedoms with which man is born—freedom of thought, freedom of religion, freedom from arbitrary arrest, freedom from taxation imposed without the consent of the governed. Law is the expression, not of the divine, but of the general, will. In essence, the "source of all sovereignty resides in the nation." Disseminated throughout France by the hundreds of thousands, it was posted up for the literate and read aloud to the illiterate; promptly translated into many languages and carried into every corner of Europe and beyond, it stimulated and strengthened ideas that had been fermenting for a century. From its very beginning, the French Revolution was for export.

THE RADICALIZATION OF
THE REVOLUTION: 1789-1793

From Absolutism to Constitutionalism

In the four months between May and August 1789 France was transformed, with the hesitant consent of the king himself, from an absolute to a constitutional monarchy. Louis XVI had demonstrated his symbolic acceptance of this revolution when he went to Paris in July to put on the revolutionary cockade—a shocking act that agitated the crowned heads of Europe as much as the French aristocracy. French aristocrats turned students of politics overnight, calculating the direction of the new government. Since between July and August 1789, some twenty thousand passports were issued, it seems plain that a sizable number of Frenchmen decided to study French affairs in the quiet of some spa abroad. One of the king's brothers, the count d'Artois, was among the first to flee; among those who followed him were not only aristocrats, but also craftsmen in the luxury trades who saw their livelihood disappearing across the borders in the silk clad persons of their patrons.[4] The émigrés, like the

---

[4] According to the best estimates, some one hundred twenty-five thousand emigrated in the course of the revolution. About 25 percent of this number were clerics; 20 percent peasants; only 17 percent nobility. Some working men, and even some members of the Constituent Assembly, disgusted with the radicalization of the revolution and the growing influence of the "mob," eventually emigrated as well. D'Artois' older brother, the count de Provence and later King Louis XVIII, fled in June 1791. See Donald M. Greer, *The Incidence of the Emigration During the French Revolution* (1951).

displaced of every period, clustered together in colonies—in Brussels, in Turin, and particularly in the little German principalities of the Rhineland along the French border. The count d'Artois and his party were untiring in their agitation to win the sympathy of Europe's rulers for the French king and in their attempt to strengthen Louis' resistance to any further encroachment on his powers. The American Revolution had already provided Europe with one object lesson; the French émigrés in the fashionable centers of Europe now increased the sense of alarm among supporters of the old order. Louis XVI's half-hearted acceptance of the Revolution meant either that he was playing for time or that he had resigned himself to the new order. In either case, monarchists everywhere should come to the support of d'Artois to bring about a proper restoration of the Bourbons to the throne of France.

The king was, indeed, besieged in Versailles—as much from within the walls, by the queen and her party of intransigents, as from without by the demands of the Assembly and the people of Paris. The possession of the king's very person was to all parties a symbol of success. While the goals of the revolution remained indistinct, the elimination of the king was not yet among them; on the contrary, the populace of Paris as earnestly desired him to join them as the aristocrats wanted him to flee abroad. By autumn 1789 the king was no longer so complaisant as he had been in mid-July. In the intervening months he had refused to approve the Declaration of the Rights of Man, refused to recognize the abolition of privileges following the renunciations of August 4, and quarrelled with the Assembly over his future veto power. While the Assembly wrangled over the place of the king and the shape of the legislature in the proposed constitution, a harvest at once late and poor was causing a shortage of flour. By mid-September Paris was in ferment. Even in normal times, a bread shortage was a serious affair, and these were not normal times. The municipality fixed a price of twelve sous for the four-pound loaf and maintained it by stationing guards at the bakeries. Crowds of women waiting at the bakeshops, already angry and hungry, were further inflamed by reports of insults offered the revolution by the queen and king in Versailles. Early on October 5, some seven thousand women armed themselves and marched off to Versailles, accompanied by agitators. Their single explicit grievance was the price of bread; their aim, as they marched, became clear: to bring "their" king to Paris.

At first, Louis XVI thought it enough to promise the crowd bread. After the queen's bedchamber was invaded toward morning and several of the royal bodyguard were killed, he decided to yield to the women's demand. On October 6 he permitted himself and his family to be escorted to Paris. The Assembly followed of its own accord ten days later. Under these painful circumstances the king ratified all the decrees of the Assembly to which he had previously refused his assent. At the same time he sent secret dispatches to his brother monarchs in Vienna and Madrid repudiating his apparent acquiescence in the changes taking place in France. His fatal policy of duplicity had begun.

The move to Paris brought Louis to the people and brought the people into politics. Where politics had before been the preserve of the deputies in either formal or informal meetings, once in Paris the business of the Assembly became the business of the man in the street. Parisians attended the meetings either as spectators or as members; in either case they lived with politics close at hand. The chief instruments of popular politics outside the meeting hall of the Assembly were the new political clubs. The most influential of these, the Society of the Friends of the Constitution, had its start as an informal group of prosperous Breton deputies who had begun to meet even before the Estates General convened. When the Assembly moved to Paris they continued their meetings, using the quarters of an old Jacobin monastery, from which their popular name derived. The original Jacobins gradually broadened their appeal by lowering club dues and establishing a network of branches across the country. By December 1790 its membership had reached a thousand. Although the Jacobin Club dominated political discussion in Paris—it formed in effect an unofficial caucus of the Assembly—it had no monopoly. The less exclusive Cordeliers,[5] appealing to workmen and shopkeepers, became the forum of the disaffected where they could give voice to their complaints against the work of the Assembly. With the king under its eye, the Constituent Assembly now addressed itself to its ostensible purpose—the making of a constitution—and to the pressing problems of restoring order and raising money. Its business was too serious not to create factions: revolutions, the offspring of fissions, produce fissions of their own. Those deputies content with the changes made so far— the Anglomaniacs—urged France to imitate the aristocratic English constitution, with its royal veto and its House of Lords. But in September, their adversaries, the radical Patriots—these radicals of 1789 were to become the reactionaries of 1792—induced the Assembly to limit the French king to a suspensive veto, which could delay but not annul legislation, and to establish a single-chamber parliament. France had come a long stretch from a society of distinct orders.

At the same time, the deputies, for all their egalitarian oratory, knew that while men are equal in rights, they are not equal in status. The Declaration of the Rights of Man had insisted on the sanctity of property. A majority in the Constituent Assembly had no intention of placing so sacred a thing as property at the mercy of the profane. The issue of the franchise thus confronted the new men of power with a serious dilemma. The deputies fervently believed in the sovereignty of the people, but, for the most part respectable property owners and well-educated professional men, they had seen, with their own eyes, the utter dependence of servants, the helpless illiteracy of peasants, the violent temper of the unemployed. To include these in the political public seemed

---

[5] Like the Jacobins the Cordelier Club took its popular name from the monastery in which it met—this one Franciscan. Its sonorous official title was Society of the Friends of the Rights of Man and of the Citizen.

sentimentality driven to the point of madness. It was Sieyès—always at hand
with the right word—who rescued the deputies from their quandary and
satisfied ideals and reality at the same time: he proposed a fundamental
distinction between "passive" and "active" citizens. All citizens would enjoy
the equal protection of the law, but only active citizens—males of twenty-five
who paid direct taxes equivalent to three days' wages every year—could vote.
This was a generous franchise; it included over four million adult Frenchmen,
three out of every five. These active citizens in turn were to vote for electors
whose property qualification was rather higher. Though on paper the franchise
remained wide, actually the government of France was not in the hands of the
potential electors but of those who could afford to serve in the electoral
assemblies which chose both the local and the national legislature. This meant
a minority of Frenchmen, about fifty thousand, who acted as electors in these
opening years of the Revolution. To radical critics, the new France appeared to
be a plutocracy speaking in the name of democracy. Maximilien Robespierre,
deputy from Arras, who was acquiring a reputation for his speeches in behalf
of democracy, vehemently objected to these electoral arrangements in the
Assembly; Jean Paul Marat, a popular Parisian journalist with a flair for name-
calling, denounced the proposed franchise as establishing an "aristocracy of
wealth."[6]

The Civil Constitution of the Clergy

The succession of dramatic events from May onward and the pervasive
uncertainty over the powers still remaining with the king and his ministers had
produced a collapse in authority. Taxes were virtually uncollectable. But,
however visionary the plans of the deputies and orators in Paris, day-to-day
government operations had to be carried on, soldiers and judges and interest
paid. The church, with its rich lands and far-flung properties, seemed an
inexhaustible source of desperately needed revenue. Acting on the accumulated grievances of centuries, the deputies saw solvency ahead, with the old
injustices set right at the same time. By no means all French ecclesiastics were
hostile to state intervention in church affairs: to the lower clergy, a guaranteed
salary seemed pure gain; to most clerics, steeped as they were in the Gallican
tradition, a certain degree of independence from Rome seemed no threat. In
fact, it was the bishop of Autun, Talleyrand, who on October 10, proposed the
nationalization of the church lands. The proposal became law in November,
and on December 19 church lands valued at four hundred million livres were
put up for sale. In expectation of new revenue arising from the sales, the
Constituent Assembly at the same time issued a mortgage bond, the *assignat*,

[6] See Alfred Cobban, *A History of Modern France,* vol. I, *The Old Regime and the Revolution,
1715-1799* (1957), 164, and L. G. Wickham Legg, *Select Documents Illustrative of the History of the
French Revolution,* vol. I (1905), 170-175. The epithet hardly seems violent, but it must be
remembered that the term "aristocrat" was acquiring some rather powerful connotations.

designed to pay the state's most exigent creditors. For some time, the value of the *assignat* held firm; in July 1790 it stood where it had stood when it was first issued—95 percent of face value. Its decline, first measured, then catastrophic, began later.

In that month, July 1790, the Assembly passed a bill that carefully redefined the relationship of church and state. This was the Civil Constitution of the Clergy. Of all the acts of the Assembly none opened such sharp divisions in the country, not only along the lines of interest but also—perhaps even more critically—along the lines of conviction. It also brought an alarmed pope into open opposition to the Revolution. In effect, the Civil Constitution made the French church into an arm of the French government. The buildings of the church became the property of the nation, its priests and bishops were to be elected by the qualified electors. The parishes and ecclesiastical districts were totally renovated. Here the Constituent Assembly had prepared the ground some months before: in December 1789, in a decisive assault on traditional loyalties and entrenched centers of power, it had destroyed France's historic divisions—its provinces, its *généralités,* its bailiwicks—and created eighty-three new rational regions, the "departments," to carry on local government. Parishes were now redesigned to conform to the new administrative units, and each department was to have one bishop, no more. This move reduced the number of bishops from one hundred thirty-five to eighty-three. These bishops, and all lower ecclesiastics, were placed on fixed salaries and under the attentive supervision of departmental authorities.

Good Catholics were torn. Many sections of the Civil Constitution seemed palatable, even statesmanlike, but the dependence of the church on the state that it decreed was far greater than the most Gallican among churchmen had foreseen. And the Assembly was decreeing the most far-reaching changes without consulting the clergy. While Louis XVI reluctantly approved the Civil Constitution in late July, resistance was open and widespread. The Assembly, seriously annoyed, made the Civil Constitution a matter of conscience; in November 1790, it insisted that each cleric swear to "uphold by every means in his power the constitution decreed by the National Assembly and accepted by the King."[7] The king, helpless, gave his assent to the oath late in December, but only seven of the bishops and less than half of the lower clergy complied. The Assembly promptly struck back: it stigmatized the holdouts as "refractory clergy" and deprived them of all clerical functions. So far, Pope Pius VI had disapproved of the Civil Constitution and the Revolution itself in private. As the division within the French clergy deepened, the pope's anxiety over the new French regime was exacerbated by upheavals in Avignon, long a papal possession where revolutionaries were pressing for reunion with France. In February 1791, Talleyrand, whom the pope had excommunicated the year before, guaranteed the apostolic succession of the constitutional clergy by

---

[7] The Civil Constitution of July, Title II, Article 21, had already exacted the same oath. The decree of November 27 simply prodded the dilatory.

consecrating new bishops. Finally, in March, Pius VI formally denounced the Civil Constitution as destructive of the Catholic religion, and the Declaration of the Rights of Man as a "shocking" establishment of unbridled "natural equality and liberty."

Every practicing Catholic in the country was drawn into the struggle. The conservative elements—women, peasants, and the pious folk of the western regions of France—sought out the refractory priests, fearing the taints of schism and excommunication that hung over the constitutional clergy. The king himself, on the first Easter after the pope had denounced the constitution, attempted to attend mass at Saint Cloud said by a refractory priest, but was held back by angry crowds. Voltaire's posthumous triumph was an ambiguous one: France was split in two.

The Road to War

Through early 1791, the divisions opened by the Civil Constitution of the Clergy renewed royalist anxieties; new contingents of the lesser nobility left the country. The king's brother in Turin, who came to be recognized as the leader of the émigrés, fervently urged European monarchs to mount a military invasion to restore the monarchy. Marie Antoinette's brother, Leopold II, now emperor (see p. 432), was regarded as a natural ally, but he refused to participate in any military adventures. The émigrés found money and support elsewhere. D'Artois moved to Coblenz to be closer to the center of preparations as plans for the attack across the Rhine advanced.

It was under these circumstances in June 1791 that the queen's party finally prevailed on the king to consider flight. It was a cumbersome scheme involving the coordination of officers and men and horses at stations along the route and depending upon the kind of timing that left little room for inevitable delays and mishaps. After a lumbering journey of twenty-four hours across France the royal party was ignominiously taken at Varennes and brought back in a slow procession to Paris. Complete with disguises, passwords, messages misunderstood, troops moved too soon or too late, couriers missing their rendezvous, a cross-country chase by a postmaster who had recognized the king, the flight had all the makings of a ludicrous comic opera. In fact it had terrible consequences. It destroyed the fiction that the king was a willing accomplice or pliant instrument of the revolution.

In the Assembly a moderate group headed by Barnave sought to save the principle of constitutional monarchy by a transparent fiction. The king's flight was described as an "abduction" and, to avoid any further difficulties during the completion of the constitution, now near, the king was temporarily suspended from office. The Assembly came to be no less than the jailer of the king. To outsiders, however, its conduct seemed timid. On July 15, the Cordeliers, headed by Danton, presented a petition to the Assembly asking that Louis be deposed and put on trial. The petition split the Jacobins, some of whom were sufficiently agitated to secede to a moderate monarchist club, the Feuillants; among them were Barnave, Bailly, and Lafayette. On July 17 at the Champ de Mars, some six thousand persons signed the Cordeliers' petition, but the demonstration turned into a massacre when the National Guard appeared. A shot rang out, the guard fired into the crowd, killing at least thirteen persons and wounding another thirty. To the Feuillants and their friends this was the preservation of order; to the radicals it became a cause for revenge—the Massacre of the Champ de Mars. Those who thought it time to stop the Revolution desperately tried to shore up the king; those who wanted to push it further began to talk of a republic.

Meanwhile, ominous news arrived from abroad. Leopold had allowed himself to be persuaded to meet with Frederick William II of Prussia to issue some statement on the French situation. Their famous Declaration of Pillnitz, issued late in August 1791, promised that the two monarchs would "not refuse to employ" the "most efficient means" of enabling Louis XVI to "establish with the most absolute freedom the foundations of a monarchical form of government." The meaninglessness of this guarantee was underlined by an escape clause, which emphasized that the signatories would only take action "if and when" all the other powers of Europe joined them—an event that Leopold, at least, did not expect to occur.

The declaration was received with greater literalness than its signatories had expected. Although Marie Antoinette, realistically enough, saw it as a betrayal, the émigrés took it as an offer of help, while the members of the Assembly chose to read it as a violent threat to the hopes of the infant Revolution. The French response to Pillnitz—aggressive rage rather than indifference or fear—was excessive, even misplaced. But it revealed the confidence with which the revolutionary leadership confronted the wrath of Europe. Indeed, undeterred by domestic division and foreign threats, the Constituent Assembly proceeded to finish the task it had assigned to itself two summers before. On September 3, it accepted the constitution; on September 14, Louis XVI obediently took his oath to it. Then, on September 30, the National Constituent Assembly dissolved. In two years, it had done an astonishing amount of demolition work. It had declared the state to be the guardian of natural rights and the servant of the sovereign people. It proposed to govern with a strong unicameral legislature, a rational, highly decentralized system of local bodies, and a hierarchical scheme of political participation that would protect the rights of all while gathering power in the hands of the qualified—that is, the propertied few. It retained the king, but dependent on annual appropriations and with only tattered remnants of his former authority. His very title—"king of the French by the grace of God and the will of the nation"—was a measure of how far France had traveled in so short a time.

Not unexpectedly, the radicalism of the new regime was circumscribed by the limited vision and the particular interests of the deputies who determined its shape. All wanted freedom, but freedom meant different things to different groups. The Constituent Assembly granted freedom to the press and the theater, full civic rights to Protestants in 1789 and (after some resistance) to Jews in 1791. But in the economic sphere the commitment to freedom and individualism resulted in the outlawing of workers' organizations. In June 1791, the Le Chapelier law forbade employers' as well as workers' associations. This destroyed, or drove underground, those rudimentary trade unions through which workers were seeking to improve their lot; it outlawed strikes as well. The enactment of such physiocratic doctrine into law was perfectly comprehensible: it opened access to all trades to everyone and definitively dissolved the encrusted gilds. Thus it clearly expressed the deputies' ideology of individualism, and their hostility to those intermediate attachments that interfered with the free individual's devotion to the common good. In 1791, it did not occur to anyone, not even the left-wing Jacobins, that this attack on special interests was in itself a form of special interest.[8]

However, when the new legislature, the Legislative Assembly, convened on October 1, 1791, the minds of the deputies were less on economic than on military matters. For the course of its short life, the Assembly was dominated by its most bellicose deputies, the Girondins, who profited from the foolish posturing and bluster of counterrevolutionaries abroad. Anything but an organized party, the Girondins were a faction of Jacobins drawn together by certain personal attachments and a degree of political agreement. Originally an informal gathering of deputies from Bordeaux, led by the silver-tongued attorney Pierre Victurnien Vergniaud, they recruited associates like the mathematician-philosophe Condorcet and the inevitable Abbé Sieyès, who were from other parts of the country. A cosmopolitan flavor was added by the adherence of a prominent Parisian hostess, Madame Roland, whose husband was a civil servant and at whose house foreign revolutionaries, including Thomas Paine, gathered to explore the future of the Revolution. The most remarkable and, from the historian's point of view, most instructive of the Girondins was Jacques Pierre Brissot. Son of a pastry cook at Chartres, Brissot had made a dubious living as a dubious political journalist; the Revolution gave him the opportunity of realizing his political schemes and personal aspirations at the same time. Only a revolutionary situation could have thrust such an ambitious mediocrity—and from a social stratum hitherto denied preferment—into a position of leadership.[9] In September, the expiring Constituent Assembly had annexed Avignon to France, thus trampling on the rights of its legal

[8] In October 1790, responding to a petition from workers in Beauvais, the spokesman of the National Assembly told the municipal officials: "The wages of workers are not within their competence, these can only be fixed by natural laws" (quoted in Alfred Cobban, *The Social Interpretation of the French Revolution* [1964], 63).

[9] Bordeaux, on the Gironde, was located in the department of the same name; hence the name of the faction. But Brissot, its best-known spokesman, after whom they were often called the Brissotins, actually sat in the Legislative Assembly for Paris. Since the Constituent Assembly had adopted, in May 1791, Robespierre's "Self-Denying Ordinance," which denied its deputies a place in the Legislative Assembly, all *its* deputies were new men. This also helps to explain, in part, Brissot's prominence.

sovereign, the papacy. In the same high-handed fashion, it had abolished the historic feudal dues owed to German princes in Alsace. Now, beginning in October, the Brissotins went beyond the provocative policy of these unilateral acts. They clamored against the émigrés, threatened unfriendly foreign monarchs that an aroused, liberty-loving French nation was ready to go to war, and preached a crusade to bring the Revolution to the world. With ingenuous naiveté, Brissot commended war as a medicine, as a surgical act. The Girondins' cry for war brought them surprising support from the government and from some of the Feuillants. The count de Narbonne, minister of war, and outside the cabinet, Lafayette, reasoned that war could only strengthen the executive; it would once again rally the nation behind the king and so restore the prestige of the monarchy. Restoration at home through aggression abroad: if the Brissotins were foolish and shallow, their conservative allies were intellectually bankrupt. Almost alone, Robespierre saw through the scheme and held firm against the rising war fever. In increasingly irritable debates with Brissot at the Jacobin Club, he argued the the émigrés posed no threat and that the Revolution's first business was at home. "No one," he said, in prophetic words, "loves an armed missionary."

Then on March 1, 1792, the queen's brother, Emperor Leopold, died, to be succeeded by his son, Francis II, who was young and eager for war. A defensive Prussian-Austrian alliance had just been concluded. The Girondins forced the Feuillant ministry out of office in March and supplanted it with their own men, including Roland. Narbonne, the advocate of war, went with them, but the dominant personality in the new cabinet, General Dumouriez, was, if anything, more bent on war than Narbonne had been, and for the same reason. Robespierre's warnings went unheard.

France declared war on Austria on April 20, 1792 ill-prepared and in a confusion of purposes: the policies officially prompting it—the liberation of Europe—were to be carried out by officers opposed to the Revolution and by ministers who hoped to use the war for the restoration of the monarchy. Dumouriez, minister of foreign affairs, an ambiguous, even sinister figure, sought to bend the situation to his personal advantage. The fears of counterrevolution which had, in part, provoked the war, had been exaggerated; Robespierre was right. But it did not take long for Prussia to join Austria, and on July 25, 1792, the two powers issued the Brunswick Manifesto, which lent plausibility to Brissot's excited pronouncements.

Ostensibly written by the duke of Brunswick, the allied commander, the document had actually been drafted in Paris, and its language had been made more virulent by émigrés. It stated the entire aim of the allied forces to be reestablishment of the rule of law and aid to Louis XVI "to exercise his legitimate authority." The manifesto warned the populace that if the royal family were harmed, "exemplary" vengeance—death and destruction—would be visited on Paris and on the "guilty rebels." The manifesto did, of course, what such threats of terror do—it redoubled revolutionary fervor and cemented the unity of the republicans. It embarrassed the men it was designed to protect, and strengthened those it was designed to frighten.

The Second Revolution

With the armies of Prussia and Austria on the frontiers of the Rhine clearly planning a march on Paris, the hardships and tensions of a country at war began to tell. As in most war emergencies, food and ordinary domestic necessities like soap and firewood became scarce and expensive. With the paper *assignats* rapidly depreciating, with the government as yet untried and unstable, with confidence in the future shaky, food became the real currency of France. While the peasants could hoard their produce and sell it, city workers with their paper money were at a disadvantage in bartering for the necessities of life. Political tensions rose and agitators flourished; yet the menace of the enemy, and the prospect of a restoration that could benefit only returning émigrés also brought mounting nationalist excitement. Troops from the provinces streamed to Paris, and local *sans-culottes* took their case against the treacherous king to the streets. The *sans-culottes* had entered French politics in July and again in October 1789; now, in the general excitement, they took an ever more active part.

The term *sans-culotte* is a social term that acquired political meaning. It referred originally to the lower, though not the lowest, orders in the cities, to men and women with modest education and modest incomes, to small shopkeepers, artisans, industrial workmen; their name literally referred to their clothing: they did not wear the *culottes,* the elegant knee-breeches. But in the course of the Revolution, *sans-culotte* became a name for politically active, generally passionate revolutionary democrats, no matter what their social origins. For them the slogan *liberté, égalité, fraternité* meant direct participation in politics, usually in endless meetings, and the translation of the new ideals into political, social, and economic reality. Now, in the early summer of 1792, they cheered the troops that marched through Paris on their way to the front, to save the country.[10]

Among these troops were recruits from Marseilles, who marched to a new song, the *Marseillaise.* With its plain denunciation of tyranny, its vivid warning against bloodthirsty foreign soldiers, its heady appeal to patriotism, the *Marseillaise* became the rallying call of the Revolution:

> Allons, enfants de la patrie,
> Le jour de gloire est arrivé,
> Contre nous, de la tyrannie,
> L'étendard sanglant est levé . . .

[10] By 1793, a rich, even a once-noble revolutionary could be a good *sans-culotte.* The counterpart was the all-purpose epithet "aristocrat," which came to mean, quite simply, enemy of the Revolution.

There had been sporadic demonstrations all during the early months of the war, as food grew scarcer and popular indignation at hoarders grew with the scarcity. Profiteers in goods imported from the colonies, such as sugar, felt the anger of Parisian housewives who invaded stores and warehouses to seize and resell the sugar at the "normal" price of twenty-five sous per pound instead of the three livres per pound charged by the profiteers. Meanwhile the provincial regiments, the *fédérés,* made common cause with the Parisian *sans-culottes.* The terms of the Brunswick Manifesto were known in Paris by August 1; shortly after calls for the abdication of Louis XVI swept through the city. By August 3, this demand was expressed by forty-seven of the forty-eight sections of Paris. On the next day, the representatives of the working-class sections, the Faubourg Saint-Antoine, threatened force if the Assembly did not depose the king by August 9.

In the early hours of the morning of August 10, representatives of the forty-eight sections of the city met at the Hôtel de Ville, suspended the municipal government, and declared a new administration, the Commune. With this, an alarm gun was fired and the tocsins throughout the city aroused the citizenry. A march on the Tuileries followed, and a sanguinary clash. In the encounter of twenty thousand Parisians and *fédérés* with the Swiss guards, misunderstandings and ill-timed orders exacerbated tensions, already high. In the event, eight hundred of the king's troops were killed, and the attackers lost heavily as well: some three hundred Parisians and ninety *fédérés* lay dead. In the confusion, the king and his family fled from their palace and threw themselves on the mercy of the Assembly. This was the *journée* of August 10, as decisive as the *journée* of July 14 had been three years before. As on Bastille Day, once again Paris had radically altered the course of events. The "second revolution" had begun.

On August 11, the Assembly recognized the Commune, surrendered the royal family to its custody, and called for elections to a new assembly, the Convention. The conditions for voting in the new elections were revolutionary, indeed; they abolished the old property qualifications and granted suffrage to every French male over twenty-one who was neither a dependent nor a domestic servant. With its king as prisoner, embroiled in a war with superior powers, the dying constitutional monarchy marched on a path of no return. Early in July, the country had been proclaimed in danger; late in July, Brunswick's troops had invaded French soil. As more and more Frenchmen enrolled for service in the war, the suspicion of domestic enemies assumed grotesque proportions. It was widely believed—and agitators like Danton and Marat did their utmost to foster that belief—that the prisons were full of royalists and traitors to the Revolution who were only waiting for the volunteers to leave Paris for the front to break jail and destroy the country from within. The grim harvest of this belief came in early September, with an attack upon prisons in Paris and in the provinces. In Paris around twelve hundred prisoners, nearly half its prison population, were summarily slaughtered—and only a quarter of them were priests, nobles, Swiss guards, or political enemies of the Revolution. The rest were ordinary criminals. The "September massacres" ushered in a new phase of the Revolution: the final overthrow of the king, the emergence of Paris under the Commune as the revolutionary vanguard, and the prosecution of the war not as a defensive action, but aggressively to win all Europe for the cause of liberty.

The Convention which met in Paris in September 1792 represented the mandate of one million Frenchmen compared with the fifty thousand who had voted for the deputies of the Legislative Assembly. Yet, despite the broadening of the electorate, the social composition of the Convention did not markedly differ from that of its predecessor. Of the seven hundred fifty deputies, nearly half were lawyers and the remainder were businessmen, doctors, landowners, constitutional clergy, artists, scientists, and local officials. In its three years of life, the Convention had only two members officially classified as working men. What did make the Convention representative was the strong local base of the deputies who came from small villages and returned there after their duties in the capital were over. A striking feature of the representation in the Convention was the invitation extended to distinguished foreigners—naturalized by decree—"whose writing has sapped the foundations of tyranny and prepared the road to liberty."[11]

The first meeting of the National Convention on September 20 coincided with the first French victory over the Prussians at Valmy, in northeastern France. It was an auspicious augury. The engagement was minor; the moral effect, decisive. Goethe, who was there, shrewdly described it as the opening of a new era in history. On September 21 the Convention carried by acclamation the formal proposition "that royalty be abolished in France."

The Convention met in a newly renovated hall in the Tuileries; its very physical arrangement, with its steeply banked seats, gave palpable form to the political division among the deputies. The Brissotins sat at the right in the lower tiers. The radical Jacobins sat to the left in the upper tiers—they were the men of the "Mountain," the Montagnards. The "Plain," a majority of the deputies, less noisy than the extremes, and less dogmatic, sat in the center and held the balance. The divisions in the Convention were, of course, more than physical; they represented sharpening differences among the deputies. The Girondins who had been in the vanguard in the Legislative Assembly urging the war and calling for a republic, now took a turn toward moderation; they grew fearful of mob rule. But they had called up spirits they could not exorcise. Robespierre did not permit them to turn back. Nor did the war: success abroad brought radicalization at home.

The victory at Valmy turned back the Prussian march on Paris and left the French free to take the initiative on other fronts. By October, French troops

---

[11] The decree included such famous men as George Washington, Alexander Hamilton, James Madison, Jeremy Bentham, and the great Swiss educational reformer Johann Heinrich Pestalozzi. But only Thomas Paine, elected deputy for Pas-de-Calais, actually took his seat.

under General de Custine, were in Germany, and on November 6, under General Dumouriez, they defeated the Austrians at Jemappes in the Austrian Netherlands. On November 14, they entered Brussels. On November 19, the Convention, responding to the heady news from the front, enacted a sweeping decree "in the name of the French nation," promising "fraternity and aid" to "all peoples wishing to recover their liberty," and charged the government to order French generals to defend all citizens who "have been, or who might be, harassed for the cause of liberty." [12] On December 15, it followed up this November decree by ordering its generals upon occupying an area to proclaim immediately the "sovereignty of the people, the suppression of all the established authorities," and the "abolition of the tithe, feudalism, and seigneurial rights."

While French armies were spreading justice and liberty according to their lights, the Convention in Paris was attempting to establish a permanent government. The most serious piece of unfinished business was the disposition of the king. Since August 10 he and the royal family had been shut up in a fortress in Paris. For several weeks the Convention debated his fate; hundreds of pamphlets on all sides of the question were printed at public expense and widely circulated. The struggle over the king was, for many, a struggle for power in the Convention; leading Girondins counseled delay, impatient Jacobins pressed for an immediate trial of "Louis Capet." At the end of November, an iron chest was discovered in the Tuileries filled with papers incriminating the king—plans for flight and correspondence with émigrés, refractory priests, and foreign diplomats. Brissotin resistance to a trial collapsed.

On December 3, the Convention decided on a trial and, allowing Louis' counsel ten days for preparation, heard his defense on December 26. In the midst of uproar and after vociferous debate on procedural matters, the deputies found Louis guilty without a dissenting vote and rejected a Girondist proposal for a popular referendum on the verdict by three to two. On the third question, then, by an absolute majority of one, 361 of the 721 deputies present voted for the king's immediate execution. [13] The closeness of the decision brought another vote on January 19 on a respite. It lost, 380 to 310. The Montagnards, the Left, had triumphed. On the morning of January 21, 1793, Louis XVI proclaimed his innocence from the scaffold—*"Peuple, je meurs innocent"*; a few minutes later he died under that new, humane device, the guillotine.

---

[12] For the decree, see John Hall Stewart, *A Documentary Survey of the French Revolution* (1951), 381.

[13] If we examine the total vote, the figure seems a little less precarious: of 749 members, 28 were absent, 321 had voted for penalties other than death, mainly imprisonment, 26 voted for death but demanded a debate on postponing the execution, 13 voted for death on condition that there be a postponement, while 361 attached no conditions to their vote for death.

THE RISE AND FALL OF
REVOLUTIONARY DEMOCRACY: 1793–1795

The Revolution and the World

The irresistible dynamism of the French Revolution had made it determined enemies from the very start. Orderly change imposed from above was one thing; revolutionary change compelled from below was something else again. The Spanish government, though committed to economic and educational reform, solved the embarrassment of news from the Revolution by sealing its frontiers against France (see p. 423). The king of Sweden, Gustavus III, who had denuded the Swedish nobility of all its power, volunteered to lead a crusade against the French revolutionaries (see p. 420). And Catherine of Russia confronted events in France with mounting fear. The fall of the Bastille won her over to the counterrevolution. After the king's flight to Varennes, she, like the Spaniards, imposed censorship; in 1792, she volunteered to join Gustavus' crusade. The execution of Louis XVI made her sick and completed her conversion. She ordered the expulsion of the French ambassador, supported émigrés, and ordered Frenchmen living in Russia to swear loyalty to "Louis XVII." The Revolution led her to reject the philosophes whose ideas she had claimed to follow and whose friendship she had courted.

Inevitably, many Europeans changed their view of the French Revolution as the Revolution itself changed. Friedrich Gentz, whose name is indissolubly linked with the reactionary years after 1815, greeted its early days as mankind's long-delayed awakening; by 1791, he opposed a Revolution which, he declared, had betrayed itself. The radicalization of the Revolution in 1792 alienated other admirers. The execution of Louis XVI alienated more. William Pitt called it "the foulest and most atrocious deed which the history of the world has yet had occasion to attest." This is significant, for Pitt was no reactionary, no friend of the émigrés. Indeed, in the mid-1780s, he had been something of a reformer, in a moderate, practical way.

The younger son of the great Chatham, Pitt had become chancellor of the exchequer at the age of twenty-two. In 1784, at twenty-four, he became prime minister and, after consolidating his hold on the cabinet and Parliament, introduced proposals for parliamentary reform. His bill provided for the abolition of thirty-six rotten boroughs [14] and for the extension of the suffrage.

---

[14] These historic anomalies were grossly overrepresented districts with few voters; with the growth of industrial cities—underrepresented or not represented at all—they became a scandal.

Finding the opposition too strong, he retreated. He was more successful with the organization of imperial government in Canada and India, spectacularly so in financial and administrative affairs. He abolished sinecures and put officials on regular salaries; he reformed the excise and the customs offices; he clarified the system of taxation. His heart was always in orderly government, notably finance.

Far from being exceptional, Pitt's reform schemes were part of a European-wide movement. Since the 1760s, as we have seen, countries from Spain to Sweden had witnessed large-scale efforts at rationalizing bureaucracies, re-vamping legal systems, and reforming taxes. This was the period of assaults on privileged bodies—on Parliament in England, the parlements in France, the nobles in the Hapsburg domains, in Sweden, in Portugal; these included attempts to widen the franchise, to eliminate noble monopoly or ownership of offices, and to reduce or abolish special privileges. Most of these efforts had been the work of royal autocrats like Joseph II or Catherine II. Elsewhere, the call for reform was sounded by movements intent on winning some political power for what in France was called the third estate. There had been political unrest in Geneva in the 1760s, in America in the 1770s, in the Austrian Netherlands, the Dutch Republic, Ireland, and Poland in the 1780s. [15] Granted that the violence, the extent, and the historic import of the French Revolution were unique; but the French Revolution occurred within a larger, fostering climate.

Not surprisingly, therefore, there were many men in many countries who greeted events in France with unconcealed joy. The great slogan, *liberté, égalité, fraternité,* spoke to an international audience: the Dutch Batavian Republic, established in 1795, was to take these words for its official motto. In England, sympathetic observers noted with satisfaction that the French were finally imitating the English. Late in 1789, the well-known dissenting minister Richard Price, gifted mathematician, rationalist theologian, and reformist political thinker, delivered an address that aroused widespread comment; Price thought that the events of 1789 in France confirmed the lesson of the events of 1689 in England: the source of sovereignty, the people, could by right "cashier" its rulers for "misconduct." Charles James Fox, the great liberal politician, consistently defended the Revolution. Thomas Paine, who had encouraged the American rebels with his *Common Sense,* now, in his *Rights of Man,* eloquently defended the natural right of any people to choose its own government, freely. And in 1792, partly drawing on radical English ideas, but much heartened by the revolution in France, Thomas Hardy, a London shoemaker, founded the London Corresponding Society, which, in alliance with similar groups in the

[15] One distinguished American historian, R. R. Palmer, has grouped these efforts under the collective name of "democratic revolution." See *The Age of the Democratic Revolution: A Political History of Europe and America, 1760-1800,* 2 vols. (1959-1964), to which we are indebted in these pages.

provinces, urged radical reforms at home and reached a wider public than the gentleman-reformers of the 1780s. Those young poets whose fame belongs to the early nineteenth century—Coleridge, Wordsworth, Southey, Landor—saw the Revolution with enthusiasm. German *Aufklärer,* young and old, hailed the Revolution as the dawn of mankind. Even the elderly poet Klopstock, wishing he had "a hundred voices" to celebrate the birth of liberty, wrote an ode to the French Revolution in April 1792. Philosophers like Kant and Fichte, Schelling and Hegel saw it as a new age, the age of philosophy. These poets and philosophers spoke for wide circles in German society. In Saxony and in the Rhineland peasants rebelled in imitation of France; German cities were crowded with more or less authentic copies of French Jacobins. At the city of Mainz, Georg Forster, university librarian and cosmopolitan intellectual, formed a pro-French political club; when in October 1792, Custine occupied the city with his army, Forster and his friends welcomed the French and cheerfully collaborated with them. In the following year, the same group sought to have their land annexed to the French Republic. Elsewhere democrats, radicals, reformers took heart. Dutch "Patriots," defeated in 1787 by a combination of the Orangist oligarchy and Prussian troops, founded underground Jacobin cells at home to prepare their country for a revolution. The Italian states were honeycombed with subversive revolutionary clubs; when Bonaparte marched into Milan in May 1796 (see p. 505), the enthusiastic welcome he received proved how revolutionary the city had become in reaction to Austrian overlordship. In the Republic of Geneva, long torn by civil contention, a radical party significantly called the *égalisateurs* made a successful coup in December 1792, proclaimed civic equality for all, and produced a democratic constitution. In restless Ireland, late in 1791, the young lawyer Wolfe Tone founded the Society of United Irishmen, an association that—true to its name and contrary to earlier Irish reform movements—welcomed Catholics as well as Protestants; it rapidly spread across the island, called for parliamentary reform and for a convention—a name that, by late 1792, reminded conservatives, and was intended to remind them, of France. Most of these movements were eventually suppressed. But they testify to the vitality of the ideas that spread from revolutionary France and to the susceptibility of the thousands who adopted them.

While the Revolution had its slogans, by 1790 the counterrevolution had its Bible: Edmund Burke's eloquent *Reflections on the Revolution in France,* an emotional rejoinder to Dr. Price's notorious address. Burke's book, though melodramatic in its defense of the queen and badly misinformed on French affairs, made an impressive philosophical point: society is not a rational business organization; the social contract is a tacit agreement among the dead, the living, and those yet unborn; long-lived institutions deserve to survive simply because they have lived long; to undo the work of centuries in a year is to overestimate the power of reason and to despise the inestimable value of tradition. The September massacres in 1792 and the execution of the king in

January 1793 seemed to confirm Burke's passionate diagnosis. Early supporters dropped away. The English poets were exceptional. Wordsworth, who had been in Paris during the September massacres, defended the establishment of the republic and the execution of Louis XVI. There were some who saw the years of terror, 1793–1794, not as essential to an evil, but as accidental to a good, thing.

Political Struggles and Civil War

In France, the execution of the king solved nothing. The way a deputy had voted on the king's fate became a political test in the acrimonious days and months that followed. It was not a wholly dependable test: the most prominent Brissotins, including Vergniaud and Brissot himself, who had voted in favor of the death sentence were now, for their earlier delaying tactics, stigmatized as "moderates"—a new word of abuse that the Montagnards used to great effect. Gutter journalists, club orators, ambitious politicians freely threw epithets like "traitor," "counterrevolutionary," "English agent" at fellow revolutionaries they disliked or distrusted. Politics became a matter of name-calling, of appeal to the streets, of outright violence. Anxiety and rage were terrible simplifiers; in May 1793, Robespierre put it very plainly: "There are now only two parties in France, the people and the enemies of the people."[16]

In retrospect, the political struggles of early 1793 came to look like a contest between two gigantic monoliths—Montagnards against Girondins. Actually, the political factions were shifting and relatively small; even on sensitive questions of economic policy, Vergniaud and Robespierre sometimes made common cause.

As usual, military reverses sharpened political animosities. The young republic had proved extraordinarily aggressive; foreign statesmen had been right to find the resolutions of the previous November and December (see p. 483) distasteful and frightening. In November, the Convention had annexed Savoy; French forces followed up their occupation of Belgium by systematically looting it and by applying revolutionary decrees in the occupied territory. In mid-November, the French had declared the Scheldt open to shipping, in clear violation of the international settlement of 1648 (see p. 254). England promptly promised the Dutch aid in case of French attack. On January 31, in an important speech, Danton called for the annexation of Belgium and justified his demand by the doctrine of "natural frontiers": France, he said, was defined by the Atlantic, the Alps, and the Rhine. The next day, Pitt voiced his indignation at France's unilateral actions: "England," he said, "will never consent that France shall arrogate the power of annulling at her pleasure and under pretence of a natural right of which she makes herself the only judge, the political system of

[16] Quoted in M. J. Sydenham, *The French Revolution* (1965), 155.

Europe, established by solemn treaties and guaranteed by the consent of all powers." On the same day, doubtless saving Pitt the trouble, France declared war on England and the Dutch Republic; war on Spain followed soon after, on March 7. Within a short time, Pitt had organized an impressive-sounding coalition against the revolutionary republic; it included France's current enemies Prussia and Austria, as well as Spain, the Dutch Republic, Russia, Sardinia, and, of course, Britain.

The precarious situation of France was made more precarious by the defection of General Dumouriez. Here was the kind of treachery that orators were always declaiming about. Once he had swept through Belgium, the Convention ordered him to move north. But the conquest of Belgium was by no means secure; by March 1, as Dumouriez advanced on the Dutch, the Belgians, incensed by the plunder of their churches, rebelled against their new masters. Within a few weeks, the Austrians had capitalized on this uprising; on March 18, at Neerwinden, and again at Louvain on March 21, they forced the French to retreat and to evacuate Belgium. Later that month, Dumouriez, anti-Jacobin at heart and appalled by the execution of Louis XVI, listened to Austrian overtures and offered to restore the constitutional monarchy under "Louis XVII." But he could not persuade his troops to join him in a march on Paris, and on April 5, followed by a few staff officers, he deserted to the Austrians. Thrown back to their own territory, the French at last made a stand at Valenciennes, while in the east, French troops fell back under pressure from the Prussians. The unconquerable revolutionary forces of the previous fall had become vulnerable armies in the spring. The Revolution was in danger; it was rescued, at least in part, by the greed, the callousness, the myopia of its enemies. Shortly after the execution of Louis XVI, the count de Provence wrote to the count d'Artois, reported their brother's death, and added that the dauphin was not likely to survive him long. "Whilst you shed tears, for those near to us," he said, "you must not forget how useful their deaths will be for the country. Comfort yourself with this idea and reflect that your son is, after myself, the heir and hope of the monarchy." [17] From such unteachable Bourbons the new regime, shaky as it was, had little to fear. Even more helpful was the preoccupation of three of the allies—Austria, Prussia, and Russia—with another partition, the second, of Poland. It came after a brave and highly effective effort on the part of Polish reformers to govern themselves more rationally than before: in 1791, under the leadership of their king, Stanislas Poniatowski, they adopted a constitution which abolished the *liberum veto*, made the kingship hereditary, and gave it adequate executive powers. In May of 1792, her hands freed after making peace with the Turks, Catherine of Russia invaded Poland to keep the old constitution, and thus her hegemony, intact. Partition was only a matter of time. Prussia insisted on its share, Austria, eager

---

[17] Quoted in J. M. Thompson, *The French Revolution* (2nd ed., 1944), 334. Thompson comments: "How these Bourbons loved one another!"

as ever, was this time kept from the trough. In January 1793 the unhappy Poles bowed to the inevitable: Russia grabbed most of the western Ukraine and most of Lithuania; Prussia grabbed Danzig, Thorn, and Great Poland. A third partition in October 1795, with Austria again a partner, would sweep Poland away. Fighting France took second place to the passion for Polish land.

Still, the Convention had good grounds for anxiety. It called for volunteers and, late in February, for three hundred thousand troops. In the far west, in the region of the Vendée, hilly, rural, deeply pious, the draft call triggered an armed rising, which by March 15 amounted to a full-fledged rebellion. And in Paris scarcity of essentials, rumors of hoarding, and the reality of high prices brought, late in February, direct action: enraged *sans-culottes* stormed the shops and terrorized their owners into selling staples at the old, low price. As the spring went on, politics in the Convention increasingly reflected pressures from the outside. This was the year of *sans-culotte* politics.

While much of the *sans-culottes'* conduct was purposeful and politically rational, the threat of hunger, the dearth of dependable news, and the contagious excitement in the streets made the *sans-culottes* particularly susceptible to radical rhetoric. Marat wrote inflammatory articles against hoarders—*accapareur* became an even more hated name than aristocrat—while a small, extremist faction, the *enragés,* shouted for death to speculators, for rationing, and for a ceiling price on food—the *maximum.*

The Convention (and this included its left-wingers like Marat) was torn. It believed in free trade, and the *sans-culottes* were demanding price controls; it was learning the need for effective government, and the *sans-culottes* were acting out the drama of direct democracy. From then on, the Convention was marked by this tragic tension.[18] By mid-March, it had decided to send eighty of its members to the provinces, to superintend recruitment of troops and to take all necessary measures against the counterrevolution—these were the famous, powerful *représentants en mission.* It also reestablished the Revolutionary Tribunal, on a firmer basis than before, to try counterrevolutionaries with suitable dispatch. On March 19, on the motion of Cambacérès (see p. 507), it officially declared those found obstructing recruitment or engaged in armed rebellion outlawed—*hors la loi.* Two days later, it decreed that each section or commune should elect a revolutionary committee of twelve members. Finally, on April 6, it created the Committee of Public Safety. The lineaments of revolutionary government were emerging, though slowly: the committee, established at the urging of Danton to strengthen the executive, did not secure its ascendancy for a few months; Danton, who dominated it, was busily seeking accommodations with the allies.

This rash of decrees left the economic front untouched. Jacques Roux, chief spokesman for the *enragés,* increased his vociferous propaganda for

[18] For a lucid survey of this tragedy, see R. R. Palmer, "Popular Democracy in the French Revolution: Review Article," *French Historical Studies,* 1 (Fall 1960), 445-469.

protection of the poor. At the same time, radical Jacobins appealed to the clubs
to purge the Convention of its disloyal members. Both had weighty consequences. Late in April, the leaders of the Mountain swallowed their economic
liberalism, made common cause with the *sans-culottes,* and on May 4 pushed
through the first *maximum,* which left the setting of ceiling prices for grain to
individual departments. The Brissotin faction, meanwhile, fearing loss of
control in the Convention, drew together in a series of ill-timed and ill-
conceived defensive maneuvers. They secured the impeachment of Marat for
signing a manifesto that openly accused the Convention of harboring counterrevolutionaries. But Marat was immensely popular in the city, and the
Revolutionary Tribunal triumphantly acquitted him; the call to cleanse the
Convention of "moderates" only grew in shrillness. It was not softened by the
Girondins' success in stirring up the provinces against the Jacobins. In May, the
cities of Marseilles, Bordeaux, and Caen joined in a call for a "federalist" revolt
against Paris. On May 30, there was a bloody clash in Lyons, and the city fell
to the anti-Jacobins. In Paris, in response, the Jacobins rallied the sections to
their side. The Central Revolutionary Committee appointed Hanriot, a good
Jacobin, commander of the National Guard, and on June 2, after two days of
confusion, the Convention, intimidated, agreed to put twenty-nine Girondin
deputies and two Girondin ministers under arrest. The Mountain had consolidated the victory it had first won in January. But its leaders acted with
circumspection, even generosity; they were not sadists. Most of the Girondins
were so lightly guarded that they made their escape to the provinces or, like
Vergniaud, stayed in Paris to carry on their fight there.

The summer proved to the Jacobins that their forbearance had been
misplaced. Reverses continued: in June, in the Vendée, the rebels took Saumur
and compelled the government to transfer badly needed troops from the Rhine
to the west. In July, the allies took the fortresses of Condé and Valenciennes and
the city of Mainz. Then, on July 13, the enthusiast Charlotte Corday brought
the danger home to the Jacobins by murdering Marat. In August, finally,
royalists turned the port city of Toulon over to the British. In the provinces, the
escaped Girondin deputies inspired a cluster of Federalist uprisings and tried to
unite the country against Paris. And in Paris itself, the *enragés,* unappeased by
the *maximum* of May, continued to harangue the Jacobins. The purged Jacobin
Convention responded in all directions. On June 24, it adopted a new
constitution—a Girondin draft hastily rewritten by Jacobins—which proclaimed new, more populist principles; it was never put into force, and perhaps
was not intended to be, but it stood as a statement of democratic aspirations.
In the following month, the radicals in the Convention pushed through a
ferocious decree against hoarding. More important, the Convention strengthened the Committee of Public Safety. Early in July, his appeasement discredited, Danton left that committee; soon after, Robespierre and two energetic and
experienced soldiers, Carnot and Prieur de la Côte d'Or, entered it. Rapidly
now, the Committee of Public Safety turned itself into a cabinet. Its members

toured the front; late in August, after some hesitation, it acted to mobilize the resources of France with the celebrated *levée en masse,* which demanded, and specified, the sacrifices all Frenchmen, young and old, must make until the republic was safe. The new government had to survive a fierce challenge on September 4 and 5; a mass demonstration of Parisian *sans-culottes,* led by the demagogic journalist Jacques Hébert and goaded by a new shortage of bread, prompted the committee to co-opt two *enragés,* Billaud-Varenne and Collot d'Herbois, to work for a general *maximum* and to press for the trial of the Girondins. On September 17, as radical pressure kept up, the Convention enacted the ominous Law of Suspects, which authorized the arrest of anyone suspected of counterrevolutionary activity. Legality had given way to the Terror. On September 29, the Convention decreed a general *maximum* to hold down wages and prices alike; a few days later, forty-five deputies—Girondins and their sympathizers—were finally put under indictment. And on October 10, Saint-Just, a flint-eyed young Jacobin speaking for the Committee of Public Safety, introduced a decisive decree that mobilized the government for the duration: "The provisional government of France," declared the first article, "will be revolutionary until the peace."

· *Revolutionary Government*

The Committee of Public Safety, which increasingly acted as the government of France, faced daunting difficulties. "Traitors" proved relatively easy to deal with: on October 9, revolutionary forces recaptured Lyons; a week later, Marie Antoinette went to the guillotine after an indecent, hasty trial, and Bordeaux returned to Jacobin control; at the end of the month, the Brissotins in government hands were guillotined. Even "tyrants" seemed vulnerable: on the day of Marie Antoinette's execution, October 16, French forces beat back the Austrians at Wattigny and thus relieved enemy pressure on the northern front.

But the fratricidal conflict between the revolutionary government and the left-wing opposition was harder to resolve. Robespierre and his associates on the Committee of Public Safety did not intend to overlook the lessons of the Hébertist uprisings on September 4 and 5: the government had to repress its wrong-headed or false friends as much as its open enemies. Freedom must wait until discipline had been reestablished. Here, it would turn out, was the tragedy of revolutionary democracy: the Mountain could not live with its supporters and would die without them. Robespierre, though by no means a dictator, had become the best-known spokesman for the Committee of Public Safety. He never doubted that there were enemies on the left and that the ultrarevolutionaries were the agents of the counterrevolutionaries. In the fall of 1793 he had an opportunity of testing his suspicions in a surprising quarter—against atheists. If there was one important issue on which revolutionaries of all stripes could agree, it was that the "Christian superstition" was at once absurd and vicious. But, if Christianity was the false religion *par excellence,* what was the true religion? Here dissensions arose. On October 5, the Convention had enacted a new revolutionary calendar designed to rationalize the year and to wipe out all traditional associations of the calendar with the hated superstition of the past. Each of the new months had thirty days; that left over five days which were designated as holidays and significantly, if rather hollowly, called *sans-culottides.* The names of the months—Brumaire, month of fog, Thermidor, month of heat—and the new arrangement of the week never became popular, but for some years revolutionary governments insisted on dating events by them. The old Gregorian calendar was not reestablished until 1806, by Emperor Napoleon I. [19] Fanatical de-Christianizers wanted to go further; they wanted to ban all religious ceremonies, compel all priests to marry, close all the churches. Robespierre opposed de-Christianization on personal and political grounds. He was a deist himself, on the Rousseauian pattern: he believed in God the creator and in a guiding providence. This doubtless figured in his opposition, but the danger that antireligious extremism might alienate the large mass of moderate believers was more important still. He ordered the committee's traveling spokesmen, the *représentants en mission,* to reduce their antireligious activities, and on November 17 (we should call it 27 Brumaire, Year II), in a famous speech to the Jacobins, he denounced atheism as the religion of aristocrats. Such fanaticism, he urged, could only aid the enemy. In December, some of the extreme de-Christianizers were arrested. Earlier in the year, Robespierre had already denounced the leading *enragés* as Austrian agents, and Jacques Roux was arrested twice. In September, the government machinery of the Terror speeded up its operations. While before then, trials had been scrupulously conducted and the death sentence handed out sparingly, both the speed of the trials and the proportion of death sentences rapidly increased. There were spectacular collective state trials, "mixed bakings" carefully arranged to

---

[19] Since the decisive *journées* of the revolution that occurred after October 1793 are still known by their revolutionary nomenclature, here, for the record, is the calendar. The decree of October 1793 named September 22, 1792, the day after the official abolition of the monarchy, the first day of Year I of the republic. The months were:

Name	Meaning of name	Dates
Vendémiaire	Month of vintage	Sept. 22–Oct. 21
Brumaire	Month of fog	Oct. 22–Nov. 20
Frimaire	Month of frost	Nov. 21–Dec. 20
Nivôse	Month of snow	Dec. 21–Jan. 19
Pluviôse	Month of rain	Jan. 20–Feb. 18
Ventôse	Month of wind	Feb. 19–Mar. 20
Germinal	Month of budding	Mar. 21–Apr. 19
Floréal	Month of flowers	Apr. 20–May 19
Prairial	Month of meadows	May 20–June 18
Messidor	Month of harvest	June 19–July 18
Thermidor	Month of heat	July 19–Aug. 17
Fructidor	Month of fruit	Aug. 18–Sept. 16

The *sans-culottides* thus fell on September 17 to 21.

increase public revulsion against the accused: suspect foreigners, unsuccessful generals, rapacious speculators, returned émigrés—and political opponents of the regime. Fouquier-Tinville, the efficient chief prosecutor, had much work to do. In October his Tribunal condemned fifty-one persons to death, in November fifty-eight, in December sixty-eight. In the provinces, meanwhile, government representatives vented wholesale vengeance on reconquered cities. After Lyons was retaken, Couthon, a member of the Committee of Public Safety and Robespierre's close associate, proposed that the houses of the rich be razed and the name of the city be wiped from the earth. It was to be called *Ville Affranchie.* And among the ruins of this "liberated city" a column was to rise bearing the legend, "Lyons made war on Liberty, Lyons is no more." But Couthon was more violent in his speech than in his acts; when Robespierre warned him that humaneness would hatch new conspiracies he asked to be transferred. His successors, Collot d'Herbois and Fouché, ex-priest and violent Jacobin, had no such scruples. Under their administration, firing squads and the guillotine carried out large numbers of executions. In the notorious *mitraillades,* the victims first had to dig their graves and then stand still to be mowed down. At Nantes, Carrier, the *représentant en mission,* had more than two thousand people drowned in the Loire in wholesale and indiscriminate murder.

The government, while reproving the actions of these extremists, acted at the same time against the "indulgents." Danton was one of these; Camille Desmoulins, Robespierre's schoolfriend and fellow Jacobin, was another. But while the extremists were merely recalled, the indulgents were arrested. Other arrests followed. In mid-March 1794, Hébert and his followers called for an insurrection against the government. By the end of March, they had been guillotined. Roux had already committed suicide in prison two months before: the *sans-culottes* had no spokesmen left. On April 5, after a short trial which he dominated until he was ruthlessly cut off, Danton also went to the guillotine. The government, it seemed, had made short work of its enemies. The king and queen were dead; so were the Brissotins, the *enragés,* the Dantonists, and most of the Hébertists. With the execution of Desmoulins, the vigorous popular press was stilled as well. In the provinces, as cheerful killers like Fouché were recalled, the Terror was relaxed; in Paris it was intensified. Attempts on Robespierre's life, coupled with the nagging fear of remaining opposition, induced Robespierre on June 10, 1794 (22 Prairial), to secure passage of a new law that gave the Revolutionary Tribunal supreme power over all "enemies of the people"; the only penalty it could impose was death. This was the beginning of the Great Terror; it led, in Paris, to thirteen hundred seventy-six executions in a month and a half.

Thus baldly summarized, the Terror seems to discredit the whole Revolution as a nightmarish orgy of madmen, a sadistic riot in the name of humanity; Robespierre and his associates seem like so many modern Caligulas, wishing that the French people had but one neck. One is reminded of Dickens' Madame Defarge, calmly knitting as she watches the guillotine do its bloody work; of

Vergniaud darkly speaking of the revolution eating its own children. But the facts are rather more complicated. There can be no excuse for murder—even one. The Terror cannot be justified by pointing out that its victims amounted to "only" about thirty-five thousand—half of them condemned to death, the rest shot or drowned without trial or dying miserably in detention. Yet the figures of the Terror give significant clues to its nature. The largest number of its victims (31 percent) were *sans-culottes;* peasants were next (28 percent), followed by the upper middle class (14 percent), the lower middle class (11 percent), the nobility (8 percent), and the clergy (7 percent). [20] Doubtless, if priests and nobles had not emigrated, the proportions would have been different, but it is clear that the guillotine struck down not merely the king of France; not merely the great chemist Lavoisier—not for being a chemist, but for being a farmer general; not merely a Girondin politician like Madame Roland, or a hapless general like Houchard, but also ordinary Frenchmen and Frenchwomen. The location of the Terror is equally instructive. Most of its victims—some 93 percent—were accused of treason or sedition, and while the laws under which the Tribunals operated were perilously vague, many of the accused had certainly been active in domestic rebellion or in aiding the enemy; it is significant that the victims of the Terror were concentrated in the rebellious west of France and in areas of intense military activity—the north and the southeast.

As these figures suggest, no single explanation will do. We may distinguish four of them, rising in complexity: character, politics, idealism, and emergency. There were Terrorists who greatly enjoyed their work, even if, as with Carrier, their previous career gave no evidence of such inclinations. Men like Fouché and Collot d'Herbois have been called men of blood, with justice. The reports they sent back from their theater of operations reek with pleasure in their ingenuity at killing and with ambitious plans for more killing in the future. Such men found willing subordinates, "drinkers of blood—*buveurs de sang*," in the provinces to do their work for them. But these killers for pleasure were always in a minority; the legislation that organized the Terror was designed at least in part to take it out of the hands of such freebooters and psychopaths.

Politics, too, played its part. Some politicians were sacrificed to the guillotine to appease other politicians. Perhaps the most prominent instance of such maneuvering was Danton. A powerful orator and energetic official, he was also callous and corrupt; in the dark September days of 1792, when the allied invasion was threatening Paris, his courage had stood France in good stead, but at the same time his connivance in the September massacres shows his character in a less flattering light. Less doctrinaire than Robespierre, he was also more amiable: he would not have fitted into Robespierre's republic of virtue.

---

[20] These figures add up to only 99 percent; 1 percent could not be determined. We are depending in these pages on Donald M. Greer's careful study, *The Incidence of the Terror During the French Revolution* (1935).

He died ostensibly because he had been involved in shady dealings, but while this was true, he died also because the *enragés* on the Committee of Public Safety insisted on it. [21]

Despite such calculation, the Terror was also the consequence of idealism. Robespierre and Saint-Just, whose power was very great when the Terror was at its height, divided the world into the forces of light and darkness. Their scheme of things had no room for honest error. Policies, or even views, that in their eyes harmed the Revolution were proof of wickedness, of complicity in a royalist plot. Saint-Just was pathologically cold-blooded; Robespierre, though, was far more complex. He was quick to accuse his enemies of treason, without a shred of evidence; he was responsible for the terrible law of 22 Prairial. But again and again he intervened to rescue potential victims from the guillotine. For some time he even supported the call of his friend Desmoulins for moderation. But he believed that terror was necessary until the enemies of virtue had been crushed and the republic of virtue secured. Virtue without terror, he said, is impotent; terror without virtue is disastrous. Robespierre— strait-laced, humorless, suspicious, the great "incorruptible"— has been called the worst kind of idealist: the man who *knows* he is right; the reformer who will sacrifice present generations to the future. There is something in this portrait. But Robespierre was also a statesman steeped in, almost overwhelmed by, practical problems. He was an honest man and a democrat, at a time when dishonesty was rife and democracy was in danger. There were men—he knew them—who profiteered from the war and battened on the poor.

And this brings us to the last cause of the Terror: the emergency. France was surrounded by very real and wholly uncompromising enemies. The Bourbons had made it perfectly clear what a restoration would mean (see p. 479). When the Committee of Public Safety established its ascendancy over the country in the fall of 1793, France had not had an effective government for more than four years. In the midst of unceasing turmoil in Paris and treachery in the provinces, the Committee of Public Safety strove to govern a large nation at war. The work of the twelve men on that committee remains impressive. They had to find new generals (the old ones had gone over to the enemy or had been guillotined), collect taxes, secure recruits, feed a large army, wrest territory from the hands of domestic and foreign enemies. In this grave emergency, Terror was a means of reestablishing control. Besides, not all the talk of treason was the fruit of a heated imagination. Toulon was turned over to the British navy by Admiral Trogoff, commander of the French Mediterranean fleet, after news had reached him that the Girondin uprisings had failed

---

[21] "The execution of the Hébertists," which occurred a week before Danton's trial, "implied that of the Dantonists also. If they were left alive after their opponents had been killed their position would be relatively stronger, and it would appear that the Committee had acted at their command. The unity of the Committee itself was also at stake, for Billaud-Varenne and Collot d'Herbois could not have been expected to accept the suppression of the extremists until the moderates were also destroyed" (Sydenham, *French Revolution*, 212).

in Normandy and Marseilles. And the uprising in the Vendée had begun with the systematic murder of numerous government officials. Radical Terror was often a response to the reactionary Terror. That reactionary Terror was soon to have its second opportunity.

Thermidor and the Thermidorians

On May 7, 1794, while his position seemed unassailable, Robespierre told the Convention that the country needed a new religion—the worship of the Supreme Being. It was essential for the establishment of virtue: "Immorality is the basis of despotism; the essence of Republicanism is virtue. The Revolution is the transition from the regime of crime to the regime of justice." [22] On June 8, in accordance with the decree passed at his instance, Robespierre presided over the first Festival of the Supreme Being. The Great Terror began two days later. In the war, meanwhile, the revolutionary armies were near victory. On May 18, General Pichegru routed the British at Tourcoing, and at the same time, Jourdan pushed forward on the northeastern front. On June 13, two weeks after a pitched naval encounter between French and British vessels, a huge food convoy, slipping past battling men-of-war, reached France unscathed. And on June 26, the French beat the Austrians in a decisive engagement at Fleurus. On July 19 they were in Brussels.

Together, these events conspired to encompass Robespierre's fall. The festival had given him undue prominence and made talk of his dictatorial pretensions plausible. The Terror had become more terrible at the very moment victories in the field made relaxation possible. Victory also permitted the Committee of Public Safety the luxury of quarreling in public. Robespierre, Couthon, and Saint-Just stood against the unreconstructed Hébertists, Billaud-Varenne and Collot d'Herbois; outside the committee, Terrorists like Fouché found themselves under attack by Robespierre and his two virtuous colleagues. A conspiracy began to form; it included moderates, but it was led by blood-stained Terrorists fearful of being outlawed: by Fouché, by Carrier, by Barras, by Tallien—men who had "pacified" the provincial cities in late 1793. Robespierre brought the plot to a head on July 26 (8 Thermidor) with an opaque and menacing speech to the Convention. He darkly spoke of a new conspiracy made up of the old combination—atheists and indulgents. He urged a final purge of traitors; pressed, he refused to give any names. This was to do the work of the plotters for them: any of the deputies might be attainted next. On the next day, the fateful 9 Thermidor, Fouché and his associates prevented Saint-Just and Robespierre from addressing the Convention and had their arrest voted. The "Plain," that silent collection of moderates who had countenanced the decimation of the Gironde, now voted against Robespierre.

---

[22] Quoted in Sydenham, *French Revolution*, 216.

For one day, the issue was in doubt. But the city did not rise: the *sans-culottes* were apathetic. Thus, by default, the people of Paris, weary at last, revenged themselves on a government that had killed their leaders and disregarded their legitimate demands. On 10 Thermidor the Republic of Virtue was dead. Robespierre, Couthon, Saint-Just, and nineteen others went to the guillotine; in the next few days, about a hundred more followed them.

The Convention survived Thermidor for over a year. A number of extremists, even though they were anti-Robespierre, were eliminated from positions of power: Billaud-Varenne and Collot d'Herbois were sent to rot in French Guiana. In long painful trials, the crimes of Carrier and his like received wide publicity. Carrier was guillotined; so was Dumas, the president of the Revolutionary Tribunal, and Fouquier-Tinville, its diligent prosecutor. Fouché barely survived the reaction he had done so much to bring about; he slipped into the protection of obscurity. With deliberate speed, the Thermidorians dismantled the machinery the Jacobins had assembled. They reduced the authority of the Committee of Public Safety, destroyed the autonomy of the Paris Commune, decentralized government, assailed Jacobins, and eventually closed down the Jacobin clubs altogether. In May 1795, they put an end to the Revolutionary Tribunal. Thousands—Girondins above all—came out of the prisons, and some émigrés returned.

The Thermidorians achieved their purposes with a new Terror, less formidable, less official, but almost as destructive as the old. In Lyons there was a small reenactment of the September massacres, as crowds stormed the prisons and lynched about a hundred Jacobin prisoners. In the southeast, at Marseilles, at Arles, at Avignon, royalist bands, self-appointed avengers, attacked whatever Jacobins they could find. One spectacular arm of the new repression was the *jeunesse dorée*. These gilded youths—draft dodgers, law clerks—in ostentatious revulsion against the egalitarian talk and dress of the Jacobins, roamed the streets in affected dress, armed with bludgeons. They invaded the offices of the remaining popular newspapers and intimidated Jacobins. The *sans-culottes* soon had good reason to regret their failure to rescue Robespierre from his enemies. The economic legislation of the Mountain had been unsatisfactory, but there had been at least a measure of price control and supervision of the food supply. The new "liberalism" of Thermidor spelled the doom of such state activity. The *maximum* was first openly disregarded; later, in December 1794, repealed. The withdrawal of the state from business brought back the speculators, the hoarders, in greater number than ever. In a final paroxysm of energy, the *sans-culottes* took to the streets once again. On April 1, 1795 (12 Germinal), a crowd broke into the Convention; significantly, its slogans included calls for bread and for the democratic constitution of 1793. It got neither. As bread supplies tightened and prices continued to mount, the *sans-culottes* repeated their demonstration on 1 Prairial (May 20, 1795). Again they invaded the Convention and briefly held the streets. Stronger this time, they shouted what they had shouted before and were sent away with promises. The next day, they were dispersed by government troops. After receiving swift and merciless punishment, the *sans-culottes* fell silent.

Thus secure, the Thermidorian Convention could address itself to making a new fundamental law for France. The Constitution of the Year III, promulgated in August, was a reminder of France's first modern constitution: the "Thermidorian Reaction" was just that—a return to early revolutionary aspirations. The franchise was as indirect and even narrower than that in the constitution of 1791: the number of electors was diminished to about twenty thousand. Its main architect, the moderate Boissy d'Anglas, candidly explained its rationale: "We must be governed by the best citizens; the best citizens are those who are most educated and most interested in the keeping of the law. Now, with very few exceptions, you will find such men only among those who possess some property."[23] One grave problem remained. The country was in a conservative, even a monarchist, mood; if few wanted the restoration of the Old Regime, most wanted the restoration of some stable order. This put the future of the delegates to the Convention, and even of the republic, in doubt. The Convention decided to protect both with the Law of the Two Thirds: two thirds of the new legislature was to be made up of themselves. This brought new uprisings, this time mainly from the Right. Barras was put in charge of the government troops; among his aides was the young general Napoleon Bonaparte. Freely using his firepower, Bonaparte dispersed the demonstrators with a "whiff of grapeshot." This was the famous "13 Vendémaire"—October 5, 1795. Bonaparte had helped to save the republic and, with it, much of the Revolution. His future role in the history of France would be rather more ambiguous.

SELECTED READINGS

The controversies over the French Revolution begin with its origins. In addition to the titles on the Old Regime cited in earlier chapters, see Douglas Dakin, *Turgot and the Ancien Régime in France* (1939), on the reforming minister of the opening years of Louis XVI; J. H. Shennan, *The Parlement of Paris* (1968), which analyzes one great center of resistance to royal power; and, for the economic origins, the authoritative studies by Ernest Labrousse, notably *La crise de l'économie française à la fin de l'ancien régime et au début de la Révolution* (1944). Labrousse's views, and those of other, mostly earlier interpreters, are conveniently summarized in Ralph W. Greenlaw, ed., *The Economic Origins of the French Revolution: Poverty or Prosperity?* (1958).

Another controversial question, still unsettled, involves the general character of the French Revolution—was it primarily French or was it part of a wider revolutionary stream? The leading proponents of the more embracing interpretation are R. R. Palmer, *The Age of the Democratic Revolution: A Political History of Europe and America, 1760-1800,* 2 vols. (1959-1964), and Jacques Godechot, *France and the Atlantic Revolution, 1770-1799* (1965). Peter Amann, ed., *The Eighteenth-Century Revolution: French or Western?* (1963), gathers these, and dissenting, views into one brief compass. One profitable way of examining this question is by looking at other countries in this

---

[23] Quoted in Georges Lefèbvre, *The Thermidorians and the Directory* (tr. 1964), 216.

era. G. P. Gooch, *Germany and the French Revolution* (1920), remains helpful, but has been largely superseded by Jacques Droz, *L'Allemagne et la Révolution française* (1949). For England, see among a large literature, Alfred Cobban, ed., *The Debate on the French Revolution, 1789-1800* (1950); Cobban, *Edmund Burke and the Revolt Against the XVIIIth Century* (ed. 1960); Thomas W. Copeland, *Our Eminent Friend Edmund Burke, Six Essays* (1949); and Carl Cone, *The English Jacobins: Reformers in Late 18th Century England* (1968).

General histories of the French Revolution are numerous. Among the more recent, the most informative are J. M. Thompson, *The French Revolution* (2nd ed., 1944) (splendidly detailed, it stops with the death of Robespierre); A. Goodwin, *The French Revolution* (1953); Norman Hampson, *A Social History of the French Revolution* (1963); and M. J. Sydenham, *The French Revolution* (1965). A classic account offering a moderate Marxist interpretation of the event as a bourgeois revolution is Georges Lefèbvre's *La Révolution française,* revised after the author's death by Albert Soboul in 1963, and now available, somewhat imperfectly translated, in two English volumes as *The French Revolution: From Its Origins to 1793* (1962) and *The French Revolution: From 1793 to 1799* (1964). Soboul's general histories of the era are not yet in English, but see his own summary, *Précis d'histoire de la Révolution française* (1962). For a general history, complete with survey of conflicting schools of interpretation, see Crane Brinton, *A Decade of Revolution* (1934). Paul Farmer, *France Reviews Its Revolutionary Origins* (1944), is also useful in this connection. The most persistent and amusing challenge to the prevailing radical interpretation of the epoch has come from Alfred Cobban, notably in *Historians and the Causes of the French Revolution* (1962) and *The Social Interpretation of the French Revolution* (1964). Students in search of documents can use Leo Gershoy's brief *The Era of the French Revolution, 1789-1799: Ten Years That Shook the World* (1957), which includes a long introductory essay; the more comprehensive *A Documentary Survey of the French Revolution* (1951) by John Hall Stewart; and J. M. Thompson, *French Revolution Documents, 1789-1794* (1948).

The year of decision, 1789, is brilliantly if a little schematically laid out in Georges Lefèbvre's *The Coming of the French Revolution* (tr. 1947). For Sieyès, see G. G. Van Deusen, *Sieyès: His life and His Nationalism* (1932), and M. Blondel's translation of Sieyès, *What Is the Third Estate?* (1964). J. H. Clapham's *The Abbé Sieyès* (1912), though old, remains valuable. Beatrice F. Hyslop, *A Guide to the General Cahiers of 1789, with Texts of Unedited Cahiers* (1936), is a useful introduction to the grievances expressed early in 1789 in writing. For the prominent early revolutionary leader, Mirabeau, see the biography by O. J. G. Welch, subtitled, *A Study of a Democratic Monarchist* (1951).

For July 14, 1789, see the authoritative study by Jacques Godechot, *The Taking of the Bastille* (tr. 1970); George Rudé's pioneering essays on *The Crowd in the French Revolution* (1959) include Bastille Day, the earlier Réveillon riots, and the most important later instances of mass action. For the Great Fear that swept France in midsummer of 1789, Georges Lefèbvre, *La grande peur de 1789* (1922), remains essential.

The Civil Constitution of the Clergy (1790) must be understood in the wider context of the relations of church to state in France. This context is provided by Alphonse Aulard, *Christianity and the French Revolution* (tr. 1927), which can be supplemented with E. E. Y. Hales, *Revolution and Papacy, 1769-1846* (1960), the first volume of Adrien Dansette, *Religious History of Modern France,* 2 vols. (tr. 1961), and the brief, lucid essay by John McManners, *The French Revolution and the Church*

(1969). Burdette C. Poland treats an important religious minority in *French Protestant-ism and the French Revolution: A Study in Church and State, Thought and Religion 1685-1815*(1957). Church-state relations bring up the hostility to the revolution. Jacques Godechot, *The Counter-Revolution: Doctrine and Action 1789-1804* (tr. 1971), is a full and judicious analysis; Donald M. Greer's statistical survey, *The Incidence of the Emigration During the French Revolution* (1951), remains useful; while Charles Tilly, *The Vendée* (1964), brings a sociologist's insights to the great counterrevolutionary insurgence in the west of France in 1793. See also, Paul Beik, *The French Revolution Seen from the Right* (1956). Agricultural France, which had its own revolution and counterrevolution, is treated in masterly fashion by Georges Lefèbvre, *Les paysans du Nord pendant la Révolution française* (2nd ed., 1959).

The study of clubs and factions in the Revolution has long been a specialty of French historians. Crane Brinton, *The Jacobins: An Essay in the New History* (1930), offers a well-documented, essentially hostile analysis of what appeared to Brinton as a movement of religious fanatics; Richard M. Brace, *Bordeaux and the Gironde, 1789-1794* (1947), is a detailed specific monograph, while M. J. Sydenham, *The Girondins* (1960), rejects simplified accounts of "Brissotins" as a unified "party." For the extremists, see R. B. Rose, *The Enragés* (1965). Biographies of leading political figures include J. M. Thompson, *Robespierre*, 2 vols. (1935), dependably summarized in Thompson, *Robespierre and the French Revolution* (1952); Louis Gottschalk, *Jean Paul Marat: A Study in Radicalism* (1927); Leo Gershoy, *Bertrand Barère, A Reluctant Terrorist* (1962); E. N. Curtis, *Saint-Just, Colleague of Robespierre* (1935). Marcel Reinhard, *Le Grand Carnot*, 2 vols. (1950-1952), is the definitive biography in French; it may be supplemented with Huntley Dupré, *Lazare Carnot, Republican Patriot* (1940). There are useful biographies by Eloise Ellery on *Brissot de Warville* (1915) and by Gita May on *Madame Roland and the Age of Revolution* (1970).

The time of war, of Jacobin dictatorship, and of the Terror, has been well surveyed. See especially the vivid portraits of those who governed France during crisis by R. R. Palmer, *Twelve Who Ruled: The Committee of Public Safety During the Terror* (1958). Donald M. Greer's statistical analysis, *The Incidence of the Terror During the French Revolution* (1935), is invaluable. To it we may add James L. Godfrey, *Revolutionary Justice: A Study of the Organization, Personnel, and Procedure of the Paris Tribunal, 1793-1795* (1951). Part of Albert Soboul's celebrated thesis on the *sans-culottes* (1958) has been translated as *The Parisian Sans-culottes in the French Revolution, 1793-1794* (1964), while John B. Sirich, *The Revolutionary Committees in the Departments of France* (1943), moves outside Paris. Rudé's *Crowd in the French Revolution* and Tilly's *Vendée*, already cited, are of special importance for this period. Seymour Harris' study of *The Assignats* (1930) traces the role of this revolutionary paper money in a French economy at war. Richard Cobb's important thesis, *Les armées révolutionnaires, instrument de la Terreur dans les départements, Avril 1793-Floréal An II*, 2 vols. (1961-1963), though accessible only in French, deserves special attention; Cobb has summarized his findings in "The Revolutionary Mentality in France, 1783-94," *History*, 17 (1957). Albert Mathiez, *La vie chère et le mouvement social sous la Terreur* (1927), on social struggles in Paris and their political consequences in the Year II has not been superseded.

For the Thermidorian Reaction see especially Georges Lefèbvre, *The Thermidorians* (tr. 1966), a masterly synthesis; two collections of essays by Albert Mathiez: *The Fall of Robespierre and Other Essays* (tr. 1927) and *After Robespierre: The Thermidorian Reaction* (tr. 1965); and Richard T. Bienvenu, ed., *The Ninth of Thermidor* (1968).

12

The Age of Napoleon

The age of Napoleon was obviously larger than the man Napoleon Bonaparte. Yet even the modern historian, averse as he is to the cult of personality, will not hesitate to apply the name of this man to his time. Napoleon left his mark on men of letters from Goethe to Byron to Stendhal, as he left it on European taste, laws, and manners, and on countries from England to Russia to Egypt. Even the irreconcilable reputations that pursue him to this day express his epoch: he was symptomatic of its aspirations, its failures, and its immense variety. He was a liberator to German Jews, an archenemy to English statesmen, an ambiguous benefactor to Italian nationalists. Did he complete, stabilize, or betray the French Revolution? The answer must be that he did all these things in turn.

NAPOLEON'S TRIUMPH:
FROM SOLDIER TO EMPEROR

The Directory: The Reluctant Republic

The Directory, which owed so much to Bonaparte's timely intervention, was inaugurated in November 1795. Its leaders were the old crowd in new clothes; the statute of the Two Thirds and the restricted franchise made the Directory a self-protective, almost a cozy arrangement. The story goes that when, after the years of turmoil, the old Abbé Sieyès was asked what he had done during the Revolution, he replied, "I survived." The Directory, in which he was to play his accustomed prominent role, was a regime of survivors. The qualities that had had greatest survival value during the previous six years were tenacity, suppleness, and a convenient memory; the most conspicuous figures in the Directory had these qualities in abundance. They tended to be rich and ostentatious, often vulgar, about their riches, for their wealth was normally of recent, usually of doubtful, origin: from profiteering and speculation. Sensuality and opulence were in vogue. This aspect of the Directory was splendidly realized in the viscount Paul François Nicolas de Barras, one of the original five directors. Born into an aristocratic family, he had survived the Revolution by being in the right place with the right remedy; he had helped to bring down Robespierre when it was time to bring him down, and now he was pushing forward young Bonaparte. Indeed, Barras' mistress, Josephine de Beauharnais, was to become Bonaparte's first wife. He was a good soldier with a fine bearing, but unscrupulous, essentially unprincipled, and wholly corrupt. Foreign diplomats discovered to their dismay that to negotiate with Barras—or with Talleyrand, the foreign minister, who matched Barras in shamelessness—meant handing out immense bribes.

Yet, while the spectacular corruptions of the Directory have been much discussed, the very genuine difficulties its directors faced have been underestimated.[1] Most of these difficulties were legacies. True, the war went on, unrest in the Vendée flared again, attempts to stabilize the currency ended in partial bankruptcy, inflation was rampant; necessities commanded fantastic prices, and starvation in the countryside was widespread. Royalists corresponded with

---

[1] This is perfectly understandable; the four years of the Directory (1795-1799) appear like an interlude between the dramatic days of the Terror before and the equally dramatic advent of Bonaparte after. Moreover, Napoleon Bonaparte later found it expedient to denigrate the regime he had overthrown, and his self-serving view was quickly adopted. Recently, historians have been suggesting a more balanced appraisal.

unreconstructed émigrés, while the old radicals—splintered, disillusioned, and powerless—desperately looked for leadership. Still, the government managed to bring prices down (partly because the harvest of 1796 was a good one), alleviate hunger by controlling the price of bread and distributing it in critical areas, effectively reorganize the tax system, pacify the Vendée, win impressive military campaigns, and stave off the powers of Europe. The constitution of the Directory flatly included annexed Belgium in France's domains; it was, thus, a regime constructed on imperialist assumptions. Despite the coalitions against it, the Directory could make those assumptions hold good, at least for some time.

Political instability proved harder to manage than the allies. The first challenge to the Directory—pathetic, but of symptomatic value and historical interest—came from the remnants of the old Left. François Emile "Gracchus" Babeuf, with a small band of fellow enthusiasts, propagated a "conspiracy of the equals." Babeuf wanted a new revolution that would accomplish what the old revolution had so miserably failed to do: break the stranglehold of the rich over the poor by nationalizing the land, imposing on everyone equal duties to work, and abolishing private property. All this was to be done by a "common administration"—which today we would call egalitarian socialism with central economic planning. His conspiracy was scheduled for May 1796; it included nebulous plans for killing the directors and winning over the troops, but it was quickly betrayed and easily suppressed. The leading conspirators were arrested and early in 1797 two of them, including Babeuf, went to the guillotine. The egalitarian fantasies of the *enragés* in the Year II remained fantasies in the Year IV.

The challenge from the Right was more widely based and more dangerous. Royalists appeared more openly than they had done for four or five years. Two of the five directors, the experienced diplomat Barthélemy and the old Terrorist General Carnot, "organizer of victory," showed increasing sympathies for the restoration of a constitutional monarchy. Stringent legislation against émigrés and their families was being relaxed, and many of them drifted back home, to strengthen sentiment for a restoration. Yet the Bourbons never made it easy for their most loyal adherents. In June 1795, the young dauphin—whom the émigrés called "Louis XVII"—died of the maltreatment he had suffered since 1793. This made the count de Provence heir to the vacant throne. With an obtuseness in no way mitigated by his years of exile or by French realities, "Louis XVIII" promptly issued the Declaration of Verona that spelled out the program of the counterrevolution in merciless detail. It called for nothing less than the total restoration of the Old Regime: restoration of confiscated property, of Catholic supremacy, of old institutions like the provinces and the parlements, and of the old privileges—the old dues, the old taxes, the old exemptions. Most French monarchists had acquired a vested interest in the abolition of these institutions and privileges and hoped for a rather more moderate return to the past than this.

Despite the unyielding foolishness of their exiled king, French monarchists scored impressive gains in the free elections held in the spring of 1797. Only a dozen of the one hundred fifty or so members of the old legislature who stood for reelection were returned; they were replaced for the most part by moderate royalists. The republic was in danger of disappearing, more peacefully than it had come. In this emergency, three of the directors, Reubell, La Reveillière-Lépeaux, and Barras, decided to forgo even the shadow of legality for the republic's sake—and their own. On 18 Fructidor (September 4, 1797), they occupied Paris, had Barthélemy arrested (Carnot eluded them), annulled most of the inconvenient election results of April, imposed censorship, and sent opposition leaders into exile. Once again Bonaparte helped to shape the course of events. He was leading the French armies in Italy, but alarmed at the prospects of a restoration—which meant an unwelcome peace—he sent General Augereau to Paris as his deputy, to guarantee the success of the coup d'etat.

The Directory: Dictatorship, Victory, Demise

Fructidor was designed to keep the old survivors in power, but its ultimate beneficiary was its servant in Italy: General Napoleon Bonaparte. Even in these early years, when little was clear to him except his unmatched ambition, there was something of the stuff of legend about him. For all his short stature he towered over other men. Born in August 1769 into the minor, impecunious nobility of Corsica, not long after France had annexed the island from Genoa, he liked to boast of his French origins ("I was born free"); but he was a Corsican nationalist and, until 1796, spelled his name in the Italian fashion: Buonaparte. A soldier's career was in his mind from his earliest days; after attending French military schools both in the provinces and in Paris, he obtained a commission in an artillery regiment in 1785. His reading in the philosophes and his youthful involvement in the cause of Corsica made him a convinced Jacobin; his moment of glory came in September 1793, when he distinguished himself in the recapture of Toulon, which counterrevolutionaries had turned over to the British. A grateful government made him a brigadier general. After a brief eclipse during Thermidor for his Jacobin associations, he emerged at Vendémiaire (see p. 498), and in March 1796, after his marriage to Josephine, he set off for Italy, in command of the French army.

The Directory, desperate for success, was the kind of regime in which a Bonaparte could flourish. In March 1795, in one of the last diplomatic triumphs of the Convention, France had breached the First Coalition, formed against her in 1792, by concluding a peace treaty with Prussia. Lesser German states followed suit; the left bank of the Rhine was retained by France, and Prussia promised neutrality. In the same year, in June, Spain also dropped out of the war. The Directory was now left with two formidable enemies: Austria and Britain. The German campaign remained inconclusive, but in Italy, Bonaparte scored lightning successes. Napoleon's Italian campaign has the breathless speed of the Revolution; and one must account for it by weeks and days, not months. He defeated the Austrians at Millesimo on April 13, 1796; the Piedmontese at Mondovi on April 22, knocking Victor Amadeus out of the war and gaining Nice and Savoy for France. On May 10, the French defeated the Austrians once again, at Lodi, and on May 15, they were in Milan. The next day, Bonaparte proclaimed the first French satellite state in Italy, the Lombard Republic. Austria's Italian allies—the papacy, Parma, Modena—were held up to ransom; priceless works of art and large sums of money made their way to Paris. Then Bonaparte's extraordinary pace slowed—a little. The fortress of Mantua held out for half a year, but the Austrians were defeated again at Arcola in November 1796 and at Rivoli in January 1797; early in February, 1797, the garrison at Mantua surrendered. By April, Bonaparte had negotiated a preliminary peace with the Austrians at Leoben. The British, meanwhile, disheartened by the cost of the war, domestic unrest, naval mutinies, and an Irish uprising, were negotiating with the French at Lille. The coup d'etat of Fructidor encouraged the negotiators to try to force stiff terms on the British, and the negotiations collapsed. Soon, in October 1797, Britain found herself alone: the Hapsburgs made peace with France at Campo Formio. It was a triumph for the Directory; the Austrians got only Venice, treacherously occupied and now just as treacherously bartered off by Bonaparte; the French got Austrian recognition of their hold on Belgium and of their new Italian creation, the Cisalpine Republic; they also got the Ionian Islands off the coast of Greece, and a promise of a congress at Rastatt to settle the complicated shifts of sovereignty consequent on French conquests on the Rhine. Italy now became a French sphere of influence arranged in a string of satellite republics: the Cisalpine, including Milan, Bologna, Ferrara, Modena, and the Romagna; the Ligurian, essentially the old Republic of Genoa; the Roman, created in early 1798; and the Parthenopean, including southern Italy, formed in January 1799. Switzerland had been turned, for good measure, into the Helvetian Republic in April 1798, and Geneva was annexed to France.

Only Britain was now left. In November 1797, Bonaparte returned to Paris, to be hailed as a conqueror and to prepare the invasion of England. Upon a reasonable assessment of British naval strength, Bonaparte soon decided that such an invasion must fail; he persuaded the directors to let him take Egypt instead. An expedition to Egypt seemed an oddly roundabout way of crippling Britain, but Bonaparte was not the only one in France to think the plan reasonable: Talleyrand, too, thought that a French conquest of Egypt might cut off Britain's trade with the East and threaten her lifeline to India. On May 19, 1798, Bonaparte sailed with a fleet of four hundred ships, a small army, and a contingent of scientists. On June 12, he surprised and took Malta; on July 1 he landed in Egypt, and on the next day, Alexandria was his. On July 22, he took Cairo: the whole expedition looked like another Italian campaign. But Napoleon found his match in Admiral Horatio Nelson. On August 1, 1798, Nelson, having missed the French fleet in the Mediterranean, surprised it anchored at

Abukir, outside Alexandria, and annihilated it. Bonaparte's campaign against the Ottomans in Syria, and further victories in Egypt in the summer of 1799, did not end his embarrassment. He seemed cut off from France.

The directors in Paris had mixed feelings about his plight. In his Italian campaign, Bonaparte had displayed unwelcome tendencies toward independence. He was conducting himself like a foreign minister with his own army and his own supplies; he put his notions into action and informed Paris later. The instrument of policy was rapidly becoming its master. That was bad enough; the impermanence of his triumphs was worse. In December 1798, Tsar Paul I—Catherine's erratic and adventurous son, who had succeeded his mother in 1796—concluded an alliance with Great Britain, and by 1799 the Second Coalition against France was in the field; it included the Austrians and Ottomans, and it scored quick victories: by May, the Russian general Suvorov was in Turin; in June, the Austrians defeated the French at Zurich; in August, at the disastrous battle of Novi, Suvorov routed the French once more. These defeats brought the specter of an invasion and, with that, troubles at home. The government found it equally difficult to raise troops and money; Jacobins were agitating on one side, royalists on the other. Then the danger of invasion receded as General Masséna drove the Russians out of Zurich in September. But the Directory faced an even more insidious danger from within. In May, Abbé Sieyès had been elected one of the directors, and he immediately began to conspire against the government he was sworn to uphold. He now wanted a regime with an energetic executive, and soon his principle, he said, was "confidence from below, power from above." This meant a coup d'etat. All he needed was a general to carry it out; in early October, Bonaparte suddenly appeared on French soil—he had left his army behind in Egypt. Clearly, he was the man, though he nearly lost his opportunity by losing his nerve for once. His coup d'etat, badly bungled, took two days to accomplish; on its second day, November 9, 1799—18 Brumaire—Napoleon Bonaparte's brother, Lucien, managed to rally the troops against the government by inventing a plot that had to be put down. The troops dispersed the legislature, and the Directory was at an end. It had been ruined by the immense costs of continued warfare, its failure to enlist the support of most Frenchmen, and its unhappy choice of leaders, like Sieyès and Bonaparte, who were more anxious to serve themselves than their government. By December, a new government, the Consulate, had taken its place. And General Bonaparte was in control.

The Consulate

Once in control—of himself and of the country—Bonaparte did not lose it again. His egotism—admirers called it self-confidence—grew beyond all bounds as flatterers told him what he needed to hear; if he believed himself to be a man of destiny, others believed it too, at least at first. Bonaparte showed a remarkable capacity for giving the nation what it wanted—peace both on the battlefield and in domestic affairs. From the beginning, he compounded his rule of the traditional, the recent, and the original so subtly that he pacified the longings of most Frenchmen and disappointed only principled Jacobins or irreconcilable émigrés. The constitution of the Year VIII, promulgated in December 1799, is a tribute to his political instincts. Its franchise was extended to universal manhood suffrage, but voters chose only "notables" whom the government could then invite to serve in some public capacity; its tribunate debated but did not vote; its legislative body voted but did not debate; its conservative senate selected the two chambers and passed on the constitution- ality of proposed legislation; and its council of state actively advised the first consul. This complex structure of the French state barely concealed, behind its Baroque facade, the concentration of autocratic power in the hands of one man—the first consul. Those sturdy classical words—tribune, senate, consu- late—evoked the manly patriotism of the Roman Republic; the appeal to "notables" was a reminder of the hierarchical Old Regime; universal suffrage combined with the indirect voting and reliance on a written constitution were devices borrowed from the Revolution; and the use of a mock constitution to screen a dictatorship links Bonaparte directly with popular dictatorships of the twentieth century. His mode of securing popular approval for this charade, the plebiscite, was another foretaste of the future; beginning in December, in open voting across the country, the French people passed on their new constitution. To no one's surprise, the plebiscite approved Bonaparte's handiwork by the overwhelming majority of 3,011,007 to 1,526. [2] Bonaparte was the heir of Sieyès' principle: *he* exercised power from above; confidence from below flowed to *him*. In selecting his closest associates, Bonaparte underscored his express desire to forget about experimentation and achieve the restoration of order: Camba- cérès, a lawyer who had sat in the Convention and voted for the execution of Louis XVI, became second consul; Lebrun, an elderly public servant with a gift for financial matters (he had assisted Maupeou in his coup d'etat against the parlements in 1771 [see p. 442]) and with a generally liberal reputation, became third consul; the sinister Joseph Fouché, a born conspirator, an old Terrorist who had turned on Robespierre just in time and who had ingratiated himself by his part in the plot of 18 Brumaire, became minister of police; while the inevitable Talleyrand reappeared as minister of foreign affairs.

One of the first acts of Bonaparte's statesmanship was to write a personal letter to George III on December 26, 1799, offering peace. The Russians, annoyed at the conduct of their allies, had already withdrawn from the Second Coalition, but neither George's ministers nor Emperor Francis II were inclined to bargain with the Corsican upstart. The war went on; Bonaparte rebuilt his

---

[2] The device is worth keeping in mind; Bonaparte would use it again, as would later rulers like Napoleon III and twentieth-century dictators. The plebiscite made it possible to combine a democratic appeal to the people with dictatorial manipulation of its timing and conduct.

army and in May 1800 rushed across the Alps into Italy; in June, in a long, bloody encounter at Marengo, the French finally carried the day against the Austrians. General Moreau meanwhile piled triumph upon triumph in the German theater; in December, at Hohenlinden, he routed the Austrians completely. The Treaty of Lunéville followed in February 1801. Substantially, it confirmed the Treaty of Campo Formio and expanded French hegemony over Italy and western Germany. Having much to lose and, for the moment, little to gain, and aided by Pitt's fall from office on a domestic issue, Bonaparte entered serious negotiations; in March 1802, he concluded the Treaty of Amiens with Britain. It returned Britain's recent conquests to France; but the islands of Trinidad (taken from Spain) and Ceylon (taken from the Dutch Batavian Republic) remained in British hands. In the eastern Mediterranean, Britain agreed to restore Malta to the Order of the Knights of Malta and to respect its independence; France in return recognized the republic of the seven Ionian Islands, returned to Turkish control. For the first time in many years, all Europe was at peace.

Bonaparte did not wait for this armistice to pacify France. He repressed the royalists in the west, independent newspapers in Paris, and for good measure, Jacobin radicals, who were no real danger to him; all this with a typical mixture of clemency and utter ruthlessness. Bonaparte was the perfect pragmatist in the derogatory sense of that word: as long as he thought measures would work, he took them. His rule is pervaded with crimes coolly committed and kindnesses well advertised. One early step, a decisive one in reducing France to order, did not require ferocity at all. The Revolution had begun with an experiment in extreme administrative decentralization; the decrees on local government of December 1789 and January 1790 had assigned wide powers to France's new departments and considerable autonomy to localities. This trust in local self-government had not survived the wars and the civil wars of the Years II and III. Now, in February 1800, Bonaparte confirmed and completed the process of centralizing administration by creating the office of prefect. The prefect headed a department; the subprefects and lesser officials were responsible to him, while he was responsible to Paris. And, in place of popular selection of public officials, Bonaparte put appointment by the central government. The ideal of local autonomy was sacrificed to the ideal of orderly administration.

The establishment of the prefects proved the first consul's most enduring achievement; his concordat with Pope Pius VII, signed after tortuous negotiations in July 1801 and ratified in September, proved the most controversial. Bonaparte's own religious convictions remain a matter of discussion; this only means that they were not strong. He was a rationalist, probably a deist. But he approached religion, as he approached everything, pragmatically. As he told his council of state: "My policy is to govern men as the great majority wish to be governed. . . . It was as a Catholic that I won the war in the Vendée, as a Moslem that I established myself in Egypt, and as an Ultramontane that I won the confidence of the Italians. If I were governing Jews, I should rebuild the temple of Solomon."[3] Bonaparte wanted a settlement with the Vatican because he judged the refractory clergy to be popular and dangerously influential in France; most Frenchmen, despite years of philosophic propaganda, remained good believers. Peace with the church would be part of the general pacification, and a religious settlement would compel many obstinate clerics to renounce their adherence to "Louis XVIII" and to rally around the Consulate.

His calculations proved correct. The concordat gave the French practically all they had asked for: the pope recognized the sale of church lands and the right of the French government to nominate bishops. France's acquisition of the old papal enclave of Avignon was passed over in silence, and since the French negotiators refused to call Catholicism the "dominant" religion or to surrender freedom of conscience, the pope had to be content with the pious declaration that "Catholicism is the religion of the great majority of French citizens"— which was true enough, and the main reason why Bonaparte had desired a concordat in the first place. The pope for his part secured repeal of some of the anticlerical legislation passed in the revolution: the French church was allowed, once again, to hold public services and to establish cathedral chapters and pious foundations. While the church had lost its land and its tithes, it had gained and kept guaranteed salaries. Thus, the church in France, the pope had reason to believe, had returned to the Roman discipline. But Bonaparte, to quiet domestic opposition to the concordat, subverted its spirit with a set of Organic Articles, published later, in April 1802. They spelled out the supremacy of the state over the church and insisted on civil marriage. To add injury to insult, the Organic Articles applied indiscriminately to Catholics and Protestants; this underscored the first consul's intention of keeping the privileges of Catholicism at a minimum. The concordat, thus unilaterally amended, was solemnly celebrated on Easter Day 1802, at Notre Dame, and Bonaparte compelled his Jacobin generals to accompany him to mass. Muttering defiance, they obeyed.

There have been interminable debates over just when Napoleon's career was at its height. One could make a strong argument for choosing the early spring of 1802.[4] Bonaparte was secure in power, self-appointed as the sole dominant figure in France for ten years. There was peace; France itself was quiet. The Consulate was seriously addressing itself to a variety of domestic matters: early in 1801, the government had begun to discuss a civil code; in April 1802, the first educational reforms went into effect. The Bank of France, founded in early 1800, helped to stabilize the currency. The distribution and collection of taxes, following reforms first laid down in the Directory, were more equitable and more efficient than before. Polite society reemerged, visitors thronged the city of Paris, prosperity was widespread. The Old Regime was dead; for most Frenchmen, this Consulate seemed like the realization of the

---

[3] Quoted in J. M. Thompson, *Napoleon Bonaparte* (1952), 188.
[4] One historian, at least, Thompson (*Napoleon Bonaparte*, 200–201), argues for this date, persuasively.

Revolution without its defects. There was no terror, no civil war, no bankrupt-cy. The abuses that had so long pervaded the fabric of French society—offices for sale, high positions monopolized by the nobility, taxes loaded on the poor and escaped by the privileged, commerce stultified by internal tariffs and manufacture by gild restrictions—had vanished, it seemed, forever. The Revolution had effected a vast redistribution of property with the confiscation of émigré lands, the sale of church properties, and the emergence of new wealth born of war and inflation. The Consulate, having made peace with England and the Vatican alike, appeared as the guarantor of this new order. In April 1802, the Consulate marked the new ease with a sweeping amnesty that included most of the émigrés. But the government made it plain that émigrés who took advantage of the amnesty and came home to swear fidelity to the Consulate would have no claim to those of their properties that had been legally handed to others. The revolutionary settlement must remain untouched.

The nation was grateful. In May 1802, prodded by Bonaparte's most assiduous courtiers, it was given an opportunity of expressing its gratitude. The Senate proposed that the first consul be reelected for another ten years; but on May 10, the Council of State proposed instead a new plebiscite to determine whether Napoleon Bonaparte should be chosen as consul for life. Bonaparte declared himself willing to sacrifice himself once more for the nation. A few outraged generals and republican intellectuals were sent off on remote assignments or kept out of Paris, and on August 2, the result of the plebiscite was announced. It allowed Bonaparte, by a vote of 3,568,885 to 8,374, to make his new sacrifice. Two days later the just-created life consul appeared with a new constitution that empowered him to appoint the other two consuls and the senators to the newly enlarged Senate. The details hardly mattered: Caesarism was at the door.

The new Consulate persisted in domestic reform. It was often of dubious quality: the civil code, developed with Bonaparte's diligent, often passionate participation, and promulgated in March 1804, was hastily drawn by relatively ignorant men. It was a supremely rationalist document, sweeping away a multiplicity of local laws and the authority of tradition in favor of general principles. It was relatively short and eminently quotable; it strengthened the laws of property in behalf of property owners; it decreed religious toleration and civil equality; it even permitted divorce. But it hedged reason and equality with conservative provisions, many of them at the insistence of Bonaparte: it gave the father extensive rights over his children, and men considerable authority over women. All were equal before the civil code, except women— and workers. The code specifically declared that in disputes over wages, courts would take the word of employer rather than that of employee.[5] This code, the

---

[5] The penal code of 1810 reiterated this inequality by strengthening the Le Chapelier law of 1791. That law, it will be recalled, had forbidden associations of labor and management alike; despite its ostensible evenhandedness, it operated mainly against workers, whose strongest weapon, the strike, it outlawed.

first of five, meant retreat from the egalitarianism of the revolution. Those who call Bonaparte a betrayer of the Revolution may appeal to these provisions. The consul retreated from republican equality in other ways. Late in May 1802, he founded a new Legion of Honor, designed to reward civic and military achievement. The legion was headed by the first consul and a grand council and was carefully organized in hierarchical, military fashion, with graduated pay and other privileges. In March 1790, the Constituent Assembly had solemnly declared the abolition of "all honorary distinctions, all power and superiority resulting from the feudal system," and in June, it had abolished hereditary nobility altogether. Now, twelve years later, Bonaparte founded new distinctions. It was Bonaparte's way of interpreting the Revolution's call, and his own, for careers open to talent.

In foreign affairs, the life consul proceeded with his celebrated energy. The fragile web of peace was soon torn. Despite the Peace of Amiens, British suspicions of Bonaparte remained acute. By late summer of 1802, suspicions had grown into tensions. The Consulate's foreign interventions had begun in 1800 in the Dutch Republic; in January 1802, Bonaparte graciously accepted the presidency of the new Italian Republic. All this activity could be justified by existing treaties. Then, in October 1802, Bonaparte turned his attention to a Switzerland torn by civil war. The British warned him; in November, George III pointedly referred to "certain states"—meaning Switzerland and Holland—in whose independence Britain had the most emphatic interest. In reply, in February 1803 and again in March, Bonaparte berated the British ambassador in violent language; Britain meanwhile refused to carry out its agreement to evacuate Malta; in May 1803 Britain declared war. Once again, French troops and ships were got ready to invade England. And in the following year, Consul Bonaparte transformed himself into Emperor Napoleon.

The Early Empire

Napoleon Bonaparte had made himself consul with a lie; he made himself emperor with a murder. He had never been above using, or even inventing, plots to advance his interests. Fouché and his secret police diligently ferreted out conspirators and exploited popular concern for Bonaparte's safety to dispose of unwelcome, if innocent, members of the opposition. On the evening of December 24, 1800, when Bonaparte was on his way to the opera, a bomb went off, killing a number of bystanders, but sparing the intended victim. The authors of the bombing were royalist extremists, but Bonaparte took this opportunity to crush the remnants of the Jacobin party. In 1804, he played the same game for higher stakes. Since the summer of 1803, an oddly assorted collection of exiled royalists, discontented republicans, and police spies had been discussing ways of overthrowing the "tyrant." Beginning in January 1804, the police made a number of arrests; by early March, most of the conspirators were in Fouché's hands. As the interrogators pieced together various confessions, it emerged that the plotters were counting on some unknown Bourbon prince to lead them to a glorious restoration of the Old Regime. But who? Suspicion fell on the young duke d'Enghien, a royal prince, the grandson of the prince de Condé, who was living in exile in Baden, not far from the French frontier. With Bonaparte's assent, he was kidnapped on March 14, brought to Paris, and secretly tried. Baden was foreign territory and the kidnapping an invasion of sovereignty; the reports brought in about the duke d'Enghien—his stealthy trips, his mysterious associates, his suspicious correspondence—were all proved palpably false at his trial, and Bonaparte knew they were false. Yet in the early morning of March 21, d'Enghien was shot.

It was easy enough to represent the event as a desperate act of self-defense—there was, after all, a genuine conspiracy, even if d'Enghien had no part in it. And as long as Bonaparte was in danger, so was France. To make his rule hereditary seemed the safest step to take. While a handful of principled republicans objected, public opinion, partly spontaneous, largely manipulated, called for Bonaparte's elevation. On May 18, the Senate, using a device reminiscent of the wily Caesar Augustus (see p. 16), combined the imperial reality with republican rhetoric. The second clause of the new constitution called Napoleon Bonaparte "First Consul of the Republic" and "Emperor of the French" in a single sentence. The inevitable plebiscite followed. It showed 3,572,329 for, only 2,569 against, the new regime. A smaller majority would have been more impressive.

Bonaparte—we must call him Napoleon I now—dramatized his accession on December 2, 1804, at Notre Dame de Paris, with a great coronation ceremony. Pope Pius VII came all the way from Rome to act his part in the rehearsed charade. He held up the imperial crown, Napoleon grasped it and placed it on his own head. It was a splendid moment for the little Corsican: Charlemagne, too, had crowned himself so. Domestically, the change of title made little difference. From 1803 on, Napoleon had surrounded himself with a court; from 1804, it became merely larger and more lavish. The new emperor created a series of resounding dignities and new titles, and a new nobility. The civil code, another product of the Consulate, was followed by related codes in the following years—a code of civil procedure, a penal code, a code of criminal procedure, and a commercial code. From 1807 on, the civil code, the most important, was deferentially called the *Code Napoléon*. For all its paternalism, this was the code by which French troops brought modernity to Europe—for what was retreat from some revolutionary principles in France was radical rationalism elsewhere.

Europe, indeed, preoccupied Napoleon I in these years as much as did France. In May 1804, while Bonaparte was preparing to make himself emperor, William Pitt had returned to office in England. He was worn with care and sherry, but he gave his remaining energies to the formation of a new coalition—the third—against French aggression. He found sympathetic support from the idealistic young Tsar Alexander I. Alexander had succeeded his unstable father,

Paul I, after a violent palace revolution in 1801. Soon, he came to think of himself as Napoleon's eastern counterpart. Bonaparte's high-handed actions in Germany, Italy, and elsewhere, and, even more, his murder of the duke d'Enghien, made Alexander all the more eager to defend Europe. In November 1804, the Russians signed a defensive treaty with the Austrians; in April 1805, they came to terms with the British. In May, Emperor Napoleon I crowned himself king of Italy and made his stepson Eugène de Beauharnais, viceroy. This was enough for the other powers; by August 1805, the Third Coalition was in being.

Napoleon, who had been ostentatiously assembling troops and ships at Boulogne for a descent on England, now just as ostentatiously turned eastward. With his troops commanded by his celebrated marshals—Ney, Davout, Lannes, Soult, Murat in Germany; Masséna in Italy—Napoleon planned to break up the coalition with lightning marches and rapid victories. He succeeded. On October 17, he compelled the Austrians under General Mack to surrender, with a large army, at Ulm, and marched on Vienna. But at sea, he faced Lord Nelson—his equal. In a melodramatic chase, the French and the allied Spanish navies had escaped British patrols in March and gathered in the West Indies, with Nelson in hot pursuit. The French plan was to draw the British navy across the Atlantic, dash back, gain control of the English channel and thus enable French troops to invade England. The scheme was risky, and Nelson too quick to let it mature. By August, Nelson had the French bottled up at Cadiz. Disappointed, Napoleon now turned his main attention to land warfare, and on October 21, 1805, after brilliant maneuvering on a sunny day, Nelson virtually destroyed the French-Spanish fleet off Cape Trafalgar. The British lost not a single ship, and only a few men, among them the national hero, Nelson himself. Napoleon made light of the debacle, but it was nothing less. Trafalgar guaranteed England the supremacy of the sea, put a permanent end to any notion of invasion, and as events were to show, frustrated Napoleon's later attempts to isolate Britain from the world (see p. 516).

On land, Napoleon had every cause for confidence. In November, when he learned of the defeat at Trafalgar, he was in Vienna, and on December 2, at Austerlitz, in Moravia, he scored his greatest victory. The French battered the allied troops, inflicting over thirty thousand casualties upon them. Austerlitz always remained Napoleon's favorite battle. With good reason: it kept the Prussians, who had been on the verge of abandoning their neutrality, out of war, and it led, in late December, to the advantageous Treaty of Pressburg with Austria.

As in other battles, so at Austerlitz, Napoleon's military prowess stemmed not from technological innovation but from tactical insight. Napoleon had a rich heritage to draw upon: his devices—the combination of line and column, for instance—and his rhetoric—the invocation of the nation in arms—belonged to the eighteenth century and to the wars of the Revolution. But Napoleon possessed unequaled skill at disposing and manipulating his forces and unsurpassed capacity for choosing the right spot to attack and to attack quickly. His insistence on mobility brought him victory after victory; he preferred light to heavy cavalry, and his armies lived off the country. Beyond his tactical skills lay his emotional appeal: he called out all the self-interest, and all the loyalty, of which his officers and men were capable. Better than anyone else, he exploited that new slogan—the career open to talents. Demonstrated fighting ability brought promotion; in Napoleon's army a private could quite literally become a field marshal. Napoleon was brilliant enough as a commander to wrest admiration not only from his associates, but from his enemies as well.

Now, at Pressburg, he used his charms on the Austrians. He got full sovereignty over Italy: Austria recognized him as king of Italy, ceded the Venetian territory they had acquired at Campo Formio eight years before, and permitted France to annex Piedmont, Parma, and Piacenza. In addition, Austria ceded important territories to Napoleon's German ally Bavaria, and agreed to recognize Bavaria and Württemberg as kingdoms, and Baden as a grand duchy.

Pressburg hastened the reorganization of Germany which had been underway for some years. In March 1803, following the provisions of the treaty of Lunéville of 1801, and at French prodding, the imperial Reichstag had simplified the map of their crazyquilt territories in an imperial recess, with the resounding German name of *Reichsdeputationshauptschluss*. It reduced the number of free cities of the empire from fifty-one to six; only two ecclesiastical principalities survived this drastic surgery. In all, some one hundred twelve sovereign units of the Holy Roman Empire disappeared and were merged into larger units. The recess was concluded under the eye of Consul Bonaparte, after undignified wrangling of German princes in Paris—a scramble for territories that made Talleyrand even richer than he already was. It benefited middle-sized states like Bavaria and Baden, made them slavishly dependent on France, and virtually destroyed the empire. Then, in 1804, anticipating its demise, Emperor Francis II officially took the title of Austrian emperor as Francis I, hoping thus to strengthen his hand in domains he could realistically control. Pressburg, as we have seen, further extended the territories of the middle-sized south German states and increased their dependence on France. In July 1806, Napoleon formed the Confederation of the Rhine and acted as its protector; it included the two new German kings—Maximilian I of Bavaria and Frederick I of Württemberg—the archduke of Baden, and most other west German rulers, tied to France by treaty and pledged to supply France with troops. In August 1806, after the members of the confederation seceded, Francis II surrendered his imperial crown, and that great anachronism, the Holy Roman Empire of the German Nation, was dead. This is what makes Napoleon Bonaparte's impact so hard to judge: abroad, however self-centered his motives, his actions often had progressive consequences.

The events of 1806 brought Prussia into the war against France. Neutral—embarrassingly so—since 1795, Prussia had been enjoying a modest age of reform under her king Frederick William III. Upon his accession in 1797, he had greatly simplified his court and given his ministers leeway for administrative changes. By 1805, the peasants on Prussia's crown lands were free, and the national debt was greatly reduced. But the foreign policy of Frederick William III was as timid as the man himself. Its only consistent point was neutrality. But in October 1806, after numerous provocations, Prussia finally went to war. A week later, at the battles of Jena and Auerstädt, the Prussian armies, those admirable instruments of Frederick the Great, were quickly and totally routed. As the French advanced across Prussia, garrison after garrison surrendered with indecent haste. By late October, Napoleon was in Berlin; by December, he had made a separate peace with the elector of Saxony; by early 1807, French troops had occupied German territory from Silesia to the Hanseatic cities. Their first check—almost unprecedented in Napoleon's stunning military career—came in early February, when Russian troops fought them to a standstill at Eylau. But in mid-June, at Friedland, the French forces compelled the Russians to retreat, and Napoleon entered Königsberg. The Treaties of Tilsit were the result. In a dramatic meeting on a raft in the middle of the river Niemen, Tsar Alexander and Emperor Napoleon decided the fate of Prussia on July 7; two days later, the Prussians meekly acceded. Prussia was reduced to half its laboriously amassed territories; only Alexander's insistence kept it on the map at all. Prussian lands between the Rhine and the Elbe were handed to Napoleon for his disposal; Saxony acquired the region around Cottbus; a new duchy of Warsaw was carved out in part from Prussian acquisitions in Poland. And both Russia and Prussia recognized the extensive redrawing of the map of Europe that Napoleon was undertaking elsewhere. In a magnificent gesture of family affection, Napoleon placed his brothers on established and yet-to-be established thrones: Joseph Bonaparte became king of Naples, Louis Bonaparte king of Holland, Jerome Bonaparte king of Westphalia;[6] and to all this, to the Confederation of the Rhine, and to Napoleon's diplomatic activities in Turkey, the signatories assented. Finally Prussia (and, in secret articles, Russia) agreed to aid France in the war against England. Napoleon's position was enviable; his control over central Europe, complete.

FROM TILSIT TO VIENNA

The Mastery of Europe

Tilsit marked an epoch in the history of Europe. Before 1807 the emperor had proved irresistible; after 1807 French successes were won against a counterpoint of resistance that would ultimately conquer. Yet the existence of that counterpoint is more apparent to historians than it was, at least immediately, to

---

[6] One brother, Lucien, was denied a kingdom; Napoleon had never been on good terms with him and had broken with him over what Napoleon regarded as an unsuitable marriage.

contemporaries. For three or four years men continued to be dazzled by the emperor's skill and good fortune. In 1809 the Austrians prematurely and overconfidently rose against him and in July were crushed at Wagram. By the Treaty of Schönbrunn, worse even than Pressburg four years earlier, Austria ceded territory to the client kingdoms and to Tsar Alexander I, who, despite his alliance with Napoleon, had remained calculatedly inactive. The principal Austrian negotiator, the new chancellor Count Klemens von Metternich, once ambassador in Paris, thereupon bought time for his country by a French alliance.

That alliance was confirmed in 1810 by a new Napoleonic triumph, his marriage to the Austrian princess Marie Louise. Josephine had proved incapable of bearing the emperor a child, and he had divorced her at the end of 1809; the hard-headed affection between the two was reflected in Josephine's successful demands for a handsome pension and the retention of her title. Napoleon's new empress gave him his heir, a son born in April 1811 and called the king of Rome, in tribute to the imperial city, which Napoleon had seized from an imprisoned pope in 1808 and incorporated, with the Papal States, into his empire the next year. Napoleon now went further in cultivating the imperial style. He flattered some of the old nobility, multiplied the new Napoleonic nobility on whose loyalty and self-interest he depended, and proclaimed his glory in monumental architecture.

The client states were kept in line. When convenience or necessity demanded, they were rearranged, and Napoleon's royal relatives and allies were shunted about. In 1808 Joseph was sent from Naples to Spain, replaced in his Italian kingdom by Caroline Bonaparte and her husband, the opportunistic and flamboyant Marshal Joachim Murat, who had ruled the grand duchy of Berg, pieced together from territories on the lower Rhine that had come to Napoleon after Austerlitz. The grand duchy of Warsaw, Napoleon's modest and not entirely sincere gesture to Polish independence—created from Prussia's Polish territories in 1807 and increased by some Austrian territory in 1809—was given Napoleon's dependent, the king of Saxony, as its puppet ruler. And when the emperor's brother Louis proved too sympathetic to the Dutch over whom he had been placed, he was unceremoniously chased from his throne in 1810. The client states were not mere conquests; they were the cutting edge of French ideals and of modernity, and to a greater or lesser degree the changes in law and institutions inspired or imposed by the French struck root. But the subjects of this vast empire also paid tribute to Napoleon—in money, in art treasures carried back to Paris, and, mercilessly, in troops.

Consolidation was the major internal task facing the Napoleonic Empire in the years after Tilsit, but, despite the victories in the field, the external challenge persisted. Great Britain, resourceful and determined, was now secure from direct assault by invasion. Napoleon was necessarily respectful of British skill and daring at sea, and he was fascinated by the casual, hard-drinking aristocrats who commanded the British army. But he comprehended British government not at all and was appalled by the freedom and scurrilousness of the British press. One thing, however, he was sure he understood: that Britain was a nation of shopkeepers.[7] Now a nation of shopkeepers was surely vulnerable to economic pressure; and, from the time of the Directory, desultory and not very effective attempts had been made at bringing Britain to its knees through economic warfare. Napoleon proposed to regularize this strategy in the Continental System.

The policy was inaugurated with the Berlin Decree in November 1806, which closed all Continental ports to British ships and goods. The British responded the next year with orders in council requiring neutral ships to be licensed in an English port, where they might also take on British goods to run the blockade. Napoleon countered with the Fontainebleau and Milan Decrees of October and December 1807, warning that any neutral ships complying with the orders in council would be treated as English. There were, in fact, few enough neutrals. The only important uncommitted maritime power caught in this paper war was the United States, and in 1807 President Jefferson tried to force France and Britain to back down by carrying an Embargo Act, which so hurt American merchants and shippers that it was soon repealed. Napoleon, playing the American card more effectively than the British, declared his readiness to make concessions, but never had to make them because the British were intransigent. The British insisted, moreover, on boarding neutral ships to find deserters from their navy, thus causing an additional grievance to the Americans, for American citizens were sometimes seized in these searches. In 1812 the United States and Britain drifted into a ridiculous and futile war, marked by some American military successes and by a British victory of sorts in the burning of Washington; but the peace that concluded this incidental embroilment in 1814 settled none of the outstanding issues between the two English-speaking nations.

British society in these years was subjected to unparalleled stresses and strains—from war, taxation, inflation, and the terrible dislocations of rapid and unplanned industrialization. French strategists calculated that a drop in English exports would provoke unrest and perhaps revolt: they were not wrong. When exports fell precipitously in late 1807 and early 1808, there was real hardship in Britain. When a newly stringent enforcement of the blockade was undertaken in 1810-1811, the difficulties within Britain triggered the savage, quasirevolutionary outbursts of violence and machine-breaking in the industrial districts known (after their mythical leader, General Ludd or King Ludd) as the Luddite riots. Had the French had the resources or will to enforce the blockade effectively and regularly, the Continental System might have gone far toward bringing Britain into negotiations. But in the end it failed.

---

[7] This famous phrase, reportedly uttered by Napoleon in his exile on St. Helena, may have originated with the Corsican patriot General Paoli; but it was also used by Adam Smith in the *Wealth of Nations* and by the American patriot Samuel Adams, both in 1776.

The British economy was far more resilient than the emperor or his advisors knew. The rapid progress of industrialization in the years when the French were preoccupied with revolution made British goods cheaper and more abundant, and increased demand for them throughout the world. Not only did the importance of the North American market continue to grow, but the Napoleonic invasion of Portugal and Spain opened the colonies of South America to British enterprise. And to a remarkable degree the Continent itself, though its importance to British commerce had been declining for more than a century, was kept open. The Baltic trade was maintained by the British seizure of Copenhagen in a daring naval raid in 1807 and by the capture of the tiny island of Heligoland in the North Sea for use as a trading base. Even the territory most directly under Napoleon's control needed British goods: internal transport on the Continent was too rudimentary and slow to allow overland supply to be substituted efficiently for transit by sea, and the coastline was too long to be regularly and closely supervised. The smugglers had a field day. In time Napoleon had to consent to a licensing system that allowed the import of colonial produce, which England was getting in increasing amounts in exchange for her stepped-up shipments to the New World. But other goods made their way through the blockade as well. Even French troops wore English cloth.

The Continental System failed in another respect. It was intended not merely as wartime strategy but as a way of strengthening the long-term prospects of the French economy against the British, but the French pursued this goal narrowly, looking on the other nations of Europe as tributaries. Had French policymakers learned from Adam Smith, they might have implemented a mutually beneficial free-trade area on the Continent. As it was, French policy offended precisely those aggressive and informed groups in the growing middle segment of European society who were, on other grounds, the best and most loyal supporters Napoleon could claim.

The Beginning of the End: Spain

Efforts to consolidate the French hold on the Continent and to bring Britain down by economic pressure dictated further French expansion. Spain had been allied to France since 1796; far overestimating Spain's strategic and economic importance, Napoleon insisted on its adherence to the Continental System. Priest-ridden, backward, and mysterious, Spain was wretchedly ruled by King Charles IV, his queen, and her favorite Manuel de Godoy. Godoy was not entirely illiberal or unenlightened, but he was fatally compromised by his taste for intrigue, his reputation (probably undeserved) as the queen's lover, and the suspicion of self-serving, even royal ambitions. Constantly working against this strange triangle was the heir to the throne, Ferdinand, who was implicated in a riot that forced his father to abdicate early in 1808. Napoleon thereupon summoned the whole royal family to Bayonne in southwestern France, badgered both Charles and Ferdinand into giving up their rights, and created a new kingdom of Spain, which he conferred on his brother Joseph. The result was a genuinely popular uprising throughout the kingdom. Joseph fled from Madrid at the beginning of August; to restore him, Napoleon had to occupy the country. Although they were successful in this immediate goal, the French found themselves facing constant guerrilla activity they could not understand. French forces had already been sent, late in 1807, to occupy Portugal, which had refused to abandon its long-standing alliance with Britain. British forces had landed and, under the command of Arthur Wellesley—later famous as the duke of Wellington—drove the French out of Portugal at the battle of Vimeiro in August 1808. A British force under Sir John Moore, sent to aid the Spanish insurgents in Madrid, was nearly cut off by the French and retreated with heavy losses to be evacuated at Corunna. But Wellesley stayed in the mountains of Portugal and let the superbly mobile French troops hurl themselves futilely time after time against his lines at Torres Vedras. Wellesley's careful preparation and patience, and a war of position, not movement, puzzled and exhausted the French; then slowly, systematically, Wellesley began to move forward into Spain. The Peninsular War had begun. "It was the Spanish ulcer," Napoleon later said ruefully, "that ruined me."

The creation of the Napoleonic kingdom of Spain brought more than an uprising and military defeat: it caused a sharp, self-conscious rejection of the cosmopolitanism for which France had come to stand and the institutions in which the French embodied their ideals. From the middle of the eighteenth century the smaller number of educated, forward-looking Spaniards to whom the term liberal was coming to be affixed, had been loyal to the enlightened monarchy of Charles III (see p. 422), and they had even managed to live with a church that, though unenlightened, was pervasive and popular and in which the highest places could still be reached by men of lowly origin. But when Napoleon dethroned the Bourbons in 1808, he forced a crisis of loyalty on the liberals. Some, the so-called *afrancesados,* saw collaboration with Joseph Bonaparte—an attractive, liberal-minded, though largely ineffectual man—as the best way of preserving a semblance of national independence and at the same time of regenerating Spain. But more of the liberals veered toward the republicanism affected by younger radicals, and in time, as they became aware of the total resistance of the church to reforming ideas, toward anticlericalism. This new radicalism, bitterly opposed to Napoleon, was grafted onto a genuinely national resistance.

In 1810, while Spain was still occupied and the British were biding their time in Portugal, the Spaniards elected a new Cortes; in it for the first time the representatives of the third estate outnumbered the nobles and clergy. In 1812, as the peninsular campaign moved forward, a constitution was adopted, which combined equality before the law, the defense of property rights, and a severely limited monarchy in a grand rhetorical scheme for which no country in Europe was ready. Taken far more seriously by liberals elsewhere than they deserved to be—the word "liberal" as a political term entered the English language from the Spanish—the Spanish reformers bequeathed a model to a generation of radical constitution-makers. But the alliance between this reforming impulse and the national resistance could not coexist for long, and ignorance, xenophobia, and clericalism proved stronger. The radical regime was threatened from the outset by opposition from the church and from a coalition of officers and conservatives, and military victory over the French doomed the reforms. In 1814 Ferdinand VII, a national hero in spite of himself, returned to rule his country with an unimaginative stupidity that provoked by turns new revolutions, French intervention, and a dreary civil war. Still, despite the confusion and cross-purposes of Spanish patriots, the Spanish example in these years is instructive. Whatever the success of reformers, whatever their obligations to native tradition, French example, or imported ideas, the struggle against Napoleonic domination and against the institutions and armies by which it was enforced, welded a new sense of nationhood, of a common culture and a shared pride, that was a potent legacy to the nineteenth century.

National Regeneration: Britain, Russia, Austria, Germany

Great Britain, the chief, most energetic, and most effective of Napoleon's enemies, changed little during these years in political and administrative structure, less perhaps than any European nation except Austria. Yet change there was; the war dictated reforms in the central administration and carried further the quest for efficiency and the reduction of useless but remunerative offices that gave the crown a major means of exerting political influence. In the income tax—instituted in 1797, revised in 1802, and heartily hated throughout the war—the government had found a modern instrument that, though it had to be given up in 1816, would be restored a quarter of a century later to remain the chief financial mainstay of British government to the present day. But William Pitt, the principal architect of such administrative reforms as were carried through, was out of office from 1801 to 1804, and in his brief second ministry from 1804 to 1806 he was completely preoccupied with the renewed war against France. In 1806 he died, exhausted, at the age of forty-seven.

The Whigs—or the most liberal-minded remnant of them—out of office since 1783, offered the only basis for a government, and, much against his will, the king agreed to a coalition known as the Ministry of All the Talents. Its most prominent figure, Charles James Fox, died late in the year, and the single notable legislative accomplishment of the ministry was the act of 1807 abolishing the slave trade, a response to a national agitation of humanitarian and religious reformers led in Parliament by Pitt's friend, the merchant and Evangelical politician William Wilberforce. An attempt to secure the traditional Whig goal of Catholic Emancipation—the right of Catholics to hold offices in the state and to sit in Parliament—the issue on which Pitt had been driven from office by the king in 1801, brought the downfall of the Talents in 1807. The governments that succeeded were made up of men who considered themselves heirs of Pitt; as they had worked his system effectively, they saw little need to change it. Headed first by an ineffectual peer, then by the colorless but competent Spencer Perceval, the government picked its way through political difficulties and somehow fought the war. Its worst political threat appeared in 1810, when King George III was declared irretrievably mad and a regency was conferred on the dissolute and incompetent prince of Wales; the prince had long dallied with the Whigs, but over the next year he rejected their claims on office, showing himself an opponent of all meaningful change. When Perceval was assassinated in 1812 (by a bankrupt who blamed his troubles on the government), his successor was another of Pitt's lieutenants, the earl of Liverpool. Liverpool's ministry was to carry Britain into the liberal era, but it was to be ten years before that promise would become apparent.

The reforming impulse that had been at work in the 1770s and 1780s and the full-blown radicalism of the early years of the French Revolution were driven underground by repressive legislation in the nineties. Among working men it survived in clandestine trade-union activity, disguised often as benefit clubs to get round the Combination Acts of 1799 and 1800, which made unions illegal. This activity in turn underlay the working-class agitations that in 1811–1812 gave rise to those episodes of machine-breaking and violence against employers associated with the effects of the Continental System. A new, more respectable, middle-class movement for parliamentary reform was organized in the city of Westminster, adjacent to London, in 1806–1807 and grew steadily throughout the remainder of the war. It drew not only on the tradition of the 1780s but on the frustration felt by some educated and ambitious men, particularly among manufacturers and members of the more radical Dissenting sects, who added dislike of the war to resentment of their continued exclusion from political participation. But neither the working-class agitation nor the Westminster movement reflected the real mood of the country. The vehement reaction against the French Revolution—so superbly if unfairly expressed by Edmund Burke in 1790—was easily transmuted into hatred of "Boney," replete with overtones of the xenophobic pride that had always characterized English patriotism.

There is, however, a more important explanation of the willingness of most Englishmen to tolerate a society so imperfect in so many ways, an explanation that goes beyond invoking patriotism, fear of radicalism, or the undoubted diffusion of prosperity in the wartime boom: England had had her revolution and was in the last analysis, as the greatest historian of nineteenth-century England has put it, a free country, "a country of voluntary obedience, of an organization freely initiated and freely accepted."[8] That lesson the entire Continent had yet to learn.

Across the Continent, in Russia, the Napoleonic era seemed to hold out greater promise for reform. The brief reign of Catherine the Great's son Paul I,

---

[8] The quotation is the concluding passage of the first volume (1913) of Elie Halévy's *A History of the English People in the Nineteenth Century,* a superb recreation of England in 1815.

from 1796 to 1801, had verged on the disastrous. Paul had come to the throne hating his mother and all she stood for. He released her prisoners, incarcerated his own, and played the autocrat in the most extreme fashion, in petty details as well as in high policy.[9] He extended the geographical sway of serfdom and harshly suppressed agrarian troubles; at the same time he offended the gentry whom his mother had cultivated by imposing limitations (scarcely enforceable but nonetheless galling to the gentry) on the amount of labor a serfowner could exact. He entered the Second Coalition precipitously at the end of 1798 and as precipitously left it in 1800, allying himself with Napoleon. When fighting the French he had extended Russian power to the Ionian Islands in the Mediterranean, where a Russian-protected republic was created under Turkish suzerainty, and to the island of Malta, when he accepted election as grand master of the Knights of Malta who had ruled there from the sixteenth century until Napoleon turned them out in 1798. When Malta was lost to the British in the tsar's change of front, he sent off an army of Cossacks to invade India. But in March 1801 a revolt of the palace guards ended in Paul's assassination; the new tsar was Paul's twenty-three-year-old son, Alexander I.

The change in rulers was received everywhere with relief. Alexander at once replaced his father's belligerency with a policy of peace, and it seemed likely that sweeping domestic changes would follow as well. The young tsar was charming, intelligent, well-informed, and ambitious to better his country. He had been educated by a Swiss philosophe, Frédéric César de La Harpe, and he early gave an earnest of his liberal intentions by declaring an amnesty for his father's political prisoners and by relaxing the censorship. He met regularly with an "unofficial committee" of liberal-minded advisors to plan how Russia might be reformed. But there was another side to Alexander's nature: he was emotional, unstable, and as prone to discouragement as he was to enthusiasm. And there was much in that huge, ungovernable country to discourage even the most determined of men. Overwhelmingly agrarian, Russia lacked any significant middle class, that source of enterprise and vision on which so much of western European progress depended. Alexander's initial hope to do something about serfdom quickly vanished when confronted with intractable reality; only a law of 1803 permitting voluntary emancipation resulted, and little was done under it. The gentry, who had hated Paul, wanted only such alterations as would restore the privileges they had gained under Catherine the Great and maintain the autocracy as they thought it had existed in the eighteenth century. There was no significant demand at any level of society for fundamental change in either society or government. And so the initial reforming impulse died out by 1804; the unofficial committee had already ceased to meet. In government some useful, even important, administrative alterations were made—the establishment of the Senate as the supreme administrative and judicial body,

[9] He is reported to have said that the person speaking to him was the only important person in the country—and only so long as the conversation lasted.

and the gradual transformation of the collegial system of administration into ministries, each with a single head. But the one lasting, broadly significant reform was in education: a number of new universities and schools were founded, and by the end of the reign the essentials of a rational, nationwide system were laid down.

Between 1807 and 1812 there was another burst of reforming activity, this time centered on the astonishing activity of M. M. Speransky. The son of a priest, Speransky had absorbed the best that could be had from the old-fashioned Scholastic education in Russian seminaries and had gone on to immerse himself in the ideas of the Enlightenment. A consummate bureaucrat and a far-sighted statesman (though entirely within the confines of autocracy), Speransky had a clear sense of the need for a rational institutional and legal structure to replace the confusion and arbitrariness that passed for tsarist autocracy. But Speransky's sense of what needed doing was better than his sense of what could be done. For all his brilliance, he had to plan and administer too much. He tried but could not carry through a codification of Russian law on the model of the French code. In 1809 he drafted a complete constitution providing for a series of legislative assemblies culminating in an indirectly elected state Duma; for a judicial administration culminating, as in the past, in the Senate; for a reformed system of local government; and for an executive capped by a Council of State made up of the tsar's most intimate advisers. But only the last survived the planning stage. Brilliant civil servants, especially when they are innovators, are rarely popular. Speransky was hated for some of his measures—notably his effort to impose written examinations or university training as qualifications for the higher ranks of the civil service. He was suspected of undue admiration for France. Above all the gentry resented his plebeian origins. In 1812 he fell, exiled to the Urals as if he were a traitor. And while he returned to St. Petersburg later in Alexander's reign, having done remarkable administrative work in Siberia, he was never again to attempt reform on so grand a scale.

Nor was Alexander. On occasion the tsar still showed signs of his early dedication to liberal ideas, but he was preoccupied with foreign affairs and sought political counsel chiefly from the reactionary Count Arakcheev, who had been his boyhood friend. His increasing withdrawal into religiosity finds its most celebrated evidence in his brief infatuation with the famous mystic, the Baroness Julie de Krüdener. In short, Alexander's fragile temperament could not bear the strains he himself had placed upon it—in vain. It is tempting to see his quarter-century's rule as a succession of lost opportunities; it is wiser to see the reign as a demonstration of futility. Liberal ideas could work marvels where the way for them had been properly prepared; they could do little to break the harsh, resistant ground of Russian society and culture.

In Austria the inclination to do nothing (or as little as possible) was superbly distilled in the outlook of Francis I, who had come to the throne in

1792, at the age of twenty-four, following the unexpected death of his father, the able and statesman-like Leopold II; he ruled until 1835. Although he maintained most of the compromises by which Leopold had sought to reverse or temper the Josephine revolution,[10] little in Francis's Austria was touched by a liberal or enlightened spirit. The serfs, with whose status and lords Joseph II had dealt so drastically, remained personally free; but because Francis had decreed that only the lord's consent could make it possible to escape the obligation of forced labor, the serfs still fell short of true peasant status. Intellectuals, especially suspect in the reaction against revolutionary ideas, were kept in hand by censorship and by strict control of schools and universities. Radical activity, like everything else, was supervised by a pervasive and, for its time quite sophisticated, police apparatus. There were breaks, however, in this cover of social and constitutional monotony. Hungary, glad enough to be freed from the hated Josephine program of Germanization, was loyal to the emperor, but a degree of patriotic independence survived in fairly regular meetings of the Hungarian Diet down to 1811, even though few grievances ever reached the stage of discussion and still fewer brought executive action. Similarly, demands for the recognition of Magyar as the language of official life and education in place of Latin and German got nowhere.

The reforming impulse flickered briefly in Austria itself in the three years after the disastrous defeat by Napoleon at Ulm in 1805 and the humiliating Peace of Pressburg. Count Philipp Stadion, a transplanted Rhinelander who was foreign minister, envisioned a national uprising among all the German peoples based on a patriotic revival and a program of genuine, if limited, reform. No solid foundation for this goal had been assured, however, when the Austrians tackled Napoleon in 1809, to end in defeat at Wagram and Schönbrunn. Stadion was at once dismissed, and reform was dismissed with him. He returned to serve under Metternich,[11] but his experiment was not repeated.

In the German lands outside Austria the situation was far different. There the French example, directly or indirectly, had a powerful impact. The parts of Germany on the left bank of the Rhine were incorporated directly into France in 1797, divided into seven departments, and ruled from Paris; much of the right bank went to make up the duchy of Berg in 1806. That the Rhineland was well prepared to welcome and retain much that was done, however alien its source, is indicated by the fact that Stadion and Metternich in Austria, Nesselrode in Russia, and the leading reformers in Prussia all came from the Rhineland—long a progressive region, it produced civil servants of fortune needed by backward states as desperate earlier rulers had needed soldiers of fortune. In northern Germany, the Napoleonic kingdom of Westphalia was

---

[10] On Joseph II and Leopold II, see pp. 426–432.
[11] On Metternich, see Ch. 13.

intended as a model of enlightened government; though much was restored in 1815, the process was irreversible. In the south, new states were created around established nuclei—Bavaria, Württemberg, and Baden were the most prominent—not merely by the accretion of petty principalities but by the ruthless ignoring of traditional boundaries and customs, by centralization, and by enlightened administration on the French model. In these parts of Germany there had been some sympathy with the efforts of Joseph II to wrench Austria into the modern world, and reforms were quickly absorbed, the more so perhaps as they were the work of native dynasties and bureaucrats who were at once enlightened, autocratic, and German. But these new creations were not undertaken as the first steps toward a united Germany; rather they were expressions of pride and ambition in separate, and for the time viable, middle-sized states. Thus the chaos of Germany was rationalized under Napoleon but not reduced to uniformity; even within the Confederation of the Rhine, that loose agglomeration of southern, western, and central German states, the variety was startling. In contrast to Bavaria or Baden, Saxony and Mecklenburg, which kept their independence by timely alliances with Napoleon, remained almost totally unchanged, even though the Saxon king, Frederick Augustus I, was required to implement the usual reforms in the grand duchy of Warsaw, which he also headed. [12]

National Regeneration: The Prussian Case

Looking back on his career, Napoleon regretted that he did not eliminate Prussia at the time of Tilsit. By detaching Prussia's western territories, leaving only its backward eastern lands, and confronting the country with occupation and a huge indemnity, he stimulated the desire for recovery and revenge; the means to attain those ends were sought in fundamental political and social reforms. In time, a reconstructed Prussia formed the base on which the ultimate solution of the German problem was founded.

Given the Prussian tradition of autocracy, a formidable civil and military bureaucracy, and a passive people, these reforms could be imposed from above. [13] Prussia's king, Frederick William III, was well-meaning but timid, preferring to rely for advice on his most intimate counselors, the cabinet secretaries, rather than on his ministers. The most prominent of his ministers was the Freiherr vom Stein, the proud descendant of a family of imperial

[12] Hence the wits of Warsaw poked fun at Frederick Augustus by calling him (alluding to the Molière farce) "*le médecin malgré lui*—the doctor in spite of himself."

[13] The late nineteenth-century English historian Sir John Seeley said, in a somewhat superior way, of the local government reforms, that the Prussian people "were commanded, not allowed, to govern themselves." A few decades later, an English historian would have been quite aware that many of the forms of English local government had originated in the Middle Ages owing to exactly the same imposition of self-government by the king, in his own interest, upon an unwilling people.

knights in the Rhineland. Stein had entered the Prussian service in 1780; by 1804 he was in charge of the general supervision of revenues, commerce, and manufactures, a task to which he brought a close knowledge of Adam Smith and the French Physiocrats and a general admiration for England. Convinced of the need for sweeping change and impatient with Frederick William's temporizing, Stein led a virtual revolt among the king ministers in 1806 and was dismissed early in 1807 for his insubordination. Stein's colleague Count Hardenberg, less imaginative and more diplomatic, persuaded the king to rely on his ministers and, in October, to recall Stein as his principal adviser. In a little over a year in office Stein initiated a series of major reforms, though he was prevented from seeing them through by Napoleon's insistence on his dismissal at the end of November 1808. [14]

During his brief hold on power, Stein reorganized the central government by removing the informal cabinet and by reorganizing the administrative structure into five ministries—interior, foreign affairs, finance, justice, and war—all organized on the French model. He wanted to unify the action of the ministries through a state council that would give collective advice to the king, hoping thus to avoid the dangers of power concentrated in the hands of a single minister—a device that surely reflects an Anglophile's awareness of the hostility in eighteenth-century England to the notion of a "prime minister." Stein was unable to carry through this second stage of his reorganization, and in 1810 the king, who temperamentally needed one man on whom he could rely, appointed the indispensable Hardenberg (a good eighteenth-century absolutist) as chancellor, an office that, later revived on a wider national level by Bismarck, has remained the pivot of German politics and administration right down to the present. Stein also increased the powers and responsibilities of provincial governments, again preferring to confide those powers to boards rather than to single officials. He did, however, provide for "high presidents" to represent the central government in the provinces, and these officials became an important part of Prussian government following 1815. Stein also initiated a sweeping reform of town governments in 1808 and hoped that at the level of the rural districts as well as in towns some representation of all ranks of society might be included. Again his departure—or perhaps the realities of the situation—prevented implementation of notions for which he was clearly indebted to his admiration of English local government.

These governmental reforms, restricted though they were in Hardenberg's politic application of them, were supplemented by military reforms carried through by Generals Scharnhorst and Gneisenau to rebuild the army so thoroughly discredited at Jena in 1806. The clear remedy for the manpower problem lay in abandoning the canton system, by which regiments could draw only on small recruiting districts—a system hampered by wholesale exemptions—and replacing it with a national system of universal service. Partly

[14] After a brief stay in Austria, Stein was summoned to become an adviser to Tsar Alexander I.

because of political problems, partly because the French put strict limits on the size of the Prussian forces, this sweeping change was postponed until 1813. But the barbarous discipline of the old Prussian army gave way to a more humane and regular system of military justice in 1808; the officer corps was opened to others than aristocrats; a new emphasis on ability and training dictated a reorganization of the war schools and a concentration on theory and planning that foreshadowed the creation of a general staff; there was, moreover, a wholesale revision of the organization of army units and of tactics.[15] Thus these years of abject defeat produced a state and an army that could cope more effectively than could the old Prussian institutions with the Napoleonic challenge. But, in Stein's view, far more sweeping social reforms were essential to a real marshaling of the nation.

The gradual reduction of ancient restrictions on the economy had gone on from the accession of Frederick William III; early in the reign, moreover, serfs on the royal estates were freed, an example followed by a handful of great landowners in East Prussia who could see the advantage of ridding themselves of the obligation to maintain their serfs and relying on hired instead of forced labor. In 1807 Stein drafted an edict decreeing the emancipation of serfs throughout what the French had left of Prussia; but his dismissal meant a less sweeping implementation and extension of these reforms than he had antici- pated or might have been able to carry into effect. The serfs obtained their legal freedom—they could, for example, now marry without the lord's consent—but their labor obligations were only gradually removed, and they were prevented by lack of capital from using more intensive agricultural techniques. The aristocratic landowners, moreover, retained special privileges through much of the century. Indeed, it was they who profited most from the reforms, not only because their estates tended to grow larger with land the peasants could not maintain, not only because the state was solicitous of their welfare and prejudices, but because what was done opened the way to more effective capitalistic exploitation of the land. And, if landowners chose not to be better capitalists, middle-class entrepreneurs could take over, for Stein did away with the old monopoly of the aristocrats on the purchase and holding of land. Far more than had been anticipated, the changes converted serfs, not into landholding peasants, but into landless laborers. A process that had taken several centuries in England was accomplished by fiat in Germany within a decade or two. The complete freeing of the industrial system, however, was not attained in practice until midcentury and later, although edicts of 1808–1811 recognized the principle, allowed most trades to be practiced by anyone who could pay the entry fee, regulated few of them, and left the gilds to survive only as voluntary institutions.

[15] The outstanding figure in this transformation was General Karl von Clausewitz, who, after helping with the reforms and serving in the field, returned to head the Kriegsakademie (war academy) from 1818 to 1830. He was the most influential military theorist of the century. His true teacher, of course, was Napoleon.

The German revival was far more sweeping and constructive in the realm of the spirit than was possible in the touchier areas of money, land, and rights. Heirs to the imposing legacy of the German Enlightenment, with its ideals of tolerance and its notions of the distinctiveness of Germany and the centrality of culture, the educated middle class and the professional classes were given a new range of educational institutions through which these ideals were propagated in ever more nationalistic forms. Stein's nominee to oversee the educational reorganization of Prussia was Wilhelm von Humboldt, the brother of the distinguished naturalist and traveler Alexander von Humboldt, and himself a literary figure of considerable importance. Humboldt remained minister of public instruction for only a little over a year, but in that year Prussia was provided with a system of *Gymnasien*, secondary schools that prepared boys for examinations for university entrance by giving them the essentials of a liberal education and rigorous intellectual discipline. In 1810, because the university at Halle had been absorbed into the Napoleonic kingdom of Westphalia, a new university was founded in Berlin; in the fields of philosophy, religion, and science, the new university was to have profound effects throughout Europe and the rest of the world. An approach to education that would nourish a distinctive German spirit had been called for in 1807–1808 in the powerful *Addresses to the German Nation*, delivered by the philosopher J. G. Fichte, who had been converted by the revolutionary and Napoleonic experience from a cosmopolitan and Francophile enthusiasm to a fervent German nationalism. Fichte saw Germany as increasingly unified by aggressive national educational institutions and by the traditions and ambitions of a common culture. To those raised in the French or English tradition, however, this fact suggests a strange and disturbing flaw: Fichte appealed to a cultural, not a political, nation; in German politics, the state still decreed, even when it was reforming, and the subject received, neither knowing nor valuing meaningful participation. Thus the legacy of the unpolitical German was transmitted in altered form, with profound effects, to the new century and to ours.

Napoleon's Fall and the Making of the Peace

After his victory over Austria at Wagram in 1809, Napoleon determined to crush Spanish resistance and to "drive the English leopard into the sea." But after Masséna's failure to penetrate the English lines in Portugal, Wellington, with deliberate initiative, attacked the French armies and in the battles of Salamanca and Vitoria in 1812 and 1813 drove them out of Spain. Wellington's way was eased by the deflection of the emperor's attention—and of a great many troops—to more pressing concerns in the east. Despite the initial show of enthusiasm, the alliance between Alexander and Napoleon concluded at Tilsit had proved little more than nominal. Neither party was particularly trustworthy, and each resented bad faith in the other. Napoleon's seizure of

Holland was in violation of the Tilsit agreements; nor did Napoleon help the tsar against the Turks, as he had promised. Worse, he had offended Alexander by supporting an independent Polish state in the grand duchy of Warsaw and by concluding an alliance and a marriage with Russia's hereditary enemy Austria. For his part, the tsar had stayed neutral during the Austrian campaign of 1809, had connived at violations of the Continental System, and was in fact consistently working against his nominal ally. By 1811 the last shred of pretense to a Franco-Russian alliance had dissolved. Metternich had noted as early as 1807 that Napoleon seemed to regard moderation as a "useless obstacle"; now the Russian impasse drove the emperor once more to a military solution. On June 24, 1812, Napoleon launched an invasion of Russia, with his Grande Armée built around a core of veterans, both officers and men, but filled out with raw recruits and unwilling draftees from occupied territories. The total number in Napoleon's forces may have reached six hundred thousand at their peak, but the ranks were quickly depleted by desertion, disease, and casualties. Napoleon could still show his old brilliance, but his leadership was sporadic. And while he could appear in Poland as a liberator, he could not imagine turning that powerful weapon—exporting the Revolution—to account in Russia: the serfs struck him as subhuman, and he feared that their liberation would touch off dreadful massacres.

The Russians made a show of resistance at Smolensk in August; early in September, at Borodino, west of Moscow, was fought the most savage and costly battle of the Napoleonic era: the French lost a quarter of their army— nearly thirty thousand—and the Russians counted casualties of twice that number.[16] But pitched battles were not to win the war for the Russians. Retreat—imposed by necessity rather than clever calculation—proved the successful strategy. On September 14, the emperor began the occupation of Moscow, the old holy city of Russia. There he planned to spend the winter and to secure reinforcements from the west. Almost at once fires broke out. "I had no idea of the wonders of this town," Napoleon wrote to his empress a few days later. "It had five hundred mansions as fine as the Elysée, with French furniture and incredible luxury, a number of imperial palaces, barracks, and magnificent hospitals. The whole place has disappeared. . . . All the small middle-class houses are of wood, and catch fire like matches. . . . The respectable inhabitants, 200,000 of them, are in despair, and are reduced to wandering wretchedly in the streets. However there is enough left for the army, which has found all kinds of valuables; in the present confusion everything is for loot."[17] Moscow was in

[16] A French officer wrote: "When it was all over I saw Napoleon riding over the battle-field; I followed him everywhere; he was beaming and rubbing his hands: 'There are five dead Russians'—he said it repeatedly with satisfaction—'to every Frenchman.' I suppose he took Germans for Russians" (Thompson, *Napoleon Bonaparte*, 333). Or perhaps generals simply prefer favorable body counts.

[17] Ibid., 335.

fact untenable. Napoleon made peace offers and waited for answers that never came. In mid-October he decided to evacuate the city. The better route to the south was barred by Russian armies; burdened with booty and short of food and transport, the remnants of the Grande Armée straggled back through Smolensk, by the route over which they had come, pursued by the Russians and harried by Cossack raiders. By skill and good fortune Napoleon escaped a trap that was closing on him at the Berezina River in November. But then the winter, long delayed, set in in earnest. Napoleon, having heard of attempts to overthrow him at home, hurried back to Paris in early December: the legend of his suffering with his troops has little foundation in fact. The ravages of cold and starvation on the army he left behind were appalling. Fewer than a hundred thousand men found their way to safety in the west. Napoleon had suffered his first major defeat.

Alexander decided to pursue the French into central Europe, a strategy encouraged by the British, who wanted certain victory; by Stein, who wanted to unify Germany; and by Alexander's own ambition to rule over Poland. Russian forces entered Prussia as liberators, and in late February and March 1813 Frederick William III was persuaded to desert his enforced alliance with the French and to join with the Russians. In June Metternich overcame his scruples against breaking the Austrian alliance with Napoleon and conquered his distrust of British goals of total victory, and the Grand Alliance was created, heavily subsidized with British money. Napoleon managed to defeat the allied armies at Dresden in late August, but in mid-October, near Leipzig, took place what has come to be known as the Battle of the Nations, in which two armies of a quarter of a million men each were engaged. Decisively defeated, Napoleon reentered France, turned on at the last moment by his Bavarian allies. The pursuit continued, and on March 30, 1814, the allied armies entered the capital, followed next day by Frederick William III and the new hero Alexander.

Piecing together the Grand Alliance had involved a number of shifting and contradictory agreements among the allies; soon after Leipzig, negotiations were begun with Napoleon. But it was not only the emperor's obstinacy over terms or his awareness of what he could and could not legitimately or politically offer France that prolonged the confusion. From the first the allies were in conflict over goals. The main outlines of the settlements finally arrived at were laid down by the British foreign secretary, Viscount Castlereagh. Castlereagh's first aim was to ensure the defeat of Napoleon so completely that neither the emperor nor France could again disturb the balance of power. Along with his political associates at home, Castlereagh preferred a restoration of the Bourbon dynasty, dethroned in 1792, though he was more willing than most British opinion to negotiate with Napoleon. Castlereagh wanted, also, to maintain a European coalition that would prevent the distortion of the balance by any single power. He was flexible on central Europe and even on Italy. But he was adamant on the restoration of Spain and Portugal and on a European guarantee of their protection from France. Like all English diplomats for at least four centuries, he insisted that territories directly across the Channel must not be allowed to fall into the possession of a major power that might threaten British security; to that end he proposed that France be kept away from Antwerp and that the southern portion of the Low Countries be given to a restored kingdom of Holland. For further security he proposed to marry Princess Charlotte of Wales, the daughter of the prince regent, to the heir to the Dutch throne. If these basic principles were granted, Britain stood ready to provide subsidies and to cede, as compensation, most of the colonies picked up during the war— from France, Holland, and Spain—to serve, in good eighteenth-century fashion, as bargaining counters. But certain strategic prizes Britain kept— Ceylon in the East, the Cape of Good Hope in southern Africa, Malta, and a protectorate over the Ionian Islands in the Mediterranean—assuring the security of the routes to India.

Metternich played a cool and cynical diplomatic game to maintain the integrity (if that is the word) of his ramshackle empire. He was won over to Castlereagh's side because of the threat posed by the willingness of Frederick William III of Prussia to defer to Alexander. Prussia was, of course, determined to regain the territory it had lost and to be compensated by territorial gains for the humiliations it, more than any other power, had suffered: to Hardenberg, the principal Prussian negotiator, it was a matter of flexibility, if not indifference, whether those gains were at the expense of the Poles or the Saxons. It was rather Alexander who posed the profound enigma and the greatest danger to allied unity. The acknowledged leader of the alliance, well advised and undoubtedly intelligent, Alexander was the only European statesman then able to grasp the importance of liberal and national movements; hence the relish with which he played the role of liberator in central and western Europe. At the same time, as he said, the burning of Moscow "had enlightened his soul," and he was entering on a deeply mystical and religious phase that was not without its impact on the Vienna settlement. Liberal and conservative, enthusiastic and calculating, generous and rigid by turns, he was predictable only when certain national or personal goals were involved, above all in Poland. He felt a personal mission to take moral charge of Poland, and he was supported by some Polish nobles who preferred him to a restoration of the Austrian or Prussian rulers they had escaped by collaborating with Napoleon. In this collision of Russian with Prussian and above all Austrian policy lay the toughest problem of the peace.

The making of a French settlement was centered on two main points: the future of Napoleon and the boundaries to which the defeated nation would be confined. In general the allies were disposed to be fairly generous. The Frankfurt Proposals were drawn up by Russia, Prussia, and Austria shortly after Leipzig and assented to by one of Castlereagh's subordinates. Castlereagh found the offer of frontiers at the Alps on the east and the Pyrenees on the south acceptable, but could not agree to a France extending to the Rhine and encompassing the Low Countries. Napoleon, hoping for better terms, remained noncommittal too long, and when his foreign minister Caulaincourt finally accepted the Frankfurt Proposals, the allies turned him down. Castlereagh was determined that no such error would be made again; negotiations brought Metternich over to the idea of limiting French frontiers more stringently, and the tsar was willing to consider that possibility, given the success of the military operations that continued during negotiations. But Napoleon would still not accept the ancient frontiers, and the tsar wavered; Castlereagh therefore gave his attention to cementing the alliance more effectively than had been done so far.

This goal was accomplished in the Treaty of Chaumont, signed on March 9, 1814. Secret articles set down specific goals that conformed to Castlereagh's intentions, above all an expanded Holland. Of more general importance was the construction of a Quadruple Alliance, to last, according to the treaty, for twenty years: the allies would act in concert to preserve the balance of power. The alliance secure, Castlereagh could return to the problem of Napoleon, whom he would allow to remain on the throne only if the chastened emperor would accept the boundaries of prerevolutionary France. At the end of March the allies were in touch with representatives of the Bourbons, and there were signs that opinion in France, or parts of it, was growing more favorable to restoration; most symptomatic and important of all, Talleyrand, that astute master of the art of surviving, had come to their aid. [18] This show of support for the Bourbons helped to convert Alexander from his enthusiasm for the candidacy of Prince Bernadotte, one of Napoleon's marshals who had been named heir to the Swedish throne, but he magnanimously agreed to offer Napoleon sovereignty over the island of Elba in the Mediterranean, a promise that Castlereagh and Metternich much disliked but that was written into the Treaty of Fontainebleau, signed on April 11. Napoleon abdicated, and on May 3 Louis XVIII entered Paris. Negotiations for a peace treaty had been opened with the Bourbons after military operations ceased in late April, and on May 30 the first Peace of Paris was signed. The French agreed to accept the frontiers of 1792 (a more generous settlement than Castlereagh had earlier insisted upon) and the main heads on which the allies had agreed at Chaumont: free navigation of the Rhine, a big Holland, an independent Switzerland, a German confederation, a divided Italy under Austrian domination, and British retention of Malta.

The French problem settled, the allies could then turn to more general European problems. Preliminary conversations were held in Paris and in London, but nothing had been made firm when the talks opened in Vienna in mid-September. Shortly thereafter the four major powers decided that all decisions would be kept in their hands; the only plenary session was the final one at which the terms were ratified. Much time was spent in discussing the organization of the congress with other, smaller powers, and those in attendance were kept under elaborate police surveillance while they were treated to

[18] On Talleyrand, see p. 474.

extensive festivities that kept them from paying close attention to business. The postponement of formal actions reflected deep divisions among the four great powers, above all over the conflict of Prussian, Russian, and Austrian ambitions concerning Poland and Saxony, ambitions on which the entire settlement of the German situation depended. The result of the deadlock was that Britain drew closer to France; when in late December the tsar insisted on beginning formal conferences on the Polish question, Castlereagh and Metternich demanded the admission of France, represented by Talleyrand, into the inner councils. Prussia was outraged and even went so far as to threaten war and to mobilize her army; the result was a treaty of alliance among Britain, Austria, and France, signed early in January 1815. Acceptance of the tsar's modified ambitions for Poland (in which some Polish territory went to both Austria and Prussia) brought him around to supporting a compromise on Saxony. France was admitted to a reconstituted committee of five; the five worked their way through to a division of Saxon territory that left part of it an independent kingdom and annexed part of it to Prussia.

While the negotiators were making gradual progress on specific provisions of the treaty, the congress was shaken by the news that on March 1 Napoleon had crossed from Elba to France and had begun a triumphal progress toward Paris. Old soldiers flocked to his standard, and by the middle of the month he was in the capital, forming a new government. Louis XVIII fled to Ghent. Of Napoleon's former allies, only Murat in Naples, who had long been negotiating with the Austrians to preserve his throne, rallied to the emperor—a decision that was to cost Murat his life. In Paris, despite the enthusiasm that had greeted him, Napoleon found much opinion dead set against the resurrection of the Napoleonic autocracy, especially since what passed for a liberal constitution had been drawn up at Alexander's insistence by the Bourbons. Napoleon responded with his own very similar constitution and assured the world that he intended to live at peace with his neighbors.

The assurance was lost on the allies at Vienna. Armies were hastily summoned, Napoleon took the field against them, and on June 18, near the Flemish village of Waterloo, Napoleon was beaten after a three-day battle. It was a narrow decision: Napoleon just failed to drive out Wellington's army and was finally routed with the last-minute help of a Prussian army under Marshal Blücher. The defeat was decisive, and after briefly toying with the idea of a dictatorship, Napoleon abdicated in favor of his son, Napoleon II. The child-king was not without supporters, but the threatened descent of the allied forces on the capital put a stop to any hesitation, and on July 8, Louis XVIII was back in his palace. Napoleon was allowed to escape to the west-coast port of Rochefort where he surrendered to the English, throwing himself on the mercy of the prince regent. After a few days on board ship in Plymouth, he was embarked on H.M.S. *Bellerophon* for the lonely island of St. Helena in the south Atlantic, where he survived a prisoner until 1821, reviewing his errors and triumphs, and spinning a legend that would stir France for fifty years and more.

The Hundred Days necessitated a new treaty of peace with France. The feelings of generosity that had inspired the first Treaty of Paris were gone from the second, concluded on November 20, 1815, which reduced France to the frontiers of 1790, transferred the Saar to Prussia, and required that France be occupied by one hundred fifty thousand troops for three to five years and pay an indemnity of 700 million francs. The new treaty was reinforced by a renewed Quadruple Alliance among the four big victorious powers. Two months earlier, however, Alexander I, from the depths of his religious conviction, had persuaded the emperor of Austria and the king of Prussia to join him in a Treaty of Holy Alliance. It was no more than an agreement that the public acts of the monarchs would be in accordance with the principles of Christianity; Castlereagh called it a "piece of sublime mysticism and nonsense." The Holy Alliance had no direct practical effect, but the fact that it was signed by the three reactionary rulers of eastern Europe made it a bogey to most liberal-minded men, the more so as they saw those rulers often acting together. The Quadruple Alliance (later expanded by adding France) was the real basis for the Concert of Europe in the postwar years, but confusion of the Concert of Europe with the Holy Alliance—by contemporaries and by historians since—gave the postwar settlement an evil reputation it did not deserve.

It has been common to discuss the provisions of the Congress of Vienna in terms of principles, some honored, some honored in the breach, and some ignored. Talleyrand, naturally, argued the case for the principle of legitimacy—the restoration of rightful rulers—which was applied in France and Naples, but legitimacy was not enforced in the many small states that simply disappeared, particularly in Germany. The force of nationalism was clearly flouted by many arrangements and is often evoked by critics of the congress; but to have recognized it would have required superhuman imagination from statesmen raised in the eighteenth century.[19] That the balance of power should be restored, that France should be isolated, that states which had lost territory to settle European problems should be compensated are not so much principles as the practical essentials of diplomatic negotiation. To be sure, there were some forward-looking provisions—an agreement on internationalizing rivers and another to put a stop to the slave trade, though the latter had to be fought for by Castlereagh, under pressure from home, and extracted from an unwilling France. The first and only plenary session at Vienna, held just before Waterloo, ratified a series of decisions that were eminently pragmatic. Taken within the limitations of the age, they were directed to solving one great problem—to destroy the Napoleonic threat and ensure against its revival—and a host of refractory conflicts of the kind that arise in any reconstruction after a major war. Some solutions worked, others did not. But the shape of Europe was by and large determined for more than a generation, and men were enabled to turn their attention to the far more novel and perplexing problems of a world at peace.

[19] For a discussion of nationalism, see Ch. 16.

SELECTED READINGS

The most extensive survey of the Napoleonic era is Georges Lefebvre, *Napoleon,* 2 vols. (1935, tr. 1969), by one of the modern masters. A briefer work of the same vintage is Geoffrey Bruun, *Europe and the French Imperium, 1799-1814* (1938), in the Langer series. More recent, though with the disadvantage of composite works, are the relevant chapters in *The New Cambridge Modern History,* vol. 9, *War and Peace in an Age of Upheaval, 1793-1830,* ed., C. W. Crawley (1965).

The best biography of Napoleon is J. M. Thompson, *Napoleon Bonaparte: His Rise and Fall* (1952). J. C. Herold's *The Mind of Napoleon* (1955) is drawn from the emperor's own words, and the same author's *Bonaparte in Egypt* (1962) deals with an episode of unusual interest. On the military side, David G. Chandler's massive and authoritative *The Campaigns of Napoleon* (1966). The fascinating legacy of Napoleon is dealt with in A. L. Guerard, *Reflections on the Napoleonic Legend* (1924) and, from a different perspective, Pieter Geyl, *Napoleon: For and Against* (1949), a study of changing views among French historians.

Owen Connelly's *Napoleon's Satellite Kingdoms* (1965) is a useful survey, and the same author has written a biography of Joseph Bonaparte under the apt title *The Gentle Bonaparte* (1968). Eli Heckscher, *The Continental System* (1922), is a study by a major economic historian. Narrower but highly sophisticated and absolutely conclusive is a formidable statistical study of the effect of the system on Britain by François Crouzet, *L'économie britannique et le blocus continental, 1806-1813,* 2 vols. (1958); it has not yet been translated. For Spain, in addition to the Connelly books, G. H. Lovett, *Napoleon and the Birth of Modern Spain,* 2 vols. (1965), is the fullest treatment, but the appropriate chapters in Raymond Carr, *Spain, 1808-1939* (1966), are excellent. On Austria, besides the general surveys of Macartney and Taylor, there are two European works on Metternich: H. Ritter von Srbik, *Metternich, der Staatsmann und der Mensch,* 2 vols. (1925), a favorable view not translated; and G. Bertier de Sauvigny, *Metternich and his Times* (1959, tr. 1962), which places that key Austrian statesman in his European setting.

On the German situation, beyond the chapters in the second volume of Hajo Holborn's general history, the best starting place is H. A. L. Fisher, *Studies in Napoleonic Statesmanship: Germany* (1903, reprinted 1968)—detailed, charmingly written, and, despite its age, authoritative. Gerhard Ritter's *Stein, eine politische Biographie* (1931, 3rd ed., 1958) remains untranslated; for an English life of the great reformer one must go back to Guy Stanton Ford, *Stein and the Era of Reform in Prussia, 1807-1815* (1922). There are valuable institutional and critical studies of Prussian reforms of more recent date: Walter M. Simon, *The Failure of the Prussian Reform Movement, 1807-1819* (1955); W. O. Shanahan, *Prussian Military Reforms, 1786-1813* (1945), and Peter Paret, *Yorck and the Era of Prussian Reform* (1966). On the intellectual background there are the chapters on the period in Leonard Krieger, *The German Idea of Freedom: History of a Political Tradition* (1957); see, too, Klaus Epstein, *The Genesis of German Conservatism* (1966), both cited before.

For Russian history in the Napoleonic era, the greatest need is for a major study of Alexander I, but much can be learned about him as well as about his principal servants in Marc Raeff, *Michael Speransky, Statesman of Imperial Russia, 1772-1839* (1957) and Patricia Kennedy Grimsted, *The Foreign Ministers of Alexander I* (1970). E. V. Tarlé, *Napoleon's Invasion of Russia, 1812* (1938, tr. 1942), is by a Soviet scholar. E. J. Knapton, *The Lady of the Holy Alliance* (1939) is of interest for the religious history of the period, but this life of the Baroness de Krüdener also touches an important side of Alexander's complex personality.

No better introduction can be found to Britain at the opening of the new century than Elie Halévy, *England in 1815* (1913, tr. 1924, and reprinted under this shortened title in 1949); it is the first volume of his masterpiece, *A History of the English People in the Nineteenth Century,* and provides a superb retrospective view of the nation and its institutions as well as a provocative interpretation of English stability in a period of revolution. The old two-volume biography of William Pitt by J. Holland Rose is now being replaced by a new life by John Ehrman, but only the first volume, *The Younger Pitt: The Years of Acclaim* (1969), covering the period to 1789, has appeared. Elizabeth Longford's *Wellington: The Years of the Sword* (1969) is the most recent biographical essay, but Wellington still awaits a major, definitive study by the lucky scholar who has a lifetime to give to the subject. The best starting point for radicalism in the period is E. P. Thompson's passionate and partisan *The Making of the English Working Class* (1963), to which should be added Carl B. Cone, *The English Jacobins: Reformers in Late 18th-Century England* (1968), cited above.

Studies of the 1815 settlement—in addition to E. Saunders, *The Hundred Days* (1964), an account of the momentous interruption of negotiations—must begin with C. K. Webster's remarkable sketch, *The Congress of Vienna, 1814-1815* (1919). A more recent work, E. V. Gulick, *Europe's Classical Balance of Power: A Case History of the Theory and Practice of One of the Great Concepts of European Statecraft* (1955) is helpful in disentangling some of the intricacies of the settlement and sets them in a schematic context.

13

The Legacy
of Revolution:
1815-1832

UNITY IN REACTION

The Congress of Vienna, like other great peace settlements before and since, has given its date, 1815, the status of a major turning point in history. But wars speed up change, and the settlements that end them end little else; they transmit to the next generation the challenge of coping with the legacy of the war years. That legacy differed widely in the different European countries after 1815, as did ways of dealing with it. Nor were the results uniform. In some countries an explosion came early, in others late, in still others not at all. But the threat of explosion was felt everywhere. Governments therefore united in their determination to prevent war by maintaining the balance of power and to preserve what remained of the social and political structure of Europe from further revolution and its consequences.

Any historical narrative of these decades poses a problem in political rhetoric and political theory. The accident of the seating arrangements of the Convention in 1792 (see p. 482), confirmed after 1814, has given us the metaphor of a political spectrum ranging in imperceptible gradations from Left to Right. But superimposed on this image, and not always congruent with it, is a far more substantive and subtle shift from the reactionary and conservative on one side to the liberal and radical on the other. These terms will appear frequently throughout this book. Sometimes they will be capitalized to indicate organized groups or political parties; sometimes they will be changed into "isms" to denote clusters of more or less consistent attitudes and policies that may end in dogma; sometimes they will be used simply as adjectives, often enough loosely. However much care historians may exercise, a political or social inclination is not always susceptible to precise terminology.

The specific content of such terms varies from country to country, even from individual to individual, and over time as well. Thus an admirer of English institutions in early nineteenth-century Prussia or in Restoration France would in all probability be a moderate liberal, well to the right of those radicals who admired the republicanism of the Convention, the moral stringencies of Robespierre, or the state-enforced egalitarianism of Babeuf. In countries such as Spain or Russia, which lacked representative institutions and suffered from economic backwardness and cultural obscurantism, liberal ideas took on the appearance of exotic growths, and it was left to radicals to advocate goals that were rapidly becoming commonplaces among unadventurous liberals in more advanced countries. Britain, the most liberal society in Europe, spawned an astonishing variety of radicalisms, compounded of long-submerged memories of resistance to the established order, of religious dissent, of admiration for American republicanism, and of class ambition. Yet much of what British radicals called for would seem impossibly conservative to socialists or even members of the Liberal party in present-day Britain; and what a mid-twentieth-century American might call liberal (a highly idiosyncratic usage, by the way) would almost certainly have been anathema to European liberals in the 1820s.

The root meanings of these political tags are worth recalling. A reactionary seeks a return to the past, as always the most utopian of dreams; a conservative concedes that some change is inevitable and seeks to temper it by conserving what is best in his inheritance. The term radical, deriving from the Latin word for root, bespeaks a determination to get back to first principles, to the root of things, and even to root out what is evil or constricting in established institutions; thus, in the nineteenth century, republicanism of the American or French variety was likely to be espoused by most radicals, at least on the Continent. But of all these words, liberal is the most protean and misleading. It signifies a concern with freedom, true, but there was no agreement on what the notion of freedom included. A liberal in economic doctrine might be either conservative or radical in his political and social views. While most liberals shared a belief in constitutions and limited monarchy, some advocated a sharp restriction of the role of the state and others, believing freedom to be more than leaving each man to pursue his own best interest, called for expanded state activity to make men free. Liberals could be stubborn and corrosive or compromising and bland, but—perhaps because their consistency lay in temperament rather than programs—they could frequently bring conservatives and radicals into strange but passionate alliances against them. There are, then, no easy answers or universally valid formulas. And it is in the three decades or so after 1815, as these terms came into general use, that their ambiguities were made manifest.

Great Britain: 1815-1822

Great Britain was a special case in the postwar years. The country treasured a political tradition that stretched back without a major break at least to the Revolution of 1688 and owed most of its institutions to a much more remote past. Englishmen prided themselves on a constitution they believed was balanced and free. The balance of which they spoke was between the king (who still ruled, though his powers were slipping away), the House of Lords, and an unrepresentative House of Commons; the freedom, though unquestioned legal fact, varied widely with one's income, status, and stake in society. In fact both central and local governments reflected the dominance of a narrow oligarchy. The functions of the central government were seen as strictly limited; there was little modern bureaucratic machinery, although some useful steps toward creating it had been taken during the war. In the localities, government rested with the country gentlemen and parsons who served as justices of the peace or with the often narrow-minded merchants who maintained their grip on unadventurous town corporations. What imaginativeness there was in social policy, as in the economy, was likely to come from private individuals—from businessmen, from a few intellectuals, from those enlightened citizens who formed new quasi-governmental bodies to better their towns, or from individuals or voluntary societies impelled by charity and humanitarianism. The political discontent that had flourished briefly in the 1770s and 1780s re-emerged after the war; it now flowed beyond the respectable classes to which it had been confined earlier and grew in urgency among the working classes because of the social and economic consequences of profound economic change. Yet the dominant mood in the country was one of thankfulness that Britain had escaped revolution and of determination (sparked by deep-seated fear) that there would be none. It would take time to learn that reforms were the best preventive.

Meanwhile, Britain's rulers tended to stick with inherited ways of doing things and with sporadic, more or less ineffectual, repressiveness as the means of dealing with discontent. Naturally, men in power or with influence on power were able to get what they wanted. In 1815 a parliament heavily dominated by landowners quickly passed a Corn Law to keep out foreign grain and to maintain the agricultural prosperity that had come with the war. In the next year the hated income tax was swept away, leaving the government to cope with a vast deficit that retention of the tax might have made manageable. But demands from workingmen to be protected from the competition of less-skilled workers went unheeded or were lost in the gulf that was growing between classes.

The cessation of wartime demand, accumulated surpluses, dislocation of markets, demobilization, and novel, uncomprehended phenomena such as the business cycle made the immediate postwar years a time of extreme difficulty. Disturbances, still responsive to preindustrial rhythms of good and bad harvests, broke out in 1816, 1817, and 1819. Some of the protest belonged to a tradition that ran back to medieval peasant revolts. Some of it was rooted in undoubted rights of Englishmen: for example, the right to meet to discuss grievances and the right to petition. But, through a cheap working-class press and the appeal of some remarkable demagogues, the political ambitions revealed in the scattered outbreaks were gradually harnessed for the cause of parliamentary reform, the cause that middle-class malcontents adhered to.

On August 16, 1819, a meeting was held in St. Peter's Fields in the northern textile center of Manchester to petition for parliamentary reform. The nervous magistrates ordered the arrest of the speaker, the famous orator Henry Hunt; the task was perforce assigned to incompetent amateurs in the local militia, for there were no police. The yeomanry struck with their swords, panic ensued, and eleven people were killed and hundreds injured. The Peterloo Massacre—so-called in ironic reference to the victory at Waterloo—scandalized the liberal-minded and created martyrs for the cause of reform. The massacre reflects, however, neither malevolence nor systematic repression by Britain's rulers. Rather, it reveals an overburdened central government and inadequate, incompetent machinery for law enforcement, both operating in traditional ways and guided by sharply constricted imagination.[1] Shortly after, the government carried the so-called Six Acts, which, in addition to speeding up trials, prohibited military drilling by civilians, temporarily restricted the right to bear arms, laid down a code for public meetings, and imposed new controls on the press. It was the high-water mark of English reaction.

In 1820 George III died and was succeeded by the prince regent as George IV, a fading roué, timid, petulant, and highly unpopular. Political discontent came to be concentrated on the monarch because he lacked admirable personal qualities and because men knew that, since his much-admired daughter Princess Charlotte had died in childbirth in 1817, his loathsome brothers would probably succeed him. This hostility was given a new focus in 1820, when the

---

[1] The home secretary, the minister principally responsible for coping with such matters, was Lord Sidmouth, who, as Henry Addington, had been prime minister when the younger Pitt was out of office in 1801–1804. He was a competent administrator within his limitations, but cautious and harried—hardly one of the monsters that contemporary radical propaganda made him and his cabinet colleagues out to be. R. J. White, in *Waterloo to Peterloo* (1957), suggests the rapid changes that left eighteenth-century men confronting nineteenth-century problems by pointing out that one member of Lord Liverpool's cabinet was robbed of his watch by a highwayman in 1786, while another was run over by a locomotive in 1830.

king forced his ministers to introduce a bill in Parliament divorcing him from his ugly, earthy wife, Caroline of Brunswick, whom he hated. Caroline, who had been leading a rather unsavory life on the Continent, returned to claim her rights as queen, and her cause was taken up by Whigs (who considered their onetime friend the king a turncoat), liberals, and radicals. So powerful was the resentment that the divorce bill had to be withdrawn, and the agitation around Caroline survived until her death in 1821. Surely few liberal causes can have coalesced around so unlikely a symbol. Yet that agitation, like the Cato Street Conspiracy of 1820—a plot hatched by a group of half-mad radicals to murder the members of the cabinet—lacked the fundamental seriousness of Peterloo. By 1822, with the return of better times, the liberal impulses that were working within Lord Liverpool's government could surface. Lord Sidmouth, the home secretary, retired, and Lord Castlereagh—that lonely architect of the European settlement—vilified and worn out, cut his own throat.

Russia: 1815-1825

The idiosyncrasy of the British situation lay in Britain's slowly evolving but still archaic institutions and in its grip, only temporarily relaxed, on an essentially liberal tradition. An equal or greater idiosyncrasy was to be found at the other extreme of Europe, in Russia, where archaic, inefficient institutions showed little sign of evolving and were tied to a powerful tradition of autocracy.

To be sure, the emperor Alexander I granted a constitution for his new Polish kingdom late in 1815; it was drafted by the tsar's old, relatively liberal friend Prince Adam Czartoryski. The gesture was more liberal than the fact, however. A ministerial council of state ruled, while the diet *(sejm)* composed of a senate of bishops and aristocratic representatives and a chamber of deputies representing towns and countryside, could only examine legislation laid before it, not introduce it. The Russian presence was maintained by occasional appearances of the tsar, who was personally popular; by an imperial commissioner; and by the tsar's eldest brother, Grand Duke Constantine, who commanded the Polish army and who ultimately chose to stay in Poland rather than succeed to the imperial throne. The imperial commissioner, N. N. Novosiltsev, another early liberal adviser to Alexander, quarreled with Czartoryski, who thereafter devoted himself to education and particularly to sustaining the admirable university at Vilna. The tsar's hints that the Poles might expect more concessions, particularly the restoration of Lithuania to Poland, came to nothing. The resulting frustration stimulated a fervid though largely impractical nationalism among Polish nobles and intellectuals, who at the outset had preferred Russian patronage to the restoration of Prussian and Austrian rule.

Alexander suggested that the Polish constitutional experiment might be repeated on a larger scale in Russia; he secretly commissioned the drafting of another Russian constitution in 1819, but it was never put into effect. The notion may have been little more than the reflex action of a vestigial commitment to liberal reform; more probably it suggests that Alexander's "constitutionalism" had from the start been no more than a concern with making his autocracy orderly and efficient. After 1812 the tsar's involvement in religion and reaction had grown steadily deeper, though his religious concerns were not without liberal aspects. The founding of the Bible Society in 1812, on the English model, led to a new translation of the Bible into modern Russian, and the society sponsored a number of schools, which borrowed their instructional techniques (with older children teaching younger) from England. The tsar's mystical bent also led to a toleration of different religions and an enthusiasm for Freemasonry, that eighteenth-century movement of liberally inclined secret societies. But far more revealing was the tsar's reliance on his chief religious advisor, Prince A. N. Golitsyn, who, as senior procurator of the Holy Synod almost from the beginning of the reign, ruled the Russian Orthodox church.

In 1816 Golitsyn also took on the responsibility for the educational system. Though benevolently inclined, like his master, toward sectarian, even enthusiastic, religious expression, Golitsyn was a disaster for Russian universities. They were systematically purged, and teaching was confined to the narrowest biblical grounds. When Golitsyn fell from favor in 1823 because he was so distrusted by the Orthodox church, the ministry of education was separated from the supervision of religious affairs. But responsibility for education was given to Admiral A. S. Shishkov, the most notable opponent of modernizing the Russian language; he held even more obscurantist views on education and strengthened the censorship machinery that was to play so important a role in the succeeding reign.

In other domestic affairs the tsar worked chiefly through his old adviser and friend, Count A. A. Arakcheev. Arakcheev and his subordinates had to cope with finances disordered by the war and with the usual reshuffling of duties among various ministries that passes for administrative reform in governments determined to do nothing. The problem of serfdom was as intractable as ever. Between 1811 and 1819 landless serfs in the Baltic provinces were given their legal freedom; denied voluntary support by landowners, however, their condition worsened. Like the Polish constitution, this experiment may also have been intended for larger application in Russia, but it was not followed up. The one large-scale social reform attempted by Arakcheev, apparently at Alexander's instigation, was the institution of military colonies. Soldiers were settled in villages of serfs and set to farming and handicrafts. In this way the government expected to save money and trouble in keeping up the military establishment, to improve farming, and generally to better the welfare of the inhabitants, soldiers and serfs alike; almost a million people were involved. But, though visitors were impressed, the colonies were hideous and hated. Because civilians other than serfs were kept out, landlords and merchants had to be dispossessed to make way for the colonies and they were insufficiently compensated. The soldiers did not like farming, and the serfs were subjected to brutal military discipline. After a hard day's work peasants resented being regimented in the interests of better health and welfare, ideas that were in any event beyond their comprehension.

What opposition there was in the reign of Alexander I grew up among younger army officers. Drawn from the aristocratic class, educated, and exposed during the Napoleonic Wars to the progressive ideas of western Europe, they had little outlet for their ambitions and their hopes for Russia other than the forming of secret societies. Much encouraged by reports of revolutions in Spain and Italy in 1820, these societies coalesced into two groups, one in the north, one in the south. Both produced draft constitutions and manifestos of reform; among them was an extremely radical social program devised by Colonel Pavel Pestel, the son of a governor general of Siberia, who became the leader of the southern group. By the end of the reign the reformers were in touch with secret societies in Poland and among the Slavs in Turkish-held territories to the southwest. But Alexander and Arakcheev had also learned a lesson from the revolutions of 1820; they were perhaps even more impressed by a mutiny in a crack St. Petersburg regiment in that same year. The tsar began to suspect a deep international revolutionary conspiracy.

By 1823 the societies were contemplating action, even the assassination of the tsar; they expected a revolution to take place in 1826. Suddenly, at the end of November 1825, Alexander died, leaving the succession in doubt. His own stated preference was for his younger brother Nicholas. Nicholas prudently acknowledged the prior claims of Grand Duke Constantine; but after Constantine rejected the crown and amid reports of conspiracies, Nicholas had himself proclaimed emperor and ordered oaths taken on December 14. The northern societies decided to act quickly by attempting to win over army units in the capital. A few thousand troops who were assembled in Senate Square in St. Petersburg refused to take the oath to Nicholas; after some fruitless attempts at persuasion, Nicholas ordered the rebels fired upon. They fled and, except for a small rising in the south at the very end of the month, the Decembrist Revolt was finished. Five of its leaders, including Pestel, were executed. The capital sentences of thirty-one others were commuted to hard labor, and eighty-seven were sent as exiles to Siberia. But many escaped with no punishment at all. Pathetic and noble, the little movement was completely divorced from the realities of Russian society and from the facts of power, which alone can give force to the invocation of ideals. The historical importance of the revolt derives from its legacy of martyrs to a long succession of Russian revolutionary movements and, more immediately, from the pretext it gave to the new emperor to rivet an even more autocratic regime upon his people.

Reaction in Austria and the Germanies

The German lands of Europe were more deeply, if variously, affected by the French Revolution and Napoleon than were Britain or Russia. But there too, though many reforms had been adopted in the national revival during the Napoleonic Wars and some of them remained, the postwar years were a time of increasing reaction.

Reaction could hardly have deepened in Austria, where immobility had been the cardinal virtue since the accession of Francis I in 1792. The years after 1815 were not easy. They brought bad harvests, inflation, the burden of demobilization, and the undercutting of a protected wartime prosperity by the appearance of English manufactured goods and grain from eastern Europe and Russia. Yet only in Hungary, traditionally restive under the Hapsburg yoke, were there suggestions of difficulties; protests in 1811–1812 against ham-handed efforts to cope with an inflated currency had led to a dissolution of the Hungarian diet, which was not summoned again until 1825. Even Austria's new Italian possessions remained relatively quiet in the troubled year of 1820. This general calm was due in part to Austria's emergence from the war as a victor, with most of its old lands restored and some important new territories (in northern Italy in particular) added. Both exhaustion and relief underlay the comfortable, bourgeois style in literature, art, and interior decoration that we have come to know as Biedermeier and that took hold in most of the German lands in the years after the war. But the lack of adventurousness in ideas as well as taste also reflects the powerful weapons of censorship and educational surveillance, which, by keeping Austria and its dependencies quiet, left Prince Metternich, the Austrian chancellor, free to pursue his role as the guarantor of order in Europe.

Charming, punctilious, intensely hardworking, the perfect courtier and the perfect bureaucrat, Metternich complemented his emperors in every aspect of their obstinate immobility. Intelligent and well-informed, perceptive and ingenious, he was an admirable diplomatic tactician, though less than completely admirable as a statesman. He was timid, and his imagination was constricted by opportunism. He was convinced that, while some rare souls (such as the English statesman George Canning) might fly into realms unknown to most men, it was his calling to walk in the prosaic regions of ordinary human action—boring perhaps, but sound. He saw the dangers that lay in any encouragement of revolution or nationality: the Austrian Empire was a political and ethnic monstrosity that Francis I himself called "a worm-eaten house"; to remove or shake any of its parts might bring the whole crashing down. Discouraging or exterminating dangerous principles would, Metternich hoped, maintain the empire and the system for his time and perhaps forever. Magnificently concealing whatever doubts he felt, he acted like a man utterly certain of his rightness. Canning, and those like him, he said a little ruefully, might fall and recover themselves twenty times; he was sure that he need never recover because his common sense would not allow him to fall. He dominated Austria and Europe for nearly forty years and was the symbol of the old regime against which the revolutionary impulse repeatedly hurled itself and over which, in 1848, it briefly triumphed.

Other German states remained absolutist in form and action but varied in the degree to which they retained Napoleonic alterations. The states that had made up the kingdom of Westphalia—Hanover (since 1815 back in the possession of the king of Great Britain), Brunswick, and Hesse—reverted to their old ways of doing things, from which Napoleon's erstwhile ally Saxony had never departed. Much of the Rhineland was now incorporated in Prussia, and its postwar history is concerned with that amalgamation. But in the new or enlarged states of south Germany—chief among them Bavaria, Württemberg, and Baden—constitutions, along the lines of the French Charter, were granted as a way to ensure effective national cohesion.

Prussia had absorbed or begun a number of important reforms in the political, social, and military spheres; the military alterations were climaxed by the adoption of universal military service in 1814. But, in contrast to the Napoleonic era, the postwar period in Prussia was largely one of regression. The Declaration of 1816 altered arrangements for the ending of serfdom much to the advantage of the landlords and speeded the conversion of serfs into laborers rather than landholding peasants. The provincial estates survived as highly conservative bodies, but, despite the appointment of Wilhelm von Humboldt as a special minister for constitutional matters, no national legislature was created and no constitution was granted. The dismissal of Humboldt in 1819 removed the last prominent spokesman for the Stein tradition; between 1815 and his death in 1822, Hardenberg, the chancellor, was increasingly isolated and complaisant. Frederick William III, restored to his natural timidity now that the wartime crisis had passed, preferred to associate with like-minded Junkers and to submit to direction from Metternich.

One new institution appeared in Germany in 1815—the Germanic Confederation, composed, under a constitution that was part of the Vienna settlement, of thirty-five states and four free cities. The eastern provinces of Prussia and the non-German lands belonging to Austria were excluded, and the foreign rulers whose possessions were included (the kings of Great Britain, Holland, and Denmark) were not bound by the pledge of mutual military aid. The Confederation was not an incipient nation but an international organization, a body essentially diplomatic in conception and function. The federal diet in Frankfurt could meet (but did so very rarely) as a plenary council, with members' votes weighted from one to four. The usual organ for Confederation business was a select council, composed for voting purposes of eleven large states and seven groups of small states; the presidency invariably went to Austria. In 1821 a common military force was organized, but little else that was forward-looking was done beyond an agreement on copyright and a guarantee, extracted by Hardenberg and Metternich, of the civil rights of Jews; otherwise, the rights of individuals were left up to the member states.

To at least a small degree, the Confederation gave political expression to a growing sentiment in favor of a unified Germany. But that sentiment found its most important expression in German intellectual life and, above all, in the universities. There the new student associations, the *Burschenschaften*, though they still countenanced the practice of dueling as proof of the students' commitment to honor, were far more serious and political than were their eighteenth-century counterparts. The first of these organizations had been founded at the University of Jena in 1815, under the influence of Ludwig Jahn, whose vigorous nationalism had found unusual expression in gymnastic organizations.[2] In 1817 the Jena students organized a demonstration at Wartburg Castle in honor of the three-hundredth anniversary of the Reformation; in restaging Luther's burning of the papal bull they burned a paper containing the names of certain reactionary authors. The alarm that this innocent demonstration caused the German governments turned to panic in 1819, when a weak-minded student named Karl Ludwig Sand, fired up by the defense of tyrannicide by a university lecturer named Karl Follen, assassinated the playwright August von Kotzebue, once a Russian official, now a Russian agent in Germany. Sand was executed, Jahn was arrested, professors were carefully watched, and Metternich persuaded the Prussian king that joint action must be taken to stamp out disorder in the universities.

The result was the Karlsbad Decrees, which imposed censorship of the press, called for regular surveillance of the universities and the removal of teachers unsympathetic to existing institutions, and set up a central investigating commission under the Confederation. Agreed upon by the major states in September 1819, the decrees were quickly forced through the Frankfurt diet and became law throughout the Confederation; they were ratified once more in the so-called Final Act of Vienna in 1820, a new fundamental law of the Confederation. Though this new legislation stemmed open dissent throughout the Confederation and strengthened Austria's hand, Metternich had to back down on one point: the south German states were allowed to keep their constitutions and legislatures, which Metternich and his adviser, Friedrich Gentz, had seen as un-German contradictions of the monarchical principle.

The results were predictable. The *Burschenschaften* were dissolved and replaced by more traditional clubs or, not very effectively, by secret societies; the universities capitulated and professors who had been politically active retreated into scholarship; some liberals went into exile;[3] what constitutional bodies remained in south Germany were drained of life. Social and political discontent was thus allowed to smolder below the surface of a placid, unadventurous society, with no way of venting itself but revolution.

[2] Called *Turnverein*, hence the sobriquet *Turnvater* Jahn, in recognition of his having fathered the groups.

[3] Karl Follen, the defender of tyrannicide, after being dismissed from the University of Jena in 1820 and from the Swiss University of Basel in 1823, emigrated to the United States, where he became the first professor of German at Harvard. The pattern was repeated again. He was dismissed from Harvard for his antislavery activities in 1835 and spent the rest of his life as a Unitarian minister and reformer.

France: 1815-1824

While Great Britain, the one inherently liberal nation in Europe, subordinated its main tradition to fear of revolution, France absorbed the legacy of the Revolution and constructed a limited, temperate system that managed to survive in essence for more than thirty years. This most important of restorations gave France time to recover from her heady dalliance with glory and to escape into the workaday world of the nineteenth century. That the confused transition was as successful as it was is surely due, more than to any other single person, to the restored king, Louis XVIII, the brother of Louis XVI. Nearly sixty at the time of his restoration and prematurely aging, this fat, unenergetic widower brought to his task goodwill and a determination to do the best he could for France. He had a reasonably acute judgment of men and events, and his natural placidity (born of self-confidence) often made him the quiet center of the storm. To these qualities, for the delectation of historians, he added (at his best) a gift for epigrammatic phrases and (at his worst) a facility for bad puns. Conciliatory though he was, on one point Louis was adamant. When a loyal supporter rushed to him with the great news, "Sire, you are king of France," he inquired icily, "Have I ever ceased to be?" In his own view the year 1814, when he ascended the throne, was the nineteenth year of his reign, dated from the mysterious disappearance of his imprisoned nephew Louis XVII; the crown he inherited was his by divine right; and what concessions he made to the intervening years or to political reality were made by grace and not in recognition of allied demands or the claims of popular sovereignty.

The issue was joined in the very terms of the Senate's proclamation. They had called Louis XVIII to the throne freely and on condition that he accept the charter, the constitution they had drafted, at their hands. "M. de Talleyrand," said the king some time later, "if I had taken an oath to that constitution, you would be sitting and I would be standing." Determined to sit, the king ingeniously dismissed the Senate's charter, arguing that its hasty drafting had left it an imperfect document; he thereupon called together the two houses of the legislature to accept a charter given of *his* free will. This charter too was a hasty production, but it did both what was necessary and what was possible. It made concessions to the Revolution by granting the rights of 1789—equality before the law, individual freedom, and freedom of thought and religion—and by allowing lands once owned by nobles and the church, confiscated by the Revolution and later purchased in good faith, to remain with their purchasers. It made peace with the Napoleonic era by carrying over intact the civil code and the centralized administrative system; titles, pensions, and decorations (such as the Legion of Honor) were retained. The state accepted all prior financial obligations, and men were promised amnesty and protection from inquisition into their thoughts or actions prior to the Restoration. There were some notable limitations. Although freedom of religion was granted and nothing was said in the Charter (as had been said in the Napoleonic concordat) about Roman

Catholicism being the religion of the great majority of Frenchmen, Catholicism was declared the state religion. Liberty of the press was potentially threatened by the requirement that published opinions conform to laws prohibiting abuses of that liberty. But on neither of these points were the British any more advanced. Nor, although the British electorate was larger (and, by virtue of its dependence on different kinds of property-holding, far more complex), was there any difference of principle between the two countries on the propriety of limiting the right to vote. Under the Charter, only those paying three hundred francs a year in direct taxes (i.e., only wealthy landlords and very wealthy bourgeois) could vote, and deputies were required to pay one thousand francs in taxes and to be at least forty years old.

The executive power was entrusted to the king; the ministers, who could sit in either chamber and could be impeached, were responsible to him alone. The legislative power was declared to rest with the king, the Chamber of Peers, and the Chamber of Deputies. The king (or his ministers) proposed laws, which they introduced in either chamber (except tax bills, which had to go to the deputies first) and which the king alone promulgated. The consent of both chambers was required for taxation, and the Charter's requirement of annual sessions was assured by limiting authorization of the land tax to one year. The king created peers; retained the right to prorogue or dissolve the Chamber of Deputies, subject to the convening of a new chamber within three months; and appointed judges, who could not be dismissed.

Historians have always spoken vaguely about an English model for this French Charter, but they have insufficiently noticed how exactly the main outlines of Restoration government reflected the theory and practice of English government in 1814. It would be at least twenty years before, in any practical way, cabinet ministers in England would be responsible to the House of Commons rather than to the king; and it would be perhaps fifty years before most Englishmen would realize that the vaunted balance of the constitution had given way to the governance of the nation by Parliament and the Commons in particular. A few minor matters aside, the chief difference between the French and English constitutions was that the French Charter set its provisions down in writing and, so to speak, froze them; English institutions and practices remained free to evolve almost unnoticed into the modern forms of parliamentary government, while official rhetoric remained stuck in 1688.

Napoleon's return to power in 1815 interrupted the progress of pacification, forced more humiliating peace terms on France, and inevitably brought demands that the guilty collaborators in the Hundred Days be exempted from the promised amnesty. Indeed, the whole question was raised again of whether the Bourbons should be brought back, for some sentiment favored Napoleon's son or the junior (Orleans) branch of the Bourbon family. That a second restoration took place is owing primarily to the astonishing activities of one man, Joseph Fouché, who had helped condemn Louis XVI to death, rose to become Napoleon's minister of police, returned to that office in the Hundred

Days, and remained to assure—by an extraordinary combination of imagination, deceit, trickery, and realism—the return of Louis XVIII and his own place (as duke of Otranto) in the king's ministry. Fouché even drew up a list of men who were to suffer for their complicity in the Hundred Days; he deserved credit for one thing, Talleyrand remarked maliciously—"he did not forget any of his friends in drawing up the list."

For a time in the summer of 1815, France was subjected not only to the outrages committed by the occupying troops (of whom the Prussians were the worst) but also to a "white terror" in the south, a spontaneous royalist quest for revenge against individuals who had collaborated with the revolutionary and Napoleonic regimes. Fouché hoped to capitalize on the reaction to such excesses by reversing field and appealing to the latent or open liberal sympathies in the country. He and Talleyrand thought they would get a Chamber of Deputies sympathetic to their opportunistic mixture of royalism and liberalism in the elections in August 1815. The elections were held in such haste, however, that no new electoral law had been passed; so they were conducted according to the Napoleonic electoral system, but with the restrictive qualifications for voting laid down in the Charter. The result was a Chamber of Deputies more royalist than the king, who called it, with a certain delight, *la Chambre introuvable*—the Chamber one could hardly have expected to find. The Chamber was determined to have done with the regicide Fouché and the apostate bishop Talleyrand. Talleyrand quickly got Fouché out of the way by sending him on a diplomatic mission while he himself, anticipating his dismissal, resigned in September, never to return to power.

Talleyrand was succeeded as president of the council (or prime minister) by a great and respected nobleman, the duke de Richelieu, an émigré who had entered the service of the tsar and became governor general of the southern provinces of Russia captured from the Turks in the time of Catherine the Great. Elie Decazes, who had risen to become prefect of police in Paris under the patronage of Fouché, took his master's place as minister of police and quickly ingratiated himself with the king, who became devoted to him. Decazes was both indispensable to the king and intolerable to the Chamber; and, because the government had great difficulty in accomplishing anything—either in moderating violence or getting government business transacted with that intractable body—Louis XVIII dissolved the Chamber in September 1816. He would not accept dictation from the legislature as to who his ministers should be.

There were three points to the political compass of the Restoration, and each attracted men of uncommon ability. The ultraroyalists—the Ultras—who had dominated the *Chambre introuvable* were not, as one might expect, mere relics from the Old Regime. In fact, the decision of Talleyrand and Fouché in 1815 to lower the age of voting and the age at which one could qualify for the Chamber brought in a horde of young reactionaries who were excluded from the more moderate Chamber elected in 1816 by a return to the former age limits. The semisecret societies that made up the *Chevaliers de la Foi*—the Knights of the Faith—had done much to create a royalist sentiment. Moreover, the Ultras could claim a powerful philosopher in the viscount de Bonald and a romantic writer and pamphleteer of genius, the viscount de Chateaubriand, who—after some sympathy with the Revolution—became an apologist for Christianity, turning his back on the Napoleonic regime he had served in its early years. On the left was a raggle-taggle of opposition, variously loyal to liberalism or republicanism, to the memory of Bonaparte, or to the prospects of the House of Orleans. Benjamin Constant was their philosopher, and the marquis de Lafayette, the veteran of both the American and French revolutions, was their most prized political possession. In the middle were the supporters of the ministries of Richelieu and Decazes, led by a group of writers called *doctrinaires*—moderating, anglicizing men, less adventurous than Constant, less high-flying than Bonald and Chateaubriand. Their most distinguished leaders, P. P. Royer-Collard, François Guizot, and the duke de Broglie, were to play prominent parts in the political life of France after 1830.

Resting on the center and trying either to placate or to isolate the extremes, the duke de Richelieu launched Restoration France on a career of moderation. He was not unsuccessful. Loans from foreign bankers allowed the huge indemnity with which the country was saddled in 1815 to be paid off within three years, and, accordingly, the Congress of Aix-la-Chapelle (see p. 555) in 1818 agreed to end the military occupation.

The difficulties of a political balancing act, complicated by rightward pressure from the allies, led Richelieu to resign in 1818; he was succeeded by a government headed by Decazes. Decazes moved, as he had long wanted to do, in a more liberal direction, notably by creating new peers and by lifting some restrictions on the press. But the liberal successes in the elections of 1819—the Charter required that one fifth of the deputies be replaced each year—alarmed even him, and he began to tinker with the electoral law. Then, early in 1820, a fanatical antimonarchist workingman assassinated the duke de Berry, the king's nephew and the one member of the senior branch of the family who, third in line for the throne, could promise an heir to carry on the line. Outraged royalists blamed Decazes and his liberalizing: "The hand that struck the blow," said Chateaubriand mordantly, "does not bear the heaviest guilt." Decazes had already realized that the Left only took advantage of his policy of conciliation; his fall in 1820 speeded a sharp turn to the right. Richelieu returned to office at the head of a rightward-leaning coalition that remained essentially sterile. In the aftermath of the assassination, a law of general security was passed permitting suspects to be detained for three months on charges of plotting against the king or the safety of the state, and a press law imposed stringent new controls that even Chateaubriand could not accept. Still, agitation continued until an abortive liberal coup and the birth of a son to the duchess de Berry, seven months after her husband's death, brought a sharp upsurge in royalist feeling.

A new, more restrictive electoral law had been passed in 1820; it created two levels of electoral colleges and gave a second vote in the upper level only to the richest of the rich. The elections of 1820 therefore produced a new influx of Ultras. In 1821 secondary schools were turned over to the church, and the press law was extended. But Richelieu's days were numbered, and at the end of 1821 he gave way to an Ultra ministry headed by the duke de Villèle, a skillful and cautious man and an admirably shrewd minister of finance. The new government set out to strengthen religion and the censorship and broke up the radical secret societies known as the *Charbonnerie,* founded at that time in imitation of the Italian *Carbonari.* [4] But the government's greatest triumph lay in the field of foreign policy. Chateaubriand, now foreign minister, secured support from the Continental powers for the French occupation of Spain to protect Ferdinand VII from the consequences of the revolutionary movement that erupted in 1820. Aware of its success, the government dissolved the Chamber, and new elections returned an overwhelmingly Ultra body. King Louis had not expected to find the *Chambre introuvable* in 1815; now he had what he called his *Chambre retrouvée*—the Chamber found again. The Ultras at once began to fall out among themselves, and Villèle dismissed Chateaubriand, thus creating a very powerful enemy. But there was no time for consequences to develop before the king, who had long been ailing, died, on September 16, 1824. He was succeeded, amid general rejoicing, by his obstinately backward-looking brother, the count of Artois, as King Charles X.

REVOLUTION AND THE CONCERT OF EUROPE

By the early 1820s the major countries of Europe seemed united in a policy of reaction. Nearly everywhere in the course of the twenties reaction deepened. There was one major, dramatic exception. Reverting to its natural, isolationist liberalism, Great Britain stood to profit from the wave of petty revolutions that began on the Continent in 1820. But Continental rulers, dyed in various hues of despotism, saw these minor and mostly unsuccessful uprisings as terrible portents that had to be put down by force.

The Spanish Example

The revolutionary movement began in Spain. Saddled with a particularly dismal and incompetent restoration, Spain, like Portugal, was deprived of resources by the breaking away of its American colonies during the Napoleonic

---

[4] The name of these secret societies meant, literally, charcoal burners.

Wars. Secret societies flourished and the army was riddled with discontent, particularly about the prospect of being shipped to America to recapture the Spanish Empire. In the years after 1815, one after another of a minority of army officers established the Spanish revolutionary tradition of the *pronunciamento,* a revolt launched by a ringing declaration of political principles in search of popular support that usually failed to materialize. On New Year's Day 1820, Major Rafael de Riego "pronounced" in Cadiz for the Constitution of 1812 (see p. 519). In February, just as Riego's effort seemed about to collapse like its predecessors, risings in a number of important northern cities assured its success: the revolution was throughout based on strength in provincial towns, with Madrid falling only tardily into line. Ferdinand VII had no choice but to take an oath to the constitution, and in March a constitutional ministry of "jailbirds"—liberals whom Ferdinand had imprisoned when he was restored in 1814—took office. The revolutionaries split at once into *moderados* and the radical *exaltados,* and, as in 1810, the situation gave opportunities to the extremists. A year later, after much backing and filling, the king dismissed the jailbirds. But his new ministry proved unable to control the Cortes—dominated as it was by *exaltados*—or the country, much of which had simply broken away under the rule of provincial juntas.

Still another ministry, appointed in February 1822 under Francisco Martínez de la Rosa, a playwright and a veteran of 1812, made some progress toward constitutional revision. Ferdinand was incapable of supporting moderate liberals, however; he undercut his new ministry by backing a royalist rising in July, sparked by loyal regiments in the army and drawing support from the church and from the population in rural areas repelled by the urban radicals. But Ferdinand was quite as incapable of boldly carrying through a coup to restore his old powers; without effective leadership, the fragmented royalism of the country could succeed against a fragmented liberalism only with the help of foreign troops. Meanwhile, the Spanish example was copied elsewhere.

Italy Against the Restoration

The near completeness of restoration in southern Europe was testimony, no doubt, to the inherent weakness of the Italian and Iberian states and to their backwardness in evolving a public opinion of any considerable extent or depth. Although the map of Italy had been reworked many times during the Napoleonic era, the peninsula knew greater stability and better government than any other of the emperor's conquests. Thus, despite growing resentment of French domination as the war drew to a close, it became increasingly difficult for educated, progressive men who had caught some glimpse of modern rational forms of government to accept a return to the past or to admit that Italy was once more, in Metternich's phrase, a "geographical expression."

During Murat's tenure at Naples, the old Kingdom of the Two Sicilies (made up of Sicily and Naples) had survived nominally on the island of Sicily itself. But Sicily was occupied by the British, who forced the unwilling Bourbon king, Ferdinand I, to accept some reforms and a constitution along the lines of the Spanish constitution of 1812. The defeat of Murat on the mainland and the British evacuation of Sicily left Ferdinand free to denounce the constitution, hound the liberals, make drastic concessions to the papacy, and lead his country—with extensive popular support or indifference—into greater and greater reaction; only the French legal reforms were retained. In the papal states not only were the French codes swept away, but so was the new-fangled practice of vaccination. Elsewhere in the restored petty states of central Italy, the situation varied: in general, French legal reforms were retained, as were some administrative practices; but these states drew their postwar characters chiefly from the personalities and inclinations of their rulers. Modena's ruler, Francis IV, was crabbed, stingy, and able, a combination that made him a particular bugbear to liberals. In Tuscany, on the other hand, Ferdinand III reintroduced an eighteenth-century despotism, but kept much from the eighteenth-century Enlightenment. He continued to exclude the Jesuits—the one Italian ruler to do so—and provided a setting in which liberal ideas could develop. This gave Florence a special place in the growth of Italian national consciousness.

It was in the north of Italy, however, that the future tensions in the peninsula were to be most clearly defined. In the enlarged kingdom of Sardinia, or Piedmont, as it was soon to be known, the restoration was ludicrously symbolized when the court of Victor Emmanuel I returned wearing eighteenth-century dress and pigtails. Modern fashions were rejected in more than clothes; Napoleonic reforms, including the law codes, were almost entirely undone. But the northwest corner of Italy could not be insulated completely from French ideas; perhaps even more to the point, Piedmont kept itself freer of Austrian influence than any other part of Italy—the battle for Italy was to be joined between the two. The immediate future, however, lay with Austria. Lombardy and Venetia were the richest, most strategic parts of the peninsula. Centered on the "Quadrilateral"—the famous four fortresses of Mantua, Verona, Peschiera, and Legnago—the new kingdom of Lombardy-Venetia, formed in 1815, was ruled despotically, directly from Vienna. From Lombardy-Venetia, Austrian influence extended—by means of dynastic ties and the collaboration of rulers and secret police—throughout Italy.

In Naples, discontent simmered more and more ominously among the educated and better-off parts of the population. Much of it was stimulated by the activities of secret societies, the most famous of them the *Carbonari*, which during the Restoration had shifted from being anti-French to being anti-Bourbon. But the repressiveness of the regime inspired new resentment among those who, however much they were opposed to the French invader and to Murat, had glimpsed the possibilities of a better state of things, above all of careers open to talents. Early in July 1820, a garrison of the Neapolitan army mutinied, and the assurance of support from the *Carbonari* led General Guglielmo Pepe to assume command of the rebels. King Ferdinand responded once more by promising a constitution on the model of the Spanish Constitution of 1812; he then fled the country and reneged on his promise the moment he was safely aboard a British cruiser at Genoa. Sicily meanwhile had risen in a separatist rebellion, proclaiming its old constitution. But the island was paralyzed by a virtual civil war among the competing groups of rebels, and the revolution there had collapsed by October. On the mainland, the constitutional government survived until General Pepe was defeated by an Austrian army in March 1821. But that intervention, requested by Ferdinand I and authorized by the Great Powers, merely set the seal on the failure of a revolution already close to collapse from internal divisions, the impracticality of the constitution, and popular indifference.

Still, the rebellion was successful enough to encourage a military rising in Piedmont in March 1821. There, despite the intent of the Great Powers to support Austrian intervention, Victor Emmanuel abdicated in favor of his brother Charles Felix. The new king was out of the country, however, and a cousin, Charles Albert, as regent, proclaimed the Spanish constitution. It lasted five days, until Charles Felix could get back to Piedmont to arrest and deport Charles Albert. The revolt was a paltry affair, but it produced an Austrian occupation, some Piedmontese exiles, and an inspiration to the fervent nationalism of a young patriot soon to be of European importance—Giuseppe Mazzini. The suppression was far more severe in the Two Sicilies, where Austrian troops remained in occupation until 1827. In the papal states, there was no rising at all, but the threat of one was dealt with sternly, especially after Pius VII was succeeded by the still more reactionary Leo XII in 1823. Spain and Italy, then, were the testing ground of the unity and determination of the great European powers.

The Concert of Europe

The diplomacy of the first third of the nineteenth century was still very much in the eighteenth-century mold. The bureaucracies of the foreign ministries were small—ranging from twenty-odd in the Foreign Office in Great Britain to over three hundred in Russia—and varied widely in ability, powers, and corruptibility. Communications were slow in the years before the railway and the telegraph, but competing networks of intelligence and counterintelligence covered the Continent, none of them more effective than Metternich's. Much therefore rested on the initiative, ingenuity, and discretion of ambassadors, less tied then than they are now to detailed instructions from their home governments. Although monarchs, foreign ministers, and ambassadors inevitably worked to serve national interests, George Canning, the British foreign minister, was putting it with a new bluntness when he prophetically described his policy, in 1823, as "Every country for itself and God for us all." Restoration diplomacy was still characterized by a genuine cosmopolitanism: French was its common language, and its practitioners were almost exclusively aristocratic. Furthermore, men from one country could still serve and bring broader views to bear on the rulers of another—the Prussian Friedrich Gentz served Metternich (himself a Rhinelander) in Austria; and high posts in the foreign service of Alexander I were held by the Corsican Pozzo di Borgo, the Greek John Capodistrias, and the Rhinelander Count Nesselrode. In the years after 1815, foreign policy in London and St. Petersburg was dominated by Castlereagh and Alexander, men of undoubted, even idealistic, Europeanism; Metternich, to protect the status quo, was impelled to take the whole Continent into account—though with the internationalism of a police-man rather than a visionary. As a result, these years left an important legacy to the increasingly nationalistic diplomacy of the nineteenth century: the concept of the Concert of Europe. This supranational community rested on the Quadruple, and later Quintuple, Alliance, was evoked in the Holy Alliance, and was given a certain reality in the postwar policies of Europe's leading statesmen. There were three more or less European postwar congresses; thereafter the Concert of Europe reappeared only fitfully through the course of the century—in 1830, in 1839, in 1856, in 1870, in 1878—sometimes to settle wars, sometimes apparently only to salvage the principle of international cooperation by ratifying essential changes. As a continuing, meaningful institution it did not survive 1822.

The Great Powers met at Aix-la-Chapelle in 1818 to terminate the allied occupation of France. In October and November of 1820, the three eastern powers—Russia, Austria, and Prussia—met again, in Troppau, with French and English observers, and resumed their deliberations early the next year in Laibach. There the diplomats had to cope with a Europe threatened by revolution, and they responded to the appeal of Ferdinand of Naples by authorizing Austrian action to put down the Italian revolts. Such a step was acceptable to Alexander, who was shifting rapidly from his interest in constitutionalism to an overriding concern with the threat to order. It was not entirely acceptable to the British, however. Castlereagh's suicide in 1822 brought the equally clever but far less cosmopolitan politician George Canning into office as foreign minister. But even before that change, the British had begun to detach themselves from the European system. At issue was the question of the interference of the Great Powers in the internal affairs of other countries.

At Troppau and Laibach the British were willing to agree to Austrian intervention in Italy; but they openly rejected the doctrine advanced by Russia, Prussia, and Austria—and for a time represented by the three as the policy of all five powers—that allied intervention would be justified in any country where illegal changes (in a word, revolution) threatened a neighbor. The failure of the royalist coup in Spain in July 1822 seemed to pose such a threat. The French, who had stationed an army of observation on the Spanish border, now proposed to set things right by invasion. Metternich was willing to support this course to keep the tsar from marching his troops across Europe. When the

Congress of Verona met in September, Castlereagh was dead, but the duke of Wellington, substituting for him, made it clear that under no circumstances would Britain take part in a collective intervention. When French action was authorized by the congress at the end of November, the duke of Wellington walked out, and any pretense to the comprehensiveness of the Concert of Europe was destroyed.

The British were consulting their own interests more than principle. Canning was quite as conservative as Castlereagh, but he was much more of a political animal, far more willing to flatter and manipulate liberal public opinion by an unabashed cultivation of the newspapers and their readers. Moreover, the Iberian peninsula was of more immediate concern to the British than Italy. To begin with, Portugal—England's "oldest ally" since the Methuen Treaty of 1703—was virtually an English fief; after the Portuguese royal family had fled to Brazil in 1807, leaving a regency at home, the country was ruled in fact by the British general Lord Beresford. Not until 1821 did King John VI return, and then only after a revolution and the adoption of a constitution, which set off a long, desultory civil war between constitutionalist and royalist forces. Meanwhile, Brazil had declared its independence and called on King John's liberal eldest son, Dom Pedro, who had remained in the colony as regent, to be its emperor. The separation of this vast new kingdom was not agreed to by King John until 1825. But it was acceptable to Castlereagh and his successors because both the monarchical principle and dynastic continuity were secured, and Metternich was willing enough to concede British paramountcy in Portugal, in return for Britain's willingness to grant a free hand to Austria in Italy.

Spain was another matter. Its American colonies had revolted and, unlike Brazil, had opted for republican governments. But the British were unwilling to see Spanish rule restored; above all they wanted South American ports kept open to all nations—an arrangement most profitable to Britain, with its control of the seas and rapidly expanding commerce and manufactures. The decision of the United States to recognize the new republics to the south made a preference for monarchy a scruple the British could no longer afford; and, having dissociated themselves from intervention in Spain and having threatened war should France decide to intervene in the Spanish colonies, Britain moved toward recognition. Conversations were held with the United States about common action to insulate the new Latin American states, but at the end of 1823 President James Monroe declared unilaterally that the United States would tolerate no interference from Europe. Moreover, his declaration foreclosed any future colonization by European states in the western hemisphere. Canning discreetly welcomed the "Monroe Doctrine"; he, like the Americans, knew that its effective enforcement lay with the British navy.

The British decision to recognize the independent republics in South America, beginning with Argentina, Mexico, and Colombia late in 1825, gave Canning the excuse to turn the whole complex transaction into a political triumph. In a famous speech at the end of 1826, he declared that the world had spilled over the boundaries it had known at the beginning of the eighteenth century: "Contemplating Spain, such as our ancestors had known her, I resolved that, if France had Spain, it should not be Spain 'with the Indies.' I called the New World into existence to redress the balance of the Old." Nor was it the balance of power alone that he secured. He had conjured up for Britain a virtual economic monopoly over South America that lasted for nearly a century. And out of the collapse of the European alliance in the 1820s, there emerged the Atlantic world—with its odd alternation of tension and cooperation between the United States and Britain—as it was known to the diplomacy of the nineteenth century.

The Balkan Tangle

The congress system—if it was a system—was also shaken by events in southeastern Europe. The Ottoman Empire was disintegrating in every respect. There were military, economic, and technological reasons for the decline of a formidable seventeenth-century empire to its nadir in the nineteenth; but the reason underlying and overriding them all was the Muslims' abhorrence for the infidel, a hatred that made the Ottomans draw back from reforms they desperately needed to undertake. At its height, the Ottoman Empire had represented the marriage between the ideals of Islam and the ideals of a warrior society. The rationale of Islam convinced rulers and soldiers alike that their wars were holy wars; it lay behind the expansive drive that gave the empire its footholds in three continents. "Firearms could be accepted," writes Bernard Lewis, "since they would be of service in the Holy War for Islam against the infidels; printing and clocks could not be accepted, since they served no such purpose, and might flaw the social fabric of Islam."[5] It was not, in fact, until the eighteenth century that printing in Turkish and Arabic was officially permitted in the empire. While Europeans increased their power over nature and their power in the world, the Ottomans lived with their sense of diminishing strength and a growing fear of their two rapacious neighbors, Austria and Russia.

This conservatism brought not only administrative chaos, but also economic crisis. The crushing burden of taxation fell mainly on the peasants. It was bad enough that the traditional Turkish agricultural techniques ensured low productivity; worse, the greedy bureaucracy pressed the peasants so hard that families abandoned whole villages to take their chances in the cities. Industry, too, fell more and more behind foreign competitors. The crafts were mostly in the hands of Christians or Jews, a sign that the dominant Muslim Turks disdained craftsmanship as a low occupation existing mainly to serve and be

[5] Bernard Lewis, *The Emergence of Modern Turkey* (1961, 2nd ed., 1968), 41. We are much indebted to this book in this section.

taxed. When European manufactured goods began to arrive in the empire, Ottoman industry was immediately placed at a severe competitive disadvantage, a development that discouraged the feeblest attempts at innovation. In trade, as in industry, the Ottoman Empire increasingly stagnated. Down to the seventeenth century, the Turks had held a monopoly on trade between East and West, but once Portuguese and English merchants penetrated to the East Indies, the Europeans were increasingly able to dispense with their Ottoman middlemen; thus another source of national income and hungrily craved revenue dried up. Even in military technology, the only area in which the Turks were willing to move at all, European developments in weaponry left the Ottoman Empire further and further behind. While the Turks had shown their preeminence in siege warfare and siege machines, the growing firepower of Western weapons made this kind of campaign obsolete. Thus the defeat at Vienna in 1683 had been one of those moments in history we rightly call a turning point; it was a symptom of a decisive weakness, as yet invisible, in the military might of the dreaded Ottomans.

The imperial government, such as it was, principally responded to the requirements of the military machine. The Turks had made hasty annexations without integrating their conquered peoples, and incessant wars demanded the uninterrupted levying of fresh troops and fresh revenue for more campaigns. As the Turks had expanded into Europe, across the littoral of northern Africa and into Arabia and Kurdistan, the cultures and, to a large measure, the governments of these territories remained intact. As early as the seventeenth century, the Kurds in northern Syria and the Druzes in Lebanon were largely self-governing. In North Africa, Algiers, Tunis, and Tripoli continued to be ruled by their hereditary beys; when the French occupied Algiers in the 1830s, the Turks barely felt the loss. Egypt had its own rulers after 1811; Anatolia, Mesopotamia, and Iraq in Asia and Rumelia in Europe all kept their local, traditional systems of rulership. And in Arabia, the Wahhabi sect took Mecca in 1803 and controlled the whole peninsula, including Yemen and Asir, though they were nominally fiefs of the empire.

Even within Constantinople itself, important minorities extracted special privileges. The Greek Christians had developed a strong community by the seventeenth century; the Jews has long acted as bankers and practiced their trades under special licenses. Colonies of Italians from Venice, Florence, and other cities and subjects of other European states, living under the legal and commercial provisions of treaties with the empire, called capitulations, effectively controlled its foreign trade. From 1654 on, the grand viziers conducted the administrative business of the empire from an official residence within Constantinople; it came to be called *Babi Ali,* the Sublime Porte, a rather ambiguous name that Europeans soon used as a synonym for the empire— much as the name of a single London street, Whitehall, is often used to stand for British government. The Ottoman bureaucratic machine was as ineffective as it was elaborate. Although in the century after the siege of Vienna the

Ottoman Empire was more and more on the defensive, it still retained the enormous military and governmental machinery it had developed during its vigorous conquering days. No better illustration of what happened to this machinery can be found than the corps of Janissaries. Originally, in the fourteenth century, they were a highly cohesive and disciplined body of slaves, recruited from the Christian peoples of the empire; they dominated the military establishment and were greatly feared by civilians, whom they regularly terrorized. Since the sixteenth century, Janissaries had been allowed to marry and to support themselves by once-forbidden trading activities. But they declined into a self-perpetuating clique—corrupt, insubordinate even with strong sultans, and dominant over weak sultans; by the end of the eighteenth century they were effective only in blocking the reforms needed to make Turkish armies successful.

On the mainland of Europe the Turks confronted the Hapsburg monarchy and Russia. The Hapsburg victories of the late seventeenth and early eighteenth centuries were not maintained at their fullest extent: Bosnia, Wallachia, and much of Serbia had been conquered in 1718 but were given up in 1739. The Russian southward drive was also abandoned, first when Peter the Great, preoccupied in the north, was defeated in 1711, and again in 1739, in consequence of the Austrian withdrawal. But Russia had gained access to the Black Sea, at Azov, in seeking to attain her natural frontiers in that area, and established an ascendancy in the Rumanian principalities of Moldavia and Wallachia. Under Catherine the Great in the late eighteenth century, the Russian southward drive began once again, this time with full success. Although Russian forces had penetrated beyond the Dniester in the west (the river that had been made the Russian frontier in the Balkans in the Treaty of Jassy in 1792), Russian ambitions were satisfied for a time by further annexations in the Black Sea area, where later they established the great port at Odessa and the naval strongholds of Sevastopol, Kherson, and Nikolaev. This expansion of Russian power and the abortive French attempt to take Egypt aroused British concern with the eastern Mediterranean, a concern that led by the end of the Napoleonic Wars to British occupation of the Ionian Islands and Corfu, off the west coast of Greece.

Sultan Selim III, who came to the Ottoman throne in 1789, had attempted to salvage his empire by two bold policies. One was an alliance with Napoleon in 1806, which, Selim hoped, would enable him to throw back the Russians; the other was an attempt at internal reform, above all of the army. The first policy came to nothing (or less than nothing) when Napoleon concluded an alliance with the sultan's principal enemy, Russia, at Tilsit. The second policy was destroyed by the resistance of the Janissaries, who forced Selim to abdicate in May 1808, strangled him, and then hampered efforts of Selim's supporters and his successor, Mahmud II, to continue the reforms. Thus by 1815 the Ottoman Empire lay in a torpor that seemed to promise only further decline. Its European provinces in the Balkans were left to cope with disintegration at the center while neither Austria nor Russia dared move boldly to conquer or partition the peninsula. This confused situation gave strong-willed men the chance to carve out domains for themselves, particularly if they were helped by distance or difficult terrain. Thus Mehemet Ali, a wily Macedonian of Albanian descent, established himself as pasha of Egypt in 1802; Ali Pasha, in the southern part of what is now Albania, and Osman Pasvan-Oglu, in the northern part of what is now Bulgaria, beginning as bandits, began to act in the empire's European lands as local rulers had long acted in the African and Asian parts of the empire.

What happened in Serbia was of an entirely different order. Of the southern Slavs, the Catholic Slovenes and Croats in the west had been largely absorbed into the Austrian Empire in the conquests of the early eighteenth century; so were some Serbs. But the Austrian withdrawal in 1739 left a sizable remnant of the old medieval Serbian kingdom under Turkish rule, and in the late eighteenth century the Serbs became newly conscious of their distinctiveness as a nationality. They were marked off from the Croats, whose language was Serbian, by their use of the Cyrillic rather than the Roman alphabet, and from both the Croats and Slovenes by their religion, which was Orthodox rather than Catholic. Still, Austrian contacts had brought some influence of Enlightenment ideas and had produced a revival of Serbian vernacular literature.

As Turkish rule decayed, the Serbs found themselves exploited more and more by petty local despots and, above all, by the Janissaries. In 1804 a rebellion broke out, led by a courageous, colorful, illiterate hog dealer named Karageorge—Black George. Fighting first against the Janissaries in the interests of the sultan, the victorious rebels failed to get him to agree to their demands and began to fight for autonomy. Once freed from their war with Russia in 1813, the Ottoman armies turned on the Serbs so successfully that Karageorge fled to Hungary. A new revolt was launched under Miloš Obrenović, who had Karageorge put to death in 1817 and who treated his other enemies with extreme cruelty. But he was clever enough to gain a degree of Serbian autonomy in 1815 and to make it final, under his own dynasty, in 1826 and 1829, without becoming deeply entangled with or absorbed in either Austria or Russia.

The Serbian revolt went more or less its own way; the later Greek uprising involved the whole European world. Greeks had come to dominate the commerce and administration of the Ottoman Empire to a remarkable degree, to the great profit of a commercial and bureaucratic aristocracy. The poorer Greeks had suffered greatly from the wars and exploitation of the seventeenth century; but by the end of the eighteenth century, the rapid growth of Greek-dominated Ottoman commerce had created a prosperity that filtered down, if not to the peasants, at any rate to the artisan classes. Contact with the West and the example of the French Revolution had, moreover, made a deep impression on those Greeks who were prosperous and well educated. They too experienced a literary renaissance, far more radical than that of the Serbs. Adamantios

Koraïs went to Paris in 1782 to study medicine and remained there; his gift to his homeland was publication of the Greek classics, with introductions in a vernacular that led to his construction of a modern Greek language. His contemporary, Rhigas Pheraios, made a double contribution: a collection of national songs and his death as a martyr in 1798 for his attempt to overthrow Turkish rule in Greece.

The dominant Greeks were too fully locked into the Ottoman system and the Orthodox church for a national uprising among them to be readily agreed upon. But it was among this primarily mercantile element that a secret Greek nationalist society, *Philike Hetairia*—Society of Friends—was organized in the Russian port of Odessa in 1814; it grew rapidly to a membership of more than one hundred thousand by 1820. In an effort to win Russian support, the leadership of the national movement was offered to John Capodistrias, a nobleman from Corfu who was serving the tsar as foreign minister; he refused. The post was then taken by a tsarist general, also Greek in origin, Alexander Ypsilanti. It was an unfortunate choice. Ypsilanti decided to move into the Danubian principalities of Moldavia and Wallachia in March 1821; his reasons for doing so are obscure—perhaps to create a diversion to allow a Greek revolution to take place, perhaps to encourage Tsar Alexander I to intervene on behalf of the Greeks. But the Rumanians of the principalities knew Greeks as Turkish administrators and exploiters and found it impossible to welcome them as liberators, the more so as Ypsilanti put the Rumanian national leader, Tudor Vladimirescu, to death after the two men had a falling out. The outcome of the expedition was far from what Ypsilanti had hoped. The rule of Phanariot Greeks[6] in the principalities was abolished, and the native Rumanian boyars returned to office. Ypsilanti himself, denounced by the tsar and Capodistrias, fled across the Austrian frontier, to be confined for seven years and then released to die in Vienna in 1828.

Despite Ypsilanti's miscalculations, a revolt engineered by the *Philike Hetairia* broke out in Greece in April 1821. Because the Turks were occupied elsewhere, the rebels had some initial successes; but when the Turks were able to turn their attention to Greece, the rebellion was put down with characteristic cruelty. Among other outrages, the Turks executed the patriarch of Constantinople, the head of the Orthodox church. This affront to Orthodoxy caused the Russians to break diplomatic relations with Turkey, and all Europe poured out its sympathy and funds: a generation of men raised on the classics saw in this divided, inept, corrupt, and perilous enterprise a rebirth of Greek civilization. Young men from England and France went out to fight, inspired by the example of the most famous poet of his time, Lord Byron, who died at Missolonghi in 1824. In 1827 the Greek forces, unable to survive their own internecine struggles, came to be commanded by Englishmen—the army under Sir Richard Church and the navy under Lord Cochrane, a brilliant sailor and radical

[6] So called from the Phanar (lighthouse) district of Constantinople, the Greek area of the city.

politician temporarily in disgrace at home; he had played a similar role in securing the independence of Chile and Brazil.[7] But Greek forces and foreign volunteers could not carry the day. Nor could the Turks. In 1826 the mutinous Janissaries were disbanded, and those in Constantinople were massacred on the sultan's orders. It would take time before a Turkish army could be organized along modern lines, and both sides needed outside intervention to succeed.

Aid came to the Turks in the form of an army sent early in 1825 by the pasha of Egypt, Mehemet Ali, and commanded by his adopted son, Ibrahim Pasha. Gradually the Greek-held fortresses gave way before this new assault. At the same time, however, intervention was being concerted on behalf of the Greeks. The first instincts of the Great Powers had been to check the Greek revolt, to maintain the status quo in Turkey, and to prevent if possible a general war between Russia and Turkey. Certainly Russia had unsatisfied grievances against Turkey: the powerful emotional link to the Orthodox religion had been savagely assaulted by the hanging of the Greek patriarch, and there was much fellow-feeling with the Greeks, quite apart from Russian strategic ambitions that might be served by support of the Greek cause. George Canning was pried out of his carefully maintained neutrality by the force of pro-Greek sympathy in Britain, by some calculation of commercial advantage, and, probably most effectively, by the likelihood of a more active Russian policy in the Balkans once Nicholas I succeeded to the throne in 1825.

In April 1826, therefore, just before the Greek stronghold of Missolonghi fell to Ibrahim's invading forces, the British and Russian governments signed the Protocol of St. Petersburg, by which they agreed to impose a settlement that would give the Greeks autonomy, which the threat of a Russian ultimatum formally attained for the Serbs and Rumanians later that year. In July 1827, during Canning's brief premiership, the protocol was converted into the Treaty of London, to which France became a party. A new article provided for sending a fleet of the three nations into Greek waters; on October 27 that fleet destroyed the Turkish and Egyptian fleets in the Battle of Navarino Bay. The Egyptians withdrew from Greece, but the sultan remained adamant and was forced to give in only by a war with Russia, which began in April 1828. By the Treaty of Adrianople, signed on September 14, 1829, Turkey lost control of the mouths of the Danube, agreed to evacuate the principalities of Moldavia and Wallachia (which, after seven years under native Rumanian princes, were now converted into virtual Russian protectorates), and again agreed to Serbian autonomy.

The Greek question was referred to Britain, France, and Russia; in the London Protocol of February 1830, they declared Greece an independent kingdom. The boundaries of the new state still had to be clarified, and the

[7] Cochrane had been accused and convicted of a stock exchange fraud, although he always maintained his innocence. In 1832 he was reinstated in the Royal Navy—no doubt helped by his succeeding to the earldom of Dundonald in 1831—where he was instrumental in securing adoption of steam power and screw propellers. See Warren Tute, *Cochrane* (1965).

question of a king was difficult to resolve, for Capodistrias had accepted the presidency of Greece in 1827 and intended to remain in that position. But in 1831 he was assassinated, and after refusals from German princes from Saxony and the house of Saxe-Coburg, the crown was offered to an enthusiast for the Greek cause, the son of the king of Bavaria; early in 1833 he entered his enlarged and guaranteed kingdom as Otto I.

Metternich, to whom the French intervention in Spain in 1823 had been so thoroughly suited, was appalled by the Greek situation, but matters escaped his control. He had hoped to keep Greece small, if Greece there must be, and free from Russian influence. Having failed to accomplish that, he had little choice but to accept the solution imposed by the three powers. Russia under a new emperor, Nicholas I, had abandoned the fitful internationalism of Alexander for a frank pursuit of national interest that, despite protestations of unity—as in the treaty concluded by the two emperors and the king of Prussia at Münchengrätz in 1833—was bound to bring Russia into conflict with Austria. The British, to whom nonintervention had proven profitable in Spain in 1823, stood to profit as well by intervention in the eastern Mediterranean. But the Russian drive into the Balkans—aiming beyond the old ambition of reaching the Black Sea to reaching the Mediterranean—stimulated in Britain a massive and growing mistrust of Russian aims and methods and a misguided but fervent hope that somehow the Ottoman Empire might be made a viable state to serve as a buffer to Russian expansion. Thus, with much bloodshed and infinite complexity, the breach in the postwar alliance was widened still more. And, as the outlines of the modern Balkans emerged, there was posed acutely that most persistent of nineteenth-century diplomatic themes, the "Eastern Question"—what, in short, would happen to the remaining Turkish possessions when "the sick man of Europe" finally died?[8]

THE REVOLUTIONS OF 1830

It has been said that nations are happy when they have no history. The 1820s, after the revolutionary ferment died away, offer little of the stuff of history in the countries of central Europe, but it is doubtful that one could call them happy. Metternich's Austria was sunk in planned and supervised torpor; its baleful influence was reflected in a somnolent Prussia and in a divided and dreary Italy. In the economy, in the universities, and among the writers and exiles, important currents of thought and action were forming, but they did not

[8] This famous phrase, though, did not come into current usage before Tsar Nicholas I spoke, in 1844, of the inevitability of the death of the Ottoman Empire. The empire proved to have a tougher constitution than any of the self-appointed physicians and heirs had anticipated.

surface until the heady decades of the thirties and forties. In Spain and Portugal the twenties saw not even those subterranean developments; deprived of most of their overseas empires and having played their part through revolution in defeating both Napoleon and the ideal of a united Europe, both countries sank into shabby civil wars. The interesting and meaningful history of Europe in the postrevolutionary twenties is confined to three countries: to Russia and Britain, the poles of a divided Europe, both of which in their characteristic ways escaped serious threat of revolution; and to France, where revolution restored a country and the Continent to life.

The Russia of Nicholas I

Alexander I had come to the throne of Russia in 1801 through a palace revolt; the succession of his brother Nicholas in 1825 touched off the Decembrist uprising. Some historians have found one explanation of the psychological puzzle of Alexander in a sense of guilt arising from his foreknowledge of the plot against his father; others have found this tantalizing possibility less convincing and certainly overworked. But there is no gainsaying the fear that the Decembrist revolt created in Nicholas I, however much he masked it. He created and maintained a system intended to root out the causes of revolution in Russia and to repress those revolutions elsewhere that escaped his preventive efforts.

This self-imposed mission was made easier by the new tsar's limited experience. He was reasonably intelligent though not well educated; his perceptive interest in painting, architecture, and music was countered by his insensitivity to literature and his distaste for philosophizing. But from childhood, his chief passion was the army. An excellent military engineer, he remained even after his accession, as Professor Riasanovsky has acutely remarked, "a junior officer at heart," fascinated by the minutiae of military life—uniforms, drill, inspections, discipline. [9] Nicholas was, however, no mere martinet. He was swift to anger and vehement in his insistence on prompt (and often disproportionate) punishment of infractions of discipline; yet he was capable of genuine magnanimity. He could not stand the sight of blood, and the punishments meted out to the Decembrists were surprisingly lenient by the standards of the time. He was scrupulously honest, devoted to his family, and, unusual for a monarch, singularly faithful to his wife. His bearing was superb: he was tall, extraordinarily handsome, and imposing—"this greatest of all earthly Potentates," as the young Queen Victoria said in 1844. His inner bearing corresponded to his outer; his passions and fears were bent to an exalted sense of duty to the Russian people and to God.

Nicholas has little of the fascination of his flawed elder brother, however. Alexander was genuinely tragic; there is justice in his being called a "crowned

[9] Nicholas V. Riasanovsky, *Nicholas I and Official Nationality in Russia, 1825-1855* (1959), 8.

Hamlet." And, for a time, to much of Europe and to his own countrymen, he was a hero. But of Nicholas we can say only that he was larger than life. In the West he became a symbol of all that is hateful in tyranny. At home, despite the official adulation, he struck terror into men's hearts: that "boa-constrictor," the intellectual Alexander Herzen called him, "buttoned up to the chin, who stifled Russia for thirty years." Yet, despite its ultimate failure in the Crimean War of the 1850s, Nicholas' rule had a certain malign success. It might even be called, with some paradox, a reforming reign: it set the forms of Russian government as they survived largely to, and in some respects after, 1917. Alexander had failed to remedy the grave defects of the autocracy he had inherited from the eighteenth century; Nicholas improved its workings and froze its forms and spirit. He was not the man to bring his country, even haltingly, into the new century that the Decembrists, in their futile way, had heralded.

The new emperor dealt first with the consequences of the uprising, deeply involving himself in the investigations and determining much of the character of the retribution (see p. 543). That done, Nicholas turned to longer-range concerns. He did not intend simply to take over the state as Alexander had left it to him. Alexander's chief adviser Arakcheev was dismissed, as were the officials who had carried out the purge of the universities. On December 6, 1826, Nicholas appointed an imposing committee to look at the whole system of government and to recommend "what is right for today, what must not be retained, and by what it is to be replaced." One of the committee's members was Speransky, now back from his Siberian exile, although the tsar had had to be satisfied by a careful investigation that Speransky was not tainted by his connections with some of the Decembrists. This committee, which lasted until 1832, was only one of a number of investigatory committees in the early part of the reign. But most of its recommendations came to little, and power came to be more and more concentrated in His Imperial Majesty's Own Chancery, an extension of personal rule that reflects Nicholas' intense involvement with the business of government.

The First Department of the Chancery was the tsar's secretariat; the Fourth, Fifth, and Sixth departments were established later in the reign for minor or temporary purposes. The remaining two departments swept far more widely, with lasting impact. The Second Department was charged with codifying the laws; the completion of its labors crowned Speransky's long and distinguished career (see p. 611). The Third Department, created in 1826, comprised the political police. Its responsibilities included intelligence, censorship, and the suppression of counterfeiting; the supervision of aliens and religious schismatics; the rooting out of corruption in local administration; and the investigation and banishment or imprisonment of state criminals. These activities were superimposed on the regular police apparatus and on the ordinary censorship, itself strengthened in 1826. Yet many of the Third Department's activities were pointless, much of its intelligence was worthless, and its administration was marked by considerable laxness. Its two chiefs in the reign—the easy-going Count Benckendorff until 1844, the positively lazy

Prince Orlov after 1844—qualified for their posts not because they were able policemen but because they were close personal friends of the tsar and regular companions on his inspection tours. Intended, as an 1829 report put it, to be "the people's moral physician," the Third Department is testimony to the existence of a deadening, paternal ideal of order, but the ideal was far from realized. For all its oppressiveness, the higher police in Nicholas' Russia was not the instrument of terror so well known in the totalitarian states of the twentieth century. [10]

The ideal of order was spelled out more fully in a memorandum prepared for the tsar toward the end of 1832 and in a circular to educational officials in April 1833. In these documents the new minister of education, Count Sergei Uvarov, formulated the doctrine that has come to be known as "official nationality"—"the joint spirit of Orthodoxy, autocracy, and nationality." In the writings of the political hacks who developed this vague concept and in the attitudes of Nicholas himself, it is clear that the second element in the trinity was dominant. Heirs and admirers of Peter the Great, Nicholas and his ministers were determined to preserve an untarnished autocracy, bolstered by religious faith and love of fatherland, as the best weapon against nineteenth-century revolution.

Reform in Britain: 1822-1832

While Russia under Nicholas I was being engineered more and more firmly into an autocratic mold, at the other end of Europe Great Britain was moving steadily toward open liberalism. We have already noted that the reaction in Britain after 1815 was a departure from the English norm, and we have seen how Canning's posture toward developments in Portugal, Spain, and Greece signaled Britain's emergence as the liberal champion in international politics (see p. 556). In domestic policy the twenties were marked by a trend toward greater freedom and efficiency. Free trade came more and more to seem the proper economic policy for a country that dominated the world's markets; hence the tariffs and navigation laws that had kept Britain's colonies enclosed in a monopolistic system were modified to give greater flexibility. In 1824 laws preventing the emigration of artisans and the export of machinery were repealed, and for many years Britain was to profit from industrializing the rest of the world. In the same year the Combination Laws of 1799 and 1800, which had prohibited the forming of trade unions, were swept away, though the wave of strikes that immediately followed brought some restraining legislation the next year. Still, the history of the British trade-union movement can be dated from 1825, however unsuccessful the early efforts at organization and however precarious the ultimate legal position of the unions (see p. 767).

[10] Questions of law and police are dealt with in a European context in pp. 611, 617.

In retrospect, the most imposing member of Lord Liverpool's government in the twenties was not Canning, but a young minister, Robert Peel. In 1812, at the age of twenty-four, he had gone to rule Ireland as chief secretary. After a spectacular success there, Peel returned to England in 1819 to chair a committee that recommended the resumption of specie payments, that is, the convertibility (which had been suspended since 1797) of paper money into gold. In 1821 Peel succeeded Lord Sidmouth as home secretary. In that post he carried through an immense task of law reform. Beginning with a reform of prisons, Peel then reorganized the jury system, speeded up trials, and removed the death penalty from a large number of minor crimes. Finally, in 1829, he instituted for the first time a professional police force in London, a force that soon became efficient and respected—the affectionate nickname "bobby," given to police officers in England, recalls the man who created them.

Peel is significant not only for what he did and for what he became, but for what he was—the son of one of England's greatest manufacturers, three generations removed from yeoman stock. He had entered the aristocratic game of politics virtually at the top, after a distinguished undergraduate career at Oxford. As a "new man" who joined the Tories, Peel demonstrates the substantial identity between the two political parties that were emerging in early nineteenth-century Britain, the Tories and the Whigs. Allegiance to one or the other was likely to be determined by family tradition, the intricacies of local politics, or a hard assessment of the probable rewards for ambition and ability—indeed, the Tories were on balance more receptive to sheer talent than were the more strongly aristocratic Whigs. Both parties in fact grew out of a generalized and nondoctrinal eighteenth-century Whiggism; the younger Pitt had never used the word "Tory," though his followers, "Mr. Pitt's friends," began to do so.

The crucial precipitant that brought parties out of the competing eighteenth-century factions or connections was the French Revolution. The early allegiance to Pitt of the once "independent" country gentlemen helped to fix the Tory tendency to support church and king, and the defection of successive groups of Whigs brought important accessions from the nobility. Thus, by 1815, the Whigs were a political remnant, long deprived of office, loyal to the memory of Charles James Fox, aristocratically disdainful of the royal family, prudently skeptical about religion; their libertarian tradition drew much support in the country, notably among the better-educated and wealthier Dissenters. But at no point in the nineteenth century were the two main English parties reflections of simple class or economic interest. Both contained noblemen, squires, bankers, merchants, and manufacturers, and neither was identified with clear advocacy of or clear resistance to reforms.

The Crown had steadily withdrawn from politics after the 1780s, a process speeded by the madness of George III after 1810 and the incompetence of his successor George IV. Administrative reform had also deprived the king and his ministers of much of the patronage that had facilitated royal or ministerial control of Parliament. Parliament, especially the House of Commons, was becoming the main focus of British politics, freed from the "influence" of the eighteenth century and not yet brought under the discipline of the modern political party. The growth of party meant a kind of polarization of politics, as opposed to the political flux of the preceding century. But it was a polarization among men in fundamental agreement, an agreement perhaps best indicated by the appearance in the 1820s of the concept of a "loyal opposition," first advanced as a happy witticism, then quickly recognized as reflecting a basic reality.

The main political issue of the 1820s was Catholic Emancipation. The question whether Roman Catholics should be allowed to hold office and to sit in Parliament might well have been solved by the slow growth of more tolerant attitudes had it not been tied so intimately to the greatest failure of British policy—Ireland. That unhappy island—the closest and so the most exploited of Britain's dependencies—had lost all autonomy in the Act of Union, which took effect on the first day of 1801. With a rapidly growing population, far beyond the resources of the island as it was then organized, Ireland was saddled with a selfish, inefficient, and largely absentee landlord class, which could not brook the idea of land reform—hence the agrarian outrages and secret organizations that so troubled the lives of the upper classes and English administrators. But the connection with England and the question of land reform became political issues only later in the century; the first Irish crisis came over religion. Peel had ruled Ireland after 1812 with firmness and a degree of enlightenment. He attempted to improve Irish education and created an Irish police as early as 1814. In that same year he also suppressed the Catholic Board, founded three years earlier to work for Catholic Emancipation, which George III had refused to allow after Pitt had promised it to the Irish in return for their accepting the Act of Union. The setback to the Emancipationist campaign was only temporary, however. In England, Catholic Emancipation found supporters in both parties; the Whigs were in agreement with Canning and Castlereagh on this as on virtually no other point. In Ireland the agitation was renewed after 1823 by a new organization, the Catholic Association, founded and led by Daniel O'Connell, a demagogue of great ability and charm.

Lord Liverpool's ministry had been able to survive, although its principal members were in disagreement over Catholic Emancipation, because the question did not affect the working of the king's government. When Lord Liverpool retired early in 1827, Canning succeeded; his coalition with the Whigs was clearly constructed on Emancipationist lines. But Canning died within a few months, and Britain did not have a settled and confident government until 1828. Then a Tory government came in, with the duke of Wellington at its head and Peel as his principal lieutenant; they were fully committed against Emancipation. In June a reconstruction of the government brought a Protestant Irish member of Parliament into a minor office; constitutional tradition required that, on taking office, he resign his seat and stand again for election, usually a pure formality. But Daniel O'Connell decided to contest the election and was overwhelmingly returned for a seat that he, as a Catholic, was ineligible to take. With civil war a grim alternative, the issue of Catholic Emancipation for the first time threatened the carrying on of the king's government. Peel, by slowly growing conviction, and Wellington, with a military man's ability to beat a necessary retreat, knew they had to concede. The king's resistance was overcome, and in 1829 these champions of Catholic exclusion carried a statute repealing the relevant sections of the seventeenth-century Test Acts. Catholics (provided they took a loyalty oath) were once more permitted to hold office and to sit in Parliament. For Ireland it meant a new and powerful role in Westminster and the possibility of redressing Irish grievances over land and the union with Britain.

A year earlier, in 1828, a statute had permitted Dissenters to hold municipal office without having to take communion from time to time in an Anglican church or having to rely on Parliament to pass acts of indemnity relieving them of the penalties they incurred by holding office. Religious disabilities were not entirely removed by these acts—Dissenters continued to face discrimination in matters such as marriage, burial, the payment of church rates, and admission to the universities. But the acts of 1828 and 1829 exploded the old assumption of identity between church and state and the consequent presumption that difference in religion must carry with it loss of privileges in civil life. The way was open for the removal of further disabilities and even to reform of the Church of England itself, when sufficient political power could be mustered. A constitutional revolution was under way, to be capped by the first great act of parliamentary reform.

Parliamentary reform had been a popular cause in the 1780s, when it was largely concerned with securing the independence of the House of Commons from government manipulation, but the example of the French Revolution had put an end to all such projects. By 1821 some of the younger Whigs had begun once more to advocate reform of Parliament, but this was overshadowed as an issue by Catholic Emancipation. After 1829, however, it could come into its own, supported by Whig tradition, by the eagerness of educated and respectable men in growing, often unrepresented towns to see their political claims recognized, and, portentously, by the direction of working-class political ambition into essentially political channels.

In 1830 a general election was necessary because of the death of George IV; Wellington and Peel emerged from it with a certain confidence, for it was still impossible then, with political parties no more than rudimentary, to tell whether an election had been won or lost until Parliament actually met and voted on an important issue. Once Parliament assembled in October, it was clear that the government was in difficulties. Reformers dominated the Commons, and Wellington offended reform sentiment by a panegyric on the unreformed constitution. Having lost the necessary ability to maneuver in a hostile Commons, Wellington's government resigned in mid-November. The new king, William IV, a bluff, popular sailor with a not quite deserved reputation as a liberal, sent for the Whig veteran Lord Grey, who formed a coalition government dominated by Whigs and committed to reform.[11]

On March 1, 1831, Lord John Russell, a younger son of the great Whig magnate the duke of Bedford, introduced a reform bill so drastic by contemporary standards as to provoke unbelieving laughter in the House of Commons. Some three weeks later it passed the Commons by a majority of one, only to be defeated on an amendment in April. Parliament was dissolved, and new elections returned a Commons overwhelmingly committed to the slogan that had dominated the elections: "The Bill, the whole Bill, and nothing but the Bill." A new bill carried easily in September, only to be rejected the next month by a broad margin in the House of Lords. Opinion in the country was savage against peers and particularly against bishops because, had the bishops voted solidly for the bill instead of almost unanimously against it, it would have carried. There were riots at Nottingham, Derby, and Bristol, and the "political unions" that had been organized among the middle and working classes mounted a huge agitation. In this tense atmosphere a third bill was introduced in December. After passing the Commons in March 1832 and its crucial second reading in the Lords in April, it was defeated on a minor amendment. Thereupon the government resigned, and the king sent for Wellington. A new, more dangerous agitation broke out, including a run on the Bank of England organized by the radical leader Francis Place: placards suddenly blossomed everywhere, urging "To stop the Duke, go for gold." After failing to form a government, Wellington agreed to use his influence to persuade other members of the House of Lords who were opposed to reform not to vote against the bill, and Grey returned to office, having got a promise from the king to create enough peers to carry the measure, if that proved necessary. Threatened by swamping, and with Wellington's statesmanlike example before them, the House of Lords at last accepted the bill and the royal assent was given in early June.

The first of the great nineteenth-century reform acts[12] changed the entire theoretical basis of the House of Commons. A redrawing of the electoral map abolished most, though not all, of the corrupt "rotten boroughs"—tiny places with few (or in one case no) voters—and the preponderance of seats in southern England was somewhat redressed. Although a number of large towns were given members for the first time, cities remained underrepresented; and the electoral boundaries were drawn so as to insulate the rural county seats from the radicalism of the towns, thus strengthening the countryside as a bastion for

---

[11] One arch-Tory was included in the cabinet as a gesture to the fanatical defenders of church privilege who, outraged by Wellington's and Peel's apostasy over Catholic Emancipation, uncharacteristically argued that a more representative Commons would never have allowed so contemptible a betrayal of principle.

[12] It was supplemented by separate acts for Scotland and Ireland, where both the context and the effects of reform were considerably different.

the agricultural interest. The reform of the franchise, a complete refashioning of an already complex system, roughly doubled the number of voters—from 400,000 to 800,000—and incorporated middle-class elements that stood for the wealth, education, and respectability of the country. Workingmen who had agitated for reform were bitterly resentful of the undemocratic character of the new arrangements, but the old oligarchical structure had been opened up and the degree of reform proved satisfactory for a generation.

A New French Revolution

It would probably have been difficult in 1824 or 1825 to predict that Charles X, the new king of France, would soon be chased from his throne by a revolution. His accession was warmly welcomed, and he was crowned with unparalleled magnificence at Rheims Cathedral on May 29, 1825. Though not so intelligent as his shrewd elder brother, Charles was imposing in appearance, generous, eager to please, and determined to succeed. He began well by vowing to maintain the Charter, by removing the censorship that had recently been imposed, and by declaring an amnesty for political offenders. But almost at once two central accomplishments of the preceding generation were threatened. The Revolution of the 1790s had abolished legal privilege and had instituted a profound secularization of society. Whatever the dogmatists of the Right might say, those steps could never be reversed. But Charles and his ministers chose to try.

It was natural enough that Charles, the most prominent of the émigrés, should want to do something for the aristocrats, just as it was natural for his right-wing ministers to placate the groups that formed their political base. It also made sense, in purely practical terms, to settle once and for all the vexed question of lands confiscated during the Revolution. To be sure, Louis XVIII had given assurances in 1814 that transactions in the nationalized lands would not be undone; but the returned émigrés continued to complain and even the holders of these lands seemed to feel that their titles to them were at least morally compromised. The former *biens nationaux* (see p. 474) tended to sell at lower prices than less doubtful property. Louis XVIII and Villèle had held back from enacting the obvious solution of an indemnity to the original owners only because of practical difficulties. Villèle thought he saw a way to finance this very expensive operation by reducing interest on outstanding government bonds (then selling well above par) and using the savings to provide the carrying charges for a new bond issue from which the indemnity would be paid. His first attempt to use this tactic failed in 1824, but in the new reign he got the principle of indemnity accepted and then set about the necessary financing. The scheme did not work as well as he had expected, not least because of the European financial crisis of 1825. Most of the seventy thousand beneficiaries got less than they had hoped for and continued to nurse their grievance, while a wider and more dangerous resentment was created among millions of citizens who had remained loyal to France but who were forced to pay to benefit a few thousand who had left. But at least the measure wiped out the distinction between confiscated and other lands and so contributed to a settling of the land market.

On the religious front the government outraged both Gallican and secularist opinion by a totally unenforceable law against sacrilege and by according legal recognition to women's religious orders—a measure that fell short of the original intention to legalize all monastic orders. This partial threat to the religious settlement of the Revolution and the Napoleonic concordat was compounded by the activities of the revived Jesuit order—a body certain to arouse the darkest (and often salacious) fears among liberals—which had established a small beachhead in seven secondary schools, disguised as seminaries to escape the secularist control of the University.

Faced with extremely vocal opposition both on the extreme Right and through the whole spectrum of the Left, Villèle made a series of miscalculations. First he unsuccessfully attempted to pass a law restricting the circulation of newspapers; then he had the king create seventy-six new peers and called a quick election, hoping to get a favorable Chamber of Deputies by catching the opposition off guard. What he got was a Chamber in which the opposition of Right and Left far outnumbered government supporters. Since Villèle could not survive as prime minister in such a situation, the king reluctantly accepted a caretaker government early in 1828. The new government, with the attractive minister of the interior, J. B. Martignac, as its principal spokesman, was forced to veer to the left, notably by restricting the Jesuits and by reiterating the importance of secular control of education. The king, disliking the drift of things and incapable of understanding the concerns and fears of the Left, began intriguing for a ministry more to his liking. Finally in early August 1829 he succeeded, disastrously. The head of the new government was Prince Jules de Polignac, formerly ambassador to Great Britain; he was an émigré, an anglophile, an Ultra, and the holder of a papal title. The minister of the interior was one of the most reactionary men in France; the minister of war was said to have betrayed Napoleon.

In May and June 1830, Polignac launched an invasion of Algiers in North Africa. There Hussein, the dey of Algiers, had long been independent of the sultan; his country had a fearsome record of piracy, which the European powers had been unable to put down. The French intervention grew directly out of a petty dispute over debts owed to two Algerian Jewish merchants who had supplied grain to Napoleonic France; the dey, who had lent the merchants money, wanted France to pay him directly. The French refusal led to strained relations, which became almost beyond bearing in 1827, when the dey struck the French consul with a flyswatter. Two years later a French ship was fired upon. On this pretext, and with the hope of gaining some prestige for the new but already shaky government, an expedition against the city of Algiers was launched and carried through to a startlingly successful conclusion in a mere twenty days.

Meanwhile, the king and Polignac were trying to cope with mounting opposition at home. In March 1830, in a stern speech from the throne, the king had made clear his intention to maintain the rights of the crown under the Charter. The Chamber respectfully pointed out that the king's ministers did not have the confidence of the country and asked for their dismissal. Instead, the king dissolved the Chamber. The outcome of elections held in late June and early July 1830 was a sweep for the opposition. Encouraged by the victory in Algiers and believing that firmness was the only answer, the king and his ministers fell back on the power given the king under the Charter to make ordinances necessary to protect the state. On July 26 Charles issued four ordinances, which drastically limited the publication of unauthorized newspapers, periodicals, and pamphlets; dissolved the newly elected Chamber (which had not yet met); altered the electoral system; and ordered new elections for September. Opposition journalists—in those days, at least, dangerous men to antagonize—decided that they would not obey the ordinance. Many workshops in Paris were closed and their workers turned out into the streets. On July 28, an uprising began in the capital; the Hôtel de Ville and the cathedral of Notre Dame were seized. Some of the royal troops mutinied and joined the insurgents, who controlled the city by the next afternoon. Some two hundred soldiers and some eighteen hundred revolutionaries were killed.

Although it was clear to nearly everyone that Charles X would have to go, it was not so clear what would take his place, a republic or another king. The skillful maneuvering of a group of moderate liberals, headed by one of the most successful of a long line of French literary statesmen, Adolphe Thiers, thrust the duke of Orléans, the head of the junior branch of the Bourbon family, into the breach. The marquis de Lafayette, who had been proposed as head of the republic by more radical insurgents, quickly rallied to this solution. Charles X first made the duke lieutenant general; then Charles abdicated on August 2 and sailed for England two weeks later. Louis-Philippe, the "citizen king"—calling himself "king of the French," not "king of France"—abandoned the traditional white flag of the Bourbons and wrapped himself in the tricolor—the red, white, and blue flag of the great Revolution and Napoleon. Louis-Philippe's investiture on August 9 made clear the contractual nature of his office, and the Charter was revised to emphasize, at least indirectly, the sovereignty of the people. Censorship and special tribunals were abolished; the age limit for voting was lowered to twenty-five; the age limit for election as a deputy was lowered to thirty; and the chambers gained the right to initiate legislation. New peers were to be created for life only, that is, their titles could not be inherited. A new electoral law lowered the franchise slightly, but the right to vote remained highly restrictive—roughly two hundred thousand persons out of thirty-five million qualified. So some things changed. But the men who ran the July Monarchy looked much like the old. The republicans and the workers who had manned the barricades were not beneficiaries of the new order. When another rising was attempted in June 1832, the bourgeois National Guard put it down mercilessly.

European Consequences

The French, or more properly the Parisian, revolution of 1830 was more dramatic than fruitful. Its principal importance may well have been as a fountainhead of republican legend and as an inspiration—magnificently embodied in Delacroix's painting *Liberty Leading the People*—to future generations of revolutionaries. But the sudden apparent success of the revolt stirred liberals and radicals across the Continent, and there were some pale attempts at imitation—with a few momentary victories. In Germany, the rulers of Brunswick, Saxony, and Hesse-Cassel were forced from their thrones, and constitutions were introduced there and in Hanover. At Metternich's instigation, a frightened Germanic Confederation accepted six articles in June 1832 that guaranteed the right of rulers to override any refusal by their legislatures to vote supplies, and enforced other antiliberal measures. In Italy, some paltry and uncoordinated uprisings in Modena, Parma, and Bologna, after brief success, were put down by Austrian intervention. In both Italy and Germany, however, liberal movements resurfaced, and the thirties and forties were a time of ferment that underlay the more significant revolutions of 1848.

In 1830 there were major uprisings in two countries. In the Russian-dominated kingdom of Poland, the limited constitution granted by Alexander I in 1815 had been steadily eroded after 1820. While the established Polish leaders discouraged a separatism that struck them as futile, patriotic and revolutionary sentiments grew among some younger army officers. This subterranean movement, much encouraged by the revolutions in western Europe, acquired a new sense of urgency when it seemed that the tsar might send troops to help the king of Holland put down the Belgian revolt. An uprising was decided on, to take place before Poland was filled with Russian soldiers. Because the viceroy, Grand Duke Constantine, was slow to act, and because the more conservative Polish leaders were irresolute, the rebels seized the Belvedere Palace in Warsaw on November 29, and the capital was soon in the hands of revolutionary crowds. A rebellious diet met in mid-December, and an independent national government was proclaimed at the end of January. The president was Prince Adam Czartoryski, a close companion of Alexander I in the early years of his reign.

A revolution of drift thus became a war, the outcome of which was never in doubt. The Russian army was hampered by problems of supply, a terrain virtually impassable in the spring thaw, and the brave and strategically skillful defense of the Polish army. At the end of May 1831, the Russian commander died of cholera; his successor was Field Marshal I. F. Paskevich, the grim veteran of the Russian campaigns against Persia in 1826–1828 and against Turkey in 1829. Paskevich at last brought the overwhelming numbers of the Russian army to bear, and Warsaw fell early in September 1831. The constitution of 1815 was withdrawn, and the Organic Statute of 1832 was put in its place; it offered a paper autonomy belied by fact. Paskevich, now prince of Warsaw, became viceroy, and a systematic suppression of Polish culture and nationality began.

The Polish rising inspired only hostility among the Russians, even among those who, like the poet Pushkin, passed for humane liberals: Polish nationalism clashed with a Russian sense of destiny and, more specifically, put an end to any tentative flexibilities that had seemed evident in the early part of the reign of Nicholas I. Many Polish intellectuals and patriots fled to the West, especially to Paris, where Prince Czartoryski held his court. The Polish cause became and remained a major emotional ingredient of liberalism and radicalism in western Europe from that time forward.

The one successful revolt in 1830 outside of France took place in Belgium, which the Vienna settlement had incorporated into an enlarged kingdom of Holland to create a barrier against French expansion. King William I, an enlightened but arbitrary man, had faced the impossible task of reconciling two widely disparate and hostile peoples. The Dutch, with a long heritage of commercial prosperity, were Protestant, well educated, and inclined to look down on their southern Catholic neighbors, so long in the possession of Austria. Believing that a big Holland could not be a barrier against the French if French influence remained predominant in Wallonia, the southern part of Belgium, William imposed Dutch administrators and, increasingly, the Dutch language on the Belgians. Although some Belgian businessmen—at that time making their country the most advanced industrial society on the Continent— were willing to support William, they fell out over commercial policy. The Dutch, a commercial nation, preferred free trade, which was anathema to the new industrialists in the south. Thus resentment among the Belgians grew, providing the tinder in which the spark of the July Revolution landed. The Belgian revolt against Dutch rule broke out in Brussels on August 25, 1830. William's elder son, sent to mediate, ordered Dutch troops out of the city early in September, and a meeting of the States General was summoned. Later in the month the city was reoccupied, only to be evacuated once again after bloody fighting; the next month the Dutch bombarded Antwerp. With no compromise possible, the Belgians declared their independence and adopted a remarkably liberal constitution.

The Great Powers assembled in London in November to confront this challenge to the Vienna settlement. Nicholas I was preoccupied with Poland; with the French behind him, the new British foreign minister, Lord Palmerston, secured recognition for an independent kingdom of Belgium. But Palmerston would not accept Louis-Philippe's second son, the duke de Nemours, as a candidate for the new throne. Agreement was reached in June 1831 on Prince

Leopold of Saxe-Coburg, who had recently refused the throne of Greece. None of the proposals of the London Conference were acceptable to the Dutch king, who held out until 1839, when at last he recognized the existence of Belgium and agreed to a boundary that was substantially the frontier of 1790. Parts of Limburg and Luxembourg were incorporated into Belgium, and the remainder of Luxembourg was made a grand duchy with the king of Holland at its head. In that same year, 1839, the Great Powers guaranteed that Belgium should remain independent and perpetually neutral, a fateful pledge that would be acted upon in 1914.

SELECTED READINGS

The two general works for the period are Frederick B. Artz, *Reaction and Revolution, 1814–1832* (1934, rev. ed., 1957) in the Langer series, and the relevant chapters in *New Cambridge Modern History*, vol. IX, *War and Peace in an Age of Upheaval, 1793–1830,* C. W. Crawley, ed., (1965).

Studies of separate national developments show that historians are likely to be found where the action is (or was); periods of stagnation, though phenomena of undoubted importance and interest, produce few monographs, and those are usually anchored to some past or future action. Aside from the ground covered in general works on Germany, for example, the only books that need be cited here are Hans Rosenberg, *Bureaucracy, Aristocracy, and Autocracy: The Prussian Experience, 1660–1815* (1958), which has some useful interpretive suggestions from a past vantage point; and Theodore S. Hamerow, *Restoration, Revolution, Reaction: Economics and Politics in Germany, 1815–1871* (1958), which is concerned with how the ground was prepared for the events of midcentury. So, too, with Italy. The single volume G. F.-H. Berkeley devotes to the period, *Italy in the Making, 1815–1846* (1932) must be compared to two volumes Berkeley devoted to events in 1846–1848 alone; the book is interesting, though, in the favorable view it takes of Charles Albert. See also George T. Romani, *The Neapolitan Revolution of 1820–21* (1950).

On Britain, where much was happening, the literature is enormous. The second volume of Elie Halévy's *History of the English People—The Liberal Awakening* (1923, tr. 1926)—covers precisely the period of this chapter in admirably clear narrative. The interpretation of the repressive period immediately after the war in E. P. Thompson, *The Making of the English Working Class* (1963) should be complemented by the more sympathetic book by R. J. White, *Waterloo to Peterloo* (1957). The best introduction to the crucial constitutional evolution of the period prior to 1830 is Richard Pares, *King George III and the Politicians* (1953), while the complexities of administration outside the central government are dealt with magisterially in Sidney and Beatrice Webb, *English Local Government,* 9 vols. (1906–1929). On the liberalizing of the 1820s, see W. R. Brock, *Lord Liverpool and Liberal Toryism, 1820 to 1827* (1941); R. L. Schuyler, *The Fall of the Old Colonial System* (1945); and the first volume of a projected two-volume life, Norman Gash's *Mr. Secretary Peel* (1961), which brings that remarkable career down to 1830. The standard account of the reform agitation is J. R. M. Butler, *The Passing of the Great Reform Bill* (1914), and the opening chapters of Norman Gash's *Politics in the Age of Peel* (1953) give an excellent summary of the provisions and the underlying assumptions of the reform.

Marc Raeff, *Michael Speransky, Statesman of Imperial Russia, 1772-1839* (1957) and Patricia Kennedy Grimsted, *The Foreign Ministers of Alexander I* (1970) are important for Russia in both reigns covered in this chapter; to them may be added Michael Jenkins, *Arakcheev: Grand Vizier of the Russian Empire* (1969). On Arakcheev's dismal experiment, see Richard Pipes, "The Russian Military Colonies, 1810-1831," *Journal of Modern History,* 22 (September 1950), 205-219. On the dramatic events of 1825, Mikhail Zetlin, *The Decembrists* (tr. 1958) is essentially portraiture, while Anatole G. Mazour, *The First Russian Revolution, 1825: The Decembrist Movement, Its Origins, Development, and Significance* (1937, 2nd ed., 1961) is a full and careful study. Other works relevant to the reign of Nicholas I will be cited in other places, but here mention should be made of two. Nicholas V. Riasanovsky, *Nicholas I and Official Nationality in Russia, 1825-1855* (1959) sweeps far more broadly than its title suggests; and Sidney Monas, *The Third Section: Police and Society in Russia under Nicholas I* (1961) is an admirable account of a central innovation of that reign.

For France in the period after 1815, one must start with G. de Bertier de Sauvigny, *The Bourbon Restoration* (1955, rev. ed., 1963, tr. 1966), which is authoritative and a delight. Daniel P. Resnick, *The White Terror and the Political Reaction after Waterloo* (1966) deals with an unhappily characteristic aftermath of revolutionary upheaval. Vincent W. Beach has written *Charles X of France* (1971). John Plamenatz, *The Revolutionary Movement in France, 1815-1871* (1952) can be supplemented by the valuable revisionist essay by David H. Pinkney, "The Myth of the French Revolution of 1830," in David H. Pinkney and Theodore Ropp, eds., *A Festschrift for Frederick B. Artz* (1964), 52-71.

On Balkan developments, besides the general works, Bernard Lewis, *The Emergence of Modern Turkey* (1961, 2nd ed., 1968) gives essential background. The Greek war was the most dramatic episode; see C. W. Crawley, *The Question of Greek Independence* (1930); C. M. Woodhouse, *The Greek War of Independence: Its Historical Setting* (1952); and Douglas Dakin, *British and American Philhellenes* (1955). The early chapters of Dakin's *The Unification of Greece, 1770-1923* (1972) provide an excellent summary of the background as well as the events of the war for independence. On Poland, the definitive work is R. F. Leslie, *Polish Politics and the Revolution of November 1830* (1956).

On the fate of the Concert of Europe, see Harold Nicolson, *The Congress of Vienna: A Study in Allied Unity, 1812-1822* (1946), and Henry A. Kissinger, *A World Restored: Metternich, Castlereagh, and the Problems of Peace, 1812-22* (1957); the latter is of particular interest inasmuch as its author became, a decade later, the principal foreign-policy adviser to President Nixon.

14

Material Circumstances: 1815-1870

COUNTRYSIDE AND TOWN

Population

In 1695 Gregory King, the most perceptive among the seventeenth-century forerunners of modern demography, estimated the population of England and Wales at 5.5 million, about double, he thought, what it had been in the year 1260. He estimated that the next doubling would take place in about 2300 and that a third doubling—to 22 million—would occur in 3500 or 3600, "in case the World should last so long"; beyond that number, however, the population could not increase because there would not be enough land to support it. Actually, the population of England and Wales doubled by 1815 and again by the 1850s. A similar pattern emerged throughout almost all of Europe.

Population statistics and their interpretations are notoriously tricky, but some impression of the magnitude of this "vital revolution" can be got from estimates that a European population of perhaps 150 million in 1750 had risen by more than two thirds of that figure, to some 260 million, a century later. Britain led the pack, reaching an average yearly rate of growth of 1.3 percent in the first half of the nineteenth century; after 1850, however, the annual rate of increase began to fall markedly. Germany and Russia, on the other hand, turned in larger average annual increases in the second half of the century than in the first. The outstanding exception in this general picture was France, where the rate of growth lagged far behind the rest of Europe in the early nineteenth century and fell to half that already low rate in the latter part of the century.[1]

Sweden took a fairly dependable census in 1749, and some other European countries, for tax or recruiting purposes, were able to provide rough estimates of their populations in the eighteenth century. Most notable in this regard was Russia, where every ten years from 1719 until 1858 "revisions" of the serf population were made available. The United States undertook the first modern general census in 1790. Britain and France followed in 1801, and in the next fifty-odd years the practice was extended throughout most of Europe. Still, much experience was required before such inquiries became statistically dependable, and similar reservations must be made about systems of registration of births and deaths. The most fruitful historical reconstruction of precensus data has gone on in France and England—the techniques are mostly those of French scholars, although English materials are more extensive—but it has been by careful, indeed painful elaboration of the situation in separate villages and regions. There is much to be said for this fragmented approach. Good local records make possible a degree of certainty denied to gross national estimates, and, as even the most advanced nations were scarcely economic and social units before the middle of the nineteenth century, enormous variations were possible from one locality to another, even between neighboring communities. These variations arose from differing geographical, climatic, and economic circumstances; from cultural and religious differences; and from perceptions of what was and was not socially acceptable within a relatively isolated cluster of families.

That the sharp rise in population was a general European phenomenon, with France the only major break in the pattern, disposes of old explanations of English population growth as a consequence of industrialization. Nor are demographers any longer convinced by explanations that rest on eighteenth-century advances in medicine (notably vaccination against smallpox) and in public health; they now argue that neither contributed much to the general well-being before the late nineteenth century. That there was a decline in mortality in the eighteenth century is certain. It was owing in part to the

---

[1] The estimate of European population (including European Russia) is based on tables in John D. Durand, "The Modern Expansion of World Population," *Proceedings of the American Philosophical Society,* III (1967), 137-159. For comparative growth rates and much other information, see E. A. Wrigley, *Population and History* (1969), especially the table on p. 185, and D. V. Glass and E. Grebenik, "World Population, 1800-1950," *Cambridge Economic History of Europe,* vol. I (1965), 56-138.

disappearance of the plague (which made its last European appearance in the south of France in 1720) and of other dreaded epidemic diseases of the past, and in part, it seems, to a general improvement of the standard of life, which allowed people, particularly children, who might have died in worse times, to survive.

It seems equally certain that there was an increase in the fertility rate, measured by the number of children born to a woman. Better food and improved living standards may have made conception more certain, while, at least among the prosperous, a new sense of well-being and of the promise of life made children seem more desirable. The eighteenth century also saw a fairly regular drop in the age at marriage, with a consequent lengthening of the childbearing period; the decay of apprenticeship, the availability of land, and the introduction of a highly productive crop, such as the potato, could make earlier marriage practicable. But whatever reasons may be adduced for a rise in fertility, the long-range trend was toward family limitation. Infanticide, uncommon in the past, became more frequent, especially among the poorest and most wretched and among poor women who engaged in casual prostitution; many children were killed through brutality or neglect, within families or in institutions; abortion was more common, apparently, than the authorities liked to think. But it seems certain that the early downturn in the French population curve and the gradual spread of limitation elsewhere was due in good part to deliberate, rational limitation; coitus interruptus was probably the most common method, since mechanical or chemical means, though advocated in England by "neo-Malthusians" from early in the nineteenth century, were not generally available until later and then were adopted largely by the middle and upper classes. They became common among working-class families only in the twentieth century.

Thinking about the question of population in the nineteenth century was guided, more than by any other writer, by the Reverend T. R. Malthus, an English clergyman determined to turn an idea derived from earlier eighteenth-century thinkers against those apostles of infinite progress, Condorcet and William Godwin. Positing the uniformity and insatiability of sexual passion and the limitation of the world's productive capacity, Malthus gave a beguiling mathematical expression to his principle of population: in the absence of restraint, he argued, population would grow at the very least by a geometrical ratio, while the food supply could increase at best in an arithmetical ratio. The terrible fate implied in this widening gap, which believers in the perfectibility of man considered only an infinitely remote, even abstract possibility, Malthus saw as an immediate threat: the "positive check" of misery and vice, which would either kill off the surplus or inhibit natural increase.

Published in 1798, Malthus' *Essay on Population* immediately seized the imagination of thoughtful and concerned men; the historian Henry Hallam said years later that anyone who would dispute the formulation of Malthus' law would dispute the multiplication table. In 1803, however, a second edition advanced a quite altered argument. Malthus now concentrated on the statistical buttressing of his theory and offered an escape that was barely perceptible in the earlier edition. He saw far more hope in the "preventive check"—not birth control, which he would have defined as vice, but abstinence from marriage until sufficient means were accumulated to support a family. In advocating what we can now see as a return to an older pattern of family dynamics, Malthus was arguing for educating people to meet their public and private responsibility, though, as he would have swept away mere palliatives like the poor laws or emigration, that education could be harsh as well as humane. In the end, it must be stressed, Malthus was trying to salvage happiness and wealth for all at the price of a limitation of numbers and a postponement of sexual gratification. He carried conviction, writing as he did amid wartime scarcity and bad harvests and when England was first encountering major problems with the poor laws. His engaging formulation of a "law" of population transformed the political economy of Adam Smith into the "gloomy science" of David Ricardo (see p. 638). But it is ironic that Malthus wrote at precisely the time when his own country was beginning to undergo economic and industrial changes that would gradually convince more ordinary people of the benefits of family limitation than were ever persuaded by the economic and moral hectoring of a couple of generations of Malthus' disciples.

Migration

However philosophers and economists might perceive the broader patterns of population movements, overpopulation—an imbalance between the number of people and the resources and employment capable of supporting them—in the end meant millions of agonizing personal and family decisions. At worst, for those without the will, strength, or means to escape, it meant staying put and suffering or starving or succumbing to disease. This happened on a monstrous scale in a famine-stricken Ireland in 1846; those who survived adopted (without knowing it) the Malthusian remedy of late marriage to an extent that has made Ireland a demographic oddity in modern Europe. A fortunate few changed trades, took advantage of a new industrial technique, or catered to some novel demand in the market. But for many, a crisis of overpopulation meant flight— the aimless panic flight that clogged the Irish roads in 1846, with corpses left along the way; migration to a nearby or distant town; or, for the boldest, emigration. Many Irish traveled to England and Scotland in the late eighteenth century to seek work during the harvest and then return; but more and more stayed. The port cities of Liverpool and Glasgow contained huge Irish populations, but they fanned out all over the country, as casual laborers doing the hard and unpleasant tasks—the digging, ditching, and scavenging that Englishmen required but hardly relished. With their physical strength, their reputation for boisterousness and violence, their alien religion, and their willingness to work for low wages, the Irish were looked on by English workingmen as a terrible threat, a threat that underlay the brawling and the discrimination. Racial stereotypes developed in those years remained to bedevil English relationships with their nearest colony for a century or more.[2]

Irishmen, when they could manage it, often chose to go to the United States or to Canada or Australia, though Canada was likely to be only a way station to complete escape, in the United States, from the hated English. A trickle became a flood in the famine years: the United States figures in 1847 stood at more than treble the thirty-odd thousand in 1844 and doubled again, to nearly a quarter of a million, in 1851. In the New World, Irish countrymen became town dwellers, transforming American urban politics and nursing bitter memories of English domination. But the Irish were only a part of a migration to America from nearly all parts of northern and western Europe that grew rapidly in the years after the Napoleonic Wars. Emigration proved a profitable business for shipowners, agents, and clever and sometimes unscrupulous entrepreneurs. It was the foundation of the prosperity of the German port of Bremen, which, having improved its facilities, capitalized on a trade its long-established neighbor Hamburg scorned. But the ports in Holland were filled with poverty-stricken Germans who had paid their money to greedy operators of riverboats on the assurance that there would be free ocean passage once they arrived, and the abuses of the emigrant trade in England led in time to the establishment of government supervision.

Most individual decisions to emigrate probably owed little—beyond some stimulation of interest—to promotional or collective activity. True, there were group movements of religious sects and of socialist enthusiasts, and some left their native lands for political reasons. But they were émigrés, not emigrants, to borrow Mack Walker's distinction.[3] Those far more numerous Germans who praised America because it had no king were really talking about escaping taxation and petty regulations, not about political theory and revolution.

The two main stimulants to emigration were the propellant effect of economic need and the experiences of those relatives or friends who had made the transition successfully; by the same token some intending emigrants were discouraged by disillusioned emigrants who returned. The economic impulse sometimes arose from a sharp crisis, as in the first wave of German emigration in the immediate postwar depression in 1816. On the other hand, it sometimes resulted from long-term changes in the economy that brought technological unemployment, as among the handloom weavers in Silesia and England in the 1840s; or that impelled the flight of the poorer rural inhabitants of Pomerania and Mecklenburg in the 1850s because the owners of the great East Prussian

---

[2] It should be said too that the Irish were an embarrassment to the sober and recessive native English Catholics; not until the 1840s did a newly aggressive church begin to provide sufficient church accommodation for the growing and increasingly Irish congregations.

[3] Mack Walker, *Germany and the Emigration, 1816–1885* (1964), 153.

estates no longer needed them. Emigration in most instances required a little capital, from savings or the sale of a no longer profitable landholding—but emigration demanded more than money. Leaving for a distant and unknown land, sacrificing friends and familiar surroundings, perhaps learning a new language took courage and faith. Emigration robbed Europe of some of its finest resources—men and women whose talents and ambition, handicapped at home, would enrich other countries, as on a much smaller scale earlier European migrations (the Huguenots, for example) had profited their host nations. The principal beneficiary was the United States.

A far larger migration, however, went from the countryside to the towns. The classical Marxist view saw the enclosures of land in eighteenth-century England (see p. 585) as thrusting yeomen and laborers into a proletariat that fed the factories of a new industrialism. It has long since been established that this was not the case, that enclosures in their initial phases were likely to increase the demand for agricultural labor; that many owner-occupiers had fallen victims to the land taxes well before the enclosure period and had sold their unprofitable holdings to provide capital for some other endeavor; and that the growing labor needs of towns were met largely by natural increase among the population already there. In an age of defective transportation, migration into a town was likely to be from the surrounding countryside, which was in all probability already closely linked to the town economically, and from which the immigrant would bring some familiarity with the forms of local life and the dialect of the region. Though London—the largest city in Europe—dominated England, the provincial towns grew rapidly with commercial and industrial prosperity, and the early nineteenth century saw both a general displacement of population to the north and midlands and the flourishing of a separate, proud, provincial culture. Four of the perhaps twenty-five European cities with populations of more than 100,000 in 1830 were in England, and the growth (and prosperity) of cities like Manchester and Birmingham, mere villages in the early eighteenth century, was phenomenal.

The Continental pattern was different. There, where distances were often greater, and where the diffusion of economic activity was slower to develop, the smaller towns remained primarily centers for regional marketing and administration; in Russia and eastern Europe they were still agricultural centers inhabited largely by peasants. The striking growth was in the capital cities. Paris, with under 600,000 in 1801, was pressing 800,000 by 1831 and topped a million by midcentury. Both Vienna and Berlin grew from around 120,000 in 1815 to 400,000 by 1848. St. Petersburg numbered about 220,000 in 1800, rose to just under half a million in the 1850s, and nearly doubled that figure in the next thirty years; Moscow, with some 241,000 in 1825 (a drop from the figure for 1811) more than trebled its size by 1882. These cities, like London, drew the fashionable and persons connected with politics and administration. Those who wished to make their way in literature, scholarship, or the arts had as a rule to set their sights on the capital. But these great cities also lured many displaced persons from the countryside because of the cities' insatiable demands for services and labor and because of expanded opportunity as new and ever more specialized employments were devised. But if the cities were magnets, they were also killers.

Towns, small or great, were hard pressed to meet the challenge of an exploding population. In Britain, town governments were almost entirely unresponsive, being confined to small oligarchical corporations with carefully circumscribed views of their proper functions; London, a congeries of jealous boroughs, had no overall governmental authority before 1888; Manchester, until 1838, had only the manorial institutions that had survived from the Middle Ages. Concerned citizens set up ad hoc authorities to look after street lighting, sanitation, and the care of the poor. But even with the best will in the world, these limited resources were insufficient to build adequate housing, to supply clean water, or to eliminate problems of sanitation and public health that were only beginning to be seen as capable of solution, while the means advanced for solving them were in dispute and often misguided. The centralist and bureaucratic institutions on the Continent offered more rational and potentially effective solutions than did the more anarchic British tradition, but even these were defeated by the very magnitude of the problems they faced. So the fashionable quarters grew side by side with festering slums, in which more and more people were crowded without amenities, privacy, or sufficient light and air. And while the wealthy might avert their gaze and live far better and safer lives than their poorer neighbors, they were not immune to the cholera transmitted through a tainted water supply or to the stench compounded of horse droppings, human excrement, rotting garbage, and smoke—that pervasive, inescapable gauge of urban civilization. Yet the people who would suffer most from conditions in towns continued to flock to them, not always in a vague, vain quest of something better, but because urban life offered them excitements and rewards—more social and psychological perhaps than material—that they could never find in the static, dependent countryside.

In time the promise of urban life was to be generally fulfilled, despite the mounting problems with which the twentieth century has had to deal. But the first half of the nineteenth century, when population skyrocketed and towns could not cope, offered mostly suffering on the way to that better life. The fact that hopes were dashed or at least postponed provoked resentment, and resentment sometimes turned to violence; hence the barricades that went up in every major European city, outside England and Russia, in 1848. Champions of the new industrialists hastened to point out that urban problems were far worse than, and quite different from, factory problems, and that urban problems, for which factory owners were often blamed, were to be laid to landlords, shortsighted and corrupt governments, and ignorance—all inheritances from the old, preindustrial world. The analysis, for all its self-interest, was right. The historian A. J. P. Taylor has put it with characteristic trenchancy: ". . . The revolutions of 1848 were not caused by the Industrial Revolution, but by its absence. Towns increased faster than the industries which provided employment and goods; and, as a consequence, their growth led to a declining standard of urban life. Industrial development, as the later history of the nineteenth century showed, is the remedy for social discontent, not its cause, and Vienna was never so revolutionary as when it was least industrialized. In Vienna a 'proletariat' of landless labourers existed, but not yet the capitalists to employ them; this was the pattern of 1848. The proletariat provided a revolutionary army, more concentrated than the universal peasantry; it, too, lacked its own leaders and found them—sure sign of economic and political backwardness—in the students of the university."[4]

Agriculture

In the census of 1851, for the first time, a majority of the population of England and Wales was reported as living in towns, though it should be remembered that probably more than half the remaining rural population was only indirectly or not at all involved in agriculture. Gradually over the next half century, the total numbers of the agricultural population declined, and its share of the population as a whole dropped steadily to a quite small percentage in the mid-twentieth century. Once more England set a pattern less dramatically repeated in most European countries over the next century. But by 1850 only Belgium had turned predominantly urban, and agriculture remained by far the largest and most important European industry, occupying something over 50 percent of the French population and just under that proportion in Germany and in the Austrian domains, though in both the latter countries the percentages increased as one moved from west to east. In Spain, Italy, and eastern Europe, the proportion of the population in agriculture was overwhelming.

The most advanced agriculture in Europe—apart from Scandinavia, where much of the population was engaged in it—was in England. There the eighteenth century saw two major alterations in agricultural life. One was a change in the pattern of landholding. Although parts of England had been enclosed—broken up into separate walled or hedged fields—since the Middle Ages, perhaps half the arable, or cultivated, land in 1700 was still farmed on the open-field system, subject to traditional though decaying manorial institutions and to often constrictive, collectively determined custom. A still considerable part of English agriculture was, however, in the hands of small owner-occupiers, colloquially called yeomen. In the eighteenth century many fac-tors—low interest rates and easier mortgages, high wartime taxes that bore heavily on those with smaller resources, the desirability of accumulating as much political influence as possible—were working in favor of large estates. The consolidation of ownership in fewer hands was eased by a new technique of enclosure. Private acts of Parliament allowed the larger landholders to

[4] A. J. P. Taylor, *The Habsburg Monarchy, 1809-1918* (Torchbook ed., 1965), 58.

compel the cooperation of their smaller neighbors who, for a variety of reasons, might have resisted enclosure by voluntary agreement. By 1830 few common fields remained. The yeomen never completely disappeared, but many of them found it more profitable, if they were efficient, to become tenant farmers, while others emigrated or moved into towns and perhaps into industry. The less fortunate declined into the growing class of landless laborers.

The eighteenth century also saw the discovery and popularization of new agricultural techniques, whose origins went back to the late seventeenth century and to practices pioneered in Holland and in the countryside around Edinburgh in Scotland. While historians used to make much of the invention of agricultural machinery, it was not until the nineteenth century that the development of the iron and engineering industries made possible the widespread use of heavy plows and such eighteenth-century ingenuities as seed drills. The great accomplishment of the eighteenth century was the devising of new crop rotations, which, by using root crops such as turnips or forage crops such as alfalfa and clover, restored nitrogen to the soil without having to allow land to lie fallow to recover its fertility naturally. These intermediate crops also provided fodder for animals, thus producing more manure for fertilization and encouraging, along with new breeding methods, the growth of stockraising and dairying.

But these advanced techniques were likely to be used only by the few big experimental farmers and by tenants whose landlords were willing to give them leases long enough to make the investment of capital worthwhile. A grasping landlord was the enemy of agricultural improvement everywhere, though to his own ultimate cost. In Ireland, where landlords were not only grasping but largely absentee, their agents responded to the intense competition for land among the growing population by subdividing holdings—with the tenants' subsistence coming increasingly from tiny potato patches—and by "rack-renting" by means of leases that had to be renegotiated every year at steadily escalating rents. By midcentury more land had been taken into cultivation—partly because of the pressure of wartime demand and partly because new techniques made possible the draining of heavy soils: the period of "high farming," with its sophisticated methods and heavy capital investment, had begun. But the country was in part dependent on imported grain, and the steady demand of farmers and landlords for tariff protection through the Corn Laws suggests how perilously exposed they were to competition from abroad. Once free trade was conceded in 1846, traditional English farming, relying heavily on grain, was protected only by distance and inadequate transportation—barriers that would fall within a generation.

Britain had long been free of any meaningful vestiges of feudal tenure; it had disappeared in France in 1789 and was shaken if not eliminated in those lands that were subjected to French law during the Napoleonic era. But the emancipation begun by Joseph II in the Hapsburg domains in the late eighteenth century was partially reversed, and that initiated by Stein in Prussia in 1807 remained incomplete (see p. 525). Thus, while France had large estates (similar to English estates) in the northern parts and a peasant economy in the center and south, the large domains of East Prussia remained substantially feudal, as did estates in Austria, Hungary, and their dependencies, until the abolition of labor services, the *robot,* in 1848. In Italy, which was exceedingly backward, highly intensive peasant cultivation or, perhaps more commonly, *métayage* (what we would call sharecropping) characterized the north and central regions, while the south retained its quasi-feudal estates. In Spain, as late as 1836, an additional brake on agricultural progress was imposed by the privileges of the *Mesta,* the corporation of stockraisers whose herds of sheep (wool was Spain's vital export) roamed the countryside. In Russia, which we shall examine later as a special case, serfdom survived until the 1860s (see p. 760).

The already extremely complex picture of Continental landholding is further complicated by innovations that slowly took hold in the nineteenth century. More land was added to the cultivated area by pushing back the sea, as in Holland, or the forest, as in Scandinavia, or by making use of heavy soils hitherto suitable only for pasture. In Russia, the late eighteenth-century acquisition of territories in the south and their subsequent settlement opened a granary of enormous potential. But in some countries, such as Italy and Switzerland, expansion was counteracted by the abandonment of mountain farms.

New crops also made their way, despite the rigidity of habits and agricultural institutions. The use of root crops to some extent eliminated fallow, but by all odds the most important root crop took hold for another reason. When wartime restrictions cut off the normal supply of cane sugar from the West Indies, the sugar beet provided a substitute and became a mainstay of agriculture in Germany, Austria, Russia, and France. Similarly, American corn (the Europeans call it maize) became an important food and forage crop in those parts of Europe that could support it climatically, notably Italy and southeastern Europe. The potato as a primary food spread nearly everywhere. But, lacking the essentially capitalistic and entrepreneurial outlook characteristic of England and deprived of the numerous and rapidly growing towns that needed specialized agriculture to provision them, agriculture on the Continent, with notable exceptions here and there, remained backward and traditional.

THE "INDUSTRIAL REVOLUTION" IN BRITAIN

To put quotation marks in the heading of this section is to make a cautionary statement well warranted by the work of two generations of economic historians. The term "industrial revolution" was the retrospective invention of an English historian, Arnold Toynbee, in the 1880s. It became hallowed by usage—and so has some claim to continued existence—with respect to the period between about 1760 and 1830 in Britain, a period when that country won an economic advantage it was to retain until the latter decades of the nineteenth century. In that period new inventions and processes transformed a small number of industries—notably cotton and iron—out of all recognition; workers in ever widening segments of the economy had to face new systems of organization and the loss of old statutory and customary protections. But much of the economy changed relatively little in this period or for some time after. The widespread adoption of the factory system or the transformation of consumption patterns by modern methods of marketing were not to be found before the late nineteenth century, when the benefits of a spreading industrialism began at last to filter down to the mass of people. A transformation that took one hundred or one hundred fifty years is not precisely a "revolution."

The New Technology

As the first industrial society, Britain has a special interest—as a phenomenon in its own right and as a model and goad to other countries. Unlike many later efforts elsewhere, British industrialization was virtually without central direction or government support; it was the aggregate of an infinite number of individual decisions, of ignorant or perceptive responses to real or presumed demands of the market. The entrepreneurs who bore the major burden of such decision-making ventured judgments about concrete situations and risked their capital in doing so. They followed self-interest—not entirely separated in their minds or in fact from the public interest—and did not pursue some abstract notion of "industrialism." They were conscious of innovation, to be sure, but if they saw themselves as revolutionary, it was in a social or intellectual, rather than an economic, sense: most of them were "new men," confident of their ultimate worthiness to share in the governance of Britain. The strength and adaptiveness of the British political system and the national vice of snobbery led some of them, and more of their sons and grandsons, to emulate and even to enter the landed classes. Mobility thus kept them from being truly revolutionary, but for a time some of them held to a faith in science and rationality and to a belief in progress that were genuinely radical. For pioneers on a course without precedents, a radical faith was nearly indispensable.

The roots of Britain's industrial development lay firmly embedded in the legal, social, and economic circumstances of the eighteenth century and earlier. Although England was small in size and population compared to most Continental countries, it was unified far earlier and so offered a larger market, unhampered by trade restrictions or customs barriers, than was to be found across the Channel. The union with Scotland, negotiated in 1707, had converted a potential competitor into a partner; although Scotland was poor in resources, it was rich in an ambitious and educated people, who contributed much to the more prosperous economy south of the border. Gilds in Britain had pretty much disappeared, except for minor ceremonial or political purposes, and the eighteenth century saw the rapid decay of apprenticeship and the old laws by which the Tudors and Stuarts had attempted to secure internal peace and a bare minimum of welfare. Although long-established industries, of which the woolen trade was the most widespread and important, displayed an exquisite complexity of traditional ways and vested interests, parts of the country were free from such restrictiveness—the West Riding of Yorkshire, where the industrialized woolen industry settled, was the best example. New industries, such as the cotton industry, were free to adopt novel modes of organization almost from the start. Eighteenth-century Britain offered its businessmen much greater potential rewards than did other countries and much more freedom to seek them.

Britain also had a sizable stratum of "middling classes" whose prosperity and confidence grew naturally out of older forms of industry and the burgeoning internal and external trade of the country. Many of them were Dissenters from the established church, still excluded from full participation in the state and debarred from certain careers that might have attracted intelligent and ambitious young men. By midcentury, some of the Dissenters, thanks to the academies founded to counterbalance their exclusion from the universities, were exposed to the most up-to-date philosophical, scientific, and theological speculation, which encouraged interest in economic and technological progress. Moreover, England's growing middle classes were less cut off from their social superiors than were their Continental counterparts.

The English aristocracy was not, in the Continental sense, a separate estate. Nobility inhered only in the actual holder of a title; his wife and children, though they might have courtesy titles, were commoners at law.[5] The early disappearance of English feudalism meant that, by the sixteenth century, the great estates of the aristocracy and their lesser untitled fellows, the gentry, were susceptible to capitalistic exploitation. By the eighteenth century landed capitalism was in full swing, encompassing the development of harbors and mineral resources; for example, the duke of Bridgewater built a canal vital to the growth of Manchester. The political stability attained after the Hanoverian dynasty came to the throne (see p. 386) in 1714 accustomed aristocrats as well as others to investing in government funds, and a willingness to invest could easily carry over, as it did in the nineteenth century, to commerce. Thus the English aristocracy was a more productive class than was the Continental nobility.

The system of primogeniture, by which estates passed intact to the eldest son, meant that the income of younger sons usually had to be supplemented by some other activity—the law, for example, or even the more respectable

---

[5] For a concise explanation of the legal position and the ranks of the peerage, see R. K. Webb, *Modern England* (1968), Appendix 2. Strictly speaking, after the Acts of Union with Scotland in 1707 and with Ireland in 1801, it was the peerage of the United Kingdom. The Scottish and Irish peerages continued their separate existence, but down to 1922 for Ireland and 1963 for Scotland only elected representatives of their orders sat in the House of Lords, whereas all peers of the United Kingdom sit there.

branches of trade, which were not held in such disdain as on the Continent. Moreover, the peerage was permeable. The usual avenues to a title were military service, politics, or the law, and the ordinary recruiting ground continued to be the gentry; but governments began to expand the peerage for political purposes toward the end of the eighteenth century. One of Pitt's many new peers was a banker, and the nineteenth century was to see the steady upward progression, to landed status and even into the aristocracy, of a growing number of businessmen. All in all, English society was more hospitable to the talents and outlook required for economic innovation than most other parts of Europe.

England was also fortunate in having a network of financial institutions that had grown up to serve the country's traders and government. At the apex of the system stood the Bank of England, founded in 1694, though it was not yet serving as the central bank it would reluctantly become during the nineteenth century. The powerful private banking firms in London and a growing number of "country banks" outside London facilitated the transfer of funds from areas where capital was in surplus to those where it was needed— in the new manufacturing districts of the north, above all. Finally, as the leading colonial power after the Seven Years' War, Britain had a flourishing overseas trade, including a substantial trade in reexports, and a largely captive market in America, which was growing more rapidly in population than any part of the world. This combination of a surging demand from abroad combined with a surging demand at home forced manufacturers to seek ways of improving their efficiency and increasing their output to take advantage of the opportunities thus offered.

New technologies and an altered scale of operation were the obvious answers. But this did not necessarily mean factory production. Adam Smith had opened *The Wealth of Nations* with an admiring description of the highly specialized division of labor to be found in the manufacture of pins. The flourishing metalworking trades in and around the midland city of Birmingham took this route of increased fragmentation and specialization. Small workshops remained the characteristic form of Birmingham industry until the end of the nineteenth century. The northern city of Sheffield, too, remained a warren of small workshops where men made cutlery much as they had done for generations, until the growth of the steel industry after 1870 converted Sheffield into a factory town. On the other hand, some industries had long been characterized by large-scale organization and extensive employment: ship-building was one, the smelting of iron was another.

The process of converting coal into coke as a replacement for increasingly scarce charcoal in smelting was discovered in the early eighteenth century, but it was slow to spread (partly because of the secretiveness of its originators). By the latter part of the century, however, the scale of iron production was impressively large, with hot-blast furnaces, puddling ovens, steam hammers, and extensive fabricating machinery. The capital cost of such equipment rose rapidly as it became more accurate and sophisticated, but the new techniques made possible a vast increase in output. The consequent lowering of prices made iron available—for building, engineering works, machinery, and consumer goods—to an extent unimaginable earlier. In 1849 the great iron works at Dowlais in Wales employed seven thousand workers in various parts of the operation, but it is important to recall that in 1851 the entire iron industry probably employed no more than eighty thousand workers. The census of that year showed twice as many people in domestic service as were employed in cotton factories.

What happened to cotton was prophetic. Imported from India since the late seventeenth century, handmade cotton calicoes were popular because they were light, easy to launder, and available in a wide variety of colorful printed patterns. It was some time before the English mastered the art of spinning and weaving cottons, partly for technical reasons, partly because the woolen industry secured some temporary protection from Parliament. But by the latter part of the eighteenth century a series of inventions took cotton spinning out of the cottages of domestic outworkers and concentrated it in factories using powered machines. Because the power was at first supplied by water, the factories were often built in out-of-the-way places, near rushing streams but far from sources of labor. The eagerness of poor law authorities to set the oversupply of London's orphans to work provided child labor for the mills. James Watt's radical improvement of the steam engine in 1769 and his later invention of a device for converting vertical into circular motion made it possible to bring the factories into the towns and thus free them from dependence on the uncertainties of water power. Factory masters, however, continued to employ large numbers of children and women, who proved cheaper and more docile than adult male workers were likely to be. The cotton industry settled largely in and around the city of Manchester, not far from Liverpool, the port through which raw cotton entered from the New World. Between 1813 and 1835 the amount of cotton spun increased six times over; by 1844 that output had increased by another two thirds. The average price per yard of cotton goods was estimated at just over threepence in 1844, whereas the same piece would have cost about fourteen times that much in 1820. Cotton calicoes, mechanically carded, spun, woven, and printed, were shipped to India at prices with which the craftsmen there could not compete, and the native Indian industry was destroyed.

Although machine spinning was quickly adapted to linen and wool, the development of satisfactory power looms lagged far behind; weaving became a factory industry only in the 1820s. Meanwhile, the enormous output of yarn was worked up by handloom weavers, outworkers who rented looms and set them up in their own cottages. Thousands of new recruits were drawn into the old and honorable trade, only to fall victims to technological unemployment when power looms were perfected, thereby creating the most famous and most investigated of early nineteenth-century industrial problems.

In contrast to the declining hand workers, factory workers were likely to prosper, most of all those workmen, such as millwrights and engineers, who could turn highly developed skills to new purposes. But the factory population paid for their prosperity by submitting to regimentation unthinkable among earlier generations of workingmen. Where once a man could set his own pace, whether in an outworker's cottage or in the organized but relatively unintegrated operation of, say, a naval dockyard, the pace in a factory was set by the steam engine that drove the machines. The factory bell began and ended the working day, and the hated overlooker, or foreman, enforced the necessary discipline by physical punishment for children, by fines or blacklisting for obstinate adults. From the cotton factories the new discipline flowed outward, as more and more industries conformed to the pattern. As schools became more common, they inculcated habits of order as well as the rudiments of literacy. And men became increasingly aware of time, an awareness given palpable form with the appearance of the railway timetable.

Indeed, it was the railway that at last drove home the radical transformation taking place in the life of an industrializing nation. Factories tucked away in remote valleys or blackening northern towns were outside the awareness of most travelers. The rapidly growing mining industry, its pits driven deeper and deeper thanks to steam pumping, was a rural phenomenon scarcely appreciated by Londoners who still spoke of "sea coal" because it came to them in ships from the northern port of Newcastle. But there was no escaping the railway: it was noisy, dirty, thrilling, even frightening, and marvelous in its speeds of twenty-five or thirty miles per hour. Contractors tunneled through hills, leveled, graded, built long viaducts across valleys, and threw bridges across rivers. Driving through towns, the railways created slums in their wake and introduced an astonishing marriage of architecture and engineering in the new phenomenon, the railway station: sometimes, like Gilbert Scott's St. Pancras station in London, evocative of a Gothic past; sometimes, especially in the great iron and glass train sheds, looking resolutely forward to modern functionalism.

The railway meant employment for signalmen, guards, and engine drivers, and for construction gangs, with their high wages and low morals; it sped people and mail from one place to another with great savings of time and money. Because goods were moved more quickly, less capital was tied up in transit, and buildings (for good or ill) could be built from other than local materials. The construction of the network demanded vast sums of money. It was said that by 1865 the capital invested in British railways was equal to half the national debt—and that meant accustoming investors to putting their money into railway stocks when hitherto they would have risked nothing but government securities. The spurts of construction and the doldrums of failure, the "railway mania" of 1844–1845, the amalgamation of lines and the search for scapegoats when such projects collapsed brought home with new meaning the alternately heady and discouraging reality of living with the cyclical fluctuations of an industrial economy.

Symbolic of the victory of industrialism as nothing else was, the railway also symbolizes what one might call an organizational revolution. New ancillary industries were spawned, from great engineering works to hotels to station bookstalls. Other enterprises declined or died: the canals so vital to early industrialization, the turnpikes through which eighteenth-century private enterprise had given England the best roads in Europe, the coaching inns for which Charles Dickens' *Pickwick Papers* (1835) was the swan song. The railway itself was not so much an invention as it was a feat of organization—the bringing together of a variety of techniques adapted from other industries (most obviously the steam engine), with a succession of solutions to technical operating problems such as braking and signaling. At the outset men continued to think in terms of the stagecoach, a model that can still be discerned in the design of English railway carriages and that, for a time, led railway proprietors to think merely of building the track and allowing customers to run their own trains. But when the Liverpool and Manchester, the first line to use locomotive power over the entire distance, opened in 1830, the company kept a monopoly of the whole operation. The railway contractors, working at home and abroad, had to muster and efficiently exploit armies of laborers on an unexampled scale, although the canal-building of the preceding half-century or so had pioneered many of the techniques.[6] The operating engineers had similarly to articulate and coordinate a highly complex and scattered enterprise, one, incidentally, that imposed a new degree of responsibility for the safety of hundreds of people on the skill and judgment of individual workingmen.

The new imperative of organization, though not entirely unknown in the preindustrial economy, affected one industry after another. The raising of capital could still be fairly casual in the first century of industrialism, relying on family or religious connections, on local merchants, landowners, or bankers, or on plowing back profits. But railways and heavy industry were increasingly organized as joint-stock companies, which could pool the resources of large numbers of investors unknown to the managers. Men had painfully to overcome the distrust of the joint-stock principle engendered in the South Sea Bubble of 1720–1721 (see p. 386) and to accept the notion of limited liability, which, if a firm failed, kept the investor from losing more than the amount of his investment.[7] The mobilization of labor, the flow of raw materials through the factory, the marketing of goods, and more sophisticated accounting were essentially organizational demands. Although it was left to the Americans in the late nineteenth century to work out the modern forms of scientific management, they were anticipated by English propagandists for industry such as Andrew Ure and by scientists such as Charles Babbage.[8]

---

[6] Hence the English term *navvies*, derived from *navigators*, for such laborers.

[7] On the evolution of joint-stock companies, see p. 212 and p. 384.

[8] Andrew Ure's *Philosophy of Manufactures* (1835) is perhaps unjustly famous for its praise of child labor. Charles Babbage's *Economy of Manufactures* (1832) is a remarkably original work; Babbage, an important mathematician, also deserves notice as the inventor of the "calculating engine," the ancestor of the modern digital computer.

The Consequences of Industrialism

Although the state took little initiative in British industrialization, its legislative and nascent regulatory powers were important both in the spread of industry and in coping with its consequences. Many of the old regulatory powers had been allowed to lapse in the eighteenth century, and the early nineteenth century saw the repeal of a number of acts no longer enforced or deemed to be constrictive: the Elizabethan legislation regulating wages and apprenticeship disappeared in 1813-1814; an act controlling wages in the uneconomic silk industry in 1824; restrictions on the export of machinery and the emigration of artisans in the same year; the "Bubble Act," which limited joint-stock company organization, in 1825; the barriers to limited liability in 1856 and 1858. The navigation laws, which had assured domination of the colonial trade to British shippers, were modified in the 1820s and finally done away with in 1849. But the state could also act positively to make the operation of the economy freer or more stable. The return to specie payment in 1819 undid the suspension of the gold standard during the wars, and the deflationary effect of the move was easily counteracted by an expanding economy. A series of acts reformed the structure of banks and the currency; another series of acts eased the incorporation of companies and, through registration, provided at least a minimum of information for potential investors.

But the often unforeseen consequences of economic change also brought the state into action with new regulations so extensive as to lead some historians to speak, anachronistically, of an early Victorian welfare state. Uncontrolled growth, some financial scandals, and far too many ghastly accidents swelled the demand for state intervention in the railway industry; there were even advocates of nationalization, though in this area Parliament declined to take bold action. The manifold problems of factories brought a more drastic response. Early humanitarian statutes in 1802 and 1819 were intended to protect the factory children; but it was not until 1833, after extensive government investigation, that inspectors were appointed to assure the enforcement of the new, more sweeping act of that year limiting hours of child labor in textile mills. In 1842, under pressure from the humanitarian reformer Lord Ashley (later Lord Shaftesbury), an act forbidding the employment of women and children in mines was carried, and one after another industry was brought under supervision.

The factory agitation reveals complex crosscurrents of opinion and interest. In general, factory regulation was supported by the workers and opposed by manufacturers, for example the Quaker John Bright—famous for his role in the anti-corn-law agitation and later for his advocacy of electoral reform. Some workers opposed regulation, however, while some progressive and prosperous manufacturers supported government regulation of labor and the imposition of safety measures such as fencing dangerous machinery— perhaps out of humanitarian concern, but sometimes to undercut less prosperous competitors. Party lines in Parliament meant little on such questions, though many rural Conservatives were eager to turn the tables on the urban factory owners who were urging the freedom of trade that landowners were likely to look upon as disastrous. The political economists were divided on the question. The celebrated J. R. McCulloch argued in favor of factory legislation, while the equally celebrated Nassau Senior, raising the specter of foreign competition, opposed limiting the working day on the dubious theoretical ground that a firm's profit was made in the last two hours of operation.

The agitation culminated in the Ten Hours Act of 1847. Though state interference with the contracts of adults was intolerable to the liberal philosophy of the time, this act and others indirectly limited the hours of adults by restricting the work of children and "young persons" between thirteen and eighteen without whom factories could not operate. Following piecemeal extension of regulation in the 1850s, a general code governing all factories and workshops was adopted with little debate in the mid-1860s. A shorter working day increased productivity and efficiency, as it turned out, and manufacturers were freed from at least one kind of undercutting by competitors willing to sweat their labor. In the long run regulation was perceived to be an advantage.

The state also tried to deal with social problems that arose from the growth of population and towns. The most intractable of these problems was poverty—whether temporary, as the result of cyclical unemployment, or permanent, among the orphaned, the aged, the ill, or the insane. The implementation of the Poor Law Amendment Act of 1834, the most important piece of British social legislation in the century, (see p. 698), brought into national prominence a famous civil servant, Edwin Chadwick, a close associate of Jeremy Bentham and the secretary to the Poor Law Commission. Chadwick turned his attention increasingly to problems of public health, which he saw as a major cause of poverty; in 1842 he produced a horrifying report on sanitary conditions in large towns. With his medical colleague Southwood Smith, Chadwick became the principal apostle of the "sanitary idea," the notion of eliminating filth by proper attention to draining, sewer construction, and the supply of pure water. Although the germ theory of disease was still far in the future, this attention to the "secondary causes" of disease made an immense contribution to the well-being of Englishmen. There was resistance, to be sure, from vested interests (among them private water companies and owners of properties where there were profitable "nuisances" such as garbage dumps); principled opposition, intensified by Chadwick's dictatorial manner, came from those who objected to the growing trend of centralization and state interference as destructive of the liberties of Englishmen: "We prefer to take our chances of cholera and the rest," the London *Times* pontificated, somewhat ungrammatically, "than be bullied into health." In 1854 the Public Health Act passed six years earlier was repealed, and Chadwick was unceremoniously dismissed from his new post at the Board of Health, never to return to office; he was a martyr to a resurgence of localism and laissez-faire and to an awareness that the crisis of the forties was over. But the sanitary idea was carried through quietly by local authorities, and by the seventies central initiative in public health became possible once more.[9]

While some enlightened manufacturers, with model villages and well-designed factories, and an enlightened government moved in paternalistic fashion to ease the lot of Britain's working population, some workers moved to help themselves. Self-help organizations—burial clubs and "friendly societies"—grew apace to provide insurance against life's calamities; savings banks were encouraged; and in 1844 the first consumers' cooperative was opened. More challenging was the trade union. Once the unions were legalized, and once they recovered from the Owenite illusion of "one big union"—an ambition savagely beaten down by the government in 1834 (see p. 682)—there gradually emerged in the forties the "new model" unionism that was to dominate the labor scene down to the 1880s. Limited to skilled laborers, usually offering insurance benefits, cautious about striking, and infinitely respectable, these unions did much to accustom workingmen to managing their own affairs (and large sums of money) and to reassure the upper classes that trade unions were not pernicious, let alone revolutionary, but a guarantee of social stability. This earliest of successful trade-union movements may seem stodgy to activist minds today. But it established a firm base from which future developments could proceed, and it eased the way for a significant injection of democracy into the English political structure through the Reform Act of 1867.

Here then were the factors making for British industrial supremacy in the hundred years or so between, roughly, the middle decades of the eighteenth and nineteenth centuries: a favorable legal framework and a complex of institutions encouraging to industrial development; an extensive, organized market; a widespread entrepreneurial spirit; technological innovation, native or borrowed; a capacity for new modes of organization; an expanded role for government; and, finally, a measure of working-class solidarity. The precise experience of Britain could not be repeated or exported, but, dominating the world in the mid-nineteenth century, Britain pointed the way and served as a challenge that ultimately was met and surpassed.

---

[9] Much was done by the new local authorities created under the Municipal Corporations Act of 1835, often by private acts of Parliament that conferred special powers on a particular local government to deal with particular problems. Especially notable was an act in 1867 that authorized Manchester to undertake slum clearance.

THE SPREAD OF INDUSTRIALIZATION

Catching Up with Britain

The transition to industrialism on the Continent came first in Belgium, a region like England in that it was small, knitted together by waterways, blessed with coal and iron deposits in close proximity, and able to draw on an impressive commercial history and a long tradition of textile manufacture. Belgium had benefited from the liberating effect of French institutions and law during the Revolutionary and Napoleonic eras, and had drawn on Dutch resources in the period when Belgium was linked to Holland. Belgium also profited from the British example and from the enterprise of British artisans and engineers. The most famous of the British emigrants was John Cockerill, brought over by two textile manufacturers to build spinning machinery; the result was a great engineering works that was soon exporting its machines throughout the Continent.

France offers an admirable example of the dangers of thinking in terms of an industrial revolution. There industrialism grew in fits and starts, and contrasts of skill and backwardness, enterprise and stodginess, make the whole picture remarkably paradoxical. Though in the eighteenth century France was the most populous and the wealthiest nation in Europe, neither the population nor the wealth was deployed in such a way as to lead to the industrial path that Britain so naturally followed. France's poor—like the poor everywhere on the Continent—were poorer than England's; France's largely peasant agriculture was unprogressive, producing little surplus capital and little demand for the products of industry. The wars of the eighteenth century, from which Britain profited, cost France dearly, and the development of its textile and iron industries was severely set back in the Revolutionary and Napoleonic eras. Thus Britain, by 1815, had acquired a margin of efficiency and cheapness that made it possible for its goods to penetrate Continental markets despite tariff walls that were thrown up against them.

At the same time legislation of the Revolutionary governments and the Empire laid the groundwork for French industrial growth, in essentials long since accomplished in England. By sweeping away internal trade barriers, archaic legal distinctions, and gild organization, a new freedom and mobility were made possible. Systematic law reform and reforms in weights, measures, and currency gave France advantages England was to be long in attaining: as only one example, the French commercial code of 1807 provided a far more flexible system of company organization than was available in England. Yet

France's market remained restricted, and even its textile industry—in every country the first to industrialize—remained wedded to the preference for fine cloths, part of the lively legacy of Colbertian mercantilism and its concentration on luxury goods (see p. 301). Hampered by a meager and awkwardly situated coal supply, the French iron industry was further slowed by the unsuitability of French coal for coking and by a relatively low demand, and so charcoal smelters were maintained in a scattered industry until very late. An act of 1842 laid down the main outlines of a national railway network, to be built by private enterprise, but capital was not readily forthcoming—the local enthusiasm so important in the English provinces was largely missing—and by 1850 only some three thousand kilometers of line were in operation.

France clearly did not have the widely diffused entrepreneurial spirit so vital in England. Too often, in their golden age between 1815 and 1848, the French bourgeoisie showed themselves little inclined to take risks. France could, however, claim two remarkable sources of enterprise not duplicated across the Channel. One lay in the system of elite and intermediate schools that came out of the Revolutionary era. Eighteenth-century France was not lacking in scientific and engineering potential: the Perier brothers, for example, opened their works at Chaillot in 1780 and so improved the steam engine that their machines, rather than British, came to dominate the Belgian and French market. Despite their emphasis on military and civil engineering, the schools developed this potential by training the skilled personnel that staffed French industry and that fanned out over the Continent and the Near East in the great age of railway building. In this resource the French were matched by the Germans, but they far outstripped the British, who in the long run were to pay dearly for their backwardness in technical education.[10]

The other unusual source of enterprise lay in a small group of men, disciples of Saint-Simonian socialism (see p. 685). They envisioned a technocratic society in which industrialists would form the new aristocracy and bankers would hold ultimate power. To an astonishing degree the Saint-Simonians made their vision reality in the middle of the nineteenth century, when the most impressive economic growth occurred in France. They played a major role in the building of French railways as well as railways all over Europe. In overcoming the conservative domination of *la haute banque* (the small cluster of largely Protestant private bankers in Paris), they developed the technique of investment banking. Investment bankers drew together capital from small and large investors and put it directly into long-term industrial investment or into temporary loans pending the marketing of the securities of a new enterprise,

---

[10] Historians have now shown that eighteenth-century English industrialism profited from the spread of scientific knowledge and that the illiterate tinker and resolute pragmatist of industrial legend were less common than was once thought. Nevertheless, England lacked the systematic, institutionalized education of Continental countries—a situation to which England's less pressing military needs certainly contributed. On schools, see p. 625.

marketing that the investment bankers themselves controlled. Unnecessary in early industrial England, where surplus funds and reinvested profits were sufficient to meet capital requirements, the French system was widely copied on the Continent. It sped up the process of capital accumulation that had taken a century or more across the Channel and almost simultaneously created a financial base, a capital market, and the industry that benefited from them.

Investment banking was not, of course, a monopoly of former Saint-Simonians; indeed the Crédit Mobilier of the Péreire brothers was quickly locked in a titanic struggle with the great international banking business founded by Nathan Meyer Rothschild, whose sons headed interlocking firms with headquarters in Paris, London, Berlin, Naples, and the home base of Frankfurt. The Rothschilds had first made their mark in floating government loans during and after the Napoleonic Wars, as did other famous international banking firms, such as Baring in London and Hope in Amsterdam, but they soon branched out to support the spreading industrialization of Europe. The involvement of French capital abroad was a credit to the imagination of the men who managed it; but to some extent it was done at the expense of the French economy itself, whose managers lacked the boldness or the appeal to draw on the full range of the capacities of their own nation.

In Germany the rapid growth in population was superimposed on two very different agrarian systems, the small peasant proprietorship of the west and the great landed estates of the east. Neither contributed greatly to the process of industrialization. The shrinking size of the peasant holdings led to emigration. The increasingly effective exploitation of the east German estates—either by the Junkers themselves or by the bourgeois owners who took over when aristocratic owners failed—produced emigrants too and also swelled the available labor supply in Saxony and Prussia. Until the late nineteenth century, the Junker aristocrats scorned commercial enterprise and the industrialists who were slowly remaking Germany. Agriculturalists first, military and civil bureaucrats second, the dominant class in Prussia slowed down the development of effective banking in the western portion of the kingdom, the progressive Rhineland, and looked skeptically for far too long on the possibility of railway development. The Germans nevertheless made more progress than the French in building railways prior to 1850, drawing in good part on British capital and experience. The pattern differed from state to state: in Baden, the Belgian example of state ownership was adopted from the start; in Prussia and most other states, private enterprise was the rule. From the beginning, however, the state played a far more active part in German economic development, thanks to the long tradition of bureaucratic direction from above. Much of the mineral development in Prussia took place in state-owned mines, and the great Prussian state-owned trading company, the Seehandlung, became deeply involved in the operation of factories and in banking, though its policy was cautious and conservative.

The outstanding characteristic of Germany, and the major barrier to effective economic development, was its lack of unity. As one newspaper put it in 1843: "Thus we have instead of one Germany, thirty-eight German states, an equal number of governments, almost the same number of courts, as many representative bodies, thirty-eight distinct legal codes and administrations, embassies, and consulates. What an enormous saving it would be, if all of that were taken care of by one central government. . . . Yet far worse than the present waste of money is the fact that in these thirty-eight states prevail as many separate interests which injure and destroy each other down to the last detail of daily intercourse. No post can be hurried, no mailing charge reduced without special conventions, no railway can be planned without each seeking to keep it in his own state as long as possible." [11] The attainment of civil and industrial freedom varied from state to state. It was largely retained in the Rhineland and those western states that had been most fully subjected to French influence. Freedom of enterprise in Prussia was implemented on the agrarian side by Stein and Hardenberg but was subsequently modified in favor of the landowners; the freeing of industry from gild control, begun by Hardenberg, was fully attained only in 1845, with unexpected consequences (see p. 732).

Even the Zollverein, the customs union launched in 1834 by Prussia and a number of north German states, though it accomplished the destruction of many customs barriers, was unable to agree on a tariff policy against the outside world that would satisfy either the protectionists or the free traders. It failed to incorporate the small, important Baltic trading states, and only after midcentury were common codes of commercial law—governing patents, for instance—painfully worked out. Thus Germany lagged far behind France or Belgium in the attainment of the legal and social conditions essential to industrial development and in the creation of a single market. In most instances where the state was involved in the economy it was a conservative, if not a regressive force, obedient to other ends than economic growth. The first Prussian child labor law in 1842, for example, was stimulated not by humanitarian concern or by managerial imagination, as in Britain, but by a report that the cities were producing children who could not meet the minimum physical qualifications for the army. It is, therefore, the more remarkable that Germany made the progress it did in introducing new technologies in the early nineteenth century. But as in all newly industrialized countries, factory industry was confined largely to textiles, and, although the Krupp family founded a famous metallurgical firm in 1827, the development of the rich mineral resources of the Ruhr valley had to wait until midcentury. Only then were the real foundations of the modern German economy laid.

Elsewhere in Europe there was some introduction of machine technology into the textile industry, and the railway age was tentatively launched,

---

[11] *Düsseldorfer Zeitung*, September 1, 1843, quoted in Theodore S. Hamerow, *Restoration, Revolution, Reaction: Economics and Politics in Germany, 1815–1871* (1958), 17.

developing quite rapidly in the sixties and seventies. But railways were not necessarily successful commercial operations; they often preceded the industries and markets that could profitably use them and were frequently undertaken solely for prestige or strategic reasons, or because aggressive financial and construction firms proved to be successful promoters. The case of Russia, though extreme, is instructive. There, to be sure, textile factories could be found in the regions around St. Petersburg and Moscow. But the iron industry in the Urals, the largest in eighteenth-century Europe, was allowed to deteriorate into a technological backwater unable to compete with the highly productive, low-cost iron industry in England. While Russian pig-iron output doubled to some 300,000 tons in the first half of the century, British output stood at more than ten times that amount on the eve of the Crimean War. When the Russians decided to build a railway from St. Petersburg to Moscow, a line not opened until 1851,[12] the rails were ordered from a state-owned foundry; but in the end the foundry could produce only a little over one percent of the requirements, and the rest had to be imported from England. The rolling stock for the line was built in Russia, in a state-owned factory operated by Americans; the locomotives and cars were simply assembled from imported parts. That factory launched a new heavy-industry sector of the Russian economy, but it symbolizes as well the technological backwardness of the country. Perpetually short of capital, Russia could produce within its own borders neither the material nor the intellectual prerequisites for effective industrialization. Its agriculture was stuck in traditional ways and locked into a stultifying system of serfdom until 1861. The bureaucratic caution with which the government was run affected the economy as well. With its enormous potential all but untapped, Russia stumbled into the Crimean War in 1854 against France and Britain (see p. 743), two industrial powers with infinitely greater resources. It is a curious reflection on the lack of awareness, even among the most advanced countries of Europe, of the advantages conferred by technology and economic growth that Russia was feared so much in the West.

The British Hegemony

The French originated the idea of an industrial exhibition, to which manufacturers came to compete for prizes for excellence in design and execution—medals that can still be seen on the labels of certain products, notably foods and brandies, that have survived the mid-twentieth-century rage for redesigning everything. But the British took the idea of the industrial exhibition and turned it into the first world's fair, the "Great Exhibition" of 1851. It was housed in

---

[12] Nicholas I disapproved of railways, believing that they would promote vagabondage; nevertheless the first Russian railway, opened in 1837, ran from St. Petersburg to the suburban village of Tsarskoe Selo, where the emperor had a summer palace and a pleasure garden. Hence the wits remarked that the fifteen-mile line ran "from capital to cabaret."

Hyde Park in London, in a brilliantly conceived pavilion of glass and iron. Prefiguring functionalism and the modern architectural engineer's use of prefabricated parts, the Crystal Palace itself proclaimed the triumph of industrialism. So did the displays inside. It must be conceded that much of the design was dreadful. Yet the multifarious objects that were displayed demonstrated the ingenuity to which machinery could be turned, often imitating the elaboration increasingly popular in contemporary craftsmanship; they also revealed the uncertain taste that a rapidly expanding middle class brought to its quest for luxury and comfort. The exhibition marks something of an epoch in British social history: despite dire predictions from the calamity-minded, large crowds of working people and their families came (often in that new device, the excursion train), proved themselves interested and good-natured, and impressed respectable England by their sobriety and good manners.

The real importance of the exhibition was wider than that, however. Though it was an exhibition of the "industry of all nations," it celebrated the triumph of British industry. Nor was Britain's victory industrial alone. Even though Britain imported more than it exported through most of the nineteenth century, an unfavorable balance of trade was converted into a highly favorable balance of payments by the services Britain provided to the world through its shipping, banking, and insurance and, increasingly, by the profits returned from overseas investments. As Andrew Ure wrote in 1835: "Nations . . . no longer send troops to fight on distant fields, but fabrics to drive before them those of their old adversaries in arms, and to take possession of a foreign mart. To impair the resources of a rival at home, by underselling his wares abroad, is the new belligerent system, in pursuance of which every nerve and sinew of the people are put upon the strain." [13] By 1851, and for a couple of decades thereafter, the British were clearly winning in that new kind of warfare. That was the one overriding economic fact in the middle decades of the nineteenth century.

SELECTED READINGS

The most comprehensive introduction to the history of European industrialization is David S. Landes, *The Unbound Prometheus: Technological Change and Industrial Development in Western Europe from 1750 to the Present* (1969). This book is an expansion of Landes' long essay in the *Cambridge Economic History of Europe,* vol. VI, *The Industrial Revolutions and After,* edited by H. J. Habakkuk and M. M. Postan (1965), 274–601. See also in the same volume of the *CEHE* Folke Dovring's "The Transformation of European Agriculture," 604–672. A brief sketch, with an interesting emphasis on the interrelationship of agricultural and industrial change is Tom Kemp, *Industrialization in Nineteenth-Century Europe* (1969). Much debate has recently centered on W. W. Rostow's controversial lectures, *The Stages of Economic Growth* (1960). For a discussion by various scholars, see W. W. Rostow, ed., *The Economics of Take-off into Sustained Growth* (1963).

[13] Ure, *Philosophy of Manufactures,* 1.

Much of the study of economic growth depends on the rapid advances being made in historical demography. A good introduction is E. A. Wrigley, *Population and History* (1969), while D. V. Glass and D. E. C. Eversley, eds., *Population in History* (1965), reprints some of the major articles on the subject. The most influential contemporary reaction to the challenge of population was the essay (1798) by T. R. Malthus, discussed in the text; the two radically different versions of the essay have been conveniently reprinted, with a valuable introduction by Gertrude Himmelfarb, in T. R. Malthus, *On Population* (1960). On migration, Walter F. Willcox, *International Migrations*, 2 vols. (1929–1931) musters detailed statistical evidence. Most of the study of emigration from Europe has been done by scholars concerned with immigration into the United States. Marcus Lee Hansen, *The Atlantic Migration, 1607–1860* (1940) is a pioneering work left incomplete by the author's death; a recent broad study is Philip Taylor, *The Distant Magnet: European Migration to the U.S.A.* (1971). The vast literature is assessed in Franklin D. Scott, *The Peopling of America: Perspectives on Immigration* (American Historical Association pamphlet, 1972). For one aspect of the situation from the standpoint of the country of origin, see Mack Walker, *Germany and the Emigration, 1816–1885* (1964).

As the first industrial nation, Britain has claimed most historical attention, from Continental scholars as well as Englishmen. An excellent brief introductory account is Phyllis Deane, *The First Industrial Revolution, 1750–1850* (1965); a fuller general survey, indeed an admirable social and intellectual history of the process as well as an economic history, is S. G. Checkland, *The Rise of Industrial Society in England, 1815–1885* (1964), also valuable for its superb mustering of bibliographical information. J. H. Clapham's *An Economic History of Modern Britain*, 3 vols. (1926–1938) is indispensable, but more useful perhaps for the amazing range of information than for broad interpretation. Another classic is the brief essay by T. S. Ashton, *The Industrial Revolution, 1760–1830* (1948, rev. ed., 1964). Ashton's *Economic History of England: The 18th Century* (1955) is important for its analysis of the "preindustrial" base. Essential for long-term trends is Phyllis Deane and W. A. Cole, *British Economic Growth, 1688–1959* (1962).

On agricultural developments: H. J. Habakkuk, "English Landownership, 1680–1740," *Economic History Review*, 10 (February 1940), 2–17; G. E. Mingay, *English Landed Society in the Eighteenth Century* (1963), and F. M. L. Thompson, *English Landed Society in the Nineteenth Century* (1963); J. D. Chambers and G. E. Mingay, *The Agricultural Revolution, 1750–1850* (1966); and Arthur Redford's classic *Labour Migration in England, 1800–1850* (1928). Books on specific industries and entrepreneurs are legion. Here are a few important ones: T. S. Ashton, *Iron and Steel in the Industrial Revolution* (1924); J. U. Nef, *The Rise of the British Coal Industry* (1932); A. Raistrick, *A Dynasty of Iron Founders: The Darbys and Coalbrookdale* (1953); W. H. B. Court, *The Rise of the Midland Industries, 1600–1838* (1938), and the same author's "Industrial Organization and Economic Progress in the Eighteenth-Century Midlands" (1946), reprinted in his *Scarcity and Choice in History* (1970), 235–249; R. S. Fitton and A. P. Wadsworth, *The Strutts and the Arkwrights, 1759–1830: A Study of the Early Factory System* (1958); D. C. Coleman, *The British Paper Industry, 1495–1860: A Study in Industrial Growth* (1958); Peter Mathias, *The Brewing Industry in England, 1700–1830* (1959); and W. G. Rimmer, *Marshalls of Leeds, Flax-Spinners, 1788–1886* (1960). The old general account of transportation is W. T. Jackman, *The Development of Transportation in England* (1916, reissued 1962). On railways, see C. Hamilton Ellis, *British Railway History: An Outline from the Accession of William IV to the Nationalisation of the*

Railways, 2 vols. (1954–1959), and the admirable sketch by Jack Simmons, *The Railways of Britain: An Historical Introduction* (1961).

The literature on financial matters is vast as well. L. S. Pressnell, *Country Banking in the Industrial Revolution* (1956) deals with a special and important aspect of English banking; Sir John Clapham wrote the official account of the major institution, *The Bank of England, a History* (1945). Leland Jenks, *The Migration of British Capital to 1875* (1927) is both authoritative and delightful, despite the somewhat forbidding sound of the subject. The history of the greatest of international banking firms, Bertrand Gille, *Histoire de la Maison Rothschild,* 2 vols. (1965–1967), is not translated.

Continental industrialization may be studied by beginning with Landes. Beyond that are J. H. Clapham, *Industrial Development in France and Germany, 1815–1914* (1936, 4th ed., 1961); and Rondo Cameron, *France and the Economic Development of Europe 1800–1914: Conquests of Peace and Seeds of War* (1914), valuable for domestic developments and for the export of French skill and capital. On Germany, Theodore S. Hamerow, *Restoration, Revolution, Reaction: Economics and Politics in Germany, 1815–1871* (1958), is useful in placing economic developments in a broader context. See also W. O. Henderson, *The State and the Industrial Revolution in Prussia* (1958). Henderson also deals with *The Zollverein* (2nd ed., 1960), as does Arnold H. Price in *The Evolution of the Zollverein* (1949). On Russia, see W. M. Pintner, *Russian Economic Policy under Nicholas I* (1967), and William L. Blackwell, *The Beginnings of Russian Industrialization, 1800–1860* (1968); the latter carefully documents the spread of industrial activity and so implies perhaps more of an "industrial revolution" than there was in the period. Essential are two fine essays in the *Cambridge Economic History of Europe,* vol. VI, cited earlier: Alexander Gerschenkron, "Agrarian Problems and Industrialization: Russia, 1861–1917," 706–800, and Roger Portal, "The Industrialization of Russia," 801–874.

15

The State
in Thought and Action:
1815-1870

THE GROUNDS OF AUTHORITY

The nineteenth century was an age of intense political argument. Some men began with concrete political issues and ended in principle; others started from philosophical, psychological, or theological premises and by deduction arrived at specific positions on the great issues of the day. The temptation is strong to seek a single thread on which debate through the entire political spectrum can be hung—to say that, in the end, they were all arguing about the French Revolution or (what may be the same thing, more abstractly put) about human nature. Many questions follow. To what extent was man a prisoner of his past, or how free was he to make his own and his society's future? Was the individual part of a larger, organic whole, or was society merely an aggregate of autonomous individuals? Was man a creature of time and specific circumstance, or was he, in essence, everywhere the same, amenable to the same prescriptions and controls? What, finally, was the nature of obligation, what made men work together and obey? Was it custom, awe, fear, self-interest, or a natural harmony? Here were the touchstones of debate for reactionaries and conservatives at one end of the spectrum and for liberals and radicals at the other.

In his magnificently oratorical plea of 1790, *Reflections on the Revolution in France,* Edmund Burke had made the case for conservatism against those who regarded society as a contract among free individuals, entitled by virtue of their original freedom to change a social order they find unjust. "Society is indeed a contract," Burke wrote, "but the state ought not to be considered as nothing better than a partnership agreement in a trade of pepper and coffee, calico or tobacco, or some other such low concern, to be taken up for a little temporary interest, and to be dissolved by the fancy of the parties. It is to be looked on with other reverence; because it is not a partnership in things subservient only to the gross animal existence of a temporary and perishable nature. It is a partnership in all science; a partnership in all art; a partnership in every virtue and in all perfection. As the ends of such a partnership cannot be obtained in many generations, it becomes a partnership not only between those who are living, but between those who are living, those who are dead, and those who are to be born. Each contract of each particular state is but a clause in the great primeval contract of eternal society, linking the lower with the higher natures, connecting the visible and invisible world, according to a fixed compact sanctioned by the inviolable oath which holds all physical and moral natures, each in their appointed place." Burke offered, not reaction, but conservatism, not retreat to an actual or imagined past, but a cautious, even skeptical approach to change that would acknowledge variety and complexity and preserve what remained valid in tradition. The rhetoric was enormously effective: translating Burke's *Reflections,* for example, converted Friedrich Gentz into an opponent of the French Revolution and won him, not merely a European reputation as a conservative publicist, but a position as adviser to Metternich. Burke's perceptions influenced many other Europeans, among them the English poet and philosopher Samuel Taylor Coleridge, and continued to inform conservative thinking long after the immediate occasion for his pamphlet had passed into history.

Eloquent though he was, Burke had an adversary who matched him in his way with words. Jean Jacques Rousseau, like Burke convinced of the power of passion over human affairs, found the source of legitimate authority not in tradition, as Burke did, but in the sovereignty of the people. "Man is born free, yet everywhere he is in chains"—with these celebrated words of the *Social Contract* (1762), Rousseau had posed the problem. Since man was born free, he might become free, and the only way to attain freedom was to give full voice to popular sovereignty. Rousseau's argument was not without obscurities, but those who advocated widening the franchise, unshackling the press, and shifting the basis of authority were appealing to Rousseau as they invoked "the people." [1]

---

[1] On the context of the writings of Burke and Rousseau, pp. 355, 359, 486.

In the early nineteenth century the dogma of popular sovereignty, a new weapon in the armory of political debate, was like an early cannon, more noisy and dramatic than effective. The direct exercise of power by the citizens of any but the tiniest community was impossible. Where representative institutions existed, they drew on only a small minority of the wealthy and established. When elections were held, they were restricted and subject to manipulation. And that invention of the French Revolution for consulting the popular will, the plebiscite, had already shown itself suspect and was not to improve its reputation in the course of the new century. Popular sovereignty was either an inflammatory bit of rhetoric or a philosophical fiction.

In the years immediately after 1815, dominated as they were by the fact of restoration and the idea of legitimacy, a very practical concern in political debate was the claim of kings to the submission of their subjects, an old theme given new force by appeals to history. Much of this looking to the past was no more than a yearning for the "good old days," a nostalgia as common among radicals (the English journalist William Cobbett, for example) or rebellious workers as it was among a threatened aristocracy. A notable Russian example was N. M. Karamzin, a poet turned historian. Hating the reforms that Speransky was attempting in government and fearing the social transformation heralded by the French Revolution and Napoleon, Karamzin launched a powerful attack on all innovation, in the guise of a defense of autocracy— though it was autocracy as Karamzin and the gentry for whom he spoke thought it had existed, not autocracy as it had really worked in the hands of living emperors and empresses. In France the viscount de Bonald, an émigré who had returned under Napoleon, undertook a more sophisticated, concentrated attack on the Revolutionary ideals of equality and popular sovereignty and on the rationalist modes of thought he blamed for having overturned the old order. Bonald's insistence on the natural hierarchy of monarchy, aristocracy, and people bound together by tradition and the cement of Catholicism looks back to the seventeenth century, though his appreciation of the organic nature of society was to carry conviction for some distinctly radical nineteenth-century thinkers, among them Saint-Simon and Auguste Comte (see p. 684).

The most striking of these theorists of reaction—and the most paradoxical—was Joseph de Maistre. A nobleman driven from his native Savoy by the French invasion of 1792, Maistre saw long service as the Sardinian ambassador in St. Petersburg. In a series of works largely composed there, he went far beyond traditionalists like Bonald. Viewing human nature as evil and corrupt and God's sovereignty as exalted and arbitrary, he not only confronted the problem of evil that had so often discomfited eighteenth-century thinkers, he seemed to glory in it. Soldiers at war and the grim figure of the executioner were doing God's work, punishing men for their sins, even when the punishment fell, with apparent injustice, on those who in the world's eyes were blameless. To keep individualism and the presumption of human reason in check, Maistre

called on established institutions, the chief of which was monarchy. But beyond
the monarchs stood the pope, to keep erring kings in line. Thus Maistre, unlike
Bonald, was a philosopher of papal power—of ultramontanism, so called
because it looks "beyond the mountains" to Rome. A son of the eighteenth
century, Maistre used reason to argue for irrationality and the centrality of
faith; the social order he prescribed was as utopian as anything created by the
hated philosophes; his "terrorist Christianity" verged on heresy or even
irreligion. A contemporary admirer had to concede that "unable to hear
anything but the voice of past centuries, that prophet of the past slept within
recollections which he took for anticipations." But there was genuine anticipation too—of a grimmer age of authoritarianism and oppression.[2]

For all their interest and influence, Bonald and Maistre were theorizing
about a subject whose outlines were shifting rapidly. To be sure, nearly all the
states of Europe remained monarchical for most of the century, but in many
countries the reality was changing; and, as monarchy was limited and forced to
share power, the traditional formulations of political philosophy grew obsolete.
François Guizot, the doctrinaire theorist, historian, and statesman of the July
Monarchy, insisted that representative government was the best way of
attaining the sovereignty of reason on earth. He argued for monarchy
in conjunction with it—historically because some form of monarchy was
known in all times and places, and pragmatically because a king personified the
community and its attributes and served as a uniting, stabilizing force superior
to the competing wills of individuals. A generation later Walter Bagehot, an
acute and skeptical English social analyst, used some of the same arguments for
monarchy. But, whereas Guizot had held that the king should play an active
political role (as his monarch Louis-Philippe did), Bagehot was writing in a time
when the independent political power of the British Crown had virtually
disappeared; thus his justification of monarchy was more psychological than
historical and just short of cynicism. In a parliamentary system, Bagehot
argued, the monarch retained only "the right to be consulted, the right to
encourage, the right to warn." Far more valuable were certain intangible
functions: the monarch embodied the religious and family sense of the nation,
guided its morality, and placed the headship of society beyond contest or the
reach of ambition. Being permanent, monarchy allowed governments to change
without damaging continuity, disguising the realities of a cabinet system from
those masses of Englishmen "not fit for an elective government." "Royalty," he
wrote, "is a government in which the attention of the nation is concentrated on
one person doing interesting actions. A republic is a government in which that
attention is divided between many, who are all doing uninteresting actions.
Accordingly, so long as the human heart is strong and the human reason weak,

[2] The quotations are from R. H. Soltau, *French Political Thought in the Nineteenth Century*
(1931), 14-24.

royalty will be strong, because it appeals to diffused feeling, and republics weak because they appeal to the understanding."[3]

The withdrawal of monarchs in parliamentary systems to the vaguer realms of influence altered but did not do away with the question of sovereignty: indeed, the place of the individual in (or against) the state became more troublesome than ever. As societies grew more populous and complex and as older patterns of deference were shattered, the state sought or had thrust upon it more functions, wider responsibilities, and more extensive control over its citizens. Ease of transportation and communication shrank time and space and, together with new administrative techniques, strengthened the hand of central governments over the localities. At the same time those who sought to explain and justify these developments tried to escape from the old value-laden terminology to a quasi-scientific objectivity. Thus in 1828 the English legal philosopher John Austin defined positive law as a series of commands from a recognized superior, carried out, under threat of sanction, by subjects habitually accustomed to obedience. It is a deceptively simple formula, useful and widely influential in facilitating analysis and reform of the law—and conducive to much subsequent criticism as well. But for the present purpose, what is important is Austin's refusal to appeal to moral considerations, the analogy of the father's authority over his children, the organic metaphor of head and members, or the pieties of natural-law theory. Austin and his friends were disciples of the philosopher Jeremy Bentham (see p. 612), who having established his reputation in his *Fragment on Government* (1776), by exploding the natural-law rhetoric of Sir William Blackstone's celebrated *Commentaries on the Laws of England* (1765–1769), had gone on to ground his legal and administrative system on the single, presumably value-free ground of utility.

Bentham became a leading radical theorist, providing a rationale for parliamentary reform and a newly efficient and responsive bureaucratic state; but the blueprints that he and his friends drew up for tidy, rational government, following their admired Continental models, were less easily domiciled in England than they would have been in any other country. Liberal Britain was characterized by a diffusion, not a focusing of power. Only gradually did the central government transcend its traditional limitations; local governments retained a high degree of autonomy; deference continued to be exacted by the upper reaches of the social hierarchy; and the country was honeycombed with innumerable voluntary organizations exercising social and political power that the presumably sovereign Parliament touched only at its peril. Ordinary

[3] The quotations are from Walter Bagehot's *The English Constitution* (1867). The role of moral leadership, which could scarcely have been attributed to Queen Victoria's uncles George IV or William IV, reflects the transformation of the English monarchy brought about by Queen Victoria and, especially, her husband Prince Albert. Bagehot's general observations may apply even more forcefully to the English royal family in the twentieth century.

Englishmen remained deeply, even belligerently, conscious of their "liberties" and proved healthily inconvenient to the advocates of extended powers for the state. And the Benthamites helped to rehabilitate Thomas Hobbes, the seventeenth-century writer, who had repelled his contemporaries by a coolly realistic insistence that sovereignty was defined solely by the ability of the sovereign to maintain himself in power.

The tension between state and individual was growing in many countries, each in its own way. The increasing disgust of Russian intellectuals with the bureaucratic rule to which they were subjected is one instance. But in Britain, political awareness and participation were spread more widely than elsewhere; hence it is fitting that the tension was most brilliantly exemplified in the writings of an Englishman, John Stuart Mill. Raised by his father, Bentham's close friend James Mill, to be a perfect Benthamite, J. S. Mill never forsook a basically utilitarian approach. But he grew more and more dissatisfied with the Benthamism he had received as a boy and drew inspiration in turn from Thomas Carlyle and Coleridge in England, from the Saint-Simonians and Auguste Comte in France. Impressed by the observations of that acute French critic Alexis de Tocqueville about the tyranny that public opinion exercised in democratic America, Mill defended the encouragement and protection of minority views on the utilitarian ground that only thus could truth ultimately be reached: *On Liberty,* published in 1859, is the century's finest and most eloquent defense of individual differences and its strongest plea for pragmatic limits to state action.

The future, however, lay more with the state than with the individual; that the victory was conceded is perhaps reflected in the decline of theorizing about the relation of the individual to the state, except in occasional purely professional discussions of philosophers. Most philosophers concerned themselves less with ultimate questions than with techniques, less with the justification of power than with the way it is exercised: political theory was being abandoned for political science. In 1859, the same year that saw the publication of *On Liberty,* a radical veteran of the revolution of 1848 protested that Germany was "sick of principles and doctrines, literary existence and theoretical greatness. What it wants is Power, Power, Power! And whoever gives it power to him will it give honor, more honor than he can imagine." [4] Six years earlier, another German, A. L. von Rochau, had first used the term *Realpolitik*—political realism. Thus was struck the keynote of an age that is still with us. But for two centuries down to about 1860 the exercise of power had been masked by an insistent, enlightened search for authoritatively grounded, universal, self-acting systems.

[4] Julius Froebel, quoted in James Joll, "Prussia and the German Problem, 1830–66," *New Cambridge Modern History,* vol. X, *The Zenith of European Power, 1830–1870* (1967), 504.

THE MACHINERY OF THE STATE

Law

In law and administration, the English Channel is wide and deep. On the Continent written, codified law reigns supreme. The civil code of France, promulgated in 1804 and supplemented by procedural, commercial, and criminal codes, provided in a few thousand clauses the rules French judges were to apply. For all the haste and arbitrariness of their construction, the codes survived unchanged during the Restoration and deeply influenced those areas of Europe most systematically brought under French control in the Napoleonic era—the Rhineland, the Low Countries, and parts of Italy. Austrian law had been codified in 1803, Prussian state law as early as 1794. Speransky's early attempt to provide Russia with a code was defeated, but after he returned from exile he was put in charge of the newly created Second Department of the tsar's Imperial Chancery, to bring some order into the chaos of Russian law. The known laws were compiled, and the resulting digest (though not strictly a code) lasted, despite its defects, as fundamental law in the Russian Empire from 1835 to the Revolution in 1917.

England's common law, though it had been brought together in a conservative synthesis in the early seventeenth century by the great jurist and statesman Sir Edward Coke, had since that time proliferated contradiction and obsolescence. Moreover, alongside the common law there had grown up the competing jurisdiction of the Court of Chancery, originally intended to provide "equity" in cases where a no longer flexible common law worked an injustice; but the Court of Chancery, even more than the three common-law courts of King's Bench, Common Pleas, and Exchequer, was famous for delay and expense. The courts relied not only on statutes but on precedents and rules established in earlier judicial decisions; thus in a very real sense the law of England owed less to legislation than it did to the collective memory of lawyers and judges enshrined in reports of cases.

By a strange irony, of the two leading philosophical approaches to the law in the early nineteenth century, one, the historical school, was centered not in England but in Germany; its leading figure was Friedrich Karl von Savigny. Through patient compilation and historical analysis, German scholars sought to comprehend the evolution of systems of laws unique to the people who produced them; the influence of the school was likely to be more conservative than critical and reformatory.

At the other pole was the rationalist school, which numbered the eighteenth-century Italian jurist Cesare Beccaria among its luminaries, but which is most prominently represented by Jeremy Bentham, in whom a number of principles of the Continental and English Enlightenment came together. A bitter opponent of natural law, Bentham proceeded from the simple psychological premise that men pursue pleasure and shun pain: it therefore remained for the legislator only to use the "felicific calculus," devising sufficient sanctions to deter evildoers and sufficient rewards to create "the greatest happiness of the greatest number." Despite the barbarous jargon in which he couched much of his thinking—in an attempt to secure a value-free language—and despite the authoritarianism and even despotism of some of the expedients that flowed from his fertile mind (for example, a scheme for a model prison, the Panopticon), Bentham's analyses, methods, and formulations are remarkably well adapted to the field of law and the associated field of administration. Until very close to the end of his life, however, he was honored more by radicals in other parts of the world than he was by his own countrymen, and his greatest influence in England probably came in the generation after his death in 1832. But England never got the codification he had pleaded for.

English law was subjected to increasing criticism from other quarters, notably from humanitarians appalled by the savagery of the criminal law. That law came under attack from lawyers and administrative reformers as well, for juries were increasingly refusing to convict, in order to escape the reckless, panicky prescribing of the death penalty: the awful deterrents were not deterring. Reform commenced in earnest in the 1820s, under Robert Peel. The application of the death penalty was drastically reduced; prisons were reformed; and the law pertaining to certain categories of crime was pruned and consolidated, a kind of partial codification. But the civil side proved far more difficult. There, piecemeal reform began to move rapidly only in the 1850s, with an important procedure act and a thorough overhauling of the law relating to matrimony. Finally, between 1873 and 1876 the main outlines of the present court system were laid down and the systems of law and equity merged. But the legislature played only a partial role in the modernization of English law; much of it, again, was accomplished by the able judges of Victoria's reign in decisions on cases that a rapidly changing society could no longer cram into inherited rules.

Administration

When it came to administering the state's business, Russia had probably the least effective apparatus of any major European nation. The size of the country and its economic backwardness were handicaps, but the machinery itself was grossly defective. Not only was the lesser official miserably underpaid, he was expected, as Professor Seton-Watson points out, "to administer laws which were cumbrous, unjust, and difficult to apply. He was obliged to support his family, often including many more or less close relatives. In these conditions, corruption was bound to flourish. Exemption from the rules, and bribes for granting the exemption, were subject to the laws of supply and demand. A market price for illegal actions was determined by economic forces. Any opportunities for placing one's relatives or friends in jobs at suitable levels of the state machine were taken." [5] Inefficiency or worse at the lower levels meant a steady flow of paper and requests for authorization upward through the hierarchy. At the center, decisions were sometimes left to ill-equipped minor officials in the ministries, while those that got beyond that level placed an intolerable burden of petty detail on the ministers and even on the tsar himself.

Although the gentry had been freed from compulsory state service in 1762, most bureaucrats still came from that class. That was no guarantee, however, that they would not be ill-educated or lazy or that they could rise above a narrow view of their class interests—for example, on the overwhelming internal problem of serfdom. They objected to the substitution of modern ministries for the old, cumbersome Petrine structure of colleges, in which decisions were made by majority vote (see p. 330); they also bitterly resented Speransky's proposal to institute examinations for entry into state service. To these difficulties were superadded those of Nicholas I's own making. To be sure, Nicholas reformed the bureaucracy, made it more efficient, and tried to keep it so by inspection. Yet he preferred to bypass the regular state machinery and use his Imperial Chancery and secret ad hoc committees. He imposed his military prejudices at every level—putting civil servants (and university students) into uniform, for example. He had able ministers at his disposal—such as Speransky or P. D. Kiselev, who did more than anyone to prepare the way for the emancipation of the 1860s; but the best-laid projects were almost invariably frustrated by ignorant opposition, lack of resources, or the general sense that the reign was a holding operation against problems that defied solution.

In the Austrian Empire, the eighteenth century had created a well-informed, effectively centralized, and imaginative bureaucracy, little troubled by corruption. This Josephinian tradition (see p. 427) did not die away. The country was ruled sensibly and evenhandedly. In some instances, as in the decision to build the great Mediterranean port of Trieste to escape exclusive dependence on the Danube as an outlet for Austrian commerce, the government even proved capable of bold strokes. But the general impression of nineteenth-century Austrian government is one of winding down. A highly centralized machine needs constant impulsion from the center, and the Austrian center was paralyzed—either by the deadening rivalry between Metternich and Count Kolowrat (see p. 709) or by the immobility and incapacity of the emperors. So the system simply ground on. "The Austrian

[5] Hugh Seton-Watson, *The Russian Empire, 1801–1917* (1967), 212.

bureaucracy," writes A. J. P. Taylor, "probably did more good than harm. It was also slow, manufactured mountains of paper, regarded the creation of new bureaucratic posts as its principal object, forgot that it dealt with human beings: these qualities are now familiar to the inhabitants of any civilized state. Still, Austrian bureaucracy was perhaps more than usually lacking in policy; and the defect was the more obvious since most of the Austrian bureaucrats were able and clear-sighted. Hartig, one of Metternich's closest colleagues, expressed the general view: 'Administration has taken the place of government.'" [6]

Prussia had turned its eighteenth-century legacy to better account than Austria. The successors of Frederick II were not what that masterful king had been, but the bureaucracy had worked its way free of the need for a continuing royal impulse. The reforms of Stein and Hardenberg early in the century were the high-water mark of this demolition of autocracy. But the reformers overreached themselves and had to arrive at an accommodation with a nobility that insisted on calling a halt to their rationalizing. But the early nineteenth-century bureaucrats were no mere timeservers. The cultural renaissance and the university reforms held up an ideal of cultivation *(Bildung)* that civil servants shared with the other professional classes and that gave them a sense of pride, independence, and superiority—much resented by the most conservative of the landed classes, who did not share these values. The civil service was not, however, a bureaucratic Eden. There was much discontent, particularly among the ambitious junior ranks, because of inadequate salaries, excessive competition for scarce places, and the deadening effect of promotion by seniority; some of this discontent found political expression in 1848. It therefore became one task of the fifties to strengthen the discipline in the service while improving its professional organization; and the conservative governments after 1848 demanded political conformity from the many officials who sat in the legislature.

Gradually over the last half of the century the civil service withdrew from active politics, as much from the nature of its job as from prudence. This did not yet mean a pure aristocracy of merit or a mandarin class divorced from the rest of society. Although entry to the service was by way of university education and examinations, the exclusiveness of Prussian society assured that Jews were not welcomed and that the great majority of the higher posts would continue to be held by nobles or those among the upper middle classes who shared with them a basic outlook. Professor Fritz Stern has referred to a pervasive "illiberalism," a cultural style emphasizing obedience and reverence to authority and the nation, rejecting tolerance and dissent, lacking what Bagehot called "the nerve" for continual discussion and frequent changes of rulers: it was, Stern argues, "a kind of civic nonage." [7] But, whatever the

---

[6] A. J. P. Taylor, *The Habsburg Monarchy, 1809-1918* (Torchbook ed., 1965), 38.
[7] Fritz Stern, *The Failure of Illiberalism: Essays on the Political Culture of Modern Germany* (1972), xlv–xlx.

shortcomings in the training of the Prussian and later the German bureaucracies, and whatever the long-range perils, English reformers admired the system and sought to obtain some of the Prussian advantages at home. And it was in Prussia that Nicholas I found his ideals best embodied: "Here is order; strict, unconditional legitimacy, no presumed omniscience and no contradictions. Everything flows, one thing from another. No one gives orders without himself having first learned to obey. No one takes precedent over another without legitimate reason. All is subordinate to one fixed aim; everything has its place. That is why it makes me feel so good to stand among these people. . . . I look on all human life merely as service; because each man serves." [8]

In France, it has been said, there are two constitutions: whatever political constitution the latest revolution has given the country and the administrative constitution created substantially by Napoleon. Of course there were obligations to the more remote past: the Napoleonic prefect mirrored the intendant of the ancient régime; the new Conseil d'Etat mirrored the old Conseil du Roi. But the Napoleonic structure, largely untouched before the advent of the Third Republic in the 1870s was more clearly defined, more rationalized, more efficient than anything France or Europe had known. The Napoleonic emphasis on the career open to talents and on the prerogatives of science found expression in a permanent civil service recruited from the technical schools founded under the Directory and the Empire. The lines of centralization and responsibility were plain; the powers of officials, particularly of the prefects, were extensive; the source of all power was clearly fixed in Paris—above all, in the ministry of the interior, to which the prefects reported. A hardheaded, carefully articulated quest for efficiency marked the administrative style, in contrast to the strict hierarchy of command in Prussia, the inertia in Austria, or the chaos in Russia. When the disastrous experiment of "national workshops" was tried during the revolution of 1848 (see p. 717) to provide work for the unemployed, the scheme was put into the hands of Emile Thomas, a young engineer. He provided himself with three assistant directors, each heading a department that was in turn subdivided into bureaus, and with a fourth assistant who had no specific assignment. The workers were assigned to squads of ten, with an elected leader; five squads made a brigade, with an elected brigadier; four brigades made up a lieutenancy; four lieutenancies a company; three companies a service; and the head of a service answered to a head of the arrondissement. From the company level up, the officers were drawn from the Ecole Centrale des Arts et Manufactures, the higher technical school founded in 1828. Had administrative rationality in itself been able to provide a meaningful policy, the experiment would have been a triumph. [9]

The ordinary law courts applied the codes in private and criminal matters.

---

[8] Quoted in Sidney Monas, *The Third Section* (1961), 11–12.
[9] The national workshops system is described in Donald C. McKay, *The National Workshops* (1935), 22–23.

But disputes in the administrative realm fell to a system of administrative tribunals culminating in the Conseil d'Etat. This was the chief consultative body of the government, where expert advice was given on the content and drafting of legislation; it was an administrative court as well. As is true of all French and Continental courts, the administrative tribunals worked by inquisitorial rather than adversary proceedings: the judge conducted the case rather than merely presiding over the clash of the parties to it. In the process a large body of judge-made administrative law has been built up, law that has become a bit more tender toward the citizen in the twentieth century than it was in the nineteenth. The founders did not foresee this growth of administrative law, but they created an administrative instrument that, for good or ill, provided the principal element of continuity throughout all the twists and turns of French political history.

How different it all was in Britain! There an amazing jumble of departments and offices, many of them dating back to the Middle Ages, survived into the early nineteenth century. The functions of some had vanished completely, except as the currency of political patronage; others had long since altered their ostensible purpose. Confusion, duplication, and pure silliness abounded, and only the most able and tireless ministers could accomplish much. By the mid-1830s, however, the picture was changing rapidly. At least from the time of the younger Pitt, old offices were being sacrificed to new notions of utility, tidiness, and efficiency; salaries were being substituted for fees, thus speeding up government business; and conditions of employment (pensions, for example) were improved to attract able people. To be sure, England never attained the degree of centralization that existed everywhere on the Continent. In the counties, the oligarchical control of the leading landowners continued until nearly the end of the century. Town governments, reformed in 1835 and given elected councils and gradually expanding powers, still levied their own taxes and were tied to the central government primarily by cooperative devices like grants-in-aid. Parliament reformed its own fact-finding and deliberative procedures, and its investigative procedures supplemented those of the Crown in laying the foundation for the legislative accomplishments of the generation after 1832; it also improved its means of holding departments accountable. New administrative commissions were created to supplement the work of the old departments, and assistant commissioners and inspectors were sent out to see that central directives were obeyed.

Masterful men were often brought in from outside the government to deal with matters on which they were expert; but what was needed was a means of making such expertise more regularly available and of freeing a sizable proportion of civil servants from the drudgery and routine to which most of them were subject. The "great evil and want," wrote one distinguished civil servant, "is that there is not within the pale of our government any adequately numerous body of efficient statesmen, some to be more externally active and answer the demands of the day, others to be somewhat more retired and meditative in order that they may take a thought for the morrow. . . . Till the government of the country shall become a nucleus at which the best wisdom in the country contained shall be perpetually forming itself in deposit, it will be, except as regards the shuffling of power from hand to hand and class to class, little better than a government of fetches, shifts, and hand-to-mouth expedients. Till a wise and constant instrumentality at work upon administrative measures (distinguished as they might be from measures of political parties) shall be understood to be essential to the government of a country, that country can be considered to enjoy nothing more than the embryo of a government." [10]

In 1854 the Trevelyan-Northcote report—named for its authors, a leading civil servant, Sir Charles Trevelyan, and Sir Stafford Northcote, a prominent Conservative politician—recommended the creation of an administrative class within the civil service. It was to be a single class, available for assignment to different departments as needed; the recruits were to be generalists, not specialists, and so the entrance examinations were to be tied to the liberal education given at Oxford and Cambridge. Except for the Foreign Office, where the need for aristocratic connections kept the service free from competition until 1919, the whole civil service came under the new system in 1870. It was no longer what James Mill had called it a generation earlier, a kind of outdoor relief for the aristocracy, though the influence of the public schools and universities made certain that civil servants would be gentlemen. Assured incomes, a large infusion of Victorian moral certainty, and a high tradition underlay the incorruptibility that was coming to characterize English government. Although government in England was less pervasive than it was on the Continent, and although it remained far more subject to political control and to the supervision of the ordinary law courts, no one could have said by 1870 what Lord Melbourne had said to the young Queen Victoria thirty years before—that bureaucracy was "something they have in France."

Police

The unique course of British bureaucratic evolution is underscored when the differing conceptions of police on the two sides of the Channel are examined. On the Continent, "police" meant more than the suppression and punishment of crime or the maintenance of civil order: it included general supervision of cleanliness and morality, the maintenance of due social subordination, the rooting out of all forms of opposition, the exercise of censorship, or, to put a positive gloss on it, the promotion of general welfare as the rulers of the age understood it. Prussia and the Austria of Joseph II offered the two best examples in eighteenth-century Europe of such a police state. But from the

[10] Sir Henry Taylor, *The Statesman* (1836), chap. 22.

founding of the ministry of police to protect the republic in 1795, the French had the most fully rationalized and developed system—one that was copied, at least in part, elsewhere. The police systems of nineteenth-century Austria and Russia—deadeningly efficient in the first case, deadeningly inefficient in the latter—were directly modeled or remodeled on the creation of Joseph Fouché. The high, or political, police, as Fouché explained it in 1805, was "the regulatory power which is felt everywhere, without ever being seen, and which at the center of the State, holds the place which the power which sustains the harmony of the celestial bodies holds in the universe, a power whose regularity strikes us although we are unable to divine the cause." [11]

The Napoleonic system was not perfect. Like all police systems, it relied heavily on informers who might be worthless as well as productive, and it was increasingly hampered by the cringing and bootlicking that, especially in authoritarian regimes, produces what inferiors think superiors want to hear. But Fouché's legacy to nineteenth-century France still exists in main outline today, its powers extended by increased specialization, the strengthening of local government, and the multiplication of social and welfare legislation and so of the supervisory powers of the police. The judiciary, or repressive, police function—the investigation and prosecution of offenses—belongs largely to the ministry of justice. The administrative, or preventive, police function, which includes most of the duties (traffic control, say, or crime prevention) that fit the Anglo-American conception, and the general police function—the far more sweeping political surveillance—come under the ministry of the interior and the prefects. [12] To the local police officials, likely to be inefficient in small communities, were added the national gendarmerie, which descended from a Revolutionary innovation—uniformed military police under the ministry of war.

With greater or lesser degrees of efficiency, then, Continental countries in the nineteenth century were police states, though the implications of the term are far more closely tied to the ideals of the Old Regime than they are to the terroristic practices of twentieth-century dictatorships. In England, by the eighteenth century, the central government had long since abandoned the pretense of exercising the general police power and was hard put to deal even with the simplest question of public order. Eighteenth-century England was riotous and violent, and the savage penalties prescribed in the criminal law may be seen as a terroristic effort to frighten wrongdoers into behavior that local authorities could not ordinarily enforce. Although some attempts had been made to improve the peace-keeping machinery in London, it was only in 1829 that Robert Peel carried an act creating the Metropolitan Police. Its command-

---

[11] Quoted in Brian Chapman, *Police State* (1970), 29-30. On Fouché, see pp. 493, 548.
[12] In Paris, the prefect's duties are divided: the prefect of the Seine exercises administrative functions; the prefect of police exercises police functions. But elsewhere in France responsibility for the two functions is united in a single official.

ers struggled to build a professional force and to establish its authority over the populace, and in time they succeeded, even winning a degree of popularity; gradually after 1839 similar police forces were built up in other parts of the country. But the English notion of police remained restricted, the inept political spying of the postwar period gradually sank of its own weight, and mid-Victorian England became a haven of freedom for thousands of refugees from Continental repression.

The Armed Forces

Those nations—first the Prussians, then the French—that had suffered the worst defeats in the Napoleonic Wars were those from which the most imaginative military reform emerged after 1815; the British and the Russians, who emerged with the greatest naval and military prestige, remained largely stuck in archaisms. To some extent this was a matter of personality. The system of seniority in both army and navy, coupled with political influence, brought veterans of the Napoleonic Wars to the top and kept them there, insulated from fresh thinking and only reluctantly responding to advances made by potential enemies. The duke of Wellington survived until 1852; he continued to think that the army he headed was incapable of improvement. In Russia, Field Marshal Paskevich, the victor in Poland in 1831, exercised a similar influence; and, in military as in civil affairs, Nicholas I was bold in minutiae and timid in essentials. [13] While Nicholas and his generals were willing to spend lavishly on defense, they failed to see that military success in the nineteenth century rested ultimately on a strong economy and industrial development. The British, more advanced economically and technologically than any nation in Europe, begrudged every penny spent on the services, above all on the army, which by jealously guarded tradition was kept small and largely occupied with garrison duty in the empire.

Enlisted men in Russia served for twenty-five years at the beginning of Nicholas' reign and for fifteen at the end. The use of conscription, spreading rapidly on the Prussian model through western Europe, was unavailable, because by law army service carried with it freedom from servitude and Russia dared not risk dissolving the system of serfdom by the short-term enlistments that elsewhere made trained reserves possible. British soldiers were also recruited for long terms and, like the Russians, subjected to savage discipline. Flogging was a basic punishment in the armed forces of both countries, and in Britain it survived more than half a century of humanitarian agitation against

---

[13] Field Marshal Radetzky, of the Austrian army, proved that age was no guarantee of stodginess. He kept himself abreast of current strategic and tactical doctrine and, in 1849, at the age of eighty-two, won a brilliant victory over the Piedmontese army at Novara. He had been born a year before Napoleon.

it. Only in the aftermath of the Crimean War did the British do anything to shorten terms of service or to humanize the life the troops led. At about the same time the navy established a true volunteer system and began to provide training, the possibility of rising in the ranks, and decent conditions aboard ship. Russian and English officers were drawn from the aristocracy, and in neither country were officers properly trained or even adequate to the tasks that fell to them—in striking contrast to the equally aristocratic Prussian officers who, whatever their limitations, were well schooled in their trade. Until 1871 commissions in the British army were purchased—a practice defended as avoiding the perils of Continental professionalism and as assuring that the army would be led by gentlemen. Abolition of purchase was rejected by the House of Lords and had to be rammed through in 1871 by a surprising use of the royal prerogative at the insistence of the forceful war minister Edward Cardwell, whose reforms launched the British army on its modern career.

The Crimean War had revealed not only the weaknesses of the British and Russian armies as fighting machines, but it had demonstrated the incapacity of the supporting and administrative services—supply, victualing, transport—on which success in modern war depends. Much was done to remedy these shortcomings, but in the matter of overall planning the Prussians continued to stay far ahead of the other European nations. Descending from reforms of the Napoleonic era, the Prussian general staff was an advisory organ subordinate to the war ministry; but the remarkable success of General Helmuth Karl von Moltke, the head of the general staff in directing the latter stages of the war against Denmark in 1864, brought control of field armies under the general staff; soon after, the chief of the general staff became the king's principal military adviser. Where war had once been a matter of the enterprise and skill of individual commanders, the new style was, as Basil Liddell Hart puts it, "more orchestral." [14] Though the concentration of planning and strategic functions in the general staff could engender a dangerous isolation and a tendency to emphasize military considerations to the exclusion of all others, the staff system seemed inescapable, given the complexity of modern warfare. After 1870 all the European armies followed suit.

In the decades between 1830 and 1870 both armies and navies began to cope with a technological revolution. At sea, the transition was being made to steam power, to iron-hulled and armor-plated ships, and to sophisticated armament that could deliver effective fire at long range. In both naval and land artillery the crucial development was the breechloading, rifled gun that fired explosive shells. At nearly every stage the French were the innovators, despite the clear lead held by Britain in all the industries on which the new techniques depended. The British had some reason for caution besides an innate conservatism; not all the new devices were successful, and some that proved

---

[14] B. H. Liddell Hart, "Armed Forces and the Art of War," *New Cambridge Modern History*, vol. X (1967), 311.

successful took long to develop into really usable form. This explains the long persistence of sail, in both naval and mercantile shipping, because sail required no fuel storage and allowed a far wider range of operations than was possible with steamships tied to a fleet of colliers and a worldwide network of coaling stations. Only the conservation of fuel by the triple-expansion steam engine and later the steam turbine assured the supremacy of steam power.[15] In the development of small arms, though the technological honors were spread more evenly, the French again had the edge; their *chassepot* rifle, in at least partial use in 1870, was superior to anything the Germans had, though superiority in weaponry could not in itself guarantee victory.

It was clear after 1870 that technological change, the use of railways in deploying troops, and the spread of conscription and reserve systems had revolutionized warfare. The navy was no longer a merchant fleet at war; the army became something other than the hunting field on serious business. New concepts in strategy and tactics reemphasized the importance of staff planning. With its vast budgetary demands and its insistence on expertise, the new warfare increased the importance of the military in the counsels of the state and started that self-propelling arms race that began in earnest after 1871 and has not yet ended.

THE MOBILIZATION OF ABILITY

Schools and Universities

The more sophisticated the technology and the political organization on which a state can draw, the more it requires effective ways of mobilizing its citizens, whether merely to indoctrinate them and so guarantee their submission, or to recruit and train them to do the specialized work that the new system demands. Educational theorists and reformers, of course, sought goals other than the good of the state. The heirs of the eighteenth-century Enlightenment believed that education would create good citizens, but they also saw in it a means of liberation from ancient prejudice and superstition. A few theorists—Rousseau, say, or Friedrich Froebel, the Swiss inventor of the kindergarten—went so far as to envision the freeing of children to respond to their own curiosity and creativity. Far more widespread was the humanitarian or religious desire to promote, by means of a basic literacy, a due knowledge of religion and (in Protestant countries) of the Bible.

The one country that had attained nearly universal literacy in the eighteenth century was Scotland, where a system of parish schools had been set

---

[15] G. S. Graham, "The Ascendancy of the Sailing Ship, 1850-1885," *Economic History Review*, 2nd ser., vol. 9 (August 1956), 74-88.

up at the very end of the seventeenth century. But the rapid growth of population and a lack of resources (notwithstanding great voluntary efforts) quickly compromised that enviable reputation in the nineteenth century. Austria devised a nationwide system of parish schools early in the new century, but they were inadequate and, given the tone of the empire under Francis I, were little more than engines to produce pious, obedient subjects. Russia, too, had secured a basic system of schools during the reign of Alexander I, but confined them to the narrowest uses. It was to Germany that one had to turn to find the most rapid development of popular education. Prussian schools flowered during the revival of the Napoleonic period, partly in response to needs of the state but also under the influence of the liberal theories of the Swiss educator Johann Heinrich Pestalozzi, popularized for a receptive Prussian audience by Fichte in his *Addresses to the German Nation* (see p. 528). Impressive progress was made as well in Scandinavia, Holland, and Switzerland.

In France, Guizot sponsored legislation to remedy the neglect of primary education by earlier regimes, and the number of primary schools increased by a third between the passage of the Guizot Law in 1833 and the revolution of 1848. The development of French education was troubled, however, by a bitter political quarrel over the role of the church. In contrast to Germany, Scandinavia, Austria, and Russia, where church and state worked together easily, the French state system, true to its Revolutionary and Napoleonic origins, was secular. In the 1820s debate raged over whether the teaching orders should be allowed to conduct schools even outside the state system. In 1850, in the aftermath of the revolution of 1848, the Falloux Law made sweeping concessions to the church; but in time the secularists were to return to the attack, and the religious question remained to bedevil French education for years to come (pp. 727, 816).

A similar quarrel in England was the rock on which foundered one after another project to create a system of primary (or "national") education. Only a few radicals went so far as to advocate a completely secular education; the issue in England lay in the irreconcilability of the church and Dissent. Early in the century two voluntary societies, one Anglican, the other largely Dissenting, were founded to build and operate schools; both for a time were wedded to the simplistic pedagogical notion—called the "monitorial system"—that older children could teach the younger, an appealing idea when trained teachers were almost nonexistent and money was in short supply. In 1833 the government began to give grants-in-aid to the societies to help with the costs of building, tying the grants to acceptance of government inspection of the schools' programs. The grants increased, and a rudimentary ministry of education set up in 1839 went beyond inspecting and encouraging to establish regular training of teachers. But it was not until 1870 that an act creating a system of state schools could be passed, and even then only to make provision where church schools were unavailable or inadequate. A few years earlier the central education authorities, for reasons of bureaucratic and educational efficiency, had made it clear that grants were contingent on the results of examinations, and the examinations were to test reading, writing, and simple calculation, no more. The schools were to produce literate and honest workers and housemaids, and the schoolteachers were to become drillmasters.

Secondary education everywhere was a high road to privilege for which privilege was virtually a precondition. Still, on the Continent, secondary education was often more penetrable and certainly better organized than it was in England. In Germany the gymnasium had emerged from the old Latin schools in the course of the eighteenth century; Prussia reorganized the schools and the examinations in the early nineteenth century, and the model was copied elsewhere in central and eastern Europe. The French counterpart of the gymnasium was the lycée, created under Napoleon; the all-important qualifying examination for higher education, the *baccalauréat,* was established in 1808. The gymnasium and the lycée alike were almost wholly classical and mathematical in their emphasis, although the Prussians provided another set of schools (Realschulen) that taught more modern subjects.

In England, as usual, there was only confusion—hundreds of endowed grammar schools, founded by pious worthies to educate local boys or even, in some instances, the poor. Some were boarding schools, some were day schools, some gave a good education, and in some the founder's intentions had been forgotten entirely. A few of the schools had undergone a development in the sixteenth and seventeenth centuries that led to their being singled out as "public schools": they took boarders, were national in their reputation and recruitment, and catered largely to the aristocracy. Yet even they suffered from routinized, dismally classical teaching, harsh discipline, and endemic rowdiness. In the early nineteenth century, some reforming headmasters appeared, the most famous of them Dr. Thomas Arnold at Rugby School. Arnold introduced a leaven of modern subjects, notably history, set and maintained a high moral tone, and devised a disciplinary system in which the power was exercised by the boys themselves. Thus was created an example—insofar as it could be separated from Arnold's compelling personality—that was followed by the other public schools, by newly founded schools, and by some old grammar schools on their way up in the world. Mid-Victorian England, then, could provide a reasonably good education for the wealthy. But the extension of secondary education (and the public school model) to a still wider range of grammar schools and to the state system was the work of the late nineteenth and twentieth centuries.[16]

---

[16] The education of girls at the secondary level was neglected throughout Europe until the latter part of the nineteenth century. In England the lead was taken by formidable ladies who headed two girls' boarding schools; they have been handsomely commemorated in verse:

> Miss Buss and Miss Beale
> Cupid's darts do not feel.
> How different from us,
> Miss Beale and Miss Buss!

The glory of the university world lay in Germany. The founding of the University of Berlin in 1810 celebrated the dawning of a national consciousness, but it was only first among equals—old and reformed or new and aggressive institutions—scattered throughout German lands. Scientific research, a theological revolution, the historical study of jurisprudence and political economy, and vital philosophical and philological contributions flowed from the German universities and stimulated an intense intellectual life in their precincts. However severe the surveillance visited on the universities by troubled governments, the modern scholarly mission continued to expand; in some respects scholarship became a haven from politics. Political repression was far more baleful in the Austrian universities or in Russia, though both nations produced students who rose above the ordinary and both could claim distinguished scholars and scientists.

In France the emphasis was far more heavily on professional training than on scholarship. To be sure, impressive research was carried on in the Institut de France—the Napoleonic substitute for the abolished (and later revived) Académie Française—and in the nonteaching Collège de France. But the old universities had been dissolved and their professional faculties gathered under the umbrella of the new Napoleonic Université de France, a kind of educational holding company that incorporated the entire structure of secondary and higher education. It was the new professional schools, however, that lent particular distinction to the French system: above all, the Ecole Polytechnique for engineers, and the Ecole Normale, which trained future secondary and university teachers. Napoleon III added the Ecole Pratique des Hautes Etudes in 1868, and the Ecole Libre des Sciences Politiques followed in 1872. But revival of a university system, relegated as it was by the Napoleonic reforms to isolated provincial faculties, began only at the very end of the nineteenth century and then was kept by war and politics from becoming really serviceable until the years after 1945.

In Scotland the eighteenth-century flowering of the universities—preternaturally modern, democratic, and professional—faded somewhat in the nineteenth century. In England the torpor of eighteenth-century Oxford and Cambridge was broken. Internal agitation for reform led to structural changes, the improvement of teaching, and the institution of honors programs, but external pressures were applied as well. In part they took the form of competition, notably from the University of London, founded as a secular institution in 1827, and from new provincial universities that were appearing by midcentury. The government investigated Oxford and Cambridge as a prelude to reforming them; new statutes in the 1850s at last allowed Dissenters full access to the two old universities, and in 1871 the remaining religious tests for the holding of fellowships (i.e., teaching posts) in the colleges were done away with. Only after 1870 did the English universities begin seriously to encourage research, often on the German model, in addition to their principal concern with teaching.

To what ends did these highly varying systems of education lead? Every system made signal contributions to the state, of course. In eastern and central Europe, the bureaucratic ambitions of the majority of students and the centrality of the universities in staffing government administration are well-known. The same may be said for the more specialized training in France. On their own evaluation, the English public schools and universities remained principally institutions for producing Christian gentlemen, for building character. And even when the cult of athletics threatened to swamp scholarship, the production of young men accustomed to lead (and, perhaps more important, to think of themselves as superior) put an indelible stamp on the civil service and on the administration of a worldwide empire.

The English universities did far less well by the professions, however. Apprenticeship remained the principal means of training lawyers and doctors, though ambitious medical students with a scientific bent often went to the Scottish universities or to the Continent. It has only been in the twentieth century that the older universities have done much about the newer professions; the "red-brick" universities founded in the nineteenth century, however, were specifically responded to the need for professional and technical training felt in the provincial towns, less hidebound and less insulated from the workaday world than the cloisters and common rooms of Oxford and Cambridge. The English failure ran right down the scale: engineers were trained in the course of working, and virtually no provision was made for training skilled workingmen or middle-level technicians in modern technology or design. France, on the other hand, had not only the Polytechnique and the Ecole Centrale des Arts et Manufactures, but also the Conservatoire des Arts et Métiers, which offered courses to artisans. The Technical Institute was founded in Berlin in 1821; it admitted boys who were at least twelve years of age and gave them two years of basic training in mathematics and scientific subjects, a course extended to three years in 1842. The creation of Peter Beuth, head of the department of trade and industry in the Prussian ministry of finance, this school was copied in other German cities and helped to assure the rapid development of German industry later in the century. Even Russia had a cluster of schools dealing in drawing, architecture, surveying, agriculture, and other branches of technology. Technical subjects were developed in the universities as well, though the results were far from adequate. But, despite warnings from parliamentary committees as early as the 1830s and despite the work of the short-lived Science and Art Department of the Board of Trade, Britain remained unsystematic and backward in developing a strong basis in technological education for its industrial supremacy. That is one reason Britain lost it.

The Intellectuals

One more development of immense importance remains to be considered: the growth in every European country of a class of people whose lives were involved principally with the intellect, a phenomenon well established before the Russians coined the word "intelligentsia" in the 1860s. This phenomenon was partly the result of expanded education, particularly at the university level, but it also flowed from a diffusion of wealth: more wealthy people came to value learning, and more people who valued learning were able to support themselves, either on inherited incomes or by mind and pen. The growth of bureaucracy also made its contributions, as did the expansion and systematization of the professions.

Although most intellectuals were formed in the universities of their countries, they were not entirely absorbed by them. Nearly as important as the universities as a foundation for the intelligentsia, and perhaps more so, was the press. In countries with large reading publics, nineteenth-century authors could actually live and live well on their writings alone, and for many more journalism provided not only a livelihood but a way of getting their ideas into circulation. In England and France the growth and mechanization of newspapers, the new rapidity of transportation and communication, and the national dedication to politics made journalism a force to be reckoned with by politicians and a profession that was rising rapidly to respectability out of eighteenth-century "scribbling." But periodical journalism and the rise of criticism as a literary form were even more important for the intelligentsia. The quarterly reviews in Britain—the *Edinburgh,* the *Quarterly,* the *Westminster*—and the monthly and weekly magazines were central in the awareness of educated men; so too the *Revue des Deux Mondes* in Paris; so too *The Bell,* published by the Russian Alexander Herzen in his London exile from 1857 to 1867 and smuggled into Russia.

The character of the intelligentsia and its structure varied from country to country. In France it was highly centralized in Paris and was involved less with educational institutions than with the salons for which the capital was famous. In Germany, the ideal of *Bildung* ("cultivation") was bred into the stratum of university men in every field of endeavor. In contrast to France, where culture was highly politicized, in Germany the intellectual—for principled as well as prudential reasons—tended to shun politics; the fate of the young Marx and his early university friends demonstrated the dangers that activist intellectuals could run (see p. 687). In England the universities became important in the perpetuation of the intellectual class but were only tangentially important in its origins. In the early nineteenth century, a number of marriages between old university and clerical families and the families of wealthy, cultivated businessmen, often from the provinces, launched a set of veritable dynasties of intellectuals. Even today Darwins, Wedgwoods, Cornfords, Huxleys, and Stracheys crop up in every corner of English intellectual and public life with far more than statistical probability. Receptive, on their own terms, to talent from outside; secure in wealth, position, and ability; accepted, even when they are critical, by society at large, this "intellectual aristocracy," as their historian has called them, offers "the paradox of an intelligentsia which appears to conform rather than rebel against the rest of society." [17]

It was in Russia that the word was coined and in Russia that the intelligentsia became most dedicated to rebellion. A good many educated men—gentry, priests' sons, outsiders who by luck or ability had penetrated the world of the universities and officialdom—began by the 1820s and 1830s to sense the enormous gulf that lay between their privilege and the overwhelming mass of their countrymen, who were kept in bondage and ignorance. These intellectuals were caught up in the remarkable literary movement in nineteenth-century Russia. Many of them nourished memories of the Decembrists (see p. 543). Some of them admired the West, plunged into liberalism and socialism, and hoped for the transformation of Russia along such Western lines as could be accommodated; others, reacting against the West, clung to Orthodoxy and a sense of Russia's distinct mission. Some of them emigrated, the most famous being Herzen, who was central in the development of Russian socialism, and M. A. Bakunin, the leading apostle of anarchism in Europe. Others stayed behind, with their circles, their little journals, and their terrible quarrels, and, above all, with the repressiveness. But the repressiveness in the long run served only to strengthen their determination to regenerate Russia and to convince them that extreme measures—violence and revolution—were the only course open to them. Few countries knew the essentially liberal common purpose that united the English intellectual aristocracy with the state and society they served; no other country experienced so terrible an alienation of a class eager to serve their people as did Russia.

SELECTED READINGS

From the vast field of the history of political thought one can choose only a few key studies. Jack Lively, ed., *The Works of Joseph de Maistre* (1971) is a selection of extracts with a helpful introduction. For French political thought, in addition to works that will be mentioned in Chapter 17, an excellent survey is R. H. Soltau, *French Political Thought in the Nineteenth Century* (1931). On Germany, see Herbert Marcuse, *Reason and Revolution: Hegel and the Rise of Social Theory* (1954); Leonard Krieger, *The German Idea of Freedom: The History of a Political Tradition* (1957); and Klaus Epstein, *The Genesis of German Conservatism* (1966), a work that comes down to 1806, left incomplete by the author's early death. On Russia, in addition to works cited in Chapters 16 and 19, see especially the long introduction in Richard Pipes, ed., *Karamzin's Memoir on Ancient and Modern Russia* (1959). On the British tradition, see Elie Halévy's classic *The Growth of Philosophical Radicalism* (1901-1904, tr. 1928). Jeremy Bentham, the fountainhead of so much British thought and action, figures centrally there, but see also the highly favorable view in Mary Peter Mack, *Jeremy Bentham: An Odyssey of Ideas* (1963), and the stern critique in Gertrude Himmelfarb, "The Haunted House of Jeremy Bentham," reprinted in her *Victorian Minds* (1968). For

---

[17] Noel Annan, "The Intellectual Aristocracy," in J. H. Plumb, ed., *Studies in Social History presented to G. M. Trevelyan* (1955), 285.

later developments, see Joseph Hamburger, *Intellectuals in Politics: John Stuart Mill and the Philosophical Radicals* (1965), and Norman St. John-Stevas, *Walter Bagehot: A Study of His Life and Thought, together with a Selection from His Writings* (1959).

Perhaps more than any other subjects treated in this book, the history of law and administration is hampered by the division of scholarship into separate national fields. On Russian law, see the chapter in Marc Raeff's *Michael Speransky, Statesman of Imperial Russia, 1772-1839* (1957). The great multivolumed *History of English Law* by Sir William Holdsworth (1903-1966) is unsatisfactory for the nineteenth century; see C. H. S. Fifoot's brief *Judge and Jurist in the Reign of Queen Victoria* (1959), and sections of W. L. Burn's fascinating *The Age of Equipoise* (1964). Bernard Schwartz's *French Administration and the Common Law World* (1954), though concerned primarily with the present, has useful comparative dimensions for the historian. Much of the history of Continental administration must be got at, at least in English, by working back from analyses of more recent periods by political scientists: F. Ridley and J. Blondel, *Public Administration in France* (2nd ed., 1969); Brian Chapman, *The Prefects and Provincial France* (1955); Charles E. Freedeman, *The Conseil d'Etat in Modern France* (1961); Robert C. Fried, *The Italian Prefects* (1963), useful in showing the influence of French and Belgian models; Herbert Jacob, *German Administration since Bismarck* (1963); J. C. G. Rohl, "Higher Civil Servants in Germany, 1890-1900," *Journal of Contemporary History*, 2 (1967), reprinted in Walter Laqueur and G. L. Mosse, eds., *Education and Social Structure in the Twentieth Century* (1967), 101-121; and, particularly, John R. Gillis, *The Prussian Bureaucracy in Crisis, 1840-1860* (1971).

British administration has been extensively studied. A good introductory survey is Emmeline Cohen, *The Growth of the British Civil Service, 1780-1939* (1941, rev. ed., 1965). For important contributions to a continuing debate on the obligation of a developing bureaucracy to practical or ideological considerations (Benthamism especially), see S. E. Finer, *The Life and Times of Sir Edwin Chadwick* (1952); Oliver McDonagh, "The Nineteenth-Century Revolution in Government: A Reappraisal," *Historical Journal*, 1 (1958), 52-67; G. Kitson Clark, "Statesmen in Disguise," ibid., 2 (1959), 19-39; and Henry Parris, "The Nineteenth-Century Revolution in Government: A Reappraisal Reappraised," ibid., 3 (1960), 17-37. A review article on the controversy by Valerie Cromwell appears in *Victorian Studies*, 9 (March 1966), 245-255.

On police, Sidney Monas, *The Third Section* (1961), cited earlier, is indispensable on the Russian situation. A valuable general interpretation of nineteenth-century Continental views is Brian Chapman, *Police State* (1970), which should be supplemented by Howard C. Payne, *The Police State of Louis Napoleon* (1966). Richard Cobb, *The Police and the People: French Popular Protest, 1789-1820* (1970) delivers more on the second part of its title than on the first but is helpful on the use of informers and the credibility of evidence so gathered. On Britain, see Leon Radzinowicz, *A History of English Criminal Law and Its Administration from 1750*, 4 vols. (1948-1968); F. C. Mather, *Public Order in the Age of the Chartists* (1960); and J. J. Tobias, *Crime and Industrial Society in the 19th Century* (1967, 2nd ed., 1971, with the title *Urban Crime in Victorian England*).

On the armed forces, in addition to works mentioned in Chapter 13 in connection with the Prussian reforms and below in connection with specific wars, see the two admirable essays on navies and armies, respectively, by Michael Lewis and B. H. Liddell Hart in the *New Cambridge Modern History*, vol. X, *The Zenith of European Power, 1830-1870*, edited by J. P. T. Bury (1967), 274-301 and 302-330. Although it is organized chiefly as a narrative of wars, Cyril Falls' *A Hundred Years of War, 1850-1950* (1953) contains both technical and institutional information. John S. Curtiss has written *The Russian Army under Nicholas I, 1825-1855* (1965).

The history of education is well served in English-language books only for England itself, for which the literature is enormous and uneven. The most recent general survey of national education is John Hurt, *Education in Evolution: Church, State, Society, and Popular Education, 1800-1870* (1971); on the growth of state secondary education, see G. A. N. Lowndes, *The Silent Social Revolution: An Account of the Expansion of Public Education in England and Wales, 1895-1935* (1937). Education for the privileged is dealt with in T. W. Bamford, *The Rise of the Public Schools* (1967), and David Newsome, *Godliness and Good Learning: Four Studies on a Victorian Ideal* (1961). A way into the transformation of the universities is provided in Sheldon Rothblatt, *The Revolution of the Dons: Cambridge and Society in Victorian England* (1968). On the differing and important situation in Scotland, see Parts 4 and 5 of L. J. Saunders, *Scottish Democracy, 1815-1840: The Social and Intellectual Background* (1950), and G. E. Davie, *The Democratic Intellect: Scotland and her Universities in the Nineteenth Century* (1961). There are two surveys, still in French, of education in France: Félix Ponteil, *Histoire de l'enseignement en France, 1789-1964* (1966), and Antoine Prost, *Histoire de l'enseignement en France, 1800-1967* (1968), to which may be added Maurice Gontard, *L'enseignement primaire en France, de la Révolution à la loi Guizot* (1959). Sections of Douglas Johnson's *Guizot, Aspects of French History, 1787-1874* (1963) are important for the subject, and the first chapter of John E. Talbott, *The Politics of Educational Reform in France, 1918-1940* (1969) is a useful retrospect.

On Russian education, see William H. E. Johnson, *Russia's Educational Heritage* (1950), and two brief surveys by Nicholas Hans, *History of Russian Educational Policy (1701-1917)* (1931) and *The Russian Tradition in Education* (1963). Technical education in Germany and Russia is touched on in the books by W. O. Henderson and W. M. Pintner, cited in the preceding chapter, and for France, see Frederick B. Artz, *The Development of Technical Education in France, 1500-1850* (1966).

On the press and the growing reading public, see Irene Collins, *The Government and the Newspaper Press in France, 1814-1881* (1959); the most recent general history for France is in the two volumes so far published (bringing the story down to 1871) of Claude Bellanger et al., *Histoire générale de la presse française* (1969). On England, see R. K. Webb, "The Reading Public," in Boris Ford, ed., *Pelican Guide to English Literature,* vol. VI, *Dickens to Hardy* (1958), 205-226; R. D. Altick, *The English Common Reader* (1957); Donald Read, *Press and People, 1790-1850;* and the anonymous five-volume *History of The Times* (1935-1952).

On the intellectual classes in Russia, see Richard Pipes, ed., *The Russian Intelligentsia* (1961), and Philip Pomper, *The Russian Revolutionary Intelligentsia* (1970). On England, see W. J. Reader, *Professional Men* (1966), and Noel Annan, "The Intellectual Aristocracy," in J. H. Plumb, ed., *Studies in Social History presented to G. M. Trevelyan* (1955), 243-287. The best first approach to the history of German education, in English, is through studies of the intellectuals, although the nineteenth century is looked at from the vantage point of the twentieth and the inevitable question of what went wrong: Fritz K. Ringer, *The Decline of the German Mandarins: The German Academic Community, 1890-1933* (1969), and the interesting essay by Friedrich Lilge, *The Abuse of Learning: The Failure of the German University* (1948).

16

Perceptions of Reality: 1815-1870

The generation of the Revolution and Napoleon may well have marked a more distinct epoch in the politics of Europe than in its intellect. Changes in cultural style are sometimes subtle, sometimes not, but when we perceive substantial differences, it is usually possible to trace their origins back far enough to cast doubt on easy invocations of a "spirit of the age" or one or another "ism." Such cultural labels are useful only when one is aware of how complex and elusive are the transformations they have come to signify. This chapter is concerned with the nature of some of those transformations.

THE MARCH OF MIND

The phrase "the march of mind" was much bandied about in England in the 1820s. It captured a common assumption that knowledge was moving steadily, relentlessly onward, and that the results could be nothing but beneficent. Not everyone agreed. In *Crotchet Castle* (1828), by the satirical novelist Thomas Love Peacock, Dr. Ffolliot, the clergyman, explains how he nearly lost his house through the march of mind—from his cook's "taking it into her head to study hydrostatics in a sixpenny tract, published by the Steam Intellect Society." She chose to read the tract in bed, naturally fell asleep, and overturned the candle, setting the curtains ablaze; disaster was prevented only by the timely appearance of the footman, who doused the flame. As for the footman's presence in the cook's room, "Sir, as good came of it, I shut my eyes and asked no questions. I suppose he was going to study hydrostatics, and he found himself under the necessity of practising hydraulics." Peacock was poking fun at the somewhat indiscriminate pursuit of self-education and the solemn efforts of such well-meaning organizations as the Society for the Diffusion of Useful Knowledge to provide cheap, "improving" reading for a newly literate public. But the joke suggests two further considerations: the march of mind meant science, and science could be unsettling and even dangerous.

The Physical Sciences

A striking change in the conceptualization and practice of science took place round about 1870. In the earlier, transitional part of the century, the scientists' heroes continued to be Newton and Bacon, and much of what was done confirmed their insights. The wave theory of light came into general acceptance about 1820 through the work of Thomas Young, a physician and fellow of the Royal Society in London, and Augustin Fresnel, a *polytechnicien* in Paris. Although their results supported the hypothesis advanced by Newton's contemporary Christian Huygens rather than that of Newton himself, by midcentury Newton's discovery of the composite nature of light had been justified and put to use in the science of spectroscopy. Even more striking confirmations came to Newton's astronomical theories, from the *Traité de mécanique céleste* published over the first quarter of the century by Pierre Laplace (whom Napoleon made a marquis) to the discovery of the planet Neptune in 1845–1846. Bacon seemed vindicated by the apparent triumphs of the experimental method, though in fact experiment was not so much a means of arriving at truth as it was a way of confirming increasingly bold hypotheses arrived at intuitively—by informed hunches, so to speak—and worked out mathematically.

The age of the gifted amateur was passing. While scientists remained astonishingly versatile, making discoveries in widely separated fields that a single mind today could only rarely comprehend, they were becoming professional in that science was their work and that work was centered increasingly in institutions. In England, the Royal Society—polite, socially desirable, and dominated by dilettantes—regained its scientific eminence only later in the century. But the Royal Institution, founded in 1799 to diffuse knowledge by public lectures and to promote practical science, was made into an important research center by two brilliant scientists—Sir Humphry Davy and Michael Faraday. The British Association for the Advancement of Science, founded in 1831, provided an important forum for the exchange of scientific views. But, the new University of London apart, the English universities began the effective pursuit of science only after 1870, with the founding of the Cavendish Laboratories in Cambridge. French science, far ahead of the rest of the world in Napoleonic days, was based on the Institut de France, the Collège de France, and the Ecole Polytechnique. But in the Restoration period these institutions were starved of funds, and by the thirties scientific leadership had clearly passed to Germany, where the universities threw enormous resources into the pursuit of science, for example, at Giessen, where the chemist Justus von Liebig had his laboratories.

The increasingly rigorous intellectual structure of science is reflected in the growth of its mathematical foundations. The mathematical giant of the early part of the century was Karl Friedrich Gauss, a retiring, conservative German who founded the theory of numbers, devised the statistical technique of the method of least squares, and laid the groundwork for mathematical statements of electrical theory. Gauss also began to question the Euclidean theorems in geometry, but the credit for developing non-Euclidean systems belongs to N. I. Lobachevsky in Russia and especially to Georg F. B. Riemann in Germany. The increasing abstractness of science can perhaps best be illustrated by following through one strand of electrical theory. In 1820, in Denmark, Hans Christian Oersted discovered that a current running through a wire affected a magnetic needle. Building on this basis, Michael Faraday in England—the finest experimentalist of his age—reversed the process and discovered induction, producing an electric current by repeated interruption of a magnetic field. Faraday's work not only made possible the development of the dynamo and the electric motor, but contributed the analytical notion of a field of force. Then, in the 1860s, the Scot James Clerk Maxwell brought his formidable mathematical powers to bear on Faraday's discoveries, making the imaginative leap to the identity of magnetic and electrical forces and perceiving that light is a special instance of an electromagnetic wave. His theoretical and mathematical hypotheses were verified by experiment, chiefly by Heinrich Hertz, in Germany; Hertz later discovered the electromagnetic waves associated with radio.

Similar conceptual genealogies can be readily traced. In the first decade of the century John Dalton, a Manchester schoolmaster active in the local literary and philosophical society, advanced an atomic hypothesis in which the essential novelty was the notion of atomic weight. The process by which elements combine was advanced by J. L. Gay-Lussac in Paris and particularly by J. J. Berzelius in Sweden, who carefully measured the atomic weights of a large number of elements. Three complementary developments in midcentury brought this phase of analytical chemistry to a climax. One was the theory of valency—the relative combining power of different atoms—contributed in the

1850s by an English chemist, Edward Frankland, and the German F. A. Kekulé. In the sixties the molecular hypothesis of the Italian Count Amadeo Avogadro, developed much earlier in the century, came to be generally accepted, and Kekulé's ring formula for benzene made it possible to visualize how the atoms within the molecule are combined. J. L. Meyer in Germany and Dmitri Mendeleev in Russia worked out the periodic law that made it possible to classify elements by "families" according to recurring properties and so to predict the discovery of elements as yet unknown. [1] The observations of the French engineer Nicolas Sadi Carnot—the son of the great military engineer of the French Revolution—led James Joule and Lord Kelvin in England and Hermann von Helmholtz in Germany to formulate the laws of thermodynamics and the concept of energy. Together with the conclusions of Clerk Maxwell, thermodynamics brought physicists by 1870 to the view that physics, which dealt with phenomena as apparently different as heat, light, and electricity, was in fact the study of various modes of the interaction of matter and energy. These highly oversimplified and partial catalogues, though they can hardly do justice to the heroic conceptual efforts of the age, at least indicate the combination of a priori, mathematical speculation with the most precise observation, the cumulative quality of scientific reasoning, and the collaborative, indeed international, character of the enterprise.

Theoretical science made notable contributions to the development of technology as well. The lectures on latent heat given by Joseph Black in Glasgow in the 1760s had helped James Watt to devise his revolutionary improvements in the old, inefficient steam engines. Sir Humphry Davy not only invented the miner's safety lamp, which saved countless lives from underground explosions, but, through his theoretical work on electrolysis, he made possible the industrial process of electroplating, to which Faraday's researches also contributed. Liebig's work on soil chemistry led in time to the use of artificial fertilizers and contributed greatly to an understanding of organic chemistry, on which so much of the chemical industry of the nineteenth century was founded. In 1828 the German Friedrich Wöhler synthesized urea, the first creation of an organic substance from inorganic components, another stimulus to both the theory and the application of organic chemistry. W. H. Perkin's discovery of coal-tar dyes in the by-products of the coking process in 1856 emancipated the textile industry from its dependence on scarce vegetable dyes. Rapidly changing technologies, increasingly obligated to theoretical science, had steadily widening impact on the lives of ordinary people—on the work they did, on the food they ate, and on the quality of their physical environment. The chemical industry and the electrical industry—the latter deeply dependent on the discoveries of Faraday and his successors—had

---

[1] Kekulé said that the benzene formula came to him while he was dozing; he saw chains of carbon atoms twisting and curling like snakes until one gripped its tail in its mouth. Mendeleev also reported that the idea of periodicity came to him in his sleep.

perhaps the most startling effect, evident throughout much of western Europe by the latter years of the nineteenth century.

New Perspectives on Man

The philosophical implications of rapid advances in physics and chemistry did not penetrate much beyond the ranks of the scientists. Developments in two other sciences, however, soon forced changed perceptions of man's place in the world on nearly every educated person. Geology made particularly rapid strides in the early decades of the century, stimulated by the intense debate between the catastrophists and the uniformitarians. Was the world as modern man knew it the result of a series of great cataclysms—earthquakes, say, or floods—that destroyed all forms of life and led to the creation of new forms, or was the world built up through the regular, slow operation of natural processes—such as deposit and erosion—that could be seen at work everywhere? The catastrophist position was, of course, more consistent with biblical narrative, but the uniformitarian hypothesis emerged victorious in Sir Charles Lyell's *Principles of Geology,* published in the early 1830s. Geological inquiry was reinforced by the speculations of the paleontologists about the origins and distribution of fossils and by the careful classification of forms of life, largely following methods laid down early in the century by Baron Cuvier, another much-honored Napoleonic scientist.

The development of biology—the name was first applied to the science of life in 1800—was bedeviled by the persistent question of the origins of the multifarious forms of life. Were species specially created, as the Bible asserted and as Cuvier (a catastrophist) and Lyell (a uniformitarian) continued to believe, or did they evolve from earlier forms of life, much as it was agreed the earth itself had evolved? The most famous of the early nineteenth-century apostles of evolution was Cuvier's colleague Jean Baptiste Lamarck. Lamarck's scientific stance originated in his rejection of the atomism and materialism that was beginning to dominate chemistry. Believing that matter, too, was subject to change and evolution, that it did not really acknowledge the unremitting sway of mathematical analysis, Lamarck insisted on an inherent principle of life realizing itself in species against the resistance of environment. Plastic tissues were adapted to form and transmit organs or types of bodily organization—hence the "inheritance of acquired characteristics" invariably associated with Lamarck's name. He was, Professor Gillispie writes, "a medley of dying echoes: a striving toward perfection; an organic principle of order over against brute nature; a life process as the organism digesting its environment; a primacy of fire, seeking to return to its own; a world as flux and as becoming."[2] The future of biology and the answer to the question of the fixity or evolution of species

[2] C. C. Gillispie, "Lamarck and Darwin in the History of Science," in Bentley Glass et al., eds., *Forerunners of Darwin, 1754–1859* (1959), 276.

was not, however, to be found in this organic, romantic, almost moral quest for an all-embracing causal system. Instead, biological phenomena came to be viewed as processes subject to much the same kind of analysis that Galileo and Newton had brought to bear on mechanics and astronomy, with a healthy respect for the limitations of human knowledge and for the hard facts that scientists confronted. In this transition Charles Darwin is of crucial importance.

Born in 1809, Darwin was already an able paleontologist and natural historian when the chance recommendation of friends led to his appointment in 1831 as the unpaid naturalist for a scientific expedition that, over five years, circumnavigated the globe aboard H.M.S. *Beagle.* In South America, on the Pacific islands, and on the coral reefs of Australia, Darwin's painstaking observations converted what had been a hobby into true scientific inquiry, gave him the material from which he elaborated his theoretical conclusions over the next twenty years, and supported his new-found belief (which he owed to reading Lyell's book) in uniformitarianism. In 1838 he read Malthus' *Essay on Population,* which gave him the notion of a competitive struggle for survival. While Darwin was publishing the results of his observations in a series of monographs and working his way toward a new interpretation of evolution, another, younger scientist, Alfred Russel Wallace, was independently arriving at similar conclusions by much the same route. In 1858 the two men presented a joint paper on the theory of natural selection. The next year Darwin brought their views to a wider public in his book *The Origin of Species.*

Starting from the obvious fact of enormous variation in species, Darwin asked not how that variation fitted into some sweeping metaphysical scheme, but by what mechanism it came about. He found the answer in the gradual emergence of small, random structural variations that proved advantageous in the struggle for existence, variations transmitted to succeeding generations and so through an entire population. The hypothesis upset the pious and repelled those scientists of the older, Lamarckian tradition, who sought more all-embracing systems of thought; it immediately attracted the adherence of others, including Lyell. Natural selection remains a hypothesis that, better than any other, satisfies the problem to be solved without resorting to explanations (such as purpose or design) that virtually no reputable scientist can now admit. The clash of the two viewpoints was encapsulated in a famous confrontation at a meeting of the British Association for the Advancement of Science in Oxford in June 1860. The anti-Darwinian case was advanced (on the basis of then reputable scientific advice) by the bishop of Oxford, Samuel Wilberforce, a son of the great antislavery advocate, William Wilberforce, and an intelligent, skillful religious politician who had earned the nickname "Soapy Sam." He was answered by the formidable Thomas Henry Huxley, an instant convert to Darwinism, a notable scientist in his own right, and a brilliant advocate. Was it, the bishop asked Huxley, through his grandfather or his grandmother that he descended from a monkey? Huxley created a furor by putting the broader issue squarely: "I asserted—and I repeat—that a man has no reason to be ashamed of having an ape for his grandfather. It there were an ancestor whom

I should feel shame in recalling, it would rather be a *man,* a man of restless and versatile intellect, who, not content with an equivocal success in his own sphere of activity, plunges into scientific questions with which he had no real acquaintance, only to obscure them by an aimless rhetoric, and distract the attention of his hearers from the real point at issue by eloquent digressions and skilled appeals to religious prejudice."[3] Not for nothing was Huxley called "Darwin's bulldog."

Two implications of first importance emerge from this encounter. One is that science is the scientist's business and that it mixes ill with moral and religious inheritances or predictions. Huxley, for all his passionate Darwinism, rejected the amoral conclusions so readily drawn from attempts in the next generation to seek wider social implications of Darwinism in a pseudoscience based on physical or racial characteristics and on a glorification of a struggle for survival in which the superior species would win (see p. 868). The other implication was even more far-reaching. The geologists had extended the history of the world by aeons; the biologists now proposed a human history running back hundreds of thousands of years. The Garden of Eden joined the Flood in the scientific dustbin; the notion of special creation was wrecked. Man became only one species of animal, evolving by small steps from lower stages in the chain of existence. The possibilities thus opened for biological science were immense; it became subject to the same scientific, even mathematical manipulation as the physical sciences, as the rapid advances made in embryology and genetics proved. And the altered place of man in the scheme of things had an emotional, moral, and aesthetic impact greater than any mental reordering since Copernicus.

Medicine

In medicine, useful diagnostic devices were introduced: the stethoscope, in use from the 1820s; the thermometer, improved by Kelvin and Helmholtz; the ophthalmoscope, invented by Helmholtz in the 1850s. Cell theory and histology developed rapidly in the 1830s and 1840s, and major advances were scored in pathology by the German doctor Rudolf Virchow, after midcentury. Still more fundamental was the work of the French chemist Louis Pasteur, who began his researches into fermentation and putrefaction in the 1850s. Pasteur's resolute vitalism—his belief in a life force, normally a drawback to scientific advance— helped to persuade him that the cause of these twin processes must be living organisms introduced from the air. The development of the germ theory, the working out of bacteriology, and the discovery of immunization techniques were accomplished by Pasteur and others, notably Robert Koch, after 1870.

---

[3] For this celebrated quotation and the way a report of the debate has come down to us, Standish Meacham, *Lord Bishop: The Life of Samuel Wilberforce* (1970), 216. The good bishop said that his nickname resulted from his being often in hot water but always emerging with his hands clean: it is not the most convincing explanation.

Pasteur's basic researches in midcentury drew the attention of the Scottish surgeon James Lister, who had become interested in the causes of the putrefaction that was an almost invariable and often fatal consequence of surgery. Lister thus arrived at the technique of antisepsis, the killing of the dangerous organisms by chemical means (carbolic acid at the outset). The complementary and more effective aseptic procedure—the most careful attention to cleanliness—had been demonstrated with remarkable results nearly a generation earlier by the Hungarian obstetrician Ignaz Semmelweiss, but he had failed to convince the profession, which was brought around only after Lister's passionate advocacy of antisepsis. Lister's discoveries, added to the development of anesthesia by two American dentists (Horace Wells and William T. G. Morton) and by the Scottish doctor James Young Simpson in the 1840s, marked the beginning of the modern era in surgery. As we have seen, a basic appreciation of the importance of public health measures had dawned on the experts by the middle of the century, but it would be some time before attacking the "secondary causes" of disease through hygiene and clean water supplies could be effected (see p. 595).

The emancipation of psychology from the philosophical interest in epistemology awaited far more detailed work on the nervous system. Pierre Cabanis, a disciple of Condillac (see p. 360), became interested during the French Revolution in the question of whether the guillotine was painful; this curiosity led him to formulate the notion of reflex action and to perceive the existence of levels of consciousness. With his contemporary Marie F. X. Bichat, whose work on tissues led him to speculation about neuropathology and psychopathology, Cabanis became the founder of physiological psychology. In England, Sir Charles Bell discovered how the sensory and motor nerves differed; the German E. H. Weber went beyond the higher sensory functions (vision, hearing, smell) that had preoccupied the philosophers to study sections of skin and muscle. Thus began the experimental psychology that was developed by an impressive group of scientists in Germany, including the ubiquitous Helmholtz, and that came of age with the founding of Wilhelm Wundt's laboratory at Leipzig in 1879 (see p. 873). The scientific concern with the workings of the mind led to some blind alleys, notably phrenology and mesmerism, though the latter, being in part concerned with the hypnotic state, was not without its importance in the prehistory of psychiatry. The humanitarianism of the age forced some improvement in the treatment of mental patients, and the most thoughtful doctors had begun to formulate the idea of mental disease, analogous to physical disease and subject to treatment and cure.

The Science of Society

The notion of a science of society, though clearly present in the eighteenth century, was given both a clearer definition and a more pressing mission by Auguste Comte, an engineer from the Polytechnique who began his philosophical career as secretary to the socialist theorist, the count de Saint-Simon (see p. 683). The two eventually parted, and Comte, while retaining a Saint-Simonian imprint, took a different route from others of the master's disciples. In his *Course of Positive Philosophy*, published between 1830 and 1842, Comte developed the persuasive hypothesis that the sciences could be classified according to their emergence from the theological through the metaphysical to the positive stage. Instead of seeking causes in supernatural sources or in abstract forces or principles, a positive science was concerned with careful observation of fact and its reduction to law. Mathematics, astronomy, and physics had long reached the positive stage; chemistry and biology were becoming positive sciences in Comte's own day. But the science of society, to which he gave the name sociology, was still stuck, as he saw it, in the metaphysical stage. To accomplish this final transition—and so to provide the integrating science that would incorporate all the rest and provide definitive guides to attaining human happiness—was the most urgent mission facing the nineteenth century.

While Comte went on to construct a utopia in his *System of Positive Polity* (1851–1854), and while some of his followers were diverted into a new "religion of humanity," the stimulus Comte gave to sociology and philosophy lay in his insistence on a scientific "positivist" view of all phenomena. But, encouraged by the still more provocative insights of Karl Marx, the sociological harvest was to come in the latter part of the century (see p. 878). The principal early nineteenth-century contributions to the science of society were the launching of the systematic study of statistics, in which the major figure is the Belgian Adolphe Quetelet, and the systematization and defense of political economy.

The roots of political economy lay deep in the eighteenth century; in the early nineteenth century the inheritance of Adam Smith was modified by Malthus' pessimistic views on population and was codified in the *Principles of Political Economy* by the English banker David Ricardo in 1817. "Classical," Ricardian economics ("the dismal science," according to its detractors) was particularly concerned with the problem of distribution, as it fell among the three essential components of an economy—land, capital, and labor—rewarded, respectively, by rent, profits, and wages. Ricardo's system was, in fact, a highly abstract schematization of English social structure.[4] But it was also a remarkably relevant analysis of the means by which scarce resources are allocated in a preindustrial or industrializing economy, so convincing in fact that Karl Marx was to derive his economics largely from the categories and problems set out by Ricardo.

The German publicist Friedrich List, notably in his *National System of Political Economy* (1841), rejected the Ricardian prescription of free trade, which he saw as an instrument for maintaining the superiority of the advanced

---

[4] The political economist in Thomas Love Peacock's *Crotchet Castle* is named Mr. Mac-Quedy—Mac Q.E.D., or son of a demonstration.

industrial nations (England above all) at the expense of the more backward. He urged the wisdom of protectionism until new industrial economies were sufficiently well established to compete in world markets. In time, other German economists reacted against the abstractness of classical economics and insisted on a historical approach, very much as the school of historical jurisprudence had attempted to supplant the analytical and critical study of law. But on the Continent as in England, classical economics remained dominant, despite much debate within the school about theoretical details and about implications of the science for public policy. In 1848, John Stuart Mill's *Principles of Political Economy* offered a definitive, imaginative, and humane restatement of what had become an orthodoxy.

At the very time that Marx—turning Ricardo on his head as he had done with Hegel—published the first volume of his *Capital* (1867) (see p. 853), the classical position of "the Manchester School" (as the classical economists were sometimes called) was coming under attack from within. The "wages fund" theory, for example, held that wages at any given time could not rise above the level predetermined by the amount of the capital available for wages divided by the number of wage earners; the implications that wages could not easily be raised and that trade unions conspired in futile violation of natural law were quickly drawn by self-interested manufacturers. In the sixties, however, the theory was proved needlessly constrictive, as wages were seen to be affected by many other factors, among them public demand for products and the bargaining power of labor. At about the same time, the labor theory of value, which Mill had expanded into the more comprehensive notion of costs of production, was undercut by the marginal utility theory advanced by W. S. Jevons. Thus by the 1870s the foundations were laid for a more sophisticated, more realistic, but necessarily more technical and professional study of economics. Classical theory, however, remains central in the awareness of economists, and its formulation was one of the major intellectual achievements of the first half of the nineteenth century.

History

In political theory, jurisprudence, and economics, we have seen that the most available and convincing counterattack on the style of thought men identified with the eighteenth century lay in history. We have seen as well the pervasiveness of an evolutionary mode of thought in the sciences of geology and biology and in the all-embracing view of the sciences advanced by Auguste Comte. This historical bent or bias can be found in any number of other sectors of late eighteenth- and early nineteenth-century culture. Architects plunged into eclecticism, drawing on a variety of past styles, notably Gothic, while designers and craftsmen plundered China and Egypt for decorative motifs. Painters found large audiences for their portrayals of imagined scenes from the past—classical recreations of events from Roman history or from current history, like Jacques Louis David's *Oath of the Horatii,* Benjamin West's *Death of General Wolfe,* and the many paintings of incidents in Napoleon's career. Above all, perhaps, one finds this historical enthusiasm in the response to the novels of Sir Walter Scott.

The most astonishing use to which the historical imagination was put was the philosophical reconstruction advanced by G. W. F. Hegel in the early decades of the nineteenth century. Immanuel Kant, it will be recalled (see p. 357), had escaped the challenge of Humean skepticism by positing an invariable set of categories imposed by the mind on sense impressions. But this certainty of knowledge was gained at the price of a distinction between things as the mind must know them and things in themselves; these, Kant declared, are unknowable. Hegel, fundamentally religious though anything but ortho- dox, was determined to conquer this distinction and make it possible to arrive at knowledge of the real world, not merely the world of appearances. He fulfilled this heroic assignment by defining the universe as the evolving product of an absolute, infinite spirit realizing itself through thought, and encompassing nature, man, man's own thought, and society. He saw this process as rational, but it is a far different rationality from that known to Hegel's eighteenth- century predecessors. All thought, divine and human—and so all history and all institutions—moves in such a way as to absorb and reconcile contradictions, contradictions that are necessary rather than avoidable. Because the infinite can apprehend its infinitude only by comprehending the finite, so every stage in thought, the thesis, carries within it an antithesis. But this contradiction is supplanted by a higher synthesis that will unite what is valid in the two contradictory elements and eliminate what is not valid; that synthesis in turn becomes a thesis, and the "dialectic" is repeated. The world-process thus becomes a gradually ascending, increasingly complex apprehension of reality, accessible to the philosopher and guaranteeing that the rational is real and the real rational—that what is, must be, but must give way in its turn to a higher synthesis.

Hegel's immense erudition made it possible for him to absorb every aspect of existence and experience into this magnificent scheme and so to give to each mode as it appeared the guarantee of necessity and beneficence. He saw man as the highest attainment yet of the divine self-consciousness emerging in nature; human history became the record of the spiritual and moral progress of man; and political forms, having evolved from natural violence through slavery to the modern state, would come to embody freedom for all. The political form that Hegel held out as an ideal for his own time was a liberal, ordered constitutional monarchy, far in advance of the Prussia of his day; but the national state was by no means an end point in a political evolution that would continue forever.

Hegel's impact on the world of the German universities was immediate, his legacy after his death in 1832 remarkably diffuse. He had his share of dreary, repetitive disciples, who led his philosophy to a dead end; his insights were turned by others to a corrosive criticism of religion. It was in this milieu, as we shall see, that Karl Marx discovered the impulse to the dialectical process in the material rather than the ideal (see p. 687). By the sixties, however, German philosophers, deeply influenced by scientific developments and tiring of ambitious system-making, were turning back to Kant. They were also beginning to specialize in one or another aspect of philosophy—ethics, aesthetics, epistemology, or metaphysics. Hegel's influence moved belatedly westward to England and America, but it was the enthusiasm of a generation, and the twentieth century saw the reestablishment of a positivist tradition and the triumph of philosophical specialization. The world after midcentury was little more propitious for Hegel than it was for Lamarck.

Even in Hegel's own time the study of history began to hamper the construction of vast, monistic, speculative enterprises. History as a literary form had reached its eighteenth-century pinnacle in Edward Gibbon (see p. 366) and continued among nineteenth-century writers who felt a similar passion to comprehend the reality—and the lessons—of past ages. Jules Michelet, for example, who studied Roman history before moving on to his life's work on the history of France, or Thomas Babington Macaulay, who brilliantly recounted the origins and consequences of the Glorious Revolution in England, were men deeply involved in their own times, and both were assuredly preaching a political message. But another view of history was increasingly in evidence. It can be traced to the manifestos of J. G. Herder in the eighteenth century; a major turning point came with Barthold Niebuhr's history of Rome, published in 1811–1812 and revised in 1827–1830. A Dane who had entered the Prussian civil service, Niebuhr began to lecture at the University of Berlin when it was founded in 1810, and from 1816 to 1823 he served as Prussian ambassador in Rome. A triumph and justification of the critical evaluation of sources, his work showed the possibilities of techniques made available by the rapid growth of philology in the late eighteenth century. But the historiographical revolution is particularly associated with Leopold von Ranke, another classicist and philologist turned historian, who joined the University of Berlin in 1824. Like Niebuhr, whom he so much admired, Ranke insisted on a scientifically critical approach to documents; even more striking is his avowed modesty of intent, a concentration on the observable that paralleled the attitude of the newer scientists. "To history has been assigned the office of judging the past, of instructing the present for the benefit of future ages. To such high offices this work does not aspire: It wants only to show what actually happened *[wie es eigentlich gewesen]*."[5]

Ranke's insistence on the primacy "of the facts, contingent and unattractive though they may be," should not be allowed to obscure his conviction that

---

[5] From the preface to *Histories of the Latin and Germanic Nations from 1494 to 1514* (1825), reprinted in Fritz Stern, ed., *The Varieties of History* (1956), 57.

history has an underlying unity and that the ultimate goal of the discipline should be a history of mankind; toward the very end of his long and amazingly productive career, indeed, he began work on a universal history. But his published work lay largely in diplomatic and political history, and the generations of historians who came under his instruction or influence often overlooked his wider vision. That insistence on the uniqueness of historical development could nevertheless have a broad humanistic scope was made evident by Ranke's student Jacob Burckhardt, who turned to cultural history without deserting historicist principles. In his masterpiece *The Civilization of the Renaissance in Italy* (1860), which moves with sovereign ease from political practice to social ideals, from humanist scholarship to urban festivals, Burckhardt gave palpable reality to the Renaissance. Other historians before him had spoken of a revival of learning and the arts in fourteenth- and fifteenth-century Italy; Burckhardt, with a scientist's knowledge and an artist's perception, pulled together the diverse strands of Italian culture to see a distinct historical period, a discovery that a century later scholars still debate. The developments in Germany were repeated in France. There the Ecole des Chartes was founded to advance the preservation and interpretation of historical documents, and the historian of the ancient world Fustel de Coulanges pursued a rigorously positivist course. But it was only about 1870 that the new methods became firmly established in England.

The first three-quarters of the nineteenth century, then, saw the emergence of what has since become the dominant scholarly view of history; it saw, too, the multiplication of the institutions and methods on which that scholarship relies: the great collections of source materials, the archives, libraries, and seminars, the monographs and learned journals. But this new, professional history separated itself increasingly from general literary culture and, like philosophy, tended to split up into specialties that kept even historians from talking to all their fellow historians.

The twin processes of professionalization and specialization, which we have seen affecting the sciences, economics, philosophy, and history, can be traced in nearly every field of knowledge. The very age that, in one country after another, saw the emergence of an intelligentsia also saw the beginnings of the fragmentation of the culture by which the intelligentsia lived. Through most of the century cultivated men could still take interest in and comprehend what was going on in most fields of learning. But by 1870 the expansion of knowledge was becoming too great for that community to last. New disciplines were created; conceptualization was outrunning ordinary mental capacities; and refinement was gained at the price of a limitation of audience. As in some instances the creation of an intellectual class brought with it an alienation of that class from the wider society, so in time the very success of the intellectuals contributed to their alienation from each other. It was a long-drawn-out process and one that continues today; knowing what we know of our own isolation, we may find the nineteenth-century origins of the breakup of the broader culture easier to discern than did contemporaries. But even men in the nineteenth century were aware of the phenomenon in which this loss of intellectual cohesiveness was first to be observed: the novel, ambiguous, self-imposed role of the artist in conflict with his new patron, the public.

THE ROMANTIC VISION

The temptation is strong to apply to romanticism the disclaiming quotation marks appropriate to the "industrial revolution." Critics and scholars differ widely, even vehemently, on the definition of romanticism and, as with industrialism, the term has been pushed backward and forward in time to an extent that provokes skepticism about its very existence. Yet, over a period of fifty or sixty years from the later years of the eighteenth century, poets and painters were abandoning the style and perceptions of their predecessors and greatly expanding the sensibilities and vocabulary of the arts. Though this new culture is shot through with contradiction and with obligation (often unacknowledged) to the rejected past, it is essential to find a few general rubrics to characterize it, and those rubrics are almost inevitably summed up as romanticism.

A Widened Sensibility

At some time around 1808 the visionary poet and painter William Blake read the discourses that Sir Joshua Reynolds had delivered over the thirty-odd years of his presidency of the Royal Academy. Blake attacked Sir Joshua's opinions in savage marginal notations. "God forbid that Truth should be Confined to Mathematical Demonstration," or again, "Here is a Plain Confession that he Thinks Mind & Imagination not to be above the Mortal and Perishing Nature. Such is the End of Epicurean or Newtonian Philosophy; it is Atheism." When Reynolds argued that, compared to nature, even the best pictures were "faint and feeble," Blake indignantly wrote, "Nonsense! Every Eye Sees differently. As the Eye, Such the Object." When Reynolds praised the facility for generalization, Blake retorted, "To Generalize is to be an Idiot. To Particularize is the Alone Distinction of Merit. General Knowledges are those Knowledges that Idiots possess." Mere enthusiasm, said Reynolds, "will carry you but a little way"; but to Blake "Meer Enthusiasm is the All in All," and he added for good measure, "Bacon's Philosophy has Ruin'd England." To show perfect beauty in its most perfect state, Reynolds maintained, one could not express the passions. "What Nonsense!" Blake shot back, "Passion & Expression is Beauty Itself. The Face that is Incapable of Passion & Experience is deformity Itself. Let it be

Painted & Patch'd & Praised & Advertised for Ever, it will only be admired by Fools." And when Reynolds urged that even amid the highest flights of fancy or imagination reason ought to prevail, Blake wrote petulantly: "If this is True, it's a devilish Foolish Thing to be an Artist."[6] In these comments are embedded four principles under which we may seek the differentiating characteristics of romanticism: the worship of nature, the primacy of feeling over reason, the preference for the particular over the general, and the unique, almost sacred mission of the artist.

The worship of nature is, of course, an eighteenth-century characteristic, whether of the cool, rational nature earlier in the century, of the artfully irregular English gardens at midcentury, or of the wilder, more terrible "sublime," that aesthetic concept which exercised an increasingly strong fascination as the century drew to a close. The romantics found a new intensity of feeling about nature, a sharper contrast between it and the artificialities or materialism of the everyday world, and they conveyed this feeling in a novel rhetoric. In 1800 William Wordsworth wrote a preface for a new edition of the *Lyrical Ballads* that he and Samuel Taylor Coleridge had brought out two years earlier. Choosing "incidents and situations from common life," Wordsworth said, the poets had attempted to describe them "in a selection of language really used by men, and, at the same time, to throw over them a certain colouring of imagination, whereby ordinary things should be presented to the mind in an unusual aspect. . . ." This language was adopted because ordinary men "hourly communicate with the best objects from which the best part of language is originally derived; and because . . . they convey their feelings and notions in simple and unelaborated expressions. Accordingly, such a language, arising out of repeated experience and regular feelings, is a more permanent, and a far more philosophical language, than that which is frequently substituted for it by Poets, who think that they are conferring honour upon themselves and their art in proportion as they separate themselves from the sympathies of men, and indulge in arbitrary and capricious habits of expression, in order to furnish food for fickle tastes and fickle appetites of their own creation." In short, the old conventions of poetic diction were to be abandoned for a heightened naturalness.

That battle was won with comparative ease in England. Wordsworth and the other romantic poets, though not unanimously admired, gained an immediate popularity and retained it, even among readers who differed from them mightily, on politics, say. Wordsworth and Coleridge had shared an initial enthusiasm for the French Revolution and even contemplated founding a utopian community in America, but both soon turned sharply to the right. Coleridge, under the influence of German philosophy and literature, abandoned literature for philosophy and social criticism that was prophetic and

[6] Geoffrey Keynes, ed., *The Complete Writings of William Blake* (1966), 445–479, passim.

profoundly influential, though few contemporaries could follow him. Words-worth moved more simply into a deep Toryism, yet his long philosophical poems, the autobiographical *The Prelude* (1805) and *The Excursion* (1814), despite an initially hostile critical reception, came to speak powerfully to his contemporaries with a sensibility that was becoming commonplace. When in 1828 John Stuart Mill suffered the crisis (what we would call a nervous breakdown) that revealed the incompleteness and futility of the intellectual world in which he had been raised (see p. 610), reading Wordsworth restored him to spiritual peace.

In France, the classical tradition was far more jealously guarded. Alfred de Vigny, Alfonse de Lamartine, and Victor Hugo, however, did much to break that tradition in the earlier part of the century, and by midcentury Charles Baudelaire brought freer form and natural language under perfect artistic control in poems that, in subject as well as technique, are poised between the romanticism they sum up and the symbolism that descends from them (see p. 894). In Germany, the Romantic writers—Novalis, the greatest talent, and the brothers August and Friedrich von Schlegel, the literary ringmasters—sought inspiration in the Middle Ages rather than in nature. But the philosopher Friedrich von Schelling, a member of their circle at Jena, devised a *Naturphilo-sophie* destined to have wide influence. He assumed the identity of nature and spirit and argued that the reality of nature might be penetrated not only by scientific observation but by intuition. Professor Riasanovsky has caught the reason for Schelling's appeal: "Everything formed a part of one glorious whole, every particle, every event, great or small, had its assigned place, and acquired a meaning and infinite connections with other components of the cosmos. Schelling offered splendid opportunities for bizarre analogies of enormous sweep. The analogies were found to be extremely valuable as a short-cut to knowledge, as an easy and systematic explanation of the universe and its mysteries: the world was not only magnificently comprehensible, but the requirements for such comprehension were fortunately not too exacting."[7] One might add, too, that such romantic philosophizing—in contrast to Hegelianism—allowed its practitioners to bypass careful logical and historical exposition and to seek wisdom by darting into the profundities of the universe, to r turn with a nugget of truth enshrined in an aphorism. Highly consonant with romantic needs, *Naturphilosophie* was eagerly received in Russia and was carried to England by Coleridge and Thomas Carlyle.

The romantic vision of nature owes far more, however, to English painters than to English poets. The rough surfaces, the brilliant touches of color, the look of incompleteness that characterized John Constable's landscapes entered French painting with Eugène Delacroix, who repainted his superb *Massacre of Chios* just before exhibiting it at the Salon of 1824 because he had seen three of Constable's pictures, among them *The Hay Wain*. In the first half of the

[7] Nicholas V. Riasanovsky, *Russia and the West in the Teaching of the Slavophiles* (1952), 16.

nineteenth century, indeed, the art of landscape painting was far more effectively cultivated in France than it was in England, where genre painting—the depiction of scenes from everyday life—flourished and where the Pre-Raphaelites of midcentury failed to recapture the naturalness of the earlier landscape painters, despite the Pre-Raphaelite insistence on the faithful rendering of detail. But one English painter, J. M. W. Turner, famous while still a young man for his imposing landscapes and seascapes in the style of the French painter Claude Lorrain, developed a mature style that quite dissolved form in color and light; largely incomprehensible to his contemporaries, these evocative paintings anticipate the work of the Impressionists in the 1860s and after and entirely transcend his period.

Another aspect of the romantic worship of nature needs to be stressed. Wordsworth justified not only the language but the subjects of the *Lyrical Ballads* by appealing to their lowly sources: "Humble and rustic life was generally chosen, because in that condition the essential passions of the heart find a better soil in which they can attain their maturity, are less under restraint, and speak a plainer and more emphatic language; because in that condition of life our elementary feelings co-exist in a state of greater simplicity, and, consequently, may be more accurately contemplated, and more forcibly communicated, because the manners of rural life germinate from those elementary feelings, and, from the necessary character of rural occupations, are more easily comprehended, and are more durable; and, lastly, because in that condition the passions of men are incorporated with the beautiful and permanent forms of nature." There was, among romantics everywhere, an intense interest in folktales and ballads, and authentic survivals were collected by enthusiasts like the brothers Jacob and Wilhelm Grimm. Wordsworth's confidence, widely shared, in the deep insight vouchsafed to ordinary people was astonishingly confirmed by the moving poems of the Scottish tenant farmer Robert Burns.

This aesthetic democracy, although it was certainly not shared by aristocrats like Alfred de Vigny, was an ingredient in the almost unanimous welcome accorded to the French Revolution by romantics everywhere; in some respects it survived even after many early enthusiasts turned on the Revolution. Even Robert Southey—linked with Wordsworth and Coleridge as one of the English "Lake poets"—retained a marked concern for education and improvement of the lower classes, despite the deep-dyed conservatism he adopted. Percy Bysshe Shelley, younger than Wordsworth, Coleridge, and Southey, remained intensely radical and, in some of the most searing verse ever written, denounced the murders at Peterloo.

The preference that Blake revealed for emotion over the reason on which the eighteenth century had so prided itself was perhaps the point at which romantics felt themselves most at variance with their predecessors. They were, for example, passionately devoted to Shakespeare and saw him in a new light.

August von Schlegel secured his literary immortality by translating Shakespeare into German, and a new, more flamboyant style of acting made the reservoirs of feeling in Shakespeare's plays more fully available to the romantic generation. In 1827, in his preface to the dramatic poem *Cromwell*, Victor Hugo wrote: "Shakespeare is the drama; and the drama, which with the same breath moulds the grotesque and the sublime, the terrible and the absurd, tragedy and comedy—the drama is the distinguishing characteristic of the third epoch of poetry, of the literature of the present day. . . ."[8] To be true to nature and to give range to feeling, the restrictive unities of time and place, so sternly imposed on the classical French stage, had to be swept away—and Hugo swept them away in his *Hernani*, which opened on February 25, 1830. The play, which violated one classical rule after another, provoked a battle between defenders and detractors and was transmuted by its author into a demand for liberty, which he called the principle of the century. It has been argued by one modern historian that the violence of English political rhetoric in the 1830s and 1840s was a result of the absorption of a debased romanticism. Audiences had acquired—from the fourth-rate imitators of great writers, particularly in the theater, and from the extemporaneous spellbinding of preachers—a taste for "the cloudy enthusiastic metaphysics, the sensational religiosity, the medievalism and the appeals to the heart"; they relished mawkishness and bombast and invocations of heroism caught in the extravagant moment of action.[9] The same influences were at work in the same way throughout Europe in the revolutionary years after 1830.

The stress on feeling joins the concern for the particular in the romantic insistence that the entire gamut of human conditions and emotions could serve as material for art. The horrors of the Gothic novel were a late eighteenth-century taste; and the Swiss painter J. H. Fuseli, who had settled in London, was plumbing depths of the imagination (for example, in *The Nightmare*, shown in 1781) with an originality that deeply impressed Blake and influenced, in debased form, much popular, ostensibly religious and historical painting in the early nineteenth century. Poets resorted to opium, and sometimes convention barely concealed the romantic fascination with the darker, largely unexplored sides of human nature—the erotic, the perverted, and the hallucinatory. The most striking visual expression of this awareness of horror and corruption is in the late etchings of the Spanish painter Francisco Goya. Even Goya's portraits of the royal family are bitterly realistic, just this side of caricature. But his recording of scenes—or comments on their essence—from the Spanish wars of liberation shock to the point of numbness. In a savage attack on contemporary mores in *Caprichos*, a series of eighty etchings published in 1799, he attained a

[8] *The Dramatic Works of Victor Hugo*, (tr. 1909), vol. 3, p. 18.
[9] G. Kitson Clark, "The Romantic Element, 1830-1850," in J. H. Plumb, ed., *Studies in Social History presented to G. M. Trevelyan* (1955), 209-239.

nightmarelike quality unequaled since Hieronymous Bosch in the fifteenth century: an inscription in one of them reads, "The dream of reason produces monsters."

In his preface to *Cromwell*, Victor Hugo maintained that the time would soon come when the grotesque would resume its rightful, minor place, subordinate to the beautiful; yet "everything tends to show its close creative alliance with the beautiful in the so-called 'romantic' period." The predominance of the grotesque over the sublime was "a spasm of reaction, an eager thirst for novelty. . . ." But the subordination of this fascination to artistic control had already been attained in that masterpiece of romantic painting, Jean Louis Géricault's *Raft of the Medusa* (1819). Drawing on an actual incident at sea in which the survivors of a wreck were abandoned on a raft by the crew who were to tow them to safety, the painting is a protest against inhumanity. The subject is agony and death. Géricault interviewed survivors, ordered a model of the raft, and spent long hours locked in the morgue with corpses. But he transcended the horror, as the magnificent composition he imposed on the subject matter proves. In the last years of his short life, he did a series of studies of the insane, whose expressions he rendered with the greatest faithfulness and compassion. Géricault's influence was profound on Delacroix, undoubtedly the greatest of the romantic painters, whose *Massacre of Chios,* already noted for its importance in extending the range of color, depicted a similarly horrifying incident in the war for Greek independence.

As the involvement with nature shaded into the emphasis on feeling, and as the concern for both demanded particularity, so all these characteristics of the romantics were caught up in their view of the personality and mission of the artist, in the end the movement's most pervasive legacy. The artist was the supreme individual, the recipient of special gifts, a man whose style, whose whole life, were inseparable from his work and his vision. The supreme instance of the artist was Lord Byron. Born in London in 1788, he succeeded to his title at the age of ten. His life, as romantic as his poetry, was a succession of escapades, scandalous even for a member of the House of Lords. Handsome, aristocratic, opinionated, he was a vigorous and sometimes vicious satirist and an outspoken political radical. Hampered by a clubfoot, he trained himself to feats of athletic skill impressive even for a whole man. It seems likely that he was involved in a love affair with his half sister; an unhappy marriage, long stretches of exile, and erotic adventures (some well publicized, some clandestine) have done much to fix the public image of the "romantic poet." His death in Greece in 1824, as a martyr to the struggle for Greek independence, came as the fitting end. The adjective "Byronic," commemorates this side of his appeal.

Concentration on Byron the man is as inevitable as it is unfortunate, for he deserves his chief recognition as a poet. While his verse is exceedingly uneven, it has, at its best, great wit, dash, clarity, and deep intensity. His youthful satire of 1809, *English Bards and Scotch Reviewers,* a riposte to unfavorable criticisms of his early poems, gave him a formidable reputation, although Byron himself singled out the first two cantos of *Childe Harold* (1812) as the poem that made him famous overnight. In 1814, when his *Corsair* appeared, fourteen thousand copies were sold in one day. Large and diverse though his output was, his brilliant and witty *Don Juan* (1819-1824) is undoubtedly his masterpiece. It takes its hero through childhood, a charming early love affair, and later adventures as a slave, a diplomat, a social lion, and a lover. Byron was the romantic artist right to the end: death kept him from finishing his poem.

Byron was not alone in pouring his life into his art and making his life art: The word artist was, for the first time, coming to be used self-consciously in the way that is now ordinary. Artists were, moreover, working in a new social context. Emancipated from the old forms of patronage, they grew increasingly dependent on the public. This new, complex, and challenging relationship produced the widest range of responses. Some, like the superbly facile English painter Sir Edwin Landseer, famous for his sentimental animal pictures, came close to selling out; others maintained a prudential public respect for their audience, confining their impatience and frustration to their private journals and correspondence. But many artists, among them some of the greatest, openly displayed cavalier or even boorish contempt for the people on whose favor they depended. In doing so—sometimes with justice, sometimes not— they were testifying to their high sense of mission and to their conviction that they were different from and superior to other mortals. They transcended the conventions by which most men lived.

To single out these characteristics of romanticism must not blind us to the qualifications that must be made in any description of the culture of the period. The romantics were not a single school and often disagreed violently with each other. The forms of classicism survived in strength throughout much of the century, although they too could carry a romantic or nostalgic spirit. This nuanced continuity with the ruling tradition of the preceding century is notable in the French painter J. A. D. Ingres and, somewhat later, in his fellow countryman, the muralist Pierre Puvis de Chavannes.[10] Architecture, deeply obligated to Greece, Rome, and the Italian Renaissance, yielded less to romanticism than to eclecticism. The architectural entrepreneur Gilbert Scott built scores of new Gothic churches in England; at St. Pancras in London he applied a Gothic station to a sweeping, contemporary cast-iron and glass train shed. But in the fifties, Scott accepted Lord Palmerston's conservative scruples and readily built the new Foreign Office in an Italianate style. When Sir Charles Barry, most at home in the Renaissance style, was commissioned to design the

[10] The greatest of Russian poets, Alexander Pushkin, is usually cited as a notable example of Byron's influence. Certainly he admired Byron. But Sir Maurice Bowra has argued Pushkin's greater debt to Shakespeare and the even more pervasive classicism of his outlook. "Pushkin," *Oxford Slavonic Papers*, vol. I (1950), 1-15.

new Houses of Parliament in 1835, he used Gothic ornament, designed by the famous Gothic theorist A. W. N. Pugin, to cover a building essentially classical in conception. When Napoleon III and his bold prefect of the Seine, Baron Haussmann, rebuilt Paris in midcentury, they turned to the Baroque of the age of Louis XIV. As Sir Nikolaus Pevsner has pointed out, nineteenth-century architecture was an art of facades, drawing on whatever style struck the architect's or patron's fancy; while there was some absorption of new materials and technologies, there was little serious reckoning with fundamental planning or with the imperatives of the new, immense city, the reconstruction of Paris being perhaps the one notable exception.[11] The outstanding characteristic of nineteenth-century architecture, then, was not romanticism but an unmistakable individualism, exciting in its greatest moments, energetic almost always. At the same time, failures of imagination were the more obvious because the classical and accepted vocabulary was no longer available to dignify the mediocre.

The dominant literary form of the nineteenth century was the novel. Novalis and Hugo wrote novels that we may call romantic; the novels of Charlotte and Emily Brontë, above all Emily Brontë's *Wuthering Heights,* must be allowed the claim; and a host of minor, popular novelists exploited the new idiom. But most outstanding novelists were compelled by the very nature of the novel to be realists, even when, as in Stendhal's *The Red and the Black,* the subject was intensely romantic. Close, indeed clinical observation is central to the novels of Jane Austen, Honoré de Balzac, Gustave Flaubert, and Charles Dickens, however different the uses to which they put it. Observation of this kind could be a vehicle for satire, social reform, didacticism, sentiment, or the recreation of history, or it could be an end in itself; but none of these purposes need have a connection with romanticism and might be antithetical to it. What the novelists of the first half of the century shared was the broadened perspective, the willingness to take a widening range of humanity and emotion as their province. In that sense they were, as we are, heirs to the bold vision of the romantics.

From Beethoven to Wagner

For a century or so after the middle of the eighteenth century the mecca of the operatic world was Paris. There "grand opera" reigned supreme. Sung throughout (in contrast to Italian opera and the French *opéra comique,* which retained spoken dialogue), formally structured with alternations of arias and accompanied recitatives, and impressively staged, grand opera had been infused with new dramatic power by Gluck (see p. 371). Maintained in force (at

---

[11] Pevsner deals with this point in his essay in the *New Cambridge Modern History,* vol. X, 136–144.

least as contemporaries saw it) by composers such as the transplanted Italian Luigi Cherubini and the transplanted German Giacomo Meyerbeer, the French tradition—both in grand opera and *opéra comique*—was widely influential, affecting Beethoven and even (in his first opera) Richard Wagner. The arid and trivial history of Italian opera had been redeemed at the end of the eighteenth century by the brilliance of Mozart's achievement. But after his tragic early death it fell back to a much lower plateau, given whatever distinction it had by Gioacchino Rossini, who produced one after another clever and popular comic opera in the second and third decades of the century. Then, following his notable effort at grand opera, *William Tell,* in 1829, Rossini retreated into a long and happy retirement, and Italian opera saw little development until Giuseppe Verdi appeared on the scene in the 1840s (see p. 902). German opera had known two late eighteenth-century masterpieces by Mozart—*The Abduction from the Seraglio* and *The Magic Flute*—but the fountainhead of the art in the nineteenth century was Carl Maria von Weber. The three large-scale operas Weber wrote before his early death in 1826—*Der Freischütz* (1821), *Euryanthe* (1824), and *Oberon* (1826)—joined romantic subjects to novel exploration of the possibilities of the orchestra. Despite the flawed librettos of the last two, Weber can be seen as the creator of the nineteenth-century music drama.

These national operatic traditions were rooted in two centuries of development. Nineteenth-century instrumental composers looked to a far more recent past. The most revealing indication of this foreshortening is that the works of J. S. Bach were almost entirely forgotten between his death in 1750 and the revival encouraged from the late 1820s by Felix Mendelssohn. Haydn and Mozart cut sharply across music history: their symphonies, concertos, sonatas, and chamber music crystallized what has come to be known as sonata form—defined most commonly in terms of a statement (in at least one movement of an instrumental work) of two contrasting but tonally related themes, which then undergo extensive development and are recapitulated at the end. In practice these "classical" composers wrote far more variously and subtly than any such abstract model implies. A recent writer, finding the essence of their style in the "symmetrical resolution of opposing forces," warns that the classical style is, "like the fugue, a way of writing, a feeling for proportion, direction, and texture rather than a pattern," [12] the musical language of a single generation. Yet so great was the respect commanded by this style that the history of nineteenth-century instrumental music could be written as a commentary on sonata form.

At the confluence of these operatic and instrumental traditions stood the titanic figure of Ludwig van Beethoven. His one opera, *Fidelio,* was first performed in 1805, then withdrawn and reworked twice to attain its final version in 1814; it descends from the French grand opera tradition, with an infusion from the genre of dramas of rescue then so popular. The larger theme

[12] Charles Rosen, *The Classical Style: Haydn, Mozart, Beethoven* (1971), 83, 30.

of the opera is a celebration of liberty, and this, together with Beethoven's use of Schiller's *Ode to Joy* as the text for the choral portion of the last movement of the Ninth Symphony, suggests an obligation to Enlightenment ideals that casts doubt on any easy labeling of Beethoven as a romantic composer. His prolific output in sonata form—nine symphonies, thirty-two sonatas and five concertos for piano, and a wide array of chamber music as well as other instrumental works—confirms his resolute classicism and his close kinship to Haydn and Mozart. Of course much was new: an amazing rhythmic impulsion, immense demands upon the technique of performers and the patience of listeners, and the difficulty of conception (to many of his contemporaries the inaccessibility) of his later works.[13] But all these innovations of genius were expressed within the formal structures he had inherited. Even when, as in the *Eroica* or *Pastoral* symphonies, Beethoven ventures moral or aesthetic allusions, the music that conveys them is subjected to the rigorous musical logic we call classical.

Beethoven's life was tragic, and, as with Byron, it has too often overshadowed his work. Born in Bonn, Beethoven settled in Vienna in good part because Haydn was there. But, with Haydn's long absence in London and given Beethoven's own rapid development, there was little of the master-pupil relationship between them; indeed, Haydn was shocked by the unconventionality and egoism of this young boor he called a "Turkish pasha." A virtuoso pianist, Beethoven quickly established a reputation so dazzling that a group of Viennese aristocrats assured him a lifetime income to prevent his being lured away by a patron elsewhere. Unkempt and often rude, solitary, afflicted at an early age with deafness, emotionally shattered by the waywardness of his nephew, Beethoven, like Byron, has helped to fix the image of the artist as we have come automatically to see it. But it is a terrible disservice to Beethoven and to the history of music to say, as one critic has done, that Beethoven's "entire artistic activity . . . is nothing but the most exhaustive expression in terms of music of his emotional world, his dreams, agitations, passions, doubts, aspirations, exaltations, and disappointments, his conflicts, tragic experiences, and joy in life. For emotions of so vast a compass and so great a variety, music as it was then was not a sufficiently flexible medium, and it was the task of Beethoven's life to recreate it and shape it to his own ends."[14] Beethoven was a musician solving musical problems—triumphantly.

With Beethoven's younger contemporaries and for a couple of generations thereafter, it is possible to speak of a romantic movement in music, though the term is used, really, for want of a better and must be thought of differently from romanticism in literature and painting. Edward Dannreuther has defined it in terms of "a tendency towards the relaxation of the laws of structure in favor of

---

[13] "He was perhaps the first composer in history to write deliberately difficult music for the greater part of his life." *Ibid.*, 385.

[14] This nonsense, and much more, from Hugo Leichtentritt, *Music, History, and Ideas* (1938), 186–187.

characteristic details, an almost total rejection of organic design on self-contained lines, and, step by step, an approach to a sketchy sort of impressionism and a kind of scene-painting—a huge piling up of means for purposes of illustration." "No doubt," he continues, "it was guilty of many excesses. . . . But, when all this has been said, it remains true that the net gain, the widening both of the range of knowledge and the scope of emotion . . . is a possession the value of which cannot be overrated." [15] Questions of form and style are at the center of the problem. Few composers could escape the gravitational pull of the classical style, to which they returned again and again, with greater or lesser skill and faithfulness, for their large-scale, serious instrumental works. Franz Schubert and Felix Mendelssohn, who reached their artistic maturity in the twenties, wrote naturally in the idiom. Two decades later, Robert Schumann, whose true gifts lay in songs and fragmentary compositions for the piano, had lost the mastery, despite four symphonies and some impressive chamber music.

The originality of the romantic period lay in other directions. Composers, following Gluck and Mozart, no longer looked kindly on the freewheeling embellishment that had been allowed to opera singers in the eighteenth century or to instrumental performers in the cadenzas of concertos. But the admiration of improvisation, if anything, increased. Composers wrote rhapsodies, fantasies, nocturnes, and other pieces that fell into no established form but that were compelling evocations of moods. The lyricism and drama of Frédéric Chopin's carefully polished music for the piano most effectively captures the sense of intimacy and spontaneity by which they set such store. Another device was the use of texts from the reigning literary romanticism, translating them into musical terms: romantic dramas served as vehicles for operas or incidental music and contemporary poems were set as songs. Today the greatest test of a singer's interpretive powers is the art song, the *Lied;* it owes more to Franz Schubert than to anyone else. In 1815, when he was only eighteen, Schubert wrote *Der Erlkönig,* a setting of Goethe's dramatic and moving poem about the death of a child, lost to the king of the elves, the erlking. This composition, it has been said, is "as incredible as Monteverdi's *Orfeo* of 1607, for the one inaugurated art song as authoritatively as the other initiated opera." [16] Yet other composers became fascinated with national characteristics. Mendelssohn's third and fourth symphonies are called "Scotch" and "Italian," but they are at most evocations of spirit. Later "nationalist" composers—Borodin and Moussorgsky in Russia, Smetana and Dvořák in Bohemia—made direct use of folk melodies and exploited nationalistic subjects in symphonic poems and operas. But to understand the boldest of the innovators one must go beyond these reflections of literary fashion and changing sensibilities to the ways in which music was performed and organized.

[15] Edward Dannreuther, *The Romantic Period* (2nd ed., 1931), 7 *(Oxford History of Music,* vol. VI).

[16] F. W. Sternfeld, "Some Aspects of the Arts in Europe: Music," in *New Cambridge Modern History,* vol. IX (1965), 245.

The first half of the nineteenth century began to offer composers resources that eighteenth-century musicians could not have imagined. Radical improvements were made in musical instruments. The piano, an eighteenth-century invention, emerged from the limited instrument for which Beethoven composed to the powerful, sonorous instrument exploited in radically new ways by Chopin, Liszt, and Schumann. Scientific design and the development of valves and key systems made possible the flexible, chromatic use of all the wind instruments, and instruments rarely used earlier became regular components of the orchestra. The pitch to which instruments were tuned rose steadily until it was standardized in 1889, thus offering greater brilliance. [17] There seems general agreement, insofar as one can venture a judgment on an age prior to recordings, that the vocal art declined while instrumental performers reached new levels of ability. Beethoven and Liszt were brilliant pianists, and the violinist Niccolò Paganini astonished his contemporaries with his virtuosity— and outraged egalitarian radicals by the fees he charged for his appearances. Orchestral players learned more easily to master difficult parts, and firm discipline was imposed by conductors, who emerged into their crucial modern role with Hans von Bülow in the mid-nineteenth century.

These new skills reflect improved music education available in the conservatories founded in the principal European cities in the first half of the century, in imitation of the Conservatoire established in Paris in 1795. Concerts, too, were institutionalized. The Gewandhaus concerts in Leipzig began in 1781; the Society of the Friends of Music in Vienna was founded in 1812; the Royal Philharmonic Society in London the following year; in Berlin the Philharmonic Society dates from 1826; the Société des Concerts du Conservatoire in Paris from 1828. All of them continue in existence. The founding of orchestras and subscription concert societies speeded up the professionalization of the art, extended it to a wider public, and offered composers technical possibilities (thanks to the new financial base) that they were quick to turn to advantage. Haydn, who had worked with a couple of dozen players in Count Esterhazy's household, was delighted with the sound made by the sixty players available to him in the London concerts in the 1790s. In 1803 Beethoven scored the *Eroica* for about thirty-five players; what might he have done with the hundred or more that Richard Strauss could take for granted a century later?

These technological and organizational changes joined with the new romantic sensibility to make possible a striking increase in color, sonority, and freedom, and composers like Hector Berlioz and Franz Liszt stood ready with musical ideas to turn the new resources to account. Berlioz's *Fantastic Symphony* in 1830 was a notable breakthrough in conception, form, and color, a fitting counterpart to Victor Hugo's *Hernani*, first performed in the same year. It is revealing of both the possibilities and the difficulties of the new musical medium that in 1844 Berlioz published the first, and long standard, treatise on

---

[17] The standard of 435 cycles had been recommended in 1858 by a French commission of six scientists and six composers, including Hector Berlioz and Giacomo Meyerbeer.

orchestration and that his impressive but uneven *Requiem* and his opera *The Trojans* require the marshaling of such vast resources that, even today when his music has been restored to a favor it was long denied, they can rarely be performed. Liszt wrote music of remarkable individuality for the piano, but his most important contribution was the invention of the "symphonic poem." In his own practice Liszt refused to go beyond intimating and elaborating upon a sentiment or a dramatic idea, but his works in this form encouraged a growing fascination with connotative, or "program," music, which reached its fullest development at the end of the century in the literal storytelling and musical imitation of nonmusical sounds in the "tone poems" of Richard Strauss.

The romantic idiom pioneered by Weber, Berlioz, and Liszt reached its climax in the work of Richard Wagner, that self-conscious, often repellent genius whose aim was to transform opera into "music drama," the *Gesamtkunstwerk*—the total work of art. The ideal was not really new. Gluck had given music and drama equal weight in his operas, and Weber insisted that his *Euryanthe* could attain its proper impact only by bringing together the "sister arts." Wagner himself began very much under the influence of French grand opera and only gradually arrived at the fusing of music and drama into a single continuum, without discrete recitatives and arias. But, in both his theoretical writing and his practice, Wagner moved from according primacy to the drama to subordinating action and poetry (he was his own librettist) to the communicative power of his music—a change ascribable at least in part to the impact upon him of the philosopher Arthur Schopenhauer (see p. 779), who argued for the superiority of music to all the other arts. The change is evident in comparing those parts of the gigantic tetralogy *Der Ring des Nibelungen* that were written in the fifties with the parts written toward the end of the sixties, when the work was performed. But the fullest perfection of Wagner's musical art was reached in *Tristan und Isolde,* the supreme achievement of romantic opera, first performed in 1859. *Tristan* offers little stage action compared with most operas, and in many places the orchestra simply overwhelms the singers: the music, not the language, conveys, with incredible power, the tragedy of this medieval tale of betrayal of trust and of guilty love that ends in the death of the lovers. The final scene, the "Liebestod," unsurpassed in its erotic, yet transfiguring intensity, is the quintessence of musical romanticism.[18] In one way or another, music lay under its spell for sixty years.

Classic and Romantic: Goethe

Romanticism, then, remains a historical problem, an undeniable cultural phenomenon whose every aspect remains subject to dispute and qualification. Perhaps the finest exemplar of this complexity is Johann Wolfgang von Goethe,

---

[18] Jack M. Stein, *Richard Wagner and the Synthesis of the Arts* (1960) is a careful analysis of this complex evolution.

a towering figure in German culture and the cherished property of all cultivated Germans, who learned to recite his lines by the hundreds and to discuss his life in the finest detail. Responsible literary historians have not hesitated to claim Goethe for the romantic movement, [19] yet Goethe himself, near the end of his long life, called the classical healthy, the romantic sick. With this pointed remark Goethe meant to record his disapproval of recent romantic authors; but the absolute dichotomy between classical and romantic does not hold, certainly not for Goethe: his classicism *was* romantic.

Goethe, that protean genius—poet, playwright, novelist, translator, aesthetician, literary critic, scientist, autobiographer—was born in Frankfurt in 1749, into a rich and civilized patrician family. He studied law, dabbled in painting, and wrote poetry; his handsome presence, irrepressible energy, and extraordinary talents made him a favorite among women and gave early promise of a great literary career. His first efforts, notably his drama in 1773, *Götz von Berlichingen,* with its vigor, its cult of feeling and adoration of freedom, placed him squarely among the rebellious young writers of the German *Sturm und Drang.* [20] But it was his first novel, *The Sorrows of Young Werther,* published in the following year, that made him famous. *Werther* is the pathetic tale of a sensitive young man ill suited to this world, repelled by bourgeois philistinism, and hopelessly in love; his suicide, with which this epistolary novel ends, seems an inescapable conclusion. Certain themes that the romantics would later develop—the alienation of the artist, the pleasures of morbidity, the dangerous proximity of love and death, the rebellious assertion of individuality—are brilliantly foreshadowed in this short book.

But if the end of *Werther* was predictable, the career of Goethe was not. He had based his novel in part on his own despairing love for an engaged girl, but writing it liberated him from despair. Indeed, all his life was a search for objectivity, a search that his respect for workmanship, his commitment to discipline, his sheer intelligence, greatly facilitated. In 1775, Goethe settled at the court of the tiny duchy of Weimar, and there he continued to live and work until his death in 1832. He wrote much at Weimar, but he also served as minister to the duke, superintended the local theater, and gathered the most striking collection of German poets and literary figures ever assembled in so small a compass. Between 1786 and 1788 he made a journey to Italy, which he later celebrated in a famous book; his Italian stay strengthened his already pronounced respect for classical themes and classical forms. His dramas of the 1780s—notably *Iphigenie auf Taurus* and *Torquato Tasso*—draw their power from their restraint, the controlled melody of their language, and their deliberate forsaking of external for internal action. Little happens in these

[19] See, for instance, René Wellek, "The Concept of Romanticism in Literary History," in Wellek, *Concepts of Criticism* (1963), 128–198.

[20] The epithet, "Storm and Stress," derived from a play of 1776 by F. M. von Klinger. The movement was noisy but short-lived. Most of its members died young; those who survived, like Goethe, transcended it.

plays—except in the minds and souls of the characters. These plays show Goethe the subtle psychologist, as his poems show him the supreme master of German lyricism.

Goethe's novels, which profoundly influenced the course of German literature, display his lyrical and psychological gifts to perfection. *Wilhelm Meister's Apprenticeship,* published in 1795-1796, records the development of a young man; it became the model of the *Bildungsroman*—the novel that traces an education in the widest possible sense: the growth of a mind, the perfection of capabilities, the cultivation of appreciation, the mastery of environment, and the maturation through experience, including that of love. A later novel, *Elective Affinities,* of 1809, is a subdued drama of love and infidelity, of the clash between convention and impulse. Together with an unending outpouring of poems and his magnificent autobiography, *Poetry and Truth,* published between 1811 and 1833, these plays and novels would have been enough to secure Goethe a supreme place in German literature.

But it is of course his *Faust* on which Goethe's ultimate claim to greatness rests; it certainly remains his best-known work. Goethe had been fascinated from his early youth with the old legend of the savant who sells his soul to the devil. He published Part One of what he called a "tragedy" in 1808; the second part, essential to the comprehension of the first, was finished very shortly before his death. Part One shows Faust, the Promethean sage, vastly ambitious and bitterly disappointed: nothing, neither philosophy nor magic, neither the contemplation of nature nor the study of Scriptures, grant him the knowledge he craves. Mephistopheles, the diabolical spirit of negation, gives him new powers, but Faust's adventures reach their sordid and pathetic climax in his seduction of Gretchen and in Gretchen's death. The longer, more elusive second part depicts Faust's adventures among the great, among spirits, among the ancients revived, his aging and his death; it chronicles Faust's redemption. In a "Prologue in Heaven," Mephistopheles had wagered the Lord that he would lead Faust to damnation, but in the end God tricks Mephisto and redeems Faust. Man, the play tells us, errs as long as he acts; but he who strives upward, seeking to live and to know, may hope for salvation.

Goethe's philosophy almost defies classification—he preached the beauty of experience and the virtue of restraint, the advantages of learning and the pleasures of spontaneity. And he embodied these divergent values in his own life. A self-respecting bourgeois, he spent most of his years at a ducal court and was ennobled there. Though in *Elective Affinities* the adulterous heroine dies, Goethe's private life was filled with similar irregularities. While he was the self-conscious presiding spirit of German literature, he was not a patriot but a true cosmopolitan, an admirer of Byron on one hand and of Napoleon on the other. His doctrine was essentially one of cultivated humanity. Only a few choice spirits could follow him there; for most, more ordinary men, Christianity had to serve as the source of moral and intellectual ideals and sanctions. In the nineteenth century Christianity proved less and less able to bear these burdens.

THE RISE AND DECLINE OF RELIGION

The nineteenth century was one of the great ages of religion, but, in its multiplicity and change, nineteenth-century religion defies easy summary. At the social and institutional level, it can be seen as undergoing extraordinary revival and growth or as suffering an unimaginable decline, depending on where the historian looks and how he measures, and perhaps on what his beliefs are. At the individual level, religion could appear sterile or profoundly creative, serene or passionate, smug or desperate, conventional or bizarre. One could find himself forever in the process of conversion or might whirl through a succession of cults and doctrines: the pilgrimages of troubled minds often ended in surprising places. But one theme pervades the whole. Insofar as it rose above a routine piety, nineteenth-century religion was locked in constant struggle.

The Crisis of Faith

Although the pattern of religious observance in earlier centuries was complex, the nineteenth century saw an indifference or hostility to the church so widespread as to be different, not only in degree but in kind. This new alienation reflected the breakup of traditional society and the loss of means for enforcing conformity to expected behavior. It stemmed too from a rapidly growing population that, particularly in towns and cities, quickly outstripped the antiquated machinery of the parish and diocesan systems, leaving generations untouched by Christian ministration or the Christian message. Most of all, the alienation grew out of the culture of the century itself, with its new stimuli and its competing doctrines and attractions. The pattern was uneven. Some parts of Europe fell away faster than others; men stopped attending church more readily than women; bourgeois skeptics, terrified of social disorder, promoted religion among the lower classes and some returned to the fold themselves. But, despite the complexity, every nineteenth-century inquiry into the state of religion revealed a bleak picture to the faithful.

Science and liberalism, too, penetrated the churches. Curiosity and scholarly conscience impelled devout men to examine the Bible as a historical document rather than the literal word of God. The study of ancient languages and the opening up of the fields of philology, anthropology, and comparative religion made men aware of startling parallels between the myths of other cultures and the biblical accounts of Christian revelation. To all this were added the unsettling hypotheses of the geologists and of Darwin. For the truly religious man, the nineteenth-century "crisis of faith" was arduous indeed.

"Being unable to accept uncertainty about the riddle of human destiny," wrote the minor French philosopher Theodore Jouffroy, "and no longer having the light of faith to resolve it, I had only the light of reason to rely upon." [21] Reason took Jouffroy, as it did many others, into philosophy, in search of a system that could offer final answers to vast questions that enlightened men of the eighteenth and twentieth centuries have tended to regard as unanswerable. Robbed of the comfortable certainties of the eighteenth century, nineteenth-century thinkers and poets fled from doubt and skepticism. Some devised surrogate religions—the Saint-Simonians in France, the Positivists in France and England. Others, intellectuals as well as the ignorant and foolish, resorted to enthusiasms (usually temporary), such as spiritualism and other dabblings in the occult. Still others took refuge in pantheism, a vague quest for certainty that something higher and grander, something divine, some Absolute pervaded the universe and gave it meaning, saving men from earth-bound materialism. No better example can be found than Alfred Tennyson, who as Britain's poet laureate, spoke again and again for the most characteristic aspirations of his countrymen.

> The sun, the moon, the stars, the seas, the hills and the plains—
> Are not these, O Soul, the Vision of Him who reigns?
>
> Is not the Vision He? tho' He be not that which He seems?
> Dreams are true while they last, and do we not live in dreams?
>
> Earth, these solid stars, this weight of body and limb,
> Are they not sign and symbol of thy division from Him?
>
> Dark is the world to thee; thyself art the reason why,
> For is He not all but thou, that hast power to feel "I am I?"
>
> Glory about thee, without thee; and thou fulfillest thy doom,
> Making Him broken gleams, and a stifled splendour and gloom.
>
> Speak to Him, thou, for He hears, and Spirit with Spirit can meet—
> Closer is He than breathing, and nearer than hands and feet.
>
> God is law, say the wise: O Soul, and let us rejoice,
> For if He thunder by law the thunder is yet His voice.
>
> Law is God, say some; no God at all, says the fool,
> For all we have power to see is a straight staff bent in a pool;
>
> And the ear of man cannot hear, and the eye of man cannot see;
> But if we could see and hear, this Vision—were it not He? [22]

---

[21] Quoted in D. G. Charlton, *Secular Religions in France, 1815-1870* (1963), 27.

[22] *The Higher Pantheism*, written for and read to the first meeting of the Metaphysical Society in London, on April 21, 1869. The Metaphysical Society was made up of philosophers, scientists, and other intellectuals who gathered to discuss the profound questions that were then of so much concern.

Those who accepted agnosticism turned their energies to scholarship, literature, social reform, or a score of other careers one is tempted to call diversions. But some theologians tried to reconcile the essentials of Christian faith with the truths that modern science and scholarship imposed.

"At present," wrote an Oxford don in 1857, "European speculation is transacted by Germans. . . . The capital of learning is in the hands of Germans, and theirs has been the enterprise which has directed it into theological channels."[23] Two currents of thought, spreading rapidly among educated Germans in the late eighteenth century, were especially fruitful for this reconciliation: romanticism and Kantianism. The "natural religion" of the eighteenth century sought to persuade finite minds of infinite majesty by pointing to the grandeur of the universe and of the discoverable laws that regulated its operation. The proofs of God's existence were external "evidences": Newtonian heavens and the exquisite, purposeful structure of the human body testified to the ingenuity and benevolence of their Creator and Governor. But analogies to natural science could not account for central Christian doctrines like the incarnation, atonement, and resurrection of the dead; belief in them depended on the authority of the Bible, until the critical researches and speculations of the nineteenth century knocked this prop away. Nor did the chilly reasoning of eighteenth-century divines resolve or even address such human realities as suffering, evil, and the sense of sin; they left untouched powerfully felt emotions like wonder, dread, and helplessness.

Here was the particular province of the romanticists. The most famous and moving statement of the emotional and aesthetic attributes of religion came from a Frenchman, the viscount de Chateaubriand. His *Genius of Christianity*, published in 1802, was an appeal, just short of sentimental, that coalesced with the growing taste for Gothic architecture and widespread fantasies about the organic, reconciled society of the Middle Ages. Robert Southey and Samuel Taylor Coleridge in England, turning their backs on their revolutionary youth, spoke similarly. But it was the German romantics, with their awareness of the wide range of feeling and of the profound limitations as well as the exaltation of the human spirit, who most effectively reinforced the growing affinity for the mystery and grandeur of religion and of Christianity in particular. Those who felt this way found Kant's denial of the possibility of absolute knowledge of phenomena convincing: they turned away from external evidences to seek the grounding of religion in the soul's sense of need.

The clearest and most important statement of this theme came from Friedrich Schleiermacher, who, after a Moravian upbringing and a rationalist education at the University of Halle, entered the romanticist circles around the Schlegels and became a professor at the new University of Berlin. Schleiermacher set little store by creeds and dogma and defined religion in terms of the

---

[23] Mark Pattison, quoted in H. R. Mackintosh, *Types of Modern Theology: Schleiermacher to Barth* (1937), 3.

utter dependence of man on God: sin thus became man's failure to realize that dependence, and the importance of Jesus lay, not in the biblical stories about him, but in His unreserved embodiment of that dependence. Schleiermacher thus enabled generations of Protestant theologians simply to dismiss as irrelevant those old items of faith that were contradicted by science and scholarship and to concentrate instead on the irreducible tendencies and yearnings of the spirit.

To Schleiermacher, then, religion was grounded in its own imperatives and not in an external science or the testimony of reason. Such an argument was anathema to Hegel, who retorted that if dependence were the central experience of Christianity, then the best Christian was a dog: the two men were uneasy colleagues at Berlin. But Hegel's own defense of religion in his philosophical system—he found Christianity superior insofar as it conformed to his perception of the unfolding of reason—had far less influence on Christian thought than did Schleiermacher or the historical schools, Catholic and Protestant, that grew up in the University of Tübingen. From Tübingen, there emerged a scholar, deeply impressed as well with the Hegelian philosophy, who did more than perhaps anyone else to bring home to ordinary educated men the revolution that had taken place in German theology. In 1835, David Friedrich Strauss published his *Life of Jesus.* While accepting the historical reality of Jesus, Strauss saw only Jesus the man, who represented the gradually unfolding perfection of humanity. The divine attributes ascribed to Jesus in the Gospels Strauss dismissed as so many results of the myth-making propensity of a primitive people, prematurely robbed of a leader who had deluded himself into believing in his divinity. Strauss lost his university post and eventually his faith. Small wonder that the *Life of Jesus,* the first of many such books, created scandal among the unthinking and fearful orthodox.

Judaism, too, was affected by the new scientific learning and biblical criticism, but perhaps even more corrosive were the spread of emancipationist legislation and the possibility (not everywhere realized) that Jews could mingle with Gentiles with increasing freedom and respect. The result was the separation of a Reform movement from the Orthodox tradition. Originating in the late eighteenth and early nineteenth centuries, Reform attained its greatest importance in mid-nineteenth-century Germany, followed by a similarly rapid growth in the United States. Reform Jews modified some beliefs concerning the Creation, for example, and the expectation of restoration to Israel, but revelation, the prophetic mission, and God's unity, omniscience, and providence were never seriously in dispute. The most important departure of the Reform movement was over observance—the dietary laws, for example—and the communal power of the rabbinate. On another front, the rabbinate came under attack from adherents of Hasidism, a late eighteenth-century pietistic movement particularly appealing to the unlearned. In time the movement's more populistic aims were modified, and Orthodoxy absorbed much of its piety and mysticism. In the long run, neither Hasidism nor Reformism seriously challenged the powerful rabbinical tradition of learning and scholarship, which has continued down to the present to serve as an intense stimulus to excellence throughout Judaism and, at one remove, in Western societies generally.

Liberal Catholicism

The road of the Catholic liberals was most difficult of all. Sectarian division and the principle of private judgment were basic in Protestantism; Catholics had to surmount both the central principle of authority and an institutional church that, with only occasional glimmers of reasonableness, stood firmly against any accommodation with new currents of thought.

No more bitter or more ironic illustration of this generalization could be found than the career of the priest Félicité Robert de Lamennais. In the period immediately after 1815, Lamennais was known as a defender of legitimism and an advocate of papal supremacy. But the French church was not ultramontane, and neither was the monarchy. In theory both were committed to the old Gallican view (see p. 100) and, as negotiations to change the concordat of 1802 had repeatedly broken down, the French church remained firmly under the extensive state control Napoleon had forced on it. The logic of Lamennais' ultramontanism forced him to turn on the monarchy he had defended so fervently; he announced his intention to "baptize the Revolution," rely on popular sovereignty, and summon the papacy to abandon its secular power and rule the world by its spiritual power.

In the freer days after the July Revolution, Lamennais and some disciples began to publish a remarkable newspaper, *L'Avenir*. When it came close to foundering because of the hostility of the Gallican bishops, Lamennais and his friends suspended publication and appealed to Pope Gregory XVI in the expectation of victory at Rome. Instead, the encyclical *Mirari Vos* in August 1832 unreservedly condemned freedom of conscience, freedom of the press, and the liberal movement in general, though without mentioning Lamennais or *L'Avenir* by name: that silence was the only thanks Lamennais got. Shocked, Lamennais submitted, but in 1834 he returned to the fray with his *Paroles d'un croyant*, a passionate plea for liberal, even quasi-socialistic beliefs. Now the papacy issued a specific condemnation; the encyclical *Singulari Nos*, issued in July of that year, called Lamennais' views "false, calumnious, rash, leading to anarchy, contrary to the Word of God, impious, scandalous, [and] errone- ous. . . ." Beaten but undaunted, Lamennais left the church the next year; his colleagues who remained chose to work in other, less controversial ways. Charles de Montalembert went into politics, aiming at the revival of the religious orders and securing a major role for the church in education; the priest Jean Baptiste Henri Lacordaire lectured in defense of Catholic doctrine; Frédéric Ozanam founded the Society of St. Vincent de Paul, a lay association for work among the poor. Liberal Catholics, successful in quiet ways during the July Monarchy, were to attain yet more prominence in England and in Germany;

but, whatever their hopes, the handwriting for Catholic liberalism was on the wall.

In 1864, Pope Pius IX appended a *Syllabus of Errors* to the encyclical *Quanta Cura*. It was a kind of index to previous papal pronouncements that was read as an unreserved rejection of every liberal impulse and accomplishment of the age. Indeed, the last proposition that the *Syllabus* condemned, in needlessly extravagant language, was that "the Roman Pontiff can and should reconcile and harmonize himself with progress, with liberalism, and with recent civilization." This salvo was followed five years later by the summoning of the first Vatican Council, which in 1870 proclaimed the pope infallible when speaking *ex cathedra* in defining doctrines concerning faith and morals. Infallibility was a terrible blow to the liberals in the church. The German historian Ignaz von Döllinger, one of the intellectual luminaries of the church and one of its great apologists, refused to accept the new doctrine and was excommunicated. But Döllinger's pupil, the English historian Lord Acton, with deep reluctance and many reservations, submitted. The legacy of this crucial moment in Roman Catholic history is very much at issue in the church today.

The Oxford Movement

Across the Channel, in England, the most striking religious movement of the 1830s was antiliberal, launched by a group of Oxford clerics in 1833 specifically to protest against the government's plans for reorganizing the Irish church and suppressing some of its dioceses. Beyond that, however, they were protesting against the virus of liberalism they saw infecting the whole of English life and against the subordination of church to state, known in England as Erastianism. The men of the Oxford Movement drew to some extent on an old tradition of English piety that was associated with advocacy of the prerogatives of the Church of England, hence the label "High Church" that was given to their partisans. In their detestation of the Reformation and their deep scholarly commitment to the so-called patristic period, the early centuries of the Christian era, the Oxford reformers emphasized the "catholic" over the national elements in the Anglican compromise. But the movement was marked as well by a hothouse quality common enough in university coteries; by the presence of a few unbalanced minds and of some *enfants terribles,* young men perfectly willing to shock their complacent compatriots; and by the literary genius and corrosive logicality of a young, formerly Evangelical don, John Henry Newman.

The men of the Oxford Movement set out their views in a series of tracts—hence Tractarians, another name by which they are known—that profoundly stirred the university world and that, in the heated religious atmosphere of the times, provoked controversy outside as well. In 1841, Tract XC, written by Newman, offered an interpretation of the already pliable Thirty-Nine Articles (see p. 159) that seemed to many to maintain no distinctions between the

Anglican and the Roman Catholic churches. The tract, condemned by the heads of the Oxford colleges and sharply criticized by the bishops, created an outcry in the country, fervently anti-Catholic as it was. The High Church emphasis on liturgy, vestments, and ecclesiastical beauty had already seemed frightening importations of "Romishness" to those accustomed to the simple and sometimes rather shabby services of most "Low Church" parsons; now there seemed a concerted campaign to undo the Reformation. Although most Tractarians remained loyal to the Anglican church, there were conversions to Rome, the most startling being Newman's own. Removed from his Oxford posts in 1841, he retired to the country to write his great *Essay on the Development of Christian Doctrine*, published in 1844, which argued an evolutionary rather than a fixed view of belief and thus implied the need for an authoritative body to pronounce upon the admissibility of given doctrines at appropriate times. Having moved closer to Rome, both intellectually and spiritually, Newman took the final step when Oxford deprived one of his Tractarian friends of his degree.

Popular Religion

In Schleiermacher, Strauss, Lamennais, and Newman we have sampled the variety of responses, liberal and antiliberal, of theologians and writers of the first order of importance in European culture. We must finally draw attention to some far more widely diffused religious movements that, in their own unsophisticated but often touching ways, were also responses to the challenge of modernity. At one level, notably in England, there was widespread resort to apocalyptic visions and to crude forms of revivalism, spurred by popular preachers, prophets, or institutions like that remarkable philanthropic organization, the Salvation Army, founded in 1878 by William Booth to bring religion and comfort to the outcast. Within the Roman Catholic church, the forms of popular devotion multiplied, notably in enthusiasm for the cult of the Virgin Mary, which, since the sixteenth century, had played an increasingly larger part in Catholic devotion. The Immaculate Conception was declared dogma in 1854, and the vision of the Virgin that came in 1858 to young Bernadette Soubirous in Lourdes, in southern France, led to the founding of the famous shrine that still attracts huge numbers of pilgrims and claims many cures. From Germany, little pietist bands migrated to the American frontier; even today in Pennsylvania and parts of the Midwest one can see their descendants, with their distinctive dress and their horses and buggies, resisting (with less and less success) the wiles of the modern world. But by far the most impressive and effective movement of popular piety occurred in England.

By the time of John Wesley's death in 1797,[24] his "Methodists" were beginning gradually to dissociate themselves from the Church of England, to

---

[24] On the early history of Methodism, see p. 403.

which Wesley himself had remained deeply loyal. The slow separation continued over perhaps half a century, a period marked by schisms within the Methodist movement: some (the "Ranters") were committed to a more emotional religion and more radical politics that suited their lower-class origins; others merely rebelled against the conservative hierarchy of the official Wesleyan "connection." At the same time, within the established church itself, there appeared in the later decades of the eighteenth century a parallel, or answering, movement known as Evangelicalism. Grounding their religious sense, as Wesley did, on experience, particularly the experience of conversion, the Evangelicals tended to be impatient with some of the forms of the visible church and found it easier than more traditional Anglicans to cooperate with the Dissenters. The most famous Evangelical layman at the turn of the century was William Wilberforce, who led the agitation against the slave trade and slavery, the former forbidden in 1807, the latter abolished in the British colonies in 1833. In the next generation, his place was taken by Lord Ashley (later Lord Shaftesbury), the most prominent English philanthropist of the century and a fervent advocate of factory legislation. The Evangelicals were also deeply concerned with public morals and the tone of society. Active in suppressing "vice" and sedition in the French Revolutionary years and always attentive to harm that might flow from indecent publications, the Evangelicals' most characteristic campaign (among many) was for observance of the Sabbath; signs of their partial victories can still be seen in the enforced sobriety of the English Sunday.

Although the Evangelicals and Methodists were not solely responsible, they contributed more than any other groups to the religious revival that swept over early nineteenth-century England, a revival marked by church-building, by missionary activity at home and abroad, by the spread of religious observances such as family prayers and Bible-reading throughout much of respectable (and even some aristocratic) society, and by a seriousness that set Victorian society sharply apart from the Continent, just as British politics was set apart by its greater infusion of moral concerns and rhetoric. By midcentury, however, Evangelicalism, dominating the so-called Low Church wing of Anglicanism, had left its great days behind. Isolated (like much of English Dissent as well) from the scientific and intellectual developments of midcentury, it did not run much beyond a now ordinary, now rabid anti-Catholicism and a somewhat externalized observance of a strict moral code: temperance or teetotalism was much more likely to characterize the religious man of the late nineteenth century than was a burning inward conviction that he had been saved by God's mercy. Yet Evangelicalism continued to contribute an impressive number of men and women to all walks of English life. Even though they were apostates from the faith of their families, they carried with them a seriousness and a dedication to wider usefulness that was rooted deep in the Evangelical inheritance.

The Victory of the Secular

What, then, were the main precipitates of this extraordinary religious ferment in the nineteenth century? In the first place, it brought a new intensity to the old struggle between church and state. In Russia, there was none of the theological excitement to be found elsewhere. Orthodoxy was a key prop in the doctrine of official nationality, and state control was riveted more and more firmly over an already docile church. Since 1824, the church had been governed by an official called the Procurator of the Holy Synod, who ran his charge as an arm of the bureaucracy. In the period of the Great Reforms in the 1860s, one church leader asked the tsar to summon a council to discuss changes in the administration of the church. "That is a weighty matter," the tsar replied. "Some day I shall summon you to discuss it with me." [25] Of course he never did, and the long rule of the procurator K. B. Pobedonostsev at the end of the century simply fixed the bureaucratic grip of the state more tightly. But even this little attempt at some alteration did not indicate a liberal spirit among the clergy: many of the leaders of the church defended serfdom almost to the end. The reign of Nicholas I, moreover, had seen a new assault on the remaining Old Believers, those schismatics whose origins lay in a passionate refusal to accept liturgical reforms in the mid-seventeenth century (see p. 325). They had been tolerated in the quasi-enlightenment of the reigns of Catherine II and Alexander I, but a new campaign against them was mounted (with characteristic inconsistency) under Nicholas I. It concentrated notably on the monastic communities in which many of the little band had found refuge, and the schism slowly withered away.

In western Europe, in contrast to Russia, the church had become militant once more, and rulers had to consider whether they could tolerate the rivalry for the loyalties of their subjects. Bismarck's political quarrel with the Roman Catholic church in the 1870s (see p. 797) was singularly artificial, but in France, where throne and altar on the one side confronted republicanism on the other, the quarrel was real and persistent. In Italy, where the papacy was nursing its grievance against the new Italian state, which had deprived the papacy of its temporal power, the faithful were told to shun participation in the affairs of the kingdom (see p. 804). In Great Britain, the state seemed triumphant. Parliament retained its full power over the Church of England, and in the seventies it undertook to put down what Low Churchmen considered the liturgical innovations and abuses (or Romanizing) of the High Churchmen. Moreover, the highest court of appeal in church cases, the Judicial Committee of the Privy Council, was a lay body; in the fifties and sixties it gave great offense to many loyal Anglicans by decisions in favor of liberal churchmen, who appeared as heretics to the orthodox. In the end, however—though as late as 1928

---

[25] Quoted in John S. Curtiss, *Church and State in Russia: The Last Years of the Empire, 1900–1917* (1940), 29.

Parliament could refuse to authorize a new prayer book drawn up by the church—the result was a compromise, and in spite of legislation and legal theory, churchmen were allowed to do pretty much what they wanted. The compromise may, however, indicate principally that the church was no longer taken so seriously.

Within the churches themselves the result of the religious ferment differed widely, as we have seen. Roman Catholicism strengthened its control over liberalizing tendencies, while the Protestant churches by and large came to accommodate themselves to the new teachings of the scientists and theologians. The continuing appeal of Catholicism and the search for other, less intellectual sources of religious satisfaction suggest that the new theology may have spoken as little to the uneducated as eighteenth-century divines had done.

One is left with an impression of tremendous activity, much of it beneficent, and some of it, though well intentioned, unfortunate. Missionary efforts reached an extraordinary peak, marching both in and out of step with European political and economic power in Asia and Africa, where in earlier centuries Christianity had made little headway. There was extensive missionary work at home as well, particularly in missions to the poor and in admirable enterprises like settlement houses. And where the religious intensity reached its widest extent, in England, few persons could have lived their lives without having had innumerable tracts thrust into their hands and many importunings from the converted, urging close attention to their spiritual health. But, despite all the proselytizing, the final impression the historian must retain is one of retreat. Christianity steadily lost adherents to agnosticism or indifference. Among many who remained conventional churchgoers, religion retained little impact; the daily lives of nominal Christians were governed more by economic imperatives and by an education that came increasingly from secular, perhaps (as in France) even militantly antireligious, institutions. Serious religion was becoming a special vocation.

This new specialization in the intellectual and emotional life of Europe is perhaps best testified to by the most profoundly religious of nineteenth-century thinkers, Sören Kierkegaard. His writings of the 1840s and 1850s— sometimes gloomy, sometimes hysterical, sometimes ecstatically prophetic— are the refraction of burning guilt, of a life of bitter, at least partly self-imposed tragedy, through the brooding of a mind genuinely poetic, darkly romantic, and profoundly (at times perversely) religious. Kierkegaard was contemptuous of the complacency with which Hegel could presume to master the universe with the resources of human reason; he went far beyond the mere relationship of dependence that Schleiermacher had posited to bring man together with God. To Kierkegaard, God's infinitude and utter difference from man could not be penetrated by reasoning, through history, or by way of the mediation of Christ. Indeed, the spectacle of God become man was inconceivable, a paradox in a world that presented nothing but paradox to finite man. Man's lot is to suffer, to know despair, the "sickness unto death" that arises from his difference from God. His only escape is through blind faith, but not a passive, accepting faith. Bearing in mind Abraham's willingness to sacrifice his son Isaac, that terrible story that so fascinated him, Kierkegaard envisioned a passionate act, a leap of faith, an "existential" commitment—a commonplace among heroes of romantic literature translated to the religious plane and made incumbent on any man who would be saved. The very romanticism of the conception should have gained Kierkegaard a wider audience in his own time, had he not written in Danish; but the rank pessimism and the intense irrationalism of his religious solutions have proved singularly influential among the neo-orthodox theologians and the existentialist philosophers of the twentieth century. In our time, dilettantism apart, theologians and philosophers are specialists, talking largely among themselves, and the European world has lost the core of Christianity around which it had been structured from its beginnings. In reaction against the eighteenth century, nineteenth-century Europe knew a kind of Indian summer of the religious spirit, but by 1870 it was perfectly clear on what course the modern intellect was set.

PEOPLES AND NATIONS

In 1835, the Académie Française, in its role as guardian of the French language, allowed the word nationality to enter the dictionary. Nationality and its variants had come into wide use round about 1830, though no one was sure exactly what they meant. As several generations of European and American historiography suggest, the difficulty of defining and accounting for nationality and nationalism is as severe as ever; the term may, indeed, present a worse tangle than romanticism.

The eighteenth century prided itself on its cosmopolitanism. At the level of the ruling aristocracy and among the philosophes and those who shared their outlook, the ideal was realized in a common style, a common literature, and (in French) a dominant language. Secure enough to be a bit patronizing, these self-conscious Europeans could even look sympathetically on exotic peoples in North Africa, Asia, and the forests of North America. Cosmopolitanism reached its fullest development and a new point of departure in J. G. Herder's celebration of the distinctiveness of cultures within the total history of mankind. Historians of modern nationalism, who almost invariably begin with Herder, have to account for the shift, over less than a century, from the cosmopolitan respect for cultural differences that Herder and his century enshrine to a narrow, aggressive, political nationalism that Friedrich Nietzsche, that good European, was to denounce as a sickness, a neurosis, of the most terrible proportions.

Herder made language the principal basis of cultural differentiation, and this notion of distinct linguistic cultures was strengthened by the rapid development of philological studies in the late eighteenth and nineteenth centuries. But the role of language was evident in more than the perceptions of scholars. The early nineteenth century saw the virtual creation of new literary languages—modern Greek, Croatian, and Serbian among them. In other countries one dialect was refined and accepted as the language of educated men: this happened in Italy, where Alessandro Manzoni, himself from Lombardy, revised his immensely influential novel *I promessi sposi*—The Betrothed—fifteen years after its first publication in 1825–1827, to conform to the Tuscan dialect, which was establishing its ascendancy. In Russia, the early years of the nineteenth century witnessed a struggle over the question of whether the language should be modernized or remain faithful to Old Church Slavonic. The battle was won by the modernizers, with the historian N. M. Karamzin (politically so conservative) at their head. Even in England, where a common literary language had long existed, the nineteenth-century public schools took one of the many accents and generalized it among the upper classes as "standard English." Everywhere scholars and enthusiasts collected folktales and legends, which gained wide popularity. Because philosophers, historians, and publicists in the nineteenth century wrote much about the nation—Fichte's *Addresses to the German Nation* are only the most celebrated of manifestos—it has been tempting to pursue nationalism as a historical force by concentrating on the history of ideas and above all on the distinctive contributions of language and literature. The late Hans Kohn put it bluntly: In eastern and central Europe, he said, "it was the poet, the philologist, and the historian who created the nationalities. . . . Europe east of the Rhine and the Alps seemed, in the stillness imposed by Metternich and Nicholas I, to slumber in the provincial drabness of small towns and in the idyllic satiety of the Biedermeier. But underneath, the foundations were being undermined, much less by any actual change of the social structure than by the dreams of the intellectuals." [26]

Much convincing evidence can be mustered to support this view, but language and literary culture are not the sole, or in many instances even the dominant, stimulus to the growth of national consciousness. The spread of literacy and the growth of newspapers and other guides of opinion did, after all, facilitate the spread of more than rediscovered epics. Religion as a force in nationalism must spring first to mind, though again the picture is not at all clear. Catholicism among the Irish was their principal bond against their hated English oppressors; it separated the Croats from the Serbs, with whom they shared a language (but not an alphabet); it helped to bring about the separation of Belgium from Holland in 1830. Belgium's national history, however, has been scarred by a conflict between Walloons and Flemings that arises primarily

[26] Hans Kohn, *Pan-Slavism: Its History and Ideology* (Vintage ed., 1953), 13.

from linguistic and cultural differences. And Switzerland, to take a thoroughly confounding example, has held together as a nation, despite a civil war fought over religion in 1847 and despite the existence of three languages within its borders.

Economic development could also play a part in determining a sense of national unity. It reinforced Belgian separatism in 1830, and in the 1850s it promoted a sense of cohesion in Italy, where particularism had survived in strength in spite of the presence of Austrian forces and the hectoring of a generation of nationalist intellectuals. The German Empire created in 1871 rested on a far more secure economic base than had been attained in 1848, when the cultural-nationalist enthusiasm of the intellectuals and professional classes had foundered on the hostility of the old ruling classes. Indeed, one historian, drawing an analogy from studies of developing countries in today's world, insists that ethnic and cultural considerations were not so much primary causes of German nationalism as they were means to legitimize the demand for unity arising from other impulses. "Nationalism in Germany, as in all societies, served both as an instrument for those who wanted to overcome economic backwardness and as a means of assuring social cohesion during the passage from traditional to modern society." [27]

Nor should one forget that particular individuals—by their charismatic appeal or by clever, even cynical calculation—could unite (and define) a national group. In Hungary the nationalist leader, Count Stephen Széchényi, encouraged economic development and the pride of his countrymen, and he defended the Magyar language against the official Latin and the common German. His successor, Louis Kossuth, cavalierly proposed to Magyarize the Slav peoples within the ancient boundaries of the Kingdom of St. Stephen (see p. 719). Cavour in Italy seized realistically on opportunities offered him by enthusiasts for Italian unity, just as Bismarck captured the German nationalist movement and turned it to his own political ends. And one must ask if the Irish nationalist movement would have taken the course it did without the brilliant maneuvering (not to say duplicity) of Charles Stewart Parnell, or if the Welsh national movement would not have petered out, its linguistic and religious grievances satisfied, were it not for the self-promoting generalship of certain liberal politicians, chief among them David Lloyd George (see p. 919).

The contours and the motive forces of national movements vary widely from place to place and over time. They all reflect a growing awareness, for whatever reasons, among a group of people that they share certain qualities, qualities that are psychologically meaningful in a particular setting. At almost any time and in almost any place in European history one finds fierce local or regional prejudices that fulfilled such psychological needs. They are likely in the first instance to be negative, defining and cementing a community in terms

[27] Robert M. Berdahl, "New Thoughts on German Nationalism," *American Historical Review*, 77 (February 7, 1972), 80. This section owes much to Berdahl's suggestive essay.

of differences from other groups, using the "foreigners" to establish a satisfying sense of superiority. Moving beyond purely xenophobic clashes between one locality and another, one of the earliest analogues of anything like a modern national consciousness may be found in sixteenth-century England, partly in assertion against the Scots, but especially in truculent resistance to Spain and the pope, a resistance that created the hardy popular tradition of English antipopery. And neither philosophers nor linguists were needed to provoke the elemental resistance of the Spaniards to the Napoleonic occupation. In England and Spain alike, such "nationalism" benefited from clearly defined frontiers, a long history of political unity that overrode still evident internal divisions, and a distinct religious tradition. But negative impulses could exist side by side with genuinely affirmative qualities—with feelings as vague as familiarity with a landscape, a familiarity that can verge on love; or with some more specific and even self-sacrificing emotion, like loyalty to a dynasty. In France at the end of the eighteenth century, the Revolution produced an amazing outpouring of national loyalty among the people. That the state helped to whip up the enthusiasm by propaganda and ceremonies does not destroy the altruistic credit due to devotion to Revolutionary ideals or to the person of Napoleon.

A glimpse of these elemental appeals can be caught in national anthems. The first appeared in England, when the Jacobite rebels of 1745 threatened to move on London: *God Save the King* was a petition for divine protection against a Scottish conquest and a Stuart restoration. The music, composed by Thomas Arne (who had written the more confident and aggressive *Rule Britannia* only a short time before), was widely borrowed, most obviously in the United States, but also in Holland, Germany, and Russia. The tune so moved Haydn when he visited London at the end of the century that he wrote the famous (and also much borrowed) Austrian hymn *Gott erhalte Franz den Kaiser,* another plea for God's support. The *Marseillaise,* carried northward during the Revolution by enthusiastic Provençal troops, was no worried appeal but a stirring exhortation to conquest, and the nineteenth-century songs breathe a new kind of defiance: *The Lion of Flanders, Croatia Has Not Yet Fallen, The Watch on the Rhine,* and *Deutschland, Deutschland über Alles.* These suggest that much of the sense of nationhood was forged in battle, perhaps even more in occupation and forced acculturation. The experiences of degradation and victory within living memory are surely far more potent than revived medieval epics and may indeed have provided the meaning that might otherwise have been hard to find in tales of battles fought long ago or fought only in some mythical kingdom. The struggle against Napoleon forced much of the new awareness of nationalism; those who fought against the French found their horizons extended far beyond their villages, in spirit as well as in fact. So too with the Poles who resisted the imposition of German or Russian officials and culture, or with those new "nationalities" in Hungary that were formed in reaction against the self-absorbed aggressiveness of the Magyars.

It is in Russia that the process of self-definition by contrast with another culture and tradition becomes most apparent. One could argue that a kind of protonationalism, similar to that in England, could be traced back at least to the sixteenth century, reinforced by the religious separation of Orthodoxy and the physical separation of distance. The dramatic course of westernization imposed on the country by Peter the Great left scars that were to be agonizingly recalled in the nineteenth century, but eighteenth-century Russia was still marked off by institutions—a more and more rigid serfdom and an increasingly bureaucratic autocracy—whose analogues in western Europe had been or were being swept away or profoundly modified in response to enlightened ideas and economic change. The influx of European ideas produced a reaction, however, in favor of what were deemed to be traditional Russian institutions, and this was crystallized in the struggle against the French. This new view is evident in the polemics and history of Karamzin (see p. 607), and the burning of Moscow enlightened the souls of more Russians than Alexander I. At the same time many other Russians, through service in the West or by reading and reflection, had also become aware of the immense superiority—legal, administrative, and moral—of many Western institutions and ideas. The Decembrist revolt was a brave if hopeless attempt to force Russia into closer conformity with Western progress, and many intellectuals in the country sympathized with such aims, though scarcely with the means: "Just look at our Russia," wrote Pushkin in elated irony when his *Eugene Onegin* found a publisher; "It seems that she really is a part of Europe, and I always thought that was some mistake of the geographers."[28] In the effort to become part of Europe, educated Russians sought inspiration and understanding from the German philosophers—Schelling and Hegel in particular—and from the burgeoning socialist movement. But Pushkin himself was torn: admiring though he was of the West and critical though he was of Russia's shortcomings, he still could not accept criticism of his country or its people and knew, from his reading and his own historical research, that Russia's path had been different in the past and had to be different in the future.

This ambivalence in the Russian intellectual outlook was suddenly revealed by the publication in 1836, in a small journal called *The Telescope*, of the "First Philosophical Letter" by P. Ya. Chadaaev. It argued that Russia had no past and no future, belonged neither to East nor West, had made no cultural contribution, and was likely to make none. "I do not know what it is in our blood that resists all true progress. At the end of it all we have not lived, we do not live now except to serve as a great lesson to distant posterity which will be able to understand it; today, whatever one may say, we are a gap in the intellectual order of things."[29] Chadaaev, a thoughtful student of religion and

---

[28] Quoted in Leonard Schapiro, *Rationalism and Nationalism in Russian Nineteenth-Century Political Thought* (1967), 52.

[29] Quoted in Riasanovsky, *Russia and the West in the Teaching of the Slavophiles*, 25.

history, had written the letter, in a passing mood of despair, in 1829; it was published without his consent. But published it was. *The Telescope* was at once closed down and its editor banished. Nicholas I personally intervened to have Chadaaev declared insane and kept under house arrest for treatment. In 1837, in his *Apology of a Madman,* Chadaaev argued that, since writing the "First Philosophical Letter" eight years before, he had come to distinguish between a patriotism that was mere love of country and a patriotism, like the English, that encompassed a glorious civilization; he now thought that Russia might create such a civilization. Russia's lack of a meaningful past might be converted into an advantage, for her people could at least confront each new idea with open minds. But however much Chadaaev might explain his conviction that Russia could find her own distinctive way, while adapting what was best from western Europe, the impact of the first letter remained, as Alexander Herzen put it, that of "a shot in the dark night."

Reinforced by the publication in 1843 of *Russia in 1839,* an extremely critical account by a French observer, the marquis de Custine, Chadaaev's letter precipitated the intense debate between the Westernizers and the Slavophiles that dominated Russian intellectual life for the next couple of decades. Chief among the Westernizers were V. G. Belinsky, who died in 1847 just before the revolutions of 1848 brought so many hopes for Western ideals crashing down, and Herzen, who spent most of his mature life in exile. They increasingly found themselves absorbed in the possibility of adapting the new socialist tradition as the means to Russia's salvation. The Slavophiles, without at all accepting the inanities promulgated by propagandists for "official nationality" (see p. 566), turned away from the West to seek answers in what was distinctively Russian— above all, perhaps, in Orthodoxy. But they also sought an answer in autocracy as they idealized it—not the bureaucratic rule of the post-Petrine emperors, but the popular patriarchal rule of the old Muscovy tsars. They were especially hopeful for such Russian institutions as the peasant commune, the *mir,* where unanimity was reached without the dissensions and reckoning of votes that characterized Western assemblies. The Slavophiles were guilty of foolish excesses (Chadaaev said that Konstantin Aksakov, one of the most prominent of them, went about dressed in the costume of the Muscovy period and was mistaken for a Persian). But, with all the faults of ideologues, they were pointing out certain home truths—that institutions cannot simply be transplanted, that historical development drives channels that are ignored at one's peril, that *samobytnost*—one's own way—can be a source of legitimate pride.

Samobytnost or the German *Volkstum* have no precise equivalents in English. The shared sense of uniqueness to which they refer has no necessary relationship with the national state, a relationship inevitably associated with our words nationality or nationalism. They could, for example, lead to wider, vaguer ambitions, such as those represented in the various supranational cultural movements—Pan-Slavism, Pan-Scandinavianism, Pan-Germanism— that cut across the more readily definable political nationalisms of late nineteenth-century Europe. In general, however, such feelings were harnessed to the national state or to smaller cultural units within larger political wholes. The Czech journalist Karel Havlíček had once embraced a cultivated Pan-Slavism, but experience turned him against it. "I learned to know Poland and I did not like it. With a feeling of hostility and pride I left the Sarmatian country, and in the worst cold I arrived in Moscow, being warmed mostly by the Slav feeling in my heart. The freezing temperature in Russia and other Russian aspects extinguished the last spark of Pan-Slav love in me. So I returned to Prague a simple Czech, even with some secret sour feeling against the name Slav which a sufficient knowledge of Russia and Poland has made suspect to me."[30] Xenophobia did not die easily.

Nationality or nationalism, then—words to be used with the greatest care—are phenomena made up of many elements, elusive, hard to define or measure, and still to be fully elucidated by historians and psychologists. But, in one way or another, the concerns of this chapter—philosophy, history, philology, romanticism, religion—were drawn into a relationship with nationalism, in which the cultural concerns strengthened the preoccupation with historical and current differences and in which the sense of difference enriched, even as it narrowed, culture. Only science seems largely to have escaped this gravitational pull. And even there, a scientific curiosity issued in the pseudoscience of race, which, tragically, captured much of the European imagination in the imperial decades after 1870.

SELECTED READINGS

Excellent brief introductory sketches of scientific developments are the essays in the relevant volumes of the *New Cambridge Modern History,* C. C. Gillispie, "Science and Technology," in vol. 9, *War and Peace in an Age of Upheaval, 1793-1830* (1965), 118-145, and A. R. Hall, "The Scientific Movement and its Influence on Thought and Material Development," in vol. 10, *The Zenith of European Power, 1830-1870* (1967), 49-75. See also Charles Singer, *A Short History of Scientific Ideas to 1900* (1959), and C. C. Gillispie's superb book, *The Edge of Objectivity: An Essay in the History of Scientific Ideas* (1960). L. Pearce Williams' *Michael Faraday, a Biography* (1965) is an excellent way into the crucial innovations in electrical theory. On chemistry, see Arnold Thackray, *Atoms and Powers: An Essay on Newtonian Matter-Theory and the Development of Chemistry* (1970); A. Clow and N. Clow, *The Chemical Revolution: A Contribution to Social Technology* (1952); and L. F. Haber, *The Chemical Industry during the Nineteenth Century* (1958). C. C. Gillispie, *Genesis and Geology: A Study in the Relations of Scientific Thought, Natural Theology, and Social Opinion in Great Britain, 1790-1850* (1951) is a strategic introduction to both scientific and religious controversy. William Coleman, *Biology in the Nineteenth Century: Problems of Form, Function, and Transformation* (1971) is a thoughtful, brief survey. [H.] Bentley Glass et al., eds., *Forerunners of Darwin, 1745-1859* (1959) is valuable for the growth of

---

[30] Kohn, *Pan-Slavism,* 24-25.

evolutionary modes of thought; see also Michael T. Ghiselin, *The Triumph of the Darwinian Method* (1969), and, for a sternly critical view, Gertrude Himmelfarb, *Darwin and the Darwinian Revolution* (1959). On medicine, see Richard H. Shryock, *The Development of Modern Medicine: An Interpretation of the Social and Scientific Factors Involved* (1936, 2nd ed., 1947), and Gardner Murphy, *An Historical Introduction to Modern Psychology* (1928, 3rd ed., 1972).

On "social science," in addition to references on socialism given in the next chapter, see W. M. Simon, *European Positivism in the Nineteenth Century: An Essay in Intellectual History* (1963), and H. B. Acton, "Comte's Positivism and the Science of Society," *Philosophy*, vol. 26 (1951), 291-310. On quantification, see Harald Westergaard, *Contributions to the History of Statistics* (1932), and Paul F. Lazarsfeld, "Notes on the History of Quantification in Sociology," *Isis*, vol. 52 (June 1961), 277-333. On classical economics, see Elie Halévy, *The Growth of Philosophic Radicalism* (1901-1904, tr. 1928); Lionel Robbins, *The Theory of Economic Policy in English Classical Political Economy* (1952); Mark Blaug, *Ricardian Economics, a Historical Study* (1958); and Donald G. Rohr, *The Origins of Social Liberalism in Germany* (1963).

The following are useful on the growth of historical consciousness and of history as a discipline: Friedrich Meinecke, *The Growth of Historicism*, 2 vols. (1936, tr. 1972); Emery Neff, *The Poetry of History* (1947); Theodore H. Von Laue, *Leopold Ranke: The Formative Years* (1950); Thomas P. Peardon, *The Transition in English Historical Writing, 1760-1830* (1933); and Duncan Forbes, *The Liberal Anglican Idea of History* (1952).

On the eighteenth-century roots of romanticism, see Walter Jackson Bate, *From Classic to Romantic: Premises of Taste in Eighteenth-Century England* (1946); Samuel Monk, *The Sublime: A Study of Critical Theories in 18th-Century England* (1935); and Marjorie Hope Nicolson, *Mountain Gloom and Mountain Glory: The Development of the Aesthetics of the Infinite* (1959). The vexed question of the definition (or existence) of romanticism, as well as reactions instinctively favorable or hostile, have affected much critical and historical writing. Arthur O. Lovejoy's destructive "On the Discriminations of Romanticisms" (1924), conveniently accessible in his *Essays in the History of Ideas* (1948), allows no coherent meaning in the name at all; but see the valiant effort at restoration by René Wellek, "The Concept of Romanticism in Literary History," and "Romanticism Reexamined," in Wellek, *Concepts of Criticism* (1963). Jacques Barzun's still useful piece of polemic definition, *Romanticism and the Modern Ego* (1943) has appeared in a new edition under the title *Classic, Romantic, and Modern* (1961). Mario Praz, *The Romantic Agony* (1930, tr. 1933, 2nd ed., 1951, 1970) deals with the "darker" impulses in romanticism and their decline into decadence later in the century. J. H. Buckley, *The Victorian Temper* (1951) examines the tension between romanticism and antiromanticism and kinds of continuities evident in nineteenth-century English literature. Emery Neff, *A Revolution in European Poetry, 1660-1900* (1941) is an unjustly neglected essay that places the romantic writers in a broad context.

On architecture, besides Nikolaus Pevsner, *An Outline of European Architecture* (7th ed., 1962), see Sir John Summerson, *English Architecture, 1500 to 1830* (1953); Kenneth Clark, *The Gothic Revival: An Essay in the History of Taste* (1928, 3rd ed., 1962); Henry Russell Hitchcock, *Early Victorian Architecture*, 2 vols. (1954); and H. S. Goodhart-Rendel, *English Architecture since the Regency: An Interpretation* (1952). On the plastic arts, see Fritz Novotny, *Painting and Sculpture in Europe, 1780-1880* (1960), and T. S. R. Boase, *English Art, 1800-1870* (1959).

From now on, any discussion of nineteenth-century music will have to begin with Charles Rosen's *The Classical Style: Haydn, Mozart, Beethoven* (1971), a brilliant analytical work by a pianist and scholar. The *New Oxford History of Music* has not yet come down to the nineteenth century; volumes VI and VII of the old series are still useful—Edward Dannreuther, *The Romantic Period* (2nd ed., 1931), and H. C. Colles, *Symphony and Drama, 1850-1900* (1934). Alfred Einstein, *Music in the Romantic Era* (1947) is a standard survey, though too broad in its application of the adjective. Jacques Barzun's *Berlioz and the Romantic Century,* 2 vols. (1950), shortened and reissued as *Berlioz and His Century: An Introduction to the Age of Romanticism* (1956), brings the concerns of an intellectual historian rather than a historian of music healthily to bear on that key figure. Curt Sachs, *The History of Musical Instruments* (1940) is a technical survey of a subject of particular interest for the nineteenth century, although the bulk of the book deals with earlier periods. Leo Schrade's *Beethoven in France: The Growth of an Idea* (1942) is an interesting account of how succeeding generations read their own concerns into the work of a great composer. For the history of a key romantic work, see Elliott Zuckerman, *The First Hundred Years of Wagner's Tristan* (1964).

On Goethe, see especially Henry Hatfield, *Goethe: A Critical Introduction* (1963, 1964), which is sensible, brief, and lucid. Barker Fairley, *A Study of Goethe* (1947) sensitively links Goethe's continuous inner struggle for health with his unremitting poetic effort toward objectivity. There is no space here to refer to studies of other artists and writers; a good many of them are noted in the bibliographical apparatus of William L. Langer, *Political and Social Upheaval, 1832-1852* (1969), and in other general works. Some mention should be made, however, of two books that show romantic artists living as romantics: E. H. Carr, *The Romantic Exiles* (1933), which deals with the circle around Alexander Herzen; and William Gaunt, *The Pre-Raphaelite Tragedy* (1942). For popular appreciation of romanticism, see particularly the chapter on the Spasmodic poets in Buckley's *Victorian Temper,* cited above, and G. Kitson Clark, "The Romantic Element, 1830-1850," in J. H. Plumb, ed., *Studies in Social History presented to G. M. Trevelyan* (1955), 209-239, which is especially concerned with effects on political attitudes.

Two excellent brief surveys deal with religion: Alec R. Vidler, *The Church in an Age of Revolution: 1789 to the Present Day* (1961), and Josef L. Altholz, *The Churches in the Nineteenth Century* (1967). H. R. Mackintosh, *Types of Modern Theology: Schleiermacher to Barth* (1937) is ample and clear. Two works by E. E. Y. Hales deal with tensions within the Roman Catholic church: *Revolution and Papacy, 1769-1846* (1960), and *Pio Nono: A Study of European Politics and Religion in the Nineteenth Century* (1954). See also Alec R. Vidler, *A Century of Social Catholicism, 1820-1920* (1964), and Peter N. Stearns, *Priest and Rebel: Lamennais and the Dilemma of French Catholicism* (1967).

On national churches, some useful information on Russia can be gleaned from the early part of John S. Curtiss, *Church and State in Russia: The Last Years of the Empire, 1900-1917* (1940), and from Robert F. Byrnes, *Pobedonostsev: His Life and Thought* (1968); see also Robert O. Crummey, *The Old Believers and the World of Anti-Christ: The Vyg Community and the Russian State, 1694-1855* (1970), which documents the tightening of state control in the nineteenth century after the relative tolerance of the eighteenth. Adrien Dansette, *Religious History of Modern France,* 2 vols. (1948, tr. 1961) is fully authoritative. See also W. O. Shanahan, *German Protestants Face the Social Question* (1954); Owen Chadwick, *The Victorian Church,* 2 vols. (1966-1970); and

G. F. A. Best, *Temporal Pillars: Queen Anne's Bounty, the Ecclesiastical Commissioners, and the Church of England* (1964), a major administrative study. The missionary movement in general is surveyed in Kenneth Scott Latourette, *A History of the Expansion of Christianity;* volumes IV–VI (1941–1944) cover the period from 1800 to 1914. For two English missionary efforts, both disastrous, the early part of L. G. Johnson, *General T. Perronet Thompson, 1783–1869: His Military, Literary, and Political Campaigns* (1957) documents the experience of an Evangelical (soon to break free) in Sierra Leone, and Owen Chadwick, *Mackenzie's Grave* (1959) movingly recounts the unsuccessful effort to plant a missionary bishopric in Central Africa.

Because the English religious revival was more important and extensive than any other, specific reference must be made to some leading studies of aspects of it. On Evangelicalism, see J. D. Walsh, "Origins of the Evangelical Revival," in G. V. Bennett and J. D. Walsh, eds., *Essays in Modern Church History, in Memory of Norman Sykes* (1966), 132–162. The controversial and critical book by Ford K. Brown, *Fathers of the Victorians* (1961) should be read along with the concise answer by Standish Meacham, "The Evangelical Inheritance," *Journal of British Studies,* vol. 3 (November 1963), 88–108, and with G. Kitson Clark's sensitive appreciation of the tradition in *The English Inheritance* (1950). On the Oxford Movement, besides J. H. Newman's essential autobiographical account, *Apologia pro Vita Sua* (1864), see Y. T. Brilioth, *The Anglican Revival* (1925), and Owen Chadwick, *The Mind of the Oxford Movement* (1960), a collection of extracts with an admirable, long introduction. Geoffrey Faber, *Oxford Apostles* (1933, rev. ed., 1936) is a skillful portrait, with some interesting psychological speculation. Torben Christensen's *Origins and History of Christian Socialism, 1848–54* (1962) is an important interpretation. R. W. Davis, *Dissent in Politics, 1780–1830: The Political Life of William Smith, M.P.* (1971) is valuable for the struggle of the Dissenters for political equality, but there is as yet nothing really satisfactory on the religious history of the Dissenting sects in the nineteenth century.

The "crisis of faith," as it relates both to scientific developments and to the challenges and competition of modern life, has been much studied. The process of "de-Christianization" has been the subject of minute examination in France, but the seminal work, Gabriel Le Bras, *Etudes de sociologie réligieuse,* 2 vols. (1955–1956), has not been translated; on the plane of intellectual history, D. G. Charlton, *Secular Religions in France, 1815–1870* (1963) is excellent. With the greater intensity of religious life in England, the challenges of science and "higher criticism" were the more widely felt. For various responses see C. C. Gillispie, *Genesis and Geology,* cited earlier in this section; J. W. Burrow, "The Uses of Philology in Victorian England" and G. F. A. Best, "Popular Protestantism in Victorian Britain" (i.e., anti-Catholicism), both in Robert Robson, ed., *Ideas and Institutions of Victorian Britain* (1967), 180–204 and 115–142; Robert M. Young et al., *The Victorian Crisis of Faith* (1970); A. O. J. Cockshut, *Anglican Attitudes: A Study of Victorian Religious Controversies* (1959), and *The Unbelievers: English Agnostic Thought, 1840–1890* (1966); Noel Annan, *Leslie Stephen* (1951); David Newsome, *The Wilberforces and Henry Manning: The Parting of Friends* (1966); Standish Meacham, *Lord Bishop: The Life of Samuel Wilberforce, 1805–1873* (1970); and K. S. Inglis, *The Churches and the Working Classes in Victorian England* (1963). Finally, Edmund Gosse, *Father and Son: A Study of Two Temperaments* (1907), is a classic autobiographical account.

On nationalism, the literature is vast and the subject at the moment is entering a state of flux. Many specific national studies will be cited or have been cited in more appropriate places; hence mention will be made here of only a few of the more famous and established general works. Much of the dominant, basically intellectualist approach derives from Friedrich Meinecke's classic *Cosmopolitanism and the National State* (1907, tr. 1970). Many of the specific studies by American scholars have derived from the influence of Carlton J. H. Hayes and his *Essays on Nationalism* (1926) and *The Historical Evolution of Modern Nationalism* (1931). More recently Hans Kohn, a European scholar who settled in the United States in the 1930s, has been the most prolific writer on the subject; see his *The Idea of Nationalism: A Study of its Origin and Development* (1943) and *Pan-Slavism: Its History and Ideology* (1953). See also Boyd C. Shafer, *Nationalism, Myth and Reality* (1955). What is said in the text about national anthems is drawn from Percy A. Scholes, *God Save the Queen! The History and Romance of the World's First National Anthem* (1954). A stimulating suggestion about a possible line of reinterpretation of the subject is Robert M. Berdahl, "New Thoughts on German Nationalism," *American Historical Review,* 77 (February 1972), 65–80.

17

The Revolutionary Impulse:
1832-1848

THE SOCIALIST CHALLENGE

From the 1820s the basic assumptions of European society—even of society as liberals and radicals hoped to see it—came under a steadily fiercer attack in the name of socialism, an entirely different mode of social organization. Socialism was different from the age-old yearnings for a better world that had led men to fancy golden ages in the past or utopias in the future. It differed, too, from earlier attempts of small bands of enthusiasts to suppress the evils they associated with distinctions in rank or the private ownership of property. Still, these old longings provided some of the emotional drive that sustained nineteenth-century socialists. So, too, did Christianity, in subtler and more complex ways. Passages in the Bible could be construed to condemn the hoarding of wealth and the sin of pride; the notion of community of property was not unknown to the Christian tradition and indeed attained specific form in the monastic ideal. The commonplaces of the European ethical code—brotherhood, service, obligation, and love—came to most men, however imperfectly, through Christianity and drove many ardent spirits to seek some new, transcendent principle of order amid chaotic change and some guarantee of justice in a world where injustice seemed to triumph. In France, Lamennais and Philippe Joseph Benjamin Buchez were openly religious socialists; in Britain, a morally imposing Christian Socialist movement flourished in the 1850s. But even among socialists who had rejected Christianity and, in particular, the church, the religious impulse and specific Christian teachings could surface, as in Wilhelm Weitling, the German tailor turned communist agitator, or, more grotesquely, in the surrogate religion practiced by the Saint-Simonians.

Another powerful stimulus to socialism lay in the French Revolution. Through it was transmitted Rousseau's belief in the innate goodness of man and the possibility of a realized community. The radical democracy of the Jacobins also fed socialist fires, as, more portentously, did the abortive conspiracy against the Directory in 1795-1796, led by Babeuf (see p. 503). One of Babeuf's close associates, Filippo Michele Buonarroti, escaped execution and survived until 1837. His history of the Babeuf conspiracy assured it a place in the consciousness of socialists and radical democrats alike, and it was through Buonarroti that Auguste Blanqui, the French agitator of the 1830s, derived the Jacobin notion of a dictatorship of the proletariat, that is, the forcible suppression of the rich and powerful in the interests of the poor until a new form of society could be brought into being. In the repressiveness of Metternich's Europe, secret societies were resorted to by all kinds of reformers—from English trade unionists to Greek nationalists to the Decembrists in Russia. But Buonarroti and his followers throve in the atmosphere of conspiracy—his biographer has called him "the first professional revolutionist"— and passed it on, almost as an end in itself, to a major socialist tradition. The main legacy of the Revolution, however, was larger than these specific doctrines or methods: the very fact that the Revolution had happened proved that society could be changed, and changed drastically.

The men who stand as the main sources of early socialist thought were, however, neither true veterans of the Revolution nor carriers of old secular or Christian ideals. Indebted to the eighteenth-century Enlightenment, they looked resolutely forward, capturing, despite sometimes astonishing naiveté, much of the essence of the industrial, bureaucratic world of our times. They often showed little comprehension of the ambitions and drives of the disciples who took up their teachings. Extraordinary, idiosyncratic men, they each pursued their goals or demons with a dogged, blinkered insensitivity to the opinion of the world; they were also or became, it must be said, slightly, or more than slightly, mad. With some condescension, Karl Marx was to label them "utopian" socialists, because their theories lacked the "scientific" basis he thought was needed to sustain a movement among the enlightened and increasingly disciplined workers of western Europe; the utopians might, he thought, be fit for Russia. But no historian of socialism can dismiss them.

Owen and English Socialism

Robert Owen was the utopian socialist most clearly identified with the industrial world of the nineteenth century. Born in Wales in 1771, he was apprenticed after a brief schooling to a linen draper in England; at the age of nineteen he had become manager of a cotton mill in Manchester. In 1800 he joined his father-in-law, David Dale, in the management of the celebrated New Lanark mills, near Glasgow in Scotland. Here Owen quickly established his reputation as a model of the enlightened, autocratic factory owner. He provided his employees with good housing, sanitation, and a store that offered quality at a low price, and with education and amusement—along with a degree of regimentation that soon weeded out the undesirables and nonconformists, leaving a community that deeply impressed a stream of visitors from home and abroad. [1]

In 1815 Owen published four essays called, significantly, *A New View of Society, or Essays on the Principle of the Formation of the Human Character:* the rationale of New Lanark was to be generalized for the world. He argued that men are creatures of their environment, a view he took from Helvétius (see p. 356), as did Bentham, who in 1813 had become a partner in the New Lanark enterprise; denying personal responsibility, Owen insisted that proper surroundings would guarantee human regeneration. In 1817 and succeeding years, prompted by the prevalent concern over poor relief, he urged the creation of cooperative villages as the basic pattern of social organization, villages of five hundred to three thousand persons constructed around a central square (they were unkindly dubbed "parallelograms of paupers"), with common kitchen, dining, and child-care facilities. Thanks to the larger yields Owen expected from cultivation by spade rather than plow, the communities would be self-sufficient in food, but he also proposed that the villages be supplied with machinery, to be kept strictly subordinated to human needs. Owen's schemes attracted attention from the wealthy and powerful, but in 1819 he alienated much respectable opinion by an open attack on organized religion; he was thus thrown back for support on the burgeoning working-class movement, where such sentiments were more acceptable.

After a stay in the United States in the midtwenties, where he founded the colony of New Harmony in Indiana, Owen returned to London to find himself the hero and in some ways the leader of a movement for "cooperation" that was growing rapidly among the working classes; in the thirties, the cooperative movement merged with a burgeoning trade unionism. In 1833 the Owenites formed the Equitable Labour Exchange, where cooperatively produced goods

---

[1] Owen made an interesting contribution to industrial discipline by his "silent monitor," a pyramidal block of wood attached to each spinning machine; each face was differently colored, and every day the supervisor would turn outward the color that represented the quality of work done and the moral condition of the employee as well; the results were recorded in a book, but the principal appeal was to the sanction of public opinion.

were to be exchanged by means of "labor notes," reflecting the labor time that went into their production; in 1834, in the Grand National Consolidated Trades Union, they attempted to create "one big union" that, embracing all the workers in the country, could attain its political and social ends by a general strike.[2] Savage government repression brought this phase of trade-union development to a sudden halt, but the cooperative enthusiasm continued, despite the stigma attached to Owen's increasingly heterodox views on religion, sex, and the family. The principal result of Owenism, however, was not the multiplication of producers' cooperatives, which Owen foresaw and which the Christian Socialists were to advocate in the fifties, but the modern consumers' cooperative movement, launched in 1844 by a little group of English Owenites in the northern textile town of Rochdale.

English socialists in the thirties and forties drew inspiration not only from Owen, but also from some now largely forgotten theorists who attacked the prevailing views of political economy derived from Smith and Ricardo. John Gray and William Thompson were both Owenites; Thomas Hodgskin was not; but they all used the labor theory of value (as did Owen) to justify the claims of labor to a fair and in fact dominant share in the yield and management of the economy, in place of the capitalists who unjustly took what the workers created. Of temporary importance in the history of English socialism, these "Ricardian socialists" were important precursors of, and in all probability contributors to, the Marxian synthesis of midcentury.

The French Socialists

In France, Owen's concerns and solutions were paralleled, far more imaginatively and profoundly and certainly more fantastically, by the doctrines of François Marie Charles Fourier. Fourier's father, a wealthy cloth merchant, had lost his fortune in the Revolution and nearly lost his life in a rising against the Jacobins. The younger Fourier was largely self-taught, and his tenuous grip on reality is shown by his habit of appearing punctually at his apartment each day at noon to await the visit of some unknown philanthropist who would endow his schemes for human perfectibility. Fourier had none of Owen's practical experience and lived the life of a near-recluse, without close friends and even without a movement from which he could draw strength, as Owen somewhat uncomprehendingly did. An apostle of Rousseau, Fourier was anti-industrial and repeatedly denounced civilization; his queer but perceptive psychology was entirely self-derived. Yet he was much like Owen in his educational insights, his rejection of religion, his criticism of the family and marriage—which he carried to a radical feminism—and his belief that the salvation of mankind lay

---

[2] The notion of the general strike, so important in trade-union and socialist history, seems to have originated in 1832 with a now obscure radical, William Benbow.

in communitarian villages he called phalansteries. He put his organizational faith not in external control of environment, but in the freeing of human instinct: the mixture of instincts varied from one individual to the next, but their liberation and proper employment would end in the attainment of perfect harmony. In thus setting out the road to perfection, Fourier sharply criticized the bourgeois dominance that had turned humanity into an antihuman path of repressiveness.

Fourier's criticisms and positive remedies got a wide hearing, despite his solitariness and despite the embroidering of his system with a fantastic cosmogony, a bizarre psychological jargon, and half-insane, half-brilliant imaginings like antilions and antiwhales and oceans turned to lemonade. During the July Monarchy, the Fourierist legacy inspired a movement, whose best-known figure was Victor Considérant. Bypassing the fantasy, Considérant called out for justice to the poor and oppressed; then, in 1848, he was caught up in a revolutionary movement for which he was ill prepared and for which he was exiled. Considérant left an inhospitable France to go to the United States, where, as in many other countries, including Russia, Fourierism had come to rest in local communitarian experiments.[3] A similar fate awaited Etienne Cabet, another disciple of Rousseau, a lawyer turned reformer, a revolutionist of 1830 who rejected the regime he had helped to install. In 1839 he published his *Voyage to Icaria;* one of the most successful of utopian novels, it also proclaimed its author's conversion to a self-styled communism. The community of Icaria was far less radical in its libertarian and sexual aspects than Fourier's phalansteries, but it was far more radical in its complete rejection of private property and its uncompromising egalitarianism. Cabet attracted a notable following among workingmen in the 1840s, but for the Icarians, too, after 1848, emigration was the only alternative. They settled in Nauvoo, Illinois, a community that had been vacated when the Mormon followers of Joseph Smith moved westward to their ultimate Zion in Utah.

The far-reaching and lasting contributions of French socialism were not, however, made by these literal utopians, but by two theoreticians who spoke more directly to the actual situation in France, although both shared the crankiness characteristic of nearly all the early socialists and although neither could bring to bear on social problems the powerful systematization that was to give ultimate victory to the German school. One was a down-at-heels aristocrat, the count de Saint-Simon, with his strange, variegated cluster of followers; the other a self-taught printer, Pierre Joseph Proudhon.

Henri de Saint-Simon was a liberal aristocrat. He served with distinction at Yorktown, supported the French Revolution, narrowly escaped the Terror,

---

[3] Fourier's ideas were closely studied in the little socialist group known in St. Petersburg as the Petrashevsky circle, which was savagely repressed in 1849; one of its members was the novelist Dostoevsky.

and acquired and lost a wife and two fortunes. In Napoleonic times he was reduced to begging for jobs as well as for official sponsorship of his scheme for reorganizing the sciences; he ended by being supported by a former servant. Round about 1814 he went beyond the scientific matters that had largely concerned him to deal with questions of the economy, constitutional organization, and international peace. His position was that of the orthodox liberal, and his closest associate was his secretary and "adopted son," Augustin Thierry, later famous as a medieval historian. In 1817 the two parted company, as Saint-Simon's developing views no longer squared with Thierry's dogmatic liberalism. "I cannot imagine association without government by someone," Saint-Simon had said to Thierry, who replied, "And I cannot imagine association without liberty." The young man's place was taken by Auguste Comte, a recently graduated engineer who proved far more sympathetic to Saint-Simon's increasingly authoritarian plans. It is difficult to tell, in either collaboration, whether the junior or the senior partner was responsible for a given idea, or indeed whether it came from some other collaborator in the Saint-Simonian circle. It is equally difficult to pinpoint Saint-Simon's passage from a position one could categorically call liberal to one that might be deemed socialist, even though the word had not been invented before his death.

It is from his liberal period that Saint-Simon derived his influential view of history as an evolution from a feudal and military society to a liberal and industrial society, an evolution marked by a clash between the classes who dominated the respective systems. Implicit in this view was his contrast between the desirable "organic" phase—in the Middle Ages or in the future industrial society—and the necessary but transitory critical phase of the eighteenth and early nineteenth centuries. As Saint-Simon inquired more deeply into the means of making society and the economy work, he departed from the enlightened individualism of Bentham and the British and French political economists to emphasize organization and hierarchy. At the same time he began openly to attack organized Christianity, losing, as Owen had done, much respectable support from bankers and businessmen; he was increasingly influenced by the arguments for an organic and structured society that he found in Maistre and Bonald. The noun "industrialism" was a Saint-Simonian invention; the *industriels* were the key to the new society, the successors of the aristocrats who had controlled the military and feudal stage and of the lawyers and metaphysicians who had dominated the critical phase. Associated with the *industriels* were the *savants,* the scientists and engineers who were the successors of the theologians. At the head of this Saint-Simonian vision of society came the bankers, who had the overview and the means necessary to determine and control the associated and complementary activities of the producers—for Saint-Simon made production the crucial activity, in contrast to the consumption that so fascinated the classical economists. Corporative and hierarchical, not democratic, industrial society nevertheless differed from former hierarchies in that the all-important administration was of things, not men: "In the old system, the people were *regimented* with respect to their leaders; in the new, they are *combined* with them. The military leaders *commanded;* the industrial leaders will only *manage.* Then the people were *subjects;* now they are *partners."* [4] At the very end of his life, Saint-Simon called for "a new Christianity," positive and scientific, that would inculcate the love of mankind as the ethical bond of industrial society.

Saint-Simon, like Bentham, attracted young men and offered them the thoughts and suggestions, often partial and ill worked out, that flowed incessantly from his fertile brain. When he died in 1825, a little band of followers were preparing to launch a periodical called *The Producer;* the principal figures among them were Saint-Amand Bazard, a veteran but disillusioned conspirator, and two bank employees, Prosper Enfantin and Olinde Rodrigues. In 1829 Bazard gave a series of lectures on Saint-Simonian doctrine that, published the next year, summarized what had been done to clarify and develop the implications of their legacy: Saint-Simonians had become harsher and harsher on liberals and had undertaken pointed critiques of lending at interest and of the inheritance of property, which they saw as devices for enslaving the workers. It was in their newspaper, the *Globe,* that the distinction between proletarian and bourgeois was drawn for the first time in the sense that it regularly assumes in socialist argument; there, too, appeared the first use of the word "socialism," by extension from Saint-Simon's idiosyncratic use of the adjective "social." [5] The Saint-Simonians had also reckoned with the vexed question of the distribution of wealth in industrial society, arriving ultimately at the motto that headed the *Globe:* "From each according to his capacity, to each capacity according to its works"—a hierarchical formulation that, as the historian Elie Halévy has argued, is nothing more than "the industrial transfiguration of the right of the strongest." But if the cleverest and strongest are to be the best paid, it is also requisite that they use their advantages to serve humankind and to exploit not men but nature. [6]

After 1830 the Saint-Simonians threw their major energies into realizing the new religion that the master had come to see as central. Drawing inspiration as well from Fourier's notion of industrial armies subduing the world, the little band created a sect and a ritual that led them into a productive missionary visit to England in 1831 and also into quarrels and schism. The cause of the split between Bazard and Enfantin—inherent in their differing tendencies toward political action and moral reform—came over the question of the emancipation

[4] Quoted in Elie Halévy, "The Economic Doctrine of Saint-Simon," in Halévy, *The Era of Tyrannies* (1938, tr. 1965), 43.

[5] The word "socialist" had occurred as early as 1827 in an Owenite publication in England, but neither noun nor concept became current until the 1830s.

[6] The quotations in this section are from two essays by Elie Halévy, written in 1907-1908 and reprinted in *The Era of Tyrannies* (1938, tr. 1965), a volume that also contains Halévy's brief appreciation of Sismondi (1933), the Swiss economist who turned on the classical economics he had helped to introduce to France and whose criticism provided still more concepts for the socialist armory.

of women. Bazard died suddenly in 1832, just before Enfantin and his associates, advocates of sexual emancipation, were tried and imprisoned for harming public morals. On his release from prison, Enfantin, whose magnetic personality had drawn a following all over Europe, set out for Egypt to find the Great Mother, the female Messiah, and also to build a canal at Suez—both projects that failed. Enfantin finally ended as an official of the Paris-Lyons-Marseilles railway. Less fanatical adherents ended in the same entrepreneurial camp: the history of French finance and banking in the Second Empire is dotted with former Saint-Simonians. Three monuments to their initiative stand out, the *Crédit Mobilier,* the bank founded by the Péreire brothers; the Cobden Treaty of 1860, providing for freer trade with England and negotiated by the former apostle Michel Chevalier; and the Suez Canal, built at last by Ferdinand de Lesseps (see p. 771). The material and institutional outcome of the movement argues that the most impressive thing about Saint-Simon and his followers was not so much their "socialism" as their grasp of the nature and requirements of industrial society. But in preaching the realization of that goal, they gave to the emerging socialist movement key parts of its vocabulary, the basic elements of its historical view, and—in contrast to the essentially liberating concerns of Fourier—a tradition of authoritarian organization.

The year 1840 saw the dramatic emergence of a new theorist, destined to have more far-reaching influence than any of those we have so far considered. It was then that Pierre Joseph Proudhon, a true workingman, a self-educated printer from Besançon, published his "first memoir" *What is Property?* His answer was simple if not original: "It is theft." Both the question and the answer terrified the bourgeoisie of the July Monarchy, and Proudhon was brought to trial for subversion. But his acquittal was a proper verdict. He had a gift for drastic and unforgettable phrases ("God is evil" was another) and for vitriolic polemics that obscured the fact that he really believed in private ownership. He rejected only what he saw as bourgeois property, the right to levy a toll on property, the right to exploit. Indeed, throughout his career Proudhon was a spokesman for the peasant and the small craftsman. He shared prejudices common among them: he hated foreigners and Jews, gloried in war, accepted slavery, and insisted on the inferiority of women. But he gave voice to the rudimentary sense of justice felt by workingmen, to its kernel of the Christian ethic, and to their utter distrust of the state. In 1848 he proposed a system of "mutualism." The state as it was known would disappear, and in its place would emerge a social organization based on free contracts: goods would be exchanged and producers paid according to their input of labor, and the whole machine would be lubricated by the provision of free and unlimited credit from a central bank.

Proudhon argued his views in two impenetrable volumes that displayed both his ignorance of the economics he presumed to criticize and his incapacity for philosophizing, notably in his misconception of the Hegelian dialectic, which he thought he was appropriating. His *System of Economic Contradictions* of 1846 bore the subtitle *The Philosophy of Poverty.* Karl Marx, who had shown some early interest in Proudhon but who had taken a dislike to him, replied with a slashingly critical rejoinder engagingly entitled *The Poverty of Philosophy.* But Marx did not destroy Proudhon, nor was this strange man ground down by the failure of 1848. When other socialists lost interest, were discredited, or fled, Proudhon (who throughout his life blew hot and cold on the subject of revolution) was able to make an uneasy peace with Napoleon III. He became the philosopher of the French labor movement and one of the major sources of the anarchist tradition.

German Socialism and Karl Marx

Compared to socialism in France and England, German socialism scarcely existed in the thirties. Among Germans who had fled to France there was a strong admiration of the democratic tradition descending from 1793, as in the poet Heinrich Heine and the young playwright Georg Büchner. Exiled working-men formed one organization after another to maintain their solidarity against the day when revolution would come to their homeland. In Germany in the late thirties, Wilhelm Weitling, a tailor from Magdeburg, proclaimed himself a communist: in these early years the terms communist and socialist were difficult to distinguish, except perhaps that communism tended to be more radical and lower class in origin. But it was not before 1842 that most Germans became aware of the socialist ferment in Paris. In that year a conservative Hegelian, Lorenz von Stein, who had been sent to Paris by the Prussian government to study these alarming developments, published his findings. Although he condemned what he had found, his careful exposition of the doctrines generalized a knowledge not only of the existence but of the structure and language of socialism—the notion of society as divided into classes, for example, or the word "proletariat." But the ultimate victory of German socialism was hatched in the unlikely nest of religious disputation, among the internecine feuds of the radical heirs of the philosopher G. W. F. Hegel. The early history of socialism culminates in the person of Karl Marx.

Marx was born in 1818 in Trier in the Rhineland. His father was a Jewish lawyer, who had converted to Christianity without much feeling of conviction either way. From this comfortable, enlightened background Marx proceeded to the university, first at Bonn, then at Berlin, where he drifted from subject to subject without much academic success but with an enormous intellectual appetite; in 1841 he took his doctorate in philosophy. In Berlin he became a member of the circle that had grown up around his teacher, the "left Hegelian" Bruno Bauer, a group known first as "The Freethinkers" and later as the "Graduates' Club." Their intense discussions benefited Marx greatly, but open radicalism ruined any prospect for an academic career; he turned instead to journalism. The complexities of the doctrinal development of the Bauer group and the precise debt Marx owed them form a highly complex subject. Suffice it to say that, after Hegel, Marx's greatest debt was to the philosopher Ludwig Feuerbach, rather more a humanitarian than the materialist he is usually called. Feuerbach rejected Hegel's transcendent God as demeaning to man, as an instrument of man's alienation from himself. From Feuerbach, Marx derived his early humanitarian concern with the problem of alienation, and Feuerbach also convinced him that Hegel was wrong in his concentration on ideas. Marx later said that he found Hegel standing on his head and set him upright by abandoning idealism for an exclusive concern with man and his welfare, a concern that Marx only later narrowed down to his belief that man's economic aspect was basic.

Marx had become editor of the *Rheinische Zeitung,* which was closed down by the censors in 1843. He then went to Paris with the express intention of studying socialism at its origin; there he became coeditor of another journal, the *Deutsch-französische Jahrbücher.* In the one issue that appeared, Marx proclaimed his conviction that German political liberation could be brought about only by the proletariat and that "the day of German resurrection will be announced by the crowing of the Gallican cock": his move from a radical liberalism to socialism had begun. He was confirmed in this course by the lifelong friendship that began in 1844 with Friedrich Engels, the son of a wealthy German cotton spinner. After a university career similar to Marx's and after exposure to the Bauer circle, Engels went to England to work in his father's factory near Manchester. The outcome of this stay was an astute book of social observation, *The Condition of the Working Classes in England in 1844,* published in 1845. In the same year the two men collaborated in a stinging attack on the Bauer group called *The Holy Family,* as in the next year Marx turned on Proudhon and began as well to attack Moses Hess, the leader of the so-called True Socialists, who had collaborated closely with Marx in his quarrels with others of his Berlin associates and who had preceded Marx and Engels into communism. The True Socialists stood guilty in Marx's eyes of a too simple sociology and a too great faith in the power of intellectual conviction rather than revolution to bring victory over the status quo in Germany. It is easy to see why a relatively simple-minded activist like Weitling could criticize Marx's "closet analysis" and consider him as having only an encyclopedic intelligence, not genius. But Marx had an extraordinary capacity to absorb the ideas of other men and to make of them a highly original synthesis. And once he had taken what he needed, once he had fitted the doctrines into their places, he almost invariably turned on his guides to demonstrate how partial, ill-informed, or faulty were their systems. The reader is torn between distaste for the compulsion and admiration for the polemical skill and the bravado.

In 1845, at the request of the Prussian government, Marx was expelled from France and found refuge in Brussels. Having added the lessons of French socialism to his amalgam of Hegel and the Berlin radicals and having become a "communist," Marx now began to move away from the Feuerbachian humanitarianism so evident in the Paris manuscripts of 1844[7] to a more narrowly materialistic interpretation of man's plight and of the motive force of history. Marx was reading the classical economists carefully, turning them handily against Proudhon. The final element in the first stage of Marx's development is provided by the radical secret societies of German workers with whom he and Engels came into close contact in Brussels, especially the League of the Just, which they joined. At the end of 1847 Marx, with Engels, drafted a program and rationale for the Communist League, which had grown out of the League of the Just; it was published as the *Manifesto of the Communist Party* in February 1848, just before the revolution broke out in Paris.

The *Communist Manifesto* (to use its popular name) derives much of its remarkable power from being a call to arms—from its opening assertion that the specter of communism is haunting Europe to its final call to the proletariat, with nothing to lose but their chains and a world to win: "Workers of all countries, unite!" The revolution is portrayed as imminent, and the means prescribed are violent. But in the long run—for the predicted revolution that so quickly came almost as quickly evaporated—the strength of this early statement of Marx's beliefs resulted from a coherent view of history that both explained how the world came to its desperate state and justified revolutionary action as the means of effecting the transformation of society. With a deterministic, essentially Hegelian evolutionism, the *Manifesto* recounted the shift from feudal to bourgeois society and predicted that the bourgeoisie would be supplanted by the proletariat, which would exercise a dictatorship, eradicating the last vestiges of bourgeois society. Finally, the state would wither away and the classless society would bring historical development to an end. The scheme would survive Marx's post-1848 abandonment of immediate revolutionary goals to receive its full theoretical development in *Capital*, the first volume of which was published in 1867 (see p. 853). For all its moral fervor and for all its denunciatory rhetoric about bourgeois family life—the *Manifesto* still recognizes that the bourgeoisie had a *necessary* role in creating the modern forms of production and, indeed, of the proletariat itself. The *Manifesto* thus displays a degree of imagination and sympathy that makes it the fountainhead of a vital tradition in sociology and of nearly the whole of economic and social history as we know it. As a political document the *Manifesto* has been, if anything, even more varied in its results. While it gave rise to the tradition of democratic socialism—a path pioneered in a sense by Marx himself—it also underlay the tradition of violent revolution by encouraging self-sacrifice in a noble, intelligible cause that will inevitably win.[8]

---

[7] These were made available only in the 1930s.

[8] Thus the *Manifesto* was first published in English by the veteran Chartist democrat George Julian Harney and translated into Russian by the anarchist Michael Bakunin.

THE FORTUNES OF LIBERALISM

The July Monarchy

In the years after 1830 France was at the center of European awareness, and not merely because France was the principal source of socialist ideas. Contemporary analysts of French politics spoke of parties of movement and resistance, and both the concept and the word *movement* were exported to other countries to indicate a wide range of agitation to the left of center. From France also came the phrase "the dangerous classes," which, with similarly elastic definition, could comprehend the threat to order from criminals and paupers as well as secret, subversive activities among revolutionaries and discontented workingmen. The reputation was in a considerable degree merited. Memories of 1793 burned brightly once more, fanned by the conviction that the people had made the revolution of 1830 and had been cheated of it. Violence seethed just below the surface of society, breaking out in an almost ritualistic series of attempts to assassinate Louis-Philippe[9] as well as in ugly demonstrations that frequently accompanied strikes and other displays of strength by the growing, though still legally proscribed, trade-union movement in Paris and in industrial centers such as Lyons.

The government dealt savagely with the radicals. A law of 1834 forbade political organizations, sparking a major rising among the silk workers in Lyons (where there had been a notable rising in 1831) and an attempt at insurrection in Paris. Both were brutally suppressed by the National Guard and the army, and the leaders were imprisoned or transported. In such an atmosphere republican and Jacobin movements, onto which forms of associationism or communism were being grafted, had necessarily to work in secret. Auguste Blanqui and Armand Barbès founded the Society of Families (i.e., small clandestine groups), and then the Society of the Seasons. In 1839 the Society of the Seasons attempted a coup in Paris, and Blanqui was thrown into prison for eight years; he was released just before the revolution of 1848. But his treatment only served to heighten the growing sense of the intolerance and injustice of a regime incapable of remedying social inequities and distress. The ambition to bring about armed insurrection, led by professional revolutionaries

---

[9] After an attempt on the king's life in 1836, a deputy asked one of the king's sons if it was appropriate to congratulate his father; he replied, "Certainly, we always do it." The threatening underworld was portrayed for wide audiences in the novels of Eugène Sue, notably *The Mysteries of Paris.*

as trustees for the exploited proletariat, was not rooted out, and it reached its ultimate expression in France in 1871; in time the method was transmitted from Blanqui to Lenin (see p. 863).

The neo-Jacobins had no monopoly on conspiracy and uprisings, however. The country still contained many unreconstructed, and perhaps even more wistful, Bonapartists. After Napoleon's son, the duke of Reichstadt (Napoleon II to his followers), died in 1832, the Bonapartist pretender became Louis Napoleon Bonaparte, the son of Napoleon's brother Louis. Banned from France, Louis Napoleon had led an adventurous life, including a dalliance with the Carbonari (see p. 551) in Italy; in 1836, deciding that his time had come, he attempted to provoke a rising in the garrison at Strasbourg. Its ludicrous failure, though a matter of real concern to the government, led only to his being packed off to the United States, although some of his co-conspirators were brought to trial. But the Napoleonic enthusiasm grew, and in 1840 the government, then led by Adolphe Thiers, attempted to bolster its claims on patriotism by bringing back the emperor's remains from St. Helena to Paris. Meanwhile, Louis Napoleon had gone from America to Switzerland and then to England; he had published a book giving his version—social and humanitarian, rather than military—of the Napoleonic mission. Impressed by the outpouring of Napoleonic sentiment, he decided to try once more, this time at Boulogne. Again the troops failed to rise, but now the government took the challenge seriously, and the pretender was condemned to life imprisonment in the fortress at Ham, which he entered on the day his uncle's ashes were interred in the magnificent tomb in the Hôtel des Invalides on the Left Bank of the Seine.

How could a country hold vigorously competing socialisms, a powerful impulse to insurrection, a violently radical press, a discontented working class, and a potent recollection of Napoleonic glory? The July Monarchy, viewed with such horror by Metternich and the tsar as embodying the hated principles of revolution and representation, in fact stood somewhere to the right of center, ruling this rebellious society with greater or lesser degrees of ineptness; it survived only until its enemies could combine to bring it down. The king was rather more a victim than a source of the difficulties. The son of Philippe Egalité—the duke of Orleans who had sympathized with the Revolution in 1789 and who was executed in the Terror—Louis-Philippe was intelligent, astute, and conciliatory. But by the forties he was aging, increasingly ineffective as a politician, and more and more determined to resist change. He was tired, occasionally petulant, and given to threats of abdication, but it must be recalled that he was constantly vilified, in frequent danger of his life, and deprived of his eldest son and heir, the duke of Orleans, by a carriage accident in 1842. Still, many regimes have easily survived with a king far less able and more set in his ways than Louis-Philippe, even in his declining years. One fundamental difficulty was the institution of monarchy itself. Widespread doubts about its legitimacy were reinforced by the growth of republican sentiments, and, perhaps worse, the effectiveness of the monarchy was compromised by uncertainty as to its proper constitutional role. Louis-Philippe, like his contemporary William IV across the Channel, intended to be an active ruler, a determination in which he was supported by a good many political leaders, while others, including Thiers in his public utterances, insisted that the king should merely reign, not rule.

Another difficulty lay in the extremely narrow political base of the regime. At the inception of the July Monarchy in 1830, only 166,000 men qualified as members of the *pays légal* (the legal country, significantly opposed to the *pays réel,* the actual country), while members of the Chamber of Deputies were drawn from an even more limited segment of society. As in England, the franchise worked differently in different places, being extremely narrow in poorer regions and more generous in wealthy regions; increasing wealth raised the electorate automatically to 241,000 in 1846. It is hard, therefore, to generalize confidently about the monopoly of political participation by the bourgeoisie or the upper bourgeoisie. As we have seen, the Revolution made little change in the composition of the Chamber, the ministries, and the administration—landowners, businessmen, lawyers, and officeholders were there in roughly the same proportions; only an increase in the numbers of those who had held office under the empire set off the post-1830 governing apparatus from its predecessors. It is true, too, that the French middle classes are difficult to pin down or to reduce to a few leading characteristics or interests. To its admirers and advocates, the bourgeoisie was large and beneficent; to its critics, it was narrow in both size and outlook; a cynic (or a historian) could easily see it as a jumble of an indefinite number of groups divided by wealth, religion, education, and business or political interests. But the exclusiveness, the irrelevance, and, in time and in some ways, the corruption of the political system were undeniable. With whatever injustice to sociological and historical truth, it was in these years that the unflattering image of the French bourgeoisie was created, caught, with powerful effect, in the savagely brilliant caricatures of Honoré Daumier. The artisans, craftsmen, and shopkeepers who had manned the barricades in 1830 and who saw their vague but potent revolutionary ideals suppressed found little difficulty in seeing truth in the picture of a grasping, narrow, single-minded class.

The narrow political base helped to produce sterility in government. There was a certain cautious liberalism in Louis-Philippe's first ministry, headed by the banker Jacques Laffitte. Laffitte was succeeded in March 1831 by another banker, Casimir Périer, who demonstrated his devotion to order by firmly suppressing the major uprising at Lyons in November. His death from cholera in May 1832, however, inaugurated an eight-year period that saw no fewer than ten ministries and four general elections. To chronicle them would be an exercise in tedium; suffice it to say that this almost classic instance of ministerial instability could occur only when the political country was completely insulated from conflicting currents of opinion in the country at large and thus removed from the need to make commitments in matters of policy. At the same time, any generalization about ministerial instability in France at any time must be read with a due appreciation of the continuity in personnel that the changes masked. In seventeen governments between 1830 and 1848, 154 available posts as minister or undersecretary were held by only sixty men.

In these shifting and uncertain combinations there was one more or less ideological position, that of the so-called *doctrinaires*, a small group of intellectual politicians dominated by two university professors, P. O. Royer-Collard and François Guizot; they emerged in the early years of the Restoration committed to the belief that the middle classes were the pivot of government. Their ideal was the *juste milieu*—the middle way, the golden mean of a constitutional monarchy, tempered by property and education, moving only gradually with due safeguards and full preparation toward wider participation. But, unlike the Whigs in England, with whom they shared many conclusions in political theory, their policy invariably came down on the side of maintaining the status quo. Aside from the law concerning primary education that Guizot carried in 1833, France in the 1830s and 1840s saw nothing like the vast program of reforms enacted across the Channel. Amid the competition of ins and outs only one notable trend in legislation appeared—the repressiveness of the laws against political organization in 1834 and of the September Laws of 1835, which sharply restricted the press.

From 1836 to 1839 the colorless and ineffective ministries of Count Molé survived with the king's favor. In March 1840 Thiers took office briefly and came close to provoking a European war over the Eastern Question (see p. 742), a show of aggressiveness that was of a piece with his organizing the great national tribute to Napoleon's memory. Thiers was dismissed in October, and a new ministry was formed, headed nominally by the Napoleonic veteran Marshal Soult, but headed in fact (and after 1847 in name) by Guizot. Guizot was a Protestant from the southern city of Nîmes, the son of a lawyer executed in 1794. Educated in Geneva, Guizot went to Paris in 1805 and soon formed powerful connections that carried him into the heart of the literary life of the capital. He wrote much on education and translated Gibbon; but it was his connections rather than his literary production that brought him an appointment first as professor of modern history at the Sorbonne in 1812 and then as secretary-general of the ministry of the interior when Louis XVIII was restored in 1814. Guizot held minor though strategic offices after 1815, but the university remained the bastion to which he could retreat when politics became inhospitable—during the Hundred Days in 1815 or after the fall of Decazes in 1820. Even this resort was denied him with the purge of the universities in 1822, and in the twenties he devoted himself largely to his historical studies, the most distinguished being his history of the English revolution from Charles I to Charles II. When he returned to the Sorbonne in 1828, he delivered a course of lectures on the history of civilization in Europe; it made him famous throughout the Continent.

As a *doctrinaire*, Guizot was propelled into the higher reaches of politics by the revolution of 1830 and maintained himself there, through various changes of ministries, by his administrative abilities and his extraordinary oratorical skill. Out of office during the Molé ministry after 1837, he combined with his political opponents, Thiers and the left-liberal lawyer Odilon Barrot, in a much criticized coalition that brought Molé down in 1839. He then went to London as ambassador, a post he held with increasing discomfort during Thiers' flamboyant tenancy of the foreign ministry. Back in France under Soult, he used his immense skills to provide a government of apparent stability for nearly eight years.

Guizot's pacific foreign policy—he held the post of foreign minister—was helped by an easy collaboration with Lord Aberdeen, his opposite number in Peel's government in Britain, and his growing determination to resist change of any sort at home was seconded by the king. Thiers, Guizot's one major rival, withdrew into a self-imposed isolation, and the new spokesman for a republican opposition, the poet Alphonse de Lamartine, bided his time, content with showy rhetoric and a principled rejection of the game of politics. The only significant trouble arose from a newly combative Catholicism, led by Montalembert, the former associate of Lamennais, determined to break the state monopoly of secondary education. But this aggressive Catholicism provoked a renewed anticlericalism and a popular outcry against the Jesuits, who, though still unauthorized, had begun to broaden their activities in the country. Guizot was not unsympathetic to Catholic demands, but it was perhaps owing more to luck than skill that an anti-Catholic education bill was withdrawn and that, at the same time, the Jesuits beat a strategic retreat. Thus, without a single accomplishment of note, other than surviving and increasing the hostility he had always inspired, Guizot and his own government emerged the victors in the general elections of 1846.

The next year Guizot insisted—no doubt with a confidence born of seeming success—that the duty of a government is to go slowly and wisely, "to maintain and to set limits." Lamartine replied that if that were the distinctive genius of a statesman, then a boundary stone would do as well. Yet more pointedly, Lamartine declared that France was bored. The enthusiasms with which the country was filled could not much longer be confined.

Britain in the Age of Peel

Great Britain after 1832 was anything but bored: the island kingdom was entering one of the most creative and exciting periods in its legislative and social history. Yet it was not an age of dominant middle-class influence, let alone the first installment of democracy that historians have sometimes incautiously implied. The Reform Act of 1832 could hardly deliver all that hopeful contemporaries expected of it. To be sure, it satisfied a far wider range of citizens than had benefited from the July Revolution in France, but it disappointed many others, while some of its results could scarcely have been predicted.

Aristocratic influence survived, though it was tempered and controlled; aristocratic dominance of high office was not to be lessened for a least a generation. The House of Lords maintained and for a time even increased its importance. Statesmanship (or prudence) led the peers to accept much new legislation that was clearly demanded in the country. At the same time, when the Lords made trouble for the Whig government of the thirties, they did so on questions like Ireland or Church reform, on which public opinion was far from unanimous, thus avoiding a coalition of interests against the upper house. Although the bishops had with one exception voted against the Reform bill, the Church of England, too, survived the assault that had begun in 1828 and 1829. Its enemies (notably the Dissenters) proved to be politically weaker than had been thought. Moreover, Sir Robert Peel and C. J. Blomfield, the bishop of London and an outstanding ecclesiastical statesman, reformed the church so as to undo some of its worst abuses and to enable it to work more effectively in a rapidly changing world. [10]

The opponents of Reform had argued that the passage of the Reform Act would upset the much-praised balance of the constitution: no king and no government, they insisted, could withstand a concerted opinion in the House of Commons, nor would the Commons be able to withstand opinion in the country. The prediction was right, though the consequences were long in developing. By the forties few members of Parliament rejected a party label, but there was as yet little government or party control of the Commons. It long remained possible for a government to be brought down by an adverse vote on an important issue, a kind of legislative control of the executive that now exists only in the pages of textbooks. This was the golden age of the individual member, who could take the initiative and bring about reforms without directly involving, or even in opposition to, the government. Parties outside Parliament were rudimentary at best, pretty much run up for elections and still subject to domination by local interests. Newspapers appealed to a growing public, which had a far greater appetite than exists today for the minutiae of political life; the most important of the papers, *The Times* of London, wielded a power that justified its nickname, "The Thunderer." [11] But there was no wholesale assault by special interests or by public opinion on Parliament, and parliamentary supremacy was established in a form that lasted convincingly until the early twentieth century.

The powers of the king were reduced sharply and quickly. Royal (which means ministerial) influence on elections and the composition of majorities in the Commons had long been shrinking (see p. 567), and the personalities of the monarchs also contributed to the decline of their office. But in 1834 William IV attempted to reassert his authority. Tired of his reforming ministry and

---

[10] On religious developments, see pp. 663, 697.

[11] Founded in 1785, *The Times* established its independence of political control early in the nineteenth century. It was the first newspaper to print on steam presses, in 1814.

troubled by divisions in the cabinet itself, he took advantage of the resignation of Lord Grey to dismiss the Whig government. Sir Robert Peel formed a new government and launched a remarkable program of legislation; but, after an election he called in 1835 to remedy his minority position in the House of Commons, he was quickly defeated in a vote in the new Commons. He resigned, and Lord Melbourne, who had succeeded Grey briefly in 1834, returned to office and carried through at least some of Peel's measures. The king's effort to behave as his father, George III, had regularly behaved was rebuffed by the voters and the Commons and was not tried again. There was, however, a curious echo. In 1837, when William IV died, Queen Victoria came to the throne. An eighteen-year-old girl, she was devoted to Lord Melbourne, her adviser, friend, and surrogate father. When Melbourne was defeated on a vote in the Commons in 1838, he resigned and the queen sent reluctantly for Peel. Peel, fearing Melbourne's continuing influence, asked the queen, as a sign of confidence, to replace her Whig ladies of the bedchamber with attendants of Conservative persuasion. The queen refused, and Peel (probably with relief) declined to take office. It was, however, only an echo: Peel was in full command after his electoral triumph in 1841. The monarch remained important as an individual throughout Victoria's long reign and remains so even today, but after 1834-1835 the government was no longer truly the king's: the king chose as his ministers not whom he wanted, but the acknowledged leaders of the majority party in the House of Commons. After half a century of evolution, "responsible government"—government answering to the Commons, not the king—was attained. [12]

Constitutional matters aside, what did the Whigs accomplish in the thirties? In 1833 slavery—declared illegal in England in 1772 and the object of fifty years of agitation—was brought to an end in the British overseas possessions; in the same year Parliament broke the monopoly of the East India Company on the China trade, leaving it only a governing corporation with no trading functions. The Whigs could not muster sufficient talent or boldness to reform government finances; they did, however, introduce penny postage in 1840—shifting the burden of payment from receiver to sender and setting a uniform rate for whatever distance a letter traveled. This reform, highly important from both a commercial and a humanitarian point of view, at first bore out its opponents' dire predictions by running up huge deficits until the country responded to the new ease and cheapness by increasing the volume of mail. [13]

[12] Queen Victoria was the daughter of George III's fourth son, the older sons having died without legitimate heirs; with her accession the crown of Hanover was separated from the crown of Great Britain. Hanover, where the Salic Law forbade the accession of a woman, fell to George III's fifth son, the duke of Cumberland, a petty tyrant in mentality.

[13] The reforms also included the invention of the adhesive postage stamp, quickly copied in other countries and giving the world a major hobby and a minor industry. But the British still proclaim their historic priority: their stamps alone bear no indication, other than the sovereign's portrait, of the country of origin.

Far more controversial than any of these measures was the reworking of England's municipal governments in 1835, along with Scottish and Irish acts in 1833 and 1840. The old, oligarchical, and often corrupt municipal corporations had rarely gone beyond their obligations to care for the town's property and to administer certain charitable trusts. Over the preceding half century or so, they had been widely supplemented by what their historians have called, rather forbiddingly, "statutory authorities for special purposes." These independent bodies, created on local initiative by private acts of Parliament, looked after newly important activities such as sewerage, street lighting, and police; indeed, one such body was the real municipal government of the city of Manchester, for the old village from which it had grown could contribute only archaic manorial institutions. Once reformed, the corporations were elected by those who paid local taxes—a far more democratic franchise than the parliamentary vote. While the powers specifically conferred by the act of 1835 were limited, the potential was there for a wide expansion of municipal activities over the next decades. It is certainly arguable that this reform was a far more significant increment of "middle-class influence" in the overall political structure than was the Reform Act of 1832.

The Whigs were far less successful with educational and religious questions. Although modest parliamentary grants were given from 1833 to assist voluntary societies in building schools, any general provision for popular education was prevented by the passions aroused in the Church of England and the Dissenting sects. The Whigs could do little to help their Dissenting supporters in other respects. The universities of Oxford and Cambridge remained closed to them, and taxes to maintain parish churches could still be levied on non-Anglicans. In 1836, however, the old requirement that marriages be performed only in Anglican churches was modified, following a scheme hit upon by Peel in his brief ministry: couples could thereafter be married in Dissenting chapels or in a civil ceremony. The problem of the established church in Ireland, which ministered only to a minority in that overwhelmingly Catholic country, split the Whig government in 1833 and helped to touch off the protest of the Oxford Movement (see p. 663). In the end, some degree of rational organization was given to a church that had found its chief justifications in its historic claims and its vast provision of ecclesiastical patronage. And Irish church reform stimulated English reforms; after 1836 the structure of the Church of England was rationalized and inequalities in income among its bishops and clergy were reduced. It also became possible to commute the payment of the tithe—the levy on agricultural produce that went to support the church or, often, the laymen who had succeeded to church property in the sixteenth century—into a money payment.

The Whigs established the first effective controls over the labor of children in textile factories (see p. 594), and they attacked a still more serious social problem, that of poverty. The cost of poor relief had mounted enormously, particularly in those parts of southern England where there were many unemployed laborers who, because of restrictive laws, could not easily move elsewhere. The injustice and degradation visited upon the poor by the old Elizabethan poor law underlay much of the rural discontent that had burst out in serious rioting and burnings in the countryside in 1830 and 1831. A major investigation was launched and issued in one of the most important pieces of legislation in nineteenth-century Britain, the Poor Law Amendment Act of 1834. The act sought to improve efficiency by making the basic administrative unit a union of parishes rather than a single parish; the elected boards of guardians for each union were subjected to central control from three commissioners in London—the "three bashaws of Somerset House" as they came to be called—and there were inspectors, or assistant commissioners, to make the control effective. The commissioners intended to care for the poor only in workhouses, instead of paying relief in money to the unemployed ("outdoor relief" as it was known); they also determined that the regimen in the workhouses should be so stringent that laborers would accept any work outside the workhouse rather than go on relief. To some extent the plan was based on theoretical recommendations emanating from Jeremy Bentham and his associates, and it worked reasonably well in the rural south. But the policy could not be strictly applied to the seasonal or cyclical unemployment characteristic of the factory districts, while some of the act's more admirable provisions were never carried into force. Thus an act of the first importance in setting a model for state administration contributed to a narrow and unimaginative view of the problem of poverty. More immediately, it touched off an outburst of hostility from those people most affected by its provisions.

The agitation against the Poor Law came together with the factory movement, the frustrated attempts at trade-union organization, Owenite socialism, and disillusion with the results of 1832 to produce the phenomenon known as Chartism. For three or four years Chartism gave the appearance of unity and concerted effort to widely differing manifestations of working-class discontent. To some extent this appearance was reinforced by the growing conviction that English society was divided into classes and that common interests held together a single "working class," which in fact comprised a bewildering variety of often antithetical types. But the upper levels of skilled workingmen in the new trades that industrialism was creating remained relatively untouched by Chartism, as were the poorest, brutalized urban dwellers. The older industrial centers—whether the factory town of Manchester, with its true proletariat, or the hardware center of Birmingham, with its small workshops and small masters—were less radical than the newer, smaller industrial towns. The people most likely to turn to Chartism were those whose way of life or very existence was threatened by industrialism—the miners and the declining numbers of domestic outworkers in the textile or metal trades. Because of an economic downturn in 1836, they were also most susceptible to the anti-Poor Law campaign.

The term "Chartism" came from a draft reform bill, the "People's Charter," put forward in 1838 by a group of radical workingmen in London; it called for universal manhood suffrage, annual elections, the secret ballot, the equalization of electoral districts, the abolition of property qualifications for membership in the House of Commons, and payment of members of Parliament. These famous "six points of the Charter" were narrowly political and traditional goals that nevertheless seemed to promise to each Chartist whatever utopia he most desired. In the case of Thomas Attwood, a Birmingham banker who had agitated for parliamentary reform in 1832, the great goal was reform of the currency; dismissed as economic nonsense by orthodox economists then, Attwood's inflationary views have received a more respectful hearing in this century. Attwood agreed to support the Charter and added the idea of a national petition to bring it to the attention of Parliament. A "People's Convention" in London would show that a truer representation of the people was possible, and a refusal of the petition would bring a general strike. The convention opened in February 1839.

Before long serious divisions had appeared in the Chartist ranks, and immediate victory was to lie with the strange figure of Feargus O'Connor, a former Irish member of Parliament who had made a name for himself by denouncing the Poor Law. A brilliant demagogue, O'Connor used his tours and speeches and his excellent newspaper, the *Northern Star,* to seize command of the movement and to pose the contrast between the "moral force" school of the London radicals headed by William Lovett and the "physical force" school, though in retrospect O'Connor's real commitment to ultimate methods is far from clear. "Missionaries" from the convention soon found that, despite the impressiveness of great mass meetings, there was little popular support for a general strike; the government had carefully prepared to deal with any disturbances; and in September the convention dissolved. In November there was an uprising on the Welsh border, a complex incident that reflected local discontents and personal frustrations more than it did a Chartist movement. The leaders of the rising, veterans of the convention, were transported to Australia; other Chartist leaders spent some time in prison; and the government, characteristically, set to investigating to find out why the uprising had occurred. Chartism, for all the appearances to the contrary, never again reached the peak of 1839. There were widespread strikes in 1842 and 1844, but the veteran Chartists were by that time pursuing widely disparate goals—among them educational reform, temperance, and religion. O'Connor carried his still loyal supporters into a visionary and quite impractical plan to provide land for the poor through a kind of lottery. Chartism left a noble legacy to later reform movements; but, for all the fear it could still evoke, as in 1848 (see p. 738), it was politically dead.

The man who had to master these diverse challenges in the forties was Sir Robert Peel. In 1834, he had signaled the conversion of his party from the old Toryism into modern Conservatism by accepting the verdict of 1832 and setting out a general policy that would accept needed changes while retaining the ancient institutions of monarchy and church. He emerged from the election of

1841 with a solid majority and a brilliantly capable cabinet, both of which he effectively controlled. The legislative accomplishment of the forties was remarkable: an act that regulated labor in the mines, excluding children from underground work, and, for the first time, bringing women within the purview of labor legislation; further factory legislation; a banking act; a basic railway act; an act easing the formation of companies. The one serious failure was an attempt in 1843 to provide a national system of schools for the poor; once again education fell victim to the objection of Dissenters to Anglican control. But all this was done in the shadow of one overriding issue, free trade.

In 1815 Parliament passed a Corn Law, which set a prohibitive tariff on imported grain to protect domestic producers. It never worked well, despite modification in later years, and the discontented agricultural interest grew more and more determined to maintain protection as a symbol of the central place that agriculture and the landed classes held in the English scheme of things. At the same time, among the economic theorists, many of the industrial and commercial interests, and a growing number of politicians, the ideal of free trade was taking hold. Half a century before, Adam Smith had despaired of ever shaking the allegiance of the merchant class to what he called "mercantilism." But by 1820 the merchants of London were petitioning for free trade, and, from the midthirties, Parliament every year received a motion for repeal of the Corn Laws—the great symbolic goal of the free traders. Peel, increasingly convinced of the necessity for free trade, launched a wholesale revision of the tariff structure in 1842 and made up the deficit by restoring the income tax that had been abolished in 1816. It was, he promised, a temporary expedient, but of course it never disappeared.

Meanwhile, a vast agitation was begun in the country, spearheaded by the Anti-Corn Law League, founded in 1839 in Manchester, the center of free-trade sentiment. After some abortive early attempts to contest elections and to provoke strikes, the League concentrated on mobilizing public opinion through a hitherto unexampled propaganda campaign and by huge rallies harangued by popular orators, often ministers who effectively coupled free trade with Christian morality. The League's outstanding figures were Richard Cobden, a Manchester manufacturer who became the principal theorist of the internationalist and pacifist consequences of free trade, and John Bright, a Quaker manufacturer from Huddersfield in Yorkshire, one of the great reform leaders and orators of the century. But, despite the amazing activities of the League, the victory had to be won in Parliament, and it was Peel who won it.

Peel found his opportunity in Ireland. In the thirties the Whigs had ruled Ireland well, thanks in good part to a scientist-administrator named Thomas Drummond, who reminded the astonished Irish landlords that property had its duties as well as its rights. In the forties the Conservatives, faced with a campaign by Daniel O'Connell (see p. 568) to repeal the Union, had to resort to forcible rule coupled with generous gestures, such as Peel's increased (and politically costly) subsidy to the training college for Irish priests. Then, in 1845, the potatoes rotted in the ground, a blight that, unlike earlier instances, recurred the next year. The resulting famine ultimately reduced the overgrown population of Ireland by about two million—a million through emigration, the rest from outright starvation or disease. It was a disaster beyond the imagination and certainly beyond the administrative capacity of the English, a tragic tale of misapplied theories, inadequate policy, and long-standing incomprehension of Ireland and its problems.

In solving the Irish population problem in the grimmest possible way, Providence also solved England's major political question. As an emergency measure, Peel lifted the tariffs on grain and made the change permanent by an act carried in May 1846, to take full effect in 1849. A number of concessions were made to the agricultural interest in the form of sharp reductions in the tariffs remaining on manufactured goods and in the taking over by the central government of certain administrative expenses that had fallen heavily on the localities. But the protectionists were not appeased. As in 1829 with Catholic Emancipation, Peel had defied the majority sentiment of his party, and disgruntled protectionists came together with the Whigs to bring Peel down. Though he remained the most powerful political figure in the country—and certainly the most popular—he was not again to return to office; he was killed in a fall from a horse in 1850. His party split, with his most devoted and talented followers forming a floating faction of "Peelites," who held the political balance for a dozen years. The remaining Conservatives were led by Lord Derby, the one minister to resign from Peel's cabinet over free trade, and by a brilliant political adventurer who had masterminded the coalition against Peel, Benjamin Disraeli.

Both Britain and France, in the years between 1830 and 1846, were exciting, but only in Britain was there steady accomplishment, which in time lessened pressures that in France were building to the flash point. How is the difference to be accounted for? It is difficult to argue anything very conclusive on the level of ideas. Neither country could claim much of an edge over the other in the area of political thought. There was, however, general agreement, then and now, that Frenchmen were far more widely aware of the European intellectual ferment than were Englishmen: the poet and social critic Matthew Arnold was only the most famous of those who lamented the intellectual backwardness of the English public, the triumph of practical over the theoretical, "the utter insensibility . . . of people to the number of ideas and schemes now ventilated on the Continent—not because they have judged them or seen beyond them, but from sheer habitual want of wide reading and thinking." [14] A little later Walter Bagehot claimed the same pervasive anti-intellectualism as an advantage when he praised English "stupidity" for

[14] In a letter of 1848, G. W. E. Russell, ed., *Letters of Matthew Arnold, 1848–1888* (1895), vol. I, 9.

protecting England from the instability of France.[15] Still, the liberal tradition was more widely accepted, more deeply felt, in England than in France. So explanations must be sought in the receptivity of the two societies to liberal doctrine and to the stage of preparedness to which they had been brought by economic development and its consequent effects on social structure and men's ambitions.

The very excitement of French intellectual debate reflects the divisions left by the great Revolution. France had been repeatedly revolutionized in its political arrangements, so that few institutions could claim the authority of long existence. Moreover, what was done in Paris had an effect on the rest of the country that was both disproportionate and insecure. Lines of governmental authority ran clearly to and from the capital, and Paris held a position in the social and intellectual life of its nation unmatched by that of any other European city. But Paris could not necessarily maintain itself when the country chose to turn against it. Although France was undergoing a striking transformation in its economic life, it had fallen behind Britain, measured on the scale of industrialism. The country remained overwhelmingly agrarian. The French urban middle classes were, for the most part, narrow in outlook and bound by a strong sense of property and status. The working classes—where they counted, in industrial centers like Paris or Lyons—were tied to archaic institutions and could escape from their social and political isolation only by occasional and futile insurrectionary outbursts.

It may be that Britain was fortunate in the timing of her long transition to industrialism. Some of the manifest social consequences were recognized and dealt with, piecemeal, before party lines and social attitudes had hardened. And while Britain's tailors, shoemakers, and printers were as radical as their French brethren, there had already been created a class of men and women, accustomed to the discipline of the new society, who stood to benefit, rather than suffer, from the new economic organization. Agrarian society in Britain had entered a long-term decline, though its principal beneficiaries, the titled and untitled landlords, retained great social prestige and much political power to the very end of the nineteenth century. A far more widely based urban middle-class culture had emerged throughout the country in the preindustrial prosperity of the eighteenth century and grew in both complexity and strength with the spread of one or another form of industrialism. Aristocratic political leaders could take a genuinely national view as well as support the interests of their own class, and they were quite willing to seek partisan advantage in advocating the goals of other groups in society. The English middle classes were restrained on the one hand by the example of a responsible aristocracy and on the other by a remarkable growth of humanitarian and religious ideals. Thus,

---

[15] Walter Bagehot, *Letters on the French Coup d'Etat of 1851* (1852), letters three and four. The letters are reprinted in Bagehot's *Historical Essays,* of which there are several editions. Bagehot, incidentally, claims the same resistance to ideas on the part of the Belgians.

the upper crust in Britain was both more permeable and less resistant than in France; in a variety of ways it stimulated and even welcomed, rather than suppressed, growth at the lower levels. The British state, though capable of neglect and injustice, was less pervasive than Continental states, and it was buffered by a complex of local governments, voluntary associations, and social hierarchies of independent authority: if it could do less less swiftly, it was also insulated from hostile reaction. Both state and monarchy were secure, except in the most abstract polemics, from fundamental question, and it was natural for political interest at all levels to be channeled into controlling existing institutions rather than into the effort to overthrow them. Yet, whatever the explanations of the differences between the two countries, it cannot be denied that the thirties and forties were a terrifying time to live through, on either side of the Channel.

Continental Liberalism: Some Small Successes

In Belgium and Switzerland, liberal victories, though less sweeping than in Britain, were permanent and heartening to liberals elsewhere. Belgium was undergoing rapid industrial development in these years, though the Belgian working classes lagged well behind those of Britain and France in their organization and self-consciousness. Belgium's bourgeois society, with a wider franchise than that in France, was divided principally on the issue of Catholic control of education, not on more fundamental matters; and King Leopold I proved able to master the situation with far more skill and flexibility than Louis-Philippe could muster in France. Belgium met the threat of revolution in 1848 by further widening of the franchise and by doing away with the tax on newspapers; the few demonstrations were easily put down.

In Switzerland, a confederation whose independence and neutrality had been guaranteed at Vienna in 1815, the twenty-two cantons were virtually independent sovereign powers, able even to conduct diplomatic relations independently, so long as they did not harm the confederation. Each canton had one vote in the federal diet, but the central government amounted to little, and local aristocracies ruled without challenge from peasants or bourgeoisie. In the late twenties and thirties, however, an aggressive liberal movement developed. Its origins lay partly in the stimulus of the movement for Greek independence, partly in ideas brought back by soldiers who had fought as mercenaries in France, partly in the growth of industry. In the early thirties agitation and riots secured new, liberal constitutions in most of the cantons. Switzerland was, moreover, a haven for German and Italian exiles, and in time radicals began to appear in Swiss politics as well. But again, as in so many countries, the central issue was religion: some cantons were predominantly Catholic and some were Protestant. In 1844 the Catholic canton of Lucerne deliberately reinstated the Jesuits, an incautious move that led to attempts by local liberals and radicals, supported by other cantons, to overthrow the Lucerne government. When these were put down, seven Catholic cantons formed a separatist league—the *Sonderbund*—a challenge to the confederation that brought yet more cantons into the hands of liberals. The liberals soon gained a majority in the federal diet, where they voted to dissolve the *Sonderbund* and expel the Jesuits. The result was a tiny war that barely lasted the month of November 1847, in which the *Sonderbund* was soundly defeated. In 1848 a new constitution, overwhelmingly accepted in an election, created an effective federal government, with a two-chamber parliament that elected the seven-man executive. The establishment of a truly unified nation, then, was a victory ascribable to the liberalism of the economically progressive northern, Protestant cantons.

The economic and political circumstances that, despite religious differences, proved hospitable to modest liberal accomplishments in Belgium and Switzerland were not to be found in Spain. Spanish liberalism had, to be sure, acquired a special position in the history of early nineteenth-century Europe, thanks to the resistance of 1810–1812 and to the constitution of the latter year, which served so many other countries as a somewhat impracticable model (see p. 519). The more moderate liberalism of the early twenties had also left its mark by arousing the forces of order, provoking French military intervention, and splitting the Concert of Europe (see p. 551). But Spanish liberalism was always something of an exotic growth; a phenomenon of radically inclined towns, it was anathema to the reactionary countryside. The situation was further complicated by a fierce regional separatism—reactionary in the Catholic royalist strongholds in Navarre and the Basque country of the northwest, radical in the rapidly growing industrial city of Barcelona, the center of the province of Catalonia. Although the liberals gained an importance out of all proportion to their numbers, they were split into factions: the radicals looked back to 1812, the moderates to the qualified constitutionalism of the early twenties. Given the lack of firm royal direction, the initiative was likely to rest with the army, which was itself divided and which could engender pronunciamentos either on behalf of or against the liberals.

Ferdinand VII continued to display no political sense at all. Incapable of supporting the moderate liberals who had rallied to him after the revolution of 1820, Ferdinand ruled through most of the twenties with ministers who harked back to the absolutism of the eighteenth century. Their sober, cautious, anticonstitutional but enlightened rule had, by the early thirties, cleaned up and reorganized government, reopened the universities, and disbanded the royal volunteers, an undoubtedly reactionary militia. This tendency to deliberate, mildly benevolent government was supported by Queen Maria Cristina, a Neapolitan princess whom the much-widowed Ferdinand had married in 1830. Maria Cristina promptly bore the king a daughter, Isabella, and it was not clear whether a woman could legally succeed to the throne. The question became acute with Ferdinand's death in 1833, when the queen mother became regent for the infant Isabella II. It was resolved only through a civil war, for reactionary sentiment in the country had crystallized around Ferdinand's ambitious and stupid brother, Don Carlos. The Carlist wars dragged on inconclusively until 1839, further complicating a succession of constitutions, pronunciamentos, and coups. In 1834 a Royal Statute much like the French Charter was promulgated, but it was unacceptable to the Exaltados, the radicals who looked back to 1812, as well as to the Progresistas, who without going as far as the Exaltados, believed in the sovereignty of the people. When a wave of provincial revolutions like those of 1820 broke out in 1835, the queen regent, advised by the British minister, gave the premiership to Juan Alvarez Mendizábal, a liberal banker just back from a dozen years of exile in London. With only some success, Mendizábal floated foreign loans, secularized church lands, and launched a program of land reform. Within a year he was dismissed in favor of a more conservative premier, only to be swept back into power (as minister of finance) in 1836 by a pronunciamento led not by officers but by sergeants. Reforming began once more; in 1837 a constituent Cortes proposed a constitution acceptable to the Progressives but not to the Moderates; and in 1839 the ministers were turned out and the Cortes was dissolved.

The queen regent was not to have her way, however. By this time the most powerful figure in the country was General Baldomero Espartero, who had defeated the Carlists at last and who brought his popularity and ambition to the cause of the Progressives. Maria Cristina called him to the premiership in 1840 and then, tired of the infighting, left the country. Espartero, declaring himself sole regent in 1841, proceeded to make enemies everywhere, even in the army and in Catalonia, which had been the main source of his support. In 1843 an uprising took place against this now apparent dictator and his unpopular clique, and he was driven from the country by his rival, General Ramon Narváez. A Moderate, Narváez secured a new constitution in 1845 that was virtually a return to the conservative Royal Statute of 1834. Narváez was never popular, and his hold on power was broken from time to time. But he dominated the Spanish scene into the sixties, his self-proclaimed liberalism degenerating into a conservative dictatorship. "I have no enemies," he is supposed to have said when he was dying, "I have shot them all."

Yet liberalism need not be identified with Progressive policies or parliamentary supremacy, and much was done in these years of military rule to bring Spain closer to the modern world. A national police force, the Civil Guard, was established; despite its unpopularity and its partiality for the landlord interest, it stood for order in a disorderly country and was no worse than the Progressive militia, which was capable of terrorism too. While the concordat with the church in 1851 abandoned some of the extreme anticlericalism of the Progressives and conceded many traditional prerogatives to the church (notably in education), it secured church recognition of past expropriations in exchange for state salaries for the secular clergy; the church was thus put on a more certain and efficient legal basis and kept from being a subversive force. The law was codified, many important public works were undertaken, and a period of economic growth and even of some prosperity was assured. Escaping the revolutionary year 1848 almost untouched, Spain postponed her revolution for twenty years. It was a liberal victory of sorts.

Portugal followed a remarkably parallel course. There was the same tension between liberal towns and a traditional, clerical countryside. The royal family, too, was split, although in this instance the reactionary uncle, Dom Miguel, was able for a time to make himself king against the claims of the seven-year-old Maria da Gloria, the daughter of Dom Pedro, the emperor of Brazil, who chose to remain in the New World and to abdicate the Portuguese throne in favor of Maria. In the end the victory of Maria over Miguel was assured by British intervention, both military, in the form of assistance to the naval force that Dom Pedro mounted to support Maria, and diplomatic, in the Quadruple Alliance arranged in 1834 among Britain, Portugal, France, and a now liberal Spain. As in Spain there was an alternation of moderate and radical constitutions and a succession of crises and ministries. The general drift was mildly liberal: the civil law and criminal law were reformed, efforts were made to improve education, and literature and the arts responded to a somewhat freer atmosphere. But Portugal remained poor and backward, with little possibility of even a modicum of political stability.

Frustrated Aspirations: Italy, the Austrian Empire, Germany

In the rest of Europe these were years of talk, not action, of frustrated ambitions and ill-starred attempts to make hopes into realities. Italy had produced one great revolutionist, Buonarroti. But, as a veteran of the 1790s, he saw France as the carrier of the new civilization (see p. 680). To his younger fellow country-men, however, this was unacceptable. They hoped to create in Italy a new nation that would inspire and lead the revolutionary movement throughout Europe. Thus a new strand, nationalism, was added to the skein of liberal ideas. Ardent spirits—above all those driven into exile after the petty revolts of 1831—were eager to overthrow the dismally efficient hegemony of Austria; they were strengthened in their resolve by a legion of writers, among them the dramatist Silvio Pellico, who in 1832 published a stirring account of his experience in Austrian prisons. While local dialects still separated peasants and workingmen in different parts of the country, educated men were increasingly bound together. Economic development forced merchants, manufacturers, and economic theorists into thinking of a country freed from artificial customs barriers and open to large-scale transportation and marketing systems. But, while the preconditions for a national solution grew, agreement on means remained as good as unattainable.

Some nationalists wanted the old claims of Rome revived, associated if possible with a liberalized Catholicism: thus could Italy be united and Europe inspired. This was the burden of Vicenzo Gioberti's *Moral and Civil Primacy of the Italians,* published in 1843. Gioberti was the most famous representative of a school known as neo-Guelphs, whose name recalled the papal party that resisted the invading Germans in medieval times. Count Cesare Balbo, in his *Hopes of Italy,* published the next year, looked, like Gioberti, to a federal solution—but under the presidency of the king of Piedmont, not the pope. Looming far larger than these writers, however, or the many poets, essayists, historians, and musicians who stimulated the growth of national consciousness, was Giuseppe Mazzini. A Genoese exile, he proclaimed that Italy's leadership of the liberal revolution in Europe would be found once she had driven out the Austrians and established a unitary republic dedicated to liberty. Mazzini too saw Piedmont as the essential base of operations, but his early attempts at insurrection there failed pitifully. He founded a secret organization known as "Young Italy," an example that inspired similar movements elsewhere, which Mazzini sought (hardly successfully) to weld into "Young Europe." In these movements and in his writings, Mazzini embodied his belief in nationality as determined by language—an ideal strongly influenced by Herder—his commitment to liberal ideals, his incurably romantic temper, and his faith in international brotherhood. The solution to the Italian problem was not to be Mazzini's—far from it. But no one contributed so much as he to the idea of an Italian nation; and no one stood so clearly as the voice of liberal nationalism for the rest of Europe, or so troubled the dreams of reactionary statesmen.

In the German lands and in the eastern domains of the Austrian emperor, the *Vormärz*—the years after the revolutions of 1830 and prior to the revolutions of March 1848—was a time of ferment, with little practical political result, though much was being accomplished in the economic sphere. In Hungary, nearly every aspect of life had been galvanized by the reforming activities and writings of Count Stephen Széchényi, whom we have already encountered as an apostle of Magyar cultural nationalism. Having seen, as a young man, the contrast between the advanced civilizations of western Europe and his own, he was a moderate liberal, an anglophile and a francophile, with a phenomenal range of interests in every way worthy of a man who numbered Benjamin Franklin among his heroes. Beyond his cultural innovations—the Academy and the Hungarian Theater—he promoted improved navigation (with steam vessels) on the Danube and the importation of machinery. He introduced horse racing and clubs (which he preferred to call casinos, to avoid the revolutionary sound of the word club) as a means of bringing the classes of Hungary's stratified society together and of enlarging their awareness of the world outside. In his writings he attacked noble privileges and advocated not only betterment of the economic lot of the peasants, but also their eventual admission to a recognized status within the constitution. And when, in 1836, the diet enabled Széchényi and his collaborators to proceed with building a bridge across the Danube to join the cities of Buda and Pest, it also authorized a first symbolic breach in the bastion of privilege by requiring that nobles pay tolls.

Although the diet of 1832–1836 was dominated by Széchényi, his ideas, and his disciples, the liberal and national movement that he launched swiftly passed after the midthirties into the hands of Louis Kossuth, one of the most prominent of nineteenth-century nationalist heroes. A minor, untitled nobleman, half-Slovak by birth, Kossuth brought to his career as a journalist and agitator something of the passion of a convert. How impressive it seemed that he, not the great nobleman Széchényi, should become the leader of his nation! But it has been argued that throughout his career Kossuth spoke for the threatened class from which he came, the minor landowners, who were under a double threat from imperial centralization and the loss of forced labor under the *robot* system. If the economic future of the gentry was bleak, a new future as the administrators of a Magyar state could be conjured up by realizing two complementary ambitions: securing autonomy for Hungary and forcing the Magyar language on the entire country, although Magyars were a minority. The latter goal was quickly attained: in 1840 Magyar was declared the official language, and in 1844 it was made the sole language of education, law, and government business, although the imperial authorities in Vienna—appalled but powerless to stem the Magyar enthusiasm of the Hungarian diet—managed to get German retained as the language of imperial correspondence. There was another significant exception: the Croatians could continue to use Latin, the old and admittedly declining official language, for another six years. But where once Magyars and Croats had stood together against Vienna, Magyar exclusiveness had unwittingly bred a Croatian national movement; its adherents ultimately joined with Serbian nationalists to work for a great South Slav state to be built on the ruins of Hapsburg domination. But, for the time being, Kossuth's journalism and oratory swept all before it.

There were nationalist stirrings in the Austrian domains as well, though they were far less impressive and advanced than those in Hungary. Polish nationalism in Galicia was confined to landlords and intellectuals. Like so many upper-class nationalists, they feared the peasants, who rose against their masters in a violent rebellion in 1846. The imperial authorities, by promising agrarian reforms, were able to turn the peasants against the Polish nationalists. [16] In Bohemia, there was a similar gap between the Czech peasantry and the Germanized upper classes, though—in partial imitation of Hungarian successes—a Czech national movement emerged. In Metternich's Austria, surprising though it seems, liberalism, not nationalism, had the better chance of bringing change. Economic development helped to spur the acceptance of liberal ideas, and these ideas were given currency in a number of trade associations and discussion groups organized among enlightened aristocrats, businessmen, and academics. Activities like these were tolerated by Metternich's rival, the minister of the interior, Count Franz Kolowrat; but Austria's flourishing intellectual life—its leading figure the playwright Franz Grillpar-

---

[16] On the course of Polish nationalism in these years, see pp. 575, 765.

zer—had still to cope with a pervasive, if erratic, censorship and constant frustration.

Metternich was capable of some cautious, administrative reforming. He was receptive to Széchényi's plans for Hungary, and he was eager to rework the imperial tariff structure to provide some counterbalance to the German customs union, the Zollverein, then pushing ahead profitably under Prussian leadership. But he was ever fearful of change and never forceful, and none of his little efforts at governmental reform succeeded; his encouragement of artificial regional distinctions in the interest of a workable federalism took a nationalist turning he could only oppose. In 1835 Francis I died; his son, Ferdinand I, who was feebleminded, required a regency, which Metternich arranged to consist of himself and the young emperor's reactionary uncle, the archduke Ludwig. Kolowrat, who had resigned in 1836 in a dispute about the sugar duties, returned to office under the patronage of the liberal archduke John and joined the regency. But this state council, as it was known, was in fact paralyzed by the intense rivalry between Kolowrat and Metternich, and immobility and half-hearted repression remained the ordinary style of Austrian government.

In Germany agricultural change, the slow growth of industry, the beginning of railway building, and the creation of the Zollverein were laying the foundations for the future German industrial system, at a high cost in social misery. Again, there was growing discussion of liberal and radical ideas, to some extent among businessmen and their publicists, but rooted mainly in Germany's imposing academic life. The more radical ideas, however, were kept underground, to surface only among the growing number of exiles abroad.

The most open success of the agitation for change during the *Vormärz* came in the wake of the revolutions of 1830-1831. On May 26-27, 1832, at Hambach in Bavaria, twenty-five thousand to thirty thousand enthusiasts from all over Germany came together for a riot of liberal and nationalist oratory. Like the Wartburg festival in 1817, it frightened the authorities of the Germanic Confederation and gave them another excuse for imposing the Six Articles, which allowed rulers to circumvent the will of their legislatures (see p. 574). But persecutions of individuals in the courts and academic dismissals swelled the ranks of émigrés and journalists, a course for which, in the long run, German reaction paid dearly.

The most notable of the exiled radicals were the leaders of the so-called Young Germany (a literary circle in no way related to Mazzini's movement): Ludwig Börne, who contributed a streamlined journalistic style to the German language, and Heinrich Heine, who added to his magnificent gifts as a lyric poet a superb talent for satire. But retribution also overtook the less radical. Two professors at the University of Freiburg, Karl von Rotteck and Karl Theodor Welcker, recognized intellectual leaders of the anglophile school of constitutional liberals, were removed from their posts in 1832. They began to compile a *Staatslexikon,* an encyclopedia of politics that enshrined in lengthy scholarly articles the accepted tenets of their school—a source book for generations of

German liberals. In Hanover in 1837, where Queen Victoria's bigoted uncle, Ernest Augustus, had become king, the University of Göttingen was purged. Among the martyrs was F. C. Dahlmann, whose *Politics,* published in 1835, was the most reasoned and philosophical of the German defenses of liberalism.

Hounded and discouraged in the thirties, both German liberals and German nationalists found new hope when Frederick William III of Prussia died in 1840, to be succeeded by his son Frederick William IV. The new king, who had grown up in the days of the French Revolution and the patriotic German reaction against Napoleon, was thought to be a liberal, and his early actions seemed to confirm this estimate. An amnesty was granted, restrictions and censorship were relaxed, and, with help from the new king, the Central Investigation Agency of the Confederation was adjourned, never to meet again. But liberal hopes were to be dashed. Frederick William IV would have no truck with the principles of the Enlightenment on which most liberal thought was predicated. He had, rather, a highly romanticized vision of a Christian king embodying the unity and will of his people, an essentially medieval ideal that could never be squared with increasingly secular and pluralistic liberal demands for the sharing of power. Frederick William, moreover, saw the realization of the national goal in the revival of the Holy Roman Empire, headed by the emperor of Austria. Small wonder that the king put off calling a meeting of representatives of the provincial diets, a meeting that Prussian liberals hoped might produce a constitution.

When he was finally prevailed upon to call a United Diet in April 1847, Frederick William IV declared that he would never allow the "natural" relationship between prince and people to be supplanted by a contractual bond. "Never will I permit a written sheet of paper to come between our God in heaven and this land, as if it were a second Providence, to rule us with its paragraphs and supplant the old sacred loyalty." [17] He would concede no normal parliamentary expectations, and in revenge the diet withheld approval of the financing of a railway between Berlin and the East Prussian city of Königsberg; even the East Prussian delegates, who certainly stood to benefit from the project, largely opposed it. After seven weeks of stalemate, the diet adjourned, and the king returned to the sentimental absolutism that incorporated his ideal. Like Louis-Philippe and Guizot in France, like Metternich in Austria, the Prussian king and his advisers, by their combination of timidity and dogmatism, left the forces of change no recourse but revolution.

SELECTED READINGS

The most extensive account of socialist ideas is G. D. H. Cole, *A History of Socialist Thought;* the first volume, *The Forerunners, 1789–1850* (1955), deals with the material in this chapter. Brief, clear, and with an admirable bibliography is George Lichtheim, *The Origins of Socialism* (1969). Sir Alexander Gray's *The Socialist Tradition, Moses to*

[17] Quoted in Theodore S. Hamerow, *Restoration, Revolution, Reaction* (1958), 91.

Lenin (1946) is amusing, sometimes perceptive (especially on the Utopians), but basically unsympathetic. On the persistence of old millennial views, see Eric Hobsbawm, *Primitive Rebels* (1959). A good introduction to the conspiratorial tradition in this period is Elizabeth L. Eisenstein, *The First Professional Revolutionist: Filippo Michele Buonarroti (1761–1839)* (1959). For a controversial interpretation of the influence of Rousseau in the socialist direction, see J. L. Talmon, *The Origins of Totalitarian Democracy* (1952).

For English socialism, there is a life of Robert Owen by G. D. H. Cole (1925), but the basic work is now J. F. C. Harrison, *Quest for the New Moral World: Robert Owen and the Owenites in Britain and America* (1969). The trade-union dimension is explored in G. D. H. Cole, *Attempts at General Union . . . 1818–1834* (1953), and Cole has also written the best available history of the cooperative movement, *A Century of Co-operation* (1945). The Ricardian socialists are the subject of H. L. Beales' brief sketch *The Early English Socialists* (1932) and of Elie Halévy's *Thomas Hodgskin* (1905, tr. 1956). The best introduction to Fourier is Nicholas V. Riasanovsky, *The Teaching of Charles Fourier* (1969), and, pending the publication of his book on Cabet and the Icarians, Christopher H. Johnson has provided an excellent article, "Communism and the Working Class before Marx: The Icarian Experience," *American Historical Review,* 76 (June 1971), 642–689. The best brief analysis of Saint-Simonian ideas is in two essays of 1907–1908 by Elie Halévy, reprinted in his *The Era of Tyrannies* (1938, tr. 1965); Frank Manuel, in addition to *The New World of Henri Saint-Simon* (1956), devotes two chapters of his *The Prophets of Paris* (1962) to the subject; the book also contains a chapter on Fourier, with some interesting psychoanalytical speculation. Proudhon has been much written about in France, notably by Georges Gurvich; see his *Proudhon, sa vie, son oeuvre* (1965). There is little in English beyond the references in the general histories of socialism and the chapter in James Joll, *The Anarchists* (1964).

On German socialism, see Carl Wittke, *The Utopian Communist: A Biography of Wilhelm Weitling, Nineteenth-Century Reformer* (1950); Sidney Hook, *From Hegel to Marx: Studies in the Intellectual Development of Karl Marx* (1950); David McLellan, *The Young Hegelians and Karl Marx* (1969); and Herbert Marcuse's *Reason and Revolution: Hegel and the Rise of Social Theory* (1954). The best introductions to Marx himself are probably Isaiah Berlin, *Karl Marx: His Life and Environment* (1939), and George Lichtheim, *Marxism: An Historical and Critical Study* (1961). On the involvement of Marx and Engels in revolutionary politics, see Oscar J. Hammen, *The Red '48ers: Karl Marx and Friedrich Engels* (1969).

Among general histories of Europe in these years, by all odds the best is William L. Langer, *Political and Social Upheaval, 1832–1852* (1969), in the Rise of Modern Europe series edited by Langer himself. Langer takes a different expository approach from that in this book, but his judgments are sound and the bibliography (some odd typographical errors apart) is a tour de force.

On France, T. E. B. Howarth has published a scholarly biography, *Citizen King: The Life of Louis Philippe* (1961). The literature in French is extensive, and much of it seems more impressed than it need be with the bourgeois aspect of the bourgeois monarchy. Two works can be singled out as particularly useful, though they remain in French: Félix Ponteil, *Les institutions de la France de 1814 à 1871* (1966), and, somewhat narrower in time, Paul Bastid, *Les institutions politiques de la monarchie parlementaire française, 1814–1848* (1954). One institution of singular importance, the National Guard, is also dealt with only in French: Louis Girard, *La garde nationale, 1814–1871* (1964). Vincent E. Starzinger, Jr., *Middlingness* (1965) is a comparison of French and English *juste milieu* theory. John Plamenatz, *The Revolutionary Movement in France, 1815–*

1871 (1952) is relevant, as are a number of books cited in the earlier part of this bibliography. But the most original and important contribution is certainly Douglas Johnson, *Guizot: Aspects of French History, 1787-1874* (1963), a revisionist work of great persuasiveness.

On Britain, volumes III and IV (the latter posthumous) of Halévy's *History of the English People* are indispensable; using their titles in the most recent English printings, they are *The Triumph of Reform, 1830-1841* (1923, tr. 1927) and *The Age of Peel and Cobden, 1841-1852* (1947). A superb introduction, from the midcentury vantage point, is G. Kitson Clark, *The Making of Victorian England* (1961); for the student who is well enough acquainted with the period to be able to appreciate an allusiveness that can be maddening even to the expert, nothing can be more challenging or rewarding than G. M. Young's amazing essay, *Victorian England: Portrait of an Age* (1936). Norman Gash's *Politics in the Age of Peel* (1953) can be supplemented with his *Reaction and Reconstruction in English Politics, 1832-1852* (1965). Works on administrative history cited in chapter 15 are important in this chapter; the classic accounts of the poor law in Sidney and Beatrice Webb's *English Local Government, 9 vols.* (1906-1929) can be supplemented by Eric C. Midwinter, *Social Administration in Lancashire, 1830-1860: Poor Law, Public Health, and Police* (1969); J. R. Poynter, *Society and Pauperism: English Ideas on Poor Relief, 1795-1834* (1969); and the important revisionist article by Mark Blaug, "The Myth of the Old Poor Law and the Making of the New," *Journal of Economic History,* 23 (June 1963), 151-184. On reform in the factories, see J. T. Ward, *The Factory Movement, 1830-1855* (1962), and Cecil Driver, *Tory Radical* (1946), a life of the agitator Richard Oastler. On Chartism, see G. D. H. Cole, *Chartist Portraits* (1941), and Asa Briggs, ed., *Chartist Studies* (1959). There are two outstanding biographies: David Williams, *The Life of John Frost* (1939), the leader of the Welsh uprising of 1839, and A. R. Schoyen's *The Chartist Challenge* (1958), on the left-wing leader G. J. Harney. There are important autobiographies by two leaders, William Lovett (1876) and Thomas Cooper (1872). Our understanding of Peel's immense accomplishment will be much advanced after the publication of the second volume of Norman Gash's biography of Peel, covering the period 1830-1850, and when William O. Aydelotte brings out his careful statistical study of voting patterns in the Parliament of the early 1840s. On the anti-Corn Law agitation, see Norman McCord, *The Anti-Corn Law League* (1958). On prefamine Ireland, see R. B. McDowell, *Public Opinion and Government Policy in Ireland, 1801-1846* (1952); J. E. Pomfret, *The Struggle for Land in Ireland, 1800-1923* (1930); and Kevin B. Nowlan, *The Politics of Repeal: A Study in the Relations between Great Britain and Ireland, 1841-1850* (1960). On the famine, see R. D. Edwards and T. D. Williams, eds., *The Great Famine, 1845-1852* (1957), a set of scholarly essays of remarkable detachment, and Cecil Woodham-Smith's passionate and superbly written *The Great Hunger* (1962).

For Spain, the best guide is Raymond Carr, *Spain, 1808-1939* (1966), and note may be taken of Edgar Holt, *The Carlist Wars in Spain* (1966). For Italy, in addition to the Berkeley volume cited in Chapter 13 and the references to be cited in Chapter 19 in connection with the unification, mention should be made of two biographies of Mazzini by G. O. Griffith (1932) and Gaetano Salvemini (1905, tr. 1957) and the more specialized study by E. E. Y. Hales, *Mazzini and the Secret Societies* (1956). For Austria and Germany, the *Vormärz* must be approached largely from the vantage point of 1848, through books cited in Chapter 18, but an exception is George Barany, *Stephen Széchényi and the Awakening of Hungarian Nationalism, 1791-1841* (1968).

18

Revolution and War:
1846-1855

THE REVOLUTIONS OF 1848

In the middle years of the forties, the politics of Continental Europe had reached the point of stagnation. Nationalism and socialism existed largely in the realm of thought, oratory, and tract-writing. Neither was a movement properly so called, but a competing collection of ambitions and remedies, rooted in moral feeling and intellectual conviction, working at cross-purposes, and riven by jealousies and exclusiveness. Liberal constitutionalism could claim only a few small victories on the Continent—in Belgium and Switzerland and in some of the south German states, notably Baden, where the liberals had overturned a government and gained enough strength in elections in 1846 to install a reforming ministry. The nominal liberalism of the Portuguese and Spanish military dictatorships did little credit to the cause. There was, to be sure, considerable enthusiasm throughout Europe when Pius IX was elected pope in June 1846 and promptly confirmed his reputation as a liberal by a series of reforms. But only in Great Britain was liberalism successfully embodied on a large scale, in Peel's reforms and in the victory of free trade; though historians now assure us that the latter owed relatively little to the activity of the Anti-Corn Law League, contemporaries saw it as the triumph of a popular movement and a heartening example to the less successful elsewhere. Generally speaking, however the mixture of principle, tradition, lethargy, timidity, and corruption might vary from country to country, the established authorities seemed firmly in control. Liberals and the other parties of movement were left to nurse their perennial hope that one day the ideas by which they set such store would sweep all before them. That this day seemed to come so suddenly in the early months of 1848 is owing, however, far more to economic and social than to political developments.

The Economic Background

The depression that began in 1846 was the worst of the century. It was also the last such disturbance to be triggered primarily by the failure of a harvest. The blight that destroyed the potato crop in Ireland in 1845 and 1846 was a general European phenomenon. Because the potato was the almost exclusive food of the Irish poor, the catastrophe there reached a horror unmatched elsewhere (see p. 701). But over the preceding half-century the potato had become increasingly important in the diet of ordinary people throughout Europe; hence the sharp rise in potato prices—there was some improvement in the harvest in 1847, but another failure in 1848—brought discontent and starvation. In the area around Caen in Normandy, the price of potatoes was four times as great in 1847 as it had been in 1844–1845, and the food riots that took place in Germany in 1847 were known as the "potato war." [1]

To this failure was added a miserable grain harvest in 1846. Europe was not as yet being fed from the vast, productive lands in Russia and North America. Deficiencies in internal transport as well as rigid marketing structures quickly worsened the crises. Flowing through the usual commercial channels, grain often went from starving countries (Ireland or East Prussia) to more prosperous regions that could pay high prices, while the repeal of the Corn Laws in England opened that wealthy and commanding market to the sale of Continental grain. It is important to realize that these same difficulties contributed to the highly uneven incidence of the agricultural depression and attendant suffering. Stockraising and dairying areas were affected later and not so severely in comparison with regions that specialized in growing grain; and it is ironic that the price of foods consumed primarily by the well-to-do—butter, for example—rose relatively little.

---

[1] The potato had been popularized in France by the eighteenth-century agronomist and chemist Antoine Augustin Parmentier. His native town erected a statue to him in, of all years, 1848, but there is a more appropriate memorial: in French cookery, potato soup is *potage Parmentier.*

To the agricultural depression was added an industrial and financial crisis emanating from Britain. Its causes lay in those mysterious factors that seemed to produce regular cyclical fluctuations in an increasingly industrial and interdependent economy. It was triggered by the collapse of the railway-building boom of the early forties. The slump in British business had immediate repercussions in those port cities, like Hamburg, that traded across the North Sea. In a relatively short time the crisis was repeated elsewhere in Europe, bringing a rash of failures and widespread unemployment. While many businessmen, particularly small traders and shopkeepers, were hard hit, the worst sufferers were the workers, whose chronic insecurity was worsened by the high prices, if not by the virtual disappearance, of their basic foods. The short-term disaster of unemployment was superimposed on the long-term decline of the artisans and handicraftsmen, whose gradual displacement by improved industrial techniques was a major ingredient in the "social question" that so troubled European peace and consciences in the forties. Here then, throughout northern, western, and central Europe, was a sudden upsurge in suffering and a sense of deep wrong, a wave of emotion and bitterness that could be appreciated by few of the wealthy and politically privileged.

The February Revolution

In France, the motley collection of leaders of the political Left came together for a new assault on the dreary and unpopular regime headed by François Guizot. Guizot had emerged victorious from the elections of 1846; he had just come through a diplomatic crisis with England over the Spanish Marriages (see p. 741); and he can perhaps be pardoned for thinking that the opposition would remain as divided and ineffective as it had been at least since 1842. The dynastic Left, headed by Adolphe Thiers and Odilon Barrot, the republican Left of Alexandre Ledru-Rollin, and the democratic and quasi-socialist working-class movement headed by Louis Blanc were deeply divided by principle and personality. But as the opposition had been defeated in an election, it was to their advantage to concert a new campaign for parliamentary reform. Very like the parliamentary reformers in England in the 1780s and the 1820s, the French Left demanded an extension of the franchise and trotted out charges of corruption. But there was also a revival of revolutionary enthusiasm, testified to and encouraged by histories of the great Revolution published by Louis Blanc, Lamartine, and Jules Michelet. In 1847 and early 1848, then, the ingredients of the political situation were not precisely what they had been five years or so before. As a political and constitutional movement, the opposition's new campaign had greater cohesiveness and credibility; what few realized was that it could set off far more sweeping demands, themselves powered by economic and social discontent.

In 1840, with no very great success, the reformers had held banquets around the country, at which local and national opposition leaders indulged in appropriate oratory, hoping to unite their supporters, educate the country, and perhaps persuade the government of the reasonableness of parliamentary reform. In 1847 they decided to try again. The first banquet was held in Paris in July 1847. Although there was a national committee, arrangements for banquets were left largely in the hands of local groups, with the result that in a number of places radicals were able to turn the planning to their advantage. Thiers, the most conservative of the opposition leaders, had dissociated himself from the movement at the outset; so had Louis Blanc, for tactical reasons. And by December 1847 it was clear that Barrot of the dynastic Left was being displaced by Ledru-Rollin of the Republicans as the principal spokesman and political beneficiary.[2]

The government was alarmed by the drift toward the radicals, and at the end of the month the king shocked the opposition by referring, in his opening speech in the Chamber of Deputies, to the "blind and hostile passions" engendered by the agitation. A banquet planned for Paris on January 19, 1848, was postponed for a month, and negotiations were begun with the government about the terms on which it would be allowed to take place. It was rescheduled for February 22, but the day before the government decided to forbid it. The leaders of the opposition overwhelmingly voted to accept the cancellation, but on the morning of February 22 a crowd dominated by radical workingmen gathered in the Place de la Madeleine, calling for Guizot's dismissal. The street agitation spread, though by evening it seemed contained by the police and the troops supporting them. The next morning, however, the crowds were larger and in an angry mood and proved beyond the capacity of the forces of order. The Municipal Guard of Paris—brutal, effective, and feared—numbered only something over three thousand men. The July Monarchy had traditionally relied on the National Guard, but it had been allowed to deteriorate in organization and morale; by 1848 far too many of the legions, bourgeois though they were, shared the general dislike of the regime they were there to protect. Since the National Guard could not be trusted and the army was disoriented and uncertain, the initiative remained in the streets. The first sacrifice was Guizot, who was dismissed on the afternoon of February 23.

The king tried at first to get a new government under Molé. But Molé failed, and so did Thiers and Barrot, to whom the king unwillingly turned. The king sought military protection from General Robert Bugeaud, recently

---

[2] The novelist Gustave Flaubert attended a banquet in Rouen. "Such taste! Such cuisine! Such wine! And such talk!" he wrote in disgust. "Nothing has done more to give me an absolute contempt for success, considering the price at which it is bought. . . . The finest works of the greatest authors would never have earned a quarter of this applause. . . . After nine hours spent before cold turkey and sucking pig in the company of my locksmith, who continually slapped me on the back at all the best parts, I came home frozen to the marrow. . . ." Georges Duveau, *1848: The Making of a Revolution* (1965, tr. 1967), 8–9. It is sad to think that the century that saw the perfection of the classic French cuisine could not rise above the level to which political dining everywhere and in any age seems condemned.

victorious in Algeria but deeply disliked at home. A clash on February 23 between a detachment of troops and a mob reinforced by renegade National Guardsmen had resulted in a number of dead and wounded; by the morning of the twenty-fourth the city was filled with barricades constructed in the narrow streets from felled trees and manned by citizens with stolen arms and torn-up paving stones. At noon on the twenty-fourth Bugeaud declared a cease-fire. Louis-Philippe abdicated and fled to England. The Tuileries palace was sacked.

Thus the monarchy, born with sudden gloriousness in July of 1830, fell with equally sudden ignominy in February of 1848. But it was not clear what was to take its place. Negotiations for a regency for Louis-Philippe's grandson quickly fell through; the sentiment in the streets, increasingly dominated by radical workingmen and carried brusquely into the Hôtel de Ville, was all for a republic. That conceded, a provisional government was formed. Its nominal president was Dupont de l'Eure, an old revolutionary veteran, but Ledru-Rollin and Lamartine took the lead. They added four colleagues from the moderate opposition—Arago, Marie, Garnier-Pagès, and Crémieux. The radical socialist group that clustered around the newspaper *La Réforme* forced the inclusion of the paper's editor, Flocon, the group's principal theorist Louis Blanc, and an obscure worker from a button factory named Alexandre Martin. A veteran of the secret societies of the thirties, Martin was called simply Albert. He was obscure then and largely silent; he is obscure now, a token gesture to the working class that the bourgeois Left could not take seriously. The effective power of the provisional government lay in the hands of Lamartine.

Lamartine, a late convert to republicanism, had played a dangerous game. He was one of the few leaders to resist the cancellation of the banquet; he would attend, he said, even though only his shadow would go with him. Now the game grew far more dangerous. The demand from the streets was for a social republic committed to the "organization of labor." The phrase was associated with Louis Blanc, the radical bourgeois journalist who had burst on the scene in 1840 with a pamphlet carrying that title. Blanc was hardly a thoroughgoing socialist, as the term was then understood. He foresaw no transformation of human character, no utopian communities, but rather the multiplication of producers' cooperatives, workshops owned by their workers, a device that had had some modest success in both France and England. But Louis Blanc was quickly named chairman of a commission to look into the labor question, known from the palace in which it met as the Luxembourg Commission. He was thus diverted into investigative and deliberative proceedings and cut off from the possibility of doing anything to realize his goals. The provisional government nevertheless appeased popular insistence on the right to work by creating "national workshops" around the city. In the workshops the unemployed would be paid two francs a day when they were laboring at make-work tasks such as excavation and grading—tasks for which most of them were unfitted—and they would be given a pittance as relief when work was not available. The national workshops were Louis Blanc's formula without the substance, a travesty of an interesting and not excessively visionary scheme. They were a source of endless expense to the government, a cause of deepening bitterness in those they were presumed to help, and a scandal to the better-off who resented supporting men they chose to consider idle.

The problem of public order was crucial. The Municipal Guard was dissolved, and a new Mobile Guard composed of volunteers was set up, as were a Popular Guard made up of former political prisoners and a refashioned National Guard open to everyone. In time—thanks no doubt to the sobering experience of a city largely out of control—these new forces came down on the side of order; even the democratized National Guard elected moderate, bourgeois officers. But the necessary reorganization and training could not be accomplished overnight, and the provisional government continued to ride the whirlwind, buffeted not only by popular aspirations but by a disastrous plunge of the economy and by renewed fears across Europe of what a revolutionary France must mean. Lamartine, as foreign minister, quietly cemented an understanding with Britain, while giving voice to fervent rhetoric about international republican brotherhood and the injustice of the settlement of 1815. So too, within the country, Lamartine acted far more realistically and conservatively than his talk would have led anyone to expect. He had in fact been terrified by the specter of social revolution that he and others had conjured up, and he was determined to have a republic without anarchy and without socialism. Balzac called him an arsonist turned fireman. The elections for a constituent assembly were held on April 23, under universal manhood suffrage. They returned a moderate republican majority, and the nation expressed its gratitude and relief at its deliverance from socialism by electing Lamartine as a deputy in ten departments.

The Austrian Empire

Given Lamartine's caution and the lack of French resources, the revolution could hardly have been forcibly exported from France. But nothing could lessen the power of the French example. Within a few weeks of those three February days, nearly the whole of the Continent—outside Belgium (where, as we have seen, timely reforms were made), Scandinavia, the Iberian peninsula, and Russia—was in the throes of revolution.

On March 3 Louis Kossuth made an impassioned speech in the Hungarian diet in Bratislava (Pressburg), attacking the Metternichian system and demanding constitutional reforms throughout the empire and autonomy for Hungary. The speech was widely talked about in Austria, and the liberal discussion groups that had grown up in Vienna in the preceding years were emboldened to petition for reform. On March 13 crowds, in which students predominated, gathered in the streets calling for Metternich's dismissal. A clash with troops resulted in casualties, rebellious workers began to emerge from the industrial suburbs, and the middle-class *Burgerwehr*—the Austrian equivalent of the French National Guard—began to defect. Metternich argued that Louis-Philippe's sacrifice of Guizot had meant the end of the dynasty; his counsel of resistance was seconded by Prince Alfred Windischgrätz, the governor of Bohemia. But the court circle chose to concede, and by evening Metternich had resigned; he fled, like all the others, to England. On March 15 the censorship was abolished, a new cabinet was appointed, and a constituent assembly was promised. A reformed national guard was created, with a special legion for students; indeed the students played a major part in keeping the ferment in Vienna alive, with increasing support from discontented workers. Confronting not only continuing demonstrations at home and the collapse of the system elsewhere in the empire, the government was unstable and ineffective. In a change of front, without waiting for the promised convention, the government promulgated a constitution on April 25 for those parts of the empire within the Germanic Confederation, with the addition of Galicia. This gesture proved unacceptable to the students and the radicals, and by mid-May the government had been forced to give in to the demand for universal suffrage and a single-chamber legislature. On May 17 the royal family fled from Vienna to Innsbruck, a move that had the intended effect of rousing moderate opinion to the danger it faced from the radicals. But efforts to put down student activity by closing the university and merging the student legion into the national guard brought the construction of barricades, and on May 26 Baron Franz von Pillersdorf, a mild liberal who had given what direction there was in the government over the preceding month, conceded the creation of a security committee, in effect a committee of public safety, the high-water mark of radical influence.

Meanwhile, the Hungarian diet had set about enacting Kossuth's program. The kingdom was thereafter to be autonomous, tied to the emperor in a personal union; the emperor would be represented by a viceroy who need refer nothing to Vienna; the diet in Bratislava was to become a parliament in Budapest with a government responsible to it; Hungary would have its own army, finance, and foreign policy. The *robot* and all remaining feudal privileges were abolished, as was noble exemption from taxation; but the interests of the gentry were served by a general provision for compensation for the loss of feudal rights and labor services and by a still restricted, though somewhat expanded, franchise. The Magyars simply assumed that the provinces of Transylvania and Croatia would be part of a unified Hungarian state: "The magic of liberty," cried Kossuth, "is stronger than nationality, faith, affinity of blood and friendship." [3] Despite Magyar enthusiasm, other nationalities did not welcome that subjection, and the court was given a chance to play one

[3] Quoted in C. A. Macartney, *The Habsburg Empire, 1790-1918* (1968), 381.

national group against another. While the emperor reluctantly assented to the Hungarian demands in the "April Laws" on the eleventh of that month (they are sometimes called the "March Laws"), the Croat leader Baron Joseph Jellačić had already been appointed governor of Croatia. On his return from Vienna, he ordered Croatian officials to have nothing to do with the Hungarian government and on April 19 broke off all relations with Budapest. The outraged Magyars had a powerful bargaining counter, however, in the need for Hungarian troops in the war that had broken out in the Austrian domains in northern Italy. The court therefore reversed itself, conceding Hungarian domination of Croatia and depriving Jellačić of all his offices.

In Bohemia, Czech reformers attempted to follow the Hungarian example, though at a considerable distance. In March, meetings in Prague petitioned for civil freedoms and other reforms; the emperor promised abolition of the *robot* in Bohemia and Moravia a year hence, conceded the equality of the Czech and German languages, promised responsible government in Prague, and referred the question of a union of Bohemia, Moravia, and Silesia to the parliament that was to meet in the summer. But the most difficult problem for the Czechs lay in their position between Vienna and the Germans, who at that time were trying to follow up their own revolutions by bringing about German unity. Resisting the pull to Germany and welcoming the adhesion of the Slovaks, whose leaders, rebuffed by the Hungarians, had fled to Prague, the Czechs turned to a program called Austro-Slavism, formulated by the historian Francis Palacký. Anti-German and anti-Magyar, Austro-Slavism envisioned a federation of Slav peoples within the Austrian empire. To that end a Congress of Slavs (rather heavily Czech in composition) was summoned to meet in Prague on June 2. It ended on June 12 with a ringing declaration of regeneration for Slavs that papered over the real divisions among the widely varying and increasingly self-conscious Slav nationalities.

By far the most dramatic response to Metternich's fall occurred in Italy; no other development within the Austrian emperor's domains so preoccupied his advisers or so paralyzed them for effective action elsewhere. The notion of Italian unity had grown apace. Italian restiveness under the despotism of the Austrians provided the ground in which nationalist ambitions could take root, and the preconditions of liberalism were becoming more and more firmly rooted in an expanding economy and in the widening horizons of Italian businessmen and intellectuals. Hence, when the news of Metternich's fall reached Milan, the capital of Lombardy, on March 17, 1848, the more radical elements at once set about planning a vast demonstration the next day to petition for reforms. The demonstration quickly got out of hand, barricades went up, and General Joseph Radetzky, the aged and able commander of the Austrian garrison, went into action. The troops at his disposal proved no match for an outraged populace, and Radetzky brought the "Five Days" to an end on March 22 by deciding to withdraw to Verona, one of the four fortresses of the Quadrilateral. On the same day Venice rose and proclaimed itself a republic.

Charles Albert, the king of Piedmont, declared war on Austria in support of the two rebellious provinces and invaded Lombardy.

Charles Albert was timid and terrified of revolution; on the other hand, he was under great pressure from liberals at home. A revolution had broken out in Sicily in January against the regime of King Ferdinand of Naples; this in turn inspired the liberals in Naples itself, and on February 10, the king was compelled to issue a constitution modeled on the French Charter of 1830. Tuscany followed suit, and on March 5 Charles Albert most reluctantly took the same step for Piedmont, having first secured absolution from his coronation oath, which he believed prevented him from thus compromising his monarchical power. Ten days later Pope Pius IX partially underlined his still lively reputation as a liberal by granting a constitution for the papal states.

Count Cavour, the principal spokesman of the Piedmontese liberals, argued that failure to intervene in Lombardy might mean that Piedmont would lose the liberated Austrian territories and might even mean the end of the dynasty. Charles Albert was not insensible to the glory that expanding his kingdom would bring and reluctantly went along with the liberals. In so doing, he was forestalling the French, whose intervention was being urged by Milanese and Venetian radicals. This matter of principle was bitterly debated in Milan between Carlo Cattaneo, the leader of the Milanese radicals, who deeply distrusted Charles Albert, and Guiseppe Mazzini, who returned from exile early in April to argue—like the Piedmontese, though for different reasons—that Italy should see to her own liberation unaided.

The Piedmontese army did nothing to cut off Radetzky's retreat. The one rash military action was taken not by Piedmontese forces but by the commander of the papal troops, General Giovanni Durando, himself a Piedmontese. Patriots had come from all over Italy to take part in the war of liberation against Austria; Naples sent troops; the papacy permitted volunteers and militia to head for Piedmont and sent regular forces to prevent an Austrian advance to the south. The pope's ministers under the new constitution were eager for a declaration of war on Austria. But the one way Pius saw to intervene—through a league of princes—came to grief over Charles Albert's unwillingness to give up anything his army might gain. Durando, however, issued a proclamation that sounded as though the pope approved the campaign against Austria and moved forward across the Po, despite the pope's clear expression of displeasure with his initiative. Pius' obligations as head of the church—Austria was, after all, a Catholic power—won out over his Italian patriotism; in an allocution to the college of cardinals at the end of April, he rejected the war and, with it, the possibility of uniting Italy under his leadership. By refusing the role in which the neo-Guelphs had cast him, and by acting in accord with his wider churchly responsibilities, Pius IX sacrificed the reputation that had led to such rejoicing over his accession in 1846. Nevertheless, on May 4, Austria broke off diplomatic relations with the papal states.

Meanwhile, Piedmontese forces had occupied Lombardy and managed even to seize Peschiera, one of the fortresses of the Quadrilateral. Gradually, from the middle of May to early July, one after another of the north Italian states voted to join in a union with Piedmont. It was the false dawn of a kingdom of Italy.

Germany

By early March the news from France had touched off a number of popular demonstrations in the states of south Germany, to which the rulers responded by installing liberal governments and undertaking some modest reforms. To some extent the way had been prepared by the inheritance of the Josephine enlightenment, by French occupation and example, and by more recent constitutionalism, which had not been entirely undermined in the pre-March era. The most drastic south German development, however, had little to do with either Paris or Vienna. In Bavaria, King Ludwig I had conceived a senile passion for a half-British, half-Creole dancer who called herself Lola Montez. Beautiful and intelligent, Lola had spent some time in the intellectual circle around the writer George Sand in Paris and was attracted to republicanism and socialism. Her radical influence was bad enough in the eyes of some Bavarians, but what brought the country together was the king's heedless doting and Lola's increasing presumption. Although the king conceded some liberal reforms in the wake of the news from Paris, the main victories of the Bavarian national protest were Lola's banishment and the king's subsequent abdication.

The revolutionary infection spread quickly to Prussia. The first manifestations occurred in Cologne. This was hardly surprising because the Rhineland, the most industrialized segment of Prussia's scattered kingdom, was suffering badly from the general economic collapse. The crowd at a huge demonstration on March 3 adopted an extremely radical set of demands, including the setting up of revolutionary committees and laws protecting labor, but the king made no move until trouble developed in Berlin. By March 13, clashes between street crowds and troops had taken place, and the king had agreed to recall at some future date the United Diet, which had ended in deadlock the preceding year. But after the news from Vienna arrived, the situation in the streets forced the king to astonishing concessions: the ending of censorship, advancing the meeting of the diet to April 2, and the promise not only of a Prussian constitution but of Prussian leadership in the movement for German unity. The announcement of these moves was well received, but the crowds began to insist on the withdrawal of the soldiers from the capital as a guarantee. For a time the king resisted, but attempts to clear the streets around the palace only angered the crowds. Barricades appeared and street fighting began. The discipline of the soldiers held, and the troops relentlessly pursued the insurgents, but the general charged with securing the city was not optimistic about an easy victory.

At last the king ordered the troops withdrawn and threw himself on the mercy of his people. He agreed to establish a civic guard; he paraded through the streets with the black, red, and gold flag that had come to symbolize a united Germany; he saluted wagons filled with the corpses of victims killed in street fighting; and, what may have been the bitterest pill, he accepted a ministry dominated by his most vocal enemies from the days of the United Diet. It was headed by the Rhenish businessman Ludolf Camphausen, with David Hansemann as minister of finance. The liberals were cautious enough. They quickly restored order, secured the government's credit, and—while conceding universal manhood suffrage in the elections for the parliament that would draft the constitution—carefully required a long residence in order to qualify for the vote and imposed indirect elections through electoral colleges. Despite these obvious efforts to exclude the vagrant, the poor, and the presumably irresponsible, the prudent constitutionalism of the liberals was totally unacceptable to the reactionary aristocratic circle who made up most of the king's friends; disapproving, they bided their time.

While the long-drawn-out process of constitutional reform was beginning in Prussia, the drive to German national unity was gathering speed. Well before the revolutions the king's one liberal-minded friend, Count Joseph Maria von Radowitz, had entered into discussions with Metternich about a possible reform of the Germanic Confederation; after the revolutions began, the federal diet summoned representatives to discuss reorganization. But these liberal representatives came under pressure from other liberals who demanded national action. The result was the summoning of an assembly known as the Vorparlament—the preparliament—in Frankfurt on March 31, to plan the organization of a national legislature. The Vorparlament was heavily dominated by delegates from the south and west and the Rhineland; only two Austrians were present. The electoral law adopted by the Vorparlament was theoretically a recommendation for universal suffrage, but, as in Prussia, it was hedged about with restrictions, most notably in the requirement that voters be "independent." This vague stipulation made it possible for local officials to exclude potentially embarrassing voters, and open and not always savory attempts were made to influence the balloting. The precautions were perhaps unnecessary, since the elections aroused surprisingly little interest; rarely did the proportion of eligible voters going to the polls exceed 50 percent—in striking contrast to the 84 percent that turned out for the French elections at about the same time.

The deliberative body that this restricted, apathetic, and politically inexperienced electorate sent to St. Paul's Church in Frankfurt included only one peasant and four master handicraftsmen; there were no industrial workers at all. The notable representation of teachers and university professors has given an unwarranted reputation to the assembly as a gathering of intellectuals, but the largest numbers were businessmen and professionals, lawyers especially. However unrepresentative it was, the Frankfurt parliament was by any standard an impressive gathering and by the criteria of a bourgeois liberal, it was well-nigh perfect. The debates, though long, were of an extremely high quality, and the actual accomplishment, as we shall see, was remarkable. That the results remained in the realm of projects rather than action was owing, not to the inherent impracticality of what was proposed, but to the lack of effective support for the assembly, whether from the states that were to make up the new nation or from popular movements. Still, few in the spring of 1848 could have foreseen the popular desertion of the cause, the apostasy of the governments, or the inability of liberal and revolutionary ideals to succeed by their inherent virtue. A revolutionized Prussia and the prospect of a greater Germany confirmed the promise that was apparent to the liberally inclined everywhere in Europe in the early days of June 1848.

THE DEFEAT OF THE REVOLUTIONS

France: A New Empire

The revolutions of 1848 had begun in France; so did the reaction. The moderate republican majority returned in the French elections of April 23 seemed to promise that the momentum of the revolution would be maintained. But the provisional government was beset by persistent problems of public order. One such difficulty was posed by the peasantry in the less prosperous central and southern parts of France. There spontaneous rural uprisings had, quite disproportionately, evoked memories of the "great fear" of 1789 (see p. 470), for the peasants still seemed a threatening rather than a conservative force. They were, however, quickly turned against the revolutionary regime by a surtax of forty-five centimes levied on landowners (and so on peasants) that went, among other things, to pay for the national workshops. Peasant insurrectionism, then, was a frightening but largely illusory specter; there was greater reality in the threat from urban radical movements, revolving around the many clubs in the capital. Yet even in these centers of activism, concentration on the minutiae of organization and political maneuvering virtually precluded broader strategic considerations, and the radical insurgency lacked really effective leadership. Moderate and conservative opinion, however, was quick to suspect the worst of those veteran conspirators, Auguste Blanqui, Armand Barbès, and Fernand Raspail. On May 15 Raspail led a crowd into the meeting hall of the National Assembly, calling for a tax on the rich to finance an army to help the Poles. Blanqui and Barbès, after counseling caution at first, joined in and were among those sentenced to life imprisonment the next year. [4]

---

[4] Blanqui, dedicated, passionate, and suffering from his long years in prison, seems to have been especially alarming to respectable contemporaries. Tocqueville, who was present on May 15, was appalled by Blanqui's appearance: "He had wan, emaciated cheeks, white lips, a sickly wicked and repulsive expression, a dirty pallor, the appearance of a moldy corpse; he wore no visible linen; an old black frock coat tightly covered his lean withered limbs; he seemed to have passed his life in a sewer and to have just left it." *Recollections* (tr. 1949), 130.

Louis Blanc, though not involved in the incident, barely escaped with his life and fled to England.

The fear and hostility that such incidents aroused came to focus on the continuing existence of the national workshops. They had proved incapable of coping with the high level of unemployment, while the radicals hoped to turn the workshops to their own advantage as a revolutionary base. Plans for phasing out the workshops had been under active consideration almost from the moment of their creation, and on May 26 Emile Thomas, the young engineer in charge, was removed from office. On May 30 a moderate law was passed, calling for the appropriation of funds to encourage public works and private employers to hire men who would no longer have access to the workshops. The government delayed implementing the scheme. Meanwhile, disorder increased and the hostility to the workshops in governing circles grew. On June 20 the assembly authorized a special committee known for its hostility to the workshops to draw up plans to bring them to an end. The proposal in the law of May 30 to send recent arrivals in Paris back to the provinces was to be put into effect, and so was a far more drastic step, discussed earlier but resisted, to enroll younger men who had entered the workshops in the army. When these moves became known to working-class leaders on June 21, they began to organize a protest for the 22nd, when the decisions were to be formally announced. The demonstration quickly escalated into street fighting. Thus began the terrible June Days—the degeneration of revolution into a short, violent civil war.

General Eugène Cavaignac—a stern, principled, conservative republican— was responsible for maintaining order; he had under his command, besides the army, the highly effective Mobile Guard and a National Guard that proved dependable after all. The fighting was savage on both sides. The insurgents, divided by Cavaignac's strategy, surrendered on June 26. To the fifteen hundred or so dead (two-thirds of them in the army and the police) were added twice that many slaughtered in the pursuit that followed the surrender; those arrested numbered at least twelve thousand, most of whom were sent to labor camps in Algeria: civilization, said Victor Hugo, was defending itself with the methods of barbarism. The violent suppression of the radicals during and after the June Days, reflecting the class hatred that had grown so swiftly since February, entered searingly into the collective memory, not only of the French, but of the entire international working-class movement.

Cavaignac was given and then resigned dictatorial powers; he was quickly named president of the council of ministers, which had succeeded the provisional government in April. His loyal firmness freed the National Assembly for its main task, the drafting of a constitution for the republic; a final version was accepted on November 4. It retained the centralized governmental structure, established a single-chamber legislature, and assured civil rights and the right to relief, though not the right to work. Two particularly fateful decisions were made. One was to retain universal manhood suffrage, which had worked so well in April; the other was to concentrate the executive power in the hands of a president, also elected by universal suffrage, for a four-year nonrenewable term.

Debates over the constitution were conducted in the shadow of a surprising figure, Louis Napoleon Bonaparte. Having been banished for one attempted coup and imprisoned for another, he had escaped from the fortress at Ham in 1846 and had returned to France at the outbreak of the revolution in February. At Lamartine's urging he had gone back to London, but through the efforts of friends was elected to the National Assembly in June. He chose to decline this opportunity, but a far more impressive call in by-elections in September brought him to Paris to take his seat in the assembly at the end of the month. He quickly announced his candidacy for the presidency, against Cavaignac and a collection of leftovers from the earlier days of the revolution— Lamartine, Ledru-Rollin, and Raspail. Without much money but with impressive personal support, with no very clear convictions but with implied promises for nearly everyone, Louis Napoleon waged a superbly skillful campaign. To the peasants he seemed certain to abolish the hated surtax, to the fearful he represented order and a rule above parties, for many he evoked the glories of the Napoleonic legend. His victory in the presidential election on December 10 was staggering—five and a half million votes to fewer than a million and a half for Cavaignac, while the others could not together muster half a million; moreover, his strength was not confined to the rural districts but brought him majorities in the towns and even in Paris.

Louis Napoleon was elected by the nation, but it was the conservative interests he had especially to placate. The leading figures in his cabinet were Odilon Barrot, that veteran of the dynastic Left under Louis-Philippe, and Count Frédéric de Falloux. Falloux, whose father had been ennobled by Louis XVIII, had been the most vocal and active critic of the national workshops; he was also a devout Catholic. The Catholics were further mollified by French military intervention to defeat the Roman republic created in February 1849 (see p. 728) and to return the pope to the Vatican. The strategy worked. In May 1849, in elections for the new assembly—the National Assembly having agreed, with some prodding, to dissolve itself—the moderate republicans, who had dominated the old body, were almost wiped out, while the various brands of monarchists (legitimists, Orleanists, and Bonapartists) won nearly five hundred seats. But the elections also indicated the persistence of notable strength on the far left, which returned about two hundred members and gave an overwhelming vote in five departments to Ledru-Rollin, who had fared so badly in the presidential election the preceding December. The radicals, incapable of biding their time, attempted a revolution on June 13. Easily put down, it resulted in the political destruction of the Left and the exile of many of its leaders, among them Victor Considérant, who joined Louis Blanc in England. Because there was little popular support for this ill-considered rising, and because a more serious one in Lyons was easily suppressed, the prince-president was at last freed of any serious threat from the left. At the end of October he felt strong enough to dismiss his cabinet and to appoint one beholden only to himself.

In the spring of 1850 the government turned to the long-standing problem of education. The expectations of the Guizot law of 1833 (see p. 622) had been far from realized; the republican government in 1848 had moved to deal with the question, but the projects advanced did not survive the June Days. Now Falloux, a partisan of church control, appointed a commission headed by Thiers who, in full flight from his liberal past, went far beyond Falloux or Montalembert in urging a restricted and clerical educational system. Under the act passed in March and famous as the Falloux Law, education was neither free nor compulsory; it was decentralized, with the clergy well represented on the governing councils. Private (i.e., church) organizations could conduct schools at both the primary and secondary levels, and a village could appoint the priest as the teacher in the state school or provide no school at all, if a church school already existed. In thus providing a political battleground for the rest of the century, the Falloux Law retreated from the ambitions of earlier educational reformers and acknowledged the need so deeply felt in a counterrevolutionary period for clerical influence and for the respect and subordination that would presumably follow from it. Yet, despite its constrictiveness, French education in the 1850s was, as a system, probably more advanced than that across the Channel in England.

A continuing show of strength by the radicals in by-elections dictated further changes in the electoral law, accomplished at the very end of May 1850. By raising the voting age and requiring three years' residence, a sweeping reduction in the electorate was brought about, of course at the lower, more radical end of the social scale. Louis Napoleon could then turn more confidently to implementing his desire to remain in power after his term expired, an ambition in which he had increasing support. Yet the constitution limited his tenure to four years, and his efforts to get the constitution revised failed in the assembly in July 1851. Plans to overthrow the constitution were therefore concerted during the parliamentary recess in the autumn. With his principal lieutenants General Leroy Saint-Arnaud, the minister of war, and the duke de Morny, the prince's half-brother, Louis Napoleon waited until the assembly reconvened and cleverly proposed the restoration of universal suffrage. They knew that the assembly would reject the proposal, but the move allowed Louis Napoleon to pose as the champion of democracy.

On the morning of December 2, 1851, the anniversary of the first Napoleon's great victory at Austerlitz, the assembly was dissolved, martial law imposed, and a referendum (under universal suffrage) ordered. Prominent political leaders were rounded up, and more were arrested when a largely royalist rump session of the assembly tried to depose the president. An anti-Bonapartist rising on the night of December 3 was dispersed the next day with a considerable loss of life, thanks to military indiscipline; the casualties were in good part among innocent spectators. Heavier resistance in the provinces, too, was repressed under martial law, and suspected offenders were dealt with by special commissions. There appeared to be general satisfaction, at home and abroad, over the coup d'état, and the referendum produced the expected triumph, although the high rate of abstention reflected a strong undercurrent of disaffection that dared not surface. The new constitution, which the plebiscite authorized the president to draw up and which was promulgated in mid-January 1852, made the council of state, the senate, and the lower house, the Corps Législatif, whose powers were sharply restricted, the creatures of Louis Napoleon. In November a second plebiscite was held to ratify the return to hereditary rule; thus, on the first anniversary of the coup d'état, France once more became an empire, under Napoleon III.

The Austrian Empire

Counterrevolution in the Hapsburg Empire began with the advantage Radetzky was able to take of Charles Albert's timidity and ineptitude; Radetzky built up his forces and defeated the Piedmontese army at Custoza on July 23–27, 1848. An armistice, repeatedly renewed, allowed negotiations to proceed throughout the autumn; as usual Charles Albert temporized. Meanwhile, an extraordinary situation arose in the papal states stretching across central Italy. The pope had long resisted demands from his liberal cabinet for war on Austria, and at last Pius thought he had found a way around his difficulties by appointing a ministry dominated by Pellegrino Rossi, who had grown up in France and who, returning as French ambassador under Guizot, had become a principal papal adviser. But Rossi, an able though unpopular administrative reformer, was assassinated in November 1848. After an uprising in Rome forced him to appoint a radical cabinet, the pope fled to the kingdom of Naples, where he promptly disavowed his new ministers. The rejected cabinet nevertheless clung to power and called a constituent assembly. A republic was declared in Rome on February 9, 1849, and the government at once set about enacting extensive social reforms. In early March Mazzini returned from exile to convert the new republic into the realization of his ideals. In late April Mazzini's forces were joined by followers of the colorful general Giuseppe Garibaldi, later to become famous for his exploits in Sicily (see p. 777). Charles Albert at last determined to act in the hope of recovering Lombardy. The result was a crushing defeat at Radetzky's hands at Novara on March 23.

Charles Albert at once abdicated. His son Victor Emmanuel II made a favorable impression on Radetzky, agreed to a peace treaty in early August, and vowed to restore royal authority in Piedmont. Radetzky wisely refrained from pressing his advantage against Piedmont and moved instead to return the rebellious grand duchy of Tuscany to its duke. But what nation was to restore the pope to his temporal authority? The papal champion proved to be France, in an intervention by Louis Napoleon that was calculated to cement Catholic support at home, while preventing a total Austrian sweep through central Italy. The initial French advance on Rome in late April was not successful, but eventually the French reduced the city. Garibaldi, who had wanted to resort to the guerrilla warfare for which he was to become so famous, lost large numbers of his forces in retreat and barely escaped himself; Mazzini, who preferred to make a glorious though hopeless defense of the republic, went once more into exile. The French commander accepted political arrangements dictated by the cardinals who represented the pope and undercut French hopes of salvaging some liberal institutions. The pope now fell completely under the influence of the stubbornly reactionary Cardinal Antonelli, and the chance that the papacy might move some distance into the modern world was lost for at least a generation.

King Ferdinand of Naples had long since reduced the rebellious Sicilians to submission, and in August 1849 the republic of Venice fell to the Austrians. The hope of Italian unity had everywhere proved premature, for no leader could muster the requisite combination of idealism and political boldness and no country was willing to sacrifice enough to assure support from another. Defeated Piedmont, under its new king, remained the one possible focus of nationalist hopes, but the war had shown decisively that Piedmont—or Italy— could not go it alone.

In Austria itself there was a foretaste of things to come when riots—an unplanned outburst from workers and students—occurred in Prague on June 12, 1848, the day the Slav Congress came to a close. Prince Windischgrätz, whose wife was shot dead while standing incautiously at a window to watch the disturbance, bombarded the city and shook the Czech patriots out of whatever separatist notions they had and into thinking prudently of working within the Austrian system. This initial advantage of the forces of order was not immediately carried to Vienna, where the security committee had undertaken an experiment along the lines of the French national workshops, with similar results. But the court returned from Innsbruck on August 12, and a new minister of public works reduced the wages paid in the national workshops. The result was a clash in late August between students and workers on one side and the government on the other, with elements of the National Guard supporting both. The victory of the government was not total, but the security committee was disbanded.

Meanwhile, a national assembly had been elected and had begun its deliberations on July 22; with the Hungarians independent and the Italian provinces in revolt, it was purely an Austrian affair. Its greatest accomplishment was unquestionably the law of September 7 that completed the emancipation of the peasantry from the *robot* and from remaining feudal dues and jurisdictions; at a stroke the danger of insurgency from the peasants was removed. The assembly then turned its attention to constitution-making. The court was, however, far more concerned to bring the Hungarian situation under control. Jellačić, the Croat leader who had been deprived of his post in June, was now restored to official favor and began a march on Hungary. But the dispatch of troops from Vienna to aid Jellačić provoked the most radical uprising of all in Vienna on October 6, led by German radicals sympathetic to Hungarian nationalism and supported by students and workers still smarting from their defeat in August. The minister of war, Count Latour, was savagely murdered. The court fled once more, this time to Olmütz in Moravia, and the capital was abandoned to a chaos of would-be ruling groups and terrorism. The rebels could survive only with outside help, and as the peasants would not respond, that could only mean the Hungarians. Kossuth was willing, but his military commander hesitated. Jellačić and Windischgrätz reached Vienna first and reduced it at the end of October after a long and difficult operation.

Late in November Prince Felix von Schwarzenberg became prime minister, and on December 2 the Emperor Ferdinand abdicated in favor of his nephew, the eighteen-year-old Francis Joseph, whose mother, the Archduchess Sophia, had long been working for that end. Formally, the accession of a new emperor was deemed to annul the April Laws, to which Ferdinand had agreed; but the Hungarians refused to accept the new emperor, arguing that they had not been consulted. In the Austro-Hungarian war that followed, the Austrian forces gained some early victories, and Budapest was occupied early in January 1849. But the Hungarians returned to the attack; they were faced in March with a government-imposed constitution that would have stripped them of all their ancient privileges and the territories over which they aspired to rule, reducing them to merely one of several lands in a centralized empire. The Hungarians at once declared the emperor deposed and launched a regency under Kossuth, a bold step followed by a successful counterattack by Hungarian forces and the retaking of Budapest in May. Vienna was now reduced to the humiliation of calling on Russia for help, help the tsar had long stood ready to provide. Overwhelmed by hundreds of thousands of Russian soldiers pouring across the frontier, the Hungarian forces retreated ably, but ultimately were surrounded. Their brilliant young commander, Arthur Görgei, chose to surrender to the Russians on August 13. He was given his freedom, which he would not have got from the Austrians; the other leaders, Kossuth among them, fled to Turkey, where British and French support enabled the sultan to refuse the extradition demanded by the Austrians and Russians. The Austrians, resentful of having had to call on the Russians, put Hungary under martial law and assigned the meting out of punishment to the brutal General Julius Haynau, who quickly became one of the specters of liberal imaginations across Europe.[5]

Schwarzenberg was, however, no mere reactionary, nor were his associates. They had no intention of returning to the inefficiencies of pre-March;

---

[5] In 1851 Haynau visited London, and like many distinguished visitors, was taken to see Barclay's huge brewery. He was set upon by the workingmen and barely escaped with his life, thus creating considerable diplomatic embarrassment for the English.

indeed, disgust with the Metternichian system had brought Alexander Bach, the chief of Schwarzenberg's aides, to the barricades in the liberal cause. But the constitutional trappings of liberalism were not the only route to efficiency. It is true that the national assembly's draft constitution, known (from the town where the assembly was then sitting) as the Kremsier constitution, had come up with some fertile suggestions: a two-house legislature in which the upper house would represent the historic diets; provincial autonomy; and the creation of new units of local government, with elected councils based on nationality. But the assembly was dismissed before it had completed its work, and on March 4, 1849, a hastily drafted constitution was promulgated from above. A legislature was provided for, though on a somewhat narrower franchise than the assembly had foreseen. But the really radical provisions lay in the imposition of a unitary system that would reduce the historic privileges of the Hungarians and stringently limit their territory by creating Croatia, Slovenia, Transylvania, and Voivodina as separate crown lands. But that constitution, never properly implemented, was revoked on New Year's Eve in 1851, and the empire returned to absolute rule with no constitution at all, a plan urged on the willing young emperor by his conservative friends at court. When Schwarzenberg died in April 1852, Count Buol succeeded him as foreign minister, but no one became prime minister; the functions of that office fell to the emperor himself. Bach, minister of the interior since 1849, ran the system. The agrarian settlement of the national assembly was not undone; indeed it had been supplemented by a wholesale redistribution of land. Nationalities were guaranteed linguistic rights, but German became the indispensable administrative language at all but the lowest levels of government. Schools, universities, and bureaucracy became more than ever instruments of Germanization. The workers were kept quiet by prosperity and police. And in 1855 a new concordat exempted the Roman Catholic church from state control, secured its property, and restored the funds raised by Joseph II's dissolution of the monasteries. To this the revolution had come—at the hands of Bach, the one-time radical.

Prussia

On May 22, 1848, a Prussian national assembly met in Berlin. Similar in composition to the Frankfurt assembly, though with more peasants and artisans and fewer intellectuals, it was intended to work with the government on the drafting of the constitution the king had promised. Taking rather more initiative than had been intended, it moved gradually to construct a liberal Prussian state; but after Camphausen's government fell in May, the assembly did not get on particularly well with his less liberal successors. Nor could it master or satisfy the agitation that continued to simmer in the streets.

There is no doubt that the Berlin workers made the March Days; the liberals and their press were full of praise for their working-class shock troops. But it soon became apparent that the risings carried far more serious and frightening implications. Throughout Germany, particularly in the south, the month of March had been punctuated by episodes of rural violence. The liberal imagination could sympathize to a degree, for hostility to landowning and aristocratic privilege was part and parcel of the liberal creed. But when the agitation spilled over into demands for peasant proprietorship, the liberals were bound by their respect for property to resist. So it was with the working classes in the towns. Despite the swift return to Germany of Karl Marx and other socialist exiles, the movement in the towns was not the rising of an industrial proletariat, nor was it particularly responsive to the analyses and prescriptions of the intellectuals. Rather, German workingmen looked back to the good old days of gilds and careful regulation of trades. The rash of machine-breaking made it clear that the workers, overwhelmingly artisans and handicraftsmen, were rebelling against the industrial freedom that had been at the very core of liberal doctrine since the era of Stein and Hardenberg and against the economic progress that, however painful the transition, was ultimately to provide salvation. But doctrinaire liberals could never accept such a return to old ways, and the workers fell into a virtual frenzy of association that kept them isolated and at cross-purposes. In Prussia, as elsewhere in Germany, the brief alliance of classes was broken.

Far more portentous were developments taking place within the confines of the court and on the great landed estates of East Prussia. The king was surrounded by a group of Junker aristocrats—serious, intelligent, and deeply reactionary—known to history as the Kamarilla. Only Count Radowitz advanced views in any way progressive, and he was isolated by Junker distrust. While stiffening the king's intention to resist the revolution, the court party and the Junkers sponsored a meeting in mid-August of a "Junker parliament," the Association for the Protection of Property; they financed an ably edited newspaper, the *Neue Preussische Zeitung,* often called the *Kreuzzeitung* because it carried the iron cross on its masthead; and they encouraged the establishment of local conservative associations in the countryside. Trumpeting loyalty to crown and church, and summoning historic and patriotic pride in traditional German institutions, this imposing movement also aimed to concert an alliance against the liberals by conciliating the lower classes. While a movement emanating from landlords could not afford to be very generous in its agrarian policy—going little beyond proposing the abolition of the landlords' judicial and police functions and the commutation of servile obligations—the landlords were able to advocate what liberal dogma would never allow, the strengthening of the traditional gild organization of industry.

The king, more and more certain of the loyalty of the countryside, was determined to resume the initiative, the more so after it became clear from discussions in the national assembly that the draft constitution would abolish divine right and do away with nobility. In October his determination was strengthened by the sharp defeat of Viennese radicalism by Windischgrätz. Not until the beginning of November, however, did the king find the man to reestablish the Prussian autocracy, his cousin Count Frederick William Brandenburg, aided as minister of the interior by the veteran bureaucrat Baron Otto von Manteuffel. A week after he took office, Brandenburg ordered the removal of the national assembly from Berlin to Brandenburg, and the next day the army entered Berlin amid a sullen but quiet populace. A few minor revolts elsewhere in the country were quickly put down. The assembly, divided and disoriented by its transplantation, appeared utterly futile; on December 1, 1848, it was dissolved, and a constitution was dictated by the government.

The new constitution steered a middle royalist course. Ministers and the army were the king's, and a royal veto and rule by decree were allowed for. But civil rights were guaranteed, and there was a legislature, rather too liberally constructed for Junker tastes, in which the lower house was to be elected by universal suffrage, without stipulation as to "independence" and with protection against interference. The government promised, and within the next year took, action to relieve the peasantry from the remaining manorial obligations and to halt the trend to freedom of industry begun a generation before by Hardenberg. The results of the elections on January 22, 1849, proved the wisdom of the government's gamble on universal suffrage and its prudence in promising the right things to the right people: it won a clear if not overwhelming victory in the lower house.

The German Problem

While Prussia was slowly returning to its old ways, the great hopes aroused by the Frankfurt assembly were being falsified. The assembly began its deliberations on May 18, 1848, balancing the claims of the three mandates it held: liberal, constitutional, and national. Without question the assembly's finest accomplishment came at the end of December 1848 with the adoption of a declaration of fundamental rights: its fifty articles proposed to sweep away the remaining forms of feudalism throughout Germany, provided for equality before the law, and guaranteed academic freedom and the other expected freedoms of association, public meeting, and the press. Not only were these rights to become basic law for Germany, but the constitutions of individual states were intended to conform to them, thus making German citizenship identical everywhere and giving meaning to the freedom of movement envisioned for the whole country. These ringing affirmations so dear to the liberal mind did not extend to the social demands of the poor, whose situation and mentality contradicted liberal assumptions. But it was a real advance to bring the Germans within hailing distance of libertarian ideals that had been commonplace in France for fifty years and in England for nearly two centuries.

Constitutional problems were less amenable to independent action by the assembly than was a program for individual rights. At the outset the assembly abolished the diet of the Confederation and substituted a new central authority, electing as its head Archduke John of Austria—John was an admirable choice, for he not only espoused liberal principles but had embodied them by marrying the daughter of a postmaster. The powers of this central authority were not defined, however, nor could they be, dependent as it was on the yielding of vital functions—such as control of the military—by the states that would make up the new empire. The states, to say the least, were disinclined to take this step. By the time a constitution was completed, almost a year later, the power vacuum created by revolution was no longer there to be filled. The Frankfurt constitution could not be swept into force; it would have to be freely accepted by the rulers or bargained for.

The most serious difficulties at Frankfurt arose from national consider-ations. Although the election of Archduke John conceded Austria's traditional primacy in German affairs, the multinational character of the Austrian Empire raised the crucial question of defining the extent of Frankfurt's creation. In the old confederation, this problem had been solved by including only the German parts of Austria. That still was the solution preferred by the "greater German"—grossdeutsch—party, whose principal strength lay in the south German states, which had always sought a counterpoise to the might of Prussia. But the simplicity of this solution was outdated. In the first place, the Czech renaissance had introduced a newly alien factor in Bohemia, hitherto always taken for German; the Czechs invited to the preparliament had declined, and Palacký's letter of refusal became the basic statement of Slav separatism as well as a call to create Austro-Slavism (see p. 720). Second, the determination of Francis Joseph, Schwarzenberg, and his associates to create a unitary empire made it impossible for Vienna to accept partial incorporation in Germany, while the notion of adding the burgeoning nationalities in the eastern parts of the emperor's domains occurred to no one. Frankfurt was thus thrown back on the "little German"—kleindeutsch—solution, which meant excluding all of Austria and, however unwillingly, accepting the leadership of Prussia.

The national scruples of the Frankfurt parliament were not always so discriminating. The events of 1848 created widespread hopes, particularly in France, that a restoration of Poland might prove possible, and a good starting place seemed to be offered by the grand duchy of Posen, administered since 1815 with some degree of autonomy by Prussia. The liberal Camphausen government in Berlin was quite willing to give up Posen and had helped to promote the Polish cause, in cooperation with the French. But Posen contained a large German population, whose resistance to the prospect of Polish domination brought the Prussian court and army around to a proposal, after some Polish uprisings had been defeated in May, to divide the duchy and to incorporate both the German parts and the mixed parts (about two-thirds of the whole) into the Confederation. The radicals at Frankfurt were appalled at this violation of Polish national aspirations, but an East German member defended "healthy national egotism," arguing against sacrificing the Germanic mission for "a few families who revel in court splendor and for a few charming mazurka dancers." [6] The assembly voted overwhelmingly to accept the proposed demarcation line and the twelve deputies from the "German" part of Posen.

The aggressive surge of German nationalism was even more strikingly demonstrated in the Schleswig-Holstein question that preoccupied the Frankfurt assembly throughout the spring and summer of 1848. The two duchies belonged to the Danish crown and contained about two-fifths of Denmark's population, but Holstein was peopled entirely by Germans and Schleswig largely so. In the arrangements of 1815, Holstein (which had been a part of the Holy Roman Empire) was incorporated into the Germanic Confederation, while Schleswig was not. But by the forties the Germans in the duchies were demanding an autonomous government and the prerogatives of their Germanness, while a newly militant Danish nationalism insisted on retaining Schleswig, which the Germans wished to add to Holstein within the Confederation. In March 1848 the Germans in the duchies set up a provisional government, only to be defeated by the Danes, who occupied the whole of Schleswig; the Germans thereupon appealed to the Confederation, which in April agreed to admit Schleswig and called for Prussian troops to be sent against the Danes.

The Prussian invasion of Denmark not only stirred Scandinavian nationalism but deeply worried both the tsar, who was appalled that the Prussian monarchy should support a revolutionary action, and the British, who were traditionally concerned with freedom of navigation into the Baltic and thus bound to resist any weakening of Denmark. Faced with this diplomatic crisis, the Prussians had to withdraw and accept Swedish mediation. The armistice of Malmö, concluded in late August between Prussia and Denmark, provided a temporary settlement favorable to the Danes—evacuation, repeal of the acts of the provisional government, and the appointment of a joint Danish-German commission to rule the duchies. In late February 1849 the Danes denounced the armistice, and a new war with Prussia ensued; it finally ended in July 1850, after Austria had brought Prussia to heel. The new armistice, however, simply left the matter an open question until it was settled by Bismarck in 1864 (see p. 786).

The Frankfurt assembly had followed the Danish imbroglio in 1848 with intense interest. The armistice of Malmö in August came as a terrible shock, as Prussia's unilateral agreement to withdraw not only violated nationalist ambitions but made it clear that one German state could take action without consultation in matters affecting them all. Early in September the assembly voted to reject the armistice, then ten days later reversed itself and accepted it by a close vote. This action gave a pretext for rioting in Frankfurt against the assembly, riots that further demonstrated the parliament's impotence, for it had to call on federal troops to protect it from the mob.

The one task that remained for the Frankfurt assembly was to complete a constitution. The federal state it envisioned would have an upper house

[6] Quoted in William L. Langer, *Political and Social Upheaval, 1832-1852* (1968), 403.

representing the states and a lower house elected through universal, direct manhood suffrage on the basis of single-member constituencies; the central government was to control foreign policy, the army, and economic matters. The constitution was accepted on March 27, 1849, and the next day the assembly voted, with no great enthusiasm, to offer the crown to Frederick William IV of Prussia. The king's private opinion of the offer was scathing—he spoke derisively of taking up the crown from the gutter and of putting on a dog collar. His public response was more circumspect: he could not accept until the German princes had approved. When the princes approved not only the choice of Frederick William but, under popular pressure, the Frankfurt constitution, he then rejected the crown because the constitution, he argued, needed drastic princely revision. Archduke John and the president of the assembly, Heinrich von Gagern, thereupon resigned; the moderate members dispersed. The more radically inclined tried to continue, first in Frankfurt, then in Stuttgart, but on June 18, 1849, the rump was turned out by Württemberg troops. Some serious uprisings had taken place in the German states outside Prussia and in the Rhineland; in Baden it proved necessary to call in Prussian troops, who dealt with the rebels severely. But the radicals who rose in May 1849 could count on little of the popular force that had carried the revolution to triumph in March 1848.

The liberated Prussian king, advised by the fertile Radowitz, still made a serious attempt at German unity. Radowitz's scheme was to create a new German empire by the voluntary adhesion of all the non-Hapsburg lands, within a larger confederation that would include the Austrian Empire. Schwarzenberg declined, however, and was increasingly able to rely on support from the tsar, who disliked the prospect of any large, unified state in central Europe and who was particularly annoyed over Prussia's role in the Schleswig-Holstein affair. The tension between the two great German nations was brought to confrontation in the small state of Hesse-Cassel. There the elector had proved unable to master a parliament he had sworn to support but wanted to dissolve, and he called on the confederation for help. In Schwarzenberg's view the confederation was the proper instrument to maintain princely power, but Hesse lay between Prussia's divided provinces, and Prussia was determined to prevent the incursion of any federal troops into this strategic area. The two German powers nearly came to war; but, with the tsar resolutely on the Austrian side, Baron von Manteuffel, then Prussian prime minister, met with Schwarzenberg at Olmütz at the end of November 1850. They agreed to abandon the plan of union and found ways of resolving the Holstein and Hessian questions. Prussia made the more drastic concessions; hence Prussian historians have always called the convention, formally known as the Punctation of Olmütz, as the "humiliation of Olmütz."

The German problem, then, was not solved. The old confederation of 1815 was restored, and many of its constituent states went back well before 1848 to find a constitutional resting place. Within Prussia, however, the constitution of

1848, revised and formally adopted in January 1850, survived (indeed until 1918). The most notable of the changes contained in the 1850 version had come about after the lower house had acted to support the Frankfurt constitution, a bold move that led to the chamber's dissolution. A new electoral law carried at the end of May 1849 retained universal suffrage, but ranked the voters of each district according to the amount each paid in taxes and then divided them into three classes. The first class, those who paid the first third of the taxes, numbered very few; the second class was somewhat larger; the bulk of moderate and small taxpayers were lumped together into the third class. As each class chose an equal number of electors who in turn chose the deputy from the district, this cumbersome system reserved the choice of a deputy to the wealthiest and so the most conservative voters. Though some conservatives worried about what might happen if the liberals became too wealthy, the political future lay with the Junkers. To be sure, they had some reason for discontent over a reforming zeal that persisted through 1850, notably in the creation of a new system of local administration that was far more centralized than most of them were willing to tolerate. But in 1853 the scheme was withdrawn in East Prussia, which returned to the pre-1848 system; the Junker estates remained independent and kept their inherent police powers, though the jurisdictional rights of trial were not restored. While the Junkers could not undo the basic agrarian reforms accomplished in the aftermath of 1848, they did regain the right to create entailed estates and so assured their continuation as a caste and as the dominant political and social force in Prussia.

The destruction of the revolution in Germany, and particularly the suppression of the last radical uprisings in the summer of 1849, sent many disillusioned partisans into exile abroad, to England and particularly to the United States.[7] The men who had fathered German socialism and communism had returned from exile to assert their leadership but were rejected. The greatest of them all, Karl Marx, had seen his predictions of imminent revolution, so stirringly advanced in the *Communist Manifesto,* falsified on all sides, though he wrote much about the events, especially in France, that was perceptive and moving. He retired to the library of the British Museum in London to consult the oracles once more.

Escaping Revolution: Britain and Russia

Two great countries of Europe escaped 1848 without serious disruption. The English, to be sure, were confronted with a threatening situation in Ireland. Daniel O'Connell had moved on after his triumphant attainment of Catholic

---

[7] The best known of the refugees in America was Carl Schurz, who escaped the suppression of the last and most successful resistance at Rastatt. He rose to become a senator and secretary of the interior in the Hayes administration; he left an important set of reminiscences.

Emancipation in 1829 to agitate for repeal of the Act of Union of 1800. Quiescent in the thirties, when he could cooperate with the Whigs and often hold the balance of political power in the House of Commons, he faced the less malleable Peel administration in the forties with a major challenge. The government met it by coercion and by bringing O'Connell to trial in 1843. Shaken by his brief imprisonment and already dying, O'Connell was finished as a political force, and the political movement passed into the hands of more radical patriots who called themselves Young Ireland. But the horror of the famine left the country in a political coma. A republican insurrection in July 1848 was easily put down, and the insurgents were transported to the colonies. Ireland remained calm in the fifties, the bitterness suppressed. The only immediate inspiration of this early drive of Irish nationalism emerged in some other nationalist movements in Europe and in the vocal hatred of England that came so naturally to Irish emigrants in the United States.

In Great Britain itself, despite the serious depression of 1846–1848, the revolutionary year passed quietly. Chartism came briefly to life once more, and Feargus O'Connor proposed a new convention. It was duly held in April 1848, and on the tenth of that month a monster demonstration was scheduled for Kennington Common, a large open space south of the Thames in London. To the fearful this promised to launch the English revolution, but the middle classes flocked to enroll as special constables to assist Wellington's troops. The march to Kennington was orderly and good-natured; the special constables far outnumbered the Chartists. The authorities forbade the marchers to return across the bridge with the petitions for reform they wanted to present to the House of Commons; they dispersed and their leaders made the journey to the Houses of Parliament in a cab. Although there were signs of tension for a few years to come, April 10, 1848, was a characteristically understated, appropriately symbolic end to the hungry forties and a prelude to the placidity and prosperity of the fifties.

At the other end of Europe, in Russia, the forties closed with scarcely a ripple inside the country. Nicholas I, "the gendarme of Europe," was appalled by the march of events.[8] He was especially concerned that there be no repetition of the uprising among the Galician Poles in 1846; in this he was fortunate. But his armies put down a rebellion in the Rumanian provinces of Moldavia and Wallachia (to which he stood protector) in June 1848, and in the summer of 1849 it was he who crushed Hungarian independence. He was the arbiter of the dispute over Schleswig-Holstein and the supporter of Austria against the erratic course of Prussia. But such forceful activity was unnecessary at home. There was, to be sure, some awareness of western European events, for censorship and police supervision had slackened a bit in the quiet times of

---

[8] The story is told that, on hearing of the events of February 24 in Paris, the tsar strode into a ball at his son's palace crying "Gentlemen, saddle your horses, a republic has been proclaimed in France!" and then swept out of the room with his retinue.

the early forties. But the interest induced among Russian intellectuals by the ferment in western Europe remained subterranean, and the outbursts in the West in 1848 merely renewed the tsar's determination to keep his empire free from infection. The last years of his reign brought an intensification of control over thought and action. Russia was not to be shaken by revolution, but by war.

TO THE CRIMEAN WAR

The Shape of Diplomacy

Between 1830 and 1848 the relations of the European states were conducted with little change in methods and assumptions. The men who worked the system continued to come from the aristocracy or, in those rare instances where they did not, quickly absorbed the cosmopolitan manner and respect for the basic goals of traditional diplomacy. The shifts and turns of European policy continued to reflect a central concern with maintaining the balance of power, despite the dogmatic conservatism with which most statesmen were inoculated and the expectation of many intellectuals that a great ideological conflict would soon take place. Men still remembered the attempts of Napoleon I at domination of the Continent and were determined to prevent any repetition. There were limits to what any one country could do to assure the peace of Europe—limits that lay in the size and effectiveness of armies and navies, in available money and industrial resources, and in the time and imagination vouchsafed to hard-pressed statesmen who had also to cope with new challenges at home. Diplomacy was therefore a matter of cooperation and conflict, of pressure and withdrawal among shifting combinations of states that were commonly conceded the honorific equality of great powers.

As a regular means of organizing this complex and elegant game, the Concert of Europe had been dead since the British withdrawal from the Congress of Verona in 1822 (see p. 556). From time to time, however, it was revived to deal with particularly vexing problems or to ratify inescapable changes. It was invoked to settle the Belgian question in 1831 and 1839; it was summoned up once more in the peace conference in Paris that ended the Crimean War in 1856. But such instances of collective action were exceptional; the more common pattern was the division of the major European states into two camps: on the one hand, the old Holy Alliance of Russia, Prussia, and Austria, united by the absolutist principle and aversion to change; on the other hand, the liberal bloc. No longer was it a question, as in the twenties, of an isolationist Britain which could, when it seemed profitable, actively "nonintervene" to support some state, like Portugal or Greece, that threatened to alter the European situation. Britain had acquired an ally in France, detached from the legitimist camp by the revolution of 1830. The Quadruple Alliance of 1834 (see p. 706), in which the two countries were joined by Portugal and Spain, was for limited purposes, but it implied a widening of the identity of diplomatic interest between the two liberal western states: in the eyes of the eastern despots, Gaul was as perfidious as Albion.

The two western nations reflected, moreover, a profound possibility for change in the future conduct of diplomacy; it lay in the growing force of public opinion. Increasingly implicit in Britain between 1815 and 1830, this new force was made explicit in the thirties and forties—a situation basically inimical to the hardheaded and sometimes cynical calculations of the older diplomacy. In the forties there emerged in Britain an aggressive yet pacifist internationalism. It was linked in the faith and rhetoric of its advocates—the most famous being the leaders of the Anti-Corn Law League, Richard Cobden and John Bright—to the glorious possibilities and the inevitability of free trade and (though much less obviously) to a universal republic of commerce that Britain would forever dominate. Self-interest was, however, subordinate to idealism, and the long-range reforming implications of the new doctrine were corrosive indeed. But successful internationalism had to wait for the twentieth century. The public opinion that was reflected in the growing number and widening circulation of newspapers and magazines and that found its voice in statesmen willingly dependent on a wider constituency was, actually, truculent and nationalistic, however much its enthusiasms might run to apparently liberal causes abroad— Greece in the 1820s, Hungary and Italy in 1848–1849, Poland always. Increasingly, public opinion in both Britain and France came to focus in hostility toward Russia, which in the person of Nicholas I embodied all that was hateful in despotism; in this symptom of what one can rightly call social pathology lay a root cause of the Crimean War.

The transitional nature of international politics in the thirties and forties is strikingly embodied in the personality and policy of Lord Palmerston. He became foreign secretary in Lord Grey's government in 1830, rather to everyone's surprise. Impeccably aristocratic—though, as his title came from an Irish peerage, he was able to remain a member of the House of Commons—he had held minor ministerial office in the succession of conservative governments that spanned the years from 1809 to 1828. As a supporter of George Canning, he was gradually detached from his Tory moorings and so found his way into Grey's Whig-dominated coalition. Although Palmerston had shown no great distinction in his earlier career, he turned in an initial triumph in the Belgian negotiations and moved with increasing authority and boldness to become one of the finest British diplomats, both in technical skill and in reputation. He served with only a brief interruption until 1841 and returned to the Foreign Office in 1847 for another four years; as home secretary from 1852 and then as prime minister he was in office much more than out until his death in 1865. Thus he outlasted Metternich, with whom he shared the limelight before 1848, to dominate European diplomacy down to the emergence of Bismarck.

A profoundly conservative force in domestic politics, Palmerston played the liberal spokesman abroad, with rather more sincerity than cynicism, for, as he saw things, Britain stood to benefit more from liberalism than to lose from it. He both meshed with British opinion and played upon it, thus carrying further a tactic that had taken its modern form with his mentor George Canning, although there is unquestionably a reminiscence of the demagoguery so successfully employed by the elder William Pitt during the Seven Years' War (see p. 401). No doubt Palmerston derived his greatest personal satisfaction from his triumph at the polls in 1857, when both Cobden and Bright were thrown out by their constituencies after waging a bitter anti-Palmerston campaign. But his most famous performance came in a self-justifying speech in the House of Commons in 1850, when he was under attack for bullying Greece to make restitution to a Portuguese Jewish usurer named Don Pacifico, whose property had been destroyed by an Athens mob. Because, as a resident of Gibraltar, Don Pacifico had a dubious claim to British citizenship, Palmerston sent a naval squadron to overawe the Greeks and, incidentally, to outrage Europe. But, he proclaimed, "as the Roman in days of old held himself free from indignity when he could say *civis Romanus sum* [I am a Roman citizen], so also a British subject, in whatever land he may be, shall feel confident that the watchful eye and the strong arm of England will protect him against injustice and wrong." Palmerston won his vote of confidence and the plaudits of the nation.

For all his courting of public opinion, Palmerston was also profoundly aware of diplomatic realities. He bullied the weak when it suited him, but he regularly conceded to the strong, unless he saw a certain victory through cleverness and bluff. Although he grew more and more anti-Russian, he was perfectly capable of working in tandem with the tsar or with the Austrians, and he quickly accepted, even welcomed, the coup d'état of Louis Napoleon as a contribution to French stability. No wonder he was so distrusted by the more consistently liberal of his countrymen, who could see beyond his speechmaking and his aggressive posturing. But so it was with all European diplomats; no one dared to dabble in anything central to the European polity. Thus Austria's hold on Italy, however sympathies might fall, remained beyond fundamental question so long as Austria could maintain it, and no one—not even Lamartine—dared move other than oratorically for that most popular of liberal and radical goals, the restoration of Poland.

Although Britain and France were willy-nilly linked together as allies, they were continually squabbling, like two siblings who can neither bear to be separated nor live together in peace. This petty rivalry, at times obscuring the fundamental agreement, lasted throughout the century. The period between the revolutions began with the two nations at loggerheads in 1831 over the choice of a king for the Belgians and ended with a showdown in 1846 over marrying off the Spanish queen and her sister. In the former case, France had to accept the British preference for Leopold of Saxe-Coburg over an Orleanist prince; in the latter, Palmerston had to swallow Guizot's triumph in securing the hand of the Spanish queen's sister for one of Louis-Philippe's sons. The rivalry was more than dynastic, however; it was bitterest, and France's defeat most humiliating, in the great Near Eastern crisis of 1839-1840. The single major diplomatic incident of the period, it drew together all the threads of a complicated fabric.

In 1831 the Eastern Question had flared up again.[9] Mehemet Ali, established as pasha of Egypt, had long coveted Syria, the large expanse of Ottoman territory at the eastern end of the Mediterranean and along the Red Sea. Late in 1831 he sent an expedition under his son Ibrahim, and the armies that the sultan, Mahmud II, sent against him were quickly routed. The Great Powers, however, were working at cross-purposes. While nearly everyone had some degree of interest in propping up the Ottoman Empire for as long as possible, for want of anything better, the French were favorably inclined to Mehemet Ali, partly because of a French involvement in Egypt that went back to Napoleonic times, partly because they had North African ambitions of their own. When intervention by the Great Powers in concert proved impossible, the sultan surprisingly turned to Russia, which sent a fleet and an army to impose a settlement in 1833. Mehemet Ali was thus prevented from destroying the Ottoman Empire, but was left in possession of Syria. Russia and Turkey then concluded the Treaty of Unkiar Skelessi. For the eight years of its life it confirmed the relations that had existed between the two states since 1829, but in the form of a defensive alliance that seemed to the Western powers to confer on Russia a special standing, even a protectorate, in relationship to Turkey. A separate article embodied Turkey's agreement to close the Dardanelles—one of the straits between European and Asiatic Turkey—to all warships in time of peace.

Throughout the thirties, as the reforms made in the Ottoman Empire in the twenties were gradually taking effect, Mahmud II prepared to retake Syria. But when war once more broke out in 1839 between sultan and vassal, the result was another resounding Turkish defeat; Mahmud's death at the moment of Mehemet Ali's victory brought Abdul Mejid, a sixteen-year-old weakling, to the throne. Concerted action to save the tottering empire was forthcoming, but the front was far from solid. Nicholas I had deserted it; Metternich had withdrawn, apparently beaten in his efforts to stage-manage the intervention; the French had all along been reluctant, given their pro-Egyptian bias. The tsar then proposed and got an effective collaboration with Palmerston. Despite anti-Russian sentiment at home and the concern of some of his associates over a possible rupture with France, Palmerston moved with superb bravado to settle things his way. Control of the eastern Mediterranean had become infinitely more important to the British with the advent of the steamship and the rapid

[9] On its emergence in the decline of the Ottoman Empire over the preceding sixty years, see p. 557.

development of both the Suez and the overland routes to India, routes they were determined should never be subject to blackmail by one power (whether Russia or France or Mehemet Ali) able to control them. The tsar for his part was quite willing to give up the Treaty of Unkiar Skelessi, which might necessitate more Russian support of the Ottoman Empire than the country had stomach or resources for; he was particularly willing to sacrifice the treaty if he could drive a wedge between Britain and France.

Taking advantage of a fortunately timed anti-Egyptian revolt in the Syrian provinces, a revolt supported by English agents and armed forces, Palmerston was able to dictate a settlement in February 1841: Mehemet Ali was confined to Egypt with a hereditary title that gave the old man some comfort amid the other, limited concessions he had to make to his overlord. But Palmerston had steered a perilous course amid the shoals of French hostility. Resenting their diplomatic isolation, under pressure from a strongly pro-Egyptian public opinion, and until the end almost consistently misinformed about the strength of Mehemet Ali's prospects, French ministers refused to accept successive stages of the settlement as it evolved. Without any clear solutions of their own, they took a stronger and stronger anti-British line. This course became more violent when Thiers succeeded Marshal Soult as head of the government in March 1840. But war with Britain was a risk Louis-Philippe could not take, and in October he dismissed his rambunctiously patriotic minister. Guizot, the new foreign minister, who as ambassador in London had opposed Thiers' extremism, climbed down. Yet despite Guizot's good intentions and those of Lord Aberdeen, Palmerston's successor at the Foreign Office in Peel's government, the defeat rankled. The early forties were punctuated by incidents between the two countries—over missionaries in Tahiti, over ambassadorial hostility in Greece, and culminating finally in the matter of the Spanish Marriages (see p. 741). But so far as the Near East was concerned, France gave in to a *fait accompli,* and Metternich at last engineered French adherence to the Straits Convention, signed by all five powers in June 1841. This document—reiterating an agreement reached among the Great Powers, without France, a year earlier—did away with the special position Russia had appeared to gain in the Ottoman Empire, under the terms of the Treaty of Unkiar Skelessi. The convention also altered the arrangements concerning the Straits: henceforward (in fact until 1923) when Turkey was at peace, no warships could pass through either the Dardanelles or the Bosporus. Once again Turkey survived, thanks to the intervention of the European powers, and the stage was set for the next chapter of the Eastern Question, the Crimean War.

The Unwanted War

The Crimean War emerged from a jumble of conflicts—an escalating distrust between Britain and Russia, trade rivalry and strategic competition, covetous uncertainty about the future of the Ottoman Empire, and the ambitions and political necessities of Napoleon III. But the pretext for the war lay in the revival of an old dispute between Latin and Orthodox Christians over the protection of shrines and churches in Jerusalem associated with events in the life of Christ and built up by pious legend into the "Holy Places." For obvious geographical reasons, far more Orthodox than Latin pilgrims visited these sites, and, in the Treaty of Kuchuk Kainarji of 1774 (see p. 437), the Russians had been allowed to build an Orthodox church and were granted the vague right to make representations on its behalf and for "those who serve it." Russian activity in the Holy Land increased in the reign of Nicholas I, while the superiority of the Latin Christians, confirmed in the eighteenth century, had clearly withered away. Seeking popularity with French Catholics, Louis Napoleon in 1850 sought concessions from the Turks to enable him to assume France's old protective role over the Roman Catholics. A petty competition for prestige quickly resulted, with the Turks making contradictory promises to both sides; the quarrel was exacerbated by the disapproval the tsar felt for the upstart emperor. [10]

In 1852 Britain got a new government, a coalition headed by the former Conservative foreign minister Lord Aberdeen, now a "Peelite." Palmerston, who became home secretary, was for a time isolated from direct responsibility for foreign affairs. Nicholas I therefore thought he could count on British neutrality; he was surely the last person in Europe who might be expected to appreciate how the force of public opinion, increasingly anti-Russian as it was in Britain, might bring pressure on a parliamentary government. Nicholas also counted on the benevolence of Austria, for he had only recently helped to put down the Hungarian revolt. Since there was some question of Napoleon's seriousness, it seemed an admirable opportunity to extract further concessions from the Ottoman Empire, which the Russians had long helped to prop up, but which seemed unlikely to survive for long. A special envoy, Prince Menshikov, was therefore sent to Constantinople early in 1853 with a series of demands. He got the Turkish foreign minister dismissed and, with the mediation of the British, reached agreement with the French about the Holy Places. But Menshikov went on to demand a treaty conferring on Russia a protectorate over all the Orthodox laymen in the Ottoman Empire, perhaps two fifths of the population. This was clearly unacceptable and, with the British back in their accustomed role of stiffening Turkish resistance, the Turks refused, precipitating the diplomatic rupture the Russians had threatened.

Russia now tried blackmail: if the treaty Menshikov had asked for were not granted, Russia would occupy the principalities of Moldavia and Wallachia,

---

[10] It was an Austrian suggestion that the monarchs address Napoleon, in whom it was easy for a legitimist to see the incarnation of revolution, as "friend," not as "brother." In the end, though, neither Prussia nor Austria had the nerve to go through with it, leaving the tsar alone to offer the insult. Some of Napoleon's advisers wanted to use the provocation to start a quarrel, but the emperor neutralized them by gracefully remarking "One puts up with brothers but chooses friends."

nominally Ottoman possessions but under Russian protection since 1829. This new threat, carried out early in July, sent British and French squadrons to Besika Bay near the Dardanelles and jarred Austria out of its indifference. The so-called Vienna note, a compromise proposed by Austria, Prussia, France, and Britain, failed when the Turks insisted on amendments, and the Russian interpretation of it as conceding her extreme demands helped to fan Western distrust. Hostilities between Russia and Turkey began at the end of October, although the Ottoman Empire had actually declared war early in the month. At the very end of November a Russian naval force wiped out a smaller Turkish squadron; the British called it the "massacre of Sinope," and it turned British public opinion hysterical. Palmerston's resignation from the cabinet and the threat of the breakup of the Peelite coalition led Aberdeen's government to agree with the French to dispatch fleets of the two nations to the Black Sea in January 1854. An ultimatum was sent in late February insisting that Russia withdraw from Moldavia and Wallachia within two months. Meanwhile, British and French efforts to draw in the Prussians and Austrians failed: Prussia had little stake in the matter and a timid king; Austria would run a serious risk in any confrontation with Russia over the shape of the Balkans and the Austrian generals were rightly hesitant. So in March 1854 the two Western powers concluded an alliance with Turkey and at the end of the month alone declared war on Russia. Through bluff, miscalculation, and political drift, a war no one in power had wanted came about. To a wide sweep of the public in Britain, however, it was immensely welcome—as a chance at last to engage and defeat the great despotic power and, as well, to purge Britain itself of the effeminacy of thirty years of peace. [11]

Except for goals that were either vague or apocalyptic, no one knew precisely what the war was being fought for. After some complications, the Austrians, French, and British agreed on August 8 to the Four Points. One of them, abandonment of the Russian claim to protect the Orthodox in the Ottoman Empire, had already been conceded by Russia. Two others—abolition of the special Russian privileges in the principalities of Moldavia and Wallachia and free navigation of the Danube—were in effect assured when the Russians, in no condition to fight a two-front war, withdrew from the principalities on the day the Four Points were agreed to. That left the demand for a revision of the Straits Convention of 1841; to put it more bluntly, was Russia to be allowed to maintain her navy in the Black Sea?

The war could not be fought in the Balkans because the Russians had withdrawn from the principalities, which were at once occupied by the Austrians under a treaty in which Turkey transferred Russian rights to them. It was fought in the Crimea because the single outstanding issue of the neutralization of the Black Sea was, it seemed, most easily resolved by seizing the Russian naval base at Sevastopol. The assignment proved anything but

[11] The war mania in England is a most interesting social and psychological phenomenon. The most famous literary expression of it is Tennyson's poem *Maud*.

easy. The allies, who landed in the Crimea in September, won three battles fairly early on—Alma on September 20, Balaklava on October 25, and Inkerman on November 5. But, while the Russians could not drive out the allies, the allies could not reduce the superb fortifications of Sevastopol and had to settle in for a winter-long siege. The operation was one for which their military administrations, at home and in the field, were utterly unprepared. The terrible suffering of the troops, the high death rate owing to disease and wretched sanitary precautions, the heroic services of Florence Nightingale and her volunteer nurses were all brought home swiftly to the British and French publics by the newspapers; this was the first war to be covered by correspondents in the modern sense and the first to have the doubtful advantage of nearly instantaneous reporting by means of the telegraph. [12]

As British bellicosity switched to a search for scapegoats, Aberdeen's government fell early in 1855 and was succeeded by one with Palmerston at its head. The new government was far more capable of waging war than Aberdeen's had been, but a peace conference began on March 15, 1855, in Vienna. The sticking point, as before, was the question of the Black Sea. As that question got nowhere at the conference table, it remained for the allies finally to capture Sevastopol in September. But that victory left no really logical place for further military efforts, and the Anglo-French alliance began to disintegrate. After some extremely complicated backstairs negotiations, the preliminaries of peace were finally agreed to on February 1, 1856. On February 25, a general congress was convened in Paris—thus conferring the ultimate accolade of international respectability on the Second Empire—to ratify what had been done in Vienna.

Although it came out of a general European congress, the Peace of Paris left many European issues untouched. Nothing was said about Poland, and nothing was said about Italy, although Napoleon had long had ambitions to remake the settlements of 1815—peaceably—and although Count Cavour, the prime minister of Piedmont, had carried his little nation into the war against the Russians to assure British and French support for his broader Italian ambitions and to obtain a voice for Piedmont in the councils of Europe. [13] Once again the Ottoman Empire survived, and once more it promised to reform. The treaty excluded both the Russians and the Austrians from Moldavia and Wallachia, which began their career as the independent buffer states of Rumania, though nominal Turkish suzerainty was retained. Freedom of navigation on the Danube, vital to Austrian commerce, was secured by the establishment of an international commission and, perhaps more to the point, by depriving Russia of southern Bessarabia, which bordered on the lower reaches of that great

---

[12] The battle of Balaklava is famous for the "Charge of the Light Brigade," immortalized in Tennyson's poem of that name: growing out of jealousies, incompetence, and misunderstanding on the part of aristocratic officers, it was a useless piece of heroism.

[13] In opposing Russia, Piedmont was in effect siding with Austria, of all nations, proving that international as well as domestic politics make strange bedfellows.

waterway. The most drastic, though in the event temporary, provision was for the neutralization of the Black Sea; no warships and no naval bases were to be allowed. Although in theory this restriction applied as much to the Ottoman Empire as to Russia, the Turks had long since ceased to dominate the Black Sea, and they could in any event maintain a fleet in the Mediterranean. But the Russians, whose policy for a hundred years had been directed to establishing themselves in the Black Sea were now denied it, and a nation that had been devoted steadfastly to the maintenance of the international settlements of 1815 became determined to overthrow the international settlement of 1856 at the earliest opportunity (see p. 790).

The Russia that agreed to the Peace of Paris on March 30, 1856, was vastly different from the nation that had launched the war three years before with a diplomatic bravado that assumed both the weakness of Turkey and the continued benevolence of its two old friends of the Holy Alliance, Prussia and Austria. There was nothing left of the Holy Alliance—though in the long run Austria was to pay dearly for its demise—and Russia had gone down to defeat. On March 2, 1855, Nicholas I had died—by some accounts a suicide, though it is more convincing to agree with Professor Seton-Watson that "he had lost the will to live, so that his powerful frame was destroyed by a minor illness."[14]

A war insignificant in motive and performance if not in casualties—for the nearly half a million deaths (from disease more than battle) were unmatched between 1815 and 1914—had shaken a great empire to its foundations, as no revolution could have done. Having escaped the revolutionary years unscathed, Russia, by the logic of its defeat in war, had to turn not only revisionist with respect to European affairs but reformist at home. It is the final irony of the upheavals that began in 1848.

SELECTED READINGS

For a general account of the revolutions, though not extending quite so far in time as this chapter, William L. Langer, *Political and Social Upheaval, 1832–1852* (1969) is excellent, both substantively and bibliographically. European coverage is also provided in François Fejtö, ed., *The Opening of an Era, 1848: An Historical Symposium* (tr. 1948). A narrower but vital subject is studied in broad perspective in William L. Langer, "The Pattern of Urban Revolution in 1848," in Evelyn M. Acomb and Marvin L. Brown, Jr., eds., *French Society and Culture since the Old Regime* (1966).

On the economic background of events in France, the central work is a volume of essays edited by Ernest Labrousse, *Aspects de la crise et de la dépression de l'économie française, 1846–1851* (1965); that so important a work has remained untranslated is curious indeed. The conclusions there should, however, be read in conjunction with the qualifications argued in Douglas Johnson, *Guizot: Aspects of French History, 1787–1874* (1963), 230–240. Since so much of the suffering of these years was related to the failure of the potato crop across Europe, mention should be made of a remarkable work, R. N.

[14] Hugh Seton-Watson, *The Russian Empire, 1801–1917* (1967), 327.

Salaman, *The History and Social Influence of the Potato,* 2 vols. (1949). Much of the work on the revolution in France is scattered in scholarly articles. Two may be mentioned in particular: Peter Amann, "The Changing Outlines of 1848," *American Historical Review,* 68 (July 1963), 938–953, a useful summary; and John J. Baughman, "The French Banquet Campaign of 1847–1848," *Journal of Modern History,* 31 (January 1959), 1–15. Georges Duveau, *1848: The Making of a Revolution* (1965, tr. 1967) is a colorful narrative. Leo A. Loubère, *Louis Blanc* (1960) is a judicious biography of a key figure, and Donald C. McKay, *The National Workshops* (1933) is indispensable. Alexis de Tocqueville's *Recollections* (1893, new tr. 1970) is a particularly important account by a contemporary, as is that in Karl Marx's brilliant reporting, later published as a book by Engels, *The Class Struggles in France, 1848–1850* (1895, with several translations).

On the general situation in the Austrian Empire, C. A. Macartney, *The Habsburg Empire, 1790–1918* (1968) is excellent. So is a more detailed study by R. John Rath, *The Viennese Revolution of 1848* (1957). Pending a further volume of George Barany's work on Széchényi, there is little in English on the Hungarian revolt, but mention may be made of Dénes A. Jánossy, *Great Britain and Kossuth* (1937). Jerome Blum, *Noble Landowners and Agriculture in Austria, 1815–1848* (1947) is essential for the agrarian reforms in the empire. Although the Polish risings of 1831 and 1863 are well treated by R. F. Leslie, the Galician uprising of 1846 awaits its historian; however, considerable emphasis is put on the importance of the Polish question in L. B. Namier's *1848: Revolution of the Intellectuals* (1944). On the Slavs, see R. W. Seton-Watson, *A History of the Czechs and Slovaks* (1943); portions of Hans Kohn, *Pan-Slavism: Its History and Ideology* (1953); and Joseph F. Zacek, *Palacký: The Historian as Scholar and Nationalist* (1970).

Italy in the years 1846–1849 is dealt with in books cited in Chapter 19, but special mention should be made of G. F.-H. Berkeley and J. Berkeley, *Italy in the Making,* vols. 2 and 3 (1936, 1940), covering June 1846–November 1848; two wonderfully readable and authoritative works by G. M. Trevelyan, *Garibaldi's Defence of the Roman Republic* (1908), and *Manin and the Venetian Revolution of 1848* (1927); and A. J. P. Taylor, *The Italian Problem in European Diplomacy, 1847–1849* (1934). Numerous works in Italian are cited in Langer.

On the Germanies, Theodore S. Hamerow, *Restoration, Revolution, Reaction* (1958) is important for social and economic context. The standard history is by Veit Valentin, *Geschichte der deutschen Revolution von 1848–1849,* 2 vols. (1930–1931); the translation is considerably and unfortunately abridged as *1848: Chapters in Germany History* (1940). On the workers' movement, see P. H. Noyes, *Organization and Revolution: Working-Class Associations in the German Revolution of 1848–1849* (1966). On the drive for unification, see Frank Eyck, *The Frankfurt Parliament, 1848–1849* (1968), and L. B. Namier, *1848,* cited above; see also William Carr, *Schleswig-Holstein, 1815–1848: A Study in National Conflict* (1963).

It is odd that the year 1848, crucial in so many ways for Great Britain, has not received direct attention from historians. Both Britain and Russia in that year must be got at largely through more general works; but for Russia special mention should be made of two studies by Isaiah Berlin. One is a series of articles, "The Marvellous Decade," *Encounter,* June, November, and December 1955, and May 1956. The other is "Russia and 1848," *Slavonic and East European Review,* 26 (April 1948), 341–360.

On the international situation in the years between 1831 and 1856, the best initial approach is through A. J. P. Taylor, *The Struggle for Mastery in Europe, 1848–1918*

(1954); the introduction is an excellent account of the assumptions on which diplomacy rested, and the first five chapters cover the complexities of international politics through 1858. H. C. F. Bell, *Lord Palmerston,* 2 vols. (1936) is full and still authoritative; but see the more recent book by Donald Southgate, *"The Most English Minister . . .": The Policies and Politics of Palmerston* (1966). The most detailed treatment is Sir Charles Webster, *The Foreign Policy of Palmerston, 1830-1841,* 2 vols. (1951). On the relationship of Palmerston to public opinion, see B. Kingsley Martin, *The Triumph of Lord Palmerston* (1924). One crisis of the period is dealt with in Ernest J. Parry, *The Spanish Marriages, 1841-1846* (1936). But the period is dominated by the Eastern Question. One may begin with M. S. Anderson, *The Eastern Question, 1774-1923* (1966), a clear, succinct account. The chief monographic studies are Vernon J. Puryear, *International Politics and Diplomacy in the Near East: A Study of British Commercial Policy in the Levant, 1834-1853* (1935), and *England, Russia, and the Straits Question, 1844-1856* (1932); Philip E. Mosely, *Russian Diplomacy and the Opening of the Eastern Question in 1838 and 1839* (1934); and J. H. Gleason, *The Genesis of Russophobia in Great Britain* (1950). On Mehemet Ali, see Henry Dodwell, *The Founder of Modern Egypt: A Study of Muhammad 'Ali* (1931).

The Crimean War must be got at largely from the English side: H. W. V. Temperley, *England and the Near East: The Crimea* (1936); J. B. Conacher, *The Aberdeen Coalition, 1852-1855: A Study in Mid-Nineteenth-Century Party Politics* (1968); Olive Anderson, *A Liberal State at War* (1967); and two compelling books by Cecil Woodham-Smith: *Florence Nightingale, 1820-1910* (1951), and *The Reason Why* (1953); the latter is a fascinating literary reconstruction (it has been attacked) of the personal conflicts that culminated in that calamitous foolhardiness celebrated by Tennyson, the charge of the Light Brigade. On the aftermath of the peace, see W. E. Mosse, *The Rise and Fall of the Crimean System, 1855-1871* (1963), and Thad W. Riker, *The Making of Roumania: A Study of an International Problem, 1856-1866* (1931).

19

Consolidation and Transformation: 1850-1871

VARIETIES OF EMPIRE

Old Empires and New

In the last quarter of the eighteenth century and the first quarter of the nineteenth, the old European empires were changed out of all recognition. Within two decades of Britain's astonishing conquests of 1763, thirteen mainland colonies in North America, her most valuable colonial possessions, had broken away. France had already been badly hurt in the competition with Britain, and the wars of 1793–1815, with Britain's command of the seas unchallenged, virtually finished France as a colonial power. The Napoleonic Wars also hurt France's unwilling allies. When Holland was occupied, its colonial possessions were seized by the British. The French occupation of Spain provoked rebellions in Spain's American colonies; and when the legitimate dynasty attempted after 1815 to reconquer the colonies by force of arms, the wars of liberation created the patchwork of Latin American republics. In the

1820s Brazil, the last monarchical outpost in Latin America, was separated from Portugal; it became a republic only in 1889. The liberation of most of the Western Hemisphere from European control was guaranteed rhetorically by the Monroe Doctrine, proclaimed by the United States in 1823, and in fact by the British navy (see p. 556).

In the early nineteenth century, the smaller European colonial powers showed little drive or imagination. The Dutch, having lost the Cape of Good Hope, abandoned the remnants of their West African trading, as did the Danes. In the East Indies, Great Britain, seeking support against a possibly resurgent France, returned the Dutch possessions: Britain contented itself with keeping Ceylon and adding that strategic plum Singapore, acquired for the East India Company in 1819 by Sir Stamford Raffles and transferred to the British Crown in 1824. But Holland concentrated on the rich island of Java, whose economy it controlled in a tight paternalism, and pretty much neglected its other holdings. Portugal clung to stretches of the coast in East and West Africa, trading into the vast hinterland and claiming dominion over it; its tiny beachheads on the west coast of India and in Macao near Hong Kong were pale reminders of former imperial grandeur. The Spanish, finally, in turmoil at home, could go little beyond routine exploitation of their last significant colonies in the West Indies—Cuba and Puerto Rico—and in the Philippines.

These same years, however, saw the creation of a "second British Empire" and the beginnings of new French overseas enterprise. Some of the enthusiasm sprang from exploration and discovery. We have already noticed in another connection the circumnavigation of the world by Louis Antoine de Bougainville in 1767–1769 (see p. 352). In the next decade, the explorations of Captain James Cook extended geographical knowledge of the Pacific and the western coasts of the Americas; by finding the fertile east coast of Australia and circumnavigating New Zealand, Cook opened those territories for eventual British settlement. Both the Bougainville and Cook expeditions were informed by a deep scientific curiosity, and the urge to know mingled with other considerations to stimulate the fabled nineteenth-century explorations that opened up the "dark continent" of Africa and began to dispel some of the profound misconceptions Europeans had about it. The most remarkable of the African explorers was the missionary David Livingstone. His journeys in the fifties and sixties extended geographical knowledge by revealing the temperate and inviting uplands of central Africa. Quite as important was his revelation of the disastrous effects on the interior tribes of the slave-trading and other depredations of half-caste Portuguese merchants and of Arab traders based on the east-coast port of Zanzibar. Livingstone's personal courage and his impassioned writings and lectures stirred wide excitement in Britain, raising hopes of easy and profitable commerce, of elimination of the slave trade, and of large-scale Christian conversion—all tasks far harder than Livingstone's sanguine vision allowed for. Perhaps it would be better to say that a world of Livingstones would have been needed to make such heroic tasks easy—but there was only one.

The impulse to explore could not alone support overseas expansion. A far more practical stimulus lay in the prestige that accrued to successful colonial powers in the eyes of other governments and possibly among disaffected citizens at home. Surely the classic example is the expedition mounted against Algiers and other North African coastal towns in the last year of the reign of Charles X (see p. 572). Piratical attacks launched from the Barbary Coast had troubled the maritime nations for years, but the capture of a few ports was not to settle matters. The reign of Louis-Philippe brought the gradual extension of French control over the hinterland, the result of a kind of unwitting inertia of motion rather than of deliberate policy. The guerrilla resistance led by a military and political genius, Abd-el-Kader, was not defeated until 1847, after long and bloody fighting that forced the French to devise entirely new tactics. By that time, however, well over one hundred thousand European settlers, half of them French, had come to the new territory. Later, Napoleon III's quest for international respect and popularity led him into a number of foreign adventures, of which the most harebrained was the effort to supplant the republican regime of Benito Juárez in Mexico by a French-supported empire under Maximilian, archduke of Austria, in 1864-1867. Spain, too, resorted to some adventurism in the sixties: the most surprising was the blighted effort to regain control of the Dominican Republic in the Caribbean in 1861-1865, and the most fateful for the future was the punitive expedition undertaken with at least temporary success and great national enthusiasm against the sultan of Morocco.

The most important motives to overseas enterprise, however, lay in trade and strategy, to which missionary endeavor provided a now harmonious, now discordant counterpoint. The interplay of trade and religious zeal is evident in China, kept in deliberate seclusion from the barbarians of the outside world by her Confucian rulers. No foreigners were allowed to enter the country; trade, dominated by the British, was permitted only through factories at the southern port of Canton. Much of the trade was in opium, grown in India originally to redress the East India Company's unfavorable balance of trade with China. To suppress the use of the drug, the Chinese government had declared the trade illicit, but it flourished following the abolition of the company's monopoly of the China trade in 1833. Disputes over restrictions on merchants and about legal jurisdiction over Europeans who committed crimes in China led to the first British war with China (the "Opium War") in 1839-1842. The Treaty of Nanking, which ended it, opened four more "treaty ports" to foreign trade and granted the privilege of extraterritoriality—that is, the right to try British nationals accused of crimes in China in British rather than Chinese courts. Similar treaties with the United States and France followed. Trade flourished, especially in the newly opened port of Shanghai; missionaries, protected by extraterritoriality, boldly penetrated the still forbidden interior. The remaining restrictions galled, and the Westerners were particularly vexed by the continued refusal of the Chinese to permit normal diplomatic relations. Between 1848 and 1865, under the weakening Ch'ing dynasty, China was reduced to the verge of anarchy by the Taiping Rebellion—a fanatical, partly Christian, partly social movement—and in 1856 a trading dispute at Canton offered an opportunity for further British action. After bombarding Canton, the British gradually mounted an invasion that reached its climax in 1860 when British and French forces occupied Peking and burned the Summer Palace. The Treaties of Tientsin in 1858, confirmed and expanded in 1860, added more treaty ports and opened the mainland to travel and to regular diplomatic relations. Meanwhile, the British had regularized relations with Siam; the French (who had joined in the China war with the British) occupied Indochina in the 1860s; and from the 1850s Japan had been opened by the initiative of the United States (see p. 841). The middle decades of the century, then, saw the economic, diplomatic, and cultural predominance of the Western powers firmly established in East Asia.

The mixture of trade and missionary enterprise in Africa was different. There the overwhelming consideration was the slave trade, declared illegal in Britain in 1807, preceded by a few years by Denmark and followed by the United States, France, and Holland. Legislation could not in itself put a stop to the trade so long as the demand for slaves continued in the United States, Cuba, and Brazil; and international cooperation to suppress the trade proved difficult to secure. The British navy bore the brunt of enforcement measures, but the long coastline of Africa thwarted its elaborate system of patrols. Efforts were made to find legitimate trade to supplement and ultimately replace the trade in men, but only the palm oil of West Africa offered much chance of expanded operations in the early part of the century, and in time it became necessary to penetrate into the interior to attempt to stifle the supply of slaves at its source. By midcentury, exploration, trading, and treaty-making were being actively pursued. Africa raised vital strategic questions as well, especially as the Suez route to the East grew in importance. Still, in the period prior to 1870, the stagnant Portuguese Empire apart, only two European powers were at all significant in Africa.

France, largely for trading reasons, pushed inland from its beachhead in Senegal in West Africa, and the strategic toehold France had been allowed to retain in the island of Réunion off the southeast coast was to become a staging area for a later appropriation of Madagascar, conceded in principle by the British when they established their primacy over the sultanate of Zanzibar farther north. Britain, entrenched in enclaves on the west coast, firmly in control at the Cape of Good Hope, and increasingly concerned with the strategic and commercial importance of the east coast, still preferred to leave initiatives to private enterprise. British governments—of whatever political complexion— became involved in the interior only reluctantly. The acquisition of the Cape in 1815 had brought Britain a somewhat unwelcome complement of Dutch settlers. Known as Boers, these sturdy, independent, slave-holding farmers, long cut off from the increasingly liberal culture of Europe, tended to push inland into territories inhabited by the Bantu. After the British abolished slavery in their colonies in 1833, Boer migration became the "Great Trek," a series of moves to the north and east. Farming apart, the economic importance of the hinterland of the Cape was not appreciated before the discovery of diamonds and gold later in the century, and the British pursuit of the trekking Boers was tentative and halfhearted. Boer movement to the east into Natal encountered fierce resistance from the Zulus, but, after defeating the Zulus, the Boers abandoned the republic they had established there and it became a British colony in 1843. In 1848 the British annexed the Boer republic north of the Orange River—a step in part owing to humanitarian concern with native interests, in part the result of the boldness of Sir Harry Smith, the governor of the Cape Colony. But this claim was abandoned in 1854, as two years earlier the British had disclaimed any pretensions to sovereignty over the Transvaal, the Boer settlement beyond the Vaal River. This voluntary renunciation of political control has been seen as the high-water mark of British anti-imperialism. But the actuality was far more complex. The evolution of the British Empire in the period before 1870 is so central to understanding the "scramble" of an imperialist Europe after 1870 and to the world of the twentieth century that it requires a special glance.

The British Empire

In a famous phrase, a late nineteenth-century historian, Sir John Seeley, referred to the British as having "conquered and peopled half the world in a fit of absence of mind." [1] It is true that the first tendency of British governments was to shrink from new colonial adventures in the hope of avoiding permanent military and governmental establishments and the permanent expense they brought with them. It is equally true that the orthodox political economy of midcentury, especially in the peaceable and cosmopolitan form preached by Richard Cobden and his disciples, opposed colonial entanglements. Ministers and civil servants were less than enthusiastic, and it was not always possible to get members of Parliament to turn out for debates on colonial subjects; but, in the very years of this supposed "anti-imperialism," a great many businessmen, economists, journalists, soldiers, and statesmen were eagerly turning their minds to the advantages and problems of empire. [2]

One thing is clear. Everyone in any position of responsibility in Britain recognized that economic power, even more than military successes, had made Britain the dominant nation in the world, and they were determined to retain that enviable position. What they disagreed about was the means. The most

---

[1] Sir John Seeley, *The Expansion of England* (1883), Lecture 1.

[2] The supervision of colonies came under the secretary of state for war and colonies, a post created in 1794; the colonies were given a separate secretaryship only in 1854. It is said that Lord Bathurst, who held the post during the long ministry of Lord Liverpool from 1812 to 1827, asked, on first arriving at his office, for a map, saying "Now let us see where these damned colonies are." It may or may not be true, and he may or may not have been making a joke.

cosmopolitan advocates of free trade were certain that Britain's position as the "workshop of the world" would keep other countries and regions tributary to Britain—a belief that the German economist Friedrich List and other Continental protectionists accepted. The advantages of free trade in assuring British superiority had been recognized in the late eighteenth century by Lord Shelburne and the younger Pitt; and, while Pitt's attempt to promote freer trade with Ireland and France had failed, the steadily growing United States market, for British investment as well as British products, was striking testimony to the correctness of this belief. So too was the rapid domination that the British secured over the economy of Latin America, a colony in all but the political sense throughout the nineteenth century. The tacit assumption at the founding of the "second British Empire" was that it would be a trading empire, without the inconveniences that seemed to arise from settlers with diverging opinions and interests.

An obvious corollary, however, was that when economics alone could not secure British interests, political or military action would be taken. The best illustration lies in India. There Clive's victory over the French at Plassey in 1757 (see p. 511) had established the East India Company in three great trading centers: Calcutta, the capital of Bengal, on the northeast coast; Madras on the southeast coast; and Bombay in the west. The company became deeply involved not only in trade but in the government of the regions subject to its control. In 1773 Parliament forced on the company a reform of the Indian courts and established a governor general in Bengal, supreme over the other two presidencies. In 1784 and 1786 legislation established a government department, the Board of Control, to supervise the activities of the company, and the powers of the governors general over their councils were increased. Thereafter, and particularly following the loss of its trading monopolies in India and China (in 1813 and 1833 respectively), the company was a governing rather than a commercial corporation; the governors-general, or viceroys, possessed immense powers, which were necessary given the vast distance from England and slow communications.

Only gradually was British control extended throughout the subcontinent, in obedience to the imperatives of diplomacy and reform. Threats from outside had inevitably to be dealt with. An invasion of the northeastern frontier led to a war with Burma in 1823–1826; mistreatment of British merchants led to another Burmese war in 1852 and to the annexation of Rangoon. Russian expansion in Central Asia led to a forward policy on the northwest frontier of India in the 1840s. While the disastrous defeat of an effort to subdue Afghanistan in 1842 kept the British from advancing beyond the frontier for another forty years, the northwestern regions of Sind and the Punjab were annexed in 1843 and 1849.[3] Within India, in the forties and early fifties, the viceroy Lord Dalhousie devised ways of taking over the states of native princes,

---

[3] Alas, there seems to be no truth in the famous story that Sir Charles Napier reported his conquest of the former with the one-word message *"Peccavi"*—I have sinned.

which, by British standards, were notoriously subject to misgovernment. And the British were determined to root out what they considered barbarous native practices, such as the burning of widows on their husbands' funeral pyres or the atrocities of a sect of ritual assassins known as Thugs. Western culture and, as far as possible, Christianity were to be substituted. The brilliant young historian and politician, Thomas Babington Macaulay, was sent to India in 1834 with specific responsibility for reforming law and education. He made it clear that he agreed with the judgment that "a single shelf of a good European library was worth the whole literature of India and Arabia" and that it would be noxious, when sound philosophy and true history could be disseminated, to allow Indian schools to continue to teach, at public expense, "medical doctrines, which would disgrace an English farrier,—Astronomy, which would move laughter in girls at an English boarding school,—History, abounding with kings thirty feet high, and reigns thirty thousand years long,—and Geography, made up of seas of treacle and seas of butter." [4]

These reforms struck deep at Indian customs, and the British disregard for Indian sensibilities rankled. In 1857 a mutiny in the Indian army spread through much of India as a rebellion against British rule. After savage fighting and terrible atrocities on both sides, it was put down; and in 1858, at the very height of the period of presumed anti-imperialism, the East India Company was dissolved, giving way to direct British rule, with a secretary of state for India in the cabinet in London, to whom the viceroy in India was immediately responsible. Some Englishmen had thought that, after long exposure to their civilizing influence, the Indians would prove able to govern themselves. The mutiny crushed that confidence. Stern, efficient, remarkably free from corruption, and totally authoritarian, British rule lasted for ninety years against a steadily mounting demand for Indian participation and, in time, resistance (see p. 1043).

India, then, offers an instance where humanitarian, economic, political, and strategic necessities inexorably drew the British into deeper and deeper involvement. The expansion of the empire in Australia and New Zealand was, on the other hand, a response to a powerful agitation at home. In the 1830s and 1840s a group known as the Colonial Reformers, drawing activist conclusions from the teachings of the political economists, urged "systematic colonization" as a means of securing British supremacy. Their principal theorist and propagandist was an able, colorful, and irascible publicist, Edward Gibbon Wakefield, who first elaborated his plan in 1829 in an anonymous pamphlet written while he was in prison for a madcap attempt to abduct and marry a rich

---

[4] Thomas Babington Macaulay's *Minute on Education* (1835), from which these quotations are taken, is worth reading both for its slashingly brilliant style as well as for its revelations of the European sense of superiority. It is conveniently available in G. M. Young, ed., *Speeches by Lord Macaulay* (1935), in the World's Classics series.

young girl. So persuasive was Wakefield's scheme—he passed the pamphlet off convincingly as the work of a settler, although he had never been in the colonies—that he gained powerful allies in Parliament and the press and awakened new interest in Australia, used until that time principally as a convict settlement. Wakefield and his friends believed that colonies should be balanced, productive replicas of society at home, not dumping grounds for its rejects. To assure an effective colonial economy, they urged that land be disposed of at a high price; land-hungry immigrants would thus be forced to work in order to accumulate the purchase price and so assure a stable labor force, which had hitherto proved almost impossible to maintain. Neither in South Australia nor in New Zealand—the colonies where the experiment was tried—did Wakefield's plan work as he wanted, and his recriminations against what he deemed obstructionism in the Colonial Office were bitter. But in both Australia and New Zealand, settlement colonies became quickly established.

How were such colonies, largely British in composition, to be governed? In 1837 rebellions broke out in Canada, both among the French colonists in Lower Canada (now Quebec) and the English colonists, many descended from American loyalist refugees, in Upper Canada (now Ontario). They were paltry risings, quickly put down, but they recalled another rebellion sixty years before and called into question the authoritarian control that had been riveted onto the two colonies when they were created in 1791—a time when the American Revolution was believed to have resulted from too much leniency. A commission was sent to investigate the Canadian rebellions; it was headed by Lord Durham, more or less the leader of the Radical party in England; Wakefield and his associate Charles Buller were among Durham's advisers. In some respects the Durham mission was a failure, partly because of Durham's own imperious personality. His plausible but futile solution to the problem of an irreconcilable Roman Catholic French population was to unite the two provinces and to force the French to modernize by swamping them with Englishmen. An act of 1840 carried out the recommendation, but in 1867 the Canadian colonies themselves worked out a federal solution to the problem of national unity. The British North America Act of that year is still the basic constitution of Canada.

With far greater insight than he displayed on the French issue, Durham urged the granting of "responsible government," that is, requiring the governor-general of Canada to choose as his ministers those politicians acceptable to the majority party of the lower house of the legislature—the very parliamentary system that had just been confirmed at home (see p. 696). The idea had been talked about as early as the 1820s among Canadian politicians eager for office. The plan was advanced independently by the Colonial Reformers as a means of securing the loyalties of British emigrants. It was not, however, an easy policy for many Englishmen to accept. One of the first moves of the Canadian government after responsible government was granted in the mid-forties was an act indemnifying the rebels of 1837 for property losses they had suffered in the uprising; in Britain that looked like rewarding treason. When responsible government was extended to the Australian colonies in the 1850s, the Australians at once adopted the heresy of protectionism and imposed tariffs on British goods. Although certain aspects of government—foreign affairs the most important—were reserved for decision in London, in most domestic matters responsible government meant self-government, whatever the Colonial Office or the British thought about it.

This devolution of sovereignty and loosening of political ties can be construed as an index of anti-imperialism, but at least in part it had the opposite effect of drawing the colonists closer to the mother country. The constitutional history of the English-speaking colonies over the century after Durham's mission is the history of the attainment of "dominion status," and much of the colonies' political history has grown from the clash between loyalty to Britain and the pursuit of national self-interest. The bond uniting these countries to Britain has been (and to some degree still is) a major international fact.

Russia's Drive to the East

As Britain expanded across the oceans, Russia moved to establish its sway in Asia. Complex, fragmented, and long-drawn-out, this massive extension of Russian control may be seen as falling into three sectors. The ambition to reach the Black Sea had brought the southern steppes and the Crimea under Russian rule in the late eighteenth century (see p. 437). This was followed by penetration of the magnificent barrier of the Caucasus Mountains into Georgia. That region, once unified in a kingdom, had long been broken into several principalities, those in the west dependent on the Ottoman Empire, those in the east dependent on Persia. At the end of the eighteenth century, the Georgians appealed for Russian help in escaping Persian attempts at reconquest, and in the first decade of the new century the annexation of Georgia was accomplished, to be confirmed after war with Persia from 1804 to 1813. A second Persian war in the late twenties assured the permanence of that incorporation and, moreover, brought Russia parts of Persian territory inhabited by Armenians, though to the west another large segment of Armenians remained subject to Ottoman rule. In the Caucasus itself, however, there were two main pockets of resistance—among the Circassians in western mountain strongholds and in Daghestan in the eastern part of the range; both peoples were Muslims. Not until 1859 was all of Daghestan brought into subjection, with the final defeat of the Circassians coming five years later. A final addition of territory, Southwest Caucasus, was made in 1878.

The second area of Russian expansion lay in the fabled lands of Central Asia. The northern tier of the region was inhabited by the three hordes of the Kazakhs, two of which had accepted Russian suzerainty in the 1730s, though the consolidation of the Russian hold on the entire territory went on throughout the reign of Nicholas I. To the south of Kazakhstan lay Turkestan, which was conquered haphazardly in the twenty years or so following 1864. As with British expansion, much of the initiative was taken by local traders or by military men in pursuit of glory, with St. Petersburg—now reluctantly, now aggressively—following suit. Afghanistan and Persia served as buffers between the Russians in Central Asia and the British in India; in both regions the competition for influence grew more intense.[5] As the positive and negative poles of a magnet are irresistibly drawn toward each other, so Britain and Russia came closer and closer to conflict. Not until the early twentieth century, under greater pressures in Europe, could they reach a tentative accommodation in the Middle East (see p. 933).

In the third sector of Russian expansion, war and competition with foreign powers played a less significant role. Peter the Great had extended the Russian grasp in Siberia as far east as the peninsula of Kamchatka on the Pacific. But this vast territory, though important for the fur trade, remained of little significance in Russian policy prior to the nineteenth century. It was, to be sure, a conveniently distant and, in some respects, unpleasant place to send exiles. But, despite the fearsome reputation of Siberia as a penal colony, the exiles in fact formed only a small part of the population. The native tribes were on the whole well treated, but the bulk of the population before the great migrations was made up of peasants who had fled from European Russia to the comparative freedom that had always survived east of the Urals; because no gentry would go there, the institution of serfdom had no reason to exist.

In the late eighteenth and early nineteenth centuries, a number of efforts were made to govern Siberia more efficiently. But it was not until the brief governorship of Speransky from 1819 to 1821, just before he returned to the center of power from which he had been banished in 1812 (see p. 523), that the real possibilities of the territory came to be appreciated and that a reasonably effective governmental structure was established. Speransky and Count P. D. Kiselev, who was at the ministry of state domains for nearly twenty years after 1837, encouraged the migration of state peasants to Siberia and further migration within Siberia from the west to the less populated east. This

---

[5] While there was a notable similarity in the strategic ideas of the two Great Powers, their methods differed. Lord Curzon, the future viceroy, quoted the Russian commander, General M. D. Skobelev, as saying: "I hold it as a principle that in Asia the duration of the peace is in direct proportion to the slaughter you inflict upon the enemy. The harder you hit them the longer they will be quiet afterwards. My system is this: to strike hard, and keep on killing till resistance is completely over; then at once to form ranks, cease slaughter, and be kind and humane to the prostrate enemy." Curzon, who was rather taken by this, contrasted it to the English method: "to strike gingerly a series of taps, rather than a downright blow; rigidly to prohibit all pillage and slaughter, and to abstain not less wholly from subsequent fraternization." Quoted in Richard A. Pierce, *Russian Central Asia, 1857-1917: A Study in Colonial Rule* (1960), 45.

movement petered out by the 1850s, when agrarian reform in European Russia became a real possibility, but after emancipation the influx into Siberia began again. Reaching a flood in the early twentieth century, it raised the total of emigrants from European Russia to something like seven million over the century from the end of the Napoleonic Wars.

Still farther east, Alaska had been opened by the explorations of Vitus Bering, a Dane in the Russian service, in the years after the death of Peter the Great. In 1798 Alaska was brought under the Russo-American Company, and Russian trading posts were established as far south as California where Fort Ross dates from 1812. But the Russians were eager to avoid conflict with the United States and Britain, and the dubious value of the North American territory, as it then appeared, led to Russian withdrawal and at last the sale of Alaska to the United States in 1867. Meanwhile, Russia grew increasingly interested in the large, sparsely settled part of China bordering on the Amur River. Taking advantage of the Chinese weakness from which the other Western powers had so greatly benefited in the 1850s, the Russians began to settle the region. In 1858 they extorted a treaty giving them possession of the left bank of the Amur to the sea. Two years later the Russians, while urging the British to attack Peking, persuaded the Chinese that they were a force for moderation, and so secured cession of the territory on the right bank of the Amur east of the Issuri River, which the earlier treaty had provided would be held in common. The Russians immediately founded a new port at the southern tip of the area and named it Vladivostok: the name meant "Ruler of the East." With the regularization of relations with Japan—following on the opening of that country in the 1850s and settled by the exchange of the Russian-held Kurile Islands for complete possession of the island of Sakhalin in 1875— Russia was established as a major Pacific power.

REFORM AND REVOLUTION

Russia: The Great Reforms

The shock given to Russia by the Crimean War and the contemporaneous beginning of a new reign made reform possible as well as necessary. Mere tinkering with the machinery of central government was not enough, and indeed little was changed at that level. What was needed was a reconstruction of society. Although it was never fully accomplished, that overhauling had to begin with the elemental problem of serfdom, a problem so vast in scope and so unpredictable in its outcome that Alexander I and Nicholas I had turned impotently away from any but the mildest palliatives.

Estimates vary, but there seem to have been in the neighborhood of eleven million privately held male serfs in 1858, something under half of the total number of male peasants. Of the nonseignorial peasantry, by far the largest number were state peasants, those resident on state-owned lands and technically, or relatively, free. Their ranks included those peasants who in one way or another had escaped reduction to serfdom, the great majority of the inhabitants of Siberia, serfs who had attained their freedom through military service or redemption, foreign colonists, and serfs of the church who became state peasants when church lands were secularized in 1764. The position of state peasants was secured and improved somewhat in the course of the nineteenth century, not only by legal enactment but through the work of the ministry of state domains, under Count P. D. Kiselev, after 1837. Another element of the nonseignorial peasantry was made up of court peasants, serfs on lands belonging to the imperial family. By the end of the eighteenth century these peasants had been freed from labor services, although the money payments that took their place gradually became more onerous. Yet, for all their privileges, state peasants and court peasants alike lived with a grim possibility, though one less threatening in the nineteenth century than before: they might be converted into serfs if the sovereign gave state or imperial lands to private individuals.

The position of serfs in private hands, as we have seen, deteriorated during the eighteenth century (see p. 413), and while in the nineteenth century efforts were made to curb the worst abuses, enforcement was usually a far cry from the decree. It is risky, however, to try to characterize the seignorial peasantry in a few generalizations. Conditions from one part of the country to another varied with the nature of the soil and the techniques of working it. In the highly productive "black soil" regions, landowners preferred to retain labor services— *barshchina;* in less productive areas and especially where domestic or even factory industry had developed, serf owners were glad enough to substitute a money payment—*obrok;* in some places both obligations were imposed. Serfs might labor in the fields, in the household, in landlord-owned factories, or, for the very wealthy, serve as actors and musicians. Concubinage was common; so was corporal punishment. The power of the gentry over their serfs was nearly unlimited, but its exercise varied from one landowner to the next, as resources, personality, education, and sense of responsibility varied. Some landlords were absentee, some were resident; a few were interested in improving agriculture, but more were interested only in improving their incomes as they fell deeper and deeper into debt. As most of the gentry construed the situation, there was no convincing economic argument for the abolition of serfdom. To the farsighted, however, reform might seem a necessary prelude to effective modernization, especially after the Crimean defeat had so forcefully demonstrated Russian backwardness. At the same time, among the better educated and more widely experienced gentry, a moral sense of the evil of serfdom gradually penetrated; by midcentury it was at least possible to discuss the problem openly. And urgency was added by an increase in peasant uprisings and rural violence.

Alexander II, better educated and milder in temper than Nicholas I, remained a convinced autocrat, given like his father to working through secret committees. He knew that he must deal with serfdom, and at the end of March 1856, echoing advice that had been given his father, he told the nobility of Moscow that it would be better to abolish serfdom from above than to wait for it to be abolished from below: Pugachev's revolt of 1773 (see p. 434) remained a terrible memory. The bureaucrats were put to work and as they canvassed alternative plans, they defined certain principles: a transition period was needed; landlords would be compensated for land given up to serfs but not for the loss of rights over their persons; peasants would be emancipated with land, at first the land immediately surrounding their houses and ultimately with a portion of the land they worked. Simply to sweep away all landlord rights would have meant a dangerous alienation of the governing class on which maintenance of the autocracy largely depended; to create a landless proletariat was unthinkable—and had had unfortunate consequences when it was tried in the Baltic provinces in 1819–1820. When slaves were freed in the United States, the got immediate legal freedom without land; the Russian solution was different, but it satisfied almost no one and created a whole new range of dangerous pressures.

The first public announcement of these principles (still rather vague) was in the so-called Nazimov Rescript in November 1857, an answer to a petition from the nobility of the province of Lithuania asking that their serfs be freed without land as had been done earlier in the Baltic provinces. While rejecting this request, the government summoned the gentry to make proposals in accordance with the principles laid down. Some of the proposals that emerged from subsequent provincial discussion were surprisingly liberal; the majority of the gentry, however, proved roundly conservative. Therefore, although a facade of gentry consultation was maintained, the government firmly kept the initiative. Despite disagreements within the government, the liberal bureaucrats, energetic and expert, carried the day.

The emancipation law was signed on February 19, 1861. Although it declared immediate freedom of serfs, it provided a two-year delay during which no change in payments or obligations was allowed; in that period surveys and the working out of details for each property could be seen to. At the end of two years, domestic serfs without land became free, but peasants on the land became "temporarily obligated" for *obrok* or for limited *barshchina*. There were only two really practicable ways to escape from this "temporary obligation." One was to accept a quarter of the maximum amount of land that separate statutes indicated for different regions of the country; these "beggar's allotments" were granted free of charge, and some clever peasants who chose that course managed to eke out a living by renting additional land. The more common escape was to redeem the amount of land permitted by statute. Not until 1881 was redemption made obligatory; until then it was accomplished by agreement with the landlord—voluntary on the landlord's part but imposed on the serf if the landlord wanted it. The state, in parlous financial condition, made no direct contribution to assist the peasants to acquire their lands. It did, however, guarantee redemption payments by advancing 80 percent of the agreed-upon sum to the landlord in interest-bearing bonds. The peasant's payments to the state for this advance extended over forty-nine years. The remaining 20 percent of the set price for the land was paid by the peasant directly to the proprietor, if peasant and proprietor reached a voluntary agreement. If, on the other hand, the landlord insisted on redemption and the peasant did not agree, the landlord got only the 80 percent advanced by the government.

Economically speaking, the principal beneficiaries of the emancipation were the landlords. They could keep at least a third of their land, and the redemption payments were set at an inflated level. Most peasants had to work outside their holdings in order to meet the payments and so were hardly freed in the sense that is understood in the agrarian reforms of western Europe. There was another sense in which the peasants' freedom was compromised. The way land was held under the new law varied with local custom: where land had been periodically reassigned by the old peasant commune, the land was transferred in its entirety to that commune and the practice of repartition continued; where land was held individually, that tenure was perpetuated, although some land was transferred to the commune to provide for landless peasants. So, while peasants escaped detailed control of their lives by landlords and were, in theory, legally free, they were in fact bound to another authority, either the old agrarian commune or a new administrative commune, which handled redemption payments, taxes, police, and other local government functions under the headship of an elected peasant elder. Permission of the commune was needed for extended absence, and the commune even retained the power to exile serious miscreants to Siberia. Court peasants and state peasants were dealt with in further legislation along similar, though generally more favorable, lines.

This cumbersome solution to a problem of staggering complexity was followed by other reforms. At the beginning of January 1864 a local government reform, gradually and never completely implemented, provided for an elected assembly *(zemstvo)*, chosen by electoral colleges of nobles, townsmen, and peasants, for each district *(uezd)* and for similar assemblies at the provincial level, chosen by the *uezd* assemblies. The assemblies met infrequently; their powers were exercised by paid executives responsible to the assemblies for supervising, among other things, communications, transportation, trade, hospitals, prisons, and schools. The zemstvos in time could number a good many practical accomplishments, but they "exercised rather than satisfied the political instincts of Russian society." [6] They were rigidly subordinated to centrally appointed provincial authorities, and the government firmly resisted the notion of a national assembly, or union of *zemstvos,* much agitated for in the early sixties by elements among the gentry.

Toward the end of 1864, a reform of the judiciary was approved and gradually extended throughout the country. The provincial courts and the courts of appeal were modeled on Western examples; a modern legal profession was created at a stroke; and, as the judges were guaranteed permanence of tenure, a remarkable degree of judicial independence developed. But the peasants were for the most part excluded from the system, and, for all their excellence, the higher courts did not manage to provide circumstances in which a convincing respect for law, as the West saw it, could take root. The educational reforms included a statute of 1863 granting the universities greater autonomy and two statutes of 1864 regulating the elementary and secondary schools. The censorship was shifted in 1865 from prior or preventive censorship to punishment for offending publications, although control of education and the censorship were strengthened once again in 1866, following an attempt on the tsar's life. Finally, in 1874, compulsory military service was inaugurated for all classes of the population, accompanied by a wholesale overhauling of the military establishment. Once serfdom was abolished, it was possible for Russia to emulate the western European system of short enlistment and maintenance of a reserve.

Thus was accomplished a sweeping, though only partial, transformation of Russian society. The onset of the period of reform was widely welcomed, even by a significant minority of the gentry. But disillusionment came quickly nearly everywhere. The peasants, confronted with statutes they could not understand, saw only infinite delay, the continuation of heavy burdens, and a steady denial of their old belief that, while serfs belonged to lords, the land belonged to serfs. The reforms were greeted with outbursts of rural violence and, in the long run more dangerous, with sullen resentment and bitterness. Although attempts were made in the reforms, and even more in their administration, to conciliate the gentry, there was resentment among the conservatives against any reform, while the liberals were alienated by the denial of the constitutionalism, on the English model, that so many of them had hoped for. The entire gentry class was united in its hatred of the bureaucracy, which, distrusting them, imposed its will. Among some intellectuals, the reforms provoked an immediate enthusiasm. The very possibility of reform was a stunning justification of their hatred of Nicholas I. Much of what was done was appealing, at least to some among them, notably the new importance given to the peasant commune, so dear to the Slavophiles as embodying a specifically Russian, orthodox spirit in contrast to the individualism of the West. But this initial enthusiasm did not last. To

---

[6] The phrase is J. M. K. Vyvyan's, in chap. 14 of the *New Cambridge Modern History,* vol. X, 377.

some extent the more radical intellectuals reacted against the harshness and incompleteness of the reforms, for they had become intensely preoccupied with achieving social justice. Competing ways of attaining this end—"nihilism," anarchism, populism, and the varieties of socialism—drew strength from this passion (see p. 805). And in the sixties, for the first time since the suppression of the Decembrists, a conspiratorial movement had sprung up in Russia, the beginning of a continuous effort to overthrow the tsarist regime.

At the same time that Russia was coping with the strenuous demands of reform at home, attempts were made to placate Russian Poland. The Poles had risen unsuccessfully against Austria in Galicia in 1846 and against Prussia in Posen in 1848; on neither occasion had Russian Poland stirred. Now, encouraged by the conciliatory policy of the new tsar and a new viceroy, Prince Michael Gorchakov, Polish nationalism flourished. Marquis Alexander Wielopolski, a veteran of the Polish uprising of 1830-1831, was appointed in 1861 to carry out reforms, including a land reform far more favorable to Polish peasants than were the contemporary Russian reforms to the serfs.[7] But the urban radicals ("the Reds") rejected any cooperation with the Russians, and the leaders of the moderates ("the Whites") did not dare to show themselves deficient in patriotism. The radicals, moreover, angered the Russians by raising demands for restoration of the Lithuanian province, which had been incorporated into Russia in the first partition in 1772. There were clashes between the Poles and Russian troops, and in 1862 attempts were made to assassinate both Grand Duke Constantine and Wielopolski.

Russian countermeasures, notably the conscription of young Poles into the army, provoked a rebellion that began on January 22, 1863. It was ineptly led and severely put down; the Poles were divided and so were the sympathies of the peasants. The peasants benefited greatly from their conversion into freeholders by the reforms finally implemented in 1864, but the long-range political goal of separating peasants from landowners was not attained. Satisfied in their agrarian demands, the peasants now found their enemy in Russian administration, forcing the Russians to resort to a systematic effort at russificiation to blot out a Polish nationalism that cut across all classes. Whatever sympathy there was in Galicia and Posen remained subterranean, and Lithuanian support for the Polish movement was brutally repressed by Count M. N. Muraviev, a former Decembrist determined to prove that he was "not one of those Muravievs who get hanged, but one of those who do the hanging." In England and France, as always, a great show of liberal enthusiasm burst forth, as futile as ever. The Polish sympathies of Alexander Herzen and Michael Bakunin actually lost them support in Russia, for the Polish uprising triggered a new surge of Russian patriotism, even among some who on internal questions were most disaffected. In the Russian Empire, then, while the Great

---

[7] Wielopolski liked to say that "reform is the vaccine for the Revolution." Quoted in R. F. Leslie, *Reform and Insurrection in Russian Poland, 1856-1865* (1963), 136.

Reforms marked the most important turning point since the reign of Peter the Great, they exacerbated old problems and opened a new era of instability.

Great Britain: The Confidence of Progress

Freed from the tensions of the "hungry forties," Britain entered a fortunate decade. Even British agriculture prospered, apparently justifying the faith in free trade that had swept away the Corn Laws and that reached its climax with the Cobden Treaty with France in 1860. The railway network was nearing completion. Established industry seemed everywhere triumphant, and new industries were being launched—chemicals, rubber, and the quantity production of steel. The fifties were not entirely untroubled—the Crimean War and the Indian Mutiny were blows to English pride and conscience—but Palmerston rode high and flattered the robust, xenophobic pride that lay not far below the surface of most of his countrymen.

Politics was in flux. The Conservatives, from whom the talented Peelites had detached themselves in 1846, were largely obscure and untried. Their leaders, Lord Derby and the novelist-politician Benjamin Disraeli, were splendid opportunists who envisioned a party that might unite Englishmen of all classes in defense of traditional values and against the more corrosive consequences of liberalism and extreme individualism. Disraeli had taken pains to assure the country that a Conservative government would not mean the return of protective tariffs, but his party was only briefly in office, on two occasions—in 1852 and in 1858-1859; both were minority governments of no great distinction or accomplishment. The midcentury decades belonged to the liberals, a term that (with an initial capital) had come to be applied increasingly to the Whig party. But the Whig-Liberals too were in disarray: the Aberdeen coalition of Whigs and Peelites fell in 1855 because it had botched the war it had blundered into. A Palmerston government succeeded; though with one brief interlude it remained in office until 1865, it could point to no stirring accomplishment. Before the election of 1859, however, the political flux was clarified by the emergence of the Liberal party, properly so-called, when the remaining Peelites—the most important being Peel's lieutenant William Ewart Gladstone—joined formally with the Whigs.

The main political issue was a new installment of parliamentary reform; the steadiest advocate of this course was Lord John Russell, although in 1837 he had declared that the reform of 1832 was final.[8] Russell's bills in the fifties—tinkering with the qualifications for voting to expand the electorate enough to garner political advantage but not so much as to endanger political stability—got nowhere. Nor did Disraeli's bill in 1859. But public opinion could not

---

[8] Hence Lord John was known as "Finality Jack," in contrast to "Radical Jack," Lord Durham. Durham's early death in 1840 deprived the Radicals, already weakened as a concerted political group, of a charismatic, though difficult, leader.

remain indifferent in the sixties. The magnificent orator John Bright, who had become famous during the Corn Law agitation in the forties, had been turned out of his seat, as had Richard Cobden, in the general election of 1857, when their pacifism could not survive Palmerston's popularity. Bright (who quickly found another seat) was now converted to the cause of parliamentary reform, which he preached with his old radical fervor.

Another strand in the growing interest in reform came from the working-men who stood most to benefit from an extension of the franchise. Skilled labor, organized increasingly into unions (see p. 596), made notable organizational advances and resisted some serious attacks. The long builders' strike of 1859, an unsuccessful attempt to get the nine-hour day, had troubled a good many people who distrusted unions in principle and disliked them even more when they disturbed industrial peace. The reputation of trade unionism was further damaged by the revelation that the saw grinders in Sheffield had used violent tactics against nonunion workers, though such methods were not typical of trade unionism as a whole. The most serious blow was delivered in 1866 in a decision by the House of Lords in its guise as the highest court of appeal. Declaring that unions were in restraint of trade and so ineligible for protection in the courts, trade unions were deprived of legal recourse against officers who embezzled their funds. A royal commission appointed to investigate the matter called for the legalization of unions, which was accomplished (somewhat grudgingly) by an act of 1870. That the unions came through the investigation so well is testimony to the statesmanship of their leaders and to the power of their middle-class allies. This increasingly confident but still threatened sector of English life mounted a major agitation after 1863 in favor of universal manhood suffrage. Labor intended to use political weapons to attain its ends.

Palmerston's death in 1865 removed the principal political obstacle to another Liberal reform bill. Russell became prime minister and, raised to the peerage as Earl Russell, went to the House of Lords. The bill was therefore introduced in the Commons in 1865 by Gladstone, whose cautious declaration the year before in favor of reform had made him the darling of the reformers. The bill was in fact quite limited. It was acceptable to radicals as a partial step, but a group of hostile Liberals known as "the Cave of Adullam" helped the Conservatives to defeat the bill and bring Russell's government down. Derby and Disraeli came in, once more in a minority, and prepared a bill of their own. Popular agitation reached a climax in the "Hyde Park Riots" of July 1866; the government had ordered the gates of the park closed to prevent a demonstration, but the press of the crowd forced down the railings and, as neither police nor troops took stern measures, there followed three days of milling about and trampling of flower beds. It was a mild affair but enough of a warning— particularly in conjunction with a sharp economic downturn—to make the government cautious about provoking the reformers.

The battle for reform was not to be fought in the streets. Disraeli introduced his bill in March 1867, yet another limited measure that promised the radical goal of household suffrage in the towns while ringing it about with stringent limitations and "fancy franchises" that gave additional votes to the highly respectable. To everyone's astonishment, in the crucial debate on the bill in August, Disraeli accepted one after another radical amendment that swept away the limitations and ended in carrying an act that enfranchised nearly all workingmen in towns, including lodgers: it was a genuine installment of democracy.

France: Liberalizing an Empire

Like Britain, France under the Second Empire threw immense energy into economic development and reaped the rewards of prosperity and confidence. For most of the period both countries could afford the luxury of being unpolitical—in Britain because the weakness of parties and the dominance of Palmerston made politics almost unnecessary, in France because an authoritarian state made political life almost impossible. The two nations cooperated in the Crimean War and the opening of China and were the only really active colonial powers in Africa. The French were more reckless in their foreign adventurism, but the British responded heartily to Palmerston's aggressive blustering. In both countries workingmen made important gains in organization, self-consciousness, and political importance, although the growth of the French labor movement, starting later, was necessarily more compressed.

Britain welcomed exiles and France, at least in the early years, created them, but the repressiveness in France did not have a seriously adverse effect on culture. Indeed there was a burst of creativity on both sides of the Channel. The literary scene was brilliant. The English were more hospitable to their rebellious painters, the Pre-Raphaelites, than the Second Empire was to the Impressionists, but in the fine arts France clearly had the edge, as it did in music. Both nations built magnificently. Private enterprise and public works were transforming the quality, the visual impact, and the smell of countryside and town. Great drainage and sanitary systems were built in the large cities. The English created Gothic town halls and dramatic railway stations; the French reconstructed Paris with broad boulevards, parks (owing much to the English example), and buildings in exuberant baroque. But behind the imposing facades that so impressed visitors, both countries created slums, and the wealth-producing railways and factories meant coal smoke and waste. The builders understood each other. When Napoleon III asked Edwin Chadwick, the English sanitary reformer, what he thought of the rebuilding of Paris, Chadwick replied: "Sir, it was said of Augustus that he found Rome brick and left it marble. May it be said of you that you found Paris stinking and left it sweet." [9]

---

[9] But not everyone understood. The German nationalist Heinrich von Treitschke sneeringly accused the English of equating soap with civilization. For both remarks, see G. M. Young, *Victorian England, Portrait of an Age* (1936), 11, 24.

Society in the two countries grew less exclusive, gayer, more tolerant, and, to some extent, more ostentatious, although the *demimonde* of Paris, as the name implies, signified a more open acceptance of sensuality than was possible in a straitlaced London, where the underworld of vice flourished amid attempts of the respectable to shut it out of mind. Horse-drawn omnibuses first appeared in the two cities at the end of the 1820s. The highly maneuverable single-horse cab patented by Joseph Aloysius Hansom in 1834 and given his name was fully established by midcentury. The first London underground line opened in 1863, but deep tubes had to await new tunneling techniques and the electric motor; the first of them was opened in London in 1890, and the Paris Metro followed ten years later. With easier transportation, shops with plate-glass windows, department stores, and modern hotels and restaurants, city life, at least in the two capitals was assuming its modern form in the decades at midcentury. It has been said that, were a young man of the upper middle class able to choose the time and place into which he would be born, he would choose to be young in mid-Victorian England; but were he inclined to raffishness, with a taste for good food and wine and a liking for the operettas of Offenbach, he might very well have chosen Paris under the Second Empire.

The authoritarian constitution and Louis Napoleon's assumption of imperial rank had been overwhelmingly ratified by the people. Between these two plebiscites, in the spring of 1852, a parliamentary election took place. Facing a widespread legitimist opposition, the government did not do so well as in the plebiscites. Still the legislature was to the new emperor's liking. The Senate, which had some important constitutional powers, was an appointed body and tame in consequence; the Corps Législatif—with some 260 members it was a mere third the size of the assembly of the Republic—met for no more than three months a year under appointed officers and was allowed to discuss only what was put before it. Even the emperor's address from the throne at the opening of a session was undebatable. The Corps Législatif would not waste time, as Louis Napoleon put it, "in vain interpellations, in frivolous accusations and in passionate struggles, the only object of which was to overthrow the ministers in order to take their place." Even the tribune, the podium from which deputies in earlier French legislatures had been accustomed to orate, was removed. A muzzled press, a pervasive police, and an effective administration were there to carry out the emperor's will.

But the emperor's will was something of a mystery. The coup d'etat had resulted from a fortunate conspiracy, and the man it benefited continued to work in secret ways. He made few pronouncements and committed little to paper; he preferred to keep negotiation and diplomacy personal and private. He depended on his old supporters and on his relatives. Among them were his old comrade in arms Persigny, a veteran of the Strasbourg adventure; his illegitimate half brother the duke de Morny, a gifted and cynical opportunist; his radical and unstable cousin Napoleon, Jerome Bonaparte's son; and Count Walewski, an illegitimate child of the great Napoleon. To that inner circle was added the new empress, the Spanish countess Eugénie de Montijo—beautiful, devoted, pious, rather dim, and an increasingly conservative influence toward the end of the reign. No single political position was shared by Napoleon's advisers, a point the emperor himself was reported to have made in jest: "The Empress is a Legitimist, Morny is an Orleanist, my cousin Napoleon is a republican, I am a Socialist; only Persigny is a Bonapartist, and he is crazy." The empire meant personal rule in the strictest sense—by a man who was a riddle to his contemporaries and who remains so to historians, who was receptive, kindly, charming, well intentioned, and too often indolent.

Napoleon was not alone in describing himself as a socialist, though others may have taken the label more seriously: when Guizot learned of the coup d'etat he exclaimed, "It is the triumph of socialism!" and the famous literary critic Sainte-Beuve called Napoleon III "Saint-Simon on horseback." The one Napoleonic statement that might be thrown into the balance—a pamphlet of 1844 titled *The Extinction of Pauperism*—is no more than a backward-looking scheme for settling the poor on wasteland. The emperor's insistence on the association of progress with order, his interest in economic development, and the prominence in the French economy of former Saint-Simonian disciples suggest that he had absorbed some influence from that powerful, widely diffused tradition. But beyond expressing a wish for general social betterment, socialism is not much help in solving the Napoleonic puzzle. The rambling, windy pamphlet, *Napoleonic Ideas,* published in 1839, is probably more rewarding: his uncle, Napoleon argued, had shown the way to reconcile order and liberty; the patron of nationality, liberation, and peace, he had provoked universal opposition only by moving too far too fast. It remained to build on the constitution the first Napoleon had hastily proclaimed after his return from Elba. "If I do not represent the French Revolution," Napoleon III told Walewski in 1859, "I represent nothing. . . . When the peoples of Europe make revolutions to obtain the blessings we possess—and which they only obtained for a brief space under the Empire as the fruit of our victories—they naturally look to me because I represent these ideas, which are not yet the common property of Europe and which have been impeded by an impious sect which confounds [17]89 with [17]93. . . . I should like you to re-read my *Idées Napoléoniennes. . . .* My convictions have not changed." [10]

Coming to power aided only by a tiny cabal, Napoleon had to create supporters. A Bonapartist party had been hurriedly thrown together in 1848, but, composed of nonentities, it dissolved prior to the elections of 1852. Elections in the first decade of the empire needed careful stage-managing, but there were simply not enough candidates with unimpeachable Bonapartist credentials to go around; hence, prefects and mayors rounded up candidates of different political lineage who possessed sufficient local standing and a potential

---

[10] Quoted in J. P. T. Bury, *Napoleon III and the Second Empire* (1964), 49. The earlier quotations are also taken from this admirable sketch.

for loyalty. Some were Orleanists; some were legitimists willing to accept the new order as the price of returning to political life; many were "new men" from the world of commerce and industry, who numbered nearly 25 percent of the members of the Corps Législatif elected in 1852, as against 10 percent under the presumably bourgeois monarchy in 1836 or the 14 percent in the republican assembly in 1848. The career open to talents was a cornerstone of the Second Empire, as of the First. Napoleon III (who said that he gloried in the position of parvenu) was, however, more likely to confer recognition on talents already proved in the world of practical affairs than to provide the means, as the first Napoleon had done, of proving those talents by ascent from nowhere. The seeds of the liberal empire were present in the very nature of the people who rallied to it. [11]

For most of the fifties all went well. The emperor conducted a somewhat erratic and aggressive foreign policy; he had, however, reached a temporary accommodation with England—an alliance by which (profiting from his uncle's errors) he set great store—and he had succeeded in isolating Austria. That the peace conference ending the Crimean War was held in Paris was a tribute to the emperor's success in restoring France to a position of the first rank. The bold economic schemes of the Saint-Simonians seemed to be paying off; the Suez Canal, built largely with French capital and under the direction of Ferdinand de Lesseps, was begun in 1859. [12] Though many republicans and other opponents of the regime were in exile, the country seemed less cowed than content.

The placid surface was not unruffled. Despite the withdrawal of the legitimists from active politics, the elections of 1857 revealed a notable opposition sentiment; five republican members were elected. In 1858 an Italian patriot named Orsini came close to assassinating Napoleon and Eugénie with a bomb. The crime worsened relations with England because the conspiracy had been hatched among exiles in London, and in 1859 England experienced a curious war scare that sent thousands into the volunteer militia to train against a French invasion for which there was no basis whatsoever. The Orsini incident also threatened to turn the emperor to the right and even to deter him from his plans to help Italy. But these consequences were averted, and shortly after the emperor and Count Cavour, the prime minister of Piedmont, concerted plans that eventually brought French cooperation in Piedmont's war against Austria, the first overt stage in the tangled process of Italian unification (see p. 777).

The Italian war of 1859 marks a turning point in the reign. It was accounted a success in France, and Napoleon's prestige rose. But he did not get everything he wanted, either for France or for Italy. Moreover, once the possibility of

[11] This point is convincingly argued in Theodore Zeldin, *The Political System of Napoleon III* (1958).

[12] The opening of the canal ten years later was an isolated triumph amid confusion and decline. It is worth noting that Verdi was commissioned to write *Aida* for a gala opera season in Cairo to celebrate completion of the canal, but the first performance did not take place until 1871.

Italian unity was clear, his willingness to accept a drastic reduction of the papal states brought a new strain into relations between the emperor and the militant French Catholics, whom he had sought to appease by going into Rome in 1849. These relations became so difficult that Napoleon refused to allow the encyclical *Quanta Cura* and the *Syllabus of Errors* (see p. 663) to be published in France; the balance began to tip toward state education and away from education dominated by the Catholic orders. French manufacturers were angered by the free-trading Cobden Treaty of 1860 negotiated by the French government partly out of conviction, partly to repair relations with England. The Mexican involvement began in 1862, steadily draining manpower and funds and ending in disaster. By the mid-sixties Bismarck, a much abler opportunist, had raised Prussia to the position of the leading Continental power. And even the economic miracle seemed insubstantial. The Crédit Mobilier, the immensely successful investment bank of the Péreire brothers, failed in 1867 and entered a long and painful reorganization; in 1868-1869 the unorthodox financing of the building of Paris, and in particular the management of its guiding spirit Baron Haussmann, came under severe parliamentary attack. Throughout the sixties Napoleon's health declined, his indolence increased, and the improvisational quality of his policies became more painfully evident.

Nevertheless, this decade of decline saw a steady liberalization of institutions. On his return from the Italian war, the emperor declared an amnesty for some 1800 political offenders. In 1860 and 1861 more moderate press laws were put into effect. The Corps Législatif obtained some real power to debate and some control over finance, powers extended yet further in 1867, when, symbolically, the orator's tribune reappeared. France had in fact seen a real resurgence of parliamentary life. The elections of 1863 returned an opposition of thirty-two, Thiers among them, a development that ended Persigny's political career because he had failed to manage the elections properly. Yet Napoleon's efforts to gain support through liberalization seemed never to work to his advantage. In 1862, for example, he subsidized the visit of some French workingmen to an exhibition in London; there they made contact with English workingmen, with the result that the First International was founded two years later (see p. 852). In 1864 strikes were legalized, and four years later French workers were given the right to unionize, with much of this legislation drawn on the English model; the equality of workers and masters before the law came to both countries in the middle of the decade. But the rapid growth of the economy had increased the stress felt by the working classes, who pursued their own ends and did not give their first loyalty to the emperor.

One difficulty lay in the men Napoleon chose to govern. The duke de Morny, his ablest minister, died prematurely in 1865, and power was exercised for far too long thereafter by the unpopular, rigid Eugène Rouher. Finally, late in 1869, in great secrecy, Napoleon made contact with one of the opposition members who had been elected in 1857, Emile Ollivier, the scion of an unimpeachably republican family, who had made an early and stormy debut in politics in 1848 when he was appointed, at the age of twenty-two, to be prefect of Marseilles. [13] Ollivier had from the first shown himself to be supple in his republicanism and willing to subordinate political dogma to a sense of social mission and nationhood. A brilliant orator, he looked to Lamartine for political inspiration, and it was not illogical—though to some it looked like treachery—to transfer his allegiance to Napoleon III. Early in January 1870, an Ollivier cabinet came into being, and in May a plebiscite ratified a new, liberal constitution; while it preserved important powers for the emperor, it came very close to providing a parliamentary regime. Napoleon's victory at the polls was impressive, testimony perhaps to the attractions of liberalism, perhaps to renewed faith in the emperor. But the new system was to have no change to prove itself. In July Napoleon's ultimate gamble carried France into war with Prussia, and his empire crumbled away (see p. 788).

Spain: A Futility of Revolutions

Spain at midcentury was nominally liberal but in fact under military rule (see p. 705). The constitution adopted by the Moderados in 1845 provided for a limited suffrage and a two-chamber Cortes that quickly came to be dominated by bureaucrats who doubled as members. Indeed, at every level of society those in a position to cadge or extort favors sought government jobs and so made possible *caciquismo*—the boss rule that determined local politics. A great gulf separated town from countryside, and the old regionalism persisted, despite theoretical centralization and the arbitrary hacking up of the country into forty-nine provinces in 1833. The state ingratiated itself with the new, aggressive, but inefficient landowners who had profited from the Progressives' confiscation of church lands in 1836; and it made its peace with the church in a concordat in 1851. But the peasants were left poverty-stricken, backward, illiterate, superstitious, and almost entirely docile. Railway construction was launched in the late 1840s, largely with French initiative and capital, but its benefits did not filter down very far on the social scale. Industry had taken hold in the Basque provinces in the northwest and, above all, in Catalonia in the northeast; but Spanish liberals angered the industrialists by their dogmatic panacea of free trade and did nothing for the workers. Thus, Spain was as far removed from the context of English or French liberalism as it was geographically remote from the rest of the Continent; Progresistas and Moderados were factions rather than parties. Spanish history in the third quarter of the nineteenth century is a succession of intrigues and palace revolts, two of which have been raised to the dignity of revolutions.

---

[13] Emile Ollivier's grandfather had named his sons Demosthenes and Aristides in good Revolutionary fashion; Demosthenes chose his son's name from the title of Rousseau's famous educational tract.

Much of this futility revolved around the monarchy. Isabella II was self-willed and self-indulgent. Married to an effeminate and reportedly impotent cousin whom she hated, she took a succession of lovers with scandalous openness. Her mother, Queen Maria Cristina, had been permitted to return from exile, and Maria Cristina's husband—a guardsman, suitably ennobled, whom she had secretly married when she was regent—was deeply involved in profiteering from railways. Isabella sought to rule with a group of loyal courtiers and with support from the church: "A royal sinner who repents on Sundays," one historian has remarked of her, "makes an ideal subject for clerical manipulation." [14] She dismissed the dictatorial Narváez in 1851, but in June 1854 discontent culminated in the *pronunciamento* of the Moderate general, Leopoldo O'Donnell. He was about to fail when, as in 1820, uprisings in provincial towns converted his initiative into a revolution. A constitution was drafted and adopted in 1856 but never put into effect. Political power shuttled from one leader to another. O'Donnell was in office from 1858 to 1863, a period in which Spain pursued an active foreign policy in Morocco, the Dominican Republic, and Mexico—ventures all futile in the end, except for producing a new hero in General Juan Prim, who soon emerged as leader of the Progressives. After 1863 Narváez, in and out of office, was once more dominant, gradually tightening his authoritarian grip. In 1868 he died; O'Donnell had died the year before. Prim, though in exile because of an abortive coup in 1866, was the one leader with any claim to authority, and on September 18, 1868, he returned to Spain, with wide support, to pronounce against the queen. As she fled, juntas in the major towns joined the revolution; a provisional government was formed; and yet another constituent Cortes was summoned.

Forced to deal sternly with radical advocates of federalism, the provisional government had to cope as well with a war for independence in the long-neglected colony of Cuba, a war that prevented Prim from keeping his promises to abolish conscription and to lower taxes. The constitution of 1869 was in essence a replay of that drafted in 1856, providing for religious freedom and universal manhood suffrage. Although much of the Left rejected the decision that monarchy was indispensable, the search for a king went on, not very successfully, for few of Europe's royal houses were eager to send candidates in quest of so dubious an inheritance. Ferdinand, a member of the little German house of Saxe-Coburg and the widower of Queen Maria of Portugal, withdrew after some consideration. Queen Isabella's brother-in-law, the duke of Montpensier, a legacy of the Spanish Marriages that had so vexed European diplomacy in 1846 (see p. 741), was acceptable to the Right but certainly not to Napoleon III, who would not allow an Orleanist on the Spanish throne. After a year of increasingly desperate searching, Prim lighted on the son of a Catholic branch of the Hohenzollern family, whose Protestant senior line were kings of Prussia. The secrecy that Prim tried to maintain to avoid a French veto was

[14] V. G. Kiernan, *The Revolution of 1854 in Spanish History* (1966), 33.

accidentally broken: "My labor is lost, the candidate lost, and God grant that is all," Prim lamented.[15] But it was far from all. Napoleon's objections to the Hohenzollern candidacy were parlayed by Bismarck into the occasion for the Franco-Prussian War, and with Prim's hopes were lost a considerable portion of French territory and the Second Empire itself (see p. 788).

A king was found at last in Amadeo of Savoy, a son of the new king of Italy. But just before Amadeo's arrival at the end of December 1870, Prim was assassinated. Though Amadeo tried his best, he abdicated early in 1873, publicly and sadly recording his inability to bring peace to the country and privately remarking, "I don't understand anything; we are in a cage of madmen."[16]

Italy and Europe

In Italian history the years between 1815 and 1870 are known as the *Risorgimento,* another of those evocative historical labels that can neither be dispensed with nor lived with comfortably. Scholars disagree not only about the significance of the *Risorgimento* but about its proper limits in substance and in time. Was cultural change an essential precondition of unification, or was unification the result only of chance and brilliant improvisation? If the *Risorgimento* is taken primarily as a cultural phenomenon, a case can be made for pushing back into the eighteenth century to find its origins; if it is seen as preeminently political, the nineteenth-century expansion of Piedmont as the nucleus of the kingdom of Italy will loom larger. Perhaps the connotations of the very word "resurgence" are an initial handicap to understanding. It suggests a vast forward movement where there were only fits and starts, false hopes, conflicts, and cross-purposes; an irresistible tide, when in fact unification was achieved by opportunism and accident; a return to past greatness, although greatness was never achieved. Still, despite the confusion, a kingdom of Italy took the place of the "geographical expression," and an important minority of Italians had glimpsed a nation that was one in more than a dynastic sense.

This transition was made against enormous handicaps. Poverty was endemic, and illiteracy, widespread in the north, was almost universal in the south. Although a standard literary Italian was emerging, most Italians spoke their native dialects and could not understand each other. Industrialism was taking hold in the north, but the peninsula was poor in natural resources, lacking in adequate transport, isolated from the main channels of international trade, and hobbled by a limited and divided internal market. Progressive agriculture, exceptional in northern and central Italy, was unknown in the south, where social conditions and a harsh, ungrateful climate had helped to

[15] Quoted in Raymond Carr, *Spain, 1808–1939* (1966), 518.
[16] Quoted in Richard Herr, *Spain* (1971), 107.

perpetuate huge quasi-feudal estates. In a mind like Giuseppe Mazzini's the heat of moral passion could dissolve such obstacles, but Mazzini's program of stimulating national consciousness among his countrymen by repeated insurrections failed almost as much in its educational as in its political purposes. It proved harder to instill *italianità* by renewing the souls of men than to bring them together against the tyranny of Austria, a tyranny that carried a new authenticity after Radetzky's victories in 1848-1849 (see p. 728). If unity was to come, it had to come through war with Austria, and it was increasingly clear that the kingdom of Piedmont—or Sardinia, as it is sometimes known—would be the pivot of the new nation.

Given Piedmont's isolation in the northwestern corner of the peninsula, and recalling the irresolution or narrowness of Piedmont's kings, one might say that the house of Savoy came to unify Italy by default; it would be more accurate to say that the dynasty's mission was thrust upon it by Count Cavour and by those patriots from other parts of Italy who, with a realism born of the wreck of 1848, began to look to Piedmont. Cavour was an enlightened landowner, born in Turin in 1810, a younger son of a noble family. It is testimony to the recentness of Piedmont's Italian credentials that, throughout his life, Cavour preferred to speak and write in French and embarrassed his associates when he spoke Italian. An admirer of Bentham in his youth, a lifelong devotee of Adam Smith and of English politics, Cavour was antipathetic to the democratic republicanism of Mazzini. When he became premier in 1852 he found his allies in the Left Center, for as a rationalist in religion as well as in economics he could not ally himself with the clerical and reactionary Right, still strong in Piedmont. He had managed his own estates and speculations well and, as minister of finance, he had managed the kingdom's business well. He found ways of financing the war in 1848-1849, paid the Austrian indemnity, and built railways. Although his budgets were out of balance, he hoped to redress matters by long-range policies for modernizing the country. But, as a contemporary pointed out, he was a Machiavelli as well as a Peel. As prime minister he continued his reforming without excessive scruples. He remained a committed parliamentarian—the constitution Charles Albert had granted in 1848 remained the basis of Italian government for nearly a century—but when it seemed necessary Cavour managed elections, put down opposition newspapers, bribed, intrigued, and double-crossed. When England and France sought to bring Piedmont into the Crimean War to protect the Italian flank of their hoped-for ally Austria, Cavour gave in to the eagerness of his king Victor Emmanuel II, put the best possible face on it, and appeared at the peace conference in Paris as a spokesman for Italy. Having contributed little to the war, Piedmont got nothing concrete out of the settlement, but an English declaration that the condition of Italy was unsatisfactory was some reward for the gesture.

Skeptical about Italian unity, Cavour was not prepared to fight for it before its time had come. His first, far less nebulous goal was to drive out Austria, adding its holdings to a Piedmont stretching across the northern tier of the peninsula. The henchman he needed stood ready in the person of Napoleon III. After some preliminary soundings, the two men met secretly in July 1858 at Plombières, a watering-place in northeastern France, and agreed that the following spring a war with Austria would be provoked; an expanded Piedmont would then enter into an Italian confederation with the Two Sicilies, a reduced papal state, and a new kingdom in central Italy. In the formal treaty of alliance concluded in January 1859, France was promised the Piedmontese provinces of Nice and Savoy on France's southeastern frontier. Cavour set out quite blatantly to provoke the Austrians and, after some delay due to sudden hesitancy on Napoleon's part, the war began.

In June 1859 the French army defeated the Austrians at Magenta and Solferino. But Cavour was already intriguing in the central Italian states and in the states of the church, a sore point with the outspoken Catholics in France; there was, moreover, some possibility that Prussia might come to the aid of the Austrians. Napoleon therefore concluded a separate truce with the Austrians, at Villafranca in July. Beside himself with rage, Cavour urged his king to continue alone; when he did not prevail he resigned. Piedmont got the major part of Lombardy, but the Austrians kept the fortresses of the Quadrilateral and Venetia, and France did not get her price of Nice and Savoy. In January 1860 Cavour was back in office with other fish to fry. He covertly supported uprisings in the duchies of Parma, Modena, and Tuscany, and in the Romagna, the northernmost part of the papal states. Cavour then proposed that if Napoleon would agree to the annexation of these states by Piedmont, the offer of Nice and Savoy would be renewed. With the English on record in favor of self-determination, plebiscites were resorted to in all the territories and in each case produced the desired vote in favor of joining Piedmont. Cavour then planned to wait until another war could bring him Venetia; meanwhile, he proposed an alliance with Naples.

At this point his hand was forced by another extraordinary figure. Giuseppe Garibaldi was a soldier of fortune, born in Nice in 1807 and early infected by Mazzinian ideals. Exiled in 1834, he fought in South America, where he schooled himself in guerrilla tactics. In 1848 he offered his services to Piedmont, but his unorthodox methods were unwelcome, and he ended by conducting the military defense of the short-lived Roman republic (see p. 728). Forced once more to leave Italy, he went to the United States, but returned to Italy in 1854. He commanded a force of volunteers in the war of 1859, but was again disappointed at the minor role he was allotted. In May 1860, with Cavour blowing alternately hot and cold, Garibaldi led a thousand red-shirted volunteers—idealistic students and revolutionaries from Italy and a motley crew of adventurers—to Sicily to support an uprising against the Bourbons that had begun in April under Mazzinian auspices. Although the "Thousand" faced a professional army of twenty-five times that number, the defenders' incompetence and Garibaldi's clever tactics brought the invaders a quick victory. They took Palermo, the capital of Sicily, at the end of the month. Claiming to rule in the name of Victor Emmanuel, Garibaldi set himself up as dictator of the island, with Francesco Crispi—a former Mazzinian and a radical who would in time change his spots—as his civilian right-hand man. The stage was now set for a struggle between Garibaldi and Cavour.

Bluff and compelling, Garibaldi easily captured men's devotion. A brilliant general, he proved to be an innocent politician. He had broken with Mazzini and showed himself a monarchist; he had compromised his reputation for radicalism by defending order and the property-owning classes against the social revolution that threatened Sicily and Naples. He despised Cavour, whose twists and turns he could not comprehend (as no one could) and who had bargained away Nice, his birthplace. Cavour, so different in temperament and personality, was willing to use but not admire Garibaldi; having little comprehension of the south, he could not appreciate Garibaldi's essential moderation in governing that region, taking him too readily as a radical threat. But Cavour had a difficult balancing act to perform. Victor Emmanuel disliked him and was drawn to Garibaldi. The English were romantically sympathetic to the Sicilian exploit, fervently antipapal, and very much at odds with France; yet Cavour could not offend Napoleon III, whose forces were supporting the pope in Rome and who was increasingly concerned at the prospect of an overgrown Piedmont. So Cavour's policy shifted violently with circumstances. After some early, underhanded encouragement of the Sicilian expedition, he attempted, perhaps halfheartedly, to stop it; then he tried to annex the island, an act that Garibaldi turned to his own account by crossing the Straits of Messina early in September to chase out the last Bourbon king of the Two Sicilies, Francis II, and to establish his dictatorship in Naples. Cavour did not want the south to fall to Piedmont on Garibaldi's terms, and he had at all costs to keep the victorious general from marching on Rome. Having convinced Napoleon that preventive action was necessary, he sent the Piedmontese army through the papal states into the south. Plebiscites held in Naples, Sicily, and the papal territories of Umbria and the Marches in the autumn of 1860 were decisive for joining with Piedmont. Outmaneuvered, Garibaldi consented to ride through the streets of Naples with Victor Emmanuel early in November and then retired to his island of Caprera. On March 17, 1861, the kingdom of Italy was proclaimed.

In June Cavour died suddenly, at the age of fifty-one. No one in the unstable ministries that followed had the requisite authority or skill to deal with the terrible problems left by this almost accidental creation of a kingdom. Plebiscites to the contrary, the south was not reconciled to northern rule. The peasants, to whom the term Italy meant nothing, were in almost constant insurrection; their social demands, overlooked, grew more intense. The long-standing southern desire for autonomy was ruthlessly thrust aside in favor of centralized rule from distant Turin. [17] Differing laws and customs in the new

[17] That the kingdom was an extended Piedmont is indicated by the fact that the king remained Victor Emmanuel II, even though, as the first king of Italy, he should have been Victor Emmanuel I. One of his ancestors had said that he would eat territory like an artichoke, piece by piece; Victor Emmanuel showed a similar appetite.

territories had to be brought into line, and a severe financial problem had to be solved. And there remained the challenges of Venetia and Rome. In 1866, disregarding a last-minute Austrian offer of Venetia in exchange for Italian neutrality, Italy chose to ally with Prussia, only to be beaten by the Austrians both on land and, despite naval superiority, at sea. But Austria lost to Prussia and handed Venetia over to France, which in turn gave it to Italy. In the same year France evacuated Rome, having received guarantees that the capital would be moved from Turin to Florence, a tacit abandonment of the ambition of the more ardent nationalists to see the capital in Rome. The Garibaldian threat to Rome had been a constant embarrassment; he tried to seize it in 1867, an action that brought the French back to defeat him and send him into a peaceful and now lasting retirement. Only when the French forces were withdrawn to fight Prussia in 1870 did Italy at last take Rome—at the very time that papal infallibility was proclaimed (see p. 663).

In almost every sense the process of Italian unification had bypassed Mazzini. Although he returned to Italy secretly on several occasions, he watched events mostly from exile. He had reluctantly reconciled himself to a monarchy in place of the republic he had hoped for, but he could not stop the centralization he loathed, and Rome, to which he had devoted such energy, escaped almost to the last. He nowhere saw the regeneration he insisted was both precondition and result of a national movement; the Italy he did see seemed to him a living lie, a corpse. He died in 1872, in Italy, while hiding under an assumed name, a fugitive to the last. Though he got full measure of posthumous recognition, it was the boldness and calculation of Garibaldi and Cavour that made the peninsula into a kingdom, a kingdom that was barely a nation and not the Italy of many men's dreams.

Germany, Austria, and Europe

In Germany in the 1850s Hegel was at a discount, his philosophy having fallen prey to the bitter quarrels of his pupils and disciples. Most practicing philosophers were turning resolutely away from grand systems to concentrate on more specific, specialized inquiries (see p. 641). But those who could not free themselves from the need for metaphysical explanation found a new guide in Arthur Schopenhauer. By this time Schopenhauer was already an old man. He had studied under Fichte and for two unsuccessful years, from 1820 to 1822, had been Hegel's colleague and rival at Berlin; his complete rejection of Hegelian idealism, at a time when it was sweeping all before it, ensured a neglect that contributed to the pessimism and misanthropy increasingly dominant in his character. Schopenhauer's principal philosophical debts were to the English empiricists and to Kant. Yet, despite his skepticism about the possibility of metaphysics, Schopenhauer recognized that larger questions persistently outran the explanatory methods of science; seeking an answer that would escape Kant's strictures, he found it in the will—that potent driving force in each individual, predetermined by circumstances, discoverable by introspection. Will, he argued, is central not only to the individual but to explaining the world.

Schopenhauer's ideas appealed to a generation that had absorbed the romantic idiom and that was farther removed than were Hegel and his pupils from the eighteenth-century adulation of reason; indeed, Schopenhauer's emphasis on irrationality—and his later recognition of the importance of sexuality—gave him an especial importance for the development of psychology. While his doctrine of the will was seminal for much late nineteenth-century thought, his philosophy has a peculiar aptness for the decade that discovered him. In Germany as elsewhere it was a time of remarkable creativity, of will made manifest in scientific triumphs as in economic conquest, and Schopenhauer's deprecation of politics underlines the apolitical cast that was even more characteristic of Germany in the fifties than of France and Great Britain. [18]

In much of Germany, and not in Prussia alone, the middle decades of the century saw a marked increase in economic innovation and accomplishment: the railway network was substantially completed; investment banking in the form pioneered in France prospered; the textile industries grew rapidly in scale and production; and the iron industry, doubling its output in the fifties and again by the mid-sixties, made the Zollverein—those states linked in a customs union since 1834—virtually self-sufficient in that basic metal. In short, these years established the structural and technological base from which the amazing expansion of the German economy after 1871 could proceed. Emigration (a tiny part of it political, most of it in quest of economic and social betterment) eased the population pressure at home; the movement from country to town went on apace. Although Germany as a whole remained overwhelmingly agrarian, the balance of the Prussian population engaged in agriculture dropped by the end of the fifties from slightly more than half to slightly less than half. Prosperity continued in the sixties, despite preoccupations with war and politics and despite two serious economic downturns after 1857 and 1866, both indications of the degree to which Germany was becoming enmeshed in the international economy. But the prosperity was not shared equally, and the lack of cohesion among Germany's increasingly self-conscious classes kept the economic revolutions from being exploited to the fullest advantage. Most of the Junker nobility, though not averse to profitable investments in industry, disdained the newer, nonagricultural forms of enterprise. A bureaucracy indoctrinated with a legalistic approach lacked comprehension and sympathy; the cultivated and creative circles of the universities and professions held aloof from a world that reeked of materialism and felt threatened by the emerging proletariat. It would be hard to imagine German Saint-Simonians; a German Tennyson is inconceivable.

---

[18] Unlike most men of the fifties, however, Schopenhauer rejected the idea of progress. The symbolic and practical meshing of Schopenhauer's teaching with the post-1848 situation is argued by Hajo Holborn, *A History of Modern Germany*, vol. III, *1840-1945* (1969), 120-121.

The geographical and economic barriers to national unity were both more evident and easier to cope with, in a psychological sense, than were those more subtle and seemingly more natural divisions among classes or cultural groupings; hence, despite the disappointments and confusions of 1848, men turned with increasing conviction to the ideal of nationality, which seemed the precondition for the sense of community that evaded the Germans at every turn: "After all the large and capital cities are linked together by the railroad, Germany will be a completely different country," wrote one enthusiast, "and the prejudices which have so splintered the German people up to now, which have so facilitated the rule of its oppressors, will have ceased to exist." [19] What might not flow from an even grander, national unity?

Nationalists were far from agreement about means. The *grossdeutsch*—greater German—solution, looking to Austria for leadership (see p. 734), was understandably attractive to southern, Catholic Germany. But it became increasingly illusory in the aftermath of 1848: Austria's German supporters were ill organized and ill supported from Vienna; the effort to create a unitary Austrian kingdom absorbed east European lands by definition beyond the ambitions of *grossdeutsch* nationalists; the resurrected Germanic Confederation was feeble; and the gulf between Austria and Prussia had been papered over unconvincingly at Olmütz. Hence, even in the heartland of *grossdeutsch* sentiment, men began, however reluctantly, to overlook the costs of a *kleindeutsch*—little German—solution; as patriots in Italy gravitated to Piedmont as the answer to the national problem, so patriots in Germany conceded primacy to Prussia. One sees this shift in the increasingly nationalist emphasis of liberal historians like F. C. Dahlmann and J. G. Droysen and even more in the next generation, in the young historian Heinrich von Treitschke. Born in 1834 in Dresden, in the *grossdeutsch* country of Saxony, Treitschke had been deeply moved by Dahlmann's lectures at Bonn in the early fifties and found his convictions reinforced by the teachings of the nationalist economist Wilhelm Roscher at Leipzig. In his own fabulously successful academic and journalistic career, Treitschke arrived at a position that allowed an easy sacrifice of means to ends, once the ends were established as morally and aesthetically desirable. His hero was Cavour—saved for Treitschke, as perhaps for historians generally, by his early death from inevitable compromises with reality. Bismarck's long, pragmatic administration of the German Empire after 1871 often found Treitschke in disagreement, but in the course of unification in the sixties the historian stood solidly behind the statesman. Others, Treitschke confessed, might find Bismarck's intrigues puzzling and repugnant, but he himself was made of "rougher stuff"; Bismarck's manifestly reasonable and moral policies "aim at what we need, they want to take a step toward the great goal of German unity, and any real man must help." [20]

[19] Quoted in Robert M. Berdahl, "New Thoughts on German Nationalism," *American Historical Review*, 77 (February 1972), 79.

[20] Quoted in Andreas Dorpalen, *Heinrich von Treitschke* (1957), 101.

The same years that saw this broadening sweep of nationalist sentiment marked the beginning of a modern working-class movement. While the artisans and handicraftsmen who had carried the 1848 revolutions into the streets survived in numbers, their traditionalist solutions were becoming increasingly outmoded by new forms of production and by the rapid spread of liberal faith. The liberals were not entirely unsympathetic to their plight, which in some ways they assimilated to the social problem generally. One radical veteran of 1848, Hermann Schulze-Delitzsch, came forward to urge the formation of cooperatives and credit unions, and the movement he launched met with considerable success. But Schulze-Delitzsch, like the English Christian Socialists, offered little to the true proletariat who, unlike the artisans, had no property beyond their labor. Efforts to form unions and to strike were unsuccessful, as such tactics usually are in the early stages of labor's growth. But socialism, which had developed less impressively in Germany than in France or England prior to 1848, now began to take firm root and with a notable difference: it was in Germany that, for the first time, socialism clearly emerged as a political movement. The John the Baptist of this new departure was one of the most startling figures to emerge in the history of socialism, a history hardly lacking in colorful personalities.

Ferdinand Lassalle, the son of a wealthy Jewish textile merchant, was born in Breslau in 1825. As a student he had thrown himself into the study of philosophy and law, but he made his first reputation through a scandal. In 1846 he took up the cause of his friend (and possibly his mistress), Countess Sophie von Hatzfeld, in a particularly lurid divorce suit. He finally won the case in 1854; in the course of it he was tried and acquitted for arranging the theft of a strongbox the countess thought contained papers helpful to her case. In the midst of all this broke the events of 1848, during which Lassalle was active in the Communist League and thrown twice into prison. Unlike many other victims of repression, he remained in Germany, and in 1859 he published a verse drama on the Peasants' Revolt. Two years later appeared his principal statement in economic and social theory, *The System of Acquired Rights,* an openly socialist attack on inherited property. A man of action rather than a thinker, Lassalle borrowed freely from Hegel, Ricardo, Louis Blanc, and Karl Marx. But the early sympathy that Marx showed for his erratic disciple did not survive a meeting of the two men in 1862: their temperaments were perhaps even more at odds than their policies. Marx had been put off by the Hatzfeld scandal, and Lassalle's egoism was too much for him. Lassalle, Marx wrote to Engels, "turns out to be not only the greatest of scholars, the deepest of thinkers, and the most inspired researcher, but also Don Juan and Cardinal Richelieu." [21]

---

[21] Quoted in Elie Halévy, *Histoire du socialisme européen* (1948), 140n. There is no good English life of Lassalle, but he was the model on which the English novelist George Meredith drew his hero in *The Tragic Comedians* (1880).

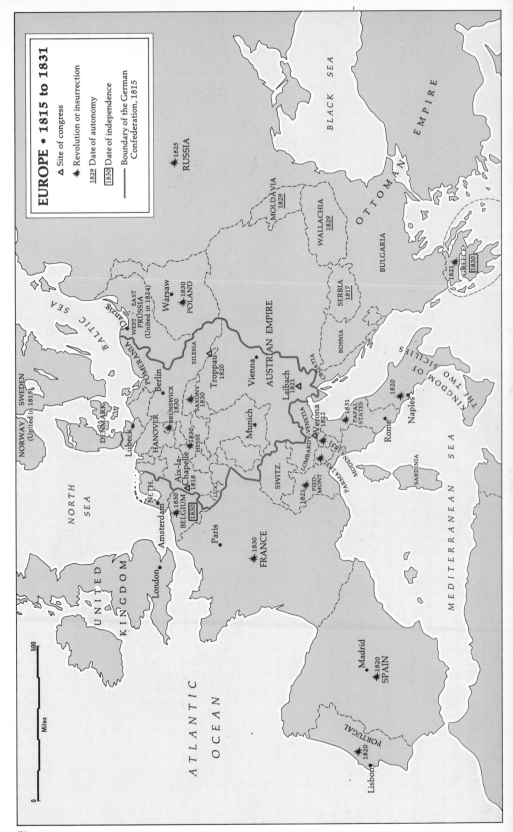

EUROPE · 1815 to 1831

△ Site of congress
✳ Revolution or insurrection
1829 Date of autonomy
[1830] Date of independence
—— Boundary of the German Confederation, 1815

BLACK SEA

OTTOMAN EMPIRE

✳ 1825 RUSSIA

MOLDAVIA 1829

WALLACHIA 1829

BULGARIA

BALTIC SEA

POMERANIA

WEST EAST PRUSSIA (United in 1824)

Danzig ✳ 1818

Warsaw 1830 POLAND

SERBIA 1817

BOSNIA

✳ 1821 GREECE [1830]

NORWAY SWEDEN (United in 1815)

DENMARK

Lübeck

HANOVER

Berlin

BRUNSWICK 1830

SAXONY 1830

SILESIA

Troppau △ 1820

Vienna AUSTRIAN EMPIRE

Laibach △ 1821

CROATIA

NORTH SEA

NETH.

Amsterdam

Aix-la-Chapelle △ 1818

1830 BELGIUM [1830]

LUX.

Munich

HESSE 1830

SWITZ.

PIED-MONT 1821

LOMBARDY-VENETIA

Verona △ 1822

PARMA 1831

MODENA 1831

1831 PAPAL STATES

Rome ●

1820 ✳ Naples

THE KINGDOM OF THE TWO SICILIES

SARDINIA

MEDITERRANEAN SEA

UNITED KINGDOM

London ●

Paris ●

✳ 1830 FRANCE

ATLANTIC OCEAN

500

Miles

0

Madrid ● ✳ 1820 SPAIN

PORTUGAL

✳ 1820 Lisbon ●

Plate 27

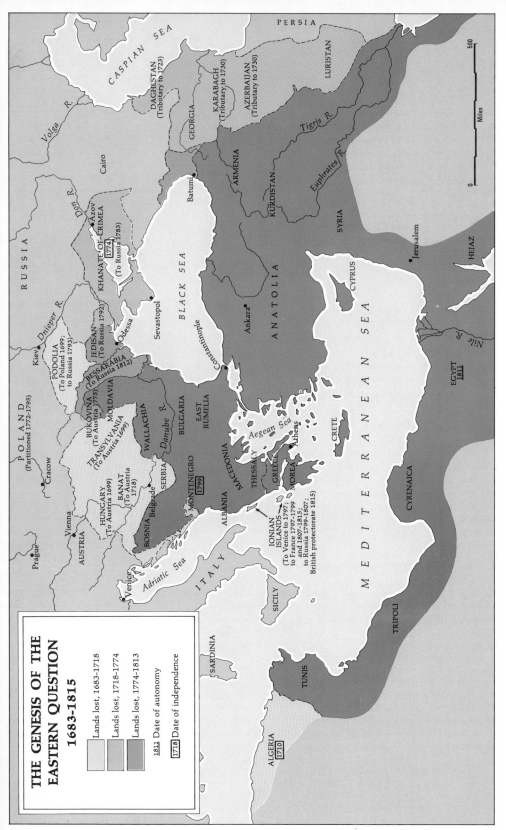

THE GENESIS OF THE
EASTERN QUESTION
1683-1815

Lands lost, 1683-1718
Lands lost, 1718-1774
Lands lost, 1774-1813

1811 Date of autonomy
1718 Date of independence

PERSIA

CASPIAN SEA

DAGHESTAN
(Tributary to 1723)

KARABACH
(Tributary to 1730)

AZERBAIJAN
(Tributary to 1730)

LURISTAN

GEORGIA

Volga R.

Cairo

Don R.

Azov

KHANATE OF CRIMEA
1774
(To Russia 1783)

ARMENIA

Tigris R.

KURDISTAN

Euphrates R.

RUSSIA

Batumi

SYRIA

Jerusalem

HEJAZ

Kiev

Dnieper R.

PODOLIA
(To Poland 1699;
to Russia 1793)

JEDISAN
(To Russia 1792)

Sevastopol

BLACK SEA

Odessa

Constantinople

Ankara

ANATOLIA

EGYPT
1811

Nile R.

POLAND
(Partitioned 1772-1795)

Cracow

BESSARABIA
(To Russia 1812)

BUKOVINA
(To Austria 1775)

MOLDAVIA

TRANSYLVANIA
(To Austria 1699)

Danube R.

WALLACHIA

BULGARIA

EAST
RUMELIA

CYPRUS

Aegean Sea

CRETE

MEDITERRANEAN SEA

Vienna

Prague

AUSTRIA

HUNGARY
(To Austria 1699)

BANAT
To Austria
1718

Belgrade

SERBIA

BOSNIA

MONTENEGRO
1799

MACEDONIA

THESSALY

GREECE

Athens

MOREA

CYRENAICA

Venice

Adriatic Sea

ITALY

ALBANIA

IONIAN
ISLANDS
(To Venice to 1797;
to France 1797-1799
and 1807-1815;
to Russia 1799-1807;
British protectorate 1815)

SICILY

TRIPOLI

SARDINIA

TUNIS

ALGERIA
1710

500

Miles

0

Plate 28

The Genesis of the Eastern Question · 1683-1815

The Ottoman failure to take Vienna in 1683 marked the beginning of a long drive to rid Europe of the Turk. The most active and successful of the European powers in the first half century of this effort was the Hapsburg Empire, assisted for a time by its allies Venice and Poland. Under Peter the Great, Russia also began to put pressure on the Ottoman Empire, with a view to reaching the warm waters of the Black Sea and so access to the Mediterranean.

By the Treaty of Carlowitz in 1699 an extensive Christian victory was registered. Venice gained footholds on the Adriatic coast and in the Greek-inhabited Peloponnesus, during the seizure of which (in 1687) the Parthenon was blown up. Poland, not very active in the war, got Podolia. Austria swept up the vast regions of Hungary and Transylvania. Russia got the coveted warm-water port of Azov, but lost it when Peter the Great suffered a defeat by the Turks in 1711.

While the Turks were recovering at Russia's expense, a new war with Austria brought further Christian gains. By the Treaty of Passarowitz in 1718 Austria got the last Turkish foothold in Hungary, the fortress of Belgrade, and parts of Serbia, Bosnia, and Wallachia; Venice kept the Ionian Islands but surrendered the Peloponnesus. The Austrians had overreached themselves, however, and in 1736 death deprived them of the incomparable generalship of Prince Eugene. They fought a war in support of Russia, but it was inconclusive. In the Treaty of Belgrade, which ended it in 1739, Austria gave up the conquests of 1718 other than the Banat. Austria's ally Russia, among other victories, had once more captured Azov, but by the parallel Treaty of Nissa was allowed to retain it only in an unfortified state. No Russian fleet could be maintained on the Black Sea, and Russian trade there could be carried on only in Turkish ships.

Under Catherine II Russia resumed its southward drive—alone—and by the Treaty of Kuchuk Kainarji of 1774 gained not only untrammeled possession of Azov and other Black Sea territories but secured the independence of the Khanate of Crimea, which was duly annexed by Russia in 1783. All that Austria gained was the small province of Bukovina in 1775—as compensation, to keep up with the Romanovs. In the latter years of the 1780s the joint war against the Ottoman Empire was resumed. The Austrians accomplished nothing and withdrew, while in the Treaty of Jassy in 1792 the Russians took more Black Sea territory extending to the River Dniester. In the Treaty of Bucharest, which ended another Russo-Turkish war in 1806-1812, they gained Bessarabia. The great commercial port of Odessa and the fortress of Sevastopol, founded toward the end of Catherine's reign, developed rapidly in the new century. Russia's control of the Black Sea was assured, and the question now was whether the Mediterranean would also be brought within the Russian orbit.

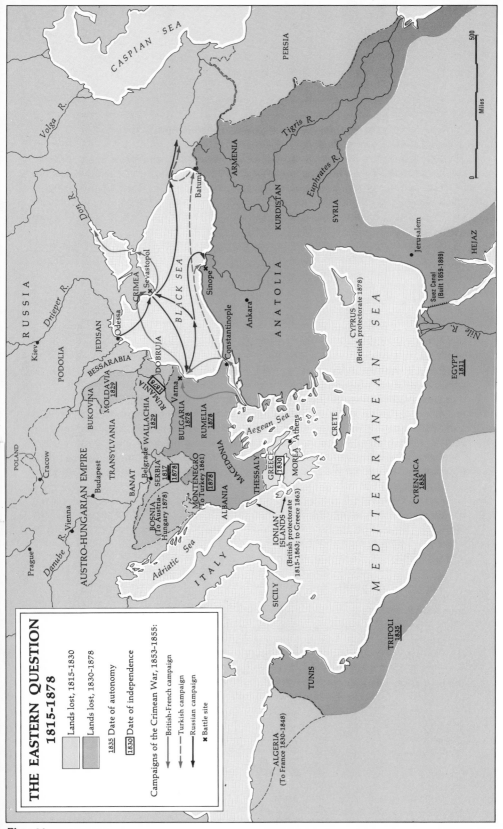

THE EASTERN QUESTION
1815–1878

Lands lost, 1815–1830

Lands lost, 1830–1878

<u>1835</u> Date of autonomy

<u>1830</u> Date of independence

Campaigns of the Crimean War, 1853–1855:

→ British-French campaign

→ Turkish campaign

→ Russian campaign

× Battle site

CASPIAN SEA

Volga R.

PERSIA

Don R.

ARMENIA

Tigris R.

Euphrates R.

KURDISTAN

Batum

SYRIA

HEJAZ

Jerusalem

Suez Canal
(Built 1859–1869)

CRIMEA
Sevastopol

BLACK SEA

Sinope

ANATOLIA

CYPRUS
(British protectorate 1878)

EGYPT
<u>1811</u>

RUSSIA

Kiev

Dnieper R.

PODOLIA

JEDISAN

Odessa

Ankara

Constantinople

Nile R.

POLAND

Cracow

BUKOVINA

BESSARABIA

MOLDAVIA
<u>1829</u>

DOBRUJA

WALLACHIA
<u>1829</u>

RUMANIA
1878

Varna

BULGARIA
1878

RUMELIA
1878

Aegean Sea

CRETE

MEDITERRANEAN SEA

TRANSYLVANIA

AUSTRO-HUNGARIAN EMPIRE

Budapest

BANAT

Belgrade

SERBIA
<u>1817</u>
1878

MACEDONIA

THESSALY

GREECE
<u>1830</u>

MOREA

Athens

CYRENAICA
<u>1835</u>

Vienna

Danube R.

Prague

BOSNIA
(To Austria-
Hungary 1878)

MONTENEGRO
(To Turkey 1861)
1878

ALBANIA

IONIAN
ISLANDS
(British protectorate
1815–1863; to Greece 1863)

Adriatic
Sea

ITALY

SICILY

TUNIS

TRIPOLI
<u>1835</u>

ALGERIA
(To France 1830–1848)

500

0

Miles

Plate 29

The Eastern Question · 1815–1878

In the nineteenth-century phase of the Eastern Question neither Austria nor Russia nor the Western powers gained large blocks of territory. The central issues had become the disintegration of the Ottoman Empire from within and the gradual emergence of the modern Balkan states. In Ottoman Europe the Serbs attained a kind of autonomy over the years from 1804 to 1817, and the successful Greek revolt in the 1820s attracted the attention and sentiment of all Europe. Another Russo-Turkish war in 1828, ending the next year with the Treaty of Adrianople, gave Russia no more than control over the mouths of the Danube, but the Turks confirmed the autonomy of Serbia, agreed to a Russian protectorate over the principalities of Moldavia and Wallachia (though both remained under Ottoman suzerainty), and conceded the autonomy of Greece. In 1830 the European powers carried matters a step further by recognizing Greek independence. In a parallel war Russia had annexed Georgia and Eastern Armenia as well as the territory occupied by the Circassians, important additions recognized by the Ottoman Empire at Adrianople.

In the thirties the sultan and Mehemet Ali, pasha of Egypt, fell out over the Egyptian seizure of Syria. The Ottoman response was the Treaty of Unkiar-Skelessi with Russia in 1833. The treaty bound the two countries to consult about matters affecting their peace and security, and also contained a secret provision that, in case Russia went to war, the Turks would close the Dardanelles, the western strait separating their European and Asiatic domains, to all foreign warships. A general settlement in 1841 gave Mehemet Ali hereditary rule of Egypt on condition that he evacuate Syria, already rebellious under the rule of his son Ibraham. The Treaty of Unkiar-Skelessi was superseded by what came to be known as the Straits Convention, which provided that the Dardanelles and the Bosporus would be closed to all warships when Turkey was at peace, thus denying the Russian Black Sea fleet access to the Mediterranean.

The Crimean War of 1854–1856 reflected the growing distrust of Russia among the Western powers. Undesired, ineptly fought, and futile, the war changed nothing in the territorial arrangements of the belligerents, other than depriving Russia of its hold over the mouths of the Danube in southern Bessarabia. Two incidental provisions of the Treaty of Paris of 1856 were especially important. Moldavia and Wallachia were confirmed as autonomous and the protectorate that Russia had exercised over them was dissolved; in 1858–1862 they came together as Rumania. Second, the Black Sea was neutralized, thus preventing even the Russians and the Turks from maintaining warships or fortifications there. In 1870, at the time of the Franco-Prussian War, Russia denounced these military and naval restrictions, and a conference of the European powers the next year lamely ratified the unilateral Russian action.

Turkish massacres among the rebellious Bulgars in 1876 led to public outcry in Britain, and the general Balkan unrest provoked a new Russo-Turkish war the next year. The Russian victory registered in the Treaty of San Stefano was revised at the Berlin Congress in 1878. Russia's ambition to create a big Bulgaria—as a Slavic-speaking people the Bulgars could be expected to follow the Russian lead—was thwarted, but Bulgarian autonomy was secured (with additional territory acquired in 1885). Serbian, Rumanian, and Montenegrin independence was formally recognized. The British gained a protectorate over the eastern Mediterranean island of Cyprus, important for British strategic interest in the Suez route to India, as was Egypt, which the British occupied in 1882. Austria-Hungary occupied and administered Bosnia, which, though still nominally under Turkish suzerainty, was coveted by the Serbs.

UNIFICATION OF GERMANY
1864–1871

Prussia before 1866

Acquired by Prussia or joined North German Confederation, 1866–1867

Incorporated in German Empire, 1871

— — — Boundary of the German Confederation, 1815

———— Boundary of the German Empire, 1871

Plate 30

FRANCE
GERMANY
SWITZERLAND
AUSTRO-HUNGARIAN EMPIRE

0   100   200
Miles

SAVOY (To France 1860)
SOUTH TYROL
LOMBARDY 1859
VENETIA 1866
Magenta ×
Peschiera □ Verona
●Milan
Solferino ×
Legnago □ ●Venice
Mantua □
PIEDMONT
DUCHY OF PARMA 1860
DUCHY OF MODENA 1860
Po R.
FRANCE
Genoa ●
●Bologna
OTTOMAN EMPIRE
NICE (To France 1860)
LUCCA (To Tuscany 1847)
Florence ●
GRAND DUCHY OF TUSCANY 1860
PAPAL STATES 1860

A D R I A T I C   S E A

CORSICA (To France)

Tiber R.
ROME 1870
●Rome

CAMPANIA
Naples ●

T Y R R H E N I A N
SEA

SARDINIA (To Piedmont)

K I N G D O M   O F   T H E   T W O   S I C I L I E S 1860

UNIFICATION OF ITALY
1815-1870

Kingdom of Sardinia at the time of the Congress of Vienna, 1815

Territory acquired, 1859-1860

Territory acquired, 1860-1870

1859 Date of annexation

Boundary of Italy, 1870

× Battle site

□ Austrian quadrilateral fortress

SICILY

M E D I T E R R A N E A N   S E A

MALTA (To Britain 1814)

Plate 31

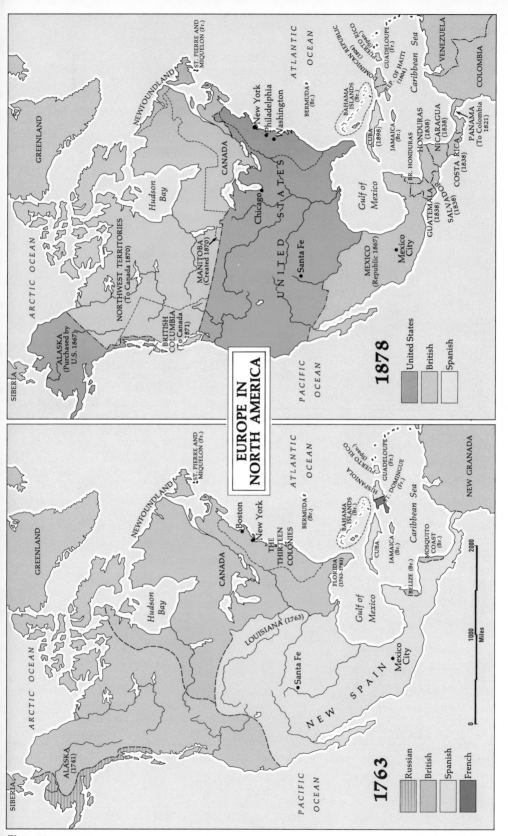

EUROPE IN NORTH AMERICA

1878

United States
British
Spanish

ARCTIC OCEAN

SIBERIA

ALASKA (Purchased by U.S. 1867)

BRITISH COLUMBIA (To Canada 1871)

NORTHWEST TERRITORIES (To Canada 1870)

MANITOBA (Created 1870)

GREENLAND

NEWFOUNDLAND

CANADA

Hudson Bay

ST. PIERRE AND MIQUELON (Fr.)

UNITED STATES

Chicago

Santa Fe

New York
Philadelphia
Washington

PACIFIC OCEAN

ATLANTIC OCEAN

BERMUDA (Br.)

BAHAMA ISLANDS (Br.)

CUBA (1898)

JAMAICA (Br.)

BR. HONDURAS

GUATEMALA (1838)

SALVADOR (1838)

HONDURAS (1838)

NICARAGUA (1838)

COSTA RICA (1838)

PANAMA (To Colombia 1821)

DOMINICAN REPUBLIC (1844)

PUERTO RICO (Span.)

GUADELOUPE (Fr.)

REP. OF HAITI (1804)

Caribbean Sea

VENEZUELA

COLOMBIA

Gulf of Mexico

MEXICO (Republic 1867)

Mexico City

1763

Russian
British
Spanish
French

ARCTIC OCEAN

SIBERIA

ALASKA (1741)

GREENLAND

NEWFOUNDLAND

CANADA

Hudson Bay

ST. PIERRE AND MIQUELON (Fr.)

THE THIRTEEN COLONIES

Boston
New York

LOUISIANA (1763)

Santa Fe

NEW SPAIN

Mexico City

FLORIDA (1763-1783)

PACIFIC OCEAN

ATLANTIC OCEAN

BERMUDA (Br.)

BAHAMA ISLANDS (Br.)

CUBA

BELIZE (Br.)

JAMAICA (Br.)

MOSQUITO COAST (Br.)

HISPANIOLA

ST. DOMINGUE (Fr.)

PUERTO RICO (Span.)

GUADELOUPE (Fr.)

Caribbean Sea

Gulf of Mexico

NEW GRANADA

0   1000   2000
Miles

Plate 32

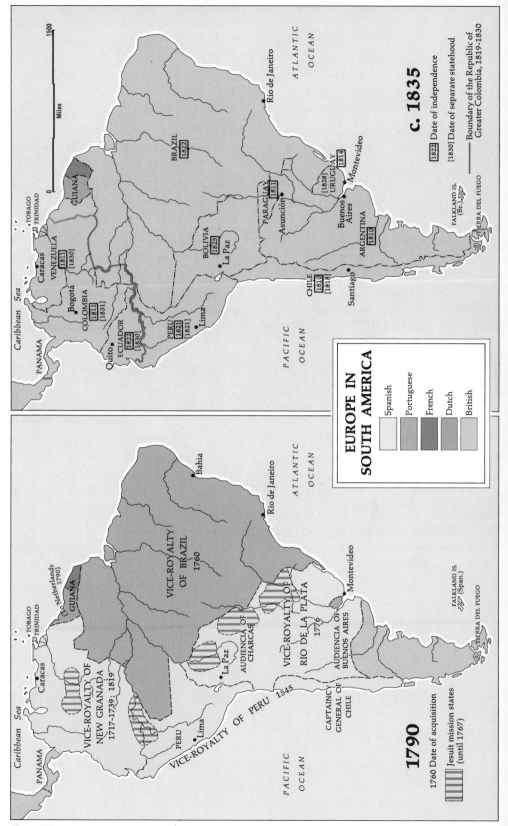

c. 1835

1822 Date of independence
[1830] Date of separate statehood
—— Boundary of the Republic of Greater Colombia, 1819–1830

Caribbean Sea

PANAMA
TOBAGO
TRINIDAD
Caracas
VENEZUELA 1811 [1830]
Bogotá
COLOMBIA 1811 [1831]
Quito
ECUADOR 1822 [1830]
GUIANA
PERU 1821 [1821]
Lima
BOLIVIA 1825
La Paz
BRAZIL 1822
PARAGUAY 1811
Asunción
CHILE 1810 [1818]
Santiago
ARGENTINA 1810
Buenos Aires
URUGUAY 1828 [1814]
Montevideo
Rio de Janeiro
ATLANTIC OCEAN
PACIFIC OCEAN
FALKLAND IS. (Br.)
TIERRA DEL FUEGO

Miles
0   1500

EUROPE IN SOUTH AMERICA

Spanish
Portuguese
French
Dutch
British

1790

1760 Date of acquisition
Jesuit mission states (until 1767)

Caribbean Sea

PANAMA
TOBAGO
TRINIDAD
Caracas
GUIANA (to Netherlands 1790)
VICE-ROYALTY OF NEW GRANADA 1717–1739; 1819
PERU
Lima
VICE-ROYALTY OF PERU 1545
AUDIENCIA OF CHARCAS
La Paz
VICE-ROYALTY OF BRAZIL 1760
Bahia
Rio de Janeiro
CAPTAINCY GENERAL OF CHILE
VICE-ROYALTY OF RIO DE LA PLATA 1776
AUDIENCIA OF BUENOS AIRES
Montevideo
ATLANTIC OCEAN
PACIFIC OCEAN
FALKLAND IS. (Span.)
TIERRA DEL FUEGO

Plate 33

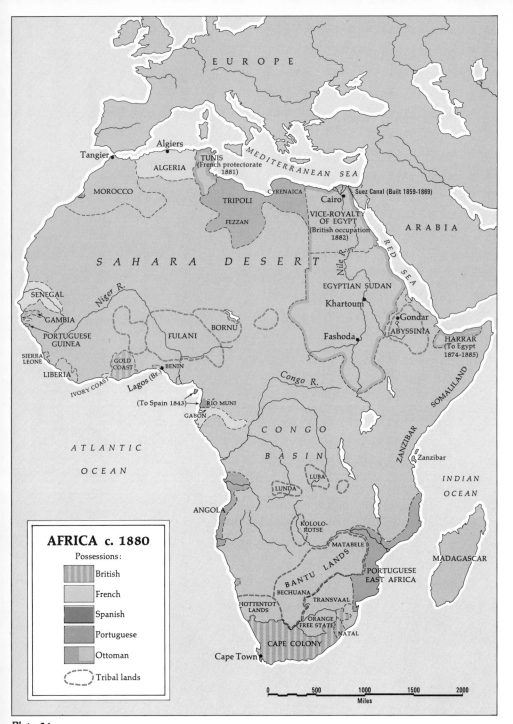

AFRICA c. 1880

Possessions:

British

French

Spanish

Portuguese

Ottoman

Tribal lands

EUROPE

MEDITERRANEAN SEA

Tangier

Algiers

ALGERIA

TUNIS
(French protectorate
1881)

MOROCCO

TRIPOLI

CYRENAICA

Cairo

Suez Canal (Built 1859-1869)

FEZZAN

VICE-ROYALTY
OF EGYPT
(British occupation
1882)

ARABIA

SAHARA DESERT

Nile R.

RED SEA

SENEGAL

Niger R.

EGYPTIAN SUDAN

GAMBIA

Khartoum

Gondar

PORTUGUESE
GUINEA

FULANI

BORNU

Fashoda

ABYSSINIA

HARRAR
(To Egypt
1874-1885)

SIERRA
LEONE

LIBERIA

GOLD
COAST

BENIN

IVORY COAST

Lagos (Br.)

(To Spain 1843)

RIO MUNI

GABON

Congo R.

SOMALILAND

ATLANTIC

OCEAN

CONGO

BASIN

ZANZIBAR

Zanzibar

INDIAN

OCEAN

LUBA

LUNDA

ANGOLA

KOLOLO-
ROTSE

MADAGASCAR

MATABELE

BANTU LANDS

PORTUGUESE
EAST AFRICA

BECHUANA

TRANSVAAL

HOTTENTOT
LANDS

ORANGE
FREE STATE

NATAL

CAPE COLONY

Cape Town

0   500   1000   1500   2000
Miles

Plate 34

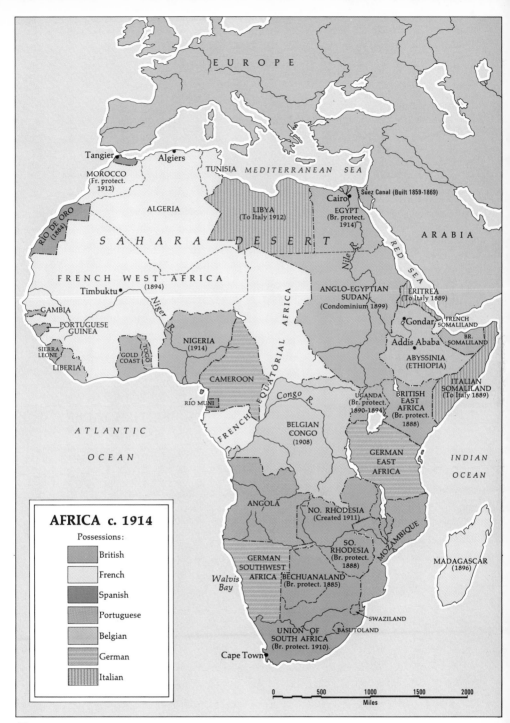

AFRICA c. 1914

Possessions:

- British
- French
- Spanish
- Portuguese
- Belgian
- German
- Italian

EUROPE

Tangier
Algiers
TUNISIA *MEDITERRANEAN SEA*
MOROCCO
(Fr. protect.
1912)
ALGERIA
LIBYA
(To Italy 1912)
Cairo
Suez Canal (Built 1859-1869)
EGYPT
(Br. protect.
1914)
ARABIA
RÍO DE ORO
(1884)
S A H A R A   D E S E R T
Nile
RED SEA
FRENCH WEST AFRICA
(1894)
Timbuktu
ANGLO-EGYPTIAN
SUDAN
(Condominium 1899)
ERITREA
(To Italy 1889)
GAMBIA
Niger R.
FRENCH
SOMALILAND
Gondar
PORTUGUESE
GUINEA
FRENCH EQUATORIAL AFRICA
Addis Ababa
BR.
SOMALILAND
SIERRA
LEONE
NIGERIA
(1914)
ABYSSINIA
(ETHIOPIA)
GOLD
COAST
TOGO
ITALIAN
SOMALILAND
(To Italy 1889)
LIBERIA
CAMEROON
UGANDA
(Br. protect.
1890-1894)
BRITISH
EAST
AFRICA
(Br. protect.
1888)
RÍO MUNI
Congo R.
BELGIAN
CONGO
(1908)
A T L A N T I C
O C E A N
GERMAN
EAST
AFRICA
I N D I A N
O C E A N
ANGOLA
NO. RHODESIA
(Created 1911)
SO.
RHODESIA
(Br. protect.
1888)
MOZAMBIQUE
MADAGASCAR
(1896)
GERMAN
SOUTHWEST
AFRICA
Walvis
Bay
BECHUANALAND
(Br. protect. 1885)
SWAZILAND
BASUTOLAND
UNION OF
SOUTH AFRICA
(Br. protect. 1910)
Cape Town

| 0 | 500 | 1000 | 1500 | 2000 |
Miles

Plate 35

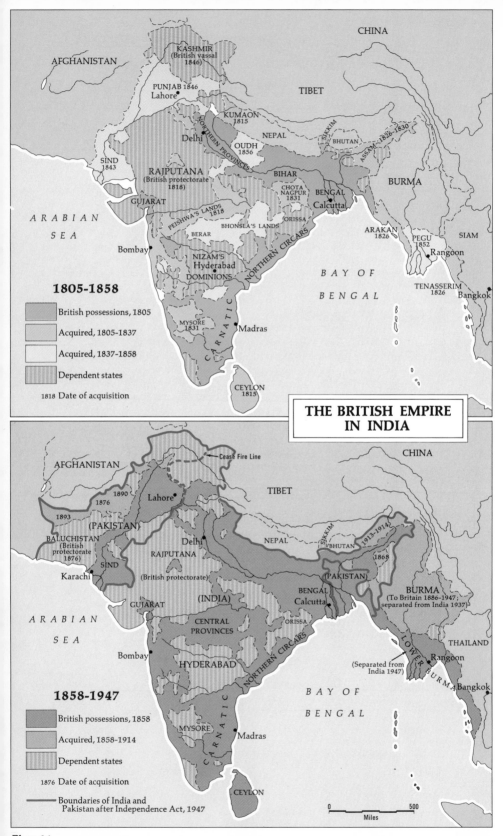

THE BRITISH EMPIRE IN INDIA

1805–1858

- British possessions, 1805
- Acquired, 1805–1837
- Acquired, 1837–1858
- Dependent states

1818 Date of acquisition

AFGHANISTAN
CHINA
KASHMIR (British vassal 1846)
PUNJAB 1846
Lahore
TIBET
KUMAON 1815
Delhi
NEPAL
OUDH 1856
SIKKIM
BHUTAN
ASSAM 1826–1830
SIND 1843
NORTHERN PROVINCES
RAJPUTANA (British protectorate 1818)
BIHAR
BURMA
GUJARAT
CHOTA NAGPUR 1831
BENGAL
Calcutta
PEISHWA'S LANDS 1818
BHONSLA'S LANDS
ORISSA
ARABIAN SEA
BERAR
NORTHERN CIRCARS
ARAKAN 1826
PEGU 1852
Rangoon
SIAM
Bombay
NIZAM'S Hyderabad
DOMINIONS
BAY OF BENGAL
TENASSERIM 1826
Bangkok
MYSORE 1831
Madras
CARNATIC
CEYLON 1815

1858–1947

- British possessions, 1858
- Acquired, 1858–1914
- Dependent states

1876 Date of acquisition

—— Boundaries of India and Pakistan after Independence Act, 1947

AFGHANISTAN
Cease Fire Line
CHINA
1890
1876
Lahore
TIBET
1893
(PAKISTAN)
BALUCHISTAN (British protectorate 1876)
Delhi
NEPAL
SIKKIM
BHUTAN
1913–1914
SIND
RAJPUTANA
1868
Karachi
(British protectorate)
(PAKISTAN)
GUJARAT
(INDIA)
BENGAL
Calcutta
BURMA (To Britain 1886–1947; separated from India 1937)
ARABIAN SEA
CENTRAL PROVINCES
ORISSA
NORTHERN CIRCARS
THAILAND
Bombay
HYDERABAD
LOWER BURMA
(Separated from India 1947)
Rangoon
BAY OF BENGAL
Bangkok
MYSORE
Madras
CARNATIC
CEYLON

0   500
Miles

Plate 36

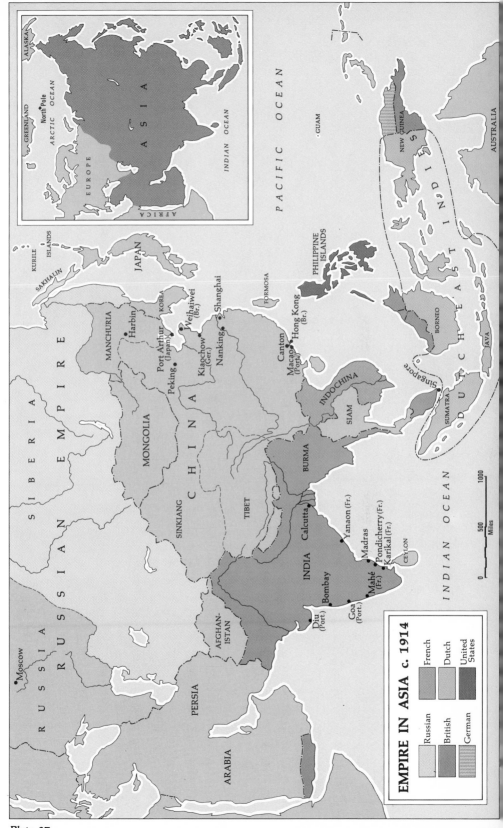

EMPIRE IN ASIA c. 1914

Russian
British
German
French
Dutch
United States

Plate 37

SCANDINAVIA

—·—·—·—1914 boundary

ARCTIC OCEAN

Narvik

ATLANTIC
OCEAN

WHITE
SEA

RUSSIA

GULF OF BOTHNIA

FINLAND
(United with Sweden
1523-1809; united with
Russia 1809-1917;
independent 1918)

NORWAY
(United with Denmark
1380-1814; united with
Sweden 1815-1904;
independent 1905)

SWEDEN

Vasa

Bergen

Christiana
(Oslo)

ÅLAND
ISLANDS

Helsingfors
(Helsinki)

Lake
Ladoga

St. Petersburg
(Leningrad 1924)

GULF OF FINLAND

Stockholm

Göteborg

GOTLAND

BALTIC SEA

Riga

ÖLAND

LITHUANIA

DENMARK

Copenhagen

Malmö

SCHLESWIG
(Denmark
to Germany
1864)

HOLSTEIN

Lübeck

Hamburg

Danzig

R U S S I A

Berlin

Warsaw

GERMANY

POLAND

AUSTRIA-HUNGARY

0   300
Miles

Plate 38

Scandinavia

No longer major powers, the Scandinavian kingdoms at the end of the eighteenth century were characterized by a growing prosperity and enlightened absolutism in government. Both in Denmark and its appendage, the once-independent kingdom of Norway, and in Sweden and its eastern territory of Finland, the abolition of serfdom provided insulation against revolutionary tremors after 1789. But the economic and strategic importance of the two states inexorably drew them into the Napoleonic Wars, despite an effort to renew the "armed neutrality" to which the Scandinavian states had belonged during the war of the American Revolution. Denmark's inclination to a French alliance brought two British bombardments of Copenhagen, in 1801 and 1807, and the loss of Norway in 1814. Sweden, which generally favored the allies, tried to buy security by choosing one of Napoleon's marshals, Jean Baptiste Jules Bernadotte, as crown prince; in 1818 Bernadotte was to become king as Charles XIV. Sweden's show of independence in allowing secret trading with Britain during the war had led to the French seizure of Swedish Pomerania, Sweden's last continental foothold, which by a series of complex diplomatic transactions came into Prussian hands in 1815. Sweden gave up Finland to Russia, which ruled its new possession as a quasi-independent grand duchy, and in compensation Sweden received Norway.

In the mid-nineteeneth century Denmark became embroiled in European diplomacy because of the cupidity felt by German nationalists toward the two German-inhabited Danish provinces of Schleswig and Holstein (see p. 735); the Danish war of 1864 detached these regions and gave them to Prussia. Otherwise, it was a century of growing prosperity and of gradually increasing liberalism. By the early twentieth century constitutional regimes were firmly established in both Sweden and Denmark, with universal suffrage (including women's suffrage in Norway as early as 1907) and a wide range of social services. Norway had attained a degree of autonomy from Denmark in 1807, and its constitution survived the union with Sweden in 1814. Nationalist sentiment grew, however, and in 1905, after a marked agitation, Norwegians declared their independence and were recognized by Sweden.

At the end of World War I, during which the three independent Scandinavian countries remained neutral, Finland won its separation from Russia, though a civil war followed between the Communist "Reds" and the conservative "Whites," with victory going to the latter under Baron Mannerheim. In World War II only Sweden managed to remain neutral. Denmark and Norway were occupied in 1940 by the Nazis, and earlier in the same year Finland had been subdued by Russia, after a valiant defense, in the "Winter War," which ended in the cession of strategic border territories to the Soviet Union; subsequently Finland was involved, in a somewhat ambiguous way, on the side of Germany. The wars proved no more than interruptions in the liberal evolution of the four states, though Finland has had to do a skillful job of tightrope walking in its relations with the Soviet Union.

Despite their small size, all four countries have made notable contributions to European culture, as the names of Kierkegaard, Ibsen, Strindberg, Munch, Grieg, and Sibelius attest. They have also contributed heavily to the peopling of North America. Their most remarkable twentieth-century cultural contribution, however, lies in architecture, urban planning, and the arts of interior design—testimony to the diffusion of prosperity and education and to the dividends that follow from a balanced and progressive political structure combined with relative insulation from the pressures and problems of the larger world.

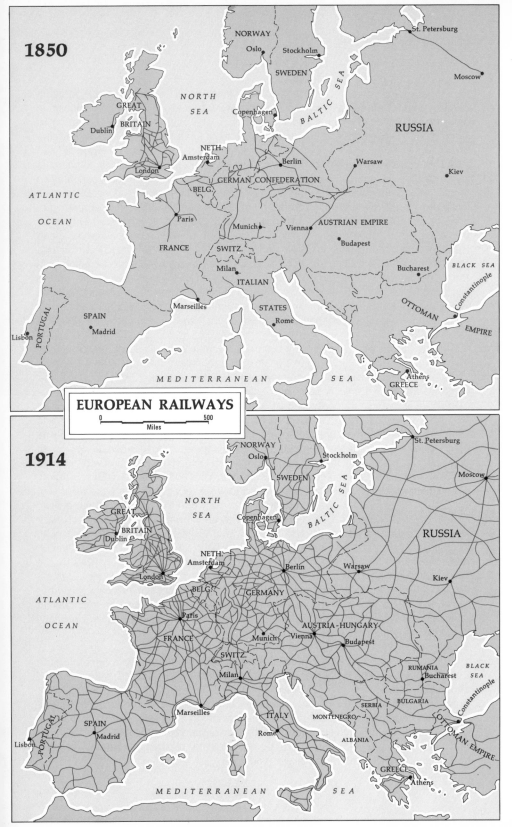

1850

NORWAY
Oslo
Stockholm
SWEDEN
St. Petersburg
Moscow

NORTH
SEA
BALTIC SEA
RUSSIA

GREAT
BRITAIN
Dublin
London

NETH.
Amsterdam
Berlin
GERMAN CONFEDERATION
Warsaw
Kiev

Copenhagen

BELG.

ATLANTIC
OCEAN

Paris
Munich
Vienna
AUSTRIAN EMPIRE
FRANCE
SWITZ.
Budapest

Milan
ITALIAN
Bucharest
BLACK SEA

Marseilles
STATES
Rome

PORTUGAL
SPAIN
Madrid
OTTOMAN
Constantinople

Lisbon

EMPIRE

MEDITERRANEAN
SEA
Athens
GREECE

EUROPEAN RAILWAYS

0   500
Miles

1914

NORWAY
Oslo
Stockholm
SWEDEN
St. Petersburg
Moscow

NORTH
SEA
BALTIC SEA
RUSSIA

GREAT
BRITAIN
Dublin
London

Copenhagen

NETH.
Amsterdam
Berlin
GERMANY
Warsaw
Kiev

BELG.

ATLANTIC
OCEAN

Paris
Munich
Vienna
AUSTRIA-HUNGARY
FRANCE
SWITZ.
Budapest

Milan
RUMANIA
Bucharest
BLACK SEA

Marseilles
SERBIA
BULGARIA
MONTENEGRO
ITALY
Rome
ALBANIA
OTTOMAN EMPIRE
Constantinople

PORTUGAL
SPAIN
Madrid

Lisbon

GREECE
Athens

MEDITERRANEAN
SEA

Plate 39

In 1863 Lassalle turned popular agitator and launched an assault on the middle classes and on Schulze-Delitzsch in particular. Cooperatives and credit unions, he argued, might lower prices but were ultimately futile, for in time they would encounter the "iron law of wages"—a term he coined for an idea lifted from Ricardo. As wages rise, so population rises, reducing real wages once again to the subsistence level. Lassalle did not reject the cooperative idea, but believed that it could work only when the economy was dominated by large units owned by the workers; then the iron law would be broken and the social problem solved. This transformation was to be accomplished by a workers' party whose political power would be irresistible. In 1863 Lassalle founded the first socialist party, the Allgemeiner Deutscher Arbeiterverein—the General German Workingmen's Society—though it numbered only a few thousand members instead of the million he had hoped for. But while he rejected the assistance of the middle classes, Lassalle tried to get the state to support the socialist transformation. In 1863–1864 he was regularly in touch with Bismarck, who at that point was willing to contemplate the possibility of bringing the working classes into the balance against the middle classes he was fighting in parliament. Lassalle was, moreover, a fervent nationalist, exulting over the unification of Italy, hoping for a similar feat in Germany, and (much to Marx's annoyance) even allowing himself a qualified admiration of Napoleon III. The result of this original and fascinating course was never to be known. In 1864 Lassalle fell passionately in love with a beautiful young woman; he was killed, at the age of thirty-nine, in a duel with his rival for her affections. With somewhat uncharacteristic generosity, Marx wrote that Lassalle had died young, "in triumph, like Achilles."

Prussia was governed after 1848 in the Junker interest—not from mere selfishness, but from high-minded if narrow principle. Baron Otto von Manteuffel, prime minister from 1850 to 1858, provided a consistent, firm control that more or less realized the ambitions of the *Kreuzzeitung* group. The repressive machinery of the state was kept in good repair and constant activity by Count Ferdinand von Westphalen, the minister of the interior—and Karl Marx's brother-in-law. The Kamarilla, that intensely conservative circle of the king's closest friends, applauded the reactionary moves of the ministry, but they also kept Frederick William IV from indulging his wilder absolutist fantasies and so the constitution and the parliament survived. These victories of the Right bred a moderate liberal opposition, however. It was led by Moritz August von Bethmann-Hollweg, who found some sympathy among members of the court, particularly from the wife of the king's brother, Prince William, and from William's son and his wife, who was a daughter of Queen Victoria. Like the *Kreuzzeitung* party, this liberal opposition came to be known from the name of its newspaper, the *Berliner Wochenblatt*—the Berlin Weekly: it was the *Wochenblatt* party.

In October 1857 Frederick William IV became mentally and physically incapacitated. His brother William, already sixty years of age, ruled in his place and a year later was made regent. With his new powers William turned out the Manteuffel government, which he despised, and brought in a group of ministers from the *Wochenblatt* party. To the small but growing band of liberals in the country the change was hailed as opening a "new era," and, despite the handicap of the three-class franchise (see p. 737) and pitifully small voter participation in elections, the first fruits were extensive liberal victories in the elections for the Landtag—the lower house of the legislature. The prince regent, as absolutist in temper as any Hohenzollern, began to wonder what he had wrought.

William's principal interest lay in reforming the army, in which he had spent his career. His chief advisers were General Edwin von Manteuffel, who as chief of the military cabinet had direct access to the sovereign, and General Albrecht von Roon, whom the regent named minister of war in 1859. The intention of the reformers was to create a thoroughly professional army. To that end they proposed to downgrade the Landwehr, the militia that had been created in the Napoleonic period precisely to form a link between army and people. The Landwehr was popular, but from the professionals' point of view it was ill disciplined, indifferently trained and officered, and too bound in its outlook to civilian life and local interests. The regular army was consequently to be enlarged and recruited for three years rather than the two that had become customary. All this would cost much more money.

Early in 1860 the government introduced an army bill, but it quickly became clear that the Landtag would not accept the proposals undiluted and that it particularly objected to the cost. Rather than compromise, Roon and the regent withdrew the bill and proposed a provisional army budget, which the parliament unwisely passed on the assurance from another minister that passage would not foreclose future reorganization and that none of the funds so appropriated would go to support the new army units already being created under the royal prerogative. The regent thereupon went on to establish the new units without parliamentary authorization. This show of contempt helped to shift the liberals sharply to the left, and in the elections in December 1861 the new Progressive party—Deutsche Fortschrittpartei, or DFP—emerged as the strongest party in the Landtag. It was committed to the maintenance of a two-year period of service and to detailed parliamentary supervision of the military budget. In May 1862 Progressive strength increased still further. While for some time the extreme reactionaries had been contemplating the possibility of a coup d'etat, others, Roon among them, sought a compromise, agreeing to the two-year term in exchange for funds to carry through the other reforms. But William I—as he was known after the death of Frederick William IV in January 1861—insisted on retaining the three-year term and, by threatening to abdicate, forced Roon to go back on the compromise he had negotiated. The parliament thereupon rejected the budget. Clearly the king's goal could be won only by the boldest moves, and it was on Roon's advice that on September 22,

1862, William I asked Otto von Bismarck to head his government. The move turned out to be even bolder than the king had anticipated. A week later Bismarck told a committee of the Landtag that the great questions of the time would be decided not by speeches and votes, "but by blood and iron."

Otto von Bismarck was born on April 1, 1815, the son of an East Prussian Junker; his mother—the daughter of a civil servant—came from a long line of academics. He was given an excellent education, but at the universities of Göttingen and Berlin in the thirties he absorbed little—except perhaps a lasting contempt for professors and professional intellectuals—and threw himself with wild abandon into student revelry and mischief. In 1838–1839 he spent a short time in the civil service, but fled from the subordination and discipline; most of the next eight years he spent on the family estates in East Prussia, where his reputation for wildness diminished not at all. He was fluent in French and English and widely read, preferring Byron and Shakespeare; he was a charming conversationalist. But whatever his cultivation and civility, the abiding impression is of violence scarcely controlled, of titanic energy, of dark brooding, of resolute determination to exercise power by gambling for the highest stakes. Bismarck was physically imposing, a naturally big man whose enormous appetite made him almost grotesque in later life. He flew into rages. When he was asked if he was really the "iron chancellor," he answered, "Far from it. I am all nerves, so much so that self-control has always been the greatest task of my life and still is." At another time he said, "Faust complains of having two souls in his breast. I have a whole squabbling crowd. It goes on as in a republic." [22] Yet, withal, he was devout, having undergone a conversion in the circle in which he met his future wife, Johanna, whom he married in 1847. He seldom attended church, but prayed daily, and the pietist tradition that had been revived in early nineteenth-century Germany gave him for the rest of his life a deep belief in God's majesty and providence. But Bismarck's actions were not dictated by God's voice; they grew from the demands of his own nature.

Bismarck emerged from his rural retirement as a delegate to the United Diet in 1847 (see p. 710), where he won a fearsome reputation as a sarcastic debater and the most extreme of conservatives. He became intimate with members of the Kamarilla and the *Kreuzzeitung* group, but was kept from any real exercise of the power he craved because of the distrust he provoked among men of all persuasions by his violent rhetoric, his outrageous positions, and his apparent inconsistencies. To his neighbors at Schönhausen he was the "mad Junker"; to William I, who turned away from him until he had no other resource, he seemed an irresponsible schoolboy. In the fifties he served in a succession of diplomatic posts, for most of the period as the Prussian delegate to the diet of the Germanic Confederation—where he consistently gave acid expression to his anti-Austrian feelings—and then as ambassador in St. Petersburg and, briefly in 1862, in Paris. He sought to expand Prussia's

[22] Quoted in A. J. P. Taylor, *Bismarck: The Man and the Statesman* (1955), Vintage ed., 12.

greatness, but he was not a German nationalist in any conventional sense. By opportunism of astonishing boldness and complexity, he brought about unification as a by-product of service to his king.

Bismarck dealt with the constitutional conflict that he inherited—after one more futile attempt at reconciliation—by simply ruling in defiance of the Landtag's disapproval; he relied on the House of Lords, some ambiguities in the constitution, and the clever juggling of revenues. He tightened the government's grip over the civil service and over the press. At last in 1866 he forced a settlement on his own terms, carrying an act of indemnity for his extraconstitutional rule. By that time his diplomatic triumphs had made him irresistible. The fiendish complexity of situations and maneuvers on the European stage in the sixties defies summary, but the main outlines, however false the relief into which they are thrown, show Bismarck's masterly ability at turning events and the missteps of lesser statesmen to his and Prussia's profit.

From the outset Bismarck was certain that Prussia's interest could be forwarded only at the expense of Austria. Shortly after he took office, the Austrian government belatedly came to the support of *grossdeutsch* enthusiasts and proposed a revision of the Confederation that would increase the weight of the smaller states, which were mostly supporters of Austria. Bismarck wrecked the scheme by the simple expedient of refusing to allow William I to attend the Congress of Princes, at which the plan was to be discussed. But the crucial gambit in his game against Austria lay in a new phase of the Schleswig-Holstein question (see p. 735). In 1863 Denmark proposed the separation of Schleswig from Holstein and the incorporation of Schleswig in the Danish state under a new constitution. This affront to German national sentiment was aggravated by the death of the Danish king and a disputed succession, for the laws of succession in the two duchies differed from those in Denmark. The diet of the Confederation was already taking military steps at the end of 1863, but Bismarck got Austria to join Prussia in a war against Denmark, which began in February 1864. Austria forfeited much support among the smaller German states by acting without the Confederation. Britain, protesting repeatedly, did not come to the Danes' assistance, and by August Denmark had conceded defeat and renounced the duchies. The Prussian armies had fought less than impressively in the earlier stages of the war, but the victory secured the reputation of General Helmuth von Moltke, chief of the Prussian general staff, who took command in the final stages.

While Bismarck wanted to annex the duchies, he proposed instead to convert the joint occupation into an arrangement under which Austria would govern Holstein and Prussia the more northerly Schleswig. This situation gave Bismarck ample opportunity to pick a quarrel with Austria subsequently. Bismarck had already secured his Russian flank for any future diplomatic or military struggle by his open expression of support for the tsar in the suppression of the Polish rebellion, which had broken out in January 1863. He concluded an alliance with Italy in April 1866, holding out Venetia as the bait. In the preceding October Bismarck had sought to reassure Napoleon III, whom he met while ostensibly on holiday at Biarritz, but the emperor proved slippery. In the end Napoleon opted for a highly advantageous agreement with Austria, which he expected to be victorious; as a reward for remaining neutral he would get Venetia along with other territorial advantages. In April 1866 Bismarck moved to capture support from German nationalists and liberals by boldly proposing his own reconstruction of the Confederation; shrewdly calculating on working-class conservatism, he offered a parliament based on, of all things, universal manhood suffrage—an about-face that created confusion in all directions. Meanwhile, Bismarck had kept up a steady barrage of complaints to Vienna, thus anesthetizing William I's somewhat inconvenient sense of rectitude; at the beginning of May the two powers had mobilized. On June 14 the federal diet voted mobilization against Prussia. The Prussian delegate thereupon declared the Confederation dissolved, and at midnight Prussian troops invaded the territory of Austria's German allies. On July 3 Moltke's forces handed a stunning defeat to the Austrian army at Königgrätz, or Sadowa, in Bohemia. It was the Seven Weeks' War; an armistice was signed at the end of July and the Treaty of Prague on August 23.

Apart from the cession of Venetia, which passed from France to Italy, Austria suffered no territorial losses in the settlement; Saxony too was protected. But the other German states were left at Prussia's disposal, and Bismarck forced the king and the military into a show of moderation. Hanover, Hesse-Cassel, Hesse-Nassau, Frankfurt, and of course Schleswig-Holstein were annexed to Prussia, and some territory was taken from Hesse-Darmstadt; the south German states of Baden, Württemberg, and Bavaria remained intact, along with Saxony; indemnities were demanded from all the defeated states. The south German states were soon linked by secret treaties to Prussia and agreed to put their armies under Prussian command in case of war. These treaties made a mockery of the scheme for a South German Confederation envisioned in the Treaty of Prague. But the North German Confederation became a reality, with a practical, highly conservative constitution completely dominated by Prussia. This constitution remained the basis of the German Empire after 1871 and lasted until 1918 (see p. 794).

The war marked the end of Austria's role as a German power. In 1860 and 1861 there had been two abortive attempts at constitutional reform to satisfy the restive Magyars, among whom leadership was passing from Kossuth to Francis Déak. In 1867 the *Ausgleich*—compromise—provided for a dual monarchy, in which the separate kingdoms of Austria and Hungary were autonomous as to internal affairs and linked in external. But it was precisely this linkage that drew Austrian concerns to the east and prevented any new assertion of Austrian influence over the south German states. The constitutional alteration, if anything, exacerbated the problem of nationalities subordinated under German and Magyar rule. Thus the *Ausgleich* marked the largest step taken in the conversion of the Hapsburg monarchy from an empire into a question.

The Franco-Prussian War

In the moment of his triumph in 1866, Bismarck hammered a table with his fist, crying "I have beaten them all! All" His domestic victories were quite as great as his foreign conquests: the national success brought not only an end to the constitutional crisis but a splintering and regrouping of parties (see p. 796). Bismarck's plans did not require the immediate provocation of France that he had visited upon Austria from the moment he assumed power; indeed, he counted on the growing prestige of the Prussian monarchy to draw the south German states into the Confederation in due time. But his coldly calculating mind saw—as did many less discriminating Germans—that one day the French would have to be dealt with. Again Bismarck profited from the weaknesses of others, in this case the frenetic bellicosity in Paris.

The sixties were a time of disaster for Napoleonic foreign policy. Rome was a standing embarrassment, coveted by Italy yet essential to French political peace. The Mexican adventure ended ingloriously in 1867. Demands that the Vienna settlement be undone had got nowhere. And France had not only backed the wrong side in 1866 but was faced with a powerful new German state abutting its frontier. Napoleon needed a victory somewhere, and after some incautious talk with Bismarck about Belgium (information Bismarck was to use later to expose French "imperialism"), his ambitions lighted on Luxembourg. This duchy was in the curious position of having the king of the Netherlands as its grand duke and a Prussian garrison, although Luxembourg, a member of the old Germanic Confederation, was specifically barred by the Treaty of Prague from joining the North German Confederation. The Dutch king was willing enough to sell his awkward possession, but Bismarck rejected his plea for Prussian approval and promptly leaked word of the proposed deal to the press. German national sentiment was outraged over French presumption, and the final disposition of Luxembourg's anomalous status—an international guarantee of its independence and neutrality, concluded in 1867—was another humiliation to Napoleon. When the news broke early in July 1870 that a Hohenzollern prince would accept the Spanish throne, French popular opinion was close to hysterical. Moreover, the new foreign minister, the duke de Gramont, was particularly volatile on the subject of the Prussian menace. After considerable confusion, the candidacy of Prince Leopold was withdrawn by his father, with the approval of William I (see p. 774). By an accident of timing this transaction took place while Bismarck was on holiday in Pomerania and the king was taking the waters at Ems, his essential decency for once out from under the control of his imperious minister. On returning to Berlin, Bismarck was appalled to learn of the withdrawal of the candidacy. A Hohenzollern on the throne of Spain would be at the very least an embarrassment to France and might well offer a strategic advantage when the war came, and so Bismarck bombarded his royal master with telegrams urging him to stand fast. But Bismarck was offered a new opportunity by a burst of foolishness in Paris that, as the late Professor Cobban remarked, appeared "to snatch war from the jaws of peace." [23]

Napoleon was ill, in great pain, and unable to pay much attention to business. The empress could lead him, and she and Gramont determined that more than mere withdrawal of the candidacy was needed. One possibility was a letter of apology from the Prussian king to the French emperor. When that, quite understandably, got nowhere, the French ambassador Count Benedetti was ordered to demand an assurance from William that the Hohenzollern candidacy would not be renewed, a piece of impertinence made worse by Benedetti's importuning William in a public park at Ems. William politely but coolly refused the assurance and when Benedetti continued to insist, the king withdrew, remarking that he had nothing further to say. He was not, however, uncordial and the two seem to have met briefly, in a friendly fashion, at the railway station that evening. A telegram giving a somewhat sharper account of the exchange was sent to Bismarck in Berlin; as he sat at dinner with Roon and Moltke, brooding over this apparent defeat for Prussian policy, Bismarck suddenly saw a way of shortening the telegram to make it sound as though the king had abruptly dismissed Benedetti. He released the edited dispatch to the press and had it liberally distributed by Prussian embassies. The news of the apparent snub brought excited crowds into the streets in Paris, singing the *Marseillaise* and crying for a march on Berlin. When the real truth about what happened at Ems was learned, there was hesitation in government circles, but second thoughts were swept away by nationalist hysteria and by the ministers' own emotions. On July 19, 1870, France declared war.

The military in France were confident in their new *chassepot* rifles, superior to the Prussian needle gun, and in the *mitrailleuse*, the ancestor of the machine gun. But some technological superiority could not make up for defective generalship and planning. Although there were errors on the Prussian side, the strategic resources they could command quickly proved their superiority. A French army under Marshal Bazaine was surrounded in the fortress at Metz, and the attempt by another army, under Marshal MacMahon and the emperor himself, to relieve Bazaine failed when they in turn were caught and decisively beaten at Sedan on September 1. As the Prussian armies moved on Paris, the Second Empire vanished. Ollivier and his ministers had been driven from office after the first French defeats. After Sedan the emperor was a captive of the Prussians, and the Bonapartist caretaker government was supplanted by a provisional government of national defense. Thus began the terrible birth pangs of the Third Republic (see p. 813). Meanwhile, Bismarck bribed the mad King Ludwig II of Bavaria to lead the south German states into the Confederation and badgered William I to take the title of German Emperor (not Emperor of Germany, which would have been an affront to the pretensions of the non-Prussian states to sovereignty), although the king was most reluctant to do so.

[23] Alfred Cobban, *History of Modern France* (1965), vol. II, 197.

But the shabbiness with which the new empire was put together was magnificently disguised in its actual proclamation on January 18, 1871—on the anniversary of the creation of the Prussian kingdom in 1701 and in the Hall of Mirrors at the Palace of Versailles, the glittering audience chamber of that fountainhead of French glory, Louis XIV.

In the peace treaties concluded shortly after, France was saddled with a huge indemnity and the loss of Alsace and half of Lorraine. There were other profiteers too. Italy had marched into Rome in September 1870, once the French had withdrawn their forces. And the Russians took advantage of the general confusion to denounce the clauses of the Treaty of Paris of 1856 that had secured the neutralization of the Black Sea. Gladstone convoked a conference of the powers in London, which ratified the Russian action. But by that time the Europe that the Great Powers had designed in 1815 had been totally transformed. Boundaries had been redrawn; Russia had suffered a humiliating defeat and was undergoing a profound internal transformation; Austria was paralyzed; and two new nation-states had been created. Now France was prostrate once more. The national and international politics of Europe were still further altered after 1870. Bismarck did more than any other statesman to bring about that alteration. For nearly twenty years longer Europe lived in the age of Bismarck.

SELECTED READINGS

The "new empires" of the early nineteenth century are dealt with in V. T. Harlow, *The Founding of the Second British Empire,* 2 vols. (1952, 1964), and, for France, in some useful works in French: Christian Schéfer, *La politique coloniale de la Monarchie de Juillet: l'Algérie et l'évolution de la colonisation française* (1928), and Paul Azan, *Conquête et pacification de l'Algérie* (1931). See also Wilfred Blunt, *Desert Hawk: Abd el-Kader and the French Conquest of Algeria* (1947). Harlow's volume has much on exploration, but the great nineteenth-century exploits and their impact at home can be followed in Philip D. Curtin, *The Image of Africa: British Ideas and Action, 1780-1850* (1964); Alan Moorehead, *The White Nile* (1960); and Robert I. Rotberg, ed., *Africa and its Explorers: Motives, Methods, and Impact* (1970). David Livingstone is given an essay in the last volume, but a fascinating portrait also emerges from Owen Chadwick, *Mackenzie's Grave* (1959). For voyages down to Cook's, J. C. Beaglehole, *The Exploration of the Pacific* (1934); for the later period, Ernest S. Dodge, *Beyond the Capes: Pacific Exploration from Captain Cook to the Challenger, 1776-1877* (1971).

On developments in the Atlantic sector of the British empire, see J. B. Brebner, *North Atlantic Triangle: The Interplay of Canada, the United States, and Great Britain* (1945); Helen Taft Manning, *The Revolt of French Canada, 1800-1835* (1962); and Chester New, *Lord Durham* (1929). R. L. Schuyler, *The Fall of the Old Colonial System* (1945) documents the dismantling of controls down to the 1870s, but see also the important article by Ronald Robinson and John Gallagher, "The Imperialism of Free Trade," *Economic History Review,* 6 (January 1953), 1-15; and Bernard Semmel, *The Rise of Free Trade Imperialism* (1970). On South Africa, see Eric A. Walker, *The Great Trek* (1934), and John S. Galbraith, *Reluctant Empire: British Policy on the South African Frontier, 1834-1854* (1963). Harlow deals extensively with the Australasian colonies.

On Russian expansion, see Robert J. Kerner, *The Urge to the Sea: The Course of Russian History* (1946); Richard A. Pierce, *Russian Central Asia, 1857-1917: A Study in Colonial Rule* (1960); Yuri Semenov, *Siberia: Its Conquest and Development* (1954, tr. 1963), a popular account; Donald W. Treadgold, *The Great Siberian Migration* (1957), which concentrates on the late nineteenth and early twentieth centuries; the Siberian sections of Marc Raeff's *Michael Speransky, Statesman of Imperial Russia 1772-1839* (1957); and George Kennan's famous exposé, *Siberia and the Exile System,* 2 vols. (1891, abridged 1958). On the American operations, see Frank A. Golder, *Russian Expansion on the Pacific, 1641-1850* (1914), and Semon B. Okun, *The Russian-American Company* (tr. 1951).

The Russian reforms at midcentury are dealt with generally in W. E. Mosse, *Alexander II and the Modernization of Russia* (1958). On the broad context of the emancipation, see G. T. Robinson's classic *Rural Russia under the Old Regime* (1932), and Jerome Blum, *Lord and Peasant in Russia from the Ninth to the Nineteenth Century* (1961). For particular discussion of the agrarian reforms, see Terence Emmons, *The Russian Landed Gentry and the Peasant Emancipation of 1861* (1968), and the same author's "The Peasant and Emancipation," in Wayne S. Vucinich, ed., *The Peasant in Nineteenth-Century Russia* (1968), a contribution that stresses peasant reactions. In the introduction to *The Politics of Autocracy: Letters of Alexander II to Prince A. I. Bariatinskii, 1857-1864* (1966), Alfred J. Rieber, the editor, argues for the centrality of military considerations following the Crimean defeat in forcing the abolition of serfdom. The views of a number of Russian scholars as well as others can be found, translated, in Terence Emmons, ed., *Emancipation of the Russian Serfs* (1970). On the response of intellectuals, see chap. 4 of Leonard Schapiro, *Rationalism and Nationalism in Russian Nineteenth-Century Political Thought* (1967). The most intensive economic analysis is Alexander Gerschenkron, "Agrarian Policies and Industrialization, 1861-1917," in the *Cambridge Economic History of Europe,* vol. VI (1965), 706-800. On the Polish situation, see R. F. Leslie, *Reform and Insurrection in Russian Poland, 1856-1865* (1963).

The best introductions to Britain at midcentury are G. F. A. Best, *Mid-Victorian Britain, 1851-1875* (1972), and G. Kitson Clark, *The Making of Victorian England* (1961). John Vincent, *The Formation of the Liberal Party, 1857-1868* (1966) is as important for the temper of politico-moral opinion in the country as it is for the narrow political meaning one would first draw from the title. On the complexities of the reform movement, see F. E. Gillespie, *Labor and Politics, 1850-1867* (1927), and the relevant essays in Royden Harrison, *Before the Socialists: Studies in Labour and Politics, 1861-1881.* For the parliamentary history of the Second Reform Act, see F. B. Smith, *The Making of the Second Reform Bill* (1966) and Maurice Cowling, *1867: Disraeli, Gladstone, and Revolution* (1967).

For a concise biography of Napoleon III, see J. M. Thompson, *Louis Napoleon and the Second Empire* (1954). Beyond the works dealing with the emperor's early career and the coup d'etat mentioned in Chapter 18, see an admirable sketch by J. P. T. Bury, *Napoleon III and the Second Empire* (1964), and two important studies by Theodore Zeldin, *The Political System of Napoleon III* (1958) and *Emile Ollivier and the Liberal Empire of Napoleon III* (1963). On economic policy, see Rondo Cameron, *France and the Economic Development of Europe, 1800-1914* (1961); A. L. Dunham, *The Anglo-French Treaty of 1860* (1930); and (for social and architectural history as well) David H. Pinkney, *Napoleon III and the Rebuilding of Paris* (1958). There is little in English on the working-class movement, but in French there is Georges Duveau, *La vie ouvrière en France sous le second empire* (1946). On foreign policy, see Emile Bourgeois and Emile Clermont,

Rome et Napoleon III, 1849–1870 (1907), and Lynn M. Case, *French Opinion on War and Diplomacy during the Second Empire* (1954). On Spain, in addition to the general works, see V. G. Kiernan, *The Revolution of 1854 in Spanish History* (1966).

The problem of defining that Italian movement, the *Risorgimento,* is dealt with in a celebrated bit of polemic, Luigi Salvatorelli, *The Risorgimento: Thought and Action* (1943, tr. 1970), and is discussed judiciously in the introduction to Derek Beales, *The Risorgimento and the Unification of Italy* (1971). Important on preparing the ground are Emiliana Noether, *Seeds of Italian Nationalism, 1700–1815* (1951) and Kent Roberts Greenfield, *Economics and Liberalism in the Risorgimento: A Study of Nationalism in Lombardy, 1814–1848* (1934, rev. ed., 1965). Raymond Grew, *A Sterner Plan for Italian Unity* (1963) deals with the activities of the Italian National Society in swinging support to Piedmont; see also W. K. Hancock, *Ricasoli and the Risorgimento in Tuscany* (1926). For the chief actors, W. R. Thayer's *The Life and Times of Cavour,* 2 vols. (1911) is still standard, and Denis Mack Smith has written a life of Garibaldi (1957), although the three volumes on Garibaldi by G. M. Trevelyan are still worth reading: in addition to that on the Roman republic cited in the previous chapter, see *Garibaldi and the Thousand* (1909) and *Garibaldi and the Making of Italy* (1911). On the politics of the struggle between the two men, see Denis Mack Smith, *Cavour and Garibaldi, 1860* (1954). Mack Smith's *Italy: A Modern History* (1959) and *Modern Sicily after 1713* (1968) are outstanding general accounts. On outside intervention, see citations under France earlier in this section and Derek Beales, *England and Italy, 1859–60* (1961).

The unification of Germany has been much studied, often in old, vast German works that have a way of turning up in not very satisfactory English abridgments, as with, notably, Heinrich Friedjung's *Der Kampf um die Vorherrschaft in Deutschland* (1897), an Austrian work that became *The Struggle for Supremacy in Germany, 1859–1866* (1935); so, too, with Erich Eyck's three-volume *Bismarck, Leben und Werk* (1941–1944), condensed as *Bismarck and the German Empire* (1950). Bismarck is well-served in original English studies, however, notably A. J. P. Taylor's *Bismarck: The Man and the Statesman* (1955), and, for this period, Otto Pflanze, *Bismarck and the Development of Germany: The Period of Unification, 1815–1871* (1963). On the broader context, see Theodore S. Hamerow, *Reaction, Revolution, Restoration* (1958), and Hamerow's two volumes titled *The Social Foundations of German Unification, 1858–1871;* the volume subtitled *Ideas and Institutions* was published in 1969, *Struggles and Accomplishments* in 1972. On the constitutional issue between Bismarck and parliament, see E. N. Anderson, *The Social and Political Conflict in Prussia, 1858–1864* (1954), and Gordon A. Craig, *The Politics of the Prussian Army, 1640–1945* (1955); see also G. G. Windell, *The Catholics and German Unity, 1866–1871* (1954).

On the diplomatic complexities of the sixties, see W. E. Mosse, *The European Powers and the German Question, 1848–1871* (1958); L. D. Steefel, *The Schleswig-Holstein Question* (1932); C. W. Clark, *Franz Joseph and Bismarck* (1934); H. Oncken, *Napoleon III and the Rhine* (1928), another abridgment of a German work published two years earlier; and L. D. Steefel, *Bismarck, The Hohenzollern Candidacy, and the Origins of the Franco-German War of 1870* (1962). On the military side, see Gordon A. Craig, *The Battle of Königgrätz: Prussia's Victory over Austria, 1866* (1964), and Michael Howard, *The Franco-Prussian War: The German Invasion of France, 1870–1871* (1961). A revealing study of one intellectual's singularly portentous reaction to these events is Andreas Dorpalen, *Heinrich von Treitschke* (1957).

20

The European State System: 1870-1900

TWO NEW POWERS: GERMANY AND ITALY

Bismarck's Reich: The Creation

In the 1860s, Bismarck had secured the ascendancy of Prussia among the German states by means of two wars. In 1870–1871, he secured the dominance of Prussia in a new Germany by means of a third. Bismarck's devotees and critics have called him a master Machiavellian. His conduct in the revolutionary year 1848, his management of the Prussian "constitutional crisis" that began in 1862, his wars against Denmark in 1864, Austria in 1866, and finally France in 1870 all seem elements in a premeditated plan for the unification of Germany, carried out with irresistible logic. In fact, Bismarck's consistent aim was service to his royal house and the aristocratic principle, an aim that meant the systematic weakening of Prussia's enemies, foreign and domestic. An opportunist of the highest order, Bismarck skillfully exploited the openings that lesser men made for him. He had few scruples. Manipulating public opinion through docile newspapers, conniving to make war, conducting two-faced diplomacy were all means ready to his hand. The creation of the new German Reich in 1871 was his supreme test.

Bismarck's Reich was, by and large, what he wanted. The empire was *kleindeutsch,* it wholly excluded the Hapsburg domains. This meant that the "third Germany," the lesser states, could no longer play off the giant Austria against the giant Prussia. The new Reich was, at the same time, a federal empire; Bavaria, Württemberg, and the other states retained a good measure of domestic autonomy. They also won a collective voice in the upper house of the federal legislature, the *Bundesrat,* to which each German state sent representatives who acted, much like diplomats, under instructions. Yet no one could doubt where the real power lay. William, king of Prussia, was William I, German emperor. The Prussian minister-president, Bismarck, was imperial chancellor. The Prussian capital, Berlin, was the imperial capital. For several decades, Munich retained supremacy in German culture; it was the center of avant-garde painters and writers. But they had no power and little prestige. Political and administrative offices clustered in Berlin.

The Bundesrat was a concession to the Germany that lay outside Prussia; the *Reichstag,* the lower house, was a concession to the Germany that wanted to season autocracy with a dash of public participation. The dash was modest; still, it galled many among the ruling orders who thought the monarchy to be of divine right, superior to the public will. The Reichstag was elected by universal manhood suffrage, and its ostensible powers were extensive. It debated most public matters; it made the laws in conjunction with the Bundesrat, which meant that it could obstruct legislation proposed by the government. And it could withhold supplies. Its members, unlike the delegates to the other house, were enjoined by the constitution to think of themselves as representatives of the nation.

Yet the Reichstag never developed into a true parliament. There were several reasons for this failure: some were inheritances from German history, some were implicit in the new constitution, and some were the consequence of Bismarck's skill. By far the largest, most populous, most industrialized of the German states was Prussia, and the Prussian legislature, unlike the Reichstag, was chosen by the notorious three-class franchise that gave political power to aristocrats, big landowners, the rich. The German liberals who might have reservations about the authoritarian character of the Reich were in no mood, and no position, to offer Bismarck any serious challenges. Their morale was low; the history of German liberalism is a history of defeat upon defeat. The great reform program of the Napoleonic era had been dismantled; the hopes of 1848 had been quickly dashed; whatever fight remained in the liberals had been beaten out of them in the years following 1862. The civil service, with its high standards and self-confidence, was relatively immune from criticism; after 1874 the military estimates were passed at seven-year intervals, which reduced the Reichstag's control over the army to a minimum. Bismarck's constitutional position was the final obstacle. As chancellor, he was responsible not to the Reichstag but to his emperor. He liked to construct majorities, but he did not need them; he could stay in office in defiance of an opposition majority. This gave Bismarck a free hand in governing his creation. The only question was what would happen to it once he had left its guidance to others.

Bismarck's Reich: Foreign Policy in the 1870s

For nearly twenty years, Bismarck presided over the Reich he had made. His policy was plain: having got what he wanted, he tried to keep what he had. In foreign policy, this meant isolating France, which was bent on *revanche* and on reacquiring the provinces of Alsace and Lorraine. It meant a system of alliances that would keep the new balance of power as stable as possible. In 1871 Bismarck declared that Germany was *saturiert*. It was all very well for Germany to announce herself a satisfied power: France was not; and in eastern Europe, Russia and Austria-Hungary could hardly contain their appetite for territory in the Balkans, left increasingly vulnerable to foreign conquests by a dying Ottoman Empire. And at home Bismarck's new defensive policy meant pacification of clamorous interests and energetic action against domestic enemies.

Bismarck's first large-scale effort at alliance-making was successful. Europe's three emperors—William I of Germany, Francis Joseph of Austria-Hungary, and Alexander II of Russia—met in September 1872. By October of the following year, a rather generally worded alliance brought them together in the "Alliance of the Three Emperors"—the *Dreikaiserbund*. Significantly, the three emperors committed themselves to act in concert against "subversive forces"; as early as September 1870, Bismarck had telegraphed the German ambassador to St. Petersburg, Prince Reuss, that "the firm closing of the ranks of the monarchist and conservative elements of Europe" was extremely desirable. [1] Actually, in contrast to the Holy Alliance, the emperors foresaw no serious action against subversives; Bismarck wanted above all to keep his eastern neighbors from forming ties with France.

France, though at first demoralized by her defeat, and burdened by the exactions of the peace treaty, was obviously a potential threat to the new Germany. The threat increased as the French, working with unforeseen energy, got rid of the occupying German troops, began to rearm, and pursued an active foreign policy. Bismarck was busy at home with his attack on Catholic clericalism, the *Kulturkampf* (see p. 796), and thought the French excessively sympathetic to his religious adversaries; news that the French had passed an aggressive-sounding army law increased tensions. Bismarck responded in characteristic fashion; he manufactured a war scare in his kept press. In April

[1] Quoted in Erich Eyck, *Bismarck and the German Empire* (1950), 190.

1875, the Berlin *Post* asked the rhetorical question "Is War in Sight?" Disingenuously disclaiming all responsibility, Bismarck drove the powers to the edge of war; but to his surprise, France, which he had tried to intimidate, rallied the powers against Germany. In face of general protests, Bismarck retreated, and the danger was past.

In the Ottoman Balkans, meanwhile, rebellion had broken out in Bosnia, and then war; by April 1877, Russian troops had moved against the Turks. Bismarck offered to act as an "honest broker," and the Congress of Berlin was the result, with Bismarck presiding; it averted general war by drastic surgery on Turkish possessions in Europe (see p. 812). For Bismarck it was a game for the sake of his empire: "It would be a triumph for our statesmanship," he candidly wrote the German crown prince Frederick William in November 1878, "if we succeeded in keeping the Eastern ulcer open and thus jarred the harmony of the other Great Powers in order to secure our own peace." [2] By late 1879 Bismarck had made a fateful decision; ruthlessly bearing down on his aged master, who resisted manfully, Bismarck drove through an alliance with Austria-Hungary. The alliance was an act of choice—a choice for Austria; in view of Austria's endemic hostility to Russia, this was diplomacy rich with menace for the future.

Bismarck's Reich: The Enemies

The mixture of quickness, penetration, and cynicism in the service of a higher cause that marked Bismarck's foreign policy governed his domestic policy as well. For some years, Bismarck enjoyed the support of the Reichstag. The largest party, the National Liberals, which commanded over a quarter of the votes, was nationalist and docile; its left wing occasionally uttered murmurs of protest against Bismarck's autocracy, but that was all. The Free Conservative party gathered up the chancellor's right-wing supporters. The Prussian Conservative party busily defended the old Prussian virtues and interests. But in 1876 it bowed to history, openly acknowledged that something had happened by changing its name to the German Conservative party, and began to support Bismarck actively. But two groups refused to fit into this consensus, the Catholic Center party and the Social Democratic party (SPD). [3] These were, in Bismarck's view, hostile to the Reich—*reichsfeindlich*. He treated them accordingly.

Bismarck's attack on Germany's Catholics was purely political. The German Center party, heir of the Catholic party in Prussia, had a delicate task; those Catholics who had favored German unification had hoped to see Catholic Austria included in the Reich. Still, even without Austria, some 37 percent of all Germany's population was Catholic. The year the Center party was founded,

[2] Ibid., 251.
[3] The initials stand for *Sozialdemokratische Partei Deutschlands*.

1870, was a fateful one: it was the year in which the Vatican Council adopted the dogma of papal infallibility. A number of German Catholics refused to accept the new dispensation and were excommunicated (see p. 663). Bismarck saw an opportunity. The Center, with about a quarter of the seats, was the second strongest party in the Reichstag. It took an inconvenient interest in the government's treatment of its Polish subjects, and its capable leader, Ludwig Windthorst, was a Hanoverian particularist—one of those who had never resigned himself to Prussia's annexation of Hanover in 1866. In 1871 Bismarck started his *Kulturkampf.* He posed as the protector of the Catholics who had been excommunicated, called the Center party disloyal, abolished the Catholic division in the Prussian Ministry of Culture, and secured a pliant *Kultusminister* to carry out his injunctions. He pacified the National Liberals (they were easily pacified) by representing his assault on Catholicism as a step toward separating state and church. But the laws proposed in 1872 and May 1873 (the notorious May Laws) were undisguised attempts to subject the church to the state. They included exceptional legislation authorizing the dissolution of Jesuit institutions and the banishment of Jesuits, state supervision of churches and the training of priests, and regulation of the jurisdiction of ecclesiastical courts. Bishops and priests who refused to recognize the May Laws were imprisoned or exiled.

But Germany, though authoritarian and arbitrary, was not a modern dictatorship. The Center party, far from being destroyed, picked up sympathy from the public and in the Reichstag. Conservatives, though anti-Catholic, disliked the anticlerical tone of the *Kulturkampf.* When Pope Pius IX died in 1878 and was succeeded by Leo XIII, Bismarck opened negotiations with the papacy and much, though not all, of the offending legislation was repealed. By 1878, the supple Bismarck foresaw the possibility of political cooperation with the Center party—the *Reichsfeind* of yesterday. And peace with the German Catholics meant war on the German socialists.

The German socialist movement was no threat to the established order. In the elections of 1871, the Social Democrats held a single seat in the Reichstag; it was occupied by their leader, August Bebel. In 1874, at the next elections, they got seven seats, a large gain, though still an insignificant number. In the following year, at Gotha, the party effected a union with Ferdinand Lassalle's old state socialist workers' association (see p. 783). The German Social Democratic party that emerged from this meeting committed itself to equality, democracy, free speech and thought, social welfare, and "cooperative control of all labor." Marx was deeply disappointed; but tepid and illogical though Marx found the Gotha program, it alarmed Bismarck.[4] In 1876 he introduced harsh penal legislation against those who incited class war; for once the National Liberals stood by their legal principles and the bill was lost. In 1878 chance gave Bismarck his opportunity. In May 1878 there was a botched attempt on William I's life; in June, there was a second one, and the shots seriously

---

[4] For Karl Marx's *Critique,* see p. 854.

wounded the aged emperor. Bismarck knew better than anyone that neither of these mad attacks was made by a socialist or countenanced by socialists. But he used the emotion they aroused to push through his antisocialist legislation. The Reichstag was dissolved; the elections gave Bismarck a comfortable majority though the Social Democrats, the ostensible villains, found their seats, which had previously risen to twelve, reduced by only three. In October Bismarck's bill "against the universally dangerous aspirations of Social Democracy" became law. It outlawed "subversive" organizations and authorized the police to ban newspapers and to close meetings. Despite these handicaps, the party prospered. Its deputies in the Reichstag retained their parliamentary immunity, and the party continued to run candidates with ever greater success. Repression, Bismarck learned, was not enough.

Bismarck's Reich: Economy and Society

However parochial his angle of vision, Bismarck understood that the world contained forces independent of his will. The point was not to deny them, but to bend them, as much as possible, to his purposes. Beginning in the 1850s the German states had undergone extensive industrialization (see p. 780); the founding of the Reich in 1871 had only increased the pace. The founding years had produced a riot of speculation and unsound enterprises. This euphoria evaporated in 1873, with a large-scale economic collapse. But this only meant that industrial production, foreign trade and investment, railroad building, and exploitation of raw materials slowed down to a more measured pace. The number of persons engaged in agriculture markedly dropped as the number engaged in industry markedly rose.

Bismarck responded by attempting to draw the working class closer to the state. His proposed social legislation was not pure cynicism; despite his political alliance with the National Liberals in the 1870s, he was not an economic liberal by conviction; he had no objection in principle to bringing the state into the economy. And then, by the end of the 1870s, he turned away from the Liberals even in politics. Around 1880 he spoke of the state's responsibility for remedying social inequities. In 1883 Germany initiated its ambitious program of social legislation with a law providing for sickness insurance; in 1884 a law on accident insurance followed; old age and disability insurance were enacted in 1889. Bismarck had to fight for this legislation every step of the way; his critics denounced it as "state socialism" and whittled away at its provisions. As a social experiment, the laws, which provided for partial contributions from employers, were a success; other countries faced with the same problems imitated the German example. As a political maneuver, the laws were a failure; in every federal election, the SPD picked up seats and increased its popular following. In 1890, a critical year in the history of Bismarck's Reich, the SPD secured nearly 1.5 million votes, three times the votes it had got in 1878, and thirty-five seats.

Bismarck did not confine the benefits of state intervention to the working class. Late in 1878 Bismarck was persuaded to reverse Germany's free trade policy and move toward protection. In 1879 he introduced legislation proposing substantial duties on industrial, as well as agricultural, imports. One of his reasons was financial: the Reich, under the constitution, could not levy direct taxes, and revenue from duties would make it less dependent on contributions from the individual states. Another reason was economic: most of the industrializing powers were shielding their new enterprises behind tariff walls, and the slump of the 1870s suggested that Germany might profitably try alternative economic policies. The third reason, in the end the most important and portentous, was political: by satisfying both the Rhenish industrialists and the East Elbian landowners, Bismarck constructed a conservative alliance that dominated policy-making in Germany from that time on. This alliance gave a peculiar shape to German industrial and agricultural organization; both grew highly concentrated and became partly the servant, partly the owner of the state. The National Liberal party, stretched on the rack between economic principle and economic self-interest, split over the tariff issue, and its influence declined while that of the conservatives in all parties increased. Here was another fateful legacy of Bismarck's policies. His much-vaunted political realism came to mean the struggle of interest groups for spoils disguised behind high-flown rhetoric.

Bismarck's conversion to imperialism was another instance of his flexibility and his readiness to protect economic interests. Despite his earlier and reiterated objections to a "colonial policy" that would saddle Germany with foreign possessions, Bismarck joined the scramble for Africa (see p. 841). By the late 1880s Germany's imperial flag flew over the small west African territories of Togo and Cameroon, over the desolate region of Southwest Africa just north of Britain's Cape Colony, and in the east, in the bleak terrain of German East Africa. As a latecomer in the imperialist competition, Germany had to be content with paltry acquisitions. In the Pacific islands, meanwhile, German gunboats supported the claims of German traders. German explorers and businessmen had ventured into these remote lands; the desire to safeguard their interests, satisfy investors in colonial trade, gain international prestige, and solidify domestic opinion behind stirring ventures—all these played their part in Bismarck's remarkable shift. In 1890 Herbert Bismarck, the chancellor's son and intimate collaborator, suggested still another reason: "When we entered upon a colonial policy, we had to reckon with a long reign of the Crown Prince. During this reign English influence would have been dominant. To prevent this, we had to embark on a colonial policy, because it was popular and conveniently adapted to bring us into conflict with England at any given moment." [5] Bismarck could not overlook the critical fact that William I was getting to be a very old man.

[5] Eyck, *Bismarck*, 275.

Bismarck's Reich Without Bismarck: The 1890s

The late 1880s were times of stormy conflict for Bismarck and of renewed triumphs. He had outlawed the Social Democrats, carried the tariff, secured the colonies, forged the conservative alliance. In 1887 he made the Reinsurance Treaty with Russia, which guaranteed mutual neutrality. In the same year he presented new army estimates, which like all these bills authorized expenditures for seven years. This "Septennate" called for a 10 percent increase; the Reichstag refused to go along. Bismarck dissolved it and campaigned by playing upon chauvinist sentiment against France and on the fear of war. In the elections the two conservative parties, with the National Liberals, formed a patriotic coalition, the "Cartel," which gave Bismarck a safe majority. The Septennate passed.

Resounding as it was, this victory was Bismarck's last. His emperor, whom he had loyally served and decisively dominated, died in 1888 at the age of ninety. His successor was Frederick III, whose consort, Victoria, was the daughter of England's Queen Victoria. Frederick III and his queen were liberals, pro-English, and thoroughly hostile to Bismarck. But when Frederick ascended the throne, he was already mortally ill with cancer of the throat; he died after a reign of ninety-nine days. He was succeeded by his son, William II, a volatile, tactless, grandiloquent martinet who took the myth of divine right seriously and never lost an opportunity to remind the country of his exalted position. His speeches were punctuated with outbursts against deputies who displeased him and with rhetorical calls for violence against socialists or other "enemies of the country." His public statements became an embarrassment. This wilful autocrat, this lover of uniforms and of his own voice, could not tolerate the aged statesman who had for too long had his own way. The two men clashed, ostensibly over policy, essentially over power. On March 18, 1890, Bismarck was induced to resign. A new Germany was on a new course.

Not much was predictable about that course, except that it would lead the country into adventures abroad. When the Russians asked to renew the Reinsurance Treaty of 1887, Germany, actively cultivating England, refused. At home, the emperor proclaimed himself the champion of labor; the antisocialist laws were allowed to lapse, and the Social Democratic party emerged from its "heroic years" of suppression and exile stronger than ever. For the socialists, certainly, the departure of Bismarck was a welcome event. But the young emperor was an inconstant ally. For all his much advertised "social" sympathies, he vowed to "crush" socialists. In November 1891 he told young Guard recruits that "the German army must be armed against the internal enemy quite as much as the foreign one. More than ever unbelief and discontent are raising their heads in our fatherland, and it may happen that you will have to shoot down, or cut down your own relatives or brothers." This was shocking talk. But it caused nothing worse than embarrassment, for discontent was not serious: times were relatively good; the depression that had recurrently attacked the German economy finally lifted around 1896.

Far more ominous than the emperor's bombast was the German naval program. Here, as elsewhere, a mixture of domestic interests and diplomatic considerations was at work. The emperor fancied himself a man of power and desired to build a fleet that would compete with Great Britain, the ruler of the sea. Shipbuilding companies saw profits, and international traders protection, from such a construction program. Strength and wealth went hand in hand. In 1897 William II put Admiral Alfred von Tirpitz into the naval office, and Germany's race for sea power was launched. When Bismarck died in 1898, an angry old man, the German Empire was in the hands of an emperor who prided himself on his "personal rule" and took chances Bismarck would have repudiated. But whose fault was it in the end? William II's indiscretions might upset intellectuals and diplomats. But the absence of any serious check to his policies was a deeper defect. It went back to the authoritarian direction of German thought, the independence and high prestige of the military, the demoralization of the liberals, and the destruction of any true politics. "Bismarck," the great German historian Theodor Mommsen rightly judged in 1902, "has broken the nation's spine." [6]

A Minor Great Power: Italy

In contrast to the unification of Germany, the unification of Italy was an inglorious affair. While Italy had heroes like Mazzini and Garibaldi and statesmen like Cavour (see p. 775), Italian politicians and patriots could not conceal that their state had grown since the 1850s in the shadow of greater powers, at the expense of the labor and the blood of others. The most disastrous policies that the new Italy would follow after 1870 sprang from this awareness and from the compensating need to show muscle, to win world prestige—to sham greatness.

The conquest of Rome in September 1870 left Italy with three intractable problems. There was first the recurrent, nagging doubt about Italy's greatness. The new state had 26.8 million inhabitants; it was thus not much less populous than the new Germany, with its 40.8 millions. But it was poor in raw materials and backward in trade. Work on the Suez Canal had been begun in Cavour's lifetime, and it had aroused high hopes for Italian shipping. But when the canal was opened in 1869, eight years after Cavour's death, these hopes proved deceptive; in 1870 only one eightieth of the tonnage passing through it was Italian. [7] A mixture of boastful diplomacy and showy grandeur, both symptoms of insecurity, wasted Italy's energies and resources. "When I think what conservatives have done in England on behalf of the poor and of agriculture," the Neapolitan historian, Pasquale Villari, wrote in 1878, "I blush with

[6] In a letter to the economist Lujo Brentano. Quoted in Albert Wucher, *Theodor Mommsen* (1956), 157.

[7] See Denis Mack Smith, *Italy: A Modern History* (rev. ed., 1969), 128.

shame. . . . It is high time that Italy began to realize that she has inside herself an enemy which is stronger than Austria. Somehow we must face up to our multitude of illiterates, the ineptitude of our bureaucratic machine, the ignorance of our professors, the existence of people who in politics are mere children, the incapacity of our diplomats and generals, the lack of skill in our workers, our patriarchal system of agriculture, and on top of all, the rhetoric which gnaws our very bones." [8] Villari's catalogue shows that the new country faced a staggering assignment. Italy was in a race with powers, such as Germany, that were endowed with superior resources, a better educated populace (Villari estimated that Italy's illiterates numbered seventeen million), a long history of discipline, and a thoroughly modern industrial plant. While many Italian politicians were men of probity and intelligence who worked hard and died poor, scandals discredited others in the late 1880s. For a country in which parliamentary politics was still a new game, this was a threatening state of affairs.

The most striking characteristic of Italian politics was government by prime ministers unhampered by party discipline or rigid political convictions. The Italian franchise was narrow; the law of 1882, which more than trebled the electorate, gave the vote to two million Italians, or 7 percent of the population. [9] The ministry was responsible to the king, and the crown reserved extensive powers to itself, notably in foreign policy. But the relations between prime minister and king on the one hand, prime minister and Chamber of Deputies on the other, depended heavily on the play of personalities. A two-party system might have answered the need of the country; this is what some anglophile reformers hoped to attain and what the political rhetoric of the day, with its "Right" and "Left" governments, seemed to imply. In fact, Italian political parties did not develop beyond rudimentary groupings; in parliament and out, constant negotiations and shifts of opinion produced short-lived coalitions. Ambitious politicians made alliances on the right or the left quite indiscriminately; a "right" ministry would include prominent "leftists" and vice versa. This is what Agostino Depretis, three times prime minister between 1876 and 1887, praised as the "transformation" of political parties. But it produced instability in the Chamber, confusion in the country, and dictatorship of the prime minister; it frustrated the political education of the Italian people. *Trasformismo* led to greatness only on the field of rhetoric.

Italy's second problem, irredentism, was intimately linked to the first. Compact and logical as the Italian state seemed after the seizure of Rome in 1870, there were *terre irredente*, unredeemed lands, that depressed patriots and worried strategists. In the northeast a triangular stretch of territory, the Trentino, was like a knife of Austrian power stuck into Italy's side. The Trentino was, for the most part, Italian in culture and language; the city that the

---

[8] Ibid., 135.
[9] Small though this seems, it meant that nearly every literate male was entitled to vote.

Austrians called Bozen the Italians persisted in calling Bolzano. Feelings ran high. Further east, Italians also made claims to the great port of Trieste. While Italian diplomats importuned their foreign counterparts with demands for these regions, politicians and generals called for war.

Italy's participation in the scramble for Africa sprang from similar motives. Italian imperialism was sporadic, dispirited, and discreditable. Since the 1860s, Italy had toyed with the economic penetration of North Africa, but it was not until Francesco Crispi became prime minister in 1887 that Italian imperialism became a serious affair, and then not in northern, but in eastern Africa. Although Crispi was sixty-seven when he took office, his energies were those of a young man. Once a member of Garibaldi's famous Thousand (see p. 777), he had put radicalism behind him and embarked on a political career in which the aggrandizement of Italy and the aggrandizement of Crispi were strangely confounded. His regime was not a total disaster. Crispi reformed prisons, humanized the criminal code, legalized strikes, and pioneered in public health. But his search for personal and national prestige came first. By 1890 he had elevated a few commercial settlements on the Red Sea into the Italian colony of Eritrea. The year before he had concluded the Treaty of Ucciali with the emperor of Ethiopia, Menelek II. In 1896, seeking to extend Italian power over the whole country, Crispi ordered his troops into Ethiopia. His motives remain unclear; what is clear is that the military campaign was managed with incredible incompetence. In March 1896 the Ethiopians routed the Italians at Aduwa, a shameful, costly defeat that ended Italian foreign ventures for a long time and Crispi's political career forever.

Italy's third problem—relations with the papacy—was nearer home. The country was officially and constitutionally Catholic; many Italians were fervent Catholics. Yet the country was deeply split on the religious issue. The leaders of the *risorgimento* were, by and large, irreligious; they were deists, Freemasons, anticlerical heretics. Many among the Italian nationalists who were good Catholics were, at the same time, opponents of the pope's secular power. The conflict between Italian nationalism and papal policy, always endemic, had become acute after 1848, after Pope Pius IX had given up whatever liberalism he had earlier professed. His outspoken encyclical of 1864, *Quanta cura*, had made it unmistakably plain that the nationalists' policy and that of the papacy were wholly irreconcilable. Among the "errors" that its *Syllabus of Errors* condemned were the cherished principles of nineteenth-century liberalism.

Italian legislators dug in their heels. In 1866 they passed a law that closed practically all Italian religious houses and confiscated their property for civic use. Marriage was made a civil ceremony, and (in open defiance of the *Syllabus of Errors*) seminarians were obliged to serve in the army. When Italian troops marched into Rome, the papacy rejected all overtures by the government. In 1871 the government offered the pope a "guarantee" which promised him sovereignty in Rome and reiterated Cavour's well-known principle of separation: "a free church in a free state—*libera chiesa in libero stato*." The papacy refused to be drawn into compromise. "No conciliation," Pius IX declared in November, "will ever be possible between Christ and Belial, between light and darkness, between truth and falsehood." [10] Disappointing those liberal Catholics who had hoped that it would take a part in promoting humanitarian causes and social legislation, the papacy withdrew into a kind of splendid domestic exile. In 1871 Pius IX issued a decree, *"Non expedit,"* which held it to be inexpedient for loyal Catholics to be active in politics. In 1874, he strengthened it to *"Non licet"*—impermissible. The accession of Pope Leo XIII in 1878 brought a new direction to papal policy. Leo's famous encyclicals on social matters, especially his *Rerum Novarum* of 1891, opened the way for Catholics across the world to work for humane, liberal political goals. But the policy of nonrecognition went on: it was not until 1929 that the papacy officially recognized Italy. But by then liberal Italy was dead (see p. 993).

TWO MULTINATIONAL EMPIRES:
RUSSIA AND AUSTRIA-HUNGARY

The two great Eastern powers, Russia and Austria-Hungary, rivals and neighbors, had much in common. They had the same potential victim on their southern or southeastern border, the Ottoman Empire. Unlike the new states, or the older Western powers, they were multinational empires with all the problems that such diversity entailed in an age of nationalism. And both had, in the 1860s, undertaken drastic surgery at home only to discover, in the 1870s and 1880s, that the surgery had not cut deep enough.

Russia: Reform, Disillusionment, Reaction

Tsar Alexander II, who had ascended the throne in 1855, was experienced, and more flexible than his father, Nicolas I. A traditionalist, faithful to the autocracy, he was open to liberal persuasion. For some years, he engaged in far-reaching experiments; the school system, the judiciary, local government, all underwent radical changes. The censorship and the secret police, though still active, relaxed their hold somewhat. And in 1861, by decree, the government emancipated the peasants. But the emancipation of Russia's serfs, as we have seen, solved few problems and created others; the nationalities settled in the sprawling Russian Empire were another inexhaustible source of trouble. The suppression of the Polish rebellion of 1863 was the signal for harsh measures against the Roman Catholic population of Poland. Russian officials resident in

---

[10] Christopher Seton-Watson, *Italy from Liberalism to Fascism, 1870–1925* (1967), 56.

Warsaw proclaimed and enforced stringent regulations intended to suppress nationalist fervor or even cultural autonomy. The church in Poland was subjected to close Russian supervision; the language used in schools and in the University of Warsaw was to be Russian. Elsewhere, especially in the Ukraine, the policy of russification was applied with new stringency. Even the Germans in the Baltic, though great favorites with the tsar, felt a new hostility. Needless to say, repression did not destroy nationalist emotions; it only drove them underground, to fester there. Russia continued to be, as it had been, an autocracy, slow moving, suspicious of Western ideas, and in the grip of a growing, almost omnipotent bureaucracy that did things in its own way, at its own speed, and, as it became a kind of class, for its own sake.

The Russian revolutionary movement, with its eccentrics, its spectrum of irreconcilable views, its utopianism, its dark strain of violence, even madness, was the appropriate plant for this soil. All those who hoped for a better Russia felt an intense and growing frustration. Before 1861 there was a widespread conviction that liberal changes would make a decisive difference. After 1861 this conviction was proved an illusion. Reform from the top seemed to benefit only those already on top; liberalism was not enough. Anarchism, nihilism, mystical revolutionary musings became the new doctrine. Still, the humane, reasonable socialism of Alexander Herzen did not lack for followers (see p. 673). After long wanderings, Herzen had settled down in London in 1852; from London, beginning in 1857, he published his influential journal, *The Bell.* Herzen advocated a certain patience with human imperfection and admiration for the Russian peasant. His slogan *"v narod!*—to the people!" aroused great enthusiasm among intellectuals and some interest even in government circles. In 1873 a movement of Populists, the *Narodniki,* took Herzen's message to the countryside. As so often, the proposed alliance between the men of words and the men of the soil whom they had idealized foundered on mutual incomprehension.

Other radicals had no patience with such "sentimentality." Michael Bakunin, the leader of the anarchist wing in the First International (see p. 852), gained a wide following with his fierce opinions and his romantic presence. In direct opposition to Marx's historical materialism, to which a number of Russian intellectuals subscribed, Bakunin preached immediate revolutionary action. Born into an aristocratic family in 1814, he found his revolutionary vocation early; during the revolutions of 1848 he was in Germany, agitating. In 1849 he was arrested, sent to Russia first and then to Siberia. In 1861 he escaped to the West, and by the end of the year he was in London with his friend Herzen. Active and impressive, he spread his message to Russia through disciples like Sergei Nechaev, a single-minded revolutionary and a ruthless, still mysterious personality. In 1869 Nechaev met Bakunin in Geneva and the two worked out the celebrated *Revolutionary Catechism.* "The revolutionary," it began, "is a lost man; he has no interests of his own, no cause of his own, no feelings, no habits, no belongings; he does not even have a name." It was a romantic, desperate vision: the revolutionary as outcast who lives, breathes only one thing, the revolution. Upon his return to Russia, Nechaev organized an underground group dedicated to terrorism; one of its most notorious acts was the murder of one of its own members for supposed treachery. [11] Bakunin, whose main inspiration was Proudhon's detestation of property and authoritarianism, had welcomed Nechaev as a magnificent fanatic; the murder he found totally hateful. Nechaev was eventually caught and imprisoned. But he continued to communicate with his circle, and after his death in 1882 he served the movement as a martyr.

All this sounds melodramatic and ineffectual. The secret police, especially alert after the attempt in 1866 on Alexander's life, closed down reading circles and progressive book shops. Some thousands of suspects were arrested; held in jail, often for years; and subjected to mass trials and arbitrary executions. But terror begot terror. Defiant of the often slow-moving and slow-witted authorities, revolutionaries succeeded in killing prominent members of the repressive machinery. In August 1878 they got a prize: the head of the notorious Third Department—the secret police. In the following year, the most uncompromising of the revolutionaries formed a terrorist group called the People's Will, determined to assassinate the tsar. Alexander II veered about. In 1880 he dismissed Dmitri Tolstoy, the reactionary minister of education who had been in office since 1866. In the same year a government commission abolished the Third Department. In addition, Alexander countenanced plans for two commissions of experts to sit with governmental bodies and an enlarged Council of State to contain, for the first time, members elected by the public. This was more than token liberalism, but far from enough for the revolutionaries. In March 1881 the tsar was murdered with a bomb. It was the work of the People's Will.

Alexander III: Prince of Reaction

On succeeding as tsar, Alexander III did not repeat what he regarded as his father's fatal mistake. There would be no nonsense about free speech, no compromise with liberalism, no popular participation in politics. Alexander III did not touch the reforms of the 1860s, but the spine of the autocracy was stiffened. Most of the new tsar's ideas and much of his policy derived from K. B. Pobedonostsev, who had been Alexander's tutor and who held the post of chief procurator of the Holy Synod. Intelligent and cultivated, Pobedonostsev rejected all modernism and Western influence; he wanted to preserve the autocracy inviolate and to extend the sway of Orthodoxy. Accordingly,

---

[11] In Dostoevsky's *The Devils* (see p. 889), this murder is explained as a diabolical device to draw the group together through collective guilt. But this interpretation must remain speculative. As Franco Venturi has justly observed: "Dostoevsky can teach us very little about Nechaev." *Roots of Revolution* (tr. 1960), xxxi.

censorship was tightened; distinguished newspapers were suppressed; a new minister of education, Delyanov, obstructed all efforts at educational reform and whipped university professors and students into line; toleration of religious sects, always precarious, dwindled away. Russification was intensified.

In his thirteen-year reign, Alexander III made many victims. The most prominent among them were the Jews. The emancipation of Russia's Jews had followed their emancipation in western Europe with slow and uncertain steps. Russian court society and the Ukrainian and Polish populations, among whom Jews were concentrated, were alike saturated with virulent anti-Jewish myths. The Jews were called the killers of Christ, strangers in the land, and (contrary to the most palpable evidence) rich bloodsuckers, fattening off the poor. They were confined to a specified region, called the Pale of Settlement, and subjected to arbitrary and severe discrimination. There were attempts, often accompanied by physical brutality, to "convert" Jewish children to the Russian Orthodox faith. The percentage of Jews compelled to serve in the army—the term was twenty-five years and, for Jews, even longer—was far higher than that of other nationalities.

For Jews, the long reign of Nicholas I had been one long nightmare. Then the nightmare had lifted. The year after his accession in 1855, Alexander II included the Jews in his general program of reform. Jews were slowly admitted to the liberal professions, and some of them received permission to settle outside the Pale. The special military service imposed on Jews was removed as well. This did not end anti-Jewish violence on the part of the populace, but it opened the prospects of a new world, if only for the most enterprising.

The assassination of Alexander II changed all this. There were pogroms against Jews, resulting in some deaths, in May 1881; there were others in 1882. While the government did not spread the rumor that the Jews had killed the tsar (as they had presumably killed the Savior), it did little to deter rioters from attacking Jewish settlements, burning down Jewish houses, raping Jewish women, and hunting Jews to death. When Dmitri Tolstoy returned to office as minister of the interior, he stopped the pogroms; violence against Jews was, as it were, nationalized. He published new residential regulations that herded Jews into enumerated towns and villages; deprived them of the vote in local elections without removing their privilege of paying local taxes; and set up quota systems limiting the number of Jewish students, lawyers, and doctors. And pogroms eventually came back, too, like a recurrent fever, though now more openly under government auspices. The great Kishinev massacre of 1903, which cost the lives of forty-seven Jews and left hundreds of them injured and thousands ruined, was instigated by a government newspaper and abetted by Viacheslav Plehve, the minister of the interior.

In time, Jews developed three attitudes to this savagery. The first was resignation and despair. The second was socialism, a movement that Russian Jews joined in increasing numbers in the fervent hope that the socialist world of the future would be free from such animality. The third was Zionism: what was more natural than for Jews to answer nationalism with nationalism? Although isolated publicists and sympathetic Gentiles had occasionally spoken of a homeland for Jews in Palestine, it was the Russian Jewish physician, Leon Pinsker, from Odessa, who brought out the first serious Zionist tract— significantly in 1882, a year of terrible Russian pogroms. His pamphlet was called *Auto-Emancipation;* written in German and published in Berlin, it appealed to secular energies, calling upon the Jews to help themselves. Significantly, too, the first classic of Zionism, Theodor Herzl's *Judenstaat* (1896), was also a response to anti-Semitism. Herzl, appalled at the reservoirs of anti-Jewish feeling tapped in France by the Dreyfus case (see p. 817), published a pamphlet in which he proposed an autonomous Jewish state under the suzerainty of the sultan. Like Pinsker, Herzl was a secularist, a thoroughly modern man. His Zionism was not religious but political. In 1897, at the first Zionist Congress in Basel, Herzl was elected president of the new Zionist Organization. Its program called for the settlement of Jewish agricultural and industrial workers in Palestine and, in the characteristic language of the day, for the "strengthening and fostering of Jewish national sentiment and conscious-ness." We have seen that terror breeds terror. In the same way, nationalism bred nationalism; Jewish nationalism was born, and has lived, as the national-ism of victims.

Austria-Hungary: A Sprawling Anachronism

By 1870-1871, the Austro-Hungarian Empire was a military disaster, a diplomatic failure, and a political anachronism. There were many who knew this, few who had any notion of how to escape the doom of second-rateness. The Italian territories—all except for that slice, the Trentino (see p. 802)—had been lost in the 1860s. Power in Germany had been lost with the triumph of Bismarck's *kleindeutsche* solution. And, in an age when nationalist sentiments were increasingly hard to resist, the Dual Monarchy resisted them with an energy worthy of a better cause.

The *Ausgleich* with Hungary (see p. 787) made things worse by appearing to make them better. It perpetuated the illusion that something was being done to cope with modern realities. The settlement of 1867 had given the Hungarians constitutional, administrative, and linguistic autonomy at home and real political power in the Dual Monarchy. In 1871 Emperor Francis Joseph made Count Gyula Andrássy, one of the architects of dualism and the Hungarian premier, his foreign minister. In the same year, negotiations with the Czech subjects of the empire broke down. This failure was in part the consequence of the Czechs' inflexibility; their leaders were not the first to discover that the man who asks for too much is likely to get nothing. But in part it stemmed from the resistance of German opinion in Austria, already shaken by Hungarian ascendancy, and from the intransigence of Andrássy, who would not grant to other nationalities the political rights he had claimed for his own. In the vocabulary of the time, he had his justification ready. "The Slavs," he said, "are not fit to govern, they must be ruled." [12] The Poles in Austrian Galicia got some much-desired concessions, including the right to use their own language in their schools and their governmental business. But the other minorities crowding the Dual Monarchy, like the Croats and Serbs and Ruthenians, were treated much like the Czechs: as political pariahs. Serious trouble awaited only a favorable opportunity.

For a time, disaster was staved off by successes in foreign policy and compromises at home. [13] In 1879 Count Eduard Taaffe became prime minister. His policy was to pacify the minorities by well-timed concessions and to strengthen the dynasty—a policy to which Francis Joseph could scarcely object. The Czechs, who had boycotted Vienna since they made their demands in 1868, now ended their splendid isolation and tried to get by good manners what they had not got by truculence. What they got was little more than nothing: the use of Czech in official business, some new schools, and even a national university. Yet when Taaffe was dismissed in 1893, the situation was one of political deadlock and imminent danger. Taaffe was let go after he had proposed a radical widening of the suffrage. It was a step, though astute in the long run, for which he could muster little support. The Dual Monarchy was run by and for the few; Austria and Hungary both were lands of immensely rich landowners face to face with poor, disfranchised peasants. And they were lands in which a single national group imposed its will on all the others. If anything, the Magyars in Hungary were more conservative than the Germans in Austria: Hungary was perhaps half non-Magyar, but the government was wholly in Magyar hands. The irritability of the empire grew more marked; in 1882 a group of Germans, though hardly an oppressed minority, launched a national-ist movement aiming to push Germanization further, especially in the Czech lands. Although that movement at first attracted a wide following, including socialists and Jews, it fell into the hands of Georg von Schönerer, an anti-Semitic demagogue, who introduced a new, ugly note into Austrian politics.

The Ottomans: The Empire as Prey

From the perspective of international politics, the third multinational giant of the east, the Ottoman Empire, was a provocation and a prey to others. The history of this inviting ruin was a paradox: the very elements that had contributed to its greatness later determined its decline. Ottoman power had reached its crest before Vienna in 1683 (see p. 318); from that moment, its empire was pushed back from its borders in Europe, Asia, and Africa (see Plate

---

[12] A. J. P. Taylor, *The Habsburg Monarchy, 1809–1918* (rev. ed. 1948), 130.
[13] For foreign policy, see p. 812.

28). For far longer than was realistic, Europeans read the single, awesome syllable "Turk" as a synonym for single, awesome power; in fact, the Ottoman Empire was from the beginning such a sprawling collection of nations and tribes that the Ottomans themselves did not use the name Turk officially until the twentieth century. And power was precisely what the empire had less and less; intermittent displays of arbitrary brutality were only the appearance of power but no substitute. The European impression of untold Ottoman wealth became equally illusory; it was a false generalization from the fabulous voluptuousness of the Ottoman court.

However much they estimated Turkish power and wealth by memories of earlier days, the European powers came to recognize the empire's increasing weakness. We have noted before the treaties that mark the main stages of its retreat: the Treaty of Carlowitz in 1699, which detached Hungary from the Ottomans; the Treaty of Kuchuk Kainarji in 1774, which gave independence to the Crimea (see p. 437). In 1775 the Turks lost Bukovina to the Austrians, and in 1812 Bessarabia to the Russians. Greece won its independence, and other Balkan dependencies were in turmoil. By the early nineteenth century, other powers were hovering by the sick man's side and waiting for his demise. If, by 1850, the Ottoman Empire was still intact, that was partly because England and France wanted to prop it up as a bulwark against Russia, partly because the Great Powers could not agree on who should get what.

But the requirements of foreign policy and the clash of unresolved greeds were not the only reasons for the Turks' survival. Although the reforming ambitions of Mahmud II were often frustrated, he seriously attempted, in a reign which lasted to 1839, to Westernize Ottoman political, administrative, and social life. Mahmud knew no Western languages, but he was eager to learn from Western ways, and he used Western advisers; his reforms, like those of Russia's Peter the Great a century earlier, extended to the very clothes his subjects and his soldiers wore. Drastic reforms like these required drastic centralization of authority, one step in which was the massacre of the Janissaries (see p. 562), a mass murder that cleared the way for reform. On Mahmud's death in 1839, his son, Abdul-Mejid, carried on his father's work. Upon his accession, his ministers issued the "Noble Rescript of the Rose Chamber," a series of reforming edicts that were given the collective name of "Reorganization," or Tanzimat. Its effects remain a matter of debate; contemporary critics were disappointed with the disparities between declared intentions and observable results. But without question the Tanzimat was an indispensable first step out from a cloistered and stagnant past.

The second step came after the Crimean War, in which the Ottomans, allied with Britain and France, had defeated the Russians (see p. 743). In 1856 a determined band of youthful reformers tried to extend Mahmud's and Abdul-Mejid's policies. They were eager to learn from the West, to import not merely privileged traders and churchmen, but also political, social, and administrative ideas. The Hatti-Humayoun, issued in 1856, was their charter. It was nothing less than the proposal to turn the Ottoman lands from a disunited, corrupt, ineffective conglomerate into a modern Western state, with toleration and access to office for everyone (instead of Muslims alone); an honest government; a modern tax system; and a humanized legal code. For some years, the reformers were in control of the country; with Sultan Abdul-Aziz, who ascended the throne in 1861, they had one of their own number in supreme authority. The Western powers were impressed by these efforts and not wholly pessimistic.

Yet, while the reforms of the *Hatti-Humayoun* were not fully implemented, they were still too drastic to please vested interests. Privileged bodies—resident Christians or traditionally powerful Muslims, traders with special concessions or border territories with near autonomy—stood to lose more from moderniza-tion than to gain. Then, too, Abdul-Aziz was profligate. By the early 1870s, when his most trusted subordinates had died, he faced the threat of adminis-trative chaos and financial bankruptcy. The Ottoman Empire was the universal debtor, and by 1876 that debtor appeared near total insolvency. In the impending chaos of that year, Abdul-Aziz was deposed. His successor, Abdul-Hamid II, was chosen by the reformers to revitalize their old policies. And for the moment, all seemed propitious: in the year of his accession, Abdul-Hamid proclaimed a constitution and called a parliament for the following year.

But by 1877, securely in power, Abdul-Hamid showed that his real inclinations were in the direction of the old-fashioned autocracy. He undid the work of his first year; he dissolved parliament, drove the reformers from the country, and ruled alone, in daily dread of assassination. He was, in his way, shrewd and (a welcome relief after his predecessor) thrifty. Nor were his actions after 1877 wholly surprising; he had proved his capacity for cruelty the year before, with the Bulgarian massacres. In 1875 a rebellion had broken out among the Ottomans' Serbian subjects; it was followed in 1876 by a rebellion among the Bulgarians. Abdul-Hamid demonstrated that foreign intervention was unnecessary by defeating the Serbs in 1876; he made foreign intervention inevitable by butchering the Bulgarians in the same year. The atrocious mass killing of some twelve thousand Christians by his troops aroused the conscience of Europe, especially that of Britain. After some hesitation, Gladstone, then leading the Liberal opposition (see p. 820), published an indignant and influential pamphlet, *The Bulgarian Horrors and the Question of the East.* While Benjamin Disraeli, the prime minister, was skeptical, some measure of British engagement in Turkey had to follow.

But Britain was not the only power to take an interest in the "Question of the East." The Russian interest in the Ottoman Empire was, if anything, more vital, and certainly far less humane. In 1870 the Russians had unilaterally torn up the clause of the 1856 Treaty of Paris that had neutralized the Black Sea (see p. 746); the act, reluctantly ratified by the other powers, was a foretaste of new Russian enterprises against the Ottoman Empire. In April 1877 Russia made war on Turkey and, in March 1878, after the fortunes of battle had shifted back and forth, the Russians imposed on the Turks the Treaty of San Stefano. It was so favorable to the Russians that a general anti-Russian war seemed likely; Austria-Hungary proposed an international congress to revise the treaty. Britain readily agreed: Disraeli had dispatched the fleet to Constantinople, while British public opinion clamored for war with the Russians. But the jingoes did not prevail. [14] At an international congress in Berlin, the Austrians picked up the right to administer the Serbo-Croat provinces of Bosnia and Herzegovina, which had been in Turkish hands since the fifteenth century; the Russians kept Batum; and, with complete disregard for burgeoning nationalist sentiments, the powers carved up Ottoman Bulgaria into three zones and gave two of these a measure of autonomy. The Treaty of Berlin was too much of a patchwork and too much of a horse trade to solve anything. But it avoided war.

One participant in the Berlin Congress was happy: Britain's prime minister, Disraeli, who obtained Cyprus for his country without firing a shot. He brought back, he said, "peace with honor." Why the island of Cyprus, in lonely splendor in the eastern Mediterranean? Disraeli's choice tells much about the direction of his real concern; he was interested in nearby Egypt, another part of the Ottoman Empire inviting intervention (see p. 844). Thus it was the weakness of the Ottomans that determined the actions of the greater powers far more than the strength of those powers. In March 1878 Lord Salisbury, about to become British foreign minister, wrote his chief, Disraeli, "I am, as you know, not a believer in the possibility of setting the Turkish government on its legs again, as a genuine reliable Power." [15] It was a tragedy for more than the Ottomans that they should have been reduced from an empire into a question.

TWO EXPERIMENTS WITH CONSERVATIVE DEMOCRACY: FRANCE AND BRITAIN

France: From the Republic of Monarchists to the Republic of Republicans

France's Third Republic was born under the most unfavorable circumstances imaginable. The French military debacle in 1870 was all the more traumatic for being so unexpected; not only the king of Italy, but most Europeans, thought the French army to be a superb fighting force. When France fell, Frenchmen fervently wanted it to rise again, but in what guise? Despite the emperor's stunning failures, Bonapartist ideas retained their popularity for years and

---

[14] The word *jingo* was added to the language through a famous music-hall ditty: "We don't want to fight; But by Jingo, if we do, we've got the men, we've got the ships, we've got the money too."

[15] C. J. Lowe, *The Reluctant Imperialists,* vol. II, *The Documents* (1967), 1.

survived Napoleon III's death in 1873. But in the end it was the republicans who triumphed, not without a good deal of assistance—partly intentional, largely unintentional—from monarchists.

French republicans made their first bid for attention and power two days after the defeat at Sedan. On September 4, Paris rose; under the leadership of the eloquent democrat, Léon Gambetta, a hastily formed emergency government proclaimed the Republic. It was a strange sight: the war was lost, but the war went on, kept alive by Gambetta's energies. He headed a Government of National Defense and moved the capital of shattered France first to Tours, then to Bordeaux; but by the end of January, when Paris had fallen, the fighting was over. In early February Gambetta was out of office. At Bismarck's insistence, Frenchmen in the same month elected a National Assembly that would have authority to conclude peace with Germany and to make a constitution for France. The elections were a repudiation of Gambetta, a vote for the peace he hoped to delay and for a monarchy he hoped to replace. Now Bismarck was ready to settle with France. On May 10, 1871, at Frankfurt, he imposed draconian conditions: the French were obliged to pay an indemnity of five billion francs (about $1 billion); sustain occupying German troops; and cede the border provinces of Alsace and Lorraine, rich in coal, iron, and textile manufacture, and largely French-speaking. The new government, under the by now very elderly statesman Adolphe Thiers, as "Chief of the Executive Power of the French Republic," began its life with a crushing deficit.

A new uprising in Paris, which erupted on March 18, added still another, even more staggering liability. To have a republic presided over by a monarchist like Thiers was not particularly paradoxical: Thiers was a liberal, his fame was secure, and his royalism gradually transmuted itself into advocacy of a republic with a strong president—himself. Thiers' France was a monarchy without a king. But the revolt in the capital, the Paris Commune, compelled Thiers to set Frenchman against Frenchman and drive a wedge of hatred between men whose single enemy until a few weeks before had been the Prussian. The Paris Commune was a tragedy, but it was rapidly converted into a political myth and exploited for partisan purposes. It did not create divisions among Frenchmen so much as dramatize them, and dramatic divisions are hard to heal. Thanks to Karl Marx's brilliant and opportune pamphlet, *The Civil War in France,* the Commune appeared to be a milestone on the march toward the proletarian revolution. Historians have noted that the conversion of the name "Communard" into "Communist" was a convenient, plausible, and widespread practice. Yet it was largely false; in March 1871 there were few Marxists in the insurrectionary capital.

The Commune of Paris did not look forward to communism so much as back to the Commune of revolutionary Paris in the Year II. It was led by proud Parisians hostile to overbearing provincials; anticlericals sick of priestly power; wounded, fiercely anti-German patriots; anarchists whose prophet was not Marx but Proudhon; and agitators encouraged by the disorders to give vent to their smoldering discontent. Thiers and the National Assembly yielded Paris to the rebels, governed from Versailles, and refused all offers of negotiation. As tensions heightened, the Communards grew irritable and pitiless; as in 1793, mobs and the government itself took revenge on prisoners for their receding hopes and mounting frustrations. The great realist painter Gustave Courbet took charge of pulling down the "militarist" Vendôme Column with its statue of Napoleon I. Worse, in May, as government troops gradually retook the city, the rebels killed hostages, including members of the old police force, numerous priests, the archbishop of Paris, and stray aristocrats. Then came vengeance on a large scale. During "Bloody Week" in May 1871, some twenty thousand Communards were unceremoniously shot down; thousands more were deported to New Caledonia. As usual, the White Terror exceeded the Red Terror in sheer savagery and the number of its victims. Having lost the war with the Prussians, the government was determined to win the civil war. It did, though for a time it seemed that the price was too high.

Yet within thirty years, after other trials, France was again a major power, a great empire, a leader in science and literature, and, above all, a stable republic. This astonishing recovery had several sources. One was stability in the midst of change: the administrative order that Napoleon I had imposed upon France remained in many respects inviolate and provided significant continuity. Another was the stupidity of monarchists and authoritarians. The leaders of the Third Republic provided its enemies with splendid opportunities for attack; but these opportunities were, with singular consistency, passed by. The first among the unexpected friends of the Third Republic were the monarchists. Try as they might, they could not unite on a candidate. The Legitimists offered the count de Chambord, grandson of France's last Bourbon king, Charles X; the Orleanists offered the count de Paris, grandson of France's last Orleanist king, Louis-Philippe. The Bonapartists, meanwhile, played their own game, hoping to bring Napoleon III back to power. One possible solution was to crown the count de Chambord first and have the younger count de Paris succeed him, but Chambord's tactless, self-centered, and public rejections of all compromise destroyed this hope. After Chambord had ruined all his chances by refusing to accept the tricolor, Thiers, with much amusement, called him "the French Washington." [16]

But Thiers, though by no means ridiculous, was the next victim of events. Ironically, it was the conservatives who voted him out of office. In by-election after by-election, republicans had won seats, and the dwindling monarchist majority in the National Assembly was near panic. Thiers had accepted the republic; the right wing wanted repression of the Left and moves toward a restoration. Since Thiers would give them neither, he had to go. In May 1873 he was defeated and promptly resigned. Marshal MacMahon, a distinguished royalist general with no particular skill in politics, followed Thiers in the presidency. His work in the legislature was done for him by the duke de

[16] David Thomson, *Democracy in France Since 1870* (5th ed., 1969), 81.

Broglie, a monarchist in search of a compromise. MacMahon's tenure, officially fixed at seven years, was designed by its engineers as a safeguard for Catholic conservatism and the prelude to a restoration. Instead, MacMahon presided over the weakening of the former and the liquidation of prospects for the latter. In the course of 1875, in a series of laws passed to move the government from its provisional to a more permanent status, France supplied itself with a patchwork of enactments that eventually served it as a constitution for sixty-five years, until 1940 (see p. 1073). Early in the year, the celebrated "Wallon Amendment" hinted at the shape of the republic to come: "The President of the Republic is elected by absolute majority vote of the Senate and the Chamber of Deputies, meeting as the National Assembly." This determined the primacy of the legislature and the ascendancy of the Chamber of Deputies over the Senate; the ascendancy of the premier over his cabinet came later.

On May 16, 1877, the famous *"seize mai,"* President MacMahon precipitated a crisis that confirmed the republicanism of the republic. Acting within his constitutional rights, he dismissed the premier, dissolved the Chamber, and appealed to the country to give him a legislature that saw things his way. Instead, the country returned an impressive republican majority. In 1879 new elections produced a Senate sympathetic to the Chamber. MacMahon, unable to govern, took the consequences: he resigned. He was followed in the presidency by Jules Grévy, an avowed republican. In eight years a handful of laws, a few governmental crises, and the accumulation of political experience had taken the republic from the monarchists. The president was rendered impotent; real power lay in the hands of the premier, who was responsible to the Chamber of Deputies, where, in order to govern, he had to secure a majority. But this majority needed to be constructed; no single party ever secured a majority at the polls, and every cabinet was therefore a coalition. Governing became a matter of trading and compromises. The country elected a new Chamber of Deputies every four years by universal male suffrage, and the premier negotiated with that body. [17] Its life was fixed and secure; a cabinet could count on a far shorter existence. Thus France became, unlike America, with its strong president, and unlike Britain, with its two-party system, a volatile parliamentary regime periodically responsible to the people. It was a system that favored skillful politicians; it was a system that worked better than it looked. Whatever its defects, by 1879 the republic was complete.

The Republic in Travail: From Boulanger to Dreyfus

If the republic was complete, it was not out of danger. Religious, social, and economic conflicts and memories of the Commune embittered political discussion. Monarchists acknowledged defeat but remained unreconciled to the

---

[17] By its lights, the Third Republic was a democracy; actually, it was a dictatorship of men over women, who did not get the vote until 1944.

republic. The split between town and country grew worse with industrialization: the French peasantry had accepted the republic and indeed profited from it; the emerging working class found itself underrepresented in the National Assembly and hamstrung by antilabor laws; trade unionism, though tolerated since the 1860s, was not legalized until 1884. Many of France's most influential officials served the republic without affection: bureaucrats, proud in their elite status, contravened with their autocratic behavior the democratic intentions of the laws. Army officers, sworn to defend the republic, were normally arch-Catholic in belief, reactionary in politics, and secretly royalist in their sentiments. On the other side were the anticlericals, disdainful of Catholic traditionalism and looking back to the French Revolution for their tradition. Beginning in 1879, this last group got its opportunity: under the sponsorship of Jules Ferry in the cabinet, the French government passed a series of school laws putting civic in the place of religious education, greatly expanding the secular school system, and forcing priests out of teaching positions. The Ferry Laws, completed in 1886, were a triumph of secularism over Catholicism; the local schoolteacher became the proverbial opponent of the local priest. The new teaching corps vastly changed the outlook of millions of young Frenchmen and helped to spread the burgeoning republican spirit. But it also kept alive angry quarrels that were to shape French politics for decades to come.

These divisions were not healed by scandals, which the sensationalist press did much to play up; with their sordid details, they confirmed those nostalgic for the glittering days of empire in their contempt for a republic apparently incapable of governing with dignity and probity. In 1887 it was discovered that the influential politician Daniel Wilson had trafficked in the coveted decoration, the Legion of Honor. To make things worse, Wilson was President Grévy's son-in-law and had conducted his business from the president's palace, the Elysée, thus covering himself in immunity and, using presidential franking privileges, thriftily saving on postage. From this rather unpleasant atmosphere emerged the Boulanger affair, a serious incident despite its ludicrous denouement. General Georges Boulanger had been appointed minister of war in early 1886; he was a republican and the candidate of the Radical party—it was the Radical politician Georges Clemenceau who had first put Boulanger forward. At first, he magnificently lived up to his reputation as a democrat; he democratized the army by a series of controversial moves, including the elimination of some prominent royalist officers. To those aching for revenge against Germany, he loomed as a potential Bonaparte. "He became the hero," as David Thomson has put it, "of revues as well as of reviews, and the music-halls sang his praises." [18] Although Boulanger lost his post in 1887, when the government fell, the Wilson scandal again focused attention on him. With abundant, enthusiastic financial backing from reactionary groups and support from a number of Radicals, Boulanger scored resounding successes at the polls: his political base, resting on

[18] Thomson, *Democracy in France*, 153.

the extreme right and the extreme left, ominously foreshadows the politics of modern dictators. But a conspiracy to make him master of Paris dismally failed; he was, after all, only a stage general, too irresponsible and too cowardly to follow his speeches with action. Ingloriously he fled abroad. That was on April 1, 1889; in September 1891 he shot himself at Brussels, on the grave of his mistress. The republic survived Boulangism, with a good deal of luck and rather less merit.

The Boulanger affair was a threat turned farce. The Dreyfus affair was a graver matter; it nearly wrecked the republic. It was a triumph—a bloody, incomplete triumph, but a triumph nonetheless—of republicanism and reason over that cancer of modern mass politics, anti-Semitism. In 1880 a French company had been formed to build a Panama canal; its officers corrupted politicians and newspapermen to win support for their scheme. In vain: by the end of the decade the company was bankrupt. A public scandal followed. Among the manipulators of the Panama Canal Company had been several Jews, and many Frenchmen feared what they called the "stranglehold" of Jews on the finances of the country. They conveniently overlooked the prominence of Protestants in the banking world—but then, the anti-Semite is immune to evidence. One instance of Jewish wickedness is welcome as "proof" of a Jewish conspiracy against the world; countless instances of Jewish probity, patriotism, self-sacrifice are equally welcome, as proof of Jewish cleverness. Anti-Semitism says nothing about Jews, but much about the strains of modern life that make such irrational beliefs not merely possible but welcome. The chief of French anti-Semites was Edouard Drumont. In 1886 he had aroused attention with his anti-Semitic diatribe, *La France juive;* from 1892 on, feeding on the Panama scandal, his anti-Semitic journal, *La libre parole,* kept the pot of hatred boiling.

In the fall of 1894, *La libre parole* had some sensational news for its readers: a Captain Alfred Dreyfus, the first Jew to join the French General Staff, had been arrested and charged with spying for the Germans. His motives seemed obscure: a rich Alsatian Jew, he had no cause to accept the pittance the Germans were paying; good cause to hate the Germans, who had stolen his province from France; and every reason for loyalty to a service hitherto closed to Jews. The only evidence against him was a torn-up memorandum, a *bordereau,* which, some experts believed, was in Dreyfus' handwriting. But his secret court-martial was swayed in part by the dark hints of Major Hubert-Joseph Henry, of Military Intelligence, concerning information so confidential that he could not show it even to the judges. In December 1894 Dreyfus was convicted and sentenced to life imprisonment; in January 1895 he was solemnly stripped of his rank. Then he was shipped to a pestilential French penal colony, Devil's Island, off the northern coast of South America.

Dreyfus stoutly proclaimed his innocence, but only his family and a handful of skeptics believed him. They probed for flaws in the evidence and, with Captain Dreyfus languishing in his tropical prison, called for a retrial. Indirectly, their cause was advanced by Major Marie-Georges Picquart, who investigated the case after Dreyfus' conviction. If anyone would save the republic, it was a man of Picquart's stamp. A loyal officer, a good Catholic, a known anti-Semite, he was convinced of Dreyfus' guilt. But he was driven by a passion for the truth, and the obstacles the authorities put in his way only spurred him on. He soon stumbled on the real writer of the *bordereau*, Commandant Esterhazy, an aristocrat of expensive habits. Henry, the officer whose words had helped to convict Dreyfus, began to forge supporting documents; Picquart was ordered away from the case. But in August 1898, faced with sure exposure, Henry confessed to his forgeries and killed himself. A new trial was inevitable. Its verdict, in September 1899, scaled heights of illogicality: by a vote of five to two, the judges declared Dreyfus guilty, but with extenuating circumstances. The president of France pardoned Dreyfus, and the family, worried over Dreyfus' health, accepted the pardon.

But the affair was out of their hands. Parties had formed; first the intellectuals, then the politicians, made Dreyfus into a towering symbol. Both parties had mixed motives: some were anti-Dreyfusards because they persisted in thinking Dreyfus guilty; others, like many French Jews, wanted the noisy case to die down; still others wanted to protect the army against all criticism, no matter how justified. Some Dreyfusards believed in justice even if it damaged established institutions: the great realist novelist, Emile Zola (see p. 884), who exposed himself to obloquy and prosecution with his brilliant diatribe, *J'accuse*, was one of these. Others, like Jean Jaurès, the respected Socialist deputy, were Dreyfusards because they saw Dreyfus' enemies—the conservatives, the army, the church—as their own. Still others mixed conviction with self-interest: France's future premier, Georges Clemenceau, was a politician in search of an issue who, at the same time, believed in the rights of man. Whatever their reasons, the Dreyfusards' triumph was total. Dreyfus himself was almost forgotten in the general struggle. In 1904 he won retrial and an acquittal; in 1906 he was reinstated and decorated with the Legion of Honor. But the Dreyfusards had more ambitious aims. They made antimilitarism and anticlericalism into irresistible slogans. In 1892 Pope Leo XIII had encouraged French Catholics to participate in politics—the famous *ralliement*, the rallying to the republic, and Catholic voices for reconciliation were still heard, though plaintively, as late as 1904. But in that year France broke off relations with the papacy, and in December 1905 a series of laic laws, harshly enforced, separated French church and state and expropriated the church. The Dreyfusards had won, but, showing their enemy no quarter, they kept open old wounds and opened new ones.

Britain after 1867: Shooting Niagara

In Britain, meanwhile, far-reaching changes caused less bitterness than in France. For over a century, perhaps since the ministry of Walpole (see p. 385),

Britain had enjoyed a reputation for political stability, for its capacity to adapt to changing conditions. Planned evolution—this was the lesson—was preferable to spontaneous revolution. If Britain ever deserved this reputation, it did so in the last third of the nineteenth century. Reforms were risky, but only a few diehards, like Thomas Carlyle, thought the risks excessive. The dour critic of Parliament, which he derisively called the "talking shop," Carlyle feared democracy as much as he hated it. But when the Conservatives put through the Reform Act of 1867, democracy was, if not complete, irresistible; this second Reform Act was a pointer to the future.

That future was explored for a decade or more in a remarkable duel between two remarkable statesmen, Disraeli and Gladstone. Early in 1868, when Lord Derby retired, Disraeli became prime minister. His appeal to the country in November was a disappointment; the voters he had done so much to enfranchise did not share his vision of Tory democracy. Confronted by a comfortable Liberal majority, Disraeli resigned and gave way to his great rival. Gladstone's Liberal ministry, which lasted until 1874, undertook a variety of reform measures, all of them compromises, all promises of more far-reaching measures to come. The government strengthened elementary schools; in 1871 it abolished all religious tests for university fellowships and did away with the purchase of army commissions. The year before, it had subjected government posts to competitive examinations[19]; the year after, it fulfilled a cherished radical demand by making the vote secret. Although political power remained largely in the hands of the peerage, the gentry, and select members of the respectable urban middle classes, democracy and the ideal of a career open to merit moved forward, step by step.

Gladstone's most conspicuous failure was the issue he had wished most fervently to solve: Ireland. That unhappy country, a sore in the side of England since the days of Oliver Cromwell, remained a sore in defiance of Gladstone's most prayerful intentions. The terrible Irish famine of 1846–1847, followed by the hopeless Irish uprising of 1848, had left increased bitterness and a new nationalism. Irishmen execrated the "United Kingdom of Great Britain and Ireland," which had been foisted on them in 1801. The Fenians, a secret Irish Republican brotherhood founded in the United States in 1858, collected enough energy and manpower to launch a small-scale assault on Canada in 1866; in 1867, Fenians blew up a London jail in which some of their brethren were held, and twelve persons died. Before this, Gladstone had already vowed to "pacify Ireland." To that end, he disestablished the Church of Ireland in 1869, leaving it to minister to the minority of Anglicans but, by breaking its ties to the state, removing the anomaly of its privileged position in an overwhelmingly Catholic country. And in 1870 he tried to aid the helpless, mainly destitute

---

[19] In the early days of civil service examinations, in the 1850s, the secretary of the treasury made sure his choice got the job by pitting him against two rivals who were known to be more stupid than anyone else. These paragons were known as the "Treasury Idiots."

Irish peasants with a Land Act, which prescribed compensation for farmers who had improved their lands and who were evicted by their greedy landlords. As time proved, the act, though well-intentioned, was not enough.

In 1874, after a substantial electoral victory, Disraeli succeeded Gladstone as prime minister and enlarged on the Liberal program. Indeed, Tory reformers had a gift for attacking social problems. In 1871 the Liberals had considerably liberalized the laws of 1824-1825 legalizing trade unions, but picketing had remained an illegal practice. In 1875 Disraeli removed that impediment to industrial action. In other acts, the Conservative government undertook to supervise the purity of foods and drugs, enabled cities to clean up slums, and consolidated a mass of statutes dealing with public health. Yet the pace of social legislation was slowing down, in part to await new problems that would exact new solutions.

Political reform, on the other hand, went on. It was in the hands of the Liberals this time. Much to Queen Victoria's disgust, the aging Disraeli—earl of Beaconsfield since 1876—gave way to Gladstone in 1880. The queen had lived in retirement since her husband's death; Disraeli, who sedulously cultivated by outrageously flattering her, won her over to his policies. To the degree that the queen came to love Disraeli, she came to dislike Gladstone. But Britain had evolved into a constitutional monarchy; the elections of 1880 gave the Liberals a solid majority, and Gladstone had to be called to form a government. In his six years of office, Gladstone now drew the logical consequences of the Reform Act of 1867 and the Ballot Act of 1872. The latter had not eliminated such unsavory practices as the bribery of electors. In 1883, after due inquiry, Parliament passed the Corrupt and Illegal Practices Act, which severely punished all undue influence and severely limited permissible expenses. With one stroke, the British had achieved the incredible: they had legislated clean and honest elections into being.

The widening of the electorate was next on the agenda of reform. In 1884 the third Reform Act, passed after vehement protests in the House of Lords, extended the vote to most agricultural workers. In 1885 a far-reaching Redistribution Act strengthened democracy further by increasing the representation of populous urban constituencies while reducing rural ones.[20] What has often been reputed to be the effect of the first Reform Act of 1832—the triumph of the middle classes—was now at hand. But it was not the middle class alone that benefited; the poor, too, could make their voices heard by having their votes counted. England had long been the very model of a deferential society;

[20] Of course, democracy was still anything but complete. It was not until 1911 that members of the House of Commons were paid (thus belatedly fulfilling an old Chartist demand); not until 1918 that the Representation of the People Act made manhood suffrage universal and gave women over 30 the vote; not until 1928 that women finally got parity with men in the franchise. The Labour government elected in 1945 eliminated members of Parliament returned from the university constituencies by the votes of graduates, who could vote there as well as in their home constituencies.

if deference survived 1885, as it did, this was more a matter of time-honored habit and educational distinctions than of legal discrimination. As the old aristocratic centers of power weakened, new centers emerged. The rise of mass politics brought with it disciplined parties. "A wide electorate need not merely be checked; it could also be cultivated." [21] In the House of Commons, party discipline grew stronger; candidates identified themselves with a program to which their party was committed; and if they were elected they were more or less compelled to cooperate with their fellow Liberals or Conservatives to realize that program. And outside the House, party organizations, though prohibited from using outright bribery, kept voters happy and in line through clubs and conferences. Joseph Chamberlain, who had gained prominence as a radical lord mayor of Birmingham and had entered Parliament in 1876, demonstrated the workings of the new organized politics in his city by making thorough canvasses of voters and constructing a political machine that reminded his opponents of nothing so much as the American party caucus.

But the picture, though bright, was not without its shadows. The great Gladstone-Disraeli duel meant rivalry without incivility, a struggle that kept political conflict within bounds. It came to an end in 1881 with Disraeli's death; while the two major parties continued their competition for voters, the old consensus was wearing thin. Optimism, both in domestic and in foreign affairs, began to give way to a new anxiety. Since 1873 England had been plagued with what came to be called "the Great Depression"; grain prices and agricultural rents dropped as cheap foreign wheat flooded into Britain. And in industry, though production continued to rise and merchants, like industrialists, made money, there was a widespread mood of dejection. The Great Depression was more a matter of lost confidence than of bankruptcies; Britain discovered that its rivals—notably the United States, the new Germany, and highly industrial-ized little Belgium—could successfully compete with British firms in the world market. Then there was Ireland—always Ireland. Once the ballot had become truly secret, Irishmen could freely vote their discontent: in the elections of 1880, they had sent sixty-one members to the Commons, all committed to home rule for Ireland; in the elections of 1885, they increased their number to eighty-six. Their leader was Charles Stewart Parnell, a Protestant landowner and a gifted parliamentarian. Their greatest ally was the aged Gladstone, who had carried a further Land Act in 1881 and who finally had been converted to home rule. But when, in 1886, he proposed a separate legislature and executive for Ireland, he could not impose his will on his party. On the crucial vote in the House of Commons, nearly a hundred of his fellow Liberals, led by Joseph Chamberlain, deserted him. In the election that followed, the country repudiated Gladstone by giving the Conservatives and the dissident anti-home-rule Liberals a huge majority. The Conservatives "solved" the Irish problem by temporizing and postponing.

[21] R. K. Webb, *Modern England from the Eighteenth Century to the Present* (1968), 396.

In any event, Britain's attention was now fastened, more than ever, on foreign affairs. Here, too, consensus was breaking down and tempers were growing short. Abroad, as at home, Disraeli and Gladstone had often done one another's work. True, the two statesmen had markedly divergent conceptions of politics. Gladstone was a moralist and a moralizer who concealed perfectly sound ideas—peace, self-determination, economy, humanitarianism, justice—behind clouds of high-flying rhetoric. Queen Victoria complained that if Mr. Gladstone consulted her at all, he addressed her as though she were a public meeting. Disraeli, a belated romantic, ostentatious dandy, and imaginative novelist (at least in his younger years), had far cooler political skills, but an equally passionate devotion to social justice; his idea of "Tory democracy," though it sounds esoteric, was actually quite simple. England, he had said in one of his novels, *Sybil* (1845), was two nations, divided between the rich and the poor; it was the task of the rich to make themselves responsible for the poor, to throw bridges across, if not to eliminate, the division. And in foreign policy, Disraeli stood for empire, as a traditional institution around which conservative sentiment could rally. When, in 1876, he persuaded Queen Victoria to adopt the grandiose title "Empress of India," this was more than a bombastic gesture. It symbolized an old (and profitable) connection, but also (and more) a new attitude toward the rest of the world. Yet that attitude and the policies that embodied it embroiled Britain in endless expense, much humiliation, a dramatic reversal in foreign policy, and war. When Queen Victoria died in 1901, after a reign of more than sixty years, her Britain was at war with the Boers in South Africa, a drawn-out and sobering affair that underscored the difficulties of navigating the ship of state in that new world of imperial Europe.

SELECTED READINGS

The titles in this section concentrate on political history. For economic history, including imperialism, see Chapter 21; for currents of thought, see Chapter 22.

For the German Reich created in 1871, the volumes by Hamerow, *Restoration, Revolution, Reaction* and *The Social Foundations of German Unification,* and by Pflanze, *Bismarck and the Development of Germany,* remain essential background. Holborn, *History of Modern Germany, 1840-1945* remains as authoritative as before. Other titles, also cited before, retain their utility for the period of 1871 to 1900, above all the relevant chapters in Craig, *Politics of the Prussian Army;* and Ramm, *Germany, 1789-1914.* Bismarck himself continues to engender controversy, well summed up in the opening chapter of Pflanze's biography, "The Bismarck Problem." Until the second volume of Pflanze's biography appears, most useful are Erich Eyck, *Bismarck and the German Empire* (1950), which is an abridgment of a three-volume, highly critical biography, published in German; the lively, somewhat perverse essay by A. J. P. Taylor, *Bismarck: The Man and the Statesman* (1955); the sober volume by Friedrich Darmstaedter, *Bismarck and the Creation of the Second Reich* (1948); and the opening two chapters of Gordon A. Craig, *From Bismarck to Adenauer: Aspects of German Statecraft* (rev. ed., 1965). Arthur Rosenberg, *The Birth of the German Republic, 1871-*

1918 (tr. 1931) is a brilliant left-wing interpretation. For Germany just after the Iron Chancellor's fall, see J. Alden Nichols, *Germany After Bismarck, the Caprivi Era, 1890-1894* (1958), and J. C. G. Röhl, *Germany Without Bismarck: The Crisis of Government in the Second Reich, 1890-1900* (1968), both valuable analyses. The increasing importance of the army in policy-making is carefully analyzed in Craig's book on the Prussian army; it may be supplemented with Lysbeth W. Muncy, *The Junker in the Prussian Administration under William II, 1888-1914* (1944) and Martin Kitchen, *The German Officer Corps, 1890-1914* (1968). Norman Rich, *Friedrich von Holstein, Politics and Diplomacy in the Era of Bismarck and William II,* 2 vols. (1965), is extremely detailed and extremely revealing. A really thorough and deep study of Emperor William II remains a desideratum in English; Michael Balfour, *The Kaiser and His Times* (1963) is the best now available.

The German socialist movement has been chronicled for these years in Vernon Lidtke, *The Outlawed Party: Social Democracy in Germany, 1878-1890* (1966) and Guenther Roth, *The Social Democrats in Imperial Germany* (1963). Interesting light is shed on the relation of economics and politics in Lamar Cecil, *Albert Ballin: Business and Politics in Imperial Germany, 1888-1918* (1967). Evelyn Anderson, *Hammer or Anvil: The Story of the German Working-Class Movement* (1945) is suggestive but partisan.

Denis Mack Smith, *Italy: A Modern History* (rev. ed., 1969), and Christopher Seton-Watson, *Italy from Liberalism to Fascism, 1870-1925* (1967), are the best recent histories. The philosopher-historian Benedetto Croce's *A History of Italy, 1871-1915* (1929), well repays reading. Other useful general accounts are Réné Albrecht-Carrié, *Italy from Napoleon to Mussolini* (1950), and Cecil J. Sprigge, *The Development of Modern Italy* (1944). These may be supplemented with more specialized histories: John A. Thayer, *Italy and the Great War: Politics and Culture, 1870-1915* (1964); Shepard B. Clough, *The Economic History of Modern Italy* (1964); A. C. Jemolo, *Church and State in Italy, 1850-1950* (tr. 1960); Robert F. Foerster, *The Italian Emigration of Our Times* (1919); and Richard Hostetter, *The Italian Socialist Movement: Origins, 1860-1882* (1958). For that strange politician, Crispi, see *The Memoirs of Francesco Crispi,* 3 vols. (tr. 1922).

The best books in English on the Russia of this period are two volumes cited elsewhere, both by Hugh Seton-Watson: *The Russian Empire* and *The Decline of Imperial Russia.* Karpovich, *Imperial Russia,* also cited, has some fine sections on this period. Werner E. Mosse, *Alexander II and the Modernization of Russia* (1958) is an excellent short overview of the emancipation period of reform; on the same subject, see the splendid monograph by Geroid T. Robinson, *Rural Russia,* cited before. For Pan-Slavism, see Michael B. Petrovich, *The Emergence of Russian Pan-Slavism, 1856-1870* (1956); for the rising radical tide, see the brilliant and thorough treatment by Franco Venturi, *Roots of Revolution* (tr. 1960). And see D. J. Footman, *Red Prelude* (1944); S. H. Baron, *Plekhanov, the Father of Russian Marxism* (1963); J. H. L. Keep, *The Rise of Social Democracy in Russia* (1963), and Leopold Haimson, *The Russian Marxists and the Origins of Bolshevism* (1955). The period of reaction during the reign of Alexander III is well treated by Robert F. Byrnes in his *Pobedonostsev, His Life and Thought* (1968). Simon M. Dubnow, *History of the Jews in Russia and Poland,* 3 vols. (tr. 1916) is essential.

Robert Kann, *The Multinational Empire: Nationalism and National Reform in the Hapsburg Monarchy, 1840-1918,* 2 vols. (1950-1964) is indispensable for Austria-Hungary, the *Ausgleich,* and subsequent political narrative; it effectively supplements the relevant chapters in Macartney's *Habsburg Empire,* cited above. See also A. J. P.

Taylor's brief and witty *The Habsburg Monarchy, 1809–1918* (rev. ed., 1948). For foreign policy, see Barbara Jelavich, *The Hapsburg Empire in European Affairs, 1814–1918* (1969).

On the Ottoman Empire, the essay by Bernard Lewis, *The Emergence of Modern Turkey* (rev. ed., 1968) says the essential in brief compass. It may be supplemented by Roderic H. Davison, *Reform in the Ottoman Empire, 1856–1876* (1963), and by Anderson, *The Eastern Question,* already cited. On the ramifications of the Suez Canal affair, see above all David S. Landes, *Bankers and Pashas: International Finance and Economic Imperialism in Egypt* (1958). For diplomacy, see W. N. Medlicott, *The Congress of Berlin and After: A Diplomatic History of the Near Eastern Settlement, 1878–1880* (rev. ed., 1963).

The literature on the French Third Republic is vast and continuously growing. Several books cited before—Gordon Wright, *France in Modern Times,* and Gagnon, *France Since 1789*—remain immensely useful as brief accounts. In addition, see the vivid and detailed history by D. W. Brogan, *France under the Republic, 1870–1939* (1940), as well as Alfred Cobban, *A History of Modern France,* vol. 3 (1965). David Thomson, *Democracy in France Since 1870* (5th ed., 1969), is a brilliant and compact analysis of the forces that made the republic. For the early events, see J. P. T. Bury, *Gambetta and the National Defense* (1936); Frank Jellinek, *The Paris Commune of 1871* (1937); and Alistair Horne, *The Fall of Paris: The Siege and the Commune, 1870–1871* (1968).

For the politics of the early republic, see again Power, *Jules Ferry and the Renaissance of French Imperialism* (1947); the early chapters of J. H. Jackson, *Clemenceau and the Third French Republic* (1948); Jackson, *Jean Jaurès: His Life and Work* (1954); and Harvey Goldberg, *A Life of Jean Jaurès* (1962). Aaron Noland, *The Founding of the French Socialist Party, 1893–1905* (1956), has much valuable material.

Among the many books on "the Affair," the most dependable are Guy Chapman, *The Dreyfus Case* (1955), and D. Johnson, *France and the Dreyfus Affair* (1967). Robert F. Byrnes, *Antisemitism in Modern France: Prologue to the Dreyfus Affair* (1950), is indispensable. There is much relevant information on the French mentality in Richard D. Challener, *The French Theory of the Nation in Arms, 1866–1939* (1955); David G. Ralston, *The Army of the Republic: The Place of the Military in the Political Evolution of France, 1871–1914* (1967); and John Anthony Scott, *Republican Ideas and the Liberal Tradition in France, 1870–1914* (1951).

For Great Britain the avalanche of books is, if anything, even more torrential than for France. Once again, R. K. Webb, *Modern England from the Eighteenth Century to the Present* (1968), provides narrative and bibliographical guidance. R. C. K. Ensor, *England, 1870–1914* (1936), though now a bit stodgy, remains full of valuable detail. The great two-volume epilogue of Elie Halévy's *History of the English People in the Nineteenth Century,* especially the first of these, *Imperialism and the Rise of Labour, 1805–1905* (tr. 1929), is a splendidly balanced account. See also the brief history by David Thomson, *England in the Nineteenth Century* (1951). The best life of Gladstone is by Sir Philip Magnus, *Gladstone: A Biography* (1954); the old three-volume standard biography by Lord Morley (1903) may still be consulted with profit. For his great opponent, see Robert Blake, *Disraeli* (1966); it has largely replaced the six-volume monument by W. F. Monypenny and G. E. Buckle, *The Life of Benjamin Disraeli, Earl of Beaconsfield* (1910–1920). Among the many biographies of Queen Victoria, Elizabeth Longford, *Queen Victoria* (1964) is the best. On the new politics, H. J. Hanham, *Elections and Party Management* (1959) is excellent. See also Trevor Lloyd, *The General Election of 1880* (1968); C. C. O'Brien, *Parnell and His Party, 1880–90* (1957); and two books by J. R. Vincent, *The Formation of the Liberal Party, 1857–1868* (1966), and *Pollbooks: How the Victorians Voted* (1967). On domestic reform, see R. J. Lambert, *Sir John Simon, 1816–1904, and English Social Administration* (1963).

On labor, the problem and the party, see H. A. Clegg, Alan Fox, and A. F. Thompson, *A History of British Trade Unions Since 1889*, vol. I, *1889–1910* (1964), which offers reliable detail and analysis. The short account by Henry Pelling, *The Origins of the Labour Party, 1880–1900* (2nd ed., 1965), and the substantial study by A. M. McBriar, *Fabian Socialism and English Politics, 1884–1918* (1962), are very informative.

21

Expanding Europe:
1870-1900

An energetic, expansive Europe has been a familiar sight since the days of Columbus and before. Earlier, we saw Europeans swarming across other continents, exploring, trading, settling, exploiting; we saw them enlarge the power of their hands and increase the ease of their lives with their inventions; we noted the growth of Europe's population. Beginning in the second half of the nineteenth century, these extensions of power, political and economic, became more dramatic than ever. The decades from 1870 to 1900 and beyond have often been called the age of the "New Imperialism." As we shall see, the name raises more difficulties than it settles. The new imperialism was not new; it was a natural modification of old policies. Nor was imperialism the sole, or even dominating reality of the time. We cannot cut it from its domestic roots, or divorce it from the lives of those who were touched by it only indirectly. The age of the new imperialism was also the age of the world economy and of the socialist challenge.

EUROPE'S WORLD

——••◦❧◦••——

Population: Advance and Retreat

The modern population explosion began sometime in the eighteenth century; it continued into the nineteenth and twentieth centuries. The causes shifted, especially in western Europe, from an increase in the birthrate to a fall in the death rate. By the 1860s the Scandinavian countries had reduced their death rate to less than twenty per thousand per year, then an enviable figure. England reached it around 1880, and the Dutch kingdom around 1890; but Italy and Austria did so only in 1910, and eastern Europe only in the 1920s and 1930s. Modern medicine and improved hygiene were finally beginning to show results.[1] Among European states, Britain grew from 22 million in 1850 to 38 million in 1900; Germany, from 35 to over 50 million in the same period. Other countries saw an equally striking growth; even France, whose declining birthrate worried many Frenchmen, registered an increase from 27 million to over 40 million in the nineteenth century. In all, Europe's population doubled between 1750 and 1850, when more than 270 million crowded into an increasingly constricted space; by 1900, it had to feed, house, and employ more than 420 million. Large agricultural countries absorbed these increases with ease; others felt the intensifying pressure of population that Malthus had predicted before 1800. At the beginning of the twentieth century, for every single Russian there were 20 Germans and 25 Britons occupying the same amount of space. But around the same time, the torrent slowed to a rivulet, and the poorer nations of Asia and Africa resumed the lead in peopling the world. The reason for this reversal was plain: the West was growing prosperous enough, and its contraceptive techniques were reliable, accessible, and acceptable enough, to permit widespread birth control. The Irish controlled their population by late marriages; elsewhere, even in Roman Catholic countries where religious prohibitions remained a powerful deterrent, other techniques had the same results. Coitus interruptus and abortion, which remained the favorite methods among the poorer urban and rural sectors, were gradually

---

[1] This information, as well as that in the rest of this section, is drawn from the lucid summary of modern scholarship by D. V. Glass and E. Grebenik, "World Population, 1800-1950," in H. J. Habbakuk and M. M. Postan, eds., *Cambridge Economic History of Europe*, vol. VI, *The Industrial Revolution and After*, Part 1 (1965), 60-138.

supplemented, though never replaced, by less disagreeable methods among the middle class. The natural consequences of sexual desire and of the biblical injunction to increase and multiply came into direct conflict with the wish to give one's children a good education and oneself a higher standard of living, wishes that could be gratified best in a small family.

While by no means everyone participated in the general accretion of wealth, this was a time of impressive improvements in living standards, even in the face of recurrent economic depressions. It was inevitable that the industrial pioneer, Britain, should sooner or later feel the hot breath of its competitors. As the British industrial plant, which called for heavy investment, began to grow obsolescent, the latercomers—Belgium, France, Japan, and, above all, Germany and the United States—could catch up. In two decades, between 1880 and 1900, Britain's share in world trade declined from 25 to 21 percent. But real wages in Britain rose—about 75 percent between 1860 and 1900. A sense of decline haunted many Englishmen in the midst of the most assertive imperialist activity, and it was grounded in reality; but the decline was really a growth relatively slower than that of competing countries.

The most spectacular of these competitors was Germany. German industrialization was well under way before 1871, but the creation of the new Reich encouraged tendencies toward expansion. Between 1871 and 1900, Germany's urban population rose from 36 to 54 percent; in the same period, coal production multiplied four times, from 38 to 150 million tons; between 1880 and 1900, German steel production increased from 1.5 to 7.4 million tons, thus overtaking Britain's production, which increased from 3.7 to only 6 million tons. The German chemical industry, stimulated by brilliant inventors and fostered by technical schools, gave the new country an undisputed lead in the manufacture of dyes and fertilizers. Yet the benefit of this phenomenal expansion was relatively restricted; the general suspicion that Germany's economic growth was fed artificially to serve future military use and present international glory is at least partially justified. While in Britain between 1876 and 1900, the average real income rose from £28 to £51 per capita per year, the corresponding rise in Germany was only from £24 to £32.[2] Yet in Germany as elsewhere, productivity and income rose, while industrial inventions promised a future in which men would labor less and earn more. This is the situation in which the idea of limiting the family to "manageable" size took firmer and firmer hold on more and more people. The promise of the goods of modern industrial civilization implied the existence of fewer people on earth to share them.

[2] For these facts, see Charles Wilson, "Economic Conditions," in H. F. Hinsley, ed., *New Cambridge Modern History,* vol. XI, *Material Progress and World Problems: 1870–1899* (1962), 52–60.

Two Great Migrations: Urbanization and Emigration

Until the time that the worry over population growth was replaced by worry over population decline, millions of Europeans found themselves obliged to find a livelihood away from their place of birth. Despite the burgeoning of cities, most Europeans in the late nineteenth century were born on the land. They could hardly stay there, though many of them did, swelling the ranks of the "invisibly unemployed," who had always hung about the rural world. But most of them migrated, some to the city, some to new lands overseas.

The greater magnet of these two, by far, was the city. Industrialization and urbanization sustained and reinforced one another: industry attracted new population; clusters of population attracted industry. The rise of the factory in place of domestic handicraft, made possible by credit, steam power, canals, and railways, encouraged the formation of industrial cities like Manchester and sprawling clusters of settlements like the Ruhr district. Old metropolitan centers developed into vast government headquarters, with their legislators, bureaucrats, soldiers, newspapermen, and social hangers-on, and with their service industries. London grew from nearly 2.5 million in 1850 to 4.5 million in 1900; the figures for Paris in the corresponding years were 1 million and 2.75 million. Prussia's capital, Berlin, had 420,000 inhabitants in 1850; by 1900, as the capital of Germany, it boasted nearly 2 million. The number of metropolises grew as much as their size: although in 1840 only London and Paris had more than 1 million inhabitants, by 1900 there were fourteen of these giants.[3] Moderate-size large cities accepted millions of newcomers as well: Germany, which gave a special name, *Grosstadt*, to cities with a population of 100,000, had eight of these in 1871; by 1914 that number had multiplied six times, to forty-eight. What the late Richard Hofstadter said about the United States holds true of European states as well: they were born in the country and moved to the city.[4]

These dry figures conceal some powerful social, economic, and political realities. The city was the longed-for goal for the adventurous artist or unemployed artisan, the natural habitat of the ambitious speculator and the modest merchant, of the social climber, the prostitute, the industrial worker. The city was a way of life at once freer and lonelier than the slower, more tradition-ridden, more familial way of the small town or village. With its ostentatious villa quarters and drab, depressing working-class districts, its perfumed parks and stinking slums, it bred radicals on the left and rioters on the right. Modern socialism is unthinkable without the modern city. It troubled

[3] Interestingly enough, most of these were outside Europe; within Europe, in addition to London and Paris, there were Berlin, Vienna, St. Petersburg, and Moscow; on the American continents there were New York, Chicago, Philadelphia, Buenos Aires, and Rio de Janeiro; and in Asia there were Tokyo, Osaka, and Calcutta.

[4] Richard Hofstadter, *The Age of Reform* (1954), 23.

many, especially poets. As one of them, William Osburn, put it in 1857, in prophetic verses read to the Leeds Philosophical and Literary Society:

> The AIRE below is doubly dyed and damned;
> The AIR above, with lurid smoke is crammed;
> The ONE flows steaming foul as Charon's Styx,
> Its poisonous vapours in the other mix.
> These sable twins the murky town invest—
> By them the skin's begrimed, the lungs oppressed.
> How dear the penalty thus paid for wealth;
> Obtained through wasted life and broken health.
>
> The one his villa and a carriage keeps;
> His squalid brother in a garret sleeps,
> HIGH flaunting forest trees, LOW crouching weeds,
> Can this be Manchester? or is it Leeds? [5]

But whether men looked upon the city with a burgher's pride or a prophet's dismay, its role in nineteenth-century Europe was to receive, and in some way to organize, Europe's burgeoning populace.

Migration from countryside or small town to the city had its risks; transplantation from country to country (which meant, chiefly, from continent to continent) had far greater risks than that. It is worth reiterating that emigration involved uprooting oneself from one's region; separating oneself from one's family, sometimes for many years; adopting new ways in a new climate and, often enough, learning a new language. The history of the great migration of the nineteenth century is filled with fantasies surpassed and expectations realized, but also with disorientation, defeat, and poignant disappointment. Let one account stand for thousands: Rabbi Isaac Mayer Wise, a leading Reform rabbi who had come to the United States from Prague in the 1840s, one day came upon a young boy sitting by the side of the road with a pack of goods beside him and crying bitterly, "I've lost my English language." Wise finally pieced together his story: the boy had recently arrived from Germany and was outfitted in the usual way with some goods to peddle. Since he knew no English he had been given a handwritten vocabulary with some indispensable phrases. It was this scrap of paper he had lost and, with it, his English language. [6]

Motives for migration varied, and its shifting patterns mirror that variety. After 1846, as we have seen, the Irish emigrated to escape starvation; after 1848, Germans emigrated to escape political reaction; in the 1880s and 1890s, east European Jews emigrated to escape onerous service in the Russian army or,

---

[5] Quoted by Asa Briggs, *Victorian Cities* (2nd ed., 1968), 139.
[6] Ruth Gay, *Jews in America: A Short History* (1965), 47.

worse, pogroms. Most of the emigrants went to find better opportunities overseas. They went everywhere and, throughout the nineteenth century, they were everywhere welcome. Between 1820 and 1930, about 62 million left Europe; but the bulk of this mass transfer of populations came between 1850 and 1914. Before that, overseas transport had been difficult and expensive; after that, country after country would open its frontiers only to "desirable" immigrants—those with scarce skills or the "right" religion and national origin. The course of the great trek overseas, beginning in perfect liberty and ending, in the 1920s, with the most severely limited and closely watched quota systems, testifies to the great retreat from liberalism in these years. When, in 1886, New Yorkers first saw the Statue of Liberty, a gift from the French, it seemed a symbol appropriate to a country that imposed practically no restrictions on immigration whatever.[7] Today, Emma Lazarus' lines, inscribed on the base of that statue, read like a nostalgic reminder of those liberal years:

> Give me your tired, your poor,
> Your huddled masses yearning to breathe free,
> The wretched refuse of your teeming shore,
> Send these, the homeless tempest-tost to me.[8]

The emigrants went everywhere, including the remote lands of Australia and New Zealand. About a tenth of them went to Canada, another tenth to Argentina, still another tenth to Asiatic Russia. But over three out of five went to the United States. Between 1861 and 1920, the United States received over 18 million immigrants; a few of them came from Canada and China, but nearly all of them from Europe. Physically and emotionally, the United States seemed ideal; the country was still empty and spawning new settlements in the South, the Midwest, the Far West; stories of the opportunities it offered, stories of its freedom, its equality, circulated widely in Europe and were confirmed by letters from the vanguard already settled there. And so they came by the millions to ease the population pressure on Europe and transform the social structure and population pattern of the United States. At first it was the Germans, the English, and the Irish who predominated. Then, as persecution mounted in eastern Europe and misery in southern Europe, the national origins of immigrants, too, changed. Austria-Hungary and Russia, which in 1865 had supplied fewer than a thousand immigrants each, supplied, respectively, 276,000 and 185,000 forty years later. And Italian immigration rose from a

[7] Until 1882, there had been no restrictions of any kind; in that year, the Chinese Exclusion Act began to discriminate against Orientals, a discrimination that was made permanent early in the twentieth century.

[8] Emma Lazarus, an American Jew born into a well-to-do family and deeply influenced by Emerson, was moved by the plight of immigrant Russian Jews to write both prose and poetry on Jewish themes.

thousand in 1865, to 100,000 in 1900, and to 221,000 in 1905. Between 1900 and 1914, more than 3 million Italians migrated to the United States. Many of these immigrants joined existing settlements to recreate as closely as they could their old environment; the fabulous "melting pot" of American legend does not wholly represent the facts, for Germans built up farming communities in Minnesota, Russian Jews streamed into the garment industry in New York, and Italians moved into the big eastern cities to do heavy physical labor. If American realities were often deeply disappointing, they were often dazzling enough to permit the old fantasies to survive. America *was* a free country, it seemed, where everyone could become a naturalized voting citizen; where discrimination was social snobbery or xenophobia but never (so long as one was white) sanctioned by law; where an immigrant might rise, as many did, to become a prosperous businessman, a powerful industrialist, a distinguished intellectual—anything but president of the United States. And the immigrants, with their skills, their customs, and their diligence, did not simply enrich themselves; they enriched America as well.

The Organization of Growth: The World Economy

Europe's economic ascendancy in those years was a stunning performance. The uneven development of the West and the rest of the world, one of the incentives for the new imperialism (see p. 839), became more marked than ever. Chemists supplied new materials and inventors new machines; enterprising companies opened new markets; imaginative employers improved productivity by rationally subdividing the work of their laborers. The effects of these devices were cumulative; they enabled the great European powers (as well as some small ones, such as Belgium) to construct and profit from what we must call a world economy. Overseas trade and overseas investments became, in the half century preceding World War I, truly global and enormously magnified. As the Western powers grew more industrialized, their dependence on the raw materials of other continents greatly increased; as Western factories improved the productivity of their machines and their men, their need for customers everywhere increased correspondingly. Surpluses were invested across the globe. British savings built Argentine railroads; the export of capital, which grew to vast magnitudes in these decades, gave European investors a share in enterprises in America, in Asia, in Africa. Economic isolation was a thing of the past; economic interdependence, with its complicated trade patterns, brought unprecedented opportunities for enrichment. But it was interdependence for evil as well as for good. The failure of a large bank, an agricultural depression, or a new labor-saving device successfully applied sent tremors across the world. And yet, in the very decades during which great powers modernized their armies and frantically built navies, Europe's bankers, industrialists, and merchants counteracted international tensions by knitting the network of the world economy ever tighter. In 1919, looking back upon the golden time before the war, the great English economist John Maynard Keynes remembered nostalgically: "The inhabitant of London could order by telephone, sipping his morning tea in bed, the various products of the whole earth, in such quantity as he might see fit, and reasonably expect their early delivery upon his doorstep; he could at the same moment and by the same means adventure his wealth in the natural resources and new enterprises of any quarter of the world, and share, without exertion, or even trouble, in their prospective fruits and advantages; or he could decide to couple the security of his fortunes with the good faith of the townspeople of any substantial municipality in any continent that fancy or information might recommend." Travel was just as free; one could easily obtain foreign currency or use gold, and simply visit any country one wanted. No European country except Russia demanded a passport. "But," Keynes adds, "most important of all," one "regarded this state of affairs as normal, certain, and permanent, except in the direction of further improvement, and any deviation from it as aberrant, scandalous, and avoidable."[9]

The Organization of Growth: The New Technology

One main reason why Europeans so misled themselves about the permanence of their prewar paradise was the overwhelming evidence that rationality, whether in abstract science, hardheaded technology, or organizational ingenuity, was solving one problem after another. It was not a time free from economic difficulties; poverty persisted, and the price of urbanization was, for many, a deterioration in the quality of their food and the healthfulness of their housing. Moreover, the Great Depression in England had its counterparts in other countries. Beginning in 1873 there was a sharp recession, bringing bankruptcies and bank failures; every dip of the business cycle produced spells of large-scale unemployment and, with it, painful destitution. But the emergence in these years of the labor movement and its twin, the socialist movement, was less a symptom of the failure of the system than an eloquent reminder that wealth was distributed unjustly (see p. 851).

The triumphs of economic rationality were highly visible. The pace of industrialization increased as the steam engine proved indispensable for more and more purposes; the striking rise in the production of coal in these decades is a measure of that pace.

[9] John Maynard Keynes, *The Economic Consequences of the Peace* (1919), 9–10.

Coal production
(Annual averages for quinquenniums—in million tons)

Period	U.K.	France	Germany	U.S.A.
1860–1864	84.9	9.8	15.4	16.7
1865–1869	103.0	12.4	23.5	26.7
1870–1874	120.7	15.1	31.8	43.1
1875–1879	133.3	16.3	38.4	52.2
1880–1884	156.4	19.3	51.3	88.7
1885–1889	165.2	20.7	60.9	115.3
1890–1894	180.3	25.4	72.0	153.3
1895–1899	201.9	29.6	89.3	189.1
1900–1904	226.8	31.8	110.7	281.0

SOURCE: William Ashworth, *A Short History of the International Economy Since 1850* (2nd ed., 1962), 21.

It is easy to match these spectacular figures by citing the multiplication of horsepower available for industrial production. In France, that power multiplied between 1860 and 1913 no less than twenty times:

Horsepower developed by fixed steam engines in France

1860	178,000 h.p.
1880	544,000 h.p.
1900	1,791,000 h.p.
1913	3,539,000 h.p.

SOURCE: Adapted from Ashworth, *International Economy*, 21.

In other countries, notably Germany and the United States, the figures were even more impressive. The production of iron and steel grew apace, as a band of inventors—Sir Henry Bessemer in England, Frederick and William Siemens in Germany and England—greatly reduced its price: in the United States, the cost of steel rails dropped from $160 a ton in 1875 to about one tenth of that price in 1898.[10] Indeed, the history of steel dramatically illustrates the interdependence of economies in these years. In 1878 two cousins, P. C. Gilchrist and S. G. Thomas, discovered a way of utilizing phosphoric iron ore in the making of steel. They were Englishmen, but it was the Germans and the French who profited from the Gilchrist-Thomas process, for it enabled them to exploit the iron ore of Lorraine, which, because of its high phosphorus content, had been unsuitable before.

Together, steam and iron produced the railway age. With its ferocious appearance and impressive utility, the steam locomotive had made its way against powerful resistance (see p. 592). For some time, England held the lead

---

[10] See Charles Wilson, "Economic Conditions," *New Cambridge Modern History,* vol. XI, 57.

with its construction, but by 1850, when there were 6,625 miles of track in Britain, the United States, with its vast territories to be spanned, had overtaken it with its 9,000 miles. Though severely challenged by river and canal transport and by coaches traveling on improved roads, the ultimate victory of the railway over its competitors was only a matter of time, finance, and construction. There were dramatic moments: in 1869 the Union Pacific and Central Pacific railroads completed the first route across the continental expanse of the United States. In 1885 the Canadian Pacific opened passenger service from Montreal to Vancouver. In 1888 the Orient Express, soon to be celebrated in travel books and spy stories, opened its run between Paris and Constantinople. In 1904 the Russians completed the Trans-Siberian Railway. The industrial revolution, exemplified by a steam engine on wheels riding on steel tracks, was making the world a smaller place.

Railway route mileage, 1840-1900

	1840	1870	1900
North America	2,954	56,106	223,454
Europe	1,818	65,192	176,179
Asia	0	5,086	37,470
South America	0	1,770	26,450
Africa	0	1,110	12,499
Australasia	0	1,097	14,922
The World	4,772	130,361	490,974

SOURCE: Adapted from Ashworth, *International Economy*, 60.

Though of vital importance in changing the contours of employment and reducing the size of the civilized world, the railway was not alone in producing this effect.[11] In Holland, in the English midlands, and in northern Germany, canals cut the time and thus the cost of transport, and the steamship made spectacular inroads in the dominance of the sailing ship: while in 1870 one merchantman in eight was powered by steam, thirty years later the proportion was over three in five. This meant cheaper transport of emigrants from Europe to America; and beginning in the 1880s, with refrigerated steamships, it meant that meat from Australia and New Zealand could enter the European market at competitive prices.

Communication kept pace with transportation. Samuel Morse demonstrated his invention, the telegraph, in 1838, and six years later the first experimental line opened between Baltimore and Washington. In 1866 Europe

[11] Although the automobile became a practicable vehicle in the 1880s and widely popular before World War I—by 1914 there were over one million cars in the United States—it did not offer serious competition to the railway, either as passenger transport or as carrier of freight, until after 1918. The same is true of the airplane; the Wright brothers made their celebrated flight at Kitty Hawk in 1903, but commercial aviation on a large scale came only after 1918.

was linked to America by Transatlantic cable. The telephone, invented by Alexander Graham Bell in 1876, offered serious technical difficulties at first; but around 1900 these had been largely overcome, and there were over one million telephones in the United States. Long-distance telephony still had to wait; the first transcontinental telephone call, between New York and San Francisco, was not made until 1915. By then, more than ten million Americans had a telephone. The wireless telegraph, the basis of radio and ship-to-shore telegraphy alike, was demonstrated successfully by Guglielmo Marconi in 1895, and in 1901 he dramatically established communications across the Atlantic Ocean, between England and Newfoundland. And, as the speed and reliability of ships, trains, and buses increased with the years, the speed and reliability of the mails increased with them. The world became a single world, not merely of commerce, but of perception as well. The speculator anxious about closing prices at a distant stock exchange, the foreign minister intent on transmitting urgent directions to a remote ambassador, the newspaperman eager to relay the latest news of faraway battles, the immigrant in America sending money or news to his family in the Russian Ukraine or southern Italy, the French manufacturer placing orders for machine tools in the United States—all of these and others found that the communications revolution had propelled them into a new world. It was a world far smaller, far better known, far more interdependent than the world of the eighteenth, let alone an earlier century. It was a world in which economic shock waves moved swiftly across the oceans, in which businessmen and statesmen had to make strategic decisions more rapidly than ever, often more rapidly than they liked. Fashions, always international, traveled quite easily now; so did socialist agitators. Regional differences were as yet little affected—the creation of uniformity was to be the work of radio, and even more, of television. But one thing was clear by 1900: the new world the communications revolution had made was one world.

The Organization of Growth: The Rationalization of Industry

Economic rationality mechanized not merely the machine, but the machinist and, to a degree, his manager as well. Ever since 1776, with Adam Smith's classic treatment of the subject in his *Wealth of Nations,* the share of the division of labor in enhancing productivity had been widely appreciated. Yet the rationalization of industry, as of management, proceeded slowly, firm by firm; there were few general principles available for general application. But as manufacturing became more and more complicated and as the easing of transport and the widening of markets made competition ever keener, managers understood that they must cut costs if they hoped to undersell their rivals. One way of doing this was, of course, to sweat labor—to work it long hours, pay the lowest possible wages, and fight protective legislation and trade unions alike. But there were other methods. The meat-packing industry in

Cincinnati around 1850 offers a dramatic approximation to such rationalization: "Live pigs were driven up an inclined plane to the top story of a building where they were slaughtered, after which each successive group of processes was carried out at a lower level, to which the carcasses dropped under their own weight, thus saving much effort. On the level they were moved in trucks and dumb-waiters and placed with the utmost regularity before those who constantly repeated the same few operations on each carcass." [12] "Taylorism," named after Frederick W. Taylor, was a sophisticated improvement over this early model. The "scientific management" he gradually introduced in America after 1900 depended on careful time and motion studies of workers and on increasing their productivity—stimulating their efforts, encouraging them to eliminate wasteful motions and costly errors—by means of incentive payments. Management, too, could be subjected to scientific observation; the organization of firms could be streamlined to reduce duplication of effort or waste of time. It is not fanciful to see the typewriter, which came into general use in the 1870s, as a symbol of this new rationality.

Even more far-reaching, and earlier, than the rationalization of the working process was the enlargement and concentration of management and of business enterprise. The 1880s and the decades that followed were the decades of trusts, of cartals, of gigantic combines that gathered, under one central management, the whole process of transforming raw materials into the finished product, from mining to manufacture to distribution to sales. Nostalgic defenders of the small workshop or the family firm lamented these develop-ments; traditional preferences for keeping profits in the family, coupled with long-standing suspicions of wild speculation [13] offered formidable resistance to the creation of these giants. But there could be no doubt that the manufacturer whose resources permitted him to buy vast quantities of materials at one time, or to make special arrangements with railroads to carry his products, or to control retail outlets that would specialize in selling his wares enjoyed a measurable economic advantage over his smaller competitor.

One way of raising the unprecedented amounts of capital required in the new world economy was to create banks especially devoted to supplying industry and merchants with funds—investment banks (see p. 598). These were more popular on the Continent than in Britain or the United States, but even in France and Germany their usefulness was circumscribed. Far more flexible in the raising of money and, from the viewpoint of management, far more docile, was the corporation. The nature of this device—a fictitious person in law—is aptly revealed by the names under which it was known in the major capitalist countries. The English called it a "joint stock company," an enterprise in which anyone might join by purchasing shares of stock; for the French it was

---

[12] Ashworth, *International Economy,* 80–81.
    [13] This goes back, along with prohibitory legislation, to the early eighteenth century, the time of the Mississippi and the South Sea bubbles.

a *"société anonyme,"* an enterprise whose thousands of part owners were truly anonymous, not knowing one another and, except for the largest shareholders, having no part whatever in the management; the Germans called it *Gesellschaft mit beschränkter Haftung,* a company with shareholders whose liability for the losses or the bankruptcy of the company was limited to the loss they would take on their own shares.

After often agonized resistance, capitalist country after capitalist country yielded to the pressure and repealed, or markedly weakened, its legislation against joint stock companies. Britain, in a series of acts, facilitated the setting up of corporations between 1844 and 1862; the French followed in 1867; the Germans between 1870 and 1872 and, with supplementary legislation, in 1892. The corporation tapped a vast reservoir of hitherto elusive capital; it could draw on the savings of thousands of small investors. All over the world, as stock exchanges boomed, shares fluctuated and changed hands every day. A rash or uninformed investor could lose his life's savings overnight; neither the issuance of stocks nor their trade was then seriously controlled. But in a time of growth, as the value of stocks appreciated and dividends came in regularly, returns on investment might be high and repeated. Besides, capital invested in shares had the advantage of liquidity: it could be turned into cash or other shares at will.

Critics of the system—populists in America, socialists in Europe—were not slow to point out that this new situation raised some unforeseen problems. They spoke harshly of "finance capitalism" and, with distrust and fear, of "the age of big business." They abhorred the rise of tycoons, of multimillionaires like John D. Rockefeller, who dominated the American oil industry; of Andrew Carnegie, who controlled American steel; of the Krupp dynasty, which practically monopolized the German armament industry. These tycoons, living in a time of little government control and no income tax, wielded enormous economic and (it was feared) corresponding political power. The laws that permitted the forming of corporations had come at a time when competition was king; as we know (see p. 700) Great Britain had taken the lead in going over to free trade in 1846, and other countries had followed. But gigantic corporations found it less strenuous and more profitable to circumvent competition than to suffer its vagaries. Nothing allayed anxiety better than a monopoly. Most Western powers expressed a certain horror of monopolies; the famous Sherman Anti-Trust Act, passed in the United States in 1890, declared illegal "every contract, combination in the form of trust or otherwise, or conspiracy, in restraint of trade or commerce." But the law was easy to evade. And, in these same years, country after country abandoned its commitment to largely unhampered international competition. Austria-Hungary was among the first to move to protection in 1874; the Russians followed in 1877; two years later, in a spectacular reversal, Bismarck joined the rush to tariffs (see p. 799). Italy had turned toward protectionism in 1878 and adopted it wholeheartedly in 1887; the United States, which had begun to protect its industry as early as

1875, raised its tariffs markedly in 1890 and then again in 1897; France, which had moved in that direction earlier, adopted the Méline tariff in 1892. Only Great Britain, despite a rising clamor to abandon free trade, held out.

These two developments—the rise of cartels and the decline of free trade—were significant aspects of a crisis through which economic liberalism was passing in these decades and from which it did not emerge unscathed. For both these developments were denials of liberal ideals. The first meant the decay of domestic competition; its advocates did not find it soothing to be told by Social Darwinists, like William Graham Sumner, that the natural result of competition was the emergence of the strongest—the monopolist—or that multimillionaire captains of industry represented the triumph of evolution. The second meant the decay of international competition; and *its* advocates were not cheered by the protectionist argument that if one country sheltered its industry and agriculture behind tariff walls, others must do so too, in self-defense. The liberal age had seen a certain withdrawal of the state from the economy; the liberal crisis saw the two brought together again in a union as close as that of seventeenth-century mercantilism.

THE "NEW IMPERIALISM"

Theories Against Facts

Critical contemporaries and, later, radical historians thought the new intimacy between state and economy most strikingly exemplified in the "new imperialism." In Lenin's famous formulation, imperialism was "the highest phase of capitalism," the bitter fruit of monopoly. Faced with falling profits in the usual markets, industrialists and financiers, whose political power had vastly increased, tried to stave off the inescapable ruin of the capitalist system by investing their capital at better rates in Africa or Asia. They maneuvered their governments into acquiring colonies they could dominate and exploit, rob of their raw materials, and convert into captive markets. Lenin published his analysis of imperialism—which was really a polemic against capitalism—in 1917; other Marxists, like Rosa Luxemburg and Rudolf Hilferding, had partially anticipated him. All these owed a great deal to the English economist J. A. Hobson, an independent-minded radical with ideas of a socialist stamp but never a Marxist. Hobson's *Imperialism: A Study*, first published in 1902, developed a persuasive underconsumption theory. The prospects of low profits at home, Hobson reasoned, forced capital to seek outlets in backward countries, where high returns could still be expected. Hobson strongly insisted and patiently demonstrated that imperialism was generally unprofitable; the only trouble was that those whom it did profit—a handful of capitalists—had power to shape and distort national policy. Thus the flag was manipulated into following trade.

Hobson was not the one who gave imperialism its bad name; it had had that before. But he fixed the connotation of the word and its reputation for decades to come. The word "imperialism" first arose in the France of Louis-Philippe and was later foisted on Napoleon III to signify his high-handed dictatorship. Thus it began as a term for the display of domestic power. In the early 1870s, when Disraeli gave voice to his new attitude toward empire, his Liberal critics tried to discredit it by burdening it with this unsavory connotation. They did not succeed in thwarting Disraeli's policies (they were in fact, as we shall see, compelled to adopt them), but only in changing the meaning of the word. Hobson made the meaning permanent.[14] There were just enough canting politicians' speeches justifying blatant aggression, enough bad imperialist poems, enough inexcusable wars, enough profiteers who acquired scandalous riches out of Chinese trade or African gold, to make Hobson's and the Marxists' theories seem plausible. Yet as a global explanation they will not work. They do not even fully explain the imperialism of those who profited from it. For decades, imperialists and anti-imperialists agreed on one point: the new imperialism was the necessary consequence of the historical situation. Imperialists called it the inescapable rivalry of world powers; anti-imperialists, the inevitable by-product of monopoly capitalism. It is only in the last few years that historians have taken a fresh look at the evidence and discovered, not an all-embracing explanation, but immense complexity.

The facts are indeed complicated. As we have emphasized, the new imperialism was in most respects an old story. European economic penetration of Asian and African countries went back to the age of the discoveries; the large-scale acquisition and exploitation of colonies under direct European rule went back to the eighteenth century (see p. 396). It is worth recalling that Disraeli intended his gesture of making Queen Victoria "Empress of India" to celebrate a century-old conquest; Disraeli took pride in being a *Conservative* prime minister. It was, then, between the poles of economic penetration and political domination that Europe's policies toward Asia and Africa oscillated. During most of the nineteenth century, commercial aggression without direct colonization was in the ascendant. This was what has been happily called the "imperialism of free trade." [15] Statesmen everywhere abhorred the very idea of annexing colonies, not because they were idealists but because it was bad business. To occupy African or Asian lands meant shoring up inefficient and corrupt administrations, subsidizing greedy potentates, and protecting irresponsible merchant adventurers. Colonies were a nuisance and an expense;

[14] See Richard Koebner and H. D. Schmidt, *Imperialism: The Story and Significance of a Political Word, 1840-1960* (1964).

[15] See John Gallagher and R. E. Robinson, "The Imperialism of Free Trade," *Economic History Review*, vol. 6, no. 1, 2nd series (1953), 1-15.

colonialism was not merely immoral but, worse, unprofitable. Yet even in the decades when these convictions dominated the minds of responsible ministers, the preferred policy often shaded insensibly into more active ventures. The "opening" of Japan by the American Commodore Matthew Perry, at a time when anti-imperialism was still the fashion, is a glaring instance of this rising activism. Perry arrived in Japanese waters in July 1853, under instructions to use, if necessary, "some imposing manifestation of power" to persuade the Japanese to abandon their traditional isolation. The threatening appearance of his steamships and his peremptory tone made their point; the treaty that in effect brought Japan into the world market was signed in March 1854.

Perry's show of force became a ritualistic gesture, a favorite device of Western statesmen to intimidate non-Western powers. Given European and American superiority in armaments, it was usually enough. Usually, but not always: the British assaults on China in the Opium War of 1839–1842 and later equally ugly incidents in the 1850s and 1860s suggest that aggressive imperialism was a perfectly plausible option in an age of anti-imperialism. "Trade with informal control if possible; trade with rule when necessary"—that was the formula for Britain, as for other countries.[16] What happened in and after the 1870s, then, was that more and more countries thought it necessary to rule. What was new about the new imperialism was the speed of its actions, the fierceness of international rivalry, and the ever-increasing unevenness in the development of the conquering and the conquered countries. In 1882 Gladstone, arch-moralist and arch-anti-imperialist, had encompassed the British occupation of Egypt; in 1883 and 1884 Bismarck, the most consistent anti-imperialist of them all, reversed his firm declaration, "As long as I am Reichskanzler, we shall not pursue a colonial policy,"[17] and committed Germany to colonies in Africa and the Pacific.

Economics of Imperialism

Surely one of the reasons for this shift was a shift in the West's economic situation. With the growing complexity of industrial production, certain raw materials, found only in Asia or Africa, assumed strategic importance. To enclose colonies in a large protected area of exclusive markets and thus stabilize domestic industry was a notion that had articulate proponents. Some of the remote regions, South Africa especially, were found to be rich in gold and diamonds, thus luring speculators and prospectors. Although opportunities for investment were uncertain, they at least appeared to be extraordinary. In the Caribbean and the Latin American mainland, German or American private

[16] Ibid., 13.
[17] The quotation is in Hans-Ulrich Wehler, "Bismarck's Imperialism, 1862–1890," *Past and Present,* 48 (August 1970), 129; and see p. 799.

companies negotiated profitable contracts in the certainty that the annulment of a concession or the murder of their traders would bring German or United States gunboats into action to protect the lives and guarantee the profits of the companies and their personnel. Some exceptional companies were rich and powerful enough to be able to dispense with the intervention of their government; the United Fruit Company, a powerful American firm, protected its vast Latin American investments, amounting in 1913 to over $82 million, by effectively monopolizing the market and by negotiating with foreign governments directly.

In Africa, Leopold II's barbaric exploitation of the Belgian Congo proved that a really determined entrepreneur could drag a good deal out of his miserable subjects. In 1878 Leopold, King of the Belgians, had founded a private company, the International Congo Association; in 1885, at an international conference in Berlin, this shapeless enterprise was transformed into the Congo Free State, with Leopold as its sovereign. Under the Berlin Act, Leopold agreed to act as the trustee and to keep the state free for free trade. He had no intention of honoring his signature; he acted as if he owned the area and stripped it without pity. He wanted to make "his" colony pay, and this meant the establishment of private monopolies and the most savage treatment of native labor. Officials sent to enforce Leopold's demands had no incentive for humanity since there were bonuses for exceeding set quotas. Workers on the rubber plantations were flogged; villages refusing to supply requisite numbers of laborers had to deliver up hostages and suffer punitive expeditions. It is true that when King Leopold heard of the blacks' sufferings, he was moved to order that their mistreatment cease. But the system he had founded proved stronger than the orders of its founder; it was not until 1908, when the Congo was taken over by the Belgian state, that the most terrible practices ended.

Still, the economic argument deserves only a modest place in the total explanation. Even Leopold's ruthless experiment in the Congo cuts two ways. For years, his enterprise was near bankruptcy; in 1890 and again in 1895 Belgium had to lend its entrepreneur-king nearly 32 million francs to keep it alive. It was only after 1901, when the Congo began to export rubber in quantities, that the venture became at all profitable. Yet, even then, Belgian investors showed not the slightest interest in the Congo. And what was true of Belgians was true of others. Between 1880 and 1900, decisive years for its imperial expansion, Britain's trade with her newly acquired colonies amounted to only 2.5 percent of her total trade, and the export of capital to these colonies remained insignificant. British investors found highly industrialized countries—Continental Europe and the United States—or the established empire— India, Australia, Canada—far less risky and far more profitable. The shift of British exports toward Africa was gradual and remained relatively small: between 1860 and 1913 it rose from 5.9 to 10.3 percent, and this figure includes more than the British colonies. "Though Britain's imperial trade was growing," William Ashworth sums up the evidence, "only a minor part of the increase was in trade with recently acquired colonies," and it is easy to argue that, "in fact, colonial commerce quite failed to repay the effort and expense put into the expansion of empire." [18] As anti-imperialists never tired of saying, imperialism did not pay, or paid only a few favored men.

In France, procolonialists berated the overwhelming majority of businessmen, industrialists, and bankers for preferring the safe home markets; in the face of mounting complaints about the cost of empire, they put their case for colonial trade and investment on the grounds of national duty. "People are not, generally speaking, conscious hypocrites," writes the French historian Henri Brunschwig. "No one holds himself in contempt for thirty years. Anyone who thinks that colonial imperialism was simply a case of capitalists snatching at profits from lucrative territories and of defenseless populations, has no idea what it was all about." [19] Such considerations do not make imperialism any better; they just make it different. And the United States? The most purely imperialist venture that this country ever undertook was its war with Spain in 1898. But the government entered it with the utmost reluctance. Despite ample provocations from the Spanish in Cuba, despite widespread clamor for war fanned, but not created, by the Hearst and Pulitzer newspapers, President Cleveland would not be drawn. And when McKinley became president in 1897, he was moved to declare war on Spain only after the American battleship *Maine* was sunk at Havana, and after he had decided that national security as well as moral indignation against Spanish oppression demanded war. But the captains of industry and the tycoons of business—the very men who, in Lenin's theory, should have led the jingoist chorus—consistently opposed this adventure. Businessmen called upon McKinley to show self-restraint, and financiers told him that the blowing up of the *Maine* should not imperil peace. These practical men knew that imperialism is costly. In 1908 the English novelist Arnold Bennett echoed a widespread view when he wrote: "In 1906 the amazing German Colonial Empire cost 180 millions of marks. A high price to pay for a comic opera, even with real waterfalls!" [20]

Imperialism had its profiteers; those who stood to make money out of imperialism often were influential men who had access to profitable inside information and to ministers, and thus to the making of policy. Sometimes they were ministers themselves. Empire provided generous employment for military men; it gave glamorous, sometimes distinguished, careers to younger sons of the English nobility or to other socially prominent, though highly unemployable, young men. Elevated talk of Europe's "cultural mission" concealed the most sordid financial dealings. In Germany the company authorized to colonize German Southwest Africa had the German government construct the railway

[18] William Ashworth, *An Economic History of England, 1870–1939* (1960), 236–237. For the figures, see *ibid.*, 143, and C. J. Lowe, *The Reluctant Imperialists,* vol. I, *British Foreign Policy, 1878–1902* (1967), 4.

[19] Henri Brunschwig, *French Colonialism, 1871–1914: Myths and Realities* (tr. 1964), 167.

[20] Arnold Bennett, "German Expansion," *Books and Persons* (1917), 31.

lines and lay down the roads, while it paid nothing for the land and made a clear profit of seven million marks when it sold its holdings.[21] Such windfalls were the by-product of empire; the remoteness of the new colony, the unfamiliarity of conditions there, the often intimate relation of officials at home with investors overseas offered splendid opportunity for manipulation. Yet the figures for trade and investment and the general attitude of the business and industrial world tell another story. As will become clearer and clearer in the pages that follow, the impulse for the new imperialism was wider, and lay deeper, than a few millions in profit for a handful of promoters.

Great Britain in Africa

A glance at the expansion into Africa of Britain, the leading imperialist power of these decades, confirms our impression of complexity. The first result of Disraeli's new assertive policy, announced early in the 1870s, was his inexpensive acquisition of Cyprus at the Berlin Congress of 1878 (see p. 812). The next, far more portentous, result was Britain's occupation of Egypt in 1882. Gladstone had orated his way into office in 1880 by an exhausting campaign in which antiimperialism had ranked high (see p. 820). Two years later he found that life is stronger than principle.

Egypt was a self-governing domain owing nominal obedience to the sultan. At midcentury Egypt flourished under the direct rule of a khedive, a successor and imitator of the celebrated Mehemet Ali (see p. 560). Egypt's staple export, cotton, was a sizable and profitable item; after 1869 the new Suez Canal opened other sources of revenue. But Khedive Ismail Pasha lacked all sense of a budget. By 1875 he was over his head in debt. Disraeli decided to profit from Ismail's bankruptcy; the Suez Canal, in which the khedive held nearly half the shares, was heavily traveled by British merchantmen and was a key link in the British route to India. In a brilliant stroke, Disraeli bought Ismail's shares in the canal for four million pounds and gave Britain effective control over the canal. The khedive's financial embarrassments were relieved for a time—but only for a time. In despair, Ismail agreed to hand over supervision of his finances to one English and one French administrator. In 1879 the two powers persuaded the sultan to depose Ismail and appoint a more pliant successor. This in turn led to a nationalist revolt in 1881, under the leadership of Colonel Arabi Pasha. With painful reluctance, Gladstone backed into action. He sent a naval squadron to Alexandria as a show of strength; this led to a massacre of Europeans, which, in response, induced the British to bombard the port city. Almost helplessly, Gladstone turned to France for cooperation, but the French, preoccupied with internal politics, refused. In September 1882 the British occupied Egypt alone. By 1883 the temporary occupation looked all but permanent.

[21] See Brunschwig, *French Colonialism*, 153.

Other ventures in colonization followed, just as complicated in origin and as unintended in consequences. In 1891 Lord Salisbury, then prime minister, said candidly of the drastic reversal of British colonial policy: "I do not exactly know the cause of this sudden revolution. But there it is." Expansionism had become popular; tales and poems of empire turned imperialism into a moral obligation—"the white man's burden." The phrase was coined by Rudyard Kipling, singer of lilting ballads, teller of exotic tales, advocate of the manly life. Kipling himself had doubts about the purity of the emotions he had done so much to inflame. In 1897, when the venerable Queen Victoria celebrated the Diamond Jubilee of her reign, he uttered a solemn warning in his famous *Recessional*:

> If, drunk with sight of power, we loose
>   Wild tongues that have not thee in awe,
> Such boastings as the Gentiles use,
>   Or lesser breeds without the Law—
> Lord God of Hosts, be with us yet,
> Lest we forget—lest we forget!

But there were powerful figures in British politics, drunk with sight of power, intent on forgetting humanity. The most striking of these was the visionary Cecil Rhodes, with his fantasy of uniting all of South Africa under British rule and opening an all-British route from the Cape to Cairo. Utterly ruthless, intensely energetic, Rhodes was not at fault if this dream did not quite become a reality. Rhodes first went to South Africa in 1870 and settled permanently in 1880; he made an immense fortune there, first in diamonds, later in gold. The discovery of unprecedented riches in the Transvaal had exacerbated relations between the British and the Boers in South Africa, already tense enough. After much bitter fighting the Boers had established the Transvaal Republic and the Orange Free State, but as prospectors discovered diamonds and gold, the British moved in on the Boer lands (see p. 753). In 1880 the Boers, having nothing to lose, rebelled, and in 1881 they humiliated English troops at the battle of Majuba Hill.

This was the position when Rhodes settled in South Africa. In 1889 he chartered the British South Africa Company; as a private entrepreneur he moved north into what is today Rhodesia. In 1890 he became prime minister of the Cape Colony. He found a tough adversary in the Afrikaner Paul Kruger, president of the Transvaal Republic, who was intent on frustrating further British encroachments and on gaining what British policy had consistently denied the Boers from the start—access to the sea. He was playing a difficult game: the fantastic mines of the Transvaal had attracted thousands of adventurers into his country. These foreigners—*uitlanders*—soon made up two thirds of the population and paid 90 percent of the taxes, but they enjoyed no political rights. Kruger fought off their demands, while Rhodes adroitly enlisted their support.

But in late 1895 Rhodes went too far. The new British colonial secretary, the imperialist Joseph Chamberlain (who had broken with the Liberals over Home Rule for Ireland), wanted to hear nothing of plots, but he encouraged Rhodes' plotting by giving him a free hand. In December Rhodes' intimate associate, Dr. Leander Starr Jameson, invaded the Transvaal with five hundred men. The Jameson Raid, designed to foment revolution in Kruger's republic, failed dismally. The men were captured, Jameson was eventually imprisoned, and Rhodes had to resign from the premiership of his colony and the directorship of his company. One consequence of the raid, and a salutary lesson in the long run, was an impetuous act by William II of Germany. When he learned of Jameson's failure, he sent Kruger a congratulatory telegram. It alerted British statesmen to the face of their real enemy in Europe. But other lessons were not learned. Though Rhodes' personal influence was lost—he died soon after, in 1902—his bellicose policy prevailed. Goaded by Chamberlain at the Colonial Office and urged on by Sir Alfred Milner, high commissioner of the Cape Colony, the British drifted into war with Kruger.

The Boer War began in October 1899 and provided imperial Britain with some unpleasant experiences. But then, African expansion had already provided such experiences before. Britain was steadily being reminded that she was not in Africa alone; her actions there aroused the hostility of competing powers. Imperialist policy, it seemed, simply extended the frontiers of conflict beyond Europe. [22] All efforts to subject the scramble for Africa to international rules had suffered shipwreck. The Berlin Conference of 1885 had secured King Leopold's assent to policies he did not intend to pursue. It had, at the same time, insisted that claims to African territory must rest on effective occupation and international notification. But this agreement did not reduce the danger of conflict; it only increased the pace of colonization. Italians, Germans, and Portuguese joined the scramble, but France and England occupied the largest, strategically most important, and potentially most rewarding territories. For France, deeply humiliated by the Germans in 1870–1871, the acquisition of empire was a matter mainly of restoring its pride at home and prestige in the world. French nationalism spilled over into French imperialism. And wherever the French went to establish or consolidate their hold in Africa, they encountered rival claimants: Italy in Tunisia; Spain, Germany, and Britain in Morocco. And it was with Britain that France almost went to war in the Sudan.

Britain's occupation of Egypt had inevitably involved it in the Sudan, to Egypt's south, and under Egypt's control. In 1881 the Sudanese had rebelled under the leadership of the Mahdi, a charismatic Muslim, who unified his forces and cut the Egyptian army to pieces. The British sent General Charles George Gordon, an immensely popular figure for his military prowess with British forces in China, to relieve the Egyptians. Besieged in Khartoum, he

---

[22] This of course had emerged very clearly in the mid-eighteenth century, when the great British-French duel was fought out across three continents. See p. 397.

needed relief himself, but when the relieving army under General Horatio Kitchener reached Khartoum in January 1885, it found that Gordon and his men had been killed two days before. It was enough to drive Gladstone from office and keep the British out of the Sudan for a decade. In 1896 Kitchener moved south once again, following the Nile upstream. This time, the British forces encountered the French, who had evolved the notion of a French belt across Africa. This, of course, ran head-on into British notions about a continuous line from Cairo to the Cape of Good Hope. The French already held most of West Africa and had penetrated deep into its center; hence Kitchener found a small French force under Captain J. B. Marchand at Fashoda on the Nile. The French had a certain case: no one was in effective occupation of this sector of the Sudan. But the British refused to yield. While Kitchener and Marchand negotiated politely, their home governments prepared for war. In the end Britain's firmness, coupled with French weakness, prevailed, and the French retreated. Early in 1899, the two powers signed an agreement recognizing Britain's bloodless victory.

Except for outraging French public opinion, the British conquest of the Sudan had been cheap. But the Boer War proved surprisingly expensive. It aroused higher emotions that anyone had expected: blatant chauvinism punctuated by scattered opposition at home, and almost universal detestation abroad. British war correspondents—among them the young Winston Churchill, then an adventurous politician, soldier, and journalist—reported home little but disaster: superior Boer forces invested British strongholds and inflicted defeats on British troops in the field. Gradually, the tide of battle turned; by October 1900 the Transvaal was once again in British hands. But victory was elusive. By the time Queen Victoria died in January 1901, the Boers had adopted guerrilla resistance, which prolonged the exhausting war still further; the British responded with sweeps through one area after another. Victory came at last in May 1902. And now Britain applied its experience to the peacemaking in the Treaty of Vereeniging. While English was the official language of the country, Dutch was permitted as an option. The treaty granted amnesty to Boers willing to swear allegiance to the British king. By 1906 a Boer, General Louis Botha, who had commanded the Boer armies, was prime minister of the Transvaal. The British, in fashioning this settlement, looked to association, not subjugation or revenge. As we know today, things did not work out as fortunately as the British had planned. But their generosity, too, was one of the faces of the new imperialism.

The Five Imperialisms

Britain's imperialist experience, though highly significant, was not typical. No single power's imperialist experience was typical; the motives of the French differed from those of the British, and the motives of the Germans differed from both. Nor should we forget, as John Gallagher and R. E. Robinson have wisely reminded us, that the victims of European imperialism were not wholly passive before the course of events. "Scanning Europe for the causes," they write, "the theorists of imperialism have been looking for the answers in the wrong places. The crucial changes that set all working took place in Africa itself. It was the fall of an old power in its north [Egypt], the rise of a new in its south [South Africa, with its gold], that dragged Africa into modern history." [23] Each of the European powers was driven on by a multiplicity of motives. We have already explored the best-known of these, the economic. We must briefly turn to four others: cultural, psychological, strategic, and social.

Beyond doubt, imperialist ventures were sustained by a chorus of approval in Western civilization, by voices expressing a strong urge for action and expansion. Not all the talk of "cultural mission" was simply a convenient excuse. Rhodes had been spurred on to his vast African dream by the imperialist fervor of John Ruskin, whom he came to know at Oxford in 1872 and whose inaugural lecture of 1870 he cherished. "There is a destiny now possible to us," Ruskin had said, "the highest ever set before a nation to be accepted or refused. We are still undegenerate in race, a race mingled of the best northern blood. . . . Will you youths of England make your country again a royal throne of kings; a sceptred isle, for all the world a source of light, a centre of peace? . . . This is what England must either do, or perish: she must found colonies as fast and as far as she is able, formed of her most energetic and worthiest men; seizing every piece of fruitful waste ground she can set her foot on." And he sweetened his call to "advance the power of England by land and sea" by pointing to its possible disinterestedness: "All that I ask of you is to have a fixed purpose of some kind for your country and for yourselves, no matter how restricted, so that it be fixed and unselfish." Kipling's verses, which Rhodes knew as well as Ruskin's declamation, carried the same welcome message for him.

Especially in England, but also in other countries, poets sang of high adventure in the imperial service and of endowing the native races, "half devil and half child," with the blessings of advanced civilization, blessings defined according to the nationality of the singer. Critics of imperialism might deride the white trader's and proconsul's civilization as a harvest of suffering and tears, but for some decades they did not command public opinion. Expansion seemed a noble venture; many philosophers celebrated imperialism as the manifestation of spiritual power in its highest form. Racist biologists swelled this self-congratulatory chorus with their scientific-sounding superstitions: whites dominated blacks because whites were superior by nature—otherwise they would not dominate them. As the English biologist Karl Pearson put it, taking

[23] John Gallagher and R. E. Robinson, "The Partition of Africa," *New Cambridge Modern History*, vol. XI, 594.

"the natural history view of mankind": a vigorous race should be "kept up to a high pitch of external efficiency by contest, chiefly by way of war with inferior races." [24] Social Darwinists blessed the grab for foreign territory and made light of its victims in the name of "nature's iron law"—all life is struggle. Philosophers of the strenuous life, like Nietzsche (see p. 870), could be misused, and activist politicians, like Theodore Roosevelt, could be correctly used, to justify punitive expeditions against hapless African tribes. The most troubling fact about these beliefs was that they were held sincerely and therefore all the more tenaciously.

Their consequences were often unfortunate—often, but not always, for there were colonial administrators who governed their territories with an eye above all to the natives' well-being. To complicate matters further, one element in this cluster of convictions was the humanitarian-religious. The English conscience, as we have seen, was deeply sensitive to the persistence of slavery and heathenism in the tropical world, and Gladstone's vigorous indignation over Turkish atrocities against the Bulgarians in 1876 persuaded many Englishmen that intervention alone could stop such massacres and raise the level of civilized conduct. As soldiers were often missionaries, missionaries were often soldiers: General Gordon, the martyr of Khartoum, was both. It has been estimated that by 1900 there were over sixty thousand missionaries in Asia and Africa, as many as there were European troops. [25] The number includes native priests, but is enormous nonetheless. Whether these men of God mainly labored toward the abolition of slavery or the advancement of national interests differed from colony to colony.

The psychological motive for imperialism was closely allied to the cultural one. An effective cultural mission proclaimed to the world that the nation mounting it was a major power. Great powers recently defeated, like France, or new powers striving for greatness, like Italy, launched into imperialism, no matter how high the cost, to restore or to create prestige on the international stage. The Italian statesman Crispi is a perfect representative of this school. French imperialists are just as striking; in 1881, J. Bébin, general secretary of the Société de Géographie at Valenciennes, joined the defeat of 1870–1871 and the need for prestige into a single imperialist prescription: it is in the French colonies, he said, that "the nation's living forces, which are beginning to feel constricted by the narrow limits of the treaty of Frankfurt, will be able to expand unhindered, and when once the events which we hope to see occur have come about, it is impossible to say where our flag will not one day fly. If a nation wishes to remain or become great, it must undertake colonization." [26] Bébin and other influential advocates of French colonial expansion knew perfectly well that imperialism was expensive; the cost of maintaining troops and officials

[24] Quoted, with evident disgust, by J. A. Hobson, *Imperialism, A Study* (1902), 163.
[25] F. H. Hinsley, "Introduction," *New Cambridge Modern History*, vol. XI, 46.
[26] Quoted in Brunschwig, *French Colonialism*, 25.

was in no way offset by new income. But the tangible price, they insisted, was worth paying—for an intangible reward.

Important as these considerations were for the British, the decisive element in their imperialism was strategy, or what they conceived to be such. Britain took an interest in Egypt because of the Suez Canal; Britain went into Egypt because a nationalist revolt threatened the country's stability; Britain stayed in Egypt and drove south into the Sudan to secure the country's further stability. This sounds self-serving and self-confirming, and it is, in part, both. [27] Similarly, anxiety about the defense of India, with its immense wealth, dictated other aggressive moves. Yet Britain's reluctance to annex still more territories was genuine enough. What complicated matters and cut off retreat was that other countries also had strategic concerns. The very fact of a scramble for Africa and Asia intensified the scramble for Africa and Asia. Some countries, such as Portugal and Italy, sought colonies in a rush because if they did not hurry no colonies would be left. Other countries, notably Britain, sought domination to prevent the domination of others. "So long as we keep other European nations out," the British said about their Niger Coast protectorate, "we need not be in a hurry to go in." [28] It was this ineluctable fact dominating the competitive state system that drove despairing pacifists to seek an international government. But though rivalry exacerbated rivalry, much imperialism was hesitant in the extreme.

Much, but by no means all. There is still one other kind of imperialism to bedevil our analysis, social imperialism. This worked in two ways. On the one hand, imperialist ventures could be used to divert attention from domestic injustice and to pacify domestic unrest by promises of greatness in colonial empire or by the lure of possible profit. This imperialism was a method for postponing, or avoiding, social reform; it commended itself especially to German policy-makers in the empire of William II. One highly placed German diplomat, Baron von Holstein, put it candidly after Bismarck's fall: "Kaiser Wilhelm's government needs some tangible success abroad which will then have a beneficial effect at home. Such a success can be expected either as a result of a European war, a risky policy on a worldwide scale, or as the result of territorial acquisitions outside Europe." [29] On the other hand, Liberal imperialists in England especially associated imperialism and the social ques-

---

[27] As L. T. Hobhouse bitterly and justly wrote in 1904: "Under the reign of Imperialism . . . blood never ceases to run. The voice of the mourner is never hushed. Of course, in every case some excellent reason has been forthcoming. We were invariably on the defensive. We had no intention of going to war. Having gone to war, we had no intention of occupying the country. Having occupied the country provisionally, we were still determined not to annex it. Having annexed it, we were convinced that the whole process was inevitable from first to last." From *Democracy and Reaction* (1904), quoted in Heinz Gollwitzer, *Europe in the Age of Imperialism, 1880-1914* (1969), 118.

[28] This quotation is in Gallagher and Robinson, "The Partition of Africa," *New Cambridge Modern History,* vol. XI, 607.

[29] Quoted in Wehler, "Bismarck's Imperialism," 152.

tion, not as a handy device to escape social betterment, but as a serious policy to promote it. Lord Rosebery, Britain's prime minister in the early 1890s, put reform first, imperialism second. Demanding better housing and education for the poor, he insisted: "Where you promote health and arrest disease, where you convert an unhealthy citizen into a healthy one, when you exercise your authority to promote sanitary conditions and suppress those which are the reverse, you in doing your duty are also working for the empire." [30] On his rare visits home, when he associated closely with Liberal imperialists, Cecil Rhodes argued in the same vein. The way to solve the social question was to provide new homes for excess population in the colonies and to rescue English markets threatened by protectionist rivals. "If you wish to avoid civil war," he told his admirer, the journalist W. T. Stead, "then you must become an imperialist." [31] It is not surprising that, much to the disgust of Marxists and anti-imperialist liberals, there were even some socialists who looked upon imperialism with anything but distaste. If expansion abroad helped to solve problems of poverty and unemployment at home, why not expand? These socialist imperialists were only a minority, if an audible one, but even without them the growth of socialist ideas, movements, and parties toward the end of the nineteenth century would have been complicated enough.

THE SOCIALIST CHALLENGE

The First International: Union and Fission

The socialist movement followed industrial capitalism like a shadow. Until the 1860s socialist ideas had been the property of isolated theorists, flaring at hectic times, such as 1848, into collective action. As capitalism expanded and matured, so did socialism. The International Workingmen's Association, better known as the First International, was just that: the first serious international association of socialists. And it was a reflection, if still pale, of the international capitalism it proposed to combat and succeed. On a deeper level, socialism was a symptom of the widening crisis of liberalism (see p. 839). Socialists were as skeptical of liberal doctrines, like free trade or free enterprise, as were conservatives and imperialists. Free enterprise, it seemed, benefited mainly the entrepreneur. As we shall see, many socialists were the heirs of political liberals who demanded social control over the means of production for the benefit of all; their views were to produce one of the many splits within the socialist camp. But most of

[30] Quoted in Bernard Semmel, *Imperialism and Social Reform: English Social-Imperial Thought, 1895-1914* (1960), 62-63.
[31] Quoted in Gollwitzer, *Age of Imperialism,* 136.

the leading theoreticians of the socialist movement—the Marxists, the anarchists, the syndicalists—harbored, each in their particular way, abiding suspicions of the state, and they called for either its immediate or its eventual abolition. These splits were to weaken the movement later, in decisive moments; but to worried conservatives in the 1870s, this weakness was less apparent than the growing strength of these "enemies of the state." In 1848 Marx and Engels had opened their *Communist Manifesto* with the bravely defiant words, "A specter is haunting Europe." A quarter of a century later, that specter was substantial enough to alarm Bismarck.

Yet for some decades socialists continued to be at a distinct disadvantage everywhere. By producing an industrial proletariat and suffering drastically from the business cycle, capitalism had created the preconditions for socialism; it gathered the shock troops of discontent in factories and slums, and it aroused humanitarian minds to seek a system less exploitative of its workers and more equitable in its rewards. Yet capitalism could hold in check the forces it had roused. Bismarck discovered in Prussia what other politicians discovered in other countries: extension of the suffrage tapped a vast pool of goodwill, or sheer deference, among the new voters, who docilely voted for conservative or, perhaps, liberal parties, but had little use for revolutionaries, no matter how moderate in tone. The veteran French socialist Louis Blanc put the matter realistically: "Universal suffrage is the instrument of order *par excellence*."[32] Timely social legislation could bind the workers more tightly to the state than repression could, though repression was always a possible threat and often an actual way of reducing socialists to obedience or silence. Finally, most activities of the trade union movement, that problematic supporter and essential mainstay of socialist parties, were still illegal.

The short, sad history of the First International is a commentary on these handicaps; it suggests that whatever optimism survived among socialists after its demise was founded on fervent hope rather than sober analysis. The doctrinaire urge to run the movement in the only "right" way—one's own—and to expel as heretics all dissenters has bedeviled socialist movements throughout their history. Fission began to destroy the First International not long after it had established a precarious unity. The International Workingmen's Association had been formed in London in 1864 by leaders of British and French trade unions, with some of Mazzini's lieutenants in attendance. Marx, who had been living in English exile since 1849, gave the inaugural address. Lauding the triumphs of the working class so far, he called for further efforts and for the eventual conquest of political power by the workers. His speech contained the seeds of conflict: it was far more radical than trade unionists would be for decades. And with his talk of seizing state power, Marx directly affronted the anarchists' doctrine that all states, including democracies, tyrannize over the worker. The anarchists' goal was not to take over, but to destroy

[32] Quoted in David Thomson, *Democracy in France Since 1870* (5th ed., 1969), 44.

the state. With each annual congress, the verbal battles between Marx and the followers of Proudhon (see p. 686) grew more pointed; when in 1868 the Russian anarchist Bakunin, wilful and noisy, joined the deliberations of the International, these disagreements became unmanageable.

Then came the eventful life and terrible death of the Paris Commune (see p. 813). Marx seized on the Commune and, in his famous *Civil War in France*, turned the debacle of the immediate past into a myth for the future. The bloodbath, he said, was "the glorious harbinger of a new society," and he hailed the revolutionary Commune itself as a model government for the working class in power because it joined the executive with the legislature. This was too much for Mazzini; it was too much for the British trade unionists in the International. Since Marx had purported to speak for the organization, they took the proper British way out: they resigned. This meant the end of the First International. At the Hague Congress of 1872, Marx succeeded in having Bakunin expelled, while Engels had the general council moved from London to New York, where it lingered on, a ghost, until 1876.

Varieties of Socialism: Marxism

Socialism survived the death of the First International. In the course of two decades, socialists absorbed the lessons of the Commune and prepared themselves for action in their countries. Marx himself and his self-effacing associate Engels elaborated the structure of their scientific socialism and simplified its teaching for the general reader. The classic of Marxian socialism was the first volume of Marx's *Capital*, which appeared in 1867. Though technical and austere, *Capital* makes its polemical point plainly enough: in the course of its evolution, capitalism is compelled by the iron laws of its very development to concentrate wealth in the hands of the few and to create increasing misery among the many. More than any other economic system, capitalism must dispose of vast sums of capital for its large-scale enterprises, its far-flung commerce, its elaborate systems of communications. Where does the capitalist system get the capital it swallows so greedily? Marx insisted that the answer was to be found in the resolution of an apparently insoluble paradox: the capitalist buys his commodities at their value and sells them at their value, but "at the end of the process" he "must withdraw more value from circulation than he threw into it at starting." The answer is this: the value of a commodity is the amount of labor embodied in it. This was the classical labor theory of value that Marx had learned from the economist David Ricardo, but Marx made his own characteristic addition: the worker is the source not merely of value but also of surplus value. The manufacturer buys the laborer at his value, which is the amount of money needed to replace him—that is to say, his subsistence. If the worker, say, produces enough to secure his survival in five hours of work, the other hours of his working day produce value that he will not receive, but will go into the pockets of his master for profit and further investment. Capital accumulation, in other words, is sweated out of the worker; it is the totality of surplus value. The idea that the rich grind the poor, that the employer exploits the worker, was by no means original with Marx. What Marx added was that the process was an inescapable part of the capitalist system and that it could be "scientifically" demonstrated. The polemical gain was enormous.

Marx sought to demonstrate not merely that exploitation was essential to capitalism, but also that capitalism was doomed. The very conditions that made for the success of capitalism made for its inevitable demise. "One capitalist always kills many . . ." Marx wrote in *Capital*. "Along with the constantly diminishing number of the magnates of capital, who usurp and monopolize all advantages of this process of transformation, grows the mass of misery, oppression, slavery, degradation, exploitation; but with this too grows the revolt of the working class, a class always increasing in numbers, and disciplined, united, organized by the very mechanism of the process of capitalist production itself. The monopoly of capital becomes a fetter upon the mode of production, which has sprung up and flourished along with, and under it. Centralization of the means of production and socialization of labor at last reach a point where they become incompatible with their capitalist integument. This integument is burst asunder. The knell of capitalist private property sounds. The expropriators are expropriated." Here was another apparent triumph of scientific socialism: it permitted Marx to predict the end of capitalism with complete confidence.

The audience for *Capital* was necessarily restricted, though it included men who would make a certain noise in history, like H. M. Hyndman and, more important, the young Lenin (see p. 862). But Marx and Engels soon found opportunities to develop their ideas in more accessible form. As Voltaire, sitting in remote Ferney, had become the grand strategist of the Enlightenment in the 1760s (see p. 359), so Marx and Engels, sitting in central London, now became the advisers and critics of young socialist movements in several countries. When the German socialists merged their two parties at Gotha in 1875, Marx condemned the program hammered out there as evasive and inconsistent. In a long private communication, he tried to drive home his doctrines with some curt memorable phrases. [33] It was utopian, he insisted, to call for equal rights as though these could be attained immediately. Even after a successful proletarian revolution, the "economic structure and the cultural development" of society must grow into a higher phase of communist society. Meantime, it will undergo a "period of revolutionary transformation" and to this, he argued, "corresponds a period of political transition during which the state can be nothing else than the revolutionary dictatorship of the proletariat." Only after this transition, when the "narrow, bourgeois horizon" has been transcended, will the new

---

[33] It was only when Engels finally published it in 1891, as *Critique of the Gotha Program*, that its influence on the newly legalized German Social Democratic party became important.

society realize the communist ideal, "From each according to his capacity: to each according to his need."

As long as this critique remained unpublished, other writings had to do the work of popularization. The best known of these, though itself not without its forbidding passages, was Engels' series of polemical articles published in 1877 and 1878. They were soon collected into a book, popularly known as the *Anti-Dühring*. Its target was Eugen Dühring, who took pride in calling himself a "German socialist" and preached virulent anti-Semitism; its essential purpose was to expound Marxist economic theory, dialectical materialism, and the conception of ideology—or "false consciousness"—which would gain prominence in twentieth-century thought. But then, after Bismarck had outlawed the German Socialist party in 1878 and driven most of its leaders underground or into exile, the discussion of theoretical questions proceeded mainly in Zurich or London. And Marx found supporters for his ideas in other countries as well, notably in Belgium and France. In 1883 three Russian exiles, G. V. Plekhanov, Vera Zasulich, and P. B. Akselrod, founded the Marxist-inspired "Liberation of Labor" group in Switzerland and began to polemicize against Russian populism; by the early 1890s, Marxist ideas were widely disseminated in Russia itself. Students and intellectuals discussed them with keen interest; in the mid-1890s, there were even some ephemeral Marxist newspapers and some tentative approaches to factory workers. Then, in December 1895, the Russian government arrested the leaders of these circles, and Russian Marxism became, more than ever, a monopoly of exiles (for its later history, see p. 862).

Varieties of Socialism: Competing Doctrines

Marxist ideas had to battle not only repressive police but also vigorous competitors for the allegiance of radical intellectuals and politically alert workingmen. Marxism itself, as it developed in its theoretical writings and its occasional pronouncements, lent itself to divergent interpretations. With its assault on all utopianism, and with its insistence that social and economic evolution must make institutions ripe for revolution before revolution can succeed, it could be read as a doctrine of evolution—peaceful revolution. In foreseeing the eventual withering away of the state, it shared the goal of the anarchists while, with its encouragement of political activity within capitalist states, it clashed directly with the most deeply felt of anarchist doctrines. Indeed, it was within the anarchist wing of the socialist movement and in its offspring and ally, the syndicalist wing, that Marxism had its fiercest rivals. It was not Bakunin alone who rejected Marx for his "authoritarianism."

The history of the socialist movement in France in these years perfectly illustrates this tangle of ideas and feelings. The representative of Marxism in France was the radical journalist Jules Guesde, who laid the foundations of the Parti Ouvrier Français in 1879. Having supported the Paris Commune and having suffered exile, Guesde was much admired; but as a convert to Marxism from anarchism, he had the convert's typical doctrinaire attitudes. He had been to see Marx in London, and he hoped to model his French party on the German Social Democrats, with their authoritarian respect for central direction. Not unexpectedly, Guesde's small party soon broke into fragments. In 1880 the anarchists walked out. In the same year, the followers of Auguste Blanqui, nostalgic for the direct action of the French Revolution, organized their Parti Socialiste Révolutionnaire, which had little program beyond direct action. Then, in 1882, the moderates rejected Guesde's unyielding theoretical position; under the leadership of Paul Brousse, they formed the rival Fédération des Travailleurs Socialistes. Its central doctrine was called *"possibilisme,"* which meant, simply, that by electing sympathetic legislators in the municipalities and to the Chamber of Deputies and by passing progressive social legislation, Brousse and his allies would convert France into a socialist country. The *possibilistes* wanted peaceful parliamentary and electoral activity in place of insurrections, secret cells, and assassinations. Their ideas found energetic and eloquent advocates among independent socialists like Alexandre Millerand and the great parliamentary leader Jean Jaurès.

Thus the French socialist movement grew up amidst the noise of competing doctrines. Then, in 1884, the French government legalized the trade unions, and the balance of socialist opinion shifted away from politics. Syndicalism took the upper hand, without driving political socialism entirely from the field. The *syndicats* were a mixture of trade union and fraternal organization, not unlike the gilds; they concerned themselves with finding employment for their members, with workers' education, and with conditions of apprenticeship. They were open to socialist ideas but hostile to politics, perhaps mainly because they were incurably suspicious of politicians, who seemed to them all rotten bourgeois anyway. Some of the most militant of the syndicalists toyed with notions of insurrection, and it took the decades of the 1880s and the 1890s to sort out the varieties of the syndicalist impulse. The successful establishment of a national federation of labor exchanges (Bourses du Travail), which emerged in 1892 from the model set up in Paris earlier, gave the unions a center for mutual aid; and in 1895, when the unions finally joined in the Confédération Générale du Travail (CGT), they could concentrate on formulating its basic ideas with fair clarity. The first article of its constitution proclaimed its autonomy: "The elements constituting the CGT will remain independent of all political schools." But if anarchist insurrectionism, Marxist revolutionism, and possibilist gradualism were all unacceptable, what course of action could the CGT safely recommend to its members? The answer emerged early in its history, in the late 1880s: it was the general strike as the supreme weapon that would transform France from a corrupt capitalist state into a purer socialist order, in which all governmental functions would be performed by the workers through their *syndicats*. The most famous exponent of these ideas, the French engineer Georges Sorel, took syndicalism to its logical conclusion; in a series of widely read articles he expounded what he called the "myth" of the general strike. Sorel—in a major contribution to sociological terminology—took myth to mean not a lie, but a grandiose idea that would rally and energize the working class for revolutionary action. Sorel put syndicalism in arresting language, but when he gathered his articles into his famous *Reflections on Violence* in 1908, he was merely restating ideas commonplace among French syndicalists for two decades. In view of such wide differences among Marxists, *possibilistes,* and syndicalists, it is not surprising that it should take until 1905 for a united Socialist party finally to emerge in France or that, when it was formed, the CGT should studiously adhere to its own antipolitical ideals and avoid any involvement with the new party.

Great Britain was even more inhospitable to the lure of Marx than France. In general it is safe to say that the sway of Marxism over the Western mind did not begin until, and after, the Russian Revolution of 1917. London was the home of Marx; to Marxism it remained relatively indifferent. Upon Marx's death in 1883, Engels loyally continued his friend's work. He brought out the second and third volumes of *Capital,* the one in 1885, and the other in 1894, the year before his own death. And he watched, with growing skepticism and contempt, the evolution of English socialism. Marx's most outspoken disciple, H. M. Hyndman, a speculator, an imperialist, a former high Tory, seemed a most unlikely recruit. Yet when he founded his radical reform group, the Democratic Federation, in 1881, he handed out to its members his book, *England for All,* which offered an epitome of Marx's economic doctrines. Unfortunately, it failed to mention their creator by name, a calculated omission that did not endear Hyndman to Marx or Engels. In 1883 he captured the writer and designer William Morris for his group; early in 1884, he changed its name to Social Democratic Federation (SDF); in the following years he ran candidates for Parliament and led tumultuous demonstrations. But Morris left the SDF in 1885 to become an anarchist, Engels remained hostile, and Hyndman alienated what supporters remained with his peculiar mixture of authoritarian leadership, political opportunism, and doctrinaire revolutionism. In any event, British opinion was not ready for Marxism, with or without Marx.

Far more characteristic of Britain's temper than the SDF and other tiny splinter groups propounding socialism was the Fabian Society, founded in 1884. Its ideas were determinedly eclectic: "Socialism," wrote Sidney Webb, one of its most famous members, in 1886, "is more than any Socialist, and its principles more than any system or scheme of reform. The Fabian Society has no such plan or scheme; we preach Socialism as a faith, as a scientific theory, as a judgment of morality on the facts of life." [34] The Fabians drew heavily on the radical liberalism associated with Jeremy Bentham and John Stuart Mill, on English Christian Socialism, on the new economics, and to some degree on a

---

[34] Sidney Webb, from a lecture printed in the characteristically named journal *The Practical Socialist*; quoted in A. M. McBriar, *Fabian Socialism and English Politics, 1884-1918* (1962), 14.

handful of Marxian ideas. Their method was propaganda, in the best sense of the word. They held discussion meetings at which the best-informed Fabians lectured on economics, politics, sociology, and aesthetics under socialism; they published pamphlets—the famous Fabian Tracts—which were inexpensive, informative, always lucid, sometimes brilliant. Gradually a doctrine emerged. The Fabians believed in state socialism, which included municipal socialism. They were collectivists, but without terror. Their distinctive strategy, which soon became famous, was known as permeation: the Fabians undertook to place their members on royal commissions and in local governments so that their views might become known, and they gave purposeful dinners for influential personages to stuff them with Fabian statistics and win them over to Fabian policies. [35]

The Fabians could expect convinced readers for their tracts and distinguished guests for their dinners because in its early decades the society boasted some remarkable members, all devoted and active—the playwright George Bernard Shaw, the novelist H. G. Wells, the social psychologist Graham Wallas, the political theorist G. D. H. Cole. Above all, there was that extraordinary pair, Sidney and Beatrice Webb. Sidney was a civil servant with a powerful analytical mind and an unsurpassed memory; Beatrice, who had been Herbert Spencer's protégé, was an energetic organizer and as fine a scholar as her husband. Malicious and inaccurate critics called the pair "two typewriters that click as one," but while the Webbs were formidable, they were as devoted to each other as to socialism. In their long years together, they wrote first-rate scholarly volumes on the history of the trade-union movement and on English local government; their suggestions and memoranda on education, the Poor Law, and social legislation in general helped to shape the British welfare state of today. But in the evolution of English labor politics, the influence of the Webbs and their Fabian Society was rather less marked. Except for George Bernard Shaw, who wanted independent political action for labor, the Fabians wanted to influence the influential, not to create new centers of influence. The Labour party that gradually emerged in Britain in the 1890s thus owed little to their intervention. It was only when the party was fully organized that the Fabians, accepting this surprising new instrument for social change, consented to give it intellectual direction.

The gradual emergence of a labor party in Britain was chiefly the work of trade unionists. We have seen that in the 1840s and 1850s "new model" unions finally struck firm roots in the highly skilled and comparatively highly paid

---

[35] The name of the society is in fact somewhat misleading. It is explained on the title page of the Fabians' first tract, "Why Are the Many Poor?" by W. L. Phillips (then the only workingman to be a member of the society). It shows a turtle and bears the motto: "For the right moment you must wait, as Fabius [called Cuncatur, the delayer, the ancient Roman general] did, most patiently, when warring against Hannibal, though many censured his delays; but when the time comes you must strike hard, as Fabius did, or your waiting will be in vain, and fruitless." This suggests an abruptness of which the Fabians were not capable; indeed, gradualism was their motto.

trades—engineers, printers, builders, and the like (see p. 596). These working-men could control entrance to their crafts through apprenticeship, afford to pay high dues in return for insurance benefits, and impress the ruling classes with their sobriety and caution. They were both politic and political. And by the seventies this approach had paid dividends, not only in well-endowed union treasuries but in a newly assured legal position for trade unions and, most important of all, in a degree of genuine respect. The seventies and eighties saw the rise of a "new unionism," with the benevolent support of the more established unionists. The most fertile field for development was found among the miners, the railwaymen, the gas workers, the textile workers, whose jobs required some skill, though hardly at the level of printers or engineers, and whose earlier efforts at organizing had been uniformly unsuccessful. Even more dramatically, the late eighties saw the extension of unionism to the compara-tively unskilled, notably the dockers, who provided far too many of the grim statistics in Charles Booth's multivolumed survey of *Life and Labour of the People of London,* which was published over a period of nearly two decades following 1886. By 1900 the trade unions could claim around two million members, perhaps a quarter of the adult male manual workers in the country. And the new unions, more amenable to socialist ideas than the old, had gained important influence on the policy and leadership of the Trades Union Congress, the labor parliament founded in 1867.

Unlike their German counterparts, English trade unions did not have to yoke themselves to a party rigidly dedicated to Marxist orthodoxy (see p. 860); unlike their French counterparts, they believed in politics as a way of advancing their interests. The traditional two-party system was an obstacle in the way of a political party speaking for labor. So was the even more traditional attitude of deference, which made English workingmen reluctant to challenge their "betters" directly. Instead, labor attempted to elect workingmen on the Liberal ticket, the Lib-Labs. In 1874 two miners were actually elected to the Commons, and through the 1880s labor was content with its Lib-Labs. In 1885 there were nine of them in parliament. But then, with the rise of the New Unionism around 1890 and with the burgeoning of socialist ideas, Lib-Labism seemed tame. In 1893, accordingly, socialists formed the Independent Labour party (ILP) and offered a socialist platform to the country; its leader, the magnetic James Keir Hardie, was a Scottish worker who was at base a Christian. The Fabians had little faith in the ILP. Nor did Britain: in the elections of 1895, when the Conservatives swept the country, the new party won not a single seat.

Then economics and politics did what propaganda had failed to do. The rise of real wages ended in the mid-1890s; labor unrest grew. So, in 1900, the Trades Union Congress established the Labour Representation Committee to extend the work of the ILP. Its record was at first disheartening: in the elections of 1900, only two Labour candidates out of fifteen entered the Commons. But in the following year, the Taff Vale decision, rendered in the House of Lords as the highest court of appeal, unified scattered energies and produced what had

eluded the most diligent socialists for decades: a Labour party. The Taff Vale
Railway Company had sued a railway union for damages done during
picketing. To the surprise of everyone, the Lords awarded the company
£23,000. The Taff Vale decision did not actually say so, but it practically
outlawed strikes, for companies with their batteries of lawyers could attack
striking unions at their most vulnerable point: their funds. Labor's response
was political organization, on a large and effective scale. In January 1906, when
the Liberals scored an impressive victory in the elections, the new Labour party
made its entry into the House of Commons—twenty-nine M.P.s strong. With
twenty-four Lib-Labs added, this made a minority that could not be ignored.
Taff Vale was reversed in the first year of the new Parliament. Radical peaceful
reform, it seemed, was on the march. The active drive for socialism in Britain
came later, after World War I.

Revisionism: The Great Debate

Whatever divided Marxists, anarchists, and syndicalists, they were all professed
revolutionaries. But while governments across the Western world set up
varying degrees of resistance to their organizations, socialists and their
bourgeois sympathizers won their way into parliaments, wherever there were
parliaments. Once there, the socialist deputies were normally isolated in
intransigent opposition. But their very presence raised a fundamental question.
Marx and Engels had not objected to political activities by their followers;
though determinists about the general course of history, they taught that the
birth of socialism can be helped or hindered by men's actions, which included
political action. Yet even for the Marxist, this question was difficult enough. To
pursue an undeviating course of revolution was to cut oneself off from effective
work in politics. To seek effective political participation was to compromise the
possibility of radically transforming all society. As trade unionists and socialist
theorists increasingly came together, if only to argue, this dilemma was
sharpened. Most trade unionists, whatever their rhetoric, wanted immediate
improvements in the workers' lot; most theorists looked to the ultimate goal.
When, in 1889, Europe's socialist parties gathered in Paris to form the Second
International, they found their deliberations dominated by this single issue—
revolution versus reform. Every three years or so they would meet and debate
it again. They would vote revolution and then go home and practice reform.

A profound crisis in Marxist theory, which became evident in the 1890s,
exacerbated this dilemma for some, but offered a way out to others. As we have
seen, it had been a tenet central to Marx's system that capitalism, in the course
of its development, must transform itself from a dynamic into a reactionary
force. As capitalism grew older, its "inner contradictions" must become ever
more apparent; their devastating symptoms were the recurrent business cycle,
the reserve army of the unemployed, the sharpening class struggle, the

disappearance of classes intermediate between the capitalist and the worker, and growing misery among the working class. In the end, as the death knell of capitalism sounded, the expropriators would be expropriated (see p. 854). But in the 1890s it became clear that, however desirable it might be to see the expropriators expropriated, capitalist development was not taking the course that Marx had so confidently predicted. There were cycles and there was unemployment, but the number of capitalists in particular, and of propertied persons in general, was growing. And far from falling into growing misery, most of the working class across Europe were improving their lot, and noticeably so. One might quibble about statistics: "real" wages are hard to measure, "propertied" is hard to define. And leading defenders of the pure doctrine, such as Karl Kautsky—"Pope" Kautsky, the arch-orthodox Marxist— insisted that the long-range tendency of capitalism was to slip into a condition of permanent crisis. There were mutterings that to doubt even a part of Marx's vision was to give comfort to the capitalist enemy and thus to subvert the coming revolution.

The critics of Marxist orthodoxy, the so-called revisionists, were unimpressed by such defenses. They liked to think that they were loyal to Marx in their own way. That is why Eduard Bernstein, their most famous representative, never liked this name. He was a Marxist of long standing and, until the revisionist controversy erupted in the late 1890s, a Marxist in good standing. During the sway of Bismarck's antisocialist legislation, he had lived in exile, first in Zurich and then in London, and had edited the illegal party's newspaper, the *Sozialdemokrat*. In London he had worked closely with Engels, and Kautsky had been his friend. When he undertook his critical examination of Marx's economic ideas he did so from within. He was guided by undeniable facts; yet none of these facts made the demise of capitalism any less certain or the triumph of socialism any less desirable. As he summed up his position in a note to himself: "Peasants do not sink; middle class does not disappear; crises do not grow ever larger; misery and serfdom do not increase. There *is* increase in insecurity, dependence, social distance, social character of production, functional superfluousness of property owners." [36] What could be a more authentic specimen of scientific socialism than this?

While it was difficult to assail Bernstein's analysis, the political lessons he drew from it opened him to fierce attack. Even in his most faithful Marxist days, Bernstein had been a partisan of democratic tactics and peaceful change; in his revisionist phase he argued that this, too, was genuine Marxism. Marx had believed in evolution; so did Bernstein. Marx had hinted at the possibility of a bloodless revolution; Bernstein now insisted that it must be won in this manner. "Democracy," he wrote, "is at the same time means and end. It is the

---

[36] See Peter Gay, *The Dilemma of Democratic Socialism: Eduard Bernstein's Challenge to Marx* (1952), 296. Bernstein wrote the article on Marx in the great eleventh edition of the *Encyclopaedia Britannica* (1911), and it is a brilliant exposition.

means of the struggle for Socialism and it is the form Socialism will take once it has been realized." Bernstein made this point in 1899, in his chief theoretical work, *Evolutionary Socialism.* [37] His forays into revisionism before this had caused some stir; his book raised a storm. In each annual congress, the German SPD debated Bernstein's ideas and, despite widespread support for revisionism, rejected them.

To party leaders like August Bebel, more interested in electoral victories than doctrinal clarity, this debate was most unwelcome. As we saw (see p. 798), even between 1878 and 1890 the outlawed SPD had increased its vote and its representation in the Reichstag. In the 1890s and after 1900, operating under the purely Marxist Erfurt program, the party was in fact acting on Bernstein's tactical advice, though it was wholly unwilling to say so. The SPD was a coalition of trade unionists, party functionaries, left-wing theorists, and a solid proportion of bourgeois voters. Reiterated public trumpeting of its revolutionary intentions seemed ill calculated to keep the coalition intact and the support growing. Yet the party continued to prosper. In the elections of 1903, it got three million votes and eighty-one mandates in the Reichstag, a gain of one million votes and twenty-five mandates over the elections of 1898; in 1912, after a temporary setback in 1907, the SPD became the largest single party in the Reichstag, with more than four million votes and one hundred ten seats. Its inner tension—a revisionist party standing on a revolutionary platform—would have its baleful effects later, during the war and after (see p. 1004). Meanwhile, the SPD was the model socialist party for all Europe, closely watched by socialists everywhere. The revisionist controversy thus had reverberations far beyond Germany's frontiers.

One of these observers was Vladimir Ilich Ulyanov, better known by his revolutionary name of Lenin. Since the 1890s, Russian Social Democrats had been carrying on an inconclusive debate over the best course to take. In Russia itself and among the Russian exiles, advocates of liberal policies confronted revolutionaries calling for a seizure of power. The debate changed character with Lenin's intervention. His brother had been executed as a revolutionary in 1887, and he himself had spent some time in Siberia. Like his fellow Marxist Plekhanov, Lenin had read Bernstein and had been appalled; what he wanted was revolution and more—a party of dedicated revolutionaries. He was freed from Siberia in 1900 and went to the West; there, in 1902, he published *What is To be Done?*, a polemic (its title deliberately borrowed from Chernyshevsky's famous novel) that deserves the closest study on the part of anyone interested in the history of communism. It begins with the kind of oversimplification that does violence to history and is ideal for political debate: there are now two tendencies in Social Democracy; the true revolutionary one, which retains Marx's teaching of the class struggle and the aim of proletarian revolution, and

[37] The original was awkwardly entitled *Voraussetzungen des Sozialismus und die Aufgaben der Sozialdemokratie;* the more felicitous title belongs to the English translation of 1909.

the other, which claims freedom to criticize Marxism. This latter "has been *stated* with sufficient precision by Bernstein, and *demonstrated* by Millerand." [38] It is a seductive tendency, this revisionism; in fact, left to itself, the working class will develop only a "trade-union consciousness," which looks to immediate and piecemeal concessions without caring for the goal, which is revolution. That is why the workers must be guided by professional revolutionaries, by "bourgeois intellectuals" whose perception of the workers' true interest is clearer than the workers' own, for these intellectuals have mastered Marxism.

The revolutionary struggle was thus to be carried on by an elite of professionals; the vague notion of a dictatorship of the proletariat receded before the precise conception of the dictatorship of the party. In 1903, when the exiled Russian socialists met, first in Brussels and then in London, they split over this dramatic departure from Marx's views. Then there were further splits. Lenin's seizure of the word *Bolshevik*—majority group—for his associates and *Menshevik*—minority group—for his adversaries was a ruthless but brilliant tactic in a complicated fight. It misrepresented not merely the relative power of the quarreling factions but the ideas of the Mensheviks: by suggesting that they belonged to the other "tendency" in Social Democracy, Lenin fathered the legend of Mensheviks as followers of Bernstein's revisionism, which they were not. Yet few in Europe were inclined to take these wrangles seriously. Only Lenin, who believed in the power of ideas as he believed in himself, thought that the time would come when his Bolsheviks would indeed be the majority. History would vindicate him—at least his prediction, if not his tactics—but only in the distant future. Down to 1914, at least, it was the time of parliamentary socialists, of peaceful labor parties. The time of revolution would come later.

SELECTED READINGS

D. V. Glass and E. Grebenik offer an excellent summary of recent studies of the population explosion in "World Population, 1800–1950", *Cambridge Economic History of Europe,* vol. VI, *The Industrial Revolution and After,* Part 1, edited by H. J. Habbakuk and M. M. Postan (1965), 60–138. T. H. Hollingsworth, *Historical Demography* (1969) has a good introduction to the field and its materials; see also Carlo M. Cipolla, *The Economic History of World Populations* (1962). A. M. Carr-Saunders, *World Population* (1936) retains its value as a general survey. On the vexed question of birth control, the brief study by J. A. Banks and Olive Banks, *Feminism and Family Planning in Victorian England* (1964) is splendid. See also the absorbing early chapters in David M. Kennedy's *Birth Control in America: The Career of Margaret Sanger* (1970).

Urbanization has recently come into the forefront of historians' discussions. H. J. Dyos, ed., *The Study of Urban History* (1968) lays out the problems on an international

---

[38] In 1899 the independent French socialist Alexandre Millerand agreed to join Waldeck-Rousseau's cabinet. His action called forth sharp criticism by the Paris Congress of the Second International in 1900 and even sharper condemnation at the 1904 congress in Amsterdam, when revisionism, "opportunism," and similar sins against revolutionary purity were rejected as calculated to keep the capitalists in power.

scale and supplies some answers in a series of revealing papers; Dyos' own "Agenda for Urban Historians," 1–46, is particularly valuable. Asa Briggs, *Victorian Cities* (2nd ed., 1968) is a series of informal and informative essays, confined to English cities and one Australian city. Wilson Smith, ed., *Cities of Our Past and Present* (1964) is a good descriptive reader on American cities. And see R. E. Dickinson, *The West European City: A Geographical Interpretation* (2nd ed., 1961).

The modern classic by Oscar Handlin, *The Uprooted* (1951), encompasses the experience of the immigrant into the United States. The prehistory of that immigration is set out in Marcus Lee Hansen, *The Atlantic Migration, 1607–1860: A History of the Continuing Settlement of the United States* (1940). Walter F. Willcox, *International Migrations*, 2 vols. (1929–1931) is a massive factual study. See also Donald R. Taft and Richard Robbins, *International Migrations: The Immigrant in the Modern World* (1955).

On the rise of a world economy, William Ashworth, *A Short History of the International Economy Since 1950* (2nd ed., 1962), is a lucid survey. Herbert Feis, *Europe: The World's Banker, 1870–1914* (1930), though old, still says the essential. Both may be supplemented with J. B. Condliffe, *The Commerce of Nations* (1950). See also J. H. Clapham, *The Economic Development of France and Germany, 1815–1914* (4th ed., 1935), and Charles P. Kindleberger, *Economic Growth in France and Britain: 1851–1950* (1964)—two solid comparative studies.

For technical improvements, see Ashworth, *Short History of the International Economy*, just cited; W. H. G. Armytage, *A Social History of Engineering* (2nd ed., 1961); the useful introductory book by T. K. Derry and T. I. Williams, *A Short History of Technology* (1961); and a fine long essay by H. J. Habbakuk, *American and British Technology in the Nineteenth Century: The Search for Labour-Saving Devices* (1962). On industrial and financial concentration, see above all Hermann Levy, *The New Industrial System: A Study of the Origins, Forms, Finance, and Prospects of Concentration in Industry* (1936).

The controversial literature on imperialism is vast and growing. Two massively detailed works by William L. Langer, *European Alliances and Alignments, 1871–1890* (2nd ed., 1950), and *The Diplomacy of Imperialism, 1890–1902*, 2 vols. (2nd ed., 1950), give the necessary facts. For a recent survey of imperialist "culture," short but informative, see Heinz Gollwitzer, *Europe in the Age of Imperialism, 1880–1914* (1969). A. P. Thornton, *Doctrines of Imperialism* (1965), and his *The Imperial Idea and Its Enemies: A Study in British Power* (1959), provide dependable surveys of ideas and policies. Richard Koebner and H. D. Schmidt, *Imperialism: The Story and Significance of a Political Word, 1840–1960* (1964) is a fascinating exploration of a significant semantic evolution. J. A. Hobson, *Imperialism: A Study*, first published in 1902, remains an indispensable document, partly for information, partly for exhibiting the liberal anti-imperialist attitude in England, partly for its place in the development of socialist theories about imperialism. For these theories, see Rosa Luxemburg, *The Accumulation of Capital* (tr. 1963), and, of course, Lenin, *Imperialism: The Highest Stage of Capitalism* (1917).

For British imperialism, the study by R. E. Robinson and John Gallagher, with Alice Denny, *Africa and the Victorians: The Official Mind of Imperialism* (1961) is indispensable and has produced widespread debate. C. J. Lowe, *The Reluctant Imperialists*, 2 vols. (1967) analyzes British foreign policy from a similar perspective; volume II contains useful documents. See also, in this connection, William Ashworth, *An Economic History of England, 1870–1939* (1960), which puts expansion into perspective. Three important essays by Bernard Semmel, *Imperialism and Social Reform: English Social-Imperial Thought, 1895–1914* (1960); *The Governor Eyre Controversy* (1962, republished in 1969 under the more explicit title *Democracy Versus Empire: The Jamaica Riots of 1865 and the Governor Eyre Controversy)*; and *The Rise of Free Trade Imperialism: Classical Political Economy, The Empire of Free Trade, and Imperialism, 1750–1850* (1970) throw much light on neglected aspects of British imperial thought and practice. Felix Gross, *Rhodes of Africa* (1956) is valuable on finances; Rita Hinden, *Empire and After: A Study of British Imperial Attitudes* (1949) is valuable on ways of thinking. And see John Evelyn Wrench, *Alfred Milner: The Man of No Illusions* (1958).

For the Germans in Africa, see W. O. Henderson, *Studies in German Colonial History* (1963), and the relevant essays in Prosser Gifford and Wm. Roger Louis, eds., *Britain and Germany in Africa: Imperial Rivalry and Colonial Rule* (1967). See also William O. Aydelotte, *Bismarck and British Colonial Policy, 1883–85* (1937), and A. J. P. Taylor, *Germany's First Bid for Colonies, 1884–1885* (1938). Hans-Ulrich Wehler, "Bismarck's Imperialism, 1862–1890," *Past and Present*, 48 (August 1970) challenges the Robinson-Gallagher thesis, at least for Germany.

The most interesting recent study of French imperialism, on the other hand, adopts that thesis: Henri Brunschwig, *French Colonialism: 1871–1914: Myths and Realities* (tr. 1964). It may be supplemented with Herbert I. Priestley, *France Overseas: A Study of Modern Imperialism* (1938); the study of a leading French advocate of expansion, Jules Ferry, by Thomas F. Power, Jr., *Jules Ferry and the Renaissance of French Imperialism* (1944); John F. Cady, *The Roots of French Imperialism in Eastern Asia* (1954); and the valuable essay by Agnes Murphy, *The Ideology of French Imperialism* (1954).

American expansionism remains a matter of controversy. After decades of sheer criticism, Ernest R. May has now produced two rather more complex studies, *Imperial Democracy* (1961), and *American Imperialism: A Speculative Essay* (1968); see also Julius W. Pratt, *Expansionists of 1898* (1936). But the returns are not all in yet. For the Italians, see Christopher Hollis, *Italy in Africa* (1941); for the Russians, see Firuz Kazemzadeh, *Russia and Britain in Persia, 1864–1914* (1968), and B. H. Sumner, *Tsardom and Imperialism in the Far and Middle East, 1880–1914* (1942).

Imperialism from the perspective of the victims deserves more work than it has had. See John Gallagher and R. E. Robinson, "The Partition of Africa," in H. F. Hinsley, ed., *New Cambridge Modern History*, vol. XI, *Material Progress and World-Wide Problems: 1870–1898* (1962), 593–640. See the fascinating psychological interpretation by O. Mannoni, *Prospero and Caliban: The Psychology of Colonization* (2nd ed., 1964), and Philip Mason, *Patterns of Dominance* (1970).

For the history of socialist ideas across the world, see the stodgy but reliable volumes by G. D. H. Cole, in his *A History of Socialist Thought*, especially vol. II, *Marxism and Anarchism, 1850–1890* (1953), and vol. III, *The Second International, 1889–1914*, 2 vols. (1955). Julius Braunthal, *History of the International*, 2 vols. (tr. 1967), and James Joll, *The Second International, 1889–1914* (1955), are clear and informative. Carl Landauer, *European Socialism*, 2 vols. (1959) is very full; George Lichtheim, *Marxism: An Historical and Critical Study* (1961) is brilliant.

For the development of socialism in Germany during Marx's last years, see Roth, *The Social Democrats in Imperial Germany* (1963), and Lidtke, *The Outlawed Party: Social Democracy in Germany, 1878–1890* (1966), both cited before. Peter Gay, *The Dilemma of Democratic Socialism: Eduard Bernstein's Challenge to Marx* (1952) is mainly relevant to the revisionist controversy of the 1890s, but deals with the earlier and later decades as well.

The complex story of French socialism is treated briefly and lucidly in David Thomson, *Democracy in France Since 1870* (5th ed. 1969) cited before; to this should be added the early chapters of Harvey Goldberg's excellent *A Life of Jean Jaurès* (1962), and Aaron Noland, *The Founding of the French Socialist Party, 1893-1905* (1956). George Lichtheim, *Marxism in Modern France* (1966) is short and suggestive. Val L. Lorwin, *The French Labor Movement* (1954) is also recommended.

Socialist thought and practice in England, never hospitable to Marxism, are well treated in Henry Pelling, *The Origins of the Labour Party, 1880-1900* (2nd ed., 1965), as in the recent exhaustive though not definitive study by A. M. McBriar, *Fabian Socialism and English Politics, 1884-1918* (1962). To this should be added Margaret Cole, *The Story of Fabian Socialism* (1961), and C. Tsuzuki, *H. M. Hyndman and British Socialism* (1961). H. A. Clegg, A. Fox, and A. F. Thompson, *History of British Trade Unionism since 1889*, vol. I (1964) is informative. E. H. Phelps Brown, *The Growth of British Industrial Relations* (1959) is essential for understanding the dynamics of trade unionism.

For the revisionist controversy, see Peter Gay, *Dilemma of Democratic Socialism*, as well as Harvey Goldberg, *Jaurès*, both just cited. See in addition, J. H. Jackson, *Jean Jaurès* (1943), and J. P. Nettl, *Rosa Luxemburg*, 2 vols. (1966), especially volume I. And for Russia, deeply involved in the revisionist controversy, there are Leopold H. Haimson, *The Russian Marxists and the Origins of Bolshevism* (1955), and Richard Pipes, *Struve: Liberal on the Left, 1870-1905* (1970), the first of a two-volume biography.

22

The Cultural Upheaval:
1870-1914

Between 1870 and 1914, the European mind changed in decisive and irrevocable ways. Philosophers and theologians, already in great agitation after the publication of Darwin's *Origin of Species* in 1859, and further agitated by the political, economic, and social ferment we have discussed, felt compelled to assimilate new knowledge and to tackle new problems. The threat or promise of secularism hung over everything. "Higher criticism," the scholarly study of the biblical texts to establish their dates and authors, dated back to the seventeenth and eighteenth centuries (see p. 337). But by the middle of the nineteenth century, the general passion for science had brought this discipline to new heights. German theologians, concentrated at the University of Tübingen, placed the New Testament into its historical context and dated it as a product of the second century. Then, in 1878, Julius Wellhausen published his *Prolegomena zur Geschichte Israels,* which advanced the hypothesis that the Pentateuch was actually a composite of four different sources. Fundamentalist believers in the literal inspiration of the Scriptures thus found themselves beleaguered not merely by scientists but by theologians as well. As late as 1881, Professor William Robertson Smith, author of a distinguished series of lectures,

The Religion of the Semites, was dismissed from his chair at the Free Church of Scotland College at Aberdeen for denying "the immediate inspiration, infallible truth and divine authority of the Holy Scriptures." Advanced theologians drew the consequences. In 1885 F. W. Farrar, a liberal Anglican cleric and author of the popular *Life of Christ,* said in a lecture to the Royal Society that "verbal infallibility could not possibly survive the birth of historic inquiry, which showed in Scripture as elsewhere an organic growth, and therefore a necessary period of immature development."[1] The intellectual transformation set in motion earlier in the century by the natural scientists was brought to its climax by theologians themselves.

At the same time, artists rebelled against the dictatorship of respectable taste on one side and against "vulgar mass society" on the other. They made a strong point of experimentation, fashioned unprecedented styles, and expressed themselves with deliberate offensiveness. Their collective effort, commonly called the "Modern Movement," crystallized in the 1890s. But its antecedents go back at least to the 1870s, and it is incomprehensible without an understanding of these earlier years.

While the Modern Movement was profuse in its works, it is far easier to sort out than the movements of thought that accompanied it. The artists and their philosophic allies sought honesty and novelty; their enemy was all too plain. "Now-a-days," wrote Bertrand Russell in 1902 to his friend, the classicist Gilbert Murray, "every impulse has to be kept within the bounds of black-coated Respectability, the living God."[2] But the winds of doctrine that blew across Europe were often wild and unpredictable, merging, as winds will, into one another. Ideas were vulgarized into slogans; scientific theories, like Darwinian evolution, became grounds for political action. Social Darwinism, a vulgar though at the time plausible doctrine, had a considerable vogue. The Social Darwinists argued, uncertainly basing themselves on Darwin's authority, that in the struggle for existence the fittest survive and that struggle, therefore, is essential for the survival of fitness. In domestic affairs, this meant a defense of the most ruthless competitive practices; in foreign affairs, it meant "realism," that is, bellicosity, aggressiveness. The distinguished biologist T. H. Huxley, who had been Darwin's most ardent and articulate defender since the publication of the *Origin of Species,* protested in 1893, in *Evolution and Ethics,* against Social Darwinism as a distortion of Darwin's theory. In vain: muscular orators like Theodore Roosevelt in the United States and poets like W. E. Henley and Rudyard Kipling in England continued to extol the strenuous life and the blessings of war.

The emergence of new political entities, large-scale migration, and the violent swings of the business cycle produced an often ugly mood among the

---

[1] Quoted in W. Neil, "The Criticism and Theological Use of the Bible, 1700–1950," in S. L. Greenslade, ed., *The Cambridge History of the Bible,* vol. III (1963), 269.

[2] Letter of December 12, 1902. *The Autobiography of Bertrand Russell,* vol. I, *1872–1914* (1967), 162.

carriers of opinion, a mood quite alien to the hopeful liberalism of midcentury. Anti-Semitism, endemic in Western society and particularly virulent in eastern Europe and Russia, assumed political significance in this period; at the very time that Jews migrated westward from the inhospitable Russian domains, fleeing extortions and pogroms, anti-Semitism became a political force in Germany, in the Hapsburg domains, and in France. As a triumphant nationalism continued to spread, Jews developed a nationalism of their own. Professional anti-Semites like Karl Lueger, the mayor of Vienna, thundered against the "corrosive influence" of the Jews; it was in this atmosphere that Theodor Herzl published *Der Judenstaat* in 1896. The Zionist Congress he founded in the following year to advance the cause of a national home for the Jews was a logical consequence (see p. 808).

Other currents of change ran deeper; less visible, they were all the more pervasive. Sexual reformers like Havelock Ellis began to break through the gentility characteristic of the nineteenth century to discuss sexual aberrations with candor and sympathy; though still extremely cautious and indirect, homosexuals timidly called for an understanding of their plight. A few of them even boldly proclaimed the superiority of their tastes to those of the conventional world. But they were exceedingly rare. Only a little more boldly, feminists continued to plead for an improvement in the condition of women. Before 1914 European women had the vote only in Norway and Finland.[3] As George Bernard Shaw, an outspoken feminist, complained in 1891, the dominant view of the "womanly woman" was that of a passive creature, a pretty doll, a submissive wife and mother who lived for others and kept herself at home. Yet, while women's rights lagged behind other causes, the half century after 1870 gave women's plight widespread notoriety.

In this atmosphere the professionalization of knowledge speeded its pace; this meant, in practice, the establishment of general standards and ever increasing specialization. It was not an accident that the great French sociologist Emile Durkheim should publish in 1893 the now classic study, *The Division of Labor in Society* (see p. 879). The organization of the rapidly growing quantity of knowledge produced the subdivision of comprehensive fields such as "natural history."[4] This process advanced considerably after 1870 because of the general adoption of a uniform scale of measurement, the so-called CGS system; its units—the centimeter, the gram, and the second—rapidly conquered country after country.

The social sciences, as always in awe of their model, the natural sciences, followed suit. Economics, for one, grew increasingly quantitative and mathe-

---

[3] In the Pacific world, New Zealand and Australia had extended the suffrage to women in 1893 and in 1902 respectively; in the United States, it was confined to nine states, mainly in the West and, at the time, politically relatively uninfluential.

[4] For example: The British Association for the Advancement of Science, founded in 1831, grouped ten sciences into six groups; almost year by year, these groups were subdivided or added to. Thus, in 1866, the section called "biology" included physiology, zoology, botany, and anthropology. In 1893, physiology split off; in 1894, anthropology; in 1895, botany.

matical, and divided itself into specialties such as international trade, finance, or money and banking. National organizations signified and further increased the new specialization and the new professional seriousness in the social sciences. Young as the discipline of sociology was, the first society of sociologists was formed in France in 1894; two years later Emile Durkheim was instrumental in founding a journal, the *Année sociologique*. Both the French organization and the French periodical served as models for sociologists in other countries. Professional journals, indeed, reflect the kind of self-consciousness to which the social sciences had attained. The first historical journal was the German *Historische Zeitschrift,* which first appeared in 1859; it was followed in 1876 by the French *Revue historique.* The *English Historical Review* and the *American Historical Review* appeared soon after: the one in 1886, the other in 1895. [5] The old Renaissance ideal of the universal man, whose passing had been noted and lamented in the eighteenth century by the philosophes, now seemed very remote. It was replaced by a new ideal, the sober specialist who knew a great deal about a strictly delimited field.

DIMENSIONS OF THOUGHT

Nietzsche: The Heroic Life

Friedrich Nietzsche's influence was far more diversified than his thought, for he used words in a special way and delighted in coining provocative aphorisms; he was the poet of philosophy. *Also Sprach Zarathustra* (1883-1885), his most quoted book, is actually a long prose poem. His thought lent itself to many parties; readers put as much into Nietzsche as they got out of him. In time, his ideas were borrowed by sinister movements, like the Nazis, whom he would have repudiated with loathing. Nietzsche's private history only helped to make him into a myth. He was born in 1844 and was trained as a classicist. For ten years he held a professorship at the University of Basel, where he was the colleague of the great Swiss historian Jacob Burckhardt. But ill health compelled him to resign his post in 1879, and after that he lived, mainly in solitude, in the Swiss mountains and northern Italy, thinking his thoughts and writing his books. Early in 1889, his mind gave way and he spent the rest of his life under the care of his sister, in almost total silence. When he went mad, he was unknown; when he died in 1900, he was widely read across Europe—widely, but not too well. Nietzsche had fallen under the spell of Arthur Schopenhauer's cosmic pessimism but transcended it. For a time, he was Wagner's friend and

---

[5] Inevitably, specialization brought further fission. The first chair of economic history anywhere was established at Harvard in 1892.

hailed Wagner's operas as the music of the future, until he came to dislike the compositions and detest the composer. In his life, as in his thought, he sought and advised independence.

Nietzsche was both critic and prophet. As critic, he looked about his native Germany and warned against its complacency and triumphant vulgarity. Germany's victory over France in 1870–1871 had exposed it to the gravest dangers. In view of his later reputation it is worth noting that what appalled Nietzsche most about modern Germany was its rising anti-Semitic movement. The anti-Semite, he said over and over again, is the stupid and envious man. In January 1889, just before his final collapse, he wrote to Burckhardt: "Have abolished William, Bismarck, and all anti-Semites."[6] Considering the course that German history was to take, this demented boast has a certain sanity. A philosophical anarchist, Nietzsche detested not only imperial Germany, but modern political systems and ideas in general. He repudiated democracy as he repudiated militarism. He thought them all pernicious—and here the critic merges into the prophet—because the modern world was in the hands of slaves. As Nietzsche saw it, Judaism and (far more important) Christianity, two great systems of slave morality, had subverted the healthy, life-affirming paganism of antiquity. And with their triumph, resentful men had clamped hypocritical moral notions such as universal love on civilization. Man's "will to power," his central urge, had been crippled. And it needed to be liberated; man must overcome himself to become truly human. Since, as Nietzsche proclaimed, "God is dead," man must make his own way in a dangerous world. For this, when all the extravagant language has been set aside, is Nietzsche's central teaching: "You shall become who you are—*Du sollst der werden, der du bist.*"

But, of course, for Nietzsche's excited admirers, the extravagant language formed part of his message. It is possible to give his doctrine an essentially benign interpretation: kindness, generosity, and love are virtues as long as they spring from strength, not weakness. But Nietzsche clothed these ideas in the most bellicose language, with metaphors drawn from battle; he spoke of "philosophizing with the hammer" and hailed the coming of the *Übermensch*— the overman, or superman. And so it is not surprising that for enthusiastic Nietzscheans weary of peace and contemptuous of modern materialism, Nietzsche appeared the prophet of brutality and war. He had deep insights into psychology—his *The Genealogy of Morals* (1887) is a splendid study of resentment; his cultural criticism is equally important. But his psychological and cultural insights, as well as his doctrine, calling for self-transcendence and an aristocracy of the spirit, were neglected. It was a tragedy for which the victim must bear some share of the responsibility.

Though influential with the educated public, Nietzsche found many critics among professional philosophers. The philosophers who came to the fore in the English-speaking countries, with their cultivated modesty and passion for

---

[6] Quoted in E. F. Podach, *The Madness of Nietzsche* (1931), 234.

clarity, seem like a direct answer to Nietzsche's splendid murkiness. But that would be a misreading. The American pragmatists found some of Nietzsche's technical ideas quite congenial, and the targets of the English philosophers were the metaphysicians of the nineteenth century, not the prophet of the twentieth. Bertrand Russell and G. E. Moore, who met as undergraduates in Cambridge in the 1890s and powerfully influenced one another, began, like all young English philosophers of the day, as disciples of the English Idealists, the neo-Hegelians T. H. Green and F. H. Bradley. Their early intellectual history is the history of their emancipation from such Teutonic doctrine. Both Russell and Moore came to distrust English Idealism, with its talk of "the Absolute," as a pallid philosophical compromise with remnants of Christianity. In a series of trenchant papers, Moore vindicated the existence of the external world, while Russell, the mathematician, demonstrated the affinity of logic and mathematics and, with his forays into social problems, the relevance of philosophy to politics. However technical their work became, both treated philosophy as the discipline that helps men to make their ideas clear and to escape from vast but empty verbal constructions. "With a sense of escaping from prison," Russell wrote of those early days, "we allowed ourselves to think that grass is green, that the sun and the stars would exist if no one was aware of them."[7]

The American rebellion against the Absolute took another form. C. S. Peirce, a gifted eccentric who had little recognition in his lifetime, laid the basis of pragmatism[8] in an epoch-making article, "How to Make Our Ideas Clear," published in the *Popular Science Monthly* in 1878. His point, quite simply, was that the truth or falsity of a statement can be determined solely by its result in action. This idea, which precipitated philosophy directly into life, found a general hearing only after William James energetically championed it. A teacher at Harvard since 1872 and a trenchant stylist, James broke away from monism into a pluralistic thought that celebrated the variousness and openness of the universe, man's freedom of choice, and the primacy of passion. "Damn the Absolute!" was his motto, and he embodied it in a series of widely read and widely appreciated works, including his *Principles of Psychology* of 1890 and his *Pragmatism* of 1907, the latter a series of lectures he characteristically subtitled "A New Name for Some Old Ways of Thinking."[9] John Dewey, like James a professor and a psychologist, took up the battle from there. He preferred the name *instrumentalism*, afraid that pragmatism had acquired too many diverse meanings, but his philosophy was in the pragmatic vein. Philosophizing, to Dewey, is intelligent activity designed to solve problems. A problem is a spur

[7] Quoted in John Passmore, *A Hundred Years of Philosophy* (1957), 207.

[8] Russell and Moore never approved of pragmatism; Russell in fact derided it as typical of America's business civilization. But here he was quite mistaken, misled by William James' use of such metaphors as "cash value."

[9] James was a notably generous man and enthusiastic about the philosophizing of others. Among the thinkers he hailed was the immensely popular French philosopher Henri Bergson, who championed feeling against reason and man's subjective perception of time and experience against arid, classifying intellect. Like James, Bergson held that if thought and experience conflict, thought must give way.

to thought; but thought makes a difference only if it seeks to solve the problem that had given rise to it. The emphasis that such a philosophy must place on experience and practicality, its affinity to science, and its hostility to metaphysics, should be obvious. Whatever divided the English and the Americans, what united them was a great ambition—to effect a reconstruction in philosophy that would rescue it from the clutches of system-making and produce, not poetic excitement, but intelligent clarity. [10]

Freud: The Hidden Dimension

William James and John Dewey were psychologists before they became philosophers; Friedrich Nietzsche was a perceptive psychologist all his life. Indeed, the nineteenth century greatly enjoyed exploring human nature. Novelists from Stendhal to Henry James and playwrights like Anton Chekhov were psychologists, amateurs perhaps but penetrating; Dostoevsky, whom Nietzsche much admired, considerably advanced men's understanding of abnormality. The word *psychology* itself had been invented in the middle of the eighteenth century by the English philosopher David Hartley, but the discipline became a science—or at least seriously aspired to that condition—in the nineteenth century. The critical point came when the intuition of novelists and philosophers was supplemented by the observations and the experiments of specialists. This transformation was in the main the work of three Germans: the pedagogue Johann Friedrich Herbart, who, early in the nineteenth century, objected to abstract generalizations about the soul and called for empirical research in psychology; the philosopher Gustav Theodor Fechner, who, in midcentury, attempted to assign quantitative value to sensations; and the physiologist Wilhelm Wundt, who performed experiments on animals and measured human reactions. Wundt's laboratory, opened at Leipzig in 1879, was the first psychological laboratory in the world. While these pioneers had theories about human nature, their significance for the history of psychology lies in their measurement of the measurable—stimuli and responses. The physiological and materialist outlook of psychologists late in the nineteenth century was neatly summarized by the German naturalist Karl Christoph Vogt, in his famous remark that the brain secretes thought as the liver secretes bile. The greatest figure in the science, Sigmund Freud, moved much further and got much deeper than that.

Freud thought himself a buccaneer, boldly exploring uncharted seas, and he was right: he discovered a new world. After his exploits, psychology, pedagogy, the social sciences, the novel, and the educated sensibility were changed forever. He was born in the Moravian town of Freiberg in 1856; his family moved to Vienna when he was four. In Vienna he remained, loving and

---

[10] *Reconstruction in Philosophy* was actually the title of a book John Dewey published in 1920.

hating the city, until the Nazis took over Austria in 1938 (see p. 1059); then he made his way to London and died there a free man, in 1939. "My parents," Freud noted in an autobiographical essay, "were Jews, and I have remained a Jew myself," but this declaration marks a cultural loyalty; Freud was an atheist who, in his later work, treated religion as an illusion and as akin to neurosis. But his being a Jew slowed up his academic career.

Freud was trained as a physician. He specialized in physiology and anatomy; in the early 1880s he turned his interest to nervous diseases and began to publish papers on neuropathology. In 1885 he went to Paris to observe the work of the great Jean Martin Charcot, whose experiments in hypnosis and investigations into the symptoms of hysteria greatly impressed Freud. After his return to Vienna Freud began his collaboration with an older Viennese physician, Josef Breuer, who had discovered that a neurotic patient could be freed of symptoms if she (or he, for men too suffered from hysteria) were put into deep hypnosis and induced to talk freely. This was the germ of free association. In 1895 Breuer and Freud published *Studies on Hysteria,* but after that their paths diverged, for Freud wanted not merely to describe hysterical symptoms, but to analyze their cause. And by the mid-1890s he was fairly confident that he understood that cause: sexual repression. This discovery was of the greatest importance because it placed a spotlight on an area of human experience that other investigators had been too genteel to explore and because it moved the explanation of mental states from physiology (where even Breuer had wanted to keep it) to psychology.

Breuer's method of curing patients through catharsis was only a step away from Freud's method, psychoanalysis. But it was a step across a chasm—how deep a chasm Freud discovered only gradually. This was the heroic period of Freud's career. He was forty in 1896, a scientist with ambitions and marked self-confidence. But the discovery that would make him famous had so far eluded him, and he was troubled by his own neurotic symptoms. For some time, until early 1897, he accepted his female patients' stories about being seduced in early life and developed a seduction theory of neurosis. Then his theory proved itself untenable. As a true scientist, he turned defeat into victory: the content of his patients' stories might be fictitious, but the fantasy that such stories represented must have a mental function. In October 1896 Freud's father died—"the most important event, the most poignant loss," he wrote, "of a man's life." It spurred him on to closer self-examination. He had analyzed one of his own dreams as early as July 1895; now, in the summer of 1897, he began his self-analysis. "It is hard for us nowadays to imagine how momentous this achievement was," writes Ernest Jones, Freud's biographer. "Yet the uniqueness of the feat remains. Once done it is done for ever. For no one again can be the first to explore those depths."[11] The first fruit of that self-analysis, the

[11] Ernest Jones, *Sigmund Freud: Life and Work,* vol. I, *The Young Freud, 1856-1900* (1953), 351.

first classic of the psychoanalytic movement, was *The Interpretation of Dreams*, published at the end of 1899. Despite its constricted program—the scientific explanation of the causes of dreams—it contains the bulk of Freud's psycho-analytical theories. Then, in 1904, came *The Psychopathology of Everyday Life*, which connected the most varied strands of conduct, including slips of the tongue, with man's unconscious. That was followed the next year by *Three Essays on the Theory of Sexuality*, which spelled out Freud's most shocking theories: his denial that sexual perverts are different in kind from "normal" people and his insistence that children have sexual feelings and wishes. Therapy and authorship went hand in hand; he published theoretical and clinical papers and case histories; in 1910, with his essay *Leonardo da Vinci*, he ventured into psychobiography; in 1913, with *Totem and Taboo*, into specula-tive cultural anthropology. Freud wrote a great deal and extremely well; he was a lucid stylist, free from all academic mannerisms or journalistic rhetoric.

Yet the immediate influence of Freud's writings was negligible; the first edition of *The Interpretation of Dreams*, a scanty six hundred copies, took eight years to sell. The international notoriety and vast influence of psychoanalysis came only after World War I. But Freud gathered a remarkable if small group of followers; to facilitate communications among them and to win new recruits, they established psychoanalytic journals, held conferences, and founded associations. Some of his disciples, like Hans Sachs, Ernest Jones, and Sandor Ferenczi, remained loyal to the teachings of the master. But between 1911 and 1913, two of them, Alfred Adler and C. G. Jung, seceded and founded their own schools of psychology. The issue that divided them from Freud was Freud's stress on sexuality.

Freud was not a pansexualist; nothing irritated him more than to be accused of holding that everything in the world was caused by sex. But Freud assigned sex—very broadly interpreted—a leading role in his system. That system is a characteristic product of the scientific mentality. There are no accidents in Freud's world; slips of the pen, or dreams, or neurotic symptoms, or sexual tastes do not just happen. If we feel them to be spontaneous and fortuitous, that is only because the mind is like an iceberg, with the main part submerged in the unconscious. There are telling moments, however, when the unconscious emerges into consciousness. Sleep is one of those: when the body is at rest, the censor normally at work screening out impermissible wishes partially relaxes and lets information through. But that censor does not relax totally; hence dreams are so strange. Dreams are expressions of repressed wishes, but the "dream work" sees to it that these wishes are distorted. Other significant clues are slips or neurotic symptoms. The repressed is not destroyed; it seeks an outlet, no matter how devious. Repression may be unfortunate— many read Freud as a sexual reformer—but *some* repression is inescapable. As the child undergoes his psychosexual development from the oral through the anal to the genital phase, he discovers in himself sexual and aggressive wishes he learns to condemn. Most notable of these is what Freud called the Oedipus complex—the longing of the boy to possess his mother and kill his father. Nearly all neurotic symptoms emerge from a failure of the child to go through all his stages and to overcome his Oedipus complex in the normal manner. [12]

Freud drew most of his material from the close observation of his patients and equally close analysis of himself, though before long psychologists subjected such Freudian ideas as dream work to experimental verification. But Freud never ceased to insist that he was aiming at a general theory of the mind; there was nothing distorting about using material derived mainly from neurotics. Freud was convinced that the mind of the mentally ill and the mentally healthy differed only in degree. In one of his three essays on sex he quoted, with approval, the German neurologist Paul Moebius: "We are all a little hysterical." Freud was a healer, and it is as a healer that his reputation spread, but more than that and above all, he was a scientist.

Einstein: The Incomprehensible Universe

Freud's ideas unsettled the Western mind. Developments in modern science were equally unsettling though, for years, only to the very few who understood them. Einstein's formula, $E = mc^2$, hit the general public only in 1945, with the news of Hiroshima. The educated manfully wrestled with popularizations of relativity and quantum theory and misinterpreted Werner Heisenberg's "uncertainty principle" to mean, not limitations on knowledge involving electrons, but horrid uncertainty everywhere. The price of specialization was the unbridgeable distance between professional scientists and laymen. With modern science, the universe became not so much unsettling as incomprehensible.

But if the professionals found the new ideas unsettling, they also found them exhilarating. The atomic theory—perfected, it seemed, in the early nineteenth century—had portrayed the world as constructed of stable building blocks. The work of Michael Faraday and, in the 1860s and 1870s, James Clerk Maxwell, had firmly established the interconnectedness of magnetism, electricity, and light. Chemistry was brought closer to physics; Dimitri Mendeleev's periodic table of the elements offered added proof for the coherent order of nature (see p. 633). These advances in science seemed purely, indeed magnificently, beneficial: the immortal names of Louis Pasteur, Robert Koch, and Paul Ehrlich testify to the uses to which medicine could put chemistry.

The first hint of trouble came with the famous Michelson-Morley experiment of 1887 on the velocity of light; contrary to all expectation, the speed of light remained constant and independent of the motion of its source.

---

[12] While Freud retained his general orientation throughout his life, his theories evolved; thus he developed the famous topography of the human mind, the id, ego, and superego, after World War I.

Then came surprising news from another area: in 1895 the German physics professor Wilhelm Roentgen discovered X rays. Following up Roentgen's work, the French physicist Antoine Henri Becquerel discovered the radioactive nature of uranium; and following *him,* Pierre and Marie Curie discovered two new radioactive elements, polonium and radium. It was strange but undeniable: elements in nature were spontaneously disintegrating. At Cambridge, meanwhile, J. J. Thomson and his assistant Ernest Rutherford discovered the electron. In 1897 Thomson could announce that the "smallest" element in nature, the "indivisible" atom, was actually a constellation of smaller units. By 1902 Rutherford offered a theory to account for radioactivity. The fabric of the universe was far more complex and far less stable than scientists had supposed.

Experimenters of genius had thrown new light, and with it, large shadows. Fortunately, theoreticians of genius were at hand. Late in 1900 Max Planck announced his unexpected and unassailable discovery that radiant energy is emitted not in continuous quantities but in discontinuous units—"Planck's constant." In 1905 a young mathematical physicist named Albert Einstein, then working in the patent office at Bern as an examiner, extended Planck's constant to light in general: there were quanta of light as there were quanta of radiant heat. In the same year, Einstein offered his explanation for the "failure" of the Michelson-Morley experiment. His Special Theory of Relativity, considerably generalized in 1915–1916, asked men to conceive the universe in a new way. Newton's conception of space and time as absolute and distinct containers, though valid enough for ordinary experience, failed to account for the world's most general characteristics. Space and time are a continuum, a fourth dimension, and both are relative to the observer. One of the most attractive elements of Einstein's theory was its elegant way of unifying hitherto disparate phenomena. Gravitation was a property of space–time. All attempts to visualize these ideas, though it has been tried, must fail; Einstein's world was that of pure mathematics. But in the papers expounding his General Theory of Relativity, Einstein had suggested ways of experimental proof. By 1919, the proof was complete and Einstein had become the Newton of the twentieth century.[13]

Max Weber: The Science of Society

Much less abstract and much less precise than the physical sciences, the sciences of society made decisive progress in these decades as well. Historians were engaged in a great debate. The German philosopher Wilhelm Windelband and his followers attempted to place history in the spectrum of the sciences by differentiating its aim of understanding concrete events from the

[13] The English critic, poet, and parodist J. C. Squire, considering Alexander Pope's famous couplet "Nature and Nature's laws lay hid in night: / God said, 'Let Newton be!' and all was light," added "It did not last: the Devil howling 'Ho, / Let Einstein be,' restored the status quo." J. C. Squire, *Collected Poems* (1959), 210.

aim of the natural sciences, which was to establish general laws. Other historians, meanwhile, did their utmost to assimilate their discipline to the natural sciences. In 1902 the English historian of antiquity, J. B. Bury, asserted in his inaugural lecture at Cambridge: "History is a science, no less and no more." One consequence of this confident expectation that history can aspire to definiteness was the emergence of cooperative history. General editors assigned to specialists chapters on subjects they knew intimately; the editors hoped that this piecework would add up to reliable knowledge. Lord Acton gathered the talent that would, between 1902 and 1912, publish one vast compendium, the *Cambridge Modern History,* while J. B. Bury was responsible for another, the *Cambridge Mediaeval History,* whose first volume appeared in 1911. In France, meanwhile, Ernest Lavisse, himself an expert on the age of Louis XIV, presided over a large collective history of France, which came out between 1900 and 1911. [14]

Probably the most impressive strides were made by the sociologists, though less in empirical investigations than in theoretical clarification. In 1904 Max Weber, disclaiming any desire of "forcing the wealth of historical life into formulas," insisted that the science of society could make progress only if that science commanded "clear, unambiguous conceptions." [15] Sociology is, in essence, the attempt to observe social conduct and institutions with some objectivity, to establish some comparative dimensions and dependable generalizations. It goes back to the Enlightenment, to Montesquieu (see p. 361). The name *sociology* itself was coined by Auguste Comte in the 1830s, but Comte was vague about what sociology was or could become. He proclaimed the ideal but contributed nothing to its realization. Beginning in the early 1860s, the English philosopher Herbert Spencer compiled a voluminous body of writing on all conceivable subjects, including economics and sociology, all based on the principle of evolution, the struggle for existence, and growing differentiation. But beyond lending support to the votaries of Social Darwinism and throwing out some suggestive ideas, his long-range contribution to sociology was limited. Others, more imaginative than Spencer and closer to reality, did more lasting work. One of these was Ferdinand Tönnies, whose epoch-making *Gemeinschaft und Gesellschaft,* published in 1887, contrasted the organic community (*Gemeinschaft*) of simpler societies with the materialistic collaboration of modern society (*Gesellschaft*). His findings could be, and were, used by reactionaries nostalgic for the imagined harmonies of medieval or even more primitive life. But Tönnies himself, in drawing this contrasting double portrait, was interested primarily in examining two types of social organization; his own political ideal, in fact, was a socialist order that would combine the best in both types of association.

---

[14] Cooperative histories are discussed in Oron J. Hale, *The Great Illusion, 1900-1914* (1971), 103-104.

[15] This is from a 1904 editorial in the German journal *Archiv für Sozialwissenschaft und Sozialpolitik,* which Weber had founded a year before with the economist Werner Sombart.

While sociology flourished in Germany, the French thought it flourished even more in their own country. As Emile Durkheim confidently said in 1900: "Sociology is a science essentially French."[16] Durkheim was certain that sociology must be a science or nothing. In his last major book, *The Elementary Forms of the Religious Life* (1912), he lamented that "as far as social facts are concerned, we still have the mentality of primitives," and he urged his fellow social scientists to recognize the "necessity of resorting to the laborious methods of the natural sciences." Durkheim exemplified his program in his books. His sociological examination of religion, which drew extensively from ethnographic reports on Australian aborigines to offer generalizations about the social function of religion, is a classic. So is his *Suicide,* published in 1897, which subjects suicide to quantitative study and elicits, from the figures and categories, a theory about social cohesion. It was the subtle undermining effects of disintegration (anomie) and the equally subtle sustaining effects of common beliefs that interested Durkheim most. He rejected psychological explanations with such vehemence that his stress on "social facts" seems excessive. But Durkheim saw man as a social animal above all; it is society that gives the individual his values and enables him, in every respect, to live. Critics have accused Durkheim of making society into a God. But his understanding of the sustaining function of society for the individual was profound, and he did much in his theoretical pronouncements and scientific monographs to advance the possibilities of the study of society.

While Durkheim did much, his German contemporary, Max Weber, did more. Born in 1863, he was called to the bar in 1889 and two years later became a professor of law at Berlin. Even at this early date, his interest in social questions was central and his erudition phenomenal. His early works include studies on Roman law and on rural workers in eastern Germany. But from the late 1890s to his death in 1920, his great work was in sociology. His life was punctuated by distressing bouts with mental illness; there were years when he could neither write nor read. Yet his output was large and impressive; it includes many essays on the methods of the social sciences, in which he championed the possibility of objectivity, and many articles on the sociology of law and religion. One of his most celebrated works (though now much disputed) was published in 1904–1905: *The Protestant Ethic and the Spirit of Capitalism.* Here Weber tried to account for the triumph of capitalism in the Protestant north by what he called "worldly asceticism," an attitude toward life that he thought was most pronounced among Calvinists. His masterpiece is *Economy and Society,* a brilliant and profound synthesis that seeks to explain social organization, legal structures, modes of domination, the role of religion, and the place of the city. Weber died before he finished it, but, even in its incomplete form, it is a vast and complex monument to the intellect and penetration of one man. *Economy and Society* and Weber's countless other writings are comprehensive efforts at sociological objectivity. But they are also

[16] Quoted in Hale, *Great Illusion,* 107.

deeply uneasy. They contain perceptions about rulership—the idea of "charismatic leadership"—whose pertinence increased in actuality after Weber's death, in the age of the dictators. But they reflect, also, the uneasiness of Weber's own time: the drift of the German empire, with its boastful vulgarity, and the problems of modernity in general.

Max Weber was not alone in anxiously analyzing the political life of his time. As early as 1896, the Italian political scientist Gaetano Mosca published a classic work on the relation of leaders to masses, *The Ruling Class,* in which he insisted that political power is always concentrated in the hands of an organized elite no matter what the constitution of the country may provide. Not long' after, the German sociologist Robert Michels analyzed what he regarded as the inescapable drift to oligarchy in all organizations whatever; his celebrated study *Political Parties,* published in 1911, elaborated an iron law of oligarchies: the most democratic of organizations must in the course of time become the tool of a minority of leaders. In England, meanwhile, the versatile social scientist Graham Wallas—sociologist, psychologist, political scientist—signally advanced the psychology of politics with several closely observant studies of the actualities of political conduct, notably in his *Human Nature in Politics* (1908) and in *The Great Society: A Psychological Analysis* (1914). For all these social scientists, no matter what their conclusions, the point was to get below the level of public oratory and theoretical professions to the actualities of social and psychological life. They were both diagnosticians and symptoms of the ferment that was at work in Europe long before World War I broke out—in art quite as much as in philosophy or politics.

1870-1890: MASTERS OF REALITY

The Public as the Enemy

As we have seen, early in the nineteenth century, artists of pen and brush alike had begun to develop tense relations with the public. Shelley's "unacknowledged legislators of the world" were unacknowledged, but not legislators. The artists answered contempt with contempt. They formed coteries of elect spirits, worked (as Stendhal put it) for the "happy few," and dreamed of the future. They painted a disparaging portrait of the "bourgeois philistine" to feed their resentment and sustain their pride. Bohemianism was rife, but this rejection of respectable modes of living was generally less a matter of choice than of necessity. Often the artist was compelled to do hated hackwork to survive. Often he starved: Renoir, who in the late 1860s was too poor to buy paints, had much company in his misery.

In the second half of the nineteenth century, the tension between artist and public grew. The avant-garde was born. [17] Several developments account for this birth, not all of them unfortunate. The literate public in Europe was changing its contours. For the long stretch of the past, it had remained stable and small: in England and Wales in the 1750s, about 51 percent of newly married persons could sign their names; half a century later, the figure had grown to only about 54 percent. But with the coming of industrial civilization, the ideal of universal education gained ground. In 1838 Leonard Horner, distinguished administrator and factory inspector, could write: "The day is happily gone by when it was necessary to debate the question, whether the lower orders should be educated at all." Yet progress remained slow. Although by 1850 literacy in England and Wales almost certainly exceeded 65 percent, perhaps half of the adult population of Europe was still illiterate—and this figure excludes Russia, where more than nine adults out of ten could not read. Yet progress was made, especially in the industrialized countries, where the increase in school attendance outstripped the increase in population. Between 1850 and 1900, even in Russia, the number of public libraries enjoyed a spectacular growth. Most of the recruits to literacy remained on a painfully low level, and confined what reading they did to the simplest tracts or the crudest newspapers. [18] After all, the large majority of their "betters", though literate, were, by any standards, badly educated. When the English critic Matthew Arnold divided the society of Victorian England into barbarians and philistines, he was speaking of its upper ranges. [19]

The literate barbarians, of whatever social position, represented a new element to be reckoned with, especially in politics. Instead of rioting, they voted. Gladstone, the most proper of politicians, catered to them in his famous "Midlothian Campaign." Late in 1879, disregarding the time-honored practice of addressing only the voters of one's own constituency, Gladstone took his case to the country with an exhausting and far-flung speaking tour. It was a shocking device, but as the elections of 1880 showed, effective. And it was to this new element, too, that another new social force, the mass press, addressed itself. Here, technological innovation preceded social and political innovation. *The Times* of London had pioneered with the steam press in 1814 and with typecasting machines in the 1850s, but it was not until the invention of the linotype machine in 1890, a great labor-saving device, that the modern press was put on a sound technological basis. The linotype swept the newspaper world within a decade. By 1900 the cost of newsprint had significantly declined, news agencies acted as collective eyes across the world for their subscribers at home, and photography was common. The new press required vast amounts of

---

[17] See Renato Poggioli, *The Theory of the Avant-Garde* (1968), a brilliant work. Poggioli sees the Impressionists as the first true avant-garde.

[18] See, for this paragraph, Carlo M. Cipolla, *Literacy and Development in the West* (1969).

[19] See R. K. Webb, "The Victorian Reading Public," in Boris Ford, ed., *Pelican Guide to English Literature*, vol. VI, *From Dickens to Hardy* (rev. ed., 1969), 205-226.

capital and spawned dynasties of publishers—Ullstein and Mosse in Germany, Harmsworth in England. These powerful houses poured out morning and evening newspapers, journals addressed to women and children, and picture magazines for all tastes, written in short sentences and racy paragraphs, and specializing in crime, sports, and gossip. The mass press did not invent the low tone of public taste; it merely made that tone more evident. Alfred Harmsworth's *Daily Mail,* a halfpenny paper he launched in London in 1896, reached a sale of one million copies in 1901, in the midst of the Boer War, and then stabilized at seven hundred thousand. Dailies like his did not simply report the news; they made it. While one should not overestimate the part of editors and publishers in molding policy, the American newspaper magnate William Randolph Hearst did more than his share to push the United States into war with Spain in 1898.

Depending on its political views, the avant-garde viewed this triumph of the vulgar with loathing or pity, but in any case as evidence that mass culture would not be denied. But it was the philistine—the public that bought paintings and attended the theater—who was the real enemy. With the decline of the private patron, the general public inherited his mantle as the arbiter of taste. And, as all sectors of the avant-garde agreed, the taste of the public was bad. [20] The public wanted pretty colors and happy endings, in a word, the kind of art that demanded no effort, shocked no sensibilities, raised no inconvenient questions. It was the French artistic establishment that refused the Impressionists entrance to the Salons; it was a respectable French critic, Albert Wolff, who could patronize a Renoir nude: "Try to explain to M. Renoir that the torso of a woman is not a mass of decomposing flesh, with green and purple patches like a corpse in a state of utter putrefaction." [21] Innovating playwrights had to make their way against the most fanatical opposition. What the public wanted and was willing to pay for was sentiment and adventure. In England the influential lending libraries, which both reflected and shaped public taste, stocked mainly romantic novels, often with a touch of piety. The best-selling writers of the time, Marie Corelli or Elinor Glyn, are little more than curiosities of cultural history today. Henryk Sienkiewicz's *Quo Vadis,* which bathed the Rome of antiquity in the light of romance, was an international success; first published in Polish in 1896, it was published in America in 1897 and in England in 1898 and sold vast quantities. The German self-taught writer Karl May tapped an inexhaustible vein with his primitive adventure tales; most of them had as their hero a superhumanly strong, much beloved German rover who encounters and vanquishes crafty adversaries all the way from Kurdistan to the Wild West.

A relatively new genre, the detective story, came to compete with more traditional bestsellers late in the nineteenth century. The English novelist

---

[20] Public patronage—commissions by states or municipalities or royalty—remained a significant factor, but the taste of these modern patrons seemed quite as bad as the taste of the general public. It is enough to think of the pompous and grandiloquent buildings and sculptures commissioned by Emperor William II.

[21] Quoted in Phoebe Pool, *Impressionism* (1967), 153. See p. 890.

Wilkie Collins had pioneered in the novel-length story of detection in his famous novel, *The Moonstone* (1868), and Collins' close friend, Charles Dickens, tried his hand at a novel of suspense in his *Mystery of Edwin Drood,* which he did not live to finish. One imaginary detective, Sherlock Holmes, the creation of Sir Arthur Conan Doyle, achieved international popularity before the turn of the century: *A Study in Scarlet,* Doyle's first Sherlock Holmes story, dates from 1887. While many of the distinguished detective novelists were British, the genre rapidly spread across the civilized world.

Realism in France and England: The Novel

In such an environment, there were several paths that advanced spirits might take. One was to renounce a public that mistook entertainment for art. The romantics had already proclaimed their distaste for the uncomprehending reader; at midcentury, Flaubert made his hatred for the bourgeoisie into a program. After he finished *Salammbô,* that strange tale of ancient Carthage, he hoped it would "(1) annoy the bourgeois, that is to say, everybody; (2) unnerve and shock sensitive people; (3) anger the archeologists; (4) be unintelligible to the ladies; (5) earn me a reputation as a pederast and a cannibal." [22] This would actually be the way of the aesthetes in the 1890s (see p. 893). But the generation of the 1870s and 1880s chose, not to deny reality, but to master it.

The chief propagandist and practitioner of the realistic novel in France was Emile Zola, but the great originator was Gustave Flaubert, whose masterpiece, *Madame Bovary,* appeared in 1857. With his cool intelligence and his absolute devotion to literature, Flaubert understood the problem of the realist with perfect clarity. It is worth noting that Flaubert disliked the name "realist" for himself. [23] He could say, "There is nothing of me in Madame Bovary," and, at the same time, "I am Madame Bovary." [24] As a realist he aimed at achieving absolute fidelity in rendering speech, dress, furniture, the countryside. At the same time, as a supremely self-conscious craftsman, he knew how hard it was to fix life upon the page. He knew, therefore, that his novel was, not reportage, but a work of art. The mastery lay in conveying the impression of life artistically. With infinite patience, revising meticulously, obsessively, Flaubert composed his tale of a small-town girl who marries a devoted, prosaic husband and is led, through her luxuriant romantic imagination, to dismal love affairs and dreary suicide. *Madame Bovary* caused a scandal: Flaubert was tried for

[22] Quoted in Philip Spencer, *Flaubert, A Biography* (1952), 160.

[23] The names that cultural historians assign to this period are admittedly tentative and often confused. In general they have called the years 1848 to 1870 an age of realism; the two decades between 1870 and 1890 an age of naturalism; and the quarter century from 1890 to the outbreak of the war in 1914, an age of Symbolism. These labels are at best moderate approximations. Movements vigorously opposed to these flourished in each period, and contemporaries often did not know if they should call themselves naturalists or realists.

[24] See Cecil Jenkins, "Realism and Reality in the Novel," in John Cruickshank, ed., *French Literature and Its Background,* vol. V, *The Late Nineteenth Century* (1969), 43.

offenses against public morals and religion. But, more important, he had invented the realistic novel. He never again achieved the same notoriety or the same success. Of his later work, the best, and the best known, is *Sentimental Education* (1869), a heavily autobiographical novel about the fortunes of a young man around the revolutionary period of 1848. When he died in 1880, he left many admirers, including Zola.

By then, the emphasis had shifted. The naturalists who came after Flaubert wanted to enlarge the canvas and enhance the lifelikeness of fiction. But they proposed a new method. As Edmond and Jules de Goncourt had put it in 1864, in the preface to their frankly experimental novel, *Germinie Lacerteux:* "Today, when the novel has assumed the methods and the duties of science, it is entitled to claim the liberties and frankness of science." [25] To that end, they adapted the pathetic life history of one of their servants and told the story of a young girl from the provinces who goes to Paris into domestic service, is seduced, takes to drink, and eventually becomes a prostitute. Emile Zola, for a time the Goncourts' disciple, pushed their program to its logical conclusion. In an avalanche of novels and critical writing probably unsurpassed in their quantity, though uneven in their quality, he tried to overcome the remote dreams of the romantics and the stylized snobbery of the neoclassicists—in a word, to make the novel into a science. He failed. Zola's work is the outpouring of a titanic energy, and it betrays the inner pressure of urgent passions inadequately disciplined by the demands his realistic doctrine imposed. Like Flaubert, Zola was not the cold anatomist he professed to be, but a poet.

As a young writer, in fact, Zola was an unashamed dreamer and undisguised moralist. Born in 1840, the son of a military engineer, he began his literary career with fairy tales and allegories. In the 1860s, in Paris, he experienced extreme poverty but also enjoyed a widespread acquaintance among painters and literati and engaged in fertile experimentation. By the end of the decade he had conceived a sweeping plan: to write a vast chronicle about a single French family. He carried out his design: between 1871 and 1893 he published twenty volumes, *Les Rougon-Macquart,* an encyclopedic saga significantly subtitled *Natural and Social History of a Family under the Second Empire.* The family and its activities are so far-flung that Zola's scheme in no way constricted his range; the best-known novels in the series—*Germinal* (1885) and *L'Assommoir* (1887)—deal, respectively, with the working class in a mining town and in Paris. In other novels, he wrote about peasants or the war of 1870-1871; his most notorious novel, *Nana* (1880), takes a working-class prostitute through a tour of the bedrooms of high society.

Many of Zola's critics have complained that he did better with the lower orders and the lower passions than with their more refined counterparts. This is true enough. He did not know the French aristocracy well enough to portray

[25] For long excerpts from this preface, see Roland N. Stromberg, ed., *Realism, Naturalism, and Symbolism: Modes of Thought and Expression in Europe, 1848-1914* (1968), 68-70.

it convincingly. As for his supposed infatuation with filth, he could reply, simply enough, that he was showing a side of life others had been too timid to confront. But what mattered most to Zola was that the novel must be a scientific work; it must disclose the workings of physiological and biological principles inherent in mankind. Jules Lemaître, reviewing *Germinal,* called it "a pessimistic epic of human animality." [26] Both halves of the remark are true. Zola was interested in animality, but he was also writing an epic. His famous set pieces (the wedding scene in *L'Assommoir* and the strike in *Germinal*) remain memorable, and so does his grand design.

Zola had his disciples in England, notably George Moore and George Gissing, whose novels were deliberate affronts to Victorian respectability and unvarnished portraits of the seamy side of life. But, in general, English fiction drew on domestic models. A great generation was leaving the stage. Dickens, the most popular of them, died in 1870. His exuberant inventiveness, his outsize characters, were much missed. William Makepeace Thackeray, the witty critic of manners, had died seven years before, in 1863. Anthony Trollope, who had achieved fame and matching fortune with his gentle novels about the rural south of England—the Barchester series—was still writing vigorously, and would write to his end in 1882. His palette darkened in his later years. He never became a pessimist, but the series of political novels he began in the late 1860s suggest a temperamentally cheerful writer honestly wrestling with a world somehow out of joint. *The Way We Live Now,* published in 1875, is a troubled and troubling novel: it recounts the invasion of Parliament by a sinister financier, Melmotte, and the spreading wake of corruption. It is a revealing book, precisely for emerging from such a sunny author: Melmotte, the villain, is a foreigner, married to a "foreign Jewess," and his natural element is the city of London. Trollope was not alone in fearing the modern metropolis as the vicious, alien destroyer of stable, traditional values.

But it will not do to make Trollope into a novelist of ideas; he was primarily a storyteller. England in general was rich in his kind. One of them, Thomas Hardy, as much poet as he was novelist, has gained something of a name as a thinker. But what he called Thomas Carlyle—"a poet with the reputation of a philosopher"—applies to him as well. His somber rural tragedies were meant to illustrate Hardy's notions about fate, but the best of them, like *Far from the Madding Crowd* (1874), which made him famous, or *The Mayor of Casterbridge* (1886), are poignant romances. As the English critic Edmund Gosse rightly asked in his review of Hardy's *Jude the Obscure* (1896): "What has Providence done to Mr. Hardy that he should rise up in the arable land of Wessex and shake his fist at his Creator?" [27] George Meredith made similar claims: a brilliant writer much given to complexity of syntax, he liked to think of himself as an

---

[26] See F. W. J. Hemmings, *Emile Zola* (2nd ed., 1966), 211.
[27] Quoted in G. D. Klingopulos, "Hardy's Tales, Ancient and Modern," in Boris Ford, ed., *The Pelican Guide to English Literature,* vol. VI, *From Dickens to Hardy* (rev. ed., 1969), 418.

intellectual and a radical. When he died in 1909, Arnold Bennett significantly hailed him as "the first of the modern school" for his professionalism and, above all, his honesty. [28] But his novels (notably *The Egoist* [1879], which takes for its theme the development of a self-centered young man), though comparatively fearless and amply witty, are best read for the stories they tell, not for their pretensions to instruct.

To place such novelists correctly, we need to read two others then active in England—George Eliot and Henry James. Both were outsiders: the first a woman using a masculine pseudonym, the second an American self-exiled in England. What sets them apart from their most accomplished competitors is their fine intelligence and their deep perception. Henry James called George Eliot "genuinely philosophic." The same compliment—for it *was* a compliment—can be returned to its author. These two were masters of deeper realities; they made the novel into a splendid instrument that subtly and courageously observed the most intricate human relationships.

George Eliot was born Mary Ann Evans, in 1819. From her early youth, she showed her sturdy and independent intellect. She lost her religious faith, moved from the Midlands—the scene of nearly all her novels—to London, and formed an illicit though permanent association with George Henry Lewes, author of the fine *Life and Works of Goethe* (1855). She was an editor and a translator; in the late 1850s, with *Scenes of Clerical Life,* she began to write novels. Several of them, *Adam Bede, The Mill on the Floss,* and *Silas Marner,* published in successive years between 1859 and 1861, became and remain the kind of novel children are still assigned in school and usually enjoy. But it is *Middlemarch,* published serially in 1871 and 1872, on which her claim to greatness rests. Its subtitle, *A Study of Provincial Life,* understates its profundity. A set of complex characters, rendered with lucid objectivity, encounter one another in a Midlands town and act out their fates, each according to his, and her, flawed character. And behind and above the characters stands the author, commenting, explaining.

Henry James, a consummate master of the art of fiction, proceeded differently. His motto was "dramatize, dramatize," and though his readers often sense the presence of the author, his characters do most of the work, enacting the story in their thoughts and their conversation. Subtle as he was, in the 1870s and 1880s his stories and novels were lucid, direct, even melodramatic, though they are always informed by James' superb intelligence. In one of his masterpieces, *The Portrait of a Lady* (1881), the heroine, Isabel Archer, discovers that her husband has a mistress by happening upon the two at conversation, with the man sitting and the woman standing. Her moment of insight, flashing upon her as she notices this breach of conventional manners, is one of the great moments in modern fiction.

The Portrait of a Lady reveals one of Henry James' central preoccupations: Isabel Archer is an American who has moved to Europe, a New World innocent

[28] Arnold Bennett, "Meredith," *New Age,* May 27, 1909, in *Books and Persons* (1917), 134.

confronting the experience (which often means the corruption) of the Old. James himself had made the pilgrimage to Europe. Born into a formidable New York family in 1843, Henry James traveled widely as a young man and felt Europe's irresistible attraction, with its rich culture, its living traditions, its literary circles. [29] In 1875, the year that he published his first novel, *Roderick Hudson,* he met Flaubert and other writers in Paris. In the following year he moved to London and, after some anguished thought, decided to settle there. He wrote, extensively and intensively, on a handful of chosen themes— cerebral ghost stories, searching tales of writers and artists, troubled novels about Americans in Europe, like his charming, small-scaled tragedy, *Daisy Miller* (1878). And he wrote superb literary criticism, marked by omnivorous reading, cultivated sensibility, and extraordinary penetration. His fiction and his criticism were intimately and deliberately linked; they served each other. No one was ever more a *writer* than Henry James. [30]

Giants from the East: Turgenev, Dostoevsky, Tolstoy

Among the men of letters Henry James met in Paris in 1875 was the Russian novelist Ivan Turgenev. The two had much in common; Turgenev, wrote James not long after, had "a poet's quarrel" with his native country—a quarrel that James found it all too easy to recognize. Turgenev, in fact, was the first of the great Russian novelists to find an appreciative public in western Europe, and for an ironic reason: he was more accessible than Dostoevsky or Tolstoy because he was less Russian than they. His themes were Russian without exception; like Henry James he found that his poet's quarrel did not prevent him from writing of his country with affection. But both physically and spiritually, Turgenev was close to the West, a quality that roused Dostoevsky to indignant fury and Tolstoy to ironic disdain. Born in 1818 into the provincial gentry, he moved about restlessly, studied in Russia and Germany, and traveled with friends. Most important, he spent long stretches of time among the literati in Paris. He also wrote like them; with all his longing for some vanished Russia, he emerges as a detached observer. He was a civilized reporter who cared, above all, for purity of expression. Like Flaubert and James, he was deeply conscious of his vocation as a writer. His elegant tales and novels deal, for the most part, with the unhappy love affairs of weak young men with strong young women, a subject that he found psychologically congenial. As more than one critic has noted, it also echoes a theme that the great Russian poet Pushkin had explored in his *Eugene Onegin.* But Turgenev's most enduring novel, *Fathers and Sons* (1862) draws on neither psychological predispositions nor literary tradition. A

---

[29] His father, Henry James, Sr., was a philosopher and religious thinker; his elder brother was William James. Of the brothers it was said: "William James is a psychologist writing like a novelist, Henry James is a novelist writing like a psychologist."

[30] For his last novels, see p. 898.

novel about contemporary Russia, it dissects the failure of ideas or, rather, of the man with one idea. The young physician Bazarov, the "hero," claims that he believes in nothing: he is a "nihilist." This was a term then current in Russia to describe radicals who professed materialism; Turgenev made it familiar across Europe. Bazarov fails, doubly so. He persuades practically no one and dies by accidentally contracting typhus in a dissection. But he fails also in a more heroic way: in his passionate humanity, he is a living refutation of the system he professes.

If Turgenev was out of his place, a French rationalist writing in Russian, Dostoevsky was out of his time. His strange novels were little read in the West until the twentieth century: when Dostoevsky died in 1881, only Russians knew him. Fyodor Dostoevsky was born in 1821 in Moscow. His father was a tyrant, his adored mother died when he was sixteen. His life was a string of failures. Love, marriage, finances, health, literary associations, all went wrong. To his psychological traumas was added, in 1849, a trauma that confirmed and exacerbated all the others. Dostoevsky belonged to a study circle that read the French socialists together; in 1849, in the wake of the panic aroused by the revolutions of 1848, the circle was closed down and its members were deported. In December 1849, after the sentence of death had been read and the victims waited to fall before the volley of gunfire, the government revealed that it had all been a ghastly joke; the actual sentence was prison. Four years of dreadful existence in Siberia followed. In 1854 Dostoevsky was released, and five years later he was permitted to return to Moscow.

His two early works, *Poor Folk* and *The Double,* both published in 1846, reveal that Dostoevsky's preoccupation with morbid themes predate that moment of imminent death. Dostoevsky was born to be the poet of suffering; what Siberia showed him was that others suffered as he did and that what is now called extreme behavior is actually quite common—in extreme circumstances. Dostoevsky's writings of the early 1860s, like those of the late 1840s, were prophetic of the quartet of immortal novels to come. In 1866 he published the first of these, *Crime and Punishment.* It was followed by *The Idiot* in 1868–1869, *The Devils* in 1871, and *The Brothers Karamazov,* widely admired as his finest achievement, in 1880. All of them dwell on the extreme behavior he had witnessed in exile and the extreme emotions he sensed in himself. They are filled with banal encounters turned menacing by sudden irrational outbursts, with moments of towering rage, with pitilessly observed instances of sadism and masochism, with passionate political and religious ravings, and with madness, murder, and suicide. These horror-laden tales seem to imprison the reader in a madhouse that the skillful author is building around him. They are hard to put down and impossible to forget. Dostoevsky was a cunning storyteller who knew how to construct scenes and to withhold information; an unmatched psychologist who commanded attention by uncovering men's deepest recesses; and, surprisingly enough, a gifted comic writer. It is only in recent decades that his terrifying fantasies have appeared to be what they were meant to be: prophetic portraits of reality.

The meaning of Dostoevsky goes beyond a novelist's talents, rare and essential as these are. There was something he urgently wished to say. His experiences, far from keeping alive any interest in political radicalism, turned him into a nationalist and a devout Christian who hated the corrosive forces—secularism, rationalism—invading Russia from the West. *The Devils,* his most savage novel, depicts the havoc wrought in a small provincial town by a few ruthless Nihilists who murder a member of their circle to tie the rest of their group together forever, but who end with arson, arrest, and suicide. The book is a harrowing portrait of fanaticism, of demonic individuals without God. It is hard to know whom Dostoevsky hated more: the radicals or the liberals who sympathized with them. *The Devils* assails both: it contains a merciless caricature of Turgenev in the shape of an affected, pretentious, ineffectual liberal poet. But Dostoevsky wanted to speak not only of crime but of redemption, not only of rebellion but of love. *The Brothers Karamazov,* which can be read as a detective story—Who killed Fyodor Karamazov?—is at bottom a religious drama that portrays the triumph of Christian innocence over clever atheism.

Compared to Dostoevsky's tempestuous genius, Tolstoy's, though vehement enough, is positively calm. His long life—born in 1828, he died in 1910—abruptly changed direction in mid career. Prey to a devastating spiritual crisis, he repudiated his writings to become an eloquent apostle of a highly personal version of Christianity. Although in his last decades he saw himself the center of a cult and the object of pilgrimages, his fame rests on his earlier work, on his long stories, and on his two masterpieces, *War and Peace* and *Anna Karenina.* These novels mark the culmination of realism. Tolstoy's crisis of the late 1870s centered around a consuming fear of death, but his novels are a celebration of life, performed with deep love and generous pity.

Offspring of a rich provincial noble family, Count Leo Nikolayevich Tolstoy had an unexceptional youth. He attended the University of Kazan, but did not study; he lived in society and led the expected life of dissipation. But it did not satisfy him, and his dissatisfaction opened the road to literary mastery. In 1847, when he was nineteen, he began to keep a diary into which he poured his plans for self-improvement and, eventually, for stories. In 1852 he published his first short novel, *Childhood,* to be followed by *Boyhood* in 1854 and *Youth* in 1857. All were largely autobiographical, but what matters most is their respect for the facts, sensitively observed and candidly reported. His experience in the Crimean War gave him further material for reflection and stories. "If you come to Sevastopol," he wrote, "with lofty notions about superhuman bravery, you will be disappointed, for all you will see is ordinary people occupied with ordinary tasks, without restlessness, haste, enthusiasm, or stoic readiness to die." [31] This vision would govern his two long novels as well.

[31] Quoted in Helen Muchnic, *An Introduction to Russian Literature* (rev. ed., 1964), 158.

Tolstoy began to write *War and Peace* in 1863; it was published serially between 1867 and 1869. Like all his writings, it underwent extensive and repeated revisions: Tolstoy's hymns to life did not reach the public as spontaneous outpourings. The canvas of *War and Peace* is vast; its form, sprawling—Tolstoy, in fact, refused to call it a novel.[32] Certainly, to call it a historical novel is to denigrate it; while its dramatic date is Russia at the time of the Napoleonic invasion, its real theme is far larger. Its true protagonists are not Napoleon (though he appears) or Russian high society (though it is brilliantly rendered) but the clash of Russia with the West, which is the clash between two ways of life and, more intimately, the fates of Pierre and Natasha and, through them, the triumph of life.

Whatever *War and Peace* may be—and a work of such dimensions creates its own form—*Anna Karenina* is unmistakably a novel. It appeared, after many revisions, in 1877, and the final version contrasts the central action—the infidelity of Anna, her life with her lover, and her suicide—with another action, quite as important—the love of Levin for Kitty and their eventual happy marriage. Here life and death confront one another directly. Anna violates all the canons of her social code, yet we can understand her. It is not a question of taking sides; her husband, Karenin, is tight-lipped and rigid, yet the reader is not invited to exculpate Anna's escapades at his expense. He, too, is a suffering human being. Yet though Anna's end is terrible—she throws herself under a train—suffering is not the only note Tolstoy strikes. In one memorable scene Levin spends the day mowing with the peasants, and in describing his sweat, his utter fatigue, his exultation at the rhythm of the scythe and the work of his muscles, Tolstoy once again pays his tribute to the kind of reality that romantics, neoclassicists, or historical novelists had entirely forgotten.

The Conquest of Light: The Impressionists

While novelists and playwrights[33] probed their way to deeper and finer perceptions of reality, a rebellious group of painters, the Impressionists, attempted the same probe on canvas. Emile Zola, who knew them well and supported them vigorously, made an explicit connection between his own realism and theirs in his enthusiastic review of their work. "Why the devil," he wrote of the Impressionists in 1866, "do you have the arrant clumsiness to paint solidly and to study nature frankly? An austere and serious kind of painting, an extreme concern for truth and accuracy. . . . You are a great blunderer, Sir, you are an artist that I like."[34] The Impressionists had their ancestors. They admired the English landscape painter John Constable who, in the 1820s, made

---

[32] See John Bayley, *Tolstoy and the Novel* (1966).
[33] For the most controversial of the playwrights working in this period, Ibsen, see 896.
[34] Quoted in Pool, *Impressionism*, 45.

meticulous studies of clouds in sunlight; the French realist Gustave Courbet who, in the 1850s, vigorously painted mundane subjects with fidelity and respect; and the Dutch watercolorist Johann Barthold Jongkind, who, in the early 1860s, painted seascapes with the light playing over boats and sand. The outlines of the name *Impressionism* are as blurred as the outlines of the Impressionists' figures on canvas. Was Edouard Manet a member of the group or a forerunner? In 1880 Zola called him a "revolutionary in form" but reserved the party name "Impressionist" for Claude Monet, Auguste Renoir, Camille Pissarro, Armand Guillaumin, "and others." Manet's historic role is clear: in 1863 he painted two scandalous canvases, *Olympia,* a reclining nude indoors, and *Déjeuner sur l'herbe,* a sitting nude outdoors, in the company of two fully clothed gentlemen. His bold handling of light and his equally bold use of the nude—a traditional subject that he treated in a new way—were inspirations for the young rebels. The storm of indignation he aroused, especially with the *Olympia* at the Salon of 1865, was only an added reason for applauding him.

In fact, 1863 is a crucial date for the history of modern art. In that year a group of young painters, refused entry to the annual official Salon, set up their own exhibition, the so-called *Salon des Refusés*. It included canvases by the young Paul Cézanne, by Manet (who showed his *Déjeuner sur l'herbe*), Pissarro, and Jongkind. Within a decade, the badge of rejection had become a badge of pride: in 1874, still offensive to the artistic establishment, the Impressionists held their first collective exhibition. One of the paintings there, Monet's luminous blue and red composition called *Impression, Sunrise,* firmly established the name of the group in the mind of the public.

The Impressionist exhibition of 1874 was a triumph only in retrospect; it was a complete failure with contemporary critics, who ridiculed the Impressionists' color, their draftsmanship, and their choice of subjects. But the paintings shown there are now display pieces in the history of art: Renoir's *La Loge,* Cézanne's *Maison du Pendu,* Monet's *Boulevard des Capucins.* Pissarro exhibited five canvases, and Edgar Degas, a frequent though somewhat inconstant ally, ten. For a decade or so, the Impressionists went from strength to strength, profiting by association and developing their individuality. Monet painted his rapidly sketched figures and boats and buildings, catching at the elusive light as it passed across surfaces. Renoir painted his ample nudes or his clothed promenaders, rendering the sun shining through the leaves, dappling their long dresses and their charming faces. Gradually, the techniques of Impressionism gained followers in other countries.

Pissarro apart, the Impressionists were painters without being intellectuals. Renoir vehemently objected to all aesthetic talk: "You construct a theory," he said, "and nature knocks it down."[35] But their principles need little elucidation—their canvases speak for them. The Impressionists were devoted to the science of light. They studied a treatise on colors by the chemist Eugène

[35] Quoted in ibid., 52.

Chevreul and experimented with the visual effects produced by the juxtaposi-
tion of complementary colors. Their object was to make the visual experience
immediate and intense; hence they used primary colors, rendered shadows a
luminous blue, and laid dabs of color next to one another on the canvas. The
Impressionists aimed at naturalness, lifelikeness. They painted out of doors—
their landscapes are not formal compositions patiently put together in the
studio, but direct impressions of what it is like to *see* the outside world. It is not
an accident that landscapes and cityscapes make up a good portion of the
Impressionists' output; even many of Renoir's nudes rest on grassy banks or
splash one another in idyllic ponds. The bustling activity of strollers, the quick
change of light and shade as clouds pass over the sun, the fluttering of flags—
this was the kind of reality the Impressionists sought to capture. This, too, is
why their pictures seem, as it were, so intent on defying composition or
prettiness. Pissarro more than his associates "posed" his haystacks or his
country lanes in accord with traditional principles. The others placed their
figures in informal, often awkward, positions and framed them with such
violent arbitrariness that houses or figures are often partially cut off by the edge
of the canvas.

Impressionism changed painting forever. But in the mid-1880s, as the
masters continued to mine their talents in rewarding but unsurprising ways, a
younger group, the Neo-Impressionists, took the science of light to its logical
conclusion. Before his early death in 1891, the extremely influential Georges
Seurat painted a small number of important canvases on which he laid on color
in small discrete dots of paint. Seurat gave up the hallmarks of the Impressionists—rapidity of work and nervousness of perception—in favor of meticulous-
ness of execution and a general impression of immobility. In Seurat's most
celebrated painting, *Un Dimanche à la Grande Jatte,* the figures stand, sit, and
promenade in well-defined patches of light and shade. But as Nikolaus Pevsner
rightly says, the scene, brilliantly atmospheric, seems like an assemblage of
"wooden toys." [36] This was one direction in which the Impressionists could
move—into perfect, permanent stillness. But other ways were open as well. The
greatest, most inventive painter of the age, Paul Cézanne, whose luminous
landscapes mark his intimacy with the Impressionists, moved, with his
experiments in composition and distortion, toward the art of the twentieth
century. The passion for the outdoors and the vibrating colors of Paul Gauguin
and Vincent van Gogh place both among the Neo-Impressionists, but both,
with their deeply private, almost religious view of art, figure, like Cézanne, as
moderns (see p. 900). Much of the work of these three was done before 1890—
the year that van Gogh committed suicide—but their impact places them in the
outbreak of modernity that occurred after 1890.

---

[36] Nikolaus Pevsner, "Art and Architecture," in F. H. Hinsley, *New Cambridge Modern
History,* vol. XI, *Material Progress and World-Wide Problems, 1870–1898* (1962), 166.

1890–1914: THE EXPLOSION OF MODERNITY
·•◦──◦•·

Aestheticism and Symbolism

The debate with "mass culture" that the romantics had begun and self-styled outcasts like Flaubert had continued was elevated, in the 1890s, into an aesthetic system in England. As early as 1873, Walter Pater, essayist and Oxford don, had electrified his public with the "Conclusion" to his *Studies in the History of the Renaissance*. All men, he wrote, are under suspended sentence of death, and so they must live, passionately, for the moment. "To burn always with this hard, gemlike flame, to maintain this ecstasy, is success in life." For Pater, this meant the fastidious "love of art for art's sake." For his followers, the "decadents" of the 1890s, it meant sensual self-indulgence and the most decisive separation of art from life.

The most complete representative of this aesthetes' rebellion was Oscar Wilde. He was also its most pathetic and most spectacular failure. Born in 1854 in Dublin, he absorbed Pater's doctrine at Oxford. Then he went on to conquer society and shone as an incomparable conversationalist. He defended his aesthetic doctrine in well-informed and eminently intelligent literary criticism; "it is to criticism," he wrote, "that the future belongs." And he embodied it in his stories and his witty paradoxical plays. "All art," he held, "is immoral," that is, remote from utility and from the humdrum reality it disdained. This is what he meant with his famous aphorism, "The first duty in life is to be as artificial as possible. What the second duty is no one has as yet discovered." Wilde had his coterie, and aestheticism its brief fling. But its journals, the short-lived *Yellow Book* and *The Savoy,* testify how specialized and constricted the movement was. Apart from *The Importance of Being Earnest* (1895) and a few other plays, its only enduring memento is a handful of Aubrey Beardsley's ominous drawings, with their monstrous, swollen, predatory females. Then, in 1895, philistine England, always in a majority even among poets and painters, struck back and crushed the aesthetic movement by crushing Oscar Wilde. After three sensational trials, he was convicted of homosexuality and imprisoned for two years. He emerged with his health broken, his reputation destroyed, and his taste unchanged: "A patriot put in prison for loving his country, loves his country," he wrote to a friend with his characteristic clarity, "and a poet in prison for loving boys, loves boys."

Wilde died in Paris in 1900. Though noisy in England, the aesthetic movement was not at home there. The English, Henry James noted in 1904, saw the principle of "beauty at any price" as a "queer high-flavoured fruit from overseas, grown under another sun than ours." James said this in an essay on the Italian novelist Gabriele d'Annunzio, whose lush novels about love and death were beginning to make something of a stir at the time. But the fathers and high priests of aestheticism were French—the Symbolist poets. [37]

The father of Symbolism, though not a full-fledged Symbolist himself, was the great French poet Charles Baudelaire. A tormented explorer of his inner states—his *spleen*—a self-conscious dandy, an evoker of perverted lust and horrid decay, yet in his own way a religious seeker, Baudelaire was an accomplished poetic craftsman and, like Flaubert, a superb hater of the bourgeoisie. He had died in 1867 and had been almost forgotten. Then, in 1884, J. K. Huysmans celebrated him in his hymn to artificiality, *A Rebours,* a splendidly absurd short novel about an aesthete who hermetically seals himself off from the world to devote himself entirely to the cultivation of his senses. In 1885 the poet Jean Moréas publicly used the name "Symbolists" and defended them against the charge of decadence, and in the following year Moréas published a manifesto in which he hailed the leaders of the Symbolist movement: Charles Baudelaire, Paul Verlaine, and Stéphane Mallarmé. One other name at least belongs on this list, that of Arthur Rimbaud, a precocious genius who briefly enjoyed—if that is the word—a tempestuous love affair with Verlaine. The lives of Rimbaud and Verlaine, complete with pistol shot, aimless vagabondage, extreme despair, and religious conversion were in themselves symbolic of the rebelliousness, the alienation, the utter unrespectability that seemed congenial to the Modern Movement. Mallarmé, it must be added, led a humdrum life; his adventures were in the mind. A teacher of English in several provincial schools, he finally came to Paris and there, beginning in 1880, he presided over his weekly literary afternoons. His output was slender; but his example, his conversation, and his essays were enormously influential. It was in the end not the temperamental outcasts but the methodical teacher who would settle the principles and lead the movement.

Symbolism was the determined effort to liberate poetry from prose and to raise poetic diction to the highest power language can attain. Poetry must cease to moralize, to tell stories, to argue or explain. Sound matters more than sense; vagueness is infinitely preferable to clarity. Walter Pater's much-quoted remark, "All art constantly aspires to the condition of music," was in essence the Symbolist position, for music was wholly pure, wholly free from the taint of meaning that adheres to words. Of all the arts, music alone guards its mysteries. It is significant that the Symbolists thought and wrote much about music. In aspiring to the condition of music, poetry would, they thought, join different arts and stimulate several senses at once. This is why the Symbolists from Baudelaire to Mallarmé worshiped Wagner: the marriage of words and

---

[37] It is interesting in this connection to note that Arthur Symons' *The Symbolist Movement in Literature* (1899) had first been called *The Decadent Movement in Literature.* With this book, Symons, editor of the *The Savoy,* introduced both Yeats and Eliot to the French Symbolists—hardly a mean achievement.

music, theme and meaning, in Wagner's operas and his ambition to create the total work of art, the Gesamtkunstwerk, struck them as nothing less than inspired. In their poetry, they attempted to make music with words. They planted, in Baudelaire's words, "forests of symbols"; they sought (as Rimbaud did) to capture pure states of consciousness to be put upon the page or (as Mallarmé did) to convey the most intense fantasies, whether aesthetic or erotic, by means of surprising verbal conjunctions, typographical experiments, and esoteric words. One may say without sarcasm that the Symbolists largely achieved their aim, even if they thought they were falling short. They rescued poetry to do its own work, "recalling," as Yeats hoped the new drama would do, "words to their ancient sovereignty." And, with their deliberate obscurity, they kept at arm's length a public unprepared to accompany them on their difficult journey.

Mallarmé died in 1898, but Symbolism did not die with him. It retained some influence at home and spread abroad to Russia and to the English-speaking world. In Ireland, Yeats felt its power. It won a foothold in Germany through Stefan George, the declared disciple of Baudelaire and Mallarmé. George was an oddity; he was endowed with great lyric gifts, a splendid profile, a vast ego, and absolutely no humor. The worshipful circle he formed around himself was as odd as he: the disciples ministered to the needs of the Master, worked themselves up into believing that they could rescue materialist modern Germany from itself, and displayed their devotion to high culture—a kind of modern Hellenism—by translating Dante, reviving the difficult poetry of Hölderlin, publishing earnest literary criticism, and staging arcane festivals in which they celebrated a beautiful young man. Some of this—the typographical affectations in their publications, the deification of George himself—appears ridiculous. Some of it—the circle's poetic preachment of the new Reich to come and the overblown biographies of heroes elevated into figures of myth—appears politically dangerous. But the circle had a positive role to play. It blew a fresh wind of literary passion into the stuffiness of the German academy; it revived poets worth reviving; and it produced some splendid lyrical poetry, notably by the Master himself. George's first book of verses, Hymnen, appeared in 1890, and he published collections at frequent intervals thereafter, distinguished by purity of diction and spiritual self-revelation. What is of particular interest about the George Circle is its peculiar mixture of isolation and involvement. George was head of a "Secret Germany," pitting cultural values against modern philistinism. His group was small, private, self-selected—an elite of elites. But as its message reached larger circles, its doctrines received some rather sinister interpretations. Almost against his will, George proved that poetry can have power. It was not quite the power he wanted. When he died in December 1933, he was, significantly enough, in Switzerland, in voluntary exile, as if to protest against the Nazis, who had come into office in January, as a ghastly caricature of his aristocratic ideals. [38]

[38] In his fate, George is like Nietzsche, whom he much admired.

Thomas Mann made this tension between art and culture into a leading theme of his fiction. Born in 1875 at Lübeck into the commercial patriciate, Mann early underwent the influence of Schopenhauer's pessimism and Nietzsche's bracing critique of modern culture; he took to writing short stories and then, in 1901, he published a large novel, *Buddenbrooks,* which made him famous. From the outset, his hallmark was irony; the author views and comments on his creations with a certain amused pity. And from the outset Mann was obsessed with the clash between art and life. *Buddenbrooks* chronicles the decay of a wealthy commercial family through several generations, but the decay plays itself out in the irreconcilable conflict between high culture and bourgeois sobriety. Art—often represented symbolically in Mann's fiction by a gift for music or by Latin origins—is ennobling but sick; commerce is dull but healthy. In Mann's *Tonio Kröger,* published in 1903, the writer-hero embodies this conflict in his person. He springs from a sober, northern, commercial family, but his mother is from "down there"—hence his "odd" first name. Literature is his vocation, but suffering and solitude are its price: art and alienation, Mann suggested, are twins. (For Mann's later career, see p. 1018.)

Criticism and Commitment

Escape into preciosity and obscurity was one way of dealing with the hated modern world. To turn and face it critically, and perhaps improve it, was another. Not all writers made a clear-cut choice: Anton Chekhov, the great Russian playwright and short-story writer, was a perfect realist, concerned less with reforming the world than with portraying it. The unpretentiousness of his poignant stories and the informality of his dialogue only conceal his mastery; the clarity of his vision has induced critics to debate endlessly what his plays in fact are. Whatever his intentions, his best four plays, notably his last, *The Cherry Orchard* (1904), remain in the standard repertory of the modern theater.[39]

Other playwrights used the stage as a platform, though the most influential of these, Henrik Ibsen, did more. Born in 1828, he tried his hand at a variety of genres before he found his voice with *Brand* (1866), the stark history of an unbending young clergyman—we would call him a fanatic—who sacrifices his mother, his wife, his child, and ultimately himself to his exacting faith. Other plays, equally stark, followed and made Ibsen a force in the naturalistic theater. In *A Doll's House* (1879), a young wife discovers, in a series of agonizing scenes, that her marriage, which she had thought happy, rests on

---

[39] "It is scarcely possible to decide . . . whether *The Cherry Orchard* is intended as a comedy or a tragedy, and similar doubts exist over the other plays: *The Seagull* (1896), *Uncle Vanya* (1899), and *The Three Sisters* (1901)." A. K. Thorlby, "Literature," *New Cambridge Modern History,* vol. IX, 149. It is fair to add that Chekhov himself insisted on calling *The Cherry Orchard* a comedy.

comfortable lies; she leaves her family to seek the answers to questions she has learned to ask. The heroine of *Ghosts* (1881) is an aging widow haunted by memories of a bad marriage that she had saved in a sacrifice to public opinion; the action begins as her son, back from abroad, reveals that he is tainted with hereditary venereal disease. His mother, honest at last, tries to give her dying son what he wants—including the maid, even though that maid is his half sister, and, in the end, the death he seeks by agreeing to feed him poison.

In these dramas and their successors—notably *The Wild Duck* (1884), *Rosmersholm* (1886), and *Hedda Gabler* (1890)—Ibsen explored the burdens of the past and the catastrophic consequences of pride, dishonesty, and the selfish probing for truth. He was a reformer, and he identified himself with Dr. Stockmann, the outspoken hero of his play, *An Enemy of the People* (1882), who holds that "the minority is always right." This, Ibsen wrote, meant not the minority of conservatives, but of those who ally themselves "most closely with the future." When *Ghosts* was published and performed, it aroused storms of protest for its "filth" and "immorality." Ibsen replied that it did not preach nihilism: "It preaches nothing at all." This, with all of Ibsen's candor and radicalism, was his own view of his work. "My task," he said late in life, "has been the description of humanity." He was writing, not propaganda, but tragedies.

Whatever Ibsen's ultimate intentions, the public took the social criticism in his plays as central. George Bernard Shaw, who in 1891 defended Ibsen against his slanderers in a lively pamphlet, *The Quintessence of Ibsenism,* interpreted Ibsen as the nemesis of cant, sham, and deadly idealism. Shaw himself was perfectly unambiguous about *his* plays: they were dramas of ideas. "My conscience," wrote Shaw, "is the genuine pulpit article: it annoys me to see people comfortable when they ought to be uncomfortable." [40] Significantly, like his fellow Fabian and fellow reformer H. G. Wells, Shaw gloried in the name of journalist.

Shaw's plays are remarkably original in form and argument alike. Born in 1856 in Dublin, Shaw came to London as a young man and started his literary career as a prolific but unsuccessful novelist; he did better as a music critic. His first play, *Widowers' Houses,* was produced in 1892. His published plays have extensive, impractical stage directions and exhaustive prefaces; they seem like dramatic novels. But they were for acting as much as for reading: by 1913, the year of *Pygmalion,* he was a famous playwright. His plays were cascades of witty talk, and nearly all of them were tendentious. They satirized greedy landlords and military greatness, physicians and imperialists. But while Shaw assaulted his audience with his ideas, his message was not single-minded. *Major Barbara* (1907) draws a sympathetic if gently ironic portrait of the Salvation Army, tackles the "woman question," and makes an unexpected hero of Undershaft,

---

[40] T. R. Barnes, "Shaw and the London Theatre," in Boris Ford, ed., *Pelican Guide To English Literature,* vol. VII, *The Modern Age* (rev. ed., 1964), 212.

the munitions maker, who recognizes that only the strong can do good and that poverty is the only crime. And Shaw's charming *Pygmalion* is a convincing, if minor, classic, which deftly develops a wholly unpolitical subject: the creation of a human being. Even the radical playwrights were not simply politicians; they were craftsmen.

Experimenters and Expressionists

Not even the novel, in flux since the eighteenth century, could escape the general mood of experimentation. Most of the novelists, like John Galsworthy in England, remained realists and social observers. But a few developed the form in striking ways. Between 1902 and 1904, Henry James, now in his "last phase," published three long, highly subtle novels: *The Wings of the Dove, The Ambassadors,* and *The Golden Bowl.* In these serpentine dramas of psychological warfare and subtle treachery, James reached for the utmost in penetration and precision. Indirection and refinement became something of an obsession with him, but whether this search for the most elusive of realities—a kind of realism beyond realism—succeeds as well as the more full-blooded tales of the 1880s remains a matter for debate.

There is no debate, on the other hand, about Marcel Proust's *Du côté de chez Swann* (1913), the first in a closely knit cycle of seven novels, *A la recherche du temps perdu—Remembrance of Things Past.* The importance of his work was not immediately acknowledged; Proust had to publish the first volume at his own expense. But since the 1920s, his complete novel has won its place as a modern classic. Marcel Proust was born in Paris in 1871, son of a physician and a rich Jewish mother. Sickly, asthmatic, dependent, he lived the life of a dilettante, published decadent short stories, and engaged in clandestine homosexual affairs. In 1905 his mother died and Proust, desolated, began to work seriously. By 1909 the shape of his task was clear; he increasingly shut himself off from society to fulfill that task. When he died in 1922, his life work was complete, though not completely revised. *A la recherche du temps perdu* is a snake biting its tail: it recounts, in the first person, the life, from childhood, of a prosperous Parisian bourgeois who, after many false starts, finally finds his vocation in literature. He decides to write a novel—it is the novel that the reader has just finished reading. Proust unrolls a rich panorama of French social life, mainly of the upper bourgeoisie, the fading aristocracy, the cocottes and parvenus who succeed in this brittle world. But the heart of Proust's drama is internal: the narrator loves, always unhappily, and finds his illusions shattered one after the other. Mistresses are unfaithful, aristocrats are ignoble, friends turn out to be secret perverts. Proust's novel is, in its ample length, a varied feast. Long reflective stretches on painting and literature, on snobbery and love, alternate with equally long analytical stretches on the power of involuntary memories, and these in turn are punctuated by long set pieces—reports of parties, objectively recounted—that are triumphs of comic invention. Proust's novel is a modern masterpiece. It is a masterpiece in its psychological penetration, its narrative skill, its musical language, its mordant humor, its sheer power to create a world. And it is modern in its experimental techniques, its games with time, and its ultimate, melancholy lesson: that we can never know anyone completely, that appearance and reality are forever at war.

It is this search for reality in another form that dominated Proust's contemporaries, the Expressionists. Expressionism is a name that loosely embraces playwrights, poets, and painters and, in the 1920s, even architects. The pioneer of the Expressionist theater was the Swedish playwright August Strindberg, who moved from realism to the experimental *Dream Play* (1902), in which he abandoned ordinary time sequences and personal identities for the unpredictable vagaries of dream life. In a gesture that was widely imitated, Strindberg deprived his characters of names and designated them simply as types—as the Stranger, the Woman. In Germany, where young playwrights could also draw on the savage social satire and sexual candor of Frank Wedekind, the Expressionists made their theater into a forum of subjectivity. Their unidentified characters scream out erotic longings and metaphysical torments. The Expressionist poets of the day, violating rhyme schemes, offending syntax, and straining at the edges of comprehensibility, treated the same themes, at the same pitch of voice.

Expressionist painting, in contrast, was richer in its vocabulary, more varied in its moods, and more lasting in its accomplishment. It depended heavily on influences from the late nineteenth century: the prophetic Breton and Tahitian scenes of Gauguin and the overwrought, mad paintings of van Gogh. Gauguin, a stockbroker, had begun as a Sunday painter and an Impressionist. In the early 1880s, he left his business to paint; later that decade he repudiated the Impressionists and sought, in company with van Gogh, a personal idiom that would translate his visions to the canvas. In 1895 he went to Tahiti to stay, and he died there in 1903. His importance for the future, as he himself rightly judged, lay less in his paintings than in his aim; he had striven to vindicate, he wrote, "the right to dare anything." [41] In the year of Gauguin's death, there was a memorial exhibition for van Gogh, another painter who had dared anything. From then on, van Gogh's explosive color, savage brushstroke, and intense objectification of passionate states became common property.

This is what the Expressionist painters saw in their masters: the courage to break away from the outside world and to draw subject matter and color alike from troubling, often unconscious, inner needs. Some of the Expressionists, like the Norwegian painter Edvard Munch, were superb technicians. Munch did naturalistic etchings, but his heart was in his brooding woodcuts, which convey the cry of loneliness, the strangling power of Woman, the bitter pangs

[41] Quoted in Pool, *Impressionism*, 207.

of jealousy. The German Expressionists—Ernst Kirchner and Emil Nolde above all—did street scenes, nudes, and religious paintings with large, quick brush-strokes, primitive modeling, and bizarre colors. All these painters grew to admire the primitive: the art of children, of madmen, of exotic peoples, of medieval craftsmen; in their enthusiasm for simplicity, they turned to that starkest of mediums, the woodcut. In France, meanwhile, Henri Matisse and his cohort, impressed by the color of van Gogh and the composition of Cézanne, produced canvases exuberant in feeling and wild in color, yet carefully controlled. The derisive name, "Wild Beasts—*les Fauves*" that an appalled critic fastened on the group, was quite inaccurate, but it stuck.

The influence of Cézanne worked in other directions as well. Cézanne had died in Aix-en-Provence, almost a recluse, in 1906. In the following fall, there were impressive retrospective shows of his work in Paris. It is not a coincidence that Cubism, a movement as historic as it was short-lived, should be born then: in his last years, Cézanne had increasingly subordinated figurative realism to painterly needs. His aim was perfect simplicity, perfect clarity. His series of "bathers," for one, distorted the figures on the canvas to make them part of a grand design. Cézanne never neglected color, but, as he advised another painter in a letter: "Deal with nature in terms of the cylinder, the sphere, the cone, all seen in perspective." [42] The founders of Cubism were Georges Braque and Pablo Picasso, although it is obvious that one cannot summarize the career of Picasso, the most protean artist of the twentieth century, by merely calling him a Cubist. He has been, all his life, an indefatigable experimenter. Born at Málaga in 1881, the son of a painter, he left Spain to settle in Paris in 1904. Once free from his academic training, he began a series of melancholy clowns and jugglers, pathetic, almost sentimental in feeling, carefully composed, and done first in pale blues, then, after 1905, in rose. His famous portraits of the American expatriate Gertrude Stein date from these years. But then, with Braque, he moved into Cubism. The two painted landscapes, portraits, still lifes—their famous guitars and bottles—by breaking up the surfaces of the object into distinct planes, and reduced their palette to dominant pale browns and greys. Later, retreating from nature still further, they took strips of newsprint and composed collages on canvas (for Picasso's later work, see p. 1014).

Although the Cubists retreated from nature, they never abandoned it; Picasso, with all his phenomenal versatility, has never been an abstract artist. But abstract art was in the air. The invention and perfection of photography made photographic realism in painting problematic; the modern stress on subjectivity put a premium on expression; the new rebelliousness against

---

[42] Because Cézanne's letter was published while the retrospective shows were going on, it had a particular impact. It is quoted in John Golding, *Cubism: A History and an Analysis, 1907-1914* (2nd ed., 1968), 64. Since Cézanne was inarticulate and self-contradictory about his aims, the precise meaning of this statement for his art remains uncertain.

established modes—there were secessions in those years, and secessions from secessions—made the most extreme experiment a realistic possibility. In 1908 the German aesthetician Wilhelm Worringer said in his dissertation, *Abstraction and Empathy,* what Oscar Wilde had said more informally twenty years before: art and nature are separate and equal. Independently of one another, several painters were groping their way toward abstraction. Then, in 1910, the Russian painter Vassily Kandinsky, working in Munich, made the decisive leap. In the following years, he did many compositions with lines, shapes, and dots that owed nothing to nature. Expression was king.

A similar development dominated design. For most of the nineteenth century, in architecture and interior design alike, clutter had been the ideal. Eclecticism was the answer to everything; structures and materials were disguised by arbitrary decoration. One way out of this riot of tastelessness was the bold, swooping design of Art Nouveau, an international movement of decorators, designers, and painters that swept across the civilized world with its imaginative curving desks and lamps, its brilliant fantasies on canvas and in glass, in iron, and in wood. Another way out was the return to the honest craftsmanship of earlier days. This is what William Morris, socialist, designer, and poet, recommended for decades; his words were echoed in England by the Arts and Crafts movement. Before Morris died in 1896, his message had become irrelevant. He had wanted beauty for all, yet he hated the machine. But modern design, to be more than the plaything of the very few—that is, the very rich—had to ally itself with the machine. By 1900 a few rebels saw this clearly. In America, the architect Louis Sullivan called for a moratorium on ornament and was building skyscrapers in Chicago that revealed the nature and form of their steel skeletons. And in England, the architect C. F. A. Voysey advocated simplicity in design for the same reason and practiced it in his white villas, his straightforward furniture, his plain tableware. To see Voysey's work was like opening a window in an unaired room.

This modern movement culminated in Germany, in large part through foreign inspiration. In 1910 two books appeared in Berlin on the American architect Frank Lloyd Wright, who long had been pleading for honesty in the use of materials. And the work of Voysey and other Britishers were made familiar to Germany through the voluminous writing of Hermann Muthesius, who had studied English housing for seven years, between 1896 and 1903, and then reported home on the new simplicity, the new freedom from decoration. In 1907, the German *Werkbund* was founded, largely under Muthesius' prodding. The program of this association was to praise honest, undecorated workmanship without denigrating the machine. The physical embodiment of this modern view came in the architecture of Walter Gropius. Appropriately, Gropius constructed a model factory for an exhibition organized in 1914 by the *Werkbund.* Functionalism is complete in that building. Decoration has almost disappeared; glass is used freely to disclose the movement of persons and open the work done inside to the light. Art and the machine, which so many moderns had thought forever irreconcilable, are here at harmony. The harmony was short-lived.

Music, 1870-1914: Toward a New Turning

For a generation after the middle of the century, European music was dominated by three towering geniuses: Richard Wagner, Giuseppe Verdi, and Johannes Brahms. Wagner's *Tristan* (1859), as we have seen, marked the pinnacle of musical romanticism (see p. 655). With regard to his conception of the *Gesamtkunstwerk,* it is difficult to know whether, in a sense, he preached better than he wrought or wrought better than he preached. For all his advocacy of a complete mingling of music and drama and for all his pretension as a dramatic poet, Wagner's music overwhelmed the other elements: few other composers have written operas, extracts from which, without the voice, have won a standard place in the repertory of symphony orchestras—and one of the few was Wagner's disciple Richard Strauss. But for a time Wagner's preaching captured the imagination of artists and the public almost as much as the music.

In 1869 *Der Ring des Nibelungen,* a cycle of four immensely complex operas based on myths of the pagan Germanic deities, was at last performed. And after the opening in 1876 of the festival theater at Bayreuth—built for Wagner by his patron, the mad King Ludwig II of Bavaria—Wagner became the center of a cult. His preaching on other than musical subjects grew steadily more unattractive, marked as it was by narrow nationalism, anti-Semitism, and portentous philosophizing. In 1880 his last opera, *Parsifal,* brought the cult to its climax. In some respects the music was as ingenious as anything he had done, in others it was thin and arid. The singularly confusing and unconvincing libretto tells a tale of redemption: it is a pseudo-Christian epic written by a former irreligious radical whose own cult had conquered him. The extravagances of the Bayreuth period turned Nietzsche, Wagner's onetime worshiper, violently against him. But however depressing the later Wagner is to contemplate from this distance in time, there is no gainsaying his influence on the generation that followed him. The debt is manifest in both the operas and the orchestral works of Richard Strauss; it is clear, too, in the works Arnold Schönberg composed prior to World War I, before he made his open break with three centuries of European musical tradition; and, although the influence is less easily discernible, it is no less profound in the epoch-making music of Claude Debussy.

But opera in Wagner's own time could also claim another master, Verdi. The very antithesis of the Wagnerian personality, this genial, contented, deeply religious man, living his mature years on his country estate, turned out one masterpiece after another with ever increasing imagination and control. His early operas of the forties are entirely within the French-Italian tradition of "grand opera"; to them he added a powerful anti-Austrian patriotic message that Italian nationalists had no trouble perceiving amid the foreign settings that got the librettos past the censors. *Rigoletto, Il Trovatore,* and *La Traviata* appeared within three years in the early fifties. They are probably—with the exception of Georges Bizet's superb realistic dramatic opera *Carmen* (1875)—the most durably popular operas in the repertory of every company. But in two works of his old age—*Otello* (1887) and *Falstaff* (1892)—Verdi realized a marriage of music and drama more convincing than anything Wagner accomplished, for all his theorizing. The tradition of grand opera, like Wagnerian romanticism, had reached its culmination; those who followed in it—notably Giacomo Puccini, whose operas also have great popularity—in fact had no place to go.

In Johannes Brahms—scholarly, retiring, melancholy—nineteenth-century music found an analogue to the phenomenon J. H. Buckley has noted in the English poet Tennyson, a deliberate subjection of romantic impulses to classic control. [43] In his respect for sonata form, Brahms goes back to Beethoven, but he lacked in some degree Beethoven's natural aptitude for the medium. Brahms' earliest, fragmentary works had quickly won Schumann's praise, and his skill as a performer gained him a wide reputation; but his first tentative essays in classic sonata form were unsuccessful, and it was not until 1876, when he was forty-three, that he ventured his first symphony. He wrote only four symphonies, but they are extraordinary compositions. Conceived on a large scale and executed with superb imagination, they also suggest, in occasional labored passages of a kind that never occur in Beethoven, a less than perfect congruence of content and form. But the mingling of discipline and feeling, the reflectiveness and the often somber colors that lead critics inevitably to use adjectives like "resigned" or "autumnal," still testify to a deep artistic integrity.

In some things Brahms has never been equaled, above all in his mastery of constructing variations on a theme: at the end of the Fourth Symphony he returns to the seventeenth-century form of the chaconne, weaving, over a motif of eight notes repeated thirty times, a stunningly unified movement that transcends the limitations the form would have imposed on a lesser genius. Many of Brahms' contemporaries were deeply committed to the symphony as the highest form of musical expression, but no one handled it so skillfully. With Peter Ilyitch Tchaikovsky, the most European of the great Russian composers of the period, or with Gustav Mahler, defects of scale, lapses of taste, and self-indulgence mar and sometimes overwhelm works otherwise distinguished by admirable musical ideas and impressive manipulative skills. The classical symphony, too, was reaching a dead end.

Three revolutionary composers—Claude Debussy, Igor Stravinsky, and Arnold Schönberg—distinguish the early years of the twentieth century. Schönberg was to attain his seminal importance only after World War I, although *Pierrot Lunaire* (1913), for soprano and orchestra, was at least a

---

[43] J. H. Buckley, *The Victorian Temper* (1951), chaps. 2 and 4.

foretaste of things to come in its evolution out of Wagnerian style and its use of *Sprechgesang*—half-sung, half-spoken text. The eldest of the three, Claude Debussy, had startled the musical world with his subtle, sensuous orchestral prelude, *The Afternoon of a Faun,* in 1892; his many works for piano were more original than anything written for that instrument since Chopin. He owes much to Wagner and to Liszt, as well as to a long chain of French influences; but the total effect of his works is modern, a clear departure from the form and vocabulary of the nineteenth century. Fragmentary, evocative but not programmatic, brilliant in color, chromatic, and rhythmically irregular, Debussy's compositions launched the musical movement known as impressionism—by an understandable analogy to the Impressionist painters—although the affiliations are quite as strong to the symbolism of fin-de-siècle poetry. The impressionist mood and style was to be found in varying degrees across Europe—Frederick Delius in England, Manuel de Falla in Spain, Maurice Ravel in France, Ottorino Respighi in Italy, and Alexander Scriabin in Russia. But Debussy was more than the inspiration of a school; he was the most fertile and influential of them all, the only impressionist who, in his explorations of new possibilities of musical language, pointed firmly toward the dissolution of the tonality and meter that had dominated Western music for so long.

Finally, there was the young Igor Stravinsky, destined to exercise over almost seventy years of the twentieth century an influence unmatched by anyone but Schönberg and to attain a popularity Schönberg would never know. In his constant experimentation, superb eclecticism, and authenticity, Stravinsky was the musical equivalent of Picasso: he taught us to hear as Picasso has taught us to see. The son of a musical family, the pupil of the Russian nationalist composer Nicolai Rimsky-Korsakov, Stravinsky made his earliest reputation as a composer for the ballet, an art to which he remained devoted throughout his life and to which he contributed more masterpieces than any other composer (or perhaps than all other composers put together). *The Firebird* of 1910 and *Petrouchka* of 1911 owe much of their orchestral color to Rimsky-Korsakov, while adding rhythmic freedom and dissonant harmonies that were clearly modern, though not yet more than a logical development from what other Russian and European composers were doing. In 1913 Stravinsky completed a ballet on the theme of a human sacrifice in pagan Russia; the *Rite of Spring* was truly revolutionary. Looking back, we can see its affinities to Stravinsky's earlier work, but in the violent dissonances and barbaric rhythms one can still feel the originality and power that provoked a riot in the Paris theater where the first performance was given. A writer who was present recalled: "A certain part of the audience, thrilled by what it considered a blasphemous attempt to destroy music as an art, and swept away with wrath, began very soon after the rise of the curtain to whistle, to make catcalls, and to offer audible suggestions as to how the performance should proceed. Others of us, who liked the music and felt that the principles of free speech were at stake, bellowed defiance. It was war over art for the rest of the evening, and the orchestra played on unheard, except occasionally when a slight lull occurred. The figures on the stage danced in time to music they had to imagine they heard and beautifully out of rhythm with the uproar in the auditorium. I was sitting in a box in which I had rented one seat. Three ladies sat in front of me and a young man occupied the place behind me. He stood up during the course of the ballet to enable himself to see more clearly. The intense excitement under which he was labouring, thanks to the potent force of the music, betrayed itself presently when he began to beat rhythmically on the top of my head with his fists. My emotion was so great that I did not feel the blows for some time. They were perfectly synchronized with the music. When I did I turned around. His apology was sincere. We had both been carried beyond ourselves." [44] The blows were more symptomatic than the apology. In the years before 1914 music and art—and perhaps wider reaches of European society as well—had been carried beyond themselves. Modern art, like the modern world, was born in violence.

SELECTED READINGS

The changing temper of the age is, of course, the subject of many books. For professionalization, see the pioneering study by W. J. Reader, *Professional Men: The Rise of the Professional Classes in Nineteenth-Century England* (1966). The rise of history as a profession is well sketched in John Higham, with Leonard Krieger and Felix Gilbert, *History* (1965), which covers the American and, more briefly, the European scene. The greatest intellectual force, Darwin, is discussed in J. C. Greene, *The Death of Adam: Evolution and its Impact on Western Thought* (1959), and Loren Eiseley, *Darwin's Century: Evolution and the Men Who Discovered It* (rev. ed., 1961). Erich Heller, *The Disinherited Mind* (1952) is a series of essays on literary figures dominated by the secularization of the world. J. Hillis Miller, *The Disappearance of God* (1963) is a sensitive study of the nineteenth-century literary mind. H. Stuart Hughes, *Consciousness and Society: The Reorientation of European Social Thought, 1890–1930* (1958) is a lucid survey.

The most authoritative treatment of Nietzsche is by Walter A. Kaufmann, *Nietzsche: Philosopher, Psychologist, Anti-Christ* (3rd ed., 1968). See also R. J. Hollingdale, *Nietzsche, The Man and His Philosophy* (1965). For English philosophy see especially John Passmore, *A Hundred Years of Philosophy* (1957), a compendious work that, despite its title, concentrates on Russell, Moore et al. Walter M. Simon, *European Positivism in the Nineteenth Century* (1963) says the essential; for William James, see the classic account by Ralph Barton Perry, *The Thought and Character of William James*, 2 vols. (1935), issued in a good one-volume version in 1948; Margaret Knight, *William James* (1950) is a helpful anthology of his psychological writings and has a long introduction.

All students of Freud must be indebted to the magisterial biography by Ernest Jones, *The Life and Work of Sigmund Freud*, 3 vols. (1953–1957); a one-volume abridgment by Lionel Trilling and Steven Marcus appeared in 1961. Philip Rieff, *Freud:*

---

[44] Carl Van Vechten, *Music after the Great War and Other Studies* (1915), 87–88.

The Mind of the Moralist (1959) is an intelligent exposition; Richard Wollheim, *Freud* (1971) offers a brilliant introduction. One of the most accessible introductions to relativity is by Albert Einstein and Leopold Infeld, *The Evolution of Physics: The Growth of Ideas from Early Concepts to Relativity and Quanta* (1938). Infeld's *Albert Einstein: His Work and Its Influence on Our World* (1950) brings a remote genius closer. Despite the recent, highly popular life by Ronald W. Clark, *Einstein: The Life and Times* (1971), Einstein still awaits his authoritative biographer. On Max Weber, see the relevant chapter in Raymond Aron, *Main Currents in Sociological Thought*, vol. II (1967), which deals at length with Pareto, Durkheim, and Weber. Reinhard Bendix, *Max Weber: An Intellectual Portrait* (1960) is straightforward. The chapter in Hughes' *Consciousness and Society*, cited above, is very helpful. Also consult the lengthy treatment by Talcott Parsons, *The Structure of Social Action* (1937). Arthur Mitzman, *The Iron Cage: An Historical Interpretation of Max Weber* (1969) offers a psychological interpretation. For Durkheim, in addition to Aron and Parsons just cited, see Harry Alpert, *Emile Durkheim and His Sociology* (1939), and the useful anthology of articles collected by Robert A. Nisbet, *Emile Durkheim* (1965), which has a long introduction.

The idea of "avant-garde" is brilliantly (though not conclusively) explored in Renato Poggioli, *The Theory of the Avant-Garde* (1968). Irving Howe, ed., *Literary Modernism* (1967) is an excellent anthology. César Graña, *Modernity and Its Discontents: French Society and the French Man of Letters in the Nineteenth Century* (ed. 1967) contains, among other things, a fine anthology of antibourgeois abuse by avant-garde writers. On the rise of the mass public, see the brief factual and informative essay by Carlo M. Cipolla, *Literacy and Development in the West* (1969). The older book by Q. D. Leavis, *Fiction and the Reading Public* (1932), is essentially a lament on the decline of English taste; it should be corrected with R. K. Webb, *The British Working Class Reader, 1790–1848: Literacy and Social Tension* (1955), and Webb's "The Victorian Reading Public," in Boris Ford, ed., *Pelican Guide to English Literature*, vol. VI, *From Dickens to Hardy* (rev. ed., 1969), 205–226. John Gross, *The Rise and Fall of the Man of Letters* (1969) is an absorbing analysis of reviewers who shaped the English public's taste. For Germany, there is now the useful but introductory study by Eda Sagarra, *Tradition and Revolution: German Literature and Society, 1830–1890* (1971). And for France, see F. W. J. Hemmings, *Culture and Society in France, 1848–1898: Dissidents and Philistines* (1971).

Any study of modern realism must begin with Erich Auerbach's masterly *Mimesis: The Representation of Reality in Western Literature* (tr. 1953), which starts with the Greeks and ends with Virginia Woolf. Linda Nochlin, *Realism* (1971) is an intelligent essay mainly, though not wholly, on realism in nineteenth-century painting. Harry Levin's civilized essay, *The Gates of Horn: A Study of Five French Realists* (1963), gives a close reading to Stendhal, Balzac, Flaubert, Zola, and Proust. Mario Praz, *The Hero in Eclipse in Victorian Literature* (1956) is a fascinating exploration of the rise of bourgeois values in English fiction; it should be supplemented with Victor Brombert, *The Intellectual Hero: Studies in the French Novel, 1880–1955* (1961). Ernest Simmons, *Introduction to Russian Realism* (1964) examines developments in Russia; Renato Poggioli, *The Poets of Russia: 1890–1930* (1960) moves ahead into Symbolism.

On some individual writers of the period, here is a selection of recommended titles: Humphry House, *The Dickens World* (1960), though brief, brilliantly sets the novelist into his world; see also George H. Ford, *Dickens and His Readers: Aspects of Novel-Criticism Since 1836* (rev. ed., 1965). For George Eliot, see Gordon S. Haight, *George*

Eliot, A Biography (1968); and Walter Allen, *George Eliot* (1964). The authoritative biography of Henry James is Leon Edel, *Henry James,* 5 vols. (1953–1972); for a short and lucid appreciation, see F. W. Dupee, *Henry James* (1951). For Zola, see Elliott M. Grant, *Zola's Germinal: A Critical and Historical Study* (1962), but above all the intellectual biography by F. W. J. Hemmings, *Emile Zola* (2nd ed., 1966).

For Russian literature, see D. S. Mirsky, *A History of Russian Literature, From Its Beginnings to 1900,* edited by Francis J. Whitfield (1958), and Helen Muchnic, *An Introduction to Russian Literature* (rev. ed., 1964), both useful guides; the latter concentrates on the nineteenth century. W. H. Bruford, *Chekhov and His Russia: A Sociological Study* (1947) moves well beyond Chekhov into Russia. On individual writers, see Avrahm Yarmolinsky, *Turgenev: The Man, His Art and His Age* (1926), and David Magarshak, *Turgenev: A Life* (1954). Dostoevsky is well served by Konstantin Mochulsky, *Dostoevsky* (tr. 1946); an anthology of critical essays edited by René Wellek, *Dostoevsky* (1962), with an informative introduction, is exceptionally useful. Ernest Simmons's biography, *Leo Tolstoy* (1946) is detailed; it should be supplemented by John Bayley's fine essay, *Tolstoy and the Novel* (1966). The best short treatment of Chekhov is by Ronald Hingley: *Chekhov: A Biographical and Critical Study* (rev. ed., 1966). See also Ernest Simmons, *Chekhov, A Biography* (1962).

On the French Impressionists, see, amid a vast literature, Phoebe Pool, *Impressionism* (1967), and John Rewald, *A History of Impressionism* (2nd ed., 1961); the latter is an exhaustive study. For the painting against which the Impressionists rebelled, see Joseph C. Sloane, *French Painting Between the Past and Present* (1951). See also George Heard Hamilton, *Manet and His Critics* (2nd ed., 1969), a fascinating essay. On individual Impressionists, see Samuel Lane Faison, *Edouard Manet, 1832–1883* (1953); John Rewald, *Camille Pissarro* (1963); Meyer Schapiro, *Paul Cézanne* (1952); William C. Seitz, *Claude Monet* (1960); and Lawrence Gowing, *Renoir* (1947).

Aestheticist and Symbolist literary criticism is authoritatively analyzed in René Wellek, *A History of Modern Criticism, 1750–1950,* vol. IV, *The Later Nineteenth Century* (1965). The best brief analysis of Pater is R. V. Johnson, *Walter Pater: A Study of his Critical Outlook and Achievement* (1961). For Oscar Wilde, see the anthology edited by Richard Ellmann, *The Artist as Critic* (1969), and for the pathetic last years of Wilde, H. Montgomery Hyde, *Oscar Wilde: the Aftermath* (1963). A. G. Lehmann, *The Symbolist Aesthetic in France, 1885–1895* (2nd ed., 1968) is informative. Arthur Symons, *The Symbolist Movement in Literature* (rev. ed., 1919) is a classic of its kind. Both can be supplemented with Antoine Adam, *The Art of Paul Verlaine* (tr. 1961); Joanna Richardson, *Verlaine: A Biography* (1971); Enid Starkie, *Rimbaud* (1962); Wilbur M. Frohock, *Rimbaud's Poetic Practice* (1963); Guy Michaud, *Mallarmé* (tr. 1965); Wallace Fowlie, *Mallarmé* (1953); and Robert Baldick, *The Life of J. K. Huysmans* (1955).

The accumulation of modernist masterpieces after 1890 is best followed through studies of individual masters. But see the general survey by G. S. Fraser, *The Modern Writer and this World* (rev. ed., 1970). For Thomas Mann, see the lucid introduction by Henry Hatfield, *Thomas Mann* (rev. ed., 1962); Erich Heller, *The Ironic German: A Study of Thomas Mann* (1958) is suggestive. For Ibsen, see, in general, Brian W. Downs, *Modern Norwegian Literature, 1860–1918* (1966), and in particular the detailed biography by Michael Meyer, *Ibsen: A Biography* (1971). For the other great Scandinavian, see Brita Mortensen and Brian Downs, *Strindberg: An Introduction to his Life and Work* (1949).

For Shaw, see Hesketh Pearson, *G.B.S.: A Full Length Portrait* (rev. ed., 1951) which is personal and well informed, and William Irvine, *The Universe of George Bernard Shaw* (1949). For Arnold Bennett, there is Dudley Baker's *Writer by Trade: A View of Arnold Bennett* (1966). H. G. Wells published a fascinating self-appraisal, *Experiment in Autobiography,* in 1934; it can be supplemented with Bernard Bergonzi, *The Early H. G. Wells* (1961). As for Proust, the biography by George D. Painter, *Proust,* 2 vols. (1959, 1965) is exhaustive but remains controversial. André Maurois' earlier *Proust: A Biography* (tr. 1950) is by no means negligible.

For developments in avant-garde painting around and after 1890, see John Rewald, *Post-Impressionism From Van Gogh to Gauguin* (2nd ed., 1962), fully documented. In addition, there are good studies by S. Løvgren, *The Genesis of Modernism: Seurat, Gauguin, Van Gogh and French Symbolism in the 1880s* (1959), a pioneering attempt; and Mark Roskill, *Van Gogh, Gauguin and the Impressionist Circle* (n.d. [1970]). See also Meyer Schapiro, *Van Gogh* (n.d.); and Robert Goldwater, *Gauguin* (n.d.). Nikolaus Pevsner, *Pioneers of Modern Design, From William Morris to Walter Gropius* (rev. ed., 1964) is an important analysis. Equally important is the valuable monograph, William Innes Homer, *Seurat and the Science of Painting* (corrected ed., 1970). Robert Schmutzler provides an extensive treatment in his *Art Nouveau* (tr. 1964).

23

The Shaking of Nations:
1900-1918

EUROPE AT THE PRECIPICE

An Uncertain Continent

In 1929 the great French historian Elie Halévy gave the Rhodes Lectures at Oxford, taking as his subject "The World Crisis of 1914–1918." His profoundly novel and stimulating generalization about the identity, or at any rate the interconnection, of war and revolution turned sharply away from the conventional diplomatic history with which his contemporaries were trying to unravel the question of how the war had come about. He would not, he said, speculate about "what such and such a sovereign, or prime minister, or foreign secretary, should, on this particular day, at this or that particular hour, have done or not done, said or not said, in order to prevent the war. Pills to cure an earthquake! The object of my study is the earthquake itself."[1] Halévy's perceptive analysis

---

[1] The lectures are reprinted in *The Era of Tyrannies* (1938, tr. 1965), and this quotation appears on p. 210.

of socialism and nationalism—those vast, impersonal, cultural forces that he saw leading inevitably to crisis—differed from the views of his more pedestrian colleagues. But they differed in grasp and imagination rather than in perspective, for he too wrote with a shattering knowledge of the outcome. Even today the notion of an inevitable clash is difficult to avoid. One senses it in the dismay with which contemporaries watched the mounting challenge of political socialism and militant syndicalism, in their sense of entrapment as one after another diplomatic incident broke on a fevered Europe. Yet it is important to remember that after the holocaust many men thought only of returning to the prewar world, submerging those chilling crises in stronger recollections of the felicity, the calm, the alluring languorousness (to borrow their metaphors) of an afternoon, an Indian summer. This selective memory—not confined to the prosperous, though it was chiefly theirs—should be recalled at the beginning of a chapter that will deal largely with futility and crisis. Earth tremors need not be cumulative warning signals; the earthquake of August 1914 was both expected and a surprise.

The history of nineteenth-century Europe can be interpreted in terms of the fortunes of liberalism or, more accurately, in terms of its failures. At the two poles were Britain and Russia: Britain, where liberal institutions and attitudes were firmly grounded and broadly accepted and where even conservatives could implement liberal policies; Russia, where autocracy remained in force and serfdom was barely abolished and where the modest constitutional ambitions of the few liberals proved both unattainable and irrelevant. The other major countries oscillated between the two extremes. In France, where false starts and setbacks had been the rule earlier in the century, the Third Republic may be considered, on balance, as a victory for the liberal tradition. In Italy and Spain, official rhetoric to the contrary, the appearance of liberal institutions was more often falsified by reality; the benefits that liberalism promised everyone in theory spread only a little distance down the social scale. Throughout central and eastern Europe, however, liberalism was most often acknowledged by its denial. Nationalists over the past century have frequently poured their emotions and strength into irredentism, the ambition to win (or win back) those "unredeemed" lands they believed to be rightfully theirs but denied them by history or diplomacy. As a developing, increasingly complex industrial economy spread across Europe—enriching some, displacing and impoverishing far more—there appeared what one might call a "social irredentism," a quest for opportunity and justice (for oneself or one's fellows) that grew with self-awareness and with the spread of education and easier communication. Some, more or less fortunate, sought to realize that goal in emigration. But for those who remained, the feeble accomplishment of nominally liberal or radical politicians or the calculated (if not cynical) welfare legislation of a Bismarck was not always enough; and the traditional armory of liberalism was inadequate to attain their ends. Far more promising were the

revolutionary movements on the left—socialism and anarchism—or the nostrums offered by a growing assortment of movements on the right, which
usually started with identifying a scapegoat (all too frequently the Jews) and
sometimes found no need to go further.

In the early years of the twentieth century these tensions grew worse. In
Russia, so monolithic and, for all its inefficiency, seemingly so eternal, there
was, as we shall see, an abortive revolution and then a last futile effort to make
the autocracy work. Even in Britain, where the Liberal party was to have its last
gloriously sweeping fling at reforming on the Victorian model, there was
disaffection with, indeed rejection of, the liberal values and institutions by
which the preceding century had set such store. Nothing so dramatic happened
on the Continent outside of Russia. It was not a heroic age: the stuff for it (or
the statesmanship) was lacking or, if present, was stymied. The gap between
ambition and accomplishment became steadily more evident, and frustration
grew apace. But, as it were, by an accident, the dynamics of diplomacy and
nationalism determined that the European crisis would be a war, not a
revolution. Little of the old Europe survived that war and its aftermath.

Southern Europe

In Portugal—that remote, backward corner of the Iberian peninsula—the late
nineteenth century had seen a quasi-parliamentary regime, with a decorous
alternation of ministries, under King Carlos I, whose extravagance made him
increasingly unpopular. In 1906 the king installed a new premier with
dictatorial powers, but after a little less than two years of this repressive regime,
the king and the crown prince were assassinated, bringing to the throne an
utterly unprepared younger son, Manoel II. Although Manoel restored constitutional government, an insurrection in October 1910 drove him from the
country and led to the establishment of a republic, the principal accomplishment of which was a fairly resolute campaign against the church, which was
formally separated from the state in 1911.

In Spain, the republic that succeeded on the abdication of King Amadeo
in 1873 (see p. 775) was an invitation to anarchy. With a rampant federalism at
one political extreme and a revived Carlism at the other, the only recourse—as
was usual in Spain—was military rule, which at least kept together an army that
had been on the verge of dissolution. At the very end of 1874 the Bourbon
dynasty was restored, in the person of Alfonso XII, Queen Isabella's seventeen-
year-old son, recalled from his military studies at Sandhurst in England. The
man who made the restoration was Antonio Cánovas del Castillo, an O'Don-
nellite supporter in 1854, who headed a Liberal Conservative (or Conservative)
party he had conjured up from the remains of the old Moderates and the Liberal
Unionists of midcentury. Cánovas created a rough copy, artificial but effective,
of the English constitutional monarchy of fifty years earlier: the king was kept

out of politics, the army was weaned away from *pronunciamentos,* the suffrage was limited, and majorities in the country were created by the species of boss rule called *caciquismo.* The two parties engaged in a decorous parliamentary minuet, the most notable instance of it in 1885, when Alfonso died prematurely and Cánovas urged the king's widow, Maria Cristina—who ruled as regent for her son Alfonso XIII, who was born the next year—to bring the Liberal opposition into office. The constitution of 1876 (which lasted until 1923) was essentially that of 1845, with an added guarantee of personal rights, including freedom of religion. Slavery was abolished in Cuba in the early eighties (it had been outlawed in Puerto Rico in 1872), and in 1890 the Liberals reintroduced universal suffrage. For a quarter of a century after the restoration Spain lived quietly, and an apparent consensus managed to keep the social threat submerged until the "disaster of 1898."

In that year Spain lost its last colonial possessions of any significance in a war with the United States. This nearly mortal blow to Spanish pride coincided with a remarkable intellectual, literary, and artistic revival whose outstanding figures were the painters Juan Gris and Pablo Picasso (though Picasso took up residence in Paris in 1904); Isaac Albéniz, Enrique Granados, and Manuel de Falla among composers; the philosophers Miguel de Unamuno and José Ortega y Gasset. To these names should be added (though he died in 1890) that unique, compelling architect, Antonio Gaudí, who worked in forms allied to but transcending Art Nouveau. In the new century some of these intellectuals—their most famous spokesman being the philosopher Unamuno—undertook a highly self-conscious examination of the faults and the meaning of Spain. But, unlike the Russian intelligentsia after the defeat in the Crimean War, they found no single evil on which they could concentrate. *Caciquismo* was an easy but relatively insignificant target, doomed in any event, and the real impact of the ideals of the "generation of '98" was felt only in the 1930s.

More immediately threatening was the rapid growth of the Spanish labor movement, unusual in Europe for the strong influence, at work in it almost at the moment of its birth in the 1870s, of Bakuninist anarchism. In the poverty-stricken, backward rural areas of the south, anarchism mingled with an ancient millenarianism to fire peasant anger and expectations of miraculous regeneration. Somewhat more surprisingly, anarchism struck root in the advanced industrial region of Catalonia, centered on Barcelona, where it merged with the syndicalism (see p. 856) that was sweeping European labor movements in the years prior to World War I. The anarchist commitment to direct, violent action began to be felt, horribly, in a series of bombings in the 1890s—twenty-one people killed at the opera in Barcelona, ten struck down during a religious procession, and Cánovas himself assassinated in 1897. In 1906 the young king Alfonso XIII and his bride were the intended targets of a bomb that killed a number of bystanders, and the able Liberal premier José Canalejas fell in 1912. The old Catalan separatism had, moreover, grown into a full-fledged movement for cultural and political nationalism. All these pressures converged in a strike that began in Barcelona on July 26, 1909. It moved through a violent campaign of arson mounted against religious orders and schools, and it ended with severe government repression and the execution, among others, of Francisco Ferrer, a wealthy supporter of the anarchist cause and the founder of a "modern school" that, until its forcible closing in 1906, had provided secularized education for workers' children. Ferrer's martyrdom helped to discredit the parliamentary regime, though it was allowed to survive for a time, thanks to the fright given to the respectable classes by the events of the "Tragic Week" and then because of the factitious prosperity brought to Spain by World War I.

In Italy, on the other hand, the early years of the twentieth century went some distance toward fulfilling the promise of the unification. The more favored parts of the peninsula prospered. New industries were taking hold, and electricity was beginning to benefit a country rich in hydroelectric resources ("white coal") but poor in other fuels. The south, still *terra incognita* to most northern politicians, remained neglected, however. It was an unproductive land, bedeviled by the cruelties of nature: an earthquake in 1908 killed perhaps 150,000. Its people were illiterate, malaria-ridden, and poverty stricken.

The new king, Victor Emmanuel III, who came to the throne after the assassination of Humbert in 1900, was a withdrawn, uninspiring man, little likely to interfere. The political scene was dominated by Giovanni Giolitti, who, a few brief intervals apart, was prime minister for the whole of the period. Giolitti was a master of the art of *trasformismo* (see p. 802), and, although his overtures to the reformist wing of the badly split Socialists failed, he enacted much of the Socialists' "minimum" program from his base in the political center. He encouraged trade unions, while dealing firmly with threatening strikes (as on the railways) and letting others exhaust themselves. Factory acts and social welfare measures were carried; wages rose; some reform of taxation was accomplished, though not the thorough overhauling Giolitti wanted; and government budgets were balanced. The conservative Pius X, a resolute enemy of modernism in the church, reigned in the Vatican from 1903 to 1914, but the more liberal spirit of his predecessor Leo XIII (see p. 818) continued to spread its beneficent influence, and Giolitti engineered closer relations with the church in a series of delicate compromises. Although Giolitti manipulated elections shamelessly,[2] he also gave the country a genuine installment of suffrage reform in 1912; the vote was given to all men over thirty, whether literate or not—a major liberal reform that would be turned against liberalism in time. Not all was well, to be sure. The country was wracked by strikes, a bumptious colonial policy contributed to international unrest and augured ill for future Italian adventurism abroad, and some syndicalist leaders were beginning to glimpse

---

[2] Giolitti reported that a mayor apologized for two antigovernment votes cast in his town and assured the premier that "the men have had such a time of it that they have emigrated to France." "I replied," said Giolitti, "that this was really too much." Quoted in Denis Mack Smith, *Italy, a Modern History* (1959, rev. ed., 1969), 221.

the possibility of capturing syndicalism for nationalist ends. But the true significance of these omens would appear only in the 1920s and 1930s. From the standpoint of 1914 they were only small clouds in a generally sunny Italian sky.

France

Between the pardon of Captain Dreyfus in 1899 (see p. 818) and the reversal of the judgment against him in 1906, the French republicans set about consolidating their victory, still only partially won, in a burst of principled vengeance. A wholesale attack on the church began with the Law of Associations of 1901, which put the authorization of "associations," that is, the religious orders, firmly under the control of the legislature. The electoral victory of republicans and Socialists in that year made it certain how the legislature would act. The premier, René Waldeck-Rousseau, shrank from sweeping measures and resigned in 1902, despite his firm majority; he was succeeded by Emile Combes, who enforced the new law sternly. In 1904 all teaching by religious orders was forbidden, and, in a calculated snub to the Vatican, President Emile Loubet was sent on a state visit to the king of Italy, with whom the pope remained officially irreconcilable; the result was a diplomatic breach with the papacy. Finally, a law of 1905 separated church and state. The concordat of 1801 (see p. 508) was abrogated, priests (and Protestant ministers and rabbis) ceased to be salaried by the state, and the churches were organized as independent corporations.

In 1906 the Radical politician Georges Clemenceau was carried into the premiership at the head of a Left coalition, but the sweeping seventeen-point program of reforms he proposed remained a dead letter. At least at the legislative level, the French state was seized with paralysis: what social welfare measures were enacted were initiated by the bureaucracy. David Thomson has argued that the year 1905 was a watershed between the generation that consolidated the republic—a consolidation capped by the final settlement of the vexed church-state issue—and the generation that had somehow to find a way of accommodating the new forces mobilized by a mature industrial society.[3] The old Left of the nineteenth century, the radicals and republicans, were left to mediate as best they could between rapidly diverging forces on the extremes. From about 1905 there was a marked resurgence of rightist sentiment in France. It drew to some extent on the old conservatives—nobility and landed proprietors displaced from politics, the church, the army—but the traditional devotion to "throne and altar" was no longer the principal motive force. A crucial infusion of numerical strength and, above all, money came to the Right from industrial and commercial circles, giving vent to their dislike of democracy and their fear of socialism and to a new nationalism, responding to the growing threat from Germany. Much of this sentiment came to focus in the movement

[3] David Thomson, *Democracy in France since 1870* (5th ed., 1969), 72-74.

built up around the newspaper *Action française,* founded at the very end of the nineteenth century and transformed into a daily paper in 1908. The paper was edited by the unscrupulous and savage journalist Léon Daudet; the guiding spirit of the movement was the literary critic Charles Maurras, theoretically a royalist, openly an atheist, uncompromisingly an anti-Semite. But Action française meant more than literary brilliance: in the Camelots du Roi, the movement organized the first of the private paramilitary gangs that were to become so dismally important in postwar Europe.

As much of wealthy and respectable France was pulled to the Right, so increasingly the working classes were drawn to the Left, which itself grew more and more extreme. Political socialism had failed to seize its opportunities. Socialists had agonized over the question of participation in bourgeois coalitions (see p. 863n), and some of them, notably Alexandre Millerand and Aristide Briand, had chosen to become ministers. Jean Jaurès, the finest mind among the independent Socialists, had been willing to defend Socialist participation in connection with the Dreyfus case; but when in 1904 the Second International imposed the obligation to abstain—a position defended in France by Jules Guesde, the chief apostle of orthodox Marxism—Jaurès conformed. While French socialism was thus kept from any direct influence on policy, French trade unionism, increasingly committed to syndicalism (see p. 856), rejected politics as well, rather more perhaps from practical disgust with the politicians than from concern for purity of doctrine. In 1907, at the Stuttgart congress of the International, a French schoolmaster, Gustave Hervé, proposed an even more extreme position—that war should be met by a general strike and that soldiers should turn the weapons put into their hands against the government. This revolutionary tactic, betraying the persistent insurrectionist appeal associated most closely with Blanqui (see p. 690), was adopted by the congress and applauded by none more warmly than Lenin. It is worth remembering, however, that Hervé himself became a fervent patriot in 1914 and survived to urge, as early as 1935, that the military hero Marshal Pétain be called upon to save the republic from itself.

Beset by strikes, increasingly polarized, its politics reduced to the sterile game of parliamentary combinations, France in the years before 1914 seemed to have lost the sense of direction that had guided it, with whatever uncertainties and disappointments, since the creation of the Third Republic.

Central Europe

The Dual Monarchy of Austria-Hungary was staggering toward its fall. Both parts were dominated by minorities, the Germans in Austria, the Magyars in Hungary; both had to cope with the discontented nationalities within their borders, a problem with which, on the whole, the Austrian part dealt more effectively. In Hungary the Magyars not only lorded it over the subject nationalities, but they continued to fight for further concessions from the Hapsburg dynasty itself. Early in the new century the Magyars had insisted that Magyar be the required language of command for Hungarian contingents in the common army. Refusing to consider such an abdication of his prerogatives, the aged Francis Joseph suspended the Hungarian constitution in 1906 and threatened to introduce universal suffrage, which would have put the Magyars in a clear minority. A compromise was reached, the Magyars backed down on the army question, the constitution was restored, and universal suffrage remained an item of the government's agenda, never to be implemented. Magyarization was riveted even more firmly on the other nationalities.

In Austria the German nationalist movement headed by Georg von Schönerer (see p. 809) continued on its demagogic way, anti-Semitic and violent, but it attracted fewer adherents than did the Christian Socialist movement headed by Karl Lueger, mayor of Vienna from 1897. Christian Socialism, too, was anti-Semitic, though rather as a tactic than as a matter of conviction, and it espoused the cause of the "little man" in Austrian society— a milieu of profound importance in forming the consciousness of a young ne'er-do-well named Adolf Hitler, then living in Vienna. Although the linguistic privileges granted to the Czechs in Bohemia in 1897 were withdrawn two years later, the overall minority position of Germans was made apparent in 1907 when the vote in Austria was given to all men aged twenty-four or over; coupled with a drawing of lines that kept electoral districts nationally homogeneous, this step produced a lower house that generously reflected the variegated makeup of the country. It is yet more characteristic that the Reichsrat had virtually no power. From 1900, under an emergency provision of the constitution of 1867, ministers had ruled Austria by decree: it was a situation in which, as A. J. P. Taylor has said, Metternich and the men of the Vormärz would have found themselves entirely at home. [4] Held together for want of any practical alternative to take its place, the Hapsburg monarchy survived and sought to survive by making and breaking bargains with whoever the ministers thought, for the moment, needed to be cultivated or dispensed with. Increasingly, however, they sought to strike a grand stroke against an outside enemy. That enemy could hardly be a powerful state, and, from 1908 on, Austria bullied Serbia (see p. 938). In doing so the Hapsburg monarchy created the circumstances that would destroy it.

In Germany, the social legislation of Bismarck's time was gradually extended until the codification of 1911 produced the most advanced system of social insurance in Europe. And while the Social Democrats, as we have seen, were deeply divided by the issue of revisionism and by the question of accommodation with bourgeois parties in parliament (see p. 860), the practical involvement of the party was far more extensive than that of the Socialists in

[4] A. J. P. Taylor, *The Habsburg Monarchy, 1809–1918* (Torchbook ed., 1965), 199.

France, notwithstanding incessant criticism from the extreme Left headed by Karl Liebknecht and Rosa Luxemburg. Surely the peak of this involvement was reached in 1913 when the Social Democrats in the Reichstag supported the army bill, a departure from their traditional antimilitarism explained readily enough by an even more traditional fear of the Russian Moloch. By that time the Social Democrats were the largest party in Germany and the largest Socialist party in Europe; in 1912 they polled over a third of the votes and won 110 seats. A future Social Democratic majority was a real possibility, a prospect that raised not only fear among adherents of the Right but serious problems about the constitutional structure of the empire and its constituent states. Alarm over the power of the Left had led a number of German states to restrict the suffrage, and Chancellor Bethmann Hollweg's intelligent recognition that the discriminatory three-class system in Prussia needed reform got nowhere; he tried to carry a modification in 1910—far from a truly democratic measure—but was forced to back away by conservative resistance, resistance reinforced by the Social Democratic victory in 1912.

At the federal level, another anomaly loomed steadily larger: the relative impotence of the Reichstag within the imperial government. The winning of responsible government was, understandably, a major ambition of the Social Democrats and, equally understandably, stoutly opposed by ministers determined to preserve the Bismarckian Reich. But far more was wrong with the inherited system than that. The cherished independence of the army meant that foreign and military policy could easily be headed in differing directions; even on the civil side officials in one part of government remained in utter ignorance of what officials in another part were doing, at a time when marching clear-eyed and in step was vital. That this ramshackle machine was incapable of meeting the demands thrust upon it by events was nevertheless not evident to the men who ran it. Indeed many of them had looked forward to Bismarck's disappearance, confident that the system could produce more consistent policy than they found in his apparent arbitrariness, his cliff-hanging, his sudden twists and turns. "After a quarter century of genius," one of them wrote, "it is a real blessing to be able to be as homely and matter of fact as other governments. Things are decided now in accordance with calculations and argument, and no longer by revelations which do not always emanate from the Holy Spirit. In the great decisive moments of a people's life, genius alone may serve, but in the regular course of affairs it causes confusion and becomes intolerable." [5] But the Bismarckian system could not work without Bismarck or someone very like him, and his successors—with the possible exception of the

---

[5] Paul Kayser, a Bismarck protégé, in 1890, quoted in Gordon A. Craig, *From Bismarck to Adenauer: Aspects of German Statecraft* (Torchbook ed., 1965), 21. The sentiment is not uncommon among lesser men who have lived in the shadow of the great: in 1922, in Britain, Stanley Baldwin was to say that Lloyd George, whose leadership of the predominantly Conservative wartime coalition was being undermined, was a great dynamic force and that a great dynamic force is a terrible thing. And perhaps there is something to it.

upright, able, though inexperienced General Leo von Caprivi, who was chancellor from 1890 to 1894—lacked the qualities that were needed. The senile and ineffectual Hohenlohe, the vain and shallow Bülow, the detached and pessimistic Bethmann Hollweg were all, in their differing ways, inadequate, whether it was a question of mastering events or of checking headstrong subordinates like Holstein or Kiderlin-Wächter in the foreign office, or of standing up to the vanity and impetuousness of William II. What under Bismarck had been masterly opportunism, pursued with infinite patience and resource, had degenerated into fitfulness and irresponsibility.

The End of Victorian England

The Liberal split in 1886 over Irish Home Rule marked the beginning of a Conservative ascendancy that lasted, with one hiatus, for twenty years. The brief interlude of Liberal rule from 1892 to 1895, though inaugurated with a bold set of proposals, in fact produced little. An Irish home rule bill passed the Commons in 1893 but was thrown out in the overwhelmingly Conservative House of Lords; the next year, his sensibilities outstripped by newer forms of liberalism, Gladstone retired, leaving his party to face a bitter internal struggle. He, like Bismarck, had trained no successor, and Joseph Chamberlain, in the eighties the most likely heir, had led the defectors over Home Rule in 1886 (see p. 821). Lord Rosebery, Gladstone's last foreign secretary, served out the government's days as prime minister, leaning to the Right and pursuing an imperialist policy not easily distinguishable from that of the Tories. Lord Salisbury, who dominated British political life from 1886 until his retirement in 1902, had made his political debut in the sixties by opposing Disraeli's opportunism and what seemed to him, as to others of his stamp, the treachery of the Second Reform Act. Intelligent, devout, aloof, Salisbury found his main preoccupation after 1886 in foreign affairs, a field in which he was technically expert. But even there he was skeptical about the future and seemed at best to be fighting a holding action;[6] what domestic reforming there was came from his nephew A. J. Balfour, whose policy of financial support for land purchase by Irish peasants went far toward solving the Irish question for a time, and from that frustrated former Liberal, Joseph Chamberlain, whose legislative monument was a workmen's compensation act in 1897.

In 1901 Queen Victoria—aged, stuffy, difficult, and beloved—died. The gaiety and the sometimes raffish conduct of the future Edward VII, while he was Prince of Wales, had been something of an embarrassment to his mother; his reign, though brief, fixed the adjective Edwardian indelibly. Its connotations— a certain elegance and opulence and a confident stance toward the world—are

---

[6] He is said to have much enjoyed the remark of the Chinese ambassador who said that he spoke as the representative of one declining empire to another.

true enough, marred though they were by the breaking of one foreign crisis after another and by mounting domestic turmoil. Balfour, who became prime minister in 1902, was a philosopher by training; he shared his uncle's cynicism and aloofness but was less able to command respect and subordination from his followers. Although the "Khaki election" of 1900, at the height of the Boer War, had given the government a comfortable majority, fate and miscalculation steadily undermined it. Trade unionists were appalled by the Taff Vale decision (see p. 859), and nearly all workingmen were hurt by the downturn in real wages in the new, more inflationary prosperity after 1896; a nascent Labour party as well as the Liberals stood to profit by their discontent. Those old allies of the Liberals, the Dissenters, were outraged by the government's major education bill in 1902, an expertly drafted compromise that gave the country state-supported secondary schools but that seemed to non-Anglicans to perpetuate the privileges of the established church; a bill intended to promote temperance by compensating proprietors of public houses for revocation of their licenses seemed to the more straitlaced a proposal to endow sin. Humanitarians were shocked by the horrors of the concentration camps of the Boer War and once again in 1905 by revelations that South African industrialists were importing Chinese coolie laborers and keeping them in degrading conditions that skirted slavery. The greatest Tory offense was Chamberlain's effort in 1904 to revive tariffs and to introduce a scheme of imperial preference. Balfour resigned in December 1905, giving way to a Liberal government that early in the new year turned all these grievances to advantage and won a sweeping electoral victory.

The Liberal task, it has been said, was making majorities out of minorities. That problem was reflected in the makeup of the cabinet. Sir Henry Campbell-Bannerman, the able victor in the struggle for the Liberal leadership that followed Gladstone's retirement, presided over a collection of Liberal Imperialists, Gladstonians, Nonconformists, a renegade Tory, and one genuine workingman, John Burns, who had long since forsaken socialism for a right-wing liberalism. The Liberal Imperialists got the lion's share of important posts: Sir Edward Grey at the Foreign Office, R. B. Haldane at the War Office, H. H. Asquith at the Exchequer. When Campbell-Bannerman retired to die in 1908, Asquith succeeded him, and the Exchequer was taken by the fiery Welsh Nonconformist David Lloyd George, a brilliant orator of unimpeachable radicalism and a superb political tactician; Lloyd George's place at the Board of Trade was taken by the former Tory, the young Winston Churchill. The son of Lord Randolph Churchill, Lord Salisbury's bête noire and leader of the Tory Democrats in the eighties, Winston Churchill had seen service in India and had been a war correspondent in South Africa; newly converted to Liberalism, he was Lloyd George's major lieutenant and competitor in introducing social reforms.

Now, after thirty years of relative quiescence, the British were once more exposed to a flurry of reforming legislation. Between 1906 and 1911 Parliament counteracted the Taff Vale decision, provided aid to children, gave miners the eight-hour day (the first legislative interference with adult male labor), established old age pensions, and set up labor exchanges to ease the getting of jobs and trade boards to regulate the so-called sweated trades, like tailoring and cigar-making, that had escaped the factory acts. In 1911 a comprehensive scheme of unemployment and health insurance (based on the Bismarckian model) was implemented, and in 1913, as a last reforming gasp, a minimum wage act for miners was passed. That all this was done and that, for the most part, it proved acceptable is testimony to the strength of the British tradition of humanitarian reform, to the sensitivity of Parliament to public opinion, and to the expertise of the civil service. But not everything that was tried succeeded. It was clear from the outset that the upper house (which Lloyd George dubbed "Mr. Balfour's poodle") would never agree to the crucial Liberal pledges to introduce Home Rule in Ireland or to disestablish the Anglican church in Wales. The Lords dared not antagonize labor and allowed the Trade Disputes Act to pass, but they rejected an education bill and a temperance bill. Moreover, the reforms cost money, and money was needed in still greater amounts for the rapidly rising expense of the arms race, above all for the naval competition with Germany. In 1909 Lloyd George introduced a budget calling for some novel taxes on land that today seem tame but that then looked confiscatory. The Lords rebelled, rejected the budget, and thus raised a major constitutional issue over control of finance and renewed an old competition between the two houses. The result was a bill in 1910 to remove the Lords' veto over legislation by providing that a bill rejected by the Lords could become law if passed by the Commons three times within two years; not even this delay was necessary for a bill that the Speaker certified as financial legislation. The Lords, as expected, refused to pass the bill, and a general election followed. Sentiment in the country was divided. The Liberal majority was cut almost to a level with the Conservatives, the balance in the house being held by eighty-two Irish nationalists and the forty Labour members, up from the twenty-nine of 1906. The budget was passed, but in the meantime King Edward had died and the new king, his son George V, insisted on another election before he would agree to the drastic step of creating new peers (perhaps as many as five hundred) to carry the Parliament bill through a hostile House of Lords. The results of the second election were almost exactly the same. The reintroduction of the Parliament bill in January 1911 brought a revolt of Conservative "diehards" and the descent on the Lords of a horde of "backwoodsmen"—Tory noblemen who rarely or never attended their house but who now flocked to save the prerogatives of their order—and only a last-minute show of statesmanship on the part of the Conservative leadership brought the upper house around to accepting the fate the Liberal government had determined upon.

This long crisis was marked by an unexampled display of obstructionism and verbal violence by Conservatives in both houses of Parliament—Asquith called it the "new style"—and it was matched by Lloyd George's bitter campaign in the country against the peers. These breaches of the essential conventions of parliamentary government led some men to ponder the fate of the country's basically liberal institutions. It was a question worth asking, for old assumptions were under constant attack in the years between 1910 and 1914. The demand for votes for women had been quietly mounted, with some success, since the middle of the preceding century: women were allowed to vote for school boards in 1870 and, by the end of the century, for local government officials. But barriers to the parliamentary franchise did not fall so easily. Constitutionalist tactics were deemed insufficient by the militant "suffragettes," led by Mrs. Emmeline Pankhurst and her two daughters Sylvia and Christabel.[7] Militant women marched, invaded the Houses of Parliament, chained themselves to fences, smashed windows, slashed paintings, set fire to mailboxes, and got a martyr when one young woman threw herself under the king's horse during the Derby at Epsom. Imprisoned, the Pankhursts and their allies went on hunger strikes, to which the government responded by permitting forcible feeding and by a grim piece of legislation, the "Cat and Mouse Act," which allowed weakened prisoners to be released and arrested again after their recovery.

A new militancy appeared as well in the trade unions. The "new unionists" had earlier rebelled against the respectable lib-labism of an older generation of workingmen (see p. 859). In the prewar years that militant socialism was reinforced by a modified syndicalism, imported to some extent from Australia, inspired in part by Continental example, and stemming as well from impatience with ordinary processes of law and by determination to defeat the growing resistance among employers. The great strikes of the railwaymen and miners failed but the dockers succeeded, and these three huge unions saw in unity the key to a wider victory. In December 1913 an industrial Triple Alliance was negotiated. Rejecting the old piecemeal opportunism, the workers planned a general strike to win a national minimum wage.

Finally there was Ireland. When Home Rule first loomed in the 1880s, Lord Randolph Churchill had threatened "to play the Orange card," that is, to use the Protestants in the northern Irish province of Ulster to defeat Catholic Irish claims to autonomy and so to preserve the empire. This was what the Tories, smarting from their defeat over the Parliament bill, did, as the third Home Rule bill made its way toward certain passage, now that the Lords could only delay but not defeat it. The generous and remarkably effective land acts of the Conservative governments had not, after all, "killed home rule with kindness," and the newly militant Irish nationalism was met by a fervent resistance from Ulstermen and their English supporters. Both sides raised private armies called

---

[7] It has been said of Mrs. Pankhurst that "it is not known . . . that she ever proposed to spend her widowhood behind any scene, if there was the slightest chance of getting in front of it"; George Dangerfield, *The Strange Death of Liberal England* (1936), 144, altogether a brilliant discussion of these troubling years.

Volunteers, both sides smuggled arms; on one occasion a Dublin mob, pursuing the soldiers who had attempted to apprehend some Catholic gunrunners, was fired upon—the "Bachelor's Walk Massacre" left three dead, thirty-eight injured, and a new fund of bitterness. The Tory leaders—Andrew Bonar Law and Walter Long (Balfour had been forced out in 1911)—pledged defiance of government and Parliament; in return Lloyd George and Churchill threatened coercion; senior army officers announced that they would refuse to serve in any action against Ulster. These threats of civil war and mutiny and this show of contempt for parliamentary processes were the more alarming when seen against a background of international tension of the gravest sort. The climax came in 1914. In June the Triple Alliance drew up its strike plans for December, and ministers promised a women's suffrage bill; in September the Home Rule bill became law. But by that time Britain was at war. The general strike did not materialize; the Home Rule bill was shelved for the duration; John Redmond, the Irish leader in the Commons, offered his country's support; and Tory rebels and militant women outdid each other in shows of patriotism.

The Crisis of Imperial Russia

Alexander III died toward the end of October 1894. The coronation of his son Nicholas II was held in mid-May 1896. In a field near Moscow half a million of his subjects had gathered for the customary distribution of gifts; badly controlled, the crowd panicked and nearly thirteen hundred people were killed in the crush and hundreds more injured. That evening the emperor and his tsarina went to a ball at the French embassy as though nothing had happened. Later, after an investigation, a police official was dismissed. In retrospect, the portent seems almost as terrible as the event itself. The autocracy was reincarnated in a new monarch, and the Romanov tradition of opulent splendor seemed more anachronistic than ever, divorced as it was from the awful reality of the deepening social crisis.

The new tsar was unintelligent, ill-educated, selfish, and weak. The chief influence on him in the first half of his reign was K. B. Pobedonostsev, the chief procurator of the Holy Synod, who had served Alexander III; then the tsar fell increasingly under the influence of his wife, a granddaughter of Queen Victoria, Princess Alice of Hesse-Darmstadt, or Alexandra Fedorovna, as she was known after her conversion to Orthodoxy. Ailing and impressionable and the mother of a hemophiliac child, the empress was prey to hysteria and the most baleful superstition. With two such guides, Nicholas was confirmed in all his prejudices—he was as anti-Semitic as his father and had a tragically exaggerated sense of Russia's civilizing mission to the East—and was strengthened in his determination to retain autocracy whole. Not only was there no legislature, there was no chancellor or prime minister. Jealousy and undercutting were rife among the ministers. Success was no guarantee of permanence—there was little agreement on what constituted success or failure, salvation or threat—and the last man to get the tsar's ear would, for the moment, be the victor.

Nicholas inherited from his father an alliance with the French, formally concluded in 1894. The diplomatic ties confirmed another linkage with the French—commercial and financial—that had been growing for some years. The capital that flowed eastward from France, and to a lesser degree from other countries, was put to work by a remarkable minister, Sergei Witte. He was of German or Dutch extraction but had been brought up as a Russian. He brought to the task of maintaining the autocracy a dedication to modernization and a degree of efficiency and persistence matched by no other tsarist minister since Speransky. Schooled as a mathematician, Witte got his early training in railway management, and when he entered the government in 1889, it was in the railway department of the ministry of finance. In 1892 he became minister of communications, charged with planning the Trans-Siberian Railway, and later in the same year he was named minister of finance, a post he held for the next eleven years. Under his supervision the railway network increased by nearly half, and the number of foreign firms doing business in the empire shot up from 16 in 1888 to 269 in 1900. The new, highly efficient metallurgical industries of the Ukraine put Russia fourth in world production of pig iron, ahead of France, and fifth in steel. Soviet calculations show the total industrial production in the eleven years of Witte's tenure of the finance ministry (using production in 1913 as the base of 100) rising from 31 to almost 64. It was done by good management, high tariffs, heavy taxes, huge exports of grain, a resolute move to the gold standard in 1897, and, above all, the deployment of foreign resources—loans, investment, and skill.

The miracle was not without its shadows. Russian agriculture felt only the burdens, not the benefits, of industrial expansion. Conditions among the industrial workers were wretched and little helped by weak protective legislation dating from the 1880s or even by the fairly extensive laws Witte enacted in 1897. There were trade unions and strikes, though both were illegal; they were responding to the recession that set in after 1900 as well as to the manner in which industrialization was brought about. Moreover, Witte and his policy inspired opposition in high places. To some of his enemies, industrialization itself was hateful, a corrupting Western novelty that threatened Russian ways—and the mounting social tension seemed to bear out the prejudice. Others resented Witte as an upstart who had, moreover, taken a Jewish wife; and his opposition to aggressive expansionism in East Asia brought him still more hatred. The tsar was convinced, and in August 1903 Witte was dismissed by being kicked upstairs.

Witte was a reformer but not a liberal. Liberalism was, however, striking roots in a small but influential segment of society. To some extent it was of native growth, the natural but repeatedly rejected demand of the local assemblies, the zemstvos, for completion of the legislative pyramid by a national assembly, a Duma. To this older tradition were added liberal ideas of more obviously Western inspiration, whose most prominent spokesmen were the distinguished historian Paul Miliukov and a recent convert from Marxism, Peter Struve. But others could see no possibility of salvation for Russia in anything short of revolution. We have already encountered the Marxism of the Social Democrats, who in their exile fell out over the vexed question of revisionism and split into the Bolshevik and Menshevik factions, with Lenin heading the former (see p. 863). By 1901 the Socialist Revolutionaries had surfaced within Russia. More closely tied to the peasants than to the industrial workers favored by the Social Democrats, they also had great appeal for the students who kept the universities in turmoil. Reviving populism and maintaining links with the apostles of anarchism, the Socialist Revolutionaries turned to violence and terror as their weapons against the hated autocracy. It is against this background of irreconcilable division that one must view the disasters of the Russo-Japanese War.

Russian interest in the Far East had increased in intensity in the nineties, encountering equally ambitious thrusts by the Japanese. In 1894 the Japanese had defeated the Chinese in a war; in the settlement that followed, Korea, Japan's natural staging area for penetration of the mainland, was made independent of Chinese suzerainty, and Japan was ceded Formosa, the Pescadore Islands, and the Liaotung peninsula, a southward extension of Manchuria that ended at the warm-water harbor of Port Arthur. Pressure from Russia, France, and Germany forced Japan to give up the Liaotung peninsula, to which the Russians soon secured a lease, in order to continue the railway imperialism that had already brought Manchuria substantially under Russian control, control that became virtual occupation after the anti-Western Boxer Rebellion in China in 1900. The Japanese, though outraged by Russian duplicity, tried patiently to negotiate the issues. In 1902 the makers of Russian foreign policy, as ever unpredictable, allowed a forward move into Korea under the guise of a commercial operation by the Yalu Company. Witte, whose interest in railways had made the earlier Eastern ventures seem appealing, had drawn back from these extreme steps—he said later that he had only wanted to take his friends to the aquarium, but they had got drunk, ended up in a brothel, and started a ruckus.[8] But he was rapidly losing influence, and St. Petersburg remained confident that Japan would not chance a fight. Its patience exhausted, Japan did just that, without a formal declaration of war, by attacking Russian warships at Port Arthur on February 9, 1904.

In every respect the war was a disaster for Russia. On land Russian forces were slowly driven out of Port Arthur and the Liaotung peninsula and severely punished in the major, bloody battle of Mukden in late February and early March 1905. The Pacific fleet suffered one misfortune after another. The Black

---

[8] Theodore H. Von Laue, *Sergei Witte and the Industrialization of Russia* (Atheneum paperback ed., 1969), 242.

Sea fleet was bottled up by the Straits Convention of 1841, which forbade the passage of the Bosporus and the Dardanelles when Russia was at war, and the Baltic fleet, which had slowly to make its way around Europe, Africa, and Asia,[9] was virtually destroyed in the battle of Tsushima Strait in May 1905. Hampered by long lines of communication and by the inadequacy of the still incomplete Trans-Siberian Railway for heavy wartime demands, Russian reinforcement in the East was difficult. Worse, the crescendo of protest and violence at home made peace imperative. The two powers accepted the mediation of President Theodore Roosevelt; Witte was called out of retirement as the Russian negotiator of the treaty concluded at Portsmouth, New Hampshire, in August. Russia came out well, though fervent Russian nationalists thought not: no indemnity was imposed, and Russia had merely to give up the Liaotung peninsula and cede the southern half of Sakhalin Island, which had been used as a prison camp. But the war was of surpassing importance in world history as the first defeat of a Western power by a non-Western power and as a revelation of the essential weakness of the Russian military colossus.

Within Russia the years after 1900 had seen the spread of disturbances in the countryside and a mounting campaign of terrorism in the cities, sparked chiefly by the Socialist Revolutionaries; in July 1904 the reactionary minister of the interior, V. K. Plehve, was assassinated.[10] The Liberals, whose demands Plehve had consistently rejected, differed in their views of the war, but they were agreed that fundamental reforms were needed and that a constitution must be secured. In November 1904, in self-conscious imitation of the French opposition in 1847 (see p. 716), they organized a series of banquets to agitate for change. Events took a more savage turn on January 22, 1905—"Bloody Sunday"—when a throng of workingmen, led by a priest and carrying icons and the tsar's portrait, marched to the square before the Winter Palace in St. Petersburg to present a petition for reform. The troops fired on the crowd, and over a hundred were killed and many hundreds more injured. Following strikes in the capital and elsewhere, the tsar agreed in February to an elected consultative assembly, but the promise, when made public in August, satisfied neither the increasingly vocal zemstvo movement nor other groups who advocated more radical solutions. Meanwhile, peasant violence grew, mutinies occurred in the forces—the most famous being the mutiny aboard the battleship *Potemkin* at Odessa in June—the universities were in tumult, and

[9] In passing through the North Sea, the fleet fired on some British fishing vessels, under the extraordinary impression that they might be Japanese. The Dogger Bank incident was one of the many trials of patience that lent so dismal an aspect to the international history of the early twentieth century.

[10] Symptomatic of the complexity of the situation was the Socialist Revolutionary leader Y. F. Azeff. Deeply implicated in the terrorism and in planning the assassinations of Plehve and of the tsar's uncle, the Grand Duke Sergei, the following February, he was throughout a police spy, a fact revealed in 1909. It has been suggested that his being Jewish may have justified those actions in his amazing double-dealing that eliminated high officials, like Plehve, who condoned or encouraged pogroms. Richard Charques, *The Twilight of Imperial Russia* (Oxford paperback ed., 1965), 83.

nationalist agitations broke out in the non-Russian provinces. A general strike in October brought the country to a standstill, and, after canvassing the notion of a military dictatorship, the tsar at last sent for Witte, making him in effect prime minister.

On October 30, a manifesto was issued guaranteeing civil liberties, promising a constitution, and sketching out a legislature, a State Duma, that would be elected on a broad franchise and that would have (the hint was vague) some supervisory control over ministers. The October Manifesto split the Liberals into the moderate Octobrists and the more radical, still dissatisfied Constitutional Democratic party, known from the initials of its name as the Kadets. Of the extremist groups, the Socialist Revolutionaries were the most successful: with their principal strength in the peasantry and their terrorist tactics, they had no need to confront the difficult theoretical problems set for the exiled factions of the Social Democrats by the events of 1905. Was this a bourgeois revolution? Could a proletarian and bourgeois revolution occur simultaneously? What attitude should be taken to the peasantry? Rival congresses of Bolsheviks and Mensheviks deliberated; Lenin refined his views on the importance of disciplined party leadership, whatever the sources of support available; and L. D. Bronstein, better known by his revolutionary name of Trotsky, began to formulate his notion of the "permanent revolution," which posited the intimate linkage of bourgeois and proletarian revolutions and the need for socialism in Russia to be secured by revolution elsewhere in Europe. Lenin returned to Russia to pursue his organizational activities after the October Manifesto. Trotsky, who had returned slightly earlier, had become the outstanding leader of the strike council, famous as the St. Petersburg Soviet, that was, until its suppression in December, a virtual alternative government.

By the end of the year the workers had little stomach left for strikes and protest, though their leaders remembered how effective these tactics had been. The last remnants of revolt were put down in December, but dealing with rural disturbances took more time and greater sternness. Official repression was seconded by the brutalities of the counterrevolutionary "Black Hundreds," private gangs whose principal victims were Jews. The Revolution of 1905 was coming to a confused and ugly end. Meanwhile, a new manifesto concerning elections had been issued. The upper chamber of the legislature was to be half appointed and half elected by established institutions—church, zemstvos, universities, and the like—while the lower house was to be chosen under a complex system of indirect suffrage, weighted carefully in favor of the peasants and against the urban workers. In May 1906, just before the Duma met and just after he had negotiated the largest French loan yet, Witte was once more dismissed. A few days later the Fundamental Laws were handed down, a constitution that restricted the powers of the Duma far more than had been allowed for in the October Manifesto and that made it clear that the autocracy would remain untouched; the government's bad faith was made transparent. When the Duma met on May 10, dominated by the Kadets, the feeling of betrayal and the fierce criticism it engendered led to deadlock and dissolution in July. The Second Duma met briefly in the spring of 1907, with similar results because, while the sharply reduced numbers of Kadets were now willing to cooperate, the revolutionary parties, which had officially boycotted the First Duma, made constructive action impossible. The Third Duma, which assembled in 1907, was elected under a new, far more conservative electoral system dominated by the propertied classes at the expense of peasants, workers, and restive nationalities; tame but not servile, it lasted its full five years.

Despite the persistence of the deep-seated social crisis, the period of the Third Duma was one of relative calm, assured by resolute suppression of all revolutionary activity. Though protest was driven underground or abroad, the country was not frozen in immobility. From the end of 1906 the prime minister was P. A. Stolypin, a provincial governor who had become minister of the interior after Witte's dismissal. Authoritarian always and brutal when necessary, Stolypin was nonetheless a reformer in his effort to preserve autocracy. What he did went far toward transforming the face of rural Russia. The Great Reforms (see p. 760) had provided two kinds of tenure—hereditary, in which ownership was vested in an individual household, and repartitional, in which the commune retained title and could periodically regrant land to the constituent families as their size and other considerations dictated. Laws of 1906 and 1910 moved toward converting all landholding into hereditary tenure, cancelled further redemption payments (already reduced under Alexander II), and encouraged the consolidation of strips in common fields into individual farms. By the time of the 1917 revolution perhaps half the peasant families had made the transition to hereditary tenure, nearly two thirds of that number since 1906. Because of the terrible difficulties imposed by geography and habit on a communal system, consolidation—unraveling what G. T. Robinson has called "that minutely patched and quilted aspect" of the countryside—made much less progress. Moreover, by vesting possession in the head of the household rather than the household itself, the family tie was loosened, as was the control of the head of the household and the commune over the comings and goings of their members. But though the rural population gained new mobility, legal distinctions that lasted to the end of the empire kept the peasantry a caste apart. There was a considerable trade in land, to the advantage of the richer and more clever: the reforms were called a "wager on the strong." Still, the growth of separate farms and the employment of wage labor created no very distinct social gulf in rural Russia, for "even among these [peasant] 'capitalists' nearly all were laborers too, in that they still knew the jerk of an unruly plow-handle and the drag of a sackful of grain between the shoulders." [11]

To the industrial impulse given by Witte, which continued its forward course, and to the agrarian reforms of Stolypin were added other liberalizing changes. The limited freedom of association granted in 1906 stimulated,

---

[11] G. T. Robinson, *Rural Russia under the Old Regime* (1932), 242.

without strictly legalizing, trade unions and strikes. While little was done to reform the church, toleration was formally conceded in 1906, and considerable progress was made in providing elementary education at state expense, a tardy recognition of public necessity that markedly raised the level of literacy. But what is to be made of all these moves? In recent years an important and deeply felt debate has taken place, particularly among historians of Russia in the United States, on precisely this head. Was imperial Russia set on a course that, without the catastrophe of World War I, would have led to a constitutional monarchy ruling over a modern, liberal society? Or was the autocracy so entrenched, society so backward, and bitterness so deep that only the drastic surgery of a true revolution could wrench the country into the modern world? It is a quarrel of a kind common enough among historians, a quarrel in which judgments of events and documents in the end differ according to the protagonists' temperaments or their disagreements about fundamental questions, say, the validity of Western-style democracy in the present day. Such differences force refinements of position, reformulation of questions, and the quest for new materials to buttress conflicting interpretations. In this case, however, there are snares—that ever enticing question of what might have happened and that equally unprovable conviction that what happened was inevitable.

The historian on the sidelines can note the main pivots of debate. Unquestionably Russia was making remarkable economic progress against enormous odds. At the same time political institutions remained rudimentary, and the dynasty, unresponsive as ever, was regarded with growing contempt. The threat of violence was constant, from all directions. Stolypin was assassinated (apparently with the connivance of the police) in 1911, and in 1912 brutal repression of a strike in the Lena gold fields in Siberia touched off a new wave of strikes. Dissatisfaction in the urban working class grew, but so did the range and sophistication of its responses. No contemporary could have predicted which party would succeed in the competition for its favor, although he might well have given odds against the Bolsheviks. Perhaps the most striking development, and the one most difficult to extrapolate from, was a marked shift in the concerns of many of the intelligentsia. Moving in the direction that Struve and others had urged in a celebrated and bitterly attacked manifesto in 1909, these intellectuals turned away from the nineteenth-century insistence on subordinating everything to the task of social renovation. Instead there was pursuit of art for its own sake and some stunningly successful experimentation. The poetry of Alexander Blok, the painting of Marc Chagall and Vassily Kandinsky, the harmonic and rhythmic innovations of Stravinsky, and—perhaps more widely influential than anything else—the creative brilliance of Serge Diaghilev's Ballet Russe (based in Paris but thoroughly Russian) made the last decade of imperial Russia an artistic glory. But, whatever the promise of all these changes, one ends with a brute fact: Russia was defeated in the Great War and could not survive the catastrophe.

THE ATMOSPHERE OF CRISIS

For Peace and War

The early years of the twentieth century were marked by what can only be called moral schizophrenia: in no age were the linked causes of peace and international cooperation more zealously pursued, and in no age were war and conflict more passionately praised or more coolly planned for. The nineteenth century had been notable for its cultivation of fraternal relations among like-minded people in different countries. The most famous instances—and among the least successful—were those socialist bodies that arrogated to themselves the name of International. But enthusiasts for all kinds of causes sought out their fellows elsewhere to exchange ideas and encouragement, their way eased by increasing affluence among the educated middle classes and by the speed of travel and communication. This new international community far surpassed the numbers (if not the fame and influence) of the cosmopolitan "family" of the philosophes and seemed likely to supplant the old community of the aristocracy as the principal bond of a European, or European-dominated, world. Much of this contact remained personal and informal, but it was reflected, too, in organizations of greater or lesser degrees of permanence. It has been calculated that, between 1815 and 1900, 164 private international bodies were set up along with 24 intergovernmental organizations; between 1900 and 1914 alone, 304 of the former and 13 of the latter were founded.[12] The complex and growing interdependence of the economy was reflected in intergovernmental organizations to coordinate communications, postal services, transportation, and legal privileges such as copyrights and patents. Scientific and social administration, in agriculture, public health, and labor problems, was rapidly moving to a higher level of generality. Not included in these figures, but quite as important if not more so, were the commercial, banking, and industrial combinations that increasingly transcended frontiers and that weighed far more heavily in the cause of peace than a couple of generations of anti-imperialist polemicists have been willing to allow.

The peace movement itself, a creation of the nineteenth century, reached its peak of positive accomplishment early in the twentieth. The first peace prize was awarded in 1901 under the will of the famous industrial chemist Alfred Nobel, the inventor of dynamite; in 1910 the Carnegie Endowment for International Peace was founded by the Scottish-American steel magnate

---

[12] F. S. L. Lyons, *Internationalism in Europe, 1815–1914* (1963), 14.

whose name it bears. At the intergovernmental level the two Hague conferences of 1899 and 1907 were failures, but modified failures. The first was summoned by Nicholas II; the second, though formally at his bidding, followed from the initiative of the Interparliamentary Union and President Theodore Roosevelt. The first conference set up a permanent court for international arbitration, and both did something to amend the Geneva Convention of 1864 on the laws of war, but the more crucial question of disarmament eluded them both. Still, their very existence was a favorable portent and confirmed the growing belief among many that war could not happen. Others, more realistic, agreed with the English pacifist Norman Angell, who argued in an immensely influential book of 1910 that, if war came, the cost would be so great that there would be no victors; war was indeed *The Great Illusion.*

At the same time Europe was plunged into a spiraling arms race that both reflected and fed a spreading militarism; in every country it ran far beyond professional military circles. To some extent the arms race was the result of technological developments and the quickening pace of obsolescence, points of especial concern to the professionals and the manufacturers of armaments. These vested interests were frequently seconded by narrowly based but powerfully focused individual visions and ambitions. No better example can be found than the competitive building of capital ships by Germany and Britain, to some extent a contest between the two masterful men who dominated the naval establishments in the two countries, Admiral Alfred von Tirpitz and Admiral Sir John Fisher, while the theoretical writings of the American admiral Alfred T. Mahan were as influential in determining views on naval strategy as the writings of Karl von Clausewitz (see p. 527n) in the early nineteenth century had been for war on land. Tirpitz turned every device of persuasion and propaganda, official and unofficial, to build a fleet large enough to deter any hostile British action, while the British, under Fisher's constant prodding, grew increasingly determined to maintain the long margin of superiority on which, traditionally, they believed their security depended. From 1898 through 1912 naval laws in the two countries underwrote the competition, a contest that from 1906 was seen primarily in terms of the all-heavy-gun battleship. The *Dreadnought* launched in that year gave its name to the type, but the battleship continued to grow in size, speed, and armament. To lay down the keels of two or four of these monsters each year, to attain a certain numerical proportion by 1914 or 1917 as current technical analysis dictated meant a frightful strain on already overburdened budgetary resources in both countries, yet taxpayers and their parliamentary representatives were willing and sporadic conversations about reductions in the programs got nowhere.

A similar competition, similarly supported, took place among armies. The German military successes of Bismarck's early years were, as we have seen (see p. 620), a stimulus to increased professionalism elsewhere, symbolized in the spread of the institution of the general staff. In many regards the German general staff still stood preeminent, though in retrospect its independence of political control and often its innocence of historical or political considerations appear tragic. The Schlieffen plan, completed in 1905 by the then chief of the general staff, was its ultimate accomplishment—a closely blinkered scheme to assure a massive and rapid total victory over France on the western front by invasion through Belgium. But staff plans in other countries pursued similar calculations, determined by geography, technology, and projections based on seemingly fixed diplomatic and military alliances. The independence of the German military establishment, though bedeviled by internal structural defects, was reinforced in the last decades of the nineteenth century by a growing sense of solidarity and mission among the officers, a feeling transmitted to those officers who were beginning to come from the middle classes, and beyond them to the country at large. In Britain, where the fear of a standing army was traditional, a figure like Lord Roberts, victor in Afghanistan and in South Africa, could become a national hero and turn his position to propaganda advantage; even in France, where the army had sadly compromised itself in the Dreyfus case, the early twentieth century saw a rise in the military spirit. Alarmist politicians helped to instill fear of the future enemy, as did a variety of popular novels depicting invasions and heroic resistance; so did misfortunes like the publication of a plan for a preventive war concocted by a former German general staff officer, General Bernhardi. Every major European country except Britain resorted to conscription and proved willing to lengthen terms of service as need dictated, while in Britain the Liberals' war minister, R. B. Haldane, undertook sweeping military reforms to enable Britain to field an expeditionary force on the Continent in support of France, thus abandoning the traditionally limited British role of naval support and financial subsidy.

A New Alignment

The external protection of Bismarck's Germany came from a superbly engineered set of diplomatic understandings (see p. 795). From Canning to Salisbury, Britain had sought protection only in the surrounding seas. But this cautious and economical intention did not prevent Britain's being dragged more and more deeply into worldwide involvements, which reached a dismal climax in the Boer War. That war, during which Britain was almost universally excoriated by its European critics, made it painfully evident that a continuation of "splendid isolation" was a dangerous illusion, once the isolation was no longer a matter of Britain's choice but of a quarantine by other countries. Britain therefore began to seek understandings or even alliances that could buttress its position in a world it no longer dominated. In 1902 an outright alliance was negotiated with Japan, an expansionist power whose interests at that time ran more or less parallel to Britain's: it was agreed that each power would come to the other's aid in case of war with two countries. But that provision was not immediately important. There were commercial advantages for both sides and, at least until the treaty was revised in 1905, there was some usefulness in a common anti-Russian front and in the rhetorical show of respect for the territorial integrity of China, where the European imperialist powers were scrambling for concessions. The treaty was more important for Japan than for Britain, however. After the humiliation of being deprived of some of its gains in 1895, Japan was now allied with the greatest power in the world and had reached great-power status itself.

More important for Britain in the long run was the protracted accommodation reached with the United States, the one country where any open sympathy had been shown for the British in South Africa—hardly surprising in view of American efforts at the time to realize "manifest destiny" in the Caribbean and the Pacific. The patient cultivation of transatlantic ties over the past half-century was bearing fruit. The English, for their part, were showing less condescension toward Americans, and many Americans, at least among the wealthy and the educated, were abandoning a touchy provincialism for anglophilia. British aristocrats repaired their fortunes by choosing American heiresses as brides, and the scholarships at Oxford established by the will of Cecil Rhodes helped to cement the notion of a worldwide English-speaking community. Despite the necessary sensitivity of American politicians to persistent popular anglophobia, particularly among Irish immigrants, a number of outstanding disputes between the two countries—some of them squabbles of venerable lineage—were quickly settled. The foundation was thus laid for the "special relationship" that has been one of the diplomatic cornerstones of the twentieth century.

Gradually, over perhaps ten years, it dawned on British statesmen and on the British public that the most likely potential enemy was not France but Germany. German economic competition had been strikingly brought home to the man in the street by a mildly protectionist act in 1887 requiring all imported goods to be labeled with the country of origin. What thus appeared a sudden flooding of the British market with German manufactures was in fact an index of the natural propensity of a prosperous country to import more and more goods. But a famous book, *Made in Germany*, published in 1896, converted a healthy symptom into an alarm. The telegram William II sent in support of the Boer president Kruger at the time of the Jameson Raid (see p. 846) was a piece of bluster that might have been absorbed; indeed to some extent it was by the emperor's own mollifying statements—Berlin jokesters liked to say that the emperor feared only God and his grandmother Queen Victoria. But a number of efforts at common action by the two powers—to collect debts in Venezuela or to assure mutual interests in China—somehow ended in misunderstanding and popular hostility. And from 1898 on there was the steady, escalating challenge of Germany's naval ambitions. As memories of the confrontation at Fashoda paled (see p. 847), it seemed wise for France and England to submerge their differences in the face of a potential threat from Germany. The way having been smoothed by an exchange of visits in 1903 between King Edward and President Loubet, a formal agreement was reached and signed on April 8, 1904. Hard bargaining settled a number of minor disputes, but the principal step was the exchange of French recognition of British paramountcy in Egypt (a French grievance since 1882) for British acquiescence in a French sphere of influence in Morocco, a concession strengthened in secret provisions that envisioned a future partition of Morocco between France and Spain. This was not quite an alliance, but a cordial understanding, an *entente cordiale;* nevertheless, from 1906 strategic talks were taking place between French and British military authorities.

Meanwhile Germany's alliances were in disrepair, to say the least. The Reinsurance Treaty with Russia had been allowed to lapse as soon as Bismarck disappeared from the scene in 1890. The Triple Alliance was only solidly an alliance of Germany and Austria-Hungary, for Italy was not bound tightly to a promise to aid Germany. [13] Thus the unthinkable resolution of Franco-British hostility came as a rude shock to Germany, whose policy-makers were already worried by the steadily closer involvement of France with Russia. While from time to time the Germans attempted to mend fences with both Russia and Britain, the course they took immediately after 1904 by way of protesting the Franco-British understanding boomeranged. It was decided to insist on protection for German interests in Morocco (such as they were) and to use this pretext to strengthen resistance among the Moroccans to the looming French control; to this end, much against his will, the emperor was sent on a formal visit to Tangier at the conclusion of his annual Mediterranean cruise in March 1905. Inflated by Moroccan enthusiasm and French touchiness into a major incident, the Kaiser's visit was followed by German insistence on an international conference to consider the status of Morocco. When the French attempted to reopen talks with Germany, the Germans refused to have anything to do with Théophile Delcassé, the foreign minister who had negotiated the Entente Cordiale, and Delcassé was sacrificed by his new, inexperienced premier Maurice Rouvier. But this apparent victory for Germany turned to defeat at the Algeciras Conference, held at a small village in southern Spain from January to April 1906. The actions agreed to, after considerable stalemate, were unimportant; the reduction of tension was perhaps accomplishment enough. But the course of the conference had demonstrated the isolation and distrust that Germany had brought upon itself by its inconstant and blustering behavior. Not only was Germany thus rudely educated, but the Entente Cordiale became yet closer and Britain opened talks with the Russians.

In patient negotiations between June 1906 and August 1907, diplomats from the two countries worked out a convention to settle conflicts that had continually flickered around the borders of Britain's crucial base in India. It was agreed that Tibet would remain under Chinese suzerainty, free from Russian or British intervention; that Afghanistan would remain independent though

[13] There is, alas, no adjectival form for two and a half.

recognized as a British sphere of influence; and that Persia—where the competition was warmest—would be divided into three zones, the southern under British and the northern under Russian influence, while the central zone was to be open to penetration by both powers. This almost too obviously limited agreement did not work very well, but despite protestations to the contrary, it was evident to everyone that it went a considerable distance toward insulating Russia from further understandings with Germany.

Still, those in command in Germany seemed not to learn. In 1908 William II granted an interview to the London *Daily Telegraph,* in which he talked openly and foolishly about German popular anglophobia and praised himself as Britain's only friend during the Boer War. This amazing piece of nonsense was cleared as to the factual accuracy of its statements by the German foreign office and the chancellor, Bülow, with no one apparently giving thought to the possible political effect. The interview caused more annoyance against Germany in Britain than anything since the Kruger telegram, and there was a corresponding outrage in Germany; in the end, despite a brilliant feat of self-justification, Bülow was forced to retire. The naval race entered a new phase of intensity at about the same time. And in 1911 Germany provoked yet another Moroccan crisis. A rebellion there had led to French and Spanish occupation of coastal regions, and, as it was clear that this would lead to complete occupation by the two Latin powers, Germany decided to insist on compensation, something the French were happy enough to discuss. But Germany astonished Europe, first by dispatching the gunboat *Panther* to the western Moroccan port of Agadir—a peculiarly threatening bargaining counter—and then by demanding the whole of the French Congo, something the French had no intention of yielding.

The British, greatly alarmed by the German show of belligerency, demanded reassurance about Germany's intentions and a part in whatever negotiations might affect Moroccan territory. But before the German foreign office could reply, Lloyd George delivered a stinging speech at the Mansion House in the City of London. He warned against a circumstance in which the only price of peace might be the "surrender of the great and beneficent position Britain has won by centuries of heroism and achievement" or by allowing Britain to be treated "as if she were of no account in the Cabinet of Nations"; such a price, he insisted, "would be a humiliation intolerable for a great country like ours to endure." [14] Talk of war swept through both countries. And while Asquith muttered mollifying words, Germany backed down. The compensation arrangement was negotiated with France, which in fact got its protectorate over Morocco, and the *Panther* was quietly withdrawn.

An upsurge of critical feeling in Britain over the narrow escape led, in early February 1912, to the Haldane mission to Berlin. Lord Haldane, formerly the

---

[14] It is only fair to say, since we are dealing with a consummate politician, that Lloyd George's alarmism was a factor in settling the national railway strike then crippling Britain.

minister of war and now lord chancellor, was an admirable choice; a philosopher as well as a lawyer, he had once acknowledged Germany as his "spiritual home"—a remark turned unfairly against him during the war. But, although the talks seemed to go well, Germany was willing to offer only minor modifications of its naval building program, while demanding in return wide colonial concessions and an assurance of British neutrality that would mean the destruction of the Entente. Thus, while Anglo-German negotiations continued on minor points for the next two years, from 1912 the Entente with France came closer to being an alliance. Although the British formally reserved some freedom of choice in the event of war, the secret naval talks that went on from late summer 1912 were cutting back British options. The crucial decision was that the British fleet would be concentrated in the Channel and North Sea, while the Mediterranean—also of major concern to the British—would become the responsibility of the French navy; the British thus took on a virtual moral commitment to defend France, whatever the circumstances, if France were threatened by Germany. Meanwhile France was drawing yet closer to Russia. At the beginning of 1912 Raymond Poincaré became the French premier; a year later he was elected president, a post that had ordinarily gone to a politically safe nonentity. That Poincaré was not. A lawyer from Lorraine, he was more fervently anti-German than his predecessors. He not only defined the relationship with Russia more broadly, but in 1914 he persuaded the British to enter into staff talks with the Russians and to disclose to them the nature of the Franco-British tie. There was some reason for German statesmen to feel encircled, though what they suspected was worse than the actuality.

The Powder Keg of Europe

Although the alliance system operated to bring the Great Powers into war in 1914, the crisis out of which that war came did not lie in that system itself or in the military and naval competition or in the clash of economic and colonial interests. The crisis was a Balkan crisis, resulting from the decay of the Ottoman and the Hapsburg empires, and inevitably engaging Russian interests. For several years around the turn of the century Russia and Austria-Hungary had worked in diplomatic tandem. The cooperation was shaken in 1903 when a bloody coup in Belgrade brought the Karageorgević dynasty back to the Serbian throne in place of the Obrenović kings; Serbia thereafter became more activist in supporting the cause of Serbs outside its own borders and looked to Russia for support. In 1906 two new appointments in Vienna signified a stiffening of Austrian resolve: Count Alois von Aehrenthal was named foreign minister, and the bellicose General Conrad von Hötzendorff became chief of staff. Both men were determined to stem the decline of Austrian prestige, and nothing seemed to threaten that prestige more than Serbian truculence and ambition.

Aehrenthal made his bold move in a curious and ill-fated collaboration with the Russian foreign minister Alexander Izvolski. The two men met secretly in mid-September 1908 and agreed that Austria would support a Russian request for an alteration of the Straits agreement of 1841 so as to allow Russian warships to enter the Mediterranean; in return the Russians would support Austria's annexation of the territories of Bosnia and Herzegovina, still nominally Turkish but administered by Austria-Hungary since 1878. Austria's proposal was dictated in part by the fact that these territories lay to the west and northwest of Serbia, which would thus be preempted from annexing them should it move toward creating an independent South Slav kingdom. The status of these territories had also been given some urgency when a revolution took place in the Ottoman Empire in the early summer of 1908 under the aegis of the "Young Turks," a group of Westernized army officers eager to regenerate their country. They forced the sultan to restore the constitution of 1876, which had survived for only a year, and it seemed possible that Turkey itself might reassert its rights in Bosnia and Herzegovina and insist that the territories send representatives to the parliament in Constantinople. The meeting with Aehrenthal over, Izvolski headed west to win support from the other Great Powers for his goals at the Straits, only to run into indifference in Paris and hostility in London. But while the Russian project came to nothing, Aehrenthal proclaimed the annexation of Bosnia and Herzegovina, at the same time that the autonomous principality of Bulgaria declared its independence of the Ottoman Empire and its transformation into a kingdom.

Austria's unilateral act outraged the Western powers, which could, however, do nothing to alter it; Turkey, though offended, was bought off the next year by an indemnity. To the furious Serbian reaction the Austrians responded by a demand that the agitation cease, a demand they were willing to back up with force. Serbia could act only with Russian support, and Russia was unprepared to risk a war so soon after the disasters of 1904–1905. Considerably embarrassed, the Russian government disavowed Izvolski's action, and Germany sent a stern demand to Russia insisting on an unequivocal acceptance of the annexation. Russia agreed, and Serbia had to give Austria the required guarantees. But the hostility to the Hapsburg Empire grew and festered among the Serbs. Germany's willingness to support Austria-Hungary, its one dependable ally, whatever the international morality of that ally's action, was perhaps the most alarming aspect of the crisis. Bismarck had once said that the Balkans were not worth the bones of a single Pomeranian grenadier. But France and Britain, discouraged by Ottoman inability to reform, had gradually withdrawn from their traditional involvement with that empire, and Germany had filled the vacuum. Now, through support of Austria, an ally gravely threatened by the breakup of the Ottoman Empire, Germany was drawn still further into the Balkan tangle.

The Young Turks, who soon fell out among themselves, proved quite as incapable as earlier sultans of making the Ottoman Empire workable or of protecting Turkish territory from the covetousness of others. As soon as the Agadir crisis was settled, Italy demanded that the new French position in Morocco be paralleled by Italian holdings in Tripoli and Cyrenaica, the colony that came to be called Libya. Italy declared war on the Ottoman Empire at the end of September 1911, seized the North African territories despite stubborn native resistance, captured some strategic islands in the eastern Mediterranean, and bombarded the Dardanelles. This desultory war was brought to an end on October 18, 1912, but on the same day the Balkan League—Serbia, Bulgaria, and Greece—declared war on Turkey, ten days after Montenegro had taken the same step. This Balkan alliance, concocted without help from the Russians, was inspired by the Italian example and by a crescendo of uprisings among the Macedonians and Albanians against their Turkish masters. The Turks managed to stop the Bulgarian armies short of Constantinople, but otherwise the war (known, with some forgetfulness, as the First Balkan War) was a military disaster for them. The peace conference summoned to London in December was faced by more than the usual task of sorting out gains and losses, for Austria had insisted that under no circumstances should Serbia be allowed access to the Adriatic Sea, although the Serbs had already seized the port of Durazzo. Austria's solution was the creation of the new nation of Albania— ethnographically correct, for the Albanians were not Slavs, though the tack was a queer one for Austria, that arch-opponent of national independence, to take. The conference quickly broke down over the Turkish refusal to give up some of the conquered territories demanded by the victors, but more fighting and pressure from the Great Powers ended in Turkish acquiescence. The Treaty of London, signed May 30, 1913, limited Turkey to a toehold on the European continent inland from Constantinople and relieved her of Crete, while the status of Albania and the other islands in the Aegean was left for determination by the powers.

The Balkan allies at once fell out. The original treaty of alliance between Serbia and Bulgaria had been ambiguous on the future of Macedonia; Serbia, denied her outlet to the sea, now wanted more of Macedonia by way of compensation. The Serbs therefore turned on the Bulgarians and were joined by Greece, Rumania, and, surprisingly, Turkey. The Second Balkan War lasted just a month, and the Treaty of Bucharest on August 10, 1913, gave Rumania southern Dobruja on the Black Sea, while most of Bulgarian Macedonia went to Serbia and Greece. By a later treaty Turkey recovered Adrianople, which had been lost to Bulgaria in the Treaty of London a few months before. The two Balkan wars left the area in turmoil. Albania had been created as an independent state at the end of 1912, but its boundaries remained in dispute and the surrounding powers in occupation of parts of it when the greater war broke out in 1914. Bulgaria and Turkey, embittered over the loss of territory, were determined to regain whatever they could by whatever bargains they could strike. Austria was particularly solicitous of the Bulgarians, as a possible counterpoise to Serbian pressure, and Germany increased its influence in

Turkey still more. Early in 1914 a crisis broke over the appointment of a German general, Liman von Sanders, as commander of the Turkish army corps at Constantinople. The Russians could hardly accept such an arrangement. The solution was to promote Liman to inspector general of the Turkish army—a post too grand to allow him to command a corps—and thus to leave him free to do what he was sent to do, modernize and train the Turkish forces.

The worst tensions, however, were those between Austria-Hungary and Serbia. Since 1907 the idea had been bruited about that Serbia might be "the Piedmont of the South Slavs," a notion certain to inflame a particularly tender Austrian memory and to arouse fears about the increasing disaffection of the Slav peoples within the empire, particularly those who were kept from any national expression by Magyar dominance. Frustrated on every front by Austrian machinations, the Serbs grew more and more shrill. On June 28, 1914, that hatred exploded in violence: while visiting Sarajevo in Bosnia, the heir to the Hapsburg throne, Francis Ferdinand, was assassinated, along with his wife, by a young Bosnian fanatic, a member of a secret terrorist organization known as the "Black Hand." Investigation soon showed that the head of Serbian military intelligence had directed the plot and that the existence of the conspiracy was known to the Serbian government, which, however, failed to take steps either to put it down or to warn the Austrians. The choice of victim has its ironies. Francis Ferdinand was deeply disliked, even feared, at home. His uncle, the aged Emperor Francis Joseph, thought the murder a judgment of God on the archduke's unsuitable marriage; others in Vienna viewed the heir apparent with alarm as both a reactionary and an activist; in Hungary he was hated for his dislike of Hungarians and his disapproval of the Compromise of 1867. If any group should have favored him it was the Slavs, because he was something of a federalist, sympathetic to "trialism," that is, to a South Slav unit within the empire analogous to Hungary.

The murder evoked widespread shock abroad and a reaction against Slav fanaticism; hence a victim whose death was welcomed by many of his countrymen, even in the highest circles, could become a convenient pretext for settling accounts with Serbia for good. Count Stephen Tisza, the Hungarian premier, opposed war at first and was brought round only by an assurance that no Serbian territory would be annexed. It was partly to help convince Tisza but also to ensure German backing in case of open conflict that Count Alexander Hoyos went to Berlin on July 5 to clear matters with Austria's ally. William II and Bethmann Hollweg both promised full German support for whatever action Austria might take against Serbia: this was the famous "blank check." Thus armed, Austria delivered a note, in effect an ultimatum, to Belgrade. It required an apology, cooperation in investigation of the crime, punishment of the guilty officials, the suppression of all newspapers and patriotic organizations hostile to Austria, and the cessation of all anti-Austrian propaganda. The note was intended to court rejection, but even though Russian support was promised, Serbia conceded on some points and temporized on others: to a relieved William II the reply looked like a nearly complete Austrian victory at no cost at all.

Austria was determined to have its war. Hostilities formally commenced on July 28, even though the Austrian army could not possibly take the field for another two weeks. Russia responded in a confused way, first ordering partial mobilization against Austria only and then total mobilization, a move that brought an ultimatum from Germany on July 31, demanding that war preparations on the German frontier be stopped. Germany could get neither a satisfactory answer from France as to its intentions nor a promise of neutrality from Britain, and Germany refused a British request to respect the neutrality of Belgium, guaranteed by the powers in 1839 (see p. 576). France and Germany ordered mobilization on August 1, and the same day Germany declared war on Russia. On August 2 the British cabinet, despite the resignation of two ministers, agreed to support France. Germany, having invaded Luxembourg, asked for the right of transit across Belgium, which was refused. On August 3 Germany declared war on both France and Belgium, and the invasion of Belgium, in accordance with the Schlieffen plan, was begun. The Germans thus gave the British interventionists a justification they were quick to turn to advantage. To the traditional British diplomatic concern over possession of the Channel ports there was added a clear moral issue. The British declared war on Germany on August 4—"for a scrap of paper" as Bethmann Hollweg contemptuously put it. With only minor hitches, the alliances worked as they were supposed to do, and World War I began.

Where did the responsibility lie? This question became crucial in the drafting of the Treaty of Versailles (see p. 964), and it has remained a lively concern of historians, who have traced the details of the war's approach with a precision that has probably been brought to no other historical question. Of Serbian provocation there can be no doubt, though it was of a kind that a confident Great Power could have ignored or dealt with less drastically. That immediate responsibility belongs more than anywhere else with Austria-Hungary's determination to assert itself seems also beyond question. Russia was confused and inept in basic policy-making and precipitate and erratic in ordering mobilization, though the latter decision must be seen against the absolute belief in military circles that victory would go to the nation that mobilized first, while mobilization once ordered—involving as it did immensely complex and extensive dispositions of men and material—could not be undone without putting a country's defenses in serious disarray.[15] Perhaps, had the British been less reticent in their commitments to France, had they been more explicit in their intention to fight for Belgium, Germany would have paused, but this argument seems less convincing now than it once did. For in the 1960s the debate has ranged particularly around the contradictory role of Germany.

[15] This point is made concisely by Michael Howard, "Reflections on the First World War," in his *Studies in War and Peace* (1971), 105-106.

Despite his bellicosity, William II did not have the nerve for war, and Bethmann Hollweg was no warmonger: why then did they give way to their tottering ally and their own militarists? The German historian Fritz Fischer and his followers have argued from the early statement of German war aims that the German leaders, including Bethmann Hollweg, were impelled by a vision of escaping from Germany's encirclement and from the threat of an industrializing Russia by means of a great central European economic unit dependent on Germany, a *Mitteleuropa* that would, ironically, revive and expand the *grossdeutsch* notion that had been abandoned in the triumph of Bismarck's unification of Germany around Prussia. However that may be, there is no doubt that Germany's sense of panic—over internal dissension, over fear of encirclement, over the disrepair of its alliances, over the possible collapse of its one remaining ally, Austria-Hungary—along with the woeful lack of unity and efficiency in the German governmental machine, created a situation in which dangerously impulsive action was possible. If the brooding, pessimistic Bethmann Hollweg was Hamlet, says Professor Fritz Stern, he was less the introspective Hamlet of legend than the prince whose strategems, undertaken despite his doubts, left the stage littered with corpses. [16]

But, recalling Elie Halévy's skepticism about the significance of what diplomats said or did (see p. 909), one must also look to those vast impersonal forces—nationalism and patriotism, social struggle and revolution—that impelled men both great and small and that created climates of opinion and domestic pressures which the most skillful and peaceable politicians could disregard at their peril. It was no simple imperialist war—many businessmen were opposed to it and knew only too well what its cost would be—but it was, or quickly became, a war of peoples moved by deeply felt, if often ill perceived, ideals and emotions. No one could know what course would have been taken by that principled opponent of war, the great French Socialist leader Jean Jaurès: the day before war was declared Jaurès was assassinated by a nationalist fanatic, a tragedy whose proportions were recognized by nearly everyone. But that austere Socialist opponent of bourgeois collaboration, Jules Guesde (see p. 915), entered the government. Under the proud banner of *union sacrée*—sacred union—the nation enlisted, submerging (for a time) its old differences. In Britain Lord Grey looked out from his window in the Foreign Office, uttering the famous remark that the lamps were going out all over Europe and wondering if they would be relit in his lifetime. But the Tory rebels and militant suffragettes who had given Grey and his cabinet colleagues so much trouble flocked to volunteer for military service or to support the men at the front. In Germany William II said he recognized no parties, only Germans. And on

---

[16] "Bethmann Hollweg and the War: The Limits of Responsibility," in Leonard Krieger and Fritz Stern, eds., *The Responsibility of Power, Historical Essays in Honor of Hajo Holborn* (1967), 252. This essay draws on the diary of Bethmann's closest aide.

August 4, General Erich von Falkenhayn, soon to be chief of the German general staff, exclaimed to Bethmann Hollweg, "Even if we end in ruin, it was beautiful."[17]

ARMAGEDDON

Stalemate

The enthusiasm, even the gaiety, with which men went to war in the summer of 1914 can to some extent be explained by the war they expected. Not many in Europe had ever known war at first hand, and those who had learned about it, the professionals, had history in mind, as well as certain dogma based on it. The ghost of Napoleon stalked the battlefields, thanks to the teachings of his admirer and near contemporary, the great military theorist von Clausewitz, but probably even more exemplary were the short, swift wars of 1864, 1866, 1870, and 1904–1905; few European military men had learned the grim lessons of the American Civil War. The Schlieffen plan, on which German strategy was unalterably fixed, was pinned to the notion of a rapid and overwhelming advance through Belgium to knock out the French army, leaving the Russian forces to the east, slower to mobilize, to be dealt with later. The French, too, put all their faith in a plunging offensive, though on their right flank and in the center of the line rather than on the left flank, where the Germans broke through. In contrast to the millions fielded by the conscript armies of the Continent, the British had a superbly trained expeditionary force of 120,000 men. Britain had rarely committed large armies to the Continent, and the BEF was expected to be sufficient, while, as in the eighteenth century, a rapid sweeping up of colonies belonging to the enemy would strengthen the British bargaining position at the conference table. No one thought the war need interfere much: it was business as usual, the British were told, and when the German industrialist Walther Rathenau asked the military commanders what provision had been made for stockpiling supplies, he was looked at incredulously.

The opening war of movement soon ground to a halt. The French offensives were thrown back in part because the chief of the German general staff, Helmuth von Moltke—the nephew but scarcely the equal of the great Bismarckian general whose name he bore—had altered the Schlieffen plan to strengthen his left wing. Thus the French right wing was not lured forward by easy victories to be cut off at its rear, but was thrown back to regroup, though

[17] Ibid., 268.

not very effectively, and to cope with the German advance in the west. That advance did not go entirely according to plan. It was held up at the bravely defended fortress of Liège in Belgium; once that barrier was passed, the German armies were hampered by inadequate or wrecked communications, insufficient supply, and poor coordination. The Belgian resistance had not been allowed for; the British army had not been expected nor was it properly assessed. Still, the German armies swept into northern France and were brought to a standstill only at the end of August 1914 in the battle of the Marne, east of Paris. In November, with the front firmly established from the sea to the Swiss frontier, the Germans attempted to break through the British lines at Ypres in Belgium, but they were unable to follow up their successes and fell back. Thereafter the war in the west became a war of position, not movement, of trenches, barbed wire, and "no-man's-land," where tens or hundreds of thousands of casualties were risked in pursuing the will-o'-the-wisp of a decisive victory, only to gain or lose a few yards: in three years the front moved no more than ten miles.

In the east the fighting was nearer to what was expected, but the results were ambiguous and confusing. No concerted plans had been made by the German and Austrian general staffs, and the Austrian General Conrad set out on his own in Galicia. Lemberg (Lvov) was a battle of ineptitudes that ended with Austria losing a third of its men and (for the time being) the province. Further north the Germans met an unexpectedly early advance of two Russian armies into East Prussia by transferring to that front, along with forces that could ill be spared in France, a relatively junior officer who had won his laurels at Liège. Because of his lack of seniority, Colonel Erich Ludendorff needed a nominal superior, and the undistinguished General Paul von Hindenburg was called out of retirement for the occasion. Ludendorff made fewer mistakes than the Russian commanders—for example, the Russians seem repeatedly to have sent radio messages without coding them. One of the Russian armies was surrounded and in good part made prisoner in the battle of Tannenberg at the end of August, and the other was driven back at the Masurian Lakes. The psychological impact of Tannenberg was enormous; it was a severe blow to both the Russians and the Allies, and in Germany it raised Hindenburg and Ludendorff to immense power and prestige—with ultimately appalling consequences (see p. 947). It also tilted the balance of German activity in 1915 to the eastern front, where the Russian conquests of Austrian territory were quickly recovered and a decisive victory was gained over the Serbians. In the west the Germans held their ground against costly Anglo-French offensives; in February 1916 they began a long assault on the famous French fortress at Verdun, an attempt to weaken the French irreparably through attrition and endless casualties. The French success in holding Verdun was a near thing, but it was greeted as a kind of deliverance.

With the advantage of a relatively compact area well served by transportation, the Germans could divert troops from one front to another with relative

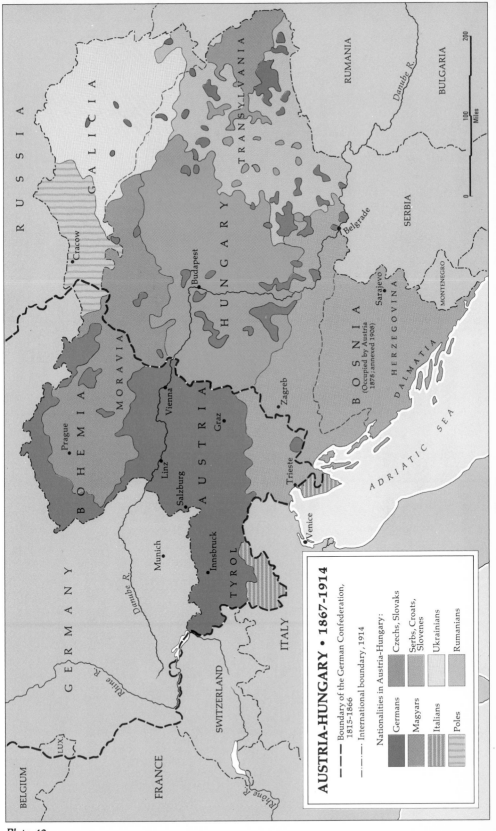

RUSSIA

GALICIA

Cracow

RUMANIA

Danube R.

BULGARIA

200

100

Miles

100

0

TRANSYLVANIA

H U N G A R Y

Budapest

Belgrade

SERBIA

MORAVIA

BOHEMIA

Prague

Vienna

Linz

Salzburg

AUSTRIA

Graz

Zagreb

Trieste

B O S N I A
(Occupied by Austria
1878; annexed 1908)

Sarajevo

HERZEGOVINA

DALMATIA

MONTENEGRO

ADRIATIC SEA

GERMANY

Danube R.

Munich

Innsbruck

TYROL

Rhine R.

SWITZERLAND

ITALY

Venice

FRANCE

BELGIUM

LUX.

Rhône R.

AUSTRIA-HUNGARY • 1867-1914

— — — Boundary of the German Confederation,
1815-1866

········ International boundary, 1914

Nationalities in Austria-Hungary:

			Czechs, Slovaks
Germans			Serbs, Croats, Slovenes
Magyars			Ukrainians
Italians			Rumanians
Poles			

Plate 40

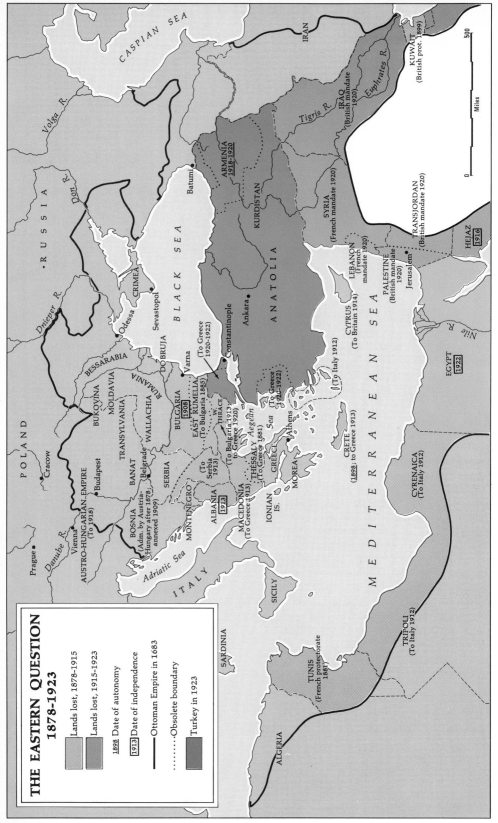

THE EASTERN QUESTION
1878–1923

Lands lost, 1878–1915
Lands lost, 1915–1923
1898 Date of autonomy
1913 Date of independence
━━━ Ottoman Empire in 1683
········· Obsolete boundary
Turkey in 1923

RUSSIA

CASPIAN SEA

Volga R.

Don R.

Dnieper R.

POLAND

Cracow

Prague

Vienna

AUSTRO-HUNGARIAN EMPIRE
(To 1918)

Budapest

TRANSYLVANIA

BUKOVINA

MOLDAVIA

BESSARABIA

RUMANIA

WALLACHIA

BANAT

Belgrade

SERBIA

BOSNIA
(Adm. by Austria-
Hungary after 1878;
annexed 1909)

MONTENEGRO

ALBANIA
1913

ITALY

SARDINIA

SICILY

TUNIS
(French protectorate
1881)

ALGERIA

TRIPOLI
(To Italy 1912)

CYRENAICA
(To Italy 1912)

CRIMEA

Sevastopol

Odessa

BLACK SEA

DOBRUJA

Varna

BULGARIA
1908

EAST RUMELIA
(To Bulgaria 1885)

THRACE

W. THRACE
(To Bulgaria 1913
to Greece 1920)

MACEDONIA
(To Greece 1913)

THESSALY
(To Greece 1881)

GREECE

MOREA

IONIAN
IS.

Athens

Aegean
Sea

CRETE
(1898; to Greece 1913)

(To
Serbia
1913)

Constantinople

(To Greece
1920–1922)

Ankara

ANATOLIA

Batumi

ARMENIA
1918–1920

KURDISTAN

IRAN

Tigris R.

Euphrates R.

IRAQ
(British mandate
1920)

KUWAIT
(British prot. 1899)

SYRIA
(French mandate 1920)

LEBANON
(French
mandate 1920)

PALESTINE
(British mandate
1920)

Jerusalem

TRANSJORDAN
(British mandate 1920)

HEJAZ
1916

EGYPT
1922

Nile R.

CYPRUS
(To Britain 1914)

(To Italy 1912)

(To Greece
1920–1922)

MEDITERRANEAN SEA

Adriatic Sea

Danube R.

Miles

500

0

Plate 41

The Eastern Question · 1885–1923

For more than two decades following 1885 no boundary changes occurred in the Balkans. But tensions that would lead to future alterations were building up: within the Ottoman Empire itself, in the covetousness with which European powers eyed the outlying parts of the empire, in the intensification of Balkan nationalism, and in the competition between the Russian and the Hapsburg Empires.

The Young Turk revolution of 1908 precipitated an action that fulfilled an old Austrian ambition—to convert the occupation of Bosnia and the adjoining region of Herzegovina into annexation, a sure barrier against the growing Serb ambition to create a great South Slav state under Serbian leadership. At the same time Bulgaria declared itself an independent kingdom. In 1911–1912 Italy seized the provinces of Tripoli and Cyrenaica in North Africa, to convert them into the colony of Libya. And in the latter year the First Balkan War broke out—a coalition of Montenegro, Serbia, Bulgaria, and Greece against Turkey, which at the war's end was left with only a toehold in Europe, at Constantinople. The Second Balkan War quickly followed; like the first it revolved around competing claims to the strategic region of Macedonia. Serbia, denied an outlet to the sea by Austria's success in the 1912 settlement in creating the new state of Albania, insisted on compensation in Macedonia at the expense of its former ally Bulgaria, which was also turned on by Greece, Rumania, and Turkey. The settlement of 1913 was largely retained after World War I, but Bulgaria's outlet to the Aegean through western Thrace was transferred to Greece. Serbia, Montenegro, and parts of the Hapsburg empire were merged into Yugoslavia, the south Slav kingdom.

World War I brought defeat to Bulgaria and Turkey, which were allied to the Central Powers, but the unfavorable territorial settlement imposed on Turkey in the Treaty of Sèvres in 1920 was redressed in the more generous Treaty of Lausanne in 1923, testimony to the Turks' successful resistance to the incursions made on their territory by Greeks and Italians and to the fact that a leader of genius, Mustapha Kemal, had at last made Turkey into a viable, modern state.

The new Turkey was not, however, interested in retaining its hold over the territories to the south. These Arab-inhabited lands had been galvanized into anti-Turkish action by the British during the war, and an incipient Arab nationalism was created. Agreements between the French and British during the war led to the carving up of the area into mandates, which ultimately became independent nations. An uncertain destiny was proposed for Palestine, however. In the Balfour Declaration of 1917 the British announced that they would favor the setting up in Palestine of a "national home" for the Jews, a decision on which much of the subsequent history of the Near East has turned.

Plate 42

EUROPE IN 1914 • THE EVE OF WAR

Triple Alliance   Triple Entente

FINLAND

Stockholm

St. Petersburg

ESTONIA

Riga

LATVIA

Moscow

LITHUANIA

Vilna

R U S S I A

Danzig

Warsaw

POLAND

Vistula R.

Cracow

Don R.

Volga R.

Dnieper R.

Dniester R.

HUNGARIAN

Budapest

EMPIRE

RUMANIA

Bucharest

Danube R.

BLACK   SEA

Sarajevo

SERBIA

Sofia

MONTENEGRO

BULGARIA

Constantinople

ALBANIA

PERSIA

O T T O M A N   E M P I R E

GREECE

Athens

CYPRUS

CRETE

S E A

EGYPT

SEA

WORLD WAR I • 1914-1918

Principal theaters of war:

- Nov. 1914-Aug. 1916
- Aug. 1916-April 1917
- April 1917-Nov. 1918

→ Allied advance

→ Advance of the Central Powers

✳ Sea battle

NORWAY

SWEDEN

British Sea Blockade

May 31-June 1, 1916

N O R T H
S E A

DENMARK

Jan. 24, 1915

BALTIC

ENGLAND

Aug. 28, 1914

London

Berlin

Poznan

NETH.

BELG.

GERMAN EMPIRE

1914

1918

LUX.

Prague

Paris

FRANCE

Munich

Vienna

SWITZ.

AUSTRO-

A T L A N T I C
O C E A N

0   500
Miles

Marseilles

1918

BOSNIA

PORTUGAL
March 1916

Madrid

SPAIN

ITALY
May 1915

Rome

M E D I T E R R A N E A N

LIBYA

WESTERN FRONT

Line of trench
warfare 1914-1917

NETHERLANDS

→ German invasion,
1914

— Maximum German
advance, 1914

--- German advance
summer, 1918

ENGLAND

Ypres

Antwerp

Brussels

Liège

B
E
L
G
I
U
M

G
E
R
M
A
N
Y

Seine R.

F
R
A
N
C
E

LUX.

Château
Thierry

Verdun

Paris

Nancy

Rhine R.

→ Allied offensive
fall, 1918

— Armistice line
Nov. 11, 1918

0   50   100
Miles

SWITZ.

Plate 43

FINLAND

St. Petersburg

Moscow

1918

Riga

1915

1915 Vilna *1918*

1914

Tannenberg *1915*

1914 Brest Litovsk *1918*

1915 *1916*

Lublin Kiev

R U S S I A

1915 Lemberg
(Lvov) *1918*

1914

1916

1918 Rostov

1918

HUNGARIAN *1918*

EMPIRE

1918

Belgrade RUMANIA *1918*
August 1916

SERBIA *1918*
July 1916

1918 BULGARIA *1918*
October 1915 BLACK SEA *1918*

ALBANIA Constantinople Bosporus

1918 Salonika *1918*

Gallipoli Trebizond

GREECE *1918* *1915* Dardanelles

October 1916

Athens OTTOMAN EMPIRE

Aleppo

S E A

1918

Jerusalem Baghdad

Cairo

EGYPT

GREAT
BRITAIN

BELG. GERMANY RUSSIA

FRANCE AUSTRIA-
HUNGARY

ITALY RUM.

SERBIA BULG.

GREECE TURKEY

☐ Allies

☐ Central
Powers

EUROPE AFTER THE TREATY OF VERSAILLES 1918-1926

Territories lost:

By Germany

By Austria

By Russia

By Bulgaria

Demilitarized zone

Boundary of new, independent nations

1918-1920 Date of independence

Plate 44

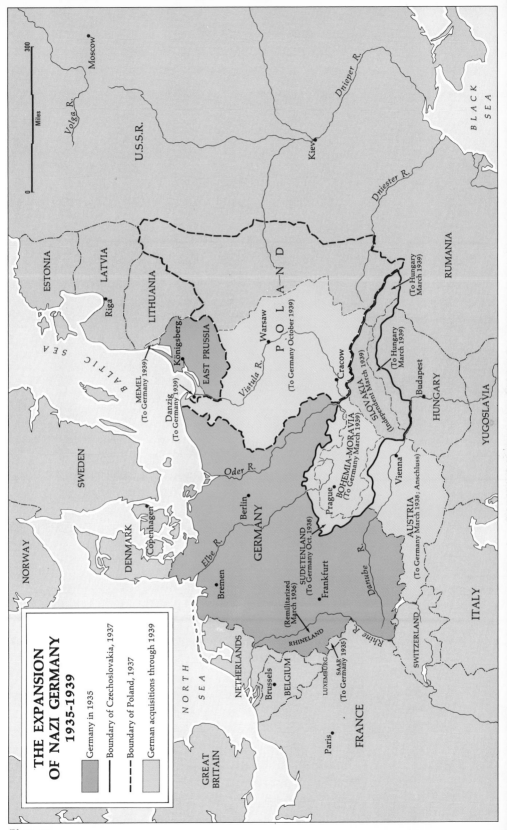

THE EXPANSION
OF NAZI GERMANY
1935-1939

Germany in 1935
———— Boundary of Czechoslovakia, 1937
– – – Boundary of Poland, 1937
German acquisitions through 1939

300

0

Miles

Moscow

Volga R.

Dnieper R.

U.S.S.R.

Kiev

Dniester R.

BLACK SEA

ESTONIA

LATVIA

Riga

LITHUANIA

MEMEL
(To Germany 1939)

Königsberg

EAST PRUSSIA

Danzig
(To Germany 1939)

Vistula R.

Warsaw

P O L A N D
(To Germany October 1939)

Cracow

(To Hungary
March 1939)

RUMANIA

(To Hungary
March 1939)

SLOVAKIA
(Independent March 1939)

Budapest

HUNGARY

YUGOSLAVIA

BALTIC SEA

SWEDEN

NORWAY

DENMARK

Copenhagen

Oder R.

Berlin

GERMANY

Elbe R.

Bremen

BOHEMIA-MORAVIA
(To Germany March 1939)

Prague

SUDETENLAND
(To Germany Oct. 1938)

Frankfurt

(Remilitarized
March 1936)

RHINELAND

Vienna

AUSTRIA
(To Germany March 1938; Anschluss)

Danube R.

Rhine R.

SWITZERLAND

ITALY

NORTH
SEA

NETHERLANDS

Brussels

BELGIUM

LUXEMBURG

SAAR
(To Germany 1935)

FRANCE

Paris

GREAT
BRITAIN

Plate 45

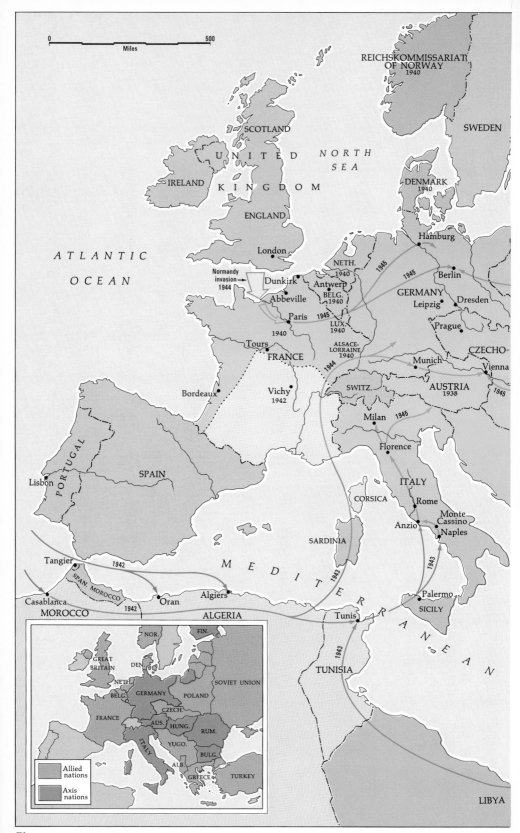

Plate 46

WORLD WAR II • 1935-1945

Maximum extent of Axis control

Controlled by Vichy France

1941 Date of Axis occupation

Allied advance

FINLAND

BALTIC SEA

Leningrad

ESTONIA

LATVIA

REICHSKOMMISSARIAT OF OSTLAND 1941

LITHUANIA

Smolensk

Moscow

U.S.S.R.

EAST PRUSSIA

Kursk

1944

1945

Warsaw

GENERAL GOVERNMENT OF POLAND 1939

1943

Kiev

Kharkov

Stalingrad

1945

REICHSKOMMISSARIAT OF UKRAINE 1941

1943

SLOVAKIA 1939

Budapest

HUNGARY

RUMANIA

1944

Rostov

CRIMEA

Yalta

CAUCASUS

Belgrade

Bucharest

BLACK SEA

YUGOSLAVIA 1941

BULGARIA

ALBANIA Annexed by Italy 1939

IRAN

GREECE 1941

TURKEY

Athens

SYRIA

CYPRUS

IRAQ

CRETE 1941

SEA

PALESTINE

1942

Tobruk

Benghasi

Alexandria

TRANS-JORDAN

El Alamein

Cairo

SAUDI ARABIA

EGYPT

North Pole

ARCTIC

ATLANTIC OCEAN

IRELAND

UNITED KINGDOM

NORWAY

SWEDEN

FINLAND

Murmansk

FRANCE

WEST GERMANY

EAST GERMANY

Berlin

Baltic Sea

LITHUANIAN S.S.R.

Riga

LATVIAN S.S.R.

ESTONIAN S.S.R.

Leningrad

URAL MTS.

Ob R.

Prague

POLAND

Warsaw

CZECH

ITALY

AUS.

Budapest

HUNG.

MOLDAVIAN S.S.R.

BELORUSSIAN S.S.R.

Minsk

Smolensk

Moscow

Kirov

UNION   OF   SOVIET

RUSSIAN   SOVIET   FEDERATED

YUGOSLAVIA

RUMANIA

Bucharest

Sofia

BULG.

UKRAINIAN S.S.R.

Kiev

Europe

Asia

Sverdlovsk

Tobolsk

GREECE

BLACK SEA

Rostov

Volgograd (Stalingrad)

Volga R.

Novosibirsk

TURKEY

GEORGIAN S.S.R.

ARMENIAN S.S.R.

AZERBAIJANIAN S.S.R.

Baku

CASPIAN SEA

Aral Sea

KAZAKH S.S.R.

Lake Balkhash

IRAN

TURKMENIAN S.S.R.

UZBEK S.S.R.

Tashkent

KIRGHIZ S.S.R.

AFGHANISTAN

TADZHIK S.S.R.

ARABIA

PAKISTAN

NEPAL

INDIA

INDIAN

0   500   1000   1500   2000

Miles

0°   20°   40°   60°   80°   100°

Plate 47

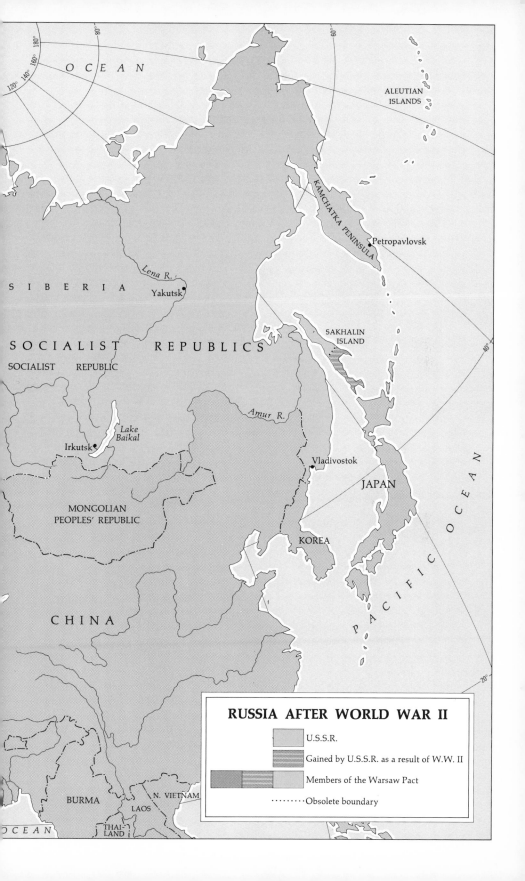

O C E A N

120° 140° 160° 180°
180°
80°

ALEUTIAN
ISLANDS

60°

KAMCHATKA PENINSULA

Petropavlovsk

Lena R.

S I B E R I A   Yakutsk

SAKHALIN
ISLAND

40°

S O C I A L I S T   R E P U B L I C S

SOCIALIST   REPUBLIC

Amur R.

Lake
Baikal

Irkutsk

Vladivostok

JAPAN

MONGOLIAN
PEOPLES' REPUBLIC

KOREA

P A C I F I C   O C E A N

C H I N A

20°

RUSSIA AFTER WORLD WAR II

U.S.S.R.

Gained by U.S.S.R. as a result of W.W. II

Members of the Warsaw Pact

·········Obsolete boundary

BURMA

N. VIETNAM

LAOS

THAI-
LAND

OCEAN

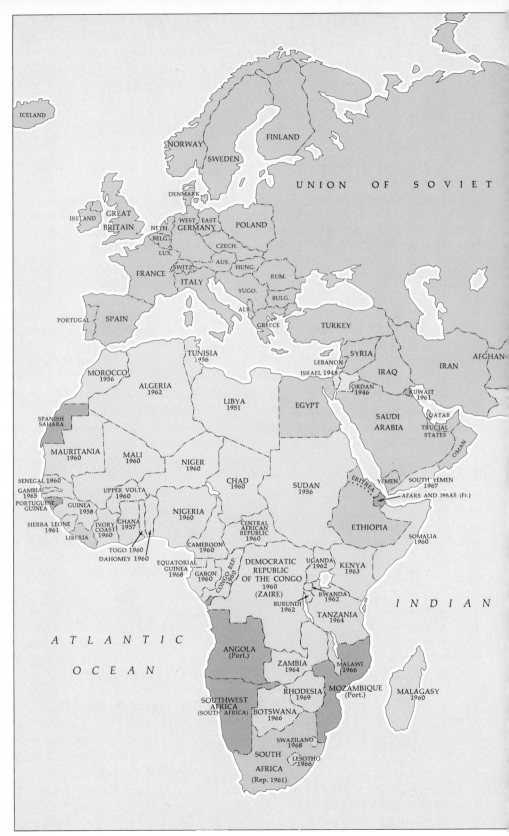

ICELAND

NORWAY
SWEDEN
FINLAND

UNION OF SOVIET

DENMARK

IRELAND
GREAT
BRITAIN
NETH.
WEST EAST
GERMANY
POLAND
BELG.
LUX.
CZECH.
FRANCE
SWITZ.
AUS.
HUNG.
ITALY
RUM.
YUGO.
BULG.
ALB.
GREECE
TURKEY

PORTUGAL
SPAIN

TUNISIA
1956
SYRIA
LEBANON
ISRAEL 1948
IRAQ
IRAN
AFGHAN.

MOROCCO
1956
ALGERIA
1962
LIBYA
1951
EGYPT
JORDAN
1946
KUWAIT
1961
SAUDI
ARABIA
QATAR
TRUCIAL
STATES

SPANISH
SAHARA

OMAN

MAURITANIA
1960
MALI
1960
NIGER
1960
CHAD
1960
SUDAN
1956
ERITREA
YEMEN
SOUTH YEMEN
1967

SENEGAL 1960
GAMBIA
1965
PORTUGUESE
GUINEA
GUINEA
1958
UPPER VOLTA
1960
AFARS AND ISSAS (Fr.)

SIERRA LEONE
1961
IVORY
COAST
1960
GHANA
1957
NIGERIA
1960
CENTRAL
AFRICAN
REPUBLIC
1960
ETHIOPIA
SOMALIA
1960

LIBERIA
TOGO 1960
DAHOMEY 1960
CAMEROON
1960

EQUATORIAL
GUINEA
1968
GABON
1960
CONGO REP.
1960
DEMOCRATIC
REPUBLIC
OF THE CONGO
1960
(ZAIRE)
UGANDA
1962
KENYA
1963

RWANDA
1962
BURUNDI
1962
TANZANIA
1964

INDIAN

ATLANTIC

OCEAN

ANGOLA
(Port.)
ZAMBIA
1964
MALAWI
1966
MOZAMBIQUE
(Port.)
MALAGASY
1960

RHODESIA
1969

SOUTHWEST
AFRICA
(SOUTH AFRICA)
BOTSWANA
1966

SWAZILAND
1968

SOUTH
AFRICA
(Rep. 1961)
LESOTHO
1966

Plate 48

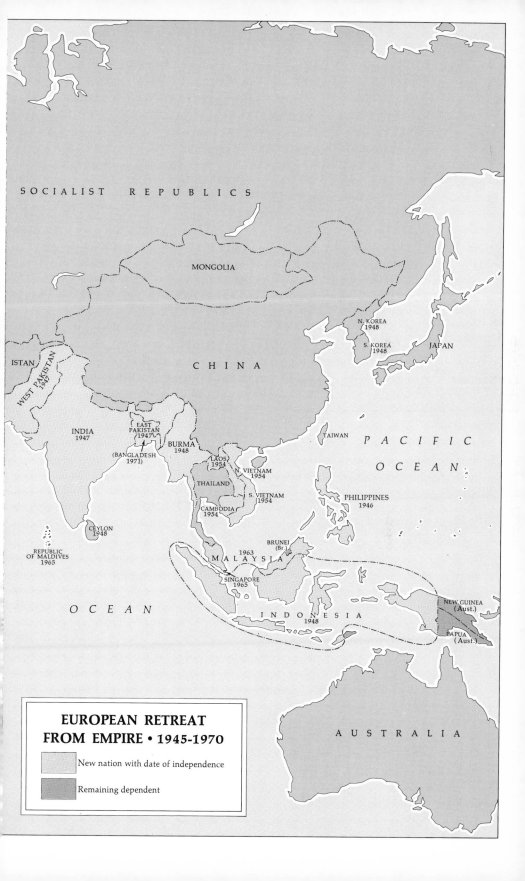

S O C I A L I S T   R E P U B L I C S

MONGOLIA

CHINA

N. KOREA
1948

S. KOREA
1948

JAPAN

TAIWAN

ISTAN

WEST PAKISTAN
1947

INDIA
1947

EAST
PAKISTAN
(1947)

(BANGLADESH
1971)

BURMA
1948

LAOS
1954

N. VIETNAM
1954

THAILAND

S. VIETNAM
1954

CAMBODIA
1954

CEYLON
1948

REPUBLIC
OF MALDIVES
1965

P A C I F I C

O C E A N

PHILIPPINES
1946

BRUNEI
(Br.)

1963

M A L A Y S I A

SINGAPORE
1965

O C E A N

I N D O N E S I A
1948

NEW GUINEA
(Aust.)

PAPUA
(Aust.)

A U S T R A L I A

EUROPEAN RETREAT
FROM EMPIRE • 1945-1970

New nation with date of independence

Remaining dependent

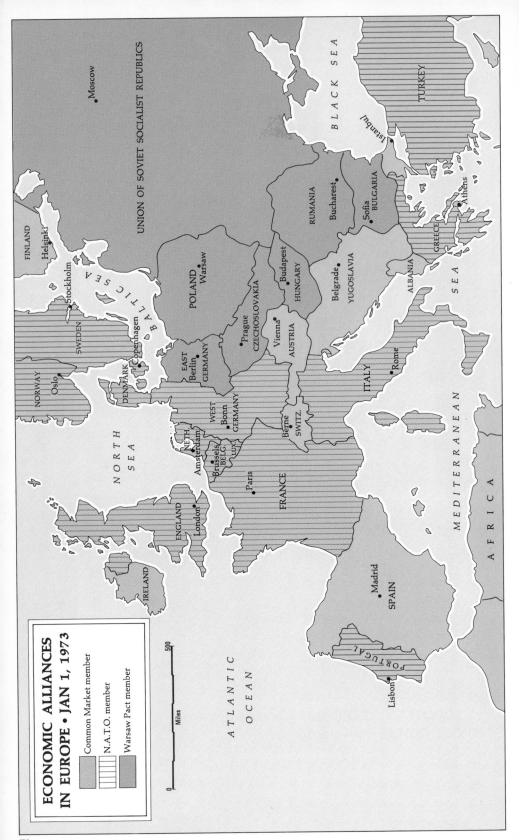

ECONOMIC ALLIANCES
IN EUROPE • JAN 1, 1973

Common Market member

N.A.T.O. member

Warsaw Pact member

Miles

0   500

UNION OF SOVIET SOCIALIST REPUBLICS

Moscow

FINLAND

Helsinki

BALTIC SEA

SWEDEN

Stockholm

NORWAY

Oslo

DENMARK

Copenhagen

POLAND

Warsaw

EAST
Berlin
GERMANY

CZECHOSLOVAKIA

Prague

WEST

Bonn

GERMANY

NETH.

Amsterdam

Brussels
BELG.

LUX.

Paris

FRANCE

ENGLAND

London

IRELAND

NORTH
SEA

ATLANTIC
OCEAN

Vienna

AUSTRIA

Budapest

HUNGARY

SWITZ.

Berne

Rome

ITALY

Belgrade

YUGOSLAVIA

ALBANIA

RUMANIA

Bucharest

Sofia
BULGARIA

GREECE

Athens

TURKEY

Istanbul

BLACK SEA

SEA

MEDITERRANEAN

AFRICA

SPAIN

Madrid

PORTUGAL

Lisbon

Plate 49

ease; the Allied theaters of war were far more scattered, and the decision to reinforce one or another of them was the more difficult as the principal French and British commanders were committed "Westerners," who believed that the war had to be won in Flanders and northern France. Both sides of course had allies and gained more. The British Empire contingents—Australians and New Zealanders (ANZACS), Canadians, Indians, and South Africans—were invaluable, in Africa, in the Near East, and on the western front. Japan, tied to Britain since 1902, proved useful in mopping up Germany's Far Eastern colonies and bases and in time was asked for help in naval patrols in the Indian Ocean and the Mediterranean. For Japan, however, the war was primarily a way to improve its already dominant position in Asia. Serbia, after repulsing early Austrian attacks with remarkable success, could not withstand the German armies sent to aid their incompetent ally; in the autumn of 1915 Serbia was knocked out of the war, though its armies regrouped at Salonika in Greece. Rumania, eager for territorial gain, joined the Allies in the late summer of 1916 but was defeated by the end of the year, its grain and oil going to swell the stores of the Central Powers. Italy, because Germany was technically the aggressor, could escape its obligations under the Triple Alliance, limited as they were to assistance in a defensive war; in 1915 Italy decided to join the Allies—or, more properly, was bribed in secret agreements promising wide territorial gains at Austria's and Turkey's expense. How worthwhile the investment was is a question. Italy tied down Austrian forces but accomplished little; in the two years after entering, Italy fought eleven battles at the River Isonzo and failed to get beyond it. The Central Powers, too, gained allies—Turkey, fatefully, at the end of 1914, and Bulgaria late in 1915.

The Central Powers operated beyond their periphery by undercover methods. They encouraged a Flemish separatist movement in Belgium, as toward the end of the war they were to encourage and then fight for separatism in the Russian Baltic provinces and the Ukraine. They aided Sir Roger Casement, the Irish nationalist, in the abortive invasion of Ireland that culminated in the rising of Easter Monday 1916 (see p. 996). Their role in Russia itself is obscure, but they willingly agreed in 1917 to facilitate Lenin's return to a Russia torn by revolution. The first diversionary effort of the Allies was directed to forcing the Dardanelles by landing in the Gallipoli peninsula in April 1915. This British effort, hotly opposed by the Westerners among the military and strongly supported by Lord Kitchener, the war minister, and Winston Churchill, the first lord of the admiralty, turned out to be almost as ill organized as the British effort in the Crimean War. The Turkish army had been remarkably improved by Liman von Sanders, and the British got nowhere. At the end of the year and in the first days of 1916 their forces were evacuated— the evacuation (as so often in British military history) being carried out superbly, without the loss of a single life.

The Gallipoli campaign had been chosen by the British over an invasion of the Balkans through the Greek port of Salonika, a move favored by Lloyd

George and also by some of the French leaders, not only to aid Serbia but to win over Bulgaria. Serbia's defeat and Bulgaria's decision to join the Central Powers did not kill the plan, which indeed gained some urgency after the failure at Gallipoli. The Greek prime minister, Eleutherios Venizelos, was eager for Allied intervention, and a secret request led to a joint Anglo-French landing at Salonika in October 1915. Greece, however, was kept by internal politics from joining the Allies until 1917, meanwhile adopting a benevolent neutrality; but Salonika remained a beachhead until 1918. Action against Turkey was begun in Mesopotamia, that part of the Near East south of Anatolia and north of the Arabian peninsula. Beginning modestly at the end of 1914 with an expedition from India to protect the oil resources in the Persian Gulf, British forces won an early and impressive victory over the Turks but were thrown back in 1916 and were under some threat in Egypt from German-led Turkish raiders. Britain and France were, however, determined to partition Asiatic Turkey, either under direct rule or through spheres of influence: the Sykes-Picot Agreement of May 1916 laid down the lines of the division. The British encouraged revolts against Turkish rule among the Arabs—a leading part being played in this by a young Oxford scholar, T. E. Lawrence, whose unorthodox ways and compelling personality helped to galvanize the Arabs into a rapidly escalating nationalism. Slowly the groundwork was laid for the victories of the last years of the war.

In the war at sea, though naval warfare had played so important a role in prewar thinking about strategy, technology, and government finance, conventional sea power counted for little. German war vessels operating in the Pacific, the South Atlantic, and the Indian Ocean did some spectacular damage in the early months of the war before they were caught, belatedly, by British or Empire ships. But for the most part Britain's Grand Fleet and Germany's High Seas Fleet stayed close to their home bases on opposite sides of the North Sea. There was only one major engagement, the battle of Jutland on May 31–June 1, 1916, and it was inconclusive: whatever the balance of losses and errors in judgment, neither fleet was beaten, and neither was much used for the remainder of the war. The dreadnought began to look like a dinosaur.

Waging war on other fronts, clandestine or not, was a way of breaking the deadlock in the West. So, more directly, was the use of new weapons or of weapons known but newly employed. One such weapon itself contributed to the deadlock. The machine gun, discounted by many military leaders, proved that a few soldiers, suitably equipped and positioned, could stop the masses of men, however vast, that had been the ideal of military leaders since Napoleon's time. Two new tactical weapons were devised to neutralize such barriers and open gaps in the lines. One was poison gas, first used by the Germans at the second battle of Ypres in April 1915; it was, however, a highly uncertain weapon, depending as it did on the direction of the wind; then, too, gas masks were quickly improved, though not before the use of gas had had a notable psychological impact on a whole generation, soldier and civilian alike. The other tactical weapon was the tank, introduced by the British, despite much official skepticism, in 1916; by the end of the war these tracked, armored vehicles—protective of their occupants, terrifying to the enemy—had come to show the power they would have in future warfare.

This was also the first war in which air power was available. Airplanes were valuable in reconnaissance, and the exploits of the "aces"—the daring pilots who fought dogfights in the air—quickly entered into legend: these roles for air power were tangential at best. On a limited scale, the war did show, however, that aircraft had an appalling future in the destruction of military installations and the harrying of civilian populations. The German zeppelins—rigid, lighter-than-air craft—raided English coastal towns in 1915-1916 and airplane raids followed. But if the war was to be brought home to civilians, and it was as no war had been before, it was best done by sea—not by the great expensive fleets of battleships and cruisers, but by the silent menace of the submarine. Britain, as an island nation, was especially vulnerable to the cutting of its supply lines, and this the Germans attempted to do early in 1915 by proclaiming the seas around Britain as a war zone in which any ship was subject to sinking. The response was a strictly enforced blockade of Germany, which got Britain—as a hundred years before—into trouble with neutrals, above all the United States. But the foolish and inhumane sinking of the British passenger liner *Lusitania* by the Germans in early May 1915, with the loss of 1,100 lives, including 139 Americans, jolted opinion in the United States out of its traditional mold and at least temporarily forced the Germans to abandon their submarine campaign. When it was resumed, after much debate, in 1916 and 1917 and declared unrestricted after February 1, 1917, it brought the United States into the war. In May 1917 the Allies belatedly adopted a countermeasure—the convoy, in which merchant ships traveled in packs guarded by destroyers. It seems astonishing in retrospect that so obvious and sensible a tactic was so long resisted by naval officers; but, as is already evident, there was little in the way of innovation in this war that was not resisted by military leaders, who were trained to fight nineteenth-century wars, not this one.

That fact helps to account for the changes in command. The first major replacement occurred in September 1914, when the ailing Moltke suffered a physical and nervous collapse; General Erich von Falkenhayn took his place and was succeeded in turn in the summer of 1916 by Hindenburg, with Ludendorff as quartermaster general. The much-criticized commander of the BEF, Sir John French, was replaced at the end of 1915 by Sir Douglas Haig. Dedicated and devout, intelligent but limited in imagination, Haig was the most committed of Westerners: his monuments are two vast offensives, at the Somme in the summer and fall of 1916, in the mud at Passchendaele, near Ypres, a year later; both were failures and each cost upward of 400,000 men. Historians still debate Haig's role. He could overlook or suppress inconvenient facts and make severe tactical misjudgments; he radiated optimism when it was scarcely warranted. He was receptive to new weapons, and, when the breakthrough he had long predicted came at last in 1918, he was skillful in turning it to advantage. Is it ironic or appropriate that his statue stands today in Whitehall, a little down the street from Charles I?[18]

With their doctrinaire commitment to offensive warfare, the French held to the dogged General Joseph Joffre until the end of 1916, when he was replaced by another advocate of the offensive, General Robert Nivelle, who also failed and would have done so, even had Haig been able to abide him or willing to serve gladly under his direction. Suffering from the terrible losses of manpower in the early campaigns—nearly one and a half million in 1915 alone—the French yielded up the main effort to the British from mid-1916; but Nivelle was not replaced until May 1917, when the famous defender of the fortress of Verdun, General Henri Philippe Pétain, succeeded him. A national hero, Pétain went as far as perhaps anyone could to restore the shattered morale of French troops; his reputation—and the defensive doctrine he represented—were to project themselves far into the future (see p. 1045). Of Russian generalship it is perhaps better not to speak. General Alexander Samsonov, with portentous symbolism, committed suicide after his army surrendered at Tannenberg in 1914; the offensive of General Alexei Brusilov in the summer of 1916 was well timed and in its initial stages well executed: it aided the Italians, pulled German forces from the Somme, and helped to bring Rumania into the war. But the initial successes could not be followed up, and delays brought the Russians up against massed German armies. Russian losses of more than a million were a terrible blow to an already shaken nation; in retrospect the campaign was Samsonov's suicide writ large.

On the Home Front

There were changes in command within governments as well, changes dictated by the very emergence of the idea of a home front. A war on such a scale and with such pressing demands on technology, labor, and industrial resources had to become a total war, with civilian populations as fully mobilized as the soldiers. Looking back, it is surprising how long the enthusiasm lasted, despite the terrible losses. The French were, of course, fighting for their homeland, a tenth of which was held by the Germans, but both the German army and the French army had long been able to rely on conscripted troops. The British, with their small, specialized professional army, had never known conscription and did not enact it until January 1916, although efforts had been made over the

[18] Haig is the general about whom most controversy rages. For opposing views, see B. H. Liddell Hart, *The War in Outline* (1936), and John Terraine in his biography, *Ordeal of Victory* (1963), and *The Western Front, 1914-1918* (1965). A balanced judgment can be found in Sir Llewellyn Woodward, *Great Britain and the War of 1914-1918* (1967), 139-142, 146-154, 256-296; the introduction sensitively describes the impact of the war—and of the quality of military leadership—on the author.

preceding six months or so to systematize the voluntary system. But that voluntary system had produced well over a million men, who were surely responding to more than that superb poster showing the old war hero Lord Kitchener, now minister of war (who from the first knew the war would be a long one), pointing sternly at the viewer over the legend "Your country needs *you!*" But ideals are not forever proof against the multiplication of death. Where there were few or no ideals, as in Russia above all, or in Austria or to some degree in Italy, crumbling morale was soon evident. But even in Germany, France, and Britain it became necessary, in Halévy's phrase, to mobilize enthusiasm, by censorship and by a steady barrage of propaganda against the enemy, a recourse the more disturbing as one moved across Europe toward the liberal West.

In the face of the material demands of war, made more stringent by the reciprocal pressures of blockade and submarine warfare, it became necessary to put entire national economies on a war footing, to ration food and raw materials, to conscript labor, to recruit women for jobs formerly closed to them, to restrict trade unionism and the resort to strikes, and even to bring trade-union leaders into government. These measures, often inefficiently, sometimes brilliantly improvised, demonstrated that the modern state possessed a coercive power in all spheres of life beyond what anyone had imagined. To some, the socialists especially, it was an experiment full of promise, not only for permanence of state control but for equality of distribution and sacrifice; to most, the extension of state power was a temporary expedient to be jettisoned as quickly as possible.

Traditional politicians, in office everywhere at the outbreak of war, failed to bring the requisite decisiveness, even ruthlessness, to this altered task: hence the new war leaders who emerged as the frightful reality began to be pressed home in 1916. In Germany Bethmann Hollweg remained chancellor until July 1917. He was not a charismatic war leader and he lacked political support, though he needed no more than the support of the emperor. Bethmann's early declaration of war aims was expansionist enough to suit all but the most rabid of pan-German imperialists: not only was the goal of *Mitteleuropa* enforced with a vengeance but, contrary to promises in the days before war began, he proposed German annexation of parts of Belgium, while what remained was to be a German satellite. The chancellor was capable, nevertheless, of both moderation and political insight. He opposed for as long as he could the resumption of unrestricted submarine warfare, and in 1917, as German will and unity crumbled and the socialist menace once more emerged, Bethmann persuaded William II to issue a decree promising replacement of the old Prussian three-class system by equal suffrage, a bold constitutional stroke he was certain would allay discontent. But he was dismissed the next day. That the emperor should reverse himself and Bethmann depart without a struggle reflects the central position that Hindenburg and Ludendorff had attained. The new suffrage was anathema to them, and its author could no longer be tolerated. The succession of nonentities following Bethmann Hollweg made it clear that the division of power between the military and civilian arms, which had so bedeviled the German polity since 1890, had been resolved into a thinly disguised military dictatorship—one that at no time showed its power so much as when in 1918, having lost the war, Ludendorff urged the making of peace, thrust the responsibility for it on a socialist civilian government, and kept his army intact and blameless.

Wartime France had a succession of governments, much as before. When the German armies made their initial advance in 1914, the high command ordered the government to Bordeaux, to which the government had fled in 1870 (see p. 813); it returned only in December. The move was disliked, and a sarcastic version of the *Marseillaise* made the rounds—calling citizens not to arms, but to the station, not to form battalions but to climb into the railway carriages. There was steady involvement, and some interference, of deputies as well as ministers in military matters, while the administration of the war effort went according to "le système D"—from the verb *se débrouiller*, to muddle through, in other words no system at all. With much of the industrial area in German hands, the French economy proved difficult to adapt to the new exigencies; the tax system was inadequate—an income tax was instituted only during the war and widely evaded—financing inept, and inflation rampant. Still, to an astonishing degree, the national will held firm.

By 1917, however, the terrible sacrifices that ordinary Frenchmen had willingly undertaken had grown too great to be borne: there were mutinies at the front and scandals at home. Still worse in patriotic eyes, sentiment for a negotiated peace—less than total victory—was increasing, even in high places. The savior France craved was found in that fierce and widely unpopular Radical politician Georges Clemenceau, who as a deputy in 1871 had refused to accept the loss of Alsace-Lorraine. Clemenceau had bitterly attacked the government ever since 1914, and in November 1917 President Poincaré overcame his hostility in the greater interest of victory and made Clemenceau premier, at the age of seventy-six. "Home policy?" Clemenceau said, "I wage war! Foreign policy? I wage war! All the time I wage war!" His method of doing it, Sir Denis Brogan has written, "was in the true Jacobin tradition, however painful such an admission would be to the self-styled heirs of the Jacobins [i.e., the Left]. He had their fanatical patriotism; he had their ruthless vigour. He had never been an amiable man and he had now so many enemies he cared little how many more he made. The acceptance of him by the Chamber was as much an abdication as the creation by the Convention, in 1793, of the Committee of Public Safety. He was a one-man committee. He had no colleagues, only useful subordinates. . . ."[19] The dictator had traitors shot (one of them the notorious woman spy Mata Hari) and the compromised brought to trial. He kept the army on a short rein, visited the front regularly, and restored morale both in the army

[19] D. W. Brogan, *The Development of Modern France (1870-1939)* (1940), 536-537.

and in the country. No one doubted at the end of 1918 that the victory belonged to Clemenceau, the "Tiger of France," no matter how much that knowledge grated.

Germany had always been a military autocracy; France had known dictators before; so it was in Britain, the home of parliamentarianism and the liberal tradition, that the war had its most startling political effects. There too the war had begun in unity, though two old-line Liberals resigned from the cabinet rather than agree to war and Ramsay MacDonald, who led the new but pivotal Labour party, resigned when his party rallied to the cause. Asquith, a superb orator and parliamentarian, presided over a tension-ridden government that was railed at by patriotic Tories who formed no part of it. In May 1915 Asquith gave in to the demand for a coalition, which included the principal Conservative leaders and Arthur Henderson of the Labour party. That summer, as the result of revelations of a shell shortage on the western front, a ministry of munitions was created; confided to the former chancellor of the exchequer David Lloyd George, it accomplished miracles of production. Lloyd George brought to his task energy, imagination, and impatience with bureaucratic channels and official conservatism. When the War Office rejected a design for a mortar that soon became standard, Lloyd George raised the money from an Indian maharajah to produce it privately; when Kitchener ventured that more than four machine guns to a battalion would be a luxury, Lloyd George told a subordinate, "Take Kitchener's maximum; square it; multiply that result by two—and when you are in sight of that, double it again for good luck."[20]

At the end of 1916, in collusion with two Tory leaders and the newspaper magnate Lord Beaverbrook, Lloyd George provoked a cabinet crisis. The end result was that Lloyd George took Asquith's place as prime minister. He at once created a war cabinet of five, including besides himself Arthur Henderson of the Labour party; Bonar Law, the Tory leader; and two brilliant authoritarians, Lord Curzon, formerly viceroy of India, and Lord Milner, who had ruled with harsh success as proconsul in South Africa after the Boer War. It was odd company for a radical Liberal, but Lloyd George was interested in action, not orthodoxy or theoretical consistency, and he was impatient of forms, even the most sacred. New ministries were created and filled with men brought in from the world of business; Parliament was increasingly ignored and policies were explained through speech-making and the press. There was discontent, though less with Lloyd George than with frustration and the endless casualty lists. Disgruntled Liberals abandoned by the prime minister were impotent. Embittered workingmen, on the other hand, turned away from official party and trade-union leadership to the radical shop stewards (many of them future Communists) to protest against the regimentation of labor; in places, notably in the shipyards on the Clyde in Scotland, the labor agitation grew into a serious

---

[20] Liddell Hart, *The War in Outline*, 73–74. In 1916 Lloyd George became minister of war, after Kitchener was lost at sea while traveling to Russia.

challenge. But with Lloyd George the whirlwind had been sown, and the harvest was victory.

The Shape of Victory

In 1917 Russia was shaken by revolution; it occurred in two stages, in March and November 1917. The Russian provisional government sought to continue the war, but Brusilov's last offensive failed in the summer and the Russian war effort collapsed. The Bolshevik revolution in November brought an armistice in December, and on March 3, 1918, the Russian representatives signed the German-dictated Treaty of Brest Litovsk, after Lenin's insistence overrode the protests of many Bolsheviks against the intolerable humiliation. Not only was Russia saddled with a huge indemnity, but the Germans insisted on the independence of Finland, the Baltic states, Poland, and the Ukraine, which they intended to constitute a buffering chain between the victorious and the defeated powers; to the southeast, Transcaucasian territory was ceded to Turkey. With these territories Russia lost more than a quarter of its population, cultivated farmland, and railways; a third of its manufactures; and most of its iron works and coal fields.

The blow to the Allies from the collapse on the eastern front was counterbalanced by the entry of the United States into the war on April 6, following on the resumption of unrestricted submarine warfare by the Germans early in 1917. But it was not until nearly a year later that American troops could be readied and got to Europe in any significant numbers. Thus the year 1917 was one of nearly unrelieved disaster for the Allies. The stalemate on the western front was only confirmed by the dismal failure of the British offensive at Passchendaele: the deadlock on the Italian front was broken by a stunning Austrian victory at Caporetto, which drove the demoralized Italian troops back from the Isonzo they had tried so many times to put behind them— in the other direction. Only in the Near East were there encouraging signs. The British forces in Mesopotamia had entered Baghdad in March; the army in Palestine, aided by the Arabs, conquered Jerusalem in early December, thus opening the way to attack Turkey directly from the south. At the end of the year, on the western front, a unified command was at last agreed upon, under the diplomatic leadership of the famous French general and military theorist Ferdinand Foch.

In the spring of 1918 Ludendorff gambled everything on an offensive in the west. German armies, with numerical superiority (thanks to transfers from the eastern front) and novel tactics, struck at one point after another in the Allied lines, almost always with success, but never enough to clinch the victory that came so close. By summer the German armies could count on reserves in neither men nor morale; in August the Allies began an advance that proved unstoppable, the more so as fresh American troops were pouring onto the

Continent, though at General Pershing's insistence they fought as separate units under American command, not as reinforcements for weary and depleted Allied forces. Movement at last began from the Allied beachhead in Salonika, and by the end of September 1918 the Bulgarian forces had been beaten and forced into an armistice. The British in Palestine moved northward in the autumn to take one after another base from Turkey, which signed an armistice on October 30. In Austria-Hungary the aged emperor Francis Joseph had died on November 21, 1916, to be succeeded by his grandnephew Charles. Charles entered into a rapidly crumbling inheritance. The Austrian army tried to repeat the triumph of Caporetto on the new Italian line at the Piave, but was repulsed with heavy losses in June 1918, and at the end of October an Italian offensive at last broke through to Vittorio Veneto, whereupon the Austrian army collapsed. A Czechoslovak republic, assured of Allied support since the summer, had already declared its independence, and the declaration of Yugoslav independence at the end of October was followed on November 1 by the creation of a separate Hungarian government.

Ludendorff, appalled by the irresistible Allied advance and close to a breakdown, demanded an armistice and the opening of talks while his army was still undefeated. In an effort at genuine constitutional innovation, a coalition government under Prince Max of Baden—upright and liberal-minded but inexperienced—took office on October 4; with the Austrians, the new government appealed to President Wilson for an armistice on the basis of the Fourteen Points Wilson had declared as American goals in January 1918 (see p. 962). At the end of October Ludendorff resigned, as military discipline collapsed and mutinies broke out in the fleet. A revolt in Munich presaged the end of the Hohenzollern dynasty; William II abdicated on November 9, fleeing to Holland. A republic was proclaimed, and on the eleventh hostilities on the western front came to an end, in accordance with an armistice signed in Marshal Foch's railway carriage in the forest of Compiègne. The terms of the armistice were harsh; but the German delegation had no choice but to accept. An armistice with Austria had been concluded on November 3, and on November 12 Emperor Charles abdicated, his empire shattered into the new "succession states." But Germany and Austria were not the only losers: the First World War was a war no one won.

THE RUSSIAN REVOLUTION

No nation, not even Austria-Hungary, was so ill prepared as Russia for the ordeal that World War I became. Despite the rapid strides made in industrialization since the last years of the nineteenth century, Russian factories could not produce even the basic requirements; transportation and communications remained inadequate. What success Russia had had in industrializing created social pressures that themselves were dangerous to the war effort. The concentration of an ill-paid and ill-used working class in large economic units made labor organization simple, however much it was hampered by official repression or by the failure of strikes; discontents could be defined and remedies proposed with lightning speed, the more so as a variety of socialist doctrines lay persuasively to hand. Agrarian problems still defied solution. Agricultural techniques remained pitifully backward: the yield of grain per acre was a third of that in Germany, half of that in France. Hated landlords continued to dominate the country; vast numbers of the peasantry still had no land of their own, despite a half-century of reforms. Yet it was from the workers and peasants, bitter with discontent and hatred, that Russia drew most of the fifteen million men called into the army and decimated in the dismal campaigns on the eastern front.

The Duma, brought into existence by the revolution of 1905, was a neutered concession to Western parliamentary forms: parties were no more than rudimentary, and political opinion was hopelessly splintered. The Duma could discuss but have little effect on policy; ministers were not responsible to it; and it could be and was dissolved whenever it became mildly inconvenient. As a mode of government, autocracy was hardly shaken by what should have been the lesson of 1905; the habit and mentality of autocracy had been touched not at all. Indeed the war made things worse. Incredibly insensitive to the sufferings of his people and his state, Nicholas II came to depend more and more on his bigoted and hysterical wife, who in turn sought counsel from Gregory Rasputin, a debauched and licentious Siberian monk, whose hypnotic powers helped to relieve the sufferings of the hemophiliac crown prince, thus confirming the belief of the royal pair that this corrupt adventurer was indeed a holy man. When the tsar ill-advisedly put himself in the place of the Grand Duke Nicholas as nominal commander in chief in 1915, his long absences threw more power into the hands of the tsarina and Rasputin. The suspicion of German influence at court was rife, the scandal of Rasputin's malign influence was shocking even by Russian standards and at the very end of 1916 Rasputin was murdered by Prince Felix Yusupov and other conspirators at court. Rasputin's importance is more symbolic than real: that he could attain such influence reflects the feebleness and moral bankruptcy of the regime. For at least a century, with rare exceptions, Russian politics and administration had functioned at a level well below that of nations to the west; the demanding test of a war on such a scale was more than the system could bear. In contrast to the West, the only savior imperial Russia could produce was utterly committed to the destruction of the regime that bred it. What happened was that the remains of the imperial system simply collapsed in 1917.

On March 8 of that year strikes began in Petrograd (as the capital had been renamed at the outset of the war); they continued the next day, augmented by raids on bakeries, amid cries for bread.[21] By the tenth an almost spontaneous general strike gripped Petrograd, and many of the soldiers sent in to maintain order sympathized with the uncontrolled masses. By the twelfth the railwaymen had cut the capital off from access to troops from the front, and even the most loyal garrison joined in the mutiny; the fortress where political prisoners were kept was stormed. At his military headquarters, the tsar dismissed as "nonsense" the frantic warnings of the president of the Duma—"that fat Rodzianko"—that unless a responsible government were formed, nothing could be saved; refusing to believe the magnitude of the crisis the tsar had tried to dissolve the Duma on the eleventh. Torn by constitutional scruples, the Duma obeyed but set up an informal committee and feebly made efforts to seek a substitute government. At the same time another governing group was established—the Soviet (council) of Workers' and Soldiers' Deputies. By the time the tsar decided on the fourteenth to commission Rodzianko to form a new ministry, two rival governments were actually functioning in Petrograd, and Moscow had gone over to the revolutionaries. On the fifteenth, in Pskov, while returning to join his family at the summer residence in Tsarskoe Seloe, the tsar yielded to entreaties from the highest military and civilian officials and abdicated, first for himself and later for his ailing son. It was intended that the royal family go to England; prevented from doing so, they were put under arrest in the summer residence and were later taken to a remote Siberian village where they were shot in the summer of 1918, incidental victims of a civil war. But such violence was not characteristic of 1917. In a chaos of disorganized, remarkably good-natured, and basically spontaneous uprisings, the Romanov dynasty came to an end, with no heroics and seemingly few regrets.

The Provisional Government formally took office on the sixteenth. Liberal and social reforms were at once instituted or promised: full civil equality for all citizens; freedom of religion, speech, and assembly; labor legislation; the independence of Poland and the autonomy of Finland; the summoning of a constituent assembly. But declaring and promising were not enacting and enforcing. The Provisional Government lacked the ability or power to reestablish order in the chaos-ridden capital, its writ ran even more uncertainly in the country; its constitutional authority was doubtful and its political base, like its vision, was narrow. It was headed by Prince George Lvov, with the able and serious Paul Miliukov as foreign minister—both belonged to the Kadet party; there were other Kadets and more conservative Octobrists and one radical, the lawyer Alexander Kerensky, as minister of justice. Kerensky was crucial, not only for his enthusiasm and oratory, but because he also belonged to the

---

[21] Imperial Russia still used the Julian calendar, which by the twentieth century was thirteen days behind the Gregorian calendar used in the West. In Russian dating the strikes began on February 23. Thus the February revolution began in March by our calendar, and the October revolution in November.

Petrograd Soviet. Closer to the masses and controlling communications and other instruments of power, the Soviet was a model for soviets established elsewhere in the country. Genuinely representative of its constituencies, thanks to frequent elections, the Soviet ranged over a spectrum of socialism, pushed further to the left as Bolsheviks began to return from their Siberian exile.

The most immediate issue facing both the Provisional Government and the Soviet was the war. On March 14 the Soviet had issued "Order No. 1," which purported to remove all authority of officers, except in actual field operations, to turn the organization of the army over to committees operating under orders from the Soviet, and to do away with the forms of hierarchy—saluting, standing at attention, titles, and the use by officers of the familiar "thou" in addressing soldiers. It seemed, with reason, to mean an end to all military discipline as it had been known, and the soldiers at the front fell into disorganization and defeatism. The Soviet favored continuing the war, which now that the tsardom was gone, could be viewed as a common democratic enterprise against the German autocracy. Anxious for the support and recognition of the Allies, the Provisional Government committed itself fully to the Allied cause. At the beginning of May Miliukov assured the Allies not only that the war would continue but that prior understandings and commitments would be honored; when these sweeping assurances provoked wide protests, Miliukov resigned. In mid-May, therefore, Kerensky became minister of war in a new government farther to the left than the first and set out to revive the fighting spirit of the troops. The Soviet insistence on a peace with "no annexations and no indemnities," taken over by the Provisional Government, had a profound effect on socialist and pacifist groups emerging in the West.

By this time, however, a new factor had entered the picture. On April 16, V. I. Lenin was welcomed at the Finland Station in Petrograd; he, his wife, and a number of associates had been carried from their Swiss exile in a sealed train across Germany. The arrangement had been made by Swiss socialists and gladly accepted by the Germans as a means of further confusing the Russian enemy; Lenin agreed to no more than to work for the repatriation of some German prisoners. In Zurich Lenin had received news of the February revolution with mounting excitement and determination, but ever since his second exile began in 1908, he had been refining his views in ways that did not at all parallel what his Bolshevik comrades elsewhere were thinking. In the "April Propositions," delivered to a meeting of the Bolshevik central committee, Lenin rejected the imperialist war, rejected any cooperation with the Provisional Government, rejected any pretense at establishing constitutional forms of government, and insisted on the abolition of private property and the distribution of land to the peasants, on worker control of factories, and on the confiding of government to the soviets. With his simple slogans of "peace, bread, and land," and "all power to the Soviets," he cut through the old debate, much agitated since March, about whether the revolution would be a bourgeois revolution and, if so, what it was to accomplish. The time had come to establish socialism, which he believed would quickly spread through proletarian uprisings in the more advanced Western countries. It was, moreover, the duty of the Bolsheviks to force through that socialist revolution; frankly recognizing their present minority status, Lenin urged constant propaganda to discredit the bourgeois government of "Lvov and Co." and to explain the Bolshevik position again and again until the party won a majority in the soviets. To many of his hearers the propositions came as a shock—to Josef Stalin and Leo Kamenev, for example, who had returned from exile prepared for cautious cooperation with the Provisional Government. But such was Lenin's authority and persuasiveness that he carried his resolutions overwhelmingly.

The proposals were prophetic, almost too much so. The Bolsheviks early won control of the Petrograd Soviet; their educational activities were soon to make them dominant in other soviets, at least in the towns. Among the peasants, insofar as they were political at all, the dominant socialism was that of the Socialist Revolutionaries. Lenin could carry their representatives with him in his call for confiscation of land but not in his proposals for organization, and the peasant uprisings that began in the spring and mounted in extent and intensity through the summer and autumn owed more to elemental land hunger and long-suppressed hatreds than to any doctrinal inspiration from above. By autumn the confiscation the Bolsheviks called for had been accomplished by local peasant committees.

In the capital the increasingly Bolshevik militants attempted an uprising, the so-called July Days—an attempt the Bolshevik central committee did all it could to prevent. The rising coincided with receipt of the news of the final failure of the Russian offensive against the Austrian and German armies. The Provisional Government, despite its weakening hold on power, suppressed the outbreak and ordered the arrest of the Bolshevik leaders: Trotsky went to prison, while Lenin escaped into hiding in Finland. Prince Lvov retired, and Kerensky now became prime minister; he replaced the defeated General Brusilov, the commander in chief, with General Lavr Kornilov.

Although his ultimate intentions are still not clear, Kornilov soon made it evident that he intended to become Russia's savior. Encouraged by Kerensky to take steps to protect the Provisional Government from an anticipated Bolshevik coup, Kornilov tried to mount his own coup by demanding the resignation of all the ministers. He could count on support from the landowners and the military officers and from most of the middle classes as well, but such support was insufficient in revolutionary times. When he learned of the challenge from his supposed protector, Kerensky ordered Kornilov to turn over his command. Kornilov refused but could not make good his promise to bring troops to Petrograd. The city mobilized to prevent the counterrevolution, and, faced with short supplies and a railway strike, the soldiers refused to follow Kornilov's orders. The victorious Kerensky now added the title of commander in chief to his other responsibilities and appealed to the Left for support, but his authority was slipping away. Trotsky, released from prison, became head of the Petrograd Soviet. Lenin, having decided that the time had come, returned secretly from Finland toward the end of October to urge on the Bolshevik central committee, despite the opposition of some of his closest associates, that an insurrection should take place at once. Again he prevailed, and it was Trotsky, that brilliant organizer, who carried the insurrection through— cleverly as the work of the soviets, not the Bolshevik central committee. On November 5, in a last-ditch attempt to save the Provisional Government, Kerensky again ordered the arrest of the Bolshevik leaders. On November 7 (October 25, old style) Red Guards seized strategic points in Petrograd, and in the early morning hours of November 8, Bolshevik-led troops stormed the Winter Palace, where the Provisional Government had taken refuge. Kerensky escaped from the capital, intending to rally the troops at the front, but he soon headed for exile; he died, a long-time resident of the United States, in 1970.

The insurrection had been timed to coincide with a second meeting of the All-Russian Congress of Soviets. Now the Bolsheviks were what their name declared, a majority party. Lenin carried a motion on immediate peace and another decreeing the immediate abolition of landlord property without compensation. Both registered accomplished facts: the military effort had collapsed, and an armistice and a humiliating peace would soon follow (see p. 950); and the peasantry had already seized the land without prompting. The remaining members of the Provisional Government were arrested, what power was left to them (and far more) passing to a council of people's commissars, headed by Lenin, with Trotsky as commissar for foreign affairs, and Stalin as commissar for nationalities. The November revolution, though more drastic than the March revolution, occurred with as little resistance and as little violence. It was done by a divided party, not yet characterized by the tight discipline that was to distinguish it in the future or that Leninist theory required. And while Lenin was to prove himself a magnificent organizer and tactician, his invaluable contribution in 1917 was, as Professor Henry L. Roberts has said, "on the level of political instinct."[22] The revolutionary regime of the Provisional Government had disintegrated as the tsarist autocracy had disintegrated. Lenin's perceptiveness brought the Bolsheviks to power, not a moment too early nor a moment too late, by strategies that were intuitive and forced on astonished colleagues by the assuredness of a demonic will. But the seizure of power in a virtual vacuum of authority was a different matter from consolidating power against a host of enemies. In that task would appear new aspects of Lenin's genius, and out of it would come an autocracy beyond the farthest imagination of a Romanov.

[22] Henry L. Roberts, in the *Columbia History of the World,* John A. Garraty and Peter Gay, eds. (1972), 998.

SELECTED READINGS

Oron J. Hale, *The Great Illusion, 1900-1914* (1971), in the Rise of Modern Europe series, is an elegant survey with an interesting emphasis on social and cultural history and with the usual essential and extensive bibliography. The period is also covered in chapters of the revised volume XII of the *New Cambridge Modern History*, C. L. Mowat, ed., *The Shifting Balance of World Forces, 1898-1945* (1968).

On Spain, in addition to the indispensable book by Raymond Carr, *Spain, 1808-1939* (1966), there is Joan Connelly Ullman's *The Tragic Week: A Study of Anti-Clericalism in Spain, 1875-1912* (1958). Denis Mack Smith, *Italy, a Modern History* (1959, rev. ed., 1969), and Christopher Seton-Watson, *Italy from Liberalism to Fascism, 1870-1925* (1967), are basic guides, and to them should be added A. William Salomone, *Italian Democracy in the Making: The Political Scene in the Giolitti Era* (1960). On France, for general narrative, see D. W. Brogan, *France under the Republic (1870-1939)* (1940), and for a stimulating interpretation, see David Thomson, *Democracy in France since 1870* (5th ed., 1969). On the emergence of the new Right, see Eugen Weber's two books, *The Nationalist Revival in France, 1905-1914* (1959), and *Action Française: Royalism and Reaction in Twentieth-Century France* (1962), the latter continuing well past the end of the period of this chapter. Harvey Goldberg's *The Life of Jean Jaurès* (1962) is essential for French socialism. Gordon Wright studies a major French politician in *Raymond Poincaré and the French Presidency* (1942). The fitfulness of German government emerges in Michael Balfour, *The Kaiser and his Times* (1964), and Norman Rich, *Friedrich von Holstein*, 2 vols. (1965). On the German socialists, see Carl E. Schorske's masterly *German Social Democracy, 1905-1917: The Development of the Great Schism* (1955).

On British developments there are two classics: the second volume of the epilogue to Elie Halévy's *History of the English People in the Nineteenth Century* (1932, tr. 1934), covering the years 1905-1915, in recent reprintings bearing the title *The Rule of Democracy;* the other is George Dangerfield's scintillating *The Strange Death of Liberal England* (1936), a controversial interpretation that holds up remarkably well. The essays in Simon Nowell-Smith, ed., *Edwardian England, 1901-1914* (1965) are excellent, as is Samuel Hynes, *The Edwardian Turn of Mind* (1968). Henry Pelling, *The Social Geography of British Elections, 1885-1910* (1967) is an important analysis. Peter Stansky, *Ambitions and Strategies: The Struggle for the Leadership of the Liberal Party in the 1890's* (1964) is an essential prelude to the Liberal resurgence. Bentley B. Gilbert, *The Evolution of National Insurance in Great Britain* (1966) deals with a major Liberal reform. Roy Jenkins, himself a prominent Labour politician, has written an admiring *Asquith* (1964), and Robert Blake has provided an authoritative biography of Balfour's successor in the Conservative leadership: *The Unknown Prime Minister: The Life and Times of Andrew Bonar Law* (1955), which in the American edition bears the equally apt title *Unrepentant Tory*. None of the biographies of Lloyd George is really satisfactory, but Kenneth O. Morgan, *Wales in British Politics, 1868-1922* (1963) provides essential background. On the crises at the end of the period, Halévy and Dangerfield are still the best guides. The books on women's suffrage are either popular or partisan, but valuable supplementary analyses on other critical fronts are F. S. L. Lyons, *The Irish Parliamentary Party, 1890-1910* (1951), and E. H. Phelps Brown, *The Growth of British Industrial Relations* (1959).

There are several admirable surveys of the last years of the Romanov dynasty: Hugh Seton-Watson, *The Decline of Imperial Russia* (1952); Richard Charques, *The Twilight of Imperial Russia* (1958); and the essays in Theofanis G. Stavrou, ed., *Russia under the Last Tsar* (1967), and in Erwin Oberländer et al., *Russia Enters the Twentieth Century, 1894-1917* (1971). Important biographical studies are Robert F. Byrnes, *Pobedonostsev: His Life and Thought* (1968); Richard Pipes, *Struve: Liberal on the Left, 1870-1905* (1970); Theodore H. Von Laue, *Sergei Witte and the Industrialization of Russia* (1963); and Howard D. Mehlinger and John M. Thompson, *Count Witte and the Tsarist Government in the 1905 Revolution* (1972). Sidney Harcave, *First Blood: The Russian Revolution of 1905* (1964) is an excellent account, but it should be remembered that Leon Trotsky wrote his own history, in differing Russian and German versions, shortly after the event; it has appeared in English translation as *1905* (1971). On the agrarian situation, see G. T. Robinson, *Rural Russia under the Old Regime* (1932), and on labor there is a very important article by Leopold H. Haimson, "The Problem of Social Stability in Urban Russia, 1905-1917," *Slavic Review*, 23 (December 1964), 619-642, and 24 (March 1965), 1-22.

On the peace movement an important work is F. S. L. Lyons, *Internationalism in Europe, 1815-1914* (1963), but militarism has been much more studied. I. F. Clarke, *Voices Prophesying War, 1763-1984* (1966) is fascinating and original. David B. Ralston, *The Army of the Republic, 1871-1914* (1967) is essential for the French situation. On Germany, see Gordon A. Craig, *The Politics of the Prussian Army, 1640-1945* (1955), and two famous books by Gerhard Ritter, *The Sword and the Scepter: The Problem of Militarism in Germany,* vol. II, *The European Powers and the Wilhelminian Reich, 1890-1914* (1960, 2nd ed., 1965, tr. 1970), and *The Schlieffen Plan: Critique of a Myth* (1956, tr. 1958). The two sides of the naval race can be seen in Arthur J. Marder, *From the Dreadnought to Scapa Flow: The Royal Navy in the Fisher Era, 1904-1919,* 5 vols. (1961-1970), and Jonathan Steinberg, *Yesterday's Deterrent: Tirpitz and the Birth of the German Battle Fleet* (1965). British diplomacy is examined in G. W. Monger, *The End of Isolation: British Foreign Policy, 1900-7* (1963), and Zara S. Steiner, *Foreign Office and Foreign Policy, 1898-1914* (1970); see also Ian H. Nish, *The Anglo-Japanese Alliance: The Diplomacy of Two Island Empires, 1894-1907* (1966). A most useful interpretation of the dynamics of policy-making in Germany in this period is the second chapter of Gordon A. Craig, *From Bismarck to Adenauer: Aspects of German Statecraft* (1958, rev. ed. 1965).

On the course of diplomacy prior to the outbreak of war, A. J. P. Taylor, *The Struggle for Mastery in Europe, 1848-1918* (1954) is an excellent general guide, while an influential interpretation is Elie Halévy, "The World Crisis of 1914-1918," reprinted in his *The Era of Tyrannies* (1938, tr. 1965), 209-247. The older important books are Sidney B. Fay, *The Origins of the World War,* 2 vols. (1928), Bernadotte E. Schmitt, *The Coming of the War, 1914,* 2 vols. (1930), and G. P. Gooch, *Before the War: Studies in Diplomacy,* 2 vols. (1936-1938). Yet more extensive is Luigi Albertini, *The Origins of the War of 1914,* 3 vols. (1942-1943, tr. 1952-1957). Briefer, more recent interpretations are Laurence Lafore, *The Long Fuse* (1965), and Joachim Remak, *The Origins of World War I* (1967). Remak has also written a dramatic account, *Sarajevo: The Story of a Political Murder* (1959). On the Balkans, see E. C. Helmreich, *The Diplomacy of the Balkan Wars, 1912-1913* (1938), Stavro Skendi, *The Albanian National Awakening, 1878-1912* (1967), and Ernest E. Ramsaur, *The Young Turks: Prelude to the Revolution of 1908* (1957). The new revisionist interpretation of Germany's role began with Fritz

Fischer, *Germany's Aims in the First World War* (1961, tr. 1967), and Fischer has pushed his argument back in a subsequent volume, not yet translated, *Krieg der Illusionen: Die deutsche Politik von 1911 bis 1914* (1969). Much of this new debate is reflected in the essays that make up Walter Laqueur and George L. Mosse, eds., *1914, The Coming of the First World War* (1966), a reprinting of vol. 3 (1966) of the *Journal of Contemporary History*. For an important reading of the context, see Henry Cord Meyer, *Mitteleuropa in German Thought and Action, 1815–1945* (1955).

On the course of the war, B. H. Liddell Hart, *The War in Outline* (1936) is an admirable brief sketch by the most influential of modern military historians. In *Ordeal of Victory* (1963), John Terraine has provided a sympathetic biography of Haig, who also dominates the essays in Terraine's *The Western Front, 1914–1918* (1965). R. R. James, *Gallipoli* (1965) is one of a number of books on that ill-fated enterprise. On the domestic impact of the war on Germany, see Gerald D. Feldman, *Army, Industry, and Labor in Germany, 1914–1918* (1966); on Austria-Hungary, see Z. A. B. Zeman, *The Break-up of the Habsburg Empire, 1914–1918: A Study in National and Social Revolution* (1961); on France, see Jere C. King, *Generals and Politicians: Conflicts between France's High Command, Parliament and Government, 1914–1918* (1951). The British domestic scene has been intensively studied, for example, Sir Llewellyn Woodward, *Great Britain and the War of 1914–1918* (1967), Arthur Marwick, *The Deluge: British Society and the First World War* (1965), and W. H. B. Court's essay, "The Years 1914–1918 in British Economic and Social History," in his *Scarcity and Choice in History* (1970); on politics, A. J. P. Taylor, *Politics in Wartime and Other Essays* (1964) is very important. Particular mention should be made of a remarkable work that is part history, part memoir, and part self-justification: Winston Churchill, *The World Crisis,* 4 vols. (1923–1929). On aspects of the diplomacy of the period, besides Fischer's first book, mentioned above, see Z. A. B. Zeman, *The Gentlemen Negotiators: A Diplomatic History of the First World War* (1971); and, for a particularly tangled situation that casts its shadow far into the future, Elizabeth Monroe, *Britain's Moment in the Middle East, 1914–1956* (1963). J. W. Wheeler-Bennett examines *Brest-Litovsk, The Forgotten Peace, 1918* (1918), and Arno J. Mayer's *Political Origins of the New Diplomacy, 1917–1918* (1959) takes a revisionist look at the Allies.

Special mention should be made of the multivolumed *Economic and Social History of the World War,* published under the auspices of the Carnegie Endowment for International Peace, Division of Economics and History. Each volume in the various national series was published under the name of its author, but most libraries will have a general entry under Carnegie Endowment.

The most concise account of events in Russia in 1917, a book remarkable for its time as well as today, is W. H. Chamberlin, *The Russian Revolution* (1935), of which volume I covers the period 1917–1918. Far more detailed is E. H. Carr, *The Bolshevik Revolution, 1917–1923,* 3 vols. (1950–1953), the introductory volumes of his *History of Soviet Russia*. See also Adam B. Ulam, *The Bolsheviks: The Intellectual, Personal, and Political History of the Triumph of Communism in Russia* (1965). The biographical approach to this subject is natural. Bertram D. Wolfe, *Three Who Made a Revolution* (2nd ed., 1956) is an excellent introduction to Lenin, Trotsky, and Stalin. Lenin is the subject of biographies by Louis Fischer (1964) and Michael Morgan (1971), and the first volume of Isaac Deutscher's three-volume biography *The Prophet Armed: Trotsky, 1879–1921* (1954), is excellent.

24

*Europe
and the World:
1919-1929*

THE RECONSTRUCTION OF EUROPE

Peacemaking

Ten days after the peace conference opened in Paris on January 18, 1919, a delegate referred in passing to the Congress of Vienna. President Wilson answered—one would guess with some emphasis—that "the present enterprise was very different from that undertaken at Vienna a century ago, and he hoped that even by reference no odour of Vienna would again be brought into their proceedings." In reporting this exchange, Sir Charles Webster, the great diplomatic historian, remarked, "Nor so far as I know was any introduced—by reference." [1] The sarcasm is well taken, for no perceptive observer in Paris in

---

[1] In the preface to the second edition of C. K. Webster, *The Congress of Vienna* (1934), 15. See also the comparison of the two settlements in Ludwig Dehio, "Versailles after Thirty-five Years," in his *Germany and World Politics in the Twentieth Century* (1955, tr. 1959), 109–123.

1919 could escape constant reminders of the general reconstruction of Europe a little over a century before. The representatives of the European states, their advisers, and the inevitable hangers-on flocked to Paris as they had descended in numbers on Vienna. Though both congresses were plenary in form, in fact the basic decisions came to be taken by four (or three) leaders of the victorious powers. In both instances the negotiators had to honor prior understandings, some of which came to light only after the proceedings began. Both settlements were compounds of conflicting aims, bargains and concessions, ingenious answers to hard problems, evasions of others, and major and minor injustices. Though Wilson wanted to keep out "the odour of Vienna," it pervaded the doings at Paris. Yet, in retrospect, the differences are the more striking.

Vienna had been dominated by a glittering array of kings and aristocrats. A hundred years of change had robbed such great figures of power and some of them even of existence. In their place at Paris were the products of twentieth-century politics, less dazzling but no less interesting. Vittorio Orlando, representing Italy in the Big Four, counted for little; he was prime minister at the end of the war by political accident, walked out when he did not get his way, returned uninvited, and fell before the deliberations were completed. The men of Vienna might have understood Georges Clemenceau, the French premier, with his tough, single-minded pursuit of French interests. Talleyrand would surely have understood David Lloyd George. Lloyd George had risen to the premiership over the wreckage of his party, had sought political allies where he could find them, had tricked and schemed, and had just won a resounding electoral triumph in a campaign notable for promises to hang the Kaiser and to squeeze Germany "until the pips squeak." Yet at Paris he was the most supple of the negotiators, the most willing to recognize Germany's rightful place, as much a Merlin on the international scene as he had been in British politics. But no one a century before could have imagined a figure like Woodrow Wilson. By profession he was a political scientist, a term that would only have puzzled the men of Vienna. Quite as novel was his moral stance. His rigid rectitude masking a taste for power, he was the product of a nineteenth-century Anglo-American culture that mingled rationalism with a powerful moral and religious impulse. Although Wilson was increasingly isolated from—and contemptuous of?—political developments at home, the wild enthusiasm that greeted his arrival in Europe in December 1918 suggested that his call for democracy, national self-determination, and a new, open diplomacy was (at that moment) what the world wanted.[2]

---

[2] "Just as Bentham, a century earlier, had taken the eighteenth-century doctrine of reason and refashioned it to the needs of the coming age, so now Woodrow Wilson, the impassioned admirer of Bright and Gladstone, transplanted the nineteenth-century rationalist faith to the almost virgin soil of international politics and, bringing it back with him to Europe, gave it a new lease of life. Nearly all popular theories of international politics between the two world wars were reflexions, seen in an American mirror, of nineteenth-century liberal thought." E. H. Carr, *The Twenty Years' Crisis, 1919–1939: An Introduction to the Study of International Relations* (Torchbook ed., 1964), 27. Carr's realist critique of the assumptions of international politics in the period makes an impelling and revealing book.

Although the diplomats at Vienna had had their advisers, like Friedrich Gentz on whom Metternich had relied, their place was taken in Paris by battalions of experts, testimony to the professionalization that had overtaken the world in the late nineteenth century. Many of them had been hard at work during the last years of the war, defining war aims and working out plans for postwar reconstruction. Whatever help could be given was warranted, for the problems facing the negotiators were formidable indeed. In 1815 victors and vanquished emerged from the war recognizable and viable monarchies, whose frontiers and possessions could be adjusted in accordance with time-honored diplomatic practice; the political complexes of Italy and Germany needed only judicious reshuffling and rationalization, while colonies were pawns in a game that was entirely European. In 1919 only the victorious Allies, though exhausted and deeply shaken by losses and internal strain, were recognizable entities; the vanquished were at, or over, the brink of chaos. Russia, the Allied power Germany had defeated, had simply withdrawn from Europe, to work out its destiny in revolution. Germany was crushed, a monarchy no longer, its institutions in flux and under threat. Austria-Hungary and the Ottoman Empire had disintegrated, the "questions" they had posed to nineteenth-century diplomats now demanding answers, not covetous fantasies. Nor could the world of the world war be treated solely from the standpoint of Europe's advantage. The United States and Japan were aggressive and, in European terms, isolationist powers with interests that did not fit into old categories; Britain's self-governing colonies, the emerging Commonwealth—Canada, South Africa, Australia, and New Zealand—insisted upon and got separate representation (within the British Empire delegation) at the peace conference and independent membership in the League of Nations; so did India, a colony still. And while the colonies of the defeated powers could be transferred, as punishment and reward, and though the extra-European possessions of Turkey remained to be carved up, the frank exercise of a prewar imperialism was no longer possible, and new methods of control had to be devised (see p. 973).

The Vienna settlement was an overtly pragmatic affair in which historians have discerned principles; at Paris principles were enunciated and historians have been left to chronicle their violation. The precise proposals of Wilson's Fourteen Points—God Almighty, Clemenceau brutally remarked, had only ten—all rested on abstract commitments to national self-determination, freedom of the seas, the freeing of trade, "open covenants openly arrived at," and collective action to preserve peace. These commitments inevitably encountered the realities of geography and politics. The postwar treaties, more than four years in the making, were compromises made under pressures diplomats of the Old Regime did not know: the shock of millions of lost and ruined lives, the long pent-up passions released in the struggle, the clash of social and political systems, the glare of publicity, and the power of a broadened public opinion—more mercurial and more threatening to political survival than the whims of any monarch. These tensions may account for the most impressive difference between the Vienna and Paris settlements—that one lasted with only minor changes for fifty years and in essence for a hundred, while the other was under attack from the outset and was destroyed in less than twenty.

The Postwar Treaties

The principal treaty to come out of Paris was the Treaty of Versailles with Germany;[3] once it was negotiated the Big Three abandoned the details of peacemaking to their subordinates. The territorial settlement of the Versailles Treaty was drastic and straightforward. Germany was to be stripped of its colonies, to return Alsace and Lorraine to France, and to surrender small bits of territory to Belgium and the new nation of Czechoslovakia; the East Baltic port of Memel was given to the Allies for future disposition. But the most sweeping loss was of Germany's eastern lands to the reconstituted state of Poland: Posen was given up while most of West Prussia went to form the so-called Polish Corridor, separating East Prussia from the Germany to which it belonged, and giving an otherwise landlocked Poland access to the sea at the free city of Danzig. Given the principle of self-determination, the territorial settlement made extensive use of plebiscites. The division of Schleswig between Germany and Denmark corresponded to a clear vote of the inhabitants of the two parts, but the effort to apply self-determination in Upper Silesia, a mining and manufacturing district seized from Poland by Frederick the Great in the eighteenth century, showed the limitations of the method. The plebiscite, held amid violence in 1921, gave a slight over-all majority to Germany, but the vote fell in such a crazy quilt of loyalties that the council of the League of Nations finally made an arbitrary decision. The British and Italians had recommended a line that fairly approximated the voting pattern, the French a vindictive boundary; by compromising between them the council added to Germany's burden of bitterness. Some temporary arrangements were imposed as guarantees of good behavior. The rich mining district of the Saar basin was to be administered by the League of Nations for fifteen years, when a plebiscite was to be held to determine its future (see p. 1050). Ownership of the mines, however, was transferred to the French, whose own mines had been severely damaged in the fighting that ranged over the northern part of their country. As another gesture to French security, the Rhineland was to be occupied for a similar period by the Allies and permanently demilitarized, though civil administration there, in contrast to the Saar, remained German. Beyond the loss of some 25,000 square miles and seven million inhabitants,

---

[3] The names of the treaties are taken from the places in the vicinity of Paris where formal signing ceremonies were held. It is worth noting (as French nationalists certainly did) that the Treaty of Versailles was the first major international agreement in which English was given equal stature with French.

Germany was also expected to pay heavy reparations; the terms were not, however, specified in the treaty. They were to be fixed by an Allied commission, and its recommendations were to form a vital part of the economic history of the postwar world (see p. 968).

Drastic though these provisions were or became, they paled beside other provisions of the treaty that reflected Allied vindictiveness and a determination (understandable enough) that Germany would never again be able to plunge Europe into war. Attempts to bring William II and other leaders of the German war effort to trial had foundered on the refusal of the Dutch to yield up the royal refugee and on the extravagance of the list of proposed victims. There was no negotiation with the German representatives; they were handed the treaty and ordered to sign it, in a ceremony held (with a nastiness like that of 1871) in the Hall of Mirrors at Versailles—it was, as the Germans never ceased reminding the world, a dictated peace. The German army was limited in size and denied the use of conscription; the German navy, to the relief of the British, was also sharply restricted. The chief source of bitterness was the unprecedented Clause 231, standing as justification at the head of the reparations section of the treaty and proclaiming a sweeping moral condemnation. Germany was required to acknowledge its guilt "for causing all the loss and damage to which the Allied and Associated Governments and their nationals have been subjected as a consequence of the war imposed upon them by the aggression of Germany and her allies." These provisions of the treaty, both vengeful and rational, were an effort to assuage French fears; in the light of a second world war and growing evidence of Germany's irresponsibility and aggressive intentions prior to 1914, historians are now inclined to see somewhat more inevitability or even justice in the draconian terms than could be admitted a generation ago. But there is another consideration to bear in mind. In the past defeated powers had lived with severe treaties; demands for revision were likely to be confined to specific grievances that might be rectified by war or diplomacy, while the passage of time could make other provisions tolerable. But from the moment the Versailles Treaty was signed, emotion and politics forced Germans to reject the entire settlement and to demand its wholesale revision. Thus Germany became a new danger to peace, while the new German government was saddled with a reputation for treachery it neither merited nor was able to throw off.

The other treaties in the settlement reflected a determination to come as close as was geographically and politically possible to a Europe rationalized by nationality, a goal brought within reach by the collapse of the old multinational states. Bulgaria's losses in the Second Balkan War of 1913 were confirmed (with minor adjustments) by the Treaty of Neuilly, signed November 27, 1919. The Treaty of Saint-Germain (September 10, 1919) left Austria a mere fragment, and the Treaty of Trianon (June 4, 1920) reduced Hungary to something over a quarter of its former size. From the severed territories two new states, Czechoslovakia and Yugoslavia, were created. But, oddly, they themselves were multinational states. The republic of Czechoslovakia, a strategically vulnerable wedge thrust into Germanic central Europe, was pieced together from Bohemia, Moravia, and part of Silesia. It was dominated by the progressive, educated Czechs—though it was dangerously close to the German frontier, the historic Czech city of Prague became the capital—and the Slovaks, a largely peasant people resentful of their subordination, were increasingly insistent on winning autonomy. The country contained large numbers of so-called Sudeten Germans on its western borders and other minorities as well—Poles, Hungarians, and Ruthenians.

Yugoslavia, the South Slav kingdom realized at last, suffered perhaps even more from internal friction. Yugoslavia's kings came from the Karageorgević dynasty of Serbia, but the dominance of the Serbs—a tough peasant people, Greek Orthodox in religion—provoked the hostility of both Croats and Slovenes, Catholic peoples from the old Hapsburg empire who considered themselves superior in their greater Westernization to the Serbs, who, independent since 1878, had led a more isolated existence. Wilsonian ideals, in short, were more easily enunciated than put into effect. "The new ordering of Europe," one historian has written, "too often involved a mere change in management: old complications re-appeared in a fresh setting. It is, for example, ironical that . . . the Yugoslav State should have comprised nine nationalities whereas the much-maligned 'Historic Hungary' of pre-war days held only seven; and the difference in attitude between a Serbian nationalist of the 1930s and a Magyar nationalist of the 1900s requires a nicety of distinction which only the most skillful exponent of political semantics could seek to explain. What was re-shaped in 1919–20 was the map of Europe, not the habits of its peoples."[4]

The biggest beneficiary of the settlement was the kingdom of Rumania. Profiting from its willingness to be wooed during the war, Rumania secured Transylvania from Hungary and Bessarabia from Russia: the country's size was doubled, and ten million people were added to its prewar population of seven million. Postwar Poland was the rectification of a century and a half of international piracy by Russia, Prussia, and Austria, but Polish ambitions were not satisfied by this belated act of justice. The new republic had troubling minority problems, including a large Jewish population, but far more dangerous were the uncertainties of Poland's frontiers, a danger complicated by the lack of any clear geographical or ethnographical demarcation as well as by Poland's high-handed behavior. In the west the Polish Corridor was a standing grievance to Germany, which it cut into two parts; and part of Silesia was disputed with Czechoslovakia. In the east, with the collapse of Russia, Poles dreamed of recapturing the lands in Lithuania, Belorussia, and the Ukraine that had once belonged to the Polish kingdom. In 1920, indeed, the Poles invaded

[4] Alan Palmer, *The Lands Between: A History of East-Central Europe since the Congress of Vienna* (1970), 173.

the Ukraine, reaching the capital at Kiev; but they were thrown back, and in the Treaty of Riga the next year they lost the Ukraine while retaining a large part of Belorussia. The independence of the little Baltic states of Estonia, Latvia, and Lithuania, first established by the Treaty of Brest Litovsk, was confirmed. Still the Poles coveted the city of Vilna, to which Lithuanians, Belorussians, and Poles all had claims, and in late 1920 a Polish expedition, connived at by the president, Marshal Joseph Pilsudski, seized the city and held it. The Poles were ultimately confirmed in their possession by the Great Powers after Lithuania, in a bit of piracy all its own, seized the German city of Memel, which under the Treaty of Versailles had been surrendered to Allied occupation.

A similar rambunctiousness was displayed in the Mediterranean. In a sharp violation of the principle of nationality, Italy had been given the German Austrian district of South Tyrol, thus gaining a "natural frontier" at the Brenner Pass—a point on which Wilson ultimately yielded to the secret Treaty of London of 1915, which had brought Italy into the war; under the Treaty of Saint-Germain Italy got Istria and the great Austrian port of Trieste at the head of the Adriatic Sea. Wilson's refusal to concede the port of Fiume as well led the Italians to walk out of the peace conference in April 1919, and in September Fiume was seized by a band of volunteers led by the poet Gabriele D'Annunzio. Left by the powers to settle the matter with Yugoslavia, Italy got the port of Zara further down the coast, and Fiume was made a free city. In 1922, however, Fiume was seized and occupied by Italy in a fascist coup, an occupation finally recognized by the Yugoslavs in 1924. The tension between the two Adriatic states remained.

The settlement of what was left of the Ottoman Empire was bedeviled by the aggressiveness of Greece. The magnetic wartime premier Eleutherios Venizelos had persuaded the powers to allow Greece to occupy the Turkish coastal city of Smyrna, an affront to Turkish pride that sparked a nationalist movement led by Mustapha Kemal. Kemal quickly established his authority over the Turkish parts of the empire, except for Constantinople, where the sultan was propped up by Allied troops. In August 1920 the sultan's government accepted the dictated Treaty of Sèvres, which sheared away the Arab regions to the south of Anatolia, provided for a neutralization of the Straits and the territory immediately adjacent, and left the Greeks in occupation at Smyrna pending a plebiscite at the end of five years. The Kemalist government established itself more firmly, made a treaty with the Soviet Union in 1921, and split the Allies by concluding agreements with France and Italy. Thus Britain alone was left supporting the sultan and the Greeks, who invaded the interior of Anatolia. After penetrating nearly to Ankara, the Greek army was routed by Mustapha Kemal, who took Smyrna and moved on Constantinople, threatening to drive out the British forces, which had landed in mid-September 1921 and were entrenched at Chanak. Lloyd George confidently appealed for military assistance from the dominions, only to be rebuffed by all of them except New Zealand, and the British intervention was abandoned. In 1923 the Treaty of Lausanne made a more favorable settlement with Turkey. The Allied evacuation of Constantinople opened the way for Kemal to proclaim the deposition of the sultan. Its capital moved to Ankara, the new Turkish republic undertook a systematic program of Westernization and secularization, thus accomplishing with the force of nationalism what the Great Powers had been unable to do with a century of reform schemes that always foundered on conservative, corrupt, Islam-dominated resistance at the sultan's court.

During the war the French and British had agreed on the carving up of the Near East, though the British confused matters considerably by conflicting promises made to various groups and leaders among the Arabs. The Kemalists, having no interest in areas that were not Turkish, willingly abandoned the suzerainty that had been at best only vaguely exercised over Arab lands. The Arabian peninsula became independent. France was given "mandates" (see p. 973) over Syria and Lebanon, and Britain over Iraq, Transjordan, and Palestine, where the British were committed by the Balfour Declaration of 1917 to establishing a national home for the Jews. Thus from the interplay of European interest and power, with a dash of moral force, emerged the problem of conflicting nationalisms that came to dominate the Near East thirty years later.

The Postwar Economy

Writing in 1919, the great British economist J. M. Keynes referred, with more truth than perversity, to "the intensely unusual, unstable, complicated, unreliable, temporary nature of the economic organization by which western Europe has lived for the last half century."[5] The war and even more the peace had made that fragility painfully evident, even though most men continued to look back to the prewar years as a time of security, prosperity, and promise that might be recaptured. The wastage wrought by the war was unprecedented— outright physical destruction in the parts of Belgium, France, and Germany that had been fought over, and in every country severe deterioration of plant and facilities through excessive use and inadequate maintenance. To the horrible toll of deaths in combat—just under a million in Britain, nearly a million and a half in France, nearly two million in Germany, and about the same number in Russia—must be added the longer-range population loss due to marriages that never took place and families that were never formed. The loss to European leadership, actual and potential, was incalculable. In the western countries, where population growth had been slowing down for some time, the demographic impact was greater than in eastern Europe and deepened the emotional shock that sprang from awareness of a "lost generation." In central

[5] J. M. Keynes, The Economic Consequences of the Peace (1920), 1.

and eastern Europe the peace settlement triggered extensive migrations—from Poland into Germany, from the eastern succession states into Hungary, from Macedonia and Thrace into Bulgaria, the agreed exchange of populations between Greece and Turkey between 1923 and 1930, and the exodus of "White Russians" escaping the Revolution and the civil war. Refugees became a major problem for the first time in over a hundred years and on an unprecedented scale. [6] At the same time the established outlets for emigration were being restricted or closed; particularly important in this regard was legislation in the United States in 1924 that discriminated sharply against European immigrants from eastern and southern Europe.

The redrawing of frontiers in the peace settlement had sweeping economic consequences, little anticipated by those who determined the shape of the new Europe. The most striking example was the shattering of the Austro-Hungarian monarchy. The port of Trieste was now Italian, and the once-unified Danube basin was broken up into separate political entities. Austria itself was a meager remnant, with more than two million of its seven million inhabitants living in Vienna, a metropolis virtually denied a hinterland; and the treaty settlement specifically forbade one means of regaining viability, a union between Austria and Germany. The war had, moreover, thrown each combatant nation on its own resources. The international specialization of production that had developed during the nineteenth century had given way to the demand for self-sufficiency, and disrupted trading patterns could not easily be reestablished. The same may be said of the pattern of capital investment abroad. The French had lost their entire investment in Russia—more than a quarter of all their foreign holdings—and an equivalent amount elsewhere. The British had sold a large proportion of their overseas investments—moving, for example, from creditor to debtor status vis-à-vis the United States—and only slowly recovered their 1913 level, at lower yields. The resources of other countries were wrecked by inflation or were required for internal rebuilding; Germany had the added burden of reparations. Japan and the United States, strengthened by the war, were able to seize and hold markets in China or in Latin America that had been virtual European preserves prior to 1914. The European share of world trade shrank permanently.

No question bedeviled the international economy of the twenties more than reparations. It was Wilson's intention that the old practice of exacting an indemnity from the defeated nation would be abandoned, but what was substituted—the notion of paying for damages, or reparations—was far more devastating. In 1921 the reparations commission set the sum due from

---

[6] In 1921 the League of Nations appointed the famous explorer, Fridtjof Nansen, then head of the Norwegian delegation, as high commissioner for refugees. He devoted the last ten years of his life, either under League or private auspices, to the work, starting with the problem of repatriating German prisoners of war in Russia and organizing famine relief for Russia. In 1922 he devised the so-called Nansen passport, widely accepted for stateless persons. Nansen won the Nobel Peace Prize in that year.

Germany at 132 billion gold marks ($33 billion). The largest amount of this bill, however, was to be payable only when the reparations commission was satisfied that Germany could afford it. The immediate obligation was defined as 2 billion gold marks annually, plus 26 percent of Germany's income from exports, the equivalent of about ten percent of Germany's national income.

Historians still debate the reality of the reparations burden and the capacity of Germany to bear it. But at the time the Germans believed that they neither could nor should pay such huge sums. And certainly there were difficulties in the way of paying them. The surplus capital of prewar days was no longer available, and if the productive capacity of the German economy was to be kept up, large-scale investment was needed at home. Plans for a capital levy were canvassed but rejected, for few Germans wanted to risk the social and economic upheaval that might follow. The German budget was seriously out of balance (thanks in part to the cost of clandestine rearming), and imports greatly exceeded exports. But even what Germany could export had increasing difficulty in finding outlets. In the Fourteen Points, Wilson had foreseen the abolition of trade barriers, but the postwar world bristled with them. The United States retreated behind raised tariff walls; Britain and France, trying to rebuild their own industries and facing a contracting economy and unemployment when the brief postwar boom disappeared, were not eager to take goods made in Germany. But it is only by the export of goods and services that any country can transfer large sums of money abroad, for only in that way can it build up the foreign credits to be offset against debts. There was, of course, one drastic and simple answer: cancellation. Germany and Russia agreed to that solution in the Treaty of Rapallo in 1922; Britain, though its foreign debts were less than the debts owed to it, suggested cancellation all around. But France, which had compensated its citizens for their war losses in expectation of recovering that expenditure, remained certain that Germany could pay, and the United States—which had lent some $11 billion (largely in goods) to Europe during the war—resolutely insisted on repayment. It took another world war and a revolution in economic thinking to impress on the United States the role incumbent on any nation that dominates the world's economy.

There seemed, then, no way of escaping the problem of reparations in the postwar world. Walther Rathenau, minister of reconstruction in Germany for a time in 1921 and foreign minister briefly in 1922, attempted to carry through on fulfillment. But in June 1922 he was assassinated—a terrible portent for the future—and his death removed the one German statesman who, for all his complexities and ambiguities, had been able to move on the reparations front and (at that time) to gain a degree of confidence in Britain and France. The state of the German economy, the imbalance in the budget, and the gap between exports and imports had long threatened the stability of the mark, and from July 1922 an inflation of incredible proportions swept the country. Germans of all stripes blamed the inflation chiefly on reparations, and while Britain was willing to agree to a moratorium, France was not. In January 1923, with

Germany technically in default and the former allies in disarray, Poincaré carried out a threat he had made the preceding August: French and Belgian troops occupied the Ruhr.[7] The Germans, in the Ruhr Valley and elsewhere, met the occupation by passive resistance. The decision was immensely costly for France and threatened the stability of the franc; in Germany it was the final blow. The inflation turned to a rout, and by November the value of German currency had dropped to more than a trillion marks to one dollar.

It is often said that the inflation, by wiping out savings, pensions, fixed interest investments, and nearly all the resources of Germany's wide range of middle classes, reduced many of them to penury, thus creating an explosive political situation. As always, the truth was more complex. To be sure, those who lived on fixed incomes were ruined, and life was terrible for the small artisan or tradesman. To own property let at rents still fixed at wartime levels or to hold mortgages was disastrous, but those who rented found their payments no more than nominal. A farmer producing goods for his own consumption and for direct sale to consumers did not do badly, and while wages in industry lagged behind prices, they rose more or less in step, thanks to trade-union pressure. Even a small income in a foreign currency could bring huge, if temporary, advantages from spiraling exchange rates, and large-scale currency speculators prospered. Above all, the great industrialists benefited; they bought up faltering or bankrupt companies, manipulated the money and credit markets, and, ignoring their stockholders, plowed back huge profits into their enterprises, while accumulating holdings in safe currencies abroad—for exchange controls did not work well. "The captains of industry," one sensitive observer has written, "were staging a capitalist variant of communist expropriation; they robbed not their 'class enemies' but the broad mass of their own supporters."[8]

But however complex the disaster, disaster it was. There were ominous internal disturbances, the most important being the attempted Putsch led by Adolf Hitler in Munich in November, another dreadful portent (see p. 1007). At last, in September, a short-lived ministry headed by Gustav Stresemann broke the passive resistance in the Ruhr and attempted to reach an accommodation with the French. In November the mark was revalued through an ingenious but complex temporary scheme and a year later a new *Reichsmark*, engineered by Dr. Hjalmar Schacht, a brilliant economist with a questionable future, made possible a period of stability and even prosperity. This turning was facilitated by acceptance of the Dawes Plan, negotiated by an international committee of

[7] The French got the reparations commission to condemn Germany for failing to meet commitments in the delivery of wood and coal, a pretext that led a British official to remark that wood had not been so misused since the Trojan horse.

[8] M. J. Bonn, *Wandering Scholar* (1949), 278. Bonn was an economic adviser during the stabilization, and his chapter on the inflation is most revealing, not only of the ambiguity of the phenomenon, but of the economic ignorance of the ministers and of the blinkered greed of the industrialists, who saw the inflation as a weapon to bring down the hated republic.

experts in 1924 to provide for more realistic reparations payments and to float an international loan—highly successful in obtaining subscribers—to buttress Germany's efforts at stabilization. Acceptance of the plan had been helped by the fall of the Poincaré government following the French elections in May, and the new French government, headed by Edouard Herriot and with the pacific Aristide Briand as foreign minister, ushered in a new era of European amity.

The war had had unprecedented effects on the structure and organization of national life in every combatant country. Centralized controls proved necessary in the rationing of scarce commodities, for consumer and industrial use alike; scarce manpower and crucial industries were regimented to a degree unimaginable before the war. Many European socialists were impressed by what had been accomplished by wartime controls, both in encouraging production and in more equitable sharing of scarce commodities. But there was a more general desire to flee from regimentation and to return to old ways. For every Walther Rathenau preaching the need for some new system to ensure more rational production and distribution there were a hundred businessmen, grown rich during the war, who wanted only to be left alone to enjoy the profits they thought would continue to roll in. Others less rich simply looked back nostalgically to the days before the war and welcomed government initiatives that translated this wistfulness into policy.

In general, economic thought remained stuck in the nineteenth century. Economists, ministers of finance, and businessmen stood by the old orthodoxies of balanced budgets, the importance of reducing indebtedness, and the proportioning of the supply of credit to the needs of trade. On no point was orthodoxy more insistent than the desirability of a return to the gold standard. Adopted in England after 1821 and generally adopted throughout Europe and North America after 1870, the gold standard had been suspended during the war and so had the automatic limitation of currency issue that the reliance on gold carries with it. Only the British had kept wartime inflation within reasonable bounds, and the postwar years provided an object lesson in the terrible consequences of uncontrollable inflation.[9] As bankers and treasury officials saw it, the better part of economic wisdom was to get back on the gold standard as quickly as it was practicable; the practicability seemed to materialize along with the easing of international tensions in the middle of the decade. Britain, inadvisedly in retrospect, led the way in 1925, at the cost of deflation and social unrest (see p. 997), and a few other countries followed its example. But a crisis was soon to develop that would destroy the shibboleth entirely.

---

[9] British prices in 1920 were about three times prewar levels but fell to perhaps twice that by 1921. In France, after a sharp wartime and postwar rise, prices were a little over three times the prewar level in 1922, but rose to seven times the 1913 index in 1926, forcing a devaluation the next year. But Austrian prices rose 14,000 times; Hungarian, 23,000; Polish, 2,500,000. In Germany, as we have seen, and in Russia, the ratios were astronomical. David Landes, *The Unbound Prometheus* (1969), 361–362.

Despite the unimaginativeness of economic thought and policy, there was considerable economic innovation in the postwar world. The period saw widespread resort to "rationalization." As managers sought economies of scale and greater efficiency in organization, certain industries came to be increasingly dominated by large quasi-monopolistic firms—the formation of Imperial Chemical Industries from a number of smaller British firms is an excellent example, as is the extraordinary position held in the German and indeed the world economy by the great chemical firm of I. G. Farben. Far more interest was shown in American methods of scientific management, which had important and not particularly welcome implications for labor. The rise of foreign competition, the failure of industries in the major European countries to recover the level of production of 1913, a shortage of capital, and technical obsolescence (particularly important in Britain) were all problems that led businessmen to think in terms of limiting competition or sharing markets by agreement, often, as with the German cartels or the English rationalization of the thirties, supported by the government.

Such a restrictive outlook was more likely to be found in the older or less adaptable basic industries, especially those that had expanded to meet wartime demand and were left by the postwar shrinkage with excess capacity and endemic unemployment. Far more aggressiveness appeared in newer industries that were transforming not only the industrial picture but the lives of ordinary people to a degree that could hardly be said of nineteenth-century industrialization. The chemical and electrical revolutions, the manufacture of automobiles and aircraft, food processing, the drastic refashioning of communications and entertainment by radio and motion pictures all presented immense opportunities that were seized and turned to account, though Europe (notably in automobiles) lagged behind the United States in catering to a mass market. Still, the new industries contributed to the sense of movement and prosperity that was coming over Europe after the middle of the twenties. But, as continued sluggishness in parts of the economy demonstrated, all was not well. The reparations questions remained unresolved, though improved; trade barriers still stood; the monetary system was inflexible; and much of Europe's prosperity depended on American loans and short-term investment and on the backwash of the unhealthy boom that was developing in the United States. Ten years after Keynes used the words, the economic system had proved itself once more to be unstable, complicated, unreliable, and temporary in nature.

The Spirit of Locarno

For about five years after the end of the war Europe was profoundly troubled. The drastic territorial alterations of the peace settlement, all but unmanageable economic dislocations, and near anarchy in international relations made a mockery of wartime hopes for a better world after the fighting stopped. The

League of Nations, the outstanding innovation of the Versailles settlement and the institution that promised more than any other to assure a peaceful world, seemed doomed almost from the start. Based on an Anglo-American model, the League had a permanent secretariat settled in Geneva, an assembly of representatives of the member nations, and a council composed at the outset of the victorious Great Powers as permanent members with four additional members elected by the assembly for three-year terms. The council was empowered to settle disputes between nations, and disputes could also be referred to the International Court of Justice sitting in The Hague. The League coordinated a wide range of international activities, thus rationalizing and expanding the international cooperation that had flourished in the prewar decades (see p. 929). Moreover, in the mandate system the League offered a means of transition from the imperialist scramble of the late nineteenth century. The colonies taken from the defeated powers were set up as "mandates," and the mandatory powers to whom they were confided were required to make regular reports to the League. In the Class A mandates of the Near East, the role of the mandatory powers (Britain and France) was intended to be advisory, looking to relatively early autonomy. Class B mandates, applying to most of the former German colonies in Africa, provided for direct administration by the mandatory powers subject to certain restrictions, such as free trade with other League members. The largest of these colonies was Tanganyika, which went to the British, and other German colonies were divided among the British, French, Belgians, and Portuguese. Finally, Class C mandates were devised for those areas deemed so backward that they could be governed by the mandatory powers as extensions of their own territory; of these, German Southwest Africa went to the Union of South Africa and the Pacific islands to Australia, New Zealand, and Japan.

The League was hampered from the outset by differing interpretations of its powers and responsibilities. The French, whose uneasiness determined much of the international history of Europe in the immediate postwar years, looked on the League solely as a device for collective security. Although the covenant of the League imposed on the council the duty of preserving the independence and territorial integrity of its members against any external aggression, and although a member committing aggression was declared to be ipso facto at war with the other members, decisive action was hampered by the requirement that the council be unanimous on all important questions. The French were eager to get procedures spelled out for imposing sanctions and proposed the creation of an independent military force under League auspices, whereas the British looked on the League as an organ of conciliation rather than coercion. The French, therefore, tended to be skeptical of the League and since isolationism in the United States prevented a proposed joint Anglo-American guarantee of French boundaries, France sought protection in arrangements outside the League—alliances with Belgium and Poland and with the countries of the so-called Little Entente: Czechoslovakia, Rumania, and Yugoslavia.

Disappointed in their principal partner across the Channel—for Britain was quickly coming around to a more relaxed view of Germany—the French also sought insurance in their own military strength and in unilateral action if necessary, of which the occupation of the Ruhr was the climactic and disastrous example.

There was, it must be said, reason enough for the French distrust of the League's capacities. When the Great Powers were in agreement, it could settle disputes between small states, as when the Greeks and Bulgarians clashed in the autumn of 1925, but when one of the Great Powers itself was involved— as in the Italian bombardment and occupation of Corfu in a dispute with Greece in 1924—the League was paralyzed. There were other severe handicaps, mostly involved with the absence of crucial states. The smaller defeated powers were admitted shortly after the League was founded, though Turkey joined only in 1932. Germany was kept out until 1926 and then was allowed to join the council only after bitter and irrelevant trading involving the claims of Spain, Brazil, and Poland to permanent seats on the council, a shabby situation that did nothing to improve the League's image in Germany. The Soviet Union denounced the League as an instrument of capitalist exploitation, while to many of the League's members—and to its first secretary general—the Bolsheviks appeared the archenemies not only of the League itself but of the values for which it stood. By the end of the twenties, however, the Soviet Union was reappraising its stand; it began to cooperate in some of the League's humanitarian activities and, in 1934, became a member. By far the most damaging abstention was that of the United States. The League covenant was a part of the Treaty of Versailles, and the United States Senate, with whose leaders Wilson had fallen out, refused to accept it without reservations that the president was unwilling to concede. The United States did take part in the International Labor Organization and it cooperated in the League's humanitarian work, but to the end it refused to join. Keeping free of this particular foreign entanglement was undoubtedly in accord with a dominant isolationist feeling within the country, but the absence of the United States seriously compromised both the moral and the practical authority of the new organization.

Yet the lack of universality in the League, its failure to settle the serious disputes that came before it, and its ignominious collapse in the 1930s should not be allowed to obscure its positive accomplishments. It effectively contributed to the control or extirpation of international problems like drug traffic and slavery. Its secretariat and the associated organizations helped to develop techniques of international administration. And because it did make a potent appeal to public opinion, it paved the way for future international organization, even though Europe was not yet ready to subordinate the interests of the nation-state to the fulfillment of larger ideals of cooperation, disarmament, and the peaceful settlement of disputes.

The occupation of the Ruhr by the French marked the peak of postwar tensions. Already, the successful conclusion of the Washington Conference in 1922 had served as a kind of harbinger of a new spirit: there the major powers had agreed to a limitation of naval armaments that would keep the capital ships of the major oceanic powers, the United States, Britain, and Japan, in a ratio of 5-5-3, with Italy and France following at 1.75. To match this feat, however limited it was, with a parallel reduction in armaments on land required some concessions to French fears of a resurgent Germany, fears justified by awareness that Germany was evading the disarmament restrictions imposed at Versailles and by the mounting criticism within Germany of the treaty itself. Two abortive efforts were made to strengthen the League. The draft treaty of mutual assistance in 1923 required the council to name the aggressor in an international dispute, whereupon the parties to the treaty would come to the aid of the victim with military force. The binding nature of these punitive actions was unacceptable to the British, respectful as they had to be of sentiment in the dominions and mindful as they were that the worldwide character of their empire would put them in the forefront of any peace-keeping operation anywhere. In 1924, with the first Labour government in power, the prime minister, Ramsay MacDonald, helped to draft the Geneva Protocol, which did not lessen British responsibilities but sought to reduce the number of instances in which the British might be called upon to act by making compulsory arbitration and disarmament preconditions of the agreement. Whether the Labour government could have carried the protocol in Parliament is a question made academic by the government's fall in September 1924.

The Conservative foreign secretary, Austen Chamberlain, thereupon negotiated a more modest understanding, the so-called Locarno Pact, aided by the willingness of the French and German foreign ministers, Briand and Stresemann, to reach an accommodation. The central provision of the Locarno Pact was acceptance of the western frontiers by Germany, France, and Belgium, which also agreed to the permanent demilitarization of the Rhineland; Britain and Italy, as presumably disinterested powers, weighed in with a guarantee of these frontiers and of the demilitarization. Although no such guarantee proved possible for the eastern frontiers, parallel treaties bound Germany and Poland and Germany and Czechoslovakia to settle disputes peacefully, while France promised the two smaller nations military assistance in case of attack. And the whole settlement was predicated on the new willingness of the French to see Germany as a member of the League of Nations. Made public at Locarno in October 1925, the treaties released what contemporaries liked to call "the Locarno spirit," a sense that genuine reduction in tension had been accomplished, that some of the worst of what were deemed injustices in the Versailles settlement had been modified, and that disputes could indeed be solved in the atmosphere of goodwill and prosperity that was spreading over Europe. But, as A. J. P. Taylor has said, the Locarno Pact was more a symbol than a cause of this spirit: "The treaty of Locarno rested on the assumption that the promises given in it would never have to be made good—otherwise the British government would not have given them." [10] It is hard to know whether Locarno

---

[10] A. J. P. Taylor, *English History, 1914–1945* (1965), 222.

should be classified with those grandiose but limited, if not meaningless, pronouncements that have come so often from world leaders meeting at so many summits in the mid-twentieth century, or whether it should be bracketed with the pieties of the Holy Alliance of 1814.

Three years later, in August 1928, the Locarno powers joined with the United States in yet another pact, this time to renounce war "as an instrument of national policy." Exceptions were allowed: Britain insisted on the exclusion of certain areas, notably Egypt; the rightfulness of wars of self-defense was so interpreted as to allow the United States to intervene in any attack in Latin America, under the Monroe Doctrine. But the principle of "outlawing war" was waved high and encouraged many people to think that a new era in world politics had truly come. The "Kellogg-Briand Pact" had no practical significance at all. In the dismal decade that followed, war remained the major instrument of national policy. The ringing principles not only proved useless; they were, in fact, all but forgotten.

THE RISE OF AUTHORITARIANISM

The New Jacobinism

For a generation after Waterloo, respectable, propertied men were terrified by the specter of Jacobinism, the impulse to change, leveling, and democracy they had seen embodied in the French Revolution and in the ambitions of domestic radicals. In the twentieth-century, the well-to-do and satisfied have been stalked by the specter of communism, or Bolshevism, to use its earlier label. True, socialism had been worrisome through much of the nineteenth century, as had the unsettling phenomenon of organized labor, but when, nearly unanimously, socialists and labor leaders rallied to the colors in 1914, they confirmed the absorption of their movements into the mainstream of European politics. Now, in Russia, revolution and civil war had created a Communist state with a ruthless completeness that staggered the imagination. Worse, enthusiasts in nearly every country were inspired by the example, and a new international organization was established to ensure that the revolution would be universal.

The Third International, founded in March 1919, grew out of Lenin's disgust with the behavior of the Second in 1914, when most of its members opted for patriotism and war; it also testified to the theoretical conviction that, while by historical accident the revolution had occurred first in Russia, its survival in so backward a country depended on the success of revolution in advanced countries. The next year the Comintern, as the Third International was known,[11] issued Twenty-one Conditions binding on Communist parties everywhere: they must rigorously adhere to the decisions of Comintern congresses; support all soviet republics and all national or colonial liberationist movements; oppose any counterrevolutionary action; use every legal or illegal means to win peasant support and to capture trade unions; organize on the principle of democratic centralism—subordinating all parliamentary activity to the directives of the central committee and maintaining a clandestine revolutionary nucleus even when the party was legalized; and purge their membership periodically in a resolute effort to isolate and defeat reformist, centrist, and pacifist tendencies. The Twenty-one Conditions precipitated the formation of national Communist parties nearly everywhere, parties that would thereafter compete with Socialists for the allegiance of the Left. Developments like these were reason enough to fear Bolshevism, but in two countries Communist risings came uncomfortably close to success. One was the so-called Spartacist revolt in Germany in January 1919 (see p. 1003), the other the short-lived Communist dictatorship established in Hungary in the spring of 1919 by Béla Kun (see p. 986). On every front, however, the threat was actually less serious than it seemed. For one thing, established governments had greater resources at their disposal than anything the reactionary governments after 1815 could muster. Moreover, the Comintern and its allies made appalling errors in tactics, trying too much too soon and behaving with an arrogance and presumption that alienated potential supporters and reinforced the arguments of their sworn enemies. And, despite the rhetoric and the constant agitation, the Bolsheviks were simply in no position to export revolution: they were too deeply engaged in ensuring their own survival.

The disintegration of the tsarist regime and the chaos and paralysis that followed had allowed one small, tightly disciplined and superbly led group, the Bolsheviks, to seize power. Their chief enemies, far more numerous, were the Socialist Revolutionaries, powerfully entrenched in the sympathies of the peasants, and the old ruling classes, especially the military officers. Effective collaboration between these two groups was impossible, and since fighting was inevitable, the reactionary officers and their motley forces—the Whites—took over all the various efforts to overthrow Bolshevik rule. To this resistance within historic Russia were added long-latent centrifugal tendencies in those lands around the borders of the old multinational Russian Empire, tendencies that asserted themselves in separatist movements or even in outright independence. While an independent Poland was a foregone conclusion, and while the Baltic states of Lithuania, Latvia, Estonia, and Finland could be brought back to

[11] One of the sorry by-products of the encounter between modern bureaucratic and journalistic trends has been a new and barbarous jargon. Nineteenth-century historians do nicely with straightforward references to ministries or commissions, colorful nicknames (Ultras, Cave of Adullam), and occasional combinations of initials (SPD). But twentieth-century histories bristle with acronyms and neologisms synthesized from the official titles of proliferating government and private agencies.

the Russian orbit neither by revolutionary attempts nor by the Red Army, the prospect of independence for the Ukraine, Belorussia, the Transcaucasus, or Siberia was intolerable and had to be put down, just as disaffection in the Russian heartland had to be crushed. In the end the solution was found in a quasi-federal system that encouraged cultural and linguistic autonomy, while binding the constituent soviet republics in a political system of democratic centralism that was in effect a dictatorship from Moscow, the new capital. But in the immediate aftermath of the Revolution the integrity of Russia was not to be won by a constitution: it was won by force of arms.

The counterrevolutionary activity of the Whites had four main centers. From the Urals, the Czech legions—former Austrian prisoners of war—were being evacuated across Siberia. A clash with the Communists led to seizure by the highly disciplined Czechs of sections of the Trans-Siberian Railway, and their efforts quickly merged with those of moderate socialists who established a short-lived republic in western Siberia. A coup in November 1918 brought the Whites into control. Admiral Alexander Kolchak was proclaimed supreme ruler of Russia, but after some early successes he was defeated in the course of 1919 and executed early in 1920. More immediately threatening was a drive, launched toward Petrograd from Estonia in the autumn of 1919, that came dangerously close to its goal, while General Anton Denikin ranged successfully over much of southern Russia and the Ukraine until he was defeated early in 1920. Only in the extreme south, in the Caucasus and the Crimea, did resistance last longer, until the end of 1920.

Military activity was scattered, highly mobile, ill provisioned, and small in scale. The most dramatic operations took place in the Ukraine, which for three years was a military and political shuttlecock. Declared independent in January 1918, the Ukraine was taken by the Bolsheviks in February and lost to a German invasion in March. When the Germans were defeated, the Ukraine once more became an independent socialist state. Reconquered by the Bolsheviks early in 1919, it was lost to General Denikin and his White forces, and when the Bolsheviks put Denikin to rout, it became the turn of the Poles, ambitious to reestablish their old, expansive kingdom. They were driven out only at the end of 1920, and the Russo-Polish frontier was finally settled in the Treaty of Riga in March 1921.

The civil war consolidated Bolshevik power. Much of that work was done for them by their enemies. The Whites invariably set about implementing reactionary policies in the territories they conquered; they implacably pursued socialists and democrats; and they insisted on the indivisibility of Russia—their rejection of any independence for Poland accounts for the fact that Polish intervention took place only after the Whites were defeated. The Bolsheviks also profited from resentment of the ineffective and confused intervention of the Allies. Small Allied forces landed at Murmansk and Archangel in the far north and moved into the Transcaucasus, while the Japanese occupied parts of eastern Siberia. At first the Allied effort was intended to revivify the struggle against the Germans in the wake of Brest Litovsk, but it slipped uncertainly into collaboration with the Whites to defeat the Bolsheviks. The armistice removed the only real excuse for Allied action, and intervention had provoked much opposition among labor and left-wing movements at home; but final evacuation was not accomplished until the early part of 1920, while the Japanese remained in occupation until late in 1922. The Bolsheviks could, however, count on more than the weakness and division of its enemies. In the areas it controlled, the Communist government accomplished far more than the Whites did in their territories, and it could tap a new vein of ideological fervor, summoning up hope for a better future, not just a return to a hated past.

Then there was the Red Army. Created as a volunteer force out of virtually nothing by Leon Trotsky, it could call upon the moral resources of the nation in arms, as the French Revolutionary generals and Napoleon had done, the more so once nationalistic fervor could be unleashed against the Polish invasion. The new army profited as well from the talents of leaders who could never have reached the social level of the officer corps in tsarist days, while some former tsarist officers of considerable ability decided, for whatever reason, to cast in their lot with the Bolsheviks. It was an ex-tsarist officer of left-socialist views, in command of irregular forces sent to the Ukraine early in 1918, who promised: "From the Baltic to the Black Sea, across the Danube towards Vienna, Berlin, Paris, and London we shall march with fire and sword, establishing everywhere Soviet power. With fire and sword we shall destroy everything which will dare to stand in our way. There will be no mercy for any of our enemies."[12] As that proclamation suggests, the ultimate weapon of the Bolshevik triumph was terror, just as it was for the men of the French Revolution when they were challenged by war and internal subversion. To some degree the elimination of enemies of the Soviet regime was accomplished by savage reprisals of the kind that occur in anarchic conditions: the former royal family, murdered in a cellar in Ekaterinburg in July 1918 as White forces converged on the town, were only the most famous victims. But to this casual violence was added a more systematic terror, the province of the secret police (the Cheka, later the GPU) headed by Felix Dzerzhinski. Stepped up after an attempt on Lenin's life at the end of August 1918, the terror so far surpassed tsarist repression as to constitute a new institutional legacy to the twentieth century.

Stringent methods were applied as well to cope with Russia's economic difficulties. Immediately after the Revolution, land was socialized. Lenin and his colleagues hoped that large-scale collective operations would result, but little that was systematic could be done, and the practical result of the destruction of large estates was that peasants took land in small, often uneconomic units. Similarly the lack of clear, developed plans led to chaos in the mines and

---

[12] Quoted in Richard Pipes, *The Formation of the Soviet Union: Communism and Nationalism, 1917-1923* (Atheneum ed., 1968), 124.

factories. The pressing demands of the civil war, the fall in industrial production, and the hoarding of grain forced a series of drastic measures known as "war communism." Workers' control gave way to factory discipline imposed by state-dominated trade unions, while management at the local level often was confided to former managers and basic planning decisions were made bureaucratically at the center. Crop surpluses, discovered by fair means or foul, were commandeered, and an incessant barrage of propaganda was launched to set the poorer peasants against the wealthier. By the spring of 1921 it was apparent that the system was not working—production remained at a fraction of its prewar level and the peasants refused to plant crops that might be seized. There were uprisings among peasants and factory workers, and in late February 1921 a mutiny broke out at the Baltic naval base at Kronstadt. It was bloodily put down, but the manifest failure of war communism brought a sharp change of direction.

While the suppression of the mutineers was under way Lenin announced the New Economic Policy (NEP). Openly confessing the bankruptcy of war communism, he now proposed to take two steps forward to communism by taking one step backward to capitalism. Internal freedom of trade was restored, individual ownership of property was assured, and a degree of private enterprise was tolerated in industry and trade, though only in small business and not (in Lenin's phrase) in "the commanding heights of the economy": basic industry remained under state control. Although crop failures in 1921 produced a terrible famine—kept from utter disaster by foreign aid, largely from the United States—the change of course produced the desired results. By 1922 Soviet agriculture was producing more food, chiefly through the agency of those rich peasants—*kulaks*—who were able, on their own land or on land leased from poorer neighbors whom they employed as laborers, to produce a surplus for sale; and by the end of the year three quarters of the retail trade was in private hands.

This partial about-face in the economic sphere was paralleled by shifts elsewhere. A more traditionalist approach to law succeeded the vague revolutionary justice that was thought to spring automatically from the revolutionary consciousness; and in 1922 new codes of civil, criminal, agrarian, and labor law were adopted, drawing on the past to some extent and relying on professional judges. Much of the experimentation of the years after 1917 was now called into question. The easing of divorce and the equality of the sexes were maintained, but a new emphasis was put on the family and on conventional sexual morality, while radical departures such as encouragement of abortion and the favoring of state orphanages over adoption came in for severe criticism and modification. An uneasy peace was made with the Orthodox church, which, after the patriarch Tikhon had submitted in 1923, was tolerated alongside "The Living Church" the Bolsheviks had conjured up in an unsuccessful attempt to lure the faithful away from their traditional religious moorings. The arts saw less experimentation and showed a greater respect for tradition. And, finally, the

Soviet Union began to turn a milder face to the outside world: foreign trade was resumed, foreign firms were invited to set up shop in the Soviet Union, and diplomatic recognition was eagerly sought. As E. H. Carr has said: "The development which, between the years 1921 and 1924, shifted the balance of emphasis from political programmes to the routine of everyday life, from iconoclastic theory to traditional practice, from revolution to organization, from visionary utopianism to hard-headed realism, from an internationalism that knew no frontiers to an astute calculation of the national interests of the USSR, affected almost every aspect of Soviet life and thought. In public affairs it brought with it a shift in emphasis from adventure to administration, from sweeping revolutionary design to the meticulous execution of day-to-day decisions." [13]

The Communist party, however, never lost control, and its revolutionary goals remained in force. Propaganda—not in the pejorative sense of the conscious resort to lies and half-truths but in the sense long known to the Vatican as the stimulating and guiding of faith—remained a duty. It became less possible than before to criticize the regime, but literature wrongly conceived was simply not published: the traditional censorship was a last, scarcely necessary resort. But the will was there. As A. V. Lunacharsky, the minister of education, put it in 1921: "We in no way shrink from the necessity of applying censorship even to belles-lettres, since under this banner and beneath this elegant exterior poison may be implanted in the still naïve and dark soul of the great mass of people, which is constantly ready to waver and, owing to the too great hardships of the journey, to throw off the hand which is leading it through the wilderness to the promised land." [14] Nevertheless, the turnabout of the NEP was a trial to the more ardent revolutionaries. Even Lenin apparently had his doubts. Although he was, as Alfred G. Meyer has said, that rare phenomenon, a revolutionary with a bureaucratic mind, Lenin wondered openly in 1922 who really ruled in Russia: "Above we have, I do not know how many, but I suppose at least some thousands, or at most some tens of thousands, of our own people. But below are hundreds of thousands of old officials inherited from the Tsar and from bourgeois society, who work in part consciously, in part unconsciously, against us." [15]

Concerns like these multiplied as it became apparent, from the end of 1921, that Lenin's health was deteriorating. In May 1922 he suffered a stroke, but a few months later was able to return to his office on a limited schedule;

---

[13] E. H. Carr, *Socialism in One Country, 1924–1926,* vol. I (Pelican ed., 1970), 33.

[14] Ibid., 76–77.

[15] Ibid., 133. Meyer's description is in *Communism* (3rd ed., 1967), 47. Lenin certainly believed that good administration would follow naturally from enlightened, rational consciousness; hence the future Communist state would need no bureaucratic apparatus because each individual would prove able to do what needed doing. This assumption led Sir Alexander Gray to the irresistible quip that "the path to Lenin's heaven is paved with good accountants." *A History of Socialist Doctrine, Moses to Lenin* (1946), 478.

he was stricken a second time in December. Now thoroughly incapacitated, except for reading and thought, he surrendered his power to a triumvirate made up of two old companions in exile, Gregory Zinoviev and Leo Kamenev, and Josef Stalin, the newly elected but still little known general secretary of the Communist party. Within the triumvirate the struggle was between Zinoviev (supported by Kamenev) and Stalin, but to one side stood the compelling figure of Leon Trotsky, the minister of war. A testament dictated by Lenin at the end of December 1922 made it clear that Stalin should be removed from the secretaryship of the party. Lenin had been appalled by Stalin's rudeness to Lenin's wife, and he was deeply concerned about the Russian chauvinism he discerned in Stalin's policy of suppressing Georgian nationalist ambitions—for Stalin, himself a Georgian, had, as immigrants often do, become more Russian than the Russians. Lenin survived until January 1924, lucid and thoughtful but removed from government, and the interregnum gave time for competing claims and ambitions to be put to the test. And when the testament was made public Stalin survived the challenge.

Zinoviev, Kamenev, and Stalin stood united for a time against a greater threat. Trotsky was the most brilliant of them all, as theorist, tactician, and administrator; he was a superb orator and had astonishing perceptiveness of what had to come. But he was resented by old-time Bolsheviks as a late recruit to the cause, and while Lenin could forgive the tardiness, others could not and raked up early anti-Lenin writings to blacken Trotsky's name. Moreover, when men were brooding on parallels to the 1790s and seeing the NEP as a Thermidorian reaction, it was easy to cast Trotsky, with his innate gifts and his strategic post as minister of war, as a potential Bonaparte. Then, late in 1924, Stalin advanced the heterodox program of "socialism in one country" against Trotsky's belief in the "permanent revolution," the standard internationalist conviction that revolution had to come everywhere in Europe to secure it in Russia. Branding this belief as leading either to fatalistic inactivity or to damaging adventurism, Stalin offered the prospect of immediate realization of socialist goals: Russia was big enough and at least potentially rich enough to create its own future without waiting for others. In January 1925, Trotsky, who throughout the crisis had failed to act when opportunity offered, resigned as commissar for war. Stalin then turned on his associates in the triumvirate. At the Fourteenth Party Congress, in December 1925, Kamenev dared to attack Stalin openly. But Stalin, in full control of the party machinery, got the adulatory speeches and the votes, and an effort of the defeated leaders to ally themselves with Trotsky in opposition came too late. In November 1927 both Trotsky and Zinoviev were expelled from the party. Zinoviev recanted, but Trotsky was exiled to Central Asia, from where he went to Turkey, France, and at last to Mexico. Partly the victim of his own shortcomings, he was thrust from power by superior political skill and power. Stalin pursued the exiled leader implacably; at last in 1940 hired assassins stole into Trotsky's Mexican house and murdered him with an axe.

The NEP had been a success: agricultural and industrial production had returned to their prewar levels, and both peasants and workers appeared reconciled to the regime that claimed to speak for them. But the NEP had triggered a profound debate about the future of Russia as a socialist and industrial state. One side argued the necessity of appeasing the peasantry and of allowing a growing and prosperous agriculture to produce not only raw materials and food for the workers but an expanding market for the output of industry and the surplus capital to invest in development. The "leftist" side of the argument, to which Trotsky adhered, argued that far more capital was required in all sectors of the economy than could ever be obtained from agriculture and from a grasping peasantry, and that continued encouragement of the agricultural sector would put the government at the mercy of the kulaks. Stalin had made no important contribution to this debate, but in 1928, his power secure, he announced the first of the Five Year Plans, aimed at the rapid development of heavy industry. The private sector tolerated under the NEP was swept away and everything subjected to the state planning commission (Gosplan). Having set goals that far outstripped what the "superindustrializers" had thought possible, Stalin moved in 1929 to a far more radical solution of the peasant problem: to enforce on the peasants the sacrifices necessary to support rapid industrialization he proposed a sweeping collectivization of agriculture, a course that caused him to break with Nikolai Bukharin, the clever theorist of the "Right Opposition" who had supported Stalin's rise to supreme power against Trotsky and his colleagues of the Left.

There was much to be said against the inefficient fragmentation of Russian peasant farming, but it is hard to justify the ill-considered haste and brutal methods of this new agricultural revolution. Collectivization was pursued without realism or planning. While officials sought a gauge of progress in counting the numbers of collectives, the peasants, fearing the new arrangements, almost ritually signalled their forced entrance into a collective by slaughtering the farm animals they had heard would be taken from them. After a spreading campaign of propaganda, the kulaks were methodically exterminated. The requisitioning techniques developed under war communism were used still more intensively; taxation was drastically raised; and beyond economic ruin lay deportation, resettlement, or execution, to say nothing of the suicides that were widely reported. By Soviet statistics the kulak population dropped from five and a half million in 1928 to 150,000 in 1934, a purge that caught many middling peasants as well, for the lines were neither easy to draw nor readily perceived by the peasants themselves. In 1930 Stalin beat a tactical retreat. In an article called "Dizzy with Success" he blamed the excesses of the collectivization drive on over-zealous lesser officials. But when the massive peasant resistance was slowed, the drive began again, and again the response was arson (that old weapon against landlord estates) and refusal to plant. Coupled with the inefficiencies of the collective farms and bad weather, the resistance brought in 1932–1933 another dreadful famine. This time the Soviet government refused to seek outside assistance, as it had done in 1921, and the toll in deaths from the famine may have risen as high as four million, in addition to the five million shot or left to live out ruined lives as a result of dekulakization. "When the head is off," Stalin said brutally, "one does not mourn for the hair."

Compared to Stalin's restructuring of Russian farming, writes the most recent historian of Russian agriculture, "the horrors described in Marx's celebrated chapter on original capital accumulation in *Capital,* or the horrors of the British industrial revolution portrayed by humanitarian historians and writers, pale into insignificance. And bleak as was the lot of the Russian peasants under serfdom in the eighteenth and nineteenth centuries, it is debatable whether it offers any parallel to the total uprooting of peasants under collectivization. Even Stalin, that 'man of steel' who spawned collectivization and spoke so blandly about the extermination of the kulaks, confessed to Winston Churchill that the terrible strain of the struggle with the peasantry exceeded that of the war." [16] Russia was set on a course of rapid and large-scale industrialization, no matter what the cost in human suffering or deprivation. The economic result was impressive within a remarkably short time (see p. 1029), but the scale of sacrifice and the methods by which it was enforced testified once again to the magnitude of the power at the disposal of the Soviet state and to the futility of resisting it, lessons soon to be enforced in yet another purge.

Reaction in Eastern Europe

The Great Powers in the West saw the states of East Central Europe as a *cordon sanitaire* sealing off the Bolshevik infection and, more traditionally, as a buffer between Russia and Germany; the main importance of these states in the interwar years may be their international role. Yet certain themes run through the internal history of all of them and may serve as a skeleton for understanding their complex development and, even more, their course during and after World War II. Two countries may be briefly noted as exceptions. Austria, as we have seen, was reduced to a fraction of its former size and was scarcely viable as an economic entity. It contained two sources of considerable tension. One was the conflict between Vienna—cosmopolitan, free-thinking, and dominated by Socialists—and the Catholic, conservative countryside; the other was Austria's now overwhelming Germanness. Prior to the Treaty of Saint-Germain, with its specific prohibition of union with Germany, Austria had declared itself part of Germany, and in 1921 the Allies had to intervene to prevent Salzburg separatists from seceding to join their great neighbor to the

---

[16] Lazar I. Volin, *A Century of Russian Agriculture: From Alexander II to Khrushchev* (1970), chaps. 9 and 10; the quotation is on p. 216.

west. But in the twenties these tensions were latent, and the decade was preoccupied with staggering problems of reconstruction. Thanks to loans and a financial administration supervised by the League of Nations, the Christian Socialist governments, representing the dominant conservative countryside, brought the new republic through its dangerous infancy.

The other, far more moving exception was Czechoslovakia. This new state was not without internal stress, manifested in Slovak and Ruthenian demands for autonomy, demands especially troublesome in Slovakia, where a narrow Catholicism reinforced cultural separatism and resentment of the more advanced and educated Czechs who dominated the administration of the region. But the western parts of the country were blessed with a prosperous industrial economy, and the Czechs displayed a political maturity found nowhere else in eastern Europe. They were fortunate, too, in having Professor T. G. Masaryk, a philosopher of distinction and a wartime hero of unquestionable stature. Responsible more than anyone else for the creation of the country, Masaryk was president from its foundation until 1935, when he was succeeded by his close friend Eduard Beneš, who as foreign minister throughout the twenties had played a vital conciliatory role in international affairs. Thus an almost providential combination of resources and leadership kept Czechoslovakia the one true—and tragic—instance of successful democracy in central and eastern Europe.

The other countries of the region were overwhelmingly agricultural. Some of them—Greece, Bulgaria, and the Serbian part of Yugoslavia—were essentially peasant economies, dominated by small holders. In Poland, Rumania, Hungary, and other parts of the old Austro-Hungarian Empire, large estates predominated. Hence land reform was a major issue in the postwar years. It was implemented with considerable effectiveness in Rumania, Czechoslovakia, and Yugoslavia and was carried still further in Bulgaria, under the dynamic agrarian leader Alexander Stamboliski. In Poland and Hungary, on the other hand, the great estates remained, despite much talk of action. But everywhere agriculture remained backward, its crops traditional, its yields low, and its markets restricted by low productivity and high cost; prosperity lay ever beyond reach. Few in the countryside were willing to copy the Russian example, and the potential agrarian interest rarely had a meaningful impact on politics.

Passions were far more likely to be stirred by the claims of minorities, whether religious, cultural, or national—difficulties exacerbated by the persistence of frontier disputes and by the extensive transfer of territories in the peace settlement. Bulgaria had to absorb large numbers of refugees from the parts of Macedonia lost to Serbia in 1913 and confirmed in Yugoslavia's possession in 1919. After the brutal murder of Stamboliski in 1923, the Internal Macedonian Revolutionary Organization (IMRO), a terrorist refugee group, simply held the country in pawn until a revolution in 1933–1934 brought in a dictatorship strong enough to liquidate them. But in general, minorities were more sinned against than sinning, and for no group were the results more tragic than for the Jews. Unimportant in the southern Balkans, the Jews were a significant proportion of the population in Rumania, Hungary, and Poland. Wealthier Jews were likely to aim for assimilation, but, dominating industry and the professions as they did, they were hated by the non-Jewish upper and middle classes, who increasingly resented the ease with which a powerful intellectual tradition enabled Jews to succeed in university and professional life. Poorer Jews were less likely to seek assimilation, and their residence in the ghetto and their clinging to traditional dress and custom made them obvious targets for abuse in the cities, while in the countryside the Jewish shopkeeper or money lender, though perhaps little more prosperous than his neighbors, nevertheless became an easy magnet for frustration and jealousy. Except for a short, sharp burst of persecution following the fall of the Béla Kun regime in 1919, Hungarian Jews fared well until the sharp rightward turn in the thirties; and Marshal Pilsudski managed to check the powerful anti-Semitic strand in Polish life until the thirties, when it once more emerged as a means of grabbing political support. But throughout the interwar period Rumania turned in a wretched record on this account; there, with particular ugliness, Jews were systematically denied the means to a livelihood and university students were encouraged to take vengeance on them. That younger Jews turned to communism as the one route of escape only increased the danger of reprisals.

To call the political history of the east European states between the wars unedifying can only be an ironic understatement. But if one cannot be edified, one can be instructed as to the irrelevance of Wilsonian hopes for democracy in societies in no way prepared to exercise it. Whether monarchy or republic, all the countries had parliamentary forms of government, democratic in some degree, inclining more toward the French model than the American or British. Two of the defeated powers went through leftist interludes. The Béla Kun government in Hungary was a full-blown Communist regime, erected after the liberal government of Count Michael Károlyi resigned in the spring of 1919 in protest against the loss of Transylvania to Rumania. While the Kun government set out to reconquer Slovakia, the Rumanians invaded to protect their gains and drove out the Communists in August. There followed a "white terror" of horrible proportions, and the Rumanian occupation was marked by the most brazen looting. The Rumanian withdrawal left what was proclaimed as a kingdom, with a vacant throne and the commander in chief of the Hungarian forces, Admiral Nicholas Horthy, as regent, a post he maintained against the desire of King Charles, the Hapsburg claimant, to return. For ten years after April 1921 Count Stephen Bethlen served as premier of a restricted, unimaginative government that was in fact a moderate dictatorship. Bulgaria's dalliance with the Left was less extreme than Hungary's, and Stamboliski's agrarian regime lasted until his murder in 1923, a crime ascribable more perhaps to his willingness to coexist with the Yugoslavs than to his economic radicalism. Stamboliski's death unleashed ten years of terroristic anarchy. The one possible constitutional focus was King Boris III, who had succeeded on the abdication of his father Ferdinand in 1918. By the mid-thirties Boris was able to establish himself as an unostentatious but effective dictator.

The pattern of royal dictatorship was repeated in both Yugoslavia and Rumania. In Yugoslavia Alexander I succeeded to the throne on the death of King Peter in 1921. The nation threatened to disintegrate because of tensions between Serbs and Croats; politics was marked by instability of the narrowest partisan variety and punctuated by violence. The Croatian leader Stephen Radić died after being shot in parliament by a Montenegrin member; the crime brought a Croatian demand for federalization so extreme that it would have reduced even the army to territorial units removed from central control. At the beginning of 1929 King Alexander proclaimed a dictatorship that failed to evoke the national patriotism he hoped for and that in its administration, despite the king's efforts, was brutal, discriminatory, and corrupt. In Rumania the twenties began with the anti-Bolshevik government of the war hero Marshal Avarescu; he was succeeded in 1922 by the Liberals, who ruled with a brief interval until 1927. In that year the Liberal leader Ion Bratianu died, and so did King Ferdinand. The heir to the throne, Carol, was in disgrace and exile because of his scandalous private life, and a regency was proclaimed for his nephew Prince Michael. The regency confided the government to Julius Maniu, head of the National Peasants' party, who proceeded to effect some agrarian reforms and to bring in foreign capital; but when Carol returned in 1930 to claim the throne and insisted on bringing his mistress Magda Lupescu with him, Maniu resigned. Carol, a flashy, shallow demagogue, was thus enabled to rule covertly through ambitious and pliable politicians until 1937 when he too proclaimed a royal dictatorship.

Greece presented the worst spectacle of political instability in eastern Europe. There King Constantine had abdicated in 1917 in favor of his son Alexander, but returned to the throne on Alexander's death in 1920; he was driven again to abdication two years later in favor of George II, a creature of the military who lasted only until the end of 1923. In 1924 a republic was proclaimed, and after considerable initial instability, the wartime premier Venizelos, who had had no great political success in the interim, returned to power for a little over four years. After yet another period of instability, George II was restored in 1935, and the next year a military dictatorship was established under General John Metaxas.

Military dictatorship in another form was imposed on Poland. There, at the creation of the republic, the great pianist Ignace Paderewski mediated between the competing factions headed by Marshal Pilsudski, a war hero with socialist leanings, and by Roman Dmowski, at the head of the National Democrats (Endeks), a conservative, anti-Semitic, nationalistic party. Pilsudski dominated the first years, sparking the invasion of the Ukraine and conniving at the seizure of Vilna but then, refusing to be hobbled by the constitution of 1921 and its relatively weak executive power, retired to his country estate. Progress was made in the next few years in solving the problems of reconstruction, but in

May 1926 Pilsudski, disgusted with parliamentary maneuvering, marched on Warsaw and, with broad support (including the Communists), established himself as dictator. He remained in that position until his death in 1935, though usually without other than his military office. He had long since abandoned his socialist tendencies and relied increasingly on industrialists and landed aristocrats; the land reform program, never very impressive, was slowed down, and the firmness of Pilsudski's rule masked an undertow of corruption. Pilsudski's patriotism and disinterestedness were beyond question, but they were not enough to lead his nation out of a morass of problems, tensions, fears, and memories. It is one of the bitter twists of history that it was for Poland, rather than Czechoslovakia, that the Western democracies were willing to go to war when the test came in 1938–1939.

The Ebb of Iberian Constitutionalism

In Portugal, despite division of opinion over the war [17] and despite a number of threats from the right, the republican regime established in 1910 (see p. 911) survived until 1926, when it was overthrown by a military coup. In 1928 an almost unknown professor of economics at the University of Coimbra, Dr. Antonio de Oliveira Salazar, became minister of finance, having specified that he would take the post only in exchange for sweeping powers to set things to rights. That was precisely what Salazar did, and although he became premier only in 1932 he had well before that established himself as the most powerful man in the country. His program for national regeneration, aside from its concern with sound finance, centered on a new party with a monopoly on legal existence. A shy, retiring scholar, Salazar tried to keep on good terms with all the nations of Europe, whatever their political complexion, and gave Portugal a cautious, unprogressive, authoritarian rule—falling well short of fascism— that lasted until his death in 1969.

In Spain, neutral during the war, the prosperity of 1914–1918 proved difficult to maintain. There was growing discontent in the army, particularly among the officers. [18] The pretext for the strike that launched the Tragic Week (see p. 913) was a protest over conscription for a war against the marauding tribes in the Moroccan hinterland of Spain's remaining North African toeholds at Ceuta and Melilla, a war that had been launched following French insistence that Spain maintain order in her Moroccan protectorate as she had agreed to do in the Algeciras Convention. The war dragged on, and by 1920 Spanish forces were being harried by the Berber tribes under their brilliant leader Abd-el-

---

[17] In 1916 Germany actually declared war on Portugal in reprisal for the seizure of some German ships in Lisbon harbor, and a small Portuguese expeditionary force fought in France.

[18] That the officer corps was ill paid and bored is hardly surprising. With perhaps fifty thousand men under arms, Spain had as many officers as France and no fewer than five hundred generals.

Krim; in July 1921 he put the Spanish forces to rout. This new blow to Spanish pride came in the midst of a mounting wave of strikes; the struggle between anarchosyndicalists, who were beginning to fall out among themselves, and employers bent on destroying the movement led to open violence. A new wave of assassinations felled yet another prime minister in May 1922 and a major syndicalist leader and the archbishop of Zaragoza the next year. On September 13, 1923, with the encouragement of the king, a *pronunciamento* was issued by General Miguel Primo de Rivera. Martial law was proclaimed and the Cortes dissolved, rendering it unable to consider a secret report on the Moroccan disaster, which, it was rumored, implicated the king. Strict censorship was imposed, and liberal critics like Unamuno were driven into exile. Thus began what Spaniards, out of bitter later experience, were to call "the gentle dictatorship."

Primo de Rivera was an unlikely dictator. Generous and emotional almost to the point of being bizarre, he insisted and no doubt believed that his extraordinary rule would last only until corruption had been purged and civilian government could be reinstalled. He accomplished much in the economic sphere; irrigation schemes, electrification, and road-building all helped to bring much of Spain with a lurch into the twentieth century, though the projects were financed by loans that ultimately threatened the stability of the currency and contributed to the dictator's fall. With French help, Primo de Rivera brought Abd-el-Krim to defeat, and at the end of 1925 he could tell a grateful country that the long Moroccan war was over. But there still remained the question of the legitimacy of his rule. He had promoted a patriotic organization, an "apolitical party," the Unión Patriótica, from 1923; after the Moroccan victory he dismissed most of his military colleagues in the government and replaced them with civilians. He placated the church and split the labor movement by instituting "corporations," mixed labor and management bodies to set wages, hours, and other working conditions. In 1927 he summoned an appointed national assembly, which met the next two years as well, carefully supervised and deprived of all power to criticize. In 1929 a new constitution provided for a single-chamber Cortes elected by universal suffrage, including women, though the executive was responsible only to the king; the constitution was to be ratified in a plebiscite in 1930. But before then Primo de Rivera had fallen, the victim of a world depression that undercut his unorthodox finance, of labor unrest that would not be stilled, of incessant criticism from liberal exiles, of student agitation so severe that the universities had had to be closed, and at last of unhappiness in the army itself. He resigned on January 28, 1930, and died two months later in Paris.

Under General Berenguer, who succeeded him, more moderate policies were adopted; the censorship was lifted, and the restoration of constitutional government was undertaken in stages. But dislike of Alfonso XIII as the author of so many of Spain's troubles mounted, and the municipal elections in April 1931 became a plebiscite on the monarchy. The results were a sweep for the

Republicans and Socialists. A revolutionary committee had been formed, and the king accepted advice from his ministers that he should leave the country. He did not abdicate: he went by automobile to Cartagena, where he embarked for Marseilles. Nothing in the vocabulary of revolution is mild enough to describe the end of the Bourbon monarchy—Spain simply became a republic. The change had its effect on some men, however. The nobleman who had tutored Alfonso XIII in polo-playing wrote that "the fall of the monarchy gave me a greater shock than any fall from a polo pony." [19]

The Birth of Fascism

Italy emerged from the war frustrated and embittered. Although its traditional enemy, the Hapsburg Empire, had been destroyed and Italy had gained its "natural frontiers," Italy did not get the territory it wanted on the Dalmatian coast, and Italians knew that their country was only honorifically a great power. The memory of the battle of Caporetto rankled; the two years of fighting—with 600,000 dead—had been far from glorious. Yet the war-weariness was not universal: many yearned for action, among them extreme nationalists, disgruntled senior officers who felt themselves victims of the politicians' compromises, and the *arditi*—the young volunteers drawn mostly from the middle class and the universities, clothed in special uniforms with black shirts, and trained for special operations that demanded boldness and risk-taking. Politics as usual—especially the politics of *trasformismo*—could do little to rid the nation of cynicism, frustration, and despair, and of the impotence depressingly revealed in the postwar governments. Francesco Nitti succeeded Orlando in June 1919. In September he had to cope with D'Annunzio's seizure of the Adriatic port of Fiume (see p. 966), which Italy had been refused in the peace settlement and which remained a sore point for nationalists. The coup was unquestionably popular: this exploit of a famous poet conjured up memories of Garibaldi, and D'Annunzio's self-indulgent demagoguery kept excitement, in Fiume and out of it, at a high pitch. Nitti did nothing to put a stop to this clearly illegal act, and indeed his government gave the venture diplomatic protection and some economic assistance. D'Annunzio's hold on the city lasted for more than a year. The aged Giolitti, who succeeded Nitti in June 1920, continued the same policy for almost six months and then, after a clash in the city ended in the death of a number of soldiers, decided to turn the invaders out, a task accomplished with ridiculous ease. [20] As one looks back, the Fiume incident is a gloomy portent, not only because it proved that lawlessness could succeed with impunity, but because it foreshadowed the psychology and techniques of totalitarianism as

---

[19] Quoted in Raymond Carr, *Spain, 1808-1939* (1966), 601.

[20] D'Annunzio, having vowed to die for Fiume, decided that inglorious Italy was not worth the sacrifice. Nitti remarked that D'Annunzio left Fiume as he left his mistresses, exploited and exhausted. Denis Mack Smith, *Italy, a Modern History* (1969), 336.

the interwar years came to know them. It also revealed the moral weakness of the parliamentary leaders and their blindness to the danger on the right.

One can understand how this miscalculation came about. In the elections of November 1919 the two largest parties were the Socialists and the new Popular party, which leaned, if it leaned at all, to the left. Politicians are impressed by numbers, which readily mask inherent weaknesses. It was probably harder to anticipate the fate of the *popolari*. The new party had come into existence after the *non expedit,* which had kept loyal Catholics from taking part in Italian politics (see p. 804), was lifted by the imaginative wartime pope Benedict XV. But Catholicism was no guarantee of agreement on a social and political program. The party lacked cohesion, and, despite an increase in its number of seats in the election of 1921 and the Liberal politicians' dependence, it was soon to decline, especially after the archconservative Pius XI came to the papal throne in 1922. The stupidity of the Socialist leaders, on the other hand, quickly neutralized their party's potential. Italian Socialists had long known the strains common to their European brethren over the vexed question of collaboration with bourgeois parties. In 1919 the "maximalists" in the party carried the day; they refused any cooperation, even against the growing threat from the Right, secure in the faith that their cause would inevitably win. Their language was violent and their abstract program revolutionary, but the Socialists did little or nothing in parliament and failed to take advantage of the unrest rooted in economic and social problems the country had failed to resolve in the decades since unification. Matters grew even worse when the left wing of the Socialists broke away late in 1920, following orders from the Third International, to form a Communist party.

For the propertied classes and the government, however, the Socialists' political futility was obscured by the threatening syndicalist turmoil, which reached a climax in the summer of 1920 in Turin, where the most militant unionism in Italy had found a leader of genius in the young Antonio Gramsci. The intransigence of the employers in the Turin metalworking trades led to a workers' occupation of the factories in August 1920; it was what fifteen years later in the United States would be known as a sit-down strike. Giolitti, as usual, let matters drift and then imposed a settlement that included concessions to the workers. But it was no syndicalist victory, for the power and impact of organized labor steadily declined thereafter. What remained was an overwhelming fear and hostility to such leftist manifestations. That hatred suffused the calm that spread over the social scene after the summer of 1919, a calm the government took as the sign of an improved national mood. It was, however, the seedbed in which a far more threatening phenomenon grew.

Benito Mussolini, born in 1883, came of peasant stock; his father was a blacksmith of radical inclination who named his son for the Mexican revolutionary hero Benito Juárez. The young Mussolini left the country in 1902 to escape conscription and held a succession of menial jobs in Switzerland; he was once arrested for begging. Two years later he returned to Italy to serve his term in the army, and eventually he drifted into left-wing journalism, having picked up syndicalist ideas and grafted them onto a tradition of extralegal action native to the Romagna from which he came. Although he began his political career as a Socialist, he broke with the party over the war, which he supported, and in Milan in 1915, with help from some big business interests he founded his own paper, *Il Popolo d'Italia.* He served briefly during the war, rising to become a corporal, and later boasted mightily about his exploits. A compulsive braggart and exhibitionist, he alternated violence with indolence, good nature, and charm; he lacked the ruthless single-mindedness of Lenin. Sharing and playing upon the postwar mood, nicely balancing bluff and notable tactical skill, he rose to power in a political system incapable of resistance.

At the outset Mussolini's prospects were not good. In March 1919, with a hundred-odd malcontents, including a number of the *arditi* with whom he had associated since the end of the war, Mussolini formed a new organization, the Fascio Italiani di Combattimento. The term *fascio,* used in the names of several veterans' organizations, meant a bundle of sticks, like those surrounding the axe that had been the symbol of the lictors in ancient Rome; the success of Mussolini's movement spawned the terms *fascist* and *fascism.* At the outset the Fascists offered something for nearly everyone, including a social program calling for participation of workers in management, increased taxes on the wealthy, and a capital levy. An impressive scattering of support was mustered, including the celebrated young conductor Arturo Toscanini, the composer Giacomo Puccini, and the futurist artist Filippo Marinetti.[21] But not a single parliamentary candidate put up by the Fascists in 1919 was elected, and the total Fascist vote was negligible. It was the first of a number of apparently crushing misfortunes from which Mussolini managed always to recover.

As program and leader escaped from their Socialist past, opportunity was offered by the intense anti-socialist mood in the country. The Fascists found it both easy and profitable to launch physical attacks on Socialists and Socialist party and newspaper offices; in 1920, the old link with the *arditi* was transmuted into a new hooliganism of gangs known as *squadristi:* to this the craving for action had come. And Mussolini profited immensely from the example of D'Annunzio. The poet's most vocal Italian supporter, Mussolini privately urged caution and prudently abandoned the enterprise when the government at last turned on it; but he shamelessly stole D'Annunzio's techniques of speech-making and stirring up a crowd: the black shirts of the *arditi* came to the Fascists through Fiume, as did the salute, the Fascist hymn, and the war cry *Eia Eia Alalà.* This violence of the Right was overlooked by the government—it did after all take on the government's chief enemies—and was actively encouraged by many local government officials. The final irony, if not crime, was Giolitti's acceptance of Fascist support in the general election of 1921; the old man, more

---

[21] Toscanini soon withdrew, outraged by a Fascist demand that he play the Fascist hymn *Giovinezza* at concerts. Marinetti fell out with the Fascists over reconciliation with the church.

wily than perceptive, assumed that fascism was a movement he could use against Socialists and Communists and then just as airily dismiss. Thirty-five Fascists entered the new parliament. After Giolitti resigned in June 1921, governments were headed by nonentities, and what initiative there was in the country passed to the Fascists; in much of the northern and central regions they were the only source of authority.

Mussolini had brought about the transformation of a movement into a political party; what he once had seen as a perpetual provincial minority group now became a claimant on power at the center. There was increasing talk of seizing power by a march on Rome; a likely occasion seemed to be the Fascist congress in Naples at the end of October 1922. The Socialists were completely neutralized, and some leftist local governments had been physically driven from power by Fascist squads; Giolitti, who might yet have mastered the situation, hung back from taking office. So Fascist mobilization proceeded, while Mussolini returned from Naples to Milan to await developments and to reassure the large industrialists who had become his backers. At last, on October 27–28, the government moved to secure Rome, where fascism had never been strong, by declaring a state of siege. King Victor Emmanuel, after agreeing to the step, changed his mind at the last minute and refused to sign the necessary document. Luigi Facta, a reluctant premier from the outset, resigned, and Giolitti's old enemy Antonio Salandra tried to bring Mussolini into a government. But Mussolini held out for an invitation to form a government himself: it came on the twenty-ninth. Mussolini traveled to Rome in a sleeping car; on the thirtieth his followers entered the capital, some on foot, most of them by truck and special train. Like everything else about fascism, the famous march on Rome turned out to be a cheap fraud.

Once in power, Mussolini set out to fulfill his promise of firm and efficient government, while trying to placate many different groups. He tried to carry on a respectable and largely pacific foreign policy, but spiced it with occasional truculence and adventurism, which appealed to the envy of nationalists and suggested the disastrous aggressiveness to come. In the new Turkish settlement at Lausanne in 1923 he got the Dodecanese Islands in the Aegean Sea; he supported the French occupation of the Ruhr, but soon was trying to bring about pacification; he seized the island of Corfu off Greece in a dispute with that country and evacuated it only in exchange for a large indemnity; he had sent forces to occupy Fiume following a local Fascist coup in 1922 and was confirmed in possession in 1924; and he was constantly embroiled with Yugoslavia and Albania. Mussolini's cabinet was a coalition in which the Fascists held relatively few posts; the church was offered new respect and old privileges. Employers were gratified to find Mussolini serious in carrying out the recommendation he had made on entering parliament in 1921 that state intervention should give way to a new dose of laissez-faire. Government expenditures were cut; land reforms and Giolitti's radical fiscal measures were shelved; taxes were lowered; and the telephone service was sold on favorable terms to private enterprise, though with a pleasing inconsistency tariffs were raised and the government came to the rescue of firms in trouble. For the moment only the workers suffered from the change in regime: the *squadristi* had wrecked the unions, strikes were impracticable, and, though it was a period of prosperity, real wages fell. Violence continued in the country, and some of it was denounced by Mussolini as "unnecessary," a matter of which he was the judge.

Only a few persons were open in voicing their doubts and fears. But there was no wholesale assault on liberties, though in 1923 the government secured reserve powers to silence the press. So too with the constitution. Directly after taking office Mussolini brought his party's leaders together as the Fascist Grand Council, the chief policy-making body; the cabinet thus became a primarily administrative organ. The *squadristi* were institutionalized, if not tamed, as a militia numbering 300,000 men. Parliament continued to sit, though Mussolini's bullying first speech made it clear that it would do so only on sufferance. The Fascists, after all, had only thirty-five members in a chamber dominated by Socialists and *popolari,* and in 1923 a new electoral law, carried by the promise of parliamentary stability and by scarcely veiled threats, gave the party receiving the largest number of votes in an election (provided it was at least 25 percent) two thirds of the seats in the chamber; elections were to be for national slates, not for members representing constituencies. The elections of April 1924 proved that the law was a needless precaution; the Fascist coalition got 65 percent of the votes cast.

At the end of May a moderate Socialist deputy, Giacomo Matteotti, in a speech of remarkable boldness, denounced the open intimidation and violence and demanded that the election be voided. A short while later Matteotti was kidnapped and murdered. That the highest officials of the Fascist party were involved was soon known, and the outraged public reaction posed a serious threat to Mussolini and the Fascists. Mussolini pleaded that the murder was the act of his enemies; the king retreated behind the limitations of a constitutional monarch (limitations he had transgressed in rejecting the advice of his ministers to declare a state of siege in 1922) and refused to hear reports of Mussolini's complicity; the Vatican newspaper praised Mussolini's resolute conduct, drawing with stunning irrelevance on the Bible to argue "Let him who is without sin cast the first stone"; the big industrialists stood firm; and a hundred deputies withdrew from parliament in an impotent gesture. The Liberals who remained in active opposition, Giolitti among them, were quite as impotent. And in January 1925 Mussolini was strong enough to avow his own responsibility for whatever had happened, and to threaten that only force would arbitrate between two such irreconcilable elements as the Fascists and the seceders. The murder created an anti-Fascist movement at last, but it was a movement possible only in exile.

The situation "clarified," as he had promised, Mussolini then moved to build up the new Fascist state. An agreement in October 1925 brought the employers' federation together with a body of tamed unionists as the sole representatives of industry, a system that left the employers relatively free while reducing a nominal syndicalism to the registration of Fascist commands. Over the next ten years, guided by the theorist Alfredo Rocco, a system was devised to allow the different sectors of industry to be governed by joint "corporations," which were in fact run by party bosses. The idea owed something to syndicalism and more to Catholic social thought; though it never amounted to much in practical terms in Italy, it passed for a novelty and aroused much interest elsewhere. The centrality of the Fascist Grand Council was secured. Mussolini, as *duce* or leader of the party, was (under the king) head of the state, and through him flowed a vast patronage, monopolized as far as possible by early adherents of the movement; it thus became the source of endless inefficiency and corruption. After a series of attempts on Mussolini's life in 1925–1926, all parties except the Fascist party were abolished, Communist leaders (including Gramsci) were imprisoned, the police were reorganized, and new procedures were worked out to deal with crime against the state.

For all the publicity given to public works projects and social welfare measures, Fascist Italy undertook little that was new and in many ways marked a retrogression from Liberal accomplishments. Despite the touting of Mussolini's vigor and forcefulness, and despite his public posturing, his regime was flabby and incompetent. Its negativism and philosophical poverty contrasted as strongly with the positive promise of Soviet dogma as did its erratic administration with Soviet ruthlessness. Nor could it compare—or stand up to—the terrible totalitarianism (the term was Mussolini's) soon to emerge in Germany. That this first Fascist was so much admired in western Europe testifies less to Mussolini's abilities and successes than to the divisive problems and querulous doubt that infected the liberal democracies.

THE WEAKNESS OF DEMOCRACY

Britain

Of all the major European nations Britain emerged from the war the strongest: loss of life was less, proportionally, than in other countries, and physically Britain had suffered only the wasting, not the ravages, of war. But its industrial plant was outmoded, and the postwar boom channeled investment into industries and areas that were less able than others to cope with the collapse in demand when it came. The British Empire was still imposing, in extent and significance, but its structure was changing and its long-range future not easy to discern. The dominions of Canada, Australia, New Zealand, and South Africa had been given internal self-government, with only a few special reservations; they had played important parts in the war and at the peace conference; and the interwar years marked still further progress toward autonomy, especially in foreign affairs. At the Imperial Conference in 1926 the British Commonwealth of Nations was defined as a free association of equal and autonomous communities, "in no way subordinate to one another in any aspect of their domestic or external affairs, though united by a common allegiance to the Crown." But the fact was known before it was defined: the rebuff given to Lloyd George when he appealed for help against the Turks at Chanak (see p. 966) had shown that the dominions would not automatically follow Britain's lead.

Dominion status had been given to Ireland by treaty in 1922, though this solution of Britain's oldest imperial problem was attained only by an arduous and bloody path. The Home Rule bill, passed in 1914 and shelved for the duration of the war, had not prevented Irish nationalist intrigues with the Germans for support. One of the conspirators, Sir Roger Casement, a former British consul, was apprehended when he landed in Ireland, on Good Friday, 1916, and the "Easter Rebellion" on the following Monday was put down; the execution of its leaders, including Casement, made them into martyrs. In the poisoned atmosphere in 1917 and 1918 the old remedy of Home Rule was insufficient. The radical Sinn Fein ("ourselves alone") party swept every seat in the election in 1918 but refused to sit in Parliament, forming themselves instead into an Irish parliament, which declared an independent Irish republic in January 1919. The Irish Republican Army, descended from the prewar Volunteers, was soon at war with British forces, a guerrilla struggle marked by terrorism and cruelty on both sides, most shockingly evident among the supplementary British forces—the "Black and Tans" and the "Auxis." When, with the statesmanship of exhaustion, a treaty was finally negotiated, the predominantly Protestant northern counties of Ulster were excluded from the Irish Free State, as the new dominion was called. This violation of the integrity of Ireland was unacceptable to the radical nationalists, who denounced the treaty and turned to fight the new Irish government in a civil war that raged through 1922, to end in May 1923 with a government victory.

In Britain, Lloyd George had won triumphant vindication in the election of 1918, but his coalition government depended heavily on Conservative support; indeed the Liberals from whom he had come had splintered into factions and never recovered their electoral strength; the official opposition, with the second largest number of seats, was now the Labour party. The economic downturn in 1920 and 1921 and a growing desire to escape from wartime regulation wrecked the extensive plans for reconstruction and social reform that were intended to make a land "fit for heroes to live in." Nor could Lloyd George accomplish any of the miracles he sought in foreign policy. The fiasco of his Greek policy and the distrust he engendered among the Tory rank and file led the Conservative party in October 1922 to pull out of the coalition. Lloyd George was thus forced to resign, and the king sent for Bonar Law, the Conservative leader, who, mortally ill, had to resign the following May. The government was now confided to Stanley Baldwin, an ironmaster turned politician, a quiet, dull man, whose comfortable and reassuring appearance masked a remarkable astuteness at political manipulation. Baldwin risked an election at the end of 1923 on the embattled question of protection, but free trade retained enough loyalty among the electorate to put the Conservatives in a minority as against Labour and the Liberals combined. The Liberals, without entering a coalition, allowed a Labour government to be formed, and in January 1924 Ramsay MacDonald became prime minister.

In 1918 the Labour party had adopted a new constitution making it possible for individuals to join directly and not merely through constituent organizations such as trade unions; the new constitution also for the first time committed the party to a socialist program, which meant above all the nationalization of basic industries. Nationalization of the ailing coal-mining industry had been recommended by a royal commission in 1920 but bypassed by Lloyd George. Labour, in a parliamentary minority, could undertake nothing so sweeping and had to content itself with improved housing legislation and the skillful performance of MacDonald in foreign affairs. Only in 1922 had MacDonald returned to the leadership of the party with which he had broken in 1914 over entry into the war. He was vain, shallow, and distrusted by many of his associates, but, impressive in appearance and oratory, he could reassure those of his countrymen who feared a Labour government. He brought down a storm of obloquy from Conservatives, however, by diplomatic recognition of the Soviet Union. Attacked in Parliament for not having prosecuted a foolish, though technically seditious, Communist journalist, MacDonald was defeated on a vote of confidence. The ensuing election was notable for the wide publicity given at the last moment to a letter (almost certainly forged) in which Zinoviev, the head of the Comintern, expressed hope for a Labour victory. Whatever the impact of the Zinoviev letter on British voters, the election brought Baldwin back into office. Winston Churchill, so long in the political wilderness, returned to the Conservative party he had deserted twenty years before and took the rather surprising post of chancellor of the exchequer.

In 1925, after receiving conflicting advice from experts, Churchill decided to return the pound to the gold standard suspended during the war and to the prewar parity with the American dollar. Because this action left British goods relatively highly priced in world markets, the need to maintain exports put additional pressure on employers to reduce costs, which they chose to do by reducing wages. Resistance to wage cuts was led by the miners, who were supported by the Trades Union Congress, and, despite long negotiations, in May 1926 Britain was subjected to a general strike. Here at last was the realization of the vaguely syndicalist threat that had foundered in 1914 on the outbreak of the war and in 1921 on trade-union disharmony. The strike lasted ten days; the miners stayed out until the end of the year. The General Strike was largely peaceable, though there were signs of growing tension and revolutionary sentiment toward the end. The government and employers won: troops and volunteers handled essential services, and Churchill, his innate combativeness aroused, was the most prominent and active opponent of the strike—organizing, speech-making, publishing a newspaper, directing the troops—a performance for which the labor movement never forgave him. In 1927, although Baldwin had spoken out against retribution, Parliament passed a severe trade-union act, outlawing sympathetic strikes or strikes intended to coerce the government, defining and forbidding intimidation, and (the only provision with practical consequences) cutting financial support of the Labour party by insisting that trade-union political contributions be voluntary for individual members. More important as a symbol than as an impediment, the act was swept away following the Labour victory in 1945.

Otherwise, Conservative legislation was useful but unspectacular—the nationalization of radio broadcasting and the production of electricity, new housing legislation, and an extensive reform of local government. A general election in 1929, interesting chiefly for an ambitious though electorally unproductive program put forward by Lloyd George and the remnant of the Liberal party, brought Labour once more into office in a minority government, just in time to face a crisis for which it was utterly unprepared.

France

British political life in the twenties, less exciting than at any time since the 1850s, fitted the national mood. So did the cautious progress on the policy front; the modes and ends of government were less central to public awareness than they had been before the war or at any time in the nineteenth century. French political life seems even less rewarding to contemplate. Perhaps the overwhelming preoccupation with external security preempted the place that domestic policy might have filled, or perhaps the nation was merely exhausted. Yet, for all the internal problems, the twenties in France were a period of remarkable stability. The writer Daniel Halévy ascribed it to the fact that rule by a bureaucracy was accepted by the masses, a coalescence of two glacial forces that allowed little scope for change.[22] The alternation of governments and parliamentary combinations, continuous with the prewar pattern, mattered little beyond the game itself. There is little point in chronicling all the ministries that followed from the vagaries of elections and votes in the Chamber, from the phasing of presidential elections, and from incidents as trival as Briand's willingness to allow Lloyd George to instruct him in golf during a conference at Cannes, an occasion that Briand's nationalist enemies used to ridicule him as

---

[22] See the quotation from Daniel Halévy in David Thomson, *Democracy in France since 1870* (5th ed., 1969), 175-176, and Thomson's discussion generally.

subservient to an Anglo-Saxon master. But the general political choice lay between the two fragments of the wartime coalition, the Bloc National and the Cartel des Gauches. When the nation recoiled from Poincaré's adventurism in the Ruhr in 1923 (see p. 970), the left-center Cartel, a coalition primarily of Radicals and Socialists, won a firm electoral victory, and Edouard Herriot became premier. Security had now given way to the internal problem of inflation, which was eating into the resources of those who depended on savings, pensions, and other forms of fixed income, a situation with which the Herriot government proved unable to cope.

This domestic crisis might ordinarily have caused serious trouble, and there was considerable agitation from the antirepublican Right. The extreme nationalist, anti-Semitic organization, the Action Française, dominated by the literary journalists Charles Maurras and Léon Daudet, had welcomed the assertiveness of the Ruhr occupation and either by word or by deed of its associated gangs, the Camelots du Roi, made trouble for its enemies; other extreme paramilitary organizations, inspired in part by Fascist successes in Italy, surfaced as well, though their time was not to come until the thirties. Meanwhile the Left, in customary fashion, had been virtually paralyzed by the emergence of Communism, forced by the demands of the Third International that Socialist parties adhere to the orthodoxy it set forth (see p. 977). French socialism was neutralized as a political force. The Confédération Générale du Travail, the national labor organization whose syndicalist activity had been so important before the war, survived, but its militancy passed to the Communist CGTU, as the Communist party broke away from the Socialists, taking with them Jaurès's great newspaper *L'Humanité*. But the Communist organizations remained small and could only bide their time.

Herriot's failure to deal with inflation brought back the Bloc National, after three brief governments headed by Briand, in July 1926. The rampant foreign policy that had characterized Poincaré's ministry of 1922–1924 was out of place in the era of Locarno, and indeed the pacific Briand remained foreign minister without interruption between 1925 and his death in 1932—under fourteen different governments. In domestic affairs Poincaré, like Baldwin across the Channel, brought a sense of stability and rectitude. Rigorous taxation, economy, budgetary reforms, and the restoration of confidence (along with regular installments of German reparations) restored the country's financial base. It was not a deflationary remedy like that carried through by Churchill in Britain; there the working classes lost, while in France they benefited. The franc was not restored to its old value, but it was stabilized at about a fifth of its prewar level, and even the middle classes, who had suffered most, proved grateful for small mercies.

In July 1929 Poincaré retired because of ill health, and the pattern of short-lived governments resumed. In itself the retirement marks no epoch and carries little justification for interrupting an account of the domestic history of France between the wars. But in October 1929 occurred two unconnected events that in retrospect make the year a watershed. Gustav Stresemann, the outstanding statesman of the German republic, died, and in New York Wall Street collapsed in panic.

The Tragedy of Weimar

History has few undoubted lessons, among them perhaps that the best intentions go awry in ways that cannot be foreseen, that evil is seductive, that crisis is always (as the psychoanalysts say) overdetermined. Of these lessons, if such they are, the history of the Weimar Republic is a veritable textbook. No experiment in democracy was more important; none failed with such terrible consequences.

Like defeated France after 1870, defeated Germany after 1918 became a republic by default. The default in Germany was, however, far more painful to assimilate. France had no single, meaningfully remembered monarchical tradition, only competing nostalgias and fantasies; but the abdication of the German Emperor William II in November 1918 tore away a working institution that—however erratically and irresponsibly it had been run—focused national loyalties and penetrated every aspect of life. Neither the Germans nor the French forty years earlier were prepared by experience to absorb an effective parliamentary government: they lacked the long apprenticeship, and were not vouchsafed the gradualism, that made the British system a virtually inimitable model. Yet the French were relatively successful in their adaptation, and the Germans were not. The French, it is true, had more time, in easier economic and political circumstances; their administrative machine—that brilliant creation of Napoleon I—was more neutrally technocratic (it had after all survived so many changes) than the equally remarkable German bureaucracy, with its mystique of service and its ideal of culture, conservative taproots not easily torn up or easily replanted in alien soil. The French, despite a deep cynicism about politics and politicians, were still political to the marrow; educated Germans, on the other hand, had been conditioned to shun politics, even to pride themselves on their distance from it—and there is a vast gulf between cynicism and disdain.

In both countries (as in all countries), deep reserves of emotion and irrationality surfaced under stress in currents antithetical to the moral and rational assumptions of liberal democracy: militarism, authoritarianism, anti-Semitism, xenophobic nationalism, ignorant pride, and fear were endemic on both sides of the Rhine. But in France these currents were met by equal or greater enthusiasms for the opposing loyalties of republicanism, its most notable advocates, perhaps, the village schoolmasters. Such loyalties barely existed in Germany; the nineteenth century had driven them into exile. Nor could the French Right muster as impressive intellectual support as the German Right; for all the brilliance of the writers of the Action Française, they remained an eccentric, minor, almost decorative, intellectual movement. In Germany critics and prophets like Paul de Lagarde in Bismarck's time or Arthur Moeller van den Bruck (to whom more than anyone else the revival of the old myth of a "Third Reich" is due) carried more conviction more widely. The admirable tradition of German scholarship in philosophy and history contained ambiguities that could be pressed into service as well. The Hegelian arsenal, even the Kantian, held different weapons from those provided by Voltaire and Rousseau. Against the respect, even worship, of the Prussian state in the histories of Ranke, Treitschke, and Friedrich Meinecke, the Germans could scarcely field historians like Guizot or Elie Halévy, with their deep appreciation of English institutions, let alone a Michelet or a Jaurès. One suspects that at bottom we are coping with the legacies of two radically different Enlightenments. But to say that is to speculate about the unprovable. Narrower, more readily isolable actions and events can explain Weimar's fate less cosmically.

William II had not wanted to abdicate; he was forced out because his departure was necessary to immediate salvation. Friedrich Ebert, the leader of the Social Democrats (SPD), and many others wanted a parliamentary monarchy, and Philipp Scheidemann's proclamation of the republic on November 9 was a tactical move to forestall more threatening developments on the left. Already an independent Bavarian republic had been proclaimed by Kurt Eisner, an Independent Socialist. The spontaneous appearance of workers' and soldiers' councils in the last days of the war promised a replay of the revolution in Russia, a promise underlined by the readiness of the extreme left wing of the German Socialist movement, the so-called Spartacists, to emulate the Bolsheviks and to channel anarchy into revolution. There was one profound difference: the Bolsheviks' theorist, Lenin, led the vanguard in action, while the Spartacist leaders, Karl Liebknecht and Rosa Luxemburg—the latter in particular at theoretical odds with Lenin about the role of the party—recognized the impossibility of a Soviet success in Germany. Following, not leading, they were martyred for their loyalty and their conviction of the tactical importance of solidarity: a white terror, as we have seen repeatedly in this book, seems even less capable than a red terror of making fine discriminations. But the threats were real in November 1918, and the men who, willy-nilly, headed the new republic had to find the means to cope with them. It was not a situation in which careful weighing of alternatives and projection of their results were possible. In the compressed perspective of crisis, when a few hours might make the difference between success and failure, the very mandate of power dictates the use of means at hand, and the odds at best are even that the means will work, even for immediate ends.

On the day of the abdication, November 9, Ebert had formed a provisional government, confirmed in power the next day by a mass meeting of the workers' and soldiers' councils and grandiloquently called a council of "people's commissars." The rhetoric was more frightening than the fact. Composed of three majority Social Democrats and three Independents, this "six-headed chancellor" proclaimed a number of social and political reforms, most of which had been discussed for some time, while employers, recognizing that the times required the sacrifice of prerogatives they had jealously guarded, made notable concessions to trade unions. But the "people's commissars" also recognized that truly fundamental alterations—such as an extensive program of nationalization urged by the radical shop stewards—were impossible under the circumstances. That did not mean, however, that the two parties were as one— far from it. On December 16, a national congress of the workers' and soldiers' councils was held in Berlin. Dominated by majority Social Democrats, the congress once more confirmed the provisional government in power until a new government should be appointed by the constituent assembly, which was to meet at the earliest possible date, January 19. A central council was appointed as a watchdog on the people's commissars, and a wildly democratic set of resolutions was carried, calling for the abolition of ranks and insignia in the armed forces, the expunging of militarism, and election of officers. Again the rhetoric bore little relation to reality. The provisional government did nothing to enforce the resolutions; the army leaders, appalled, not only ignored the directives but showed their contempt for them. When another naval mutiny split the sympathies of the six, the Independents withdrew on December 29, to be replaced by three Social Democrats.

Meanwhile a far more significant alliance had been forged. On November 10, the day after the creation of the republic and the day before the armistice, telephone calls between Ebert and General Wilhelm Groener, Ludendorff's successor as first quartermaster general, cemented an understanding between the provisional government and the army. Although the forces were honey-combed with discontent—the navy far more than the army—and although there was no guarantee that discipline could be imposed or that units would fight when ordered, the officers were determined to retain both their old image of themselves as the elite of the nation and their power within the state. Uneasily eyeing the eastern frontier as well as the anarchy at home, Ebert had little choice but to accept the offer of help from the one quarter where it was most securely available. When the government was reconstructed at the end of the year, the central council chose Gustav Noske, of the SPD, as one of the commissars. Seeing himself as the bloodhound the situation required, Noske not only strengthened the alliance with the military but authorized the use of the free corps—volunteer units that had coalesced around certain officers and that drew on former soldiers whose taste for military life was undiminished, nationalists and adventurers, and some more unsavory types. If regular soldiers could not be counted on to fire on workingmen in a confrontation, the free corps could. Ultimately the government and regular army officers—and the Allies—insisted on the disbandment of the free corps; they were a malign necessity at best, a terrifying harbinger in retrospect.

The free corps had their way against the radical and Communist uprisings that punctuated the troubled months after the armistice. The sharpest of these encounters occurred in January 1919. When the Social Democrats attempted to purge the Prussian government, one Independent Socialist official refused to resign; his ouster led to massive demonstrations in his support and to an uprising of the Spartacus League, which, on December 30 had transformed itself into the Communist party. By January 12 the ruthlessness of the free corps had destroyed the insurrection a week after it had begun; on January 15 Liebknecht and Luxemburg, who had joined the uprising to protect their leadership and to mediate in what they saw as a hopeless course, were brutally murdered by the officers who were assigned to take them to prison. On February 21 Kurt Eisner, the radical Bavarian separatist, was also murdered. The government that succeeded him in that troubled state proved incapable of controlling its followers and fled before a Communist republic set up in early April. It was in turn brought down with violence at the beginning of May by government troops and free corps.

In the midst of bloodshed and near chaos the constructive work had gone on. The elections to the constituent assembly had given the Social Democrats by far the largest delegation, 163 seats. The Independents had a mere 22, one more than the new People's party, a combination leaning to big business and the Right and dominated by Gustav Stresemann. In the middle were the Catholic Center party, with 89 seats; the new, intellectually impressive Democratic party, with 75; and the old Conservatives, now the National People's party, with 42. The assembly met in Weimar, Goethe's city and a center of eighteenth-century cosmopolitanism that, more to the point, was a safe distance from the turmoil of Berlin. Ebert was elected president, and in a remarkably short time the constitution was agreed to; it was formally adopted on July 31 and put into effect on August 11. A federal form of government was retained, although the constituent states had less power than under the empire and the upper house, the Reichsrat, retained only a suspensive veto. Extensive civil rights were guaranteed, and the political reforms already granted— universal suffrage and responsible government—were kept, while democracy was reinforced by those ubiquitous nostrums of early twentieth-century political thought, proportional representation, initiative, and referendum. The lower house, the Reichstag, thus elected sat for four years. But the president was to be no British monarch, nor even a French president, nor was he subject to the checks that limit an American president. Elected for a seven-year term, he could select and dismiss the chancellor and, under the famous Article 48, could take the executive power into his own hands and rule by decree in case of disruption of or danger to public security and order.

By the time the constituent assembly had completed its work, the first government Ebert had appointed had fallen, for the chancellor, Scheidemann, was unwilling to accept responsibility for accepting the *Diktat* of the Versailles Treaty, a task shouldered by the ministry of Gustav Bauer. But the Bauer government fell in the aftermath of the Kapp Putsch, the first determined right-wing effort to overthrow the republic, on March 13–17, 1920. The course of the republic, moderate though it was, had caused profound discontent among conservatives, nationalists, and the military caste. Discontent increased among military men when the decision was made to disband the free corps. The commander of one of the more notorious of these groups, the Ehrhardt Brigade, refused to accept the order and, with the encouragement of his superior, General Walther von Luttwitz, marched on Berlin. Fearing (through calculation or conviction) to set one part of the army against another, General Hans von Seeckt, the head of the troop office (a substitute for the banned general staff) counseled inaction, and the government prudently withdrew, first to Dresden, then to Stuttgart. The Ehrhardt Brigade moved into Berlin, where Wolfgang Kapp, a former civil servant turned nationalist politician, was named chancellor; Luttwitz was made head of the army. The Kapp Putsch, widely welcomed by the Right, was brought to an end not by a divided army but by a general strike called in response to a government request for a boycott of the insurgent government. When the collapse of the Putsch was assured, the strike ended, except in the Ruhr, where it was taken over by Communists and mounted into a new revolutionary attempt violently put down by the army. There was no purge of those involved in the Putsch, but there were other casualties: Noske was dropped from the cabinet for his indulgence of the military, and General Reinhardt, who had tried seriously to cooperate with the republican government, retired. He was succeeded by the complex and skillful Seeckt.

The Weimar coalition of Social Democrats, Democrats, and Center was destroyed by the first general elections under the new constitution, held on June 6, 1920, to replace the constituent assembly with a new Reichstag. The number of Center party seats fell slightly, but the vote for the Social Democrats and the Democrats plummeted, while the Nationalists and the People's party improved their showing greatly. The Independent Socialist vote too went up, reflecting a disenchantment in the SPD with their leadership, and in October a majority of a convention of Independent Socialists voted to join the tiny Communist party of the Spartacists under conditions laid down by the Comintern, leaving the right-wing Independents to return to the Social Democratic fold. With an eye to the Left, the chastened Social Democrats held aloof from government after 1920, except for brief participation in 1921–1922 and 1923, until 1928. The republic the Socialists had created was handed over to the Center and the Right.

One government followed rapidly on another, and all of them had to deal with three great, often interrelated problems. One was the construction of an army within the stringent limits imposed by the Treaty of Versailles. This was Seeckt's domain, masterfully ruled. The hundred thousand men that the treaty allowed were enlisted for long terms, superbly trained, and destined to be the cadre of a much larger army once the treaty restrictions could be thrown off; other ways of circumventing the restrictions were found, including the use of training grounds in the Soviet Union. Another problem, already extensively discussed, revolved around the complex questions of reparations, inflation, and "accommodation" with the rest of Europe (see p. 969). The major events in this complex were the Treaty of Rapallo in 1922, which, with Seeckt's enthusiastic endorsement, secured Germany against the Russian threat; the French occupation of the Ruhr, passive resistance, the inflation, and the currency stabilization carried out in connection with the Dawes Plan in 1924; and the Locarno treaties and Germany's reentry into the inner councils of Europe. Rapallo and the early attempts at accommodation were linked with Walther Rathenau; from 1923 the restoration of Germany to internal stability and a degree of external respect was the work chiefly of Gustav Stresemann, who from his moorings in the near-reactionary People's party (and after a very brief dalliance with the Kapp Putsch), moved toward a statesmanlike centrism that appalled increasingly vocal elements on the right.

It was among the latter that the third great problem of Weimar was to be found—the endemic violence in postwar German society. Less easy to define than the other two problems, that problem found no one with a solution to offer and, more tragically, many in positions of high authority (judges, for example) to condone. The barbarous murders of Liebknecht and Luxemburg, the cool killing of Eisner, were replayed not only in notorious political assassinations—Matthias Erzberger (who had signed the treaty) in 1921, Rathenau in 1922—and in an attempt on Scheidemann's life shortly before, but also in countless, anonymous atrocities in the suppression of Communist uprisings and in the activities of the semiofficial, irregular militia that guarded the eastern frontiers. Patriotic and nationalistic organizations sprouted everywhere; the most famous and widespread was the *Stahlhelm*—Steel Helmet—a patriotic veterans' organization, but it was outstripped by openly paramilitary organizations dedicated to the overthrow of the republic and to seeking revenge for Versailles, organizations counted on by the army for reinforcement when the time came.

Nowhere were such movements more in evidence than in Bavaria. In that southern, Catholic country, never effectively integrated into the Reich, the independent Socialist republic of Eisner and the soviet regime that followed his death provoked a sharp turn to the right at the very time the Kapp Putsch came to failure in Berlin. In Bavaria were to be found unreconciled elements of the disbanded free corps; there Ehrhardt and his followers fled; there the murders of Erzberger and Rathenau were plotted.[23] There too in 1919 a young, embittered ex-corporal—Austrian by birth and a frustrated (because incompetent) artist—joined the founders of a tiny nationalist workers' party; the next year it was renamed the National Socialist German Workers' Party, the NSDAP, or, more familiarly, the Nazis. In it Adolf Hitler found his vocation and soon became the party's acknowledged leader. With help from sympathetic

[23] Were there murder gangs in Bavaria? the chief of police of Munich was asked. "Yes," he replied, "but not enough of them."

industrialists and with secret funds from the army, the party acquired a newspaper, the *Völkischer Beobachter;*[24] and the superb organizing abilities of Captain Ernst Röhm (whose work for the Nazis while on active service was tolerated by the army until 1923) produced yet another paramilitary organization, the *Sturmabteilung*—Storm Troopers—the brown-shirted SA, which Röhm saw as his contribution to national preparedness, although Hitler insisted on using it as his own political militia. Like the *squadristi* in Italy, the SA broke up meetings, terrorized opponents, and created a wide impression of strength. To what end? The socialist leanings of the party's founders, useful enough to Hitler in starting out, soon went by the boards, though in the mid-twenties he was ready to make an alliance of convenience with Gregor and Otto Strasser, who advocated extensive socialist reforms.[25]

Miserable in his youth, a failure and drifter in his young manhood, Hitler had built up within him a terrible stock of hatred, hatred that sought conventional targets, above all the Jews. His transplantation to Germany made him a fervent *grossdeutsch* nationalist, and his arduous and, to him, inspiriting service in the army made him eager to avenge defeat. That he had not a single original idea, that he could attract only adventurers, stupid or calculating rich men, and third-rate intellects were handicaps he could turn to advantage. He claimed to be a man of the people, to have suffered as the people suffered, and to know them—because for years he traveled about speaking to whatever audiences he could find—better than any other politician in the country. He trained himself, after a bad start, to be a demagogic orator of fantastic, mesmerizing skill. He controlled and used his own hysteria to advantage, he exploited his followers' violence, he urged and practiced the technique of the "big lie." With his propagandistic techniques perfected, he needed only a crisis. All forms of discontent, Alan Bullock has written, "were grist to his mill; there was as much room in his Party for the unemployed ex-officer like Göring and Hess, or the embittered intellectual like Rosenberg and Goebbels, as for the working man who refused to join a trade union or the small shopkeeper who wanted to smash the windows of the big Jewish department stores. Ambition, resentment, envy, avidity for power and wealth—in every class—these were the powerful motive forces Hitler sought to harness. He was prepared to be all things to all men, because to him all men represented only one thing, a means to power."[26]

[24] *Beobachter* is readily translated as *Observer,* but the indispensable German adjective *völkisch* has—one may say happily—no equivalent in English. It implies an irrationalist notion of the people (akin perhaps to the Russian but not the American usage of populist) with distinct racial overtones. Historians feel pretty generally forced to leave the word in German.

[25] Hitler logic, in a speech in 1922: "Whoever is prepared to make the national cause his own to such an extent that he knows no higher ideal than the welfare of his nation; whoever has understood our great national anthem, *Deutschland, Deutschland über Alles,* to mean that nothing in the wide world surpasses in his eyes this Germany, people and land, land and people—that man is a Socialist." Quoted in Alan Bullock, *Hitler, A Study in Tyranny* (rev. ed., 1962), 76.

[26] Ibid.

In the early twenties, however, Hitler's success was only local, and the fitfulness of his movement is owing to his dependence for national impact on the course of Bavarian separatism. In the fall of 1923, as Stresemann's firmness began to check the twin disasters of the Ruhr occupation and the inflation, Hitler determined to force the hand of the Bavarian leaders. On November 8, as they were addressing their supporters in a large beer hall in Munich, six hundred armed SA men surrounded the building. Hitler, inside the hall, fired a shot at the ceiling, strode to the platform, and announced the beginning of a revolution. By a series of outrageous lies about what had already been accomplished by his forces in Munich and Berlin, he forced a kind of common front with the Bavarian rulers and for good measure added old General Ludendorff, who in his cranky way was a notorious backer of right-wing causes aimed at avenging the defeat he more than anyone had brought on his country. As the meeting ended in confusion, Hitler lost control of his new allies. He attempted next day to recover by a march with Ludendorff and his party associates through the city. The march ended with gunfire from loyal government troops. Hitler fled, leaving behind twelve dead comrades, while the old general marched on, bravely erect, to submit to arrest and to be acquitted by a Bavarian court. Hitler, who turned his trial for treason into a brilliant, destructive performance of self-justification, was sentenced to five years in prison and served nine months. Bavarian officials kept him from being deported to Austria—he did not become a German citizen until 1932—and he devoted the years after his release to rebuilding his party and to creating a national base. But after the beer-hall Putsch most Germans who knew of Hitler assumed that he was finished; when Hitler's friend, the Bavarian minister of justice, persuaded the minister-president of the state to lift the ban on the Nazis and their paper, his chief remarked, "The wild beast is checked. We can afford to loosen the chain." It was a fair enough conclusion. The return of prosperity robbed Hitler of the misery he needed to work upon, and the nearly unreadable book he had dictated in prison—a windy statement of his beliefs and program called *Mein Kampf*—sold few copies.

In an era dominated by Stresemann, amid a succession of ministries, two political events need to be noted. One was the election of a new president, made necessary by the death of Friedrich Ebert in February 1925. The victor, in a closely fought election, was the old war hero Field Marshal von Hindenburg, then in his seventy-eighth year. He was the Nationalist candidate, supported in the runoff election by the Nazis, whose own candidate Ludendorff had got less than one percent of the vote. The other event was the Reichstag election of 1928, which registered the nation's satisfaction by reducing the representation of the Nationalists and the already tiny number of seats held by the Nazis, while increasing the vote for the Social Democrats. In June 1928 the SPD returned to power, dominating a governing coalition that still included Stresemann, who after some hesitation took the plunge into an alliance that his political origins might well have prevented in a less courageous man. In 1929, the Kellogg-Briand pact, concluded in August 1928, was accepted by Germany; the French withdrew their last occupation forces from the Rhineland, after much temporizing; and the Young Plan, worked out by an international committee of experts, was agreed upon to provide a still more reduced, more realistic, and highly specific schedule for German reparations payments, extending to 1988. The plan was violently attacked in Germany by the Nationalists and the Nazis, now close political allies thanks in part to the machinations of the Nationalist newspaper tycoon Alfred Hugenberg; a constitutional referendum was resorted to, which the plan's opponents lost. The plan was thereupon accepted by the Reichstag and signed by Hindenburg in March 1930. But Stresemann, worn out by his endeavors, in ill health, and under constant attack, had died the preceding October. Conservative though he · was, he had given the Socialists their last chance. The coalition was at an end, and the republic would soon follow.

SELECTED READINGS

Raymond J. Sontag, *A Broken World, 1919-1939* (1971) is a lucid survey of the highly complex interwar years, with the bibliographical excellence characteristic of the Langer series. The relevant chapters of volume XII of the *New Cambridge Modern History—The Shifting Balance of World Forces, 1898-1945,* C. L. Mowat, ed. (rev. ed., 1968)—are uneven. Those on the wars and diplomatic history generally are excellent, but the history of most of the European countries is forced into omnibus chapters that deny their authors scope and frustrate effective organization.

For a narrative of international history in the period, it would be hard to better E. H. Carr, *International Relations Between the Two World Wars, 1919-1939* (rev. ed., 1947), which should be supplemented by his critical analysis, *The Twenty Years' Crisis, 1919-1939: An Introduction to the Study of International Relations* (1939, 2nd ed. 1946). Gordon A. Craig and Felix Gilbert, eds., *The Diplomats, 1919-1939* (1953), a large volume of excellent essays, surveys a gallery of diplomats and the contexts and approaches within which they worked. A useful collection of articles and extracts of recent vintage is Hans W. Gatzke, ed., *European Diplomacy Between Two Wars, 1919-1939* (1972). For a full account of the peace conference, see H. W. V. Temperley, *A History of the Peace Conference of Paris,* 6 vols. (1920-1924); Harold Nicolson (who also wrote on the Congress of Vienna) has written *Peacemaking, 1919* (1935). For contrasting views of one ghost at the conference, see John M. Thompson, *Russia, Bolshevism, and the Versailles Peace* (1966), and Arno J. Mayer, *Politics and Diplomacy of Peacemaking: Containment and Counterrevolution at Versailles, 1918-1919* (1967). An instant, brilliant, and highly unfavorable view that became a historical force in its own right is J. M. Keynes, *The Economic Consequences of the Peace* (1920), to which may be contrasted Etienne Mantoux, *The Carthaginian Peace, or the Economic Consequences of Mr. Keynes* (1946). The best introduction to the economic history of the period is chapter 6, "The Interwar Years," in David S. Landes, *The Unbound Prometheus* (1969).

Henry R. Winkler, *The League of Nations Movement in Great Britain, 1914-1919* (1952) is important for the origins of the League. For its history, generally, see F. P. Walters, *A History of the League of Nations,* 2 vols. (1952). On two incidents in which the League was involved, see James Barros, *The Corfu Incident of 1923: Mussolini and the League of Nations* (1965), and *The League of Nations and the Great Powers: The Greek-Bulgarian Incident, 1925* (1970). See also Robert H. Ferrell, *Peace in Their Time: The Origins of the Kellogg-Briand Pact* (1952).

E. H. Carr's massive *History of Soviet Russia* continues through the twenties: *The Interregnum, 1923-1924* (1954); *Socialism in One Country, 1924-1926,* 3 vols. (1958); and (with R. W. Davies) *Foundations of a Planned Economy, 1926-1929,* of which the two parts of volume I appeared in 1969 and 1971. The two relevant volumes of Isaac Deutscher's superb biography of Trotsky are entitled *The Prophet Unarmed: Trotsky, 1921-1929* (1959), and *The Prophet Outcast: Trotsky, 1929-1940.* Deutscher's *Stalin, a Political Biography* (1949, 2nd ed., 1966) is less detailed and less satisfactory. Monographs of particular interest are Robert V. Daniels, *The Conscience of the Revolution: Communist Opposition in Soviet Russia* (1960); Richard Pipes, *The Formation of the Soviet Union: Communism and Nationalism, 1917-1923* (1954, rev. ed., 1964); and Alexander Erlich, *The Soviet Industrialization Debate, 1924-1928* (1960). Of particular importance for this chapter is Lazar I. Volin, *A Century of Russian Agriculture: From Alexander II to Khrushchev* (1970).

An excellent country-by-country survey is S. J. Woolf, ed., *European Fascism* (1969). Ernst Nolte, *Three Faces of Fascism: Action Française, Italian Fascism, German Nazism* (tr. 1965) is a difficult and challenging philosophical analysis. See also F. L. Carsten, *The Rise of Fascism* (1967), and Hans Rogger and Eugen Weber, eds., *The European Right: A Historical Profile* (1965). On Mussolini, Sir Ivone Kirkpatrick, *Mussolini: A Study in Power* (1964) is the standard biography. The relationship between the Italian state and big business is analyzed in Roland Sarti, *Fascism and the Industrial Leadership in Italy, 1919-1940: A Study in the Expansion of Private Power under Fascism* (1971). On Eastern Europe, in addition to the Woolf volume cited above, see Hugh Seton-Watson, *Eastern Europe Between the Wars, 1918-1941* (1946).

There are some admirable surveys of the British scene: C. L. Mowat, *Britain between the Wars, 1918-1940* (1955); A. J. P. Taylor, *English History, 1914-1945* (1965); and W. N. Medlicott, *Contemporary England, 1914-1964* (1967). A high-spirited social history is provided by Robert Graves and Alan Hodge, *The Long Weekend* (1940). Essential for an understanding of politics are Trevor Wilson, *The Downfall of the Liberal Party, 1914-1935* (1966); R. W. Lyman, *The First Labour Government, 1924* (1957); and *Baldwin, A Biography* by Keith Middlemass and John Barnes (1970). For a clear sketch of a crucial imperial development, see R. M. Dawson, *The Development of Dominion Status* (1937). On France, as for all periods after 1870, see D. W. Brogan, *France under the Republic (1870-1939)* (1940), and David Thomson, *Democracy in France since 1870* (5th ed., 1969), to which may be added Geoffrey Bruun, *Clemenceau* (1943), and J. H. Jackson, *Clemenceau and the Third Republic* (1959), although most of Clemenceau's career falls before the period covered in this chapter.

More scholarly attention has been given to Germany than to any other European country in the twenties. Pride of place must go to Erich Eyck, *A History of the Weimar Republic,* 2 vols. (tr. 1962). Basically biographical in approach are Klaus Epstein, *Matthias Erzberger and the Dilemma of German Democracy* (1959); J. P. Nettl, *Rosa Luxemburg,* 2 vols. (1966); David Felix, *Walther Rathenau and the Weimar Republic: The Politics of Reparations* (1971); the sketch of Rathenau in James Joll, *Intellectuals in Politics: Three Biographical Essays* (1960); Andreas Dorpalen, *Hindenburg and the Weimar Republic* (1964); Henry A. Turner, *Gustav Stresemann and the Politics of*

Weimar (1963); and Hans W. Gatzke, *Stresemann and the Rearmament of Germany* (1954). On the army, see Gordon A. Craig, *The Politics of the Prussian Army, 1640–1945* (1955), and F. L. Carsten, *The Reichswehr and Politics, 1918–1933* (1966). The frightening appearance of paramilitarism is dealt with in R. G. L. Waite, *Vanguard of Nazism: The Free Corps Movement in Postwar Germany, 1918–1923* (1952). The currents of thought that underlay the discontent with Weimar and the emergence of Nazism are dealt with in three important books: Fritz Stern, *The Politics of Cultural Despair: A Study in the Rise of the Germanic Ideology* (1961); George L. Mosse, *The Crisis of German Ideology: Intellectual Origins of the Third Reich* (1966); and P. J. G. Pulzer, *The Rise of Political Anti-Semitism in Germany and Austria* (1964). A. J. Nicholls, *Weimar and the Rise of Hitler* (1968) is a conveniently brief sketch. Finally, there is a fine biography, *Hitler, a Study in Tyranny* by Alan Bullock (rev. ed., 1962).

25

A New Time
of Troubles:
1929-1939

CULTURE BETWEEN THE WARS

The Shock of Armageddon

In high culture, as in so much else, World War I marked the agonizing end of
a scintillating epoch. Like many other human beings, artists and writers too
responded with despair, rage, or withdrawal; for its part, with a fine impartial-
ity, the war destroyed bearers of high culture as it destroyed workers, farmers,
and professional soldiers. The young English poet Rupert Brooke died on his
way to the Dardanelles; the unorthodox French Catholic writer Charles Péguy,
the promising German painters Franz Marc and August Macke were killed at
the front. Wilfred Owen, whose unsentimental poems movingly evoked the
terror and effectively debunked the glory of war, fell in action on November 4,
1918, a week before the general armistice. Many artists saw the war and its
aftermath, revolution, as an unaccustomed invitation to politics; they were
overwhelmed by the fierce conviction that this must not happen again. The

great German architect Walter Gropius, on leave from the front as the German revolution broke out in November 1918, suddenly understood the significance of the nightmare through which he had passed. "This is more than just a lost war," he remembers saying to himself. "A world has come to an end. We must seek a radical solution to our problems."[1]

Gropius' own solution to the emergence of a new world proved of lasting significance for Western civilization. Himself an imaginative architect who had designed some unconventional buildings before the war, Gropius in early 1919 became director of a new kind of school, the Bauhaus, which employed not merely brilliant designers and architects, but remarkable modern painters like Lyonel Feininger, Vassily Kandinsky, and Paul Klee. Its ideal was to elevate craftsmanship into art, to accept machine civilization without surrendering to ugliness or shoddiness. The Bauhaus produced the common objects of modern mass culture—chinaware, lamps, furniture, even advertising—along with private houses and factories, all free of showy clutter, sham decoration, or vulgar eclecticism. The spare, clean Bauhaus designs, modern without being either inaccessible or cheap, retain their appeal and their influence to this day. Much of that influence was to be abroad: the Nazis closed the Bauhaus in 1933.

Other artists had experienced the full gravity of events before the peace. Dadaism, one of the few real innovations in high culture after 1914, flourished as a visceral protest against the uselessness, the stupidity, the utter horror of world war. The extravagant experiments and "public hell-raising"[2] for which the Dadaists became notorious had some prewar precursors among artists intent on "spitting in the eye of the bourgeoisie," but the movement developed its real momentum as a direct protest against the mutual and seemingly interminable mass slaughter. Early in 1916, the German poet Hugo Ball founded the first Dadaist nightclub in Zurich, the Cabaret Voltaire; its aim, he said, was "to draw attention across the war and patriotism, to those few independent spirits who live for other ideals."[3] Ball and his associates performed outlandish dances and read poems that, in their more conventional passages, sounded like the frenetic outpourings of the Expressionists, but normally eluded sense altogether:

> zimzim urallala zimzim urallala zimzim zanzibar zimzalla zam
> elifantolim brussala bulomen brussala bulomen tromtata
> veio da bang bang affalo purzami affalo purzamai lengado tor
> gangama bimbalo glandridi glassala zingtata impoalo ögrogööö
> viola laxato viola zimbrabim viola uli paluji maloo

This was the kind of chant with which Ball entertained, even electrified, his audiences. The lesson of all this pointedly pointless activity was plain: the most

---

[1] See Walter Gropius, *Scope of Total Architecture* (ed. 1962), 19.
[2] This is part of the definition of Dada offered by one of the founders of the movement, Hans Richter. See his *Dada: Art and Anti-Art* (1965), 11.
[3] Ibid., 15.

telling comment on an outrageous and meaningless world was to produce outrageous and meaningless art—or, rather, anti-art.

Dada attracted some adventurous and talented spirits, including the Alsatian sculptor Hans Arp, the German poet Richard Huelsenbeck, the Rumanian artist-of-all-works Tristan Tzara, the French painter Francis Picabia; Dadaists founded branches in Berlin, Paris, New York, and elsewhere and grew more raucously political as the war dragged on. One of the most gifted recruits Dadaism enlisted was Marcel Duchamp, who as early as 1913 had outraged stodgy viewers at the Armory Show in New York with his semiabstract monochromatic painting of a figure in several positions, the celebrated *Nude Descending a Staircase.* With such "ready-mades" as the bicycle wheel fastened onto a kitchen stool, or with such impudent sneers at high art as the Mona Lisa onto which he penciled a fine mustache and a small Vandyke beard, Duchamp gave form to the despairing and aggressive Dadaist pronouncement: "Dada means nothing."

Nonsensical poems, farfetched collages, disrespectful paintings, and public antics were political commentaries on a civilization killing and killing in the name of freedom, decency, and culture. But Dadaists also went into political protest directly: "Dada is German Bolshevism,"[4] they proclaimed in Berlin during the revolutionary period. And George Grosz, who had participated in the Dadaist movement in the course of the war, after the war used his considerable if constricted gifts to draw savage caricatures that juxtaposed maimed veterans and obese war profiteers, revolting prostitutes and imbecilic Prussian officers.

Dada, an effervescence born of a terrible moment, could not last; but it left some splendid monuments and intensified a rebellious attitude, and it helped to father an artistic movement in the 1920s, Surrealism, that marks yet another genuine innovation of these troubled decades. Surrealism began not in painting but in poetry; its creator, the French poet André Breton, published the first Surrealist manifesto in 1924 and included among his supporters other poets. But he was soon joined by painters—the Italian Giorgio di Chirico, the German Max Ernst, the Belgian René Magritte, the Frenchman Yves Tanguy, and the Spaniard Salvador Dali, this last of the group the most flamboyant and the most given to self-advertising. For some painters and poets Surrealism had the same meaning and demanded the same technique: the depiction of dreams, the capture of random associations, the outpouring of automatic writing unchecked and uncensored by ordinary restraints. As they themselves were aware, the Surrealists produced works that sounded and looked like Freudian doctrine made graphic. Tanguy's impossible lunar landscapes, Dali's equally impossible encounters of detached mustaches with melting watches, the overt, sometimes oppressive erotic content of their canvases illustrated, often in a rather cheap

[4] See George Heard Hamilton, *Painting and Sculpture in Europe, 1880-1940* (1967), 248.

and merely decorative way, the disoriented world in which these modern artists lived and suffered.

Continuities: Primitivism, Abstraction, Expressionism

Suffering and disgust are the leading themes for the Modern Movement in the 1920s. But though their intensity sometimes rose to new heights and their preoccupation grew more explicitly political, the private impulses and stylistic solutions of the moderns reached back to the decades before the world war—to their own earlier work, or to the Tahitian fantasies of Gauguin, the wild impasto of van Gogh's canvases, the passion for form in Cézanne's landscapes, the candid sensuality of Wedekind's plays, the objectified nightmares of Strindberg's dramas and Munch's lithographs (see p. 899). The distortions that figure in Picasso's paintings and etchings of the 1920s and 1930s had their direct ancestry in his prewar experiments, notably in a painting he had completed in 1907, the *Demoiselles d'Avignon.* Its five nudes, their faces and figures heavily outlined, starkly simplified, and grossly distorted, owe something at least to the African sculptures Picasso knew and liked, much to Picasso's tireless imagination and to his patient, long-drawn-out exploration of a wide variety of artistic styles. Indeed, many of the aesthetic problems that puzzled artists after the war had emerged before 1914. Paul Klee (to give but one instance), that prolific producer of small and immensely imaginative watercolors, drawings, and collages, veered in his work of the 1920s and 1930s between principles he had developed before 1910—a curious and incongruous mixture of spontaneity and skill. In 1909 he had paid tribute to the superior artistic insight of "children, madmen, and savages," and even perpetrated that old cliché normally attributed to the philistine helpless before a modern work of art: "The pictures my little Felix paints," Klee said, "are better than mine, which all too often have trickled through the brain." At the same time, he was wholly unwilling to attribute his art to chance or to the unconscious. "Will and discipline," he insisted, "are everything." And he added, "If my works sometimes produce a primitive impression, this 'primitiveness' is explained by my discipline. . . . It is no more than economy; that is the ultimate professional awareness, which is to say, the opposite of primitiveness."[5] Like other moderns, Klee, the self-styled primitive, was also an old-fashioned craftsman.

Similar continuities dominate other styles and other media. The best known abstract painters of the 1920s and 1930s, Vassily Kandinsky and Piet Mondrian, who both ascribed their search for artistic purity to religious emotions, had matured as artists much earlier: Kandinsky had been painting wholly nonobjective canvases by 1910 (see p. 901), while Mondrian was working his way toward abstraction deliberately and slowly in the years around

[5] Quoted in Robert Goldwater, *Primitivism in Modern Art* (rev. ed., 1967), 199-201.

1913; his famous grids did not appear until the 1920s. In the same way, Expressionist poets, playwrights, sculptors, architects, and painters continued to produce in the rhetorical, declamatory vein that had fully emerged by 1910 and even before. What made the 1920s such a crucial decade for high culture was no essential novelty of forms or themes, but the profusion of excellence. The war in many ways had simply compelled the suspension of work begun before.

Moderns As Classics

In 1930 Sinclair Lewis received the Nobel Prize for literature. He was the first American to be so distinguished, but the award was greeted with dismay by literary critics, not because Lewis was an American, but because his satirical novels, though amusing caricatures of small-town bourgeois society, scarcely deserved such a signal honor. By then it was well known that the Nobel Prize for literature eluded some of the most important of the moderns and often fell into the lap of minor authors. Some writers doubtless were left out because they died too soon: Henry James in 1916, Marcel Proust in 1922, though his great serial novel *A la recherche du temps perdu* continued to appear volume by volume through the twenties (see p. 898). But death gave no excuse for overlooking James Joyce, who lived until 1941. Joyce, born in Dublin in 1882, was a lifelong, almost a professional exile: he left behind traditional ways of writing, his Catholic religion, and his Ireland to live in Trieste, in Paris, and in Zurich. After publishing, in 1907, a volume of interesting if minor poems, *Chamber Music,* he made his mark in 1914 with a collection of short stories, *Dubliners,* which brilliantly evoke the atmosphere of his native city and the elusive moods of his characters. His first novel, the largely autobiographical *Portrait of the Artist as a Young Man,* published two years after his stories, confirmed his mastery and extended his reputation. But it was with *Ulysses,* begun in 1914 and completed in 1921, that Joyce entered the pantheon of the classic novelist.

Ulysses is one of the boldest books in the history of literature. At the time of its publication in 1922, its frank eroticism and scatological detail made it scandalous to the respectable; it was not until 1933 that, through an epoch-making court order, the novel was permitted to be distributed legally in the United States. From our perspective, however, it is not the presumed obscenity of *Ulysses* that constitutes its boldness. The scene of the book is the Dublin that Joyce knew so intimately and remembered so well. Its time span is less than twenty-four hours—from the morning of one June day to the next. Its protagonists are Leopold Bloom, a middle-aged Jew, Stephen Dedalus, a rebellious young Irish teacher (he had been the hero, as a child and adolescent, of Joyce's earlier novel), and Mollie Bloom, Leopold's sensual wife. Mollie dominates much of the novel though she does not appear until the long last scene, an internal monologue recounting Leopold's wooing and her unsentimental surrender: "he kissed me under the Moorish wall and I thought well as well him as another and then I asked him with my eyes to ask again yes and then he asked me would I yes to say yes my mountain flower and first I put my arms around him yes and drew him down to me so he could feel my breasts all perfume yes and his heart was going like mad and yes I said yes I will Yes." "The book," Joyce said, "must end with the most positive word in the human language." [6]

Ulysses, indeed, unlike most other avant-garde writing of the time, is a celebration of life; Leopold Bloom and Stephen Dedalus, the one a father in search of a son, the other a son in search of a father, encounter each other late at night, perhaps to become friends, after a day filled with quite ordinary experiences. Joyce renders those experiences—thoughts, feelings, and above all sensations, the pleasures of eating, looking, talking, defecating, indulging in erotic fantasies—with a luxuriant bouquet of styles, brilliant imitations of earlier manners of writing, deftly reported speech, imaginative renderings of thoughts, streams of consciousness that report private soliloquies. Joyce had complete control over this profusion. He patterned the whole on the *Odyssey* and carefully plotted each scene, placing each under the sign of a color, a season, a number, an organ of the body—the reader of *Ulysses,* though he is likely to find it an overwhelming experience simply to read the book, can profit from a key. [7] Joyce's last novel, *Finnegans Wake* (1939) positively requires such a key. A sprawling panorama, the novel evokes, with broken, labyrinthine sentences, obscure images, recondite symbols, and multilingual puns, the mind of a sleeper in the course of a night. The difficulties of *Ulysses,* considerable as they are, pale before the formidable demands of *Finnegans Wake.*

One of Joyce's most appreciative early readers was another exile, T. S. Eliot, though Eliot, for his own purposes, chose to view Joyce's use of the *Odyssey* as "giving significance to the immense panorama of futility and anarchy which is contemporary history." This interpretation is less apt as a commentary on Joyce's work than on Eliot's own. Born in St. Louis in 1888, Eliot studied at Harvard and in Europe and began living in England in 1914. He established his early reputation with his editorship of avant-garde magazines in London, his perceptive literary criticism, and his very first book of poems, *Prufrock and Other Observations* (1917). Then, in 1922, Eliot tried to encompass the "immense panorama of futility and anarchy which is contemporary history" with an ambitious poem bearing the revealing title, *The Waste Land.* Witty, learned, often difficult, *The Waste Land* is doubtless the most influential poem of our century. It offers a disenchanted vision of a civilization without faith or hope and evokes a world, as the critic Northrop Frye has put it,

---

[6] See Richard Ellmann, *James Joyce* (1959), 536.

[7] While there have been several interpretations of the book, the most authoritative is Richard Ellmann, *Ulysses on the Liffey* (1972).

"without laughter, love, or children."[8] In it, and the poems that followed, notably *The Hollow Men* of 1925, Eliot displayed an unsurpassed ear for the language, a striking capacity for juxtaposing the ordinary words of colloquial speech with allusions to obscure religious and esoteric literatures, and the commonplace experiences of commonplace people with vast symbols. Like his fellow American and fellow exile Ezra Pound, from whom he learned much and to whom he dedicated *The Waste Land,* Eliot at this stage found his poetic material in what he scorned as the sheer materialism, the hollowness and alienation, of modern culture. These impulses continued to inform his later work, but with a difference: in 1927 he became a British subject and joined the Anglican church. His later poetry and the verse plays he began to write in the 1930s abundantly attest both to his critical and his religious convictions.

His literary and cultural criticism are just as eloquent. Eliot's poetry cannot be separated from his activities as a literary critic and commentator on society— though we can admire the first while having our doubts about the second and deploring the third. For as a critic of other poets and of modern society, Eliot gained an ascendancy over lesser minds that was not always salutary. His poetic ideal of impersonality and admiration for tradition, articulated in a number of widely read lectures, pointed the way to a fruitful modern classicism, but his pronouncements on Milton, Kipling, Goethe, the Elizabethan dramatists, though normally suggestive and often learned, were as dogmatic as they were provisional; hence Eliot left his faithful followers stranded when he changed his mind (as he did about Goethe and Milton) and said so in public. Most unfortunate of all—and most difficult for his many admirers to justify—were his political views, which stemmed from his consistent "struggle against Liberalism." This led him to cherish a naïve vision of an earlier Christian culture, to neglect the Fascist and Nazi threats to civilization, and to use the Jew as the symbol for all he detested: modernity, rootlessness. When he won that supreme accolade, the Nobel Prize, in 1948, it was for his poetry rather than his politics.

The same prize had come to another great and problematic modern poet, William Butler Yeats, a quarter of a century before, in 1923. Yeats, the son of a gifted painter, was born near Dublin in 1865 and began his poet's career with verse dramas in the late 1880s. Yeats in his long life—he died in 1939—held pronounced views on art, on society, and on religion. He did not despise the popular arts, but was uncomfortable with the prevailing vulgarity and veered between attempts to reach the general public and a declared loyalty to the avant-garde, with its defiance of the mass market and insistence on difficulty. He wrote plays to be performed in the Irish National Theatre, which he helped to found in 1901; he associated, in Dublin, Paris, and London, with other masters of modern literature, and between 1922 and 1928 he was a member of the Irish senate. A mystic, he belonged to theosophical societies, practiced automatic writing, and wrote occult prose and poetry.

[8] Northrop Frye, *T. S. Eliot* (rev. ed., 1968), 48.

But Yeats was many things, and many things went into his poetry: his dabbling in the occult; his uncertain social thought, which found expression at one time in moderate Irish nationalism, at another in glancing sympathy for Italian fascism, and at still others in outright distaste for all politics; his fascination with the possibility of symbolism in poetry; and his casual but memorable diction. Yeats, in his variety, is a poet to discover; "he is the only modern writer I know of," the English critic G. S. Frazer wrote in the early 1960s, "whose reputation has steadily risen in the twenty years since his death."[9] That verdict still holds true today.

Joyce, Eliot, and Yeats were only the most conspicuous of old masters who made the 1920s such a great decade in the arts and in literature. Thomas Mann was another. While Mann had found his style, and most of his themes, before 1914, it was 1914 that presented him with his ideal subject: it shed new light on the years—so blithe and so unaware, it seemed in retrospect, of the coming judgment—that preceded Armageddon. Other writers had shared Mann's vision: Henry James, shaken to the depths of his being by August 1914, thought that the outbreak of war devalued all that had gone before as mere "treacherous years," while George Bernard Shaw anatomized the prewar period in the very title of his play as a *Heartbreak House*. Mann portrayed this complacent, doomed society in his best-known novel, *The Magic Mountain,* published in 1924. The action takes place in a Swiss sanatorium for sufferers from tuberculosis; ever intent on symbolism, Mann found the deceptive condition of the tubercular—the flush of health, the perpetual slight hectic fever, the capacity to be up and about—the perfect analogue for the Europe before 1914. The novel is a long—many think overlong—debate among spokesmen for various views of life; its protagonist, young Hans Castorp, who comes to the sanatorium as a visitor and remains as a patient, is the innocent from the plains who learns about the complexities of love and death, their fatal entanglement and ultimate incompatibility, in the sophisticated heights.

Sophisticated as Mann's spokesmen were, *The Magic Mountain* is anything but inaccessible; it even became a best seller. But in music the sophistication of new composers came to mean the alienation of the wider public, accustomed as it was to the compositions of the classical or the romantic schools. For many, the swollen constructions of Gustav Mahler—those interminable symphonies played by enlarged orchestras—or the more accessible works of Debussy and Ravel were about as "modern" as music could safely become. Stravinsky, whose prewar ballet scores had startlingly heralded the advent of modern music, turned after the war (and after his exile from Russia) to a neoclassicism that frequently relied upon sonata form and grew steadily more cosmopolitan in its emphasis on past musical and literary traditions. Thus the ballets *Apollo Musagètes* (1928) and *Perséphone* (1934) and the imposing choral work *Oedipus Rex* (1927) turn to Greek literature for inspiration, and the moving *Symphony*

[9] G. S. Fraser, *The Modern Writer and His World* (ed. 1970), 275.

of Psalms (1930), its text drawn from the Bible, bespeaks the devoutness of the composer. Stravinsky was also a master at turning the works of past composers to his own uses: the musical themes of the ballets *Pulcinella* (1920) and *The Fairy's Kiss* (1928) are drawn, respectively, from Pergolesi and Tchaikovsky—a magnificent and loving eclecticism that is shared, as we have seen, by those other modern traditionalists Picasso and Joyce. The Hungarian composer Béla Bartók made a similar transition from the expressionism of his wartime works to the neoclassicism of his sonatas and string quartets of the 1920s and 1930s. But, for all their allegiance to tradition, these compositions, with their complexities and dissonances, struck audiences generally as baffling and even unpleasant. Stravinsky always retained wide respect (though chiefly for his colorful early works), but Bartók was woefully neglected until the 1940s, at the very end of his life. Another neoclassicist, the influential German theorist and teacher Paul Hindemith, insisted on the role of composer as craftsman and found his astonishingly prolific output derided as *Gebrauchsmusik*—utility music.

The separation of composer from audience was even more marked in the case of Arnold Schönberg, Anton Webern, and Alban Berg, the leaders of a school whose music was about as far toward the opposite pole as could be imagined from that of their fellow Viennese, Mahler. Before the war, surfeited with the overripe products of the German romantic decadence, the satirical and acerbic French composer Erik Satie had called, in a remark to Claude Debussy, for "our own music—if possible without sauerkraut."[10] This was precisely the kind of music the great trio came to provide. Schönberg, scholarly, patient, and extraordinarily experimental, had moved away from traditional tonalities before the war; *Pierrot Lunaire* of 1912 was the culmination of an atonal period that in retrospect appears as a long and tentative interlude, issuing at last, after the war, in his "breaking through all past aesthetic"[11] with the twelve-tone system, or serial music, as it is now more generally known. Serial composers abandoned the notion that any one of the twelve notes in the chromatic scale could claim primacy over any other, and the system, in its strictest application, required that a motif use each of the twelve tones before any one was repeated. Coupled with immensely ingenious architectural devices—inversions, mirror images, and the like, conceits that owe much to a scholarly fascination with the contrapuntal composers of the seventeenth and earlier centuries—serialism produced works of unquestioned intellectual appeal to those who were prepared to understand. It was a satisfaction akin to that derived by scholars from the abstruse monographs of their colleagues or provided to the mathematically literate by the elegant expositions of the physicists and astronomers. Neither scholars nor scientists wrote for general readers, unless they were

---

[10] Quoted from Joseph Machlis, *Introduction to Contemporary Music* (1961), in Oron J. Hale, *The Great Illusion, 1900–1914* (1971), 161.

[11] Quoted in Francis Routh, *Contemporary Music: An Introduction* (1968), 87.

deliberately popularizing; the ordinary concert goer was without the mental equipment to experience the pleasure a trained musician might find in serialism, pleasure that might be as great in reading and analyzing the score of the work as in listening to it. It is a measure of the immensity of this new task set to audiences that today even the most difficult works of Stravinsky or Bartók find quite general appreciation, while receptivity for most serial works remains confined to a very small public. The price of being in the avant-garde had come increasingly to be the sacrifice of popularity; it was a price these stern seekers after musical truth seemed all too ready to pay.

The Popular Arts

Detached comment, lonely experimentation, and (as in the novels of Hermann Hesse) contemplation and flight from Western civilization were familiar artistic responses to the shattered world of the 1920s. But there were two bridges between high and popular culture: satire and politics. The tone of the culture of the 1920s was, for many, a tone of desperate gaiety. In the United States, the "noble experiment" of Prohibition generalized the habit of drinking and reduced respect for law; it was out of this hectic atmosphere that there emerged the books of the "lost generation"—Ernest Hemingway's early novels and F. Scott Fitzgerald's minor classic *The Great Gatsby* (1925). In Europe, in the great capital cities, life acquired a stridency that was profitable to profiteers, liberating for provincials, heady for the young, and horrifying to more conservative spirits. Stefan Zweig later remembered that Berlin in the early 1920s "was transformed into the Babylon of the world. Bars, amusement parks, honky-tonks sprang up like mushrooms." His earlier experience in Austria seemed by contrast "a mild and shy prologue to this witches' sabbath; for the Germans introduced all their vehemence and methodical organization into the perversions. Along the entire Kurfürstendamm powdered and rouged young men sauntered and they were not all professionals; every high school boy wanted to earn some money and in the dimly lit bars one could see government officials and men of the world of finance tenderly courting drunken sailors without any shame. Even the Rome of Suetonius had never known such orgies as the pervert balls of Berlin, where hundreds of men costumed as women and hundreds of women as men danced under the benevolent eyes of the police. In the general collapse of all values, a kind of madness gained hold particularly in the bourgeois circles which until then had been unshakeable in their probity. Young girls bragged proudly of their perversion, to be sixteen and still under suspicion of virginity would have been considered a disgrace in any school of Berlin at that time." [12] Zweig was doubtless overstressing the corruption of life in Berlin, but the frenzy of the 1920s—a reflection of the disaster just over and

[12] Stefan Zweig, *The World of Yesterday: An Autobiography* (1943), 313.

the continuing uncertainty about politics, the future, the very shape of morality—was real and widespread enough. It was in this atmosphere that satirical novelists found their targets: Aldous Huxley, notably in *Point Counter Point* (1928), poured a kind of exuberant comic venom over a civilization that had lost all direction, all meaning. Four years later, in *Brave New World,* Huxley pioneered in what was to become a favorite expression of growing pessimism, the anti-Utopia, which portrays a perfect, and perfectly horrible, mechanical society of the future. Even bleaker, because even more talented, was Evelyn Waugh; his first short novel, *Decline and Fall,* published in 1928, set the pattern for other satirical, equally hopeless novels to come: *Vile Bodies* appeared in 1930 and, four years later, *A Handful of Dust,* the title an evocation of T. S. Eliot's chilling line from *The Waste Land:* "I will show you fear in a handful of dust."

Satire implied detachment, or the will to detachment; there were writers who could not remain content with such a passive role. Erich Maria Remarque's pacifist novel *All Quiet on the Western Front* (1929) was an enormous success in Germany and roused the Nazis and their allies to ugly demonstrations; it was typical of a large number of novels designed for a wide audience, and, as events were to show, as ineffective as it was popular. Perhaps the most interesting German playwright to emerge in the 1920s, Bertolt Brecht, was just as unable to shape history, but it was not for want of trying. Born in Augsburg in 1898, Brecht had seen the world war at first hand as a medical orderly. It had proved a searing experience, and it haunted him into the uneasy years of peace. He became a pacifist and a satirist: his early *Legend of the Dead Soldier* tells a tale about a soldier's corpse, which is exhumed, dressed up, and pronounced fit for further service; the poem brilliantly exploits the depth of Brecht's disillusionment and his almost instinctive mastery over colloquial language. In the early 1920s, Brecht wrote several extravagant and scandalous plays in the highly charged idiom of the Expressionists. But the vogue of Expressionism was fading, and in any event Brecht's real talents lay elsewhere, in the so-called epic theater. With this portentous term Brecht meant to signalize his rejection of the drama as emotional treat, spiritual uplift, or light distraction; all these, Brecht said contemptuously, are forms of "culinary theater." He did not want his audiences to leave the theater as satisfied consumers, but as intelligent beings—thinking. One way of prompting thought was to keep the action on the stage distinct from the emotions in the hall, to prevent the audience, in other words, from identifying itself with the suffering or the triumphant hero; this was Brecht's famous *Verfremdungseffekt*—the estrangement effect. By the mid-twenties, as he experimented with these ideas, he had come under Marxist influence, though it was not until about 1930 that he accepted Communist discipline. The most lasting production of these years of increasing commitment was Brecht's *Threepenny Opera,* for which the avant-garde composer Kurt Weill wrote the music. Set to simple tunes that amateurs could master, this adaptation of John Gay's eighteenth-century comedy, *The Beggar's Opera,* was a nihilistic fable about crime and corruption; Brecht supplied it with a wholly incredible happy ending, which only underscores the cynicism of his brilliant, cool lyrics that sing of the ubiquity of greed, the economic basis of ethics, and the impossibility of love in this world.

The premiere of the *Threepenny Opera* was in 1928. It is an ominous date. Speculation, presaging depression, was wild, fascism was entrenched in Italy, the Nazis were making serious gains among the German electorate. Poets and painters, playwrights and novelists went into the thirties more as victims than as actors. Some, like Brecht, Mann, and Grosz, were to survive this terrible time in exile; others, like Ezra Pound, compounded their voluntary exile by embracing the Fascist cause. But in any event, the time for high culture was past, the time of propaganda was at hand. Mass culture, against which the avant-garde railed in its reviews and its manifestos, was not a new thing in the 1920s. The technical inventions that had made possible the mass press and the rapid dissemination of news and photographs all dated back to the nineteenth century (see p. 881). The 1920s saw a radical improvement in techniques, especially in two media that were to gain immense popularity and, in the hands of skillful propagandists, considerable political significance: the motion picture and the radio.

The invention of the motion picture dates in its primitive form to the 1870s and to the celluloid film of Thomas Alva Edison, first commercially produced in the early 1890s. In America and in France, thousands of little shops and halls were converted into "nickelodeons" in which one-reel silent films were shown to rapidly growing audiences. Primitive in technique, simple in story, melodramatic in acting, films were an immediate success. By 1915, the year of D. W. Griffith's epoch-making film, *The Birth of a Nation,* motion pictures were grown up; they were carefully edited and of substantial length. Finally, after prolonged experimentation, Hollywood produced the first full-fledged talking film, *The Jazz Singer,* in 1927, with Al Jolson in the title role. The age of the "silents," and of those movie stars who could not adapt to the new medium, was over.

One way for the film to go was from entertainment to art. In the interwar years, a group of great cameramen, scriptwriters, and directors, working in the major Western countries and in the young Soviet Union, brought to the motion picture new talents and unexpected new possibilities. Among the enduring productions of these heroic decades was the hour-long German film *The Cabinet of Dr. Caligari* (1920), with its Expressionist sets, bizarre story, and gripping coherence; among the geniuses of the genre were the Russian director Sergei Eisenstein, who raised the pageant into the realm of high art; the English director Alfred Hitchcock, who performed the same service for the suspense film; and that versatile performer Charlie Chaplin—scriptwriter, composer, director, and actor in one—who made himself immortal as the little man, forever defeated by the world and forever returning to combat.

But as the costs, and the potential, of the movies enormously increased with the arrival of the "talkies," the motion picture also moved in two other directions: big business and political propaganda. A medium that could produce the sardonic and misanthropic humor of a W. C. Fields and the zany adventures of the Marx Brothers cannot be all bad. Yet, excursions into high quality apart, for the studio moguls in the United States, the commercial motive was overriding, practically exclusive. In the early 1920s, as film merchants moved out to the favorable climate of Hollywood, California, they established powerful corporations to grind out motion pictures by the hundreds and to monopolize their distribution. The few independent producers discovered that they could not compete with the resources Hollywood had assembled. By the time the talking picture arrived, a pattern was set that was not to be challenged, let alone broken, until the 1950s: a handful of giant studios tied up directors, scriptwriters, cameramen, and, most important, that salable commodity, the star, with lush long-term contracts and ground out trivial but irresistible entertainment. In the midst of the depression of the 1930s, the low quality of this mass entertainment became particularly evident, and the intellectuals who despised "the movies" but loved the "film" could only slake their thirst for quality by seeking out fine foreign imports. In the hands of Metro-Goldwyn-Mayer, Warner Brothers, or Paramount, Hollywood became truly a "dream factory." [13]

The German pattern was somewhat different. The monopoly was more blatant there; the dominant company, UFA, [14] was vast and powerful and had close connections with right-wing politicians, journalists, and bankers. Significantly, UFA had been founded in the midst of war, in 1917, to make German propaganda; when, after the defeat, the company came into private hands, the hands were those that had pushed Germany into military adventure in the first place. The directors of UFA were not averse to making money, and in their search for international prestige (which meant, of course, international markets) they sometimes gave talented directors a free hand. But politics was rarely far from their minds; such eminently popular ventures as the series of motion pictures celebrating Frederick the Great of Prussia and the soldierly virtues proved that one could be commercial and political at the same time.

The similar potentialities of radio were explored during the same period. Nothing demonstrates the capacity of industrial culture to adapt itself to technological innovation better than the history of the radio. The first commercial broadcasting station in the world, KDKA in Pittsburgh, started to transmit regular programs of music and talk in 1920. Two years later, there were more than five hundred such stations in the country: "Radio," John A. Garraty has noted, "became a giant industry almost overnight. By 1930, 12 million families owned sets, by 1938, 40 million—soon the United States had far more radios than families." [15] Elsewhere, developments were slower, but still rapid enough. Like the motion picture industry, the radio industry was an

---

[13] The term is Hortense Powdermaker's. See *Hollywood, The Dream Factory* (1950).
[14] The initials stand for Universum Film A.G. (i.e., *Aktiengesellschaft*—corporation).
[15] John A. Garraty, *The American Nation Since 1865* (1966), 449.

ambiguous blessing. In the United States, advertisers discovered the un-matched drawing power of that much-criticized, endlessly joked-about radio sales pitch, the commercial. In their search for the audiences whose purchases would pay for the large sums that commercial time on radio extorted from advertisers, manufacturers of toothpaste, chewing gum, deodorants, or break-fast cereals pitched the programs they sponsored at the lowest possible level. Europe, where owners of radio sets subscribed a monthly sum for the privilege of listening, was free from the curse of the commercial. But it was not free from the political potential of radio. In Britain, the creation of the British Broadcast-ing Corporation in 1926 was a step toward guaranteeing quality of programs and fairness in political coverage; under the stern, dour directorship of John (later Lord) Reith, the BBC became an instrument in a high-minded campaign to bring culture and high moral standards to the masses. In the United States, Congress first undertook to regulate radio in 1927, then returned to the problem in 1934, with the creation of the Federal Communication Commission. But, in a sense, radio was passive: it transmitted the golden voices of political orators as well as those of popular singers; and in dictatorships—as Hitler and Joseph Goebbels, his propaganda minister, readily saw—the clever manipula-tion of the radio, reinforced by ruthless censorship of all dissenting views, was intensely useful. Popular culture, debased and debasing in the democracies, became an arm of political manipulation in the totalitarian systems of the 1930s.

Popular Entertainment: Jazz and Sports

The totalitarians, indeed, could use almost anything for their purposes, and what they could not use they stamped out. Jazz, that uniquely American contribution to the history of music, was an instance of the latter: the Nazis, in particular, railed against "nigger music," first ridiculing and then prohibiting it. Sports, since the late nineteenth century the great passion of millions everywhere, was an instance of the former; the Olympic games of 1936, held in Hitler's Berlin, were exploited as a showcase for the Nazi regime, which demonstrated its presumed capacity to govern by showing its capacity to build stadiums and to win in competition.

Jazz, however critics choose to define it, originated among American blacks, though probably with obscure roots in African music. While nearly all of the immortal performers of jazz—"Jelly Roll" Morton, Charlie Parker, "Duke" Ellington, Louis Armstrong—have been black, much of their audience has been white, and often sophisticated: a connoisseur of jazz might happily sit in a smoke-filled nightclub delighting in Armstrong's trumpet and the next night attend a concert of chamber music in rather tamer conditions. The first noteworthy American center of jazz was New Orleans, though distinct schools also grew up in St. Louis and Chicago. One ingredient in that complex musical form called jazz was ragtime—rhythmical and repetitive music based on the piano; another was the blues—far more informal, inviting improvisation and normally including vocal interludes. By the 1920s, there were famous jazz bands in the United States and famous soloists; by the 1930s, approving and disapproving Europeans alike identified jazz with America, and often, America with jazz. Roquentin, the protagonist of Jean-Paul Sartre's existentialist novel *Nausea*, is haunted by a line from an American jazz recording.

Though jazz became the musical idiom of millions through radio and phonograph records, the numbers who could experience the pleasure of hearing and seeing an actual performance by fine jazz musicians were relatively small, confined as those performances were to little clubs, dances, and (occasionally) concerts. Sports, on the other hand, could entertain vast masses at the same time. The origins of the modern industry of sports were anything but benign: in Germany, after the disasters of the Napoleonic Wars, dismayed patriots like Friedrich Ludwig Jahn (see p. 546) started gymnastic clubs designed to toughen the bodies of young Germans and awaken their love for the fatherland at the same time. Later in the nineteenth century, the select English public schools developed a craze for competitive sports, to "build character" and encourage "manliness." By the 1880s, at Rugby and Harrow and the other public schools, how a boy did on the cricket field was more important—not merely to himself and his classmates but often to his teachers—than his performance in the classroom. The intellect, the proponents of this new anti-intellectualism insisted, was not everything. In France, after its dismal defeat in 1870 at the hands of the Germans, gymnastics and competitive sports were both promoted by militant patriots intent on revenge.

The growing popularity of spectator sports, in which the few sweated for the gratification of the many, brought its own class differentiations: sports that could be played only before small audiences and were essentially clean—like tennis—were for the upper classes; more massive and more messy combats, like baseball, soccer, and boxing, were by and large reserved for the lower orders. Spectators at cricket matches conversed, sat down, and had tea; spectators at soccer games shouted, stood up, and had fights. By the twentieth century, many favorite sportsmen were professionals, capable and hard-working entertainers playing to tens of thousands of spectators. And these players were as open to deification, and in the same way, as were movie stars.

Yet the cult of the amateur persisted; it stood behind Baron de Coubertin's revival of the ancient Greek Olympic games. The first modern Olympics, held symbolically in Athens in 1896, brought together the world's finest amateur athletes, who took an oath to compete cleanly and to care more for sportsmanship than for victory. From then on, interrupted only by great wars, the Olympic games have been held every four years, to pit sprinters and long-distance runners, discus throwers and high jumpers against one another, the implacable clock, and the objective tape measure. Designed to unite the nations in friendly competition, the games have often produced ill will instead. The committees in charge of keeping the Olympics pure have sometimes made unpopular decisions in disqualifying athletes they deem to be professionals; this is what happened in 1932 to the great Finnish long-distance runner Paavo Nurmi, who had won six gold medals in the three preceding games. And at least on one memorable occasion, the Olympic games have helped to shatter a racist myth. In 1936, the American Jesse Owens demonstrated the athletic prowess of blacks—which the Nazis had denied—by winning four gold medals, for the one hundred meters, the two hundred meters, the broad jump, and the 4-x-100-meter relay race. In the politicized twentieth century, not even sports could escape political implications.

AN UNEQUAL CONFRONTATION

Depression

On October 24, 1929, "Black Thursday," a wave of panic selling hit the New York Stock Exchange. The following days were worse, and a succession of shocks continued into the next month. From the beginning of September to the middle of November, the *New York Times* index of the prices of industrial shares fell by more than half; in the summer of 1932, it stood at about an eighth of what it had registered three years earlier. In actuality the stock market was late in indicating the onset of trouble. The boom of the mid-twenties had come to an end in 1928: American investment in Europe had already begun to decline, and production was cut back to cope with swollen inventories. But the momentum of speculation, helped on by low margin requirements, had shielded investors from realizing what was happening; the very artificiality of the system made the collapse more shattering. The Great Depression of the thirties was no mere cyclical downturn of the kind the industrial world had known and (with difficulty) absorbed for more than a century. Nor was it a long-term crisis of confidence and readjustment of expectations such as had occurred in Britain between 1873 and 1896, and to which economists have long pinned the same label. After 1929 in the United States and in Europe after 1931, the economy literally contracted: prices fell, production was slashed, and unemployment soared—the most searing of all experiences for those who lived through it. Taking 1929 as 100, the index of production in 1932 stood at 84 in Britain, 72 in France, 67 in Italy, and 53 in Germany and the United States. [16]

The causes, as always, were many. The recovery from the depletion and dislocation of the war was clearly artificial. The sagging of world prices of

---

[16] The New York stock market figures are from John Kenneth Galbraith, *The Great Crash, 1929* (1955, 3rd ed., 1972), 146; the production index figures are from W. Arthur Lewis, *Economic Survey, 1919-1939* (1949), quoted in Raymond J. Sontag, *A Broken World, 1919-1939* (1971), 202.

agricultural products throughout the decade contributed to a fall in demand. The speculative fever had grown, and in no way more unhealthily than in the flight of "hot money" from one temporary shelter to another in quest of huge profits to be made from tiny fluctuations in interest rates. The European economy had developed unevenly, and the imbalance was made worse by the startling inflow of American capital, which was just as startlingly reversed in 1928 in response to the contraction that set in within the United States. Net exports of American capital were less than $200 million in 1926 and, after rising to more than $1 billion in 1928, fell back to $200 million in 1929. Credit, unwisely expanded, was lethally cut back; prices of shares and goods fell precipitously; and obligations, optimistically entered into, could not be met. "In a highly integrated economy," writes David Landes, "this kind of collapse builds up in mass and momentum like an avalanche or a sandslide. Each man calls upon his debtors for help in meeting the claims of his creditors, so that even the healthiest enterprises are hard pressed to meet the demands that crowd in upon them. So it was in the United States; so it was in Europe. The weaker firms, the swollen industrial empires with watered stock and large debts went first; but they dragged some of the strongest companies down with them." [17]

As in all economic crises, the incidence varied. The Soviet Union remained completely insulated. But Japan, like Russia a newly industrializing power, relying on its own resources and helped by a deliberately inflationary policy, was so fully integrated into the world economy that it was seriously buffeted. In France, tariff protection, the relatively small scale of French industry, and the impressive reserves accumulated in the twenties postponed the blow and spread it out into a gradual decline, but the end point by the mid-thirties was disaster. Britain, having never risen so high nor recovered so well as Germany in the twenties, did not have so far to fall. There was variation within a given country too. Areas of heavy industry suffered most—the Ruhr Valley in Germany, Britain's mining, steel, and shipbuilding centers—while contraction was less severe where the economy rested on consumption items like tobacco and food processing. And as the industrial countries fell into depression, the countries that supplied them with raw materials and foodstuffs followed. Indeed they suffered more, for the terms of trade—the ratio of prices paid for goods sold as against prices paid for goods bought—turned in favor of manufacturing countries and against the suppliers of raw materials.

Crisis in industry and the financial markets inevitably shook the banking structure. Nowhere did banks fail to the extent that they did in the United States, but then nowhere were they so decentralized. A banking crisis hit Europe first in Vienna in 1931, but the Creditanstalt, the largest and most respected of Viennese banks, was rescued from insolvency by loans from abroad, and similar swift action shored up the German banks whose turn came next. The crisis made a shambles of international trade and wrecked the

[17] *The Unbound Prometheus* (1969), 372.

international monetary system that was being so painfully rebuilt in the years following the war. One consequence was the ending of reparations payments, a decision taken at the Lausanne Conference in 1932; the war debts to the United States, which that country would not or could not forgive, simply went by default. In 1931 Britain abandoned the gold standard reerected at such cost in 1925, and the pound was allowed to find a new, more favorable relationship to other currencies and so to lower the cost of British goods to foreign buyers. Other countries that had followed the British example in returning to gold now followed Britain's lead in abandoning it; though gold remained important in settling international accounts, it no longer stood in any simple relationship to the maintenance of national currencies. In 1933, in a last effort to restore the international system that had worked automatically before 1914, a world monetary conference was convened in London. The conference probably had little chance of devising a policy for joint action, but what chance it had was torpedoed when President Franklin D. Roosevelt announced a drastic, unilateral devaluation of the dollar.

If the search for solutions can be summed up in a word, it is autarky—self-sufficiency or, more brutally, selfishness—a reliance on domestic resources rather than imports, a search for national solutions without taking into account their effects elsewhere. Most governments, even with their new perspective, were hamstrung by their allegiance to old financial orthodoxies; J. M. Keynes' epochal *General Theory of Employment, Interest, and Money* was not published until 1936, and time was needed for its prescriptions to penetrate beyond the ranks of younger professional economists. But there were anticipations of Keynesianism in controlled currencies, exchange regulations, and deficit financing—commonplace now but abhorrent then—as governments were forced to learn that they could take the initiative in the economy and direct it successfully, above all to cope with the terrible social problem of unemployment, which doubled in Britain (to almost 2,700,000) between 1929 and 1931, trebled in Germany (to 6,000,000) between 1929 and 1932, and in the latter year reached 15,000,000 for Europe as a whole. [18]

More traditional nationalist policies were resorted to as well. In 1930 the United States legislated the highest tariff in its long protectionist history; in 1932 even Britain abandoned free trade, though softening the new protectionist course with a scheme of "imperial preference"—coordinating tariff policies with the Commonwealth nations—adopted at the Ottawa Conference of that year. Cartelization—agreements between firms to fix prices and share markets—was long familiar in Germany and was pressed further. It was echoed in the "rationalization" that British industry and government turned to to solve problems of excess capacity and antiquated plant as well as in the codes of fair practices adopted, industry by industry, under the National Recovery Administration of the American New Deal, a device in which many contemporaries

[18] Ibid., 373.

saw similarities to the corporative state, then so highly touted in Fascist Italy. Marketing schemes, import quotas, public works, government subsidies to private enterprise (as with the building of the British liner *Queen Mary*), and direct aid to distressed areas were other expedients tried, with varied results. Britain responded more quickly than any major nation; Germany and the United States needed preparation for war and war itself to recover, a remedy that only the United States survived. But recovery did not easily wipe away the remembered sight of bread lines, the sense of hopelessness, or the radicalization of intellectuals as well as proletarians. Many were prepared to say that the capitalist order had broken down at last; many more had reason to believe them.

The Soviet Example

From all this the Soviet Union stood apart. Statistics were hard to come by, and what there were were hardly trustworthy; the same may be said of firsthand reports. Outside the Soviet Union men filtered what they learned about it through screens of fear and prejudice, of dogma and all-dissolving enthusiasm. But the work of a generation of economic analysts and historians has told us most of what we will ever know about the Soviet "miracle" in the thirties, and what they tell us at first glance must underline the faith of those who believed that Russia had indeed found an alternative way to economic progress. As production in other industrial countries fell, production in the Soviet Union rose fantastically. The first Five Year Plan, inaugurated at the beginning of October 1928, was pronounced complete and a success at the end of 1932; the second Five Year Plan ran from 1933 through 1937, the third from 1938 until it was interrupted by war in 1941. It is estimated that in the ten years after 1928 the gross national product, in terms of 1928 prices, grew by just under 12 percent per year and at about half that rate—still a remarkable performance—if 1937 prices form the base. However inflated the official claims, it is certain that the Soviet Union advanced in one after another sector of the economy from the most backward of Great Powers to the forefront, ranking in some areas (electric power, say, or machine production) with or close behind the United States, Britain, and Germany.[19]

On a closer look the miracle begins to dissolve, in part. The growth was uneven—overwhelmingly in heavy industry, to the sacrifice of consumer goods and the standard of living of ordinary citizens. Housing was in desperately short supply, what goods were available were often shoddy and expensive, and even in the areas of greatest advance there were inelasticities and crudities. No other nation but Britain and, in its differing way, Japan had industrialized largely

[19] Robert W. Campbell, *Soviet Economic Power: Its Organization, Growth and Challenge* (1960, 2nd ed., 1966), 123-124.

from its own resources; Britain had the luxury of a long period of prior capitalist accumulation and an industrial revolution lasting nearly a century, while Japan did not take on a social revolution at the same time.[20] Granted the lead established in the last decades of imperial Russia and allowing for the contributions of foreign capital—confiscated at the Revolution without compensation—still the accomplishment within ten years was remarkable. It encompassed not only the expansion of existing industry but the building of whole new industrial complexes in European Russia and in the distant Central Asian and Siberian provinces, secure from military seizure in another war. The greatest single failure was to be found on the farms (see p. 983), but even there—by paying the collectives far less than the market price and absorbing the difference—the state forced agriculture to swell the capital accumulation that powered industrialization. And with the good harvest of 1934, it was possible for a time to abolish the rationing of food.

In 1936 a new constitution was adopted for the Soviet Union. It provided for a two-house legislature—the Supreme Soviet, elected by universal, equal suffrage and divided into a Soviet of the Union, representing all citizens, and a Soviet of Nationalities, reflecting the federal nature of the state. Although supreme power lay with that legislature, its powers were delegated between sessions (in practice very short) to a presidium, while actual administration was confided to a council of ministers, the cabinet. But what impressed those in the West who judged the constitution by what it said were the social and civil guarantees: the right to work and to be maintained in old age and in illness; the right to leisure, through regulation of working hours and provision of facilities; the right to be educated, to speak freely, to exercise the classic civil freedoms of press, conscience, and assembly; the inviolability of person, home, and correspondence; and the complete equality of women. To be sure, the right of association was stated to be "in conformity with the interests of the working people," and citizens were assigned the duty not only of observing laws, but of maintaining labor discipline, performing public duties honestly, and respecting "the rules of socialist society." Every citizen had the duty of protecting socialist property, and persons offending against such property were by constitutional fiat "enemies of the people." Universal military service was required, and treason, as everywhere, was laid down as the most heinous of crimes.

These last provisions were qualifications enough for those who cared to read them, but much more was left unsaid. There was no mention of the role of the Communist party as a parallel and intertwined government that in the last instance was superior. There was no mention of the secret police—the Cheka of revolutionary days, which, after reincarnations as GPU and OGPU, emerged in 1934 as the NKVD, and which by the end of the thirties could count millions of people in its labor camps. Already in the twenties the early experimentation in society and the arts had been reined in; in the thirties the

---

[20] Japan drew significantly on foreign capital prior to World War I—again like Russia—but not after.

emphasis was on narrow, preferably technical education (invaluable, of course, for industrialization), on conformity to the canons of "socialist realism," and on glorification of the Russian past, even at its most tyrannical.

If demonstration were needed of Soviet totalitarianism, it was to be found in the great purge that went on between 1934 and 1938. The purge began with the murder of Sergei Kirov, the party boss in Leningrad; the murder then appeared to be the work of rightist enemies, but now is believed to have implicated Stalin himself. Three show trials were held in full publicity, heightened by the spectacle of one after another of the accused pleading guilty to crimes they had never committed; having so pleaded they were sentenced to be shot. In this way were eliminated all the remaining Old Bolsheviks and all the past and possible future critics or rivals of Stalin, the Trotskyites (Trotsky himself survived in exile until he was murdered in 1940), and even the officials who conducted the purge in its early stages. The purge reached far down into the ranks of officialdom, wiping out a large proportion of the higher officers in the army and removing or imprisoning key managerial personnel; since survival might depend on timely accusation of someone else, the police were flooded with denunciations. Any police system gives some opportunity to the unscrupulous and the vicious. In a liberal society the tendency is checked in varying degrees by tradition, organizational controls, an independent judiciary, and public opinion. In a totalitarian state, where those limiting factors scarcely exist, the opportunity given to the opportunistic, the mean and criminal, or the psychopathic is immense, and the methods of terror become ends in themselves. One NKVD man liked to boast that, if he had Karl Marx to interrogate, he could make him confess to being an agent of Bismarck.

Executions and incarcerations ran into the millions. Yet the system continued to turn up occupants for posts that fell vacant, and the first loyalty of these new men was to Stalin—or to survival and the prudence it inculcated. The trials had an intense fascination for contemporaries, and psychologists and novelists (notably Arthur Koestler in *Darkness at Noon*) have tried to explain the self-abasement to which the victims were, almost without exception, reduced. Torture, threats to family, and relentless, unending questioning are only part of the answer; as important, though harder to grasp, is the mentality of the dedicated party member, who sees himself as the pawn of history and the party as the sole guide to truth. The phenomenon was known to the medieval church and to absolute monarchs, among them, significantly, the tsars of Russia. The growing suspicion as years passed that the truth about the purge was far worse than appeared on the surface was borne out when, following Stalin's death in 1953, Nikita Khrushchev denounced the "cult of personality" and accused Stalin of monstrous crimes; what Khrushchev said has been documented independently as well. That the purge secured Stalin's personal power, as it had not been secured before, is unquestionable. That it was related either to his preparation for war or to the quest for efficiency in management is far more dubious; indeed it must have seriously interfered with both. We know now that much of the impulse lay in Stalin's personality—dark, violent, and increasingly paranoid. The wider acceptance of the result—in Russia and abroad—testifies both to an inability to believe in terror on so vast a scale and to a compulsion to believe in the beneficence of the Soviet alternative, compared to what had gone before in Russia or to what existed elsewhere.

While the Soviet Union was being thus violently transformed, it presented conflicting but increasingly ingratiating faces to other nations. Ideally, in a socialist world, there would be no need for ministries of foreign affairs and their functionaries. In the real world of the twenties the post of foreign minister was held by Georgi Chicherin, a cultivated Menshevik of gentry stock; starting with the Treaty of Rapallo with Germany, which so surprised Europe in 1922, Chicherin sought recognition and by the mid-twenties had got it from most states other than those in eastern Europe and the United States, the latter falling belatedly into line in 1933. In the thirties, particularly with the rise of an expansionist menace in Japan and Germany, Soviet foreign policy, then directed by Maxim Litvinov, went far toward entering fully into the world of diplomacy: military alliances were undertaken with Czechoslovakia and France, and nonaggression pacts were concluded with a number of other countries. In 1934 the Soviet Union entered the League of Nations, which it had so long denounced as an agency of imperialism. The Comintern, the international arm of the Soviet Union, was less in evidence in the thirties than in the early twenties, but Communist parties in nearly every country followed the line laid down in Moscow with singular faithfulness. The standing contrast in both internal and external matters between stated principle and actual practice, indeed between practice and practice, made it difficult for any other nation to trust the Soviet Union, though some of them, increasingly beleaguered, felt the need of what support that puzzling power could—or might—give in a crisis. In a Europe torn between democracy in decay and fascism on the march, the fitfulness of Soviet policy adds a special dimension to the nightmarishness of the decade.

Fascism In The Thirties

The history of fascism in the thirties—even assuming that agreement is possible on the meaning of the term—need detain us little. Mussolini's Italy, about whose claim to be a fascist state there is no doubt, lurched from ineptitude to absurdity and back again. The Duce's bombast continued to attract a kind of indulgent fondness from the Italians, and the hectoring and sloganeering were accepted fatalistically or overlooked: "I am the most disobeyed man in history," the dictator cried when he fell in 1943;[21] the realization was late in dawning. Some worthwhile art had come out of Italy in the twenties, and objective scholarship was still possible; but in the thirties culture became more drearily conformist, professors knuckled under, and the

[21] Denis Mack Smith, *Italy, a Modern History*, 435.

minority who retained their integrity either emigrated (like the great atomic physicist Enrico Fermi) or retreated into silence to wait for better days. The regime could point to a few significant public works like the famous highways, the *autostrade,* but for all the theorizing about corporatism, no solution was found for the problems of the backward south or for the depression, which hit Italy early. Workingmen and their families benefited from the official recreational organization, the Dopolavoro, but real wages continued to shrink, and in time Mussolini shifted from praising Fascist prosperity to preaching the virtues of an austere life. Some big businessmen did well, but the state of Italian industry as a whole was parlous and certainly no very effective base for a war effort. Every level of government was suffused with corruption, known to almost everyone but Mussolini.

Hitler borrowed from Mussolini, who was flattered; though Mussolini continued to think of himself as the superior leader, he began in time to borrow from Hitler, in no way more depressingly than in the imposition of a policy of racial purity, halfheartedly but still tragically applied. And in the last years of the decade Mussolini, physically and mentally deteriorating, began to return to some of the socialist, or at any rate antibourgeois, attitudes of his youth, the vulgar showiness of earlier years giving way to an equally vulgar plebeianism. Inside its borders Fascist Italy in the thirties is unedifying and of little importance; externally, as we shall see, it was quite as unedifying but very important indeed.

The authoritarian regimes of eastern Europe (see p. 984) drifted gradually to the right; whether fascist or not is a question for continuing scholarly debate. One sharper movement needs to be noticed, the establishment in Austria in 1932 of a clerical-corporative regime that probably deserves the epithet. A fascist organization, the Heimwehr, founded in 1927, became an auxiliary militia; parties were abolished, or as the Austrian leaders would have it, transcended. The chancellor, Dr. Engelbert Dollfuss, was murdered in 1934 by Austrian Nazis, but the regime survived under Dr. Kurt von Schuschnigg until he was browbeaten into submission by Hitler in 1938 and his country incorporated into the German Reich (see p. 1059). Fascism and nazism were not synonymous. All the eastern European countries, however one wants to label them and whatever accommodations they were forced to make, were anti-German, the despair of the native Nazi movements within their borders. And the Nazi victories, when they came, assured that the long-term future of those countries would be found in a very different quarter.

The Triumph of Nazism

The authoritarian regimes of eastern Europe were, in origin and evolution, drably continuous with what had gone before. Italian fascism glorified will and vigor, but, save for the tragic outcome, would have to be deemed comically out of phase with its axioms. In Germany there was revolution—sharp, determined, ruthless, complete, partly accidental, and almost totally misunderstood until too late.

Hitler's Nazi party (NSDAP) had achieved a certain respectability and a platform through alliance with the nationalist opposition in the campaign against the Young Plan in 1929 (see p. 1008). It began to draw on wider resources for its funds, including big business, though only a few industrial magnates were committed wholeheartedly to it and more (like businessmen making political contributions in the United States) were prudently backing all sides. With the sudden descent of depression the public appeal of nazism rose rapidly, and so did the numbers of its recruits. Yet few could imagine that Hitler offered a viable political alternative: the conviction that he was insubstantial and would not last or that he could be turned to the purposes of others gave him his opportunity.

Stresemann's death in 1929 removed the linchpin of the Great Coalition of the Social Democratic party (SPD) and the Center party that governed Germany in its last fully republican phase. When the government finally fell from internal dissension at the end of March 1930, Hindenburg turned to a Center politician, Heinrich Brüning, a stolid conservative. Differences with the Reichstag led Brüning to call for a new legislature; held in mid-September, the elections had results shocking to the propertied and the timid. The SPD did well, keeping 143 seats; the parties of the Center and Right—including the Nationalists, led by the newspaper and film magnate Alfred Hugenberg—did poorly. The gap was filled by the Communists, with 77 seats, and the Nazis, with 107 as against the 12 they had won in 1928; between them the two revolutionary parties won almost a third of the vote. Without a workable majority, Brüning invoked Article 48 of the Weimar constitution allowing him to rule by decree. An orthodox economist, Brüning pinned his hopes for German recovery on the ending of reparations, but this could not be pushed so soon after the adoption of the Young Plan or in the midst of a crisis of foreign confidence, in part the result of the election, that was causing a run on the mark. A bold proposal made early in 1931 to create an Austro-German customs union was technically illegal under the Treaty of St. Germain with Austria, and while that was open to interpretation, French and Czech hostility was not and the project came to nothing. A banking crisis was surmounted with help from abroad, but Brüning could not accept devaluation as a way to lower the cost of German exports; instead he cut prices, wages, and social benefits, which increased public disaffection. The cabinet was reshuffled in the autumn of 1931, but the business leaders Hindenburg wanted in it refused and the president grew more and more distrustful of his government.

A presidential election was scheduled for March 1932; Hitler, still on record as committed to attaining power legally, announced that he would be a candidate. There was no obvious competitor to put up against him, and hopes to avoid the problem by briefly extending the term of the aged Hindenburg came to nothing. Hindenburg led the poll, with just under a majority; Hitler came in second with 30 percent of the vote. In the runoff, a bold campaign and the poor showing of other parties raised Hitler's vote to nearly 37 percent, while Hindenburg got a bare majority. The government almost at once issued a decree banning the Nazi SA, the Storm Troopers, but at the last moment General Kurt von Schleicher, the political officer in the ministry of defense, changed his mind and began to maneuver to have the ban repealed, in part because he could thus ingratiate himself with the Nazis in the hope of neutralizing them. Brüning resigned at the end of May, unable to get Hindenburg's assent to a project of agrarian reform; Schleicher, who had the old field marshal's ear, stood ready with a new government, headed by a shallow, slippery, right-wing aristocrat, Franz von Papen.

The ban on the Nazi organizations was lifted, but the Nazis showed themselves conspicuously ungrateful; they also profited from the still further deflationary measures the new government adopted. New elections were called for the end of July, and the subsequent parliamentary deadlock, in which no majority was possible, meant the continuation of a presidential cabinet, that is, one relying solely on Hindenburg's support. But what was to be done with the Nazis, who had more than doubled their seats, to 230? Hitler refused to enter the cabinet in a subordinate position, insisting on full power, which Hindenburg publicly refused. Hitler's lieutenant Hermann Göring, elected president of the Reichstag, at once entertained a Communist motion of no confidence. Papen had a letter of dissolution already prepared; the parliament thus got no further than passing the censure overwhelmingly, and the new elections were held on November 6. The Communist representation went up, that of the Nazis declined, testimony perhaps to fear engendered by the agitation they had mounted; the Nazi votes apparently went to the other right-wing groups.

Schleicher now maneuvered Papen out of office and himself into it, and Papen took his revenge by opening negotiations with Hitler. Schleicher tried to court popularity by making concessions to the trade unions, but failed to win their support and by the same token alienated conservative circles and the president. Schleicher resigned and on January 30, 1933, after much soul-searching, Hindenburg allowed himself to be persuaded to appoint Hitler chancellor. The three Nazis in the cabinet were surrounded by nine conservatives as a guarantee against any radical departures, and the wire-pullers sat back to await the inevitable discrediting of the Nazis in power. New elections were set for March 5.

On February 27, at the height of a campaign marked by constant Nazi propaganda and terrorism, the Reichstag building was burned; a young Dutch ex-Communist was found on the scene. The fire, probably set by the Nazis, was turned into a weapon against the Communists and made the pretext for an emergency decree the next day. On March 5 only the Communist vote fell significantly, and even then Communists and Social Democrats together accounted for about a third of the votes; the other parties roughly held their own. The Nazis got only 44 percent of the votes, thanks to an unprecedentedly high turnout at the polls. But minority status meant nothing; not even Hugenberg's Nationalists were called upon to provide a bare majority, for parliamentary rule was to be dispensed with. On March 23, with only Social Democrats dissenting, the government was given dictatorial powers by an enabling act "to relieve the distress of the people and of the Reich." Armed with these powers and beholden to no one, Hitler moved swiftly against the institutions that might hamper or threaten his purposes. The checks and balances of federalism were absorbed into a unitary system by the process that came to be known euphemistically as *Gleichschaltung*—roughly rendered as "coordination." Trade unions were destroyed and replaced by a labor front, in time replete with an organization known as Strength Through Joy, an imitation of the Italian Dopolavoro, to occupy the workers' leisure and secure their gratitude. By summer the political parties had been dissolved, by force or consent, and on July 14 the NSDAP was made the sole party in Germany. The purging or subjection of universities and the regimentation of culture proceeded somewhat more slowly, but as early as May 1933 there were public book-burnings and in time art deemed "decadent" was denounced and destroyed. Scientists, scholars, and artists in increasing numbers fled into exile. Many others remained, silent, though some, including such distinguished musicians as Richard Strauss and the conductor Wilhelm Furtwängler, at least formally cooperated in the organizational schemes imposed on German intellectual life. Whether from conviction or opportunism, philosophers, historians, and lawyers joined in glorifying Nazism and in tracing its alleged roots in the Germanic tradition or helped to devise philosophical justifications for the course the dictatorship took.

The churches proved more difficult. Both Catholic and Protestant churches were in the main gratified by the advent of Hitler. A concordat was negotiated with the Vatican in the summer of 1933, but Hitler had no intention of carrying out that agreement any more than he would respect other treaties. The resulting tension with Rome led to such protests as the placing of books by the Nazi cultural chief, Alfred Rosenberg, on the Index and a sharp attack on the principles of National Socialism in a papal encyclical in 1937. The papacy was caught in ambiguity, however, supporting Hitler's territorial annexations, accepting the war, and playing a curiously cautious part during it, the latter the crux of much recent controversy.[22] Still, more Catholics than Protestants became active in the political resistance. Most Protestant churchmen had never been reconciled to the republic and welcomed the restoration of authority. The Protestant friendliness toward the new order was quickly cooled by Nazi successes in reorganizing the church and imposing an official bishop, and by the attempt to insert an Aryan restriction in the church constitution. The Protestants' resistance was less likely than the Catholics' to be political; they sought,

[22] Notably in Rolf Hochhuth's play *The Deputy.*

rather, to survive and to preach as they wanted. But there were Protestant martyrs: the Berlin pastor Dr. Martin Niemöller, close to the Nazis at first but arrested in 1936; and two theologians of great distinction, the Swiss Karl Barth, removed from his professorship at Bonn, and Dietrich Bonhoeffer, shot during the war. In the end the Nazis decided against a headlong confrontation with the Christian churches; they cultivated their appalling neopaganism and put a reckoning with Christianity high on the list of postwar priorities.

Big business survived relatively unshaken. Extensive controls were imposed, not only to fight the depression but to make possible the rapid progress of rearmament; until 1937, when he protested that rearmament was proceeding too rapidly for economic health, Dr. Hjalmar Schacht, who had restored the mark in 1925, was responsible for the impressive accomplishments of state finance. Corporatism never went so far in Germany as it did in the show-window industrial reorganization of Italy, for German industry was already highly structured in cartels, efficient and amenable to understandings at the highest level. So, too, with the army, at least at first: the officers welcomed rearmament and the promise of escape from the Versailles restrictions, as most of them welcomed the evaporation of the republic. In 1934 they accepted a pledge of personal loyalty to Hitler. But Hitler rejected the restraining hand the army wanted to place on his eager expansionism after 1936, and in 1938 the two top commanders were purged on trumped-up charges and dependable hacks substituted. Hitler's old comrade-in-arms and, for a time, heir apparent, Hermann Göring, was imposed on the German air force, the Luftwaffe. Göring's ostentation and presumption were much resented by old-line officers, and there was rejoicing among them when his air strategy miscarried during the war and he fell into comparative disgrace.

It was in part to conciliate the army that Hitler moved in 1934 to purge the Nazi party itself. The principal target was the SA, whose ambitious leader Ernst Röhm, that veteran of the free corps and an early recruit to Hitler's cause, had urged a coup d'état while his master was still committed to legal means. Now the SA threatened to rival the army itself. At the end of June in that year Röhm and an uncertain number of other leaders of the SA were rounded up and shot; in Röhm's case, his well-known homosexuality was one of the crimes of which he was accused. But while the attack fell mainly on the SA, there were other strategically chosen victims as well, among them General von Schleicher, Hitler's predecessor as chancellor, and Gregor Strasser, the organizing genius of the party in the twenties and the principal spokesman for the now-forgotten socialist side of Nazism. The example of the purge was known to be admired by Stalin, though Hitler's victims numbered no more than a couple of hundred. The SA, shown its place, continued in existence, but its humbling marks the rise of the notorious SS *(Schutzstaffeln)*, Hitler's own elite guard, whose founding dated from 1929 and which was headed by Heinrich Himmler, the precise, methodical, mild-mannered schoolmaster's son who had found in Hitler a leader to whom he could give himself unreservedly. In time an expanded SS came to absorb all the police functions of the country, including the dreaded secret police, the Gestapo; through its grimly named Death's Head division, the SS also manned the concentration camps.

With enemies and potential rivals eliminated, the supremacy of the party had been established over the state; when Hindenburg died in August 1934, Hitler combined the presidency and the chancellorship. Thus everything culminated in the *Führer*—the leader who intuitively knew what was best for his people. To what ends was this awesome power directed? To the restoration of Germany, to the destruction of the Versailles settlement, to a new imperialism that would win *Lebensraum*—room in which a vigorous Germany could expand. Nazi philosophy and rhetoric are singularly cloudy, but through them—perhaps because of them—one can see the rejection of nearly every good, other than material progress, that Western man, with whatever disagreements, had worked for for centuries. Not only were the goals of liberals abandoned but so were the restraints and civilities with which conservatives or even most reactionaries had tempered their allegiance to a lost, regretted, past. For the Nazis the past did not exist, and even the "Nordic" myths enshrined at Bayreuth or celebrated in the party festivals at Nuremberg were perverted. What the Third Reich stood for, said one loyal professor, was "blood against formal reason; race against purposeful rationality; honor against profit; unity against individualistic disintegration; martial virtue against bourgeois security; the folk against the individual and the mass." [23] In that mystical evocation of the *Volk* the Nazis found excuses for their worst excesses—from the neopagan rituals, to the glorification of the mindless thuggery of which youth can be capable, to the quest for racial purity and the sadism to which it gave rein.

In its thoroughness, its pretension to scientific truth, and its horror, the insistence on racial purity—the most characteristic trait of Nazism—goes far beyond any modern anti-Semitism and far beyond any nineteenth-century racial thinking that was not certifiable as insane. Those who had viewed the Nazi movement in the twenties as just another anti-Jewish crusade were sadly mistaken. Systematic harrying of the Jews began immediately after the assumption of power in 1933. In the Nuremberg Laws of 1935 Jews were deprived of citizenship and made mere subjects, and the most detailed definitions were laid down as to what constituted Jewishness and as to crimes and penalties for, for example, marriage and sexual relationships between persons of different races. Perhaps because of the restraining influence of Schacht, no immediate steps were taken against the economic and professional life of German Jews, but in 1938 the campaign was begun to deprive Jews of their means of livelihood. All Jewish-owned businesses and financial holdings of more than five thousand marks had to be registered; Jews were excluded from certain trades, and gradually the prohibitions were extended to nearly all

---

[23] Ernst Krieck, quoted in Franz Neumann, *Behemoth: The Structure and Practice of National Socialism, 1933-1944* (Torchbook ed., 1966), 464.

forms of economic activity. Special stamps were required on passports; the names of Jewish children had to be chosen from a legislated list (which did not include many of the most common Jewish names) or if the name were not from the list Israel or Sarah had to be added. Some of this regulation and legislation found a pretext in the murder of a German diplomat in Paris by a young Polish Jew, whose parents had been cruelly used when Germany expelled Jews to a Poland that had turned them out and would not have them back. But the legislation had been long preparing. A more direct result of the murder was the terror of the night of November 9–10, 1938, when Jewish stores and homes were wrecked and looted and Jews maltreated and murdered. Far more was shattered than the shop windows that gave the outrage its bitterly ironic name, *Kristallnacht*—the night of crystal. By 1939 Nazi leaders were saying openly that the ultimate goal was the complete elimination of German Jewry. The pledge could be interpreted away, but eugenic legislation had been enacted at the outset of the regime; it was clear that the Jews were only one class, though the worst, of defectives who had to be purged from the new order. And elimination meant elimination.

Sensing these events now, vicariously and with the knowledge of the outrages that were yet to come, one asks numbly how it could have happened. How could the German people, who had made such magnificent contributions to Western civilization, have tolerated crimes whose actual perpetrators are perhaps more comprehensible to the historian and the student of psychopathology than are the bystanders. How could even the victims fail to grasp what was happening and bound to happen? Victims of any disaster can sometimes react with disbelief, even with wild, almost comic detachment: that too may be pathological or a profound defense. But bystanders may be truly ignorant, can choose to know or not, can suspect but not believe, or may profit in one way or another, salve their consciences, and forget.

In 1936 Elie Halévy, whose perspicuous objectivity has so often figured in these pages, surveyed the European scene and concluded that the world was entering on a new era of tyrannies. [24] He was brought to that conclusion by a then novel and unpopular perception that the governmental systems of the Soviet Union, Italy, and Germany—followed at some distance by the no longer apologetic regimes of eastern Europe—in fact had many characteristics, and even their essence, in common. There were differences, to be sure, above all the allegiance of communism to a rationally based dogma, as opposed to intuition and will, and the Communist dedication to a long-range goal of freedom and anarchy, not submission. But Halévy claimed no vision beyond the transitional period of dictatorship, a transition to the perfect society perhaps destined to last a century or two. In the Russia he saw he could descry only similarities in

[24] Halévy's propositions and the discussion of them by him and his colleagues are reprinted in *The Era of Tyrannies* (1938, tr. 1965), 265–316.

methods to those of fascism and nazism, similarities imposed by the conditions of the modern world. Perhaps—only perhaps—Halévy was wrong in his grand design, as he was assuredly wrong in overestimating the "socialist" side of the Italian and German systems. But his perceptions of positive identities were reinforced by something else—the dashing of his temperate optimism about the possible success of liberalism, severely threatened in France and even doubtful in his beloved England. To that side of the equation of the thirties we must now turn.

The Crisis Of The Third Republic

Secure in its prosperity, France watched the sudden onset of depression in Germany and the United States with a certain smugness. Though French exports began to shrink from 1930, price supports and import quotas cushioned the impact of the world depression until nearly the middle of the decade. Then French governments confronted a major financial crisis at the same time that they faced a renewed threat to their external security from Nazi Germany. And over all loomed a crisis of political confidence that presaged the fall of the Third Republic. Prosperity had plastered over deep divisions in French society; the old debates had been adjourned but not forgotten.

At the end of 1933 a warrant was issued against Serge Alexandre Stavisky, a disreputable financier accused of fraud in the flotation of a vast bond issue, heavily subscribed to by reputable financial institutions, for, of all things, a municipal pawnshop in the small southwestern town of Bayonne. It was soon learned that Stavisky had been repeatedly in and out of trouble with the law, but never prosecuted, presumably because powerful friends were deputies. In January 1934 Stavisky was found dead—a suicide or murdered; in late February the body of a high police official was found horribly mangled on a railway track—murdered, probably, or a suicide. For the Right, with the Action Française at their head, there was no question that these deaths were connected, whatever the official explanations. And the case that the Right made with such outrage and glee found sympathetic echoes among the Communists, who had their own reasons to denigrate the Republic, and among ordinary men and women whose suspiciousness of politicians was never far below the surface: "The 'Republic of Pals' meant that rigorously honest men were on good terms with fairly honest men who were on good terms with shady men who were on good terms with despicable crooks."[25] The Stavisky scandal brought the government down. A new government, headed by a younger Radical Socialist, Edouard Daladier, of whom much was hoped, began investigations, muffed them, made some quixotic firings and transfers, and so, when

---

[25] D. W. Brogan, *The Development of Modern France* (1940), 660.

it first met the Chamber of Deputies on February 6, 1934, provoked a street riot major in scale and alarming in import.

For more than two years France seemed to teeter on the brink of civil war. The rightist gangs that had made their appearance in the twenties were reinforced by others, all of them now taking on an openly fascist aura and program and demanding the regeneration of a corrupt nation. Gaston Doumergue, who succeeded Daladier in the wake of the February riots, tried but failed to get alterations in the constitution to strengthen the executive as against the Chamber, among them the possibility (as in Britain) of requiring elections when the Chamber turned out a government. Pierre Flandin, Doumergue's successor in 1935, sought and failed to get special powers to deal with the growing financial crisis. Flandin gave way to Pierre Laval, in office from May 1935 to January 1936; with his ambiguous foreign policy we shall shortly deal. The long paralysis of the government had, however, given rise to a new phenomenon. From early in the twenties, the estrangement between Socialists and Communists had been complete, for, whatever accommodations individual Communists might have to make with the system when they held local office, the first loyalty of the party ran to Moscow, not to Paris. Now, faced with the threat of native fascism as well as the menace of nazism abroad, the parties of the Left—Socialists, Communists, Radical Socialists—came together in a Popular Front; in the elections of 1936, it won a majority in the Chamber.

On June 5, in the midst of a rash of sit-down strikes in the factories, the new government took office; it was headed by Léon Blum, a distinguished lawyer and intellectual, much respected by many but hated by the Right as a symbol (he was a Jew) of the Left; early in 1936 he had been savagely beaten by a gang of right-wing hoodlums. The new government moved with commendable energy, of a kind not seen since the war: in the so-called Matignon Agreement, Blum imposed an industrial settlement on the employers, including compulsory collective bargaining and wage increases. Legislation went further and established the forty-hour week and paid vacations. The Bank of France was brought under firm government control, the armaments industries were nationalized, and the right-wing paramilitary organizations, declared illegal by parliament at the very end of 1935, were at last dissolved. But the labor settlement was inflationary, and rising costs and rumors of devaluation led speculators to withdraw their funds from France, thus ensuring the predicted danger to the franc. In October 1937 Blum devalued the franc; then, drawing back from more extreme measures to control the economy, he declared a pause in reforming to give the country a chance to get moving again. Stable only under the specific threats of 1935–1936, the Popular Front now disintegrated, in good part over disagreements about the Spanish civil war (see p. 1052). Blum fell in June. A reconstituted government was forsaken by the Socialists early in 1938, and in March Blum returned briefly with a new Popular

Front government but failed. He gave way to Daladier, whose fateful ministry belongs to the history of foreign policy.

Britain: The National Government

In Britain the minority Labour government that came into office in June 1929 had almost at once to confront the world economic crisis. Virtually paralyzed for domestic legislation, unable even to repeal the vindictive trade-union act the Conservatives had carried in the aftermath of the General Strike of 1926, hampered by tenaciously held principles of orthodox finance, the Labour government could neither solve the unemployment problem nor retain the confidence of the financiers abroad, whose support proved necessary to save the pound or the gold standard. In August 1931, unwilling to agree to the conditions the bankers laid down—economy, increased taxes, reduced unemployment benefits—the government decided to resign. But Ramsay MacDonald emerged from his audience with King George V as prime minister of a coalition "National Government," with Stanley Baldwin and Neville Chamberlain as his senior colleagues: it was regarded by the labor movement as an act of unparalleled treachery, but the country supported the new government overwhelmingly in an election in October. Meanwhile, the bankers' demands had been met, and the government was forced to abandon the gold standard and to devalue the pound, which it had been formed to save. Protective tariffs soon followed (see p. 1028), along with schemes to help the ailing economy, but the improvement that gradually manifested itself (outside some stubbornly resistant pockets of industrial ruin and unemployment) seems to have come less from government effort than from forces within the economy itself, notably a housing boom that owed only part of its stimulus to government subsidies. On MacDonald's resignation in 1935 Baldwin became prime minister, and the National Government, a predominantly Conservative coalition, came solidly through an election in November. In 1937 Baldwin retired to the House of Lords, and his place as prime minister was taken by Neville Chamberlain, who had distinguished himself as an administrator at the Home Office and the Exchequer. Under him, the National Government carried Britain into a new war.

In retrospect the British government may be seen as having acquitted itself well enough in the thirties, though few of the unemployed and underpaid would have shared that evaluation at the time. Though the government was not exciting, it was not unadventurous, and it had strong support in the country. But there was ferment and disillusion all the same. The country seemed to awaken far more quickly than did the government to the dangers posed by the dictators. Increasingly, the spokesman for the policy of preparedness that the government came only belatedly to adopt was Winston Churchill, excluded from the National Government, distrusted and even hated by labor for his provocative role in the return to gold and the subsequent General Strike in 1925–1926. Many British subjects were utterly disillusioned with the capitalist system and bitter about the failure of the Labour party to act boldly to change it; the disillusionment extended to a questioning of the whole parliamentary and even democratic system. Britain spawned its own fascist movement under Sir Oswald Mosley, a former socialist and Labour minister, and saw an even larger number of its intellectuals turn to communism. It was perhaps to be expected that those arch-planners Sidney and Beatrice Webb would return from a visit to Russia smitten with what they called in the title of their book, published in 1936, *A New Civilization,* but many less rigorously authoritarian minds inclined in the same direction. The book that probably had more impact than any other of this kind was John Strachey's *The Coming Struggle for Power,* published in 1932; it is worth noting that, shortly before, Strachey—a member of one of England's most distinguished literary families—had joined with Mosley in founding the short-lived New Party, from which one moved to combative Marxism, the other to fascism. But the crisis of confidence in Britain did not approach that in France, and in retrospect the British resistance to the Nazis after 1939 seems as predictable as the fall of France.

The British Commonwealth

The twenties and thirties were years of rapid evolution in the British Empire and, as part of it was known after 1926, the Commonwealth of Nations (see p. 996). In 1931 the grandiloquently named Statute of Westminster made the legal changes necessary to ensure the independent existence of the Commonwealth countries—the former dominions of Canada, Australia, New Zealand, the Union of South Africa, and the Irish Free State, the last soon to abandon its name for the Gaelic form, Eire. In India, too, some progress was made against considerable odds. There a nationalist movement had grown up in the 1880s, centered on the Indian National Congress; it had split between advocates of a moderate evolutionary course and advocates of violence. In 1917 the British government announced its intention of associating Indians increasingly with the government of the subcontinent, with a view to the ultimate attainment of responsible government, in other words dominion status. But, as so often happens in gradualist reforms, concessions were made when they were already outstripped by demands and expectations. An act of 1919 made Indian provincial governments responsible for certain functions within their domain, while the British governor retained final authority in others—a division of responsibility known as dyarchy. In 1935 a constitution was proposed that would have given full responsible government in the provinces; the states of the native princes were to be brought within a federal structure; and the principle of dyarchy was to be applied at the federal level. But this next-to-last step to dominion status was rejected by the Congress party, although the party entered the elections of 1937 and won power in a number of states. Still the constitution never went into effect, and the governor general remained in full control of a unitary government.

Two new forces had entered the Indian picture. One was the charismatic figure of Mohandas K. Gandhi, who dominated the Congress movement for more than a quarter-century after 1920. Gandhi's advocacy of nonviolent refusal to cooperate was a new tactic, reflecting profound inner conviction on his part and offering inspiration not only to Indians but to nationalists in other parts of the world and to many admirers in the West. The other force was an Islamic militancy enshrined in the Muslim League, founded in the 1920s and from the thirties led by M. A. Jinnah: the Muslims insisted increasingly that the state must be based on religion and refused to accept the idea of the unitary India envisioned by the Hindu-dominated Indian National Congress. Thus was prepared the confrontation that, after the war, led the British to transfer power to two successor states, India and Pakistan, the first major step in a European-wide retreat from empire (see p. 1098).

Finally, it may be best to view as an imperial problem a crisis of the mid-thirties involving the British throne. King George V, much admired, died early in 1936; the colorful and attractive Prince of Wales—whose glamorous public life had been so much a part of the gaiety of the interwar years—succeeded as Edward VIII. It was at once known (though not through the discreet British press) that he was in love with an American divorcee, Mrs. Wallis Simpson. The king was determined to marry Mrs. Simpson or to step down; Baldwin tried as firmly to prevent the marriage, which he believed would damage the throne and so both national and imperial unity. In the end the king abdicated, to marry and retire from Britain as duke of Windsor. The episode engaged the attention of the world, but its long-range significance seems to be its reaffirmation of the constitutional principle that the king must accept the advice of his ministers in all matters whatsoever. The new king, Edward's brother George VI, proved an admirably correct and beloved monarch, a focus for loyalty in the Common-wealth. To judge from the popular press, it must be said that the world has remained grateful that one major state has remained a monarchy, headed by, in Bagehot's phrase, "an interesting person doing interesting things."

TOWARD CONFLICT

The thirties confronted the liberal nations of western and central Europe with a steadily mounting external threat to their security. It arose from Germany's ruthless discarding of morality, both national and international, and from a new aggressiveness on the part of Fascist Italy, to which was added a brutal display of imperialism in East Asia by the empire of Japan. A succession of crises far surpassed in scale and violence the diplomatic incidents that had caused the mounting tension of the decade prior to 1914. The nations that had to cope with this new international situation were, as we have seen, preoccupied with economic disaster and internal division. They were, moreover, in the grip of— and paralyzed by—two other fears, the fear of communism and the fear of war.

The fear of communism was only in part a consequence of the successful Bolshevik revolution and the triumphant rise of a totalitarian Soviet Union to the status of a major industrial nation. Fearful though that new power was, and puzzling as were its moves on the international stage, a Communist Russia was as much a symbol as a threat. In 1937 the future British foreign minister Lord Halifax told Hitler that he had "not only accomplished great things in Germany itself, but that through the extirpation of Communism in his own country had also erected a barrier in Western Europe, and that therefore Germany rightly had to be considered as a Western bulwark against Communism."[26] In the imaginations of many in the middle and upper classes, the challenge of communism ran far beyond the rather mindless though sometimes organizationally impressive agitations of native Communist parties. It encompassed the threat of socialism, notwithstanding the timidity and respectability of nearly all European socialists; it was seen in the occasional militancy of labor, in the demand for social benefits and the higher taxes that would follow, and in the loss of habitual respect for the accustomed superiority of those who liked to think of themselves as "the ruling classes." Any show of authority that countered this challenge was welcome, whatever inconveniences or crudities might accompany it.

The fear of war was self-evident in a generation that had known the trenches and the casualty lists of 1914–1918: nearly every village had a monument with a long roll of names as a standing reminder of what war meant. In some the fear of war meant a militant pacifism, the rejection of war in any guise, and the denunciation of arms manufacturers as "merchants of death." The most celebrated expression of this sentiment (along with dashes of social disgust and youthful disrespect) was the motion carried by a wide margin in the Oxford Union (the university debating society) early in 1933, that "this House will in no circumstances fight for its King and Country." On the political side fear of war was reflected in a refusal to give high priority to rearmament when so many other demands had to be met in a depression-ridden society; internationally it meant the ultimately futile but fervent quest for disarmament or, failing that, for embargoes on shipments of arms to belligerents; militarily it meant cautiousness in strategy and in weighing risks. France's frantic search for security in the twenties had given her a large, well-equipped army as well as a series of alliances, but, backed by the prestige of Marshal Pétain, France had gone over to a defensive strategy, enshrined in the immense chain of

---

[26] Quoted in Karl Dietrich Bracher, *The German Dictatorship: The Origins, Structure, and Effects of National Socialism* (1969, tr. 1970), 306.

fortifications on the northeastern frontier known as the Maginot Line. Beyond such caution there lay only the League of Nations as a resource: never completed and clearly successful only in minor matters, the League failed every real test that was put to it and so was reason for yet more caution, not hope.

The Far East

Japan, in the half-century after her "opening up," moved systematically to become a modern industrial power, though without greatly altering the traditional social or governmental structure, especially at the local level. The Chinese, on the other hand, were the Ottomans of East Asia: their empire too was a question that had long looked as though it might be answered in much the same way. China's emperors, from the alien Manchu dynasty, had become fanatical defenders of traditional Chinese culture and coupled their ineptitude with a refusal to entertain any serious or consistent efforts at reform; the civil service was hidebound and corrupt; the economy developed almost not at all; and what rationality there was was to be found in the British administration of the customs. The British were the most important of the Western trading nations, based on their own colony of Hong Kong, the great port of Shanghai, and other treaty ports; they were established in India and Malaya, and their domination of Burma had been recognized by the Manchus. Other nations too carved out imperialist enclaves, whether colonies, protectorates, spheres of influence, or leases: Japan in Korea, the French in Indochina, the Russians in Manchuria, the Germans in Kiaochow with rights to exploit the province of Shantung. The United States, coming late to the game, took what advantages it could (extraterritoriality, for example) and invoked the "open door," the right of all nations to trade equally in the leased territories, a piece of rhetoric to which the firmly established imperialist powers agreed. The Sino-Japanese War of 1894–1895 had shown the impossibility of Chinese resistance to a modern state bent on conquest; the international suppression of the fanatical anti-Western "Boxer" uprising in 1900–1901 confirmed that paralysis.

In 1908 the emperor died; so did the dowager empress Tzu Hsi, who had so long been the malign opponent of any modernization. In 1911–1912 the repeated attempts of the Westernized Sun Yat-sen to expel the Manchus at last succeeded. But this revolution, like that of the Young Turks, was uncertain in direction and incapable of definitively reversing the downward course of China or of restoring a unity eroded by the de facto autonomy of provincial warlords. Sun's victory had been made possible only by the collaboration of the military leader Yüan Shih-k'ai, who had deserted from the Manchus and who was rewarded for his timely intervention by being made president of the new republic. Yüan, authoritarian in temper and ambitious to found a new dynasty, outlawed the Kuomintang, the party Sun had founded. But Yüan's death in 1916 reversed the course to parliamentary rule, with the Kuomintang, once more legal, as the dominant party.

Chaos in China offered particularly fertile ground for the old ambitions of Japan, which early in 1915 presented a list of Twenty-one Demands, which, if accepted, would have assured Japan's predominant position on the mainland, not only in the territories Japan either held on lease or coveted but in Chinese administration. Japan backed down from the most sweeping political claims but came out of World War I with the substance of its territorial desires confirmed, in Manchuria and in the former German-dominated province of Shantung. China had entered the war in 1917, and its case for restoration of sovereign rights was brilliantly presented at the peace conference by V. K. Wellington Koo. But it was only at the Washington Conference in 1922 that any formal acknowledgment was made by the Great Powers of the justice of China's goals. Japan emerged from the Washington Conference with its position clearly weakened. At American insistence the Anglo-Japanese alliance was replaced by a virtually meaningless four-power treaty among Japan, Britain, France, and the United States. All nine powers present formally recognized Chinese sovereign rights and the country's territorial integrity, though the means of implementing these concessions in principle were left vague. In a separate agreement Japan agreed to restore Chinese sovereignty over the former German holdings, with adjustments to be made for Japan's investment in railways and other enterprises there; Britain paralleled this agreement by giving up its rights in the leased port of Weihaiwei, thus assuring China full control of Shantung. But, promising though these agreements were thought to be, events in the twenties made fulfilling them difficult, especially for Japan.

One very pressing reason for the reluctance of the Great Powers to give up their special privileges lay in the anarchy that seemed a perpetual threat in China. In 1924, however, a real prospect appeared that China might be effectively governed by the Chinese. In that year Sun Yat-sen accepted aid and advisers from the Soviet Union—which had disclaimed all imperialist interests in China but which asserted a strong ideological concern—and with this assistance Sun reorganized the Kuomintang as a powerful, centralized nationalist organization. Sun died the next year, a hero who even in death was to serve (albeit ambiguously) as an inspiration to the varieties of Chinese nationalism. The leadership of the movement passed to General Chiang Kai-shek. From his base in Canton, Chiang marched north, successfully occupied Peking in June 1928, and transferred the seat of government to Nanking. To the Western powers this promising development seemed to justify at least a partial carrying out of the principles laid down at the Washington Conference. Chiang's regime was recognized by the powers, many of the foreign concessions were given up or their future sacrifice negotiated or promised, and by 1930 China had gained control of its own tariff administration. Extraterritoriality, however, remained: the willingness to concede supervision of foreign nationals to the courts of a former dependency was, as usual, the touchiest and most crucial concession to be made in withdrawing from empire.

Japan saw these developments differently from the Western nations. Despite its dominant position in Asia and the western Pacific, Japan still felt some humiliation as a result of Western machinations. The Japanese recalled the gains in China they had had to give up in 1895 at the insistence of Russia, France, and Germany; the Anglo-Japanese alliance had been sacrificed; though the halting of construction of naval bases under the Washington naval agreement in 1922 left Japan supreme in Asian waters, the legislated inferiority in capital ships rankled; and neither at the Paris peace conference nor later was Japan able to get a declaration of racial equality, which foundered on the susceptibilities of Australia, New Zealand, and the United States, where Asian immigration was both feared and legislated against. Now the prospect of a unified and assertive China threatened to remove the confusion from which Japan had benefited, both economically and politically. A resurgent China, able to control its own economic destiny, threatened the major outlet for Japanese goods. The Kuomintang was not in fact at one on policy: Chiang Kai-shek represented the right wing of the movement and in 1929 there was actually an armed clash between Chinese and Soviet forces. But, whatever its weaknesses, the successful establishment of the government in Nanking exacerbated the problem of Manchuria, where the Japanese were firmly entrenched and which formed their most important mainland market. The Chinese asserted their rights over Manchuria at the end of 1928, and the Chinese rulers of that province—though it was essentially autonomous—had rallied to the Nanking government. The Japanese government tried to negotiate its differences with the Chinese, but the power of the military was growing in Japan and the onset of the depression weakened the ability of the civilian government to resist. On September 18, 1931, the army forced the government's hand by launching an attack on Chinese troops from its base in the southern Manchurian railway zone.

To many in the West, Japan's long-established rights in Manchuria notwithstanding, this action was naked aggression, in violation of the League Covenant and the recently concluded Kellogg-Briand Pact. The League powers, however, were preoccupied with their own concerns, without the means of confronting Japan in the western Pacific, and unable to rely on the United States for any help other than words. Hopeful that the aggression might be brought to an end within Japan itself, they took no action beyond appointing an investigatory commission headed by Lord Lytton, a former viceroy of India. In its report in October 1932 the Lytton Commission recommended that Manchuria remain an integral part of China, while respecting the treaty rights of other nations. By that time, however, the Japanese had occupied all of Manchuria and had replied to a boycott of Japanese goods by attacking Shanghai from the sea. A more chauvinistic government had come into power in Tokyo, and in February 1932 Japan had recognized a puppet government in Manchuria, now rechristened Manchukuo. Early in 1933 the League assembly adopted the so-called Stimson Doctrine, put forward by the American secretary of state a year earlier, denying recognition to any state where the regime had been changed by force in violation of the Kellogg-Briand Pact. This moral sanction meant no more to Japan than the League's acceptance of the Lytton report. On May 27, 1933, Japan announced that it would withdraw from the League of Nations. No action was taken against the aggressor, and China conceded Japanese control of the occupied areas.

Collective Security on Trial

Europeans could draw some comfort from the fact that Manchuria was, as one French statesman put it, a long way away. Little comfort could be drawn from the failure of the disarmament conference held under League auspices in 1932–1933, at the very time that Japan was consolidating its gains in Manchuria. No agreement could be reached on ways of limiting weapons or on the kinds of weapons that would be regulated; and efforts to provide a controlled revision of the disarmament clauses and other aspects of the Treaty of Versailles by means of a treaty among Italy, Britain, France, and Germany got nowhere. British opinion was oscillating between a resolute pacifism and concern over the new direction Germany was taking; the French were dead set against any compromising of their security; across the Atlantic the American government could urge international cooperation in disarmament at almost the same time that it was wrecking the possibility of international cooperation on the monetary front and showing nothing more clearly than its determination to remain isolated from the quarrels of Europe. The proposals for an agreement with Germany were stiffened to provide parity in armaments after four years, but in the meantime close supervision would be required, along with dismantling of the illegal rearmament that everyone knew was taking place in Germany. After some temporizing, Hitler took a leaf from the Japanese book and announced on September 14, 1933, that Germany would withdraw not only from the disarmament conference but from the League of Nations. The quest for "collective security" through the League and its agencies was a demonstrated futility.

There was, however, another possible tack, an older style of diplomacy through bilateral or multilateral treaty arrangements. This course was taken by Louis Barthou, the French foreign minister in the Doumergue cabinet, which came into office in the wake of the riots of February 6, 1934. Concerned over British wavering, Barthou seized the opportunity presented by Hitler's blood purge in June and by the virtual ending of cooperation of the German and Russian armies to begin discussions with the Soviet Union, which was about to join the League of Nations. Barthou's aim was an "Eastern Locarno," a guarantee of the frontiers that had escaped the sureties of 1925. Then on October 9, 1934, Croatian terrorists assassinated King Alexander of Yugoslavia when he was on a visit to Marseilles; Barthou, who was with the king, died in the attack.

The new foreign minister was Pierre Laval, a former leftist who had long been moving opportunistically to the right; Laval retained office under Pierre Flandin, who succeeded Doumergue as premier in November, and in May 1935

Laval himself became premier. Laval continued the alliance policy, cultivating Mussolini and getting British support for a guarantee of the frontiers of eastern Europe. Laval also tried to avoid giving offense to Germany. He interposed no objection to the plebiscite in early 1935 (provided for at Versailles) that overwhelmingly reunited the Saar Basin, which France had held since 1919, with Germany; he also hinted that he would be willing to consider revisions of the postwar settlement. Hitler responded brutally in March 1935 by openly rejecting the limitations on rearmament and by reintroducing conscription and announcing the existence of an air force, both forbidden under the treaty. Hitler's action precipitated a series of agreements that had been in gestation for some time—between France and Russia; between Russia and Czechoslovakia; and among Britain, France, and Italy. This last understanding, called the "Stresa front" from the Italian town where it was concluded in April 1935, was quickly put to the test.

Ethiopia

However repellent was Mussolini's dictatorship within Italy, on the international stage he had been more or less on his best behavior since the mid-twenties. But Mussolini's rise to power had been based on an aggressive nationalism or, more accurately, on a widely diffused feeling that Italy had been cheated of her just due, by fate, by the war, or (more convincingly) by the machinations of the other powers. [27] The prewar seizure of Libya—a pretty piece of international piracy—was matched in the first years of Fascist power by a frenetic pursuit of territory or influence: the seizure of Fiume; an incident (settled by the League and a conference of ambassadors) in which Italy occupied Corfu in a dispute with Greece; constant interference in Albania and Yugoslavia, in much of which the greater European nations were willing, rather condescendingly, to indulge the Fascist state. By 1934, with the example of a contemptuously resurgent Germany before him, Mussolini prepared to return to his earlier, instinctive stance as an international bully.

Italian covetousness had long been drawn to Ethiopia, that independent, backward, heterodox Christian kingdom in Africa, inland from the east-coast Italian colonies of Eritrea and Somaliland and from French and British Somaliland, which separated the two Italian possessions. Once before, in 1895, the Italians had tried to take the kingdom, only to be decisively beaten early the next year in the battle of Aduwa, near the Eritrean border. Now, a clash at the oasis of Wal Wal, near Somaliland, on December 5, 1934, was used as a pretext for wiping away the stain of Aduwa and for carrying further Italy's outdated ambitions to be a great colonial power. Laval, desperate to keep Italy as an ally

---

[27] It is revealing of the weight Italy carried that an Italian demand early in 1899 for a treaty port in China was successfully repulsed.

and none too scrupulous about means, gave his blessing to the enterprise in January 1935. In June the British proposed that Italy might settle for some Ethiopian territory along the Somaliland border, a transfer Britain would facilitate by giving Ethiopia a corridor to the sea through British territory; coming from what seemed to most Italians a satiated colonial power, the offer was treated with studied contempt. In October, at last, the Italian forces invaded Ethiopia. The League of Nations branded Italy an aggressor and imposed sanctions: no arms were to be sent to Italy, no loans were to be made, imports from Italy were embargoed, and certain exports to Italy were forbidden. But the forbidden shipments did not include coal, steel, or the all-essential oil, without which, Mussolini confessed, the invasion could not have lasted a week; the Suez Canal remained open to Italian vessels. Would the League adopt the more drastic sanctions? If it did, Mussolini had assured the world the action would mean war, and Britain and France knew that war meant they would have to fight it.

Laval clung to the remnants of the Stresa front as a means of political and perhaps national survival; in any event a nation so divided as France was at that time could scarcely fight. In Britain the situation was more complex. There the German revelations of what dictatorship really meant had produced a shift in public opinion, encapsulated in the "Peace Ballot," a wide sampling of public opinion taken in the autumn of 1934 and in which over eleven million British subjects took part. The results, known in the summer of 1935, showed an overwhelming sentiment for disarmament but also strong support for economic sanctions and (by a smaller margin) for collective military steps against an aggressor. In the autumn, at a Labour party conference, the militant trade-union leader Ernest Bevin launched a bitter attack on the pacifism of the party's leader, the saintly George Lansbury, and drove him from office. Facing a general election, the National Government could not ignore this swing in opinion, and the lead the British took in opposing Italy at Geneva can be largely ascribed to political calculation. Certainly most members of the government lacked conviction, and, yet more to the point, they knew that the British services were not sufficiently equipped to fight. Fear of what Fascist retaliation could mean, above all to the fleet in the Mediterranean and so to the lifeline to the East, kept Britain from taking the final plunge.

In retrospect it may appear that the salutary results of stopping aggression would have been worth even a severe risk; at the time, and without benefit of hindsight, the British calculation must be deemed a rational one. There then arose the question of extricating the country from its awkward posture. The elections in November gave the National Government a resounding victory; in December the new and relatively untried foreign secretary, Sir Samuel Hoare, headed for a holiday in Switzerland. On the way he stopped in Paris, where a group of subordinate diplomats from Britain and France had been working on the problems raised by the Ethiopian crisis. Laval, the French premier, had already been in touch with Mussolini about a plan that would turn large portions of Ethiopia over to Italy and make much of the rest a sphere of influence; he persuaded Hoare to join him in a formal proposal to that effect. Before the British cabinet could act, Laval leaked the terms of the agreement to the press, hoping thereby to prevent any British dilution of the Hoare-Laval pact. So flagrant a case of selling out caused a sharp revulsion in British opinion; the cabinet prudently rejected the agreement and Hoare was forced to resign, to be succeeded by the young Anthony Eden who, as minister for League of Nations affairs, had gained wide popularity. But Britain was distracted by the death of King George V early in 1936 and then by the abdication crisis (see p. 1044) and, with all of Europe, by the alarming decision of Nazi Germany to remilitarize the Rhineland (see p. 1066). Unable to agree on any action, the League stood by while the Italian army (not too scrupulous to use poison gas) mopped up the Ethiopians; the annexation of that unhappy country was proclaimed in May, and in July the sanctions were voided. It was the last significant act of the League of Nations, an act of futility if not of suicide. The Stresa front lay in ruins, and, though early in 1936 the French Chamber of Deputies voted to ratify the Russian alliance, the significant negative vote— stimulated no doubt by the prospect of an imminent Popular Front victory in France—made the French paralysis palpable. Then, in this miserable situation, came a new blow, a civil war in Spain.

Spain

The provisional government that succeeded the Spanish monarchy on April 14, 1931, was a somewhat disparate coalition of party leaders knitted together in the northern border town of San Sebastian on August 17, 1930. Formed for a revolution, it had become the unwitting beneficiary of the elections that sent the king packing. At its head was a moderate liberal Niceto Alcalá Zamora; the most prominent of the leaders proved to be Manuel Azaña, of the small Republican Action party. The constitution adopted in early December provided for a single-chamber legislature, to which the ministry was responsible; the president, elected by an electoral college for a single six-year term, was given powers to appoint and dismiss ministries, to exercise a veto, and to dissolve the Cortes, though if the Cortes elected after a second dissolution decided the action was unnecessary, the president would be forced out of office. Suffrage was universal, including women; hence the second republic was a vital instrument in politicizing the Spanish people.

The constitution also declared the separation of church and state and added to that startling innovation a hotly contested clause bringing the religious orders under strict control. Finding this unacceptable, Alcalá Zamora resigned, but was elected as president of the republic with the support of Azaña, the new premier. The new government undertook an ambitious and reasonably successful program: the top-heavy military establishment was reduced by generous financial inducements to surplus officers to resign; the hated Civil Guard was returned to serving as a rural police, its place in towns being taken by a resolutely republican Assault Guard; and, in an extremely skillful maneuver, a statute granting effective autonomy was carried for Catalonia, where separatism had long been rife but where republican loyalties now grew quickly. But a moderate liberal government could yield little encouragement to stringent socialists, and no government could have satisfied the anarchosyndicalists, who were so strong in the Spanish labor movement. The plan for much-needed agrarian reform was small in scale, underfinanced, and riddled with exceptions; it helped neither the rural poor nor the government's reputation with reformers. The granting of Catalan autonomy and the sympathetic ear the government gave to other regional movements offended the centralizers and many Castilians. Almost constant strikes and anarchist demonstrations bespoke the dissatisfaction of the labor movement and provoked growing resistance among the employers, while government enforcement of public order outraged the anarchists yet more. Above all there was anticlericalism. The opening weeks of the republic were marred by violent outbursts against church buildings, priests, and nuns; that the government was slower than it might have been to take action branded it as inimical to religion, which in some ways it was, though its reputation was worse than the reality. The late summer of 1932 saw a futile, small-scale revolt led by General José Sanjurjo, and there was a steady growth of both conservative and Catholic feeling.

This shift to the right was registered impressively in the elections in November 1933, following the president's dismissal of Azaña; only Catalonia went against the trend. The new government was headed by Alejandro Lerroux, long the head of the Radical party, a member of the San Sebastian coalition, and a supreme opportunist with an unsavory reputation for corruption. The largest party, however, was the CEDA,[28] headed by José María Gil Robles, a Catholic corporatist and advocate of constitutional revision who was reputed (unjustly) to be an admirer of the way Dollfuss had managed things in Austria. Alcalá Zamora's distrust of Gil Robles kept him from becoming premier, but in early October 1934 the CEDA got three cabinet seats as the price of parliamentary support for Lerroux. This was the signal for uprisings and strikes around the country, culminating briefly in a declaration of Catalan independence, at once overborne, and more bitterly in the protracted strike of the anarchist and Communist miners in the province of Asturias on the northern coast, a strike that was put down with extreme cruelty.

The year 1935 saw deterioration in all directions, marked especially by the heedless violence of various youth groups associated with established political parties. As elsewhere in Europe, many of these were fascist or proto-fascist; the most celebrated of them was the Falange, founded in 1933 by José Antonio

---

[28] The initials stand for Confederación Española de Derechas Autónomas—the Spanish Confederation of Autonomous Parties of the Right.

Primo de Rivera, the flamboyant and compelling son of the late dictator. The discovery of corruption among Lerroux's associates gave Alcalá Zamora his opportunity. Lerroux resigned, and, rather than call on Gil Robles, the president dissolved the Cortes. The Socialists and the various Republican parties, at last able to submerge their differences in a Popular Front, won the election; Azaña returned as premier. But the government was not what had been hoped. The most impressive labor leader in the country was the Socialist Francisco Largo Caballero, who had been minister of labor in the early years of the republic. He had taken the Socialists out of the coalition in 1933, and now, having swung leftward into ever greater doctrinal purity, he refused to enter the government or to permit the Socialists to do so: it was a display of demagoguery that gave little promise of justifying Largo's reputation among his followers as the Spanish Lenin to Azaña's Kerensky. The new Cortes took advantage of the constitutional weapon it held over the president on a second dissolution and forced Alcalá Zamora out of office, putting Azaña in his place. The results were tragic. Disturbances continued to mount, violence in both talk and action increased, and disaffection in the army was obvious. Azaña had transferred the most prominent of rightist generals to distant places, one of them, General Francisco Franco, to the Canary Islands. But plotting among the officers grew and was assured of support from the Falange and, ominously, from Germany. The rising was already planned, with Generals Sanjurjo (the head of the abortive *pronunciamento* of 1932), Emilio Mola Vidal, and Franco as the key figures. On July 12 Falangists shot a Republican officer of the Assault Guard; that night some of his fellows, in search of any prominent victim on the Right, seized and killed a well-known politician, José Calvo Sotelo. Here was a pretext. On July 17 the garrison at Melilla, in Morocco, rose; the next day, from the Canaries, General Franco announced the army's intention to preserve the country from anarchy. The civil war had begun.

The split in the country was substantially that evident at least from the eighteenth century. The Insurgents, or Nationalists, held the arid, agricultural area in the west; they could count on the traditionalism—indeed the Carlism (see p. 705)—in the northern mountain fastnesses of Navarre; and they quickly conquered the major towns in the southern province of Andalusia, the beachhead for an operation mounted from Spanish Morocco. The Republicans held the three major cities of Madrid, Valencia, and Barcelona, with the more prosperous, agricultural eastern half of Spain and the northern coastal strip. Workers, revolutionaries, some peasants, and leftward-leaning intellectuals rallied to the republic; the church, the army, landowners, and much of the middle class flocked to the Insurgents. As usual, liberals had really no place to go. General Sanjurjo was killed in an airplane accident at the outset, and General Franco emerged as the principal Nationalist leader, taking the title "head of the state"; the temporary capital was established at Burgos, north of Madrid. In the Republican areas anarchistic tendencies quickly surfaced in spontaneously formed militia units, rural cooperatives, workers' committees in factories, and governing committees in towns. The government had had no time to establish authority and was ignored until, in early September, Azaña called on Largo Caballero to head it; two months later he persuaded the anarchosyndicalists to join him. The principal military goal of the Insurgents was Madrid. The Republican government fled to Valencia, but the attack on Madrid failed, and the battle line remained west of the city for the rest of the war. [29] On both sides, everywhere, the release of pent-up passions and hatreds meant dreadful atrocities—drumhead courts, indiscriminate murder, and torture, far more extensive on the Nationalist side than on the Republican. In a sober weighing of necessarily uncertain statistics, Gabriel Jackson concludes that out of a total of just under 600,000 deaths attributable to all aspects of the war, the Republicans were responsible for 20,000 deaths in *paseos,* the Nationalists for ten times that many. [30]

The war was not to be won by Spaniards alone. From the very beginning the Insurgents could count on extensive support from Italy and Germany. German planes made it possible for the Nationalists to ferry the essential troops from Africa to Spain, despite a Republican naval blockade, German tanks supported the ground forces. German air power provided steady bombing support; on April 26, 1937, occurred the indiscriminate bombing of the Basque town of Guernica, to test what effect terror could have on civilians—a terrible foretaste of what all Europe could expect three years later. The Italians provided "volunteers" in numbers, ground troops that, despite some early reverses, were important supplements for the Nationalists, who could count on far fewer volunteers than the Republicans. The Republican government, immediately on learning of the rising, had telegraphed for help from the French. Léon Blum, then heading the Popular Front government, responded positively at first but was forced to back away by his realization of the depth of resistance to intervention in his sadly divided country and, even more, by the refusal of the British to act.

The two liberal states proposed a general nonintervention agreement. Italy and Germany signed and continued their aid to Franco; the Soviet Union signed and openly intervened on the Republican side. That the sole assistance from a foreign government came to the Republicans from Russia posed terrible problems. Largo Caballero found it increasingly difficult to hold his government together against Communist insistence on control; when he resigned in May 1937, he was succeeded by the able Socialist Juan Negrín. Negrín hoped to win support from the West, but even when that hope proved futile, he continued to fight—despite growing defeatism among his colleagues and despite the extent to which he appeared to be under Communist control—at least in the

---

[29] From the battle for Madrid came a phrase in the language. General Mola announced that four columns of Nationalist troops were converging on the capital, but that he could rely as well on a "fifth column" of sympathizers inside the city.

[30] Gabriel Jackson, *The Spanish Republic and the Civil War, 1931–1939* (1965), *Dar un paseo* is the approximate equivalent of the English phrase "taking for a ride."

hope of staving off defeat until the coming of a general European war (which he clearly foresaw) that would merge the Republican cause with that of the enemies of Hitler and Mussolini. But the Nationalist forces moved slowly toward victory. The Basque country in the north fell in the summer of 1937, Barcelona at the beginning of 1939, and with the surrender of Madrid at the close of March, the civil war was at an end. The Italian and German volunteers, now seasoned in battle, withdrew for business elsewhere.

There had been one other source of outside assistance—young men from France, Britain, the United States, and other countries who formed the International Brigades fighting on the Republican side. Motivated by an intense idealism and decimated in battle, these volunteers demonstrated the tremendous emotional appeal that the Republican cause held for many liberals and the entire Left in the Western democracies, an appeal that survives today, a full generation later, in many minds and hearts. The Spanish civil war was the emotional watershed of the thirties, more decisive for the Left, perhaps— precisely because it was so concentrated and dramatic—than the more random development of the Nazi menace. To many the civil war demonstrated the shabbiness of established governments and carried further the disillusion that flowed from World War I and that was compounded by the revelations of patent injustice in the Great Depression. It also made possible belief in a just war; fighting in a good cause could once more be imagined, and so the civil war contributed to something it would have been risky to predict in 1933—the unanimity of purpose in the greater war to come. As in 1810-1812 and 1820- 1823, a Spanish trauma was an event of wide European significance. But the scale of horror had increased out of all proportion. Goya left chilling visions of the degradation of Napoleonic Spain; because those who remember the thirties will die, the enduring monument to the agony of twentieth-century Spain, and perhaps of all mankind, is the frozen scream of Picasso's *Guernica*.

Nazi Aggression

By the mid-thirties most intelligent Europeans had come to see the Treaty of Versailles as a mistake and an injustice; despite a continuing concern for security, they were in varying degrees resigned to alterations of the settlement in Germany's favor. But even that most pliable of Frenchmen, Pierre Laval, had drawn the line at one concession: the remilitarization of the Rhineland, that rich industrial area, so crucially poised to threaten France. Keeping the Rhineland free of arms was not only the work of Versailles; it had been freely accepted by Germany in the Locarno pact. It was, therefore, a special blow when Hitler, using the pretext of the Franco-Russian alliance, denounced Locarno on March 7, 1936, and proclaimed the return of German troops to the Rhineland. The French threatened military reprisals but, divided and unable to draw on British support, did nothing. It is often said that the Rhineland crisis offered the democracies their last real chance to stop Hitler. But this is to speak knowing that Hitler acted against the urgings of his military advisers and that German rearmament had not gone so far as the West had thought. What the Western leaders did know was their own military weakness, the genuine reluctance of their people, and the horror of war, any war. What precisely could have been done? And might not any action, even if successful, only have deepened German bitterness and ensured a later explosion?

At a stroke Hitler had sharply altered the balance of power in Europe. It was further altered by the transformation of the pattern of alliances. The Little Entente of Czechoslovakia, Rumania, and Yugoslavia, one anchor of French security since the early twenties, was falling into decay. The Stresa front had crumbled in Ethiopia. The Spanish civil war was soon to convince the Russians of the worthlessness of their alliance with France. And as the encirclement of Germany by the painfully elaborated system of French security collapsed, Germany achieved new and threatening relationships beyond its borders. The Anglo-German naval agreement of 1935 was far less than Hitler had hoped for; in *Mein Kampf* he had envisioned a broad alliance with Britain as a counter-poise against Germany's real enemy, France. Yet the agreement, which lasted until Hitler denounced it in 1939, was some modest reassurance to the British and a sharper irritant to the French. From 1936 negotiations were under way, often over the heads of the German foreign office, between Germany and Italy and Germany and Japan. A "gentlemen's agreement" reduced tension between Germany and Italy over Austria, and the secret Berlin Protocols established at least nominal policy agreements on other points of mutual interest. This rapprochement was not enough to prevent Mussolini from dallying with Britain in another gentlemen's agreement early in 1937, to preserve the situation in the Mediterranean, but it did allow Mussolini to boast of the "Rome-Berlin axis," a pivot that in time became a trap. The Anti-Comintern pact with Japan seemed to Hitler and his personal advisers to offer security against Russia, the more so after Japan renewed the war against China in July 1937 and became increasingly embroiled with the Soviet Union in Manchuria. Germany soon ceased its aid to China and recognized Manchukuo.

With seeming effortlessness, Hitler was turning things his way. It must be emphasized, however, that he took gambler's risks of the utmost boldness, that the success of his initiatives and their congruence with his long-stated and constantly reiterated goals were the result of brilliant opportunism rather than of timetables and careful planning. This is not to deny the constancy of his long-range intentions or his willingness to use whatever means, including war, to attain them. On this point, considerable debate has recently taken place around the so-called Hossbach Memorandum, dated November 5, 1937, the record taken down by Hitler's adjutant, Colonel Hossbach, of a meeting of Hitler and Göring with the foreign minister Konstantin von Neurath and the chiefs of the military and naval services. Once more Hitler expounded his old theme of *Lebensraum:* it had, he said, to be found in Europe, not in colonies or foreign trade, and be won by war, not later than 1943-1945, while the military balance was still in Germany's favor; Austria and Czechoslovakia were the announced victims.

In *The Origins of the Second World War* (1961), A. J. P. Taylor has advanced the interpretation, more than a little perverse, that Hitler was only an opportunist, in the traditional mold of European statesmen, whose wild talk was bluff and whose victories were offered him by the supine leaders of the Western democracies. Because in this view the enunciation of long-range goals was insubstantial—it is significant that Taylor generally depreciates the role of ideas in history—the Hossbach Memorandum is played down; indeed in a later riposte to a critic Taylor regrets that he even mentioned it. It is far more convincing to take the general statement of goals seriously and to recognize that the ways of reaching them were improvised as opportunity offered: there was no fixed timetable, true, and options were kept open to the very end, but the very fact that Hitler knew *what* he wanted, if not precisely when or how, provided the purposefulness and consistency that enabled him to seize and keep the initiative, while the rest of Europe's statesmen floundered. Against him France and Britain could offer only appeasement—that shorthand term, now so laden with guilty connotations, for a piecemeal policy that mixed, in remarkably equal quantities, realistic assessment of possibilities, genuine idealism, and failure of nerve.[31]

Austria, we have seen, was at least a quasi-fascist state, but the native Nazi movement could be satisfied with nothing less than complete control and reunion with Germany. It was Hitler's intention that this be accomplished peaceably through the Austrian Nazi leader Artur Seyss-Inquart. The Austrian chancellor, Kurt von Schuschnigg, had indeed made concessions to Seyss-Inquart as a hedge against the more radical Austrian Nazis, who were constantly making trouble with a view to provoking suppression so severe that German intervention would follow. On February 12, 1938, Schuschnigg reluctantly visited Hitler at his Bavarian mountain retreat in Berchtesgaden; there, after being subjected to hours of verbal abuse, Schuschnigg agreed to the demands Hitler made of him under threat of invasion: full freedom of action for the Austrian Nazis, who were to be included in the ruling party, the

---

[31] The German chief of staff, Field Marshal Werner von Blomberg, communicated his own understanding of policy to the army in December 1937. If the political situation failed to develop favorably, he said, then a move against Czechoslovakia (Operation Green) might have to be postponed for years. "If, however, a situation arises which, owing to Britain's aversion to a general European War, through her lack of interest in the Central European problem and because of a conflict breaking out between Italy and France in the Mediterranean, creates the probability that Germany will have to face no other opponent than Russia on Czechoslovakia's side, then operation Green will start *before* the completion of Germany's full preparedness for war. The military objective . . . is still the speedy occupation of Bohemia and Moravia with the simultaneous solution of the Austrian question in the sense of incorporating Austria into the German Reich. In order to achieve the latter aim military force will only be required if other means do not lead or have not led to success." Quoted in Christopher Thorne, *The Approach of War, 1938-9* (1967), 41. The first chapter of that book also provides a concise and admirably balanced interpretation of "appeasement."

Fatherland Front; complete congruence of foreign policies; and, as the crucial tactical step, the inclusion of Seyss-Inquart in the cabinet as minister of the interior—the most valuable post from which to direct a takeover. When Schuschnigg returned to Vienna, however, his determination stiffened, and on Wednesday, March 9, he called for a plebiscite four days later to decide the country's future as a "free and German, independent and social, Christian and united Austria."

The announcement forced Hitler into military action. German troops were massed for assault on Friday morning, and by Friday evening Schuschnigg had made all the concessions, including a postponement of the plebiscite. By that time, however, Hitler had ordered his army forward, and a last-minute appeal from Seyss-Inquart to stay the invasion was rejected. At dawn on March 12 the troops moved across the frontier in an operation so ill prepared that hundreds of army vehicles broke down on the way to Vienna. That afternoon Hitler returned to his native land to proclaim it a province of the Third Reich. On April 14, a plebiscite accepted the annexation—the *Anschluss*—by a vote of more than 99.75 percent.

Hitler's next territorial move was better planned, but what he could scarcely have anticipated was the extent to which he would be aided by the Western leaders. The *Anschluss* had suddenly altered the entire defense posture of Czechoslovakia for the worse. It now faced Germany on a third side, and the crescendo of demands from the Sudeten Germans along the western frontier went far beyond the autonomy that had long been their goal. The centrifugal force of nationality, the weakness built into Czechoslovakia from its creation in 1919, encouraged the Slovaks and Ruthenians to make demands only less advanced and vocal than those of the Germans, while Hungary and Poland stood by, jackal-like, to take what they could. The dominant Czech majority, led by Eduard Beneš—Masaryk's friend and president of the republic since 1935—were determined to resist the partition of their country. The Sudeten leader, Konrad Henlein, negotiated with the government during the summer; but in the end, strengthened not only by Hitler but by the favorable impression he had made on the special British emissary Lord Runciman, Henlein stuck by the extreme demands he had made in his Karlsbad program in April, which included full equality and autonomy for the Sudeten Germans, reparations for grievances, and freedom to preach their Germanism and the German ideology.

The Czechs had entered the spring crisis confident in their alliances; Russia and France both pledged support, and Neville Chamberlain hinted that Britain might not stand idly by while France went to war. At the same time Chamberlain was convinced that it was not worth fighting, as he said later in some anguish, over a quarrel "between people of whom we know nothing." He was seconded in this feeling by his foreign minister Lord Halifax;[32] by Sir

---

[32] Anthony Eden had resigned in February 1938 in protest against Chamberlain's insistence on making an agreement with Italy.

Nevile Henderson, the incredibly inept British ambassador in Berlin; by Sir Horace Wilson, the government's chief industrial adviser and Chamberlain's closest confidant; by an influential part of the British press; and by Georges Bonnet, the foreign minister in the new French cabinet headed by Edouard Daladier. The choice of the icy Runciman as mediator was a signal of how things would go, and Beneš was left little choice but to accept Runciman's advice to concede nearly everything Henlein asked for. This concession was made in early September, rejected by the Sudeten leader as insufficient, and followed up by a wildly threatening speech from Hitler on September 12, a speech that touched off rioting in the Sudetenland.

In a dramatic move, Chamberlain flew to Germany for an interview with Hitler at Berchtesgaden on September 15. Hitler was violent in his denunciation of the Czechs and their mistreatment of the Germans but remained vague about the precise terms on which he would accept the reunion of the Sudeten Germans with the Reich; the formula forced on the Czechs by the British and French was the cession of all areas in which the German population numbered more than half. The Czechs tried to resist but could not withstand what amounted to an ultimatum to accept or be abandoned. On September 22, as irregular German forces were already raiding across the frontier, Chamberlain returned to Germany for another interview with Hitler, this time at Bad Godesberg. He was astonished to find Hitler's demands raised and his timetable moved up; Hungarian and Polish claims could not be ignored, Hitler said, and so he insisted on plebiscites, not only in the Sudetenland but elsewhere. Now the Czechs mobilized, and in Britain preparations were made for war—trenches were dug, gas masks were issued, and the fleet was mobilized at the initiative of Duff Cooper, first lord of the admiralty, who later resigned in disgust over the government's supineness.

Still Chamberlain's determination to avoid war remained, and Hitler hinted that further efforts to persuade the Czechs might be worthwhile. The device was a four-power conference of Germany, France, Britain, and Italy, a conference convened at the formal suggestion of Mussolini. After two days of talks at Munich on September 29 and 30, the Godesberg terms were substantially conceded—occupation of the Sudetenland during October, plebiscites, the satisfaction of Poland and Hungary, and a four-power guarantee of what was left of Czechoslovakia. The Czech delegates were called in and told what they must do. Beneš agreed to the decision and resigned. In a private talk with Hitler, Chamberlain got the chancellor to sign a document promising that Germany and Britain would never go to war again. As Chamberlain stepped from his aircraft in England he waved the signed paper, crying that he had brought back "peace in our time"; later, echoing Disraeli after the Berlin congress of 1878, he said he had won "peace with honor." The relief nearly everywhere was immense and Chamberlain was cheered wildly; in France the crowds greeted a skeptical Daladier with flowers.

The optimism in London was matched by a more cynical optimism in Berlin: Munich had proved conclusively to Hitler that Chamberlain would not fight. While Chamberlain and his close advisers seized at every straw, Germany held off signing the guarantee, foreseen at Munich, of the remaining Czechoslovak state; by January Germany was bombarding the Czech government with humiliating demands—for a road across the country under German control, for the aligning of foreign policies, for Czech action against Jews consistent with the Nuremberg Laws. Early in March the Czech government deposed Monsignor Josef Tiso, the president of the newly autonomous region of Slovakia, for working for Slovakian independence. Tiso turned to the Germans, and Emil Hácha, the Czech president, was summoned to Berlin and forced to sign away the fate of his country into German safekeeping. On March 15 Czechoslovakia was dismembered. Slovakia declared its independence, to survive as a German protectorate; Ruthenia (renamed Carpatho-Ukraine), autonomous since Munich, became independent just long enough to be seized in heavy fighting by Hungary. German forces occupied Bohemia and Moravia and incorporated them into the Reich—which was not, after all, to be limited to Germans. Britain and France did nothing to help the Czechs. True, at the end of March, the two Western democracies assured Poland of aid in case of German attack—with reason, for Germany had seized Memel from Lithuania on March 21, and early in April Mussolini was to follow suit and find a pretext for invading and seizing Albania. But long after Britain's guarantees to Poland, Rumania, and Greece, British diplomats continued to negotiate with both Germany and Italy. The British even negotiated, most unwillingly, with the Soviet Union.

In Moscow, however, the Western-oriented foreign minister Maxim Litvinov had been replaced in early May by V. M. Molotov, and even as Anglo-French-Soviet conversations continued, the Russians were consulting with the Germans. On August 23, a Nazi-Soviet pact was signed in Moscow. Whether Stalin saw it as a genuine accommodation sweetened by a division of spoils or as a way of buying time in a perfidious world we shall probably never know. But the effect on the West of this joining of two sworn enemies was shattering, not least to Western Communists. At the same time the pressures that Germany had been bringing to bear on Poland over Danzig and the Polish Corridor reached the stage of crisis. The British government strengthened its guarantee to Poland and was given extensive powers by Parliament; once more preparations for war began in earnest. On September 1, pleading Polish rejection of sixteen demands presented to Poland the day before and taking advantage of the usual trumped-up incidents, Germany invaded Poland. Two days later Britain and France delivered ultimatums and then, receiving no reply, declared war on Germany. "Everything that I have worked for," Chamberlain told the House of Commons, "everything that I have hoped for, everything that I have believed in during my public life, has crashed in ruins."

SELECTED READINGS

For the artistic-literary protest emerging during World War I, see Hans Richter, *Dada: Art and Anti-Art* (1965), a fascinating account and anthology; Surrealism, its heir, is well treated in Herbert Read, ed., *Surrealism* (1936). André Breton's testimony, especially in *What Is Surrealism?* (tr. 1936) is very valuable. So is M. Nadeau, *The History of Surrealism* (tr. 1965). For these and related movements, see the appropriate chapters in George Heard Hamilton, *Painting and Sculpture in Europe, 1880–1940* (1967). The best book on the modern "primitives" is Robert Goldwater, *Primitivism in Modern Art* (2nd ed., 1967). For Picasso, amid a vast and still rapidly growing literature, see Alfred H. Barr, Jr., *Picasso: Fifty Years of His Art* (1946); and Pierre Daix, *Picasso* (tr. 1965). For some other major painters of the period, see Jean Guichard-Meili, *Matisse* (tr. 1967); and G. Di San Lazzaro, *Klee: A Study of His Life and Work* (tr. 1957). The Centennial Exhibition Catalogue published by the Solomon R. Guggenheim Museum, *Piet Mondrian, 1872–1944* (1971), is splendidly informative; see also Michel Seuphor, *Piet Mondrian, Life and Work* (1956). Robert L. Herbert, ed., *Modern Artists on Art* (1964) is a valuable collection of statements on their art by such modern masters as Klee, Kandinsky, Le Corbusier et al.

Critical studies of modern literature abound. G. S. Fraser, *The Modern Writer and His World* (3rd ed., 1970) deftly sets the stage. Other general treatments include Leon Edel, *The Modern Psychological Novel* (1964); Raymond Williams, *Drama from Ibsen to Eliot* (1952); Randall Jarrell, *Poetry and the Age* (1955); George Watson, *The Literary Critics* (2nd ed., 1972); and C. M. Bowra, *The Heritage of Symbolism* (1943). See also Cleanth Brooks, *Modern Poetry and the Tradition* (1939), a great document of its day. Among studies of individual writers, see Richard Ellmann, *James Joyce* (1959), the standard biography; and Ellmann, *Ulysses on the Liffey* (1972), an elegant and persuasive interpretation of Joyce's most famous book. For Eliot, see the brief essay by Northrop Frye, *T. S. Eliot* (2nd ed., 1968); Allen Tate, ed., *T. S. Eliot: The Man and His Work* (1966), a collection of essays as adoring as they are informative; George Williamson, *A Reader's Guide to T. S. Eliot: A Poem-by-Poem Analysis* (1955), a useful introduction. For Yeats, see Richard Ellmann, *Yeats: The Man and the Mask* (1948), and Ellmann, *The Identity of Yeats* (1954), both illuminating.

American culture of the 1920s is outlined in Alfred Kazin, *On Native Grounds: An Interpretation of Modern American Prose Literature* (1956), Part II; F. J. Hoffman, *The Twenties* (1955); and, for the author of Babbitt, Mark Schorer, *Sinclair Lewis* (1961), a bulky biography. For the English counterpart, in addition to the lucid chapters in Fraser, just cited, Boris Ford, ed., *The Modern Age*, vol. VII of *The Pelican Guide to English Literature* (ed. 1964); and Frank Swinnerton, *The Georgian Literary Scene, 1910–1935* (rev. ed., 1969). Peter Gay, *Weimar Culture: The Outsider as Insider* (1968) offers an assessment of the hectic cultural life of the Weimar Republic. German literature is treated compendiously in Jethro Bithell, *Modern German Literature, 1880–1938* (2nd ed., 1946). For the stage, see H. F. Garten, *Modern German Drama* (1959); and for Brecht in particular, Martin Esslin, *Brecht: The Man and His Work* (1959), and John Willett, *The Theatre of Bertolt Brecht* (1959).

For the film, see the bulky history by Paul Rotha, *The Film Till Now* (rev. ed., 1967); Richard Griffith and Arthur Mayer, *The Movies* (1957); and Richard Schickel, *Movies: The History of an Art and an Institution* (1964). The history of British radio is brilliantly recorded in Asa Briggs, *The History of Broadcasting in the United Kingdom*, vol. I, *The Birth of Broadcasting* (1961), vol. II, *The Golden Age of Wireless* (1965), vol. III, *The War of Words* (1970). For the United States, see Erik Barnouw, *A History of Broadcasting in the United States*, 2 vols. (1965, 1968).

Good histories of jazz include Sidney Finkelstein, *Jazz: A People's Music* (1948); and Rudi Blesh, *Shining Trumpets* (1946). Historical investigation of sports as a cultural activity is still in its infancy. See meanwhile, R. D. Binfield, *The Story of the Olympic Games* (1948); and the pioneering article by Eugen Weber, "Gymnastics and Sports in *Fin-de-Siècle* France: Opium of the Classes," *American Historical Review*, 76 (February 1971), 70-98.

On developments in the economy in the thirties, the best introduction remains David S. Landes, *The Unbound Prometheus: Technological Change and Industrial Development in Western Europe from 1750 to the Present* (1969), chapter 6, and the multitude of works cited there. On the depression, John Kenneth Galbraith, *The Great Crash, 1929* (1955, 3rd ed., 1972) is good sense and good fun on a sober subject. Lionel Robbins, *The Great Depression* (1934) is a work by a major economist written shortly after the events. Goronwy Rees, *The Great Slump: Capitalism in Crisis, 1929-1933* (1972) is superficial and popular in approach and style.

Two famous and differing analyses of the phenomenon of totalitarianism, embracing fascism and the Soviet experiment alike, are Hannah Arendt, *The Origins of Totalitarianism* (1951, 2nd ed., 1958) and Elie Halévy, *The Era of Tyrannies: Essays on Socialism and War* (1938, tr. 1965). Although only the last section of the Halévy book, from which the title is drawn, directly addresses the phenomenon in the thirties, the whole book forms a coherent argument about the linkage of socialism and war to the emergence of authoritarianism. Two indictments are addressed to Stalin's purge in the thirties. Robert Conquest, *The Great Terror: Stalin's Purge of the Thirties* (1968) is highly detailed, but the story is dreadful enough without Conquest's exaggerated rhetoric. Far more interesting is Roy Medvedev, *Let History Judge: The Origins and Consequences of Stalinism* (tr. 1971), the work of a Soviet historian who dared to follow up the leads given by Khrushchev in his denunciation of Stalin at the twentieth party congress, with the result that the book has been circulated only in typescript in the Soviet Union and published abroad. On fascism in the thirties the books cited in the preceding chapter will serve, both for Italy and eastern Europe, but to them may be added Charles F. Delzell, *Mussolini's Enemies: The Italian Anti-Fascist Resistance* (1961).

In addition to titles cited in Chapter 24 for Hitler and the Nazi party, a number of books deal with the Nazi exercise of power. Citing W. S. Allen, *The Nazi Seizure of Power: The Experience of a Single German Town, 1930-1935* (1966) is self-explanatory. Karl Dietrich Bracher, *The German Dictatorship: The Origins, Structure, and Effects of National Socialism* (1969, tr. 1970) is the most judicious and penetrating analysis, and the four essays in Helmut Krausnick et al., *Anatomy of the SS State* (1965, tr. 1968) are of great value. Franz Neumann, *Behemoth: The Structure and Practice of National Socialism, 1933-1944* (1942, rev. ed. 1944), remains interesting, if controversial. More specialized studies include George L. Mosse, ed., *Nazi Culture: Intellectual, Cultural, and Social Life in the Third Reich* (1969), a collection of documents with commentary; Z. A. B. Zeman, *Nazi Propaganda* (1964); J. S. Conway, *The Nazi Persecution of the Churches, 1933-1945* (1969); and Gunther Lewy, *The Catholic Church in Nazi Germany* (1964).

Beyond the works already mentioned as basic for France, notice should be taken of a remarkable account by a perceptive English journalist, Alexander Werth, *The Twilight of France, 1933-1940* (1942), and of James Joll's *The Decline of the Third Republic* (1959). Joel Colton has provided an excellent biography in *Léon Blum,*

Humanist in Politics (1966). Again, for general works on Britain reference may be had to the list of readings for Chapter 24, but of special interest for the thirties are Neal Wood, *Communism and British Intellectuals* (1959), and a trio of biographies: Alan Bullock, *The Life and Times of Ernest Bevin,* vol. I., *Trade Union Leader, 1881–1940* (1960); Keith Feiling, *The Life of Neville Chamberlain* (1946); and Iain MacLeod, *Neville Chamberlain* (1961). The first is definitive, the latter two are not but contain much of interest.

On the background of Far Eastern developments, see Akira Iriye, *After Imperialism: The Search for a New Order in the Far East, 1921–1931* (1965), and on the crucial situation in the early thirties, see Christopher Thorne, *The Limits of Foreign Policy: The West, the League, and the Far Eastern Crisis of 1931–1933* (1972). On Mussolini's rambunctious past, see Alan Cassels, *Mussolini's Early Diplomacy* (1970), as well as the two books by James Barros cited in the preceding chapter. George W. Baer deals authoritatively with *The Coming of the Italian-Ethiopian War* (1967). The title of another book by James Barros is sufficient comment on its subject: *Betrayal from Within: Joseph Avenol, Secretary-General of the League of Nations, 1933–1940* (1969). Three books by Stanley G. Payne deal fully and effectively with the context of events in Spain: *Politics and the Military in Modern Spain* (1967), *Falange: A History of Spanish Fascism* (1962), and *The Spanish Revolution: A Study of the Social and Political Tensions that Culminated in the Civil War in Spain* (1970). Also important for the background are Edward Malefakis, *Agrarian Reform and Peasant Revolution in Spain: Origins of the Civil War* (1970), and Richard A. H. Robinson, *The Origins of Franco's Spain: The Right, the Republic and Revolution, 1931–1936.* All three authors are represented, with others, by essays in Raymond Carr, ed., *The Republic and the Civil War in Spain* (1971). On the war itself the fullest account is Hugh Thomas, *The Spanish Civil War* (1961), but the most balanced assessment is Gabriel Jackson, *The Spanish Republic and the Civil War, 1931–1939* (1965), to which should be added Jackson's record, in *Historian's Quest* (1969), of his own encounter with Spain in writing the earlier book. Peter Stansky and William Abrahams, *Journey to the Frontier: Julian Bell and John Cornford, Their Lives and the 1930s* (1966), studies two English volunteers who fought and died on the Republican side.

Gerhard L. Weinberg has published the first of two volumes on German diplomacy of the period: *The Foreign Policy of Hitler's Germany: Diplomatic Revolution in Europe, 1933–36* (1971) is of signal importance. A. J. P. Taylor put the cat among the pigeons with *The Origins of the Second World War* (1961, rev. ed. 1963). The principal critiques, with Taylor's answers, are reprinted in Esmonde M. Robertson, ed., *The Origins of the Second World War: Historical Interpretations* (1971). The most lucid and convincing interpretation, much relied upon in this chapter, is Alan Bullock's British Academy lecture, "Hitler and the Origins of the Second World War" (1967), reprinted in the Robertson collection and, perhaps more conveniently and certainly more attractively, in Hans W. Gatzke, ed., *European Diplomacy between Two Wars, 1919–1939* (1972). Two older studies of the immediate origins of the war are L. B. Namier, *Diplomatic Prelude, 1938–1939* (1948), and John W. Wheeler-Bennett, *Munich: Prologue to Tragedy* (1948). But it would be difficult to better the clarity and good sense of Christopher Thorne's succinct *The Approach of War, 1938–9* (1967).

Epilogue:
Out of the Crucible

WORLD WAR II

The German Ascendancy

On September 1, 1939, German armies invaded Poland. On September 27, after a splendid but futile resistance, Warsaw surrendered. Ten days earlier, Russian forces had intervened to secure the share of Poland promised to the Soviet Union in a secret protocol that accompanied the Nazi-Soviet pact of August. The Russian move was logical, given the swiftness of Germany's success with the technique of lightning war, the *Blitzkrieg*. The Blitzkrieg was not a German invention. The strategy of combining a highly mobile, massed tank force with closely coordinated air support had been worked out in the interwar years chiefly by British theorists and planners, notably Major General J. F. C. Fuller and Captain B. H. Liddell Hart, and was taken up in France by a bold-thinking, solitary colonel named Charles de Gaulle. But it was the Germans, rather than the French and British, who learned the lessons first.[1] Defeat in World War I and the restrictions imposed by the Treaty of Versailles gave a special importance to innovative thinking and careful training of what forces the Germans were allowed; younger officers like Heinz Guderian quickly appreciated the possibilities in the new doctrines. And in Poland the German army proved the effectiveness of these novel tactics. The Polish air force was destroyed on the ground, the Polish army was thrown into confusion, and German Stuka dive bombers—their attacks made more fearsome by the piercing whistles on their wings—generalized the terror and destruction that had been tried on a small scale in Spain (see p. 1055).

The guarantees that France and Britain had given Poland proved useless. Undermanned and underequipped, the British could have done nothing; the large armies of France were hobbled by uncertainty of purpose and by the defensive doctrine to which the country's military leaders were wedded—in striking contrast to World War I. Hitler had early given orders for a similar knockout blow against France, but the timetable had to be set back until the following spring. What action there was after the fall of Poland was confined to the East. There the Soviet Union, seeking ever more security, negotiated tight and favorable arrangements with the Baltic states of Latvia, Lithuania, and Estonia. Failing to get similar political and territorial concessions from Finland, the Russians invaded that country at the end of November, and for a time the world was treated to the heartening spectacle of a tiny, valiant nation besting a great military power. In time, thanks to a change in the Russian command and the overwhelming force of numbers, the Winter War ended with Finland's acceptance of the Russian terms in March 1940. In the West, where all remained quiet, men talked about the "Phony War" and the *Sitzkrieg,* and on April 4 Neville Chamberlain exulted publicly that Hitler had "missed the bus."

British hopes of relieving the Finns had foundered on the refusal of the Norwegians and Swedes to give transit rights across the northern tier of Scandinavia. When Finnish resistance collapsed, the British retained an active interest in Norway, not least because in the winter months Swedish iron ore made its way to Germany through the ice-free Norwegian port of Narvik. Accordingly, the British developed plans for mining Norwegian coastal waters, an action begun on April 8. The next day, by sea and air, German forces invaded Norway, seizing its principal towns; Denmark was swept up at the same time. The Norwegian army fought back bravely, but could only delay the ultimate German occupation. The local Nazi boss, Vidkun Quisling, at once proclaimed himself head of the new Norwegian government, but his intense

---

[1] In his chapter on the war in volume XII of the *New Cambridge Modern History* (*The Shifting Balance of World Forces, 1898-1945* [1968], 738) Liddell Hart quotes, with what seems a certain bitter satisfaction, his old bête noire, Lord Haig, the World War I commander, in 1925: "I am all for using aeroplanes and tanks, but they are only accessories to the man and the horse, and I feel sure that as time goes on you will find just as much use for the horse—the well-bred horse—as you have ever done in the past."

unpopularity with his countrymen caused the Germans to bypass him until 1942, when on Hitler's orders he was put in charge: Quisling's memorial is the entry of his name into the language as a synonym for traitor. In response to Norwegian appeals, small British forces landed but were quickly withdrawn; at Narvik, however, a force of British, French, and Poles managed to hold on until full-scale war in France forced its withdrawal in early June.

The Norwegian episode at last brought down Neville Chamberlain in a vote of confidence in the House of Commons. Many Conservative members either voted against him or abstained, and in the debate one Tory dissident, Leo Amery, witheringly revived the contemptuous dismissal Oliver Cromwell had addressed to the Rump Parliament in 1653: "Depart, I say, and let us have done with you. In the name of God, go!" Chamberlain won the vote by a slight margin, but no prime minister can survive such drastic desertion within his own party. Chamberlain resigned, recommending that Lord Halifax succeed him, a choice that, despite Halifax's record of appeasement, was welcome to many. But Winston Churchill, who had been made first lord of the admiralty at the outbreak of war, remained silent when asked if he would serve under Halifax, and Churchill—so long the champion of resistance to the dictators—was indispensable. Halifax pleaded that it would be inappropriate to have a peer as prime minister, and Churchill assumed the office on May 10, 1940. In October he succeeded Chamberlain as leader of the Conservative party, which had so long distrusted him as a maverick; he was to guide its destinies for another fifteen years.

On the day Churchill was appointed, the Blitzkrieg began in the West. The situation was—or seemed—different from Poland: the Germans could not claim any great superiority over the Allies in numbers or materiel. But the defenders were hopelessly outclassed in organization, strategy, and generalship. Holland was out of the war by May 15; the previous day drastic German bombing had levelled much of the port of Rotterdam. Belgium held out until May 28, when King Leopold III ordered his army to surrender; the Belgian ministers, like the Dutch, escaped to carry on as a government-in-exile in London; but, unlike the Dutch queen Wilhelmina, Leopold chose to remain behind, a decision that seriously compromised his authority.[2] British and French forces had moved north into Belgium to stiffen the resistance there, but in a late and surprising alteration of strategy, the main thrust of the attack on France came at Sedan when German armored (*Panzer*) divisions plunged through a region always regarded as virtually impassable to tanks—the hilly and wooded Ardennes, which lay between the Belgian salient (where the Germans, according to the Schlieffen plan had concentrated their attack in 1914) and the heavily fortified Maginot line farther east. By May 20 the German

---

[2] Leopold, a "voluntary prisoner," won popularity at first, but it quickly faded. He went into exile when Belgium was liberated, was allowed to return in 1950 by a relatively narrow margin in a popular referendum, and abdicated when his son Baudouin came of age in 1951.

columns had reached the sea at Abbeville, cutting off the bulk of the Anglo-French forces. The French premier, Paul Reynaud, who had succeeded Daladier in March, replaced the cautious General Maurice Gamelin with the aged General Maxime Weygand and brought Pétain into the cabinet as vice premier. But changes in command could do nothing to remedy the critical situation caused by a shortage of mobile reserves, lack of proper planning, and the confusion that followed the lightning German attack. An Allied effort to move south to cut the German lines failed, but the Germans hesitated in their counterthrust to the north, a curious and much-debated decision that allowed time for the evacuation of 200,000 British troops and about two-thirds as many French troops from the Channel port of Dunkirk. Arms and equipment were left behind, but there were astonishingly few losses of personnel; brilliant execution and a good measure of luck turned a defeat into what passed for a victory in those dark days.

On June 11, as the German armies headed for Paris, the French government abandoned the capital, first for Tours and then for Bordeaux. On June 16, the French cabinet voted to request an armistice. They had rejected Churchill's surprising last-minute proposal for a Franco-British union, as they continued to reject the notion of escape to North Africa to carry on as a government-in-exile. Reynaud resigned and was succeeded by Marshal Pétain, who had stood firm at Verdun but now surrendered. The armistice was signed on June 22 in the forest of Compiègne, in the same railway car in which Foch had accepted the German surrender in 1918. A famous photograph shows Hitler doing a little dance of triumph.

The stunning success of German arms in France put to Hitler the dilemma of where to move next. His stated purpose of obtaining *Lebensraum* could be fulfilled only in the East, a fact that comported well with his detestation of Slavs and Jews, and in late July 1940 Hitler ordered his generals to begin planning for war with the Soviet Union. But Britain had not collapsed as he had expected when France fell, and it now appeared that Britain would have to be neutralized before the grander continental design could succeed. Plans for an invasion were hurriedly thrown together. Admiral Raeder insisted, rightly, that the precondition of success was air supremacy, which Göring rather casually guaranteed would be provided by the German air force, the *Luftwaffe*, which he commanded. Throughout the summer the scale of German air attacks on Britain mounted, and in mid-August began the contest between the Luftwaffe and the Royal Air Force that Churchill was to name the Battle of Britain. The Germans had a slight numerical edge in both bombers and fighters; the RAF, with its Hurricanes and Spitfires, had the advantage in speed and armament. While the Luftwaffe had been singularly successful in its supporting role in the Blitzkrieg, it had not engaged in purely aerial battle, and even operating from bases in France it was still at something of a disadvantage when pitted against British planes operating over their own airfields. The Germans had made great strides in perfecting radar and effective ground control, but they failed to assess properly British progress in that field, progress the British continued to make while the Germans began to lag behind. Göring added his own strategic blunders, not only discounting radar stations as vital targets, but interrupting a series of attacks on RAF bases at just the critical point, in order to bomb aircraft factories and cities, where results could be meaningful only in the future if at all. By mid-September, as German losses mounted, the invasion plans were postponed indefinitely and, in fact, forever. Churchill's famous tribute to the RAF—"never in the field of human conflict was so much owed by so many to so few"—was deserved: not only was the military victory a turning point—despite the punishment that London and other cities continued to take from German bombers—but the psychological benefit to a beleaguered nation and to its allies and admirers was incalculable.

It is not really true that, as is sometimes said, Britain stood alone against Hitler after the fall of France. Canada, Australia, and New Zealand—formally and practically independent nations but tied to Britain in the Commonwealth—went to war willingly and promptly in 1939. The South African parliament voted to join by a relatively narrow majority and then only with the stipulation that its forces be confined to Africa. In India, where the constitution of 1935 had not been implemented, the viceroy acted alone to carry the colony into the war, without the slightest consultation with Congress party leaders; this technically correct but politically insensitive step committed Indian troops in the West, though India was soon to be threatened more directly from another quarter. Moreover, under the impact of events and with careful nudging from President Franklin D. Roosevelt, the regnant isolationism in the United States began to crumble. Congress lifted the embargo on arms sales toward the end of 1939, and transactions were put on a strict "cash and carry" basis. Giving new priority to defense of the western hemisphere, the president asked for and got an expansion of American forces and a selective service act. In September 1940 the United States gave fifty antiquated destroyers to Britain in exchange for rights to install American bases in British territories in the western Atlantic, and in March 1941 the Lend-Lease Act, passed by wide margins in both houses of Congress, authorized wide latitude in supplying arms to any country "whose defense the president deems vital to the defense of the United States." In the spring of 1941 that meant Britain.

The fall of France touched off a series of drastic shifts in the Balkans and eastern Europe. The Soviet Union incorporated the Baltic republics of Latvia, Lithuania, and Estonia. Rumania, that profiteer of the 1919 settlement, yielded to Russian demands for Bessarabia and northern Dobruja, while German pressure forced Rumania to cede territory to Hungary and Bulgaria. In the autumn of 1940 Germany occupied what was left of Rumania to secure the oil fields, and over the next several months Rumania, Hungary, Bulgaria, and Yugoslavia joined the Berlin-Rome-Tokyo pact—the Axis—which had been concluded on September 27, 1940. In Yugoslavia, however, joining the Axis provoked a coup d'etat and a return to neutrality in March 1941, an action that brought a swift German invasion.

Farther south, in Greece, a more serious stumbling block was created by the bungling of Germany's junior European partner. On June 10, 1940, a month after the German attack in the west and two weeks before the French capitulation, Italy had declared war on France. Like Hitler, Mussolini had gone to war as opportunity offered, well ahead of the date—round about 1942—by which he expected to be ready. Italian forces were unable to move until June 21, and when the war ended next day had pushed no more than a hundred yards into the French territory they hoped to gain. In October Italy demanded the use of Greek bases; when they were refused, the Italians invaded Greece from their newly established staging area in Albania, without notifying Hitler of their intentions. The Greek army quickly threw the Italians back, a resistance that offered the British a chance to honor one of their commitments in eastern Europe. They established themselves on the Greek island of Crete and soon sent an expeditionary force (which they could ill spare) from Africa to the Greek mainland. The wretched showing of Mussolini's forces brought German intervention, and the subjection of Yugoslavia in mid-April 1941 was followed within a week by a German takeover in Greece. Had the British been able to hold on in Crete, the German timetable for invading Russia might have been seriously upset, but in the latter days of May, the Germans seized Crete in a parachute invasion.[3] German superiority in the air not only forced British withdrawal from the island but inflicted heavy naval losses as well. The British had been able to do little to obstruct the creation of Greater Germany in central and eastern Europe, and Hitler confirmed the date originally set for the attack on Russia.

Britain could, however, confront the weaker Axis power in another theater of war. Italy was entrenched in Libya and Britain in Egypt; sensing both the possibility and the importance of a victory, Churchill ordered reinforcements to North Africa at the very height of the Battle of Britain. Taking the initiative, the Italians seized British Somaliland on the east coast in August 1940 and invaded Egypt from Libya shortly after. In December, however, British armor returned the blow and drove the Italians back across the desert; by February 1941 the British were in possession of the Libyan port of Tobruk and had taken more than 100,000 Italians prisoner. Once more Hitler had to intervene; he did so with an armored division under General Erwin Rommel, a committed Nazi (unlike many of his fellow officers) and a brilliant tactician who had distinguished himself in the Panzer attack on France. Within a few weeks of opening his African campaign at the beginning of April 1941, Rommel had thrown the British back on their Egyptian bases, though the garrison at Tobruk managed to hold out with help from the Mediterranean fleet. Yet in Germany's overall

---

[3] On both sides fears and fantasies had exaggerated what airborne troops might accomplish. The operation in Crete was costly and difficult and was not repeated.

strategy North Africa was a sideshow, and the opening of the Russian campaign blunted Rommel's effectiveness. The two armies confronted each other without much movement until the end of the year.

However temporary, the British success against the Italians in Africa, like the Battle of Britain, had given the few remaining enemies of Hitler an important psychological boost. Two more terrible blows were to fall in 1941, however. On June 22, Barbarossa—the code name for the Germans' Russian operation—began. The Blitzkrieg technique was now to be tried on a scale far greater than anything attempted before, with four million men, more than three thousand tanks, and five thousand aircraft. The attack was not concentrated as it had been in Poland or the West. Rather, the Germans undertook three sweeps—northward to Leningrad, southward through the Ukraine toward the Caucasus and its oil fields, and in the center toward Moscow. There was ground for objection to so ambitious a strategy, but Hitler's intuitive decisions had been so successful earlier that he met no serious opposition from his professional advisers. Trusting to his invincible forces, his "inspired" leadership, and his expectation of an instantaneous collapse of the Soviet regime, Hitler predicted, and demanded, victory within three months. It seemed at first as though he would get it. Leningrad was besieged; Smolensk fell in July, Kiev in September. The Red Army had lost more than two million men, most of them taken prisoner, and its equipment had been reduced to a pitiful remnant. Much of Russia's industry had fallen into German hands, along with some of its richest agricultural land. There was panic in Moscow, but the regime remained secure. Russia had great resources to call upon. New industry in the Urals and Siberia could make up losses, and, as the Germans advanced, more than 1500 factories in the west were dismantled and painfully carried east to be reassembled; some of them were back in operation within four months. German forces were stretched over vast spaces, and, thanks to assurance from a spy in Tokyo that the Japanese would not attack from Manchuria, Stalin could bring reinforcements west from the Asiatic frontier. Finally, winter, an invariable ally of defenders in that part of the world, came early that year. In his confidence, Hitler had made no preparations for a winter campaign—even in such elementary matters as adequate clothing for troops or antifreeze for army vehicles—and he refused advice to withdraw to a defensible winter line and to postpone the knockout blow until the next year. When a Soviet counterattack blunted the Nazis' drive on Moscow in early December, Hitler ordered his units to establish winter quarters where they were: they would be supplied by air.

The second blow against Britain and its allies came from Japan. There a decision had been made to cut through the tensions with the United States that had mounted steadily since 1937: they were resolved in a surprise air attack on the great American naval base at Pearl Harbor in Hawaii on December 7, 1941. Within a few days Japanese forces had landed in the Philippines, in Malaya, and in the Dutch East Indies. Hong Kong fell on Christmas day; in February the great naval base of Singapore succumbed to a land attack—an eventuality the designers of its fortifications had never anticipated; the last resistance in the Philippines came to an end in the spring; and the Japanese threat, overextended though the supply lines were, came perilously close to India, where one dissident political faction was quite prepared to welcome the Japanese as liberators from the British *raj.* The war was now genuinely a world war. Pearl Harbor brought American opinion around to full belligerency—and on two fronts, for Hitler at once declared war on the United States. He had not calculated that the United States would decide to give the European war priority over recovery in the Pacific.

The Nature of the War: Leadership

World War II was a total war; every resource and nearly every person in the belligerent countries were ultimately caught up in it and bent to its necessities. World War I, with its conscript armies, its gradual resort to regimentation of the economy, and its novel techniques of mobilizing opinion, had set the pattern, but the new war implemented that pattern with a completeness and ruthlessness unimaginable a quarter of a century earlier. In every sense, the modern state had come into its own, and that was far from an unmixed blessing. Yet, though the war was in the last analysis a clash of technologies and bureaucracies, leadership and personality retained a vital importance.

That this should be so with respect to the German war effort is obvious: the Nazi state, after all, culminated in the all-wise *Führer,* and his intuitive grasping of diplomatic and military opportunity had proved itself, in a grotesque parody of pragmatism, by one victory after another. The concentration of so much power in the hands of one man was peculiarly appropriate to Germany, where what independence of political spirit had developed in the nineteenth century had been largely neutralized or snuffed out. A civilian bureaucracy ground on, tolerant of ineptitude and cross-purposes, with its central ethic of service to the state perverted to unspeakable purposes; a military bureaucracy, more accustomed to a sense of separateness, nevertheless acquiesced in the humiliation of some of its best representatives and accepted the negation of its informed professional judgments. But while Hitler's results seemed to justify his means, his unique position and personality helped to make the German war effort chaotic and, in the end, no match for the more complete—and more rational—organization of his enemies.

Hitler had always been surrounded by second-rate (or worse) visionaries and by incompetents and thugs. The war gave this repellent crew new opportunities and power. Göring's self-indulgence, inconstancy, and ineptitude were scandalous; yet he commanded a vital branch of the military and dabbled in other matters as well. The SS, under that fastidious pedant Heinrich Himmler, was allowed to grow not only into an army coequal to and competitive with the regular army, the *Wehrmacht,* but into a virtual state within the state. Brutes were given free rein in disposing of Jews, Slavs, and other undesirables, and some of them, like the functionary Adolf Eichmann—made notorious by his capture and execution by Israel in the 1960s—proved that bureaucratic routine can do as much to forward sadism as to check it. Yet even though Germany tolerated the rise of such persons, Hitler found it necessary or convenient to isolate the traditionally authoritative groups. Distrusting, even hating, the professional army—"the only Masonic order that I haven't yet dissolved"[4]—Hitler established his own military cabinet, the *Oberkommando der Wehrmacht* (OKW) under the pliant and mediocre General Wilhelm Keitel, to keep the professionals at bay. This division in the supreme command, applied in the most haphazard manner, perpetuated the improvisational character of military decision making, which seemed capable of only short-run effectiveness. This failure on the military side was paralleled by a refusal to commit the nation's entire economy to the war. In the late thirties, observers everywhere had thought that Germany was on a complete war footing; in fact, it was so only at the very end of the war and then without fully effective central direction. Well into the war Hitler preferred "armament in breadth" to "armament in depth"; he remained certain of quick victories and wanted to be able to shift his resources as varying needs dictated. After Hitler decided early in 1942 to move to a full war economy, the responsibility for its management was increasingly exercised by Albert Speer, an architect who shared aesthetic and political judgments with his master; but Speer was never to have the extent of power he wanted or needed. He had to put up with interference from Göring; certain more radical Nazi bureaucrats prevented him from subordinating production of consumer goods to the production of armaments; he lost to the same bureaucrats on the disposition of labor from occupied countries, which he would have preferred to use in the countries themselves instead of importing what amounted to slave labor to man German factories; he had no control over naval production until 1943 or over aircraft until 1944; and the SS escaped him to the end.

Hitler was a master without mastery; he took the successes of a lucky gambler for the rewards of genius. He was, assuredly, intelligent; he was interested not only in strategy but in the details of military technology. But when the tide began to turn against him, he could not respond with the rationality that is needed to cope with frustration and defeat. From 1942 he was deteriorating both physically and mentally; having spread tragedy everywhere, he himself ended in insane melodrama.

Two thirds of defeated France was occupied and ruled directly by the Germans. The remaining third, in the south and east, was ruled from the famous spa at Vichy by a government headed by Marshal Pétain, aged,

---

[4] Quoted in Michael Howard, *Studies in War and Peace* (1971), 112.

obstinate, and cunning. In 1940 and again from 1942 to 1944 the principal executive power was in the hands of Pierre Laval, who had cut such a sorry figure in the politics of the thirties; in the interval, when Laval was out of favor with the marshal, the dominant minister was Admiral Jean Darlan, for whom a curious future was in store. At last, though in only a remnant of the country, the French Right got the authoritarian, corporative regime it had wanted, and in 1942 Daladier, Blum, and Gamelin were brought to trial at Riom to demonstrate their treasonable responsibility for France's defeat. But the leaders of the Vichy regime were themselves so obviously implicated that the show trial was quickly abandoned. Shabby from the outset, Vichy became a mere facade after 1942 when the Germans occupied all of France in response to the Anglo-American invasion of North Africa. French collaboration with the Nazis had been the rule from the outset; now it increased. In one respect, however, Vichy's nationalism was a saving grace. It enacted anti-Semitic laws but insisted on handling its own Jewish problem; hence, French Jews suffered less than Jews in other countries from the horrors of the Nazis' "final solution." But Jews were deported in increasing numbers, and Vichy's complicity is clear.

France did, however, produce a new leader of genius in Charles de Gaulle. An advocate of the offensive in a defensive era, in 1939 he was an obscure general, scarcely known within military circles. Disobeying orders, he escaped to England; on June 18, 1940 he broadcast an appeal not to surrender, and after the French defeat, he sought to rally his countrymen to the "Free French" movement. But the auguries were not favorable. The most important parts of the French empire supported Vichy, though some of the African colonies and the small holdings in the Pacific and India turned to de Gaulle. An unknown, with unknown backing, de Gaulle had difficulty establishing his credibility with the British and a nearly insuperable obstacle to overcome in the hostility of the Americans, Roosevelt foremost among them. The American government had chosen to work with Vichy in the hope of keeping it from close collaboration with the Nazis, and, although the policy had finally to be abandoned, the Americans found de Gaulle hard to comprehend and harder to take; he was, it is true, a difficult and egoistic man, who saw himself embodying the destiny of France. In late 1941 his forces seized St. Pierre and Miquelon at the mouth of the St. Lawrence River, a Vichyite island outpost with a Gaullist population. Washington had wanted Canada to take the colony but London was willing enough to see it fall to the Gaullists. When the Americans invaded North Africa late in 1942 they chose to deal first with Admiral Darlan, who happened to be in Algiers on personal business, and, after Darlan's assassination, tried to set up the ineffective General Giraud as an alternative to de Gaulle. But by that time a growing resistance movement in France was turning to de Gaulle, and by 1944 his position as head of a liberated France was secure. But he never forgave the snubs, and the Anglo-American partnership was repaid in kind twenty years later.

Of all the wartime leaders of the major combatant powers, Winston Churchill was the most accessible and the most fully human, though he was certainly larger than life. It would be easy enough to chronicle his flaws: he could be tyrannical as well as charming with subordinates; he could play his own advisers off against the professionals;[5] he was perhaps too fascinated with the minutiae of military operations and certainly convinced of his own strategic insight. Some of his attitudes might seem to have disqualified him for the leadership of a functioning democracy at war in the mid-twentieth century: the last of the great Victorians, he did not, as he said, become his majesty's first minister to preside over the liquidation of the British Empire; he had earned the distrust of labor by his role in the General Strike of 1926 (see p. 998); and from the time of his advocacy of Allied intervention in Russia in 1919 he had been resolutely anti-Communist. But he brought to his task a genuine commitment to a kind of Tory democracy and a long schooling in parliamentary debate and tactics. His keen intelligence was coupled with an extraordinary sense of humor. His rhetoric itself was a major weapon of war, with its slightly archaic cadences and its unforgettable phrases: in our sadly unrhetorical age, only de Gaulle can be ranked with him.

Toward the end of the war, earlier than the Americans, Churchill began to suspect Stalin's ultimate intentions and accordingly sought to counter the growth of Soviet power. At the outset of the wartime alliance with Russia, he had been willing to make great concessions, in resources and territory, to Russian fears and ambitions. In the war Churchill was fighting, and in his circumstances, an ally was an ally: he told his private secretary that if Hitler had decided to invade Hell, he would at least make a favorable reference to the Devil in the House of Commons. And in that can be found the overriding consistency of his wartime leadership: victory over Germany was his single purpose.[6] The British political system made available to him an extraordinary array of talent from the civil service, the political parties, and the universities, and from the trade-union movement. For all his quixotic devotion to his own enthusiasms, he could accept criticism and advice, admit error, and back a superb set of commanders and fellow ministers. He galvanized his colleagues into action as no one else could have done, and he did the same for the British people. In his first speech to the House of Commons after becoming prime minister he put it bluntly: "I have nothing to offer but blood, toil, tears and sweat. You ask, What is our policy? I will say: It is to wage war, by sea, land, and air, with all our might and with all the strength that God can give us. . . .

[5] The most curious and perhaps most fateful of these relationships was with Professor F. A. Lindemann (later Lord Cherwell), a controversial Oxford don who became Churchill's principal scientific adviser and a vocal advocate of strategic bombing.

[6] One could almost rest the case on his superb and invariable mispronunciation of the word *Nazi. Nazzy* is about as close as one can come phonetically, but no combination of letters can capture the mixture of loathing and contempt the word conveyed in his delivery of it.

You ask, What is our aim? I can answer in one word: Victory—victory at all costs, victory in spite of all terror; victory, however long and hard the road may be." Under Churchill's leadership, Britain was better—and also more freely— organized for victory than any other nation.

To praise the organization of the British war effort is not to depreciate the heroic accomplishment of the Soviet Union, but the differences are startling. There is first—as always with Russia—the difference in scale: in sheer magnitude, both of the task assigned and the results achieved, the Russians performed prodigies beyond any other country. The scope of the initial German victories reflected more than poor Russian planning and surprise; many troops were reluctant to fight, as is indicated by the enormous number taken prisoner, while in some areas the German armies were welcomed as liberators. The old nationalistic impulses in the border regions had not been eliminated and no doubt there were memories of the injustices and horrors of the social revolution forced on the countryside in the early 1930s (see p. 983). No one could maintain that the Soviet war effort was a voluntary regimentation, like that in Britain or to a lesser extent in the United States. Yet the control of the Soviet state remained unshaken in the areas where the Germans did not penetrate, and the mobilization of labor and industry was complete, effective, and admirably planned: American and British aid was important to the Soviet success in the field, but it came primarily in the form of food, clothing, and vehicles; Russia substantially rearmed itself. Moreover, the war soon became voluntary in that it became nationalist: the Russians still call it the "Great Patriotic War." German atrocities in the occupied regions assured the growth of an underground resistance and a steadily escalating fund of bitterness and determination. Psychologically even more than militarily, 1941–1942 was a repetition of 1812.

The role of Josef Stalin is puzzling and contradictory. He bears much of the responsibility for the early defeats: the disaffection of the populace at the outset reflected in part his policy on social, economic, and nationality questions; the unpreparedness of the army followed directly from Stalin's sweeping purge of the officer corps and his confiding of commands to the politically dependable; trapped by his devious diplomacy of 1939, he was unwilling to heed warnings about the imminence of the German attack. In the early days of the war he was silent.

When at last he spoke on July 3 there were no Churchillian fireworks. From a dry, measured assessment of the danger the country faced he moved on to describe the malevolence of the enemy and to recall the ordeals of 1812 and World War I; he ended with a call for total resistance and a strategy of scorched earth. To sustain patriotic fervor Stalin later made remarkable concessions: in words that came strangely from a follower of Marx and Lenin he praised nationalism; with equal oddity he encouraged a revival of the Russian Orthodox Church. He cashiered the political generals, put able professionals in their place, and, although he was himself commander in chief, took careful soundings of his military advisers and trusted them. Unlike Hitler or Churchill, Stalin never visited the front; indeed throughout the war he remained in the Kremlin, that symbol of Russian power that Hitler had ordered blown up when Moscow was taken. There, as his biographer says, "he went on, day after day, throughout four years of hostilities—a prodigy of patience, tenacity, and vigilance, almost omnipresent, almost omniscient."[7] Despite his early errors or even doubts, his leadership was never challenged and was exercised with a remarkable grasp of minutiae in every direction. His remoteness may have contributed as much as the official propaganda to create the near-deification that was his at the end of the war. Both Stalin and Churchill came to embody not only their countries' wills to victory but their respective national virtues as they were seen in wartime. But Churchill was unceremoniously thrown out of office in 1945 by an electorate determined to make a new world; immune from such vagaries, Stalin projected the fears, passions, and resolution of wartime into the postwar era. His dethronement would come only after his death, and then ambiguously.

Franklin D. Roosevelt was the one great leader in the fight against the Axis who failed to survive the war. In the United States his image was to be cast forward for at least a generation, but, though he was admired in Europe, his impact was less than that of Woodrow Wilson in 1918–1919. Roosevelt was a patrician turned democratic politician, a combination of qualities that helped to underpin the close relationship that quickly grew up between him and Churchill. The social welfare legislation and the increase in state intervention of the New Deal era had led the president's opponents to brand him a socialist and a dictator. He was neither, by any stretch of the imagination: the New Deal was an effort to prop up a sadly defective American capitalism by reforms of a kind that advanced European countries had known for a long time; the Roosevelt administration was a chaos of competing leaders and strategies among which the president served as an immensely skilled broker. To be sure, he had an extraordinary charismatic hold on the electorate, as much on those who hated him as on the vast majority that in 1940 had returned him for an unprecedented third term. Indeed, it was more as a politician than as a leader in the Stalin or Churchill mold that Roosevelt affected the war and his own country's effort in it. He thought that his consummate political gifts could be exercised as effectively on his partners at the summit as he could exercise them at home. He sought accommodation and genuinely pinned his hopes on a supranational world order to cope with postwar problems. But his statement of goals was less precise than Wilson's and, for good or evil, his idealism lacked Wilson's evangelistic passion. He did not make up the deficiency with an appreciation of the dynamics of European power, which Stalin and Churchill

---

[7] Isaac Deutscher, *Stalin, a Political Biography* (1960), 467.

profoundly understood, or with the historical sensibility that Churchill possessed to a supreme degree. Moreover, by the time of the Yalta Conference early in 1945 he was in poor health, and Harry S. Truman, who became president on Roosevelt's death in April 1945, was unprepared for his task, however quickly he grew into it. Thus neither Roosevelt nor his successor exercised the kind of leadership that we associate with the European states and recognize by giving the names of Stalin, Churchill, and Hitler priority over all their subordinates. Roosevelt had, it is true, led the nation toward involvement, no small task in an isolationist era, but Hitler and the Japanese leaders finished the conversion of American sentiment that the president had started. The mobilization of the greatest and most advanced industrial power on earth was the work of many hands.

The Nature of the War: Technology

World War II was above all a war of technologies, of scientific, managerial, and industrial resources and methods. In some respects the techniques and possibilities of World War I were carried to their fullest development. The infantry and artillery fought with weapons of new sophistication and power, aided by improved telephonic and radio communication that made coordination more certain. The tanks that spearheaded the Blitzkrieg were a far cry from the crude vehicles of 1916; still more advanced were the mammoth Sherman tanks, produced in the United States and used by all the Allies, on the Russian front as well as in North Africa and western Europe. There were some surface naval engagements early in the war—the most famous being the cornering and scuttling of the German "pocket battleship" *Graf Spee* in Montevideo harbor— and there were some dramatic sinkings of famous ships with serious loss of life. But far more important was the further development of submarine warfare as a weapon of blockade, countered as before by convoys (though that lesson had to be learned once again by both British and Americans) and by new antisubmarine procedures, notably the invention of sonar tracking and the use of microwave radar in the latter stages of the war to detect the undersea raiders. The American navy took the lead in developing the techniques of amphibious warfare, so important in the "island-hopping" campaigns devised by the American leaders, General Douglas MacArthur and Admiral Chester Nimitz: Japan's control of the western Pacific was broken and the noose tightened by seizing strategic Japanese strongholds while bypassing the less important and leaving them cut off from supplies. In the west these new methods of coordinated assaults from the sea were put to use in North Africa, southern France, Italy, and, on the greatest scale of all, in Normandy.

The weapon whose potential was demonstrated in World War I and most fully developed in World War II was the military airplane. Here, despite the apparent initial advantage of the Germans, the productive capacity of the Allies proved most valuable in the end. The increasing range of bombers and fighters and the sophisticated means of bringing them to their targets meant a war of unexampled destructiveness. And, as ever since World War I a debate has raged over trench warfare, with its shocking waste of soldiers' lives to gain a few yards in a futile offensive, so debate rages over the effectiveness of bombing in World War II. Advocates of air power recognize that modern war is less a conflict between rival armies than between the productive capacities that sustain those armies; it is a characteristic of total war that destruction is visited more on civilians than on the military. But questions have been raised about the proportion of means to ends, about undertaking incredibly expensive operations to achieve results that in many instances prove misconceived or impermanent. In purely military terms no one could deny the effectiveness of support aircraft in clearing the way for ground troops: that was demonstrated in the Blitzkrieg, in the amphibious operations in the Pacific, and in the successive "second fronts" in Europe and Africa. The bombing of targets in the rear—railway junctions, depots, and factories—was less likely to succeed. Sometimes spectacular accomplishments were turned in, as in the crucial delay of German atomic research by the destruction in 1943 of the Norwegian factory on which German scientists depended for their supply of heavy water. But factories were camouflaged or went underground and, if hit, were, like the railways, often quickly back in action. Britain's industrial capacity increased steadily despite the interruptions of bombing, and it was a long time before German industry was crippled.

The main pivot of debate, however, is the resort to strategic, or area, bombing. Here bombers aimed only incidentally at targets of immediate or secondary military significance; the purpose was rather to shake civilian morale. Terroristic bombing had been an adjunct of the Blitzkrieg in Poland, and even the possibility of the bombing of English cities led to panicky evacuation, seriously endangering morale. Stanley Baldwin's somber warning early in the 1930s that the bomber would always get through had been taken to heart. In fact, after the initial exposure, bombing seemed to stiffen morale and determination rather than to undermine it; this was as true of the steady bombing of London in 1940–1941 as of the gratuitous "Baedeker raids," which the Luftwaffe launched in 1940 on historic and scenic English towns of no military importance. The scale of bombing of German cities toward the end of the war greatly surpassed what the Luftwaffe had visited on Britain; Allied incendiary bombs generated "firestorms," virtual hurricanes with winds of over a hundred miles per hour and temperatures of more than 1000° centigrade, which nothing could withstand, not even those taking refuge in shelters. A week of raids on Hamburg in July–August 1943 demonstrated their potential for destructiveness. The bombing of Dresden in February 1945, a city the Germans were by then unable to defend from air attack, came after an erroneous report that German armor was being moved by rail through the city; when the error was pointed out, British and American bomber headquarters failed to agree on cancellation of the raids. Estimates place casualties in Dresden at twice the number that died in the atomic bombing of Hiroshima later that year; yet the railways were back in action in four days and the industrial plants scarcely touched. The question of military effectiveness—certainly greater with precision bombing, for all its difficulties, than with area bombing—merges insistently into a profound problem in ethics.

Morally, then, there was nothing new when toward the end of the war, the world got a glimpse of the warfare of the future; scientifically and psychologically, the implications were immense. The Germans had developed the V-1 "buzz-bombs," in fact pilotless aircraft directed by radio from their launching stations; by 1944 they had V-2s, true rockets travelling at supersonic speeds and descending noiselessly on their targets; against them no defense was then possible, and for a time Britain suffered severely. But in 1945 the Americans won the race to create the atomic bomb, which turned a scientific discovery of the first importance—induced atomic fission accompanied by the release of incredible amounts of energy—to military purposes. Extended to the thermo-nuclear (or hydrogen) bomb after the war and tied to rocketry as a delivery system, the atomic bomb was to dominate defense debates and expenditures in the postwar world and to have a pervasive effect on men's awareness and expectations. But the war in Europe came to an end in a display of more conventional warfare on a scale the world had never before seen and may never see again.

The Winning of the War

The war aims of the Allies were, as we have seen, reduced to a word: Victory. This simplicity was ambiguously reinforced when Churchill and Roosevelt met at Casablanca in January 1943 and pronounced for "unconditional surrender" as the only terms on which they would make peace. The two statesmen had earlier drafted the Atlantic Charter—so called because the meeting took place on a ship anchored off Newfoundland, in Placentia Bay, in August 1941—disclaiming territorial gain for themselves, calling for self-determination with respect to forms of government in liberated countries, and looking forward to some form of postwar international organization. These hurriedly drafted pieties were useful enough, no doubt, and it would be difficult to take exception to them. It is different with the call at Casablanca, about which argument has swirled ever since. If no such sweeping demand had been made, might the war have ended sooner, with a Europe less completely wrecked and less polarized? Or, more pathetically, might more moderate terms have strengthened the hand of those lonely men working within Germany to oppose, and even to eliminate, Hitler? However that may be, the proponents of unconditional surrender—and Roosevelt was a far more enthusiastic advocate than Churchill—had compelling psychological and political reasons. The tide had only begun to turn, and the second front Stalin demanded so insistently was far in the future. Unconditional surrender was a gesture of determination and an assurance of trustworthiness. Both Americans and British feared that Russia might make a separate peace, while American dealings with Vichy in France and with Darlan in North Africa were a source of uneasiness to Stalin. Then, too, after 1918 Germany had been able to maintain that its armies had not been beaten but had been stabbed in the back.

The history of wartime diplomacy is also vexed—inevitably, given the course of the postwar world—with regard to the difficult relations between Russia and the Anglo-American partners. When the Germans attacked the Soviet Union, both Britain and the United States at once rallied to the Russian side, and Stalin went so far as to suggest that he might accept American troops fighting on Russian soil under American commanders. But, for all the willingness of Churchill and Roosevelt to concede much to Stalin, and for all the public assurances of mutual admiration and support, the collaboration was uneasy and troubled. At Teheran in November 1943 the three leaders met with a considerable degree of success. The British and Americans were at last able to promise a cross-Channel invasion—for which Stalin had been clamoring since 1942—in the spring of 1944, and Stalin agreed to join in the war against Japan once the European conflict was ended; there was preliminary talk about a future world organization, the germ of the United Nations. But no agreement was reached there, nor at Yalta in February 1945, on the fundamental question of the disposition of eastern Europe. Nor was there agreement on the disposition of Germany, on which the three powers had earlier seemed in rather general accord.

Although Churchill was alert to the threat that Soviet power might pose to western Europe, he had been willing in a separate meeting with Stalin to agree to an arbitrary division of responsibility in eastern Europe, a division that Stalin seemed to respect when he refrained from intervening to support Greek Communists in a civil war that broke out in that country in 1944 and that found the Americans and British on the anticommunist side. The situation was most troubled with respect to Poland, where Stalin insisted on the frontier attained in 1940—ultimately modified to conform to a slightly altered version of the 1920 "Curzon line"—with Poland to be compensated by the gift of German territory to the west. But it was impossible to get the Polish government-in-exile to agree, the more so after the truth became known about the Katyn massacre. In 1943 the Nazis announced that they had found mass graves in Katyn Forest, near Smolensk, graves containing some 4,000 bodies of murdered Polish soldiers. Nazi propagandists set the number at 10–12,000 and accused the Russians of the crime, but almost instinctively Western opinion reacted by blaming the Nazis for the killings. It became increasingly clear on investigation that the Nazi allegations, if not the figures, were correct. More than 15,000 Polish soldiers, more than half of them officers, had been taken in 1939 and interned in three Russian prison camps, which were closed down in 1940. The bodies of about a third of the prisoners were found in the pits in Katyn; the rest have never been accounted for. A Polish demand that the atrocity be investigated by the Red Cross was used by Stalin as a pretext for breaking relations with the government-in-exile. When the Russian armies began at last to move west, a Russian-dominated Communist government would be installed in Poland.

The winter of 1941–1942 saw the Russian front fairly stabilized, with the Germans, despite some small Soviet victories, in possession of vast tracts of Russian territory. In the summer of 1942 the principal German effort was launched toward the Caucasus, where the first oil fields were taken in early August. Then, in order to cut vital supply routes, the Germans directed an attack on the industrial city of Stalingrad, on the Volga. The Russians defended the city bitterly, house by house, and soon launched a huge pincer movement against the invaders, as Hitler, once more contravening the advice of his generals, insisted that his forces remain in the city. The battle raged through the winter until February 2, 1943, when Field Marshal von Paulus surrendered his army—or what was left of it. The Russians took something over 100,000 Germans prisoner; five times that many had been killed. A southward move by Russian armies forced Hitler at last to retreat from the Caucasus and the Crimea, but he mustered sufficient German strength to launch yet a third offensive in the summer of 1943. The Germans recaptured Kharkov, which the Red Army had won back after Stalingrad, and drove toward Kursk. But the Soviet armies quickly stopped the offensive and, drawing on the strength made available by Russian industrial recovery and by massive aid from the United States, began to pursue the retreating Germans in a drive that would stop only in Berlin.

The African theater revealed a similar see-saw in the fortunes of battle. Rommel had indeed reversed the successful British pursuit of the Italians in 1941, but a British winter offensive relieved the garrison at Tobruk and pressed on to Benghazi. In May 1942 Rommel returned to the attack, this time seizing Tobruk and pursuing the British deep into Egypt, where they made their stand at El Alamein, some sixty miles from Alexandria. Beginning in late October, the British Eighth Army, headed by General Sir Bernard Montgomery, with General Sir Harold Alexander in the supreme command in Cairo, began an attempt to break the German lines. This they accomplished on November 1–2 in a battle that the British were to see as the turning point of the war, as the Russians (with as much or more justice) viewed Stalingrad. A week later a joint Anglo-American landing took place in Morocco and Algeria in northwestern Africa; the two offensives met in Tunis in May 1943. Rommel had tried one last desperate move to defeat his enemies on both sides, but he failed and was invalided home. Though his African campaigns ended in failure, Rommel remains one of the most fascinating figures of the war; he gained immense respect from the succession of remarkable British commanders who opposed him. He displayed his talents once more in defending a German Europe from invasion, but ultimately he came to question Hitler's orders and to oppose him. When the plot to assassinate Hitler failed (see p. 1086) Rommel was one of many officers who knew of it and died in consequence; he shot himself on the *Führer's* command. If nazism did not by its very nature exclude the possibility, Rommel would be the one figure on the Axis side who might claim the status of tragedy.

From their African victories, the Allies turned to invade Sicily in July 1943; on July 25 Mussolini was forced to resign, to be succeeded by Marshal Pietro Badoglio, who negotiated an armistice with the Allies in early September. But Hitler would permit no such easy victories. As he had ordered the whole of France occupied in November 1942, now in September 1943 his forces moved into Italy. The next month the Allies crossed to the mainland and seized Naples but were stopped at a line below the famous abbey of Monte Cassino south of Rome, a stalemate that a costly amphibious landing at Anzio, behind that line, in January 1944 failed to break. In May the Allied advance began once again, and Rome and Florence were taken during the summer. Thereupon the Italian front was stabilized, and the principal action moved elsewhere.

For months southern England had been made into a staging area, not only for the British army but for a million and a half Americans and all their equipment and supplies. Churchill had pleaded a shortage of amphibious landing craft in explaining to Stalin the delays in opening the second front, but now there were four thousand of them, more than a thousand naval vessels, and 7,500 aircraft for direct support of the invasion, as well as 3,500 bombers. On June 6, 1944, "D-day," the invasion of Normandy began. Two hundred thousand men stormed the heavily defended shore on the first day; ten days later more than three times that many were in France; within two months two million fighting men had landed. On August 15, the Allies mounted another amphibious operation on the Mediterranean coast of France. In early September Belgium was liberated; shortly after, Allied forces crossed the frontier into Germany. German defenses were strong, however, and the battle slowed; in December the Germans counterattacked in Luxembourg in the so-called Battle of the Bulge, a surprise that the Americans were finally able to repulse. It was the Nazis' last gesture. The early months of 1945 saw a steady advance on Germany from American, British, and French forces on the west and from Russian forces in the east. Because the Russian advance had swept Bulgaria, Rumania, Yugoslavia, Hungary, and Poland into the Soviet orbit, Churchill was eager to beat the Russians to Berlin, but Eisenhower refused, without direct orders that never came, to pursue what he saw as a political rather than a military objective. Stalin suspected a feint, but American troops were stopped at the Elbe, and in mid-April a million and a half Russian troops began to move on Berlin.

The liberation of Europe gradually revealed the deepening horror that the Nazi "New Order" had imposed on the Continent. German leaders had been open enough about their intentions from the outset, though the goals were consistent neither in their enunciation nor in their fulfillment. The conquered territories were to be plundered and colonized with racially pure and aggressive Germans, while the inferior native inhabitants were shunted farther east and barely kept alive, to become German slave labor or to be exterminated. With somewhat less completeness the Nazis applied the same techniques to the subject nations in western Europe: Holland, Belgium, and even France supplied their quotas of forced labor, and Hitler himself intervened to quash a plan that Speer had worked out with Vichy's minister of production for a coordinated economy in which France would remain autonomous. It is estimated that two million of the five million Soviet prisoners taken by the Germans died in captivity, while another million remain unaccounted for; and maltreatment brought death in similar proportions to the hordes of laborers rounded up and used for manning German factories and building the defenses against invasion in France.

Nazi racialism reached a kind of absurd obscenity in German efforts to separate those people in a subject population who, because of their "Nordic appearance" were deemed worthy of Germanization. But there was no inconsistency or arbitrariness in the treatment meted out to Jews. A "final solution" was put into ruthless execution: none were to be left. Jews and other victims were being gassed in 1941, and the pace mounted until at Auschwitz toward the end of the war twelve thousand persons per day could be disposed of in efficient gas chambers and crematoria. The exact toll of the concentration camps will never be known; at least six million Jews must have died in one way or another, in or out of the camps. Hitler ordered the camps destroyed as the end of the war neared, but the Allied advance was too swift, and the truth was borne in on the world. Reports or rumors of genocide had often been dismissed as atrocity stories like those churned out by the propaganda machines in World War I. The Germans may not have been Huns in 1914-1918; they were worse than Huns in 1941-1945.

The terror of Nazi rule provoked occasional uprisings. The most remarkable was that in Warsaw in 1944, on orders from the provisional government of Poland, which had sprung into existence as the Germans retreated. The rising lasted from the beginning of August to the beginning of October, but in the end the Germans prevailed in almost their last military success. The aid the Poles needed to win came too uncertainly from the West—the airlifting of supplies was about all that was possible—while the Russian forces on the outskirts of the city were unable, or possibly unwilling, to help; Polish casualties amounted to at least two hundred thousand. Paris rose on August 17 as Allied armies approached; its citizens fought the Germans on the streets. Hitler, outraged, ordered the city destroyed, orders the German military governor refused to obey. Despite some Allied reluctance, a French division under the Gaullist general Jacques Leclerc was sent ahead to take the city, where de Gaulle arrived on August 25, 1944.

But sporadic risings were less important than the more diffused and steadily growing accomplishment of the resistance movements that sprang up in every occupied country. The Resistance had materialized almost at once in

Yugoslavia, where the mountainous terrain permitted concealment, but a split developed early between the Chetniks of General Draža Mihajlović, a Serbian monarchist, and the partisans headed by the secretary of the Yugoslav Communist party, Josip Broz, who called himself Tito. By 1943 it was apparent that Tito's forces were the more effective and dependable, and the Allies threw their weight behind them. In Greece a similar split led to civil war in 1944, ending in the victory of the monarchists, with British backing. Such splits were often likely to occur as the Resistance spread from country to country, for men swept up in an initially patriotic enterprise also brought with them a determination that the old society they had known—which could readily be blamed for its collapse in the face of the Nazi menace—must be renovated from top to bottom. Thus the Resistance was as much a source of division as of unity. But far more important were the positive contributions of the Resistance to the undercutting of German rule and to the maintenance of will to oppose the Nazis and hope that one day the nightmare would be over. The hiding of victims of Nazi persecution or of secret agents, sabotage, and assassination were the most dramatic manifestations; fugitive but steadily growing clandestine publications and secret radio transmitters were as valuable and as dangerous.[8] The Resistance attracted those who had been misfits in ordinary life and who could find excitement and justification in the subterranean battle; it also attracted men who had been famous and well-off, even gentle and retiring, who fought for their beliefs and for humanity against inhumanity. In both extremes as well as among more ordinary citizens there was heroism and a willingness to court danger and even martyrdom—which came, for example, to the great French medievalist Marc Bloch. The boon to the Allies was immense. It is said that, at their height, Yugoslav partisans tied down fifteen German divisions; Eisenhower maintained that the French Resistance shortened the Allied campaign after D-day by two months.

There was opposition within the homelands of the Axis as well. In Italy, once Russia entered the war, the Resistance was at first the province of the Communists, though they were joined by recruits from the Christian Democratic party, the heirs to the Popular party of the World War I era (see p. 991), which was revived in 1942. After the Allies invaded Italy and Mussolini was overthrown in 1943, the Resistance became more widespread. From 1944 it was surprisingly unified, the Communists having decided to cooperate with Badoglio's government and to leave the future of the monarchy a question to be decided after the war. A daring rescue by German soldiers in August 1943 freed Mussolini from captivity, and he was installed as the puppet head of a German-dominated government in the occupied territory of northern Italy. Mussolini sought scapegoats (even among the Germans) for his downfall and had executed as many of his former associates as he could reach, including his son-in-law and former foreign minister Galeazzo Ciano, who was shot in the

---

[8] Particular mention should be made of the importance in occupied Europe of the sober, factual, and credible broadcasts of the BBC.

back as a traitor. In April 1945, as the Allied advance proceeded, Mussolini attempted to escape to Switzerland with his mistress; they were recognized by partisans, taken, and shot. Their mutilated bodies were hanged upside down in a public square in Milan, the city where Mussolini had begun his political career thirty-odd years before.

Resistance was harder in Germany than anywhere else—and rarer. It took hold among a few idealists, students or devout Christians like the theologian Dietrich Bonhoeffer, shot by the Nazis in 1944. A Communist cell, the Rote Kapelle, which dated from before the war, was uncovered and exterminated in 1942, as was a student group known as the White Rose the next year. But the most remarkable of German resistance movements was to be found among conservative officers, whose sense of honor and professional integrity were outraged by Hitler and what he stood for. Attempts on Hitler's life were planned and then abandoned for lack of opportunity. But on July 20, 1944, Colonel Claus von Stauffenberg planted a bomb in Hitler's headquarters; it went off, as a previous bomb had not, but Hitler was only slightly wounded. Stauffenberg, having heard the explosion, flew to Berlin and proclaimed Hitler's death. Retribution on the conspirators and the much wider circles that had knowledge of the plot was swift: some five thousand were executed, including more than fifty general staff officers and men of the stature of Rommel and Admiral Wilhelm Canaris. Always small and ill-supported from abroad, the German Resistance posed no danger for the rest of the war.

On April 30, 1945, Hitler committed suicide, as did his mistress Eva Braun, to whom he had been married only a few hours before. According to Hitler's testament, power in the state was turned over to Grand Admiral Karl Doenitz; by Hitler's orders, his body and his wife's were burned in the underground bunker of the Chancellery, as the Russians approached the city.

The official end to the war in Europe was declared to be May 8, 1945. After a long, brilliant, predominantly American campaign across the Pacific, the war with Japan abruptly ended after two atomic bombs were dropped, one on Hiroshima on August 6, the second on Nagasaki on August 9. On August 8, true to his promise at Yalta, Stalin had brought the Soviet Union into the war. On August 10, the Japanese government sued for peace, and the formal surrender took place aboard the U.S.S. *Missouri* on September 2.

A NEW EUROPE IN A NEW SETTING

World War II took more lives and wrought more destruction than any conflict or man-made calamity in the past. Figures are highly speculative, but the fact that in an age of statistics allowable error may be reckoned in millions or tens of millions of dead is itself a challenge to the imagination. In Russia alone as many as twenty million may have died, more than all the dead in World War I and more than all the dead in the rest of Europe in World War II. Poland, it is said, lost 15 percent of its population—nearly six million in all, about half of them Jews. Four and a half million Germans died and a million and a half Yugoslavs, two thirds of them in the Resistance. The toll was somewhat more than half a million in France, somewhat less in Rumania and Hungary, in Italy and Britain. To the total dead of perhaps thirty million must be added millions of refugees, who had been deported by the Nazis or who fled or were forced to emigrate in the months immediately after the end of the war—crammed into ruined cities or huddled together in makeshift camps. The plight of the refugees reached a special intensity for those who had somehow escaped the assembly-line murder of the Nazi New Order and who faced their liberation without family, country, or property, sometimes without even a sense of identity, having known horrors that would long recur in dreams.

The human and material devastation was worst in eastern Europe, where for sheer magnitude of suffering Russia stood as a case apart. Of the major western nations, however, only Germany suffered greater losses than in World War I. Everywhere else in the West losses were visited far more on civilians than on soldiers—a marked change from the situation thirty years earlier—and material destruction was nearly everywhere, not merely at the front, on a scale few could have imagined before 1939. Yet, however grim the losses, however evident the wreckage, however shocking the barbarity, the impact of World War II on European awareness was far less shattering than World War I. To some extent this paradox can be explained by the simple fact that it was a *second* war and one long expected and feared: few illusions remained to be broken, while some initial fears proved groundless. Moreover, losses among the elites of the European nations were lower than in 1914–1918, and it is elites who ordinarily define and transmit the awareness of a war that later generations sense. It is true, too, at least for the victors, that the second war retained throughout a clearly discernible, not a merely rhetorical, moral purpose; they perceived the enemy as evil, and in the end the evil proved not only true but far worse than had been thought. The European conscience has long wrestled with the idea of just war; in this instance the idea was fully applicable.

More than in World War I men came to fight for a historic sense of distinctive nationality and for a genuine impulse to human decency. It seemed, moreover, that, with new political machinery and sufficient will, these ideals (often engendered in the Resistance) could be realized in a postwar world. In that sense the totality of the war was an advantage: men shared risks as well as resources, creating community rather than destroying it. After 1919 European politics had been at the mercy of revolution or eroded by disillusion and bitterness; after 1945 Europe saw a true politics of reconstruction. This was helped by the fact that, in contrast to 1919, the United States did not turn its back on Europe, and its vast resources were brought to bear through the Marshall Plan (see p. 1094). Significantly, the European birth rate soared. Though Europeans were poor, war-weary, and daunted by the magnitude of the tasks they faced, they seemed to glimpse the promise of life as their fathers had been unable to do.

Reconstruction in Western Europe

In countries that Germany had defeated and occupied, scores were settled in the days immediately following liberation. We have already seen the ugly end to which Mussolini came. In France Laval and Petain were sentenced to death, though de Gaulle commuted the old marshal's sentence to life imprisonment. For nearly a year after November 1945, in Nuremberg, a court of nine judges drawn from the Allied countries, sat in judgment on the major German war criminals. A few were acquitted (von Papen was one), some (Speer among them) were given long prison terms, and twelve were sentenced to death, though Göring committed suicide before the sentence could be carried out. Goebbels had already died, a suicide, with his master in the bunker in Berlin, and Himmler had killed himself shortly after. In all the belligerent countries on the Continent thousands of others, less eminent, suffered for collaboration or, in some instances, for enmities made in a fragmented Resistance. Nearly everywhere the period of retribution was short; only in Germany did recrimination drag on—in "denazification" proceedings conducted by the occupying forces, an inevitably bureaucratic process that depended on endless questionnaires and that was eventually abandoned as an unworkable, or at any rate unconvincing, exercise.

As the British war effort had been more fully integrated and consistent than that of any other nation, so reconstruction in Britain was pursued more systematically than elsewhere. There was widespread agreement in all segments of the political spectrum that fundamental reforms could not be delayed. Planning had begun early in the war—its most famous instance being Sir William Beveridge's report on full employment and social services—and an act of 1944 overhauled the entire state educational system, at last providing secondary education for all to the age of fifteen. Sensing opportunity in the mood of the country, the Labour party withdrew from the coalition government, and July 5, 1945 saw the first general election in ten years. The result was a Labour sweep, with a majority over all the other parties of nearly 150. Admiration for Churchill as a war leader did not carry over to Churchill—or his party—as the instrument for rebuilding society. The new prime minister was Clement Attlee, leader of the Labour party since 1934 and deputy prime minister during the war. A quiet, seemingly unassertive man, he proved to have strength, authority, and great political skill—all of which he needed to preside over his colorful and aggressive cabinet. Three of the ministers, perhaps, stand out above the rest: Ernest Bevin, long the head of the transport workers' union and a superb wartime minister of labor, became foreign secretary; Aneurin Bevan, a combative Welsh miner and Churchill's most vocal critic during the war, took the crucial post of minister of health; and Sir Stafford Cripps, a brilliant, highly placed lawyer, a passionate socialist, and a devout Christian who—first at the Board of Trade and after 1947 at the Exchequer—ruled the British economy.

With the tightest parliamentary discipline, the new government carried through the social security proposals foreseen in the Beveridge Report, established a national health service with nationalized hospitals and doctors salaried by the state, and legislated the most effective control over land use, in both town and country, of any European nation. The commitment to state ownership of basic industries—Labour party policy since 1918—was redeemed by nationalization of the mines, most public utilities, the railways and other modes of transport, including long-distance trucking, and, in 1949, steel. The government kept prices down, encouraged or forced exports, carefully channeled investment, and met the immense costs of social services and the rebuilding of industry through high taxes. Priorities were enforced by stringent controls on everyday life, in a regime of austerity little different from wartime. The remarkable display of civic discipline proved the strength of the nineteenth-century tradition of orderliness and respect, voluntarily accepted, that had made Britain unique in Europe. There was virtually no black market and remarkably little grumbling.

In 1950, after five years of the most intense legislative activity, a general election left Labour with a scarcely workable majority of six. The next year the Conservatives under Churchill returned to office. There were changes. Austerity, only slightly softened in the last years of Labour rule, had disappeared by 1954: thanks in good part to Marshall aid (see p. 1094) the country could begin to enjoy prosperity; though that prosperity was insecurely based, it was convincing enough for the electorate to keep the Tories in power for thirteen years. The Conservatives abandoned direct economic controls in favor of indirect controls, of which the money supply was the most important. Because the economy was not strong and because imports and capital investment increased sharply in response to demand, inflation became a problem and the country fell into periodic crises, made worse by skittishness on the part of foreign speculators who transferred huge sums into and out of the country as the stability of the pound seemed to dictate. The government, alternately putting on the brakes and encouraging economic expansion, made rational planning by businessmen difficult; its resort to short-run solutions for long-term problems supported the charge that Conservative policy was no more than improvisation. But the Conservatives scarcely touched the welfare state Labour had created. The Tories undid the nationalization of steel—the most controversial of socialist measures, which the Labour government had been able to carry only by further restricting the suspensive veto of the House of Lords—although Labour renationalized the industry shortly after returning to office in 1964. The Conservatives also partially denationalized trucking and set up a commercial television service to compete with the BBC. Even Labour began to have second thoughts about socialism, strictly defined, and the willingness of Hugh Gaitskell, Attlee's successor as leader, to abandon nationalization as a general panacea induced intense intraparty debates and a degree of political paralysis that helped the Tories to remain in office.

Belgium, Holland, and the Scandinavian countries also managed to keep firm control over long pent-up demand and to relieve, slowly, the terrible shortages of goods. But in France and Italy attempts to check the black market and inflation were virtually total failures. Rising prices, unemployment, and glaring contrasts between rich and poor strengthened the emotional appeal of the Left, already charged by passions unleashed during the war. But not even in France and Italy (let alone elsewhere in western Europe) did the Communist parties come close to taking power, and they were soon denied even a share in it everywhere. The Socialists formed major parliamentary blocs in France and Italy, but they could not make common cause with the Communists and, as is far too evident in the history of political socialism, were likely to quarrel and splinter and lose much of their potential effectiveness. Over most of western Europe, except for Scandinavia and for a time Britain, the dominant politics of the postwar era were those of the Center and the Center-Right.

Italy needed a new constitution. Though it retained the allegiance of a small percentage of voters, fascism was swept away. So was the monarchy, in 1946. Victor Emmanuel III had abdicated, hoping to save the throne for his son Humbert II, but a referendum made Italy a republic, with an honorific president chosen by the two houses of the legislature, an elected senate, and a truly independent judiciary; the substance of Mussolini's concordat with the papacy in 1929 was confirmed and agreed to even by the Communists, then on their best behavior. Italian parliamentarianism, still an amalgam of numerous parties and shifting coalitions, was dominated by the relatively conservative Christian Democrats, who were never stronger than under the leadership of Alcide De Gasperi between 1945 and 1953. De Gasperi's anti-Fascist credentials were impeccable. He had been imprisoned briefly in the late twenties; then in 1943, from his refuge as a librarian in the Vatican, he quietly began to re-establish the Catholic *popolari* (see p. 991), cooperating closely with the Resistance. He stood to the left of most of his party and forced on them the lesson that all Italy was soon to learn: that priority must be given to economic and social problems, not to the pursuit of sham prestige and inefficient authoritarianism that had characterized the Fascist era. The government enacted social security measures, undertook genuine land reform, and even made progress in the backward south, though the rapid spread of prosperity in the industrial north widened the gap between the two regions still more.

In France General de Gaulle had been the beneficiary of the national upsurge in the Resistance and of the joyfulness of the liberation; for well over a year he ruled as head of a provisional government, made up of all parties, with the assistance of a nominated consultative assembly. De Gaulle was scrupulously correct in dealing with his political allies and in the preparations for launching a Fourth Republic; a constituent assembly was elected in October 1945. But he was never happy with the political process or with the weakness of the executive power on which most French parliamentarians insisted. Well before the new republic was formed, in January 1946, de Gaulle resigned in a dispute with Socialists over the military budget and retired to his country estate to bide his time. He was to wait for more than twelve years. In May 1946 the draft constitution, which embodied the old Radical ideal of a nearly omnipotent single chamber, was rejected in a popular vote. A revised constitution, finally adopted in October, provided a tamed upper house—the Council of the Republic—and a National Assembly in place of the old Chamber of Deputies. With such slight alterations, it was the Third Republic warmed over; if anything, the instability of governments was greater than ever. The Communists regularly got the largest vote, but cabinets were dominated by shifting combinations of Socialists and representatives of a new party that had risen suddenly from nowhere to immense electoral strength: the Popular Republican Movement (MRP), another Christian Democratic party with impressive Resistance credentials. Its chief figure was Georges Bidault. In France, as in Italy, the dominant party at the Center was aware that much needed doing to renovate the country. Already under de Gaulle construction of an extensive welfare state had begun; it was carried through in a sweeping system of social security, along with nationalization of coal, gas, and electricity.

German reconstruction was the most dramatic of all. Its cities wrecked, its people decimated, Germany was divided by the Allies into four zones of occupation—the British in the north and west, the Americans in the south, the French (in a concession to de Gaulle) in a small area in the southwest, the Russians in the east; a quadripartite division was repeated in the city of Berlin, which fell entirely within the Russian zone. In the realities of the occupation lay the origins, even the certainty, of the ultimate division of the country. The Russians, understandably enough, were merciless in their demands for reparation; having milked the part of Germany under their control, they proceeded to incorporate it into the Soviet bloc they were forming in eastern Europe and to impose a Communist government. In the west, as early as 1946 the British and the Americans agreed to a joint administration of their zones—the so-called Bizone—and in 1948 the French joined as well. The map of Germany was redrawn, not only by a westward shift of the eastern frontier to the benefit of Poland (which had lost lands to Russia in the east), but by reordering the internal geography of the country as well. Historic Prussia, that sprawling aggregation of territories, simply disappeared, and while some historic units (such as Bavaria) remained, the states that made up the part of Germany under Western control were largely administrative creations of roughly equal size.

Political parties were far stronger and more resilient in Germany than in France or Italy. The Social Democratic party was reborn as an aggressive and unified movement under a new leader, Kurt Schumacher, long a prisoner of the Nazis, who brought both reputation and passion to the cause. But, once again, the dominant party was a Center-Right combination, the Christian Democratic party, a revival of the old Center party of Bismarckian days. Its leader was Konrad Adenauer, already sixty-nine. He had made his political debut before 1914; he had been of some importance in the Weimar Republic, having been briefly considered in one change of governments as a possible chancellor, but he made his principal reputation as the progressive mayor of the Rhineland city of Cologne. While he had kept clear of the Nazis, he had also managed to avoid worse treatment than two prison terms. Chosen by the Americans immediately after the war as the politician with whom they could most effectively deal, Adenauer moved swiftly to establish his ascendancy. When the three western zones were joined in 1948, the new constitution of the Federal Republic of Germany was essentially that of Weimar with new safeguards—a purely honorific president with no emergency powers. In the elections in August 1949 the Christian Democrats narrowly won out over the Social Democrats, and Adenauer became chancellor. He remained in office until 1963. A superb debater, a clever politician, and a tough negotiator, he inspired confidence at home and abroad. At the same time he was dictatorial and often contemptuous of his associates, qualities that became more marked as he advanced in age.[9] But, more than any one man, Adenauer created the West Germany that exists today, and it was he, with General de Gaulle, who confirmed a course of Franco-German cooperation that (it is safe to say) no one could have imagined at any point in the past century.

The Economic Base

Journalists writing about the postwar economics of Europe have been addicted to the word miracle. Despite all the qualifications that must be made—the persistence of poverty, unevenness of development, currency crises, mild cyclical downturns—it is hard not to grant the term validity. A couple of tables will give the miracle substance:

Gross Domestic Product, 1948–1963	
Compound Annual Rates of Growth (%)	
Austria	5.8
Belgium	3.2
Denmark	3.6
France	4.6
Germany	7.6
Italy	6.0
Netherlands	4.7
Norway	3.5
Sweden	3.4
Switzerland	5.1
United Kingdom	2.5

[9] In his admirable appreciation, "The Statecraft of Konrad Adenauer" (in *From Bismarck to Adenauer: Aspects of German Statecraft* [1965], 95–117), Gordon A. Craig notes a probably apocryphal story about a member of a delegation from the lower house, the Bundestag, who told the Chancellor, "*Herr Bundeskanzler,* we have not come here just to say 'Amen' and 'Ja' to everything you propose." Adenauer answered: "Gentlemen, 'Amen' is not necessary—'Ja' will do fine."

Rates of Growth of Productivity

Rates of Growth of Output,
Per Head of Population (%)

	1870–1913	1948–1962
Belgium	1.8	2.2
Denmark	2.1	2.8
France	1.4	3.4
Germany	1.8	6.8
Italy	0.7	5.6
Norway	1.4	2.9
Sweden	2.3	2.6
United Kingdom	1.3	2.4

SOURCE: Adapted from M. M. Postan, *An Eco-nomic History of Western Europe, 1945-1964* (1967), 12, 17. Domestic product differs from the more commonly cited Gross National Product in that it excludes income from and payments to other countries.

And since the mid-sixties the pace has been maintained.

Some of the sources of this remarkable accomplishment lay in the prewar era—in certain technologies developed then (the first synthetic fibers, for example) that came into their own only after the war; in the increasing boldness and sophistication of economic thinking, notably under the influence of J. M. Keynes (see p. 1028); and in the very experience of the depression, which had shattered so many of the old economic verities. Some sources are to be found in the war itself—in the forced growth, despite extensive destruction, of certain sectors of national economies; in the total mobilization of resources; in the complex interplay of intellectual and managerial enterprise that flowered in wartime operations research and that maintained its impetus on a broader scale in the field we now know as research and development. The creation, following the Bretton Woods Conference in 1944, of the International Bank for Recon-struction and Development (better known as the World Bank) and the International Monetary Fund provided a means for channeling resources from richer countries to poorer ones and for maintaining some kind of equilibrium on the international monetary front. Although the monetary system has taken some hard knocks in recent years, the very determination to seek international solutions for the problems of a world economy was and remains salutary.

All this suggests sharp alterations in patterns of thought compared with those of 1919, when the dominant longing was to get back to the prewar world: not many people in 1945, even among the rich, could have wanted their prewar world restored in its completeness. There is no better—indeed finer—example of this new temper than the role played by the United States, which had emerged from the war richer than ever and with a military strength and political power far beyond what it could claim in 1939. To be sure, the first American actions, once the war ended, were not encouraging: immediately after the victory over Japan, the Truman administration abruptly terminated lend-lease. This proved a particular blow to the British, who now were required to pay even for goods that were, as the phrase had it, in the pipeline—ordered, that is, but not yet delivered. The United States offered Britain a loan, though grudgingly and on far less generous terms than Britain asked for and needed. Then the United States changed front. In an address at Harvard University in June 1947, General George C. Marshall, the distinguished wartime chief of staff who became secretary of state in January of that year, urged the European nations to decide on their needs and priorities so that the United States could provide assistance in a systematic way. The offer was made to all countries alike, but after some hesitation the countries of the Soviet bloc followed Russian orders and declined to take part. In April 1948 President Truman signed an act creating the Economic Cooperation Administration. The participating nations responded with the Organization for European Economic Cooperation (OEEC) to coordinate the aid program, encourage modernization of European industry, and improve international trade, and the European Payments Union (EPU) to facilitate financial settlements among its members. Over the next four years the United States sent abroad more than $22 billion, most of it in outright gifts; the recipients of the largest shares were Britain, France, and—chosen with an unusual mixture of altruism and calculation—Germany. Whatever the declared or ulterior purposes of the Marshall Plan, no objective observer can deny the large element of American generosity or the crucial lift the program gave to European economies. By the early fifties they were able largely to stand by themselves, as is indicated by an impressive rise in the volume of European exports.

Volume of Exports, 1890–1960

	Compound Annual Rates of Growth (%)		
	1890–1913	1913–1950	1950–1960
Belgium	3.5	0.2	7.7
France	2.8	1.1	7.2
Germany	5.1	-2.5	15.8
Italy	– –	1.4	11.8
Netherlands	4.6	1.2	10.0
Sweden	3.8[a]	1.9	5.5
Switzerland	– –	0.3	7.8[b]
United Kingdom	2.1	0.2	1.9
Western Europe	3.2	0.1	7.0

[a]1893–1913 [b]1950–1959

SOURCE: Adapted from David S. Landes, *The Unbound Prometheus: Technological Change and Industrial Development in Western Europe from 1750 to the Present* (1969), 512.

It is clear from the tables that the performance of European countries varied widely. So did the means of implementing goals on which they all agreed—encouragement of exports, promotion of growth, maintenance of employment. In Germany and Italy the ministers responsible for the economy prided themselves on their orthodox finance and their reliance on the mechanisms of the free market. France, on the other hand, led all the other western European nations in developing a comprehensive planning structure; this economic strategy remained rudimentary at best in Germany, and Britain did not adopt it—although its economy was closely supervised—until 1963. Britain and France gave high priority to social welfare, Germany less so. The British were far more innovative in education than any Continental country, though they continued to lag behind, as they had done in the nineteenth century, in advanced technical education. In these immensely complicated and contradictory patterns observers can find confirmation for almost any hypothesis ingenuity or dogma may suggest. [10] It seems likely, however, that psychological and social determinants are as significant in the outcome as economic factors. Certainly Britain's poor showing is grounded primarily on attitudes enshrined in its venerable and fragmented trade unionism, in managerial sluggishness (despite brilliant exceptions), and in a persistent and by now irrelevant hankering after past glories in the world of diplomacy.

In the long run, the most important economic current in the postwar world may prove to be its internationalism. The OEEC was intended to facilitate a lowering of tariffs and so provide all countries with access to a larger market. But in 1950 a far more radical international experiment was launched when the French foreign minister, Robert Schuman, proposed the establishment of a European Coal and Steel Community. Basic industries like coal and steel, it could be argued, lend themselves particularly well to integration and economies of scale. [11] But there was also a political motive: German heavy industry, the source of so much mischief in the past, would be merged into a large international combine with an administration—the High Authority—independent of the governments of the constituent states and, with its own income, literally sovereign in its own sphere. Bringing together France, Germany, Italy, Belgium, the Netherlands, and Luxembourg, the Community began operation in 1952 under the presidency of Jean Monnet, who had established the planning authority in France immediately after the war and who was the guiding spirit of a new breed of international civil servants dedicated to economic cooperation. To ease the transition, the Community made concessions to inefficient and

[10] In *The Unbound Prometheus,* chapter 7, David S. Landes provides an admirable sampling of economists' views on key issues in interpreting the postwar European economy.

[11] M. M. Postan, in *An Economic History of Western Europe,* 110, illustrates the latter by citing the increasing size of three generations of nylon-producing plants built by Imperial Chemical Industries. The plant built in the 1950s could produce seven to eight times the output of its predecessor but still only half as much as its successor. As the optimum size of an operation grows with changing technology, access to larger markets becomes indispensable. Thus the British chemical industry was in the forefront of supporters of British entry into the Common Market.

high-cost plants, but gradually rationalization of the industry was attained. By 1963 output had doubled over 1951, without a significant addition to the labor force, while prices in the Community (in contrast to other countries) remained relatively stable, beginning to rise only toward the end of the decade.

In March 1957 the six nations of the Community signed the Treaty of Rome; from the beginning of 1958 they were joined in the European Economic Community (EEC), better known as the Common Market: the integration of the Coal and Steel Community was to be extended to the economy as a whole. The existence of a large market unimpeded by tariff barriers, it was reasoned, would not only encourage economies of scale but stimulate innovation and increased efficiency through competition. The planners foresaw the elimination of all tariffs in twelve to fifteen years and steadily increasing freedom of movement for capital and labor—the last a matter of considerable importance, for Europe was witnessing extensive migration of labor from countries like Italy, where there was a surplus, to France and Germany, where the demand for labor could not be met. Exceptions could be made for underdeveloped areas like the south of Italy, for member countries experiencing temporary crises, and, most significant of all, for agriculture, which presented the greatest difficulties in arriving at common policies. But by 1968 the tariff walls had been demolished, and the general prosperity of the Common Market—despite unevennesses in specific national development—seems established.

Britain was offered membership in the Coal and Steel Community at its inception, but declined, fearful of what the sovereign power of the High Authority might mean. When the Common Market appeared sure of success, the British took the lead in organizing the European Free Trade Area (EFTA), a much looser customs grouping that, besides Britain, included Norway, Sweden, Denmark, Switzerland, Austria, and Portugal—the "Outer Seven" as opposed to the "Inner Six." There was a certain lack of conviction about EFTA, which became more evident when Britain applied to enter the Common Market in 1962, only to be rebuffed by General de Gaulle. He was mistrustful of the Anglo-Saxons and uneasy (as he and his advisers might properly be) about the uncertain state of the British economy; moreover, Britain had an entirely different system of agricultural price supports, while its long-standing ties of sentiment and material interest to the countries of the Commonwealth— particularly those great suppliers of meat and wool, Australia and New Zealand—posed serious difficulties. Ten years later, however, a new British application was successful, both in negotiations with the Common Market countries and in surmounting a growing hostility at home; the beginning of 1973 marked the expansion of the Common Market to include not only Britain but Ireland and Denmark as well. The move will require some drastic readjustments within Britain; whether the treatment will cure the many ills of the British economy is one of the most interesting questions to be answered in the decade of the seventies.

The Ebb and Flow of Empire

As Europe, tentatively and with much hesitation, submerged its traditional nationalism in a new internationalism, nationalism was striking root in those parts of the world that Europe had long dominated with little challenge. We have noted the early growth of a nationalist movement in India (see p. 1043) and more tentative steps in that direction in the Near East. But in most of Africa and Asia the interwar years had seen little restiveness. The effect of the war was electrifying. The European powers had simply committed their colonial possessions to the struggle without regard to local opinion. Some of their territories in Asia were occupied by the Japanese; there, and even more in Africa, European armies fought over the lands of subject peoples guided only by a Europe-oriented strategy. Even more corrosive was the spectacle of one imperial power after another going down to defeat. France, Belgium, and Holland collapsed almost at once; Britain was seriously threatened in Europe and could not hold its Asian colonies against Japanese aggression. Italy, that blustering and ineffective latecomer to the imperialist game, was simply destroyed as a colonial power. Only Portugal, a neutral in the war, survived into the new age with its holdings substantially intact; India seized Portugal's tiny enclaves in the subcontinent in 1961, but Angola and Mozambique are colonies still, paternally and uninventively ruled—poor, backward, and restless anachronisms.

Italy's African colonies, occupied by the Allies during the war, were turned over to the United Nations for disposition. In 1949 the UN decided that Libya should have its independence, which was attained two years later; and Eritrea was given to Ethiopia. While Somaliland was returned to Italy as a trust territory,[12] it became independent as Somalia in 1960. The Dutch, returning to their Indonesian possessions after the war, failed to negotiate a mutually satisfactory settlement with the nationalists, who had grown much stronger during the Japanese occupation. Intent on keeping their profitable colonies, the Dutch went to war for them, but in the end they had to abandon the struggle. In 1949 Indonesia became independent, to face a chaotic and bloody future. The same fate was in store for the vast Belgian holdings in the Congo. There the immediate postwar years brought little challenge to Belgian rule, but in 1959 rioting broke out, and the next year the Belgians decided to abandon their claims. The Belgian presence in the Congo had meant blood and tears (see p. 842); their absence meant the same, but from different causes: nationalism or tribalism could be as destructive as imperialism. Civil war set leader against leader, province against province, tribe against tribe. Withdrawal from empire seemed invariably to involve grim choices—military stalemate or internal chaos: the British and French confronted both in their vast colonial holdings.

---

[12] This is the new name devised for the mandates the Great Powers had held under the League of Nations.

Striking a balance of success and failure in the records of the two greatest imperial powers is therefore a difficult exercise.

On the whole, the British retreated from empire with better grace and less difficulty than the French. Even Churchill had been forced in 1942 to offer the Indians independence after the war, but the Indians rejected his terms, and it was not until the Labour party came into office, committed as it was to the dismantling of empire, that the matter was settled. The stumbling block to an easy transfer of power in India was the growth of separatism among the Muslims, an ambition for autonomy that could be satisfied only by partition. But that solution was unacceptable to the Hindus in the Congress party. When the British decided to leave, no matter what the consequences, the Congress party was forced to accept the partition they hated, and on August 15, 1947, two new nations, India and Pakistan, came into being. Despite the skill with which India's last viceroy, Lord Mountbatten, had prepared for the transition, communal war broke out between Hindus and Muslims. The slaughter was terrible, and in January 1948 Gandhi himself was assassinated by a Hindu fanatic, crazed by the statesman's willingness to see India divided. Tension between the two nations continued, but, despite their enmity, they continued as members of the British Commonwealth, whose definition was found to be sufficiently elastic to include not only nonwhite nations but republics, such as India became shortly after independence, followed by Pakistan in 1956. In time Pakistan fell victim to internal division and in 1971 a civil war led to the splitting off of East Pakistan as the new nation of Bangla Desh. Ceylon and Burma achieved independence in 1948 without internal strife; the former chose to stay in the Commonwealth and the latter departed into neutralism.

The British found relatively little difficulty in granting independence to Ghana (the former Gold Coast) in 1957 or to Nigeria in 1960 or in time to other, smaller colonies in West Africa; almost entirely black in population and leadership, these colonies had developed nationalist movements that could take over the efficient structures of British administration with considerable ease. Yet the strains of independence showed: Ghana was exposed to the corruption of one-man rule by the charismatic Kwame Nkrumah, Nigeria soon suffered from the endemic tribal rivalries among its three sections, and almost all the new nations ended in some form of military dictatorship. In east, central, and south Africa, however, the presence of whites made decolonization more difficult. Kenya contained a large number of white settlers, determined to stay. That determination impelled the British to support them against the terroristic activity of the secret society of the Mau Mau in the years between 1952 and 1956, and Kenyan independence was attained only in 1963. Southern Rhodesia had another large complement of white settlers, who shared the white supremacist views that were increasing in strength among the dominant Boer population in the Union of South Africa. An attempt to federate Northern and Southern Rhodesia and Nyasaland failed, and the two black nations of Northern Rhodesia and Nyasaland withdrew to face an uncertain economic future under the names of Zambia and Malawi, while Southern Rhodesia, more and more at odds with British governments, finally chose to declare its independence in 1967 and maintain the old dominance of whites over blacks by manipulation of the suffrage, by intimidation, and by force. On a tour of South Africa in 1960, Harold Macmillan, British prime minister from 1957 to 1963, had dared to speak frankly about "winds of change," but his plea did not impress the Boers, committed as they were to a stringent policy of separation of the races—*apartheid*. In 1961 South Africa chose to leave the Commonwealth to become a republic and a scarcely concealed police state. The South Africans' racial policies and their suppression of dissent almost justify the Boer War in retrospect.

Even the more successful instances of British withdrawal were likely to produce awkwardnesses. Colonial administrations and governments in London, concerned to protect their handiwork and to assure an orderly transfer, wanted to move far more slowly than seemed proper, or even conscionable, to colonial nationalists. In the end the British usually had to give in, and often it happened that native leaders moved directly from jail to the seat of government. But the British sometimes faced challenges from sources other than a powerful and impatient nationalism. In Malaya, where Chinese formed a significant part of the population, a Communist guerrilla movement, supported from Communist China, had to be put down before it seemed safe to confer independence. That meant a long, difficult jungle war, successfully concluded only in 1957, when Malaysia entered the Commonwealth. Elsewhere, conflicts between hostile groups of native populations induced the home government to delay the granting of independence in the hope that reconciliation might be effected. Thus in Cyprus the British served as a buffer between Greek and Turkish patriots; each group wanted union with its respective homeland, and Greek terrorism—against the British as well as Turks—became a commonplace. For four years, from 1956 to 1960, the island was under military rule, but statesmanship at last prevailed and yet another new nation joined the Commonwealth.

By all odds the most fateful British problem lay in Palestine, a British mandate since the end of World War I. Here Britain had to balance its moral commitment to support a national home for the Jews against a long-standing involvement (and fascination) with the Arabs, a tie reinforced by the crucial need for oil and by the general military and diplomatic importance of the Near East. The Arabs feared the growth of the Jewish population, and in 1939, with wartime necessities in view, the British put a strict limit on Jewish immigration. In the aftermath of the war, as a result of the Nazis' slaughter of the Jews, the Zionist ideal became irresistible to hundreds of thousands of Jews displaced from their homelands and to others who found it impossible to live in a Europe stained with such terrible memories. The pressure on the British—from their contradictory obligations to humanity and the imperatives of diplomacy as well as from their American allies—became unbearable. Beset by Jewish terrorists in the postwar years as they had been by Arab terrorists in the late thirties, the British simply announced in May 1948 that they would withdraw, turning the problem over to the United Nations. The UN decided to partition Palestine, carving out the new Jewish state of Israel and leaving the remainder of the country to be absorbed by Jordan. Again there was war: Israel was born in military triumph.

In the mid-fifties an objective observer would have declared Egypt to be one of the successes of British policy. Nominally independent since 1922, Egypt had been dealt with during the war pretty much as British strategy dictated. In 1952, when a revolution under General Mohammed Neguib drove King Farouk from the throne, the British took the change in their stride; two years later they agreed to pull out the troops they had long maintained in the Suez Canal zone. But this retreat removed a buffer between Israel and Egypt, and Egypt under Colonel Gamal Abdel Nasser, who had supplanted Neguib, was assuming the leadership of an Arab world whose chief enemy was the new Jewish state. Moreover, Nasser began to play a game common among the emerging nations in the era of the Cold War (see p. 1103)—bidding for financial support from the competing world powers, in this case for funds to build a great dam at Aswan on the Nile. A joint Anglo-American venture seemed likely when suddenly John Foster Dulles, the American secretary of state, notified Nasser that the United States would not take part. Nasser's outraged reaction was to seize the Suez Canal on July 26, 1956.[13] Although, rather to the surprise of everyone in the West, the Egyptians proved perfectly capable of operating the canal efficiently, French and British opinion alike was deeply offended by Nasser's high-handed action. In deep secrecy, the leaders of the two nations, Guy Mollet and Anthony Eden, concerted action with Israel, which was planning a pre-emptive strike against Egypt. The Israeli invasion began at the end of October and quickly proved victorious. The British and French, with singular ineffi-ciency, launched their invasion of Egypt from the Mediterranean in early November. The outspoken objections of the United States, Soviet threats, and indignation around the world brought a quick withdrawal of the joint forces and the issuance of a face-saving communiqué to the effect that the invasion's purpose was accomplished. The damage to the prestige of both imperial powers was immense. Despite wide but far from unanimous support for the venture at home, the Suez fiasco deprived Britain and France of whatever moral authority they had left in the Near East. For Britain it was the last gasp of the imperial spirit.

Eden's role is hard to assess. A brilliant diplomat with an admirable record of recognizing and resisting the Nazi threat, he was in this instance imprisoned by his memory of Munich. Surely he was right in his conviction that one must

---

[13] Egypt ultimately built the dam with Soviet help. But gratitude is short, and in 1972 Nasser's successor, Anwar Sadat, expelled most of the Russians stationed in Egypt. For the earlier history of the canal, see pp. 771 and 844.

"stand up to dictators," but Nasser was not Hitler. Moreover, Eden acted in secrecy and without consulting his professional advisers, making plain the power that inheres in the office of a modern prime minister, even in the best-functioning parliamentary democracy. Shortly after the Suez episode Eden resigned. He was succeeded by Harold Macmillan, who, though he had been involved in Suez, rebuilt his party's shattered morale and moved from one triumph to another—but in domestic politics. The demolition of empire went on with quickened pace; in 1966, with striking appropriateness, the Colonial Office, created in 1794 to govern Britain's overseas possessions, was abolished.

The French were to have an even more difficult time of it. Like the British, they had relatively little trouble in freeing the black-dominated territories of Equatorial Africa; Tunis and Morocco proved more awkward, but the problems were resolved between 1954 and 1956, although in Morocco there was bloodshed. In two parts of their empire, however, the French fought long and bitter wars, with singular consequences not only for the empire but for France itself. In Indochina, Cambodia and Laos presented no serious obstacles to decolonization, but Vietnam, the eastern region of the peninsula, proved far more intractable. Chinese pressure from the north competed with a native nationalism led by Ho Chi Minh, himself a Communist but one inclined to act independently of both Moscow and Peking. The French were disposed to reach an agreement with Ho, but in 1946 a local French military commander ordered bombardment of the port of Haiphong, starting a conflict in which the French became mired more and more deeply. For seven years the war dragged on. It was fiercely unpopular in France, for it was costly in human wastage and drained the resources of an economy that could ill spare them. By supporting Ho Chi Minh's conservative opponents, the French drove Ho into the arms of the great Communist powers; the United States, viewing this colonial struggle from the vantage point of the Cold War, urged continued French resistance. But in May 1954 the French army suffered a decisive defeat at Dien Bien Phu. In France, the disaster brought a bold and inspiring leader into office as premier, the independent Radical Pierre Mendès-France. Mendès-France had long insisted that the war must be brought to an end, and in July 1954 a conference at Geneva determined on a partition of Vietnam, with Ho Chi Minh established in the north and the former emperor Bao Dai as head of state in the south. Vietnam was not to disappear from European, or even more from American, awareness, but the French at least had been cut free from an impossible tangle.

A badly shaken Fourth Republic was at once plunged into a worse tragedy in Algeria. The country presented special problems: the oldest of the major French colonies, Algeria contained about a million white settlers. Though only half of them were French in origin and though most of them had spent their entire lives in Algeria, they were passionately patriotic. In 1954, encouraged by the imminence of a settlement in Tunis and Morocco, Algerian nationalists rebelled. The French, just freed in Indochina, determined to suppress the rising—a decision, it must be said, in which Mendès-France played a major part: Algeria was to remain "forever French." The resulting war, far worse than that in East Asia, involved the French people more directly. Conscripts were sent to fight in Africa, a step the government had not dared to take for Vietnam; emotions were deeply engaged; and sensational revelations were published about the torture and bestiality practiced by fighting men on both sides of the conflict. In time terrorism became endemic in France itself. As with Indochina, a savior proved necessary; he was, once again, General de Gaulle, called back from retirement in 1958 not only to solve the Algerian crisis but—as a condition of his accepting the call—to bring the Fourth Republic to an end. A new and hastily drafted constitution, overwhelmingly endorsed in a referendum, created the Fifth Republic. The most striking innovation was the strengthening of the presidency, an institutional change de Gaulle had wanted in 1945 and had not been able to extract. As he worked it, the presidency was more like a monarchy: de Gaulle ruled above the political battle, and his cabinet was dominated by experts rather than politicians.

On Algeria de Gaulle played a waiting game, marked by skillful and devious maneuvering compelled by the fierce resistance to decolonization on the part of French colonials and the French army. Not until 1962 could de Gaulle bring the Algerian tragedy to an end, and then he did so on the rebels' terms. The Europeans in Algeria felt betrayed—it was, after all, among the believers in *Algérie française* that de Gaulle's return to power had first been agitated—and so did their many sympathizers in France. But by 1962 the nation was weary of war, and de Gaulle had created an aggressive and disciplined party supporting his intrinsically authoritarian rule. Entrenched in power, de Gaulle could set about his long-postponed mission of regenerating France and securing its proper place in the world, an effort that coincided with a marked upsurge in the French economy. Working with Adenauer, de Gaulle cemented the Franco-German friendship; working against Britain[14] and the United States, de Gaulle enforced his intention to keep France to some degree independent of the great power blocs of the Cold War, an intention borne out by the vast and expensive French effort to develop an independent nuclear striking force—the *force de frappe.* Sometimes inspiring, often crotchety, always confident, grand in gesture, and memorable in style, de Gaulle towered over the Europe of the sixties, the last of the generation of great war leaders. Then, in May 1968, a surge of domestic discontent, sparked by student rioting, brought a stern lecture from de Gaulle to his rebellious countrymen. He ordered new elections. Although a year before he had won re-election only in a runoff, he now swept all before him. But he had more in mind. He demanded a further referendum on a plan for decentralizing French administration. In April 1969 the proposals

---

[14] Notably in his veto of Britain's entry into the Common Market in 1963 (see p. 1096). De Gaulle's delight in cocking a snook at the Anglo-Saxons led him on a visit to the French Canadian province of Quebec in 1967 to endorse the separatism advocated by a small group of radicals. His cry of *"Vive le Québec libre"* was infuriating to Canadians. But if de Gaulle made a blunder, it was done grandly; he never recanted.

lost by a narrow margin. Decisively but not petulantly, de Gaulle retired to the country; his prime minister, Georges Pompidou, succeeded the general in the presidency, and France remained Gaullist even without de Gaulle. In 1970 he died. Without his gigantic presence, France has followed a less independent or idiosyncratic course in a world that will not allow much glory to any man or nation.

The Cold War

As the traditional imperial powers retreated from empire, two new empires emerged. The advance of Soviet troops in the last year of the war had brought the countries of eastern Europe into the Russian orbit. All of these states had had authoritarian governments before the war (see p. 986). Their conversion into what were called, with curious redundancy, "people's democracies" varied in timing and method, but in the end was always the same. In only one of the states was a Communist movement fully in the ascendant—in Yugoslavia, where Tito's partisans formed a genuinely popular movement. Elsewhere the immediate future seemed likely to lie with the peasant parties, for these countries were overwhelmingly agrarian. Moreover, some brilliant leaders had emerged, among them Ferenc Nagy in Hungary and Stanislaw Mikolajczyk in Poland. Czechoslovakia was a case apart: more advanced industrially than the others and more Western in its cultural orientation, it had the famous Eduard Beneš as its president. But Beneš, recalling the betrayal of his country in 1938–1939, had little enough reason to be grateful to the western nations, and he, like other east European leaders, sought to collaborate with the Communists in what had been known before the war as a popular front. It was soon clear, however, that Stalin thought of these as interim regimes at best. In Bulgaria in January 1945 Communist pressure forced out unacceptable ministers; the next year the monarchy had been abolished and a dictatorial Communist regime installed. One by one the Russians brought the other eastern European states to heel, dissolved the coalitions, and installed puppet regimes, guaranteeing their unanimity by Soviet might.

Czechoslovakia, the last state to maintain its independence, succumbed to a coup d'etat in February 1948; the tragedy was heightened by the murder or suicide of the foreign minister, Jan Masaryk, the son of the nation's founder. From 1949 the German Democratic Republic was painfully built on the ruined base of the Russian zone of occupation. This broadening conformity was counterbalanced by the expulsion of Yugoslavia from the Soviet bloc in June 1948—the fruit of Tito's immense strength, which allowed him to take an independent line, and of Russia's growing mistrust. The suspicion of "Titoism" or of any deviation from the Moscow line in other states brought instant action, and there were notable purges within the Communist leadership. In the interwar years the Soviet Union had resented the role of eastern Europe as a *cordon sanitaire* against the spread of Bolshevik ideas. Now, ironically, the region was once more a *cordon sanitaire*—against the penetration of Western ideas. But would it also be a springboard for a new attack on the West?

In a famous speech at Westminster College in Fulton, Missouri in March 1946, Winston Churchill warned that an "iron curtain" had descended across Europe, and called for an open alliance of his country and the United States to oppose the Communist threat. Many Western liberals found the speech puzzling, even outrageous; they were imbued with recollections of the heroic Soviet performance in the war and many of them felt a lingering sentimentality about Communism, reacting instinctively to the old cry of "no enemies to the left." But Churchill was only giving voice to a reality that he and other Western leaders had increasingly feared from the latter years of the war. His challenge was eagerly taken up in the United States, prepared as it was by tradition to oppose the imposition of alien rule upon an unwilling people and convinced as it was of the merits, almost the sacredness, of what publicists called, with some exaggeration, the free enterprise system. Many residents of the United States were refugees from Communist rule; many more citizens traced their descent by a generation or two to those nations that now were under Soviet domination. There were, then, sound political reasons why an accommodation with the Russians would be difficult and even more compelling military and strategic reasons why the United States, with its new-found sense of power or even omnipotence, would want to gain dependable allies for a possible confrontation. While American aid to western Europe (see p. 1094) sprang in part from real altruism, the United States was also strengthening the governments of western Europe to resist Russian military incursion (if it came to that), and the much greater likelihood that native Communist parties would seize power if popular discontent were fanned by economic collapse.

The European retreat from empire put a whole new range of burdens on the United States, burdens it shouldered willingly but not always wisely. In 1947, in proclaiming what came to be known as the Truman Doctrine, President Truman took over from Britain responsibility for the defense of Greece and Turkey against subversion from within or without and declared that the United States "would support free peoples who are resisting subjugation by armed minorities or by outside pressure." Thus in 1958 American forces intervened in Lebanon, underlining the growing American involvement in the Near East: the United States was heavily committed, emotionally and politically, to the cause of Israel, but it was deeply concerned as well about continued access to the vast oil resources in Arab hands. The demise of the French empire in Indochina left the United States with another responsibility, a modest commitment at first that grew inexorably as Americans came to grips with the challenge of communism in a China they had never possessed but believed that, somehow, they had lost. Fear of China and determination to resist Communist pressure had already led the United States and its allies, formally constituted as a United Nations force, into war in South Korea in 1950, to repel the incursions of that small nation's northern and Communist twin. And in time the United States drifted into full-scale war in Vietnam. The American fear of the Soviet Union and China was matched by often hysterical fear of Communist subversion at home. These fears were intensified by the ending of the American monopoly of atomic and nuclear weapons as first the Soviet Union and then China learned how to make these deadly bombs.

The Cold War, both for Americans and Russians, was related to the need for security, a need reinforced in both nations by the experience of World War II. What resulted was a division of the world into spheres of influence, delimited by confrontations or tacit agreement in one area after another. At Yalta and Potsdam the two powers had been unable to agree on a common German policy; by 1949 they accepted a de facto partition of Germany, despite all their rhetoric about the ultimate goal of reunification. The sharpest clashes came over Berlin—a partitioned city surrounded by Soviet-dominated territory. The most dramatic instance occurred in 1948 when the Russians closed off access to the city, and West Berlin was supplied by an Allied, chiefly American, air lift—an operation of staggering scope and technical proficiency. But there were many more Berlin crises, arising out of calculated provocation by the Russians for often obscure purposes, and they always resulted in serious talk of war and redoubled American efforts at military preparedness. The Americans sponsored military and political alliance systems—the highly effective North Atlantic Treaty Organization (NATO) founded in Europe in 1949, the abortive Baghdad Pact in the Middle East, and the longer-lived but ultimately futile Southeast Asia Treaty Organization (SEATO). In 1955 the Russians responded with the Warsaw Pact, to bind together the nations of eastern Europe. And even to the point of ridicule, the two world powers sought to outbid each other for the allegiance of newly emerging nations, by offering military, economic, and technical assistance and by seeking to establish friendly governments and to maintain them in power.

Even at the height of the Cold War, however, accommodation proved possible. Treaties with Italy, Hungary, Rumania, Bulgaria, and Finland were hammered out in 1947 and a treaty with Austria as late as 1955, triumphs of patience that history books scarcely mention. But it is an interesting commentary on the nature of modern war and diplomacy that no general congress, like that of Versailles or Vienna, ended World War II. The fighting stopped, ad hoc arrangements were made, the powers pushed as far as they dared and settled for what they could get. Clausewitz's famous definition of war as diplomacy carried on by other means might well be reversed in the postwar world: diplomacy was war carried on by other means.

Formally, much of this conflict has been transferred to the United Nations, founded at a conference in San Francisco in 1945. In structure the UN resembles the League of Nations. It has an able and dedicated secretariat, with its headquarters in New York; an assembly, though with more authority than the assembly of the League; and three councils instead of one. The Trusteeship

Council and the Economic and Social Council have remained relatively unimportant, and attention has focused on the Security Council, where the five permanent members—the United States, Great Britain, France, the Soviet Union, and China (since 1971 Communist China rather than the Nationalist regime in Taiwan)—contend. The UN has done some valuable work in mediating disputes, notably in Africa and the Near East. But, as was true of the League, little can be done to settle a major question on which the great powers disagree, for Council decisions are subject to veto. There is no veto in the Assembly, and the decision that the UN would intervene in Korea resulted from reference to the Assembly while the Russians were boycotting the Security Council. The greater authority that seems to inhere in the office of secretary general, as compared to the League, is a legacy from the brilliant diplomat and administrator Dag Hammarskjöld, who held the office from 1953 until he was killed in an air crash while on a peace mission to the Congo in 1961. As the UN approaches the age at which the League expired, it seems, despite its financial difficulties and some condescending comment, set to survive as a talking ground. Winston Churchill liked to say that "jaw-jaw is better than war-war"; it is hard to differ from him in an age when war could mean nuclear destruction.

Although, in its early stages, the polarization of Europe (and of much of the rest of the world) was grounded in self-interest, the need for such arrangements seemed less pressing, especially to the lesser partners, as they increased in prosperity and confidence. Europeans talked about becoming a "Third Force," independent of the two superpowers; the non-European nations met at Bandung in Indonesia in 1955 and proclaimed a policy of neutralism; de Gaulle, as soon as he was able, took a markedly independent line and in 1966 withdrew French troops from NATO and ordered NATO bases out of France within a year. Nations in the Soviet bloc tried to take an independent line: East Germany in 1953, Hungary in 1956, Poland in 1956 and 1970, and, most significant and moving of all, Czechoslovakia in 1968. The Soviet Union had accepted the deviation of Yugoslavia and contented itself with vilifying Marshal Tito, but it could not accept displays of independence and put them down by armed force if local Communists lost control. The struggles of political leaders like Imre Nagy in Hungary or Alexander Dubček in Czechoslovakia and the resistance of ordinary citizens against Soviet tanks contain the stuff of heroism and tragedy. Although the Russian suppression of the Hungarian rising was almost overlooked in the outrage the world felt over the Suez incident, which occurred at exactly the same time, no one could overlook the crushing of Czechoslovakia. Displays of brute force to suppress what seemed legitimate aspirations of nations still loyal to socialism caused a marked erosion of support for the Soviet Union even among its sympathizers in Western countries. Many Communists defected from their parties, and some Western Communist parties ventured to criticize Soviet policy. If the United States is imperialist, it has had subtler means at its disposal—outside Asia, at any rate.

The history of the Cold War cannot be divorced from the personality and legacy of Josef Stalin. Postwar Russia saw the dreariest of conformities re-established under the supervision of Andrei Zhdanov, Stalin's right-hand man. After Zhdanov's death in 1948, the younger men who moved into power were for the most part bureaucrats, trained under the Stalinist regime, dedicated to routine, and prudent by instinct. Hence Russian isolation from the West increased steadily, as did Stalin's isolation within Russia, an isolation that, as he possessed supreme power, gave free rein to the suspicion and despotism that had characterized so much of his rule. When Stalin died in 1953, amid rumors of plots and signs of a new burst of anti-Semitism, he was succeeded by a directory of five: Georgi Malenkov, Nicolai Bulganin, V. M. Molotov (the foreign minister), Lavrenti Beria (head of the secret police), and Nikita Khrushchev. Malenkov emerged as the dominant figure. Soon Beria was driven out and executed, but when Malenkov resigned under pressure in 1955, he was not executed but merely sent to manage a power plant in Kazakhstan. The ultimate beneficiary of the struggle was Khrushchev, an engaging and ram-bunctious though fundamentally serious man. On February 25, 1956, in a speech before the Twentieth Party Congress, Khrushchev launched a stinging attack on the "cult of personality," which he blamed for many of the nation's failures, and on Stalin, whom he declared guilty of heinous crimes. Within Russia and outside it, this drastic departure inaugurated a "thaw"; it became possible for Western scholars and tourists to visit the Soviet Union with comparative ease and even for some carefully chosen Soviet citizens to travel abroad. Diplomatic and commercial relations with other countries became warmer, the more so as a split developed between the Soviet Union and the aggressive and distinctive Communist regime of Mao Tse-tung in China. In 1960 Khrushchev actually visited the United States, and in 1961 it was possible for Khrushchev and President John F. Kennedy to meet, though (like many summit meetings) it was a failure. Matters quickly grew worse. In 1961 the division of Europe was symbolized by the building of a wall between East and West Berlin to prevent East Germans from fleeing to the West, and in October 1962 tension reached its peak when United States intelligence discovered that Russia was installing guided missile sites in nearby Cuba, which had recently undergone a successful Communist revolution led by Fidel Castro. President Kennedy, gambling on the Russian desire to avoid a conflict, ordered the American navy to intercept Soviet supply ships. He won his gamble: the ships turned back. This triumph of American policy was an embarrassment to Khrushchev at home, and he was saddled with other problems too, not least the Sino-Soviet quarrel. In 1964 he fell, going into retirement and anonymity so deep that his death in 1971 was not reported in the Soviet press. He was succeeded by Alexei Kosygin as premier and Leonid Brezhnev as first secretary of the party.

In the course of the sixties, the hostility between the United States and the Soviet Union gradually waned, though both sides gave much cause for mutual distrust and though competition could remain intense in the arms race, with its guided missiles and enlarged navies, and in such dramatic and expensive undertakings as space exploration. At the same time the reputation of both powers declined, as much because independent nations no longer needed their support as because of catastrophic blunders like the Russian interventions in Hungary and Czechoslovakia or the American intervention in Vietnam. By the late sixties, Russian leaders had conceded some independence of policy to the East European countries, and one—the poor and isolated state of Albania— showed its contempt for the Soviet Union by transferring its allegiance to China. One may speak, almost exactly, of a Cold War generation: it is too soon to know what patterns the world will assume in its wake.

THE POSTWAR SPIRIT

Culture in the East

Historians and scholars in other disciplines have observed that the systems of the East and the West have many points of convergence—similarities that arise from the very nature of modern industrial and bureaucratic society. Among them are the pervasiveness of bureaucracy (not merely in the state but in industry and education); new hierarchies arising from the imperatives of management and of intellect; the quest for efficiency and rational organization, with their correlative of accountability. Industrial society—its contours first adumbrated by the Saint-Simonians (see p. 684)—depends on certain bour-geois and liberal virtues such as rationality, forethought, and organization, virtues that writers and artists, intent on their private missions, increasingly came to see as vices. Yet for all these convergences, it remains true that, on the purely cultural side, the Iron Curtain is as clear a demarcation as it is in politics, diplomacy, and economics. Perhaps by now it is even clearer.

The consolidation of the Russian Revolution in the early twenties put an end to much of the experiment and intellectual ferment that had arisen before World War I and that was given new impetus by the liberation of 1917 (see p. 980), and Stalin's rule made certain that art and intellect would be bent to the purposes of Soviet society, as he narrowly defined them. The reaffirmation of the Stalinist system after 1945, enforced by Zhdanov and his successors, kept Russian culture drearily conformist. In the thaw after 1953 the West became aware of breaks in this apparent uniformity. The first, and most eagerly consumed, Soviet export was in the performing arts; there the Soviet system of rigorous training and special privilege for the talented produced superb executants—in ballet (long a Russian specialty), in musical performance, and quite as impressively in athletics. Ballet and instrumental playing are relatively unpolitical, but, not surprisingly, the Russians showed themselves to best advantage in the classical repertory rather than in creation. For all their excellence, the Sadler's Wells Ballet (later the Royal Ballet) in London and the New York City Ballet in the United States could not claim the overall technical perfection of Russian dancers; but the Russians could offer no modern choreography remotely approaching the genius of Frederick Ashton in London or that greatest of modern masters—trained in Russia and an exile from the 1920s—George Balanchine in New York. The works that secured Sergei Prokofiev his place as the greatest of modern Russian composers were written mostly in Paris; his compositions after his return to Russia in 1932, though prolific, lack the originality of the earlier work, though two of his ballet scores (*Lieutenant Kije* and *Romeo and Juliet*) are attractive and popular. In 1934, Dmitri Shostakovich, second to Prokofiev in international stature, had to accept a harsh rebuke from Soviet critics for his opera *Lady Macbeth of Mzensk*, and, like Prokofiev, he has known other periods of official disfavor. It is questionable that any of his symphonies—even the much-acclaimed Seventh, written during the siege of Leningrad in World War II, approaches the high-spirited charm of his First Symphony (1925) or of his satirical ballet, *The Golden Age*, written in 1930.

The impressiveness of Russian science was dramatically borne in on the West by the swiftness with which the country entered the atomic age after the war and by Russia's winning the first stage of the race in space exploration with the launching of *Sputnik*, the first orbiting satellite, in 1958. Russian theoretical science can count some triumphs as well. But in intellectual disciplines that might carry political implications, the pressures mount—now since the thaw even more visibly than before. Boris Pasternak, famous as a poet before the Revolution, had occupied himself with translations during the Stalin era; then in 1958 his *Dr. Zhivago,* a novel in the Russian epic tradition, was published abroad. Implicitly critical of the Soviet regime, it brought down the wrath of the authorities, and Pasternak was forbidden to go to Stockholm to receive the Nobel Prize for literature, which was awarded to him (prudently for his poetry) in 1958; Pasternak could have accepted the prize only on pain of permanent exile, something he could not contemplate. Alexander Solzhenitsyn's first novel, *One Day in the Life of Ivan Denisovich*—a compelling account of life in a prison camp drawn from his own experience—was published only after direct intervention by Khrushchev, who must have found it valuable in his de-Stalinization campaign. Solzhenitsyn's subsequent novels—*The First Circle, Cancer Ward,* and *August 1914*—have circulated in Russia only in clandestine editions (*Samizdat*), though they have been published, to wide acclaim, abroad. The Nobel Prize came to Solzhenitsyn in 1970; it is some measure of progress, though perhaps not much, that, unlike Pasternak, he was permitted to accept it, though *in absentia;* his letter of acceptance is a moving appeal for intellectual freedom. But Solzhenitsyn could bring himself to abandon neither his country nor the myriad associations that inevitably cluster about a writer's native ground and language, welcome though he would have been in exile. In his moral heroism, Solzhenitsyn towers over his contemporaries; but he is not alone, for other writers, some historians among them, have dared to court official disapproval in pursuit of their art and truth as they see it. Except in medicine, theoretical science, and some aspects of the performing arts, Soviet intellectual life is dominated by wariness and conformity, a situation in which rewards and privilege are likely to go to the mediocre but dependable. To a greater or lesser degree, the culture of the satellite states of eastern Europe has followed suit.

Culture in the West

In western Europe, World War II produced nothing like the artistic legacy of World War I, another measure of the differing impact of the two cataclysms. In the visual arts one exception was the series of sensitive drawings of wartime scenes by the great British sculptor Henry Moore, serving as an official war artist. The literature of the Resistance—an important though necessarily transient phenomenon—found its most notable figure in the French novelist and playwright Albert Camus, whose career was cut tragically short in 1960 by a fatal automobile accident. His novel, *The Plague,* is an enduring monument to his existentialist thought and the decency of his impulses. The message of the novel, poignant and pointed, is a call for innocence in a world steeped in indifference and barbarity—man must firmly refuse to be his fellow man's hangman. Though many popular novels dealt with the war, few approached the distinction with which, two decades before, writers had recaptured and assessed the collapse of the world of 1914. There was even little of the satire. Nor did the postwar years share that need for innovation, resolute or desperate, that touched so many artists in the twenties (see p. 1011). The giants of prewar culture, now in their old age but still producing—Mann and Eliot, Stravinsky and Schönberg, the incredibly versatile Picasso—continued to dominate the Western sensibility. Many of the men and women who might have given new vitality to the culture of the postwar years were lost to Europe—some through death in the war, many in concentration camps or by suicide, and many more through emigration. Through sheer numbers and the extent of its institutional and financial resources, the United States came to play a far larger role in Western culture than it had ever played before, in science above all, but in painting and architecture and many areas of scholarship as well. The proportion is beyond calculation, but this transatlantic flowering owes much to the direct contribution or to the teaching or example of European intellectuals who fled from Nazism and other despotisms to the freedom of the United States, where many of them found a permanent home.

Building on the conceptual foundations established in earlier decades, and profiting from new technical resources like the computer or the electron microscope, scientists have gone from strength to strength. A generation that can count phenomenal advances in medical knowledge and practice, startling cosmological speculations, or the unravelling of the complex mechanisms of heredity cannot be accused of travelling in well-worn paths. Social scientists and historians can claim few such advances, though, especially in social history, much stimulating and important work has been and continues to be done. But scholarship, with its growing sophistication of method and increasing arcaneness of language, has intensified the specialization that began to appear in the later nineteenth century and to produce the fragmentation of a once unified culture. In *The Two Cultures and The Scientific Revolution,* a famous lecture given in 1959, the English scientist and novelist C. P. Snow lamented the gulf in understanding that had grown between scientific and literary endeavor. Snow has been much attacked, especially for taunting humanists with their ignorance of the simplest laws of science. But he may well have understated the case: there are many more than two cultures, and lines between disciplines seem more formidable barriers in the intellectual world than national frontiers.

Philosophy offers a striking instance of this insulation. As philosophers in Britain and the United States reflected upon their mission in the years after the war, they found the most seminal book to be the *Tractatus Logico-Philosophicus,* first published (in German) in 1921 by the Viennese philosopher Ludwig Wittgenstein. Wittgenstein had studied with Bertrand Russell in Cambridge before World War I and was deeply indebted as well to G. E. Moore (see p. 872); after nearly a decade in Austria, teaching in elementary schools, he returned to Cambridge in 1929, remaining there until he died in 1951. Wittgenstein and his followers believed language, its uses and abuses, to be the principal concern of philosophy. "The right method of philosophy would be this: to say nothing except what can be said, i.e. the propositions of natural science, i.e. something that has nothing to do with philosophy: and then, always, when someone else wishes to say something metaphysical, to demonstrate to him that he had given no meaning to certain signs in his propositions." After quoting this passage, Professor John Passmore remarks: "Philosophy, on this view, is not a theory but an activity: the activity of making clear to people what they can, and what they cannot, say." [15] Critics charge that this school of linguistic analysis abandons the time-honored philosophical enterprise—inquiry into man's deepest questions—for a modern scholasticism; and few can deny that, for all the virtues inherent in criticism and for all the benefits that flow from careful scrutiny of language, philosophical discussion today is almost entirely confined to professionals.

In the years immediately after the war, however, another philosophical school burst into wider prominence. Existentialism was essentially the creation in the 1920s of two German philosophers, Martin Heidegger and Karl Jaspers, though its roots go back nearly a century to the radical theological and moral perceptions of Sören Kierkegaard (see p. 667). Frankly irrationalist, the existentialists were preoccupied with the absurdity of life, confronting, as it does, every individual with agonizing experiences like fear and despair and with the necessity of making moral choices when no clear grounds for those choices exist. A younger French philosopher, Jean Paul Sartre, adding a dash of idiosyncratic psychoanalysis, expounded this philosophical attitude in memorable works of fiction. After the war, and following his discovery of Marxism, Sartre's prose became more difficult and abstract—more Teutonic, one might say—and his thought more directly political than it had been in the late 1930s. But the relevance of his views to men's existence seemed confirmed by the irreducible choices posed by World War II and by Sartre's own experience in the Resistance. His major philosophical treatise, *Being and Nothingness,* appeared in 1943, and his literary works continued to carry his message to a wide public. For a time after the war Sartre ranked as a leading intellectual in the Western world; he was lionized, quoted, and eagerly read or listened to by men and women for whom his combination of despair and moral stringency had a special appeal. But existentialism proved to be a fashion, taken up and dropped, and dropped in part because Sartre's insistence on commitment led him at times to approximate a Stalinist line; it was over politics that Sartre broke in 1950 with his friend Albert Camus.

Whatever the intrinsic merits of Sartre's philosophizing, the cultural historian may profitably contemplate the wide extent and the transient nature of his popularity. For a time Sartre answered a need intensely felt among people whom traditional literary, philosophical, or scholarly resources had ceased to serve. Other writers, then or later, performed a similar function. In the thirties a distinguished ancient historian, Arnold J. Toynbee, began to publish *A Study of History,* a ponderous multivolumed work that claimed to interpret and explain the rise and fall of civilizations. Made accessible in a one-volume abridgment in 1946, Toynbee's work was hailed in many quarters as a major achievement, and once again an author was sought after, interviewed, and listened to with respect as he pronounced upon the health of our society and culture and on many other topics. Historians were quick to point out that the history on which Toynbee based his theories was badly flawed and that his deterministic pattern was in fact a vehicle for religious prophecy. But changed needs or fashion, not historians' criticism, undercut his authority in the end. Lewis Mumford, an able critic of society, technology, and urban planning, also edged more and more into prophecy, though his audience and fame were probably never so large, or so transient, as Toynbee's. In later years a similar enthusiasm swept up the distinguished Marxist philosopher Herbert Marcuse.

For many, though not for all, these enthusiasms are surrogate religions. The main religious traditions also sought to revivify their message in the postwar world. Fundamentalist sects had grown steadily in England and the United States for at least a century, but they attracted people of relatively little education and sophistication. For the more cultivated, Protestantism found a new appeal through Neo-Orthodoxy, whose most uncompromising exponent was the Swiss theologian Karl Barth. While it had nothing in common with the biblical literalism of the fundamentalists, Neo-Orthodoxy called for a return to the essentials of Protestant tradition—faith rather than reason, obedience to divine authority, and, for Barth at any rate, something akin to predestination. But authority in religion was to have no easy time of it. The cautious conservatism of Pope Pius XII reflected a Roman Catholic church free from serious internal questioning, although some liberal impulses working beneath the surface came into view. The most striking of these manifestations was the worker-priest movement in France. Priests went to live among factory workers without revealing their identity until they had established themselves as friends and equals. The priests were more often radicalized than the workers were converted, and the papacy at last suppressed the movement, welcomed though it had been by the French hierarchy.

The suppression of the worker-priests was announced in 1959 by a new pope, John XXIII, who, in view of his advanced age, had been elected in the general expectation that he would be a caretaker. He occupied the papal throne for less than five years, but in that brief time, this simple, direct, warmhearted man won the respect, even the love, of men and women far removed from the church he ruled. Moreover, after a conservative start, he began a liberalization of the church that is still in process. He issued encyclicals calling for world peace, aid to backward nations, and compassion for the poor; he summoned the second Vatican Council in 1962, the first such conclave since the declaration of papal infallibility by the Vatican Council in 1870 (see p. 663). Vatican II was to finish its deliberations in 1965 under another pope, Paul VI, who, though he made dramatic public appeals for peace and travelled abroad in the interests of ecumenicism—meeting publicly, for example, with the heads of the Greek Orthodox and the Anglican churches—proved to be a prudent reformer at best. Still, Vatican II authorized revision of the liturgy and the use of the vernacular in place of Latin in much of the mass, qualified the absolute power of the papacy and the papal curia by associating bishops more closely with decision making in the church, and, after much debate, absolved Jews of responsibility for the death of Christ and pronounced in favor of religious liberty. The *aggiornamento*—the bringing up to date—of the Roman Catholic church begun by John XXIII will be long in the working out; its continued resistance to birth control remains a critical obstacle to its full reconciliation with the practical morality of the modern world. Yet it seems likely that the 1960s will be as crucial in the history of the church as were the 1560s, when the deliberations of the Council of Trent (see p. 169) were completed, though this time the tide seems to be running in the opposite direction.

Culture High and Low

In serious art the postwar world can mark few (some would say, no) monuments of the stature of *Ulysses* or *The Waste Land*, the paintings of the Cubists or Surrealists, or the atonal compositions of Schönberg and his school. The reading public was plied, as always, with popular successes (and failures) written to old formulas, except that now sex loomed far larger and was treated far more explicitly than was possible even in the interwar years. Some popular novels had pretensions to art, but serious writing came to be more and more narrowly confined, both in conception and in audience. A small group of French writers—Alain Robbe-Grillet, Michel Butor, and Nathalie Sarraute—proclaimed the "anti-novel", which abandoned the old requisites of narrative and plot for uncompromising introspection or the patient description of surfaces. In England, where the old literary forms continued in strength, there was much acclaim for the novels and plays of a group dubbed "the angry young men," obsessively preoccupied with the persistence of the traditional class structure, and writing passionately, in a realistic vein, about the human failures English society induces. But perhaps the esoteric and chilling novels of Ivy Compton-Burnett—in which the action is carried in cryptic, often unnatural and strangely witty conversation—are more significant than the ranting protagonists of John Osborne's dramas: her novels have become the almost exclusive property of a cult.

English music regained a European stature it had not had since the eighteenth century. One undoubted master, Ralph Vaughan Williams, was bringing his career to a close in the postwar years with a series of remarkably venturesome symphonies, as Benjamin Britten was reaching the height of his powers. Particularly skilled in writing for voice, Britten is probably the most successful living opera composer; his *War Requiem*, a setting of poems by Wilfred Owen (see p. 1011) is a work of the first importance. In France Olivier Messiaen and the younger Pierre Boulez have been far more experimental, though Messiaen's appeal has been limited by the curious metaphysical purposes he sees as underlying his music, as Boulez' is limited by difficulty. Nearly everywhere the dominant mode of composition has become serialism, derived from the influence of Schönberg. Another group of composers has turned to electronic instruments, but they, like the serialists, are restricted to a small, highly knowledgeable audience. In them, the separation between artist and public, long in the making, seems almost complete.

Although painting has moved from one fashion of abstraction to another, it has proved far more accessible to the public than much contemporary writing or composing; the same holds true for sculpture, which has undergone a notable revival. Especially in abstract painting, as the names of Jackson Pollock and Robert Motherwell attest, America has repaid some of its long-standing cultural debt to Europe. The School of New York—including besides Pollock and Motherwell such European-born artists as Arshile Gorky, Mark Rothko, and the great teacher Hans Hofmann—has been as influential in London or Paris as at home. It carried the cerebral experimentation and emotional freedom of such earlier masters as Cézanne or Matisse or Kandinsky into abstract expressionism, a style that owes nothing to the objective world and everything to color and design.

No art has had greater opportunities than architecture, with a continent to be rebuilt and with steadily growing demands for new offices, schools, factories, and housing. Again the giants—Frank Lloyd Wright, Le Corbusier, Mies van der Rohe, Gropius—cast their shadows and their principles forward. All of them produced masterpieces in the postwar years, and younger architects have followed their teachings or have reacted against them. Among the notable innovators is the Italian structural engineer Pier Luigi Nervi, whose elegant and breathtaking use of concrete in stadiums and public buildings has had wide influence since the 1930s. But the demands of clients, the stringencies of economics, and the inevitable rarity of first-rank talent have left the architectural record mixed. With few exceptions, the rebuilding of European cities has been an exercise in lost opportunities.

One popular entertainment—the motion picture—has been transmuted into an art form on a scale scarcely imaginable in the interwar years. Here Europe was pre-eminent, for the monopoly of Hollywood on American film production began to suffer from the weaknesses inherent in the star system, from business management that adapted with difficulty to changed conditions, and from the threat posed to a high-cost industry by the new medium of television. Immediately after the war, a number of "neo-realist" Italian films— Vittorio de Sica's *Shoeshine* and *Bicycle Thief* and Roberto Rossellini's *Open City*—proclaimed anew the artistic potential of the film. But the Italian film industry lost its impetus for a dozen years or so, and leadership passed to France, with the work of inventive directors like Alain Resnais, François Truffaut, and Jean-Luc Godard, and to Sweden, where Ingmar Bergman's brooding fables explored poetic and symbolic possibilities of the medium with singular persuasiveness. The principal innovation in entertainment, however, was in the advent and rapid spread of television. Though subject to the same controls and manipulation and the same political exploitation as radio (see p. 1023), television brought athletic contests and highly paid entertainers directly into the home at little cost in money or personal inconvenience to the viewer. The uncounted cost lies in the threat to literacy—who wants to read if he can watch?—and the sacrifice of common experience to experience in isolation; although ambiguous in its significance for individuals, the effect is generally disastrous for those parts of the entertainment industry that rely on live audiences. Every European state to some degree subsidizes the higher forms of art—opera, ballet, theater, the symphony orchestra—but television and the steadily improving technology of recording confront the performing arts with a perplexing future.

Popular music evolved quickly through one style after another, each with its cluster of highly paid performers who in many cases fell from fame as quickly as they reached it. Jazz played a less prominent role after the war than before, though its derivatives and imitations captured wide audiences. In the early sixties the world—highbrow and lowbrow alike—was startled by a singing group of four working-class boys from Liverpool called The Beatles. The simplistic rhythm, the melodic poverty, and the banal lyrics of the "rock" they performed before screaming teenagers were a far cry from the sophistication and infinite subtlety of jazz at its best, though, before they disbanded at the end of the decade, the Beatles had begun to penetrate to a higher musical and literary level. But the insistent, incantatory effect of the new style and the strident celebration in its lyrics of peace, drugs, and sexual freedom had an elemental appeal to a generation of young people facing a confused and threatening world. In the long run, however, the significance of the Beatles and their imitators may lie less in the revolution they made in popular musical taste or in the styles of clothing and appearance they inspired than in their immense success as a business enterprise: the earnings of the Beatles and other English groups abroad formed a not insignificant item in the British balance of payments. But there is more to the business than money. The reliance of rock music on amplification is neatly symbolic, as is the increase in the volume of sound compared to the gentle crooning of popular singers in the thirties. In live performance as in television, a whole technology is interposed between the performers and the direct experience of their work by an audience; in some respects—and this is true of films as well—the technology has become an end in itself. Even the performers are manufactured; they are the creatures of managers, arrangers, technicians, press agents, and the entrepreneurs of the world of show business. With such resources even a little talent can be brightly packaged and profitably marketed.

The nineteenth century was an age of domestic music-making, and though the standard of performance could not have been high among the young ladies for whom piano-playing and singing were genteel accomplishments, even serious composers provided simple compositions for home consumption. While television has introduced high standards of professionalism to passive spectators at home, a reverse phenomenon is just as evident—amateur musicians, often little better than Victorian young ladies in attainments, perform in public, and some manage to turn professional: the Beatles, after all, began their career as amateurs.

The Puzzle of Prosperity

The history traced in this book has been marked by a number of "revolutions," turning points in European awareness, economy, and social structure that are also pivots of historical debate—the Renaissance, the Reformation, the scientific revolution, the industrial revolution, and political and social revolutions in

England, America, France, Russia, and elsewhere. Perhaps to a future historian the last half of the twentieth century will take its place in this company as the revolution of prosperity. Though no one now can predict its results, it may prove to be not beneficent alone, but corrosive and destructive beyond the fears of most people today. Already we are becoming aware of the penalties of abundance: the population explosion, the exhaustion of natural resources, the upsetting of the delicate ecological balance in nature, the blight of our cities, the burden of waste—both the polluting effluents of industry and the discarding of goods by those who can afford to be heedless. Rational planning and the steady development of new technologies may provide ways of coping with all these threats, but the political cost of the effort may prove high. Marx and Engels had hoped that control over people would give way to control over things; we have reason to fear that control over things all too often brings control over people in its train.

There are social as well as material and environmental consequences of prosperity. The spread of wealth and abundance was envisioned by nineteenth-century adherents of classical liberalism and of socialism alike. But liberals and socialists assumed that certain virtues—the willingness to work, pride in craftsmanship, respect for law, and civility—would continue unchallenged and might indeed be strengthened by the new dispensation. They believed, too, that society would function far more effectively than in the past, as illegitimate authority came to be replaced by authority arising from ability and opportunity. However individualistic their philosophy, no nineteenth-century liberals saw anarchy as a boon. Even anarchists never believed that social order would be unnecessary, but only that it would become voluntary. If many socialists were willing to contemplate a period of authoritarian rule, this proletarian dictatorship was only to effect a transition to a rational, fully reconciled, and fully efficient society. Few of them, however moved they were by passions and frustration, would have predicted or desired dropping out from society, a flight from politics, a quest for personal satisfaction with no measure beyond the satisfaction itself, or the erosion of decency. Without deprecating the immense benefits that the postwar years have brought to masses of men, they made problems more acute, or at least more visible, than ever. These problems form part of the new order of difficulties everyone faces in getting an education, choosing a career, earning a living, raising children, and coping with the day-to-day business of getting through the world.

European conservatives and a good many radicals have talked unhappily about the Americanization of Europe. In one sense the term is accurate: American power and priorities have long held sway over the politics of western Europe. But while that dominance is diminishing, what remains is the growing and more persistent dominance rooted in America's superior wealth and in the seemingly irresistible tendencies to industrial and commercial amalgamation. American ownership of European firms and resources poses a far greater threat to European autonomy than American exports; and against that threat the

Common Market is a somewhat uncertain counterpoise.[16] But the term Americanization is more generally used to sum up what Europeans like to think is the American style: diffused wealth, an insatiable demand for material goods, and a discontent with established manners and social structures. Here the accusation misfires; it is not so much that America has offered an example, or a lure, as that prosperity, which America has known longer and more securely than Europe, seems to bring new values and new desires, even to Europeans. Ease of travel and communication only whets the appetite for change: hence the profound, and often profoundly justified, protests of the 1960s against the perpetuation of privilege, against outmoded and insufficient education, against traditional politics, against war.

Three of these protest movements—of blacks, students, and women— deserve particular attention. Although, like many other rebellions in the past, they came at a time of improvement and widening prosperity, they cannot for that reason be dismissed as irrelevant or unnecessary; rather, they reflected the rising hopes that follow naturally in such encouraging circumstances as well as the repeated disappointments that accompany any great leaps forward. Because these three movements shared rhetoric and tactics and drew strength from such successes as one or another of them attained, they have been taken for aspects of a single phenomenon of protest, giving the decade a vivid, often lurid, coloration. There have been many accounts of each of them, but no satisfactory synthesis has as yet been constructed, nor is one likely to appear until we have achieved a longer perspective. One thing, though, is clear: while the demands for black power, students' rights, and women's liberation are normally lumped together as single movement, they are distinct in their historical origins, as they are in their class base and in their ultimate aims.

Largely confined to the United States, the black protest movement was an explosion of rage too long delayed and too long suppressed. When slavery was abolished in the United States in the 1860s, the word had been "this is the negro's hour." A hundred years later, blacks did not think that their hour had been much advanced. The promise of legal equality, economic opportunity, and social acceptance was indeed closer to redemption than ever before—a fact that owes much to the patient and self-sacrificing efforts of generations of civil rights workers, both black and white. But its fulfillment seemed too desperately slow in coming, and white resistance was proving too stubborn and too devious to be any longer tolerable. Militancy grew in the established organizations and found new expression among the Black Muslims and Black Panthers, with their insistence on racial self-segregation and their preoccupation with black identity.

The student movement, in contrast, was a worldwide contagion, an avalanche of demonstrations against grievances part imagined, part trivial, and

---

[16] This threat is the concern of Jean-Jacques Servan-Schreiber's important book, *The American Challenge* (1968).

part serious and justified. Some observers have asked whether universities were the right targets for the wrath of the young, since so much of the protest—chiefly that against American involvement in Vietnam—was directed at policies in which institutions of higher learning had played or could play only a marginal role. Ambiguous in its conception, the student movement has also been ambiguous in its results. In the United States where it all began, it was overwhelmingly a middle-class phenomenon, and seems to have lost momentum as the danger of being drafted into a hated war receded, though it left universities shaken in confidence and financing. But, for all the "restructuring" that was undertaken, American universities, like British universities, remained committed to substantially the same purposes and the same ways of realizing them as before the agitation began. In other countries the game was for higher and highly political stakes, and the future of some universities as untrammeled institutions of higher learning is now in doubt—in Germany above all, a bitter irony given the extent to which the modern scholarly mission and the contours of academic freedom were defined in that country in the nineteenth century.

The congeries of women's movements, hastily grouped under the single and confining rubric of Women's Liberation, has the longest history of the three. It is particularly a phenomenon of the Atlantic world and was tied closely from its organizational beginnings in the 1840s to the parallel campaigns for the abolition of slavery and control of drink. Only after the 1860s did it come to concentrate on a single issue, passionately fought for in both Britain and America: women's suffrage. Attained in the United States in 1918 and in two stages in Britain, in 1918 and 1928, the goal of votes for women had been anticipated in Australia, New Zealand, and Scandinavia, and even in Britain and America in certain local elections. In countries where the demand was less evident or where the fear of church influence was strong—in France, Italy, and Switzerland—the suffrage was extended to women only after World War II. In the postwar world, perhaps in part the result of widened access to education and leisure, women found new grievances in the economic, social, domestic, and sexual spheres. Here again, prosperity offered a puzzle. Longest in the making, Women's Liberation has, at least so far, turned in a highly uneven record of accomplishment; certainly it has made no progress to match what was done for women by two world wars, when men were suddenly forced to turn to women for tasks that had been closed to them and that they performed splendidly. But improvements in male attitudes toward women and the gradual reduction in economic inequities suggest the imminence of further progress, slow though advances against entrenched habits must always be.

Despite the differences among these three movements, and despite the internal splintering to which they were all subject, two things can be said about all three together. First, they all began in the United States and so reflect the inextricable connection of America to Europe and the growing and probably permanent cultural prominence of the United States in European affairs.

Second, they all share in a quest for community, a search that represents rejection of the fragmentation and isolation of modern life.

It remains uncertain to what extent governments can remedy discontents that are social and cultural at base, given the ineradicable irrationality of the human mind, the limitations of political methods, the uncertainties of social analysis, and the immensity of scale attained by both society and its problems in the present century. The task of reform will certainly be far more difficult if society loses its cohesion, and there are signs that this is precisely what is happening. In place of the personal autonomy—the full self-development of the individual—that has been the noble goal of generations of political philosophers and moralists, we seem to be falling into a new privatism. Despite their resemblance, privatism is not autonomy; it is autonomy gone bad, a turning inward that devalues personal relationships, compromises citizenship, and leaves individuals to their own resources, facing both success and failure without the traditional supports that in the past have helped to make reality tolerable. The old are left to themselves, in isolation or in segregated communities; children know less of childhood and are abandoned to their peers or to schools alone for their education. Thus the old interaction among generations disappears, creating a far more fundamental generation gap—one in the very structure of our society—than disagreement between young and old over ideas and morals, a disagreement that has existed ever since there were parents and children. What can be done to ease the psychological barrenness in a mere aggregate of privatized individuals is a question to which there is no easy answer. Again, the state may not have the answer, and what solutions it may be able to muster may contradict the dearest assumptions of Western culture.

Few historians will seriously argue that the study of history can offer answers to problems that are in some ways utterly new in the world's experience. Since the eighteenth century, history has aspired to be a kind of science, and, as a science, it confines itself to speculation on what is observable within its field of inquiry, in this case the past. History has not, therefore, attempted to suggest specific lines of policy for the future, for neither its materials nor its techniques allow the kind of confident extrapolation in human affairs to which some other social sciences pretend; but this modesty of purpose does not rule out the usefulness of the discipline. History deals with humankind in all its aspects, in despair and creation, in defeat and victory, in cravenness and heroism. It records mankind's appalling failures—this book is full of the terrible things human beings have done to one another—but its occasional triumphs as well. If some historians have served first their class or their nation, or if they have kept alive their own prejudices or those comfortable myths men like to believe about themselves, others have helped to expose self-interest and prejudice and to penetrate the myths, and so have served as physicians to society—a function as important now as at any time in the history of history.

History shares a paradox with other sciences: it is precisely when it has least aspired to be directly relevant that it has been most fruitful. The point of history, the great nineteenth-century historian Jacob Burckhardt said, is not be clever for today but to be wise forever; wisdom may lie in the remote and accidentally discovered as much as in what is consciously sought. Thus it is precisely as a science, serving no master but itself, that we may judge history worthy of study. It is in the completeness and variety of history, not in its subjection to temporary or partisan purposes, that it offers to the present a usable past.

SELECTED READINGS

The broadest account of World War II, one that gives commendable attention to its social and cultural consequences, is Gordon Wright, *The Ordeal of Total War, 1939-1945* (1968), another volume in the Rise of Modern Europe series; the bibliography is extensive and excellent. Peter Calvocoressi and Guy Wint, *Total War: Causes and Courses of the Second World War* (1972) is an admirable account on a huge scale, with emphasis on the military side and about equal attention given to the war in Europe and the war in the Pacific. B. H. Liddell Hart, *History of the Second World War* (1971) was published posthumously; here the emphasis is almost entirely on military developments. There are interesting reflections in some of Michael Howard's essays reprinted in his *Studies in War and Peace* (1971). As British intelligence was particularly successful in fooling the Nazis, reference should be made to J. C. Masterman, *The Double-Cross System in the War of 1939 to 1945* (1972). Memoirs of participants are legion; two, however, particularly deserve mention here, for their importance and their literary quality: Winston Churchill, *The Second World War,* 6 vols. (1948-1953) and the *War Memoirs* of Charles de Gaulle (tr. 1958-1960), the latter appearing in several editions with varying titles. Albert Speer's self-serving *Inside the Third Reich* (1970) is important for the German war effort. For lurid and depressing but fully authoritative accounts of the end of the Axis, see F. W. Deakin, *The Brutal Friendship: Mussolini, Hitler, and the Fall of Italian Fascism* (1962) and H. R. Trevor-Roper, *The Last Days of Hitler* (1947). On the greatest tragedy of the war the most exhaustive account is Raul Hilberg, *The Destruction of the European Jews* (1961), and there is particular poignancy in an analysis of the fall of France by the great historian Marc Bloch, who died in the Resistance: *Strange Defeat: A Statement of Evidence Written in 1940* (tr. 1949).

H. Stuart Hughes, *Contemporary Europe, A History* (3rd ed., 1971) is a deservedly standard survey of the period since 1914, but it is particularly valuable for the period after World War II, for which guides are not easy to come by. See also R. C. Mowat, *Ruin and Resurgence, 1939-1965* (1966) and Maurice Crouzet, *The European Renaissance since 1945* (1970), a suggestive interpretation, though rather solemnly condescending in tone at times; Crouzet's carefully selected lists of readings are valuable. On the economic recovery of postwar Europe, the last chapter of David S. Landes, *The Unbound Prometheus: Technological Change and Industrial Development in Western Europe from 1750 to the Present* (1969) is excellent; more detailed, and indispensable, is M. M. Postan, *An Economic History of Western Europe, 1945-1964* (1967). Important analyses of the nature of present-day economic institutions and their consequences are Andrew

Shonfield, *Modern Capitalism* (1965) and John Kenneth Galbraith, *The Affluent Society* (1958).

Contemporary Britain has produced many critical analyses, some close to self-flagellation. The best guide to the workings of the country is Anthony Sampson, *A New Anatomy of Britain* (rev. ed. 1971). For narrative, see W. N. Medlicott, *Contemporary England, 1914-1964* (1967), while Samuel H. Beer, *British Politics in the Collectivist Age* (1965) is a stimulating interpretation. On Germany, Ralf Dahrendorf, *Society and Democracy in Germany* (1968) is an important essay. French developments have attracted an able battery of historians; the most valuable results are John Ardagh, *The New French Revolution: A Social and Economic Study of France, 1945-1968* (1968); Gordon Wright, *The Reshaping of French Democracy* (1948); Dorothy Pickles, *Algeria and France: From Colonialism to Cooperation* (1963) and *The Fifth French Republic: Institutions and Politics* (2nd ed., 1962); Philip M. Williams, *French Politicians and Elections, 1951-1969* (1970) and (with Martin Harrison), *Politics and Society in de Gaulle's Republic* (1972). On Eastern Europe, see R. W. Pethybridge, *A History of Post-War Russia* (1966); Alec Nove, *The Soviet Economy* (2nd ed., 1965); Robert Lee Wolff, *The Balkans in our Time* (1956); and two books by Hugh Seton-Watson, *The East European Revolution* (3rd ed., 1956) and *From Lenin to Khrushchev: The History of World Communism* (1960). For international affairs, Peter Calvocoressi, *World Politics since 1945* (1968) is a useful survey. A balance on the Cold War may be struck with Stephen E. Ambrose, *The Rise to Globalism, 1938-1970* (1971) and Herbert Feis, *From Trust to Terror: The Onset of the Cold War, 1945-1950* (1970). Withdrawal from empire has not been satisfactorily treated as a general phenomenon, but Dorothy Pickles' book on Algeria, cited above, is valuable for one instance, and Elizabeth Monroe, *Britain's Moment in the Middle East, 1914-1956* (1963) helps to place another set of developments in context. John Strachey's *The End of Empire* (1959) is a suggestive essay by a thoughtful and important British politician, particularly interesting in view of the importance in the thirties of Strachey's powerful Marxist manifesto, *The Coming Struggle for Power* (1932), noted in Chapter 25 of the text.

On postwar culture, some of the books cited in Chapter 25 are relevant. In addition, Gregory Battcock, ed., *The New Art* (1966) is a convenient anthology of articles on postwar painting. Dore Ashton, *A Reading of Modern Art* (rev. ed., 1971) critically examines modern painting and sculpture. Martin Esslin, *The Theatre of the Absurd* (1961) gives a lucid account of Beckett, Ionesco, Genet, and other Modernist playwrights. The brief survey by Peter Demetz, *Postwar German Literature: A Critical Introduction* (1970) is authoritative. For the French antinovel, see Maurice Nadeau, *The French Novel since the War* (tr. 1967), and John Sturrock, *The French New Novel: Claude Simon, Michel Butor, Alain Robbe-Grillet* (1969). Morris Philipson, ed., *Aesthetics Today* (1961) is a compendious anthology of contemporary philosophies of art. Edgar Wind, *Art and Anarchy* (1963) is a stimulating, argumentative essay on modern art by a great art historian. Beyond that the only sensible recommendation is to read the novels, see the plays, look at the paintings, listen to the music, and go to the movies.

General Bibliography

In the selected readings we appended to each chapter, we emphasized appropriate monographs. But we had occasion as well to refer to more general histories—individual volumes in collaborative ventures or multivolume national histories, and separate surveys covering single countries over longer or shorter periods of time. We think it useful to list here, with brief comments, some of these general works and to add some others.

Among the great collaborative histories, several are particularly useful. There is, first, the series edited by William L. Langer, begun in 1936 and still not quite complete; though called The Rise of Modern Europe, it is popularly known as the Langer series. Each of its volumes is written by a specialist and each devotes considerable space to social, intellectual, religious, economic, and literary, as well as political, history. Without wishing to make invidious discriminations, we consider the following volumes as outstanding: Myron P. Gilmore, *The World of Humanism, 1453-1517* (1952); Walter L. Dorn, *Competition for Empire, 1740-1763* (1940); William L. Langer, *Political and Social Upheaval, 1832-1852* (1969); Oron J. Hale, *The Great Illusion, 1900-1914* (1971); and Gordon Wright, *The Ordeal of Total War, 1939-1945* (1968).

The New Cambridge Modern History was begun in 1957; of the fourteen volumes only the thirteenth, which will be devoted to the period following 1945, remains to be published. Completed (with that exception) over a period of little more than a decade—a remarkable record for a work on so large a scale—the NCMH is more consistently authoritative as regards recent scholarship than the Langer series, some volumes of which date back to the 1930s. At the same time, the Langer series has the advantage that each volume is by one scholar and so gains in consistency of performance and point of view. The separate volumes of the NCMH, bulky and informative, are subdivided among many contributors, and the only attempt at a total conspectus (often a summary) is in the introductory chapter provided by the editor of each volume. Special mention should be made of volume XIV, a superb historical atlas, which for most purposes supersedes all others, although on certain points the old standby, William R. Shepherd, *Historical Atlas* (rev. ed., 1956) is still worth consulting.

Another important series, edited by J. H. Plumb, is called The History of Human Society; it stresses, as the general title indicates, social in company with political history. Among its best volumes so far are J. H. Parry, *The Spanish Seaborne Empire* (1966), which covers the period from the conquests in the fifteenth century to the decline in the eighteenth; and Charles R. Boxer, *The Dutch Seaborne Empire, 1600–1800* (1965). We should also mention A General History of Europe, edited by Denys Hay, a set of trim volumes each covering a century or more and particularly alert to available documentation and to the social structure of Europe in the period under discussion. All the volumes so far published are worth reading: A. H. M. Jones, *The Decline of the Ancient World* (1966); Christopher Brooke, *Europe in the Central Middle Ages, 962–1154* (1964); Denys Hay, *Europe in the Fourteenth and Fifteenth Centuries* (1966); H. G. Koenigsberger and G. L. Mosse, *Europe in the Sixteenth Century* (1968); M. S. Anderson, *Europe in the Eighteenth Century, 1713–1783* (1961); F. L. Ford, *Europe, 1780–1830* (1970); H. Hearder, *Europe in the Nineteenth Century, 1830–1880* (1966); and John Roberts, *Europe, 1880–1945* (1967).

There are many volumes of selections from books, scholarly articles, documents, and debates; they are of varying merit but even the better ones are far too numerous to mention here. A number of pamphlet series have also been devised, offering banquets of conflicting interpretation, summaries of leading views, and normally excellent bibliographies. Among these aids, Problems in European Civilization, the so-called Heath series, is particularly helpful; it now comprises many volumes. Between 1957 and 1970 the American Historical Association published a series of pamphlets, most of which took a bibliographical approach to the history of various countries or regions and to particular periods and problems for the more important countries. That series—usually called the Service Center pamphlets—though now largely out of print is generally available in libraries and can be useful if one keeps in mind how quickly outdated bibliography becomes. It is now being supplanted by a new series, called AHA Pamphlets, which are narrative, critical essays covering many problems and periods in the world's history; select bibliographies are included.

For the economic history of Europe, see the great Cambridge Economic History of Europe, under the general editorship of M. M. Postan and H. J. Habakkuk; like the New Cambridge Modern History, this venture subdivides each of its volumes among specialists. Of particular interest to the student of modern European history are volume IV, *The Economy of Expanding Europe in the Sixteenth and Seventeenth Centuries* (1967), edited by E. E. Rich and C. H. Wilson; and volume VI (in two parts), *The Industrial Revolutions and After* (1965), edited by Postan and Habakkuk. Among general economic histories of Europe, see Herbert Heaton, *Economic History of Europe* (rev. ed., 1948) and Shepard B. Clough and Charles W. Cole, *Economic History of Europe* (3rd ed., 1952). The general history of economic thought has not been dealt with synoptically in recent years, but there is the classic survey by Charles Gide and Charles Rist, *A History of Economic Doctrines* (rev. ed., 1948), and *A History of Economic Thought* (3rd ed., 1954) by the distinguished Marxist economist Eric Roll. A more recent guide to an immensely complex subject is T. W. Hutchison, *A Review of Economic Doctrines, 1870–1929 (2nd ed., 1962).* G. D. H. Cole, *A History of Socialist Thought,* 5 vols. (1953–1960) is pedestrian but thorough; Carl Landauer, *European Socialism: A History of Ideas and Movements from the Industrial Revolution to Hitler's Seizure of Power,* 2 vols. (1959) is useful.

On the history of science, see Herbert Butterfield, *The Origins of Modern Science, 1300–1800* (rev. ed., 1957); Marie Boas Hall, *The Scientific Renaissance, 1450–1630* (1962); A. R. Hall, *The Scientific Revolution, 1500–1800* (2nd ed., 1966); and Charles J. Singer, *A Short History of Scientific Ideas to 1900* (1959). Mention should also be made of Thomas S. Kuhn, *The Structure of Scientific Revolutions* (2nd ed., 1970), an essay immensely influential not only for the writing of history of science but of history generally. Closely related both to science and economics, and highly important, is the history of technology. Here the best place to go for detailed information is *History of Technology,* edited by Charles Singer and others; the five volumes, published between 1954 and 1958, bring the narrative down to 1900.

The history of philosophy is excellently served by the distinguished Jesuit writer F. C. Copleston in *A History of Philosophy;* volumes III through VIII (1953–1966) trace developments from William of Occam to Bertrand Russell. Emile Bréhier published a two-volume *History of Philosophy* in 1926–1932; the three parts of the first volume of the original French edition deal with the Middle Ages and the Renaissance, the four parts of the second with the period since the seventeenth century. A translation into English has been published in seven volumes in 1963–1969. On political thought there is nothing to match George H. Sabine's magnificent survey, *A History of Political Theory* (3rd ed., 1951). The history of theology, on the other hand, is badly served. But a classic in that stern and demanding field of history of ideas illuminates a central concept informing both philosophy and theology: Arthur O. Lovejoy, *The Great Chain of Being: A Study in the History of an Idea* (1936). Lovejoy's *Essays in the History of Ideas* (1948) also deserve close attention.

The arts are fortunate in a great series, not quite complete as yet but far along. This is the Pelican History of Art, edited by Nikolaus Pevsner. Amid the many fine volumes, we may single out Rudolf Wittkower, *Art and Architecture in Italy, 1600–1750* (2nd ed., 1965); Anthony Blunt, *Art and Architecture in France, 1500–1700* (2nd ed., 1970); George Heard Hamilton, *Painting and Sculpture in Europe, 1880 to 1940* (1967); and Henry-Russell Hitchcock, *Architecture, Nineteenth and Twentieth Centuries* (1958). On architecture, Nikolaus Pevsner, *An Outline of European Architecture* (7th ed., 1963) is an indispensable guide. An extremely bold and highly personal synthesis, in which the visual arts dominate, was offered in a television series made by the British Broadcasting Corporation, written and narrated by the distinguished art historian Kenneth Clark (Lord Clark); prints of the films are available to colleges and museums and the text of the narration has been published under the title of the series, *Civilisation* (1969). See also Lionello Venturi, *History of Art Criticism* (rev. ed., tr. 1964). For music there is Paul Henry Lang's broadly conceived *Music in Western Civilization* (1941) and Donald Jay Grout, *A History of Western Music* (1960). Most of the Norton History of Music has already been published: Gustave Reese, *Music in the Renaissance* (rev. ed., 1959); Manfred F. Bukofzer, *Music in the Baroque Era, from Monteverdi to Bach* (1947); and Alfred Einstein, *Music in the Romantic Era* (1947). The best guide to more recent trends is Francis Routh, *Contemporary Music: An Introduction* (1968).

A good introduction to literary trends across Europe is Emery Neff, *A Revolution in European Poetry, 1660–1900* (1940), but most histories do not venture outside national traditions. The Oxford History of English Literature, edited by F. P. Wilson and Bonamy Dobrée, is not yet complete but will reach twelve volumes. Boris Ford, ed., The Pelican Guide to English Literature, is complete in seven volumes (1955–1965), each volume being made up of essays by specialists, whereas the volumes of the Oxford series have single authors. René Wellek has published four volumes of *A History of Modern Criticism, 1750–1950* (1955–1965), with one more yet to come.

There are many histories of individual countries, and choices are hard to make. Some of the titles that follow have already been mentioned, while others will be new to the reader. For England, the Oxford History of England, edited by Sir George Clark, is serviceable. While the quality of individual volumes varies somewhat, the following are most useful: J. B. Black, *The Reign of Elizabeth, 1558–1603* (2nd ed., 1959); J. Steven Watson, *The Reign of George III, 1760–1815* (1960); Sir Llewellyn Woodward, *The Age of Reform, 1815–1870* (2nd ed., 1962); Sir Robert Ensor, *England, 1870–1914* (1936, but very much worth reading still); and A. J. P. Taylor's brilliant *English History, 1914–1945*

(1965). The Pelican History of England, in eight volumes, is short, popular, pointed, surprisingly comprehensive, and highly recommended; for the period of this book, see S. T. Bindoff, *Tudor England* (1950); Maurice Ashley, *England in the Seventeenth Century* (1952); J. H. Plumb, *England in the Eighteenth Century* (1950); and David Thomson, *England in the Nineteenth Century* (1950). A new series, The History of British Society, edited by E. J. Hobsbawm, stresses social history almost to the exclusion of politics; two of the volumes, J. F. C. Harrison, *The Early Victorians, 1832-51* (1971), and Geoffrey Best, *Mid-Victorian Britain, 1851-75* (1971) are untraditional and interesting. For a general history of the period after 1760, see R. K. Webb, *Modern England, from the Eighteenth Century to the Present* (1968). There is an admirable two-volume history of Scotland: W. C. Dickinson and G. S. Pryde, *A New History of Scotland* (1961-1962); the dividing point is 1603. J. C. Beckett, *The Making of Modern Ireland* (1966) is a good introduction, and see also the interesting, essentially Marxist interpretation in Erich Strauss, *Irish Nationalism and British Democracy* (1951). The British economy is surveyed impressively in Sir John Clapham, *A Concise Economic History of Britain, from the Earliest Times to 1750* (1949) and W. H. B. Court, *A Concise Economic History of Britain, from 1750 to Recent Times* (1954). There is also the lucid survey by D. L. Keir, *Constitutional History of Modern Britain since 1485* (9th ed., 1969). Finally, any student who has mastered the fundamental outlines of English history should consider as mandatory reading W. C. Sellar and R. J. Yeatman, *1066 and All That*, written in the early 1920s and reprinted many times since; it is a brilliant comic history, unequalled anywhere.

For a general history of France, stressing social developments in the broadest possible sweep, see Georges Duby and Robert Mandrou, *A History of French Civilization from the Year 1000 to the Present* (tr. 1964). Among histories of France after the age of Louis XIV, Alfred Cobban, *A History of Modern France,* 3 vols. (new ed., 1963-1965) is remarkable for its economy, its wit, and its judgment. Gordon Wright, *France in Modern Times, 1760 to the Present* (1960) is far superior to the ordinary textbook. Paul A. Gagnon, *France since 1789* (rev. ed., 1972) is lucid and persuasive. For the span of the Third Republic, the narrative account by D. W. Brogan, *The Development of Modern France (1870-1939)* (1940) would be hard to better. For a survey of economic developments in the modern period, see Shepard B. Clough, *France, A History of National Economics, 1789-1939* (1939).

The best-known long history of the Dutch is P. J. Blok, *History of the People of the Netherlands,* 5 vols. (tr. 1898-1912), very comprehensive in narration and facts, but quite old-fashioned in approach and judgment. More modern histories are B. H. M. Vlekke, *Evolution of the Dutch Nation* (1945), and G. J. Renier, *The Dutch Nation, an Historical Study* (1944), which ends, however, with the early nineteenth century. Henri Pirenne, one of the great figures in the history of history, published his *Histoire de Belgique* in five volumes between 1907 and 1920, bringing the story down to 1799. While there are a few more recent brief general histories of Belgium, there is nothing that can rank with this classic in scale or authority.

Modern Spain is admirably served by J. H. Elliott, *Imperial Spain, 1469–1716* (1963); Richard Herr, *The Eighteenth-Century Revolution in Spain* (1958); and Raymond Carr, *Spain, 1808–1939* (1966), the last a volume in the Oxford History of Modern Europe. Richard Herr has also published a brief one-volume sketch, *Spain* (1971), which is a useful guide, though the emphasis is on the more recent period. For Portugal, H. V. Livermore, *A New History of Portugal* (1966). General histories of modern Italy include Denis Mack Smith, *Italy: A Modern History* (2nd ed., 1969), which is vigorous and informative; Christopher Seton-Watson, *Italy from Liberalism to Fascism, 1870–1925* (1967) is sober and equally informative. Shepard B. Clough has traced *The Economic History of Modern Italy* (1964). For the longer span see H. Hearder and D. P. Waley, eds., *A Short History of Italy* (1963) and Luigi Salvatorelli, *A Concise History of Italy* (tr. 1939), both helpful for introductory purposes.

The most compendious and dependable history of Germany after the Middle Ages is Hajo Holborn, *A History of Modern Germany,* 3 vols. (1959–1969). See also Marshall Dill, Jr., *Germany, A Modern History* (1961); Koppel S. Pinson, *Modern Germany: Its History and Civilization* (rev. ed. 1966); and the witty, idiosyncratic interpretation by A. J. P. Taylor, *The Course of German History* (1946), which takes up the story after Napoleon. Holborn necessarily deals with Austria. In addition, see Friedrich Heer, *The Holy Roman Empire* (tr. 1968). The Hapsburg world is impressively treated by C. A. Macartney in *Hungary, A Short History* (1962) and, for the period since the French Revolution, in *The Habsburg Empire, 1790–1918* (1969). For the same period as the latter work, A. J. P. Taylor's *The Habsburg Monarchy, 1809–1918* (1948) provides a contrasting point of view.

The Scandinavian countries are covered in Ragnar Svanstrom and C. F. Palmstierna, *A Short History of Sweden* (tr. 1934); Stewart Oakley, *A Short History of Sweden* (1966); Karen Larsen, *A History of Norway* (1948); and J. H. S. Birch, *Denmark in History* (1938). See, in addition, Stanley M. Toyne, *The Scandinavians in History* (1948). Poland is dealt with in a collaborative work, *The Cambridge History of Poland,* edited by W. F. Reddaway and others; volume I (1950) covers the period from the origins to 1696, volume II (1951) from 1697 to 1935. Oscar Halecki, *A History of Poland* (3rd ed. 1966) is a single-volume survey by the dean of Polish historians living in the United States. Among histories of Russia, Bernard Pares, *History of Russia* (rev. ed. 1953) is more old-fashioned than Nicholas V. Riasanovsky's excellent *History of Russia* (2nd ed. 1969). James H. Billington, *The Icon and the Axe* (1966) is an interpretative survey of Russian culture. Jerome Blum, *Lord and Peasant in Russia, from the Ninth to the Nineteenth Century* (1961) takes a vitally important problem through a long span of time. See also P. I. Liashchenko, *History of the Russian National Economy to the 1917 Revolution* (tr. 1949).

Hugh Seton-Watson, *The Russian Empire, 1801-1917* (1967), a volume in the Oxford History of Modern Europe, is very full and judicious.

On southeastern Europe, see Bernard Lewis, *The Emergence of Modern Turkey* (1961) for the essential Ottoman context. William H. McNeill, *Europe's Steppe Frontier, 1500-1800* (1964) is a fascinating interpretation. For a clear and valuable survey, see L. S. Stavrianos, *The Balkans since 1453* (1958).

Writers on the papacy have tended to concentrate on the Middle Ages, but there is the series of forty volumes by Ludwig von Pastor, *The History of the Popes from the Close of the Middle Ages* (tr. 1938-1953), literally a chronicle that comes down to 1799. More immediately useful is the Pelican History of the Church, edited by Owen Chadwick. Of the five volumes, the three that touch on the modern period have been published: Owen Chadwick, *The Reformation* (1964); Gerald R. Cragg, *The Church and the Age of Reason, 1648-1789* (1960); and Alec R. Vidler, *The Church in an Age of Revolution* (1961).

On international relations, the volumes of the Langer series are excellent first guides. But particular mention should be made of Garrett Mattingly's imposing *Renaissance Diplomacy* (1955) and A. J. P. Taylor's volume in the Oxford History of Modern Europe, *The Struggle for Mastery in Europe, 1848-1918* (1954). M. S. Anderson's *The Eastern Question, 1774-1923* (1966) is an extremely useful survey of one of the major diplomatic issues in modern times.

Finally, a few books on history deserve mention. Friedrich Meinecke, *Historism* (1936, tr. 1972) is a classic, though far from the final word. A good study of the professionalization of the discipline is John Higham, with Leonard Krieger and Felix Gilbert, *History* (1965). And Marc Bloch's *The Historian's Craft* (tr. 1953) says better than anything else what it is we are about and how one of the greatest of historians viewed his mission.

Index

Birth and death dates are given for all persons mentioned in the text, including a few historians whose works have attained the status of classics. Dates are also given for the reigns of kings and the pontificates of popes, but regnal dates are given only for queens when they ruled in their own right. A query (?) indicates an approximate but reasonably certain date; to avoid ambiguity it appears after a birth date but before a death date. Where dates are less certain, c. (for circa) is used, and occasionally we can only note a date of death or (with fl., for *floruit*, flourished) the time when the person comes to our attention.

Names are given in the form that is most convenient with respect to usage in the text. It is not possible to take into account variations in spelling or (save very occasionally) translation. Titles of nobility present great complexities that vary from country to country; they are given here in the simplest form consistent with the text and common usage. Fuller information for most names in this index can be derived (as can pronunciation) from *Webster's Biographical Dictionary* or the *Columbia Encyclopedia*. Beyond those handy brief references one may resort to the great national encyclopedias or biographical dictionaries.

The index is constructed to facilitate reviewing as well as the usual checking of references. The absence of identification other than birth and death dates for an individual allows a student to test his knowledge and to check back if his memory has slipped. For more important subjects a student can easily construct little informal outlines by using index entries to help fix in his mind what he has learned. To that end, analytical entries are provided for certain key concepts like bureaucracy or centralization or armies, making possible a review outline or an essay cutting across national boundaries. Entries for major countries or institutions—such as France, England, the Roman Catholic Church—are handled somewhat differently. Every substantive entry in the text is noted in the index, but identifying phrases are used only for major references; these phrases and the pages to which they pertain appear in chronological sequence, set off by semicolons from the briefer or secondary references.

EUROPE AFTER WORLD WAR II

Zones of occupation, 1949 :

British
French
American
Russian

500   1000
Miles

ARCTIC

ICELAND

NORWAY
SWEDEN
Oslo
Stockholm

SCOTLAND
UNITED
NO.
IRELAND
Edinburgh
Belfast
IRELAND
Dublin
KINGDOM
ENGLAND

NORTH
SEA

DENMARK
Copenhagen

BALTI

Lübeck
Hamburg
Danzi

London
NETHERLANDS
Amsterdam
Thames R.
The Hague
See inset
Berlin
Bremen

ATLANTIC
OCEAN

Antwerp
Brussels
BELGIUM
WEST
GERMANY
EAST
Bonn
Leipzig
Elbe R.
Oder R.
POLAN

Paris
LUX.
Frankfurt
Prague
Crac

Loire R.
Rhine R.
Danube R.
CZECHOSLOVAK
Brno

FRANCE
Zürich
Berne
SWITZ.
Munich
Vienna
AUSTRIA
Budapest
HUNGA

Bordeaux

Rhône R.
Milan
Venice
Zagreb
YUGOSLAV

PORTUGAL
Tagus R.
Madrid
Ebro R.
SPAIN
Lisbon

Barcelona
Marseilles
Nice
CORSICA
ITALY
ADRIATIC SEA

Cordoba
Seville
Gibraltar

SARDINIA
Rome
Naples
ALBAN

MEDITERRANEAN

Palermo
SICILY

MOROCCO
ALGERIA
AFRICA
TUNISIA

Genoa

Arctic Circle